The United States Government Manual 2006/2007

Office of the Federal Register

National Archives and Records Administration

Revised June 1, 2006

Raymond A. Mosley,
Director of the Federal Register.

Allen Weinstein,
Archivist of the United States.

On the cover: The *Phalaenopsis* orchid that graces this year's cover of *The United States Government Manual 2006–2007* is just one of many exquisite displays showcased at the United States Botanic Garden (Botanic Garden).

The Botanic Garden, located at the foot of the U.S. Capitol in Washington, DC, is a national treasure that captivates our collective spirit with its unique aura of elegance and repose due to its vast, magnificent plant collection.

The Botanic Garden proper consists of three locations: the newly renovated Conservatory, which showcases a beautiful and fascinating living plant museum; Bartholdi Park, which serves as a home landscape demonstration garden and showcases innovative plant combinations in a variety of styles and design themes; and the Production Facility, which is used for growing and storing plants for propagation, for the maintenance of the collection, or for display in upcoming annual shows. Construction is also underway for a National Garden west of the Conservatory, scheduled to open in October 2006.

The current Botanic Garden was inspired by American naval officer and explorer Charles Wilkes, commander of the United States Exploring Expedition to the South Seas from 1838–1842, who amassed an extensive collection of live and dried specimens of plants and seeds from around the globe that were previously unknown to the United States. The expedition greatly advanced the field of science in the United States.

Located on the National Mall across from the U.S. Capitol along First Street SW., between Maryland Avenue and C Street, visitors can marvel at the exhibits that include over 25,000 living specimens.

For sale by the Superintendent of Documents, U.S. Government Printing Office
Internet: bookstore.gpo.gov Phone: toll free (866) 512–1800; DC area (202) 512–1800
Fax: (202) 512–2250 Mail: Stop SSOP, Washington, DC 20402–0001

ISBN 0–16–051455–X

[redacted]

The Botanic Garden is open every day of the year, including Federal holidays. Admission to all public areas of the Botanic Garden is free. It is ADA compliant and offers full accessibility for those with special needs. The Conservatory offers pay phones with TTY capability and wheelchairs. Sign language interpreters are available by advance reservation; telephone 202–226–4082.

For more information on the Botanic Garden, visit its Web site at http://www.usbg.gov or call 202–225–8333.

We thank the Creative Services artists at the U.S. Government Printing Office for their assistance in developing this elegant cover.

Preface

As the official handbook of the Federal Government, *The United States Government Manual* provides comprehensive information on the agencies of the legislative, judicial, and executive branches. The *Manual* also includes information on quasi-official agencies; international organizations in which the United States participates; and boards, commissions, and committees.

A typical agency description includes a list of principal officials, a summary statement of the agency's purpose and role in the Federal Government, a brief history of the agency, including its legislative or executive authority, a description of its programs and activities, and a "Sources of Information" section. This last section provides information on consumer activities, contracts and grants, employment, publications, and many other areas of public interest.

The 2006/2007 *Manual* was prepared by the Presidential and Legislative Publications Unit, Office of the Federal Register, under the supervision of Gwendolyn J. Henderson. Alfred W. Jones was Managing Editor; Stephen J. Frattini was Chief Editor, assisted by Ashley Merusi.

The Federal Register and Its Special Editions

The *Manual* is published as a special edition of the *Federal Register* (*see* 1 CFR 9.1). Its focus is on programs and activities. Persons interested in detailed organizational structure, the regulatory documents of an agency, or Presidential documents should refer to the *Federal Register* or one of its other special editions, described below.

Issued each Federal working day, the *Federal Register* provides a uniform system for publishing Presidential documents, regulatory documents with general applicability and legal effect, proposed rules, notices, and documents required to be published by statute.

The *Code of Federal Regulations* is an annual codification of the general and permanent rules published in the *Federal Register.* The *Code* is divided into 50 titles that represent broad areas subject to Federal regulation. The *Code* is kept up to date by the individual issues of the *Federal Register.*

The *Weekly Compilation of Presidential Documents* serves as a timely, up-to-date reference source for the public policies and activities of the President. It contains remarks, news conferences, messages, statements, and other Presidential material of a public nature issued by the White House during the week reported.

A companion publication to the *Weekly Compilation* is the *Public Papers of the Presidents,* which contains public Presidential documents and speeches in convenient book form. Volumes of the *Public Papers* have been published for every President since Herbert Hoover, with the exception of Franklin D. Roosevelt, whose papers were published privately.

Other Office of the Federal Register Publications

The Office of the Federal Register publishes slip laws, which are pamphlet prints of each public and private law enacted by Congress. Slip laws are compiled annually as the *United States Statutes at Large.* The *Statutes* volumes contain all public and private laws and concurrent resolutions enacted during a session of Congress;

recommendations for executive, legislative, and judicial salaries; reorganization plans; proposed and ratified amendments to the Constitution; and Presidential proclamations. Included with many of these documents are sidenotes, U.S. Code and statutes citations, and a summary of their legislative histories.

Publication Availability

The publications of the Office of the Federal Register are available for sale by writing to the following address:

Superintendent of Documents
P.O. Box 371954
Pittsburgh, PA 15250–7954

Publications are also available for sale through the Government Printing Office online bookstore at http://bookstore.gpo.gov, the Government Printing Office bookstore located in Washington, DC, and the retail sales outlet in Laurel, MD. Telephone inquiries should be directed to 202–512–1800.

Electronic Services

The Office of the Federal Register maintains an Internet site for public law numbers, the Federal Register's public inspection list, and information on the Office and its activities at www.archives.gov/federal-register. This site also contains links to the texts of *The United States Government Manual*, public laws, the *Weekly Compilation of Presidential Documents*, the *Federal Register*, and the *Code of Federal Regulations* (both as officially published on a quarterly basis and a new unofficial, daily updated version, the e-CFR) in electronic format through *GPO Access*. For more information about these online publications, contact Electronic Information Dissemination Services, U.S. Government Printing Office. Phone, 202–512–1530, or 888–293–6498. Internet, www.gpoaccess.gov. E-mail, gpoaccess@gpo.gov.

Further Information

Information on *The United States Government Manual* and other publications of the Office of the Federal Register may be obtained by writing to the following address:

Office of the Federal Register
National Archives and Records Administration
Washington, DC 20408

Inquiries should be directed by phone to 202–741–6000, faxed to 202–741–6012, or e-mailed to fedreg.info@nara.gov.

Contents

The Declaration of Independence

In Congress, July 4, 1776.

The unanimous Declaration of the thirteen united States of America,

When in the Course of human events, it becomes necessary for one people to dissolve the political bands which have connected them with another, and to assume among the powers of the earth, the separate and equal station to which the Laws of Nature and of Nature's God entitle them, a decent respect to the opinions of mankind requires that they should declare the causes which impel them to the separation.—We hold these truths to be self-evident, that all men are created equal, that they are endowed by their Creator with certain unalienable Rights, that among these are Life, Liberty and the pursuit of Happiness.—That to secure these rights, Governments are instituted among Men, deriving their just powers from the consent of the governed,—That whenever any Form of Government becomes destructive of these ends, it is the Right of the People to alter or to abolish it, and to institute new Government, laying its foundation on such principles and organizing its powers in such form, as to them shall seem most likely to effect their Safety and Happiness. Prudence, indeed, will dictate that Governments long established should not be changed for light and transient causes; and accordingly all experience hath shown, that mankind are more disposed to suffer, while evils are sufferable, than to right themselves by abolishing the forms to which they are accustomed. But when a long train of abuses and usurpations, pursuing invariably the same Object evinces a design to reduce them under absolute Despotism, it is their right, it is their duty, to throw off such Government, and to provide new Guards for their future security.—Such has been the patient sufferance of these Colonies; and such is now the necessity which constrains them to alter their former Systems of Government. The history of the present King of Great Britain is a history of repeated injuries and usurpations, all having in direct object the establishment of an absolute Tyranny over these States. To prove this, let Facts be submitted to a candid world.—He has refused his Assent to Laws, the most wholesome and necessary for the public good.—He has forbidden his Governors to pass Laws of immediate and pressing importance, unless suspended in their operation till his Assent should be obtained; and when so suspended, he has utterly neglected to attend to them.—He has refused to pass other Laws for the accommodation of large districts of people, unless those people would relinquish the right of Representation in the Legislature, a right inestimable to them and formidable to tyrants only.—He has called together legislative bodies at places unusual, uncomfortable, and distant from the depository of their public Records, for the sole purpose of fatiguing them into compliance with his measures.—He has dissolved Representative Houses repeatedly, for opposing with manly firmness his invasions on the rights of the people.—He has refused for a long time, after such dissolutions, to cause others to be elected; whereby the Legislative powers, incapable of Annihilation, have returned to the People at large for their exercise; the State remaining in the mean time exposed to all the dangers of invasion from without, and convulsions within.—He has endeavored to prevent the population of these States; for that purpose obstructing the Laws for Naturalization of Foreigners; refusing to pass others to encourage their migration hither, and raising the conditions of new Appropriations of Lands.—He has obstructed the Administration of Justice, by refusing his Assent to Laws for establishing Judiciary powers.—He has made Judges dependent on his Will alone, for the tenure of their offices, and the amount and payment of their salaries.—He has erected a multitude of New Offices, and sent hither swarms of Officers to harrass our people, and eat out their substance.—He has kept among us, in times of peace, Standing Armies, without the Consent of our legislatures.—He has affected to render the Military independent of and superior to the Civil power.—He has combined with others to subject us to a jurisdiction foreign to our constitution, and unacknowledged by our laws; giving his Assent to their Acts of pretended Legislation:—For quartering large bodies of armed troops among us:—For protecting them, by a mock Trial, from punishment for any Murders which they should commit on the Inhabitants of these States:—For cutting off our Trade with all parts of the world:—For imposing Taxes on us without our Consent:—For depriving us in many cases, of the benefits of Trial by Jury:—For transporting us beyond Seas to be tried for pretended offences:—For abolishing the free System of English Laws in a neighbouring Province, establishing therein an Arbitrary government, and enlarging its Boundaries so as to render it at once an example and fit instrument for introducing the same absolute rule into these Colonies:—For taking away our Charters, abolishing our most valuable Laws, and altering fundamentally the Forms of our Governments:—For suspending our own Legislatures, and declaring themselves invested with power to legislate for us in all cases whatsoever.—He has abdicated Government here, by declaring us out of his Protection and waging War against us.—He has plundered our seas, ravaged our Coasts, burnt our towns, and destroyed the lives of our people.—He is at this time transporting large Armies of foreign Mercenaries to compleat the works of death, desolation and tyranny, already begun with circumstances of Cruelty & perfidy scarcely paralleled in the most barbarous ages, and totally unworthy the Head of a civilized nation.—He has constrained our fellow Citizens taken Captive on the high Seas to bear Arms against their Country, to become the executioners of their friends and Brethren, or to fall themselves by their Hands.—He has excited domestic insurrections amongst us, and has endeavoured to bring on the inhabitants of our frontiers, the merciless Indian Savages, whose known rule of warfare, is an undistinguished destruction of all ages, sexes and conditions. In every stage of these Oppressions We have Petitioned for Redress in the most humble terms: Our repeated Petitions have been answered only by repeated injury. A Prince, whose character is thus marked by every act which may define a Tyrant, is unfit to be the ruler of a free people. Nor have We been wanting in attentions to our Brittish brethren. We have warned them from time to time of attempts by their legislature to extend an unwarrantable jurisdiction over us. We have reminded them of the circumstances of our emigration and settlement here. We have appealed to their native justice and magnanimity, and we have conjured them by the ties of our common kindred to disavow these usurpations, which, would inevitably interrupt our connections and correspondence. They too have been deaf to the voice of justice and of consanguinity. We must, therefore, acquiesce in the necessity, which denounces our Separation, and hold them, as we hold the rest of mankind, Enemies in War, in Peace Friends.—

WE, THEREFORE, the Representatives of the UNITED STATES OF AMERICA, in General Congress, Assembled, appealing to the Supreme Judge of the world for the rectitude of our intentions, do, in the Name, and by Authority of the good People of these Colonies, solemnly publish and declare, That these United Colonies are, and of Right ought to be **FREE AND INDEPENDENT STATES;** that they are Absolved from all Allegiance to the British Crown, and that all political connection between them and the State of Great Britain, is and ought to be totally disolved; and that as Free and

Independent States, they have full Power to levy War, conclude Peace, contract Alliances, establish Commerce, and to do all other Acts and Things which Independent States may of right do.—And for the support of this Declaration, with a firm reliance on the protection of Divine Providence, we mutually pledge to each other our Lives, our Fortunes and our sacred Honor.

John Hancock
Button Gwinnett
Lyman Hall
Geo. Walton
Wm. Hooper
Joseph Hewes
John Penn
Edward Rutledge
Thos. Heyward, Jr.
Thomas Lynch, Jr.
Arthur Middleton
Samuel Chase
Wm. Paca
Thos. Stone
Charles Carroll of Carrollton
George Wythe
Richard Henry Lee
Th. Jefferson

Benj. Harrison
Thos. Nelson, Jr.
Francis Lightfoot Lee
Carter Braxton
Robt. Morris
Benjamin Rush
Benj. Franklin
John Morton
Geo. Clymer
Jas. Smith
Geo. Taylor
James Wilson
Geo. Ross
Caesar Rodney
Geo. Read
Tho. M: Kean
Wm. Floyd
Phil. Livingston
Frans. Lewis

Lewis Morris
Richd. Stockton
Jno. Witherspoon
Fras. Hopkinson
John Hart
Abra. Clark
Josiah Bartlett
Wm. Whipple
Saml. Adams
John Adams
Robt. Treat Paine
Elbridge Gerry
Step. Hopkins
William Ellery
Roger Sherman
Sam. Huntington
Wm. Williams
Oliver Wolcott
Matthew Thornton

The Constitution of the United States

We the People of the United States, in Order to form a more perfect Union, establish Justice, insure domestic Tranquility, provide for the common defence, promote the general Welfare, and secure the Blessings of Liberty to ourselves and our Posterity, do ordain and establish this Constitution for the United States of America.

Article I

Section 1. All legislative Powers herein granted shall be vested in a Congress of the United States, which shall consist of a Senate and House of Representatives.

Section 2. The House of Representatives shall be composed of Members chosen every second Year by the People of the several States, and the Electors in each State shall have the Qualifications requisite for Electors of the most numerous Branch of the State Legislature.

No Person shall be a Representative who shall not have attained to the Age of twenty five Years, and been seven Years a Citizen of the United States, and who shall not, when elected, be an Inhabitant of that State in which he shall be chosen.

Representatives and direct Taxes shall be apportioned among the several States which may be included within this Union, according to their respective Numbers, which shall be determined by adding to the whole Number of free Persons, including those bound to Service for a Term of Years, and excluding Indians not taxed, three fifths of all other Persons. The actual Enumeration shall be made within three Years after the first Meeting of the Congress of the United States, and within every subsequent Term of ten Years, in such Manner as they shall by Law direct. The Number of Representatives shall not exceed one for every thirty Thousand, but each State shall have at Least one Representative; and until such enumerations shall be made, the State of New Hampshire shall be entitled to chuse three, Massachusetts eight, Rhode-Island and Providence Plantations one, Connecticut five, New-York six, New Jersey four, Pennsylvania eight, Delaware one, Maryland six, Virginia ten, North Carolina five, South Carolina five, and Georgia three.

When vacancies happen in the Representation from any State, the Executive Authority thereof shall issue Writs of Election to fill such Vacancies.

The House of Representatives shall chuse their speaker and other Officers; and shall have the sole Power of Impeachment.

Section 3. The Senate of the United States shall be composed of two Senators from each State, chosen by the Legislature thereof, for six Years; and each Senator shall have one Vote.

Immediately after they shall be assembled in Consequence of the first Election, they shall be divided as equally as may be into three Classes. The Seats of the

Senators of the first Class shall be vacated at the Expiration of the second Year, of the second Class at the Expiration of the fourth Year, and of the third Class at the Expiration of the sixth Year, so that one third may be chosen every second Year; and if Vacancies happen by Resignation, or otherwise, during the Recess of the Legislature of any State, the Executive thereof may make temporary Appointments until the next Meeting of the Legislature, which shall then fill such Vacancies.

No Person shall be a Senator who shall not have attained to the Age of thirty Years, and been nine Years a Citizen of the United States, and who shall not, when elected, be an Inhabitant of that State for which he shall be chosen.

The Vice President of the United States shall be President of the Senate, but shall have no Vote, unless they be equally divided.

The Senate shall chuse their other Officers, and also a President pro tempore, in the Absence of the Vice President, or when he shall exercise the Office of President of the United States.

The Senate shall have the sole Power to try all Impeachments. When sitting for that Purpose, they shall be on Oath or Affirmation. When the President of the United States is tried, the Chief Justice shall preside: And no Person shall be convicted without the concurrence of two thirds of the Members present. Judgment in Cases of Impeachment shall not extend further than to removal from Office, and disqualification to hold and enjoy any Office of honor, Trust or Profit under the United States: but the Party convicted shall nevertheless be liable and subject to Indictment, Trial, Judgment and Punishment, according to law.

Section 4. The Times, Places and Manner of holding Elections for Senators and Representatives, shall be prescribed in each State by the Legislature thereof; but the Congress may at any time by Law make or alter such Regulations, except as to the Places of chusing Senators.

The Congress shall assemble at least once in every Year, and such Meeting shall be on the first Monday in December, unless they shall by Law appoint a different Day.

Section 5. Each House shall be the Judge of the Elections, Returns and Qualifications of its own Members, and a Majority of each shall constitute a Quorum to do business; but a smaller Number may adjourn from day to day, and may be authorized to compel the Attendance of absent Members, in such Manner, and under such Penalties as each House may provide.

Each House may determine the Rules of its Proceedings, punish its Members for disorderly Behaviour, and, with the Concurrence of two thirds, expel a Member.

Each House shall keep a Journal of its Proceedings, and from time to time publish the same, excepting such Parts as may in their Judgment require Secrecy; and the yeas and Nays of the Members of either House on any question shall, at the Desire of one fifth of those Present, be entered on the Journal.

Neither House, during the Session of Congress, shall, without the Consent of the other, adjourn for more than three days, nor to any other place than that in which the two Houses shall be sitting.

Section 6. The Senators and Representatives shall receive a Compensation for their Services, to be ascertained by Law, and paid out of the Treasury of the United States. They shall in all Cases, except Treason, Felony and Breach of the Peace, be privileged from Arrest during their Attendance at the Session of their respective Houses, and in going to and returning from the same; and for any Speech or Debate in either House, they shall not be questioned in any other Place.

No Senator or Representative shall, during the Time for which he was elected, be appointed to any civil Office under the Authority of the United States, which shall have been created, or the Emoluments whereof shall have been encreased during such time; and no Person holding any Office under the United States, shall be a Member of either House during his Continuance in Office.

Section 7. All Bills for raising Revenue shall originate in the House of Representatives; but the Senate may propose or concur with Amendments as on other Bills.

Every Bill which shall have passed the House of Representatives and the Senate, shall, before it become a Law, be presented to the President of the United States; If he approve he shall sign it, but if not he shall return it, with his Objections to that House in which it shall have originated, who shall enter the Objections at large on their Journal, and proceed to reconsider it. If after such Reconsideration two thirds of that House shall agree to pass the Bill, it shall be sent, together with the Objections, to the other House, by which it shall likewise be reconsidered, and if approved by two thirds of that House, it shall become a Law. But in all such Cases the Votes of both Houses shall be determined by yeas and Nays, and the Names of the Persons voting for and against the Bill shall be entered on the Journal of each House respectively. If any Bill shall not be returned by the President within ten Days (Sundays excepted) after it shall have been presented to him, the Same shall be a Law, in like Manner as if he had signed it, unless the Congress by their Adjournment prevent its Return, in which Case it shall not be a Law.

Every Order, Resolution, or Vote to which the Concurrence of the Senate and House of Representatives may be necessary (except on a question of Adjournment) shall be presented to the President of the United States; and before the Same shall take Effect, shall be approved by him, or being disapproved by him, shall be repassed by two thirds of the Senate and House of Representatives, according to the Rules and Limitations prescribed in the Case of a Bill.

Section 8. The Congress shall have Power To lay and collect Taxes, Duties, Imposts and Excises, to pay the Debts and provide for the common Defence and general Welfare of the United States; but all duties, Imposts and Excises shall be uniform throughout the United States;

To borrow Money on the Credit of the United States;

To regulate Commerce with foreign Nations, and among the several States, and with the Indian Tribes;

To establish an uniform Rule of Naturalization, and uniform Laws on the subject of Bankruptcies throughout the United States;

To coin Money, regulate the Value thereof, and of foreign Coin, and fix the Standard of Weights and Measures;

To provide for the Punishment of counterfeiting the Securities and current Coin of the United States;

To establish Post Offices and post Roads;

To promote the Progress of Science and useful Arts, by securing for limited Times to Authors and Inventors exclusive Right to their respective Writings and Discoveries;

To constitute Tribunals inferior to the supreme Court;

To define and punish Piracies and Felonies committed on the high Seas, and Offences against the Law of Nations;

To declare War, grant Letters of Marque and Reprisal, and make rules concerning Captures on Land and Water;

To raise and support Armies, but no Appropriation of Money to that Use shall be for a longer Term than two Years;

To provide and maintain a Navy;

To make rules for the Government and Regulation of the land and naval Forces;

To provide for calling forth the Militia to execute the Laws of the Union, suppress Insurrections and repel Invasions;

To provide for organizing, arming, and disciplining, the Militia, and for governing such Part of them as may be employed in the Service of the United States, reserving to the States respectively, the Appointment of the Officers, and the Authority of training the Militia according to the discipline prescribed by Congress;

To exercise exclusive Legislation in all Cases whatsoever, over such District (not exceeding ten Miles square), as may, by Cession of particular States, and the Acceptance of Congress, become the Seat of the Government of the United States, and to exercise like Authority over all Places purchased by the Consent of the Legislature of the State in which the Same shall be for the Erection of Forts, Magazines, Arsenals, dock-Yards, and other needful Buildings;—And

To make all Laws which shall be necessary and proper for carrying into Execution the foregoing Powers, and all other Powers vested by this Constitution in the Government of the United States, or in any Department or Officer thereof.

Section 9. The Migration or Importation of such Persons as any of the States now existing shall think proper to admit, shall not be prohibited by the Congress prior to the Year one thousand eight hundred and eight, but a Tax or duty may be imposed on such Importation, not exceeding ten dollars for each Person.

The Privilege of the Writ of Habeas Corpus shall not be suspended, unless when in Cases of Rebellion or Invasion the public Safety may require it.

No Bill of Attainder or ex post facto Law shall be passed.

No Capitation, or other direct, Tax shall be laid, unless in Proportion to the Census or Enumeration herein before directed to be taken.

No Tax or Duty shall be laid on Articles exported from any State.

No Preference shall be given by any Regulation of Commerce or Revenue to the Ports of one State over those of another: nor shall Vessels bound to, or from, one State, be obliged to enter, clear, or pay Duties in another.

No money shall be drawn from the Treasury, but in Consequence of Appropriations made by Law; and a regular Statement and Account of the Receipts and Expenditures of all public Money shall be published from time to time.

No Title of Nobility shall be granted by the United States: And no Person holding any Office of Profit or Trust under them, shall, without the Consent of the Congress, accept of any present, Emolument, Office, or Title, of any kind whatever, from any King, Prince, or foreign State.

Section 10. No State shall enter into any Treaty, Alliance, or Confederation; grant Letters of Marque and Reprisal; coin Money; emit Bills of Credit; make any Thing but gold and silver Coin a Tender in Payment of Debts; pass any Bill of Attainder, ex post facto Law, or Law impairing the Obligation of Contracts, or grant any Title of Nobility.

No State shall, without the Consent of the Congress, lay any Imposts or Duties on Imports or Exports, except what may be absolutely necessary for executing it's inspection Laws: and the net Produce of all Duties and Imposts, laid by any State on Imports or Exports, shall be for the Use of the Treasury of the United States; and all such Laws shall be subject to the Revision and Controul of the Congress.

No State shall, without the Consent of Congress, lay any Duty of Tonnage, keep Troops, or Ships of War in time of Peace, enter into any Agreement or Compact with another State, or with a foreign Power, or engage in War, unless actually invaded, or in such imminent Danger as will not admit of delay.

Article II

Section 1. The executive Power shall be vested in a President of the United States of America. He shall hold his Office during the Term of four Years, and, together with the Vice President, chosen for the same Term, be elected, as follows

Each State shall appoint, in such Manner as the Legislature thereof may direct, a Number of Electors, equal to the whole Number of Senators and Representatives to which the State may be entitled in the Congress: but no Senator or Representative, or Person holding an Office of Trust or Profit under the United States, shall be appointed an Elector.

The Electors shall meet in their respective States, and vote by Ballot for two Persons, of whom one at least shall not be an Inhabitant of the same State with themselves. And they shall make a List of all the Persons voted for, and of the Number of Votes for each; which List they shall sign and certify, and transmit sealed to the Seat of the Government of the United States, directed to the President of the Senate. The President of the Senate shall, in the Presence of the Senate and House of Representatives, open all the Certificates, and the Votes shall then be counted. The Person having the greatest Number of Votes shall be the President, if such Number be a Majority of the whole Number of Electors appointed; and if there be more than one who have such Majority, and have an equal Number of Votes, then the House of Representatives shall immediately chuse by Ballot one of them for President: and if no Person have a Majority, then from the five highest on the List the said House shall in like Manner chuse the President. But in chusing the President, the Votes shall be taken by States, the Representation from each State having one Vote; A quorum for this Purpose shall consist of a Member or Members from two thirds of the States, and a Majority of all the States shall be necessary to a Choice. In every Case, after the Choice of the President, the Person having the greatest Number of Votes of the Electors shall be the Vice President. But if there should remain two or more who have equal Votes, the Senate shall chuse from them by Ballot the Vice President.

The Congress may determine the Time of chusing the Electors, and the Day on which they shall give their Votes; which Day shall be the same throughout the United States.

No Person except a natural born Citizen, or a Citizen of the United States, at the time of the Adoption of this Constitution, shall be eligible to the Office of President; neither shall any Person be eligible to that Office who shall not have attained to the Age of thirty five Years, and been fourteen Years a Resident within the United States.

In Case of the Removal of the President from Office, or of his Death, Resignation, or Inability to discharge the Powers and Duties of the said Office, the Same shall devolve on the Vice President, and the Congress may by Law provide for the Case of Removal, Death, Resignation or Inability, both of the President and Vice President, declaring what Officer shall then act as President, and such Officer shall act accordingly, until the Disability be removed, or a President shall be elected.

The President shall, at stated Times, receive for his Services, a Compensation, which shall neither be encreased nor diminished during the Period for which he shall have been elected, and he shall not receive within that Period any other Emolument from the United States, or any of them.

Before he enter on the Execution of his Office, he shall take the following Oath or Affirmation:—"I do solemnly swear (or affirm) that I will faithfully execute the Office of President of the United States, and will to the best of my Ability, preserve, protect and defend the Constitution of the United States."

Section 2. The President shall be Commander in Chief of the Army and Navy of the United States, and of the Militia of the several States, when called into the actual

Service of the United States; he may require the Opinion, in writing, of the principal Officer in each of the executive Departments, upon any Subject relating to the Duties of their respective Offices, and he shall have Power to grant Reprieves and Pardons for Offences against the United States, except in Cases of Impeachment.

He shall have Power, by and with the Advice and Consent of the Senate, to make Treaties, provided two thirds of the Senators present concur; and he shall nominate, and by and with the Advice and Consent of the Senate, shall appoint Ambassadors, other public Ministers and Consuls, Judges of the supreme Court, and all other Officers of the United States, whose Appointments are not herein otherwise provided for, and which shall be established by Law: but the Congress may by Law vest the Appointment of such inferior Officers, as they think proper, in the President alone, in the Courts of Law, or in the Heads of Departments.

The President shall have Power to fill up all Vacancies that may happen during the Recess of the Senate, by granting Commissions which shall expire at the End of their next Session.

Section 3. He shall from time to time give to the Congress Information of the State of the Union, and recommend to their Consideration such Measures as he shall judge necessary and expedient; he may, on extraordinary Occasions, convene both Houses, or either of them, and in Case of Disagreement between them, with Respect to the Time of Adjournment, he may adjourn them to such Time as he shall think proper; he shall receive Ambassadors and other public Ministers; he shall take Care that the Laws be faithfully executed, and shall Commission all the Officers of the United States.

Section 4. The President, Vice President and all civil Officers of the United States, shall be removed from Office on Impeachment for, and Conviction of, Treason, Bribery, or other High Crimes and Misdemeanors.

Article III

Section 1. The judicial Power of the United States, shall be vested in one supreme Court, and in such inferior Courts as the Congress may from time to time ordain and establish. The Judges, both of the supreme and inferior Courts, shall hold their Offices during good Behaviour, and shall, at stated Times, receive for their Services, a Compensation, which shall not be diminished during their Continuance in Office.

Section 2. The judicial Power shall extend to all Cases, in Law and Equity, arising under this Constitution, the Laws of the United States, and Treaties made, or which shall be made, under their Authority;—to all Cases affecting Ambassadors, other public Ministers and Consuls;—to all Cases of admiralty and maritime Jurisdiction;—to Controversies to which the United States shall be a Party;—to Controversies between two or more States; between a State and Citizens of another State;—between Citizens of different States;—between Citizens of the same State claiming Lands under Grants of different States, and between a State, or the Citizens thereof, and foreign States, Citizens or Subjects.

In all Cases affecting Ambassadors, other public Ministers and Consuls, and those in which a State shall be Party, the supreme Court shall have original Jurisdiction. In all the other Cases before mentioned, the supreme Court shall have appellate Jurisdiction, both as to Law and Fact, with such Exceptions, and under such Regulations as the Congress shall make.

The Trial of all Crimes, except in Cases of Impeachment, shall be by Jury; and such Trial shall be held in the State where the said Crimes shall have been committed; but when not committed within any State, the Trial shall be at such Place or Places as the Congress may by Law have directed.

Section 3. Treason against the United States, shall consist only in levying War against them, or in adhering to their Enemies, giving them Aid and Comfort. No Person shall be convicted of Treason unless on the Testimony of two Witnesses to the same overt Act, or on Confession in open Court.

The Congress shall have Power to declare the Punishment of Treason, but no Attainder of Treason shall work Corruption of Blood, or Forfeiture except during the Life of the Person attainted.

Article IV

Section 1. Full Faith and Credit shall be given in each State to the public Acts, Records, and judicial Proceedings of every other State. And the Congress may by general Laws prescribe the Manner in which such Acts, Records and Proceedings shall be proved, and the Effect thereof.

Section 2. The Citizens of each State shall be entitled to all Privileges and Immunities of Citizens in the several States.

A Person charged in any State with Treason, Felony, or other Crime, who shall flee from Justice, and be found in another State, shall on Demand of the executive Authority of the State from which he fled, be delivered up, to be removed to the State having Jurisdiction of the Crime.

No person held to Service or Labour in one State, under the Laws thereof, escaping into another, shall, in Consequence of any Law or Regulation therein, be discharged from such Service or Labour, but shall be delivered up on Claim of the Party to whom such Service or Labour may be due.

Section 3. New States may be admitted by the Congress into this Union; but no new State shall be formed or erected within the Jurisdiction of any other State; nor any State be formed by the Junction of two or more States, or Parts of States, without the Consent of the Legislatures of the States concerned as well as of the Congress.

The Congress shall have Power to dispose of and make all needful Rules and Regulations respecting the Territory or other Property belonging to the United States; and nothing in this Constitution shall be so construed as to Prejudice any Claims of the United States, or of any particular State.

Section 4. The United States shall guarantee to every State in this Union a Republican Form of Government, and shall protect each of them against Invasion; and on Application of the Legislature, or of the Executive (when the Legislature cannot be convened) against domestic Violence.

Article V

The Congress, whenever two thirds of both Houses shall deem it necessary, shall propose Amendments to this Constitution, or, on the Application of the Legislatures of two thirds of the several States, shall call a Convention for proposing Amendments, which, in either Case, shall be valid to all Intents and Purposes, as Part of this Constitution, when ratified by the Legislatures of three fourths of the several States, or by Conventions in three fourths thereof, as the one or the other Mode of Ratification may be proposed by the Congress; Provided that no Amendment which may be made prior to the Year One thousand eight hundred and eight shall in any Manner affect the first and fourth Clauses in the Ninth Section of the first Article; and that no State, without its Consent, shall be deprived of its equal Suffrage in the Senate.

Article VI

All Debts contracted and Engagements entered into, before the Adoption of this Constitution, shall be as valid against the United States under this Constitution, as under the Confederation.

This Constitution, and the Laws of the United States which shall be made in Pursuance thereof; and all Treaties made, or which shall be made, under the Authority of the United States, shall be the supreme Law of the Land; and the Judges in every State shall be bound thereby, any Thing in the Constitution or Laws of any State to the Contrary notwithstanding.

The Senators and Representatives before mentioned, and the Members of the several State Legislatures, and all executive and judicial Officers, both of the United States and of the several States, shall be bound by Oath or Affirmation, to support this Constitution; but no religious Test shall ever be required as a Qualification to any Office or public Trust under the United States.

Article VII

The Ratification of the Conventions of nine States, shall be sufficient for the Establishment of this Constitution between the States so ratifying the Same.

done in Convention by the Unanimous Consent of the States present the Seventeenth Day of September in the Year of our Lord one thousand seven hundred and Eighty seven and of the Independence of the United States of America the Twelfth *In witness whereof We have hereunto subscribed our Names,*

G^{o} Washington—Presid^{t}
and deputy from Virginia

New Hampshire	John Langdon Nicholas Gilman
Massachusetts	Nathaniel Gorham Rufus King
Connecticut	Wm Saml Johnson Roger Sherman
New York	Alexander Hamilton
New Jersey	Wil: Livingston David Brearley. Wm Paterson. Jona: Dayton
Pennsylvania[1]	B Franklin Thomas Mifflin Robt Morris Geo. Clymer Thos FitzSimons Jared Ingersoll

[1] Spelled with one "n" on the original document.

	James Wilson Gouv Morris
Delaware	Geo: Read Gunning Bedford jun John Dickinson Richard Bassett Jaco: Broom
Maryland	James McHenry Dan of St Thos Jenifer Danl Carroll
Virginia	John Blair— James Madison Jr.
North Carolina	Wm Blount Richd Dobbs Spaight. Hu Williamson
South Carolina	J. Rutledge Charles Cotesworth Pinckney Charles Pinckney Pierce Butler.
Georgia	William Few Abr Baldwin

Amendments

(*The first 10 Amendments were ratified December 15, 1791, and form what is known as the Bill of Rights*)

Amendment 1

Congress shall make no law respecting an establishment of religion, or prohibiting the free exercise thereof; or abridging the freedom of speech, or of the press; or the right of the people peaceably to assemble, and to petition the Government for a redress of grievances.

Amendment 2

A well regulated Militia, being necessary to the security of a free State, the right of the people to keep and bear Arms, shall not be infringed.

Amendment 3

No Soldier shall, in time of peace be quartered in any house, without the consent of the Owner, nor in time of war, but in a manner to be prescribed by law.

Amendment 4

The right of the people to be secure in their persons, houses, papers, and effects, against unreasonable searches and seizures, shall not be violated, and no Warrants shall issue, but upon probable cause, supported by Oath or affirmation, and particularly describing the place to be searched, and the persons or things to be seized.

Amendment 5

No person shall be held to answer for a capital, or otherwise infamous crime, unless on a presentment or indictment of a Grand Jury, except in cases arising in the land or naval forces, or in the Militia, when in actual service in time of War or public danger; nor shall any person be subject for the same offence to be twice put in jeopardy of life or limb; nor shall be compelled in any criminal case to be a witness against himself, nor be deprived of life, liberty, or property, without due process of law; nor shall private property be taken for public use, without just compensation.

Amendment 6

In all criminal prosecutions, the accused shall enjoy the right to a speedy and public trial, by an impartial jury of the State and district wherein the crime shall have been committed, which district shall have been previously ascertained by law, and to be informed of the nature and cause of the accusation; to be confronted with the witnesses against him; to have compulsory process for obtaining witnesses in his favor, and to have the Assistance of Counsel for his defence.

Amendment 7

In Suits at common law, where the value in controversy shall exceed twenty dollars, the right of trial by jury shall be preserved, and no fact tried by a jury, shall be otherwise re-examined in any Court of the United States, than according to the rules of the common law.

Amendment 8

Excessive bail shall not be required, nor excessive fines imposed, nor cruel and unusual punishments inflicted.

Amendment 9

The enumeration in the Constitution, of certain rights, shall not be construed to deny or disparage others retained by the people.

Amendment 10

The powers not delegated to the United States by the Constitution, nor prohibited by it to the States, are reserved to the States respectively, or to the people.

Amendment 11

(*Ratified February 7, 1795*)

The Judicial power of the United States shall not be construed to extend to any suit in law or equity, commenced or prosecuted against one of the United States by Citizens of another State, or by Citizens or Subjects of any Foreign State.

Amendment 12

(*Ratified July 27, 1804*)

The Electors shall meet in their respective states, and vote by ballot for President and Vice-President, one of whom, at least, shall not be an inhabitant of the same state with themselves; they shall name in their ballots the person voted for as President, and in distinct ballots the person voted for as Vice-President, and they shall make distinct lists of all persons voted for as President, and of all persons voted for as Vice-President, and of the number of votes for each, which lists they shall sign and certify, and transmit sealed to the seat of the government of the United States, directed to the President of the Senate;—The President of the Senate shall, in the presence of the Senate and House of Representatives, open all the certificates and the votes shall then be counted;—The person having the greatest number of votes for President, shall be the President, if such number be a majority of the whole number of Electors appointed; and if no person have such majority, then from the persons having the highest numbers not exceeding three on the list of those voted for as President, the House of Representatives shall choose immediately, by ballot, the President. But in choosing the President, the votes shall be taken by states, the representation from each state having one vote; a quorum for this purpose shall consist of a member or members from two-thirds of the states, and a majority of all the states shall be necessary to a choice. And if the House of Representatives shall not choose a President whenever the right of choice shall devolve upon them, before the fourth day of March next following, then the Vice-President shall act as President, as in the case of the death or other constitutional disability of the President.—The person having the greatest number of votes as Vice-President, shall be the Vice-President, if such number be a majority of the whole number of Electors appointed, and if no person have a majority, then from the two highest numbers on the list, the Senate shall choose the Vice-President; a quorum for the purpose shall consist of two-thirds of the whole number of Senators, and a majority of the whole number shall be necessary to a choice. But no person constitutionally ineligible to the office of President shall be eligible to that of Vice-President of the United States.

Amendment 13

(*Ratified December 6, 1865*)

Section 1. Neither slavery nor involuntary servitude, except as a punishment for crime whereof the party shall have been duly convicted, shall exist within the United States, or any place subject to their jurisdiction.

Section 2. Congress shall have power to enforce this article by appropriate legislation.

Amendment 14

(*Ratified July 9, 1868*)

Section 1. All persons born or naturalized in the United States, and subject to the jurisdiction thereof, are citizens of the United States and of the State wherein they reside. No State shall make or enforce any law which shall abridge the privileges or immunities of citizens of the United States; nor shall any State deprive any person of life, liberty, or property, without due process of law; nor deny to any person within its jurisdiction the equal protection of the laws.

Section 2. Representatives shall be apportioned among the several States according to their respective numbers, counting the whole number of persons in each State, excluding Indians not taxed. But when the right to vote at any election for the choice of electors for President and Vice President of the United States, Representatives in Congress, the Executive and Judicial officers of a State, or the members of the Legislature thereof, is denied to any of the male inhabitants of such State, being twenty-one years of age, and citizens of the United States, or in any way abridged, except for participation in rebellion, or other crime, the basis of representation therein shall be reduced in the proportion which the number of such male citizens shall bear to the whole number of male citizens twenty-one years of age in such State.

Section 3. No person shall be a Senator or Representative in Congress, or elector of President and Vice President, or hold any office, civil or military, under the United States, or under any State, who, having previously taken an oath, as a member of Congress, or as an officer of the United States, or as a member of any State legislature, or as an executive or judicial officer of any State, to support the Constitution of the United States, shall have engaged in insurrection or rebellion against the same, or given aid or comfort to the enemies thereof. But Congress may by a vote of two-thirds of each House, remove such disability.

Section 4. The validity of the public debt of the United States, authorized by law, including debts incurred for payment of pensions and bounties for services in suppressing insurrection or rebellion, shall not be questioned. But neither the United States nor any State shall assume or pay any debt or obligation incurred in aid of insurrection or rebellion against the United States, or any claim for the loss or emancipation of any slave; but all such debts, obligations and claims shall be held illegal and void.

Section 5. The Congress shall have power to enforce, by appropriate legislation, the provisions of this article.

Amendment 15

(*Ratified February 3, 1870*)

Section 1. The right of citizens of the United States to vote shall not be denied or abridged by the United States or by any State on account of race, color, or previous condition of servitude.

Section 2. The Congress shall have power to enforce this article by appropriate legislation.

Amendment 16

(*Ratified February 3, 1913*)

The Congress shall have power to lay and collect taxes on incomes, from whatever source derived, without apportionment among the several States, and without regard to any census or enumeration.

Amendment 17

(*Ratified April 8, 1913*)

The Senate of the United States shall be composed of two Senators from each State, elected by the people thereof for six years; and each Senator shall have one vote. The electors in each State shall have the qualifications requisite for electors of the most numerous branch of the State legislatures.

When vacancies happen in the representation of any State in the Senate, the executive authority of such State shall issue writs of election to fill such vacancies: *Provided,* That the legislature of any State may empower the executive thereof to make temporary appointments until the people fill the vacancies by election as the legislature may direct.

This amendment shall not be so construed as to affect the election or term of any Senator chosen before it becomes valid as part of the Constitution.

Amendment 18

(*Ratified January 16, 1919. Repealed December 5, 1933 by Amendment 21*)

Section 1. After one year from the ratification of this article the manufacture, sale, or transportation of intoxicating liquors within, the importation thereof into, or the exportation thereof from the United States and all territory subject to the jurisdiction thereof for beverage purposes is hereby prohibited.

Section 2. The Congress and the several States shall have concurrent power to enforce this article by appropriate legislation.

Section 3. This article shall be inoperative unless it shall have been ratified as an amendment to the Constitution by the legislatures of the several States as provided in the Constitution, within seven years from the date of the submission hereof to the States by the Congress.

Amendment 19

(*Ratified August 18, 1920*)

The right of citizens of the United States to vote shall not be denied or abridged by the United States or by any State on account of sex.

Congress shall have power to enforce this article by appropriate legislation.

Amendment 20

(*Ratified January 23, 1933*)

Section 1. The terms of the President and Vice President shall end at noon on the 20th day of January, and the terms of Senators and Representatives at noon on the 3d day of January, of the years in which such terms would have ended if this article had not been ratified; and the terms of their successors shall then begin.

Section 2. The Congress shall assemble at least once in every year, and such meeting shall begin at noon on the 3d day of January, unless they shall by law appoint a different day.

Section 3. If, at the time fixed for the beginning of the term of the President, the President elect shall have died, the Vice President elect shall become President. If a President shall not have been chosen before the time fixed for the beginning of his term, or if the President elect shall have failed to qualify, then the Vice President elect shall act as President until a President shall have qualified; and the Congress may by law provide for the case wherein neither a President elect nor a Vice President elect shall have qualified, declaring who shall then act as President, or the manner in which one who is to act shall be selected, and such person shall act accordingly until a President or Vice President shall have qualified.

Section 4. The Congress may by law provide for the case of the death of any of the persons from whom the House of Representatives may choose a President whenever the right of choice shall have devolved upon them, and for the case of the death of any of the persons from whom the Senate may choose a Vice President whenever the right of choice shall have devolved upon them.

Section 5. Sections 1 and 2 shall take effect on the 15th day of October following the ratification of this article.

Section 6. This article shall be inoperative unless it shall have been ratified as an amendment to the Constitution by the legislatures of three-fourths of the several States within seven years from the date of its submission.

Amendment 21

(*Ratified December 5, 1933*)

Section 1. The eighteenth article of amendment to the Constitution of the United States is hereby repealed.

Section 2. The transportation or importation into any State, Territory, or possession of the United States for delivery or use therein of intoxicating liquors, in violation of the laws thereof, is hereby prohibited.

Section 3. This article shall be inoperative unless it shall have been ratified as an amendment to the Constitution by conventions in the several States, as provided in the Constitution, within seven years from the date of the submission hereof to the States by the Congress.

Amendment 22

(*Ratified February 27, 1951*)

Section 1. No person shall be elected to the office of the President more than twice, and no person who has held the office of President, or acted as President, for more than two years of a term to which some other person was elected President shall be elected to the office of the President more than once. But this Article shall not apply to any person holding the office of President when this Article was proposed by the Congress, and shall not prevent any person who may be holding the office of President, or acting as President, during the term within which this Article becomes operative from holding the office of President or acting as President during the remainder of such term.

Section 2. This article shall be inoperative unless it shall have been ratified as an amendment to the Constitution by the legislatures of three-fourths of the several States within seven years from the date of its submission to the States by the Congress.

Amendment 23

(*Ratified March 29, 1961*)

Section 1. The District constituting the seat of Government of the United States shall appoint in such manner as the Congress may direct:

A number of electors of President and Vice President equal to the whole number of Senators and Representatives in Congress to which the District would be entitled if it were a State, but in no event more than the least populous State; they shall be in addition to those appointed by the States, but they shall be considered, for the purposes of the election of President and Vice President, to be electors appointed by a State; and they shall meet in the District and perform such duties as provided by the twelfth article of amendment.

Section 2. The Congress shall have power to enforce this article by appropriate legislation.

Amendment 24

(*Ratified January 23, 1964*)

Section 1. The right of citizens of the United States to vote in any primary or other election for President or Vice President, for electors for President or Vice President, or for Senator or Representative in Congress, shall not be denied or abridged by the United States or any State by reason of failure to pay any poll tax or other tax.

Section 2. The Congress shall have power to enforce this article by appropriate legislation.

Amendment 25

(*Ratified February 10, 1967*)

Section 1. In case of the removal of the President from office or of his death or resignation, the Vice President shall become President.

Section 2. Whenever there is a vacancy in the office of the Vice President, the President shall nominate a Vice President who shall take office upon confirmation by a majority vote of both Houses of Congress.

Section 3. Whenever the President transmits to the President pro tempore of the Senate and the Speaker of the House of Representatives his written declaration that he is unable to discharge the powers and duties of his office, and until he transmits to them a written declaration to the contrary, such powers and duties shall be discharged by the Vice President as Acting President.

Section 4. Whenever the Vice President and a majority of either the principal officers of the executive departments or of such other body as Congress may by law provide, transmit to the President pro tempore of the Senate and the Speaker of the House of Representatives their written declaration that the President is unable to discharge the powers and duties of his office, the Vice President shall immediately assume the powers and duties of the office as Acting President.

Thereafter, when the President transmits to the President pro tempore of the Senate and the Speaker of the House of Representatives his written declaration that no inability exists, he shall resume the powers and duties of his office unless the Vice President and a majority of either the principal officers of the executive department or of such other body as Congress may by law provide, transmit within four days to the President pro tempore of the Senate and the Speaker of the House of Representatives their written declaration that the President is unable to discharge the powers and duties of his office. Thereupon Congress shall decide the issue, assembling within forty-eight hours for that purpose if not in session. If the Congress, within twenty-one days after receipt of the latter written declaration, or, if Congress is not in session, within twenty-one days after Congress is required to assemble, determines by two-thirds vote of both Houses that the President is unable to discharge the powers and duties of his office, the Vice President shall continue to discharge the same as Acting President; otherwise, the President shall resume the powers and duties of his office.

Amendment 26

(*Ratified July 1, 1971*)

Section 1. The right of citizens of the United States, who are eighteen years of age or older, to vote shall not be denied or abridged by the United States or by any State on account of age.

Section 2. The Congress shall have the power to enforce this article by appropriate legislation.

Amendment 27

(*Ratified May 7, 1992*)

No law, varying the compensation for the services of the Senators and Representatives, shall take effect, until an election of Representatives shall have intervened.

THE GOVERNMENT OF THE UNITED STATES

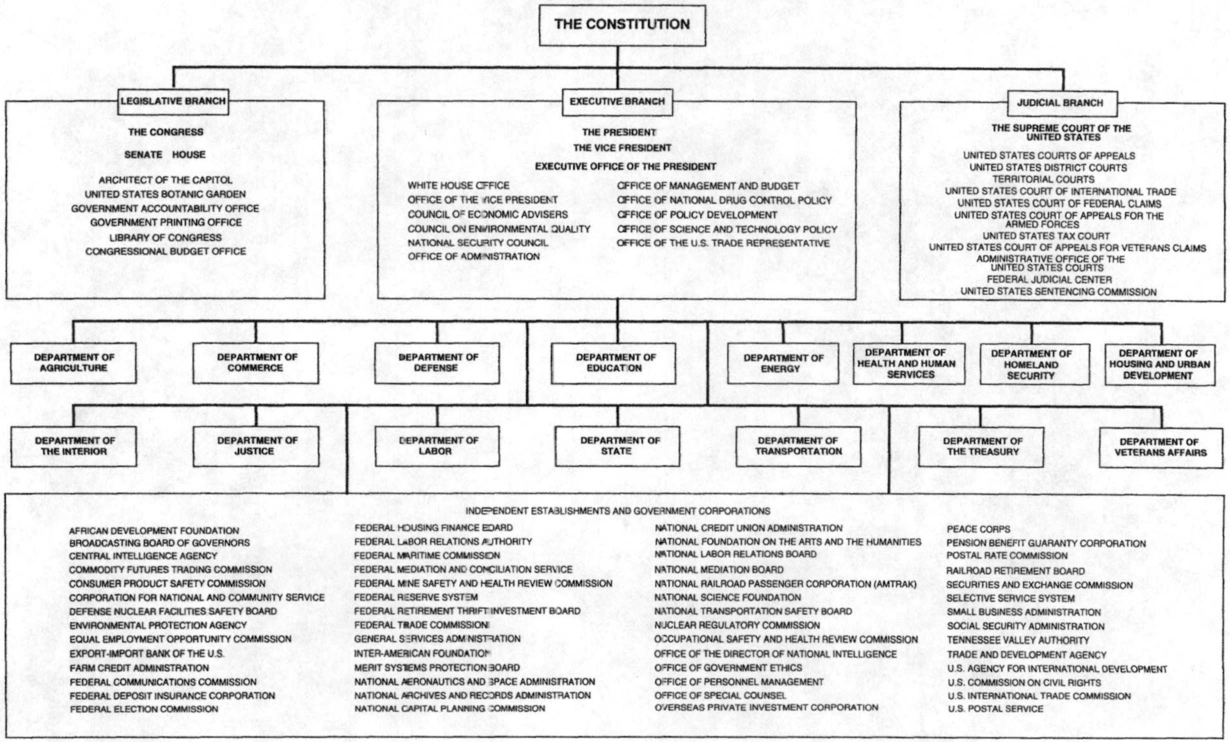

Legislative Branch

LEGISLATIVE BRANCH

CONGRESS

One Hundred and Ninth Congress, Second Session

The Senate

The Capitol, Washington, DC 20510
Phone, 202–224–3121. Internet, www.senate.gov.

President of the Senate (Vice President of the United States)	DICK CHENEY
President pro tempore	TED STEVENS
Majority Leader	BILL FRIST
Minority Leader	HARRY REID
Secretary of the Senate	EMILY REYNOLDS
Sergeant at Arms	BILL PICKLE
Secretary for the Majority	DAVID J. SCHIAPPA
Secretary for the Minority	MARTIN PAONE
Chaplain	BARRY BLACK

The House of Representatives

The Capitol, Washington, DC 20515
Phone, 202–225–3121. Internet, www.house.gov.

The Speaker	J. DENNIS HASTERT
Clerk	KAREN L. HAAS
Sergeant at Arms	WILSON L. LIVINGOOD
Chief Administrative Officer	JAMES M. EAGEN III
Chaplain	REV. DANIEL P. COUGHLIN

The Congress of the United States was created by Article I, section 1, of the Constitution, adopted by the Constitutional Convention on September 17, 1787, providing that "All legislative Powers herein granted shall be vested in a Congress of the United States, which shall consist of a Senate and House of Representatives."

The first Congress under the Constitution met on March 4, 1789, in the Federal Hall in New York City. The membership then consisted of 20[1] Senators and 59 Representatives.

[1]New York ratified the Constitution on July 26, 1788, but did not elect its Senators until July 15 and 16, 1789. North Carolina did not ratify the Constitution until November 21, 1789; Rhode Island ratified it on May 29, 1790.

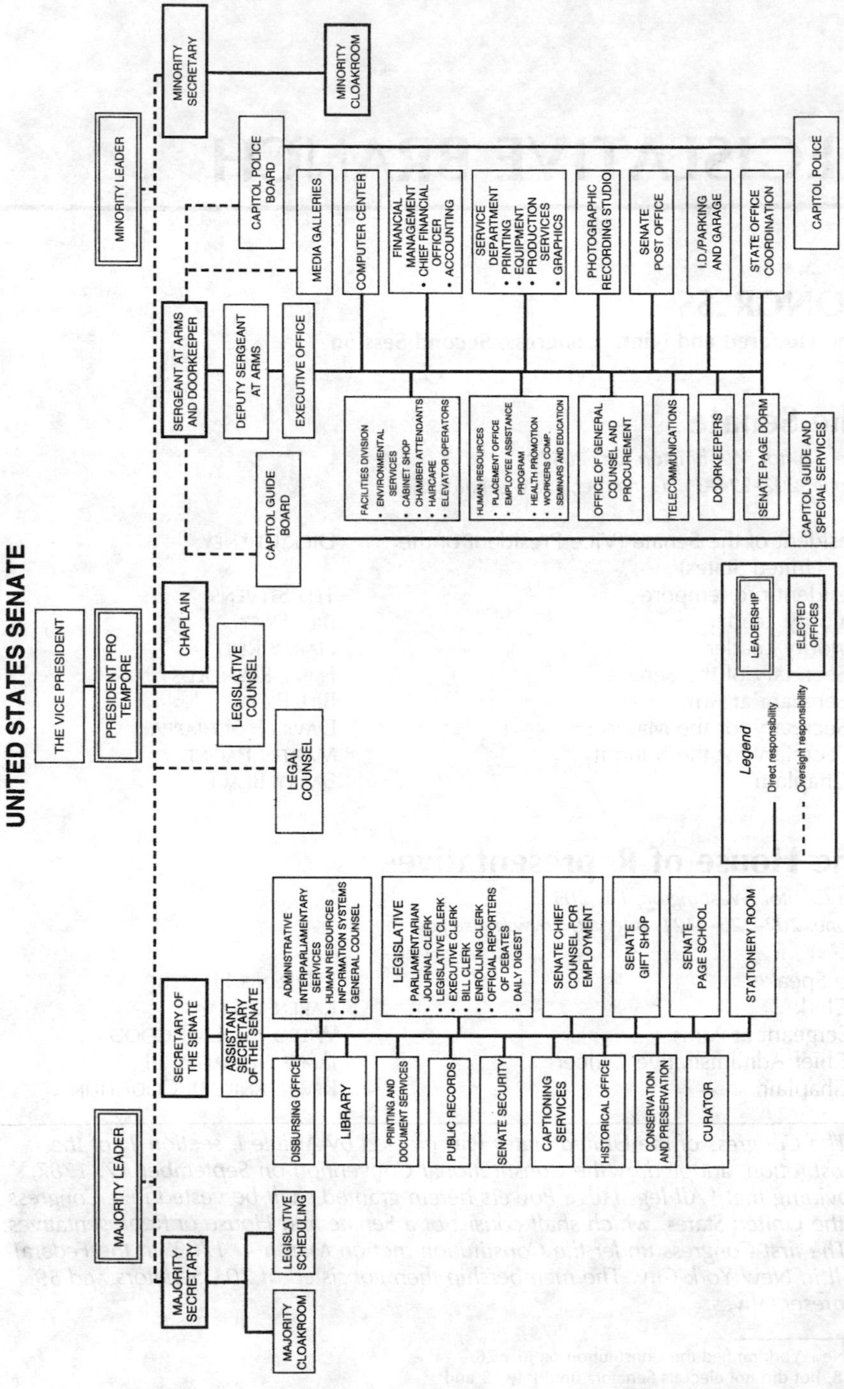
UNITED STATES SENATE
THE VICE PRESIDENT
PRESIDENT PRO TEMPORE
MAJORITY LEADER
MINORITY LEADER
MAJORITY SECRETARY
MAJORITY CLOAKROOM
LEGISLATIVE SCHEDULING
SECRETARY OF THE SENATE
ASSISTANT SECRETARY OF THE SENATE
ADMINISTRATIVE
• INTERPARLIAMENTARY SERVICES
• HUMAN RESOURCES
• INFORMATION SYSTEMS
• GENERAL COUNSEL
LEGISLATIVE
• PARLIAMENTARIAN
• JOURNAL CLERK
• LEGISLATIVE CLERK
• EXECUTIVE CLERK
• BILL CLERK
• ENROLLING CLERK
• OFFICIAL REPORTERS OF DEBATES
• DAILY DIGEST
SENATE CHIEF COUNSEL FOR EMPLOYMENT
SENATE GIFT SHOP
SENATE PAGE SCHOOL
STATIONERY ROOM
DISBURSING OFFICE
LIBRARY
PRINTING AND DOCUMENT SERVICES
PUBLIC RECORDS
SENATE SECURITY
CAPTIONING SERVICES
HISTORICAL OFFICE
CONSERVATION AND PRESERVATION
CURATOR
CHAPLAIN
LEGISLATIVE COUNSEL
LEGAL COUNSEL
SERGEANT AT ARMS AND DOORKEEPER
DEPUTY SERGEANT AT ARMS
EXECUTIVE OFFICE
CAPITOL GUIDE BOARD
CAPITOL POLICE BOARD
FACILITIES DIVISION
• ENVIRONMENTAL SERVICES
• CABINET SHOP
• CHAMBER ATTENDANTS
• HAIRCARE
• ELEVATOR OPERATORS
HUMAN RESOURCES
• PLACEMENT OFFICE
• EMPLOYEE ASSISTANCE PROGRAM
• HEALTH PROMOTION
• WORKERS COMP.
• SEMINARS AND EDUCATION
OFFICE OF GENERAL COUNSEL AND PROCUREMENT
TELECOMMUNICATIONS
DOORKEEPERS
SENATE PAGE DORM
CAPITOL GUIDE AND SPECIAL SERVICES
MEDIA GALLERIES
COMPUTER CENTER
FINANCIAL MANAGEMENT
• CHIEF FINANCIAL OFFICER
• ACCOUNTING
SERVICE DEPARTMENT
• PRINTING
• EQUIPMENT
• PRODUCTION SERVICES
• GRAPHICS
PHOTOGRAPHIC RECORDING STUDIO
SENATE POST OFFICE
I.D./PARKING AND GARAGE
STATE OFFICE COORDINATION
CAPITOL POLICE
MINORITY SECRETARY
MINORITY CLOAKROOM
Legend
Direct responsibility
Oversight responsibility
LEADERSHIP
ELECTED OFFICES

HOUSE OF REPRESENTATIVES

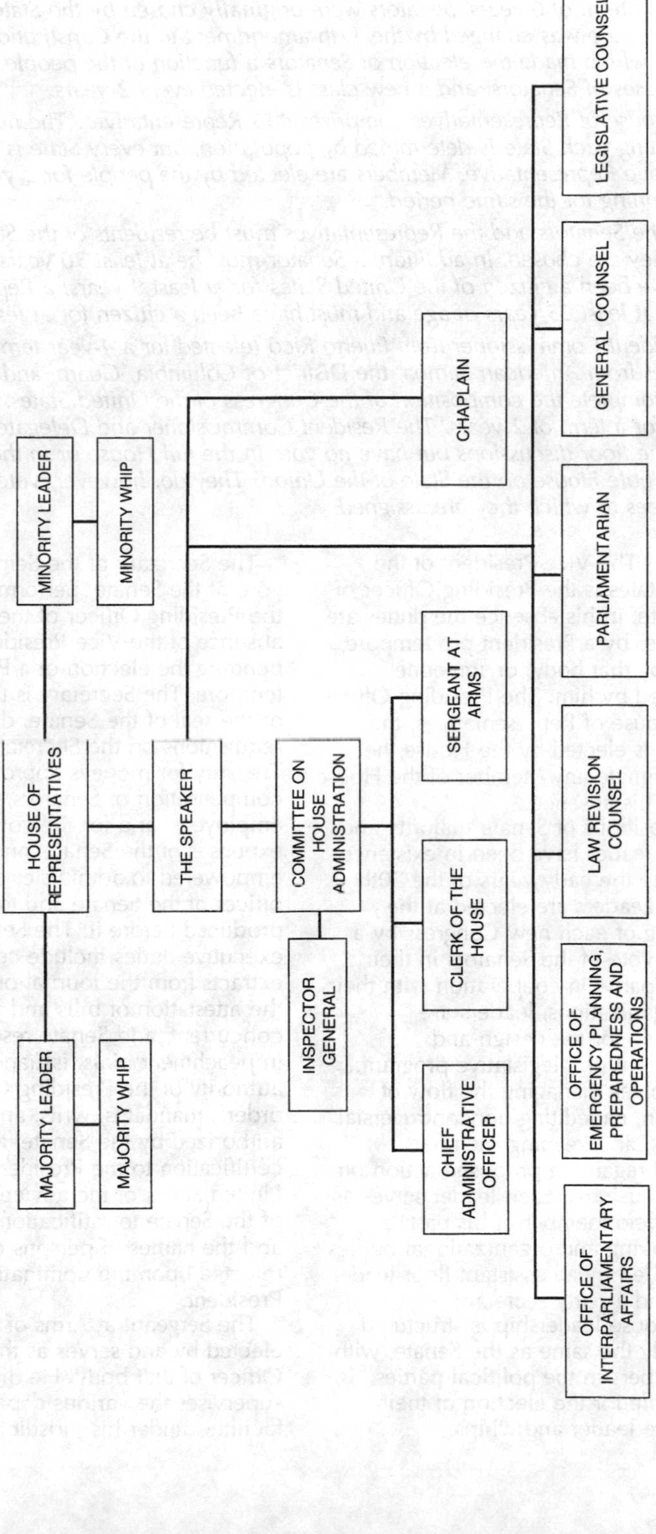

The Senate is composed of 100 Members, 2 from each State, who are elected to serve for a term of 6 years. Senators were originally chosen by the State legislatures. This procedure was changed by the 17th amendment to the Constitution, adopted in 1913, which made the election of Senators a function of the people. There are three classes of Senators, and a new class is elected every 2 years.

The House of Representatives comprises 435 Representatives. The number representing each State is determined by population, but every State is entitled to at least one Representative. Members are elected by the people for 2-year terms, all terms running for the same period.

Both the Senators and the Representatives must be residents of the State from which they are chosen. In addition, a Senator must be at least 30 years of age and must have been a citizen of the United States for at least 9 years; a Representative must be at least 25 years of age and must have been a citizen for at least 7 years.

A Resident Commissioner from Puerto Rico (elected for a 4-year term) and Delegates from American Samoa, the District of Columbia, Guam, and the Virgin Islands complete the composition of the Congress of the United States. Delegates are elected for a term of 2 years. The Resident Commissioner and Delegates may take part in the floor discussions but have no vote in the full House or in the Committee of the Whole House on the State of the Union. They do, however, vote in the committees to which they are assigned.

Officers The Vice President of the United States is the Presiding Officer of the Senate; in his absence the duties are taken over by a President pro tempore, elected by that body, or someone designated by him. The Presiding Officer of the House of Representatives, the Speaker, is elected by the House; he may designate any Member of the House to act in his absence.

The positions of Senate majority and minority leader have been in existence only since the early years of the 20th century. Leaders are elected at the beginning of each new Congress by a majority vote of the Senators in their political party. In cooperation with their party organizations, leaders are responsible for the design and achievement of a legislative program. This involves managing the flow of legislation, expediting noncontroversial measures, and keeping Members informed regarding proposed action on pending business. Each leader serves as an *ex officio* member of his party's policymaking and organizational bodies and is aided by an assistant floor leader (whip) and a party secretary.

The House leadership is structured essentially the same as the Senate, with the Members in the political parties responsible for the election of their respective leader and whips.

The Secretary of the Senate, elected by vote of the Senate, performs the duties of the Presiding Officer of the Senate in the absence of the Vice President and pending the election of a President pro tempore. The Secretary is the custodian of the seal of the Senate, draws requisitions on the Secretary of the Treasury for moneys appropriated for the compensation of Senators, officers, and employees, and for the contingent expenses of the Senate, and is empowered to administer oaths to any officer of the Senate and to any witness produced before it. The Secretary's executive duties include certification of extracts from the Journal of the Senate; the attestation of bills and joint, concurrent, and Senate resolutions; in impeachment trials, issuance, under the authority of the Presiding Officer, of all orders, mandates, writs, and precepts authorized by the Senate; and certification to the President of the United States of the advice and consent of the Senate to ratification of treaties and the names of persons confirmed or rejected upon the nomination of the President.

The Sergeant at Arms of the Senate is elected by and serves as the Executive Officer of that body. He directs and supervises the various departments and facilities under his jurisdiction. He is also the Law Enforcement and Protocol Officer. As Law Enforcement Officer, he has statutory power to make arrests; to locate absentee Senators for a quorum; to enforce Senate rules and regulations as they pertain to the Senate Chamber, the Senate wing of the Capitol, and the Senate Office Buildings. He serves as a member of the Capitol Police Board and as its chairman each odd year; and, subject to the Presiding Officer, maintains order in the Senate Chamber. As Protocol Officer, he is responsible for many aspects of ceremonial functions, including the inauguration of the President of the United States; arranging funerals of Senators who die in office; escorting the President when he addresses a Joint Session of Congress or attends any function in the Senate; and escorting heads of state when they visit the Senate.

The elected officers of the House of Representatives include the Clerk, the Sergeant at Arms, the Chief Administrative Officer, and the Chaplain.

The Clerk is custodian of the seal of the House and administers the primary legislative activities of the House. These duties include accepting the credentials of the Members-elect and calling the Members to order at the commencement of the first session of each Congress; keeping the Journal; taking all votes and certifying the passage of bills; and processing all legislation. Through various departments, the Clerk is also responsible for floor and committee reporting services; legislative information and reference services; the administration of House reports pursuant to House rules and certain legislation including the Ethics in Government Act and the Lobbying Disclosure Act of 1995; the distribution of House documents; and administration of the House Page Program. The Clerk is also charged with supervision of the offices vacated by Members due to death, resignation, or expulsion.

The Sergeant at Arms maintains the order of the House under the direction of the Speaker and is the keeper of the Mace. As a member of the U.S. Capitol Police Board, the Sergeant at Arms is the chief law enforcement officer for the House and serves as Board Chairman each even year. The ceremonial and protocol duties parallel those of the Senate Sergeant at Arms and include arranging the inauguration of the President of the United States, Joint Sessions of Congress, visits to the House of heads of state, and funerals of Members of Congress. The Sergeant at Arms enforces the rules relating to the privileges of the Hall of the House, including admission to the galleries, oversees garage and parking security of the House, and distributes all House staff identification cards.

Committees The work of preparing and considering legislation is done largely by committees of both Houses of Congress. There are 16 standing committees in the Senate and 19 in the House of Representatives. The standing committees of the Senate and the House of Representatives are shown in the list below. In addition, there are two select committees in each House and various congressional commissions and joint committees composed of Members of both Houses. Each House may also appoint special investigating committees. The membership of the standing committees of each House is chosen by a vote of the entire body; members of other committees are appointed under the provisions of the measure establishing them.

Each bill and resolution is usually referred to the appropriate committee, which may report a bill out in its original form, favorably or unfavorably, recommend amendments, report original measures, or allow the proposed legislation to die in committee without action.

Standing Committees of the Congress

House Committee	Room[1]	Senate Committee	Room[2]
Agriculture	1301	Agriculture, Nutrition, and Forestry	SR–328A
Appropriations	H218	Appropriations	S–128
Armed Services	2120	Armed Services	SR–228

Standing Committees of the Congress—Continued

House Committee	Room [1]	Senate Committee	Room [2]
Budget	309	Banking, Housing, and Urban Affairs	SD–534
Education and the Workforce	2181	Budget	SD–624
Energy and Commerce	2125	Commerce, Science, and Transportation	SD–508
Financial Services	2129	Energy and Natural Resources	SD–364
Government Reform	2157	Environment and Public Works	SD–410
Homeland Security	H2–176		
House Administration	1309		
Franking Commission:			
Majority	1309		
Minority	1216		
International Relations	2170	Finance	SD–219
Judiciary	2138	Foreign Relations	SD–450
Publications	B29		
Resources	1324	Homeland Security and Governmental Affairs	SD–340
Rules	H312	Health, Education, Labor, and Pensions	SD–428
Minority	234		
Science	2320		
Small Business	2361		
Standards of Official Conduct	HT2	Judiciary	SD–224
Office of Advice and Education	HT2		
Transportation and Infrastructure	2165	Rules and Administration	SR–305
Veterans' Affairs	335	Small Business and Entrepreneurship	SR–428A
Ways and Means	1102	Veterans' Affairs	SR–412

[1] Room numbers with three digits are in the Cannon House Office Building, four digits beginning with 1 are in the Longworth House Office Building, and four digits beginning with 2 are in the Rayburn House Office Building. Room numbers preceded by H or HT are in the House wing of the Capitol Building. Rooms preceded by an LA are in the John Adams Building of the Library of Congress.

[2] Room numbers preceded by S are in the Senate wing of the Capitol Building; those preceded by SD are in the Dirksen Office Building; those preceded by SR are in the Russell Office Building; and those preceded by SH are in the Hart Office Building.

Congressional Record Proceedings of Congress are published in the *Congressional Record,* which is issued each day when Congress is in session. Publication of the *Record* began March 4, 1873. It was the first record of debate officially reported, printed, and published directly by the Federal Government. The Daily Digest of the *Congressional Record,* printed in the back of each issue of the *Record,* summarizes the proceedings of that day in each House, and each of their committees and subcommittees, respectively. The Digest also presents the legislative program for each day and, at the end of the week, gives the program for the following week. Its publication was begun March 17, 1947.

Sessions Section 4 of Article I of the Constitution makes it mandatory that "The Congress shall assemble at least once in every Year. . . ." Under this provision, also, the date for convening Congress was designated originally as the first Monday in December, "unless they shall by Law appoint a different Day." Eighteen acts were passed, up to 1820, providing for the meeting of Congress on other days of the year. From 1820 to 1934, however, Congress met regularly on the first Monday in December. In 1934 the Twentieth Amendment changed the convening of Congress to January 3, unless Congress "shall by law appoint a different day." In addition, the President, according to Article II, section 3, of the Constitution "may, on extraordinary Occasions, convene both Houses, or either of them, and in Case of Disagreement between them, with Respect to the Time of Adjournment, he may adjourn them to such Time as he shall think proper. . . ."

Powers of Congress Article I, section 8, of the Constitution defines the powers of Congress. Included are the powers to assess and collect taxes—called the chief power; to regulate commerce, both interstate and foreign; to coin money; to establish post offices and post roads; to establish courts inferior to the Supreme Court; to declare war; and to raise and maintain an army and navy. Congress is further empowered "To provide for calling forth the Militia to execute the Laws of the Union, suppress Insurrections and repel Invasions;" and "To make all Laws which shall be necessary and proper for carrying into Execution the foregoing Powers, and all other Powers vested by this Constitution in the Government of the United States, or in any Department or Officer thereof."

Amendments to the Constitution Another power vested in the Congress is the right to propose amendments to the Constitution, whenever two-thirds of both Houses shall deem it necessary. Should two-thirds of the State legislatures demand changes in the Constitution, it is the duty of Congress to call a constitutional convention. Proposed amendments shall be valid as part of the Constitution when ratified by the legislatures or by conventions of three-fourths of the States, as one or the other mode of ratification may be proposed by Congress.

Special Powers of the Senate Under the Constitution, the Senate is granted certain powers not accorded to the House of Representatives. The Senate approves or disapproves certain Presidential appointments by majority vote, and treaties must be concurred in by a two-thirds vote.

Special Powers of the House of Representatives The House of Representatives is granted the power of originating all bills for the raising of revenue. Both Houses of Congress act in impeachment proceedings, which, according to the Constitution, may be instituted against the President, Vice President, and all civil officers of the United States. The House of Representatives has the sole power of impeachment, and the Senate has the sole power to try impeachments.

Prohibitions Upon Congress Section 9 of Article I of the Constitution also imposes prohibitions upon Congress. "The Privilege of the Writ of Habeas Corpus shall not be suspended, unless when in Cases of Rebellion or Invasion the public Safety may require it." A bill of attainder or an ex post facto law cannot be passed. No export duty can be imposed. Ports of one State cannot be given preference over those of another State. "No money shall be drawn from the Treasury, but in Consequence of Appropriations made by Law. . . ." No title of nobility may be granted.

Rights of Members According to section 6 of Article I, Members of Congress are granted certain privileges. In no case, except in treason, felony, and breach of the peace, can Members be arrested while attending sessions of Congress "and in going to and returning from the same. . . ." Furthermore, the Members cannot be questioned in any other place for remarks made in Congress. Each House may expel a Member of its body by a two-thirds vote.

Enactment of Laws All bills and joint resolutions must pass both the House of Representatives and the Senate and must be signed by the President, except those proposing a constitutional amendment, in order to become law, or be passed over the President's veto by a two-thirds vote of both Houses of Congress. Section 7 of Article I states: "If any Bill shall not be returned by the President within ten Days (Sundays excepted) after it shall have been presented to him, the Same shall be a Law, in like Manner as if he had signed it, unless the Congress by their Adjournment prevent its Return, in which Case it shall not be a Law."

When a bill or joint resolution is introduced in the House, the usual procedure for its enactment into law is as follows:

—assignment to House committee having jurisdiction;

—if favorably considered, it is reported to the House either in its original form or with recommended amendments;

—if the bill or resolution is passed by the House, it is messaged to the Senate and referred to the committee having jurisdiction;

—in the Senate committee the bill, if favorably considered, may be reported in the form as received from the House, or with recommended amendments;

—the approved bill or resolution is reported to the Senate, and if passed by that body, is returned to the House;

—if one body does not accept the amendments to a bill by the other body, a conference committee comprised of Members of both bodies is usually appointed to effect a compromise;

—when the bill or joint resolution is finally approved by both Houses, it is signed by the Speaker (or Speaker pro tempore) and the Vice President (or President pro tempore or acting President pro tempore) and is presented to the President; and

—once the President's signature is affixed, the measure becomes a law. If the President vetoes the bill, it cannot become a law unless it is re-passed by a two-thirds vote of both Houses.

Electronic Access Specific information and legislation can be found on the Internet at http://thomas.loc.gov, http://clerk.house.gov, or www.senate.gov.

Publications The *Congressional Directory,* the *Senate Manual,* telephone directories for the U.S. Senate and the House of Representatives, and the *House Rules and Manual* may be obtained from the Superintendent of Documents, Government Printing Office, Washington, DC 20402. Internet, www.gpoaccess.gov/databases.html.

Senators

[Republicans in roman (55); Democrats in italic (44); Independents in bold (1); total, 100]

Room numbers preceded by SR are in the Russell Office Building (Delaware and Constitution Avenues); those preceded by SD are in the Dirksen Office Building (First Street and Constitution Avenue); and those preceded by SH are in the Hart Office Building (Second and C Streets). Members' offices may be reached by phone at 202–224–3121.

Name	State	Room
Akaka, Daniel K	Hawaii	SH141
Alexander, Lamar	Tennessee	SH302
Allard, Wayne	Colorado	SD521
Allen, George	Virginia	SR204
Baucus, Max	Montana	SH511
Bayh, Evan	Indiana	SR463
Bennett, Robert F	Utah	SD431
Biden, Joseph R., Jr	Delaware	SR201
Bingaman, Jeff	New Mexico	SH703
Bond, Christopher S	Missouri	SR274
Boxer, Barbara	California	SH112
Brownback, Sam	Kansas	SH303
Bunning, Jim	Kentucky	SH316
Burns, Conrad R	Montana	SD187
Burr, Richard	North Carolina	SR217
Byrd, Robert C	West Virginia	SH311
Cantwell, Maria	Washington	SH717
Carper, Thomas R	Delaware	SH513
Chafee, Lincoln D	Rhode Island	SR141A
Chambliss, Saxby	Georgia	SR416
Clinton, Hillary Rodham	New York	SR476
Coburn, Tom	Oklahoma	SR172
Cochran, Thad	Mississippi	SD113
Coleman, Norm	Minnesota	SH320
Collins, Susan M	Maine	SD461
Conrad, Kent	North Dakota	SH530
Cornyn, John	Texas	SH517
Craig, Larry E	Idaho	SH520
Crapo, Mike	Idaho	SD239
Dayton, Mark	Minnesota	SR123
DeMint, Jim	South Carolina	SR340
DeWine, Mike	Ohio	SR140
Dodd, Christopher J	Connecticut	SR448
Dole, Elizabeth H	North Carolina	SD555
Domenici, Pete V	New Mexico	SH328
Dorgan, Byron L	North Dakota	SH322
Durbin, Richard J	Illinois	SD332
Ensign, John	Nevada	SR356

Senators—Continued

[Republicans in roman (55); Democrats in italic (44); Independents in bold (1); total, 100]

Room numbers preceded by SR are in the Russell Office Building (Delaware and Constitution Avenues); those preceded by SD are in the Dirksen Office Building (First Street and Constitution Avenue); and those preceded by SH are in the Hart Office Building (Second and C Streets). Members' offices may be reached by phone at 202–224–3121.

Name	State	Room
Enzi, Mike	Wyoming	SR379A
Feingold, Russell D	Wisconsin	SH506
Feinstein, Dianne	California	SH331
Frist, Bill	Tennessee	SH509
Graham, Lindsey O	South Carolina	SR290
Grassley, Charles E	Iowa	SH135
Gregg, Judd	New Hampshire	SR393
Hagel, Chuck	Nebraska	SR248
Harkin, Tom	Iowa	SH731
Hatch, Orrin G	Utah	SH104
Hutchison, Kay Bailey	Texas	SR284
Inhofe, James M	Oklahoma	SR453
Inouye, Daniel K	Hawaii	SH722
Isakson, Johnny	Georgia	SR120
Jeffords, James M	Vermont	SD413
Johnson, Tim	South Dakota	SH136
Kennedy, Edward M	Massachusetts	SR317
Kerry, John F	Massachusetts	SR304
Kohl, Herb	Wisconsin	SH330
Kyl, Jon	Arizona	SH730
Landrieu, Mary L	Louisiana	SH724
Lautenberg, Frank	New Jersey	SH324
Leahy, Patrick J	Vermont	SR433
Levin, Carl	Michigan	SR269
Lieberman, Joseph I	Connecticut	SH706
Lincoln, Blanche L	Arkansas	SD355
Lott, Trent	Mississippi	SR487
Lugar, Richard G	Indiana	SH306
Martinez, Mel	Florida	SH317
McCain, John	Arizona	SR241
McConnell, Mitch	Kentucky	SR361A
Menendez, Robert	New Jersey	SH502
Mikulski, Barbara A	Maryland	SH503
Murkowski, Lisa	Alaska	SH709
Murray, Patty	Washington	SR173
Nelson, Bill	Florida	SH716
Nelson, E. Benjamin	Nebraska	SH720
Obama, Barack	Illinois	SH713
Pryor, Mark	Arkansas	SD257
Reed, Jack	Rhode Island	SH728
Reid, Harry	Nevada	SH528
Roberts, Pat	Kansas	SH109
Rockefeller, John D., IV	West Virginia	SH531
Salazar, Ken	Colorado	SH702
Santorum, Rick	Pennsylvania	SD511
Sarbanes, Paul S	Maryland	SH309
Schumer, Charles E	New York	SH313
Sessions, Jeff	Alabama	SR335
Shelby, Richard C	Alabama	SH110
Smith, Gordon	Oregon	SR404
Snowe, Olympia J	Maine	SR154
Specter, Arlen	Pennsylvania	SH711
Stabenow, Debbie	Michigan	SH133

Senators—Continued

[Republicans in roman (55); Democrats in italic (44); Independents in bold (1); total, 100]

Room numbers preceded by SR are in the Russell Office Building (Delaware and Constitution Avenues); those preceded by SD are in the Dirksen Office Building (First Street and Constitution Avenue); and those preceded by SH are in the Hart Office Building (Second and C Streets). Members' offices may be reached by phone at 202–224–3121.

Name	State	Room
Stevens, Ted	Alaska	SH522
Sununu, John E	New Hampshire	SR111
Talent, James M	Missouri	SR493
Thomas, Craig	Wyoming	SD307
Thune, John	South Dakota	SR383
Vitter, David	Louisiana	SH516
Voinovich, George V	Ohio	SH524
Warner, John W	Virginia	SR225
Wyden, Ron	Oregon	SD230

Representatives

[Republicans in roman (231); Democrats in italic (201); Independents in bold (1); vacancy (2); total, 435]

Room numbers with three digits are in the Cannon House Office Building (New Jersey and Independence Avenues), four digits beginning with 1 are in the Longworth House Office Building (between South Capitol Street and New Jersey Avenue on Independence Avenue), and four digits beginning with 2 are in the Rayburn House Office Building (between First and South Capitol Streets on Independence Avenue). Members' offices may be reached by phone at 202–225–3121. The most current listing of House Members can be found on the Internet at http://clerk.house.gov.

Name	State (District)	Room
Abercrombie, Neil	Hawaii (1)	1502
Ackerman, Gary L	New York (5)	2243
Aderholt, Robert B	Alabama (4)	1433
Akin, W. Todd	Missouri (2)	117
Alexander, Rodney	Louisiana (5)	316
Allen, Thomas H	Maine (1)	1127
Andrews, Robert E	New Jersey (1)	2439
Baca, Joe	California (43)	328
Bachus, Spencer	Alabama (6)	442
Baird, Brian	Washington (3)	1421
Baker, Richard H	Louisiana (6)	341
Baldwin, Tammy	Wisconsin (2)	1022
Barrett, J. Gresham	South Carolina (3)	1523
Barrow, John	Georgia (12)	226
Bartlett, Roscoe G	Maryland (6)	2412
Barton, Joe	Texas (6)	2109
Bass, Charles F	New Hampshire (2)	2421
Bean, Melissa L	Illinois (8)	512
Beauprez, Bob	Colorado (7)	504
Becerra, Xavier	California (31)	1119
Berkley, Shelley	Nevada (1)	439
Berman, Howard L	California (28)	2221
Berry, Marion	Arkansas (1)	2305
Biggert, Judy	Illinois (13)	1317
Bilirakis, Michael	Florida (9)	2408
Bishop, Rob	Utah (1)	124
Bishop, Sanford D., Jr	Georgia (2)	2429
Bishop, Timothy H	New York (1)	1133
Blackburn, Marsha	Tennessee (7)	509
Blumenauer, Earl	Oregon (3)	2446
Blunt, Roy	Missouri (7)	217
Boehlert, Sherwood	New York (24)	2246

Representatives—Continued

[Republicans in roman (231); Democrats in italic (201); Independents in bold (1); vacancy (2); total, 435]

Room numbers with three digits are in the Cannon House Office Building (New Jersey and Independence Avenues), four digits beginning with 1 are in the Longworth House Office Building (between South Capitol Street and New Jersey Avenue on Independence Avenue), and four digits beginning with 2 are in the Rayburn House Office Building (between First and South Capitol Streets on Independence Avenue). Members' offices may be reached by phone at 202–225–3121. The most current listing of House Members can be found on the Internet at http://clerk.house.gov.

Name	State (District)	Room
Boehner, John A	Ohio (8)	1011
Bonilla, Henry	Texas (23)	2458
Bonner, Jo	Alabama (1)	315
Bono, Mary	California (45)	405
Boozman, John	Arkansas (3)	1519
Boren, Dan	Oklahoma (2)	216
Boswell, Leonard L	Iowa (3)	1427
Boucher, Rick	Virginia (9)	2187
Boustany, Charles W., Jr	Louisiana (7)	1117
Boyd, Allen	Florida (2)	1227
Bradley, Jeb	New Hampshire (1)	1218
Brady, Kevin	Texas (8)	428
Brady, Robert A	Pennsylvania (1)	206
Brown, Corrine	Florida (3)	2444
Brown, Henry E., Jr	South Carolina (1)	1124
Brown, Sherrod	Ohio (13)	2332
Brown-Waite, Ginny	Florida (5)	414
Burgess, Michael C	Texas (26)	1721
Burton, Dan	Indiana (5)	2185
Butterfield, G.K	North Carolina (1)	413
Buyer, Steve	Indiana (4)	2230
Calvert, Ken	California (44)	2201
Camp, Dave	Michigan (4)	137
Campbell, John	California (48)	2402
Cannon, Chris	Utah (3)	2436
Cantor, Eric	Virginia (7)	329
Capito, Shelley Moore	West Virginia (2)	1431
Capps, Lois	California (23)	1707
Capuano, Michael E	Massachusetts (8)	1530
Cardin, Benjamin L	Maryland (3)	2207
Cardoza, Dennis A	California (18)	435
Carnahan, Russ	Missouri (3)	1232
Carson, Julia	Indiana (7)	1535
Carter, John R	Texas (31)	408
Case, Ed	Hawaii (2)	115
Castle, Michael N	Delaware (At Large)	1233
Chabot, Steve	Ohio (1)	129
Chandler, Ben	Kentucky (6)	1504
Chocola, Chris	Indiana (2)	510
Clay, William Lacy	Missouri (1)	131
Cleaver, Emanuel	Missouri (5)	1641
Clyburn, James E	South Carolina (6)	2135
Coble, Howard	North Carolina (6)	2468
Cole, Tom	Oklahoma (4)	236
Conaway, K. Michael	Texas (11)	511
Conyers, John, Jr	Michigan (14)	2426
Cooper, Jim	Tennessee (5)	1536
Costa, Jim	California (20)	1004
Costello, Jerry F	Illinois (12)	2269
Cramer, Robert E. (Bud), Jr	Alabama (5)	2368
Crenshaw, Ander	Florida (4)	127

Representatives—Continued

[Republicans in roman (231); Democrats in italic (201); Independents in bold (1); vacancy (2); total, 435]

Room numbers with three digits are in the Cannon House Office Building (New Jersey and Independence Avenues), four digits beginning with 1 are in the Longworth House Office Building (between South Capitol Street and New Jersey Avenue on Independence Avenue), and four digits beginning with 2 are in the Rayburn House Office Building (between First and South Capitol Streets on Independence Avenue). Members' offices may be reached by phone at 202–225–3121. The most current listing of House Members can be found on the Internet at http://clerk.house.gov.

Name	State (District)	Room
Crowley, Joseph	New York (7)	312
Cubin, Barbara	Wyoming (At Large)	1114
Cuellar, Henry	Texas (28)	1404
Culberson, John Abney	Texas (7)	1728
Cummings, Elijah E	Maryland (7)	2235
(Vacancy)	California (50)	2350
Davis, Artur	Alabama (7)	208
Davis, Danny K	Illinois (7)	1526
Davis, Geoff	Kentucky (4)	1541
Davis, Jim	Florida (11)	409
Davis, Jo Ann	Virginia (1)	1123
Davis, Lincoln	Tennessee (4)	410
Davis, Susan A	California (53)	1224
Davis, Tom	Virginia (11)	2348
Deal, Nathan	Georgia (10)	2133
DeFazio, Peter A	Oregon (4)	2134
DeGette, Diana	Colorado (1)	1527
Delahunt, William D	Massachusetts (10)	2454
DeLauro, Rosa L	Connecticut (3)	2262
DeLay, Tom	Texas (22)	242
Dent, Charles W	Pennsylvania (15)	502
Diaz-Balart, Lincoln	Florida (21)	2244
Diaz-Balart, Mario	Florida (25)	313
Dicks, Norman D	Washington (6)	2467
Dingell, John D	Michigan (15)	2328
Doggett, Lloyd	Texas (25)	201
Doolittle, John T	California (4)	2410
Doyle, Michael F	Pennsylvania (14)	401
Drake, Thelma D	Virginia (2)	1208
Dreier, David	California (26)	233
Duncan, John J., Jr	Tennessee (2)	2267
Edwards, Chet	Texas (17)	2264
Ehlers, Vernon J	Michigan (3)	1714
Emanuel, Rahm	Illinois (5)	1319
Emerson, Jo Ann	Missouri (8)	2440
Engel, Eliot L	New York (17)	2161
English, Phil	Pennsylvania (3)	1410
Eshoo, Anna G	California (14)	205
Etheridge, Bob	North Carolina (2)	1533
Evans, Lane	Illinois (17)	2211
Everett, Terry	Alabama (2)	2312
Farr, Sam	California (17)	1221
Fattah, Chaka	Pennsylvania (2)	2301
Feeney, Tom	Florida (24)	323
Ferguson, Mike	New Jersey (7)	214
Filner, Bob	California (51)	2428
Fitzpatrick, Michael G	Pennsylvania (8)	1516
Flake, Jeff	Arizona (6)	424
Foley, Mark	Florida (16)	104
Forbes, J. Randy	Virginia (4)	307
Ford, Harold E., Jr	Tennessee (9)	325

Representatives—Continued

[Republicans in roman (231); Democrats in italic (201); Independents in bold (1); vacancy (2); total, 435]

Room numbers with three digits are in the Cannon House Office Building (New Jersey and Independence Avenues), four digits beginning with 1 are in the Longworth House Office Building (between South Capitol Street and New Jersey Avenue on Independence Avenue), and four digits beginning with 2 are in the Rayburn House Office Building (between First and South Capitol Streets on Independence Avenue). Members' offices may be reached by phone at 202–225–3121. The most current listing of House Members can be found on the Internet at http://clerk.house.gov.

Name	State (District)	Room
Fortenberry, Jeff	Nebraska (1)	1517
Fossella, Vito	New York (13)	1239
Foxx, Virginia	North Carolina (5)	503
Frank, Barney	Massachusetts (4)	2252
Franks, Trent	Arizona (2)	1237
Frelinghuysen, Rodney P	New Jersey (11)	2442
Gallegly, Elton	California (24)	2427
Garrett, Scott	New Jersey (5)	1318
Gerlach, Jim	Pennsylvania (6)	308
Gibbons, Jim	Nevada (2)	100
Gilchrest, Wayne T	Maryland (1)	2245
Gillmor, Paul E	Ohio (5)	1203
Gingrey, Phil	Georgia (11)	119
Gohmert, Louie	Texas (1)	508
Gonzalez, Charles A	Texas (20)	327
Goode, Virgil H., Jr	Virginia (5)	1520
Goodlatte, Bob	Virginia (6)	2240
Gordon, Bart	Tennessee (6)	2304
Granger, Kay	Texas (12)	440
Graves, Sam	Missouri (6)	1513
Green, Al	Texas (9)	1529
Green, Gene	Texas (29)	2335
Green, Mark	Wisconsin (8)	1314
Grijalva, Raúl M	Arizona (7)	1440
Gutierrez, Luis V	Illinois (4)	2367
Gutknecht, Gil	Minnesota (1)	425
Hall, Ralph M	Texas (4)	2405
Harman, Jane	California (36)	2400
Harris, Katherine	Florida (13)	116
Hart, Melissa A	Pennsylvania (4)	1024
Hastert, J. Dennis	Illinois (14)	235
Hastings, Alcee L	Florida (23)	2353
Hastings, Doc	Washington (4)	1323
Hayes, Robin	North Carolina (8)	130
Hayworth, J.D	Arizona (5)	2434
Hefley, Joel	Colorado (5)	2372
Hensarling, Jeb	Texas (5)	132
Herger, Wally	California (2)	2268
Herseth, Stephanie	South Dakota (At Large)	331
Higgins, Brian	New York (27)	431
Hinchey, Maurice D	New York (22)	2431
Hinojosa, Rubén	Texas (15)	2463
Hobson, David L	Ohio (7)	2346
Hoekstra, Peter	Michigan (2)	2234
Holden, Tim	Pennsylvania (17)	2417
Holt, Rush D	New Jersey (12)	1019
Honda, Michael M	California (15)	1713
Hooley, Darlene	Oregon (5)	2430
Hostettler, John N	Indiana (8)	1214
Hoyer, Steny H	Maryland (5)	1705
Hulshof, Kenny C	Missouri (9)	412

Representatives—Continued

[Republicans in roman (231); Democrats in italic (201); Independents in bold (1); vacancy (2); total, 435]

Room numbers with three digits are in the Cannon House Office Building (New Jersey and Independence Avenues), four digits beginning with 1 are in the Longworth House Office Building (between South Capitol Street and New Jersey Avenue on Independence Avenue), and four digits beginning with 2 are in the Rayburn House Office Building (between First and South Capitol Streets on Independence Avenue). Members' offices may be reached by phone at 202–225–3121. The most current listing of House Members can be found on the Internet at http://clerk.house.gov.

Name	State (District)	Room
Hunter, Duncan	California (52)	2265
Hyde, Henry J	Illinois (6)	2110
Inglis, Bob	South Carolina (4)	330
Inslee, Jay	Washington (1)	403
Israel, Steve	New York (2)	432
Issa, Darrell E	California (49)	211
Istook, Ernest J., Jr	Oklahoma (5)	2404
Jackson, Jesse L., Jr	Illinois (2)	2419
Jackson-Lee, Sheila	Texas (18)	2435
Jefferson, William J	Louisiana (2)	2113
Jenkins, William L	Tennessee (1)	1207
Jindal, Bobby	Louisiana (1)	1205
Johnson, Eddie Bernice	Texas (30)	1511
Johnson, Nancy L	Connecticut (5)	2409
Johnson, Sam	Texas (3)	1211
Johnson, Timothy V	Illinois (15)	1229
Jones, Stephanie Tubbs	Ohio (11)	1009
Jones, Walter B	North Carolina (3)	422
Kanjorski, Paul E	Pennsylvania (11)	2188
Kaptur, Marcy	Ohio (9)	2366
Keller, Ric	Florida (8)	419
Kelly, Sue W	New York (19)	2182
Kennedy, Mark R	Minnesota (6)	1415
Kennedy, Patrick J	Rhode Island (1)	407
Kildee, Dale E	Michigan (5)	2107
Kilpatrick, Carolyn C	Michigan (13)	1610
Kind, Ron	Wisconsin (3)	1406
King, Peter T	New York (3)	436
King, Steve	Iowa (5)	1432
Kingston, Jack	Georgia (1)	2242
Kirk, Mark Steven	Illinois (10)	1717
Kline, John	Minnesota (2)	1429
Knollenberg, Joe	Michigan (9)	2349
Kolbe, Jim	Arizona (8)	237
Kucinich, Dennis J	Ohio (10)	1730
Kuhl, John R. (Randy), Jr	New York (29)	1505
LaHood, Ray	Illinois (18)	1424
Langevin, James R	Rhode Island (2)	109
Lantos, Tom	California (12)	2413
Larsen, Rick	Washington (2)	107
Larson, John B	Connecticut (1)	1005
Latham, Tom	Iowa (4)	2447
LaTourette, Steven C	Ohio (14)	2453
Leach, James A	Iowa (2)	2186
Lee, Barbara	California (9)	1724
Levin, Sander M	Michigan (12)	2300
Lewis, Jerry	California (41)	2112
Lewis, John	Georgia (5)	343
Lewis, Ron	Kentucky (2)	2418
Linder, John	Georgia (7)	1026
Lipinski, Daniel	Illinois (3)	1217

Representatives—Continued

[Republicans in roman (231); Democrats in italic (201); Independents in bold (1); vacancy (2); total, 435]

Room numbers with three digits are in the Cannon House Office Building (New Jersey and Independence Avenues), four digits beginning with 1 are in the Longworth House Office Building (between South Capitol Street and New Jersey Avenue on Independence Avenue), and four digits beginning with 2 are in the Rayburn House Office Building (between First and South Capitol Streets on Independence Avenue). Members' offices may be reached by phone at 202–225–3121. The most current listing of House Members can be found on the Internet at http://clerk.house.gov.

Name	State (District)	Room
LoBiondo, Frank A	New Jersey (2)	225
Lofgren, Zoe	California (16)	102
Lowey, Nita M	New York (18)	2329
Lucas, Frank D	Oklahoma (3)	2342
Lungren, Daniel E	California (3)	2448
Lynch, Stephen F	Massachusetts (9)	319
McCarthy, Carolyn	New York (4)	106
McCaul, Michael T	Texas (10)	415
McCollum, Betty	Minnesota (4)	1029
McCotter, Thaddeus G	Michigan (11)	1632
McCrery, Jim	Louisiana (4)	2104
McDermott, Jim	Washington (7)	1035
McGovern, James P	Massachusetts (3)	430
McHenry, Patrick T	North Carolina (10)	224
McHugh, John M	New York (23)	2333
McIntyre, Mike	North Carolina (7)	2437
McKeon, Howard P. (Buck)	California (25)	2351
McKinney, Cynthia	Georgia (4)	320
McMorris, Cathy	Washington (5)	1708
McNulty, Michael R	New York (21)	2210
Mack, Connie	Florida (14)	317
Maloney, Carolyn B	New York (14)	2331
Manzullo, Donald A	Illinois (16)	2228
Marchant, Kenny	Texas (24)	501
Markey, Edward J	Massachusetts (7)	2108
Marshall, Jim	Georgia (3)	515
Matheson, Jim	Utah (2)	1222
Matsui, Doris O	California (5)	2310
Meehan, Martin T	Massachusetts (5)	2229
Meek, Kendrick B	Florida (17)	1039
Meeks, Gregory W	New York (6)	1710
Melancon, Charlie	Louisiana (3)	404
(Vacancy)	New Jersey (13)	2238
Mica, John L	Florida (7)	2313
Michaud, Michael H	Maine (2)	437
Millender-McDonald, Juanita	California (37)	2445
Miller, Brad	North Carolina (13)	1722
Miller, Candice S	Michigan (10)	228
Miller, Gary G	California (42)	1037
Miller, George	California (7)	2205
Miller, Jeff	Florida (1)	324
Mollohan, Alan B	West Virginia (1)	2302
Moore, Dennis	Kansas (3)	1727
Moore, Gwen	Wisconsin (4)	1408
Moran, James P	Virginia (8)	2239
Moran, Jerry	Kansas (1)	2443
Murphy, Tim	Pennsylvania (18)	322
Murtha, John P	Pennsylvania (12)	2423
Musgrave, Marilyn N	Colorado (4)	1507
Myrick, Sue Wilkins	North Carolina (9)	230
Nadler, Jerrold	New York (8)	2334

Representatives—Continued

[Republicans in roman (231); Democrats in italic (201); Independents in bold (1); vacancy (2); total, 435]

Room numbers with three digits are in the Cannon House Office Building (New Jersey and Independence Avenues), four digits beginning with 1 are in the Longworth House Office Building (between South Capitol Street and New Jersey Avenue on Independence Avenue), and four digits beginning with 2 are in the Rayburn House Office Building (between First and South Capitol Streets on Independence Avenue). Members' offices may be reached by phone at 202–225–3121. The most current listing of House Members can be found on the Internet at http://clerk.house.gov.

Name	State (District)	Room
Napolitano, Grace F	California (38)	1609
Neal, Richard E	Massachusetts (2)	2266
Neugebauer, Randy	Texas (19)	429
Ney, Robert W	Ohio (18)	2438
Northup, Anne M	Kentucky (3)	2459
Norwood, Charlie	Georgia (9)	2452
Nunes, Devin	California (21)	1017
Nussle, Jim	Iowa (1)	303
Oberstar, James L	Minnesota (8)	2365
Obey, David R	Wisconsin (7)	2314
Olver, John W	Massachusetts (1)	1111
Ortiz, Solomon P	Texas (27)	2470
Osborne, Tom	Nebraska (3)	507
Otter, C.L. (Butch)	Idaho (1)	1711
Owens, Major R	New York (11)	2309
Oxley, Michael G	Ohio (4)	2308
Pallone, Frank, Jr	New Jersey (6)	420
Pascrell, Bill, Jr	New Jersey (8)	2464
Pastor, Ed	Arizona (4)	2465
Paul, Ron	Texas (14)	203
Payne, Donald M	New Jersey (10)	2209
Pearce, Stevan	New Mexico (2)	1607
Pelosi, Nancy	California (8)	2371
Pence, Mike	Indiana (6)	426
Peterson, Collin C	Minnesota (7)	2159
Peterson, John E	Pennsylvania (5)	123
Petri, Thomas E	Wisconsin (6)	2462
Pickering, Charles W. (Chip)	Mississippi (3)	229
Pitts, Joseph R	Pennsylvania (16)	221
Platts, Todd Russell	Pennsylvania (19)	1032
Poe, Ted	Texas (2)	1605
Pombo, Richard W	California (11)	2411
Pomeroy, Earl	North Dakota (At Large)	1501
Porter, Jon C	Nevada (3)	218
Price, David E	North Carolina (4)	2162
Price, Tom	Georgia (6)	506
Pryce, Deborah	Ohio (15)	204
Putnam, Adam H	Florida (12)	1213
Radanovich, George	California (19)	438
Rahall, Nick J., II	West Virginia (3)	2307
Ramstad, Jim	Minnesota (3)	103
Rangel, Charles B	New York (15)	2354
Regula, Ralph	Ohio (16)	2306
Rehberg, Dennis R	Montana (At Large)	516
Reichert, David G	Washington (8)	1223
Renzi, Rick	Arizona (1)	418
Reyes, Silvestre	Texas (16)	2433
Reynolds, Thomas M	New York (26)	332
Rogers, Harold	Kentucky (5)	2406
Rogers, Mike	Michigan (8)	133
Rogers, Mike	Alabama (3)	514

Representatives—Continued

[Republicans in roman (231); Democrats in italic (201); Independents in bold (1); vacancy (2); total, 435]

Room numbers with three digits are in the Cannon House Office Building (New Jersey and Independence Avenues), four digits beginning with 1 are in the Longworth House Office Building (between South Capitol Street and New Jersey Avenue on Independence Avenue), and four digits beginning with 2 are in the Rayburn House Office Building (between First and South Capitol Streets on Independence Avenue). Members' offices may be reached by phone at 202–225–3121. The most current listing of House Members can be found on the Internet at http://clerk.house.gov.

Name	State (District)	Room
Rohrabacher, Dana	California (46)	2338
Ros-Lehtinen, Ileana	Florida (18)	2160
Ross, Mike	Arkansas (4)	314
Rothman, Steven R	New Jersey (9)	2303
Roybal-Allard, Lucille	California (34)	2330
Royce, Edward R	California (40)	2202
Ruppersberger, C.A. Dutch	Maryland (2)	1630
Rush, Bobby L	Illinois (1)	2416
Ryan, Paul	Wisconsin (1)	1113
Ryan, Tim	Ohio (17)	222
Ryun, Jim	Kansas (2)	1110
Sabo, Martin Olav	Minnesota (5)	2336
Salazar, John T	Colorado (3)	1531
Sánchez, Linda T	California (39)	1007
Sanchez, Loretta	California (47)	1230
Sanders, Bernard	Vermont (At Large)	2233
Saxton, Jim	New Jersey (3)	2217
Schakowsky, Janice D	Illinois (9)	1027
Schiff, Adam B	California (29)	326
Schmidt, Jean	Ohio (2)	238
Schwartz, Allyson Y	Pennsylvania (13)	423
Schwarz, John J.H. (Joe)	Michigan (7)	128
Scott, David	Georgia (13)	417
Scott, Robert C	Virginia (3)	1201
Sensenbrenner, F. James, Jr	Wisconsin (5)	2449
Serrano, José E	New York (16)	2227
Sessions, Pete	Texas (32)	1514
Shadegg, John B	Arizona (3)	306
Shaw, E. Clay, Jr	Florida (22)	1236
Shays, Christopher	Connecticut (4)	1126
Sherman, Brad	California (27)	1030
Sherwood, Don	Pennsylvania (10)	1131
Shimkus, John	Illinois (19)	513
Shuster, Bill	Pennsylvania (9)	1108
Simmons, Rob	Connecticut (2)	215
Simpson, Michael K	Idaho (2)	1339
Skelton, Ike	Missouri (4)	2206
Slaughter, Louise McIntosh	New York (28)	2469
Smith, Adam	Washington (9)	227
Smith, Christopher H	New Jersey (4)	2373
Smith, Lamar S	Texas (21)	2184
Snyder, Vic	Arkansas (2)	1330
Sodrel, Michael E	Indiana (9)	1508
Solis, Hilda L	California (32)	1725
Souder, Mark E	Indiana (3)	2231
Spratt, John M., Jr	South Carolina (5)	1401
Stark, Fortney Pete	California (13)	239
Stearns, Cliff	Florida (6)	2370
Strickland, Ted	Ohio (6)	336
Stupak, Bart	Michigan (1)	2352
Sullivan, John	Oklahoma (1)	114

Representatives—Continued

[Republicans in roman (231); Democrats in italic (201); Independents in bold (1); vacancy (2); total, 435]

Room numbers with three digits are in the Cannon House Office Building (New Jersey and Independence Avenues), four digits beginning with 1 are in the Longworth House Office Building (between South Capitol Street and New Jersey Avenue on Independence Avenue), and four digits beginning with 2 are in the Rayburn House Office Building (between First and South Capitol Streets on Independence Avenue). Members' offices may be reached by phone at 202–225–3121. The most current listing of House Members can be found on the Internet at http://clerk.house.gov.

Name	State (District)	Room
Sweeney, John E	New York (20)	416
Tancredo, Thomas G	Colorado (6)	1130
Tanner, John S	Tennessee (8)	1226
Tauscher, Ellen O	California (10)	1034
Taylor, Charles H	North Carolina (11)	339
Taylor, Gene	Mississippi (4)	2311
Terry, Lee	Nebraska (2)	1524
Thomas, William M	California (22)	2208
Thompson, Bennie G	Mississippi (2)	2432
Thompson, Mike	California (1)	231
Thornberry, Mac	Texas (13)	2457
Tiahrt, Todd	Kansas (4)	2441
Tiberi, Patrick J	Ohio (12)	113
Tierney, John F	Massachusetts (6)	120
Towns, Edolphus	New York (10)	2232
Turner, Michael R	Ohio (3)	1740
Udall, Mark	Colorado (2)	240
Udall, Tom	New Mexico (3)	1414
Upton, Fred	Michigan (6)	2183
Van Hollen, Chris	Maryland (8)	1419
Velázquez, Nydia M	New York (12)	2241
Visclosky, Peter J	Indiana (1)	2256
Walden, Greg	Oregon (2)	1210
Walsh, James T	New York (25)	2369
Wamp, Zach	Tennessee (3)	1436
Wasserman, Debbie Schultz	Florida (20)	118
Waters, Maxine	California (35)	2344
Watson, Diane E	California (33)	125
Watt, Melvin L	North Carolina (12)	2236
Waxman, Henry A	California (30)	2204
Weiner, Anthony D	New York (9)	1122
Weldon, Curt	Pennsylvania (7)	2466
Weldon, Dave	Florida (15)	2347
Weller, Jerry	Illinois (11)	108
Westmoreland, Lynn A	Georgia (8)	1118
Wexler, Robert	Florida (19)	213
Whitfield, Ed	Kentucky (1)	301
Wicker, Roger F	Mississippi (1)	2455
Wilson, Heather	New Mexico (1)	318
Wilson, Joe	South Carolina (2)	212
Wolf, Frank R	Virginia (10)	241
Woolsey, Lynn C	California (6)	2263
Wu, David	Oregon (1)	1023
Wynn, Albert Russell	Maryland (4)	434
Young, C.W. Bill	Florida (10)	2407
Young, Don	Alaska (At Large)	2111
	Delegates	
BORDALLO, MADELEINE Z	Guam	427
CHRISTENSEN, DONNA M.	Virgin Islands	1510
FALEOMAVAEGA, ENI F.H	American Samoa	2422
NORTON, ELEANOR HOLMES	District of Columbia	2136

Representatives—Continued

[Republicans in roman (231); Democrats in italic (201); Independents in bold (1); vacancy (2); total, 435]

Room numbers with three digits are in the Cannon House Office Building (New Jersey and Independence Avenues), four digits beginning with 1 are in the Longworth House Office Building (between South Capitol Street and New Jersey Avenue on Independence Avenue), and four digits beginning with 2 are in the Rayburn House Office Building (between First and South Capitol Streets on Independence Avenue). Members' offices may be reached by phone at 202–225–3121. The most current listing of House Members can be found on the Internet at http://clerk.house.gov.

Name	State (District)	Room
Resident Commissioner		
FORTUÑO, LUIS G	Puerto Rico	126

For further information concerning the United States Senate, contact the Secretary of the Senate, The Capitol, Washington, DC 20510. Phone, 202–224–2115. Internet, www.senate.gov. For further information concerning the House of Representatives, contact the Clerk, The Capitol, Washington, DC 20515. Phone, 202–225–7000. Internet, http://clerk.house.gov.

ARCHITECT OF THE CAPITOL

U.S. Capitol Building, Washington, DC 20515
Phone, 202–228–1793. Internet, www.aoc.gov.

Architect of the Capitol	ALAN M. HANTMAN
Special Assistant to the Architect of the Capitol	MICHAEL G. TURNBULL
Director, Architecture Division	BRUCE ARTHUR
Director, Construction Division	GARY VAWTER
Director of Engineering	SCOTT BIRKHEAD
Director of Facilities Planning and Programming	TERRELL EMMONS
Director of Project Management	WILLIAM WEIDEMEYER
Director of Congressional and External Relations	(VACANCY)
Chief Administrative Officer	DAVID FERGUSON, *Acting*
Director, Human Resources Management Division	REBECCA TISCIONE
Director, Equal Employment Opportunity	PATRICIA BROWN
Director, Information Resources Management	STAN KIRK
Curator	BARBARA WOLANIN
Communications Officer	EVA MALECKI
Congressional Liaison	BRYAN H. ROTH
Head, Procurement Division	CYNTHIA BENNETT
Inspector General	ARTHUR L. MCINTYE
Director of Safety, Fire, and Environmental Programs	SUSAN ADAMS
Director, Safety and Environmental Division	LARRY DENICOLA
Safety Officer	CHARLES BOWMAN
Chief Financial Officer	(VACANCY)
Budget Officer	MARILYN WILES
Accounting Officer	TIMOTHY MACDONALD
Director, Financial Management Systems Division	RUSS FOLLIN
General Counsel	PETER KUSHNER
Chief Operating Officer	STEPHEN AYERS, *Acting*

Director, Labor Relations and Collective Bargaining	MARGARET COX
Senior Landscape Architect	MATTHEW EVANS
Superintendent, House Office Buildings	FRANK TISCIONE
Superintendent, Senate Office Buildings	LAWRENCE R. STOFFEL
Superintendent, Library of Congress Buildings and Grounds	GREGORY SIMMONS, *Acting*
Superintendent, U.S. Capitol	CARLOS ELIAS
Superintendent, Capitol Grounds	GLENN MARSHALL
Director, U.S. Botanic Garden	HOLLY H. SHIMIZU
Superintendent, U.S. Supreme Court	MARC FRAMPTON
Director, U.S. Capitol Power Plant	MARK WEISS

The Architect of the Capitol is responsible for the care and maintenance of the U.S. Capitol and the buildings and grounds acrosss the Capitol complex. The agency is charged with implementing construction, renovation, conservation, and landscape improvement projects as authorized by the Congress.

The Architect of the Capitol is charged with operating and maintaining the buildings of the Capitol complex committed to his care by Congress. Permanent authority for the care and maintenance of the Capitol was established by the act of August 15, 1876 (40 U.S.C. 162, 163). The Architect's duties include the mechanical and structural maintenance of the Capitol, the conservation and care of works of art in the building under the Architect's jurisdiction, the upkeep and improvement of the Capitol grounds, and the arrangement of inaugural and other ceremonies held in the building or on the grounds.

In addition to the Capitol, the Architect is responsible for the upkeep of all of the congressional office buildings, the Library of Congress buildings, the U.S. Supreme Court building, the Thurgood Marshall Federal Judiciary Building, the Capitol Power Plant, the Capitol Police headquarters, and the Robert A. Taft Memorial. The Architect performs his duties in connection with the Senate side of the Capitol, the Senate office buildings, and the operation of the Senate restaurants subject to the approval of the Senate Committee on Rules and Administration. In matters of general policy in connection with the House office buildings and the Capitol Power Plant, his activities are subject to the approval and direction of the House Office Building Commission. The Architect is under the direction of the Speaker in matters concerning the House side of the Capitol. He is subject to the oversight of the Committee on House Administration with respect to many administrative matters affecting operations on the House side of the Capitol complex. In addition, the Architect of the Capitol serves as the Acting Director of the U.S. Botanic Garden under the Joint Committee on the Library.

The position of Architect of the Capitol was historically filled by Presidential appointment for an indefinite term. Legislation enacted in 1989 provides that the Architect is to be appointed for a term of 10 years by the President, with the advice and consent of the Senate, from a list of three candidates recommended by a congressional commission. Upon confirmation by the Senate, the Architect becomes an official of the legislative branch as an officer and agent of Congress; he is eligible for reappointment after completion of his term. The present Architect, Alan M. Hantman, is the 10th to hold this position since the office was established in 1793 and the first to be appointed in accordance with the new procedure.

Recent and ongoing projects carried out by the Architect of the Capitol include construction of the Capitol Visitor Center; the restoration of the U.S. Botanic Garden Conservatory;

conservation of murals and decorative paintings in the Capitol; completion of the murals in the first-floor House corridors; improvement of speech-reinforcement, electrical, and fire-protection systems in the Capitol and congressional office buildings; work on security improvements within the Capitol complex; renovation, restoration, and modification of the interiors and exteriors of the Thomas Jefferson and John Adams Buildings of the Library of Congress and provision of off-site book storage facilities for the Library; and management oversight of the Thurgood Marshall Federal Judiciary Building.

For further information, contact the Office of the Architect of the Capitol, U.S. Capitol Building, Washington, DC 20515. Phone, 202–228–1793. Internet, www.aoc.gov.

UNITED STATES BOTANIC GARDEN

Office of Executive Director, 245 First Street SW., Washington, DC 20024
Phone, 202–226–8333. Internet, www.usbg.gov.

Conservatory, 100 Maryland Avenue SW., Washington, DC 20024
Phone, 202–225–6670

Production Facility, 4700 Shepherd Parkway SW., Washington, DC 20032
Phone, 202–226–4780

Director (Architect of the Capitol)	Alan M. Hantman
Executive Director	Holly H. Shimizu

The United States Botanic Garden informs visitors about the aesthetic, cultural, economic, therapeutic, and ecological importance of plants to the well-being of humankind.

The U.S. Botanic Garden has artistic displays of plants, exhibits, and educational programs promoting botanical knowledge through the cultivation of an ordered collection of plants; fostering plant conservation by acting as a repository for endangered species; and growing plants for the beautification of the Capitol complex. Uniquely situated at the heart of the U.S. Government, the Garden seeks to promote the exchange of ideas and information relevant to its mission among national and international visitors and policymakers.

The Garden's collections include orchids, epiphytes, bromeliads, carnivorous plants, ferns, cycads, cacti, succulents, medicinal plants, rare and endangered plants, and plants valued as sources of food, beverages, fibers, cosmetics, and industrial products.

The U.S. Botanic Garden's facilities include the Conservatory, Bartholdi Park, an administration building, and an off-site production facility. The Conservatory, one of the largest structures of its kind in this country, re-opened on December 11, 2001, after undergoing major renovation that required more than 4 years to complete. In addition to upgraded amenities for visitors, it features 12 exhibit and plant display areas. A new facility, the National Garden, is currently under construction on a three-acre site just west of the Conservatory.

Outdoor plantings are showcased in Bartholdi Park, a home landscape demonstration area located across from the Conservatory. Each of the displays is sized and scaled for suitability in an urban or suburban setting. The gardens display ornamental plants that perform well in this region arrayed in a variety of styles and themes. Also located in this park is Bartholdi Fountain, created by

Frédéric Auguste Bartholdi (1834–1904), sculptor of the Statue of Liberty.

The Garden's staff is organized into horticulture, operations, administration, and public programs divisions. Programs for the public are listed in a quarterly calendar of events and also on the Garden's Web site. A horticultural hotline is available to answer questions from the public.

The U.S. Botanic Garden was founded in 1820 under the auspices of the Columbian Institute for the Promotion of Arts and Sciences, an organization that was the outgrowth of an association known as the Metropolitan Society, which received its charter from Congress on April 20, 1818. The Garden continued under the direction of the Institute until 1837, when the Institute ceased to exist as an active organization.

In June 1842, the U.S. Exploring Expedition under the command of Captain Charles Wilkes returned from its 4-year voyage with a wealth of information, artifacts, pressed-plant specimens, and living plants from around the world. The living plants were temporarily placed on exhibit on a lot behind the old Patent Office under the care of William D. Brackenridge, the Expedition's botanist. By November 1842, the plants were moved into a greenhouse built there with funds appropriated by Congress. Subsequently, the greenhouse was expanded with two additions and a small growing area to care for the burgeoning collection. In 1843, stewardship of the collection was placed under the direction and control of the Joint Committee on the Library, which had also assumed responsibility for publication of the results of the Expedition. Expansion of the Patent Office in 1849 necessitated finding a new location for the botanical collections.

The act of May 15, 1850 (9 Stat. 427), provided for the relocation of the Botanic Garden under the direction of the Joint Committee on the Library. The site selected was on the National Mall at the west end of the Capitol Grounds, practically the same site the Garden occupied during the period it functioned under the Columbian Institute. This site was later enlarged, and the main area continued to serve as the principal Garden site from 1850 to 1933, when the Garden was relocated to its present site.

Although the Government had assumed responsibility for the maintenance and stewardship of the plant collection in 1842, the two functions were divided between the Commissioner of Public Buildings and the Joint Committee on the Library, respectively. In 1856, in recognition of their increasing stature, the collections and their associated operations and facilities were officially named the United States Botanic Garden, and the Joint Committee on the Library assumed jurisdiction over both its direction and maintenance (11 Stat. 104). An annual appropriation has been provided by Congress since 1856.

Presently, the Joint Committee on the Library exercises its supervision through the Architect of the Capitol, who has held the title of Acting Director since 1934.

For further information concerning the United States Botanic Garden, contact the Public Programs Division, 245 First Street SW., Washington, DC 20024. Phone, 202–225–8333. Plant Hotline, 202–226–4785. Internet, www.usbg.gov. E-mail, usbg@aoc.gov.

GOVERNMENT ACCOUNTABILITY OFFICE

441 G Street NW., Washington, DC 20548
Phone, 202–512–3000. Internet, www.gao.gov.

Comptroller General of the United States — DAVID M. WALKER

Chief Operating Officer	GENE L. DODARO
Chief Administrative Officer	SALLYANNE HARPER
Deputy Chief Administrative Officer	ANTHONY CICCO
General Counsel	ANTHONY GAMBOA
Teams:	
Managing Director, Acquisition and Sourcing Management	KATHERINE SCHINASI
Managing Director, Applied Research and Methods	NANCY KINGSBURY
Directors	THOMAS J. MCCOOL, BARRY SELTSER
Chief Accountant	ROBERT DACEY
Chief Economist	(VACANCY)
Chief Statistician	(VACANCY)
Chief Technologist	KEITH RHODES
Chief Actuary	JOSEPH APPLEBAUM
Managing Director, Defense Capabilities and Management	HENRY L. HINTON, JR.
Managing Director, Education, Workforce, and Income Security	CYNTHIA M. FAGNONI
Managing Director, Financial Management and Assurance	JEFFREY C. STEINHOFF
Managing Director, Forensic Audits and Special Investigations	GREGORY D. KUTZ
Managing Director, Financial Markets and Community Investments	RICHARD J. HILLMAN
Managing Director, Health Care	MARJORIE KANOFF
Managing Director, International Affairs and Trade	JACQUELYN WILLIAMS-BRIDGERS
Managing Director, Information Technology	JOEL WILLEMSSEN
Managing Director, Natural Resources and Environment	ROBERT A. ROBINSON
Managing Director, Physical Infrastructure	PATRICIA A. DALTON
Managing Director, Strategic Issues	J. CHRISTOPHER MIHM
Managing Director, Homeland Security and Justice	NORMAN J. RABKIN
Support Functions:	
Managing Director, Congressional Relations	GLORIA JARMON
Managing Director, Opportunity and Inclusiveness	RONALD STROMAN
Managing Director, Public Affairs	PAUL ANDERSON
Managing Director, Quality and Continuous Improvement	TIMOTHY BOWLING
Managing Director, Strategic Planning and External Liaison	HELEN HSING
Managing Director, Field Offices	JOHN ANDERSON, JR.
Inspector General	FRANCES GARCIA
Mission Support Offices:	
Chief Information Officer	ANTHONY CICCO
Controller/Administrative Services Office	GEORGE STRADER
Chief Human Capital Officer	JESSE HOSKINS
Managing Director, Knowledge Services	CATHERINE TETI

Managing Director, Professional Development Program	DAVID CLARK
Chair, Personnel Appeals Board	MICHAEL W. DOHENY

The Government Accountability Office is the investigative arm of the Congress and is charged with examining all matters relating to the receipt and disbursement of public funds.

The Government Accountability Office (GAO) is an independent, nonpartisan Agency that works for Congress. GAO is often called the "congressional watchdog" because it investigates how the Federal Government spends taxpayer dollars. The GAO was established as the General Accounting Office by the Budget Accounting Act of 1921 (31 U.S.C. 702). It was renamed the Government Accountability Office pursuant to the GAO Capital Reform Act of 2004 (31 U.S.C. 702 note; 118 Stat. 881).

Activities

GAO gathers information to help Congress determine how effectively executive branch agencies are doing their jobs. GAO's work routinely answers such basic questions as whether Government programs are meeting their objectives or providing good service to the public. Ultimately, GAO ensures that Government is accountable to the American people. To that end, GAO provides Senators and Representatives with the best information available to help them arrive at informed policy decisions—information that is accurate, timely, and balanced. GAO supports congressional oversight by:

—evaluating how well Government policies and programs are working;

—auditing Agency operations to determine whether Federal funds are being spent efficiently, effectively, and appropriately;

—investigating allegation of illegal and improper activities; and

—issuing legal decisions and opinions.

With virtually the entire Federal Government subject to its review, GAO issues a steady stream of products—more than 1,000 reports and hundreds of testimonies by GAO officials each year. GAO's familiar "blue book" reports meet short-term immediate needs for information on a wide range of Government operations. These reports also help Congress better understand issues that are newly emerging, long term in nature, and with more far-reaching impacts. GAO's work translates into a wide variety of legislative actions, improvements in Government operations, and billions of dollars in financial benefits for the American people.

For further information, contact the Office of Public Affairs, Government Accountability Office, 441 G Street NW., Washington, DC 20548. Phone, 202–512–4800. Internet, www.gao.gov.

GOVERNMENT PRINTING OFFICE

732 North Capitol Street NW., Washington, DC 20401
Phone, 202–512–0000. Internet, www.gpo.gov.

Office of the Public Printer:

Public Printer	BRUCE R. JAMES
Deputy Public Printer	WILLIAM H. TURRI
Chief of Staff	ROBERT C. TAPELLA
Deputy Chief of Staff	MARIA LEFEVRE

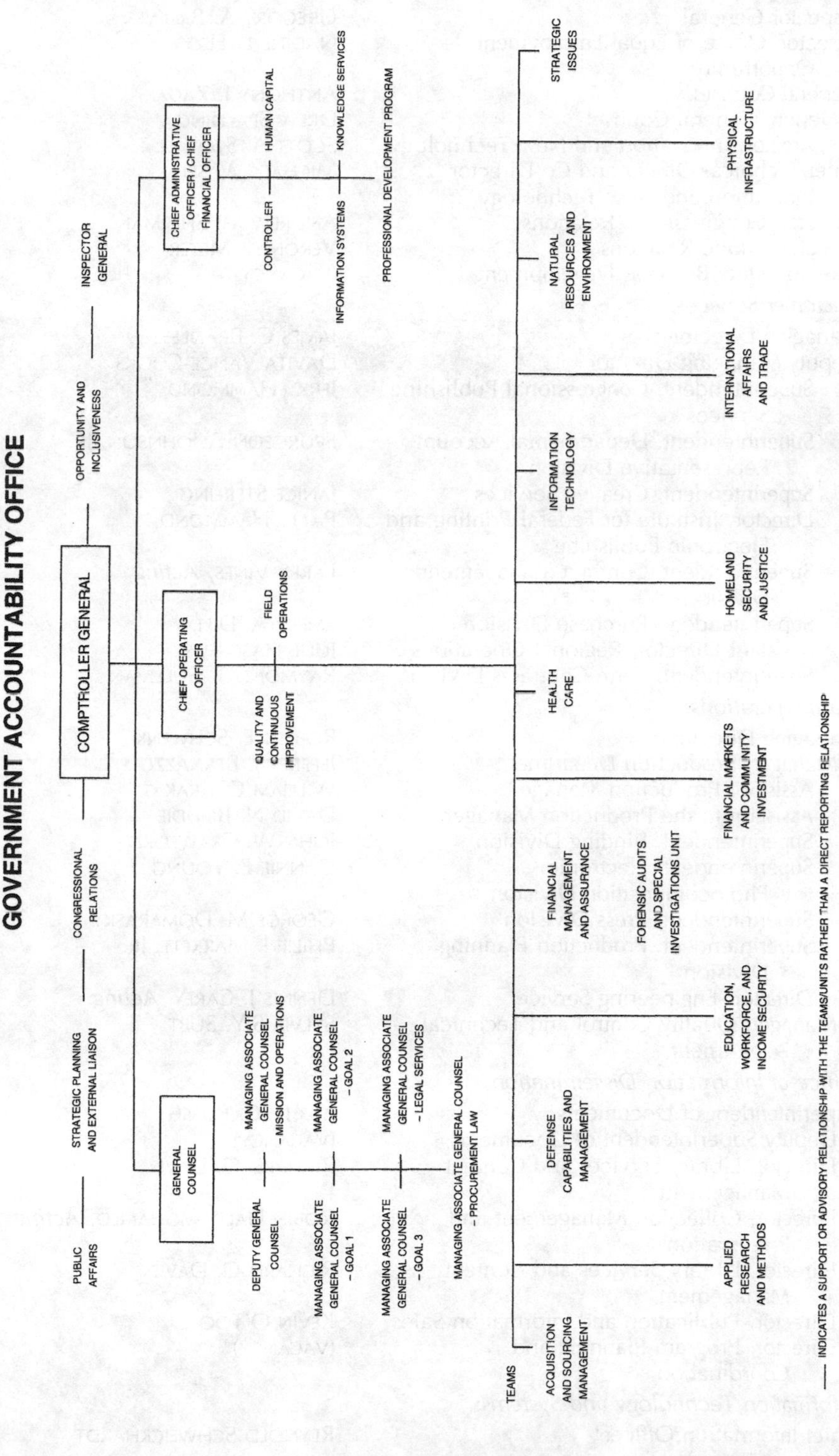
GOVERNMENT ACCOUNTABILITY OFFICE
PUBLIC AFFAIRS
STRATEGIC PLANNING AND EXTERNAL LIAISON
CONGRESSIONAL RELATIONS
COMPTROLLER GENERAL
OPPORTUNITY AND INCLUSIVENESS
INSPECTOR GENERAL
GENERAL COUNSEL
CHIEF OPERATING OFFICER
CHIEF ADMINISTRATIVE OFFICER / CHIEF FINANCIAL OFFICER
DEPUTY GENERAL COUNSEL
MANAGING ASSOCIATE GENERAL COUNSEL - MISSION AND OPERATIONS
MANAGING ASSOCIATE GENERAL COUNSEL - GOAL 1
MANAGING ASSOCIATE GENERAL COUNSEL - GOAL 2
MANAGING ASSOCIATE GENERAL COUNSEL - GOAL 3
MANAGING ASSOCIATE GENERAL COUNSEL - LEGAL SERVICES
MANAGING ASSOCIATE GENERAL COUNSEL - PROCUREMENT LAW
QUALITY AND CONTINUOUS IMPROVEMENT
FIELD OPERATIONS
CONTROLLER
HUMAN CAPITAL
INFORMATION SYSTEMS
KNOWLEDGE SERVICES
PROFESSIONAL DEVELOPMENT PROGRAM
TEAMS
ACQUISITION AND SOURCING MANAGEMENT
APPLIED RESEARCH AND METHODS
DEFENSE CAPABILITIES AND MANAGEMENT
EDUCATION, WORKFORCE, AND INCOME SECURITY
FINANCIAL MANAGEMENT AND ASSURANCE
FORENSIC AUDITS AND SPECIAL INVESTIGATIONS UNIT
FINANCIAL MARKETS AND COMMUNITY INVESTMENT
HEALTH CARE
HOMELAND SECURITY AND JUSTICE
INFORMATION TECHNOLOGY
INTERNATIONAL AFFAIRS AND TRADE
NATURAL RESOURCES AND ENVIRONMENT
PHYSICAL INFRASTRUCTURE
STRATEGIC ISSUES
— INDICATES A SUPPORT OR ADVISORY RELATIONSHIP WITH THE TEAMS/UNITS RATHER THAN A DIRECT REPORTING RELATIONSHIP

Inspector General	GREGORY A. BROWER
Director, Office of Equal Employment Opportunity	NADINE L. ELZY
General Counsel	ANTHONY J. ZAGAMI
Deputy General Counsel	DREW SPALDING
Co-Director, Innovation and New Technology	SCOTT A. STOVALL
Chief Technical Officer and Co-Director, Innovation and New Technology	MICHAEL WASH
Director, Congressional Relations	ANDREW M. SHERMAN
Director, Public Relations	VERONICA METER
Director, New Business Development	(VACANCY)
Customer Services:	
Managing Director	JAMES C. BRADLEY
Deputy Managing Director	DAVITA VANCE-COOKS
Superintendent, Congressional Publishing Services	JERRY HAMMOND
Superintendent, Departmental Account Representative Division	SPURGEON F. JOHNSON, JR.
Superintendent, Creative Services	JANICE STERLING
Director, Institute for Federal Printing and Electronic Publishing	PATTY HAMMOND
Superintendent, Contract Management Division	LARRY VINES, *Acting*
Superintendent, Purchase Division	EMERY A. DILDA
Assistant Director, Regional Operations	JULIE HASENFUS
Superintendent, Term Contracts Division	RAYMOND T. SULLIVAN
Plant Operations:	
Managing Director	ROBERT E. SCHWENK
Manager, Production Department	JEFFREY J. BERNAZZOLI
Assistant Production Manager	WILLIAM C. KRAKAT
Assistant to the Production Manager	DAVID N. BODDIE
Superintendent, Binding Division	JOHN W. CRAWFORD
Superintendent, Electronic Photocomposition Division	DANNIE E. YOUNG
Superintendent, Press Division	GEORGE M. DOMARASKY
Superintendent, Production Planning Division	PHILIP J. MARKETT, JR.
Director, Engineering Service	DENNIS J. CAREY, *Acting*
Manager, Quality Control and Technical Department	SYLVIA S.Y. SUBT
Office of Information Dissemination:	
Superintendent of Documents	JUDITH C. RUSSELL
Deputy Superintendent of Documents	(VACANCY)
Director, Library Services and Content Management	RICHARD G. DAVIS
Director, Collection Management and Preservation	ROBIN HAUN-MOHAMED, *Acting*
Director, Library Services and Content Management	RICHARD G. DAVIS
Director, Publication and Information Sales	KEVIN O'TOOLE
Director, Program Planning and Coordination	(VACANCY)
Information Technology and Systems:	
Chief Information Officer	REYNOLD SCHWEICKHARDT

Deputy Chief Information Officer	BRUCE C. O'DELL
Manager, Electronic Systems Development Division	RICHARD G. LEEDS, JR.
Manager, Graphic Systems Development Division	JOEL E. REEVES
Director, Plans/Policies/Program Support	MELVIN C. ELEY
Human Capital:	
Human Capital Officer	WILLIAM T. HARRIS
Deputy Chief Human Capital Officer	RAFAEL E. LANDRAU
Director, Office of Labor and Employee Relations	NEIL H. FINE
Director, Workforce Development Education and Training	STEVEN L. PATRICK
Director, Occupational Health and Environmental Services	(VACANCY)
Finance and Administration:	
Chief Financial Officer	STEVEN T. SHEDD
Comptroller	WILLIAM L. BOESCH, JR.
Director, Office of Budget	WILLIAM M. GUY

The mission of the Government Printing Office is to inform the Nation by producing, procuring, and disseminating printed and electronic publications of the Congress as well as the executive departments and establishments of the Federal Government.

The Government Printing Office (GPO) opened for business on March 4, 1861. GPO's duties are defined in title 44 of the U.S. Code. The Public Printer, who serves as the head of GPO, is appointed by the President and confirmed by the Senate.

Activities

Headquartered in Washington, DC, with a total employment of approximately 2,500, GPO is responsible for the production and distribution of information products and services for all three branches of the Federal Government. GPO is the Federal Government's primary centralized resource for gathering, cataloging, producing, providing, authenticating, and preserving published information in all its forms. GPO's 1.5-million-square-foot complex is the largest information processing, printing, and distribution facility in the world.

While many of our Nation's most important products, such as the *Congressional Record* and *Federal Register,* are produced at GPO's main plant, the majority of the Government's printing needs are met through a long-standing partnership with America's printing industry. GPO procures between 600 and 1,000 print-related projects a day through private sector vendors across the country, competitively buying products and services from thousands of private sector companies in all 50 States. The contracts cover the entire spectrum of printing and publishing services and are available to fit almost any firm from the largest to the smallest.

GPO disseminates Federal information products through a sales program, distribution network of more than 1,250 Federal libraries nationwide, and via GPO Access. More than 286,000 Federal Government document titles are available to the public at www.gpoaccess.gov.

Printed copies of many documents, ranging from Supreme Court opinions to reports from the Bureau of Labor Statistics, may also be purchased as follows:

—To order in person, please visit the GPO Main Bookstore at 710 North Capitol Street NW., Washington, DC, (corner of North Capitol and H Streets) from 8 a.m. to 4 p.m., e.s.t.

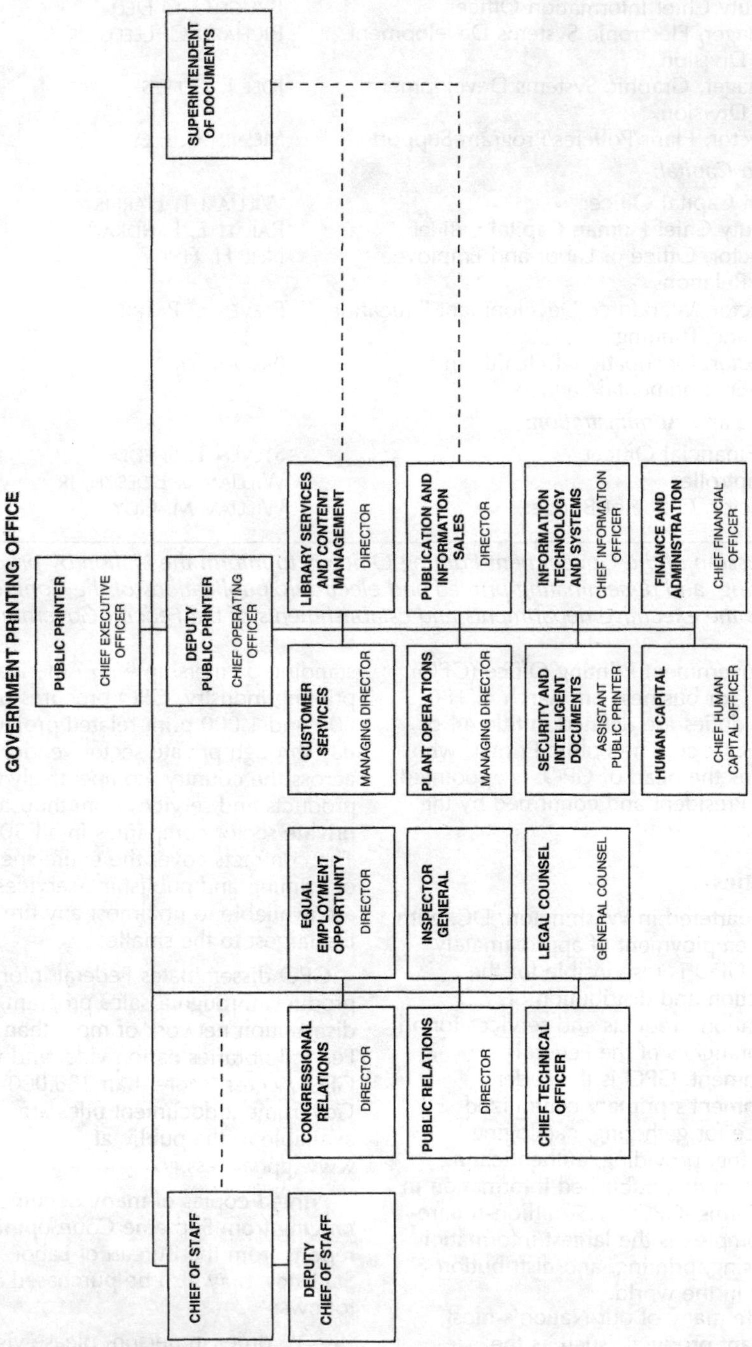
GOVERNMENT PRINTING OFFICE
PUBLIC PRINTER
CHIEF EXECUTIVE OFFICER
DEPUTY PUBLIC PRINTER
CHIEF OPERATING OFFICER
SUPERINTENDENT OF DOCUMENTS
CHIEF OF STAFF
DEPUTY CHIEF OF STAFF
CONGRESSIONAL RELATIONS
DIRECTOR
EQUAL EMPLOYMENT OPPORTUNITY
DIRECTOR
CUSTOMER SERVICES
MANAGING DIRECTOR
LIBRARY SERVICES AND CONTENT MANAGEMENT
DIRECTOR
PUBLIC RELATIONS
DIRECTOR
INSPECTOR GENERAL
PLANT OPERATIONS
MANAGING DIRECTOR
PUBLICATION AND INFORMATION SALES
DIRECTOR
CHIEF TECHNICAL OFFICER
LEGAL COUNSEL
GENERAL COUNSEL
SECURITY AND INTELLIGENT DOCUMENTS
ASSISTANT PUBLIC PRINTER
INFORMATION TECHNOLOGY AND SYSTEMS
CHIEF INFORMATION OFFICER
HUMAN CAPITAL
CHIEF HUMAN CAPITAL OFFICER
FINANCE AND ADMINISTRATION
CHIEF FINANCIAL OFFICER

—To order online, visit the GPO Online Bookstore at http://bookstore.gpo.gov.

—To order by phone or inquire about an order, call 866–512–1800 or, in the Washington, DC, metro area, call 202–512–1800 from 7 a.m. to 9 p.m., e.s.t.

—To order by fax, dial 202–512–2104.

—To order by e-mail, send inquiries to contactcenter@gpo.gov.

—To order by mail, write to Information Dissemination (Superintendent of Documents), P.O. Box 371954, Pittsburgh, PA 15250–7954.

All orders require prepayment by VISA, MasterCard, American Express, or Discover/NOVUS credit cards, check, or SOD deposit account.

Sources of Information

Congressional Relations Congressional relations matters, phone, 202–512–1991.

Public Relations Public relations inquiries, phone, 202–512–1957. Fax, 202–512–1998.

Contracts Commercial printers interested in Government printing contract opportunities should direct inquiries to Customer Services, Government Printing Office, Washington, DC 20401. Phone, 202–512–0111. Internet, www.gpo.gov/procurement/index.html.

GPO Access User Support Phone, 202–512–1530.

GPO Offices Nationwide

Office	Address	Telephone
Atlanta, GA	Suite 110, 1888 Emery St., 30318–2542	404–605–9160
Charleston, SC	2825 Noisette Blvd., 29405	843–743–2036
Boston, MA	28 Court Square, 02108–2504	617–720–3680
Chicago, IL	Suite 810, 200 N. LaSalle St., 60601–1055	312–353–3916
Columbus, OH	Suite 112–B, 1335 Dublin Rd., 43215–7034	614–488–4616
Dallas, TX	Rm. 731, 1100 Commerce St., 75242–0395	214–767–0451
Oklahoma City, OK	Suite 100, 3420 D Ave., Tinker AFB, OK 73145–9188	405–610–4146
San Antonio, TX	Suite 2, 1531 Connally St., Lackland AFB, TX 78236–5514	210–675–1480
Denver, CO	Rm. D–1010, Bldg. 53, Denver Federal Center, 80225–0347	303–236–5292
Hampton, VA	Suite 400, 11836 Canon Blvd., Newport News, VA 23606–2555	757–873–2800
San Diego, CA	Suite 109, 2221 Camino Del Rio S., 92108–3609	619–497–6050
New York, NY	Rm. 709, 201 Varick St., 10014–4879	212–620–3321
Philadelphia, PA	Suite A–190, 928 Jaymore Rd., Southampton, PA 18966–3820	215–364–6465
Pittsburgh, PA	Rm. 501, 1000 Liberty Ave., 15222–4000	412–395–6929
RAPID RESPONSE CENTER	GPO Regional Printing Procurement Office, Rm. C825, Stop RRC, 732 North Capitol St. NW., Washington, DC 20401.	202–512–2240
San Francisco, CA	Suite I, 536 Stone Rd., Benicia, CA 94510–1170	707–748–1970
Seattle, WA	4735 E. Marginal Way S., Federal Center South, 98134–2397	206–764–3726

GPO Bookstore

City	Address	Telephone
Washington, DC, area:		
Central Office	710 N. Capitol St. NW.	202–512–0132

For further information, contact Public Relations, Government Printing Office, 732 North Capitol Street NW., Washington, DC 20401. Phone, 202–512–1957. Fax, 202–512–1998.

LIBRARY OF CONGRESS

101 Independence Avenue SE., Washington, DC 20540
Phone, 202–707–5000. Internet, www.loc.gov.

Librarian of Congress	James H. Billington
Deputy Librarian of Congress	Donald L. Scott

Chief of Staff	JoAnn Jenkins
Associate Librarian for Library Services	Deanna Marcum
Associate Librarian for Human Resources Services	Dennis Hanratty
Director, Congressional Research Service	Daniel P. Mulhollan
Register of Copyrights and Associate Librarian for Copyright Services	Marybeth Peters
Law Librarian	Rubens Medina
General Counsel	Elizabeth Pugh
Inspector General	Karl Schornagel
Chief, Collections Access, Loan, and Management Division	Steven Herman
Library of Congress Trust Fund Board	
Chairman (Librarian of Congress)	James H. Billington
(Secretary of the Treasury)	John W. Snow
(Chairman, Joint Committee on the Library)	Vernon Ehlers
(Vice Chairman, Joint Committee on the Library)	Ted Stevens
Members	Ruth Altshuler, Edwin L. Cox, Elisabeth De Vos, J. Richard Fredericks, Leo Hindery, John Kluge, Tom Luce, Bernard Rapoport, B. Francis Saul II, Anthony Welters

The Library of Congress is the national library of the United States, offering diverse materials for research including the world's most extensive collections in many areas such as American history, music, and law.

The Library of Congress was established by act of April 24, 1800 (2 Stat. 56), appropriating $5,000 "for the purchase of such books as may be necessary for the use of Congress . . . ." The Library's scope of responsibility has been widened by subsequent legislation (2 U.S.C. 131–168d). The Librarian, appointed by the President with the advice and consent of the Senate, directs the Library.

The Library's first responsibility is service to Congress. As the Library has developed, its range of service has come to include the entire governmental establishment and the public at large, making it a national library for the United States.

Activities

Collections The Library's extensive collections are universal in scope. They include books, serials, and pamphlets on every subject and in a multitude of languages, and research materials in many formats, including maps, photographs, manuscripts, motion pictures, and sound recordings. Among them are the most comprehensive collections of Chinese, Japanese, and Russian language books outside Asia and the former Soviet Union; volumes relating to science and legal materials outstanding for American and foreign law; the world's largest collection of published aeronautical literature; and the most extensive collection in the Western Hemisphere of books printed before 1501 A.D.

The manuscript collections relate to manifold aspects of American history and civilization, and include the personal papers of most of the Presidents from George Washington through Calvin Coolidge. The music collections contain volumes and pieces—manuscript and published—from classic works to the newest popular compositions. Other materials available for research include maps and views; photographic records

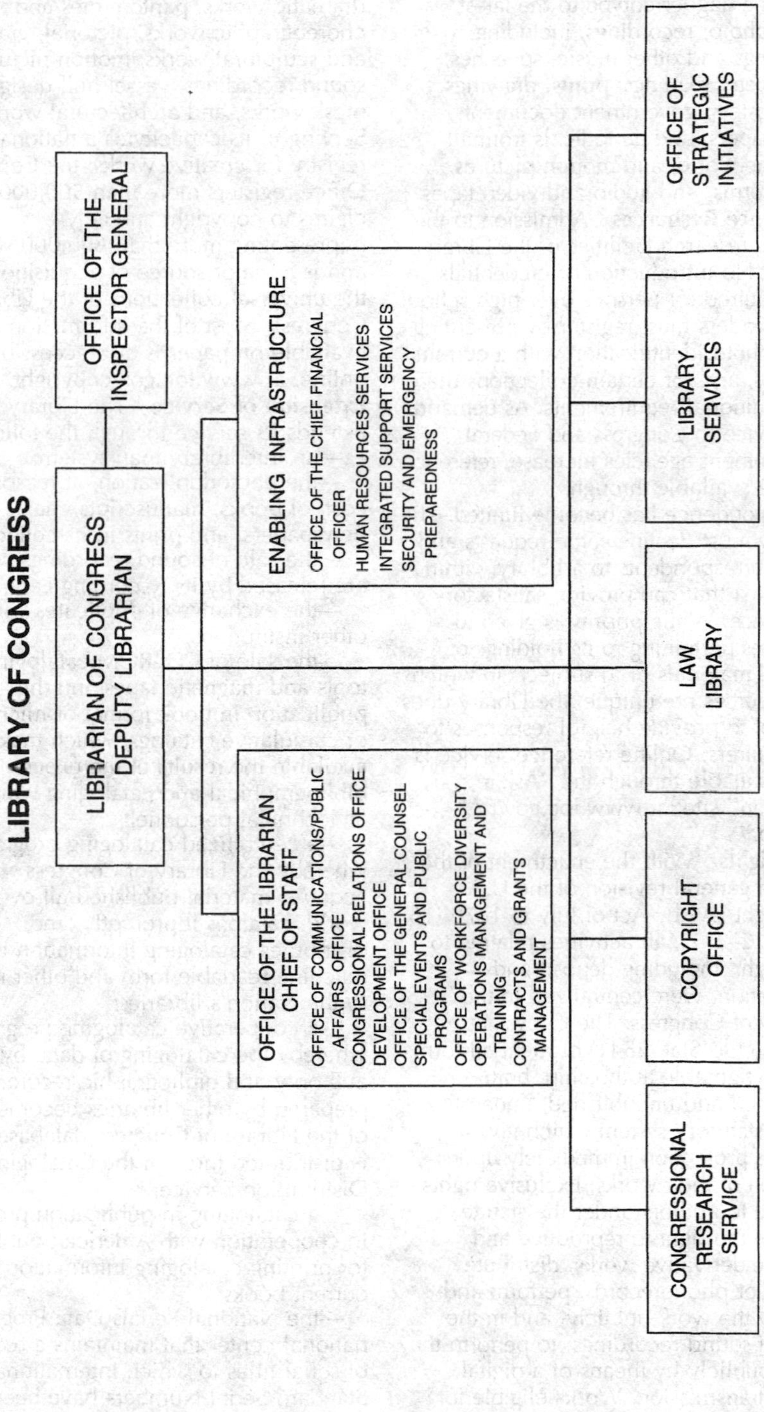
LIBRARY OF CONGRESS
LIBRARIAN OF CONGRESS
DEPUTY LIBRARIAN
OFFICE OF THE
INSPECTOR GENERAL
OFFICE OF THE LIBRARIAN
CHIEF OF STAFF
OFFICE OF COMMUNICATIONS/PUBLIC AFFAIRS OFFICE
CONGRESSIONAL RELATIONS OFFICE
DEVELOPMENT OFFICE
OFFICE OF THE GENERAL COUNSEL
SPECIAL EVENTS AND PUBLIC PROGRAMS
OFFICE OF WORKFORCE DIVERSITY
OPERATIONS MANAGEMENT AND TRAINING
CONTRACTS AND GRANTS MANAGEMENT
ENABLING INFRASTRUCTURE
OFFICE OF THE CHIEF FINANCIAL OFFICER
HUMAN RESOURCES SERVICES
INTEGRATED SUPPORT SERVICES
SECURITY AND EMERGENCY PREPAREDNESS
CONGRESSIONAL RESEARCH SERVICE
COPYRIGHT OFFICE
LAW LIBRARY
LIBRARY SERVICES
OFFICE OF STRATEGIC INITIATIVES

from the daguerreotype to the latest news photo; recordings, including folksongs and other music, speeches, and poetry readings; prints, drawings, and posters; government documents, newspapers, and periodicals from all over the world; and motion pictures, microforms, and audio and video tapes.

Reference Resources Admission to the various research facilities of the Library is free. No introduction or credentials are required for persons over high school age. Readers must register by presenting valid photo identification with a current address, and for certain collections there are additional requirements. As demands for service to Congress and Federal Government agencies increase, reference service available through correspondence has become limited. The Library must decline some requests and refer correspondents to a library within their area that can provide satisfactory assistance. While priority is given to inquiries pertaining to its holdings of special materials or to subjects in which its resources are unique, the Library does attempt to provide helpful responses to all inquirers. Online reference service is also available through the "Ask a Librarian" site, at www.loc.gov/rr/askalib.

Copyrights With the enactment of the second general revision of the U.S. copyright law by Act of July 8, 1870 (16 Stat. 212–217), all activities relating to copyright, including deposit and registration, were centralized in the Library of Congress. The Copyright Act of 1976 (90 Stat. 2541) brought all forms of copyrightable authorship, both published and unpublished, under a single statutory system which gives authors protection immediately upon creation of their works. Exclusive rights granted to authors under the statute include the right to reproduce and prepare derivative works, distribute copies or phonorecords, perform and display the work publicly, and in the case of sound recordings, to perform the work publicly by means of a digital audio transmission. Works eligible for copyright include literary works (books and periodicals), musical works, dramatic works, pantomimes and choreographic works, pictorial, graphic, and sculptural works, motion pictures, sound recordings, vessel hull designs, mask works, and architectural works. Serving in its capacity as a national registry for creative works, the Copyright Office registers more than 500,000 claims to copyright annually (representing more than 800,000 works) and is a major source of acquisitions for the universal collections of the Library of Congress. Most of the information available on paper is also accessible online, at www.loc.gov/copyright.

Extension of Service The Library extends its service through the following:

—an interlibrary loan system;

—the photoduplication, at reasonable cost, of books, manuscripts, maps, newspapers, and prints in its collections;

—the sale of sound recordings, which are released by its Recording Laboratory;

—the exchange of duplicates with other institutions;

—the sale of CD–ROM cataloging tools and magnetic tapes and the publication in book format or microform of cumulative catalogs, which make available the results of the expert bibliographical and cataloging work of its technical personnel;

—a centralized cataloging program whereby the Library of Congress acquires material published all over the world, catalogs it promptly, and distributes cataloging information in machine-readable form and other means to the Nation's libraries;

—a cooperative cataloging program whereby the cataloging of data, by name authority and bibliographic records, prepared by other libraries becomes part of the Library of Congress database and is distributed through the Cataloging Distribution Service;

—a cataloging-in-publication program in cooperation with American publishers for printing cataloging information in current books;

—the National Serials Data Program, a national center that maintains a record of serial titles to which International Standard Serial Numbers have been assigned and serves, with this file, as the United States Register; and

—the development of general schemes of classification (Library of Congress and Dewey Decimal), subject headings, and cataloging, embracing the entire field of printed matter.

Furthermore, the Library provides for the following:

—the preparation of bibliographical lists responsive to the needs of Government and research;

—the maintenance and the publication of cooperative publications;

—the publication of catalogs, bibliographical guides, and lists, and of texts of original manuscripts and rare books in the Library of Congress;

—the circulation in traveling exhibitions of items from the Library's collections;

—the provision of books in braille, electronic access to braille books on the Internet, "talking books," and books on tape for the blind and the physically handicapped through 134 cooperating libraries throughout the Nation;

—the distribution of its electronic materials via the Internet; and

—the provision of research and analytical services on a fee-for-service basis to agencies in the executive and judicial branches.

Congressional Research Service Congress created the Congressional Research Service (CRS) to serve its needs for nonpartisan and objective research and analysis of legislative policy issues. CRS provides timely, confidential, and authoritative research and analysis to Members, committees, and their staff. The Service provides comprehensive support in foreign policy, economics, law, science, political science, and social policy. CRS also covers the operations and procedures of both Chambers, legislative processes for the Federal budget and appropriations, and all constitutional issues, including separation of powers, war powers, impeachment, and electoral procedures.

CRS analysts, attorneys, and information specialists work closely with Members and committees to explain policy problems, develop options and legislative proposals, conduct legal analysis of pending legislation, deliver testimony before congressional committees, prepare products on current legislative issues, write confidential memoranda, and provide personal consultations. The Service also conducts seminars on public policy and legal issues as well as training in the legislative and budget processes.

For further information, call 202–707–5700.

American Folklife Center The Center was established in the Library of Congress by Act of January 2, 1976 (20 U.S.C. 2102 *et seq.*). It supports, preserves, and presents American folklife by receiving and maintaining folklife collections, scholarly research, field projects, performances, exhibitions, festivals, workshops, publications, and audiovisual presentations. The Center has conducted projects in many locations across the country, such as the ethnic communities of Chicago, IL; southern Georgia; a ranching community in northern Nevada; the Blue Ridge Parkway in southern Virginia and northern North Carolina; and the States of New Jersey, Rhode Island, and Montana. The projects have provided large collections of recordings and photographs for the Archive of Folk Culture. The Center administers the Federal Cylinder Project, which is charged with preserving and disseminating music and oral traditions recorded on wax cylinders dating from the late 1800s to the early 1940s. A cultural conservation study was developed at the Center, in cooperation with the Department of the Interior, pursuant to a congressional mandate. Various conferences, workshops, and symposia are given throughout the year.

The *Folklife Center News,* a quarterly newsletter, and other informational publications are available upon request. Many Center publications and a number of collections are available online through the Internet, at www.loc.gov/folklife.

The American Folklife Center maintains and administers the Archive of Folk Culture, an extensive collection of ethnographic materials from this country and around the world. It is the national repository for folk-related recordings, manuscripts, and other unpublished materials. The Center's reading room contains over 3,500 books and periodicals; a sizable collection of magazines, newsletters, unpublished theses, and dissertations; field notes; and many textual and some musical transcriptions and recordings. The American Folklife Center also administers the Veterans History Project. Established by Congress in 2000, the purpose of the Veterans History Project is to record and preserve for future generations the first-person accounts of war veterans, including Members of Congress.

For further information, call 202–707–5510.

Center for the Book The Center was established in the Library of Congress by an act of October 13, 1977 (2 U.S.C. 171 *et seq.*), to stimulate public interest in books, reading, and libraries, and to encourage the study of books and print culture. The Center is a catalyst for promoting and exploring the vital role of books, reading, and libraries—nationally and internationally. As a partnership between the Government and the private sector, the Center for the Book depends on tax-deductible contributions from individuals and corporations to support its programs.

The Center's activities are directed toward the general public and scholars. The overall program includes reading promotion projects with television and radio networks, symposia, lectures, exhibitions, special events, and publications. More than 90 national educational and civic organizations participate in the Center's annual reading promotion campaign.

All 50 States and the District of Columbia have established statewide book centers that are affiliated with the Center for the Book in the Library of Congress. State centers plan and fund their own projects, involving members of the State's "community of the book," including authors, readers, prominent citizens, and public officials who serve as honorary advisers.

For further information, contact the Center for the Book. Phone, 202–707–5221. Fax, 202–707–0269. E-mail, cfbook@loc.gov.

National Film Preservation Board The National Film Preservation Board, established by the National Film Preservation Act of 1992 (2 U.S.C. 179) and reauthorized by the National Film Preservation Act of 2005 (2 U.S.C. 179n), serves as a public advisory group to the Librarian of Congress. The Board works to ensure the survival, conservation, and increased public availability of America's film heritage, including advising the Librarian on the annual selection of films to the National Film Registry and counseling the Librarian on development and implementation of the national film preservation plan. Key publications are *Film Preservation 1993: A Study of the Current State of American Film Preservation, Redefining Film Preservation: A National Plan*, and *Television and Video Preservation 1997: A Study of the Current State of American Television and Video Preservation.*

For further information, call 202–707–5912.

National Sound Recording Preservation Board The National Sound Recording Preservation Board, established by the National Recording Preservation Act of 2000 (2 U.S.C. 1701 note), includes three major components: a National Recording Preservation Advisory Board, which brings together experts in the field, a National Recording Registry, and a fundraising foundation, all of which are conducted under the auspices of the Library of Congress. The purpose of the Board is to create and implement a national plan for the long-term preservation and accessibility of the Nation's audio heritage. It also advises the Librarian on the selection of culturally, aesthetically, or historically significant sound recordings to be included on the National Recording Registry. The national recording preservation program will set standards for future private and public preservation efforts and will be conducted in conjunction with the state-of-the-art National Audio-Visual Conservation Center the Library is developing in Culpeper, VA.

For further information, call 202–707–5856.

Preservation The Library provides technical information related to the preservation of library and archival material. A series of handouts on various preservation and conservation topics has been prepared by the Preservation Office. Information and publications are available from the Office of the Director for Preservation, Library of Congress, Washington, DC 20540–4500. Phone, 202–707–1840.

Sources of Information

Books for the Blind and Physically Handicapped Talking and braille books and magazines are distributed through 134 regional and subregional libraries to blind and physically handicapped residents of the United States and its territories. Qualified users can also register for Web-Braille, an Internet-based service. Information is available at public libraries throughout the United States and from the headquarters office, National Library Service for the Blind and Physically Handicapped, Library of Congress, 1291 Taylor Street NW., Washington, DC 20542–4960. Phone, 202–707–5100.

Cataloging Data Distribution Cataloging and bibliographic information in the form of microfiche catalogs, book catalogs, magnetic tapes, CD–ROM cataloging tools, bibliographies, and other technical publications is distributed to libraries and other institutions. Information about ordering materials is available from the Cataloging Distribution Service, Library of Congress, Washington, DC 20541–4910. Phone, 202–707–6100. TDD, 202–707–0012. Fax, 202–707–1334. E-mail, cdsinfo@mail.loc.gov.

Library of Congress card numbers for new publications are assigned by the Cataloging in Publication Division. Direct inquiries to CIP Division, Library of Congress, Washington, DC 20540–4320. Phone, 202–707–6372.

Contracts Persons seeking to do business with the Library of Congress should contact Contracts and Logistics Services, Room 325, John Adams Building, Washington, DC, 20540–9410. Phone, 202–707–0419.

Copyright Services Information about the copyright law (title 17 of the U.S. Code), the method of securing copyright, and copyright registration procedures may be obtained by writing to the Copyright Office, Library of Congress, 101 Independence Avenue SE., Washington, DC 20559–6000. Phone, 202–707–3000. Copyright information is also available through the Internet at www.loc.gov/copyright. Registration application forms may be ordered by calling the forms hotline at 202–707–9100. Copyright records may be researched and reported by the Copyright Office for a fee; for an estimate, call 202–707–6850. Members of the public may use the copyright card catalog in the Copyright Office without charge. The database of Copyright Office records cataloged from January 1, 1978, to the present is available through the Internet at www.loc.gov/copyright/rb.html. The Copyright Information Office is located in Room LM–401, James Madison Memorial Building, 101 Independence Avenue SE., Washington, DC 20559–6000, and is open to the public Monday through Friday, 8:30 a.m. to 5 p.m. e.s.t., except Federal holidays.

Employment Employment inquiries should be directed to Human Resources Services, Library of Congress, 101 Independence Avenue SE., Washington, DC 20540–2200. Vacancy announcements and applications are also available from the Employment Office, Room LM–107, 101 Independence Avenue SE. Phone, 202–707–4315. Internet, www.loc.gov/hr/employment.

Photoduplication Service Copies of manuscripts, prints, photographs, maps, and book material not subject to copyright and other restrictions are available for a fee. Order forms for photo reproduction and price schedules are available from the Photoduplication Service, Library of Congress, 101 Independence Avenue SE., Washington, DC 20540–4570. Phone, 202–707–5640.

Publications A list of Library of Congress publications, many of which are of interest to the general public, is available through the Internet at www.loc.gov. A monthly *Calendar of Events,* listing programs, and exhibitions at the Library of Congress can be mailed regularly to persons within 100 miles of Washington, DC. Make requests to Office Systems Services, Mail and Distribution Management Section, Library of Congress, 101 Independence Avenue SE., Washington, DC 20540–9441.

Reference and Bibliographic Services Guidance is offered to readers in identifying and using the material in the Library's collections, and reference service is provided to those with inquiries who have exhausted local, State, and regional resources. Persons requiring services that cannot be performed by the Library staff can be supplied with names of private researchers who work on a fee basis. Requests for information should be directed to the Reference Referral Service, Library of Congress, 101 Independence Avenue SE., Washington, DC 20540–4720. Phone, 202–707–5522. Fax, 202–707–1389.

Research and Reference Services in Science and Technology Reference specialists in the Science, Technology, and Business Division provide a free service in answering brief technical inquiries entailing a bibliographic response. Requests for reference services should be directed to the Science, Technology, and Business Division, Library of Congress, Science Reference Section, 101 Independence Avenue SE., Washington, DC 20540–4750. Phone, 202–707–5639. Internet, www.loc.gov/rr/scitech.

Research Services in General Topics Federal Government agencies can procure directed research and analytical products on foreign and domestic topics using the collections of the Library of Congress through the Federal Research Division. Science, technology, humanities, and social science topics of research are conducted by staff specialists exclusively on behalf of Federal agencies on a fee-for-service basis. Requests for service should be directed to the Federal Research Division, Marketing Office, Library of Congress, Washington, DC 20540–4840. Phone, 202–707–3909. Fax, 202–245–3920.

For further information, contact the Public Affairs Office, Library of Congress, 101 Independence Avenue SE., Washington, DC 20540–8610. Phone, 202–707–2905. Fax, 202–707–9199. Internet, www.loc.gov.

CONGRESSIONAL BUDGET OFFICE

Second and D Streets SW., Washington, DC 20515
Phone, 202–226–2600. Internet, www.cbo.gov.

Director	DONALD B. MARRON, *Acting*
Deputy Director	DONALD B. MARRON
Special Assistant to the Director	EDWARD DAVIS
General Counsel	ROBERT P. MURPHY
Assistant Director for Business, Management, and Information Services	STEPHEN A. WEIGLER
Associate Director for Communications	MELISSA MERSON
Associate Director for Research and Reports	ARLENE HOLEN
Assistant Director for Budget Analysis	ROBERT A. SUNSHINE
Assistant Director for Health and Human Resources	BRUCE VAVRICHEK
Assistant Director for Macroeconomic Analysis	ROBERT A. DENNIS
Assistant Director for Microeconomic Studies	JOSEPH KILE

Assistant Director for National Security — J. MICHAEL GILMORE
Assistant Director for Tax Analysis — G. THOMAS WOODWARD

The Congressional Budget Office provides the Congress with economic analyses of alternative fiscal, budgetary, and programmatic policy issues, and with information and estimates required for the congressional budget process.

The Congressional Budget Office (CBO) was established by the Congressional Budget Act of 1974 (2 U.S.C. 601), which also created a procedure by which the United States Congress considers and acts upon the annual Federal budget. This process enables the Congress to have an overview of the Federal budget and to make overall decisions regarding spending and taxing levels and the deficit or surplus these levels incur.

Activities

Economic Forecasting and Fiscal Policy Analysis The Federal budget affects and is affected by the national economy. The Congressional Budget Office provides the Congress with biannual forecasts of the economy and analyses of economic trends and alternative fiscal policies.

Scorekeeping Under the budget process, the Congress establishes (by concurrent resolution), targets for overall expenditures, budget authority and budget outlays, and broad functional categories. The Congress also establishes targets for the levels of revenues, the deficit or surplus, and the public debt. The Office "keeps score" for the Congress by monitoring the results of congressional action on individual authorization, appropriation, and revenue bills against the targets specified in the concurrent resolution.

Cost Projections The Office prepares multiyear cost estimates for carrying out any public bill or resolution reported by congressional committees. As soon as practicable after the beginning of each fiscal year, CBO also provides multiyear projections on the costs of continuing current Federal spending and taxation policies.

Annual Report on the Budget The Office is responsible for submitting to the House and Senate Budget Committees each year a report on fiscal policy that includes alternative spending and revenue levels and baseline projections of the Federal budget.

Federal Mandates To better assess the impact of laws on State, local, and tribal governments and the private sector, the Congress passed the Unfunded Mandates Reform Act of 1995. The act amends the Congressional Budget Act to require CBO to give authorizing committees a statement about whether reported bills contain Federal mandates. If the 5-year direct costs of an intergovernmental or private-sector mandate exceed specified thresholds, CBO must provide an estimate of those costs (if feasible) and the basis of the estimate.

Budget-Related Studies The Office undertakes studies requested by the Congress on budget-related areas. This service is provided in the following order of priority to the House and Senate Budget Committees, the House and Senate Appropriations Committees, the Senate Finance Committee, and the House Ways and Means Committee, and all other congressional committees.

For further information, contact the Management, Business, and Information Services Division, Congressional Budget Office, Second and D Streets SW., Washington, DC 20515. Phone, 202–226–2600. Fax, 202–226–2714. Internet, www.cbo.gov.

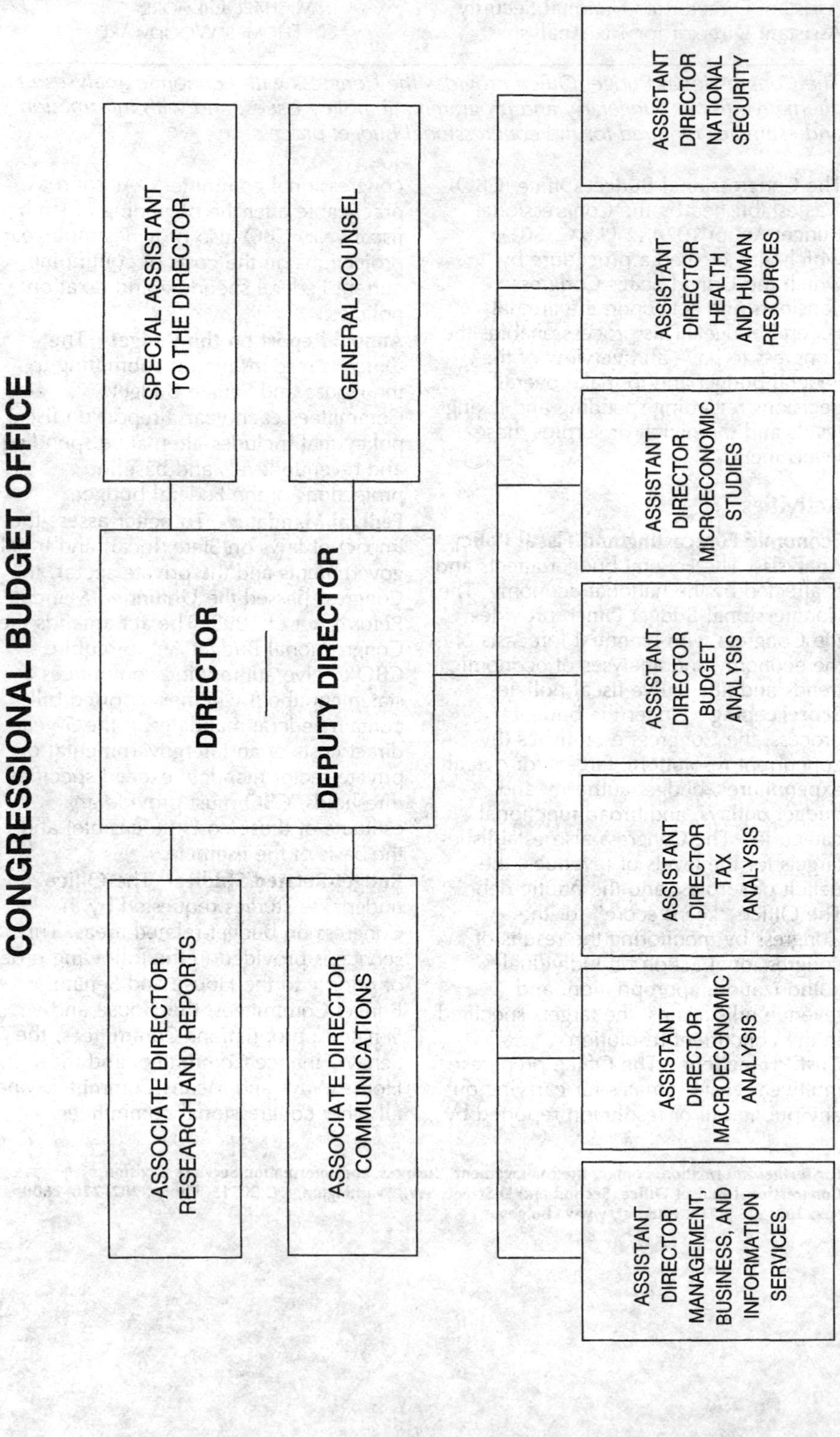
CONGRESSIONAL BUDGET OFFICE
SPECIAL ASSISTANT TO THE DIRECTOR
GENERAL COUNSEL
DIRECTOR
DEPUTY DIRECTOR
ASSOCIATE DIRECTOR RESEARCH AND REPORTS
ASSOCIATE DIRECTOR COMMUNICATIONS
ASSISTANT DIRECTOR NATIONAL SECURITY
ASSISTANT DIRECTOR HEALTH AND HUMAN RESOURCES
ASSISTANT DIRECTOR MICROECONOMIC STUDIES
ASSISTANT DIRECTOR BUDGET ANALYSIS
ASSISTANT DIRECTOR TAX ANALYSIS
ASSISTANT DIRECTOR MACROECONOMIC ANALYSIS
ASSISTANT DIRECTOR MANAGEMENT, BUSINESS, AND INFORMATION SERVICES

Judicial Branch

JUDICIAL BRANCH

THE SUPREME COURT OF THE UNITED STATES

United States Supreme Court Building
One First Street NE., Washington, DC 20543
Phone, 202–479–3000. Internet, www.supremecourtus.gov.

Members:

Chief Justice of the United States	JOHN G. ROBERTS, JR.
Associate Justices	JOHN PAUL STEVENS, ANTONIN SCALIA, ANTHONY M. KENNEDY, DAVID H. SOUTER, CLARENCE THOMAS, RUTH BADER GINSBURG, STEPHEN G. BREYER, SAMUEL A. ALITO, JR.

Officers:

Administrative Assistant to the Chief Justice	SALLY M. RIDER
Clerk	WILLIAM K. SUTER
Court Counsel	SCOTT S. HARRIS
Curator	CATHERINE E. FITTS
Director of Budget and Personnel	(VACANCY)
Director of Data Systems	DONNA CLEMENT
Librarian	JUDITH GASKELL
Marshal	PAMELA TALKIN
Public Information Officer	KATHLEEN L. ARBERG
Reporter of Decisions	FRANK D. WAGNER

Article III, section 1, of the Constitution of the United States provides that "[t]he judicial Power of the United States, shall be vested in one supreme Court, and in such inferior Courts as the Congress may from time to time ordain and establish."

The Supreme Court of the United States was created in accordance with this provision and by authority of the Judiciary Act of September 24, 1789 (1 Stat. 73). It was organized on February 2, 1790. Article III, section 2 of the Constitution defines the jurisdiction of the Supreme Court.

The Supreme Court is comprised of the Chief Justice of the United States and such number of Associate Justices as may be fixed by Congress, which is currently fixed at eight (28 U.S.C. 1). The President nominates the Justices with the advice and consent of the Senate. Article III, section 1, of the Constitution further provides that "[t]he Judges, both of the supreme and inferior Courts, shall hold their Offices during good Behaviour, and shall, at stated Times, receive for their Services, a Compensation, which shall not be diminished during their Continuance in Office."

Court officers assist the Court in the performance of its functions. They include the Administrative Assistant to the Chief Justice, the Clerk, the Reporter of Decisions, the Librarian, the Marshal, the Director of Budget and Personnel, the Court Counsel, the Curator, the Director of Data Systems, and the Public Information Officer.

Appellate Jurisdiction Appellate jurisdiction has been conferred upon the Supreme Court by various statutes under the authority given Congress by the Constitution. The basic statute effective at this time in conferring and controlling jurisdiction of the Supreme Court may be found in 28 U.S.C. 1251, 1253, 1254, 1257–1259, and various special statutes. Congress has no authority to change the original jurisdiction of this Court.

Rulemaking Power Congress has from time to time conferred upon the Supreme Court power to prescribe rules of procedure to be followed by the lower courts of the United States.

Court Term The term of the Court begins on the first Monday in October and lasts until the first Monday in October of the next year. Approximately 8,000 cases are filed with the Court in the course of a term, and some 1,000 applications of various kinds are filed each year that can be acted upon by a single Justice.

Access to Facilities The Supreme Court is open to the public from 9 a.m. to 4:30 p.m., Monday through Friday, except on Federal holidays. Unless the Court or Chief Justice orders otherwise, the Clerk's office is open from 9 a.m. to 5 p.m., Monday through Friday, except on Federal legal holidays. The library is open to members of the bar of the Court, attorneys for the various Federal departments and agencies, and Members of Congress.

For further information concerning the Supreme Court, contact the Public Information Office, United States Supreme Court Building, One First Street NE., Washington, DC 20543. Phone, 202–479–3211. Internet, www.supremecourtus.gov.

Lower Courts

Article III of the Constitution declares, in section 1, that the judicial power of the United States shall be invested in one Supreme Court and in "such inferior Courts as the Congress may from time to time ordain and establish." The Supreme Court has held that these constitutional courts ". . . share in the exercise of the judicial power defined in that section, can be invested with no other jurisdiction, and have judges who hold office during good behavior, with no power in Congress to provide otherwise."

United States Courts of Appeals The courts of appeals are intermediate appellate courts created by act of March 3, 1891 (28 U.S.C. ch. 3), to relieve the Supreme Court of considering all appeals in cases originally decided by the Federal trial courts. They are empowered to review all final decisions and certain interlocutory decisions (18 U.S.C. 3731; 28 U.S.C. 1291, 1292) of district courts. They also are empowered to review and enforce orders of many Federal administrative bodies. The decisions of the courts of appeals are final except as they are subject to review on writ of certiorari by the Supreme Court.

The United States is divided geographically into 12 judicial circuits, including the District of Columbia. Each circuit has a court of appeals (28 U.S.C. 41, 1294). Each of the 50 States is assigned to one of the circuits. The territories and the Commonwealth of Puerto Rico are assigned variously to the first, third, and ninth circuits. There is also a Court of Appeals for the Federal Circuit, which has nationwide jurisdiction defined by subject matter. At present each court of appeals has from 6 to 28 permanent circuit judgeships (179 in all), depending upon the amount of judicial work in the circuit. Circuit judges hold their offices during good behavior as provided by Article III, section 1, of the Constitution. The judge senior in commission who is under 70 years of age (65 at inception of term), has been in office at least 1 year, and has not previously been chief judge, serves as the chief judge of the circuit for a 7-year term. One of the justices of the Supreme Court is assigned as circuit justice for each of the 13 judicial circuits. Each court of appeals normally hears cases in panels consisting of three judges but may sit *en banc* with all judges present.

The judges of each circuit (except the Federal Circuit) by vote determine the size of the judicial council for the circuit, which consists of the chief judge and an equal number of circuit and district judges. The council considers the state of Federal judicial business in the circuit and may "make all necessary and appropriate orders for [its] effective and expeditious administration . . ." (28 U.S.C. 332). The chief judge of each circuit may summon periodically a judicial conference of all judges of the circuit, including members of the bar, to discuss the business of the Federal courts of the circuit (28 U.S.C. 333). The chief judge of each circuit and a district judge elected from each of the 12 geographical circuits, together with the chief judge of the Court of International Trade, serve as members of the Judicial Conference of the United States, over which the Chief Justice of the United States presides. This is the governing body for the administration of the Federal judicial system as a whole (28 U.S.C. 331).

United States Court of Appeals for the Federal Circuit This court was established under Article III of the Constitution pursuant to the Federal Courts Improvement Act of 1982 (28 U.S.C. 41, 44, 48), as successor to the former United States Court of Customs and Patent Appeals and the United States Court of Claims. The jurisdiction of the court is nationwide (as provided by 28 U.S.C. 1295) and includes appeals from the district courts in patent cases; appeals from the district courts in contract, and certain other civil actions in which the United States is a defendant; and appeals from final decisions of the U.S. Court of International Trade, the U.S. Court of Federal Claims, and the U.S. Court of Appeals for Veterans Claims. The jurisdiction of the court also includes the review of administrative rulings by the Patent and Trademark Office, U.S. International Trade Commission, Secretary of Commerce, agency boards of contract appeals, and the Merit Systems Protection Board, as well as rulemaking of the Department of Veterans Affairs; review of decisions of the U.S. Senate Select Committee on Ethics concerning discrimination claims of Senate employees; and review of a final order of an entity to be designated by the President concerning discrimination claims of Presidential appointees.

The court consists of 12 circuit judges. It sits in panels of three or more on each case and may also hear or rehear a case *en banc*. The court sits principally in Washington, DC, and may hold court wherever any court of appeals sits (28 U.S.C. 48).

Judicial Circuits—United States Courts of Appeals

Circuit	Judges	Official Station
	District of Columbia Circuit	
(*Clerk*: Mark J. Langer; *Circuit Executive*: Jill C. Sayenga; Washington, DC)	*Circuit Justice*	
	Chief Justice John G. Roberts, Jr.	
	Circuit Judges	
	Douglas H. Ginsburg, *Chief Judge*	Washington, DC
	David Bryan Sentelle	Washington, DC
	Karen LeCraft Henderson	Washington, DC
	A. Raymond Randolph	Washington, DC
	Judith W. Rogers	Washington, DC
	David S. Tatel	Washington, DC
	Merrick B. Garland	Washington, DC

Judicial Circuits—United States Courts of Appeals—Continued

Circuit	Judges	Official Station
	Janice Rogers Brown	Washington, DC
	Thomas B. Griffith	Washington, DC
	Brett M. Kavanaugh	Washington, DC
	(2 vacancies)	
	First Circuit	
Districts of Maine, New Hampshire, Massachusetts, Rhode Island, and Puerto Rico (*Clerk*: Richard C. Donovan; *Circuit Executive*: Gary Wente; Boston, MA)	*Circuit Justice*	
	Justice David H. Souter	
	Circuit Judges	
	Michael Boudin, *Chief Judge*	Boston, MA
	Juan R. Torruella	San Juan, PR
	Bruce M. Selya	Providence, RI
	Sandra L. Lynch	Boston, MA
	Kermit V. Lipez	Portland, ME
	Jeffrey R. Howard	Concord, NH
	Second Circuit	
Districts of Vermont, Connecticut, northern New York, southern New York, eastern New York, and western New York (*Clerk*: Roseann B. MacKechnie; *Circuit Executive*: Karen G. Milton; New York, NY)	*Circuit Justice*	
	Justice Ruth Bader Ginsburg	
	Circuit Judges	
	John M. Walker, Jr., *Chief Judge*	New Haven, CT
	Dennis G. Jacobs	New York, NY
	Guido Calabresi	New Haven, CT
	Jose A. Cabranes	New Haven, CT
	Chester J. Straub	New York, NY
	Rosemary S. Pooler	Syracuse, NY
	Robert D. Sack	New York, NY
	Sonia Sotomayor	New York, NY
	Robert A. Katzmann	New York, NY
	Barrington D. Parker, Jr.	White Plains, NY
	Reena Raggi	New York, NY
	Richard C. Wesley	New York, NY
	Peter W. Hall	New York, NY
	Third Circuit	
Districts of New Jersey, eastern Pennsylvania, middle Pennsylvania, western Pennsylvania, Delaware, and the Virgin Islands (*Clerk*: Marcia M. Waldron; *Circuit Executive*: Toby D. Slawsky; Philadelphia, PA)	*Circuit Justice*	
	Justice David H. Souter	
	Circuit Judges	
	Anthony J. Scirica, *Chief Judge*	Philadelphia, PA
	Dolores Korman Sloviter	Philadelphia, PA
	Jane R. Roth	Wilmington, DE
	Theodore A. McKee	Philadelphia, PA
	Marjorie O. Rendell	Philadelphia, PA
	Maryanne Trump Barry	Newark, NJ
	Thomas L. Ambro	Wilmington, DE
	Julio M. Fuentes	Newark, NJ
	D. Brooks Smith	Duncansville, PA
	D. Michael Fisher	Pittsburg, PA
	Franklin S. Van Antwerpen	Easton, PA
	Michael A. Chagares	Newark, NJ
	Fourth Circuit	
Districts of Maryland, northern West Virginia, southern West Virginia, eastern Virginia, western Virginia, eastern North Carolina, western North Carolina, middle North Carolina, and South Carolina (*Clerk*: Patricia S. Connor; *Circuit Executive*: Samuel W. Phillips; Richmond, VA)	*Circuit Justice*	
	Chief Justice John G. Roberts, Jr.	
	Circuit Judges	
	William W. Wilkins, Jr., *Chief Judge*	Greenville, SC
	H. Emory Widener, Jr.	Abingdon, VA
	James Harvie Wilkinson III	Charlottesville, VA
	Paul V. Niemeyer	Baltimore, MD
	Karen J. Williams	Orangeburg, SC
	M. Blane Michael	Charleston, WV
	Diana Gribbon Motz	Baltimore, MD
	William B. Traxler, Jr.	Greenville, SC
	Robert B. King	Charleston, WV
	Roger L. Gregory	Richmond, VA

Judicial Circuits—United States Courts of Appeals—Continued

Circuit	Judges	Official Station
	Dennis W. Shedd	Columbia, SC
	Allyson K. Duncan	Raleigh, NC
	(3 vacancies)	
	Fifth Circuit	
Districts of northern Mississippi, southern Mississippi, eastern Louisiana, middle Louisiana, western Louisiana, northern Texas, southern Texas, eastern Texas, and western Texas (*Clerk*: Charles R. Fulbruge III; *Circuit Executive*: Gregory A. Nussel; New Orleans, LA)	*Circuit Justice*	
	Justice Antonin Scalia	
	Circuit Judges	
	Edith H. Jones, *Chief Judge*	Houston, TX
	Carolyn Dineen King	Houston
	E. Grady Jolly	Jackson, MS
	Patrick E. Higginbotham	Dallas, TX
	W. Eugene Davis	Lafayette, LA
	Jerry Edwin Smith	Houston, TX
	Jacques L. Wiener, Jr.	New Orleans, LA
	Rhesa H. Barksdale	Jackson, MS
	Emilio M. Garza	San Antonio, TX
	Harold R. DeMoss, Jr.	Houston, TX
	Fortunado P. Benavides	Austin, TX
	Carl E. Stewart	Shreveport, LA
	James L. Dennis	New Orleans, LA
	Edith Brown Clement	New Orleans, LA
	Edward C. Prado	San Antonio, TX
	Priscilla R. Owen	Austin, TX
	(vacancy)	
	Sixth Circuit	
Districts of northern Ohio, southern Ohio, eastern Michigan, western Michigan, eastern Kentucky, western Kentucky, eastern Tennessee, middle Tennessee, and western Tennessee (*Clerk*: Leonard Green; *Circuit Executive*: James A. Higgins; Cincinnati, OH)	*Circuit Justice*	
	Justice John Paul Stevens	
	Circuit Judges	
	Danny J. Boggs, *Chief Judge*	Louisville, KY
	Boyce F. Martin, Jr.	Louisville, KY
	Alice M. Batchelder	Medina, OH
	Martha Craig Daughtrey	Nashville, TN
	Karen Nelson Moore	Cleveland, OH
	Ransey Guy Cole, Jr.	Columbus, OH
	Eric L. Clay	Detroit, MI
	Ronald Lee Gilman	Memphis, TN
	Julia Smith Gibbons	Memphis, TN
	John M. Rogers	Lexington, KY
	Jeffrey S. Sutton	Columbus, OH
	Deborah L. Cook	Akron, OH
	David W. McKeague	Lansing, MI
	Richard A. Griffin	Traverse City, MI
	(2 vacancies)	
	Seventh Circuit	
Districts of northern Indiana, southern Indiana, northern Illinois, central Illinois, southern Illinois, eastern Wisconsin, and western Wisconsin (*Clerk*: Gino J. Agnello; *Circuit Executive*: Collins T. Fitzpatrick; Chicago, IL)	*Circuit Justice*	
	Justice John Paul Stevens	
	Circuit Judges	
	Joel M. Flaum, *Chief Judge*	Chicago, IL
	Richard A. Posner	Chicago, IL
	Frank H. Easterbrook	Chicago, IL
	Kenneth F. Ripple	South Bend, IN
	Daniel A. Manion	South Bend, IN
	Michael S. Kanne	Lafayette, IN
	Ilana Diamond Rovner	Chicago, IL
	Diane P. Wood	Chicago, IL
	Terence T. Evans	Milwaukee, WI
	Ann C. Williams	Chicago, IL
	Diane S. Sykes	Milwaukee, WI
	Eighth Circuit	
Districts of Minnesota, northern Iowa, southern Iowa, eastern Missouri,	*Circuit Justice*	
	Justice Samuel A. Alito, Jr.	

Judicial Circuits—United States Courts of Appeals—Continued

Circuit	Judges	Official Station
western Missouri, eastern Arkansas, western Arkansas, Nebraska, North Dakota, and South Dakota (*Clerk*: Michael Ellis Gans; *Circuit Executive*: Millie B. Adams; St. Louis, MO)	*Circuit Judges*	
	James B. Loken, *Chief Judge*	Minneapolis, MN
	Roger L. Wollman	Sioux Falls, SD
	Morris S. Arnold	Little Rock, AR
	Diana E. Murphy	Minneapolis, MN
	Kermit E. Bye	Fargo, ND
	William Jay Riley	Omaha, NE
	Michael J. Melloy	Cedar Rapids, IA
	Lavenski R. Smith	Little Rock, AR
	Steven M. Colloton	Des Moines, IA
	Raymond W. Gruender	St. Louis, MO
	Duane Benton	Kansas City, MO
	Ninth Circuit	
Districts of northern California, eastern California, central California, southern California, Oregon, Nevada, Montana, eastern Washington, western Washington, Idaho, Arizona, Alaska, Hawaii, Territory of Guam, and District Court for the Northern Mariana Islands (*Clerk*: Cathy A. Catterson; *Circuit Executive*: Gregory B. Walters; San Francisco, CA)	*Circuit Justice*	
	Justice Anthony M. Kennedy	
	Circuit Judges	
	Mary M. Schroeder, *Chief Judge*	Phoenix, AZ
	Harry Pregerson	Woodland Hills, CA
	Stephen Reinhardt	Los Angeles, CA
	Alex Kozinski	Pasadena, CA
	Diarmuid F. O'Scannlain	Portland, OR
	Pamela A. Rymer	Pasadena, CA
	Andrew J. Kleinfeld	Fairbanks, AK
	Michael D. Hawkins	Phoenix, AZ
	Sidney R. Thomas	Billings, MT
	Barry G. Silverman	Phoenix, AZ
	Susan P. Graber	Portland, OR
	M. Margaret McKeown	Seattle, WA
	Kim M. Wardlaw	Pasadena, CA
	William A. Fletcher	San Francisco, CA
	Raymond C. Fisher	Pasadena, CA
	Ronald M. Gould	Seattle, WA
	Richard A. Paez	Pasadena, CA
	Marsha S. Berzon	San Francisco, CA
	Richard C. Tallman	Seattle, WA
	Johnnie B. Rawlinson	Las Vegas, NV
	Richard R. Clifton	Honolulu, HI
	Jay S. Bybee	Las Vegas, NV
	Consuelo Maria Callahan	Sacramento, CA
	Carlos T. Bea	San Francisco, CA
	Milan D. Smith, Jr.	Pasadena, CA
	(3 vacancies)	
	Tenth Circuit	
Districts of Colorado, Wyoming, Utah, Kansas, eastern Oklahoma, western Oklahoma, northern Oklahoma, and New Mexico (*Clerk*: Elisabeth A. Shumaker; *Circuit Executive*: David J. Tighe; Denver, CO)	*Circuit Justice*	
	Justice Stephen G. Breyer	
	Circuit Judges	
	Deanell Reece Tacha, *Chief Judge*	Lawrence, KS
	Paul J. Kelly, Jr.	Santa Fe, NM
	Robert H. Henry	Oklahoma City, OK
	Mary Beck Briscoe	Lawrence, KS
	Carlos F. Lucero	Denver, CO
	Michael R. Murphy	Salt Lake City, UT
	Harris L. Hartz	Albuquerque, NM
	Terrence L. O'Brien	Cheyenne, WY
	Michael W. McConnell	Salt Lake City, UT
	Timothy M. Tymkovich	Denver, CO
	(2 vacancies)	
	Eleventh Circuit	
Districts of northern Georgia, middle Georgia, southern Georgia, northern Florida, middle Florida, southern Florida, northern Alabama, middle Alabama, southern Alabama	*Circuit Justice*	
	Justice Clarence Thomas	
	Circuit Judges	
	J.L. Edmondson, *Chief Judge*	Atlanta, GA
	Gerald B. Tjoflat	Jacksonville, FL
	R. Lanier Anderson III	Macon, GA

Judicial Circuits—United States Courts of Appeals—Continued

Circuit	Judges	Official Station
(*Clerk*: Thomas K. Kahn;	Stanley F. Birch, Jr.	Atlanta, GA
Circuit Executive:	Joel F. Dubina	Montgomery, AL
Norman E. Zoller;	Susan H. Black	Jacksonville, FL
Atlanta, GA)	Edward E. Carnes	Montgomery, AL
	Rosemary Barkett	Miami, FL
	Frank Mays Hull	Atlanta, GA
	Stanley Marcus	Miami, FL
	Charles R. Wilson	Tampa, FL
	William H. Pryor, Jr.	Birmingham, Al

Federal Circuit—Washington, DC

Circuit Justice
Chief Justice John G. Roberts, Jr.

Chief Judge
Paul R. Michel

Judges
Pauline Newman
Haldane Robert Mayer
Alan D. Lourie
Randall R. Rader
Alvin A. Schall
William C. Bryson
Arthur J. Gajarsa
Richard Linn
Timothy B. Dyk
Sharon Prost
(vacancy)

Clerk: Jan Horbaly
Administrative Services Officer: Ruth A. Butler

United States District Courts The district courts are the trial courts of general Federal jurisdiction. Each State has at least one district court, while the larger States have as many as four. Altogether there are 89 district courts in the 50 States, plus the one in the District of Columbia. In addition, the Commonwealth of Puerto Rico has a district court with jurisdiction corresponding to that of district courts in the various States.

At present, each district court has from 2 to 28 Federal district judgeships, depending upon the amount of judicial work within its territory. Only one judge is usually required to hear and decide a case in a district court, but in some limited cases it is required that three judges be called together to comprise the court (28 U.S.C. 2284). The judge senior in commission who is under 70 years of age (65 at inception of term), has been in office for at least 1 year, and has not previously been chief judge, serves as chief judge for a 7-year term. There are altogether 645 permanent district judgeships in the 50 States and 15 in the District of Columbia. There are 7 district judgeships in Puerto Rico. District judges hold their offices during good behavior as provided by Article III, section 1, of the Constitution. However, Congress may create temporary judgeships for a court with the provision that when a future vacancy occurs in that district, such vacancy shall not be filled. Each district court has one or more United States magistrate judges and bankruptcy judges, a clerk, a United States attorney, a United States marshal, probation officers, court reporters, and their staffs. The jurisdiction of the district courts is set forth in title 28, chapter 85, of the United States Code and at 18 U.S.C. 3231.

Cases from the district courts are reviewable on appeal by the applicable court of appeals.

Territorial Courts Pursuant to its authority to govern the Territories (art. IV, sec. 3, clause 2, of the Constitution), Congress has established district courts in the territories of Guam and the Virgin Islands. The District Court of the Canal Zone was abolished on April 1, 1982, pursuant to the Panama Canal Act of 1979 (22 U.S.C. 3601 note). Congress has also established a district court in the Northern Mariana Islands, which presently is administered by the United States under a trusteeship agreement with the United Nations. These Territorial courts have jurisdiction not only over the subjects described in the judicial article of the Constitution but also over many local matters that, within the States, are decided in State courts. The district court of Puerto Rico, by contrast, is established under Article III, is classified like other "district courts," and is called a "court of the United States" (28 U.S.C. 451). There is one judge each in Guam and the Northern Mariana Islands, and two in the Virgin

Islands. The judges in these courts are appointed for terms of 10 years.

For further information concerning the lower courts, contact the Administrative Office of the United States Courts, Thurgood Marshall Federal Judiciary Building, One Columbus Circle NE., Washington, DC 20544. Phone, 202–502–2600.

United States Court of International Trade This court was originally established as the Board of United States General Appraisers by act of June 10, 1890, which conferred upon it jurisdiction theretofore held by the district and circuit courts in actions arising under the tariff acts (19 U.S.C. ch. 4). The act of May 28, 1926 (19 U.S.C. 405a), created the United States Customs Court to supersede the Board; by acts of August 7, 1939, and June 25, 1948 (28 U.S.C. 1582, 1583), the court was integrated into the United States court structure, organization, and procedure. The act of July 14, 1956 (28 U.S.C. 251), established the court as a court of record of the United States under Article III of the Constitution. The Customs Court Act of 1980 (28 U.S.C. 251) constituted the court as the United States Court of International Trade.

The Court of International Trade has jurisdiction over any civil action against the United States arising from Federal laws governing import transactions. This includes classification and valuation cases, as well as authority to review certain agency determinations under the Trade Agreements Act of 1979 (19 U.S.C. 2501) involving antidumping and countervailing duty matters. In addition, it has exclusive jurisdiction of civil actions to review determinations as to the eligibility of workers, firms, and communities for adjustment assistance under the Trade Act of 1974 (19 U.S.C. 2101). Civil actions commenced by the United States to recover customs duties, to recover on a customs bond, or for certain civil penalties alleging fraud or negligence are also within the exclusive jurisdiction of the court.

The court is composed of a chief judge and eight judges, not more than five of whom may belong to any one political party. Any of its judges may be temporarily designated and assigned by the Chief Justice of the United States to sit as a court of appeals or district court judge in any circuit or district. The court has a clerk and deputy clerks, a librarian, court reporters, and other supporting personnel. Cases before the court may be tried before a jury. Under the Federal Courts Improvement Act of 1982 (28 U.S.C. 1295), appeals are taken to the U.S. Court of Appeals for the Federal Circuit, and ultimately review may be sought in appropriate cases in the Supreme Court of the United States.

The principal offices are located in New York, NY, but the court is empowered to hear and determine cases arising at any port or place within the jurisdiction of the United States.

For further information, contact the Clerk, United States Court of International Trade, One Federal Plaza, New York, NY 10278–0001. Phone, 212–264–2814.

Judicial Panel on Multidistrict Litigation The Panel, created by act of April 29, 1968 (28 U.S.C. 1407), and consisting of seven Federal judges designated by the Chief Justice from the courts of appeals and district courts, is authorized to temporarily transfer to a single district, for coordinated or consolidated pretrial proceedings, civil actions pending in different districts that involve one or more common questions of fact.

For further information, contact the Clerk, Judicial Panel on Multidistrict Litigation, Room G–255, Thurgood Marshall Federal Judiciary Building, One Columbus Circle NE., Washington, DC 20002–8041. Phone, 202–502–2800.

Special Courts

The Supreme Court has held that ". . . Article III [of the Constitution] does not express the full authority of Congress to create courts, and that other

Articles invest Congress with powers in the exertion of which it may create inferior courts and clothe them with functions deemed essential or helpful in carrying those powers into execution." Such courts, known as legislative courts, have functions which ". . . are directed to the execution of one or more of such powers and are prescribed by Congress independently of section 2 of Article III; and their judges hold office for such term as Congress prescribes, whether it be a fixed period of years or during good behavior." Appeals from the decisions of these courts, with the exception of the U.S. Tax Court and the U.S. Court of Appeals for the Armed Forces, may be taken to the U.S. Court of Appeals for the Federal Circuit. Appeals from the decisions of the Tax Court may be taken to the court of appeals in which judicial circuit the case was initially heard. Certain decisions of the U.S. Court of Appeals for the Armed Forces are reviewable by writ of certiorari in the Supreme Court.

United States Court of Federal Claims The U.S. Court of Federal Claims has jurisdiction over claims seeking money judgments against the United States. A claim must be founded upon the United States Constitution; an act of Congress; the regulation of an executive department; an express or implied-in-fact contract with the United States; or damages, liquidated or unliquidated, in cases not sounding in tort. Judges in the U.S. Court of Federal Claims are appointed by the President for 15-year terms, subject to Senate confirmation. Appeals are to the U.S. Court of Appeals for the Federal Circuit.

For further information, contact the Clerk's Office, United States Court of Federal Claims, 717 Madison Place NW., Washington, DC 20005–1086. Phone, 202–357–6400.

United States Court of Appeals for the Armed Forces This court was established under Article I of the Constitution of the United States pursuant to act of May 5, 1950, as amended (10 U.S.C. 867). Subject only to certiorari review by the Supreme Court of the United States in a limited number of cases, the court serves as the final appellate tribunal to review court-martial convictions of all the Armed Forces. It is exclusively an appellate criminal court, consisting of five civilian judges who are appointed for 15-year terms by the President with the advice and consent of the Senate. The court is called upon to exercise jurisdiction to review the record in all cases:

—extending to death;

—certified to the court by a Judge Advocate General of an armed force or by the General Counsel of the Department of Transportation, acting for the Coast Guard; or

—petitioned by accused who have received a sentence of confinement for 1 year or more, and/or a punitive discharge.

The court also exercises authority under the All Writs Act (28 U.S.C. 1651 (a)).

In addition, the judges of the court are required by law to work jointly with the senior uniformed lawyer from each armed force, the Chief Counsel of the Coast Guard, and two members of the public appointed by the Secretary of Defense, to make an annual comprehensive survey and to report annually to the Congress on the operation and progress of the military justice system under the Uniform Code of Military Justice, and to recommend improvements wherever necessary.

For further information, contact the Clerk, United States Court of Appeals for the Armed Forces, 450 E Street NW., Washington, DC 20442–0001. Phone, 202–761–1448. Fax, 202–761–4672. Internet, www.armfor.uscourts.gov.

United States Tax Court This is a court of record under Article I of the Constitution of the United States (26 U.S.C. 7441). Currently an independent judicial body in the legislative branch, the court was originally created as the United States Board of Tax Appeals, an independent agency in the executive branch, by the Revenue Act of 1924 (43 Stat. 336) and continued by the Revenue Act of 1926 (44 Stat. 105), the Internal Revenue Codes of 1939, 1954, and 1986. The name was changed to the Tax Court of the United States by the Revenue Act of 1942 (56 Stat. 957), and the Article I status and change in name to United States Tax Court were effected by the Tax Reform Act of 1969 (83 Stat. 730).

The court is composed of 19 judges. Its strength is augmented by senior judges who may be recalled by the chief judge to perform further judicial duties and by special trial judges who are appointed by the chief judge and serve at the pleasure of the court. The chief judge is elected biennially from among the 19 judges of the court.

The matters over which the Court has jurisdiction are set forth in the various sections of title 26 of the U.S. Code.

At the option of the individual taxpayer, simplified procedures may be utilized for the trials of small tax cases, provided that in a case conducted under these procedures the decision of the court would be final and not subject to review by any court. The jurisdictional maximum for such cases is $50,000 for any disputed year.

All decisions, other than small tax case decisions, are subject to review by the courts of appeals and thereafter by the Supreme Court of the United States upon the granting of a writ of certiorari.

The office of the court and all of its judges are located in Washington, DC. The court conducts trial sessions at various locations within the United States as reasonably convenient to taxpayers as practicable. Each trial session is conducted by a single judge or a special trial judge. All proceedings are public and are conducted judicially in accordance with the court's Rules of Practice and the rules of evidence applicable in trials without a jury in the U.S. District Court for the District of Columbia. A fee of $60 is prescribed for the filing of a petition. Practice before the court is limited to practitioners admitted under the court's Rules.

For further information, contact the Administrative Office, United States Tax Court, 400 Second Street NW., Washington, DC 20217–0002. Phone, 202–521–0700. Internet, www.ustaxcourt.gov.

United States Court of Appeals for Veterans Claims The United States Court of Veterans Appeals was established on November 18, 1988 (102 Stat. 4105, 38 U.S.C. 7251) pursuant to Article I of the Constitution, and given exclusive jurisdiction to review decisions of the Board of Veterans Appeals. The court was renamed the United States Court of Appeals for Veterans Claims by the Veterans Programs Enhancement Act of 1998 (38 U.S.C. 7251 note). The court may not review the schedule of ratings for disabilities or actions of the Secretary in adopting or revising that schedule. Decisions of the Court of Appeals for Veterans Claims may be appealed to the United States Court of Appeals for the Federal Circuit.

The court consists of seven judges appointed by the President, with the advice and consent of the Senate, for 15-year terms. One of the judges serves as chief judge.

The court's principal office is in the District of Columbia, but the court can also act at any place within the United States.

For further information, contact the Clerk, United States Court of Appeals for Veterans Claims, Suite 900, 625 Indiana Avenue NW., Washington, DC 20004–2950. Phone, 202–501–5970. Internet, www.vetapp.gov.

Other Courts There have also been created two courts of local jurisdiction for the District of Columbia: the District of Columbia Court of Appeals and the Superior Court.

Business of the Federal Courts

The business of all the Federal courts described here, except the Court of Appeals for the Armed Forces, the Tax Court, the Court of Appeals for Veterans Claims, and the District of Columbia courts, is discussed in detail in the text and tables of the *Annual Report of the Director of the Administrative Office of the United States Courts (1940–2001).*

ADMINISTRATIVE OFFICE OF THE UNITED STATES COURTS

One Columbus Circle NE., Washington, DC 20544
Phone, 202–502–2600

Director	LEONIDAS RALPH MECHAM
Associate Director	CLARENCE A. LEE, JR.
Chief, Office of Audit	JEFFERY J. LARIONI
Assistant Director, Office of Judicial Conference Executive Secretariat	LAURA C. MINOR
Assistant Director, Office of Legislative Affairs	CORDIA A. STROM
General Counsel	WILLIAM R. BURCHILL, JR.
Chief, Office of Management, Planning and Assessment	CATHY A. MCCARTHY
Assistant Director, Office of Public Affairs	DAVID A. SELLERS
Assistant Director, Office of Human Resources	CHARLOTTE G. PEDDICORD
Chief, Court Personnel Management Division	TONYA M. DEANES, *Acting*
Chief, Fair Employment Practices Office	TRUDI M. MORRISON
Chief, Business Technology Optimization Division	CHARLES C. WILBURN, *Acting*
Chief, Benefits Division	CYNTHIA A. ROTH, *Acting*
Chief, Judges Compensation and Retirement Services Office	CAROL S. SEFREN
Chief, Policy and Strategic Initiatives Office	ALLEN BROWN
Assistant Director, Office of Finance and Budget	GEORGE H. SCHAFER
Chief, Accounting and Financial Systems Division	PHILIP L. MCKINNEY
Chief, Budget Division	JAMES R. BAUGHER
Chief, Financial Analysis Staff	PENNY JACOBS FLEMING
Assistant Director, Office of Information Technology	MELVIN J. BRYSON, JR.
Chief, Information Technology Applications Development Office	WENDY R. FITE
Chief, Information Technology Security Office	ROBERT N. SINSHEIMER
Chief Technology Officer	RICHARD D. FENNELL
Chief, Information Technology Infrastructure Management Division	CRAIG W. JENKINS
Chief, Information Technology Project Coordination Office	ROBERT D. MORSE
Chief, Information Technology Systems Deployment and Support Division	HOWARD J. GRANDIER
Chief, Information Technology Policy Staff	TERRY A. CAIN
Assistant Director, Office of Court Administration	NOEL J. AUGUSTYN
Chief, Appellate Court and Circuit Administration Division	GARY A. BOWDEN
Chief, Bankruptcy Court Administration Division	GLEN K. PALMAN
Chief, Court Administration Policy Staff	ABEL J. MATTOS
Chief, Office of Court Administration Technology Division	GARY L. BOCKWEG

Chief, District Court Administration Division	ROBERT LOWNEY
Chief, Electronic Public Access Program Office	MARY M. STICKNEY
Assistant Director, Office of Judges Programs	PETER G. MCCABE
Chief, Bankruptcy Judges Division	FRANCIS F. SZCZEBAK
Chief, Article III Judges Division	MARGARET A. IRVING
Chief, Magistrate Judges Division	THOMAS C. HNATOWSKI
Chief, Rules Committee Support Office	JOHN K. RABIEJ
Chief, Statistics Division	STEVEN R. SCHLESINGER
Assistant Director, Office of Internal Services	DOREEN G.B. BYDUME
Chief, Administrative Services Division	IRIS GUERRA
Chief, Personnel Division	CHERI THOMPSON REID
Chief, Information and Technology Services Division	JOHN C. CHANG
Chief, Procurement Management Division	WILLIAM A. ROEDER
Assistant Director, Office of Facilities and Security	ROSS EISENMAN
Chief, Judiciary Emergency Preparedness Office	WILLIAM J. LEHMAN
Chief, Security and Facilities Policy Staff	MELANIE FESS GILBERT
Chief, Court Security Office	EDWARD M. TEMPLEMAN
Chief, Space and Facilities Division	DEBRA L. WORLEY
Assistant Director, Office of Probation and Pretrial Services	JOHN M. HUGHES
Chief, Program Administration Division	ANNE BEATTY
Chief, Criminal Law Policy Staff	JAMES C. OLESON
Chief, Special Projects Office	NANCY LEE BRADSHAW
Chief, Probation and Pretrial Services Technology Division	NICHOLAS B. DISABATINO
Assistant Director, Office of Defender Services	THEODORE J. LIDZ

The Administrative Office of the United States Courts is charged with the nonjudicial, administrative business of the United States Courts, including the maintenance of workload statistics and the disbursement of funds appropriated for the maintenance of the U.S. judicial system.

The Administrative Office of the United States Courts was created by act of August 7, 1939 (28 U.S.C. 601). The Office was established November 6, 1939. Its Director and Deputy Director are appointed by the Chief Justice of the United States after consultation with the Judicial Conference.

Administering the Courts The Director is the administrative officer of the courts of the United States (except the Supreme Court). Under the guidance of the Judicial Conference of the United States the Director is required, among other things, to do the following:

—supervise all administrative matters relating to the offices of clerks and other clerical and administrative personnel of the courts;

—examine the state of the dockets of the courts, secure information as to the courts' need of assistance, and prepare and transmit quarterly to the chief judges of the circuits statistical data and reports as to the business of the courts;

—submit to the annual meeting of the Judicial Conference of the United States, at least 2 weeks prior thereto, a report of the activities of the Administrative Office and the state of the business of the courts;

—fix the compensation of employees of the courts whose compensation is not otherwise fixed by law;

—regulate and pay annuities to widows and surviving dependent children of judges;

ADMINISTRATIVE OFFICE OF THE UNITED STATES COURTS

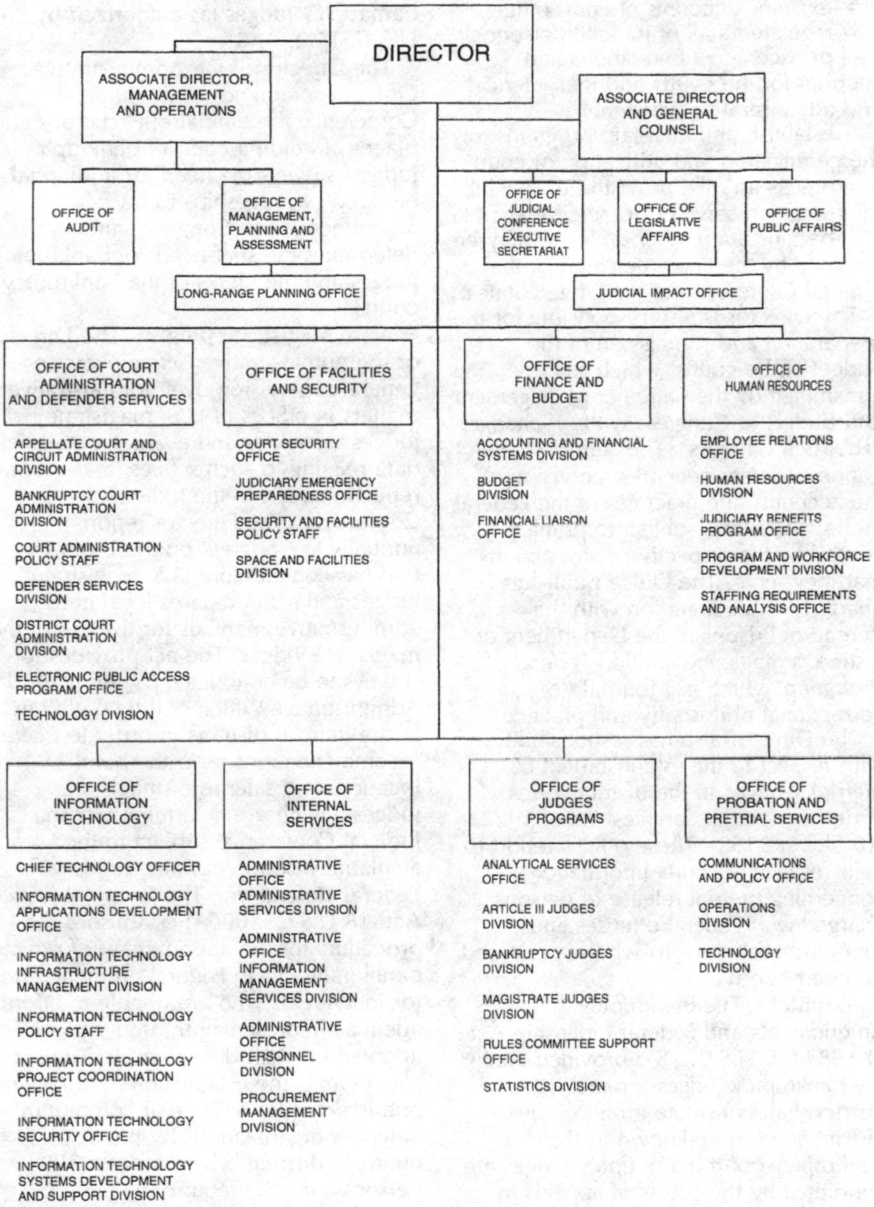
DIRECTOR
ASSOCIATE DIRECTOR, MANAGEMENT AND OPERATIONS
ASSOCIATE DIRECTOR AND GENERAL COUNSEL
OFFICE OF AUDIT
OFFICE OF MANAGEMENT, PLANNING AND ASSESSMENT
LONG-RANGE PLANNING OFFICE
OFFICE OF JUDICIAL CONFERENCE EXECUTIVE SECRETARIAT
OFFICE OF LEGISLATIVE AFFAIRS
OFFICE OF PUBLIC AFFAIRS
JUDICIAL IMPACT OFFICE
OFFICE OF COURT ADMINISTRATION AND DEFENDER SERVICES
APPELLATE COURT AND CIRCUIT ADMINISTRATION DIVISION
BANKRUPTCY COURT ADMINISTRATION DIVISION
COURT ADMINISTRATION POLICY STAFF
DEFENDER SERVICES DIVISION
DISTRICT COURT ADMINISTRATION DIVISION
ELECTRONIC PUBLIC ACCESS PROGRAM OFFICE
TECHNOLOGY DIVISION
OFFICE OF FACILITIES AND SECURITY
COURT SECURITY OFFICE
JUDICIARY EMERGENCY PREPAREDNESS OFFICE
SECURITY AND FACILITIES POLICY STAFF
SPACE AND FACILITIES DIVISION
OFFICE OF FINANCE AND BUDGET
ACCOUNTING AND FINANCIAL SYSTEMS DIVISION
BUDGET DIVISION
FINANCIAL LIAISON OFFICE
OFFICE OF HUMAN RESOURCES
EMPLOYEE RELATIONS OFFICE
HUMAN RESOURCES DIVISION
JUDICIARY BENEFITS PROGRAM OFFICE
PROGRAM AND WORKFORCE DEVELOPMENT DIVISION
STAFFING REQUIREMENTS AND ANALYSIS OFFICE
OFFICE OF INFORMATION TECHNOLOGY
CHIEF TECHNOLOGY OFFICER
INFORMATION TECHNOLOGY APPLICATIONS DEVELOPMENT OFFICE
INFORMATION TECHNOLOGY INFRASTRUCTURE MANAGEMENT DIVISION
INFORMATION TECHNOLOGY POLICY STAFF
INFORMATION TECHNOLOGY PROJECT COORDINATION OFFICE
INFORMATION TECHNOLOGY SECURITY OFFICE
INFORMATION TECHNOLOGY SYSTEMS DEVELOPMENT AND SUPPORT DIVISION
OFFICE OF INTERNAL SERVICES
ADMINISTRATIVE OFFICE ADMINISTRATIVE SERVICES DIVISION
ADMINISTRATIVE OFFICE INFORMATION MANAGEMENT SERVICES DIVISION
ADMINISTRATIVE OFFICE PERSONNEL DIVISION
PROCUREMENT MANAGEMENT DIVISION
OFFICE OF JUDGES PROGRAMS
ANALYTICAL SERVICES OFFICE
ARTICLE III JUDGES DIVISION
BANKRUPTCY JUDGES DIVISION
MAGISTRATE JUDGES DIVISION
RULES COMMITTEE SUPPORT OFFICE
STATISTICS DIVISION
OFFICE OF PROBATION AND PRETRIAL SERVICES
COMMUNICATIONS AND POLICY OFFICE
OPERATIONS DIVISION
TECHNOLOGY DIVISION

—disburse moneys appropriated for the maintenance and operation of the courts;

—examine accounts of court officers;

—regulate travel of judicial personnel;

—provide accommodations and supplies for the courts and their clerical and administrative personnel;

—establish and maintain programs for the certification and utilization of court interpreters and the provision of special interpretation services in the courts; and

—perform such other duties as may be assigned by the Supreme Court or the Judicial Conference of the United States.

The Director is also responsible for the preparation and submission of the budget of the courts, which shall be transmitted by the Office of Management and Budget to Congress without change.

Probation Officers The Administrative Office exercises general supervision of the accounts and practices of the Federal probation offices, subject to primary control by the respective district courts that they serve. The Office publishes quarterly, in cooperation with the Bureau of Prisons of the Department of Justice, a magazine entitled *Federal Probation,* which is a journal "of correctional philosophy and practice."

The Director also has responsibility with respect to the establishment of pretrial services in the district courts under the Pretrial Services Act of 1982 (18 U.S.C. 3152). These offices report to their respective courts information concerning pretrial release of persons charged with Federal offenses and supervise such persons who are released to their custody.

Bankruptcy The Bankruptcy Amendments and Federal Judgeship Act of 1984 (28 U.S.C. 151) provided that the bankruptcy judges for each judicial district shall constitute a unit of the district court to be known as the bankruptcy court. Bankruptcy judges are appointed by the courts of appeals in such numbers as authorized by Congress and serve for a term of 14 years as judicial officers of the district courts.

This act placed jurisdiction in the district courts over all cases under title 11, United States Code, and all proceedings arising in or related to cases under that title (28 U.S.C. 1334). The district court may provide for such cases and proceedings to be referred to its bankruptcy judges (as authorized by 28 U.S.C. 157).

The Director of the Administrative Office recommends to the Judicial Conference the official duty stations and places of holding court of bankruptcy judges, surveys the need for additional bankruptcy judgeships to be recommended to Congress, and determines the staff needs of bankruptcy judges and the clerks of the bankruptcy courts.

Federal Magistrate Judges The Director of the Administrative Office exercises general supervision over administrative matters in offices of U.S. magistrate judges, compiles and evaluates statistical data relating to such offices, and submits reports thereon to the Judicial Conference. The Director reports annually to Congress on the business that has come before U.S. magistrate judges and also prepares legal and administrative manuals for the use of the magistrate judges. The act provides for surveys to be conducted by the Administrative Office of the conditions in the judicial districts in order to make recommendations as to the number, location, and salaries of magistrate judges, which are determined by the Judicial Conference subject to the availability of appropriated funds.

Federal Defenders The Criminal Justice Act (18 U.S.C. 3006A) establishes the procedure for the appointment of private panel attorneys in Federal criminal cases for individuals who are unable to afford adequate representation, under plans adopted by each district court. The act also permits the establishment of Federal public defender or Federal community defender organizations by the district courts in districts where at least 200 persons annually require the appointment of counsel. Two adjacent districts may be combined to reach this total.

Each defender organization submits to the Director of the Administrative Office an annual report of its activities along with a proposed budget or, in the case of community defender organizations, a proposed grant for the coming year. The Director is responsible for the submission of the proposed budgets and grants to the Judicial Conference for approval. The Director also makes payments to the defender organizations out of appropriations in accordance with the approved budgets and grants, as well as compensating private counsel appointed to defend criminal cases in the United States courts.

Sources of Information

Information may be obtained from the following sources:

Bankruptcy Judges Division. Phone, 202–502–1900.

Budget Division. Phone, 202–502–2100.

Defender Services Division. Phone, 202–502–3030.

General Counsel. Phone, 202–502–1100.

Human Resources Division. Phone, 202–502–3100.

Judicial Conference Executive Secretariat. Phone, 202–502–2400.

Legislative Affairs Office. Phone, 202–502–1700.

Magistrate Judges Division. Phone, 202–502–1830.

Office of Probation and Pretrial Services. Phone, 202–502–1610.

Public Affairs Office. Phone, 202–502–2600.

Statistics Division. Phone, 202–502–1440.

For further information, contact one of the offices listed above, Administrative Office of the United States Courts, Thurgood Marshall Federal Judiciary Building, One Columbus Circle NE., Washington, DC 20544. Phone, 202–502–2600. Internet, www.uscourts.gov.

FEDERAL JUDICIAL CENTER

Thurgood Marshall Federal Judiciary Building,
One Columbus Circle NE., Washington, DC 20002–8003
Phone, 202–502–4000. Internet, www.fjc.gov.

Director	BARBARA J. ROTHSTEIN
Deputy Director	JOHN S. COOKE
Director, Education Division	BRUCE M. CLARKE
Director, Systems Innovation and Development Office	TED E. COLEMAN
Director, Research Division	JAMES B. EAGLIN
Director, Interjudicial Relations Office	MIRA GUR-ARIE
Director, Federal Judicial History Office	BRUCE A. RAGSDALE
Director, Communications Policy and Design Office	SYLVAN A. SOBEL

The Federal Judicial Center is the judicial branch's agency for policy research and continuing education.

The Federal Judicial Center was created by act of December 20, 1967 (28 U.S.C. 620), to further the development and adoption of improved judicial administration in the courts of the United States.

The Center's basic policies and activities are determined by its Board, which is composed of the Chief Justice of the United States, who is permanent Chair of the Board by statute, and two judges of the U.S. courts of appeals, three judges of the U.S. district courts, one bankruptcy judge, and one magistrate judge, all of whom are elected for 4-year terms by the Judicial Conference of the United States. The Director of the Administrative Office of the United States Courts is also a permanent member of the Board.

Pursuant to statute, the Center carries out the following duties:

—develops and administers orientation and continuing education programs for Federal judges, Federal defenders, and nonjudicial court personnel, including probation officers, pretrial services officers, and clerks' office employees;

—conducts empirical and exploratory research and evaluation on Federal judicial processes, court management, and sentencing and its consequences, usually for the committees of the Judicial Conference or the courts themselves;

—produces research reports, training manuals, satellite broadcasts, video programs, computer based training, and periodicals about the Federal courts;

—provides guidance and advice and maintains data and records to assist those interested in documenting and conserving the history of the Federal courts; and

—cooperates with and assists other agencies and organizations in providing advice to improve the administration of justice in the courts of foreign countries.

Sources of Information

Information may be obtained from the following divisions and offices:

Director and Deputy Director. Phone, 202–502–4162, or 202–502–4164. Fax, 202–502–4099.

Research. Phone, 202–502–4071. Fax, 202–502–4199.

Education. Phone, 202–502–4110. Fax, 202–502–4088.

Communications Policy and Design. Phone 202–502–4250. Fax, 202–502–4077.

Federal Judicial History. Phone, 202–502–4181. Fax, 202–502–4077.

Information Services. Phone, 202–502–4153. Fax, 202–502–4077.

International Judicial Relations. Phone, 202–502–4161. Fax, 202–502–4099.

Human Resources. Phone, 202–502–4165. Fax, 202–502–4099.

Systems Innovation and Development. Phone, 202–502–4223. Fax, 202–502–4288.

Electronic Access Selected Federal Judicial Center publications, including access to its Federal judicial history databases and selected educational resources, are available through the Internet at www.fjc.gov.

Publications Single copies of most Federal Judicial Center publications are available free of charge. Phone, 202–502–4153. Fax, 202–502–4077.

For further information, contact the Federal Judicial Center, Thurgood Marshall Federal Judiciary Building, One Columbus Circle NE., Washington, DC 20002–8003. Phone, 202–502–4000. Internet, www.fjc.gov.

UNITED STATES SENTENCING COMMISSION

Suite 2–500, South Lobby, One Columbus Circle NE., Washington, DC 20002–8002
Phone, 202–502–4500. Internet, www.ussc.gov.

Chair	RICARDO H. HINOJOSA
Vice Chairs	RUBEN CASTILLO, WILLIAM K. SESSIONS III, JOHN R. STEER
Commissioners	BERYL A. HOWELL, MICHAEL E. HOROWITZ, (VACANCY)
Commissioners (*ex officio*)	EDWARD F. REILLY, JR., MICHAEL J. ELSTON
Staff Director	JUDITH W. SHEON
Deputy Staff Director	KENNETH P. COHEN
General Counsel	(VACANCY)
Public Affairs Officer	MICHAEL COURLANDER
Director of Administration and Planning	SUSAN L. WINARSKY
Director and Chief Counsel of Training	PAMELA G. MONTGOMERY
Director of Legislative and Governmental Affairs	LISA A. RICH, *Acting*

Director of Monitoring	J. DEON HAYNES, *Acting*
Director of Policy Analysis	LOUIS W. REEDT, *Acting*
Special Counsel	JANEEEN M. GAFFNEY, *Acting*

The United States Sentencing Commission develops sentencing guidelines and policies for the Federal court system.

The United States Sentencing Commission was established as an independent agency in the judicial branch of the Federal Government by the Sentencing Reform Act of 1984 (28 U.S.C. 991 *et seq.* and 18 U.S.C. 3551 *et seq.*). The Commission establishes sentencing guidelines and policies for the Federal courts, advising them as to the appropriate form and severity of punishment for offenders convicted of Federal crimes.

The Commission is composed of seven voting members appointed by the President with the advice and consent of the Senate for 6-year terms, and two nonvoting members. One of the voting members is appointed Chairperson.

The Commission evaluates the effects of the sentencing guidelines on the criminal justice system, advises Congress regarding the modification or enactment of statutes relating to criminal law and sentencing matters, establishes a research and development program on sentencing issues, and performs other related duties.

In executing its duties, the Commission promulgates and distributes to Federal courts and to the U.S. probation system guidelines to be consulted in determining sentences to be imposed in criminal cases, general policy statements regarding the application of guidelines, and policy statements on the appropriate use of probation and supervised release revocation provisions. These sentencing guidelines and policy statements are designed to further the purposes of just punishment, deterrence, incapacitation, and rehabilitation; provide fairness in meeting the purposes of sentencing; avoid unwarranted disparity; and reflect advancement in the knowledge of human behavior as it relates to the criminal justice process.

In addition, the Commission provides training, conducts research on sentencing-related issues, and serves as an information resource for Congress, criminal justice practitioners, and the public.

Sources of Information

Electronic Access Commission information and materials may be obtained through the Internet, at www.ussc.gov.

Guideline Application Assistance Helpline Phone, 202–502–4545.

Public Information Information concerning Commission activities is available from the Office of Publishing and Public Affairs. Phone, 202–502–4590.

For further information, contact the Office of Publishing and Public Affairs, United States Sentencing Commission, Suite 2–500, South Lobby, One Columbus Circle NE., Washington, DC 20002–8002. Phone, 202–502–4590. Internet, www.ussc.gov.

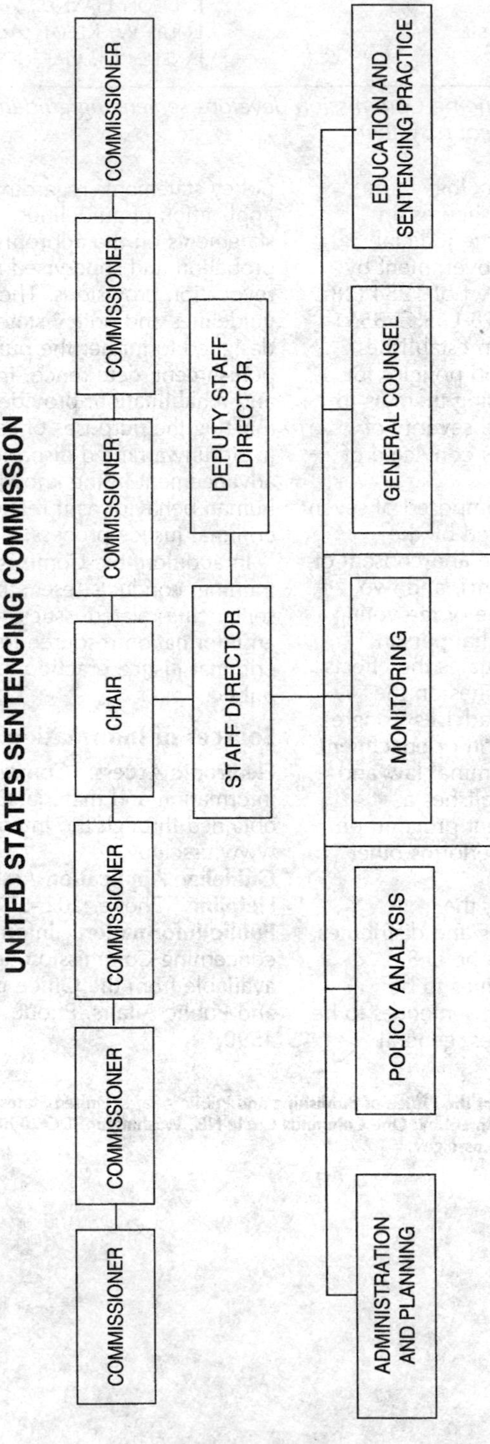
UNITED STATES SENTENCING COMMISSION
COMMISSIONER
COMMISSIONER
COMMISSIONER
CHAIR
COMMISSIONER
COMMISSIONER
COMMISSIONER
STAFF DIRECTOR
DEPUTY STAFF DIRECTOR
ADMINISTRATION AND PLANNING
POLICY ANALYSIS
LEGISLATIVE AND GOVERNMENTAL AFFAIRS
MONITORING
SPECIAL COUNSEL
GENERAL COUNSEL
EDUCATION AND SENTENCING PRACTICE

Executive Branch

EXECUTIVE BRANCH

THE PRESIDENT OF THE UNITED STATES

THE PRESIDENT OF THE UNITED STATES — GEORGE W. BUSH

Article II, section 1, of the Constitution provides that "[t]he executive Power shall be vested in a President of the United States of America. He shall hold his Office during the Term of four Years, . . . together with the Vice President, chosen for the same Term . . . ." In addition to the powers set forth in the Constitution, the statutes have conferred upon the President specific authority and responsibility covering a wide range of matters (United States Code Index).

The President is the administrative head of the executive branch of the Government, which includes numerous agencies, both temporary and permanent, as well as the 15 executive departments.

The Cabinet

The Cabinet, a creation of custom and tradition dating back to George Washington's administration, functions at the pleasure of the President. Its purpose is to advise the President upon any subject, relating to the duties of the respective offices, on which he requests information (pursuant to Article II, section 2, of the Constitution).

The Cabinet is composed of the Vice President and the heads of the 15 executive departments—the Secretaries of Agriculture, Commerce, Defense, Education, Energy, Health and Human Services, Homeland Security, Housing and Urban Development, Interior, Labor, State, Transportation, Treasury, and Veterans Affairs, and the Attorney General. Additionally, in the Bush administration, Cabinet-level rank has been accorded to the Chief of Staff to the President; the Administrator, Environmental Protection Agency; the Director, Office of Management and Budget; the Director, Office of National Drug Control Policy; and the U.S. Trade Representative.

THE VICE PRESIDENT OF THE UNITED STATES

THE VICE PRESIDENT — DICK CHENEY

Article II, section I, of the Constitution provides that the President "shall hold his Office during the Term of four Years . . . together with the Vice President . . . ." In addition to his role as President of the Senate, the Vice President is empowered to succeed to the Presidency, pursuant to Article II and the 20th and 25th amendments to the Constitution.

The executive functions of the Vice President include participation in Cabinet meetings and, by statute, membership on the National Security Council and the Board of Regents of the Smithsonian Institution.

EXECUTIVE OFFICE OF THE PRESIDENT

Under authority of the Reorganization Act of 1939 (5 U.S.C. 133–133r, 133t note), various agencies were transferred to the Executive Office of the President by the President's Reorganization Plans I and II of 1939 (5 U.S.C. app.), effective July 1, 1939. Executive Order 8248 of September 8, 1939, established the divisions of the Executive Office and defined their functions. Subsequently, Presidents have used Executive orders, reorganization plans, and legislative initiatives to reorganize the Executive Office to make its composition compatible with the goals of their administrations.

The White House Office

1600 Pennsylvania Avenue NW., Washington, DC 20500
Phone, 202–456–1414. Internet, www.whitehouse.gov.

Assistant to the President and Chief of Staff	JOSHUA B. BOLTEN
Assistant to the President, Chief of Staff to the Vice President, and Counsel	DAVID S. ADDINGTON
Assistant to the President and Deputy Chief of Staff	JOSEPH W. HAGIN
Assistant to the President and Deputy National Security Adviser	JACK D. CROUCH II
Assistant to the President and Press Secretary	TONY SNOW
Assistant to the President and Staff Secretary	RAUL F. YANES
Assistant to the President for Communications	NICOLLE WALLACE
Assistant to the President for Homeland Security and Counterterrorism	FRANCES FRAGOS TOWNSEND
Assistant to the President for Legislative Affairs	CANDIDA PEROTTI WOLFF
Assistant to the President for National Security Affairs	STEPHEN J. HADLEY
Assistant to the President for Presidential Personnel	LIZA WRIGHT RENNER
Assistant to the President for Speechwriting	WILLIAM J. MCGURN
Assistant to the President, Deputy Chief of Staff, and Senior Adviser	KARL C. ROVE
Counsel to the President	HARRIET E. MIERS
Counselor to the President	DANIEL J. BARTLETT
Deputy Assistant to the President and Adviser to the Chief of Staff	STEVEN S. MCMILLIN
Deputy Assistant to the President and Chief of Staff to the First Lady	ANITA B. MCBRIDE
Deputy Assistant to the President and Deputy Director of Communications for Policy and Planning	CATHERINE J. MARTIN

Deputy Assistant to the President and Deputy Director of Communications for Production	SCOTT N. SFORZA
Deputy Assistant to the President and Deputy to the Senior Adviser	BARRY S. JACKSON
Deputy Assistant to the President for Appointments and Scheduling	MELISSA S. BENNETT
Deputy Assistant to the President and Director of Advance	TODD W. BEYER
Deputy Assistant to the President and Director of Public Liaison	RHONDA N. KEENUM
Deputy Assistant to the President and Director of Strategic Initiatives	PETE H. WEHNER
Deputy Assistant to the President and Director of USA Freedom Corps	DESIREE T. SAYLE
Deputy Assistant to the President and Director, Intergovernmental Affairs	RUBEN S. BARRALES
Deputy Assistant to the President and Deputy National Security Adviser	FARYAR SHIRZAD
Deputy Assistants to the President for Legislative Affairs	WILLIAM DOUGLAS BADGER, BRIAN C. CONKLIN, SEAN B. O'HOLLAREN
Deputy Assistant to the President for Management and Administration	LINDA M. GAMBATESA
Special Assistant to the President and Director of Media Affairs	JEANIE S. MAMO
Special Assistant to the President and White House Social Secretary	JANET LEA BERMAN
Special Assistant to the President for Cabinet Liaison	HEIDI MARQUEZ SMITH

The White House Office serves the President in the performance of the many detailed activities incident to his immediate office.

The staff of the President facilitates and maintains communication with the Congress, the individual Members of the Congress, the heads of executive agencies, the press and other information media, and the general public.

The various Assistants to the President assist the President in such matters as he may direct.

Office of the Vice President of the United States

Eisenhower Executive Office Building, Washington, DC 20501
Phone, 202–456–7549

Assistant to the Vice President, Chief of Staff to the Vice President, and Counsel	DAVID S. ADDINGTON
Assistant to the Vice President for National Security Affairs	JOHN HANNAH
Deputy Chief of Staff to the Vice President	CLAIRE O'DONNELL
Counsel to the Vice President	SHANNEN COFFIN

Assistant to the Vice President for Legislative Affairs	Brenda Becker
Assistant to the Vice President for Domestic Policy	Neil Patel
Assistant to the Vice President for Political Affairs	Mel Raines
Assistant to the Vice President for Homeland Security Affairs	Bruce Miller
Assistant to the Vice President and Staff Secretary	Derrick Morgan
Assistant to the Vice President and Director of Advance	Troy McNichols
Deputy Assistant to the Vice President and Director of Scheduling	Elizabeth Kleppe
Press Secretary to the Vice President	Lea Anne McBride
Chief of Staff to Mrs. Cheney	Cece Boyer
Director of Correspondence for the Vice President	Susan Posey
Deputy Assistants to the Vice President for National Security Affairs	Samantha Ravich, Joe Wood
Executive Assistant to the Vice President	Debbie Heiden

The Office of the Vice President serves the Vice President in the performance of the many detailed activities incident to his immediate office.

Council of Economic Advisers

1800 G Street NW., Washington, DC 20502
Phone, 202–395–5084. Internet, www.whitehouse.gov/cea.

Chairman	Edward P. Lazear
Members	Katherine Baicker, Matthew J. Slaughter
Chief of Staff	Gary D. Blank

The Council of Economic Advisers primarily performs an analysis and appraisal of the national economy for the purpose of providing policy recommendations to the President.

The Council of Economic Advisers (CEA) was established in the Executive Office of the President by the Employment Act of 1946 (15 U.S.C. 1023). It now functions under that statute and Reorganization Plan No. 9 of 1953 (5 U.S.C. app.), effective August 1, 1953.

The Council consists of three members appointed by the President with the advice and consent of the Senate. One of the members is designated by the President as Chairman.

The Council analyzes the national economy and its various segments; advises the President on economic developments; appraises the economic programs and policies of the Federal Government; recommends to the President policies for economic growth and stability; assists in the preparation of the economic reports of the President to the Congress; and prepares the Annual Report of the Council of Economic Advisers.

For further information, contact the Council of Economic Advisers, 1800 G Street NW., Washington, DC 20502. Phone, 202–395–5084. Internet, www.whitehouse.gov/cea.

Council on Environmental Quality

722 Jackson Place NW., Washington, DC 20503
Phone, 202–395–5750 or 202–456–6224. Fax, 202–456–2710. Internet, www.whitehouse.gov/ceq.

Chairman	JAMES CONNAUGHTON
Chief of Staff	BRYAN HANNEGAN
General Counsel	DINAH BEAR
Deputy General Counsel	EDWARD BOLING
Associate Director for Communications	MICHELLE ST. MARTIN
Associate Director for Agriculture and Public Lands	GREG SCHILDWACHTER
Associate Director for NEPA Oversight	HORST GRECZMIEL
Associate Director for Natural Resources	KATHY COPELAND
Associate Director for Toxics and Environmental Protection	ELIZABETH STOLPE
Associate Director for Congressional Affairs	ASHLEY COHEN

The Council on Environmental Quality formulates and recommends national policies to promote the improvement of the quality of the environment.

The Council on Environmental Quality (CEQ) was established within the Executive Office of the President by the National Environmental Policy Act of 1969 (NEPA) (42 U.S.C. 4321 *et seq.*). The Environmental Quality Improvement Act of 1970 (42 U.S.C. 4371 *et seq.*) established the Office of Environmental Quality (OEQ) to provide professional and administrative support for the Council. The Council and OEQ are collectively referred to as the Council on Environmental Quality, and the CEQ Chair, who is appointed by the President and confirmed by the Senate, serves as the Director of OEQ.

The Council develops policies which bring into productive harmony the Nation's social, economic, and environmental priorities, with the goal of improving the quality of Federal decisionmaking. As required by NEPA, CEQ evaluates, coordinates, and mediates Federal activities; advises and assists the President on both national and international environmental policy matters. In addition, it oversees Federal agency and department implementation of NEPA.

For further information, contact the Information Office, Council on Environmental Quality, 722 Jackson Place NW., Washington, DC 20503. Phone, 202–395–5750. Fax, 202–456–2710. Internet, www.whitehouse.gov/ceq.

National Security Council

Eisenhower Executive Office Building, Washington, DC 20504
Phone, 202–456–1414

Members:	
The President	GEORGE W. BUSH
The Vice President	DICK CHENEY
The Secretary of State	CONDOLEEZZA RICE
The Secretary of Defense	DONALD H. RUMSFELD
Statutory Advisers:	
Director of National Intelligence	JOHN D. NEGROPONTE
Chairman, Joint Chiefs of Staff	GEN. PETER PACE, USMC
Standing Participants:	
The Secretary of the Treasury	JOHN W. SNOW
Chief of Staff to the President	JOSHUA B. BOLTON
Counsel to the President	HARRIET E. MIERS
Assistant to the President for National Security Affairs	STEPHEN J. HADLEY
Assistant to the President for Economic Policy	ALLAN B. HUBBARD
Officials:	
Assistant to the President for National Security Affairs	STEPHEN J. HADLEY
Assistant to the President for National Security Affairs and Deputy National Security Adviser	JACK D. CROUCH II
Executive Secretary	V. PHILLIP V. LAGO

The National Security Council was established by the National Security Act of 1947, as amended (50 U.S.C. 402). The Council was placed in the Executive Office of the President by Reorganization Plan No. 4 of 1949 (5 U.S.C. app.).

The National Security Council is chaired by the President. Its statutory members, in addition to the President, are the Vice President and the Secretaries of State and Defense. The Chairman of the Joint Chiefs of Staff is the statutory military adviser to the Council, and the Director of the Central Intelligence Agency is its intelligence adviser. The Secretary of the Treasury, the U.S. Representative to the United Nations, the Assistant to the President for National Security Affairs, the Assistant to the President for Economic Policy, and the Chief of Staff to the President are invited to all meetings of the Council. The Attorney General and the Director of National Drug Control Policy are invited to attend meetings pertaining to their jurisdictions; other officials are invited, as appropriate.

The Council advises and assists the President in integrating all aspects of national security policy as it affects the United States—domestic, foreign, military, intelligence, and economic—in conjunction with the National Economic Council.

For further information, contact the National Security Council, Old Executive Office Building, Washington, DC 20504. Phone, 202–456–1414.

Office of Administration

Eisenhower Executive Office Building
725 Seventeenth Street NW., Washington, DC 20503
Phone, 202–456–2861

Special Assistant to the President and Director of the Office of Administration	JOHN STRAUB
Chief Operations Officer	SANDY EVANS
Director for Equal Opportunity	CLARA PATTERSON
Director for Office of Security and Emergency Preparedness	JAMES KNODELL
General Counsel	VICTOR BERSEN
Chief Information Officer	THERESA PAYTON

The Office of Administration was formally established within the Executive Office of the President by Executive Order 12028 of December 12, 1977. The Office provides administrative support services to all units within the Executive Office of the President. The services provided include information, personnel, technology, and financial management; data processing; library and research services; security; legislative liaisons; and general office operations such as mail, messenger, printing, procurement, and supply services.

For further information, contact the Office of the Director, Office of Administration, Washington, DC 20503. Phone, 202–456–2861.

Office of Management and Budget

Executive Office Building, Washington, DC 20503
Phone, 202–395–3080. Internet, www.whitehouse.gov/omb.

Director	ROBERT J. PORTMAN
Deputy Director	AUSTIN SMYTHE, *Acting*
Deputy Director for Management	CLAY JOHNSON III
Executive Associate Director	AUSTIN SMYTHE
Administrator, Office of Federal Procurement Policy	(VACANCY)
Administrator, Office of Information and Regulatory Affairs	(VACANCY)
Assistant Deputy Director for Administration	LAUREN E. WRIGHT, *Acting*
Assistant Director for Budget	ELIZABETH ROBINSON
Assistant Director for Legislative Reference	JAMES J. JUKES
Associate Director for Communications	(VACANCY)
Associate Director for Economic Policy	JAMES D. FOSTER
Associate Director for Human Resource Programs	(VACANCY)
Associate Director for General Government Programs	(VACANCY)
Associate Director for Information Technology and E-Government	KAREN EVANS

Associate Director for Legislative Affairs	MARGARET STEWART
Associate Director for National Security Programs	JOSEPH BOWAB
Associate Director for Natural Resource Programs	DAVID ANDERSON
Controller, Office of Federal Financial Management	LINDA COMBS
General Counsel	(VACANCY)

The Office of Management and Budget evaluates, formulates, and coordinates management procedures and program objectives within and among Federal departments and agencies. It also controls the administration of the Federal budget, while routinely providing the President with recommendations regarding budget proposals and relevant legislative enactments.

The Office of Management and Budget (OMB), formerly the Bureau of the Budget, was established in the Executive Office of the President pursuant to Reorganization Plan No. 1 of 1939 (5 U.S.C. app.).

The Office's primary functions are:

—to assist the President in developing and maintaining effective government by reviewing the organizational structure and management procedures of the executive branch to ensure that the intended results are achieved;

—to assist in developing efficient coordinating mechanisms to implement Government activities and to expand interagency cooperation;

—to assist the President in preparing the budget and in formulating the Government's fiscal program;

—to supervise and control the administration of the budget;

—to assist the President by clearing and coordinating departmental advice on proposed legislation and by making recommendations effecting Presidential action on legislative enactments, in accordance with past practice;

—to assist in developing regulatory reform proposals and programs for paperwork reduction, especially reporting burdens of the public;

—to assist in considering, clearing, and, where necessary, preparing proposed Executive orders and proclamations;

—to plan and develop information systems that provide the President with program performance data;

—to plan, conduct, and promote evaluation efforts that assist the President in assessing program objectives, performance, and efficiency;

—to keep the President informed of the progress of activities by Government agencies with respect to work proposed, initiated, and completed, together with the relative timing of work between the several agencies of the Government, all to the end that the work programs of the several agencies of the executive branch of the Government may be coordinated and that the moneys appropriated by the Congress may be expended in the most economical manner, barring overlapping and duplication of effort; and

—to improve the economy, efficiency, and effectiveness of the procurement processes by providing overall direction of procurement policies, regulations, procedures, and forms.

Sources of Information

Employment Various civil service examinations and registers are used for filling positions, such as economist, budget examiner, and management analyst. Inquiries on employment should be directed to the Human Resources Division, Office of Administration, Washington, DC 20500. Phone, 202–395–1088.

Inquiries Contact the Office of Administration, Office of Management and Budget, New Executive Office Building, Washington, DC 20503. Phone, 202–395–3080. Fax, 202–395–3504. Internet, www.whitehouse.gov/omb.

Publications *The Budget of the U.S. Government* and *The Budget System and*

OFFICE OF MANAGEMENT AND BUDGET

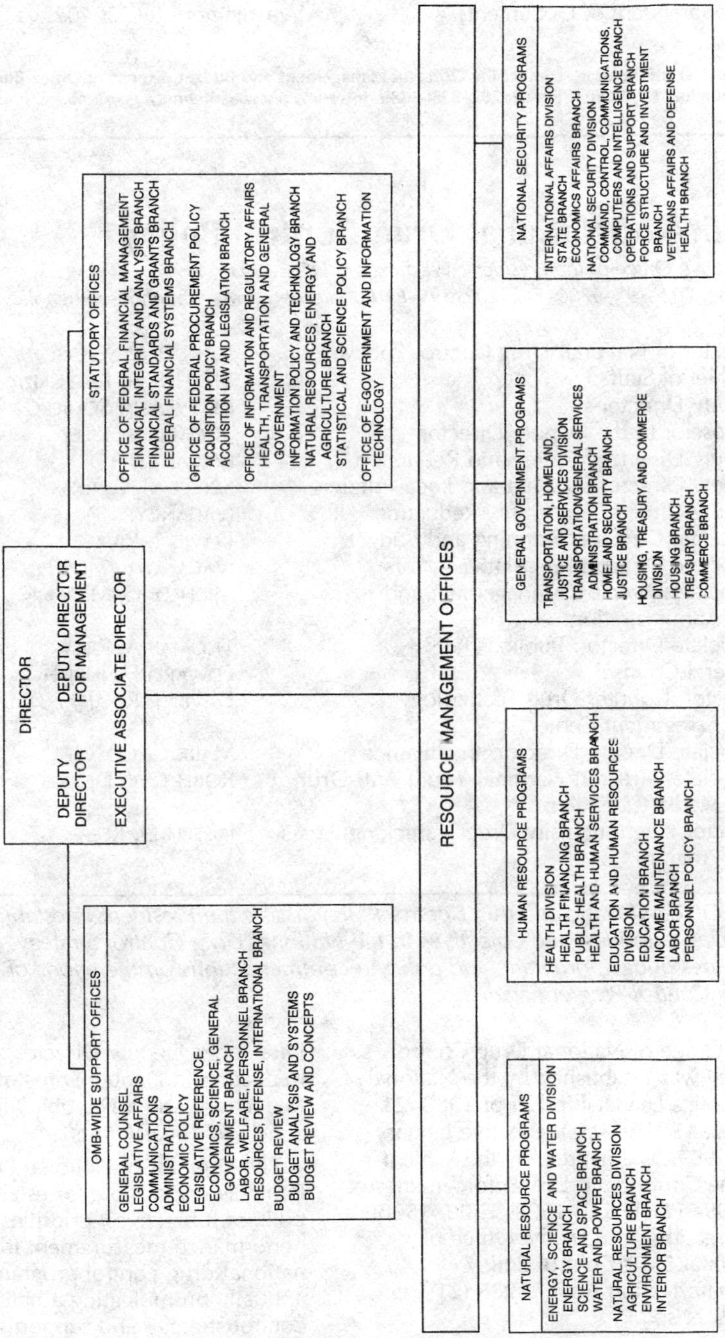
DIRECTOR
DEPUTY DIRECTOR
DEPUTY DIRECTOR FOR MANAGEMENT
EXECUTIVE ASSOCIATE DIRECTOR
OMB-WIDE SUPPORT OFFICES
GENERAL COUNSEL
LEGISLATIVE AFFAIRS
COMMUNICATIONS
ADMINISTRATION
ECONOMIC POLICY
LEGISLATIVE REFERENCE
ECONOMICS, SCIENCE, GENERAL GOVERNMENT BRANCH
LABOR, WELFARE, PERSONNEL BRANCH
RESOURCES, DEFENSE, INTERNATIONAL BRANCH
BUDGET REVIEW
BUDGET ANALYSIS AND SYSTEMS
BUDGET REVIEW AND CONCEPTS
STATUTORY OFFICES
OFFICE OF FEDERAL FINANCIAL MANAGEMENT
FINANCIAL INTEGRITY AND ANALYSIS BRANCH
FINANCIAL STANDARDS AND GRANTS BRANCH
FEDERAL FINANCIAL SYSTEMS BRANCH
OFFICE OF FEDERAL PROCUREMENT POLICY
ACQUISITION POLICY BRANCH
ACQUISITION LAW AND LEGISLATION BRANCH
OFFICE OF INFORMATION AND REGULATORY AFFAIRS
HEALTH, TRANSPORTATION AND GENERAL GOVERNMENT
INFORMATION POLICY AND TECHNOLOGY BRANCH
NATURAL RESOURCES, ENERGY AND AGRICULTURE BRANCH
STATISTICAL AND SCIENCE POLICY BRANCH
OFFICE OF E-GOVERNMENT AND INFORMATION TECHNOLOGY
RESOURCE MANAGEMENT OFFICES
NATURAL RESOURCE PROGRAMS
ENERGY, SCIENCE AND WATER DIVISION
ENERGY BRANCH
SCIENCE AND SPACE BRANCH
WATER AND POWER BRANCH
NATURAL RESOURCES DIVISION
AGRICULTURE BRANCH
ENVIRONMENT BRANCH
INTERIOR BRANCH
HUMAN RESOURCE PROGRAMS
HEALTH DIVISION
HEALTH FINANCING BRANCH
PUBLIC HEALTH BRANCH
HEALTH AND HUMAN SERVICES BRANCH
EDUCATION AND HUMAN RESOURCES DIVISION
EDUCATION BRANCH
INCOME MAINTENANCE BRANCH
LABOR BRANCH
PERSONNEL POLICY BRANCH
GENERAL GOVERNMENT PROGRAMS
TRANSPORTATION, HOMELAND, JUSTICE AND SERVICES DIVISION
TRANSPORTATION/GENERAL SERVICES ADMINISTRATION BRANCH
HOMELAND SECURITY BRANCH
JUSTICE BRANCH
HOUSING, TREASURY AND COMMERCE DIVISION
HOUSING BRANCH
TREASURY BRANCH
COMMERCE BRANCH
NATIONAL SECURITY PROGRAMS
INTERNATIONAL AFFAIRS DIVISION
STATE BRANCH
ECONOMICS AFFAIRS BRANCH
NATIONAL SECURITY DIVISION
COMMAND, CONTROL, COMMUNICATIONS, COMPUTERS AND INTELLIGENCE BRANCH
OPERATIONS AND SUPPORT BRANCH
FORCE STRUCTURE AND INVESTMENT BRANCH
VETERANS AFFAIRS AND DEFENSE HEALTH BRANCH

Concepts are available for sale by the Superintendent of Documents, Government Printing Office, Washington, DC 20402.

For further information, contact the Office of Management and Budget, Executive Office Building, Washington, DC 20503. Phone, 202–395–3080. Internet, www.whitehouse.gov/omb.

Office of National Drug Control Policy

Executive Office of the President, Washington, DC 20503
Phone, 202–395–6700. Fax, 202–395–6708. Internet, www.whitehousedrugpolicy.gov.

Director of National Drug Control Policy	JOHN P. WALTERS
Chief of Staff	STEPHEN A. KATSURINIS
Deputy Director	MARY ANN SOLBERG
Counselor to the Deputy Director	THOMAS A. RILEY
Deputy Director for Demand Reduction	(VACANCY)
Deputy Director for State and Local Affairs	SCOTT M. BURNS
Deputy Director for Supply Reduction	(VACANCY)
Associate Director, Planning and Budget	DAVID J. RIVAIT
Associate Director, Legislative Affairs	(VACANCY)
Associate Director, Management and Administration	MICHELE C. MARX
Associate Director, Public Affairs	THOMAS A. RILEY
General Counsel	EDWARD H. JURITH
Director, Counter-Drug Technology Assessment Center	DAVID J. RIVAIT, *Acting*
Associate Deputy Director, Intelligence	MARK C. COOMER
Associate Director, National Youth Anti-Drug Media Campaign	ROBERT W. DENNISTON
Director, High-Intensity Drug Trafficking Areas Program	JOSEPH D. KEEFE

The Office of National Drug Control Policy assists the President in establishing policies, priorities, and objectives in the National Drug Control Strategy. It also provides budget, program, and policy recommendations on the efforts of National Drug Control Program agencies.

The Office of National Drug Control Policy was established by the National Narcotics Leadership Act of 1988 (21 U.S.C. 1501 *et seq.*), effective January 29, 1989, as amended by the Violent Crime Control and Law Enforcement Act of 1994 (21 U.S.C. 1502, 1506, 1508) and reauthorized by the Office of National Drug Control Policy Reauthorization Act of 1988 (21 U.S.C. 1701, *et seq.*).

The Director of National Drug Control Policy is appointed by the President with the advice and consent of the Senate. The Director is assisted by a Deputy Director, a Deputy Director for Demand Reduction, a Deputy Director for Supply Reduction, and a Deputy Director for State and Local Affairs.

The Director of National Drug Control Policy is responsible for establishing policies, objectives, priorities, and performance measurement for the national drug control program, and for annually promulgating a national drug control strategy and supporting annual reports and an annual national drug control program budget to be submitted to the Congress by the President. The Director advises the President regarding necessary changes in the organization, management, budgeting, and personnel allocation of Federal agencies involved in drug enforcement activities and is also responsible for notifying Federal agencies if their policies are not in compliance with their responsibilities under the National Drug Control Strategy. Additionally, the Office has direct programmatic responsibility for the Drug-Free Communities Program, the National Youth Anti-Drug Media Campaign, the various programs under the Counter-Drug Technology Assessment Center, and the High Intensity Drug Trafficking Areas Program.

Sources of Information

Employment Inquiries regarding employment should be directed to the Personnel Section, Office of National Drug Control Policy. Phone, 202–395–6695.

Publications To receive publications about drugs and crime, to get specific drug-related data, to obtain customized bibliographic searches, and to find out about data availability and other information resources that may meet your needs, contact the Drugs and Crime Clearinghouse. Phone, 800–666–3332. Fax, 301–251–5212. E-mail, askncjrs@aspensys.com. Internet, www.whitehousedrugpolicy.gov.

For further information, contact the Office of National Drug Control Policy, Executive Office of the President, Washington, DC 20503. Phone, 202–395–6700. Fax, 202–395–6708. Internet, www.whitehousedrugpolicy.gov.

Office of Policy Development

Domestic Policy Council

Room 469, Eisenhower Executive Office Building, Washington, DC 20502
Phone, 202–456–5594

Assistant to the President for Domestic Policy	WALTER KARL ZINSMEISTER
Deputy Assistant to the President for Domestic Policy	TEVI D. TROY

National Economic Council

Room 235, Eisenhower Executive Office Building, Washington, DC 20502
Phone, 202–456–2800

Assistant to the President for Economic Policy and Director, National Economic Council	ALLAN B. HUBBARD
Deputy Assistant to the President for Economic Policy and Deputy Director, National Economic Council	KEITH B. HENNESSY
Special Assistants to the President for Economic Policy	CHARLES P. BLAHOUS, LISA E. EPIFANI, JEFFREY F. KUPFER

The Office of Policy Development is comprised of the Domestic Policy Council and the National Economic Council, which are responsible for advising and assisting the President in the formulation, coordination, and implementation of domestic and economic policy. The Office of Policy Development also provides support for other policy development and implementation activities as directed by the President.

Domestic Policy Council

The Domestic Policy Council was established on August 16, 1993, by Executive Order 12859. The Council oversees development and implementation of the President's domestic policy agenda and ensures coordination and communication among the heads of relevant Federal offices and agencies.

National Economic Council

The National Economic Council was created on January 25, 1993, by Executive Order 12835, to coordinate the economic policymaking process and provide economic policy advice to the President. The Council also ensures that economic policy decisions and programs are consistent with the President's stated goals, and monitors the implementation of the President's economic goals.

Office of Science and Technology Policy

New Executive Office Building, 725 17th Street NW., Washington, DC 20502
Phone, 202–456–7116. Fax, 202–456–6021. Internet, www.ostp.gov.

Director	JOHN H. MARBURGER III
Associate Director for Science	(VACANCY)
Associate Director for Technology	RICHARD M. RUSSELL
Executive Secretary for the National Science and Technology Council	TED WACKLER
Executive Director for the President's Committee of Advisors on Science and Technology	CELIA MERZBACHER

The Office of Science and Technology Policy was established within the Executive Office of the President by the National Science and Technology Policy, Organization, and Priorities Act of 1976 (42 U.S.C. 6611).

The Office serves as a source of scientific, engineering, and technological analysis and judgment for the President with respect to major policies, plans, and programs of the Federal Government. In carrying out this mission, the Office advises the President of scientific and technological considerations involved in areas of national concern, including the economy, national security, health, foreign relations, and the environment; evaluates the scale, quality, and effectiveness of the Federal effort in science and technology; provides advice and assistance to the President, the Office of Management and Budget, and Federal agencies throughout the Federal budget development process; and assists the President in providing leadership and coordination for the research and development programs of the Federal Government.

For further information, contact the Office of Science and Technology Policy, New Executive Office Building, 725 17th Street NW., Washington, DC 20502. Phone, 202–456–7116. Fax, 202–456–6021. Internet, www.ostp.gov.

Office of the United States Trade Representative

600 Seventeenth Street NW., Washington, DC 20508
Phone, 202–395–3230. Internet, www.ustr.gov.

United States Trade Representative	ROBERT J. PORTMAN
Deputy U.S. Trade Representatives (Washington)	KARAN K. BHATIA, SUSAN C. SCHWAB
Deputy U.S. Trade Representative (Geneva)	PETER F. ALLGEIER
Special Textile Negotiator	SCOTT D. QUESENBERRY
General Counsel	JAMES MENDENHALL
Chief Agricultural Negotiator	RICHARD T. CROWDER
Assistant U.S. Trade Representative for Administration	FRED AMES
Assistant U.S. Trade Representative for Agricultural Affairs	JAMES MURPHY
Assistant U.S. Trade Representative for Southeast Asia, Pacific, and Pharmaceutical Policy	BARBARA WEISEL
Assistant U.S. Trade Representative for Congressional Affairs	JUSTIN J. MCCARTHY
Assistant U.S. Trade Representative for Economic Affairs	DAVID A. WALTERS
Assistant U.S. Trade Representative for Environment and Natural Resources	MARK LINSCOTT
Assistant U.S. Trade Representative for Europe and the Middle East	SHAUN DONNELLY
Assistant U.S. Trade Representative for Industry, Market Access and Telecommunications	MEREDITH BROADBENT
Assistant U.S. Trade Representative for Intergovernmental Affairs and Public Liaison	TIFFANY M. MOORE
Assistant U.S. Trade Representative for Japan, Korea, and APEC Affairs	WENDY CUTLER
Assistant U.S. Trade Representative for China	TIMOTHY STRATFORD
Assistant U.S. Trade Representative for South Asian Affairs	DOUGLAS HARTWICK
Assistant U.S. Trade Representative for Monitoring and Enforcement	DANIEL BRINZA
Assistant U.S. Trade Representative for Africa	FLORIE LISER
Assistant U.S. Trade Representative for Policy Coordination	CARMEN SURO-BREDIE
Assistant U.S. Trade Representative for Services and Investment	CHRISTINE BLISS, *Acting*
Assistant U.S. Trade Representative for Intellectual Property Rights	VICTORIA ESPINEL, *Acting*
Assistant U.S. Trade Representative for Trade and Labor	LEWIS KARESH

Assistant U.S. Trade Representative for World Trade Organization (WTO) and Multilateral Affairs	DOROTHY DWOSKIN
Assistant U.S. Trade Representative for the Americas	EVERETT EISSENSTAT
Assistant U.S. Trade Representative for Public and Media Affairs	CHRISTIN BAKER
Assistant U.S. Trade Representative for Trade Capacity Building	MARY RYCKMAN

The United States Trade Representative is responsible for directing all trade negotiations of and formulating trade policy for the United States.

The Office of the United States Trade Representative was created as the Office of the Special Representative for Trade Negotiations by Executive Order 11075 of January 15, 1963. The Trade Act of 1974 (19 U.S.C. 2171) established the Office as an agency of the Executive Office of the President charged with administering the trade agreements program.

The Office is responsible for setting and administering overall trade policy. It also provides that the United States Trade Representative shall be chief representative of the United States for the following:

—all activities concerning the General Agreement on Tariffs and Trade;

—discussions, meetings, and negotiations in the Organization for Economic Cooperation and Development when such activities deal primarily with trade and commodity issues;

—negotiations in the U.N. Conference on Trade and Development and other multilateral institutions when such negotiations deal primarily with trade and commodity issues;

—other bilateral and multilateral negotiations when trade, including East-West trade, or commodities is the primary issue;

—negotiations under sections 704 and 734 of the Tariff Act of 1930 (19 U.S.C. 1671c and 1673c); and

—negotiations concerning direct investment incentives and disincentives and bilateral investment issues concerning barriers to investment.

The Omnibus Trade and Competitiveness Act of 1988 codified these prior authorities and added additional authority, including the implementation of section 301 actions (regarding enforcement of U.S. rights under international trade agreements).

The Office is headed by the United States Trade Representative, a Cabinet-level official with the rank of Ambassador, who is directly responsible to the President. There are three Deputy United States Trade Representatives, who also hold the rank of Ambassador—two located in Washington and one in Geneva. The Chief Agricultural Negotiator also holds the rank of Ambassador.

The United States Trade Representative serves as an *ex officio* member of the Boards of Directors of the Export-Import Bank and the Overseas Private Investment Corporation, and serves on the National Advisory Council for International Monetary and Financial Policy.

For further information, contact the Office of Public Affairs, Office of the United States Trade Representative, 600 Seventeenth Street NW., Washington, DC 20506. Phone, 202–395–3230. Internet, www.ustr.gov.

Departments

DEPARTMENT OF AGRICULTURE

1400 Independence Avenue SW., Washington, DC 20250
Phone, 202–720–4623. Internet, www.usda.gov.

SECRETARY OF AGRICULTURE	MIKE JOHANNS
Deputy Secretary	CHARLES F. CONNER
Under Secretary for Farm and Foreign Agricultural Services	J.B. PENN
Deputy Under Secretaries	FLOYD GAIBLER, (VACANCY)
Administrator, Farm Service Agency	TERESA C. LASSETER
Administrator, Foreign Agricultural Service	MICHAEL W. YOST
Administrator, Risk Management Agency	ELDON F. GOULD
Under Secretary for Food, Nutrition, and Consumer Services	ERIC M. BOST
Deputy Under Secretary	KATE COLER
Administrator, Food and Nutrition Service	ROBERTO SALAZAR
Executive Director, Center for Nutrition Policy and Promotion	ERIC HENTGES
Under Secretary for Food Safety	RICHARD RAYMOND
Deputy Under Secretary	CURT MANN
Administrator, Food Safety and Inspection Service	BARBARA MASTERS
Under Secretary for Natural Resources and Environment	MARK E. REY
Deputy Under Secretaries	MERLYN CARLSON, DAVE TENNY
Chief, Forest Service	DALE BOSWORTH
Chief, Natural Resources Conservation Service	BRUCE KNIGHT
Under Secretary for Research, Education, and Economics	GALE A. BUCHANAN
Deputy Under Secretary	MERLE D. PIERSON
Administrator, Agricultural Research Service	EDWARD B. KNIPLING
Administrator, Cooperative State Research, Education, and Extension Service	COLIEN HEFFERAN
Administrator, Economic Research Service	SUSAN E. OFFUTT
Administrator, National Agricultural Statistics Service	RON BOSECKER
Under Secretary for Rural Development	THOMAS DORR
Deputy Under Secretary	AL JOHNSON
Administrator, Rural Business-Cooperative Service	JACKIE GLEASON
Administrator, Rural Housing Service	RUSSELL DAVIS
Administrator, Rural Utilities Service	JAMES ANDREW

Assistant Secretary for Congressional Relations	LINDA A. STRACHAN
Deputy Assistant Secretary	ARLEN LANCASTER
Under Secretary for Marketing and Regulatory Programs	CHUCK LAMBERT, *Acting*
Deputy Under Secretary	CHUCK LAMBERT
Administrator, Agricultural Marketing Service	LLOYD C. DAY
Administrator, Animal and Plant Health Inspection Service	RON DEHAVEN
Administrator, Grain Inspection, Packers, and Stockyards Administration	JAMES LINK
Assistant Secretary for Administration	BOYD K. RUTHERFORD
Deputy Assistant Secretary	PETER J. THOMAS
Chairman, Board of Contract Appeals	HOWARD A. POLLACK
Judicial Officer	WILLIAM G. JENSON
Chief Judge, Administrative Law Judges	MARC HILLSON
Director, Office of Ethics	RAYMOND SHEEHAN
Director, Office of Human Capital Management	(VACANCY)
Director, Office of Operations	PRISCILLA B. CAREY
Director, Office of Procurement and Property Management	WARREN R. ASHWORTH
Director, Office of Small and Disadvantaged Business Utilization	JAMES E. HOUSE
Director, Conflict Resolution and Prevention Center	DALE GENTRY
Assistant Secretary for Civil Rights	(VACANCY)
Deputy Assistant Secretary	ANNABELLE ROMERO
Associate Assistant Secretary	CLYDE THOMPSON
Director, Office of Civil Rights	SADHNA G. TRUE
Director, Office of Outreach	GLADYS VAUGHN
Chief Information Officer	DAVE COMBS
Deputy Chief Information Officer	JERRY E. WILLIAMS
Chief Financial Officer	CHARLES CHRISTOPHERSON
Deputy Chief Financial Officer	PATRICIA HEALY
General Counsel	MARC L. KESSELMAN
Deputy General Counsel	J. MICHAEL KELLY
Inspector General	PHYLLIS K. FONG
Deputy Inspector General	KATHLEEN S. TIGHE
Director, Office of Communications	TERRI TEUBER
Chief Economist	KEITH COLLINS
Deputy Chief Economist	JOSEPH GLAUBER
Director, Office of Risk Assessment and Cost-Benefit Analysis	JAMES SCHAUB
Chairman, World Agricultural Outlook Board	GERALD BANGE
Director, Global Change Program Office	WILLIAM HOHENSTEIN
Director, Office of Energy Policy and New Uses	ROGER CONWAY
Director, National Appeals Division	ROGER J. KLURFELD

Director, Office of Budget and Program Analysis	SCOTT STEELE
Director, Office of the Executive Secretariat	BRUCE BUNDICK

[For the Department of Agriculture statement of organization, see the *Code of Federal Regulations,* Title 7, Part 2]

The Department of Agriculture works to improve and maintain farm income and to develop and expand markets abroad for agricultural products. The Department helps to curb and to cure poverty, hunger, and malnutrition. It works to enhance the environment and to maintain production capacity by helping landowners protect the soil, water, forests, and other natural resources. Rural development, credit, and conservation programs are key resources for carrying out national growth policies. Department research findings directly or indirectly benefit all Americans. The Department, through inspection and grading services, safeguards and ensures standards of quality in the daily food supply.

The Department of Agriculture (USDA) was created by act of May 15, 1862 (7 U.S.C. 2201).

In carrying out its work in the program mission areas, USDA relies on the support of departmental administration staff, as well as the Office of the Chief Financial Officer, Office of the Chief Information Officer, Office of Communications, Office of Congressional and Intergovernmental Relations, Office of the Inspector General, and the Office of the General Counsel.

Rural Development

USDA's rural development mission is to assist rural Americans to increase their economic opportunities and improve their quality of life. To accomplish this, USDA works to foster new cooperative relationships among Government, industry, and communities. As a capital investment bank, USDA provides financing for rural housing and community facilities, business and cooperative development, telephone and high-speed Internet access, electric, water, and sewer infrastructure. Approximately 800 rural development field offices, staffed by 7,000 employees, provide frontline delivery of rural development loan and grant programs at the local level.

Rural Business-Cooperative Programs

To meet business credit needs in underserved areas, USDA rural development business programs are usually leveraged with commercial, cooperative, or other private sector lenders. USDA's business programs are as follows:

Business and Industry Guaranteed Loans This program helps create jobs and stimulates rural economies by providing financial backing for rural businesses. Loan proceeds may be used for working capital, machinery and equipment, buildings and real estate, and certain types of debt refinancing.

Business Enterprise These grants help public bodies, nonprofit corporations, and federally recognized Indian tribal groups finance and facilitate development of small and emerging private business enterprises located in rural areas. Grant funds can pay for the acquisition and development of land and the construction of buildings, plants, equipment, access streets and roads, parking areas, utility and service extensions, refinancing, and fees for professional services, as well as technical assistance and related training, startup costs and working capital, financial assistance to a third party,

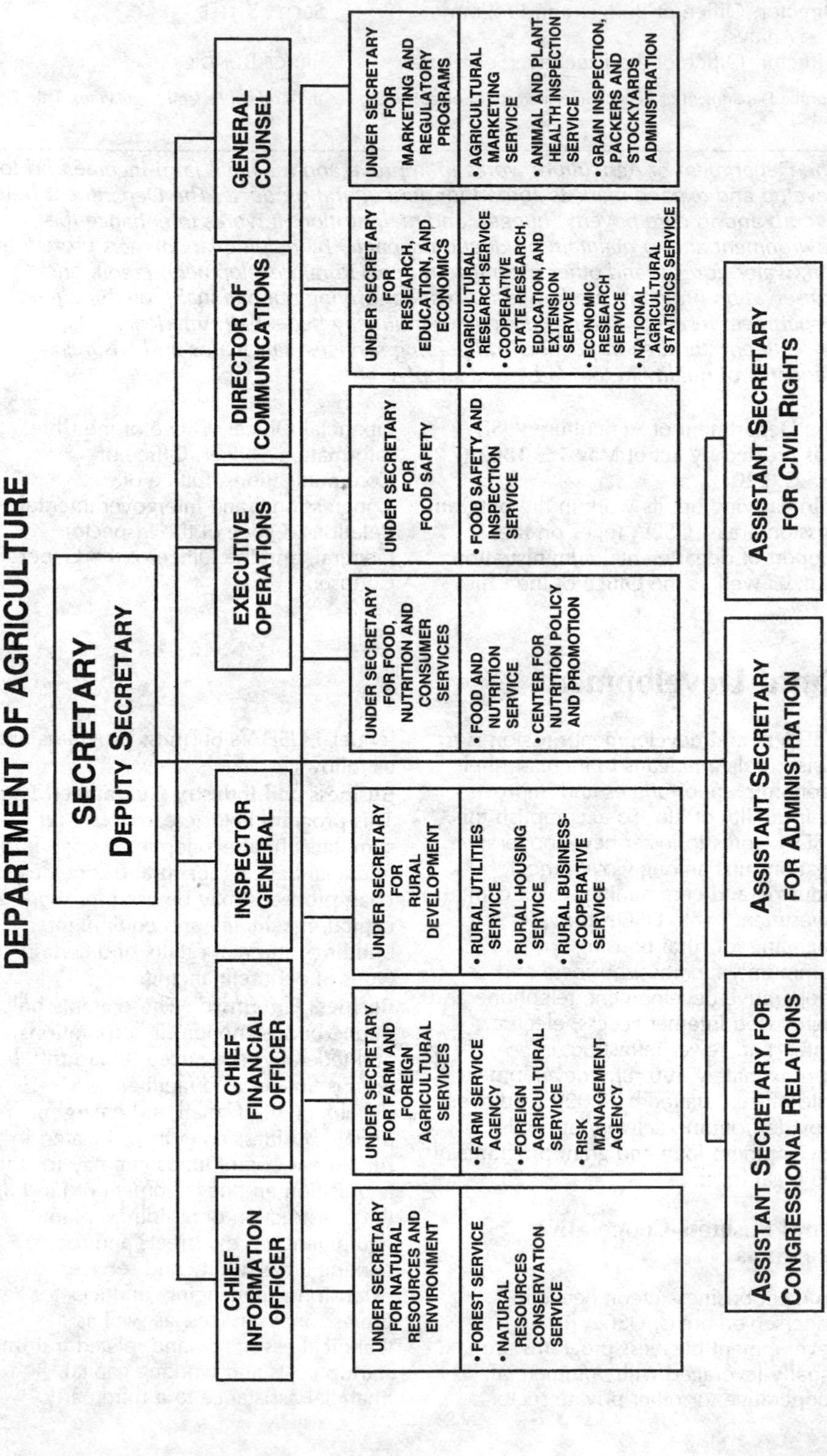
DEPARTMENT OF AGRICULTURE
SECRETARY
DEPUTY SECRETARY
CHIEF INFORMATION OFFICER
CHIEF FINANCIAL OFFICER
INSPECTOR GENERAL
EXECUTIVE OPERATIONS
DIRECTOR OF COMMUNICATIONS
GENERAL COUNSEL
UNDER SECRETARY FOR NATURAL RESOURCES AND ENVIRONMENT
• FOREST SERVICE
• NATURAL RESOURCES CONSERVATION SERVICE
UNDER SECRETARY FOR FARM AND FOREIGN AGRICULTURAL SERVICES
• FARM SERVICE AGENCY
• FOREIGN AGRICULTURAL SERVICE
• RISK MANAGEMENT AGENCY
UNDER SECRETARY FOR RURAL DEVELOPMENT
• RURAL UTILITIES SERVICE
• RURAL HOUSING SERVICE
• RURAL BUSINESS-COOPERATIVE SERVICE
UNDER SECRETARY FOR FOOD, NUTRITION AND CONSUMER SERVICES
• FOOD AND NUTRITION SERVICE
• CENTER FOR NUTRITION POLICY AND PROMOTION
UNDER SECRETARY FOR FOOD SAFETY
• FOOD SAFETY AND INSPECTION SERVICE
UNDER SECRETARY FOR RESEARCH, EDUCATION, AND ECONOMICS
• AGRICULTURAL RESEARCH SERVICE
• COOPERATIVE STATE RESEARCH, EDUCATION, AND EXTENSION SERVICE
• ECONOMIC RESEARCH SERVICE
• NATIONAL AGRICULTURAL STATISTICS SERVICE
UNDER SECRETARY FOR MARKETING AND REGULATORY PROGRAMS
• AGRICULTURAL MARKETING SERVICE
• ANIMAL AND PLANT HEALTH INSPECTION SERVICE
• GRAIN INSPECTION, PACKERS AND STOCKYARDS ADMINISTRATION
ASSISTANT SECRETARY FOR CONGRESSIONAL RELATIONS
ASSISTANT SECRETARY FOR ADMINISTRATION
ASSISTANT SECRETARY FOR CIVIL RIGHTS

production of television programs targeted to rural residents, and rural distance learning networks.

Business Opportunities This program promotes sustainable economic development in rural communities with exceptional needs. Funds are provided for technical assistance, training, and planning activities that improve economic conditions. Applicants must be located in rural areas.

Renewable Energy and Efficiency Loans and Grants This program encourages agricultural producers and small rural businesses to create renewable and energy-efficient systems.

Cooperative Development These grants finance the establishment and operation of centers for cooperative development. The primary purpose of this program is to enhance the economic condition of rural areas through the development of new cooperatives and improving operations of existing cooperatives, and encourage the development of value-added ventures.

Cooperative Opportunities and Problems Research This program encourages research, funded through cooperative agreements, on critical issues vital to the development and sustainability of agricultural and other rural cooperatives as a means of improving the quality of life in America's rural communities.

Cooperative Program This program helps farmers and rural communities become self-reliant through the use of cooperative organizations. Studies are conducted to support cooperatives that market farm products, purchase production supplies, and perform related business services. These studies concentrate on the financial, organizational, legal, social, and economic aspects of cooperative activity. Technical assistance and research is provided to improve cooperative performance in organizing new cooperatives, merging existing cooperatives, changing business structures, and developing strategies for growth. Applied research is conducted to give farmers and rural communities expert assistance pertaining to their cooperatives. The program also collects and publishes statistics regarding the role and scope of cooperative activity in U.S. agriculture. A bimonthly magazine, *Rural Cooperatives*, reports current developments and research for cooperative management leadership.

Economic Development These loans and grants finance economic development and job creation projects based on sound economic plans in rural areas. Loans and grants are available to any eligible USDA electric or telecommunications borrower to assist in developing rural areas from an economic standpoint, to create new job opportunities, and to help retain existing employment. Loans at zero interest are made primarily to finance business startup ventures and business expansion projects. Grants are made to eligible telephone and electric utilities to establish revolving loan programs operated at the local level. The revolving loan program provides capital to nonprofit entities and municipal organizations to finance business or community facilities which promote job creation in rural areas, for facilities which extend or improve medical care to rural residents, and for facilities which promote education and training to enhance marketable job skills for rural residents.

Intermediary Relending These loans finance business facilities and community development projects in rural areas. The Service lends these funds to intermediaries, which in turn provide loans to recipients who are developing business facilities or community development projects.

Sheep Industry The National Sheep Industry Improvement Center promotes strategic development activities to strengthen and enhance the production and marketing of sheep and goat products in the United States. It works to improve infrastructure and business development, market and environmental research, and designs unique responses to the needs of the industries for their long-term sustainable development. The Center's board of directors oversees its activities and operates a revolving fund for loans and grants.

Technology Transfer This program provides information to farmers and other rural users on a variety of sustainable agricultural practices that include both cropping and livestock operations. It offers reliable, practical information on production techniques and practices that reduce costs and that are environmentally friendly. Farmers can request such information by telephone at 800–346–9140.

For further information, contact the Rural Development, Legislative and Public Affairs Staff, Stop 0705, Department of Agriculture, 1400 Independence Avenue SW., Washington, DC 20250–0320. Phone, 202–720–4323.

Rural Housing Programs

Rural Development provides affordable rental housing, homeownership opportunities, and essential community facilities to rural Americans through a broad array of direct loan, guarantee, and grant programs. Rural residents and communities may inquire about any of these programs through local and State rural development offices. It also provides financial and management assistance through the following services:

—guaranteed single-family housing (SFH) loans which guarantee loans made by commercial lenders to moderate-income rural residents with sufficient income and acceptable credit, who may lack the downpayment to secure a loan without assistance;

—direct SFH loans made available to people with incomes less than 80 percent of area median, to build, purchase, and repair rural homes;

—home improvement and repair loans and grants for owner-occupants to remove health and safety hazards from a home;

—mutual self-help housing technical assistance grants for nonprofit organizations and public bodies to help groups of six to eight very low- and low-income families to build their own homes by providing "sweat equity" which reduces the families' mortgages;

—rural housing site loans for private or public nonprofit organizations to purchase sites for the development of housing for very low- and low-income families;

—direct and guaranteed multi-family housing loans for private nonprofit corporations, consumer cooperatives, State or local public agencies, and individuals or organizations operating on a nonprofit or limited profit basis to provide rental or cooperative housing in rural areas for persons of very low, low, and moderate income;

—farm labor housing loans and grants enabling farmers, public or private nonprofit organizations, or units of local government to build, buy, or rehabilitate farm labor housing;

—housing preservation grants made to a public body or public/private nonprofit organization to provide assistance to homeowners and landlords to repair and rehabilitate housing for very low- and low-income families in rural areas;

—housing for the homeless, SFH real estate-owned (REO) property to nonprofit organizations or public bodies for transitional housing for the homeless and to the Federal Emergency Management Agency to house families affected by natural disasters; and

—community program loans, direct and guaranteed loans and grants for public and quasi-public bodies, nonprofit associations, and Indian tribes for essential community facilities such as health care centers, public safety buildings and vehicles, and child care centers.

For further information, contact the Rural Development, Legislative and Public Affairs Staff, Stop 0705, Department of Agriculture, 1400 Independence Avenue SW., Washington, DC 20250–0320. Phone, 202–720–4323.

Rural Utilities Programs

Rural Development assists rural electric and telecommunications utilities in obtaining financing and administers a nationwide water and waste loan and grant program to improve the quality of life and promote economic development in rural America. A total of 890 rural electric and 800 rural telecommunications utilities in 47 States, Puerto Rico, the Virgin Islands, Guam, the Republic of the Marshall Islands, the Northern Mariana Islands, and the

Federated States of Micronesia have received financial assistance. It also provides assistance through the following programs:

—The electric program provides loans for improving electric service to persons in rural areas, including construction of electric generating plants and transmission and distribution lines to provide reliable electric service.

—The telecommunications program provides telephone service and high-speed Internet access in rural areas.

—The water and waste direct and guaranteed loan program provides assistance to develop water and wastewater systems, including solid waste disposal and storm drainage, in rural areas, cities, and towns.

—Water and waste disposal grants assist in reducing water and waste disposal costs to a reasonable level for users of the system.

—Emergency community water assistance grants provide assistance to rural communities experiencing a significant decline in quantity or quality of drinking water.

—Technical assistance and training grants are available to nonprofit organizations to provide rural water and waste system officials with technical assistance and training on a wide range of issues relating to the delivery of water and waste service to rural residents.

—Solid waste management grants are available for nonprofit organizations and public bodies to provide technical assistance and training to rural areas and towns to reduce or eliminate pollution of water resources and improve planning and management of solid waste facilities.

—The rural water circuit rider technical assistance program provides, through the National Rural Water Association, technical assistance to rural water systems to solve operational, financial, and management problems.

—The distance learning and telemedicine program provides assistance to help rural schools and health care providers invest in telecommunications facilities and equipment to bring to rural areas educational and medical resources that otherwise might be unavailable.

—Rural Development also guarantees loans from the Department of the Treasury's Federal Financing Bank (FFB), which it lends to borrowers, primarily for large-scale electric and telecommunication facilities. It may also guarantee electric and telecommunications loans from private sources.

For further information, contact the Rural Development Legislative and Public Affairs Staff, Department of Agriculture, Stop 0705, 1400 Independence Avenue SW., Washington, DC 20250–0320. Phone, 202–720–4323.

Marketing and Regulatory Programs

This mission area includes marketing and regulatory programs other than those concerned with food safety.

Agricultural Marketing Service

The Agricultural Marketing Service (AMS) was established by the Secretary of Agriculture on April 2, 1972, under the authority of Reorganization Plan No. 2 of 1953 (5 U.S.C. app.) and other authorities. The Service administers standardization, grading, certification, market news, marketing orders, research and promotion, and regulatory programs.

Market News The Service provides current, unbiased information to producers, processors, distributors, and others to assist them in the orderly marketing and distribution of farm commodities. Information is collected on supplies, shipments, prices, location, quality, condition, and other market data on farm products in specific markets and marketing areas. The data is disseminated nationally via the Internet and other electronic means and is shared with several countries. The Service also assists other countries in developing their own marketing information systems.

Standardization, Grading, and Classing Nearly 600 grade standards have been established for some 230 agricultural commodities to help buyers and sellers trade on agreed-upon quality levels. Standards are developed with the benefit of views from those in the industries directly affected and others interested. The Service also participates in developing international commodity standards to facilitate trade.

Grading and classing services are provided to certify the grade and quality of products. These grading services are provided to buyers and sellers of live cattle, swine, sheep, meat, poultry, eggs, rabbits, fruits, vegetables, tree nuts, peanuts, dairy products, and tobacco. Classing services are provided to buyers and sellers of cotton and cotton products. These services are mainly voluntary and are provided upon request and for a fee. The Service is also responsible for testing seed.

Laboratory Testing The Service provides microbiological, chemical, and other scientific laboratory support to its commodity and food procurement programs, testing peanuts for aflatoxin, and testing seeds for germination and purity. The Agency also carries out quality assurance and safety oversight activities for its milk market laboratories, resident grading programs, and State and private laboratory programs.

The Service also administers the Pesticide Data Program which, in cooperation with States, samples and analyzes 33 agricultural commodities for pesticides residue. It shares residue test results with the Environmental Protection Agency and other public agencies.

Food Quality Assurance Under a governmentwide quality assurance program, AMS is responsible for the development and revision of specifications used by Federal agencies in procuring food for military and civilian uses. The Service coordinates and approves certification programs designed to ensure that purchased products conform to the specification requirements.

Regulatory Programs The Service administers several regulatory programs designed collectively to protect producers, handlers, and consumers of agricultural commodities from financial loss or personal injury resulting from careless, deceptive, or fraudulent marketing practices. Such regulatory programs encourage fair trading practices in the marketing of fruits and vegetables, require truth in seed labeling and in advertising. The Service provides voluntary laboratory analyses of egg products, and monitors the disposition of restricted shell eggs—eggs that are a potential health hazard.

Marketing Agreements and Orders The Service administers marketing agreements and orders to establish and maintain orderly marketing conditions for certain commodities. Milk marketing orders establish minimum prices that handlers or distributors are required to pay producers. Programs for fruits, vegetables, and related specialty crops like nuts and spearmint oil promote product quality control and help stabilize supplies and market prices. In some cases, they also authorize research and market development activities, including advertising supported by assessments that handlers pay. Through the orderly marketing of commodities facilitated by these programs, the interests of both producers and consumers are protected.

Plant Variety Protection Program The Service administers a program that provides for the issuance of certificates of plant variety protection. These certificates afford developers of novel varieties of sexually reproduced plants exclusive rights to sell, reproduce, import, or export such varieties, or use them in the production of hybrids or different varieties for a period of 20 years for non-woody plants and 25 years for woody plants.

Research and Promotion Programs The Service monitors certain industry-sponsored research, promotion, and information programs authorized by Federal laws. These programs provide farmers and processors with a means to finance and operate various research, promotion, and information activities for cotton, potatoes, eggs, milk and dairy products, beef, pork, honey, watermelon, mushrooms, soybeans, blueberries, avocados, peanuts, and popcorn.

Transportation Programs The Service is also responsible for the promotion of an efficient transportation system for rural America that begins at the farm gate and moves agricultural and other rural products through the Nation's highways, railroads, airports, and waterways, and into the domestic and international marketplace. To accomplish this, AMS conducts economic studies and analyses of these systems, and represents agricultural and rural transportation interests in policy and regulatory forums. To provide direct assistance to the transportation community, AMS supplies research and technical information to producers, producer groups, shippers, exporters, rural communities, carriers, governmental agencies, and universities.

Organic Standards The Service, with the assistance of the National Organic Standards Board, develops national organic standards.

Other Programs Other marketing service activities include financial grants to States for marketing improvement projects. The Agency also has responsibility for the conduct of studies of the facilities and methods used in the physical distribution of food and other farm products; for research designed to improve the handling of all agricultural products as they move from farm to consumers; for increasing marketing efficiency by developing improved operating methods and facilities; and for certifying equipment for processing, handling, and distributing dairy, poultry, and meat products.

Pesticide Recordkeeping Program The Agricultural Marketing Service manages the Pesticide Recordkeeping Program in coordination with State agencies, the National Agricultural Statistics Service, and the Environmental Protection Agency. The Service has developed educational programs and works with State agencies in inspecting applicator records.

For further information, contact the Public Affairs Staff, Agricultural Marketing Service, Department of Agriculture, Room 3510, South Agriculture Building, Stop 0273, Washington, DC 20250. Phone, 202–720–8998 or visit the Web site at www.ams.usda.gov.

Animal and Plant Health Inspection Service

[For the Animal and Plant Health Inspection Service statement of organization, see the *Code of Federal Regulations,* Title 7, Part 371]

The Animal and Plant Health Inspection Service (APHIS) was reestablished by the Secretary of Agriculture on March 14, 1977, pursuant to authority contained in 5 U.S.C. 301 and Reorganization Plan No. 2 of 1953 (5 U.S.C. app.).

The Service was established to conduct regulatory and control programs to protect and improve animal and plant health for the benefit of man and the environment. In cooperation with State governments, the agency administers Federal laws and regulations pertaining to animal and plant health and quarantine, humane treatment of animals, and the control and eradication of pests and diseases. Regulations to prevent the introduction or interstate spread of certain animal or plant pests or diseases are also enforced by the Service. It also carries out research and operational activities to reduce crop and livestock depredation caused by birds, rodents, and predators.

Biotechnology Regulatory Services (BRS) Biotechnology regulatory officials are responsible for regulating the importation, movement, and field release of genetically engineered plants, insects, microorganisms, and any other known organism or potential plant pest.

BRS regulations are designed to ensure that genetically engineered organisms, such as herbicide-tolerant cotton or virus -resistant papayas, are just as safe for agriculture and the environment as traditionally bred crop varieties. In regulating biotechnology, BRS works in concert with the Environmental Protection Agency and the Food and Drug Administration, agencies that also play important roles in protecting agriculture, a safe food supply, and the environment. BRS involvement begins when a person or organization wishes to import, move across a State line, or field-test a genetically engineered plant. These activities are subject to the BRS permitting and notification system.

Plant Protection and Quarantine (PPQ) Plant protection officials are responsible for programs to control or eradicate plant pests and diseases. These programs are carried out in cooperation with the States involved, other Federal agencies, farmers, and private organizations. Pest control programs use a single tool or a combination of pest control techniques, both chemical and nonchemical, which are both effective and safe.

PPQ officials develop Federal regulations and policies that prohibit or restrict the entry of foreign pests and plants, plant products, animal products and byproducts, and other materials that may harbor pests or diseases. These regulations and policies, in conjunction with inspections conducted by the Department of Homeland Security's Customs and Border Protection (CBP) help protect agricultural production and natural resources from pests and diseases. CBP maintains inspection services at all major sea, air, and land border ports of entry into the United States. PPQ continues to be present at many of these locations to take regulatory action on prohibited or restricted products that are found.

Veterinary Services Animal health officials are responsible for programs to protect and improve the health, quality, and marketability of U.S. animals and animal products. The programs are carried out through cooperative links with States, foreign governments, livestock producers, and other Federal agencies.

Service officials exclude, control, and eradicate animal pests and diseases by carrying out eradication and control programs for certain diseases, providing diagnostic services, and gathering and disseminating information regarding animal health in the United States through land, air, and ocean ports. They also certify as to the health status of animals and animal products being exported to other countries, and respond to animal disease incursions or epidemics which threaten the health status of U.S. livestock and poultry.

The Service also administers a Federal law intended to ensure that all veterinary biological products, whether developed by conventional or new biotechnological procedures, used in the diagnosis, prevention, and treatment of animal disease are safe, pure, potent, and effective. The Service regulates firms that manufacture veterinary biological products subject to the act, including licensing the manufacturing establishment and its products, inspecting production facilities and production methods, and testing products under a surveillance program.

Animal Care The Service administers Federal laws concerned with the humane care and handling of all warm-blooded animals bought, sold, and transported in commerce and used or intended for use as pets at the wholesale level, or used or intended for use in exhibitions or for research purposes. The agency also enforces the Horse Protection Act of 1970, which prohibits the soring of horses at shows and sales.

International Services Service activities in the international arena include conducting cooperative plant and animal pest and disease control, eradication, and surveillance programs in foreign countries. These programs provide a first line of defense for the United States against threats such as screwworm, medfly, foot-and-mouth disease, and other exotic diseases and pests. The Service also provides international representation concerning sanitary and phytosanitary technical trade issues, and manages programs for overseas preclearance of commodities, passengers, and U.S. military activities.

Wildlife Services Wildlife services officials cooperate with States, counties, local communities, and agricultural producer groups to reduce crop and livestock depredations caused by birds, rodents, and predators. Using methods and techniques that are biologically sound, environmentally acceptable, and economically feasible, they participate in efforts to educate and advise farmers and ranchers on proper uses of control methods and techniques; suppress serious nuisances and threats to public health and safety caused by birds, rodents, and other wildlife in urban and rural communities; and work with airport managers to reduce risks of bird strikes. In addition, they conduct research into predator-prey relationships, new control methods, and more efficient and safe uses of present methods such as toxicants, repellants and attractants, biological controls, scare devices, and habitat alteration.

For further information, contact Legislative and Public Affairs, Animal and Plant Health Inspection Service, Department of Agriculture, Washington, DC20250. Phone, 202–720–2511.

Grain Inspection, Packers, and Stockyards Administration

The Grain Inspection, Packers, and Stockyards Administration (GIPSA) was established in 1994 to facilitate the marketing of livestock, poultry, meat, cereals, oilseeds, and related agricultural products, and to promote fair and competitive trading practices for the overall benefit of consumers and American agriculture. The Agency's mission is carried out in two different segments of American agriculture. The Federal Grain Inspection Service provides the U.S. grain market with Federal quality standards and a uniform system for applying them. The Packers and Stockyards Programs (P&SP) enforces the Packers and Stockyards Act of 1921 (P&S Act), 7 U.S.C. 181 *et seq.*, to promote fair and competitive marketing environments for the livestock, meat, and poultry industries. GIPSA also certifies State central filing systems for notification of liens against farm products. GIPSA is responsible for establishing official U.S. standards for grain and other assigned commodities, and for administering a nationwide official inspection and weighing system.

Inspection The United States Grain Standards Act requires that, with some exceptions, all U.S. export grain be officially inspected. At export port locations, inspection is performed by GIPSA or by State agencies that have been delegated export inspection authority by the Administrator. For domestic grain marketed at inland locations, the Administrator designates private and State agencies to provide official inspection services upon request. Both export and domestic services are provided on a fee basis.

Weighing Official weighing of U.S. export grain is performed at port locations by GIPSA or by State agencies that have been delegated export weighing authority by the Administrator. For domestic grain marketed at inland locations, the weighing services may be provided by GIPSA or by designated private or State agencies. Weighing services are provided on a fee basis, upon request.

Standardization The Administration is responsible for establishing, maintaining, and revising official U.S. standards for corn, wheat, rye, oats, barley, flaxseed, sorghum, soybeans, triticale, sunflower seed, canola, and mixed grain. It is authorized to perform applied research to develop methods to improve accuracy and uniformity in grading grain. It is also responsible for standardization and inspection activities for rice, dry beans, peas, lentils, hay, straw, hops, and related processed grain commodities. Although standards no longer exist for hay, straw, and hops, GIPSA maintains inspection procedures for and retains authority to inspect these commodities.

Methods Development The Administration's methods development activities include applied research or tests that produce new or improved techniques for measuring grain quality. Examples include new knowledge gained through study of how to establish the framework for real-time grain inspection and develop reference methods to maintain consistency and standardization in the grain inspection system, and the comparison of different techniques for evaluation of end-use quality in wheat.

Packers and Stockyards Activities The P&S Act prohibits unfair, deceptive, anti-competitive, and fraudulent practices by market agencies, dealers, packers, swine contactors, and live poultry dealers in those particular industries. The P&S Act protects producers and poultry growers by requiring most regulated entities to obtain bonds and meet strict payment requirements. To protect unpaid cash sellers of livestock, packers are subject to trust provisions which require that livestock and related investments or proceeds from meat, meat food products, or livestock products derived from them be held in trust for unpaid sellers until payment is made in full. A similar provision exists for live poultry dealers to protect growers. P&SP analyzes all trust and bond claims as a courtesy to the regulated industries. It is also responsible for the Truth-in-Lending Act and the Fair Credit Reporting Act as each relates to persons and firms subject to the P&S Act. P&SP carries out the Secretary's responsibilities under section 1324 of the Food Security Act of 1985 pertaining to State-established central filing systems to pre-notify buyers, commission merchants, and selling agents of security interests against farm products. GIPSA administers the section of the statute commonly referred to as the "Clear Title" provision, and certifies qualifying State systems.

For further information, contact the Grain Inspection, Packers, and Stockyards Administration, Department of Agriculture, Washington, DC 20250. Phone, 202–720–0219.

Food Safety

Food Safety and Inspection Service

The Food Safety and Inspection Service (FSIS) was established by the Secretary of Agriculture on June 17, 1981, pursuant to authority contained in 5 U.S.C. 301 and Reorganization Plan No. 2 of 1953 (5 U.S.C. app.).

Meat, Poultry, and Egg Products Inspection Federal meat and poultry inspection is mandatory for cattle, calves, swine, goats, sheep, lambs, horses (and other equines), chickens, turkeys, ducks, geese, and guineas used for human food. FSIS provides for the inspection of each animal or bird at slaughter and processed products during various stages of production.

FSIS regulates the processing and distribution of meat and meat products, poultry and poultry products, and egg products, to ensure that those products moving in intrastate, interstate, and foreign commerce are wholesome, unadulterated, and properly labeled and packaged. Through its inspection process, FSIS also prevents the movement or sale of meat, poultry, and egg products in interstate or foreign commerce which are unwholesome, adulterated or misbranded. FSIS tests samples of egg products and meat and poultry products for microbial and chemical contaminants to monitor trends for enforcement purposes.

FSIS monitors livestock upon arrival at federally inspected facilities; conducts voluntary reimbursed inspection for rabbits, other domestic food animals, bison, other exotic food animals, ratites, and certain egg products not covered by the inspection law; and ensures that inedible egg products and inedible products from meat or poultry, such as offal rendered for animal feed, are properly identified and isolated from edible products.

Each product label must be approved by FSIS before they can be sold. FSIS monitors meat and poultry products in storage, distribution, and retail channels; and takes necessary compliance actions to protect the public, including detention of products, voluntary product recalls, court-ordered seizures of products, administrative withdrawal of inspection, and referral for criminal prosecution. FSIS also conducts State programs for the inspection of meat and poultry products sold in intrastate commerce.

FSIS maintains a toll-free meat and poultry hotline (phone, 888–674–6854, TTY, 800–256–7072) to answer questions in English and Spanish about the safe handling of meat, poultry, and egg products. The hotline's hours are Monday through Friday, from 10 a.m. to 4 p.m., Eastern Time, year-round. An extensive selection of food safety messages, in English and Spanish, is also available at the same number 24 hours a day.

In 2004, FSIS launched "Ask Karen," a Web-based virtual representative tool that provides answers to consumer questions about food safety. "Ask Karen" is available 24 hours a day, 7 days a week at www.fsis.usda.gov/Food_Safety_Education/Ask_Karen/.

For further information, contact the Director, Food Safety Education Staff, Food Safety and Inspection Service, Department of Agriculture, Beltsville, Maryland 20705. Phone, 301–504–9605. Fax, 301–504–0203. Internet, www.fsis.usda.gov. E-mail, MPHotline.fsis@usda.gov.

Food, Nutrition, and Consumer Services

The mission of Food, Nutrition, and Consumer Services is to reduce hunger and food insecurity, in partnership with cooperating organizations, by providing access to food, a healthful diet, and nutrition education to children and needy people in a manner that supports American agriculture.

Food and Nutrition Service

The Food and Nutrition Service (FNS) administers the USDA food assistance programs. These programs, which serve one in six Americans, represent our Nation's commitment to the principle that no one in this country should fear hunger or experience want. They provide a Federal safety net to people in need. The goals of the programs are to provide needy persons with access to a more nutritious diet, to improve the eating habits of the Nation's children, and to help America's farmers by providing an outlet for distributing foods purchased under farmer assistance authorities.

The Service works in partnership with the States in all its programs. State and local agencies determine most administrative details regarding distribution of food benefits and eligibility of participants, and FNS provides commodities and funding for additional food and to cover administrative costs. FNS administers the following food assistance programs:

—The Food Stamp Program provides food benefits through State and local welfare agencies to needy persons to increase their food purchasing power. The benefits are used by program participants to buy food in retail stores approved by the Food and Nutrition Service to accept and redeem the benefits.

—The Special Supplemental Nutrition Program for Women, Infants, and Children (WIC) improves the health of low-income pregnant, breastfeeding, and nonbreastfeeding postpartum women, and infants and children up to 5 years of age by providing them with specific nutritious food supplements, nutrition education, and health care referrals.

—The WIC Farmers' Market Nutrition Program provides WIC participants with increased access to fresh produce. WIC participants receive coupons to purchase fresh fruits and vegetables from authorized farmers.

—The Commodity Supplemental Food Program provides a package of foods monthly to low-income pregnant, postpartum, and breastfeeding women, their infants and children under age 6, and the elderly. Nutrition education is also provided through this program.

—The National School Lunch Program supports nonprofit food services in elementary and secondary schools and in residential child-care institutions. More than half of the meals served through these institutions are free or at reduced cost.

—The School Breakfast Program supplements the National School Lunch Program by supporting schools in providing needy children with free or low-cost breakfasts that meet established nutritional standards.

—The Special Milk Program for Children provides milk for children in those schools, summer camps, and child-care institutions that have no federally supported meal programs.

—The Child and Adult Care Food Program provides cash and commodities for meals for preschool and school-aged children in child-care facilities and for functionally impaired adults in facilities that provide nonresidential care for such individuals.

—The Summer Food Service Program for Children helps various organizations get nutritious meals to needy preschool and school-aged children during the summer months and during school vacations.

—The Emergency Food Assistance Program provides State agencies with commodities for distribution to food banks, food pantries, soup kitchens, and other charitable institutions throughout the country, with administrative funds to assist in distribution.

—The Food Distribution Program on Indian Reservations and the Trust Territories provides an extensive package of commodities monthly to low-income households on or near Indian reservations in lieu of food stamps. This program is administered at the local level by Indian tribal organizations or State agencies.

—The Nutrition Program for the Elderly provides cash and commodities to States for meals for senior citizens. The food is delivered through senior citizen centers or meals-on-wheels programs.

—The Nutrition Assistance Programs for Puerto Rico and the Northern Marianas are block grant programs that replace the Food Stamp Programs in these two territories and provide cash and coupons to resident participants.

—The Nutrition Education and Training Program grants funds to States for the development and dissemination of nutrition information and materials to children and for training of food service and teaching personnel.

For further information, contact the Public Information Officer, Food and Nutrition Service, Department of Agriculture, Alexandria, VA 22302. Phone, 703–305–2286. Internet, www.usda.gov/fns.htm.

Center for Nutrition Policy and Promotion

The Center coordinates nutrition policy in USDA and provides overall leadership in nutrition education for the American public. It also coordinates with the Department of Health and Human Services in the review, revision, and dissemination of the *Dietary Guidelines for Americans*, the Federal Government's statement of nutrition policy formed by a consensus of scientific and medical professionals.

For further information, contact the Office of Public Information, Center for Nutrition Policy and Promotion, Suite 200, 1120 20th Street NW., Washington, DC 20036–3406. Phone, 202–418–2312. Internet, www.cnpp.usda.gov.

Farm and Foreign Agricultural Services

Farm Service Agency

The Farm Service Agency (FSA) administers farm commodity, disaster, and conservation programs for farmers and ranchers, and makes and guarantees farm emergency, ownership, and operating loans through a network of State and county offices.

Farm Commodity Programs FSA manages commodity programs such as the direct and countercyclical program, commodity and livestock disaster programs, marketing assistance loan programs, noninsured crop disaster assistance programs, and the tobacco transition payment program. It administers commodity loan programs for wheat, rice, corn, grain sorghum, barley, oats, oilseeds, peanuts, upland and extra-long-staple cotton, and sugar. FSA provides operating personnel for the

Commodity Credit Corporation (CCC), a Government-owned and -operated organization. CCC provides short-term loans using the commodity as collateral. These loans provide farmers with interim financing and facilitate orderly marketing of farm commodities throughout the year.

Farm Loan Programs FSA makes and guarantees loans to family farmers and ranchers to purchase farmland and finance agricultural production. These programs help farmers who are temporarily unable to obtain private commercial credit. These may be beginning farmers who have insufficient net worth to qualify for commercial credit, who have suffered financial setbacks from natural disasters, or who have limited resources with which to establish and maintain profitable farming operations.

Noninsured Crop Disaster Assistance Program (NAP) NAP provides catastrophic crop loss protection for crops not covered by Federal crop insurance. Crops that are eligible include commercial crops grown for food and fiber, floriculture, ornamental nursery products, Christmas tree crops, turfgrass sod, seed crops, aquaculture (including ornamental fish such as goldfish), and industrial crops. Losses resulting from natural disasters not covered by the crop insurance policy may also be eligible for NAP assistance. NAP does not include trees grown for wood, paper, or pulp products.

Other Emergency Assistance There are FSA programs to assist farmers who encounter natural disasters from drought, flood, freeze, tornadoes, and other natural calamities. Eligible producers can be compensated for crop losses, livestock feed losses, and tree damage, and for the cost of rehabilitating eligible farmlands damaged by natural disaster. Low-interest loans for eligible farmers can help cover production and physical losses in counties declared disaster areas.

The largest component of USDA disaster assistance is the Crop Disaster Program (CDP), which has provided more than $3 billion in financial relief to farmers, ranchers, foresters, and other agricultural producers who incurred losses because of recent adverse weather conditions.

Conservation Programs FSA's conservation programs include enhancement of wildlife habitat and water and air quality. The Conservation Reserve Program is the Federal Government's single-largest environmental improvement program on private lands. It safeguards millions of acres of topsoil from erosion, improves air quality, increases wildlife habitat, and protects ground and surface water by reducing water runoff and sedimentation. In return for planting a protective cover of grass or trees on vulnerable property, the owner receives a rental payment each year of a multi-year contract. Cost-share payments are also available to help establish permanent areas of grass, legumes, trees, windbreaks, or plants that improve water quality and give shelter and food to wildlife.

Commodity Operations FSA's commodity operations facilitates the storage, management, and disposition of commodities used to meet humanitarian needs abroad. FSA's commodity operations also administers the United States Warehouse Act (USWA) which authorizes the Secretary of Agriculture to license warehouse operators who store agricultural products. Warehouse operators that apply must meet the USDA standards established within the USWA and its regulations. Under the milk price support program, the Commodity Credit Corporation buys surplus butter, cheese, and nonfat dry milk from processors at announced prices to support the price of milk. These purchases help maintain market prices at the legislated support level, and the surplus commodities are used for hunger relief both domestically and internationally. FSA's commodity operations also coordinates with other Government agencies to provide surplus commodities for various programs and also purchases commodities for the National School Lunch Program and other domestic feeding programs.

For further information, contact the Public Affairs Branch, Farm Service Agency, Department of Agriculture, Stop 0506, 1400 Independence Avenue SW., Washington, DC 20250. Phone, 202–720–5237. Internet, www.fsa.usda.gov.

Commodity Credit Corporation

The Commodity Credit Corporation (CCC) stabilizes, supports, and protects farm income and prices, assists in maintaining balanced and adequate supplies of agricultural commodities and their products, and facilitates the orderly distribution of commodities.

CCC carries out assigned foreign assistance activities, such as guaranteeing the credit sale of U.S. agricultural commodities abroad. Major emphasis is also being directed toward meeting the needs of developing nations. Agricultural commodities are supplied and exported to combat hunger and malnutrition and to encourage economic development in developing countries. In addition, under the Food for Progress Program, CCC supplies commodities to provide assistance to developing democracies.

For further information, contact the Information Division, Foreign Agricultural Service, Department of Agriculture, Stop 1004, 1400 Independence Avenue SW., Washington, DC 20250. Phone, 202–720–7115. Fax, 202–720–1727.

Risk Management Agency

The Risk Management Agency (RMA), via the Federal Crop Insurance Corporation (FCIC), oversees and administers the crop insurance program under the Federal Crop Insurance Act.

Crop insurance is offered to qualifying producers through 16 private sector crop insurance companies. Under the new Standard Reinsurance Agreement (SRA), RMA provides reinsurance, pays premium subsidies, reimburses insurers for administrative and operating costs and oversees the financial integrity and operational performance of the delivery system. RMA bears much of the noncommercial insurance risk under the SRA, allowing insurers to retain commercial insurance risks or reinsure those risks in the private market.

In 2006, the Federal crop insurance program is expected to provide producers with more than $44 billion in protection on approximately 246 million acres through about 1.2 million policies. There are 22 insurance plans available and 26 active pilot programs in various stages of development.

RMA is also working closely with the private sector to find new and innovative ways to provide expanded coverage. This includes risk protection for specialty crops, livestock and forage, and rangeland and pasture. Thus, RMA is able to reduce the need for ad hoc disaster bills and available coverage caused by long-term production declines that result from extended drought in many areas.

Additional information about RMA can be found on its Web site (www.rma.usda.gov), including agency news, State profiles, publications, announcements on current issues, summaries of insurance sales, pilot programs, downloadable crop policies, and agency-sponsored events. The site also features online tools, calculators, and applications.

For further information, contact the Office of the Administrator, Risk Management Agency, Department of Agriculture, Stop 0801, 1400 Independence Avenue SW., Washington, DC 20250. Phone, 202–690–2803. Internet, www.rma.usda.gov.

Foreign Agricultural Service

The Foreign Agricultural Service (FAS) works to improve foreign market access for U.S. products, to build new markets, to improve the competitive position of U.S. agriculture in the global marketplace, and to provide food aid and technical assistance to foreign countries.

FAS has the primary responsibility for USDA's activities in the areas of international marketing, trade agreements and negotiations, and the collection and analysis of international statistics and market information. It also administers the USDA's export credit guarantee and food aid programs. FAS helps increase income and food availability in developing nations by mobilizing expertise for agriculturally led economic growth.

FAS also enhances U.S. agricultural competitiveness through a global network of agricultural economists, marketing experts, negotiators, and other specialists. FAS agricultural counselors, attachés, trade officers, and locally employed FAS staff stationed in over 90 countries support U.S. agricultural interests and cover 140 countries.

In addition to agricultural affairs offices in U.S. embassies, agricultural trade offices also have been established in a number of key foreign markets and function as service centers for U.S. exporters and foreign buyers seeking market information.

Reports prepared by our overseas offices cover changes in policies and other developments that could affect U.S. agricultural exports. FAS staff in U.S. embassies around the world assess U.S. export marketing opportunities and respond to the daily informational needs of those who develop, initiate, monitor,and evaluate U.S. food and agricultural policies and programs.

In addition to data collection, FAS also maintains a worldwide agricultural reporting system based on information from U.S. agricultural traders, remote sensing systems, and other sources. Analysts in Washington, DC, prepare production forecasts, assess export marketing opportunities, and track changes in policies affecting U.S. agricultural exports and imports.

FAS programs help U.S. exporters develop and maintain markets for hundreds of food and agricultural products, from bulk commodities to brand name items. Formal market promotion activities are carried out chiefly in cooperation with agricultural trade associations, State-regional trade groups, small businesses, and cooperatives that plan, manage, and contribute staff resources and funds to support these efforts. FAS also provides guidance to help exporters locate buyers and provides assistance through a variety of other methods. This includes supporting U.S. participation in several major trade shows and a number of single-industry exhibitions each year.

For further information, contact the Public Affairs Division, Foreign Agricultural Service, Stop 1004, 1400 Independence Avenue, SW., Department of Agriculture, Washington, DC 20250-1004. Phone, 202–720–7115. Fax, 202–720–1727. Internet, http://www.fas.usda.gov.

Research, Education, and Economics

This mission area's main focus is to create, apply, and transfer knowledge and technology to provide affordable food and fiber, ensure food safety and nutrition, and support rural development and natural resource needs of people by conducting integrated national and international research, information, education, and statistical programs and services that are in the national interest.

Agricultural Research Service

The Agricultural Research Service (ARS) conducts research to develop and transfer solutions to agricultural problems of high national priority. It provides information access and dissemination to ensure high-quality safe food and other agricultural products; assess the nutritional needs of Americans; sustain a competitive agricultural economy; enhance the natural resource base and the environment; and provide economic opportunities for rural citizens, communities, and society as a whole.

Research activities are carried out at 103 domestic locations (including Puerto Rico and the U.S. Virgin Islands) and 5 overseas locations. Much of this research is conducted in cooperation with partners in State universities and experiment stations, other Federal agencies, and private organizations. National Programs, headquartered in Beltsville, MD, is the focal point in the overall planning and coordination of ARS' research programs. Day-to-day management of the respective programs for specific field locations is assigned to eight area offices.

National Agricultural Library

The National Agricultural Library (NAL) is the primary resource in the United States for information about food, agriculture, and natural resources, and serves as an electronic gateway to a widening array of scientific literature, printed text, and agricultural images. The Library serves USDA and a broad customer base including policymakers, agricultural specialists, research scientists, and the general public. The library works with other agricultural libraries and institutions to advance open and democratic access to information about agriculture and the Nation's agricultural knowledge.

Information is made available through Web sites, loans, photocopies, reference services, and literature searches. NAL maintains public reading rooms in the South Building at USDA Headquarters, District of Columbia, and at the main library in the Abraham Lincoln Building, Beltsville, Maryland.

The library maintains more than 63,000 Web pages and in 2004 delivered more than 54 million direct customer services throughout the world via its Web site (www.nal.usda.gov).

NAL's eight national information centers are specialized gateways to science-based information in key areas of agriculture, including alternative farming systems (www.nal.usda.gov/afsic), animal welfare (www.nal.usda.gov/awic), food and nutrition (www.nal.usda.gov/fnic), food safety (www.nal.usda.gov/foodsafety), rural revitalization (www. nal.usda.gov/ric), technology transfer (www.nal.usda.gov/ttic), and water quality (www.nal.usda.gov/wqic). These centers collaborate with other organizations throughout the Government to provide timely, accurate, comprehensive, and in-depth coverage within their subject areas.

In addition to its own Web-based services, the Library maintains the following Governmentwide Web portals: www.science.gov, www.nutrition.gov, and www.invasivespecies.gov.

NAL's AGRICOLA (AGRICultural OnLine Access) bibliographic database, http://agricola.nal.usda.gov, contains more than 4 million citations to agricultural literature with links to the full text of many publications. NAL provides a broad base of users with no-cost access to this information.

NAL is also part of the AgNIC Alliance (Agriculture Network Information Center), www.agnic.org, which is a distributed collaboration of over 55 institutions to meet local, national, and international needs in a cost-effective manner.

For further information, contact the Public Affairs Officer, USDA National Agricultural Library, 10301 Baltimore Avenue, Beltsville, MD 20705–2351. Phone, 301–504–1668. Fax, 301–504–7042. E-mail, director@nal.usda.gov. Internet, www.nal.usda.gov.

Cooperative State Research, Education, and Extension Service

The Cooperative State Research, Education, and Extension Service (CSREES) links the research and education resources and activities of USDA and works with academic and land-grant institutions throughout the Nation. In cooperation with its partners and customers, CSREES advances a global system of research, extension, and higher education in the food and agricultural sciences and related environmental and human sciences to benefit people, communities, and the Nation.

CSREES's programs increase and provide access to scientific knowledge; strengthen the capabilities of land-grant and other institutions in research, extension, and higher education; increase access to and use of improved communication and network systems; and promote informed decisionmaking by producers, consumers, families, and community leaders to improve social conditions in the United States and around the world. These conditions include improved agricultural and other economic enterprises; safer, cleaner water, food, and air; enhanced stewardship and management of natural resources; healthier, more responsible and more productive individuals, families, and communities; and a stable, secure, diverse, and affordable national food supply.

CSREES provides research, extension, and education leadership through programs in plant and animal systems; natural resources and environment; economic and community systems; families, 4–H, and nutrition; competitive research and integrated research, education, and extension programs and awards management; science and education resources development; and information systems and technology management.

CSREES's partnership with the land-grant universities is critical to the effective shared planning, delivery, and accountability for research, higher education, and extension programs.

For further information, contact the Communications Staff, Cooperative State Research, Education, and Extension Service, Department of Agriculture, 1400 Independence Avenue SW., Washington, DC 20250–2207. Phone, 202–720–4651. Fax, 202–690–0289. E-mail, CSREES@csrees.usda.gov. Internet, www.csrees.usda.gov.

Economic Research Service

The mission of the Economic Research Service (ERS) is to inform and enhance public and private decisionmaking on economic and policy issues related to agriculture, food, the environment, and rural development.

Activities to support this mission and the following goals involve research and development of economic and statistical indicators on a broad range of topics including, but not limited to, global agricultural market conditions, trade restrictions, agribusiness concentration, farm and retail food prices, foodborne illnesses, food labeling, nutrition, food assistance programs, worker safety, agrichemical usage, livestock waste management, conservation, sustainability, genetic diversity, technology transfer, rural infrastructure, and rural employment. Research results and economic indicators on such important agricultural, food, natural resource, and rural issues are fully disseminated to public and private decisionmakers through published and electronic reports and articles; special staff analyses, briefings, presentations, and papers; databases; and individual contacts. Through such activities, ERS provides public and private decisionmakers with economic and related social science information and analysis in support of the Department's goals of enhancing economic opportunities for agricultural producers; supporting economic opportunities and quality of life in rural America; enhancing the protection and safety of U.S. agriculture and food; improving U.S. nutrition and health; and enhancing the natural resource base and environment. More information on ERS's program is contained on the ERS Web site (www.ers.usda.gov).

For further information, contact the Information Services Division, Economic Research Service, Department of Agriculture, Washington, DC 20036–5831. Phone, 202–694–5100. Fax, 202–694–5641.

National Agricultural Statistics Service

The National Agricultural Statistics Service (NASS) prepares estimates and reports on production, supply, price, chemical use, and other items necessary for the orderly operation of the U.S. agricultural economy.

The reports include statistics on field crops, fruits and vegetables, dairy, cattle, hogs, sheep, poultry, aquaculture, and related commodities or processed products. Other estimates concern farm numbers, farm production expenditures, agricultural chemical use, prices received by farmers for products sold, prices paid for commodities and services, indexes of prices received and paid, parity prices, farm employment, and farm wage rates.

The Service prepares these estimates through a complex system of sample surveys of producers, processors, buyers, and others associated with agriculture. Information is gathered by mail, telephone, personal interviews, and field visits.

NASS is responsible for conducting the Census of Agriculture. The Census of

Agriculture is taken every 5 years and provides comprehensive data on the agricultural economy down to the county level. Periodic reports are also issued on aquacultures, irrigation, and horticultural specialties.

The Service performs reimbursable survey work and statistical consulting services for other Federal and State agencies and provides technical assistance for developing agricultural data systems in other countries.

For further information, contact the Executive Assistant to the Administrator, National Agricultural Statistics Service, Department of Agriculture, Washington, DC 20250–2000. Phone, 202–720–2707. Fax, 202–720–9013.

Natural Resources and Environment

This mission area is responsible for fostering sound stewardship of 75 percent of the Nation's total land area. Ecosystems are the underpinning for the Department's operating philosophy in this area in order to maximize stewardship of our natural resources. This approach ensures that products, values, services, and uses desired by people are produced in ways that sustain healthy, productive ecosystems.

Forest Service

[For the Forest Service statement of organization, see the *Code of Federal Regulations,* Title 36, Part 200.1]

The Forest Service was created by the Transfer Act of February 1, 1905 (16 U.S.C. 472), which transferred the Federal forest reserves and the responsibility for their management from the Department of the Interior to the Department of Agriculture. The mission of the Forest Service is to achieve quality land management under the sustainable, multiple-use management concept to meet the diverse needs of people. It's objectives include:

—advocating a conservation ethic in promoting the health, productivity, diversity, and beauty of forests and associated lands;

—listening to people and responding to their diverse needs in making decisions;

—protecting and managing the national forests and grasslands to best demonstrate the sustainable, multiple-use management concept;

—providing technical and financial assistance to State and private forest landowners, encouraging them toward active stewardship and quality land management in meeting their specific objectives;

—providing technical and financial assistance to cities and communities to improve their natural environment by planting trees and caring for their forests;

—providing international technical assistance and scientific exchanges to sustain and enhance global resources and to encourage quality land management;

—assisting States and communities in using the forests wisely to promote rural economic development and a quality rural environment;

—developing and providing scientific and technical knowledge, improving our capability to protect, manage, and use forests and rangelands; and

—providing work, training, and education to the unemployed, underemployed, elderly, youth, and the disadvantaged.

National Forest System The Service manages 155 national forests, 20 national grasslands, and 8 land utilization projects on over 191 million acres in 44 States, the Virgin Islands, and Puerto Rico under the principles of multiple-use and sustained yield. The Nation's tremendous need for wood and paper products is balanced with the other vital, renewable resources or benefits that the national forests and grasslands provide: recreation and natural beauty, wildlife habitat, livestock forage, and water supplies. The guiding principle is the greatest good to the greatest number in the long run.

These lands are protected as much as possible from wildfire, epidemics of disease and insect pests, erosion, floods, and water and air pollution. Burned areas get emergency seeding treatment to prevent massive erosion and stream siltation. Roads and trails are built where needed to allow for closely regulated timber harvesting and to give the public access to outdoor recreation areas and provide scenic drives and hikes. Picnic, camping, water-sport, skiing, and other areas are provided with facilities for public convenience and enjoyment. Timber harvesting methods are used that will protect the land and streams, assure rapid renewal of the forest, provide food and cover for wildlife and fish, and have minimum impact on scenic and recreation values. Local communities benefit from the logging and milling activities. These lands also provide needed oil, gas, and minerals. Rangelands are improved for millions of livestock and game animals. The national forests provide a refuge for many species of endangered birds, animals, and fish. Some 34.6 million acres are set aside as wilderness and 175,000 acres as primitive areas where timber will not be harvested.

Forest Research The Service performs basic and applied research to develop the scientific information and technology needed to protect, manage, use, and sustain the natural resources of the Nation's forests and rangelands. The Service's forest research strategy focuses on three major program components: understanding the structure and functions of forest and range ecosystems; understanding how people perceive and value the protection, management, and use of natural resources; and determining which protection, management, and utilization practices are most suitable for sustainable production and use of the world's natural resources.

Manpower Programs The Service operates the Youth Conservation Corps and the Volunteers in the National Forests programs and participates with the Department of Labor on several human resource programs that involve the Nation's citizens, both young and old, in forestry-related activities. Included in these programs are the Job Corps and the Senior Community Service Employment Program. These programs annually accomplish millions of dollars worth of conservation work, while providing participants with such benefits as training, paid employment, and meaningful outdoor experience.

For further information, contact the Office of Communications, Forest Service, Department of Agriculture, P.O. Box 96090, Washington, DC 20090–6090. Phone, 202–205–8333.

Field Offices—Forest Service

Region/Station/Area	Address
	National Forest System Regions—Regional Forester
1. Northern	Federal Bldg. (P.O. Box 7669), Missoula, MT 59807
2. Rocky Mountain	740 Simms St., P.O. Box 25127, Lakewood, CO 80225
3. Southwestern	517 Gold Ave. SW., Albuquerque, NM 87102
4. Intermountain	324 25th St., Ogden, UT 84401
5. Pacific Southwest	630 Sansome St., San Francisco, CA 94111
6. Pacific Northwest	333 SW. 1st Ave., P.O. Box 3623, Portland, OR 97208
8. Southern	1720 Peachtree Rd. NW., Atlanta, GA 30367
9. Eastern	310 W. Wisconsin Ave., Milwaukee, WI 53203
10. Alaska	Federal Office Bldg. (P.O. Box 21628), Juneau, AK 99802
	Research Stations—Director
Forest Products Laboratory	1 Gifford Pinchot Dr., Madison, WI 53705
North Central	1992 Folwell Ave., St. Paul, MN 55108
Northeastern	Suite 200, 100 Matson Ford Rd., P.O. Box 6775, Radnor, PA 19087–4585
Pacific Northwest	333 SW. 1st Ave., P.O. Box 3890, Portland, OR 97208
Pacific Southwest	800 Buchanan St., P.O. Box 245, Albany, CA 94710
Rocky Mountain	240 W. Prospect Ave., Fort Collins, CO 80526
Southern	200 Weaver Blvd., P.O. Box 2860, Asheville, NC 28802
	State and Private Forestry Areas—Director
Northeastern	Suite 200, 100 Matson Ford Rd., P.O. Box 6775, Radnor, PA 19087–4585
International Institute of Tropical Forestry	UPR Experimental Station Grounds, Botanical Garden, Call Box 25000, Rio Piedras, PR 00928

Natural Resources Conservation Service

[For the Natural Resources Conservation Service statement of organization, see the *Code of Federal Regulations,* Title 7, Parts 600 and 601]

The Natural Resources Conservation Service (NRCS), formerly the Soil Conservation Service, has national responsibility for helping America's farmers, ranchers, and other private landowners develop and carry out voluntary efforts to conserve and protect our natural resources.

Conservation Technical Assistance This is the foundation program of NRCS. Under this program, NRCS provides technical assistance to land users and units of government for the purpose of sustaining agricultural productivity and protecting and enhancing the natural resource base. This assistance is based on the voluntary cooperation of private landowners and involves comprehensive approaches to reduce soil erosion, improve soil and water quantity and quality, improve and conserve wetlands, enhance fish and wildlife habitat, improve air quality, improve pasture and range condition, reduce upstream flooding, and improve woodlands.

Emergency Watershed Protection Program This program provides emergency assistance to safeguard lives and property in jeopardy due to sudden watershed impairment by natural disasters. Emergency work includes quickly establishing a protective plant cover on denuded land and stream banks; opening dangerously restricted channels; and repairing diversions and levees. An emergency area need not be declared a national disaster area to be eligible for help under this program.

Environmental Quality Incentive Program This program assists producers with environmental and natural resource conservation improvements on their agricultural lands. One-half of the available funds are for conservation activities related to livestock production. Technical assistance, cost-share payments, incentive payments, and education focus on priority areas and natural resource concerns identified in cooperation with State technical committees, including such areas as nutrient management, pest management, and grazing land management.

Farmland Protection Program (FPP) This program protects soil by encouraging landowners to limit conversion of their farmland to nonagricultural uses. States, Indian tribes, or local governments administer all aspects of acquiring lands that are in the FPP, except when it is more effective and efficient for the Federal Government to do so.

Forestry Incentives Program This program helps to increase the Nation's supply of products from nonindustrial private forest lands. This also ensures more effective use of existing forest lands and, over time, helps to prevent shortages and price increases for forest products. The program shares the cost incurred by landowners for tree planting and timberstand improvement.

National Cooperative Soil Survey The National Cooperative Soil Survey provides the public with local information on the uses and capabilities of their soils. The published soil survey for a county or other designated area includes maps and interpretations that are the foundation for farm planning and other private land use decisions as well as for resource planning and policy by Federal, State, and local governments. The surveys are conducted cooperatively with other Federal, State, and local agencies and land grant universities. The Service is the national and world leader in soil classification and soil mapping, and is now expanding its work in soil quality.

Plant Materials Program At 26 plant materials centers across the country, NRCS tests, selects, and ensures the commercial availability of new and improved conservation plants for erosion reduction, wetland restoration, water quality improvement, streambank and riparian area protection, coastal dune stabilization, biomass production, carbon sequestration, and other needs. The Plant Materials Program is a cooperative effort with conservation districts, other Federal and State agencies, commercial businesses, and seed and nursery associations.

Resource Conservation and Development Program This program (RC&D) is a locally driven program—an opportunity for civic-oriented groups to work together sharing knowledge and resources in solving common problems facing their region. The program offers aid in balancing the environmental, economic, and social needs of an area. A USDA coordinator helps each designated RC&D council plan, develop, and carry out programs for resource conservation, water management, community development, and environmental enhancement.

Rural Abandoned Mine Program This program helps protect people and the environment from the adverse effects of past coal-mining practices and promotes the development of soil and water resources on unreclaimed mine land. It provides technical and financial assistance to land users who voluntarily enter into 5- to 10-year contracts for the reclamation of eligible land and water.

Small Watersheds Program The program helps local sponsoring groups to voluntarily plan and install watershed protection projects on private lands. These projects include flood prevention, water quality improvement, soil erosion and sediment reduction, rural and municipal water supply, irrigation water management, fish and wildlife habitat enhancement, and wetlands restoration. The Service helps local community groups, government entities, and private landowners working together using an integrated, comprehensive watershed approach to natural resource planning.

Snow Survey and Water Supply Forecasting Program This program collects snowpack moisture data and forecasts seasonal water supplies for streams that derive most of their water from snowmelt. It helps farm operators, rural communities, and municipalities manage water resources through water supply forecasts. It also provides hydrometeorological data for regulating reservoir storage and managing streamflow. The Snow Supply Program is conducted in the Western States and Alaska.

Watershed Surveys and Planning This program assists Federal, State, and local agencies and tribal governments in protecting watersheds from damage caused by erosion, floodwater, and sediment and conserves and develops water and land resources. Resource concerns addressed by the program include water quality, water conservation, wetland and water storage capacity, agricultural drought problems, rural development, municipal and industrial water needs, upstream flood damages, and water needs for fish, wildlife, and forest-based industries. Types of surveys and plans include watershed plans, river basin surveys and studies, flood hazard analysis, and flood plain management assistance. The focus of these plans is to identify solutions that use land treatment and nonstructural measures to solve resource problems.

Wetlands Reserve Program Under this program, USDA purchases easements from agricultural land owners who voluntarily agree to restore and protect wetlands. Service employees help these owners develop plans to retire critical wetland habitat from crop production. The primary objectives are to preserve and restore wetlands, improve wildlife habitat, and protect migratory waterfowl.

Wildlife Habitat Incentives Program This program provides financial incentives to develop habitats for fish and wildlife on private lands. Participants agree to implement a wildlife habitat development plan, and USDA agrees to provide cost-share assistance for the initial implementation of wildlife habitat development practices. USDA and program participants enter into a cost-share agreement for wildlife habitat development, which generally lasts a minimum of 10 years from the date that the contract is signed.

For further information, contact the Management Services Division, Natural Resources Conservation Service, Department of Agriculture, P.O. Box 2890, Washington, DC 20013. Phone, 202–690–4811.

Graduate School, U.S. Department of Agriculture

Fourteenth Street and Independence Avenue SW., Washington, DC 20250
Phone, 888–744–4723

Executive Director	JERRY ICE
Deputy Executive Director	LYNN EDWARDS

The Graduate School was established by act of May 15, 1862 (7 U.S.C. 2201). It is a continuing education school offering career-related training to adults. Courses are planned with the assistance of Government professionals and specialists. The Graduate School's objective is to improve Government services by providing needed continuing education and training opportunities for Government employees and agencies.

The faculty is mostly part-time and is drawn from throughout Government and the community at large. They are selected because of their professional and specialized knowledge and experience and thus bring a practicality and experience to their classrooms.

The school does not grant degrees but does provide planned sequences of courses leading to certificates of accomplishment in a number of occupational and career fields important to government. Training areas include management, auditing, computer science, communications, foreign language, procurement, financial management, and others.

For further information, contact the Communications Office, Graduate School, U.S. Department of Agriculture, Room 270, 600 Maryland Avenue SW., Washington, DC 20024. Phone, 888–744–4723.

Sources of Information

Consumer Activities Educational, organizational, and financial assistance is offered to consumers and their families in such fields as rural housing and farm operating programs, improved nutrition, family living and recreation, food stamp, school lunch, donated foods, and other food programs.

Contracts and Small Business Activities To obtain information about contracting or subcontracting opportunities, attending small business outreach activities, or how to do business with USDA, contact the Office of Small and Disadvantaged Business Utilization. Phone, 202–720–7117. Internet, www.usda.gov/da/smallbus.html.

Employment Most jobs in the Department are in the competitive service and are filled by applicants who have established eligibility under an appropriate examination administered by the Office of Personnel Management or Department Special Examining Units. General employment information is available at www.usajobs.opm.gov.

Whistleblower Hotline Persons wishing to register complaints of alleged improprieties concerning the Department should contact one of the regional offices or the Inspector General's whistleblower hotline. Phone, 800–424–9121 (toll free, outside Washington, DC); 202–690–1622 (within the Washington, DC, metropolitan area); or 202–690–1202 (TDD). Fax, 202–690–2474.

Reading Rooms Located at each USDA agency at addresses indicated in the preceding text.

Speakers Contact the nearest Department of Agriculture office or county Extension agent. In the District of Columbia, contact the Office of Public Liaison, Office of Communications, Department of Agriculture, Washington, DC 20250. Phone, 202–720–2798.

For further information concerning the Department of Agriculture, contact the Office of Communications, Department of Agriculture, Washington, DC 20250. Phone, 202–720–4623. Internet, www.usda.gov.

DEPARTMENT OF COMMERCE

Fourteenth Street and Constitution Avenue NW., Washington, DC 20230
Phone, 202–482–2000. Internet, www.doc.gov.

SECRETARY OF COMMERCE	CARLOS M. GUTIERREZ
Chief of Staff and Counselor to the Secretary	CLAIRE E. BUCHAN
Deputy Chief of Staff	JOSEPH V. SCHWAN II
Director, Office of White House Liaison	CHRISTY SIMON
Director, Executive Secretariat	TRACEY S. RHOADES
Deputy Secretary of Commerce	DAVID A. SAMPSON
Director, Office of Small and Disadvantaged Business Utilization	LAJUENE DESMUKES
Chief Information Officer	KAREN HOGAN, *Acting*
Deputy Chief Information Officer	KAREN HOGAN
General Counsel	JOHN J. SULLIVAN
Deputy General Counsel	DAVID M. BEARDEN
Assistant General Counsel for Administration	BARBARA S. FREDERICKS
Assistant General Counsel for Legislation and Regulation	MICHAEL A. LEVITT
Assistant General Counsel for Finance and Litigation	JOAN B. MAGINNIS
Chief Financial Officer and Assistant Secretary for Administration	OTTO J. WOLFF
Deputy Assistant Secretary for Administration	JEFFERY K. NULF
Director for Security	RICHARD YAMAMOTO
Deputy Director for Security	DAVID K. BELL
Director, Office of Budget	BARBARA A. RETZLAFF
Deputy Director	(VACANCY)
Director for Management and Organization	JOHN J. PHELAN III
Director, Office of Civil Rights	SUZAN J. ARAMAKI
Deputy Director	(VACANCY)
Deputy Chief Financial Management Officer and Director for Financial Management	LISA CASIAS, *Acting*
Deputy Director for Financial Systems	TERESA COPPOLINO
Deputy Director for Financial Policy	(VACANCY)
Director for Human Resources Management	DEBORAH JEFFERSON
Deputy Director	WILLIAM FLEMING
Director for Administrative Services	CHERIE A. STALLMAN
Deputy Director	(VACANCY)
Director for Acquisition Management	MICHAEL S. SADE
Assistant Secretary for Legislative and Intergovernmental Affairs	NATHANIEL F. WIENECKE, *Acting*
Director for Legislative and Intergovernmental Affairs	KAREN SWANSON-WOLF
Deputy Assistant Secretary for Trade Legislation	(VACANCY)
Director for Intergovernmental Affairs	ELIZABETH DIAL

Inspector General	JOHNNIE E. FRAZIER
Deputy Inspector General	EDWARD L. BLANSITT
Counsel to the Inspector General	ALLISON C. LERNER
Assistant Inspector General for Auditing	JOHN M. SEEBA
Assistant Inspector General for Investigations	ELIZABETH T. BARLOW
Assistant Inspector General for Systems Evaluation	JUDITH J. GORDON
Assistant Inspector General for Inspections and Program Evaluations	JILL A. GROSS
Assistant Inspector General for Administration	JESSICA RICKENBACH
Director, Office of Public Affairs	E. RICHARD MILLS
Press Secretary	DAN NELSON
Director, Office of Business Liaison	DANIEL MCCARDELL
Deputy Directors	JENNIFER ANDBERG, ROBERT OLLISON, JR.

ECONOMICS AND STATISTICS ADMINISTRATION

Department of Commerce, Washington, DC 20230
Phone, 202–482–3727

Under Secretary for Economic Affairs	(VACANCY)
Deputy Under Secretary	ELIZABETH R. ANDERSON, *Acting*
Associate Under Secretary for Management	KIM WHITE
Associate Under Secretary for Communications	ELIZABETH R. ANDERSON
Chief Economist	KEITH HALL
Director, Bureau of the Census	CHARLES L. KINCANNON
Director, Bureau of Economic Analysis	J. STEVEN LANDEFELD

BUREAU OF INDUSTRY AND SECURITY

Department of Commerce, Washington, DC 20230
Phone, 202–482–2721

Under Secretary for Industry and Security	DAVID H. MCCORMICK
Deputy Under Secretary	MARK FOULON
Assistant Secretary for Export Administration	(VACANCY)
Assistant Secretary for Export Enforcement	DARRYL W. JACKSON

ECONOMIC DEVELOPMENT ADMINISTRATION

Department of Commerce, Washington, DC 20230
Phone, 202–482–2309

Assistant Secretary for Economic Development	SANDY K. BARUAH
Deputy Assistant Secretary	BENJAMIN ERULKAR
Deputy Assistant Secretary for Management Services and Chief Financial Officer	MARY C. PLEFFNER

INTERNATIONAL TRADE ADMINISTRATION

Department of Commerce, Washington, DC 20230
Phone, 202–482–3917

Under Secretary for International Trade	FRANKLIN L. LAVIN
Deputy Under Secretary	MICHELLE O' NEILL

Assistant Secretary for Import Administration	DAVID SPOONER
Assistant Secretary for Market Access and Compliance	DAVID BOHIGIAN
Assistant Secretary for Manufacturing and Services	ALBERT FRINK
Assistant Secretary for Trade Promotion and Director of the U.S. and Foreign Commercial Service	ISRAEL HERNANDEZ
Chief Financial Officer and Director of Administration	LINDA CHEATHAM
Chief Information Officer	RENEE MACKLIN

MINORITY BUSINESS DEVELOPMENT AGENCY

Department of Commerce, Washington, DC 20230
Phone, 202–482–5061. Internet, www.mbda.gov.

National Director, Minority Business Development Agency	RONALD N. LANGSTON
Deputy Director	(VACANCY)

NATIONAL OCEANIC AND ATMOSPHERIC ADMINISTRATION

Department of Commerce, Washington, DC 20230
Phone, 202–482–2985. Internet, www.noaa.gov.

Under Secretary for Oceans and Atmosphere	VICE ADM. CONRAD C. LAUTENBACHER, JR., USN (RET.)
Assistant Secretary for Oceans and Atmosphere and Deputy Administrator	JAMES R. MAHONEY
Deputy Assistant Secretary for Oceans and Atmosphere	TIMOTHY R.E. KEENEY
Deputy Under Secretary for Oceans and Atmosphere	JOHN J. KELLY, JR.
Chief Financial Officer	MAUREEN E. WYLIE
Chief Administrative Officer	WILLIAM BROGLIE
Assistant Administrator for Fisheries Service	WILLIAM T. HOGARTH
Assistant Administrator for Ocean Services and Coastal Zone Management	RICHARD SPINRAD
Assistant Administrator for Environmental Satellite, Data, and Information Service	GREGORY W. WITHEE
Assistant Administrator for Weather Service	D.L. JOHNSON
Assistant Administrator for Oceanic and Atmospheric Research	RICHARD D. ROSEN

NATIONAL TELECOMMUNICATIONS AND INFORMATION ADMINISTRATION

Department of Commerce, Washington, DC 20230
Phone, 202–428–1840.

Assistant Secretary for Communications and Information	JOHN M.R. KNEUER, *Acting*
Deputy Assistant Secretary	JOHN M.R. KNEUER
Chief Counsel	KATHY D. SMITH
Associate Administrator for Spectrum Management	FREDERICK R. WENTLAND

Associate Administrator for Policy Analysis and Development	ERIC R. STARK
Associate Administrator for International Affairs	FIONA ALEXANDER, *Acting*
Associate Administrator for Telecommunications and Information Applications	BERNADETTE A. MCGUIRE-RIVERA
Associate Administrator for Telecommunication Sciences	ALAN VINCENT

U.S. PATENT AND TRADEMARK OFFICE

2121 Crystal Drive, Arlington, VA 22202
Phone, 703–305–8341. Internet, www.uspto.gov.

Under Secretary for Intellectual Property and Director of the U.S. Patent and Trademark Office	JON W. DUDAS
Deputy Under Secretary and Deputy Director	STEPHEN M. PINKOS
Commissioner for Patents	JOHN J. DOLL
Commissioner for Trademarks	LYNNE G. BERESFORD

TECHNOLOGY ADMINISTRATION

Department of Commerce, Washington, DC 20230
Phone, 202–482–1575

Under Secretary for Technology	ROBERT C. CRESANTI
Deputy Under Secretary	JO GANN, *Acting*
Assistant Secretary for Technology Policy	(VACANCY)
Director, National Institute of Standards and Technology	WILLIAM A. JEFFREY
Director, National Technical Information Service	ELLEN HERBST

The Department of Commerce encourages, serves, and promotes the Nation's international trade, economic growth, and technological advancement. The Department provides a wide variety of programs through the competitive free enterprise system. It offers assistance and information to increase America's competitiveness in the world economy; administers programs to prevent unfair foreign trade competition; provides social and economic statistics and analyses for business and government planners; provides research and support for the increased use of scientific, engineering, and technological development; works to improve our understanding and benefits of the Earth's physical environment and oceanic resources; grants patents and registers trademarks; develops policies and conducts research on telecommunications; provides assistance to promote domestic economic development; and assists in the growth of minority businesses.

The Department was designated as such by act of March 4, 1913 (15 U.S.C. 1501), which reorganized the Department of Commerce and Labor, created by act of February 14, 1903 (15 U.S.C. 1501), by transferring all labor activities into a new, separate Department of Labor.

Office of the Secretary

Secretary The Secretary is responsible for the administration of all functions and authorities assigned to the Department of Commerce and for advising the President on Federal policy and programs affecting the industrial and commercial segments of the national economy. The Secretary is served by the

DEPARTMENT OF COMMERCE

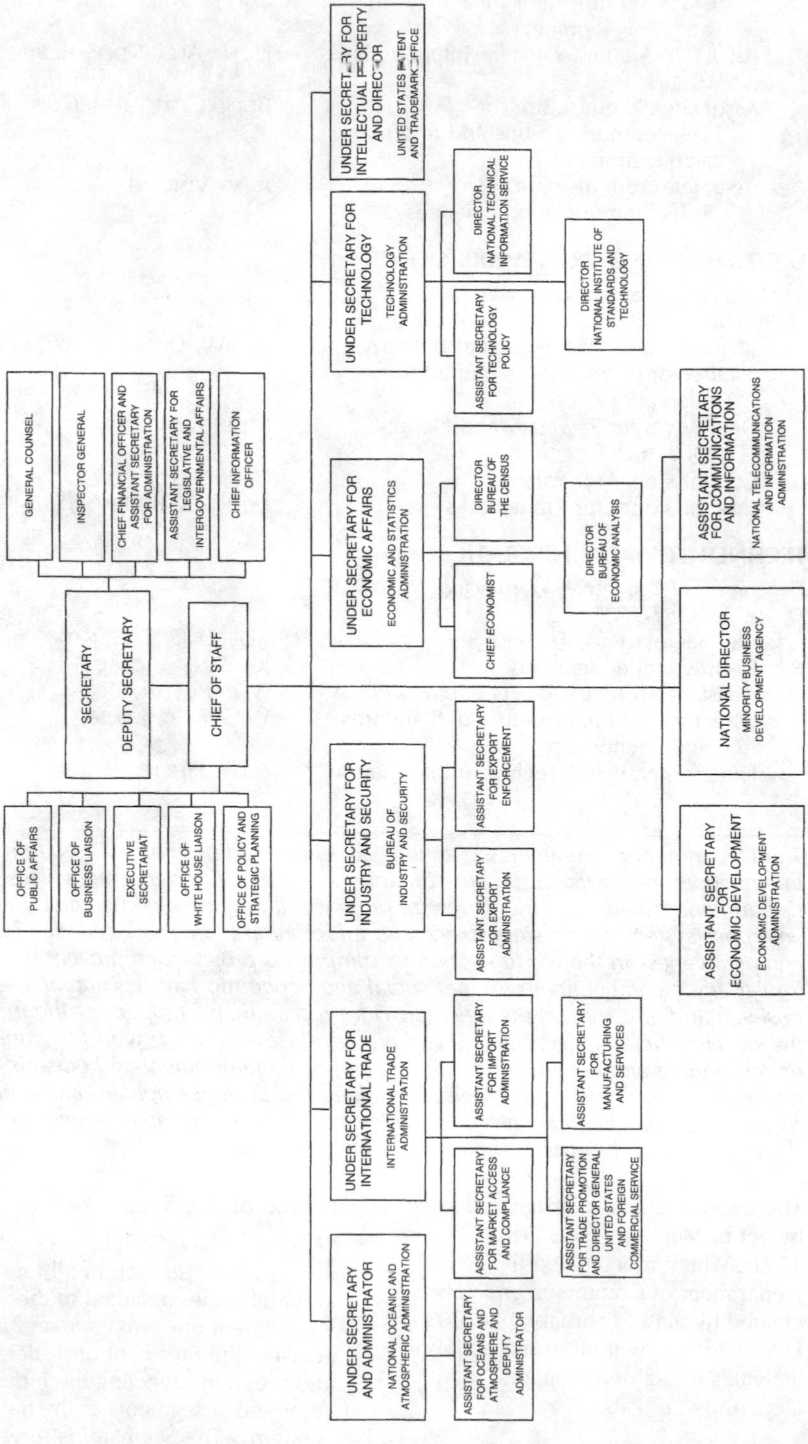

offices of Deputy Secretary, Inspector General, General Counsel, and the Assistant Secretaries of Administration, Legislative and Intergovernmental Affairs, and Public Affairs. Other offices whose public purposes are widely administered are detailed below.

Business Liaison The Office of Business Liaison directs the business community to the offices and policy experts who can best respond to their needs by promoting proactive, responsive, and effective outreach programs and relationships with the business community. It also informs the Secretary and Department officials of the critical issues facing the business community, informs the business community of Department and administration initiatives and priorities, as well as information regarding Department resources, policies, and programs, and provides general assistance to the business community.

For further information, call 202–482–1360.

Economics and Statistics Administration

The Economics and Statistics Administration (ESA) provides broad and targeted economic data, analyses, and forecasts for use by Government agencies, businesses, and others, as well as develops domestic and international economic policy. The Under Secretary is the chief economic adviser to the Secretary and provides leadership and executive management of the Bureau of the Census and the Bureau of Economic Analysis.

ESA provides key business, economic, and international trade information products that American business and the public can use to make informed decisions through STAT.USA®.

For further information, contact the Economics and Statistics Administration, Department of Commerce, Washington, DC 20230. Phone, 202–482–3727.

Bureau of the Census

[For the Bureau of the Census statement of organization, see the *Federal Register* of Sept. 16, 1975, 40 FR 42765]

The Bureau of the Census was established as a permanent office by act of March 6, 1902 (32 Stat. 51). The major functions of the Census Bureau are authorized by the Constitution, which provides that a census of population shall be taken every 10 years, and by laws codified as title 13 of the United States Code. The law also provides that the information collected by the Census Bureau from individual persons, households, or establishments be kept strictly confidential and be used only for statistical purposes. The Census Bureau is responsible for:

—the decennial censuses of population and housing;

—the quinquennial censuses of State and local governments, manufacturers, mineral industries, distributive trades, construction industries, and transportation;

—current surveys that provide information on many of the subjects covered in the censuses at monthly, quarterly, annual, or other intervals;

—compilation of current statistics on U.S. foreign trade, including data on imports, exports, and shipping;

—special censuses at the request and expense of State and local government units;

—publication of estimates and projections of the population;

—publication of current data on population and housing characteristics; and

—current reports on manufacturing, retail and wholesale trade, services, construction, imports and exports, State and local government finances and employment, and other subjects.

The Census Bureau makes available statistical results of its censuses, surveys, and other programs to the public through printed reports, CD–ROMs and DVDs, the Internet and other media, and prepares special tabulations sponsored and paid for by data users. It also produces statistical compendia, catalogs, guides, and directories that are useful in locating information on specific subjects. Upon request, the Bureau makes searches of decennial census records and furnishes certificates to individuals for use as evidence of age, relationship, or place of birth. A fee is charged for searches.

For further information, contact the Marketing Service Office, Bureau of the Census, Department of Commerce, Washington, DC 20233. Phone, 301–763–INFO (4636). Fax, 301–457–3842.

Field Organization—Bureau of the Census

Regional Office (Areas Served)	Address
Atlanta, GA (AL, FL, GA)	Suite 3200, 101 Marietta St. NW., 30303–2700
Boston, MA (CT, MA, ME, NH, NY (all counties not listed under the New York Regional Office), PR, RI, VI, and VT)	Suite 301, 4 Copley Pl., 02117–9108
Charlotte, NC (KY, NC, SC, TN, VA)	Suite 106, 901 Center Park Dr., 28217–2935
Chicago, IL (IL, IN, WI)	Suite 5501, 2255 Enterprise Dr., Westchester, IL 60154
Dallas, TX (LA, MS, TX)	Suite 800S, 8585 Stemmons N. Fwy., 75237–3836
Denver, CO (AZ, CO, MT, NE, ND, NM, NV, SD, UT, and WY)	Suite 100, 6900 W. Jefferson Ave., Lakewood, CO 80235–2032
Detroit, MI (MI, OH, WV)	Suite 100, 1395 Brewery Park Blvd., 48207–2635
Kansas City, KS (AR, IA, KS, MN, MO, OK)	1211 North 8th St., 66101–2129
Los Angeles, CA (CA (counties of Fresno, Imperial, Inyo, Kern, Kings, Los Angeles, Madera, Mariposa, Merced, Monterey, Orange, Riverside, San Benito, San Bernardino, San Diego, San Luis Obispo, Santa Barbara, Tulare, and Ventura), HI)	Suite 300, 15350 Sherman Way, Van Nuys, CA 91406–4224
New York, NY (NJ (counties of Bergen, Essex, Hudson, Middlesex, Morris, Passaic, Somerset, Sussex, Union, and Warren), NY (counties of Bronx, Kings, Nassau, New York, Queens, Richmond, Rockland, Suffolk, and Westchester))	Suite 800, 395 Hudson St., 10014
Philadelphia, PA (DC, DE, MD, NJ (all counties not listed under the New York Regional Office), PA)	Suite 504, 833 Chestnut St., 19107–4405
Seattle, WA (AK, CA (all counties not listed under the Los Angeles Regional Office), ID, OR, WA)	Suite 3800, 601 Union St., 98101–1074

Bureau of Economic Analysis

[For the Bureau of Economic Analysis statement of organization, see the *Federal Register* of Dec. 29, 1980, 45 FR 85496]

The Bureau of Economic Analysis (BEA) promotes a better understanding of the U.S. economy by providing the most timely, relevant, and accurate economic accounts data in an objective and cost-effective manner. BEA's economic statistics are closely watched and provide a comprehensive picture of the U.S. economy. BEA prepares national, regional, industry, and international accounts that present essential information on such issues in the world economy.

BEA's national economic statistics provide a comprehensive look at U.S. production, consumption, investment, exports and imports, and income and saving. The international transactions accounts provide information on trade in goods and services (including the balance of payments and trade), investment income, and government and private finances. In addition, the accounts measure the value of U.S. international assets and liabilities and direct investment by multinational companies.

The regional accounts provide data on total and per capita personal income by region, State, metropolitan area, and county, and on gross State product. The industry economic account provides a detailed view of the interrelationships between U.S. producers and users and the contribution to production across industries.

For further information, contact the Public Information Office, Bureau of Economic Analysis, Department of Commerce, Washington, DC 20230. Phone, 202–606–9900. Fax, 202–606–5310. Internet, www.bea.gov. E-mail, customerservice@bea.gov.

For further information, contact the Economics and Statistics Administration, Department of Commerce, Washington, DC 20230. Phone, 202–482–3727.

Bureau of Industry and Security

[For the Bureau of Industry and Security statement of organization, see the *Federal Registers* of June 7, 1988, 53 FR 20881 and April 26, 2002, 67 FR 20630]

The mission of the Bureau of Industry and Security (BIS) is to advance U.S. national security, foreign policy, and economic objectives by ensuring an effective export control and treaty compliance system and promoting continued U.S. strategic technology leadership. BIS activities include regulating the export of sensitive goods and technologies in an effective and efficient manner; enforcing export control, antiboycott, and public safety laws; cooperating with and assisting other countries on export control and strategic trade issues; assisting U.S. industry to comply with international arms control agreements; and monitoring the viability of the U.S. defense industrial base and seeking to ensure that it is capable of satisfying U.S. national and homeland security needs.

Export Administration The Office of the Assistant Secretary for Export Administration is responsible for export licenses, treaty compliance, treaty obligations relating to weapons of mass destruction, and the defense industrial and technology base. The primary objectives are to determine the items requiring export licenses for reasons of national security, nonproliferation, foreign policy, and short supply; ensure that approval or denial is consistent with economic and security concerns; act as the liaison with the business community to ensure its compliance with regulations; represent the Department in interagency and international fora relating to export controls; ensure the availability of industrial resources for national defense under the authority of the Defense Production Act; and assess the security consequences for the United States of various trade activities.

Export Enforcement The Office of the Assistant Secretary for Export Enforcement enforces dual-use export controls for reasons of national security, nonproliferation, counterterrorism, foreign policy, and short supply, enabling exporters to take advantage of legal export opportunities while ensuring that illegal exports will be detected and either prevented or investigated and sanctioned. The Office also ensures prompt, aggressive action against restrictive trade practices such as boycotts; reviews visa applications of foreign nationals to prevent illegal technology transfers; and conducts cooperative enforcement activities on an international basis.

Office of International Programs The Office of International Programs provides technical assistance to nations lacking effective export and transit control systems. These nations are identified as potential locations for export or transit of nuclear, chemical, biological or radiological weapons, missile delivery systems, or the commodities, technologies, or equipment that could be used to design or build such weapons or their delivery systems.

Field Offices—Bureau of Industry and Security

Field Area	Address
Export Enforcement	
Boston, MA	Rm. 350, 10 Causeway St., 02222
Dallas, TX	Suite 622, 525 S. Griffin St., 75202
Hillside, IL	Suite 350, 4415 W. Harrison St., 60162
Houston, TX	Suite 250, 15355 Vantage Pkwy. West, 77032
El Segundo, CA	Suite 720, 222 N. Sepulveda Blvd., 90245
Fort Lauderdale, FL	Suite 2060, 200 E. Las Olas Blvd., 33301
Herndon, VA	Suite 1125, 381 Elden St., 20170

Field Offices—Bureau of Industry and Security—Continued

Field Area	Address
Irvine, CA	Suite 310, 2601 Main St., 92714–6299
San Jose, CA	Suite 250, 96 N. 3d St., 95112–5519
Staten Island, NY	Suite 104, 1200 South Ave., 10314
Export Administration	
Newport Beach, CA	Suite 345, 3300 Irvine Ave., 92660
San Jose, CA	Rm. 605, 111 N. Market St., 6th Fl., 95113

For further information, contact the Bureau of Industry and Security, Office of Public Affairs, Room 3897, Fourteenth Street and Constitution Avenue NW., Washington, DC 20230. Phone, 202–482–2721.

Economic Development Administration

The Economic Development Administration (EDA) was created in 1965 under the Public Works and Economic Development Act (42 U.S.C. 3121) as part of an effort to target Federal resources to economically distressed areas and to help develop local economies in the United States. It was mandated to assist rural and urban communities that were outside the mainstream economy and that lagged in economic development, industrial growth, and personal income.

The Administration provides grants to partners (States, regions, and communities) across the Nation to help create wealth and minimize poverty by promoting a favorable business environment to attract private capital investment and higher skill, higher wage jobs through world-class capacity building, planning, infrastructure, research grants, and strategic initiatives. Through its grant programs, the Administration seeks to utilize public sector resources in a manner that leverages investment by the private sector to create an environment where the private sector risks capital, and job opportunities are created.

Public works and development facilities grants support infrastructure projects that foster the establishment or expansion of industrial and commercial businesses, supporting the retention and creation of jobs.

Planning grants support the design and implementation of effective economic development policies and programs, by local development organizations, in States and communities. EDA funds a network of over 300 planning districts throughout the country.

Technical assistance provides for local feasibility and industry studies, management and operational assistance, natural resource development, and export promotion. In addition, EDA funds a network of university centers that provides technical assistance.

Research, evaluation, and demonstration funds are used to support studies about the causes of economic distress and to seek solutions to counteract and prevent such problems.

Economic adjustment grants help communities adjust to a gradual erosion or sudden dislocation of their local economic structure. Economic assistance provides funding for both planning and implementation to address economic change.

The Trade Adjustment Assistance program helps U.S. firms and industries injured as the result of economic globalization. A nationwide network of Trade Adjustment Assistance Centers offers low-cost, effective professional assistance to certified firms in developing and implementing recovery strategies.

Regional Offices—Economic Development Administration

Region (Areas Served)	Address
Atlanta, GA (AL, FL, GA, MS, NC, SC, TN)	Suite 1820, 401 W. Peachtree St. NW., 30308–3610

Regional Offices—Economic Development Administration—Continued

Region (Areas Served)	Address
Kentucky	Suite 200, 771 Corporate Dr., Lexington, 40503–5477
Austin, TX (AK, NM, OK, TX)	Suite 100, 504 Lavalle St., 78701–2858
Louisiana	Rm. 1025, 500 Poydras St., New Orleans, 70130
Chicago, IL (IN, MI, WI)	Suite 855, 111 N. Canal, 60606–7204
Minnesota	Rm. 104, 515 W. 1st St., Duluth, MN 55802
Ohio	Rm. 740, 200 N. High St., Columbus, OH 43215
Denver, CO (CO, SD, UT)	Rm. 632, 1244 Speer Blvd., 80204
Iowa and Nebraska	Rm. 823, 210 Walnut St., Des Moines, IA 50309
Kansas and Missouri	Suite C, 101 Park DeVille Dr., Columbia, MO 65203
Montana, North Dakota, and Wyoming	Rm. 123, 301 S. Park Ave., P.O. Box 578, Helena, MT 59601
Philadelphia, PA (CT, NJ, NY, PA, PR, RI, VT,).	Suite 140 S., Independence Sq. W., 19106
Delaware, District of Columbia, Maryland, and Virginia.	Rm. 474, 400 N. 8th St., Richmond, VA 23240–1001
Massachusetts and New Hampshire	Rm. 3503, Federal Bldg., 55 Pleasant St., Concord, NH 03301–5089
New York and Vermont	Suite 104, 620 Erie Blvd. W., Syracuse, NY 13204–2442
Pennsylvania	525 N. Broad St., W. Hazelton, 18201–1107
West Virginia	Rm. 411, 405 Capital St., Charleston, 25301–1727
Seattle, WA (AZ, WA)	Rm. 1890, 915 2d Ave., 98174
Alaska	Suite 444, 510 L St., Anchorage, 99501–7594
California (Northern) and Oregon	Suite 244, One World Trade Ctr., 121 SW. Salmon St., Portland, OR 97204
California (Central)	Suite 411, 801 I St., Sacramento, CA, 95814
California (Coastal)	709 Martinelli St., Watonville, CA, 95076
California (Southern)	Suite 1675, 5777 W. Century Blvd., Los Angeles, CA 90045
Hawaii, Guam, American Samoa, Marshall Islands, Micronesia, Northern Marianas and Republic of Palau.	Rm. 5180, Federal Bldg., 300 Ala Moana Blvd., P.O. Box 50264, Honolulu, HI 96850
Idaho and Nevada	Rm. 146, 304 N. 8th St., Boise, ID 83702

For further information, contact the Economic Development Administration, Department of Commerce, Washington, DC 20230. Phone, 202–482–2900. Fax, 202–273–4723.

International Trade Administration

[For the International Trade Administration statement of organization, see the *Federal Register* of Jan. 25, 1980, 45 FR 6148]

The International Trade Administration (ITA) was established on January 2, 1980, by the Secretary of Commerce to promote world trade and to strengthen the international trade and investment position of the United States.

ITA is headed by the Under Secretary for International Trade, who coordinates all issues concerning trade promotion, international commercial policy, market access, and trade law enforcement. The Administration is responsible for nonagricultural trade operations of the U.S. Government and supports the trade policy negotiation efforts of the U.S. Trade Representative.

Import Administration The Office of the Assistant Secretary for Import Administration defends American industry against injurious and unfair trade practices by administering efficiently, fairly, and in a manner consistent with U.S. international trade obligations the antidumping and countervailing duty laws of the United States. The Office ensures the proper administration of foreign trade zones and advises the Secretary on establishment of new zones; oversees the administration of the Department's textiles program; and administers programs governing watch assemblies, and other statutory import programs.

Market Access and Compliance The Office of the Assistant Secretary for Market Access and Compliance advises on the analysis, formulation, and implementation of U.S. international economic policies and carries out programs to promote international trade, improve access by U.S. companies to overseas markets, and strengthen the international trade and investment position of the United States. The Office analyzes and develops recommendations for region- and country-specific international economic, trade, and investment policy strategies and objectives. In addition, the Office is responsible for implementing, monitoring, and enforcing foreign compliance with bilateral and multilateral trade agreements.

Manufacturing and Services The Assistant Secretary for Manufacturing and Services advises on domestic and international trade and investment policies affecting the competitiveness of U.S. industry and carries on a program of research and analysis on manufacturing and services. Based on this analysis and interaction with U.S. industry, the Assistant Secretary develops strategies, policies, and programs to strengthen the competitive position of U.S. industries in the United States and world markets. The Assistant Secretary manages an integrated program that includes both industry and economic analysis, trade policy development and multilateral, regional, and bilateral trade agreements for manufactured goods and services; administers trade arrangements (other than those involving AD/CVD proceedings) with foreign governments in product and service areas; and develops and provides business information and assistance to the United States on its rights and opportunities under multilateral and other agreements.

Trade Promotion and U.S. and Foreign Commercial Service The Assistant Secretary for Trade Promotion and Director General of the U.S. and Foreign Commercial Service directs ITA's export promotion programs, develops and implements a unified goal-setting and evaluation process to increase trade assistance to small- and medium-sized businesses, directs a program of international trade events, market research, and export-related trade information products and services; and directs programs to aid U.S. firms to compete successfully for major projects and procurements worldwide. ITA provides a comprehensive platform of export assistance services to support U.S. firms who enter or expand their presence in overseas markets, including counseling, trade events, and outreach services through 109 export assistance centers located in the United States and 158 posts located in 83 countries throughout the world.

Export Assistance Centers—International Trade Administration

Address	Director/Manager	Telephone	Fax
Alabama (Rm. 707, 950 22d St. N., Birmingham, 35203)	George Norton	205–731–1331	205–731–0076
Alaska (Suite 1770, 431 W. 7th Ave., Anchorage, 99501)	Chuck Becker	907–271–6237	907–271–6242
Arizona (Suite 970, 2901 N. Central Ave., Phoenix, 85012)	(Vacancy)	602–640–2513	602–640–2518
(166 W. Alameda, Tucson, 85701)	Eric Nielsen	520–670–5540	520–791–5413
Arkansas (Suite 700, 425 W. Capitol Ave., Little Rock, 72201).	(Vacancy)	501–324–5794	501–324–7380
California (Suite 166, 2100 Chester Ave., Bakersfield, 93301).	Glen Roberts	661–637–0136	661–637–0156
(550 E. Shaw Ave., Fresno, 93710)	Eduardo Torres	559–227–6582	559–227–6509
(84–245 Indio Springs Dr., Indio, 92203–3499)	Cynthia Torres	760–342–4455	760–342–3535
(Suite 121, 2940 Inland Empire Blvd., Ontario, 91764)	Fred Latuperissa	909–466–4134	909–466–4140
(Suite 509, 350 S. Figueroa St., Los Angeles, 90071)	Rachid Sayouty	213–894–4231	213–894–8789
(Suite 975, 11150 Olympic Blvd., Los Angeles, 90064)	Julieanne Hennessy	310–235–7104	310–235–7220
(Suite 316A, 411 Pacific St., Monterey, 93940)	Chris Damm, *Acting*	408–641–9850	408–641–9849
(Suite 305, 3300 Irvine Ave., Newport Beach 92660)	Mary Delmege, HUB Director.	949–660–1688	949–660–1338
(Suite 630N, 1301 Clay St., Oakland, 94612)	Rod Hirsch	510–273–7350	510–273–7352
(Suite 200, 440 Civic Center Dr., San Rafael, 94903)	Elizabeth Krauth	415–492–4546	415–492–4549
(2d Fl., 917 7th St., Sacramento, 95814)	George Tastard	916–498–5155	916–498–5923
(Suite 230, 6363 Greenwich Dr., San Diego, 92122)	Matt Andersen	619–557–5395	619–557–6176
(14th Fl., 250 Montgomery St., San Francisco, 94104)	Stephan Crawford	415–705–2300	415–705–2297
((Silicon Valley) Suite 550, 152 N. 3d St., San Jose, 95113–5591).	Greg Mignano, HUB Director.	408–271–7300	408–271–7306
(Suite 550, 152 N. 3d St., San Jose, 95113–5591)	Joanne Vilet	408–271–7300	408–271–7306
((Ventura County) 333 Ponoma St., Port Hueneme, 93041).	Gerald Vaughn	805–488–4844	805–488–7801
Colorado (Suite 680, 1625 Broadway, Denver, 80202)	James Kennedy	303–844–6001	303–844–5651
Connecticut (Suite 903, 213 Court St., Middletown, 06457–3346).	Carl Jacobsen	860–638–6950	860–638–6970
Delaware (Served by the Philadelphia, Pennsylvania, Export Assistance Center).			

Export Assistance Centers—International Trade Administration—Continued

Address	Director/Manager	Telephone	Fax
District of Columbia (Served by the Arlington, Virginia (Northern Virginia) Export Assistance Center).			
Florida (Suite 704, 14010 Roosevelt Blvd., Clearwater, 33762).	George Martinez	727–893–3738	727–893–3839
(Suite 1600, 200 E. Las Olas Blvd., Ft. Lauderdale, 33301).	John McCartney	954–356–6640	954–356–6644
(3 Independent Dr., Jacksonville, 32202–5004)	Jorge Arce	904–232–1270	904–232–1271
(Suite 203, 5835 Blue Lagoon Dr., Miami, 33126–3009)	Linda Santucci	305–526–7425	305–526–7434
(P.O. Box 5115, Deltona, 32728–5115)	Kenneth Mouradian	407–968–8122	
(Suite 201, Atrium Bldg., 325 John Knox Rd., Tallahassee, 32303).	Michael Higgins	850–942–9635	850–922–9595
Georgia (Suite 105, 75th St. NW., Atlanta, 30308)	Thomas A. Stauss	404–897–6090	404–897–6085
(Suite 202, 111 E. Liberty St., Savannah, 31401)	Joseph Kramer	912–652–4204	912–652–4241
Hawaii (Rm. 214, 521 Ala Moana Blvd., Honolulu, 96813)	Paul Tambakis	808–522–8040	808–522–8045
Idaho (2d Fl., 700 W. State St., Boise, 83720)	Amy Benson	208–364–7791	208–334–2783
Illinois (Suite 2440, 200 W. Adams St., Chicago, 60606)	Mary N. Joyce, HUB Director.	312–353–8045	312–353–8120
(Rm. 141, Jobst Hall, 922 N. Glenwood Ave., Peoria, 61606).	Shari Stout	309–671–7815	309–671–7818
(Suite 212, 28055 Ashley Cir., Libertyville, 60048)	Robin F. Mugford	847–327–9082	847–247–0423
(515 N. Court St., Rockford, 61103)	Patrick Hope	815–987–8123	815–963–7943
Indiana (Suite 106, 11405 N. Pennsylvania St., Carmel, 46032).	Mark Cooper	317–582–2300	317–582–2301
Iowa (Suite 100, 700 Locust St., Des Moines, 50309–3739)	Allen Patch	515–288–8614	515–288–1437
Kansas (Suite 300, 209 E. William, Wichita, 67202–4012)	A.J. Anderson	316–263–4067	316–263–8306
Kentucky (4th Fl., 140 E. Main St., Lexington, 40507)	Sara M. Moreno	859–225–7001	859–225–6501
(Rm. 634B, 601 W. Broadway, Louisville, 40202)	Peggy Pauley, *Acting*	502–582–5066	502–582–6573
(Suite 240, 2292 S. Hwy. 27, Somerset, 42501)	(Vacancy)	606–677–6160	606–677–6161
Louisiana (Suite 2710, 2 Canal St., New Orleans, 70130)	Donald Van De Werken	504–589–6546	504–589–2337
(Business Education Bldg. 119H, One University Pl., Shreveport, 71115–2399).	Patricia Holt	318–676–3064	318–676–3063
Maine (c/o Maine Int'l Trade Ctr., 511 Congress St., Portland, 04101).	Jeffrey Porter	207–541–7400	207–541–7420
Maryland (Suite 300, 300 W. Pratt St., Baltimore, 21202)	William Burwell	410–962–4539	410–962–4529
Massachusetts (WTC, Suite 307, 164 Northern Ave., Boston, 02210).	Jim Cox	617–424–5990	617–424–5992
(WTC, Suite 307, 164 Northern Ave., Boston, 02210)	Dorothy Zur Muhlen-Tomaszeska.	617–424–5990	617–424–5992
Michigan (Suite 1104, 211 W. Fort St., Detroit, 48226)	Sara Coulter	313–226–3650	313–226–3657
(Suite 311–C, 401 W. Fulton St., Grand Rapids, 49504)	Thomas Maguire	616–458–3564	616–458–3872
(Suite 1300 W., 250 Elizabeth Lake Rd., Pontiac, 48341)	Richard Corson	248–975–9600	248–975–9606
((Ypsilanti) Suite 306G, 300 W. Michigan Ave., c/o Eastern Michigan University, Owen, 48197).	Paul Litton	734–487–0259	734–485–2396
Minnesota (Suite 2240, 45 S. 7th St., Minneapolis, 55402)	Ryan Kanne	612–348–1638	612–348–1650
Mississippi (Suite 255, 175 E. Capitol St., Jackson, 39201)	Carol Moore	601–965–4130	601–965–4132
Missouri (Suite 520, 8235 Forsyth Ctr., St. Louis, 63105)	Randall J. LaBounty	314–425–3302	314–425–3381
(Suite 650, 2345 Grand, Kansas City, 64108)	Regina Heise	816–426–6285	816–426–6292
Montana (P.O. Box 7487, Missoula, 59807)	Mark Peters	406–542–6656	406–542–6659
Nebraska (11135 "O" St., Omaha, 68137)	Meredith Bond	402–597–0193	402–597–0194
Nevada (400 Las Vegas Blvd. S., Las Vegas, 89101)	Tony Michalski	702–366–9406	702–366–0688
(16th Fl., 1 E. 1st St., Reno, 89502)	Bill Cline	775–784–5203	775–784–5343
New Hampshire (17 New Hampshire Ave., Portsmouth, 03801–2838).	Susan Berry	603–334–6074	603–334–6110
New Jersey (Suite 1505, 744 Broad St., Newark, 07102)	Carmela Mammas	973–645–4682	973–645–4783
(P.O. Box 820, 20 W. State St., Trenton, 08625–0820)	Rod Stuart	609–989–2100	609–989–2395
New Mexico (1100 St. Francis Dr., c/o NM Dept. of Economic Development, Santa Fe, 87505–4147).	Sandra Necessary	505–827–0350	505–827–0263
New York (Rm. 1304, 111 W. Huron St., Buffalo, 14202)	James Mariano	716–551–4191	716–551–5290
(Suite 904, 163 W. 125th St., Harlem, 10027)	K.L. Fredericks	212–860–6200	212–860–6203
((Long Island) Rm. 109, Harriman Hall, SBDC Stony Brook Univ., Stony Brook, 11794–3777.	Kenneth Reidbord	631–897–9349	631–632–7176
(40th Fl., 20 Exchange Pl., New York, 10007)	William Spitler	212–809–2675	212–809–2687
(Suite 710, 400 Andrews St., Rochester, 14604)	Erin Cole	585–263–6480	585–325–6505
((Westchester) Suite 209, 707 Westchester Ave., White Plains, 10604).	Joan Kanlian	914–682–6712	914–682–6698
North Carolina (Suite 435, 521 E. Morehead St., Charlotte, 28202).	Samuel P. Troy, HUB Director.	704–333–4886	704–332–2681
(Suite 435, 521 E. Morehead St., Charlotte, 28202)	Greg Sizemore	704–333–4886	704–332–2681
(2nd Fl., 342 N. Elm St., Greensboro, 27401)	John Schmonsees	336–333–5345	336–333–5158
((Triangle) Suite 110, 10900 World Trade Blvd., Raleigh, 27617).	Debbie Strader	919–715–7373	919–715–7777
North Dakota (Served by the Minneapolis Export Assistance Center).			
Ohio (17th Fl., One Cascade Plz., Akron, 44308)	Ricardo Pelaez	330–237–1264	330–375–5612
(Suite 2650, 36 E. 7th St., Cincinnati, 45202)	(Vacancy)	513–684–2944	513–684–3227

Export Assistance Centers—International Trade Administration—Continued

Address	Director/Manager	Telephone	Fax
(Suite 700, 600 Superior Ave. E., Cleveland, 44114)	Michael Miller, HUB Director.	216–522–4750	216–522–2235
(Suite 700, 600 Superior Ave. E., Cleveland, 44114)	Susan Whitney	216–522–4750	216–522–2235
(Suite 1400, 280 N. High St., Columbus, 43215)	Roberta Ford	614–365–9510	614–365–9598
(300 Madison Ave., Toledo, 43604)	Robert Abrahams	419–241–0683	419–241–0684
Oklahoma (Suite 330, 301 NW. 63d St., Oklahoma City, 73116).	Ronald L. Wilson	405–608–5302	405–608–4211
(Suite 1400, 700 N. Greenwood Ave., Tulsa, 74106)	Jim Williams	918–581–7650	918–581–6263
Oregon (Suite 242, One World Trade Ctr., 121 SW. Salmon St., Portland, 97204.	Scott Goddin	503–326–3001	503–326–6351
Pennsylvania (Suite 850, P.O. Box 11698, 228 Walnut St., Harrisburg, 17108–1698).	Deborah Doherty	717–221–4510	717–221–4505
(The Curtis Ctr., Suite 580 West, Independence Sq. W., Philadelphia, 19106).	Joseph Hanely, HUB Director.	215–597–6101	215–597–6123
(The Curtis Ctr., Suite 580 West, Independence Sq. W., Philadelphia, 19106).	Michael Lally	215–597–6101	215–597–6123
(Suite 2950, 425 6th Ave., Pittsburgh, 15222)	Lynn Doverspike	412–664–2800	412–664–2803
Puerto Rico (10th Fl., Midtown Bldg., 420 Ponce de Leon Ave., San Juan (Hato Rey), 00918).	Maritza Ramos	787–766–5555	787–766–5692
Rhode Island (One W. Exchange St., Providence, 02903)	Keith Yatsuhashi	401–528–5104	401–528–5067
South Carolina (Suite 201-C, 5300 International Blvd., North Charleston, 29418).	Phil Minard	843–760–3794	843–760–3798
(Suite 1720, 1201 Main St., Columbia, 29201)	Ann Watts	803–765–5345	803–253–3614
(Suite 109, Bldg. 1, 555 N. Pleasantburg Dr., Greenville, 29607).	Denis Csizmadia	864–271–1976	864–271–4171
South Dakota (Rm. 122, Madsen Ctr., Augusta College, 2001 S. Summit Ave., Sioux Falls, 57197).	Cinnamon King	605–330–4264	605–330–4266
Tennessee (Suite 300, 601 W. Summit Hill Dr., Knoxville, 37902–2011).	George Frank	865–545–4637	865–545–4435
(Suite 348, Buckman Hall, 650 East Pkwy. S., Memphis, 38104).	(Vacancy)	901–323–1543	901–320–9128
(Suite 100, 3d Fl., 211 Commerce St., Nashville, 37201)	Dean Peterson	615–259–6060	615–259–6064
Texas (2d Fl., 1700 Congress, Austin, 78701)	Karen Parker	512–916–5939	512–916–5940
(808 Throckmorton St., Fort Worth, 76102)	Mark Weaver	817–392–2673	817–392–2668
(Suite 530, 15600 JFK Blvd., Houston, 77002)	Duaine Priestley	281–449–9402	281–449–9437
((North Texas) Suite 220, 1450 Hughes Rd., Grapevine, 76051).	Daniel Stewart	817–310–3744	817–310–3757
(Suite 360, 203-A St. Mary's St., San Antonio, 78205)	Daniel Rodriguez	210–228–9878	210–228–9874
((South Texas) Suite 4, 6401 S. 36th St., McAllen, 78503)	(Vacancy)	956–661–0238	956–661–0239
((West Texas) Rm. 1303, 1400 FM 1788, Midland, 79707–1423).	Steve Recobs	432–552–2490	432–552–3490
Utah (Suite 331, 9690 South 300 West, Sandy, 84070)	David Fiscuss	801–255–1871	801–255–3147
Vermont (6th Fl., National Life Bldg., Montpelier, 05620–0501).	Susan Murray	802–828–4508	802–828–3258
Virginia ((Northern Virginia) Suite 1225, 1401 Wilson Blvd., Arlington, 22209).	Ann Grey	703–235–0331	703–524–2649
(Suite 412, P.O. Box 10026, 400 N. 8th St., Richmond, 23240–0026).	Eric McDonald	804–771–2246	804–771–2390
Washington (Suite 320, 2601 4th Ave., Seattle, 98121)	Diane Mooney	206–553–5615	206–553–7253
(Suite 400, 801 W. Riverside Ave., Spokane Regional Chamber of Commerce, Spokane, 99201).	Janet Daubel	509–353–2625	509–353–2449
(Suite 410, 950 Pacific Ave., Tacoma, 98402)	Young Oh	253–593–6736	253–383–4676
West Virginia (Suite 807, 405 Capitol St., Charleston, 25301)	(Vacancy)	304–347–5123	304–347–5408
(316 Washington Ave., Wheeling Jesuit University NTTC, Wheeling, 26003).	James F. Fitzgerald	304–243–5493	304–243–5494
Wisconsin (Rm. 596, 517 E. Wisconsin Ave., Milwaukee, 53202).	Paul D. Churchill	414–297–3473	414–297–3470
Wyoming (Served by the Denver Export Assistance Center).			
National Director (Rm. 3810 HCH Bldg., 14th and Constitution Ave. NW., Washington, DC 20230).	Thomas McGinty	202–482–3940	202–501–4007

For further information, contact the International Trade Administration, Department of Commerce, Washington, DC 20230. Phone, 202–482–3917.

Minority Business Development Agency

[For the Minority Business Development Agency statement of organization, see the *Federal Register* of Mar. 17, 1972, 37 FR 5650, as amended]

The Minority Business Development Agency was established by Executive order in 1969. The Agency develops and coordinates a national program for minority business enterprise.

The Agency was created to assist minority businesses in achieving effective and equitable participation in the American free enterprise system and in overcoming social and economic disadvantages that have limited their participation in the past. The Agency provides national policies and leadership in forming and strengthening a partnership of business, industry, and government with the Nation's minority businesses.

Business development services are provided to the minority business community through three vehicles: the minority business opportunity committees which disseminate information on business opportunities; the minority business development centers that provide management and technical assistance and other business development services; and electronic commerce which includes a Web page on the Internet that will show how to start a business and use the service to electronically match business with contract opportunities.

The Agency promotes and coordinates the efforts of other Federal agencies in assisting or providing market opportunities for minority business. It coordinates opportunities for minority firms in the private sector. Through such public and private cooperative activities, the Agency promotes the participation of Federal, State, and local governments, and business and industry in directing resources for the development of strong minority businesses.

National Enterprise Centers—Minority Business Development Agency

Region	Address	Director	Telephone
Atlanta, GA	Suite 1715, 401 W. Peachtree St. NW., 30308–3516	Robert Henderson	404–730–3300
Chicago, IL	Suite 1406, 55 E. Monroe St., 60603	Eric Dobyne	312–353–0182
Dallas, TX	Suite 7B23, 1100 Commerce St., 75242	John Iglehart	214–767–8001
El Monte, CA	Suite 455, 9660 Flair Dr., 91713	Maria Accosta	818–453–8636
New York, NY	Suite 3720, 26 Federal Plz., 10278	Heyward Davenport	212–264–3262
Philadelphia, PA	Rm. 10128, 600 Arch St., 19106	Alfonso C. Jackson	215–597–9236
San Francisco, CA	Rm. 1280, 221 Main St., 94105	Linda Marmolejo	415–744–3001

For further information, contact the Office of the Director, Minority Business Development Agency, Department of Commerce, Washington, DC 20230. Phone, 202–482–5061. Internet, www.mbda.gov.

National Oceanic and Atmospheric Administration

Department of Commerce, Washington, DC 20230
Phone, 202–482–2985. Internet, www.noaa.gov.

[For the National Oceanic and Atmospheric Administration statement of organization, see the *Federal Register* of Feb. 13, 1978, 43 FR 6128]

The National Oceanic and Atmospheric Administration (NOAA) was formed on October 3, 1970, by Reorganization Plan No. 4 of 1970 (5 U.S.C. app.).

NOAA's mission entails environmental assessment, prediction, and stewardship. It is dedicated to monitoring and assessing the state of the environment in order to make accurate and timely forecasts to protect life, property, and natural resources, as well as to promote the economic well-being of the United States and to enhance its environmental security. NOAA is committed to protecting America's ocean, coastal, and living marine resources while promoting sustainable economic development.

National Weather Service

The National Weather Service (NWS) provides weather, water and climate warnings, forecasts and data for the United States, its territories, adjacent waters, and ocean areas. NWS data and products form a national information database and infrastructure used by Government agencies, the private sector, the public, and the global community to protect life and property and to enhance the national economy. Working with partners in Government, academic and research institutions and private industry, NWS strives to ensure their products and services are responsive to the needs of the American public. NWS data and information services support aviation and marine activities, wildfire suppression, and many other sectors of the economy. NWS supports national security efforts with long- and short-range forecasts, air quality and cloud dispersion forecasts, and broadcasts of warnings and critical information over the 800-station NOAA Weather Radio network.

For further information, contact the National Weather Service, Attention: Executive Affairs, 1325 East-West Highway, Silver Spring, MD 20910–3283. Phone, 301–713–0689. Fax, 301–713–0049. Internet, www.nws.noaa.gov.

National Environmental Satellite, Data, and Information Service

The National Environmental Satellite, Data, and Information Service (NESDIS) operates the Nation's civilian geostationary and polar-orbiting environmental satellites. It also manages the largest collection of atmospheric, geophysical, and oceanographic data in the world. From these sources, NESDIS develops and provides, through various media, environmental data for forecasts, national security, and weather warnings to protect life and property. This data is also used to assist in energy distribution, the development of global food supplies, the management of natural resources, and in the recovery of downed pilots and mariners in distress.

For further information, contact the National Environmental Satellite, Data, and Information Service, 1335 East-West Highway, Silver Spring, MD 20910–3283. Phone, 301–713–3578. Fax, 301–713–1249. Internet, www.noaa.gov/nesdis/nesdis.html.

National Marine Fisheries Service

The National Marine Fisheries Service (NMFS) supports the management, conservation, and sustainable development of domestic and international living marine resources and the protection and restoration of healthy ecosystems. NMFS is involved in the stock assessment of the Nation's multi-billion-dollar marine fisheries, protecting marine mammals and threatened species, habitat conservation operations, trade and industry assistance, and fishery enforcement activities.

For further information, contact the National Marine Fisheries Service, 1315 East-West Highway, Silver Spring, MD 20910. Phone, 301–713–2239. Fax, 301–713–2258. Internet, kingfish.ssp.nmfs.gov.

National Ocean Service

The National Ocean Service (NOS) works to balance the Nation's use of coastal resources through research, management, and policy. NOS monitors the health of U.S. coasts by examining how human use and natural events impact coastal ecosystems. Coastal communities rely on NOS for information about natural hazards so they can more effectively reduce or eliminate the destructive effects of coastal hazards. NOS assesses the damage caused by hazardous material spills and works to restore or replace the affected coastal resources. Through varied programs, NOS protects wetlands, water quality, beaches, and wildlife. In addition, NOS provides a wide range of navigational products and data that assist vessels' safe movement through U.S. waters and provides the basic set of information that establishes the latitude, longitude, and elevation framework necessary for the Nation's surveying, navigation, positioning, and mapping activities.

For further information, contact the National Ocean Service, Room 13231, SSMC 4, 1305 East-West Highway, Silver Spring, MD 20910. Phone, 301–713–3070. Fax, 301–713–4307. Internet, www.nos.noaa.gov.

Office of Oceanic and Atmospheric Research

The Office of Oceanic and Atmospheric Research (OAR) carries out research on weather, air quality and composition, climate variability and change, and coastal and Great Lakes ecosystems. OAR conducts and directs its research programs in coastal, marine, atmospheric, and space sciences through its own laboratories and offices, as well as through networks of university-based programs across the country.

For further information, contact the Office of Oceanic and Atmospheric Research, Room 11627, 1315 East-West Highway, Silver Spring, MD 20910. Phone, 301–713–2458. Fax, 301–713–0163. Internet, www.oar.noaa.gov.

NOAA Marine and Aviation Operations

NOAA also maintains a fleet of ships and aircraft under the auspices of its NOAA Marine and Aviation Operations (NMAO). These are used for scientific, engineering, and technical services, as well as to serve as research platforms for gathering critical marine and atmospheric data in support of a number of NOAA's research programs. This includes flying "hurricane hunter" aircraft into nature's most turbulent storms to collect data critical to hurricane research.

For further information, contact NOAA Marine and Aviation Operations, Room 12857, 1315 East-West Highway, Silver Spring, MD 20910–3282. Phone, 301–713–1045.

Field Organization—National Oceanic and Atmospheric Administration

Organization	Address/Telephone	Director
National Weather Service		
Headquarters	Attention: Executive Affairs, 1325 East-West Hwy., Silver Spring, MD 20910–3283. Phone, 301–713–0689. Fax, 301–713–0610.	D.L. Johnson
Office of Climate, Water, and Weather Service.	1325 East-West Hwy., Silver Spring, MD 20910–3283. Phone, 301–713–0700. Fax, 301–713–1598.	Dennis H. McCarthy
Office of Science and Technology	1325 East-West Hwy., Silver Spring, MD 20910–3283. Phone, 301–713–1746. Fax, 301–713–0963.	Greg Mandt
Office of Hydrologic Development	1325 East-West Hwy., Silver Spring, MD 20910–3283. Phone, 301–713–1658. Fax, 301–713–0003.	Gary M. Carter
Office of Systems Operations	1325 East-West Hwy., Silver Spring, MD 20910–3283. Phone, 301–713–0165. Fax, 301–713–0657.	John McNulty
National Centers for Environmental Prediction.	5200 Auth Rd., Camp Springs, MD 20746–4304. Phone, 301–763–8016. Fax, 301–763–8434.	Louis W. Uccellini
Eastern region	630 Johnson Ave., Bohemia, NY 11716–2626. Phone, 516–244–0100. Fax, 516–244–0109.	Dean P. Gulezian
Southern region	Rm. 10A26, 819 Taylor St., Fort Worth, TX 76102–6171. Phone, 817–978–2651. Fax, 817–334–4187.	X. William Proenza
Central region	7220 NW 101st Terrace, Kansas City, MO 64153–2371. Phone, 816–891–8914x600. Fax, 816–891–8362.	Lynn Maximuk
Western region	Rm. 1210, 125 S. State St., Salt Lake City, UT 84138–1102. Phone, 801–524–5722. Fax, 801–524–5270.	Vickie L. Nadolski
Alaska region	Rm. 517, 222 W. 7th Ave., Anchorage, AK 99513–7575. Phone, 907–271–5136. Fax, 907–271–3711.	Laura Furgione
Pacific region	Suite 2200, 737 Bishop St., Honolulu, HI 96813. Phone, 808–532–6416. Fax, 808–532–5569.	Jeff LaDouce
Office of the Federal Coordinator for Meteorological Services and Supporting Research.	1500 Ctr., 8455 Colesville Rd., Silver Spring, MD 20910–3315. Phone, 301–427–2002.	Samuel Williamson

Field Organization—National Oceanic and Atmospheric Administration—Continued

Organization	Address/Telephone	Director
National Marine Fisheries Service		
Headquarters	1315 East-West Hwy., Silver Spring, MD 20910. Phone, 301–713–2239. Fax, 301–713–2258.	William T. Hogarth
Alaska region	P.O. Box 21668, Juneau, AK 99802–1668. Phone, 907–586–7221. Fax, 907–586–7249.	James W. Balsiger
Alaska Fisheries Science Center	Bin C15700, Bldg. 4, 7600 Sand Point Way NE., Seattle, WA 98115. Phone, 206–526–4000. Fax, 206–526–4004.	Douglas DeMaster
Northwest region	Bin C15700, Bldg. 1, 7600 Sand Point Way NE., Seattle, WA 98115–0070. Phone, 206–526–6150. Fax, 206–526–6426.	D. Robert Lohn
Northwest Fisheries Science Center	2725 Montlake Blvd. E., Seattle, WA 98112. Phone, 206–860–3200. Fax, 206–860–3217.	Usha Varanasi
Northeast region	1 Blackburn Dr., Gloucester, MA 01930. Phone, 978–281–9250. Fax, 978–281–9371.	Patricia Kurkul
Northeast Fisheries Science Center	166 Water St., Woods Hole, MA 02543. Phone, 508–548–5123. Fax, 508–495–2232.	John Boreman
Southeast region	263 13th Ave. South, St. Petersburg, FL 33701. Phone, 727–824–5301. Fax, 727–824–5320.	Roy Crabtree
Southeast Fisheries Science Center	75 Virginia Beach Dr., Miami, FL 33149. Phone, 305–361–5761. Fax, 305–361–4219.	Nancy Thompson
Southwest region	Suite 4200, 501 W. Ocean Blvd., Long Beach, CA 90802. Phone, 562–980–4001. Fax, 562–980–4018.	Rodney McInnis
Southwest Fisheries Science Center	P.O. Box 271, 8604 La Jolla Shores Dr., La Jolla, CA 92038. Phone, 858–546–7067. Fax, 858–546–5655.	William Fox
Pacific Islands region	Suite 1110, 1601 Kapiolani Blvd., Honolulu, HI 96814. Phone, 808–944–2280. Fax, 808–973–2941.	William Robinson
Pacific Islands Fisheries Science Centers.	2570 Dole Ave., Honolulu, HI 96822–2396. Phone, 808–983–5303. Fax, 808–983–2901.	Samuel Pooley
National Environmental Satellite, Data, and Information Service		
Headquarters	1335 East-West Highway, Silver Spring, MD 20910. Phone, 301–713–3578. Fax, 301–713–1249.	Gregory W. Withee
Integrated Program Office	Rm. 1450, 8455 Colesville Rd., Silver Spring, MD 20910. Phone, 301–427–2070.	John Cunningham
Satellite operations	Rm. 0135, 5200 Auth Rd., Suitland, MD 20746. Phone, 301–817–4000. Fax, 301–457–5175.	Kathleen A. Kelly
Satellite data processing and distribution.	Rm. 1069, 5200 Auth Rd., Suitland, MD 20746. Phone, 301–457–5120. Fax, 301–457–5184.	Richard Barazotto
Research and applications	NOAA Science Center, 5200 Auth Rd., Camp Springs, MD 20233. Phone, 301–763–8127. Fax, 301–763–8108.	Marie Colton
Systems development	1335 East-West Hwy., Silver Spring, MD 20910. Phone, 301–713–0100. Fax, 301–713–3599.	Gary K. Davis
National Climatic Data Center	151 Patton Ave., Asheville, NC 28801–5001. Phone, 828–271–4476. Fax, 828–271–4246.	Tom Karl
National Geophysical Data Center	RL–3, 325 Broadway, Boulder, CO 80303–3328. Phone, 303–497–6215. Fax, 303–497–6513.	Christopher Fox
National Oceanographic Data Center	1315 East-West Hwy., Silver Spring, MD 20910. Phone, 301–713–3303. Fax, 301–713–3300.	(Vacancy)
National Ocean Service		
Headquarters	Rm. 13632, 1305 East-West Hwy., Silver Spring, MD 20910. Phone, 301–713–3074. Fax, 301–713–4269.	(Vacancy)
International Programs	Rm. 5651, 1315 East-West Hwy., Silver Spring, MD 20910. Phone, 301–713–3078. Fax, 301–713–4263.	Clement Lewsey, *Acting*
NOAA Coastal Services Center	2234 S. Hobson Ave., Charleston, SC 29405–2409. Phone, 843–740–1200. Fax 843–740–1224.	Margaret A. Davidson
Center for Operational Oceanographic Products and Services.	Rm. 6633, 1305 East-West Hwy., Silver Spring, MD 20910. Phone, 301–713–2981. Fax, 301–713–4392.	Michael Szabados
National Centers for Coastal Ocean Science.	Rm. 8211, 1305 East-West Hwy., Silver Spring, MD 20910. Phone, 301–713–3020. Fax, 301–713–4270.	Gary C. Matlock
Coast survey	Rm. 6147, 1315 East-West Hwy., Silver Spring, MD 20910. Phone, 301–713–2770. Fax, 301–713–4019.	Capt. Roger L. Parsons, NOAA
National Geodetic Survey	Rm. 8657, 1315 East-West Hwy., Silver Spring, MD 20910. Phone, 301–713–3222. Fax, 301–713–4315.	Charles W. Challstrom

Field Organization—National Oceanic and Atmospheric Administration—Continued

Organization	Address/Telephone	Director
Office of Response and Restoration	Rm. 4389, 1305 East-West Hwy., Silver Spring, MD 20910. Phone, 301–713–2989. Fax, 301–713–4387.	David M. Kennedy
Ocean and coastal resource management.	Rm. 10414, 1305 East-West Hwy., Silver Spring, MD 20910. Phone, 301–713–3155. Fax, 301–713–4012.	Eldon Hout
Office of Oceanic and Atmospheric Research		
Headquarters	Rm. 11627, 1315 East-West Hwy., Silver Spring, MD 20910. Phone, 301–713–2458. Fax, 301–713–0163.	Richard Spinrad
Climate Programs Office	Rm. 1225G, 1100 Wayne Ave., Silver Spring, MD 20910–5603. Phone, 301–427–2089. Fax, 301–427–2082.	Chester A. Koblinsky
Earth System Research Laboratory	Rm. 2204, Bldg. 24, 325 Broadway, Boulder, CO 80303. Phone, 303–497–3134. Fax, 303–497–5340.	Alexander E. MacDonald, *Acting*
Air Resources Laboratory	Rm. 3151, 1315 East-West Hwy., Silver Spring, MD 20910. Phone, 301–713–0684, ext. 100. Fax, 301–713–0295.	Richard S. Artz, *Acting*
Atlantic Oceanographic and Meteorological Laboratory.	4301 Rickenbacker Causeway, Miami, FL 33149. Phone, 305–361–4300. Fax, 305–361–4449.	Robert Atlas
Climate Diagnostics Center	Rm. 247, RL3, 325 Broadway, Boulder, CO 80303. Phone, 303–497–6878. Fax, 303–497–7013.	(Vacancy)
Geophysical Fluid Dynamics Laboratory.	P.O. Box 308, Princeton University Forrestral Campus, Princeton, NJ 08452. Phone, 609–452–6503. Fax, 609–987–5070.	Ants Leetmaa
Great Lakes Environmental Research Laboratory.	2205 Commonwealth Blvd., Ann Arbor, MI 48105. Phone, 734–741–2244. Fax, 734–741–2003.	Stephen Brandt
National Severe Storms Laboratory	1313 Halley Circle, Norman, OK 73069. Phone, 405–366–0426. Fax, 405–366–0472.	James Kimpel
Pacific Marine Environmental Laboratory.	Bin C 15700, Bldg. 3, 7600 Sand Point Way NE., Seattle, WA 98115. Phone, 206–526–6800. Fax, 206–526–6815.	Eddie N. Bernard
National Undersea Research Program	Rm. 11350, 1315 East-West Hwy., Silver Spring, MD 20910. Phone, 301–713–2427. Fax, 301–713–1967.	Barbara S.P. Moore
National Sea Grant College Program	Rm. 11716, 1315 East-West Hwy., Silver Spring, MD 20910. Phone, 301–713–2448. Fax, 301–713–0799.	Leon Cammen, *Acting*
Office of Research and Technology Applications.	Rm. 11464, 1315 East-West Hwy., Silver Spring, MD 20910. Phone, 301–713–3565. Fax, 301–713–4100.	Joe Bishop
Chief Financial Officer	Rm. 6805, 14th St. and Constitution Ave. NW., Washington, DC 20230. Phone, 202–482–0917.	William E. Wylie
Chief Administrative Officer	Rm. 8431, 1305 East-West Hwy., Silver Spring, MD 20910. Phone, 301–713–0836.	William Broglis
Budget Office	Rm. 6114, 14th St. and Constitution Ave. NW., Washington, DC 20230. Phone, 202–482–4600.	Steven I. Gallagher
Finance Office	20020 Century Blvd., Germantown, MD 20874–1143. Phone, 301–444–2132.	Jon Alexander
Real Property Management	Rm. 4162, 1305 East-West Hwy., Silver Spring, MD 20910. Phone, 301–713–0836.	(Vacancy)
Environment, Compliance and Safety Office.	Rm. 5555, MPO Bldg. 1, 325 Broadway, Boulder, CO 80305–3228. Phone, 303–497–6219.	Ezekiel Dennison
Logistics Staff Office	Rm. 8553, East-West Hwy., Silver Spring, MD 20910. Phone, 301–713–3551.	Anthony Fleming
Office of Civil Rights	Rm. 12222, 1305 East-West Hwy., Silver Spring, MD 20910. Phone, 301–713–0500.	Al Corea
Audit and Internal Control Branch	Rm. 10662, 1315 East-West Hwy., Silver Spring, MD 20910. Phone, 301–713–1150.	Mack Cato
Budget Office	Rm. 6114, 14th St. and Constitution Ave. NW., Washington, DC 20230. Phone, 202–482–4600.	Steven I. Gallagher
Finance Office	20020 Century Blvd., Germantown, MD 20874–1143. Phone, 301–444–2132.	R.J. Dominic
Human Resources Management Office	Rm. 12434, 1305 East-West Hwy., Silver Spring, MD 20910. Phone, 301–713–0530.	Eduardo J. Ribas
Chief Information Officer	Rm. 10452, 1315 East-West Hwy., Silver Spring, MD 20910. Phone, 301–713–9600.	Carl Staton

Field Organization—National Oceanic and Atmospheric Administration—Continued

Organization	Address/Telephone	Director
Acquisition and Grants Office	Rm. 6300, 1305 East-West Hwy., Silver Spring, MD 20910. Phone, 301–713–0325.	Helen Hurcombe
NOAA Marine and Aviation Operations		
Headquarters	Rm. 12857, 1315 East-West Hwy., Silver Spring, MD 20910–3282. Phone, 301–713–1045.	Rear Adm. Samuel P. DeBow, Jr., NOAA
Marine and Aviation Operations Center.	Rm. 12857, 1315 East-West Hwy., Silver Spring, MD 20910–3282. Phone, 301–713–1045.	Rear Adm. Richard Behn, NOAA
Marine Operations Center Atlantic	439 W. York St., Norfolk, VA 23510–1114. Phone, 757–441–6776.	Capt. Gary Bulmer, NOAA Commanding Officer
Marine Operations Center Pacific	1801 Fairview Ave. E., Seattle, WA 98102. Phone, 206–553–4764.	Capt. John Clary, NOAA
Aircraft Operations Center	7917 Hangar Loop Dr., MacDill AFB, FL 33621–5401. Phone, 813–828–3310.	Capt. Steve Kozak, NOAA Commanding Officer
Commissioned Personnel Center	1315 East-West Hwy., Silver Spring, MD 20910. Phone, 301–713–1045.	Capt. Jon Bailey, NOAA

For further information, contact the Office of Public Affairs, National Oceanic and Atmospheric Administration, Department of Commerce, Washington, DC 20230. Phone, 202–482–4190.

National Telecommunications and Information Administration

[For the National Telecommunications and Information Administration statement of organization, see the *Federal Register* of June 5, 1978, 43 FR 24348]

The National Telecommunications and Information Administration (NTIA) was established in 1978 by Reorganization Plan No. 1 of 1977 (5 U.S.C. app.) and Executive Order 12046 of March 27, 1978 (3 CFR, 1978 Comp., p. 158), by combining the Office of Telecommunications Policy of the Executive Office of the President and the Office of Telecommunications of the Department of Commerce to form a new agency reporting to the Secretary of Commerce.

The Administration's principal responsibilities and functions include:

—serving as the principal executive branch adviser to the President on telecommunications and information policy;

—developing and presenting U.S. plans and policies at international communications conferences and related meetings;

—prescribing policies for and managing Federal use of the radio frequency spectrum;

—serving as the principal Federal telecommunications research and engineering laboratory, through NTIA's Institute for Telecommunication Sciences (ITS), headquartered in Boulder, CO;

—providing grants through the Technology Opportunities Program for demonstration projects to promote the widespread availability of digital network technologies in the public and nonprofit sectors, which will help stimulate economic development, improve learning at all levels, improve delivery of health care, strengthen public safety efforts, and allow greater access for citizens to nationwide information resources; and

—providing grants through the Public Telecommunications Facilities Program to extend delivery of public telecommunications services to U.S. citizens, to increase ownership and management by women and minorities, and to strengthen the capabilities of existing public broadcasting stations to provide telecommunications services.

For further information, contact the National Telecommunications and Information Administration, Department of Commerce, Washington, DC 20230. Phone, 202–482–1551. Internet, www.ntia.doc.gov.

Patent and Trademark Office

[For the Patent and Trademark Office statement of organization, see the *Federal Register* of Apr. 14, 1975, 40 FR 16707]

The patent system was established by Congress ". . . to promote the progress of . . . the useful arts. . ." The registration of trademarks is based on the commerce clause of the U.S. Constitution.

The Patent and Trademark Office (PTO) examines applications for patents to determine if the applicants are entitled to patents and grants the patents when they are so entitled. The patent law provides for the granting of patents in three major categories: utility patents, design patents, and plant patents. The term of a design patent is 14 years from the date of grant. It also issues statutory invention registrations, which have the defensive but not the enforceable attributes of a patent. It also processes international applications for patents.

PTO registers and renews trademarks. A trademark includes any distinctive word, name, symbol, device, or any combination thereof adopted and used or intended to be used by a manufacturer or merchant to identify his goods or services and distinguish them from those manufactured or sold by others. Trademarks are examined by the Office for compliance with various statutory requirements to prevent unfair competition and consumer deception.

In addition to the examination of patent and trademark applications, issuance of patents, and registration of trademarks, the Patent and Trademark Office:

—sells printed copies of issued patents and trademark registrations;

—records and indexes documents transferring ownership;

—maintains a scientific library and search files with access to technical information documents, including U.S. and foreign patents and U.S. trademarks;

—provides research facilities for the public;

—hears and decides appeals from prospective inventors and trademark applicants;

—participates in legal proceedings involving the issue of patents or registration of trademarks;

—advocates strengthening intellectual property protection worldwide;

—compiles the *Official Gazettes*, a weekly notice of patents issued and trademarks registered by the Office, including other information; and

—maintains a roster of patent agents and attorneys qualified and recognized to practice before the Office.

Patents and trademarks may be reviewed and searched at PTO in over 80 patent and trademark depository libraries throughout the country and online. The patent system fosters innovation, investment in developing and marketing inventions, and prompt disclosure of technological information.

For further information, contact the Office of Public Affairs, Patent and Trademark Office, Washington, DC 20231. Phone, 703–305–8341. Internet, www.uspto.gov. The Office's operations are located at 2121 Crystal Drive, Arlington, VA 22202.

Technology Administration

The Technology Administration (TA) was established by Congress in 1988 (15 U.S.C. 3704) and was directed to work with U.S. industry to maximize technology's contribution to U.S. economic growth by maintaining and improving key components of the Nation's technological infrastructure; fostering the development, diffusion, and adoption of new technologies and leading business practices; creating a business and policy environment conducive to innovation; and disseminating technical information.

The Technology Administration serves as a policy portal for the technology community to the executive branch. Led by the Under Secretary for Technology, TA fulfills its broad responsibilities through its three component organizations: the Office of Technology Policy, the National Institute of Standards and Technology, and the National Technical Information Service.

Office of Technology Policy

Through analytical reports and memoranda, briefings and congressional testimony, the Office of Technology Policy (OTP) provides national, State, and local policymakers with information and deeper understanding of trends and policy implications of new technologies, business models and practices, and the implications for U.S. competitiveness of technology policy issues. OTP serves as the U.S. Government's technology ambassador to industry, frequently meeting with innovative leaders and entrepreneurs to better understand their needs and concerns and to represent TA's technology policies and agenda. OTP also assists others across America—from managers of traditional industries to regional economic development leaders to middle school students—to better understand and appreciate the importance of technology and innovation to America's future. In its advocacy role, OTP helps shape policies that support a vibrant national innovation infrastructure and the interests of entrepreneurs and technologists in Federal policymaking circles.

For further information, call 202–482–5687.

National Institute of Standards and Technology

The National Institute of Standards and Technology (NIST) operates under the authority of the National Institute of Standards and Technology Act (15 U.S.C. 271), which amends the Organic Act of March 3, 1901 (ch. 872), that created the National Bureau of Standards (NBS) in 1901. In 1988, Congress renamed NBS as NIST and also established the Regional Centers for the Transfer of Manufacturing Technology (15 U.S.C. 278k) and the Advanced Technology Program (15 U.S.C. 278n). The National Quality Program was established and its functions were assigned to NIST by the Malcolm Baldrige National Quality Improvement Act of 1987 (15 U.S.C. 3711a).

NIST develops and disseminates measurement techniques, reference data, test methods, standards, and other infrastructural technologies and services required by U.S. industry to innovate and compete in global markets. In addition to its core measurement, testing, and standards functions, NIST also conducts several extramural programs, including the Advanced Technology Program, to stimulate the development of high-risk, broad-impact technologies by U.S. firms; the Manufacturing Extension Partnership, to help smaller firms adopt new manufacturing and management technologies; and the Baldrige National Quality Program, to help U.S. businesses and other organizations improve the performance and quality of their operations by providing clear standards and benchmarks of quality.

NIST is a non-regulatory Federal agency within the Commerce Department's Technology Administration. NIST's mission is to develop and promote measurement, standards, and technology to enhance productivity, facilitate trade, and improve the quality of life. Major program areas include measurement and standards laboratories that perform research in the areas of electronics, electrical engineering, manufacturing engineering, chemical science and technology, physics, materials science and engineering, building and fire research, and information technology.

For further information, call 301–975–NIST (301–975–6478). Fax, 301–926–1630. E-mail, inquiries@nist.gov. Internet, www.nist.gov.

National Technical Information Service

The National Technical Information Service (NTIS) operates a central clearinghouse of scientific and technical information that is useful to U.S. business and industry. NTIS collects scientific and technical information; catalogs, abstracts, indexes, and permanently archives the information; disseminates products in the forms and formats most useful to its customers; develops electronic and other new media to disseminate information; and provides information processing services to other Federal agencies, without appropriated funds. NTIS's revenue comes from these sources: the sale of technical reports to business and industry, schools and universities, State and local government offices, and the public at large; and from services to Federal agencies that help them communicate more effectively with their employees and constituents.

The NTIS collection of more than 3 million works covers a broad array of subjects and includes reports on the results of research and development and scientific studies on manufacturing processes, current events, and foreign and domestic trade; business and management studies; social, economic, and trade statistics; computer software and databases; health care reports, manuals, and data; environmental handbooks, regulations, economic studies, and applied technologies; directories to Federal laboratory and technical resources; and global competitive intelligence. The collection also includes audiovisual training materials in such areas as foreign languages, workplace safety and health, law enforcement, and fire services.

Information products in the NTIS collection are cataloged in the *NTIS Bibliographic Database,* which is available online through commercial vendors, on CD–ROM from NTIS, and for recently acquired materials, via FedWorld, NTIS online information network (Internet, www.ntis.gov).

For further information, or to order NTIS products, call the NTIS sales desk at 800–553–NTIS (6847) or visit the NTIS Web site at www.ntis.gov. For information on dissemination services for other agencies, call 703–605–6181.

For further information about the Technology Administration, contact the Office of Technology Policy, U.S. Department of Commerce, Room 4814C HCHB, Washington, DC 20230. Phone, 202–482–1575. Internet, www.ta.doc.gov.

Sources of Information

Age and Citizenship Age search and citizenship information is available from the Personal Census Search Unit, Bureau of the Census, National Processing Center, P.O. Box 1545, Jeffersonville, IN 47131. Phone, 812–218–3046.

Economic Development Information Clearinghouse The EDA will host on its Web site the Economic Development Information Clearinghouse, an online depository of information on economic development (Internet, www.doc.gov/eda).

Employment Information is available electronically through the Internet, at www.doc.gov/ohrm. Phone, 202–482–5138.

The National Oceanic and Atmospheric Administration has field employment offices at the Western Administrative Support Center, Bin C15700, 7600 Sand Point Way NE., Seattle, WA 98115 (phone, 206–526–6294); 325 Broadway, Boulder, CO 80303 (phone, 303–497–6332); 601 East Twelfth Street, Kansas City, MO 64106 (phone, 816–426–2056); and 200 World

Trade Center, Norfolk, VA 23510–1624 (phone, 757–441–6516).

Environment The National Oceanic and Atmospheric Administration conducts research and gathers data about the oceans, atmosphere, space, and Sun, and applies this knowledge to science and service in ways that touch the lives of all Americans, including warning of dangerous weather, charting seas and skies, guiding our use and protection of ocean and coastal resources, and improving our understanding and stewardship of the environment which sustains us all. For further information, contact the Office of Public and Constituent Affairs, National Oceanic and Atmospheric Administration, Room 6013, Fourteenth Street and Constitution Avenue NW., Washington, DC 20230. Phone, 202–482–6090. Fax, 202–482–3154. Internet, www.noaa.gov.

Patent and Trademark Office The Office has priority programs for advancement of examination of certain patent applications where the invention could materially enhance the quality of the environment of mankind. For further information, contact the Commissioner for Patents, Office of Petitions, Washington, DC 20231. Phone, 703–305–9282.

Inspector General Hotline The Office of Inspector General works to promote economy, efficiency, and effectiveness and to prevent and detect fraud, waste, abuse, and mismanagement in departmental programs and operations. Contact the Hotline, Inspector General, P.O. Box 612, Ben Franklin Station, Washington, DC 20044. Phone, 202–482–2495, or 800–424–5197 (toll free). TTD, 202–482–5923, or 800–854–8407 (toll free). Fax, 202–789–0522. Internet, www.oig.doc.gov. E-mail, hotline@oig.doc.gov.

Publications The titles of selected publications are printed below with the operating units responsible for their issuance. These and other publications dealing with a wide range of business, economic, environmental, scientific, and technical matters are announced in the weekly *Business Service Checklist,* which may be purchased from the Superintendent of Documents, Government Printing Office, Washington, DC 20402. Phone, 202–512–1800.

Bureau of the Census Numerous publications presenting statistical information on a wide variety of subjects are available from the Government Printing Office, including the following: *Statistical Abstract of the U.S.; Historical Statistics of the United States, Colonial Times to 1970; County and City Data Book, 1994;* and *State and Metropolitan Area Data Book, 1997–1998.*

Employment opportunities, data highlights, large data files, access tools, and other material are available on the World Wide Web. Internet, www.census.gov. E-mail, webmaster@census.gov.

Bureau of Economic Analysis The *Survey of Current Business* (Monthly Journal) is available from the Government Printing Office. Current and historical estimates, general information, and employment opportunities are available on BEA's Web site at www.bea.gov. For more information, contact the Public Information Office. Phone, 202–606–9900. E-mail, webmaster@bea.gov.

Bureau of Industry and Security The Bureau's Web site (Internet, www.bis.doc.gov) provides information for the U.S. business community, including export news, general, subject and policy fact sheets, updates to the Export Administration regulations, Bureau program information, e-FOIA information, and export seminar event schedules. Publications available on the site include the Bureau's annual report, foreign policy controls report, and international diversification and defense market assessment guides. The Government Printing Office, in conjunction with the Bureau, has created a Web site that contains an up-to-date database of the entire export administration regulations, including the commerce control list, the commerce country chart, and the denied persons list (Internet, www.access.gpo.gov/bis/index.html). The Outreach and

Educational Services Division has offices in Washington, DC (phone, 202–482–4811; fax, 202–482–2927) and on the West Coast (phone 949–660–0144, or 408–351–3378; fax, 949–660–9347, or 408–351–3355). For enforcement-related questions, contact the partnership-in-security hotline (phone, 800–424–2980).

International Trade Administration The Administration maintains a Web site, (Internet, www.trade.gov), which offers the single best place for individuals or firms seeking reports, documents, import case/regulations, texts of international agreements like NAFTA and GATT, market research, and points of contact for assistance in exporting, obtaining remedies from unfair trading practices, or receiving help with market access problems. Customers are able to review comprehensive information on how to export, search for trade information by either industry or by country, learn how to petition against unfairly priced imports, and obtain information on a number of useful international trade related products like overseas trade leads and agent distributor reports. The Web site also features e mail addresses and locations for trade contacts in Washington, overseas, in major exporting centers in the United States, and in other parts of the Federal Government.

Minority Business Development Agency Copies of *Minority Business Today* and the *BDC Directory* may be obtained by contacting the Office of Business Development. Phone, 202–482–6022. Comprehensive information about programs, policy, centers, and access to the job matching database, is available through the Internet at www.mbda.gov.

National Institute of Standards and Technology *Journal of Research; Publications of the Advanced Technology Program and Manufacturing Extension Partnership Program; Handbook of Mathematical Functions; Experimental Statistics; International System of Units (SI); Standard Reference Materials Catalog; Specifications, Tolerances, and Other Technical Requirements for Weighing and Measuring Devices Handbook;* and *Uniform Laws and Regulations Handbook* are available from the Government Printing Office.

National Technical Information Service To place an order, request the *Catalog of NTIS Products and Services.* For other general inquiries, contact the NTIS Sales Desk from 8 a.m. to 8 p.m. (eastern standard time) (phone, 800–553–NTIS; fax, 703–321–8547; TDD, 703–605–6043; Internet, www.ntis.gov).

To inquire about NTIS information services for other Federal agencies, call 703–605–6540.

National Oceanic and Atmospheric Administration The Administration provides technical memoranda, technical reports, monographs, nautical and aeronautical charts, coastal zone maps, data tapes, and a wide variety of raw and processed environmental data. Information on NOAA products is available through the Internet at www.noaa.gov. Contact the Office of Public and Constituent Affairs, Fourteenth Street and Constitution Avenue NW., Washington, DC 20230. Phone, 202–482–6090. Fax, 202–482–3154.

National Telecommunications and Information Administration Several hundred Technical Reports, Technical Memoranda, Special Publications, Contractor Reports, and other information products have been published by NTIA or its predecessor agency since 1970. The publications are available from the National Telecommunications and Information Administration, Department of Commerce, Washington, DC 20230 (phone, 202–482–1551); or the National Telecommunications and Information Administration, Institute for Telecommunication Sciences, Department of Commerce, Boulder, CO 80302 (phone, 303–497–3572). Electronic information can be obtained from the NTIA homepage (Internet, www.ntia.doc.gov).

Patent and Trademark Office *General Information Concerning Patents, Basic Facts About Trademarks, Official Gazette of the United States Patent and Trademark Office,* and *Attorneys and*

Agents Registered To Practice Before the U.S. Patent and Trademark Office are available from the Government Printing Office. Publications can be accessed through the Internet at www.uspto.gov. File transfer protocol, ftp.uspto.gov. Phone, 703–308–HELP, or 800–PTO–9199.

Small Business The Office of Small and Disadvantaged Business Utilization (OSDBU) was established under the authority of Public Law 95–507. It is responsible for promoting the use of small, small-disadvantaged, (8a), HUBZone, veteran-owned, service-disabled-veteran-owned, and women-owned businesses. It also assists such businesses in obtaining contracts and subcontracts with the Department of Commerce and its prime contractors. The goals of OSDBU are to institutionalize the use of small businesses and to fully integrate them into the Department of Commerce's competitive base of contractors. Phone, 202–482–1472. Internet, www.doc.gov/osdbu.

For further information concerning the Department of Commerce, contact the Office of Public Affairs, Department of Commerce, Fourteenth Street and Constitution Avenue NW., Room 5040, Washington, DC 20230. Phone, 202–482–3263. Internet, www.doc.gov.

DEPARTMENT OF DEFENSE

Office of the Secretary, The Pentagon, Washington, DC 20301–1155
Phone, 703–545–6700. Internet, www.defenselink.mil.

SECRETARY OF DEFENSE	DONALD H. RUMSFELD
Deputy Secretary of Defense	GORDON ENGLAND
The Special Assistant	PAUL W. BUTLER
Special Assistant to the Deputy Secretary of Defense	DAVE PATTERSON
Special Assistant to the Secretary of Defense for White House Liaison	JIM O'BEIRNE
Special Assistant to the Secretary and Deputy Secretary of Defense for Protocol	MARY CLAIRE MURPHY
Executive Secretary	CAPT. WILLIAM P. MARRIOTT, USN
Under Secretary of Defense for Acquisition, Technology, and Logistics	KENNETH J. KRIEG
Principal Deputy Under Secretary of Defense for Acquisition, Technology, and Logistics	MICHAEL W. WYNNE
Deputy Under Secretary of Defense (Acquisition and Technology)	MICHAEL W. WYNNE
Deputy Under Secretary of Defense (Logistics and Materiel Readiness)	(VACANCY)
Director, Defense Research and Engineering	RONALD M. SEGA
Assistant to the Secretary of Defense for Nuclear and Chemical and Biological (NCB) Defense Programs	DALE E. KLEIN
Deputy Under Secretary of Defense (Installations and Environment)	PHILLIP GRONE
Deputy Under Secretary of Defense (Advanced Systems and Concepts)	SUE C. PAYTON
Deputy Under Secretary of Defense (Industrial Policy)	SUZANNE D. PATRICK
Deputy Under Secretary of Defense (International Technology Security)	(VACANCY)
Deputy Under Secretary of Defense (Laboratory and Basic Sciences)	(VACANCY)
Deputy Under Secretary of Defense (Science and Technology)	CHARLES HOLLAND
Director, Small and Disadvantaged Business Utilization	FRANK M. RAMOS
Under Secretary of Defense for Policy	DOUGLAS J. FEITH
Principal Deputy Under Secretary of Defense for Policy	RYAN HENRY
Assistant Secretary of Defense (International Security Affairs)	PETER W. RODMAN
Assistant Secretary of Defense (Special Operations and Low-Intensity Conflict)	THOMAS W. O'CONNELL

Assistant Secretary of Defense (Homeland Defense)	PAUL F. MCHALE
Assistant Secretary of Defense (International Security Policy)	(VACANCY)
Deputy Under Secretary of Defense (Technology Security Policy/Counter Proliferation)	LISA BRONSON
Deputy Under Secretary of Defense (Near East and South Asian Affairs)	(VACANCY)
Deputy Under Secretary of Defense (Asian and Pacific Affairs)	RICHARD P. LAWLESS, JR.
Under Secretary of Defense for Personnel and Readiness/Chief Human Capital Officer	DAVID S.C. CHU
Principal Deputy Under Secretary of Defense for Personnel and Readiness	CHARLES S. ABELL
Assistant Secretary of Defense (Health Affairs)	WILLIAM WINKENWERDER
Assistant Secretary of Defense (Reserve Affairs)	THOMAS F. HALL
Deputy Under Secretary of Defense (Program Integration)	JEANNE FITES
Deputy Under Secretary of Defense (Readiness)	PAUL W. MAYBERRY
Deputy Under Secretary of Defense (Civilian Personnel Policy)	(VACANCY)
Deputy Under Secretary of Defense (Military Personnel Policy)	(VACANCY)
Deputy Under Secretary of Defense (Military Community and Family Policy)	JOHN M. MOLINO
Deputy Under Secretary of Defense (Plans)	GAIL H. MCGINN
Deputy Under Secretary of Defense (Equal Opportunity)	(VACANCY)
Under Secretary of Defense (Comptroller)/Chief Financial Officer	TINA W. JONAS
Principal Deputy Under Secretary (Comptroller)	ROBERT J. HENKE
Deputy Chief Financial Officer	TERRI A. MCKAY
Deputy Under Secretary of Defense (Management Reform)	ROBERT J. HENKE
Deputy Under Secretary of Defense (Resource Planning and Management)	DAVID L. NORQUIST
Deputy Under Secretary of Defense (Financial Management)	THOMAS B. MODLY
Under Secretary of Defense (Intelligence)	STEPHEN CAMBONE
Deputy Under Secretary of Defense (Counterintelligence and Security)	CAROL HAAVE
Deputy Under Secretary of Defense (Intelligence and Warfighting)	LT. GEN. WILLIAM G. BOYKIN, USA
Deputy Under Secretary of Defense (Policy, Requirements, and Resources)	LETITIA LONG
Deputy Under Secretary of Defense (Preparation and Warning)	THOMAS BEHLING
Assistant Secretary of Defense (Networks and Information Integration)/Chief Information Officer	(VACANCY)

Assistant Secretary of Defense (Legislative Affairs)	(VACANCY)
Assistant Secretary of Defense (Public Affairs)	J. DORRANCE SMITH
General Counsel	WILLIAM J. HAYNES II
Director, Operational Test and Evaluation	(VACANCY)
Inspector General	JOSEPH E. SCHMITZ
Assistant to the Secretary of Defense (Intelligence Oversight)	(VACANCY)
Director of Administration and Management	MICHAEL B. DONLEY
Director, Net Assessment	ANDREW W. MARSHALL
Director, Force Transformation	(VACANCY)
Director, Program Analysis and Evaluation	(VACANCY)

Joint Chiefs of Staff

Chairman	GEN. PETER PACE, USMC
Vice Chairman	GEN. ADM. EDMUND P. GIAMBASTIANI, JR., USN
Chief of Staff, Army	GEN. PETER J. SCHOOMAKER, USA
Chief of Naval Operations	ADM. MICHAEL G. MULLEN, USN
Chief of Staff, Air Force	GEN. T. MICHAEL MOSELEY, USAF
Commandant, Marine Corps	GEN. MICHAEL W. HAGEE, USMC

Joint Staff

Director	LT. GEN. WALTER L. SHARP, USA
Vice Director	MAJ. GEN. SCOTT S. CUSTER, USAF
Director for Manpower and Personnel—J–1	REAR ADM. DONNA L. CRISP, USN
Director, Intelligence—J–2	REAR ADM. DAVID J. DORSETT, USN
Director for Operations—J–3	LT. GEN. JAMES T. CONWAY, USMC
Director for Logistics—J–4	LT. GEN. CLAUDE V. CHRISTIANSON, USA
Director for Strategic Plans and Policy—J–5	LT. GEN. VICTOR E. RENUART, JR., USA
Director for Command, Control, Communications, and Computer Systems—J–6	LT. GEN. ROBERT M. SHEA, USMC
Director for Operational Plans and Interoperability—J–7	REAR ADM. RICHARD J. MAUDLIN, USN
Director for Force Structure, Resources, and Assessment—J–8	VICE ADM. EVAN M. CHANIK, USN

[For the Department of Defense statement of organization, see the *Code of Federal Regulations,* Title 32, Chapter I, Subchapter R]

The Department of Defense is responsible for providing the military forces needed to deter war and protect the security of our country.

The major elements of these forces are the Army, Navy, Marine Corps, and Air Force, consisting of about 1.4 million men and women on active duty. They are backed, in case of emergency, by the 1.3 million members of the Reserve and National Guard. In addition, there are about 700,000 civilian employees in the Defense Department.

Under the President, who is also Commander in Chief, the Secretary of Defense exercises authority, direction, and control over the Department, which includes the separately organized military departments of Army, Navy, and Air Force, the Joint Chiefs of Staff providing military advice, the combatant commands, and defense agencies and field activities established for specific purposes.

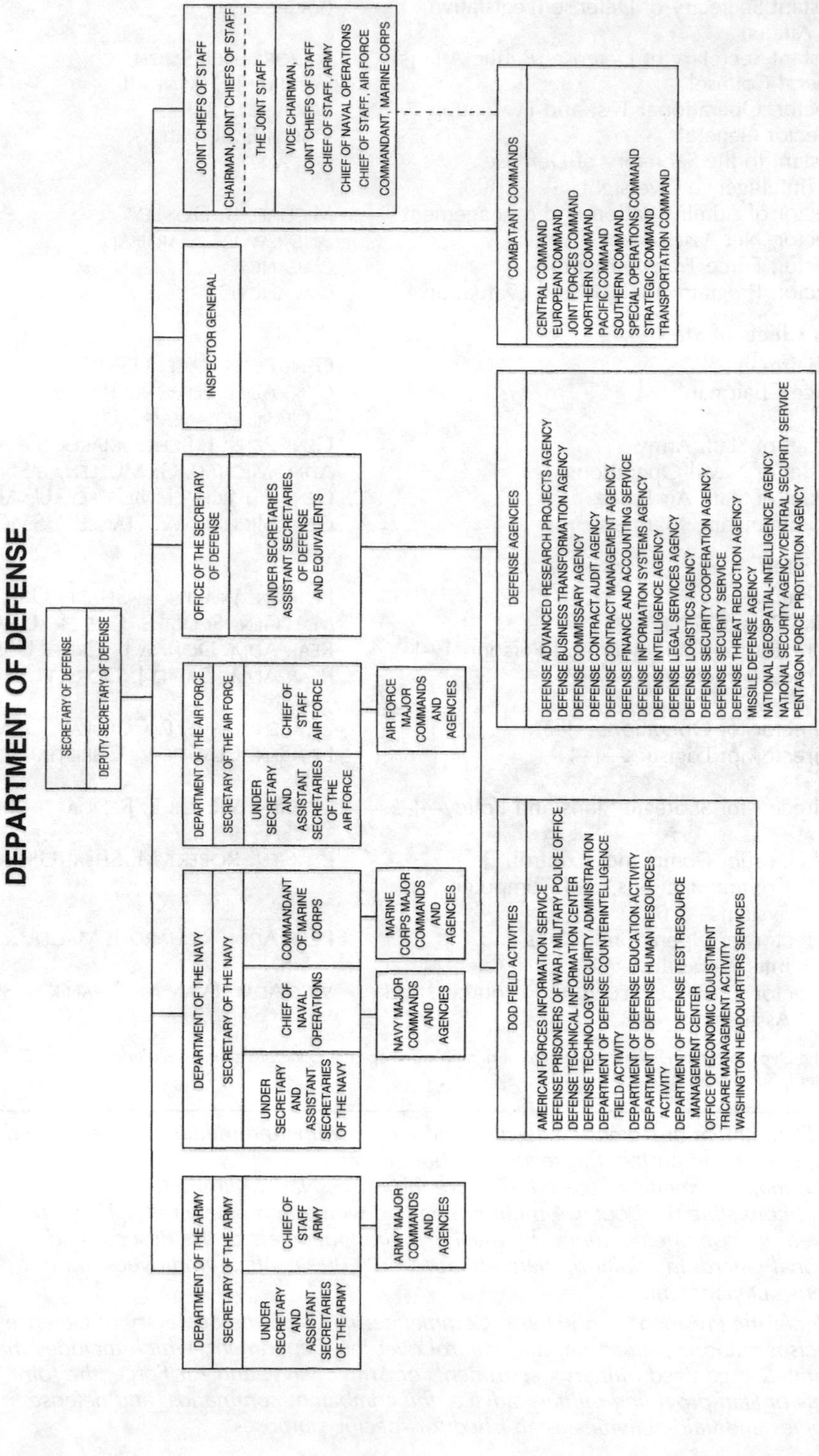
DEPARTMENT OF DEFENSE
SECRETARY OF DEFENSE
DEPUTY SECRETARY OF DEFENSE
JOINT CHIEFS OF STAFF
CHAIRMAN, JOINT CHIEFS OF STAFF
THE JOINT STAFF
VICE CHAIRMAN, JOINT CHIEFS OF STAFF
CHIEF OF STAFF, ARMY
CHIEF OF NAVAL OPERATIONS
CHIEF OF STAFF, AIR FORCE
COMMANDANT, MARINE CORPS
INSPECTOR GENERAL
OFFICE OF THE SECRETARY OF DEFENSE
UNDER SECRETARIES ASSISTANT SECRETARIES OF DEFENSE AND EQUIVALENTS
DEPARTMENT OF THE AIR FORCE
SECRETARY OF THE AIR FORCE
UNDER SECRETARY AND ASSISTANT SECRETARIES OF THE AIR FORCE
CHIEF OF STAFF AIR FORCE
AIR FORCE MAJOR COMMANDS AND AGENCIES
DEPARTMENT OF THE NAVY
SECRETARY OF THE NAVY
UNDER SECRETARY AND ASSISTANT SECRETARIES OF THE NAVY
CHIEF OF NAVAL OPERATIONS
COMMANDANT OF MARINE CORPS
NAVY MAJOR COMMANDS AND AGENCIES
MARINE CORPS MAJOR COMMANDS AND AGENCIES
DEPARTMENT OF THE ARMY
SECRETARY OF THE ARMY
UNDER SECRETARY AND ASSISTANT SECRETARIES OF THE ARMY
CHIEF OF STAFF ARMY
ARMY MAJOR COMMANDS AND AGENCIES
COMBATANT COMMANDS
CENTRAL COMMAND
EUROPEAN COMMAND
JOINT FORCES COMMAND
NORTHERN COMMAND
PACIFIC COMMAND
SOUTHERN COMMAND
SPECIAL OPERATIONS COMMAND
STRATEGIC COMMAND
TRANSPORTATION COMMAND
DEFENSE AGENCIES
DEFENSE ADVANCED RESEARCH PROJECTS AGENCY
DEFENSE BUSINESS TRANSFORMATION AGENCY
DEFENSE COMMISSARY AGENCY
DEFENSE CONTRACT AUDIT AGENCY
DEFENSE CONTRACT MANAGEMENT AGENCY
DEFENSE FINANCE AND ACCOUNTING SERVICE
DEFENSE INFORMATION SYSTEMS AGENCY
DEFENSE INTELLIGENCE AGENCY
DEFENSE LEGAL SERVICES AGENCY
DEFENSE LOGISTICS AGENCY
DEFENSE SECURITY COOPERATION AGENCY
DEFENSE SECURITY SERVICE
DEFENSE THREAT REDUCTION AGENCY
MISSILE DEFENSE AGENCY
NATIONAL GEOSPATIAL-INTELLIGENCE AGENCY
NATIONAL SECURITY AGENCY/CENTRAL SECURITY SERVICE
PENTAGON FORCE PROTECTION AGENCY
DOD FIELD ACTIVITIES
AMERICAN FORCES INFORMATION SERVICE
DEFENSE PRISONERS OF WAR / MILITARY POLICE OFFICE
DEFENSE TECHNICAL INFORMATION CENTER
DEFENSE TECHNOLOGY SECURITY ADMINISTRATION
DEPARTMENT OF DEFENSE COUNTERINTELLIGENCE FIELD ACTIVITY
DEPARTMENT OF DEFENSE EDUCATION ACTIVITY
DEPARTMENT OF DEFENSE HUMAN RESOURCES ACTIVITY
DEPARTMENT OF DEFENSE TEST RESOURCE MANAGEMENT CENTER
OFFICE OF ECONOMIC ADJUSTMENT
TRICARE MANAGEMENT ACTIVITY
WASHINGTON HEADQUARTERS SERVICES

The National Security Act Amendments of 1949 redesignated the National Military Establishment as the Department of Defense and established it as an executive department (10 U.S.C. 111), headed by the Secretary of Defense.

Structure

The Department of Defense is composed of the Office of the Secretary of Defense; the military departments and the military services within those departments; the Chairman of the Joint Chiefs of Staff and the Joint Staff; the combatant commands; the defense agencies; DOD field activities; and such other offices, agencies, activities, and commands as may be established or designated by law, or by the President or the Secretary of Defense.

Each military department is separately organized under its own Secretary and functions under the authority, direction, and control of the Secretary of Defense. The Secretary of each military department is responsible to the Secretary of Defense for the operation and efficiency of his department. Orders to the military departments are issued through the Secretaries of these departments or their designees, by the Secretary of Defense, or under authority specifically delegated in writing by the Secretary of Defense or provided by law.

The commanders of the combatant commands are responsible to the President and the Secretary of Defense for accomplishing the military missions assigned to them and exercising command authority over forces assigned to them. The operational chain of command runs from the President to the Secretary of Defense to the commanders of the combatant commands. The Chairman of the Joint Chiefs of Staff functions within the chain of command by transmitting the orders of the President or the Secretary of Defense to the commanders of the combatant commands.

Office of the Secretary of Defense

Secretary of Defense The Secretary of Defense is the principal defense policy adviser to the President and is responsible for the formulation of general defense policy and policy related to DOD, and for the execution of approved policy. Under the direction of the President, the Secretary exercises authority, direction, and control over the Department of Defense.

Acquisition, Technology, and Logistics The Under Secretary of Defense for Acquisition, Technology, and Logistics is the principal staff assistant and adviser to the Secretary of Defense for all matters relating to the DOD Acquisition System; research and development; modeling and simulation; systems engineering; advanced technology; developmental test and evaluation; production; systems integration; logistics; installation management; military construction; procurement; environment, safety, and occupational health management; utilities and energy management; business management modernization; document services; and nuclear, chemical, and biological defense programs.

Intelligence The Under Secretary of Defense for Intelligence is the principal staff assistant and adviser to the Secretary and Deputy Secretary of Defense for intelligence, intelligence-related matters, counterintelligence, and security. The Under Secretary of Defense for Intelligence supervises all intelligence and intelligence-related affairs of DOD.

Networks and Information Integration The Assistant Secretary of Defense (Networks and Information Integration) is the principal staff assistant and adviser to the Secretary and Deputy Secretary of Defense for achieving and maintaining information superiority in support of DOD missions, while exploiting or denying an adversary's ability to do the same. The Assistant Secretary of Defense (NII) also serves as the Chief Information Officer.

Personnel and Readiness The Under Secretary of Defense for Personnel and Readiness is the principal staff assistant and adviser to the Secretary of Defense for policy matters relating to the structure and readiness of the total force. Functional areas include readiness; civilian and military personnel policies, programs, and systems; civilian and military equal opportunity programs; health policies, programs, and activities; Reserve component programs, policies, and activities; family policy, dependents' education, and personnel support programs; mobilization planning and requirements; language capabilities and programs; and the Federal Voting Assistance Program. The Under Secretary of Defense (Personnel and Readiness) also serves as the Chief Human Capital Officer.

Policy The Under Secretary of Defense for Policy is the principal staff assistant and adviser to the Secretary of Defense for policy matters relating to overall international security policy and political-military affairs and represents the Department at the National Security Council and other external agencies regarding national security policy. Functional areas include homeland defense; NATO affairs; foreign military sales; arms limitation agreements; international trade and technology security; regional security affairs; special operations and low-intensity conflict; stability operations; integration of departmental plans and policies with overall national security objectives; drug control policy, requirements, priorities, systems, resources, and programs; and issuance of policy guidance affecting departmental programs.

Additional Staff In addition, the Secretary and Deputy Secretary of Defense are assisted by a special staff of assistants, including the Assistant Secretary of Defense for Legislative Affairs; the General Counsel; the Inspector General; the Assistant Secretary of Defense for Public Affairs; the Assistant to the Secretary of Defense (Intelligence Oversight); the Director of Administration and Management; the Under Secretary of Defense (Comptroller)/Chief Financial Officer; the Director of Operational Test and Evaluation; Director, Force Transformation; Director, Net Assessment; Director, Program Analysis and Evaluation; and such other officers as the Secretary of Defense establishes to assist him in carrying out his duties and responsibilities.

Joint Chiefs of Staff

Joint Chiefs of Staff

The Joint Chiefs of Staff consist of the Chairman; the Vice Chairman; the Chief of Staff of the Army; the Chief of Naval Operations; the Chief of Staff of the Air Force; and the Commandant of the Marine Corps. The Chairman of the Joint Chiefs of Staff is the principal military adviser to the President, the National Security Council, and the Secretary of Defense. The other members of the Joint Chiefs of Staff are military advisers who may provide additional information upon request from the President, the National Security Council, or the Secretary of Defense. They may also submit their advice when it does not agree with that of the Chairman. Subject to the authority of the President and the Secretary of Defense, the Chairman of the Joint Chiefs of Staff is responsible for:

—assisting the President and the Secretary of Defense in providing for the strategic direction and planning of the Armed Forces;

—allocating resources to fulfill strategic plans;

—making recommendations for the assignment of responsibilities within the Armed Forces in accordance with and in support of those logistic and mobility plans;

—comparing the capabilities of American and allied Armed Forces with those of potential adversaries;

—preparing and reviewing contingency plans that conform to policy guidance from the President and the Secretary of Defense;

—preparing joint logistic and mobility plans to support contingency plans; and

—recommending assignment of logistic and mobility responsibilities to the Armed Forces to fulfill logistic and mobility plans.

The Chairman, while so serving, holds the grade of general or admiral and outranks all other officers of the Armed Forces.

The Vice Chairman of the Joint Chiefs performs duties assigned by the Chairman, with the approval of the Secretary of Defense. The Vice Chairman acts as Chairman when there is a vacancy in the office of the Chairman, or in the absence or disability of the Chairman. The Vice Chairman, while so serving, holds the grade of general or admiral and outranks all other officers of the Armed Forces except the Chairman of the Joint Chiefs of Staff.

Joint Staff

The Joint Staff, under the Chairman of the Joint Chiefs of Staff, assists the Chairman and the other members of the Joint Chiefs of Staff in carrying out their responsibilities.

The Joint Staff is headed by a Director who is selected by the Chairman in consultation with the other members of the Joint Chiefs of Staff and with the approval of the Secretary of Defense. Officers assigned to serve on the Joint Staff are selected by the Chairman in approximate equal numbers from the Army, Navy, Marine Corps, and Air Force.

Combatant Commands

The combatant commands are military commands with broad continuing missions maintaining the security and defense of the United States against attack; supporting and advancing the national policies and interests of the United States and discharging U.S. military responsibilities in their assigned areas; and preparing plans, conducting operations, and coordinating activities of the forces assigned to them in accordance with the directives of higher authority. The operational chain of command runs from the President to the Secretary of Defense to the commanders of the combatant commands. The Chairman of the Joint Chiefs of Staff serves as the spokesman for the commanders of the combatant commands, especially on the administrative requirements of their commands.

Combatant Commands

Command	Address	Commander
Central	USCENTCOM, 7115 S. Boundary Blvd., MacDill AFB, FL 33621–5101.	Gen. John P. Abizaid, USA
European	USEUCOM, APO AE 09705	Gen. James L. Jones, Jr., USMC
Joint Forces	USJFCOM, Suite 200, 1562 Mitscher Ave., Norfolk, VA 23551–2488.	Gen. Lance Smith, USAF
Pacific	USPACCOM, Box 64028, Camp H.M. Smith, HI 96861–4028.	Adm. William J. Fallon, USN
Southern	USSOUTHCOM, 3511 NW. 91st Ave., Miami, FL 33172	Gen. Bantz J. Craddock, USA
Northern	USNORTHCOM, Suite 116, 250 S. Peterson Blvd., Peterson AFB, CO 80914–3010.	Adm. Timothy J. Keating, USN
Special Operations	USSOCOM, 7701 Tampa Point Blvd., MacDill AFB, FL 33621–5323.	Gen. Bryan D. Brown, USAF
Strategic	USSTRATCOM, Suite 2A1, 901 SAC Blvd., Offutt AFB, NE 68113–6000.	Gen. James E. Cartwright, USMC
Transportation	USTRANSCOM, Rm. 339, 508 Scott Dr., Scott AFB, IL 62225–5357.	Gen. Norton A. Scwartz, USAF

Field Activities

American Forces Information Service The American Forces Information Service (AFIS) provides internal communications program support to U.S. military forces worldwide to promote and sustain military unit and individual readiness, situational awareness, quality of life, and morale; trains public affairs, broadcast, and visual information professionals for DOD; and provides military commanders and combat forces with news, features, photography, videography, news clippings, and other internal command information products and services. AFIS provides internal communications policy guidance and oversight for departmental periodicals and pamphlets, military command newspapers, the broadcast elements of the military departments, DOD audiovisual matters, and public affairs and visual information training.

For further information, contact the American Forces Information Service, Department of Defense, Suite 300, 601 North Fairfax Street, Alexandria, VA 22314–2007. Phone, 703–428–1200. Internet, www.defenselink.mil/afis.

Counterintelligence The DOD Counterintelligence Field Activity was established in 2002 to build a Defense counterintelligence (CI) system that is informed by national goals and objectives and supports the protection of DOD personnel and critical assets from foreign intelligence services, foreign terrorists, and other clandestine or covert threats. The desired end is a transformed Defense CI system which integrates and synchronizes the counterintelligence activities of the Military Departments, Defense Agencies, Joint Staff, and Combatant Commands.

For further information, contact the Department of Defense Counterintelligence Field Activity, Crystal Square 5, Suite 1200, 1755 Jefferson Davis Highway, Arlington, VA 22202–3537. Phone, 703–699–7799.

Defense Technical Information Center The Defense Technical Information Center (DTIC) is a Field Activity in the office of the Under Secretary of Defense (Acquisition, Technology, and Logistics), operating under the authority, direction, and control of the Director, Defense Research and Engineering. DTIC is the premier provider of DOD scientific and technical information and supports DOD research, development and engineering, and studies programs. DTIC's collections include technical reports, summaries of research in progress, defense technology transfer agreements, and DOD planning documents.

For further information, contact the Defense Technical Information Center, Fort Belvoir, VA 22060–6218. Phone, 800–225–3842. Internet, www.dtic.mil/dtic/index.html.

Defense Technology Security Administration The Defense Technology Security Administration (DTSA) is the central DOD point of contact for development and implementation of technology security policies governing defense articles and services and dual-use commodities. DTSA administers the development and implementation of DOD technology security policies on international transfers of defense-related goods, services, and technologies to ensure that critical U.S. military technological advantages are preserved; transfers that could prove detrimental to U.S. security interests are controlled and limited; proliferation of weapons of mass destruction and their means of delivery is prevented; diversion of defense-related goods to terrorists is prevented; legitimate defense cooperation with foreign friends and allies is supported; and the health of the defense industrial base is assured.

For further information, contact the Deputy Under Secretary of Defense for Technology Security Policy and National Disclosure Policy, Defense Pentagon, Washington, DC 20301–2900. Phone, 703–325–3294. Fax, 703–325–6467. Internet, www.defenselink.mil/policy/sections/policy_offices/dtsa/index.html

Education The Department of Defense Education Activity (DODEA) was established in 1992. It consists of two subordinate organizational entities: the Department of Defense Dependents Schools (DODDS) and the Department of Defense Domestic Dependent Elementary and Secondary Schools (DDESS). DODEA formulates, develops, and implements policies, technical guidance, and standards for the effective management of Defense dependents education activities and programs. It also plans, directs, coordinates, and manages the education programs for eligible dependents of U.S. military and civilian personnel stationed overseas and stateside; evaluates the programmatic and operational policies and procedures for DODDS and DDESS; and provides education activity representation at meetings and deliberations of educational panels and advisory groups.

For further information, contact the Department of Defense Education Activity, 4040 North Fairfax Drive, Arlington, VA 22203–1635. Phone, 703–588–3200. Internet, www.dodea.edu.

Human Resources and Manpower The Department of Defense Human Resources Activity (DODHRA) was established to support departmental and congressionally mandated programs in the benefits, readiness, and force protection areas. DODHRA collects, maintains, and analyzes manpower, personnel, training, and financial data; establishes and maintains data and systems used to determine entitlements to DOD benefits; and manages civilian personnel administrative services for the Department. It performs long-term programmatic research and analysis to improve DOD personnel security systems, administers the Federal responsibilities of the Uniformed and Overseas Citizens Absentee Voting Act, advises the DOD on matters and policies relating to women in the Armed Forces, and provides program and policy support on sexual assault issues and language capabilities.

For further information, contact the Department of Defense Human Resources Activity-Headquarters, Suite 200, 4040 Fairfax Drive, Arlington, VA 22203–1613. Phone, 703–696–1036. Internet, www.dhra.osd.mil.

Health Care The TRICARE Management Activity (TMA) was formed in 1998 from the consolidation of the TRICARE Support Office (formerly Civilian Health and Medical Program of the Uniformed Services (CHAMPUS) headquarters), the Defense Medical Programs Activity, and the integration of health management program functions formerly located in the Office of the Assistant Secretary of Defense for Health Affairs. The mission of TMA is to manage TRICARE; manage the Defense Health Program appropriation; provide operational direction and support to the Uniformed Services in the management and administration of the TRICARE program; and administer CHAMPUS.

For further information, contact the TRICARE Management Activity, Suite 810, Skyline 5, 5111 Leesburg Pike, Falls Church, VA 22041–3206. Phone, 703–681–1730. Fax, 703–681–3665. Internet, www.tricare.osd.mil.

Test Resource Management The Defense Test Resource Management Center is a DOD field activity under the authority, direction, and control of the Under Secretary of Defense for Acquisition, Technology, and Logistics. The Center plans for and assesses the adequacy of the major range and test facility base to provide adequate testing in support of development, acquisition, fielding, and sustainment of defense systems; maintains the test and evaluation resources strategic plan; administers the central test and evaluation investment program and the DOD test and evaluation science and technology program; and maintains awareness of other test and evaluation facilities and resources, within and outside the DOD, and their impact on DOD requirements.

Prisoners of War and Missing Personnel The Defense Prisoner of War/Missing Personnel Office (DPMO) was established in 1993 to provide centralized management of prisoner of war/missing personnel affairs within the DOD. DPMO's primary responsibilities include: leadership for and policy oversight over all efforts to account for Americans still missing from past conflicts and the recovery of and accounting for those who may become isolated in hostile territory in future conflicts. The Office also provides administrative and logistical support to the U.S.-Russia Joint Commission on POW/MIAs; conducts research and analysis to help resolve cases of those unaccounted for; examines DOD documents for possible public disclosure; and, through periodic consultations and other appropriate measures, maintains viable channels of communications on POW/MIA matters between DOD and Congress, the families of the missing, and the American public.

For further information, contact the Defense Prisoner of War/Missing Personnel Office, 2400 Defense Pentagon, Washington, DC 20301–2400. Phone, 703–699–1160. Fax, 703–602–4375. Internet, www.dtic.mil/dpmo.

Economic Adjustment The Office of Economic Adjustment is a DOD field activity under the authority, direction, and control of the Under Secretary of Defense for Acquisition, Technology, and Logistics. The Office is responsible for planning and managing the Department's defense economic adjustment programs and for assisting Federal, State, and local officials in cooperative efforts to alleviate any serious social and economic side effects resulting from major departmental realignment or other actions.

For further information, contact the Office of Economic Adjustment, Department of Defense, Suite 200, 400 Army Navy Drive, Arlington, VA 22202–4704. Phone, 703–604–6020.

Washington Headquarters Washington Headquarters Services (WHS), established as a DOD Field Activity on October 1, 1977, is under the authority, direction, and control of the Director of Administration and Management. WHS provides a wide range of administrative and operational services to the Office of the Secretary of Defense, specified DOD components, selected other Federal Government activities, and the general public. Such support includes contracting and procurement; Defense facilities management; Pentagon renovation and construction; directives and records management; financial management; human resource services for executive, political, military, and civilian personnel; personnel security services; advisory boards and commissions; legal services and advice; IT and data systems support; enterprise IT infrastructure services; and planning and evaluation functions.

For further information, contact the Administration and Program Support Directorate, Washington Headquarters Services, 1155 Defense Pentagon, Washington, DC 20301–1155. Phone, 703–601–2553. Internet, www.whs.pentagon.mil.

Sources of Information

Audiovisual Products Certain Department of Defense productions on film and videotapes, CD–ROMs, and other audiovisual products such as stock footage and still photographs are available to the public. An up-to-date, full-text searchable listing of the Department's inventory of film, videotape, and interactive multimedia titles is available on the Internet. For information and obtaining productions, contact the following sources:

—For newer productions, contact the National Technical Information Service, 5285 Port Royal Road, Springfield, VA 22161 (phone, 800–553–6847 or 703–605–6000), or the defense visual information site (Internet, dodimagery.afis.osd.mil, and select "Central DoD Production Databases@DAVIS/DITIS").

—For older productions, contact the Motion Picture, Sound, and Video Branch (NWDNM), National Archives and Records Administration, 8601 Adelphi Road, College Park, MD 20740–6001. Phone, 301–713–7050. For general inquiries, phone 800–234–8861 or 301–713–6800 or e-mail Inquiry@nara.gov.

—For stock footage, still photographs, and CD–ROMs, contact the Defense Visual Information Center, 23755 Z Street, Riverside, CA 92518–2070. Phone, 909–413–2515. Internet, www.dodimagery.afis.osd.mil, and select ''Records Center Servers@DVIC'').

There is usually a fee charged for the Department's audiovisual and multimedia products.

Contracts and Small Business Activities Contact the Director, Small and Disadvantaged Business Utilization, Office of the Secretary of Defense, 3061 Defense Pentagon, Washington, DC 20301–3061. Phone, 703–588–8631.

DOD Directives and Instructions Contact the Executive Services and Communications Directorate, Washington Headquarters Services, 1155 Defense Pentagon, Washington, DC 20301–1155. Phone, 703–601–4722.

Electronic Access Information about the following offices is available as listed below:

Office of the Secretary of Defense: www.defenselink.mil.
Joint Chiefs of Staff: www.dtic.mil/jcs.
Central Command: www.centcom.mil.
Combatant commands: www.defenselink.mil/pubs/almanac/unified.html.
European Command: www.eucom.mil.
Joint Forces Command: www.jfcom.mil.
Pacific Command: www.pacom.mil.
Northern Command: www.northcom.mil.
Southern Command: www.southcom.mil.
Special Operations Command: www.socom.mil.
Strategic Command: www.stratcom.mil.
Transportation Command: www.transcom.mil.

Employment Positions are filled by a variety of sources. Positions filled competitively are advertised at https://storm.psd.whs.mil/cgi-bin/apply.pl. Assistance in applying for positions is available from the Employment Information Center at 866–205–4975 or by writing to: Human Resources Directorate, Washington Headquarters Services, 1155 Defense Pentagon, Washington, DC 20301–1155.

Speakers Civilian and military officials from the U.S. Department of Defense are available to speak to numerous public and private sector groups interested in a variety of defense-related topics, including the global war on terrorism. Requests for speakers should be addressed to the Director for Community Relations and Public Liaison, 1400 Defense Pentagon, Room 2C546, Washington, DC 20310–1400, or by calling 703–695–2733.

Pentagon Tours Information on guided tours of the Pentagon may be obtained by writing to the Director, Pentagon Tours, 1400 Defense Pentagon, Room 2C546, Washington, DC 20310–1400 or calling 703–695–7778 or by sending an e-mail to tourschd.pa@osd.mil. Internet, www.defenselink.mil/pubs/pentagon.

Defend America Web Site The Defend America Web site, which can be found at http://defendamerica.mil, is produced by the Department of Defense and devoted to educating people on the global war on terrorism. This site features up-to-date news, photographs, briefings and more information from authoritative Defense Department sources.

For further information concerning the Department of Defense, contact the Director, Directorate for Public Inquiry and Analysis, Office of the Assistant Secretary of Defense for Public Affairs, 1400 Defense Pentagon, Washington, DC 20301–1400. Phone, 703–428–0711. Internet, www.defenselink.mil and www.defendamerica.mil.

DEPARTMENT OF THE AIR FORCE

1690 Air Force Pentagon, Washington, DC 20330–1670
Phone, 703–697–6061. Internet, www.af.mil.

SECRETARY OF THE AIR FORCE	MICHAEL W. WYNNE
Under Secretary of the Air Force	RONALD M. SEGA
Deputy Under Secretary (International Affairs)	BRUCE S. LEMKIN
Assistant Secretary (Manpower, Reserve Affairs, Installations, and Environment)	MICHAEL DOMINGUEZ
Assistant Secretary (Installations, Environment and Logistics)	NELSON F. GIBBS
Assistant Secretary (Financial Management and Comptroller of the Air Force)	JOHN G. VONGLIS
Assistant Secretary (Acquisition)	(VACANCY)
Assistant Secretary (Warfighting Integration and Chief Information Officer)	LT. GEN. MICHAEL W. PETERSON
General Counsel	MARY L. WALKER
Inspector General of the Air Force	LT. GEN. RONALD F. SAMS
Administrative Assistant to the Secretary	WILLIAM A. DAVIDSON
Auditor General of the Air Force	ROBERT E. DAWES
Director, Legislative Liaison	MAJ. GEN. DANIEL J. DARNELL
Director, Public Affairs	COL. MICHELLE D. JOHNSON
Chief of Staff	GEN. T. MICHAEL MOSELEY
Vice Chief of Staff	JOHN D.W. CORLEY
Assistant Vice Chief of Staff	LT. GEN. ARTHUR J. LICHTE
Deputy Chief of Staff (Plans and Programs)	LT. GEN. STEPHEN G. WOOD
Deputy Chief of Staff (Personnel)	LT. GEN. ROGER A. BRADY
Deputy Chief of Staff (Air and Space Operations)	LT. GEN. RONALD E. KEYS
Deputy Chief of Staff (Warfighting Integration)	LT. GEN. WILLIAM T. HOBBINS
Deputy Chief of Staff (Installations and Logistics)	LT. GEN. DONALD J. WETEKAM
Chief Master Sergeant of the Air Force	CMSGT. GERALD R. MURRAY
Chief of Safety	MAJ. GEN. MAURICE L. MCFANN
Director of Test and Evaluation	JOHN T. MANCLARK
Chairman, USAF Scientific Advisory Board	MARK J. LEWIS
Air Force Historian	CLARENCE R. ANDEREGG
Chief Scientist of the Air Force	ALEXANDER H. LEVIS
Chief, Air Force Reserve	LT. GEN. JOHN A. BRADLEY
Director, National Guard Bureau	LT. GEN. DANIEL JAMES III
Surgeon General of the Air Force	LT. GEN. GEORGE PEACH TAYLOR, JR.
Chief of the Chaplain Service	MAJ. GEN. CHARLES C. BALDWIN
Judge Advocate General	MAJ. GEN. JACK L. RIVES

The Department of the Air Force is responsible for defending the United States through control and exploitation of air and space.

The Department of the Air Force (USAF) was established as part of the National Military Establishment by the National Security Act of 1947 (61 Stat. 502) and came into being on September 18, 1947. The National Security Act Amendments of 1949 redesignated the National Military Establishment as the Department of Defense, established it as an executive department, and made the Department of the Air Force a military department within the Department of Defense (63 Stat. 578). The Department of the Air Force is separately organized under the Secretary of the Air Force. It operates under the authority, direction, and control of the Secretary of Defense (10 U.S.C. 8010). The Department consists of the Office of the Secretary of the Air Force, the Air Staff, and field organizations.

Secretary The Secretary is responsible for matters pertaining to organization, training, logistical support, maintenance, welfare of personnel, administrative, recruiting, research and development, and other activities prescribed by the President or the Secretary of Defense.

Air Staff The mission of the Air Staff is to furnish professional assistance to the Secretary, the Under Secretary, the Assistant Secretaries, and the Chief of Staff in executing their responsibilities.

Field Organizations The major commands, field operating agencies, and direct reporting units together represent the field organizations of the Air Force. These are organized primarily on a functional basis in the United States and on an area basis overseas. These commands are responsible for accomplishing certain phases of the worldwide activities of the Air Force. They also are responsible for organizing, administering, equipping, and training their subordinate elements for the accomplishment of assigned missions.

Major Commands

The Continental U.S. Commands

Air Combat Command This Command operates Air Force bombers and CONUS-based, combat-coded fighter and attack aircraft. It organizes, trains, equips, and maintains combat-ready forces for rapid deployment and employment while ensuring strategic air defense forces are ready to meet the challenges of peacetime air sovereignty and wartime air defense.

Air Force Materiel Command This Command advances, integrates, and uses technology to develop, test, acquire, and sustain weapons systems. It also performs single-manager continuous product and process improvement throughout a product's life cycle.

Air Mobility Command This Command provides airlift, air refueling, special air mission, and aeromedical evacuation for U.S. forces. It also supplies forces to theater commands to support wartime tasking.

Air Force Reserve Command This Command supports the Air Force mission of defending the Nation through control and exploitation of air and space. It plays an integral role in the day-to-day Air Force mission and is not a force held in reserve for possible war or contingency operations.

Air Force Space Command This Command operates space and ballistic missile systems, including ballistic missile warning, space control, spacelift, and satellite operations.

Air Force Special Operations Command This Command provides the air component of U.S. Special Operations Command, deploying specialized air power and delivering special operations combat power.

Air Education and Training Command This Command recruits, assesses, commissions, educates, and trains Air Force enlisted and officer personnel. It provides basic military training, initial and advanced technical training, flying training, and professional military and degree-granting professional education. The Command also conducts joint, medical service, readiness, and Air Force security assistance training.

Major Commands

Command	Address	Commander
Air Combat Command	Langley AFB, VA 23665–2788	Gen. Ronald E. Keys
Air Education and Training Command	Randolph AFB, TX 78150–4324	Gen. William R. Looney
Air Force Materiel Command	Wright-Patterson AFB, OH 45433–5001	Gen. Bruce Carlson
Air Force Reserve Command	Robins AFB, GA 31098–1635	Lt. Gen. John A. Bradley
Air Force Space Command	Peterson AFB, CO 80914–4020	Lt. Gen. Frank G. Klotz
Air Force Special Operations Command	Hurlburt Field, FL 32544–5273	Lt. Gen. Michael W. Wooley
Air Mobility Command	Scott AFB, IL 62225–5310	Gen. Duncan J. McNabb

Overseas Commands

Pacific Air Forces The Command is responsible for planning, conducting, and coordinating offensive and defensive air operations in the Pacific and Asian theaters.

United States Air Forces in Europe The Command plans, conducts, controls, coordinates, and supports air and space operations to achieve United States national and NATO objectives.

Overseas Commands

Command	Address	Commander
Pacific Air Forces	Hickam AFB, HI 96853–5420	Gen. Paul V. Hester
U.S. Air Forces in Europe	APO AE 09094–0501	Gen. William T. Hobbins

Field Activities

Air National Guard The Center performs the operational and technical tasks associated with manning, equipping, and training Air National Guard units to required readiness levels.

Base Closures The Agency serves as the Federal real property disposal agent and provides integrated executive management for Air Force bases in the United States as they are closed under the delegated authorities of the Base Closure and Realignment Act of 1988 and the Defense Base Closure and Realignment Act of 1990.

Communications The Agency ensures that command, control, communications, and computer systems used by USAF warfighters are integrated and interoperable. It develops and validates C^4 architectures, technical standards, technical reference codes, policies, processes and procedures, and technical solutions, supporting information superiority through technical excellence.

Emergency Preparedness The Office is responsible for Air Force-related national security emergency preparedness functions, including military support to civil authorities, civil defense, and law enforcement agencies and planning for continuity of operations during emergencies.

Engineering The Agency maximizes Air Force civil engineers' capabilities in base and contingency operations by providing tools, practices, and professional support for readiness, training, technical support, management practices, automation support, vehicles and equipment, and research, development, and acquisition consultation.

Environmental Quality The Center provides the Air Force with services in environmental remediation, compliance, planning, and pollution prevention, as well as construction management and facilities design.

Flight Standards The Agency performs worldwide inspection of airfields, navigation systems, and instrument approaches. It provides flight standards to develop Air Force instrument requirements, and certifies procedures and directives for cockpit display and navigation systems. It also provides air traffic control and airlift procedures and evaluates air traffic control systems and airspace management procedures.

Historic Publications The Office researches, writes, and publishes books and other studies on Air Force history and provides historical support to Air Force headquarters.

Historical Research The Agency serves as a repository for Air Force historical records and provides research facilities for scholars and the general public.

Intelligence The Agency provides intelligence services to support Air Force operations through flexible collection, tailored air and space intelligence, weapons monitoring, and information warfare products and services.

Medical Operations The Agency assists the USAF Surgeon General in developing plans, programs, and policies for the medical service, aerospace medicine, clinical investigations, quality assurance, health promotion, family advocacy, bioenvironmental engineering, military public health, and radioactive material management.

Modeling and Simulation The Agency implements policies and standards and supports field operations in the areas of modeling and simulation.

News The Agency gathers information and packages and disseminates electronic and printed news and information products. It manages and operationally controls Air Force Internal Information, the Army and Air Force Hometown News Service, the Air Force Broadcasting Service, and the Air Force Armed Forces Radio and Television outlets worldwide; operates the Air Force hotline; and provides electronic information through the Air Force bulletin board and the Internet.

Nuclear Weapons Monitoring The Air Force Technical Applications Center monitors compliance with various nuclear treaties. It provides real-time reporting of nuclear weapons tests and operates a global network of sensors and analytical laboratories to monitor foreign nuclear activity. It conducts research and development of proliferation detection technologies for all weapons of mass destruction.

Real Estate The Agency acquires, manages, and disposes of land for the Air Force worldwide and maintains a complete land and facilities inventory.

Weather Services The Service provides centralized weather services to the Air Force, Army joint staff, designated unified commands, and other agencies, ensuring standardization of procedures and interoperability within the USAF weather system and assessing its technical performance and effectiveness.

Field Operating Agencies

Agency	Address	Commander/Director
Air Force Center for Environmental Excellence	San Antonio, TX	Paul A. Parker
Air Force Civil Engineer Support Agency	Tyndall AFB, FL 32403–5319	Col. Gus G. Elliott
Air Force Command and Control and Intelligence, Surveillance, Reconnaissance Center	Langley AFB, VA 23665–2788	Maj. Gen. Charles E. Croom, Jr.
Air Force Communications Agency	Scott AFB, IL 62225–5206	Col. Robert Steele
Air Force Frequency Management Agency	Alexandria, VA	Col. Louis G. Jakowatz III
Air Force Historical Research Agency	Maxwell AFB, AL 36112–6424	Col. Richard Rauschkolb
Air Force Inspection Agency	Kirtland AFB, NM 87117–5670	Col. Thomas F. Berardinelli
Air Force Logistics Management Agency	Maxwell AFB, AL 36112–6424	Col. Seann P. Cassidy
Air Force News Agency	San Antonio, TX 78226	(Vacancy)
Air Force Personnel Center	Randolph AFB, TX 78150–4451	Maj. Gen. Anthony F. Przybyslawski
Air Force Real Property Agency	Arlington, VA	Kathryn Haldorson
Air Force Safety Center	Kirtland AFB, NM 87117–5670	Maj. Gen. Maurice L. McFann
Air Force Services Agency	Randolph AFB, TX 78150–4451	Col. Timothy J. Hanson
Air Force Weather Service	Scott AFB, IL 62225–5206	Col. John M. Lanicci

Direct Reporting Units

Air Force Communication and Information Center The Center applies information technology to improve operations processes and manages all Air Force information technology systems.

Air Force Doctrine Center The Center develops and publishes basic and operational level doctrine for the Air Force. It provides USAF input into joint and multinational doctrine development, ensures that Air Force doctrine is consistent with policy and joint doctrine, and serves as the Air Force's primary source of expertise for military operations other than war doctrine and strategy development as well as training, education, exercises, and simulations.

Air Force Operational Test and Evaluation Center The Center plans and conducts test and evaluation procedures to determine operational effectiveness and suitability of new or modified USAF systems and their capacity to meet mission needs.

Air Force Security Forces Center The Center ensures quick and effective security responses to protect U.S. personnel around the globe.

Eleventh Wing The Wing provides support for Headquarters Air Force and other Air Force units in the National Capital Region, including day-to-day operations of Bolling Air Force Base. The Wing plans and directs the Air Force Band and the Air Force Honor Guard support to ceremony activities of the Air Force Chief of Staff, the Air Force Secretary, the White House, and Arlington National Cemetery.

U.S. Air Force Academy The Academy provides academic and military instruction and experience to prepare future USAF career officers. Graduates receive Bachelor of Science degrees in 1 of 26 academic majors and commissions as second lieutenants.

Direct Reporting Units

Unit	Address	Commander
Air Force District of Washington	Bolling AFB, Washington, DC 20332–0101	Maj. Gen. Robert Smolen
Air Force Doctrine Center	Maxwell AFB, AL 36112–6335	Maj. Gen. Bentley B. Rayburn
Air Force Operational Test and Evaluation Center	Kirtland AFB, NM 87117–5558	Maj. Gen. Felix Dupre'
Air Force Security Forces Center	Lackland AFB, TX 78236–5226	Brig. Gen. Richard A. Coleman, Jr.
U.S. Air Force Academy	CO 80840–5001	Lt. Gen. John W. Rosa, Jr.

For further information concerning the Department of the Air Force, contact the Office of the Director of Public Affairs, Department of the Air Force, 1690 Air Force Pentagon, Washington, DC 20330–1670. Phone, 703–697–6061. Internet, www.af.mil.

DEPARTMENT OF THE ARMY

The Pentagon, Washington, DC 20310
Phone, 703–695–6518. Internet, www.army.mil.

SECRETARY OF THE ARMY	FRANCIS J. HARVEY
Under Secretary of the Army	PRESTON M. GREEN
Assistant Secretary of the Army (Acquisition, Logistics, and Technology)	CLAUDE M. BOLTON, JR.
Assistant Secretary of the Army (Civil Works)	JOHN PAUL WOODLEY, JR.
Assistant Secretary of the Army (Financial Management and Comptroller)	VALERIE L. BALDWIN
Assistant Secretary of the Army (Installations and Environment)	KEITH EASTIN
Assistant Secretary of the Army (Manpower and Reserve Affairs)	DANIEL DENNING, *Acting*
General Counsel	(VACANCY)
Administrative Assistant to the Secretary of the Army	SANDRA RILEY
Chief Information Officer/G–6	LT. GEN. STEVEN W. BOUTELLE
Inspector General	MAJ. GEN. STANLEY E. GREEN
Auditor General	PATRICK FITZGERALD, *Acting*
Deputy Under Secretary of the Army	(VACANCY)
Deputy Under Secretary of the Army (Operations Research)	WALTER W. HOLLIS
Chief of Legislative Liaison	MAJ. GEN. GALEN JACKMAN
Chief of Public Affairs	BRIG. GEN. VINCENT BROOKS
Director, Small and Disadvantaged Business Utilization	TRACEY L. PINSON

Office of the Chief of Staff:

Chief of Staff, United States Army	GEN. PETER J. SCHOOMAKER
Vice Chief of Staff	GEN. RICHARD A. CODY
Director of the Army Staff	LT. GEN. JAMES A. CAMPBELL
Vice Director of the Army Staff	BRIG. GEN. LEO A. BROOKS, JR.

Army Staff:

Deputy Chief of Staff, G–1	LT. GEN. JOHN F. KIMMONS
Deputy Chief of Staff, G–2	LT. GEN. KEITH B. ALEXANDER
Deputy Chief of Staff, G–3/5/7	LT. GEN. JAMES J. LOVELACE, JR.
Deputy Chief of Staff, G–4	LT. GEN. ANNE E. DUNWOODY
Deputy Chief of Staff, G–8	LT. GEN. DAVID F. MELCHER
Chief, Army Reserve	LT. GEN. JAMES R. HELMLY
Chief, National Guard Bureau	LT. GEN. H. STEVEN BLUM
Chief of Engineers	LT. GEN. CARL A. STROCK
The Surgeon General	LT. GEN. KEVIN C. KILEY
Assistant Chief of Staff for Installation Management	LT. GEN. DAVID BARNO
Chief of Chaplains	MAJ. GEN. DAVID H. HICKS
Provost Marshall General	MAJ. GEN. DONALD J. RYDER
Judge Advocate General	MAJ. GEN. SCOTT C. BLACK

Director, Army National Guard	Lt. Gen. Clyde A. Vaughn
Major Army Commands:	
Commanding General, U.S. Army Materiel Command	Gen. Benjamin Griffin
Commanding General, U.S. Army Corps of Engineers	Lt. Gen. Carl A. Strock
Commanding General, U.S. Army Forces Command	Gen. Dan K. McNeill
Commanding General, U.S. Army Medical Command	Lt. Gen. Kevin C. Kiley
Commanding General, U.S. Army Space and Missile Defense Command	Lt. Gen. Larry J. Dodgen
Commanding General, U.S. Army Special Operations Command	Lt. Gen. Robert W. Wagner
Commanding General, U.S. Army Training and Doctrine Command	Gen. William S. Wallace
Commanding General, 8th U.S. Army	Lt. Gen. Charles C. Campbell
Commanding General, U.S. Army Pacific	Lt. Gen. John M. Brown III
Commanding General, U.S. Army Europe and 7th Army	David D. McKiernan
Subordinate Commands:	
Commanding General, U.S. Army Military Surface Deployment and Distribution Command	Brig. Gen. Charles W. Fletcher, Jr.
Commanding General, U.S. Army South	Brig. Gen. Paul F. Keen
Headquarters-Direct Reporting Units:	
Commanding General, U.S. Army Military District of Washington	Maj. Gen. Guy C. Swan III
Commanding General, U.S. Army Criminal Investigation Command	Maj. Gen. Donald J. Ryder
Commanding General, U.S. Army Intelligence and Security Command	Maj. Gen. John DeFreital III

The mission of the Department of the Army is to organize, train, and equip active duty and reserve forces for the preservation of peace, security, and the defense of our Nation. As part of our national military team, the Army focuses on land operations; its soldiers must be trained with modern arms and equipment and be ready to respond quickly. The Army also administers programs aimed at protecting the environment, improving waterway navigation, flood and beach erosion control, and water resource development. It provides military assistance to Federal, State, and local government agencies, including natural disaster relief assistance.

The American Continental Army, now called the United States Army, was established by the Continental Congress on June 14, 1775, more than a year before the Declaration of Independence. The Department of War was established as an executive department at the seat of government by act approved August 7, 1789 (1 Stat. 49). The Secretary of War was established as its head. The National Security Act of 1947 (50 U.S.C. 401) created the National Military Establishment, and the Department of War was designated the Department of the Army. The title of its Secretary became Secretary of the Army (5 U.S.C. 171). The National Security Act Amendments of 1949 (63 Stat. 578) provided that the Department of the Army be a military department within the Department of Defense.

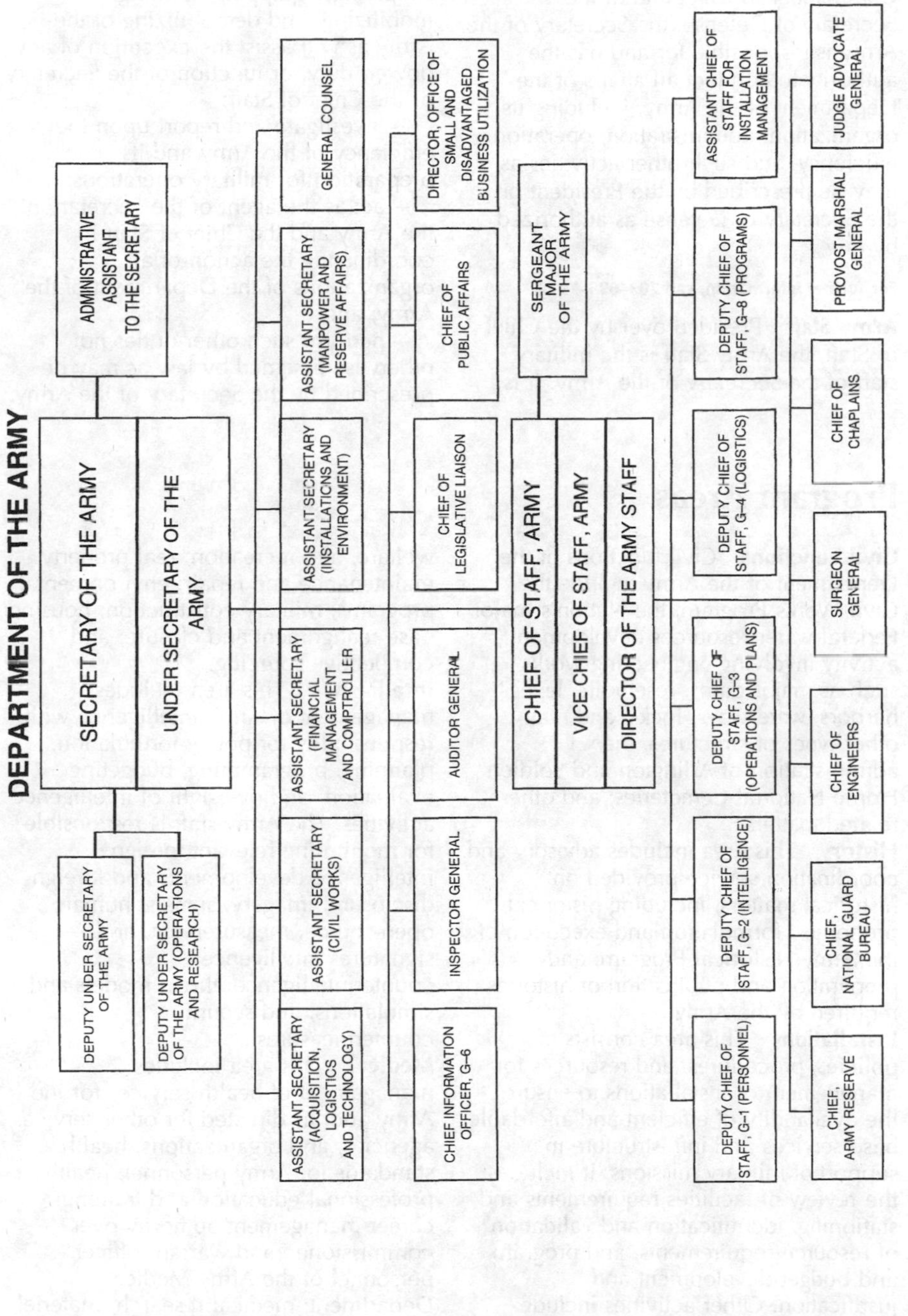
DEPARTMENT OF THE ARMY
SECRETARY OF THE ARMY
UNDER SECRETARY OF THE ARMY
ADMINISTRATIVE ASSISTANT TO THE SECRETARY
DEPUTY UNDER SECRETARY OF THE ARMY
DEPUTY UNDER SECRETARY OF THE ARMY (OPERATIONS AND RESEARCH)
ASSISTANT SECRETARY (ACQUISITION, LOGISTICS AND TECHNOLOGY)
ASSISTANT SECRETARY (CIVIL WORKS)
ASSISTANT SECRETARY (FINANCIAL MANAGEMENT AND COMPTROLLER)
ASSISTANT SECRETARY (INSTALLATIONS AND ENVIRONMENT)
ASSISTANT SECRETARY (MANPOWER AND RESERVE AFFAIRS)
GENERAL COUNSEL
CHIEF INFORMATION OFFICER, G–6
INSPECTOR GENERAL
AUDITOR GENERAL
CHIEF OF LEGISLATIVE LIAISON
CHIEF OF PUBLIC AFFAIRS
DIRECTOR, OFFICE OF SMALL AND DISADVANTAGED BUSINESS UTILIZATION
CHIEF OF STAFF, ARMY
VICE CHIEF OF STAFF, ARMY
DIRECTOR OF THE ARMY STAFF
SERGEANT MAJOR OF THE ARMY
DEPUTY CHIEF OF STAFF, G–1 (PERSONNEL)
DEPUTY CHIEF OF STAFF, G–2 (INTELLIGENCE)
DEPUTY CHIEF OF STAFF, G–3 (OPERATIONS AND PLANS)
DEPUTY CHIEF OF STAFF, G–4 (LOGISTICS)
DEPUTY CHIEF OF STAFF, G–8 (PROGRAMS)
ASSISTANT CHIEF OF STAFF FOR INSTALLATION MANAGEMENT
CHIEF, ARMY RESERVE
CHIEF, NATIONAL GUARD BUREAU
CHIEF OF ENGINEERS
SURGEON GENERAL
CHIEF OF CHAPLAINS
PROVOST MARSHAL GENERAL
JUDGE ADVOCATE GENERAL

Secretary The Secretary of the Army is the senior official of the Department of the Army. Subject to the direction, authority, and control of the President as Commander in Chief and of the Secretary of Defense, the Secretary of the Army is responsible for and has the authority to conduct all affairs of the Department of the Army, including its organization, administration, operation, efficiency, and such other activities as may be prescribed by the President or the Secretary of Defense as authorized by law.

For further information, call 703–695–7922.

Army Staff Presided over by the Chief of Staff, the Army Staff is the military staff of the Secretary of the Army. It is the duty of the Army Staff to perform the following functions:

—prepare for deployment of the Army and for such recruiting, organizing, supplying, equipping, training, mobilizing, and demobilizing of the Army as will assist the execution of any power, duty, or function of the Secretary or the Chief of Staff;

—investigate and report upon the efficiency of the Army and its preparation for military operations;

—act as the agent of the Secretary of the Army and the Chief of Staff in coordinating the action of all organizations of the Department of the Army; and

—perform such other duties not otherwise assigned by law as may be prescribed by the Secretary of the Army.

Program Areas

Civil Functions Civil functions of the Department of the Army include the Civil Works Program, the Nation's major Federal water resources development activity involving engineering works such as major dams, reservoirs, levees, harbors, waterways, locks, and many other types of structures; the administration of Arlington and Soldiers' Home National Cemeteries; and other related matters.

History This area includes advisory and coordination service provided on historical matters, including historical properties; formulation and execution of the Army Historical Program; and preparation and publication of histories required by the Army.

Installations This area consists of policies, procedures, and resources for management of installations to ensure the availability of efficient and affordable base services and infrastructure in support of military missions. It includes the review of facilities requirements and stationing, identification and validation of resource requirements, and program and budget development and justification. Other activities include support for base operations; morale, welfare, and recreation; real property maintenance and repair; environmental programs; military construction; housing; base realignment and closure; and competitive sourcing.

Intelligence This area includes management of Army intelligence with responsibility for policy formulation, planning, programming, budgeting, evaluation, and oversight of intelligence activities. The Army staff is responsible for monitoring relevant foreign intelligence developments and foreign disclosure; imagery, signals, human, open-source, measurement, and signatures intelligence; counterintelligence; threat models and simulations; and security countermeasures.

Medical This area includes management of health services for the Army and, as directed for other services, agencies, and organizations; health standards for Army personnel; health professional education and training; career management authority over commissioned and warrant officer personnel of the Army Medical Department; medical research, materiel development, testing and evaluation;

policies concerning health aspects of Army environmental programs and prevention of disease; and planning, programming, and budgeting for Army-wide health services.

Military Operations and Plans This includes Army forces strategy formation; mid-range, long-range, and regional strategy application; arms control, negotiation, and disarmament; national security affairs; joint service matters; net assessment; politico-military affairs; force mobilization and demobilization; force planning, programming structuring, development, analysis, requirements, and management; operational readiness; overall roles and missions; collective security; individual and unit training; psychological operations; information operations; unconventional warfare; counterterrorism; operations security; signal security; special plans; table of equipment development and approval; nuclear and chemical matters; civil affairs; military support of civil defense; civil disturbance; domestic actions; command and control; automation and communications programs and activities; management of the program for law enforcement, correction, and crime prevention for military members of the Army; special operations forces; foreign language and distance learning; and physical security.

Reserve Components This area includes management of individual and unit readiness and mobilization for Reserve components, comprised of the Army National Guard and the U.S. Army Reserve.

Religious This area includes management of religious and moral leadership and chaplain support activities throughout the Department; religious ministrations, religious education, pastoral care, and counseling for Army military personnel; liaison with the ecclesiastical agencies; chapel construction requirements and design approval; and career management of clergymen serving in the Chaplains Branch.

Major Army Commands

Eighth U.S. Army Eighth U.S. Army provides forces to the commander of the U.S. Forces Korea who in turn provides them to the commander of the Republic of Korea/U.S. Combined Forces Command.

For further information, contact Eighth U.S. Army. Phone, 011–82–279–13–6544. Internet, http://8tharmy.korea.army.mil.

U.S. Army Corps of Engineers The U.S. Army Corps of Engineers (USACE) provides engineering, construction management, and environmental services in peace and in support of the global war on terror. In Iraq, USACE soldiers and civilians are responsible for constructing training facilities, military bases, police and fire stations, and rehabilitating or building schools and clinics. In Afghanistan, USACE personnel are working to reform the security sector and military construction for coalition forces. The civil works program includes navigation, flood damage reduction, recreation, hydropower, environmental regulation, and other missions. The military program includes construction of Army and Air Force facilities, base realignment and closure activities, installation support, military contingency support, environmental restoration, strategic mobility, and international activities. USACE provides real estate acquisition, management, and disposal for the Army and Air Force, and researches and develops advanced technology for mobility/countermobility, force protection, and sustainment engineering. It also supports several Federal agencies and responds to natural disasters and other emergencies as the Nation's primary engineering agency.

For further information, contact USACE. Phone, 202–761–0011. Internet, www.usace.army.mil.

U.S. Army Europe and 7th Army The U.S. Army Europe and 7th Army provides the principal land component for the U.S. European Command (EUCOM). U.S. Army Europe (USAREUR) forms, trains, and projects expeditionary forces and JTF-capable headquarters to prosecute joint and combined operations throughout a 91-country area. As the U.S. Army's largest forward-deployed expeditionary force, USAREUR supports NATO and U.S. bilateral, multinational, and unilateral objectives. It supports U.S. Army forces in the European command area; receives and assists in the reception, staging, and onward movement and integration of U.S. forces; establishes, operates, and expands operational lines of communication; ensures regional security, access, and stability through presence and security cooperation; and supports U.S. combatant commanders and joint and combined commanders.

For further information, contact USAREUR. Phone, 011–49–6221–39–4100. Internet, www.hqusareur.army.mil.

U.S. Army Forces Command The U.S. Army Forces Command (FORSCOM) trains, mobilizes, deploys, sustains, transforms, and reconstitutes conventional forces, providing relevant and ready land power to combatant commanders worldwide in defense of the Nation at home and abroad.

For further information, contact FORSCOM. Phone, 404–464–5023. Internet, www.forscom.army.mil.

U.S. Army Materiel Command The U.S. Army Materiel Command (AMC) is the Army's principal materiel developer. AMC's missions include the development of weapon systems, advanced research on future technologies, and maintenance and distribution of spare parts and equipment. AMC works closely with Program Executive Offices, industry, academia, and other military services and Government agencies to develop, test, and acquire equipment that soldiers and units need to accomplish their missions.

For further information, contact AMC. Phone, 703–806–8010. Internet, www.amc.army.mil.

U.S. Army Medical Command The U.S. Army Medical Command (MEDCOM) is responsible for worldwide Army Medical Department policy, planning, and operations. Through six Regional Medical Commands, MEDCOM oversees Army medical centers, hospitals, and the Fisher Houses. It's also responsible for 32 Army and DOD Executive Agencies and operates the U.S. Army Medical Department Center and School, the U.S. Army Medical Research and Materiel Command, and the U.S. Army Center for Health Promotion and Preventive Medicine. MEDCOM's mission includes providing the vision, direction, and long-range planning for Army medicine; developing and integrating doctrine, training, leader development, organization, materiel, and soldier support for the Army health service system; allocating resources, analyzing health services utilization, and conducting performance assessments; and coordinating and managing graduate medical education programs at Army Medical Centers.

For further information, contact MEDCOM/OTSG. Phone, 703–681–3000. Internet, www.armymedicine.army.mil.

U.S. Army Pacific The U.S. Army Pacific (USARPAC) provides trained and ready forces in support of military operations and peacetime engagements in the Asia-Pacific area. USARPAC carries out a cooperative engagement strategy known as the Theater Security Cooperation Program with the 43 Asian and Pacific nations within or bordering its area of responsibility. These countries include the Philippines, Thailand, Vietnam, Japan, Mongolia, Russia, China, South Korea, India, Bangladesh, Australia, New Zealand, Marshall Islands, and Papua New Guinea.

For further information, contact USARPAC. Phone, 808–438–1393. Internet, www.usarpac.army.mil.

U.S. Army Special Operations Command The U.S. Army Special Operations Command (USASOC) trains, equips, deploys, and sustains Army special operations forces for worldwide special operations supporting regional combatant commanders and country ambassadors. USASOC soldiers deploy to numerous countries conducting missions such as peacekeeping, humanitarian assistance, demining, and foreign internal defense. USASOC includes special forces, rangers, civil affairs, psychological operations, special operations aviation, and signal and support.

For further information, contact USASOC. Phone, 910–432–3000. Internet, www.usasoc.soc.mil.

U.S. Army Space and Missile Defense Command The U.S. Army Space and Missile Defense Command (SMDC) serves as the Army's specified proponent for space and national missile defense and operational integrator for theater missile defense. SMDC coordinates, integrates, and/or executes combat development, materiel development, technology, and advanced research and development for missile defense and space programs. It also serves as the Army Service Component Command, the primary land component for the U.S. Strategic Command. SMDC's mission includes space operations, information operations, global strike, integrated missle defense, and command and control, communications, computers, intelligence, surveillance, and reconnaissance. In addition, SMDC serves as a primary research and development organization for the Missile Defense Agency. From its headquarters in Arlington, Virginia, SMDC also oversees a number of Army elements around the globe, ensuring missile defense protection for the Nation and deployed forces, and facilitates access to space assets and products.

For further information, contact SMDC. Phone, 703–607–1873. Internet, www.smdc.army.mil.

U.S. Army Training and Doctrine Command Headquartered in Fort Monroe, Virginia, the U.S. Army Training and Doctrine Command (TRADOC) recruits, trains, and educates the Army's soldiers; develops leaders; supports training in units; develops doctrine; establishes standards; and builds the future Army. TRADOC operates schools and centers at Army installations. TRADOC's priorities are recruiting a quality all-volunteer force; providing rigor and relevance in training and leader development; fostering innovation; preparing the Army for joint operations; and developing the future forces.

For further information, contact TRADOC. Phone, 757–788–4465. Internet, www.tradoc.army.mil.

Subordinate Commands

U.S. Army Military Surface Deployment and Distribution Command The U.S. Army Military Surface Deployment and Distribution Command (SDDC) provides global surface deployment command and control and distribution operations to meet national security objectives for DOD. This requires a presence in 24 ports worldwide as DOD's single-port manager, transportation, traffic-management services, deployment planning and engineering, and development of new technologies. SDDC is also the link between DOD shippers and the commercial surface transportation industry.

For further information, contact SDDC. Phone, 703–428–3207. Internet, www.sddc.army.mil.

U.S. Army South The U.S. Army South (USARSO) is a major subordinate command of the U.S. Army Forces Command, Fort McPherson, Georgia, and is the Army Service Component Command of the U.S. Southern Command. USARSO executes and is responsible for all Army operations within the U.S. Southern Command's area (Central and South America and the Caribbean Islands). USARSO seeks to build regional cooperative security and increase hemispheric cooperation by planning and executing multilateral exercises and carrying out humanitarian aid, peacekeeping, engineering, and medical assistance exercises. USARSO maintains a deployable headquarters at Fort Sam Houston, Texas, where they conduct strategic and operational planning.

For further information, contact the USARSO Public Affairs Office. Phone, 210–295–6388. E-mail, usarsowebmaster@samhouston.army.mil. Internet, http://usarso.army.mil.

Headquarters-Direct Reporting Units

U.S. Army Military District of Washington The U.S. Army Military District of Washington (MDW) provides force protection, conducts official and public events on behalf of the Nation's civilian and military leadership, and furnishes administrative, legal, and support services for assigned installations. MDW provides the core command and staff for the Joint Force Headquarters-National Capital Region. It is also responsible for planning, coordinating, and maintaining situational awareness and, as directed, employing forces for homeland defense and defense support to civil authorities in the National Capital Region to deter, prevent, and defeat threats.

For further information, contact the U.S. Army Military District Public Affairs Office. Phone, 202–685–6249. E-mail, mdwweb@fmmc.army.mil. Internet, www.mdw.army.mil.

U.S. Army Criminal Investigation Command The U.S. Army Criminal Investigation Command (CID) is a law enforcement agency that supports the Army in peacetime and during war. CID special agents conduct criminal investigations and protective service operations worldwide.

For further information, contact CID Headquarters Public Affairs Office. Phone, 703–806–0376. Internet, www.cid.army.mil.

U.S. Army Intelligence and Security Command The U.S. Army Intelligence and Security Command (INSCOM) is a multi-discipline, values-based intelligence organization that conducts and supports relevant intelligence, security, and information operations for Army, joint, and combined forces.

For further information, contact the INSCOM Public Affairs Office. Phone, 703–428–4553. Internet, www.inscom.army.mil.

United States Military Academy

West Point, NY 10996

Superintendent	LT. GEN. WILLIAM J. LENNOX, JR.
Commandant of Cadets	BRIG. GEN. CURTIS M. SCAPARROTTI
Dean of the Academic Board	BRIG. GEN. PATRICK FINNEGAN

The United States Military Academy is located at West Point, NY. The course is of 4 years' duration, during which the cadets receive, besides a general education, theoretical and practical training as junior officers. Cadets who complete the course satisfactorily receive the degree of Bachelor of Science and a commission as second lieutenant in the Army.

For further information, contact the Public Affairs Office, United States Military Academy, West Point, NY 10996. Phone, 845–938–4261. For information about Military Academy admission criteria and policies, contact the Office of the Registrar, United States Military Academy, West Point, NY 10996.

Sources of Information

Arlington and Soldiers' and Airmen's Home National Cemeteries For information write to the Superintendent, Arlington National Cemetery, Arlington, VA 22211–5003. Phone, 703–607–8545.

Army Historical Program For information concerning the Army Historical Program, write to the U.S. Army Center of Military History, Collins Hall, 103 Third Avenue, Fort Lesley J.

McNair, Washington, DC 20319–5058. Phone, 202–685–2714. Fax, 202–685–4570. Internet, www.army.mil/cmh. Information on historic buildings preservation and reuse is available through the Office of Historic Properties. Phone, 703–692–9892.

Civilian Employment For information, visit the Army civilian personnel Web site (Internet, www.cpol.army.mil) or contact the civilian personnel advisory center at the desired Army installation.

Contracts Contract procurement policies and procedures are the responsibility of the Deputy for Procurement, Office of the Assistant Secretary of the Army (Acquisition, Logistics, and Technology), Room 2E532, The Pentagon, Washington, DC 20310–0103. Phone, 703–695–6154.

Environment Contact the Public Affairs Office, Office of the Chief of Public Affairs Headquarters, Department of the Army, Washington, DC 20314–1000 (Phone, 202–761–0010); the Army Environmental Center (Internet, http://aec.army.mil/usaec/); or the Army Environmental Policy Institute (Internet, www.aepi.army.mil).

Films, Videotapes, and Videodiscs Requests for loan of Army-produced films should be addressed to the Visual Information Support Centers of Army installations. Unclassified Army productions are available for sale from the National Audiovisual Center, National Technical Information Service, 5285 Port Royal Road, Springfield, VA 22161. Phone, 800–553–NTIS. Internet, www.ntis.gov/nac.

Freedom of Information and Privacy Act Requests Requests should be addressed to the Information Management Officer of the Army installation or activity responsible for the requested information.

Military Surface Deployment and Distribution Command Information concerning military transportation news and issues is available electronically through the Internet, www.mtmc.army.mil.

Public Affairs and Community Relations For official Army information and community relations, contact the Office of the Chief of Public Affairs, Department of the Army, Washington, DC 20310–1508. Phone, 703–697–5081. During nonoffice hours, call 703–697–4200.

Publications Requests should be addressed to either the proponent listed on the title page of the document or the Information Management Officer of the Army activity that publishes the requested publication. Official texts published by Headquarters, Department of the Army, are available from the National Technical Information Service, Department of Commerce, Attn: Order Preprocessing Section, 5285 Port Royal Road, Springfield, VA 22161–2171. Phone, 703–487–4600. Internet, www.ntis.gov. If it is uncertain which Army activity published the document, forward the request to the Publishing Division, Army Publishing Directorate, Room 1050, 2461 Eisenhower Avenue, Alexandria, VA 22331–0301. Phone, 703–325–6292. Internet, www.apd.army.mil.

Research Industry may obtain information on long-range research and development plans concerning future materiel requirements and objectives from the Commander, U.S. Army Research Development and Engineering Command, Attn: AMSRD–PA, Bldg. E5101, 5183 Blackhawk Road, Aberdeen Proving Ground, MD 21010–5424.

Small Business Activities Assistance for small businesses and minority educational institutions to enhance their ability to participate in the Army contracting program is available through the Office of Small and Disadvantaged Business Utilization, Office of the Secretary of the Army, 106 Army Pentagon, Room 3B514, Washington, DC 20310–0106. Phone, 703–697–2868.

Speakers Civilian organizations desiring an Army speaker may contact a nearby Army installation or write or call the Community Relations Division, Office of the Chief of Public Affairs, Department of the Army, Washington, DC 20310–1508. Phone, 703–697–5081. Requests for Army Reserve speakers may be addressed to HQDA (DAAR–PA),

Washington, DC 20310–2423, or the local Army Reserve Center. Organizations in the Washington, DC, area desiring chaplain speakers may contact the Chief of Chaplains, Department of the Army, Washington, DC 20310–2700. Phone, 703–601–1140. Information on speakers may be obtained by contacting the Public Affairs Office, Office of the Chief of Engineers, Washington, DC 20314, or the nearest Corps of Engineer Division or District Office.

Military Career and Training Opportunities Information on all phases of Army enlistments and specialized training is available by writing to the U.S. Army Recruiting Command, 1307 Third Avenue, Fort Knox, KY 40121–2725. For information about career and training opportunities, contact the appropriate office listed below:

Army health professions: Headquarters U.S. Army Recruiting Command, Health Services Directorate (RCHS–OP), 1307 Third Avenue, Fort Knox, KY 40121–2725. Phone, 502–626–0367. E-mail, Tanya.Beecher@usarec.army.mil. Internet, www.healthcare.goarmy.com.

Army National Guard training opportunities: Army National Guard, NGB–ASM, 1411 Jefferson Davis Highway, Arlington, VA 22202–3231. Phone, 703–607–5834. Internet, www.arng.army.mil.

Army Reserve training opportunities for enlisted personnel and officers: Army Reserve Personnel Command, One Reserve Way, St. Louis, MO 63132–5200. Phone, 314–592–0000 or 800–318–5298. Internet, www.goarmyreserve.com.

Army Reserve Officers' Training Corps (ROTC): U.S. Army Cadet Command, Recruiting, Retention and Operations Directorate, ATCC-OP, 55 Patch Road, Fort Monroe, VA 23651. Phone, 757–788–3770. Or, contact a professor of military science or Army ROTC Advisor at the nearest college or university offering the program in your area. Internet, www.armyrotc.com.

Chaplain Recruiting Branch HQ: U.S. Army Recruiting Command, Attn: RCRO- SM-CH, 1307 Third Avenue, Fort Knox, KY 40121–2726. Phone, 502–626–0722 or 866–684–1571. Fax, 502–626–1213. Internet, www.chaplain.goarmy.com.

Judge Advocate General's Corps: Department of the Army, Judge Advocate Recruiting Office, 1777 North Kent Street, Suite 5200, Rosslyn, VA 20124–2194. Phone, 866–ARMY–JAG. Internet, www.law.goarmy.com.

U.S. Military Academy: Director of Admissions, United States Military Academy, Building 606, West Point, NY 10996. Phone, 845–938–4041. Internet, www.usma.edu.

For further information concerning the Department of the Army, contact the Office of the Chief of Public Affairs, Headquarters, Department of the Army, Washington, DC 20310–1508. Phone, 703–697–5081. Internet, www.army.mil.

DEPARTMENT OF THE NAVY

The Pentagon, Washington, DC 20350
Phone, 703–697–7391. Internet, www.navy.mil.

SECRETARY OF THE NAVY	DONALD C. WINTER
Director, Office of Program Appraisal	THOMAS TESCH
Special Assistant for Acquisition and Business Reform	DOUGLAS COMBS
Under Secretary of the Navy	DIONEL M. AVILES
Director, Small and Disadvantaged Business Utilization	NANCY J. TARRANT
Auditor General of the Navy	RICHARD A. LEACH
Director, Naval Criminal Investigative Service	DAVID L. BRANT
Chief of Information	REAR ADM. TERRY L. MCCREARY, USN
Chief Information Officer	DAVID M. WENNERGREN
Chief of Legislative Affairs	REAR ADM. MARK FERGUSON, USN
General Counsel	ALBERTO J. MORA
Principal Deputy General Counsel	FRANK R. JIMENEZ
Deputy General Counsel	WILLIAM R. MOLZHAN
Naval Inspector General	VICE ADM. RONALD A. ROUTE, USN
Judge Advocate General of the Navy	REAR ADM. JAMES E. MCPHERSON, JAGC, USN
Deputy Judge Advocate General	REAR ADM. BRUCE E. MACDONALD, JAGC, USN
Assistant Secretary of the Navy (Financial Management and Comptroller)	RICHARD GRECO, JR.
Deputy	ASHLEY GODWIN
Director, Office of Budget	REAR ADM. BRUCE B. ENGELHARDT, USN
Director, Office of Financial Operations	MARK E. EASTON
Assistant Secretary of the Navy (Manpower and Reserve Affairs)	WILLIAM A. NAVAS, JR.
Deputy Assistant Secretary (Reserve Affairs)	HARVEY C. BARNUM
Deputy Assistant Secretary (Total Force Transformation)	ANITA K. BLAIR
Deputy Assistant Secretary (Civilian Human Resources)	PATRICIA C. ADAMS
Deputy Assistant Secretary (Manpower Analysis and Assessment)	RUSSELL BELAND
Deputy Assistant Secretary (Military Personnel Policy)	ANITA K. BLAIR
Director, Naval Council of Personnel Boards	COL. MARSHA L. CULVER, USMC
Executive Director, Board for Correction of Naval Records	W. DEAN PFEIFFER
Assistant Secretary of the Navy (Installations and Environment)	B.J. PENN

Principal Deputy	WAYNE ARNY
Deputy Assistant Secretary (Shore Resources)	RICHARD O. THOMAS
Deputy Assistant Secretary (Safety)	CONNIE K. DEWITTE
Deputy Assistant Secretary (Environment)	DONALD SCHREGARDUS
Assistant Secretary of the Navy (Research, Development, and Acquisition)	JOHN J. YOUNG, JR.
Chief of Naval Research	REAR ADM. JAY M. COHEN, USN
Principal Deputy	(VACANCY)
Deputy Assistant Secretary (Air Programs)	WILLIAM BALDERSON
Deputy Assistant Secretary (C41/Space Programs)	GARY A. FEDERICI
Deputy Assistant Secretary (Littoral and Mine Warfare Programs)	ROGER SMITH
Deputy Assistant Secretary (Ship Programs)	ALLISON STILLER
Deputy Assistant Secretary (Integrated Warfare Systems)	ANNE SANDEL
Deputy Assistant Secretary (Management and Budget)	CAPT. ERIC R. WILSON, USN
Program Executive Officers/Direct Reporting Program Managers	REAR ADM. WILLIAM COBB, USN; REAR ADM. PHIL DAVIS, USN; REAR ADM. DENNIS M. DWYER, USN; REAR ADM. GIB GODWIN, USN; REAR ADM. CHARLES HAMILTON, USN; REAR ADM. STEVE ENEWOLD, USN; REAR ADM. DAVE VENLET, USN; THOMAS LAUX; REAR ADM. TIMOTHY HEELY, USN; GARY BREEDLOVE; REAR ADM. WILLIAM LANDAY, USN; REAR ADM. JOHN BUTLER, USN; REAR ADM. CHARLES BUSH, USN; STEVEN EHRLER; DENNIS BAUMAN; CARL SIEL; COL. MIKE BROGAN, USMC; RONALD ROSENTHAL; REAR ADM. CHARLES B. YOUNG, USN; LORRAINE WILSON

U.S. Navy

Chief of Naval Operations	ADM. MICHAEL G. MULLEN, USN
Vice Chief of Naval Operations	ADM. ROBERT WILLARD, USN
Deputy Chief, Manpower, Personnel, Traning and Education	VICE ADM. JOHN C. HARVEY, JR., USN
Director of Naval Intelligence	REAR ADM. ROBERT B. MURRETT, USN
Deputy Chief, Fleet Readiness and Logistics	VICE ADM. JUSTIN D. MCCARTHY, USN
Deputy Chief, Plans, Policy and Operations	VICE ADM. JOHN G. MORGAN, JR., USN
Deputy Chief, Warfare Requirements and Programs	REAR ADM. MARK J. EDWARDS, USN
Deputy Chief, Resources, Requirements and Assessments	VICE ADM. LEWIS W. CRENSHAW, JR., USN
Director, Navy Staff	VICE ADM. ANN RONDEAU, USN

Director of Naval Nuclear Propulsion Program	ADM. KIRKLAND H. DONALD, USN
Director of Test and Evaluation and Technology Requirements	REAR ADM. JAY M. COHEN, USN
Surgeon General of the Navy	VICE ADM. DONALD C. ARTHUR, MC, USN
Director of Naval Reserve	VICE ADM. JOHN G. COTTON, USN
Chief of Chaplains of the Navy/Director of Religious Ministries	REAR ADM. LOUIS V. IASIELLO, CHC, USN
Assistant Chief, Information Technology	VICE ADM. JAMES D. MCAUTHUR, JR., USN
Major Shore Commands:	
Commander, Naval Air Systems Command	VICE ADM. WALTER B. MASSENBURG, USN
Commander, Naval Network and Space Operations Command	REAR ADM. JOHN P. CRYER III, USN
Commander, Naval Facilities Engineering Command	REAR ADM. MICHAEL K. LOOSE, CEC, USN
Commander, Naval Legal Service Command	REAR ADM. JAMES E. MCPHERSON, JAGC, USN
Commander, Naval Meteorology and Oceanography Command	REAR ADM. TIMOTHY MCGEE, USN
Commander, Naval Sea Systems Command	VICE ADM. PHILLIP M. BALISLE, USN
Commander, Naval Supply Systems Command	REAR ADM. JUSTIN D. MCCARTHY, SC, USN
Commander, Space and Naval Warfare Systems Command	REAR ADM. KENNETH D. SLAGHT, USN
Commander, Naval Warfare Development Command	REAR ADM. JOHN M. KELLY, USN
Chief, Bureau of Medicine and Surgery	VICE ADM. DONALD C. ARTHUR, MC, USN
Commander, Naval Education and Training Command	VICE ADM. KEVIN MORAN, USN
Chief of Naval Personnel	VICE ADM. GERALD L. HOEWING, USN
Commander, Office of Naval Intelligence	CAPT. TONY COTHRON, USN
Director, Strategic Systems Program	REAR ADM. CHARLES B. YOUNG, USN
Commander, Navy Installations Command	VICE ADM. ROBERT T. CONWAY, JR., USN
Major Fleet Commands:	
Commander, U.S. Atlantic Fleet	ADM. WILLIAM J. FALLON, USN
Commander, U.S. Pacific Fleet	ADM. WALTER F. DORAN,USN
Commander, U.S. Naval Forces Europe	ADM. MICHAEL G. MULLEN, USN
Commander, Military Sealift Command	REAR ADM. DAVID L. BREWER III, USN
Commander, Naval Forces Central Command	VICE ADM. DAVID C. NICHOLS, USN
Commander, Naval Reserve Force	VICE ADM. JOHN G. COTTON, USN
Commander, Naval Special Warfare Command	REAR ADM. JOSEPH MAGUIRE, USN
Commander, Operational Test and Evaluation Force	REAR ADM. DAVID ARCHITZEL, USN

U.S. Marine Corps

Commandant of the Marine Corps	Gen. Michael W. Hagee, USMC
Assistant Commandant of the Marine Corps	Gen. William L. Nyland, USMC
Sergeant Major of the Marine Corps	Sgt. Maj. John L. Estrada, USMC
Director, Marine Corps Staff	Col. J.L. Welsh, USMC
Director, Command, Control, Communications, and Computers	Brig. Gen. John R. Thomas, USMC
Deputy Commandant for Aviation	Lt. Gen. Michael A. Hough, USMC
Deputy Commandant for Installations and Logistics	Lt. Gen. Richard L. Kelly, USMC
Deputy Commandant for Manpower and Reserve Affairs	Lt. Gen. H.P. Osman, USMC
Deputy Commandant for Plans, Policies, and Operations	Lt. Gen. Jan C. Huly, USMC
Deputy Commandant for Programs and Resources	Lt. Gen. Robert Magnus, USMC
Counsel for the Commandant	Robert D. Hogue
Director of Administration and Resource Management	Albert A. Washington
Deputy Director of Human Intelligence, Defense Intelligence Agency	Brig. Gen. M.E. Ennis, USMC
Director of Marine Corps History and Museums	Col. John W. Ripley, USMC (Ret.)
Director of Public Affairs	Brig. Gen. Mary Ann Krusa-Dossin, USMC
Director, Special Projects Directorate	Joel P. Eissinger, USMC
Legislative Assistant to the Commandant	Brig. Gen. John F. Kelly, USMC
Chaplain of the Marine Corps	Rear Adm. Robert F. Burt, CHC, USN
Marine Corps Dental Officer	Capt. William G. Reynolds, DC, USN
Medical Officer of the Marine Corps	Rear Adm. Thomas Cullison, MC, USN
President, Permanent Marine Corps Uniform Board	Col. James B. Laster, USMC
Commanding General, Marine Corps Recruiting Command	Brig. Gen. Walter E. Gaskin, USMC
Commanding General, Marine Corps Combat Development Command	Lt. Gen. James N. Mattis, USMC
Commander, Marine Corps Systems Commands	Brig. Gen. William D. Catto, USMC
Commander, Marine Corps Base, Quantico	Col. James M. Lowe, USMC

[For the Department of the Navy statement of organization, see the *Code of Federal Regulations,* Title 32, Part 700]

The primary mission of the Department of the Navy is to protect the United States, as directed by the President or the Secretary of Defense, by the effective prosecution of war at sea including, with its Marine Corps component, the seizure or defense of advanced naval bases; to support, as required, the forces of all military departments of the United States; and to maintain freedom of the seas.

The United States Navy was founded on October 13, 1775, when Congress enacted the first legislation creating the Continental Navy of the American

DEPARTMENT OF THE NAVY

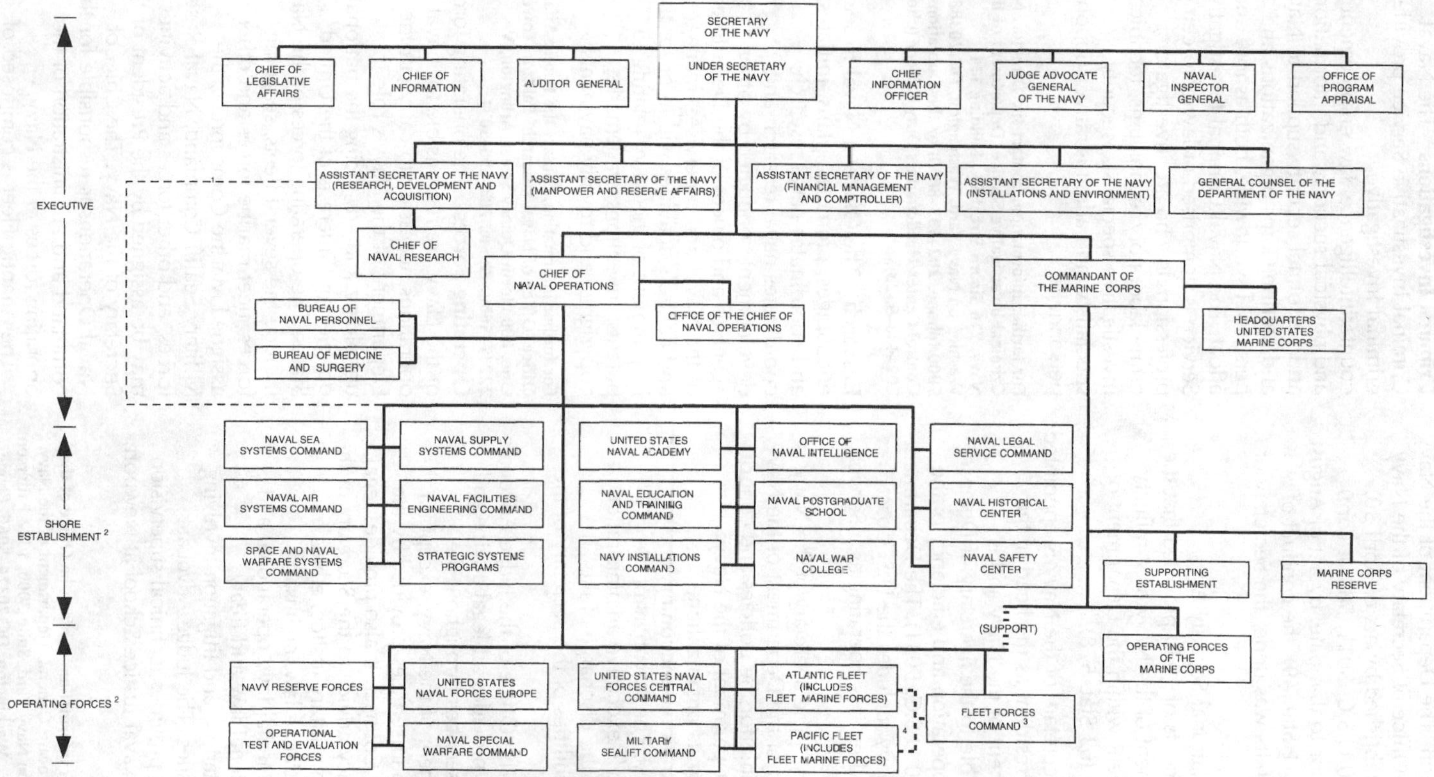

[1] Systems commands and SSP report to ASN (RDA) for acquisition matters only.
[2] Also includes other Echelonn 2 commands and subordinate activities under the command or supervision of the designated organizations.
[3] Additional duty for Commander, U.S. Atlantic Fleet.
[4] For Interdeployment Training Cycle purposes, Commander, Fleet Forms Command Controls LANFLT and PACFLT assets.

Revolution. The Department of the Navy and the Office of Secretary of the Navy were established by act of April 30, 1798 (10 U.S.C. 5011, 5031). For 9 years prior to that date, by act of August 7, 1789 (1 Stat. 49), the conduct of naval affairs was under the Secretary of War.

The National Security Act Amendments of 1949 provided that the Department of the Navy be a military department within the Department of Defense (63 Stat. 578).

The Secretary of the Navy is appointed by the President as the head of the Department of the Navy and is responsible to the Secretary of Defense for the operation and efficiency of the Navy (10 U.S.C. 5031). The Department of the Navy includes the U.S. Coast Guard when it is operating as a Service in the Navy.

Secretary The Secretary of the Navy is the head of the Department of the Navy, responsible for the policies and control of the Department of the Navy, including its organization, administration, functioning, and efficiency. The members of the Secretary's executive administration assist in the discharge of the responsibilities of the Secretary of the Navy.

Legal The Office of the Judge Advocate General provides all legal advice and related services throughout the Department of the Navy, except for the advice and services provided by the General Counsel. It also provides legal and policy advice to the Secretary of the Navy on military justice, ethics, administrative law, claims, environmental law, operational and international law and treaty interpretation, and litigation involving these issues. The Judge Advocate General provides technical supervision for the Naval Justice School at Newport, RI.

For further information, contact the Office of the Judge Advocate General, Department of the Navy, Washington Navy Yard, Suite 3000, 1322 Patterson Avenue SE., Washington, DC 20374–5066. Phone, 202–685–5190.

Criminal Investigations The Naval Criminal Investigative Service provides criminal investigative, counterintelligence, law enforcement and physical security, and information and personnel security support to Navy and Marine Corps organizations and personnel worldwide, both ashore and afloat. The Naval Criminal Investigative Service is comprised of law enforcement professionals who are investigators, crime laboratory technicians, technical investigative specialists, security specialists, and administrative support personnel.

For further information, contact the Director, Naval Criminal Investigative Service, Department of the Navy, 716 Sicard Street SE., Building 111, Washington Navy Yard, Washington, DC 20388–5000 (phone, 202–433–8800) or the Operations Control Center/Headquarters Duty Officer (phone, 202–433–9323).

Research The Office of Naval Research encourages, promotes, plans, initiates, and coordinates naval research; coordinates naval research and development conducted by other agencies and offices of the Department of the Navy; and supervises, manages, and controls activities within or for the Department of the Navy relating to patents, inventions, trademarks, copyrights, and royalty payments.

For further information, contact the Public Affairs Office, Office of Naval Research, Ballston Tower One, 800 North Quincy Street, Arlington, VA 22217–5660. Phone, 703–696–5031.

Operating Forces The operating forces of the Navy are responsible for naval operations necessary to carry out the Department of the Navy's role in upholding and advancing the national policies and interests of the United States. The operating forces of the Navy include the several fleets, seagoing forces, fleet marine forces and other assigned Marine Corps forces, the Military Sealift Command, Naval Reserve forces, and other forces and activities as may be assigned by the President or the Secretary of the Navy. The Chief of Naval Operations is responsible for the command and administration of the operating forces of the Navy.

The Atlantic Fleet is composed of ships, submarines, and aircraft that operate throughout the Atlantic Ocean and Mediterranean Sea.

The Naval Forces, Europe, includes forces assigned by the Chief of Naval Operations or made available from either the Pacific or Atlantic Fleet to operate in the European theater.

The Pacific Fleet is composed of ships, submarines, and aircraft operating throughout the Pacific and Indian Oceans.

The Military Sealift Command provides ocean transportation for personnel and cargo of all components of the Department of Defense and, as authorized, for other Federal agencies; operates and maintains underway replenishment ships and other vessels providing mobile logistic support to elements of the combatant fleets; and operates ships in support of scientific projects and other programs for Federal agencies.

Other major commands of the operating forces of the Navy are the Naval Forces Central Command, Operational Test and Evaluation Force, Naval Special Warfare Command, and Naval Reserve Force.

Activities

Air Systems The Naval Air Systems Command provides material support to the Navy and Marine Corps for aircraft, airborne weapon systems, avionics, related photographic and support equipment, ranges, and targets.

For further information, contact the Commander, Naval Air Systems Command, 47123 Buse Road, Patuxent River, MD 20670–1547. Phone, 301–757–1487.

Coast Guard The Commandant of the Coast Guard reports to the Secretary of the Navy and the Chief of Naval Operations when the Coast Guard is operating as a service in the Navy, and represents the Coast Guard before the Joint Chiefs of Staff. During such service, Coast Guard operations are integrated and uniform with Department of the Navy operations to the maximum extent possible. The Commandant of the Coast Guard organizes, trains, prepares, and maintains the readiness of the Coast Guard for the performance of national defense missions, as directed. The Commandant also maintains a security capability; enforces Federal laws and regulations on and under the high seas and waters subject to the jurisdiction of the United States; and develops, establishes, maintains, and operates aids to maritime navigation and ice breaking and rescue facilities, with due regard to the requirements of national defense.

Computers and Telecommunications
The Naval Network and Space Operations Command (NNSOC) was formed in July 2002 by the merger of elements of Naval Space Command and Naval Network Operations Command. The command operates and maintains the Navy's space and global telecommunications systems and services, directly supports war fighting operations and command and control of naval forces, and promotes innovative technological solutions to war fighting requirements. NNSOC enables naval forces to use information and space technologies and expertise to achieve and maintain knowledge superiority essential for dominating the battle space.

For further information, contact the Commander, Naval Network and Space Operations Command, 5280 Fourth Street, Dahlgren, VA 22448–5300. Phone, 540–653–6100.

Education and Training The Naval Education and Training Command provides shore-based education and training for Navy, certain Marine Corps, and other personnel; develops specifically designated education and training afloat programs for the fleet; provides voluntary and dependents education; and participates with research and development activities in the development and implementation of the most effective teaching and training systems and devices for optimal education and training.

For further information, contact the Commander, Naval Education and Training Command, Department of the Navy, Naval Air Station Pensacola, 250 Dallas Street, Pensacola, FL 32508–5220. Phone, 850–452–2713.

Facilities The Naval Facilities Engineering Command provides material and technical support to the Navy and

Marine Corps for shore facilities, real property and utilities, fixed ocean systems and structures, transportation and construction equipment, energy, environmental and natural resources management, and support of the naval construction forces.

For further information, contact the Commander, Naval Facilities Engineering Command and Chief of Civil Engineers, Washington Navy Yard, 1322 Patterson Avenue SE., Suite 1000, Washington, DC 20374–5065. Phone, 202–685–1423.

Intelligence The Office of Naval Intelligence ensures the fulfillment of the intelligence requirements and responsibilities of the Department of the Navy.

For further information, contact the Commander, Office of Naval Intelligence, Department of the Navy, 4251 Suitland Road, Washington, DC 20395–5720. Phone, 301–669–3001.

Manpower The Bureau of Naval Personnel directs the procurement, distribution, administration, and career motivation of the military personnel of the regular and reserve components of the U.S. Navy to meet the quantitative and qualitative manpower requirements determined by the Chief of Naval Operations.

For further information, contact the Bureau of Naval Personnel, Department of the Navy, Federal Office Building 2, Washington, DC 20370–5000. Phone, 703–614–2000.

Medicine The Bureau of Medicine and Surgery directs the provision of medical and dental services for Navy and Marine Corps personnel and their dependents; administers the execution and implementation of contingency support plans and programs to provide effective medical and dental readiness capability; provides professional and technical medical and dental service to the fleet, fleet marine force, and shore activities of the Navy; and ensures cooperation with civil authorities in matters pertaining to public health disasters and other emergencies.

For further information, contact the Bureau of Medicine and Surgery, Department of the Navy, 2300 E Street NW., Washington, DC 20373–5300. Phone, 202–762–3211.

Oceanography The Naval Meteorology and Oceanography Command and the Naval Observatory are responsible for the science, technology, and engineering operations which are essential to explore the ocean and the atmosphere and to provide astronomical data and time for naval and related national objectives. To that end, the naval oceanographic program studies astrometry, hydrography, meteorology, oceanography, and precise time.

For further information, contact the following offices: Oceanographer of the Navy, U.S. Naval Observatory, 3450 Massachusetts Avenue NW., Washington, DC 20392–1800. Phone, 202–762–1026; Commander, Naval Meteorology and Oceanography Command, 1100 Balch Blvd., Stennis Space Center, MS 39529–5005. Phone, 228–688–4188; and Superintendent, Naval Observatory, 3450 Massachusetts Avenue NW., Washington, DC 20392–5100. Phone, 202–762–1438.

Sea Systems The Naval Sea Systems Command provides material support to the Navy and Marine Corps and to the Departments of Defense and Transportation for ships, submarines, and other sea platforms, shipboard combat systems and components, other surface and undersea warfare and weapons systems, and ordnance expendables not specifically assigned to other system commands.

For further information, contact the Commander, Naval Sea Systems Command, 1333 Isaac Hull Avenue SE., Washington Navy Yard, DC 20376–1010. Phone, 202–781–1973.

Space and Naval Warfare The Space and Naval Warfare Systems Command provides technical and material support to the Department of the Navy for space systems; command, control, communications, and intelligence systems; and electronic warfare and undersea surveillance.

For further information, contact the Commander, Space and Naval Warfare Systems Command, 4301 Pacific Highway, San Diego, CA 92110–3127. Phone, 619–524–3428.

Strategic Systems The Office of Strategic Systems Programs provides development, production, and material support to the Navy for fleet ballistic missile and strategic weapon systems, security, training of personnel, and the installation and direction of necessary supporting facilities.

For further information, contact the Director, Strategic Systems Programs, Department of the Navy, Nebraska Avenue Complex, 287 Somers Court NW., Suite 10041, Washington, DC 20393–5446. Phone, 202–764–1608.

Supply Systems The Naval Supply Systems Command provides supply management policies and methods and administers related support service systems for the Navy and Marine Corps.

For further information, contact the Commander, Naval Supply Systems Command, 5450 Carlisle Pike, P.O. Box 2050, Mechanicsburg, PA 17055–0791. Phone, 717–605–3565.

Warfare Development The Navy Warfare Development Command plans and coordinates experiments employing emerging operational concepts; represents the Department of the Navy in joint and other service laboratories and facilities and tactical development commands; and publishes and disseminates naval doctrine.

For further information, contact the Commander, Navy Warfare Development Command, 686 Cushing Road, Sims Hall, Newport, RI 02841. Phone, 401–841–2833.

United States Marine Corps

Commandant of the Marine Corps,
Headquarters, U.S. Marine Corps, 2 Navy Annex, Washington, DC 20380–1775
Phone, 703–614–1034. Internet, www.usmc.mil.

The United States Marine Corps was established on November 10, 1775, by resolution of the Continental Congress. Marine Corps composition and functions are detailed in 10 U.S.C. 5063.

The Marine Corps, which is part of the Department of the Navy, is the smallest of the Nation's combat forces and is the only service specifically tasked by Congress to be able to fight in the air, on land, and at sea. Although marines fight in each of these dimensions, they are primarily a maritime force, inextricably linked with the Navy to move from the sea to fight on land.

The Marine Corps conducts entry-level training for its enlisted marines at two bases, Marine Corps Recruit Depot, Parris Island, SC, and Marine Corps Recruit Depot, San Diego, CA. Officer candidates are evaluated at Officer Candidate School at Marine Corps Combat Development Command, Quantico, VA. Marines train to be first on the scene to respond to attacks on the United States or its interests, acts of political violence against Americans abroad, disaster relief, humanitarian assistance, or evacuation of Americans from foreign countries.

Marine Corps Districts

District	Address
1st	1605 Stewart Ave., Garden City, NY 11530–4761
4th	Bldg. 54, Suite 3, New Cumberland, PA 17072–0806
6th	Marine Corps Recruit Depot, P.O. Box 19201, Parris Island, SC 29905–9201
8th	Bldg. 10, Naval Support Activity, New Orleans, LA 70142
9th	3805 E. 155th St., Kansas City, MO 64147–1309
12th	3704 Hochmuth Ave., San Diego, CA 92140–5191

For further information, contact the Division of Public Affairs, Headquarters, U.S. Marine Corps, 2 Navy Annex, Washington, DC 20380–1775. Phone, 703–614–1034. Internet, www.usmc.mil.

United States Naval Academy

Annapolis, MD 21402–5018
Phone, 410–293–1500. Internet, www.usna.edu.

The United States Naval Academy is the undergraduate college of the naval service. Through its comprehensive 4-year program, which stresses excellence in academics, physical education, professional training, conduct, and honor, the Academy prepares young men and women morally, mentally, and physically to be professional officers in the Navy and Marine Corps. All graduates receive a bachelor of science degree in 1 of 19 majors.

For further information concerning the United States Naval Academy, contact the Superintendent, United States Naval Academy, 121 Blake Road, Annapolis, MD 21402–5018.

Sources of Information

Civilian Employment Information about civilian employment with the Department of the Navy can be obtained from the Office of the Deputy Assistant Secretary of the Navy for Civilian Human Resources Web site, www.donhr.navy.mil. Information about civilian employment opportunities in the Washington, DC, metropolitan area can be obtained from the Secretariat/ Headquarters Human Resources Office, Navy Annex, Room 2510, Washington, DC 20370–5240. Phone, 703–693–0888.

Consumer Activities Research programs of the Office of Naval Research cover a broad spectrum of scientific fields, primarily for the needs of the Navy, but much information is of interest to the public. Inquiries on specific research programs should be directed to the Office of Naval Research (Code 10), 800 North Quincy Street, Arlington, VA 22217–5660. Phone, 703–696–5031.

Contracts and Small Business Activities Information about small businesses, minority-owned businesses, and labor surplus activities can be obtained from the Office of Small and Disadvantaged Business Utilization (SADBU), 720 Kennon Street SE., Room 207, Washington Navy Yard, DC 20374–5015. Phone, 202–685–6485.

Environment For information on environmental protection and natural resources management programs of the Navy and Marine Corps, contact the Assistant Secretary of the Navy (Installations and Environment), Environment and Safety, 1000 Navy Pentagon, Room 4A686, Washington, DC, 20350–1000. Phone, 703–693–5080.

General Inquiries Navy and Marine Corps recruiting offices, installation commanders, and Commanding Officers of Marine Corps Districts (see listing in the preceding text) can answer general inquiries concerning the Navy and Marine Corps and their community and public information programs.

The Department of the Navy Office of Information provides accurate and timely information about the Navy so that the general public, the press, and Congress may understand and assess the Navy's programs, operations, and needs. The Office also coordinates Navy participation in community events and supervises the Navy's internal information programs, 1200 Navy Pentagon, Room 4B463, Washington, DC 20350–1200. Phone, 703–695–0965.

Speakers and Films Information can be obtained on speakers, films, and the Naval Recruiting Exhibit Center. For information on the above Navy items, contact the Office of Information, Department of the Navy, 1200 Navy Pentagon, Room 4B463, Washington, DC 20350–1200. Phone, 703–695–0965. For information on above Marine

Corps items, contact the Commandant of the Marine Corps, Headquarters, U.S. Marine Corps (PHC), Room 5E774, The Pentagon, Washington, DC 20380–1775. Phone, 703–614–4309.

Tours To broaden the understanding of the mission, functions, and programs of the Naval Observatory, regular night tours and special group day tours are conducted. The night tours are by reservation only and are given on alternating Monday nights. Information concerning activities of the observatory and public tours may be obtained by writing to the Superintendent, United States Naval Observatory, 3450 Massachusetts Avenue NW., Washington, DC 20392–5420. Phone, 202–762–1438.

Marine Corps Military Career and Training Opportunities The Marine Corps conducts enlisted personnel and officer training programs; provides specialized skill training; participates in the Naval Reserve Officers Training Corps Program for commissioning officers in the Marine Corps; provides the Platoon Leaders Class program for commissioning officers in the Marine Corps Reserve to college freshmen, sophomores, or juniors and the Officer Candidate Class program for college graduates or seniors.

Information about these programs is available at most civilian educational institutions and Navy and Marine Corps recruiting stations. Interested persons also may write directly to the Marine Corps Recruiting Command, 3280 Russell Road, Quantico, VA 22134–5103. Phone, 703–784–9454. Information about Marine Corps Reserve opportunities can be obtained from local Marine Corps recruiting stations or Marine Corps Reserve drill centers. Interested persons may also write directly to the Director, Reserve Affairs, 3280 Russell Road, Suite 507, Quantico, VA 22134–5103. Phone, 703–784–9100.

For further information concerning the Navy, contact the Office of Information, Department of the Navy, 1200 Navy Pentagon, Washington, DC 20350–1200. For press inquiries, phone 703–697–7391 or 703–697–5342. Internet, www.navy.mil. For further information regarding the Marine Corps, contact the Director of Public Affairs, Headquarters, U.S. Marine Corps, 2 Navy Annex (Pentagon 5D773), Washington, DC 20380–1775. Phone, 703–614–1492.

DEFENSE AGENCIES

Defense Advanced Research Projects Agency

3701 North Fairfax Drive, Arlington, VA 22203–1714
Phone, 703–526–6630. Internet, www.darpa.mil.

Director	ANTHONY J. TETHER
Deputy Director	ROBERT LEHENY

The Defense Advanced Research Projects Agency is a separately organized agency within Department of Defense and is under the authority, direction, and control of the Under Secretary of Defense (Acquisition, Technology & Logistics). The Agency serves as the central research and development organization of the Department of Defense with a primary responsibility to maintain U.S. technological superiority over potential adversaries. It pursues imaginative and innovative research and development projects and conducts demonstration projects that embody technology appropriate for joint programs, programs in support of deployed forces, or selected programs of the military departments. To this end, the Agency arranges, manages, and directs the performance of work connected with assigned advanced projects by the military departments, other Government agencies, individuals, private business entities, and educational or research institutions, as appropriate.

For further information, contact the Defense Advanced Research Projects Agency, 3701 North Fairfax Drive, Arlington, VA 22201–1714. Phone, 703–526–6630. Internet, www.darpa.mil.

Defense Business Transformation Agency

1851 South Bell Street, Room 1002, 10th Floor, Arlington, VA 22240
Phone, 703–607–3370. Internet, www.dod.mil/dbt and www.dod.mil/bta.

Co-Directors	PAUL A. BRINKLEY, THOMAS B. MODLY

The Defense Business Transformation Agency (BTA) was established on October 7, 2005. BTA is jointly managed by the Deputy Under Secretary of Defense for Business Transformation and the Deputy Under Secretary of Defense for Financial Management, while operating under the auspices of the Office of the Under Secretary of Defense for Acquisition, Technology, and Logistics. Its mission is to guide the transformation of business operations throughout DOD and to deliver enterprise-level capabilities that align to warfighter needs. BTA serves as a catalyst for and provides direct support to the greater business transformation effort across the DOD.

For further information, please contact the Defense Business Transformation Agency. Phone, 703–607–3370. Internet, www.dod.mil/dbt/contact.html.

Defense Commissary Agency

1300 "E" Avenue, Fort Lee, VA 23801–1800
Phone, 804–734–8253. Internet, www.commissaries.com.

Director	(VACANCY)
Chief Executive Officer	PATRICK NIXON
Chief Operating Officer	SCOTT SIMPSON
Director, Headquarters Operations	THOMAS KINSEY

The Defense Commissary Agency was established in 1990 and is under the authority, direction, and control of the Under Secretary of Defense for Personnel and Readiness and the operational supervision of the Commissary Operating Board. The Agency provides an efficient and effective worldwide system of commissaries that sell quality groceries and household supplies at low prices to members of the Armed Services community. This benefit satisfies customer demand for quality products and delivers exceptional savings while enhancing the military community's quality of life. This Agency supports the morale and peace of mind of deployed combat personnel, who know their families have secure and affordable access to American products. It works closely with its employees, customers, and civilian business partners to satisfy its customers and to promote the commissary benefit. The benefit fosters recruitment, retention, and readiness of skilled and trained personnel.

Sources of Information

Employment The following information is available on the Defense Commissary Agency's Web site at www.commissaries.com or by calling the following telephone numbers: employment (703–603–1600); small business activities (804–734–8742/8529); contracting for resale items (804–734–8884/8885); and contracting for operations support and equipment (804–734–8165/8519). Also the publication "A Business Guide for Marketing to the Defense Commissary Agency" is available online by selecting "About us/Business with DeCA/Marketing/Business Guide."

For further information, contact the Defense Commissary Agency. Phone, 804–734–8253/8998 or 800–699–5063x48998. Internet, www.commissaries.com.

Defense Contract Audit Agency

Suite 2135, 8725 John J. Kingman Road, Fort Belvoir, VA 22060–6219
Phone, 703–767–3200. Internet, www.dcaa.mil.

Director	WILLIAM H. REED
Deputy Director	APRIL G. STEPHENSON

The Defense Contract Audit Agency was established in 1965 and is under the authority, direction, and control of the Under Secretary of Defense (Comptroller)/Chief Financial Officer. The Agency performs all necessary contract audit functions for DOD and provides accounting and financial advisory services to all Defense components responsible for procurement and contract administration. These services are provided in connection with the negotiation, administration, and settlement of contracts and subcontracts. They include evaluating the acceptability of costs claimed or proposed by contractors and reviewing the efficiency and economy of contractor operations. Other Government agencies may request the Agency's services under appropriate arrangements.

The Agency manages its operations through 5 regional offices responsible for approximately 81 field audit offices throughout the United States and overseas. Each region is responsible for the contract auditing function in its assigned area.

Regional Offices—Defense Contract Audit Agency

Region	Address	Director	Telephone
Central	6321 E. Campus Circle, Irving, TX 75063–2742	Francis P. Summers, Jr.	972–753–2513
Eastern	Suite 300, 2400 Lake Park Dr., Smyrna, GA 30080–7644.	Paul Phillips	770–319–4400
Mid–Atlantic	Suite 1000, 615 Chestnut St., Philadelphia, PA 19106–4498.	Michael Steen	215–597–7451
Northeastern	Suite 300, 59 Composite Way, Lowell, MA 01851–5150	Edward Nelson	978–551–9715
Western	Suite 300, 16700 Valley View Ave., La Mirada, CA 90638–5830.	Christopher Andrezze	714–228–7001

For further information, contact the Executive Officer, Defense Contract Audit Agency, Suite 2135, 8725 John J. Kingman Road, Fort Belvoir, VA 22060–6219. Phone, 703–767–3265. Internet, www.dcaa.mil.

Defense Contract Management Agency

6350 Walker Lane, Alexandria, VA 22310–3241
Phone, 703–428–1700. Internet, www.dcma.mil.

Director	(VACANCY)
Deputy Director	KEITH ERNST

The Defense Contract Management Agency was established by the Deputy Secretary of Defense in 2000 and is under the authority, direction, and control of the Under Secretary of Defense (Acquisition, Technology, and Logistics). It is responsible for DOD contract management in support of the military departments, other DOD components, the National Aeronautics and Space Administration, other designated Federal and State agencies, foreign governments, and international organizations, as appropriate.

For further information, contact the Public Affairs Office, Defense Contract Management Agency, 6350 Walker Lane, Alexandria, VA 22310–3241. Phone, 703–428–1969. Internet, www.dcma.mil.

Defense Finance and Accounting Service

Room 920, Crystal Mall 3, Arlington, VA 22240–5291
Phone, 703–607–2616. Internet, www.dfas.mil or https://mypay.dfas.mil.

Director	ZACK E. GADDY
Principal Deputy Director	BRIG. GEN. BELINDA PINCKNEY, USA

The Defense Finance and Accounting Service was established in 1991 under the authority, direction, and control of the Under Secretary of Defense (Comptroller)/Chief Financial Officer to strengthen and reduce costs of financial management and operations within DOD. The Service is responsible for all payments to servicemembers, employees, vendors, and contractors. It provides business intelligence and finance and accounting information to DOD decisionmakers. It is also responsible for preparing annual financial statements for DOD and for the consolidation, standardization, and modernization of finance and accounting requirements, functions, processes, operations, and systems in the Department.

For further information, contact Defense Finance and Accounting Service Corporate Communications, Room 924, Crystal Mall 3, Arlington, VA 22240–5291. Phone, 703–607–1083. Internet, www.dod.mil/dfas.

Defense Information Systems Agency

P.O. Box 4502, Arlington, VA 22204–4502
Phone, 703–607–6900. Internet, www.disa.mil.

Director	LT. GEN. CHARLES E. CROOM, JR., USAF
Vice Director	MAJ. GEN. MARILYN QUAGLIOTTI, USA
Chief of Staff	BRIG. GEN. MARK S. BOWMAN, USA

Established originally as the Defense Communications Agency in 1960, the Defense Information Systems Agency (DISA), is under the authority, direction, and control of the Assistant Secretary of Defense (Command, Control, Communications, and Intelligence). The Agency is responsible for planning, developing, fielding, operating, and supporting command, control, communications, and information systems that serve the needs of the President, Vice President, the Secretary of Defense, the Joint Chiefs of Staff, the combatant commanders, and other DOD components under all conditions of peace and war.

For further information, contact the Public Affairs Office, Defense Information Systems Agency, P.O. Box 4502, Arlington, VA 22204–4502. Phone, 703–607–6900. Internet, www.disa.mil or www.disahomejs.html.

Defense Intelligence Agency

The Pentagon, Washington, DC 20340–5100
Phone, 703–695–0071. Internet, www.dia.mil.

Director	(VACANCY)
Deputy Director	WILLIAM HUNTINGTON

The Defense Intelligence Agency (DIA) was established in 1961 and is under the authority, direction, and control of the Under Secretary of Defense for Intelligence. Its mission is to provide timely, objective, and cogent military intelligence to warfighters, force planners, and defense and national security policymakers. DIA obtains and reports information through its field sites worldwide and the Defense Attaché System; provides timely all-source intelligence analysis; directs Defense Human Intelligence programs; operates the Joint Intelligence Task Force for Combating Terrorism and the Joint Military Intelligence College; coordinates and facilitates Measurement and Signature Intelligence activities; manages and plans collection from specialized technical sources; manages secure DOD intelligence networks; and coordinates required intelligence support for the Secretary of Defense, Joint Chiefs of Staff, Combatant Commanders, and Joint Task Forces.

For further information, contact the Public Affairs Office, Defense Intelligence Agency, Washington, DC 20340–5100. Phone, 703–695–0071. Internet, www.dia.mil.

Defense Legal Services Agency

The Pentagon, Washington, DC 20301–1600
Phone, 703–695–3341. Internet, www.defenselink.mil/dodgc.

Director (General Counsel, Department of Defense)	WILLIAM J. HAYNES II
Principal Deputy Director (Principal Deputy General Counsel)	DANIEL J. DELL'ORTO

The Defense Legal Services Agency was established in 1981 and is under the authority, direction, and control of the General Counsel of the Department of Defense, who also serves as its Director.

The Agency provides legal advice and services for specified DOD components and adjudication of personnel security cases for DOD and other assigned Federal agencies and departments. It also provides technical support and assistance for development of the Department's legislative program; coordinates positions on legislation and Presidential Executive orders; provides a centralized legislative and congressional document reference and distribution point for the Department; maintains the Department's historical legislative files; and administers programs governing standards of conduct and alternative dispute resolution.

For further information, contact the Administrative Officer, Defense Legal Services Agency, The Pentagon, Washington, DC 20301–1600. Phone, 703–697–8343. Internet, www.defenselink.mil/dodgc.

Defense Logistics Agency

Suite 2533, 8725 John J. Kingman Road, Fort Belvoir, VA 22060–6221
Phone, 703–767–6200. Internet, www.dla.mil.

Director	VICE ADM. KEITH W. LIPPERT, SC, USN
Vice Director	MAJ. GEN. LOREN M. RENO, USAF

The Defense Logistics Agency (DLA) is under the authority, direction, and control of the Under Secretary of Defense for Acquisition, Technology, and Logistics. It supports both the logistics requirements of the military services and their acquisition of weapons and other materiel. The Agency provides logistics support and technical services to all branches of the military and to a number of Federal agencies. Agency supply centers consolidate the requirements of the military services and procure the supplies in sufficient quantities to meet their projected needs. The Agency manages supplies in eight commodity areas: fuel, food, clothing, construction material, electronic supplies, general supplies, industrial supplies, and medical supplies.

Field Activities—Defense Logistics Agency

Activity	Commander
Defense Distribution Center	Col. Michael J. Lally, USA
Defense Energy Support Center	Richard Connelly
Defense Logistics Information Service	Col. John Fitzgerald, USMC
Defense National Stockpile Center	Cornel A. Holder
Defense Reutilization and Marketing Service	Col. Patrick O'Donnell, USA
Defense Supply Centers:	
Columbus	Rear. Adm. Charlie Lilli, SC, USN
Philadelphia	Brig. Gen. Jesse R. Cross, USA
Richmond	Rear Adm. Mark F. Heinrich, SC, USN
Document Automation and Production Service	Stephen Sherman
DLA Europe	Col. Paul F. Abel, Jr., USA
DLA Pacific	Col. Christopher Iskra, USA
DLA Central	Col. Franklin K. Jones, USA

Sources of Information

DOD Surplus Sales Program Questions concerning this program should be addressed to DOD Surplus Sales, International Sales Office, 74 Washington Avenue North, Battle Creek, MI 49017–3092. Phone, 877–352–2255.

Employment For the Washington, DC, metropolitan area, all inquiries and applications concerning the Agency's job recruitment program should be addressed to Human Resources, Customer Support Office, 3990 East Broad Street, Building 11, Section 3, Columbus, OH, 43213–0919. Phone, 877–352–4762.

Environment For information concerning the Agency's program, contact the Staff Director, Environmental and Safety, Defense Logistics Agency, Attn: DSS–E, 8725 John J. Kingman Road, Fort Belvoir, VA 22060–6221. Phone, 703–767–6278.

Procurement and Small Business Activities For information, contact the Director, Small and Disadvantaged Business Utilization, Defense Logistics Agency, Attn: DB, 8725 John J. Kingman Road, Fort Belvoir, VA 22060–6221. Phone, 703–767–0192.

For further information, contact the Defense Logistics Agency, Suite 2533, 8725 John J. Kingman Road, Fort Belvoir, VA 22060–6221. Phone, 703–767–6200. Internet, www.dla.mil.

Defense Security Cooperation Agency

2800 Defense Pentagon, Washington, DC 20301–2800
Phone, 703–601–3700. Internet, www.dsca.mil.

Director	LT. GEN. JEFFREY B. KOHLER, USAF
Deputy Director	RICHARD MILLIES

The Defense Security Cooperation Agency was established in 1971 and is under the authority, direction, and control of the Under Secretary of Defense (Policy). The Agency executes the traditional security assistance functions such as military assistance, international military education and training, and foreign military sales, as well as program management responsibilities for humanitarian assistance, demining, and other DOD programs.

For further information, contact the Defense Security Cooperation Agency, 2800 Defense Pentagon, Washington, DC 20301–2800. Phone, 703–601–3700. E-mail, lpa-web@dsca.mil. Internet, www.dsca.mil.

Defense Security Service

1340 Braddock Place, Alexandria, VA 22314–1651
Phone, 703–325–9471. Internet, www.dss.mil.

Director	(VACANCY)
Chief Operating Officer/Chief Information Officer	JANICE HAITH
Chief, Office of Congressional and Public Affairs	CARYL CLUBB

The Defense Security Service (DSS) is under the authority, direction, and control of the Under Secretary of Defense for Intelligence. DSS ensures the safeguarding of classified information used by contractors on behalf of the Department of Defense and 22 other executive branch agencies under the National Industrial Security Program; oversees the protection of conventional arms, munitions, and explosives in the custody of DOD contractors; evaluates the protection of selected private sector critical assets and infrastructures (physical and cyber-based systems) and recommends measures needed to maintain operations identified as vital to DOD; makes clearance determinations for industry and provides support services for DOD Central Adjudicative Facilities; and provides security education, training, and proactive awareness programs for military, civilian, and cleared industry to enhance their proficiency and awareness of DOD security policies and procedures. DSS also has a counterintelligence office to integrate counterintelligence principles into security countermeasures missions and to support the national counterintelligence strategy.

Operating Locations and Centers—Defense Security Service

Region/Center	Director
Regional Headquarters	
Northern (495 Summer St., Boston, MA 2210)	Alfred Buccigrosso
Capital (Crystal Plaza 5, Suite 1100, 02211 S. Clark St., Arlington, VA 22202)	Stephen Hampton
Southern (Pembroke 5, Suite 525, 293 Independence Blvd., Virginia Beach, VA 23462–5400)	Timmy Sartin
Western (Suite 2026, 1149 W. 19th St., Gardena, CA 90248)	John Whitecotton
Security Education Training and Awareness (881 Elkridge Landing Rd., Linthicum, MD 21090–2902)	Thomas Mauriello
Defense Industrial Security Clearance Office (Suite 400, 2780 Airport Square, Columbus, OH 43219–2268)	John W. Faulkner

For further information, contact the Defense Security Service, Office of Congressional and Public Affairs, 1340 Braddock Place, Alexandria, VA 22314–1651. Phone, 703–325–9471. Internet, www.dss.mil.

Defense Threat Reduction Agency

8725 John J. Kingman Road, MS 6201, Ft. Belvoir, VA 22260–5916
Phone, 703–325–2102. Internet, www.dtra.mil.

Director	JAMES A. TEGNELIA
Deputy Director	MAJ. GEN. TRUDY H. CLARK, USAF

The Defense Threat Reduction Agency (DTRA) was established in 1998 and is under the authority, direction, and control of the Under Secretary of Defense for Acquisition, Technology, and Logistics. The DTRA mission is to reduce the threat posed by weapons of mass destruction (WMD). DTRA covers the full range of WMD threats (chemical, biological, nuclear, radiological, and high explosive), bridges the gap between the warfighters and the technical community, sustains the nuclear deterrent, and provides both offensive and defensive technology and operational concepts to the warfighters. DTRA reduces the threat of WMD by implementing arms control treaties and executing the Cooperative Threat Reduction Program. It uses combat support, technology development, and chemical-biological defense to deter the use and reduce the impact of such weapons. It prepares for future threats by developing the technology and concepts needed to counter the new weapons of mass destruction threats and adversaries.

For further information, contact the Public Affairs Office, Defense Threat Reduction Agency, 8725 John J. Kingman Road, MS 6201, Fort Belvoir, VA 22060–5916. Phone, 703–767–5870. Internet, www.dtra.mil.

Missile Defense Agency

The Pentagon, Washington, DC 20301–7100
Phone, 703–695–6420. Internet, www.acq.osd.mil/mda/.

Director	LT. GEN. HENRY A. OBERING III, USAF
Deputy Director	MARVIN K. MCNAMARA, USA
Executive Director	PATRICIA SANDERS
Chief of Staff	COL. DAVID WOLF, USA

[For the Missile Defense Agency statement of organization, see the *Code of Federal Regulations,* Title 32, Part 388]

The Missile Defense Agency's (MDA) mission is to establish and deploy a layered ballistic missile defense system to intercept missiles in all phases of their flight and against all ranges of threats. This capability will provide a defense of the United States, deployed forces, allies, and friends. MDA is under the authority, direction, and control of the Under Secretary of Defense for Acquisition, Technology, and Logistics. MDA manages and directs the DOD's ballistic missile defense acquisition programs and enables the Services to field elements of the overall system as soon as practicable. MDA will develop and test technologies and, if necessary, use prototype and test assets to provide early capability. Additionally, MDA will improve the effectiveness of deployed capabilities by implementing new technologies as they become available or when the threat warrants an accelerated capability.

For further information, contact the Human Resources Directorate, Missile Defense Agency, Washington, DC 20301–7100. Phone, 703–693–1744. Internet, www.acq.osd.mil/mda/.

National Geospatial-Intelligence Agency

4600 Sangamore Road, Bethesda, MD 20816–5003
Phone, 301–227–7300. Internet, www.nga.mil.

Director	LT. GEN. JAMES R. CLAPPER, JR., USAF (RET.)
Deputy Director	JOANNE O. ISHAM

The National Geospatial Intelligence Agency (NGA), formerly the National Imagery and Mapping Agency, was established in 1996 and is under the authority, direction, and control of the Under Secretary of Defense for Intelligence. NGA is a DOD combat support agency and a member of the national intelligence community. NGA's mission is to provide timely, relevant, and accurate geospatial intelligence in support of our national security. Geospatial intelligence means the use and analysis of imagery to describe, assess, and visually depict physical features and geographically referenced activities on the Earth. Headquartered in Bethesda, MD, NGA has major facilities in the Washington, DC, Northern Virginia, and St. Louis, MO, areas with NGA support teams worldwide.

For further information, contact the Public Affairs Office, National Geospatial-Intelligence Agency, 4600 Sangamore Road, Bethesda, MD 20816–5003. Phone, 301–227–2057. Fax, 301–227–3920. Internet, www.nga.mil.

National Security Agency/Central Security Service

Fort George G. Meade, MD 20755–6000
Phone, 301–688–6524. Internet, www.nsa.gov.

Director	(VACANCY)
Deputy Director	LT. GEN. KEITH B. ALEXANDER

The National Security Agency (NSA) was established in 1952, and the Central Security Service (CSS) was established in 1972. It is under the authority, direction, and control of the Under Secretary of Defense for Intelligence. As the Nation's cryptologic organization, the Agency employs the Nation's premier codemakers and codebreakers. It ensures an informed, alert, and secure environment for U.S. warfighters and policymakers. The cryptologic resources of NSA/CSS unite to provide U.S. policymakers with intelligence information derived from America's adversaries while protecting U.S. Government signals and information systems from exploitation by those same adversaries.

For further information, contact the Public Affairs Office, National Security Agency/Central Security Service, Fort Meade, MD 20755–6272. Phone, 301–688–6524. Internet, www.nsa.gov.

Pentagon Force Protection Agency

Director	(VACANCY)
Deputy Director	ROBERT W. TAYLOR

The Pentagon Force Protection Agency (PFPA) was established in May 2002 in response to the events of September 11, 2001, and subsequent terrorist threats facing the DOD workforce and facilities in the National Capital Region (NCR). It is under the authority, direction, and control of the Director, Administration and Management, in the Office of the Secretary of Defense. The Agency provides force protection, security, and law enforcement for the people, facilities, infrastructure, and other resources at the Pentagon Reservation and for DOD activities and facilities within the NCR that are not under the jurisdiction of a military department. Consistent with national strategy on combating terrorism, PFPA addresses the full spectrum of threats, including chemical, biological, and radiological agents, through a strategy of prevention, preparedness, detection, and response to ensure that the DOD workforce and facilities in the NCR are secure and protected.

For further information, contact the Pentagon Force Protection Agency, Washington, DC 20301. Phone, 703–693–3685. Internet, www.pfpa.mil.

JOINT SERVICE SCHOOLS

Defense Acquisition University

Fort Belvoir, VA 22060–5565
Phone, 703–805–3360. Internet, www.dau.mil.

President	FRANK J. ANDERSON, JR.

The Defense Acquisition University, established pursuant to the Defense Acquisition Workforce Improvement Act of 1990 (10 U.S.C. 1701 note), serves as the DOD center for acquisition, technology, and logistics training; performance support; continuous learning; and knowledge sharing. The University is a unified structure with five regional campuses and the Defense Systems Management College-School of Program Managers, which provides executive and international acquisition training. The University's mission is to provide the training, career management, and services that enable the acquisition, technology, and logistics community to make smart business decisions and deliver timely and affordable capabilities to warfighters.

For further information, contact the Director, Operations Support Group, Defense Acquisition University, Fort Belvoir, VA 22060–5565. Phone, 800–845–7606. Internet, www.dau.mil.

Joint Military Intelligence College

Defense Intelligence Analysis Center, Washington, DC 20340–5100
Phone, 202–231–5466. Internet, www.dia.mil/jmic.html.

President	A. DENIS CLIFT
Deputy to the President	COL. KURT KLINGENBERGER, USAF
Provost	RONALD D. GARST

The Joint Military Intelligence College (previously the Defense Intelligence College) was established in 1962. It is a joint service educational institution serving the intelligence community and operates under the authority of the Director, Defense Intelligence Agency. Its mission is to educate military and civilian intelligence professionals and conduct and disseminate relevant intelligence research. The College is authorized by Congress to award the bachelor of science in intelligence (BSI) and master of science of strategic intelligence (MSSI). Courses are offered to full-time students in a traditional daytime format and for part-time students in the evening, on Saturday, and in an executive format (one weekend per month and a 2-week intensive summer period).

For further information, contact the Admissions Office, MCA–2, Joint Military Intelligence College, Defense Intelligence Analysis Center, Washington, DC 20340–5100. Phone, 202–231–5466 or 202–231–3319. Internet, www.dia.mil/jmic.html.

National Defense University

Building 62, 300 Fifth Avenue, Fort McNair, Washington, DC 20319–5066
Phone, 202–685–3922. Internet, www.ndu.edu.

President	LT. GEN. MICHAEL M. DUNN, USAF
Senior Vice President	JOHNNIE CARSON
Vice President for Administration/Chief Operating Officer	CLYDE M. NEWMAN

THE NATIONAL WAR COLLEGE

Building 61, 300 D Street, Fort McNair, Washington, DC 20319–5078
Phone, 202–685–3674. Fax, 202–685–6461. Internet, www.ndu.edu/ndu/nwc/nwchp.html.

Commandant	REAR ADM. RICHARD D. JASKOT, USN
Dean of Students/Executive Officer	COL. MARK B. PIZZO, USMC (RET.)
Dean of Faculty and Academic Programs	COL. TIMOTHY A. RAINEY, USA

INDUSTRIAL COLLEGE OF THE ARMED FORCES

Building 59, 408 Fourth Avenue, Fort McNair, Washington, DC 20319–5062
Phone, 202–685–4337. Internet, www.ndu.edu/ndu/icaf.

Commandant	MAJ. GEN. FRANCES C. WILSON, USMC

JOINT FORCES STAFF COLLEGE

Norfolk, VA 23511–1702
Phone, 757–443–6200. Internet, www.jfsc.ndu.edu.

Commandant	MAJ. GEN. KENNETH J. QUINLAN, USA

INFORMATION RESOURCES MANAGEMENT COLLEGE

Building 62, 300 Fifth Avenue, Fort McNair, Washington, DC 20319–5066
Phone, 202–685–6300. Internet, www.ndu.edu/irmc.

Director	ROBERT D. CHILDS

National Defense University

The National Defense University was established in 1976 and incorporates the following colleges and programs: the Industrial College of the Armed Forces, the National War College, the Joint Forces Staff College, the Information Resources Management College, the Institute for National Strategic Studies, the Center for Hemispheric Defense Studies, the Africa Center for Strategic Studies, the Near East South Asia Center for Strategic Studies, the National Security Education Program, the School for National Security Executive Education, the Center for the Study of Weapons of Mass Destruction, the Center for Technology and National Security Policy, the International Student Management Office, the Office of Reserve Affairs, Capstone, the Secretary of Defense Corporate Fellows Program, the Regional International Outreach Program, the Institute for Homeland Security Studies, and the NATO Staff Officer Orientation Course.

The mission of the National Defense University is to educate military and civilian leaders through teaching, research, and outreach in national security strategy, national military strategy, and national resource strategy; joint and multinational operations; information strategies, operations, and resource management; acquisition; and regional defense and security studies.

For further information, contact the Human Resources Directorate, National Defense University, Building 62, 300 Fifth Avenue, Fort McNair, Washington, DC 20319–5066. Phone, 202–685–2169. Internet, www.ndu.edu.

The National War College

The National War College provides education in national security policy to selected military officers and career civil service employees of Federal departments and agencies concerned with national security. It is the only senior service college with the primary mission of offering a course of study that emphasizes national security policy formulation and the planning and implementation of national strategy. Its 10-month academic program is an issue-centered study in U.S. national security. The elective program is designed to permit each student to tailor his or her academic experience to meet individual professional development needs.

For further information, contact the Department of Administration, The National War College, Building 61, Room G20, 300 D Street, Fort McNair, Washington, DC 20319–5078. Phone, 202–685–3674. Internet, www.ndu.edu/nwc.

Industrial College of the Armed Forces

The Industrial College of the Armed Forces is an educational institution that prepares selected military and civilians for strategic leadership and success in developing our national security strategy and in evaluating, marshalling, and managing resources in the execution of that strategy. The College offers an education in the understanding of the importance of industry to our national security strategy, and more importantly the resource component of national security. The rigorous, compressed curriculum, completed in two semesters, leads to a master of science degree in national resource strategy.

For further information, contact the Director of Operations, Industrial College of the Armed Forces, Building 59, 408 Fourth Avenue, Fort McNair, Washington, DC 20319–5062. Phone, 202–685–4333. Internet, www.ndu.edu/icaf.

Joint Forces Staff College

The Joint Forces Staff College (JFSC) is an intermediate- and senior-level joint college in the professional military education system dedicated to the study of the principles, perspectives, and techniques of joint operational-level planning and warfare. The mission of JFSC is to educate military officers and other national security leaders in joint, multinational, and interagency operational-level planning and warfighting, and to instill a primary commitment to joint, multinational, and interagency teamwork, attitudes, and perspectives. The College accomplishes this mission through four schools: the Joint Advanced Warfighters School, the Joint and Combined Warfighting School, the Joint Continuing and Distance Education School, and the Joint Command, Control, and Information Operations School.

For further information, contact the Directorate of Academic Affairs, Joint Forces Staff College, 7800 Hampton Boulevard, Norfolk, VA 23511–1702. Phone, 757–443–6185. Fax, 757–443–6034. Internet, www.jfsc.ndu.edu.

Information Resources Management College

The Information Resources Management College provides graduate-level courses in information resources management (IRM). The College prepares leaders to direct the information component of national power by leveraging information and information technology for strategic advantage. The College's primary areas of concentration include policy, strategic planning, leadership/management, process improvement, capital planning and investment, performance- and results-based management, technology assessment, architecture, information assurance and security, acquisition, domestic preparedness, transformation, e-

Government, and information operations.

For further information, contact the Registrar, Information Resources Management College, Building 62, 300 Fifth Avenue, Fort McNair, Washington, DC 20319–5066. Phone, 202–685–6300. Internet, www.ndu.edu/irmc.

Uniformed Services University of the Health Sciences

4301 Jones Bridge Road, Bethesda, MD 20814–4799
Phone, 301–295–3770. Internet, www.usuhs.mil.

President	CHARLES L. RICE
Dean, School of Medicine	LARRY LAUGHLIN
Dean, Graduate School of Nursing	PATRICIA A. HINTON-WALKER

Authorized by act of September 21, 1972 (10 U.S.C. 2112), the Uniformed Services University of the Health Sciences was established to educate career-oriented medical officers for the Military Departments and the Public Health Service. The University currently incorporates the F. Edward Hebert School of Medicine (including graduate and continuing education programs) and the Graduate School of Nursing.

Students are selected by procedures recommended by the Board of Regents and prescribed by the Secretary of Defense. The actual selection is carried out by a faculty committee on admissions and is based upon motivation and dedication to a career in the uniformed services and an overall appraisal of the personal and intellectual characteristics of the candidates without regard to sex, race, religion, or national origin. Applicants must be U.S. citizens.

Medical school matriculants will be commissioned officers in one of the uniformed services. They must meet the physical and personal qualifications for such a commission and must give evidence of a strong commitment to serving as a uniformed medical officer. The graduating medical student is required to serve a period of obligation of not less than 7 years, excluding graduate medical education.

Students of the Graduate School of Nursing must be commissioned officers of the Army, Navy, Air Force, or Public Health Service prior to application. Graduate nursing students must serve a commitment determined by their respective service.

For further information, contact the President, Uniformed Services University of the Health Sciences, 4301 Jones Bridge Road, Bethesda, MD 20814–4799. Phone, 301–295–3770. Internet, www.usuhs.mil.

DEPARTMENT OF EDUCATION

400 Maryland Avenue SW., Washington, DC 20202
Phone, 800–USA–LEARN (toll free). Internet, www.ed.gov.

SECRETARY OF EDUCATION	MARGARET SPELLINGS
Chief of Staff	DAVID DUNN
Assistant Secretary for Communication and Outreach	KEVIN F. SULLIVAN
Assistant Secretary for Planning, Evaluation and Policy Development	TOM LUCE
General Counsel	KENT TALBERT, *Acting*
Inspector General	JOHN P. HIGGINS, JR.
Assistant Secretary for Legislation and Congressional Affairs	TERRELL HALASKA
Deputy Secretary	RAYMOND SIMON
Chief Financial Officer	(VACANCY)
Chief Information Officer	MICHELL CLARK, *Acting*
Assistant Secretary for Management	MICHELL CLARK
Assistant Secretary for Civil Rights	STEPHANIE JOHNSON MONROE
Chief Operating Officer for Federal Student Aid	THERESA A. SHAW
Under Secretary	(VACANCY)
Director, Institute of Education Sciences	GROVER J. WHITEHURST
Assistant Secretary for Elementary and Secondary Education	HENRY L. JOHNSON
Assistant Secretary for Postsecondary Education	SALLY STROUP
Assistant Secretary for Special Education and Rehabilitative Services	JOHN HAGER
Assistant Secretary for Vocational and Adult Education	HERIBERTO GONZALEZ, *Acting*
Director, Office of English Language Acquisition, Language Enhancement, and Academic Achievement for Limited English Proficient Students	KATHLEEN LEOS
Deputy Under Secretary, Office of Safe and Drug Free Schools	DEBORAH PRICE
Deputy Under Secretary, Office of Innovation and Improvement	(VACANCY)

The Department of Education establishes policy for, administers, and coordinates most Federal assistance to education. Its mission is to ensure equal access to education and to promote educational excellence throughout the Nation.

The Department of Education was created by the Department of Education Organization Act (20 U.S.C. 3411) and is administered under the supervision and direction of the Secretary of Education.

Secretary The Secretary of Education advises the President on education plans, policies, and programs of the Federal

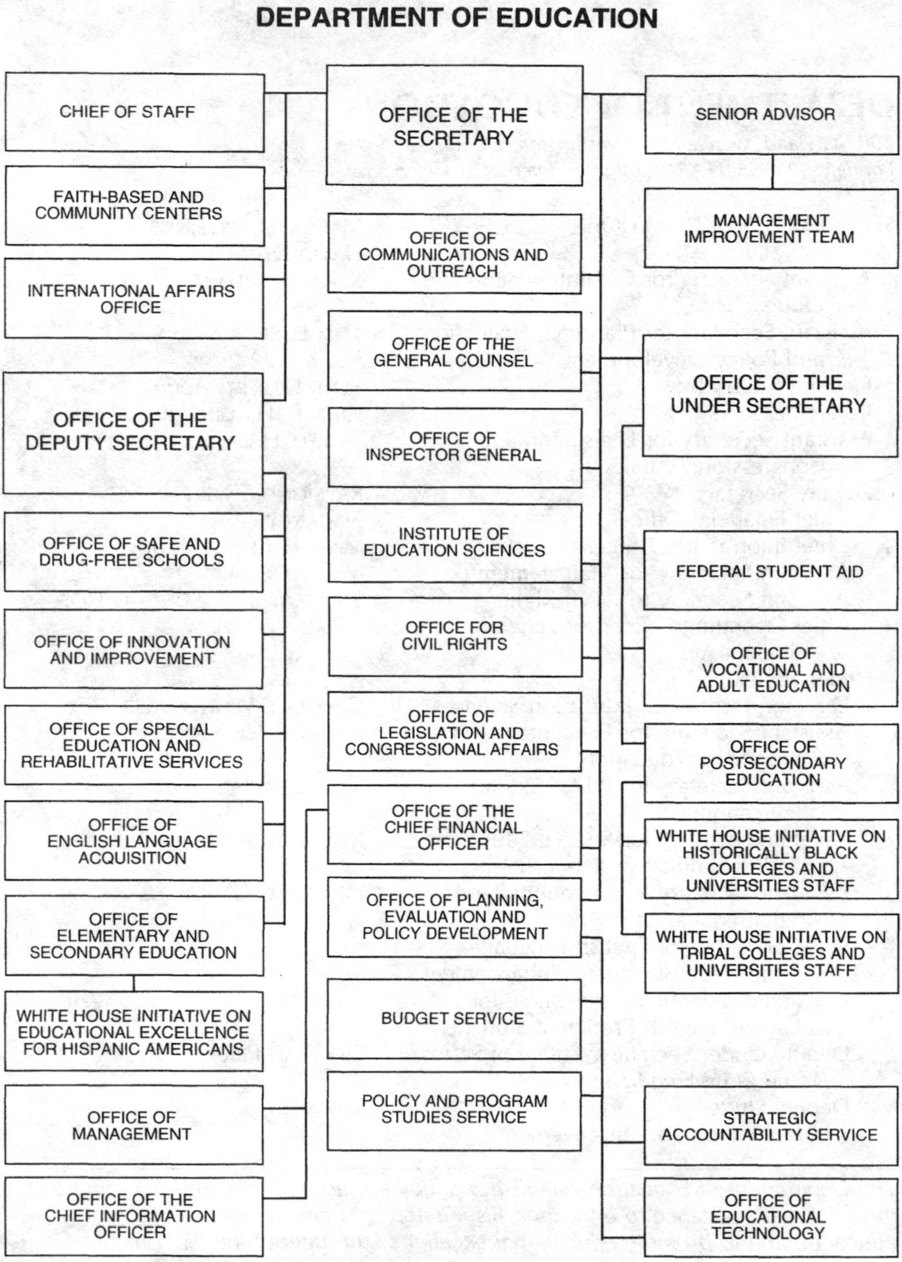
DEPARTMENT OF EDUCATION
CHIEF OF STAFF
OFFICE OF THE SECRETARY
SENIOR ADVISOR
FAITH-BASED AND COMMUNITY CENTERS
MANAGEMENT IMPROVEMENT TEAM
OFFICE OF COMMUNICATIONS AND OUTREACH
INTERNATIONAL AFFAIRS OFFICE
OFFICE OF THE GENERAL COUNSEL
OFFICE OF THE UNDER SECRETARY
OFFICE OF THE DEPUTY SECRETARY
OFFICE OF INSPECTOR GENERAL
OFFICE OF SAFE AND DRUG-FREE SCHOOLS
INSTITUTE OF EDUCATION SCIENCES
FEDERAL STUDENT AID
OFFICE OF INNOVATION AND IMPROVEMENT
OFFICE FOR CIVIL RIGHTS
OFFICE OF VOCATIONAL AND ADULT EDUCATION
OFFICE OF SPECIAL EDUCATION AND REHABILITATIVE SERVICES
OFFICE OF LEGISLATION AND CONGRESSIONAL AFFAIRS
OFFICE OF POSTSECONDARY EDUCATION
OFFICE OF ENGLISH LANGUAGE ACQUISITION
OFFICE OF THE CHIEF FINANCIAL OFFICER
WHITE HOUSE INITIATIVE ON HISTORICALLY BLACK COLLEGES AND UNIVERSITIES STAFF
OFFICE OF ELEMENTARY AND SECONDARY EDUCATION
OFFICE OF PLANNING, EVALUATION AND POLICY DEVELOPMENT
WHITE HOUSE INITIATIVE ON TRIBAL COLLEGES AND UNIVERSITIES STAFF
WHITE HOUSE INITIATIVE ON EDUCATIONAL EXCELLENCE FOR HISPANIC AMERICANS
BUDGET SERVICE
OFFICE OF MANAGEMENT
POLICY AND PROGRAM STUDIES SERVICE
STRATEGIC ACCOUNTABILITY SERVICE
OFFICE OF THE CHIEF INFORMATION OFFICER
OFFICE OF EDUCATIONAL TECHNOLOGY

Government and serves as the chief executive officer of the Department, coordinating and overseeing all Department activities, providing support and encouragement to States and localities on matters related to education, and focusing the resources of the Department and the attention of the country on ensuring equal access to education and promoting educational excellence throughout the Nation.

Activities

Institute of Education Sciences The Institute of Education Sciences was formally established by Education Sciences Reform Act 2002. The Institute includes national education centers focused on research, statistics, and evaluation, and is the mechanism through which the Department supports the research activities needed to improve education policy and practice.

Elementary and Secondary Education The Office of Elementary and Secondary Education directs, coordinates, and formulates policy for the Department's activities relating to early childhood, elementary, and secondary education. Included are grants and contracts to State educational agencies and local school districts, postsecondary schools, and nonprofit organizations for the education of disadvantaged, migrant, and Indian children; enhancement of State student achievement assessment systems; improvement of reading instruction; impact aid; technology; and after-school learning programs. The Office also focuses on providing children with the readiness skills and support they need in early childhood so they are ready to learn when they enter school, and on improving the quality of teachers and other instructional staff.

English Language Acquisition The Office of English Language Acquisition, Language Enhancement, and Academic Achievement for Limited English Proficient Students helps children who are limited in their English, including immigrant children and youth, attain English proficiency, develop high levels of academic attainment in English, and meet the same challenging State academic content and student academic achievement standards that all children are expected to meet.

Federal Student Aid Federal Student Aid partners with postsecondary schools and financial institutions to deliver programs and services that help students finance their education beyond high school. This includes administering postsecondary student financial assistance programs authorized under Title IV of the Higher Education Act 1965, as amended. The Title IV programs collectively represent the Nation's largest source of financial aid for postsecondary students, providing $73 billion in aid to over 10 million students attending more than 6000 institutions in fiscal year 2005.

Innovation and Improvement The Office of Innovation and Improvement (OII) oversees competitive grant programs that support innovations in the educational system and disseminates the lessons learned from these innovative practices. OII also helps coordinate policies related to parental options and choice. OII administers, coordinates, and recommends programs and policy for improving the quality of activities designed to support and test innovations throughout the K–12 system in areas such as parental choice, teacher quality, use of technology in education, and arts in education. OII encourages the establishment of charter schools through planning, start-up funding, and approaches to credit enhancement for charter school facilities. OII also encourages the expansion of parental options and information in the public schools through magnet schools, public school choice, and supplemental educational services, and by working with community organizations to inform parents of their school choice options. OII serves as the Department's liaison and resource to the nonpublic education community, oversees the Family Policy Compliance Office, and manages the Fund for the Improvement of Education.

Postsecondary Education The Office of Postsecondary Education (OPE) formulates Federal postsecondary education policy and administers programs that address critical national needs in support of their mission to increase access to quality postsecondary education. To increase access to postsecondary education, OPE develops policy for Federal student financial programs and support programs that reach out to low-income, first-generation college students and communities. OPE also supports programs that strengthen the capacity of colleges and universities serving a high percentage of disadvantaged students and improve teacher quality. OPE recognizes accrediting agencies that monitor academic quality, promote innovation in higher education, and improve and expand American educational resources for international studies and services.

Safe and Drug-Free Schools The Office of Safe and Drug-Free Schools (OSDFS) administers, coordinates, and recommends policy for improving drug and violence prevention programs. OSDFS, in partnership with State and local educational agencies and public and private nonprofit organizations, supports and provides funding for efforts to create safe schools, respond to crises, prevent drug and alcohol abuse, ensure the health and well-being of students, and teach students good citizenship and character. The Office coordinates Department efforts in these areas with other Federal agencies and also leads the Department of Education's homeland security efforts. OSDFS also participates in the formulation and development of program policy, legislative proposals, and developing administration policies related to violence and drug prevention. The Office drafts program regulations, advises the Secretary on the formulation of comprehensive school health education policy, and develops a national research agenda with other Federal agencies. OSDFS also administers the Department's character, citizenship, and civic education programs; gives guidance on correctional education issues; and provides financial assistance to States and local entities implementing correctional education programs.

Special Education and Rehabilitative Services The Office of Special Education and Rehabilitative Services (OSERS) provides leadership to ensure that people with disabilities have services, resources, and equal opportunities to learn, work, and live as fully integrated, contributing members of society. OSERS supports programs that serve millions of children, youth, and adults with disabilities. It coordinates the activities of the Office of Special Education Programs in administering IDEA (the Individuals with Disabilities Education Act), which works to help States provide quality early intervention services and educational opportunities to help infants, toddlers, children, and youth with disabilities achieve their goals. OSERS supports State vocational rehabilitation and independent living programs that give people with disabilities the education, job training, and job placement services they need to gain meaningful employment and independent lives. It supports research and technological programs that are crafting blueprints for a barrier-free, inclusive society. OSERS supports Gallaudet University, the National Technical Institute for the Deaf, the American Printing House for the Blind, and the Helen Keller National Center.

Vocational and Adult Education The Office of Vocational and Adult Education administers grant, contract, and technical assistance programs for vocational-technical education and for adult education and literacy.

Regional Offices Each regional office serves as a center for the dissemination of information and provides technical assistance to State and local educational agencies and other institutions and individuals interested in Federal educational activities. Offices are located in Boston, MA; New York, NY; Philadelphia, PA; Atlanta, GA; Chicago, IL; Dallas, TX; Kansas City, MO; Denver, CO; San Francisco, CA; and Seattle, WA.

Federally Aided Corporations

American Printing House for the Blind

P.O. Box 6085, Louisville, KY 40206
Phone, 502–895–2405. Internet, www.aph.org.

President	TUCK TINSLEY III
Chairman of the Board	W. JAMES LINTNER, JR.

Founded in 1858 as a nonprofit organization, the American Printing House for the Blind (APH) received its Federal charter in 1879 when Congress passed the Act to promote Education of the Blind. This Act designates APH as the official supplier of educational materials adapted for students who are legally blind and who are enrolled in formal educational programs below the college level. Materials produced and distributed by APH include textbooks in Braille and large type, educational tools such as Braille typewriters and microcomputer software and hardware, teaching aides such as tests and performance measures, and other special supplies. The materials are distributed through allotments to the States to programs serving individuals who are blind.

For further information, contact the American Printing House for the Blind, P.O. Box 6085, Louisville, KY 40206. Phone, 502–895–2405. Internet, www.aph.org.

Gallaudet University

800 Florida Avenue NE., Washington, DC 20002
Phone, 202–651–5000. Internet, www.gallaudet.edu.

President, Gallaudet University	I. KING JORDAN
Chairman, Board of Trustees	GLENN B. ANDERSON

Gallaudet University received its Federal charter in 1864 and is currently authorized by the Education of the Deaf Act of 1986, as amended. Gallaudet is a private, nonprofit education institution providing elementary, secondary, undergraduate, and continuing education programs for persons who are deaf. The University offers a traditional liberal arts curriculum for students who are deaf, and graduate programs in fields related to deafness for students who are deaf and students who are hearing. Gallaudet also conducts a wide variety of basic and applied deafness research and provides public service programs for persons who are deaf and for professionals who work with persons who are deaf.

Gallaudet University is accredited by a number of accrediting bodies, among which are the Middle States Association of Colleges and Secondary Schools, the National Council for Accreditation of Teacher Education, and the Conference of Educational Administrators of Schools and Programs for the Deaf.

Laurent Clerc National Deaf Education Center Gallaudet's Laurent Clerc National Deaf Education Center operates elementary and secondary education programs that are federally funded, on the main campus of the University—the Kendall Demonstration Elementary School and the Model Secondary School for the Deaf. These programs are authorized by the Education of the Deaf Act of 1986 (20 U.S.C. 4304, as amended) for the primary purpose of developing, evaluating, and disseminating model curricula, instructional techniques and strategies, and materials that can be used in a variety of educational environments serving individuals throughout the Nation who are deaf or hard of hearing. The Education of the Deaf Act requires the programs to include students preparing for postsecondary opportunities other than college and students with a broad spectrum of needs, such as students who are lower achieving academically, come from non-English-speaking homes, have secondary disabilities, are members of minority groups, or are from rural areas.

Model Secondary School for the Deaf The school was established by act of October 15, 1966 (20 U.S.C. 693), which was superseded by the Education of the Deaf Act of 1986. The school provides day and residential facilities for secondary-aged students from across the United States from grades 9 to 12, inclusively.

Kendall Demonstration Elementary School The school became the Nation's first demonstration elementary school for the deaf by act of December 24, 1970 (20 U.S.C. 695). This act was superseded by the Education of the Deaf Act of 1986. The school is a day program for students from the Washington, DC, metropolitan area from the age of onset of deafness to age 15, inclusively, but not beyond the eighth grade or its equivalent.

For further information, contact the Public Relations Office, Gallaudet University, 800 Florida Avenue NE., Washington, DC 20002. Phone, 202–651–5505. Internet, www.gallaudet.edu.

Howard University

2400 Sixth Street NW., Washington, DC 20059
Phone, 202–806–6100. Internet, www.howard.edu.

President — H. PATRICK SWYGERT

Howard University was established by act of March 2, 1867 (14 Stat. 438). It offers instruction in 12 schools and colleges, as follows: the colleges of arts and sciences; dentistry; engineering, architecture, and computer sciences; medicine; pharmacy, nursing, and allied health sciences; the graduate school; the schools of business; communications; divinity; education; law; and social work. In addition, Howard University has research institutes, centers, and special programs in the following areas: cancer, child development, computational science and engineering, international affairs, sickle cell disease, and the national human genome project.

For further information, contact the Office of University Communications, Howard University, 2400 Sixth Street NW., Washington, DC 20059. Phone, 202–806–0970. Internet, www.howard.edu.

National Institute for Literacy

Suite 730, 1775 I Street NW., Washington, DC 20006
Phone, 202–233–2025

Director — SANDRA L. BAXTER, *Acting*

The National Institute for Literacy leads the national effort towards a fully literate America. By building and strengthening national, regional, and State literacy infrastructures, the Institute fosters collaboration and innovation. Its goal is to ensure that all Americans with literacy needs receive the high-quality education and basic skills services necessary to achieve success in the workplace, family, and community.

National Technical Institute for the Deaf

Rochester Institute of Technology

52 Lomb Memorial Drive, Rochester, NY 14623
Phone, 716–475–6853 (voice/TDD). Internet, www.ntid.edu.

President, Rochester Institute of Technology	ALBERT J. SIMONE
Vice President, National Technical Institute for the Deaf	T. ALAN HURWITZ

The National Technical Institute for the Deaf (NTID) was established by act of June 8, 1965 (20 U.S.C. 681) to promote the employment of persons who are deaf, by providing technical and professional education. The National Technical Institute for the Deaf Act was superseded by the Education of the Deaf Act of 1986 (20 U.S.C. 4431, as amended October 7, 1998). The U.S. Department of Education maintains a contract with the Rochester Institute of Technology (RIT) for the operation of a residential facility for postsecondary technical training and education for individuals who are deaf. The purpose of the special relationship with the host institution is to give NTID's faculty and students access to more facilities, institutional services, and career preparation options than could be otherwise provided by a national technical institute for the deaf standing alone.

NTID offers a variety of technical programs at the certificate, diploma, and associate degree levels. Degree programs include majors in business, engineering, science, and visual communications. In addition, NTID students may participate in approximately 200 educational programs available through the Rochester Institute of Technology. Students who are deaf that enroll in NTID or RIT programs are provided a wide range of support services and special programs to assist them in preparing for their careers, including tutoring, counseling, notetaking, interpreting, specialized educational media, cooperative work experience, and specialized job placement. RIT and NTID are both accredited by the Middle States Association of Colleges and Secondary Schools.

NTID also conducts applied research in occupational- and employment-related aspects of deafness, communication assessment, demographics of NTID's target population, and learning processes in postsecondary education. In addition, NTID conducts training workshops and seminars related to deafness. These workshops and seminars are offered to professionals throughout the Nation who employ, work with, teach, or otherwise serve persons who are deaf.

For further information, contact the Rochester Institute of Technology, National Technical Institute for the Deaf, Department of Recruitment and Admissions, Lyndon Baines Johnson Building, 52 Lomb Memorial Drive, Rochester, NY 14623–5604. Phone, 716–475–6700. Internet, www.ntid.edu.

Sources of Information

Inquiries on the following information may be directed to the specified office, Department of Education, 400 Maryland Avenue SW., Washington, DC 20202.

Contracts and Small Business Activities Call or write the Office of Small and Disadvantaged Business Utilization. Phone, 202–245–6301.

Employment Inquiries and applications for employment, and inquiries regarding the college recruitment program, should be directed to the Human Resources Group. Phone, 202–401–0553.

Organization Contact the Executive Office, Office of Management. Phone, 202–401–0690. TDD, 202–260–8956.

For further information, contact the Information Resources Center, Department of Education, Room 5E248 (FB–6), 400 Maryland Avenue SW., Washington, DC 20202. Phone, 800–USA–LEARN. Internet, www.ed.gov.

DEPARTMENT OF ENERGY

1000 Independence Avenue SW., Washington, DC 20585
Phone, 202–586–5000. Internet, www.energy.gov.

SECRETARY OF ENERGY	SAMUEL W. BODMAN
Deputy Secretary	CLAY SELL
Under Secretary for Science	RAYMOND L. ORBACH
Under Secretary of Energy	DAVID K. GARMAN
Assistant Secretary, Fossil Energy	JEFFREY D. JARRETT
Assistant Secretary, Energy Efficiency and Renewable Energy	ALEXANDER KARSNER
Director of Nuclear Energy, Science, and Technology	R. SHANE JOHNSON, *Acting*
Administrator, Energy Information Administration	GUY F. CARUSO
Director of Science	RAYMOND L. ORBACH
Assistant Secretary, Environmental Management	JAMES RISPOLI
Director of Civilian Radioactive Waste Management	EDWARD F. SPROAT III
Under Secretary for Nuclear Security and Administrator for National Nuclear Security Administration	LINTON F. BROOKS
Deputy Administrator for Defense Programs	THOMAS P. D'AGOSTINO
Deputy Administrator for Defense Nuclear Nonproliferation	JERALD S. PAUL, *Acting*
Deputy Administrator for Naval Reactors	ADM. KIRKLAND H. DONALD, USN
Deputy Under Secretary for Counterterrorism	STEVEN AOKI, *Acting*
Chief Financial Officer	SUSAN J. GRANT
Chief Human Capital Officer	JEFF T.H. PON
Chief Information Officer	THOMAS N. PYKE
General Counsel	DAVID R. HILL
Inspector General	GREGORY H. FRIEDMAN
Assistant Secretary, Congressional and Intergovernmental Affairs	JILL L. SIGAL
Assistant Secretary, Environment, Safety, and Health	C. RUSSEL SHEARER, *Acting*
Assistant Secretary, Policy and International Affairs	KAREN HARBERT
Director, Public Affairs	ANNE W. KOLTON
Director of Economic Impact and Diversity	THERESA ALVILLAR SPEAKE
Director of Hearings and Appeals	GEORGE B. BREZNAY
Director of Human Capital Management	CLAUDIA A. CROSS
Director of Intelligence and Counterintelligence	ROLF MOWATT-LARSSEN
Director of Management	INGRID KOLB

Executive Director, Secretary of Energy Advisory Board Support Office	MICHAEL RICHARD
Defense Nuclear Facilities Safety Board Liaison	MARK B. WHITAKER
Director of Security and Safety Performance Assurance	GLENN S. PODONSKY
Director of Legacy Management	MICHAEL W. OWEN
Director of Electricity Delivery and Energy Reliability	KEVIN M. KOLEVAR

FEDERAL ENERGY REGULATORY COMMISSION

888 First Street NE., Washington, DC 20426
Phone, 202–502–8055. Internet, www.ferc.gov.

Chairman	JOSEPH T. KELLIHER
Commissioners	NORA MEAD BROWNELL, SUEDEEN KELLY, (2 VACANCIES)

The Department of Energy's mission is to foster a secure and reliable energy system that is environmentally and economically sustainable; to be a responsible steward of the Nation's nuclear weapons; to clean up the Department's facilities; to lead in the physical sciences and advance the biological, environmental, and computational sciences; and to provide premier scientific instruments for the Nation's research enterprise.

The Department of Energy (DOE) was established by the Department of Energy Organization Act (42 U.S.C. 7131), effective October 1, 1977, pursuant to Executive Order 12009 of September 13, 1977. The act consolidated the major Federal energy functions into one Cabinet-level Department.

Secretary The Secretary decides major energy policy and planning issues; acts as the principal spokesperson for the Department; and ensures the effective communication and working relationships with Federal, State, local, and tribal governments and the public. The Secretary is the principal adviser to the President on energy policies, plans, and programs.

Defense Nuclear Facilities Safety Board Liaison The Office of the Departmental Representative to the Defense Nuclear Facilities Safety Board (DNFSB) manages the Department's interaction with DNFSB as mandated by law, including achievement of the mutual goal of ensuring protection of public and employee health and safety and the environment by appropriate and timely resolution of DNFSB recommendations and concerns.

For further information, contact the Departmental Representative to the Defense Nuclear Facilities Safety Board. Phone, 202–586–3887.

Intelligence and Counterintelligence
The Office of Intelligence and Counterintelligence ensures that all departmental intelligence information requirements are met and that the Department's technical, analytical, and research expertise is made available to support U.S. intelligence efforts. The Office develops and implements programs to identify, neutralize, and deter foreign government or industrial intelligence activities directed at or involving Department programs, personnel, facilities, technologies, classified information, and sensitive information. The Office ensures effective use of the U.S. Government's intelligence apparatus in support of DOE's need for information on foreign energy situations and hostile threats, information on global nuclear weapons development, nonproliferation, and foreign hydrocarbon, nuclear, and other energy production and consumption.

DEPARTMENT OF ENERGY

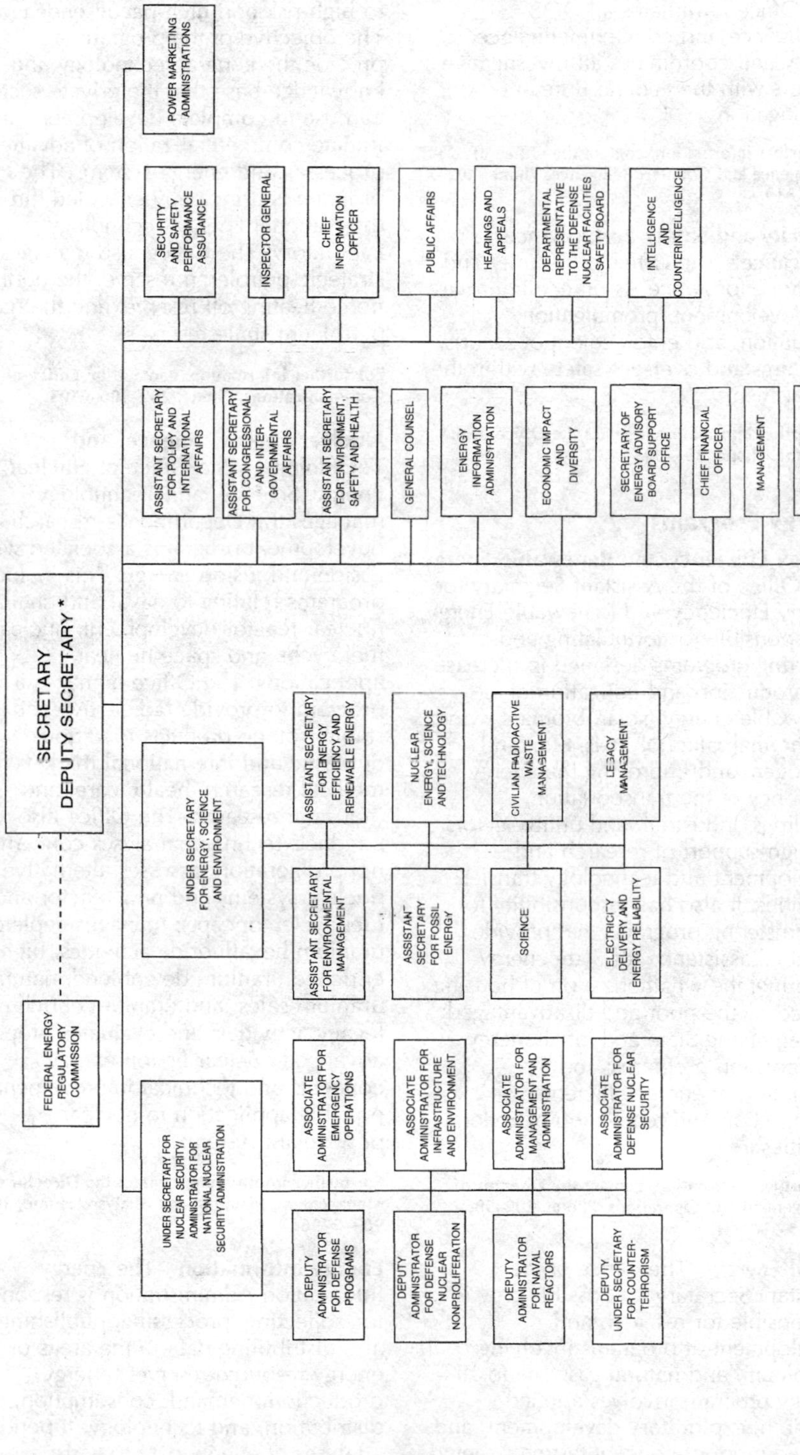

* The Deputy Secretary also serves as the Chief Operating Officer.

The Office formulates all DOE intelligence and counterintelligence policy and coordinates all investigative matters with the Federal Bureau of Investigation.

For further information, contact the Office of Intelligence and Counterintelligence. Phone, 202–586–2610.

Security and Safety Performance Assurance The Office of Security and Safety Performance Assurance improves the development, promulgation, evaluation, and enforcement of security programs and oversees safety within the Department.

For further information, contact the Office of the Director. Phone, 301–903–3777.

Energy Programs

Energy Efficiency and Renewable Energy The Office of the Assistant Secretary for Energy Efficiency and Renewable Energy is responsible for formulating and directing programs designed to increase the production and utilization of renewable energy (solar, biomass, wind, geothermal, alcohol fuels, etc.) and hydrogen, and improving the energy efficiency of the transportation, buildings, industrial, and utility sectors through support of research and development and technology transfer activities. It also has responsibility for administering programs that provide financial assistance for State energy planning; the weatherization of housing owned by the poor and disadvantaged; implementing State and local energy conservation programs; and the promotion of energy efficient construction and renovation of Federal facilities.

For further information, contact the Director of Management and Operations. Phone, 202–586–6768.

Fossil Energy The Office of the Assistant Secretary for Fossil Energy is responsible for research and development of programs involving coal, petroleum, and natural gas. The fossil energy program involves applied research, exploratory development, and limited proof-of-concept testing targeted to high-risk and high-payoff endeavors. The objective of the program is to provide the general technology and knowledge base that the private sector can use to complete development and initiate commercialization of advanced processes and energy systems. The program is principally executed through the National Energy Technology Laboratory. The Office also manages the strategic petroleum reserve, the northeast home heating oil reserve, and the naval petroleum shale reserves.

For further information, contact the Office of Communications. Phone, 202–586–6503.

Nuclear Energy, Science, and Technology The Office of Nuclear Energy, Science, and Technology manages the Department's research and development programs associated with fission and fusion energy. This includes programs relating to naval and civilian nuclear reactor development, nuclear fuel cycle, and space nuclear applications. The Office manages a program to provide radioactive and stable isotope products to various domestic and international markets for medical research, health care, and industrial research. The Office also conducts technical analyses concerning nonproliferation; assesses alternative nuclear systems and new reactor and fuel cycle concepts; manages depleted uranium hexafluoride activities, highly enriched uranium downblend, natural uranium sales, and uranium enrichment legacy activities; and evaluates proposed advanced nuclear fission energy concepts and technical improvements for possible application to nuclear powerplant systems.

For further information, contact the Director of Management, Planning and Analysis. Phone, 301–903–3796.

Energy Information The Energy Information Administration is responsible for collecting, processing, publishing, and distributing data in the areas of energy resource reserves, energy production, demand, consumption, distribution, and technology. It performs analyses of energy data to assist government and nongovernment users in understanding energy trends.

For further information, contact the Director, National Energy Information Center. Phone, 202-586-6537.

Electricity Delivery and Energy Reliability The Office of Electricity Delivery and Energy Reliability leads a national effort to modernize and expand America's electricity delivery system. The Office is responsible for the enhanced security and reliability of the energy infrastructure and facilitates the recovery from disruptions to energy supply.

For further information, contact the Office of the Director. Phone, 202-586-1411.

Nuclear Security Programs

Nuclear Security The National Nuclear Security Agency (NNSA) was created by Congress through the National Defense Authorization Act for Fiscal Year 2000 to bring focus to the management of the Nation's defense nuclear security programs. Three existing organizations within the Department of Energy—Defense Programs, Defense Nuclear Nonproliferation, and Naval Reactors—were combined into a new, separately organized and managed agency within DOE, headed by an Administrator who reports to the Secretary. The NNSA is responsible for strengthening United States security through military application of nuclear energy and by reducing the global threat from terrorism and weapons of mass destruction.

For further information, contact the Associate Administrator for Management and Administration. Phone, 202-586-8454.

Defense Activities The Office of the Deputy Administrator for Defense Programs directs the Nation's nuclear weapons research, development, testing, production, and surveillance program. It is also responsible for the production of the special nuclear materials used by the weapons program within the Department and the management of defense nuclear waste and byproducts. The Office ensures the technology base for the surety, reliability, military effectiveness, and credibility of the nuclear weapon stockpile. It also manages research in inertial confinement fusion.

For further information, contact the Associate Administrator for Management and Administration. Phone, 301-586-8454.

Naval Reactors The Office of the Deputy Administrator for Naval Reactors manages and performs research, development, design, acquisition, specification, construction, inspection, installation, certification, testing overhaul, refueling, operations procedures, maintenance, supply support, and ultimate disposition of naval nuclear propulsion plants.

For further information, contact the Deputy Administrator for Naval Reactors. Phone, 703-603-5502.

Nuclear Nonproliferation The Office of the Deputy Administrator for Defense Nuclear Nonproliferation directs the development of the Department's policy, plans, procedures, and research and development activities relating to arms control, nonproliferation, export controls, international nuclear safety and safeguard, and surplus fissile materials inventories elimination activities.

For further information, contact the Associate Administrator for Management and Administration. Phone, 202-586-8454.

Environmental Quality Programs

Civilian Radioactive Waste Management The Office of Civilian Radioactive Waste Management is responsible for implementation of the Nuclear Waste Policy Act of 1982, as amended (42 U.S.C. 10101 *et seq.*), which provides for the development of a permanent, safe geologic repository for disposal of spent nuclear fuel and high-level radioactive waste.

For further information, contact the Director for Human Resources. Phone, 202-586-5975.

Environmental Management The Office of the Assistant Secretary for Environmental Management manages safe cleanup and closure of sites and facilities; directs a safe and effective waste management program, including storage and disposal of transuranic, and mixed low- and high-level waste; and develops and implements an applied research program to provide innovative technologies that yield permanent cleanup solutions at reduced costs.

For further information, contact the Director of Resource Management. Phone, 202–586–2661.

Legacy Management The Office of Legacy Management manages the Department's post-closure responsibilities and ensures the future protection of human health and the environment. The Office has control and custody of legacy land, structures, and facilities and is responsible for maintaining them at levels suitable for long-term use.

For further information, contact the Director of Property Management and Community Assistance. Phone, 202–586–3751.

Science Program

The Office of Science supports basic research that underpins DOE missions in national security, energy, and environment; constructs and operates large scientific facilities for the U.S. scientific community; and provides the infrastructure support for 10 national laboratories. In terms of basic research, the Office of Science provides over 40 percent of Federal support to the physical sciences (including 90 percent of Federal support for high energy and nuclear physics), the sole support to select sub-fields of national importance, such as nuclear medicine, heavy element chemistry, and magnetic fusion, and support for the research of scientists and graduate students located in universities throughout the Nation. Office of Science support for major scientific user facilities, including accelerators, synchrotron light sources, and neutron sources, means that more that 18,000 scientists per year are able to use these state-of-the-art facilities to conduct research in a wide range of fields, including biology, medicine, and materials.

For further information, contact the Associate Director of Resource Management. Phone, 301–903–4944.

Federal Energy Regulatory Commission

The Federal Energy Regulatory Commission (FERC) is an independent agency within the Department of Energy which regulates the interstate transmission of electricity, natural gas, and oil. FERC has retained many of the functions of the Federal Power Commission, such as setting rates and charges for the transportation and sale of natural gas and the transportation of oil by pipelines, as well the valuation of such pipelines. FERC also reviews proposals to build liquefied natural gas terminals and interstate natural gas pipelines as well as licensing hydropower projects. FERC is composed of five members appointed by the President of the United States with the advice and consent of the Senate. FERC Commissioners serve 5-year terms and have an equal vote on regulatory matters. One member is designated by the President to serve as both Chairman and FERC's administrative head.

For further information, contact the Office of External Affairs. Phone, 202–502–8004 or 866–208–FERC. Fax, 202–208–2106. Internet, www.ferc.gov.

Operations and Field Offices

The vast majority of the Department's energy and physical research and development, environmental restoration, and waste management activities are carried out by contractors who operate Government-owned facilities. Management and administration of Government-owned, contractor-operated facility contracts are the major responsibility of the Department's five operations offices and three special purpose field offices.

Department operations offices provide a formal link between Department headquarters and the field laboratories and other operating facilities. They also manage programs and projects as assigned from lead headquarters program offices. Routine management guidance, coordination, oversight of the operations and field offices, and daily specific program direction for the operations offices is provided by the appropriate Assistant Secretary, Office Director, or program officer.

The service center and eight site offices are part of the National Nuclear Security Administration (NNSA) and provide operations oversight and contract administration for NNSA site activities, acting as the agency's risk acceptance for the site. The site offices are responsible for the following functions: the safe and secure operation of facilities under the purview of NNSA; supporting NNSA programs to ensure their success in accordance with their expectations; and ensuring the long-term viability of the site to support NNSA programs and projects.

Operations, Field and Site Offices—Department of Energy

Office/Address	Telephone
Operations Offices	
Chicago, IL (9800 S. Cass Ave., Argonne, IL 60439–4802)	630–252–2110
Idaho Falls, ID (850 Energy Dr., 83401–1563)	208–526–5665
Oak Ridge, TN (P.O. Box 2001, 37831–8763)	423–576–4444
Richland, WA (P.O. Box 550, 825 Jadwin Ave., 99352–0550)	509–376–7395
Savannah River, SC (P.O. Box A, Aiken, SC 29802–0900)	803–725–2405
Field Offices	
Carlsbad, NM (4021 National Parks Hwy, 88220)	505–234–7330
Miamisburg, OH (P.O. Box 3020, 45343–3020)	937–865–3977
Rocky Flats, CO (P.O. Box 928, Golden, CO 80402–0928)	303–966–2025
Site Offices	
Kansas City, MO (P.O. Box 41020, 64141–3202)	816–997–3341
Las Vegas, NV (P.O. Box 98518, Las Vegas, NV 89193–8518)	702–295–3211
Livermore, CA (Rm. 700N, 1301 Clay St., Oakland, CA 94612)	510–637–1800
Los Alamos, NM (528 35th St., 87544)	505–667–5491
NNSA Service Center, NM (P.O. Box 5400, Albuquerque, NM87185–5400)	505–845–6050
Pantex, TX (P.O. Box 30030, Amarillo, TX 79120)	806–477–3000
Savannah River, SC (Attn: S. Green, HRM&DD, P.O. Box A, Aiken, SC 29802)	803–725–2405
Y12, TN (P.O. Box 2050, Oak Ridge, TN 07001)	423–576–4444

Power Administrations

The marketing and transmission of electric power produced at Federal hydroelectric projects and reservoirs is carried out by the Department's four Power Administrations. Management oversight of the Power Administrations is the responsibility of the Deputy Secretary.

Bonneville Power Administration The Administration markets power produced by the Federal Columbia River Power System at the lowest rates, consistent with sound business practices, and gives preference to public entities.

In addition, the Administration is responsible for energy conservation, renewable resource development, and fish and wildlife enhancement under the provisions of the Pacific Northwest Electric Power Planning and Conservation Act of 1980 (16 U.S.C. 839 note).

For further information, contact the Bonneville Power Administration, 905 NE. Eleventh Avenue, Portland, OR 97232–4169. Phone, 503–230–5101.

Southeastern Power Administration The Administration is responsible for the transmission and disposition of surplus electric power and energy generated at reservoir projects in the States of West Virginia, Virginia, North Carolina, South Carolina, Georgia, Florida, Alabama, Mississippi, Tennessee, and Kentucky.

The Administration sets the lowest possible rates to consumers, consistent with sound business principles, and gives preference in the sale of such power and energy to public bodies and cooperatives.

For further information, contact the Southeastern Power Administration, 1166 Athens Tech Road, Elberton, GA 30635–6711. Phone, 706–213–3805.

Southwestern Power Administration
The Administration is responsible for the sale and disposition of electric power and energy in the States of Arkansas, Kansas, Louisiana, Missouri, Oklahoma, and Texas.

The Southwestern Power Administration transmits and disposes of the electric power and energy generated at Federal reservoir projects, supplemented by power purchased from public and private utilities, in such a manner as to encourage the most widespread and economical use. The Administration sets the lowest possible rates to consumers, consistent with sound business principles, and gives preference in the sale of power and energy to public bodies and cooperatives.

The Administration also conducts and participates in the comprehensive planning of water resource development in the Southwest.

For further information, contact the Southwestern Power Administration, Suite 1600, Williams Center Tower One, One West Third Street, Tulsa, OK 74103–3532. Phone, 918–595–6601.

Western Area Power Administration
The Administration is responsible for the Federal electric power marketing and transmission functions in 15 Central and Western States, encompassing a geographic area of 1.3 million square miles. The Administration sells power to cooperatives, municipalities, public utility districts, private utilities, Federal and State agencies, and irrigation districts. The wholesale power customers, in turn, provide service to millions of retail consumers in the States of Arizona, California, Colorado, Iowa, Kansas, Minnesota, Montana, Nebraska, Nevada, New Mexico, North Dakota, South Dakota, Texas, Utah, and Wyoming.

The Administration is responsible for the operation and maintenance of transmission lines, substations, and various auxiliary power facilities in the aforementioned geographic area and also for planning, construction, and operation and maintenance of additional Federal transmission facilities that may be authorized in the future.

For further information, contact the Western Area Power Administration, 12155 West Alameda Parkway, Lakewood, CO 80228–2802. Phone, 720–962–7000.

Sources of Information

Consumer Information For information on the consumer impact of Department policies and operations and for other DOE consumer information, call 202–586–1908.

Contracts and Small and Disadvantaged Business Utilization Activities Information on business opportunities with the Department and its contractors is available electronically through the Internet, at www.pr.doe.gov/prbus.html. For information on existing DOE awards, call 202–586–9051.

Electronic Access Information concerning the Department is available through the Internet at www.energy.gov.

Employment Most jobs in the Department are in the competitive service. Positions are filled through hiring individuals with Federal civil service status, but may also be filled using lists of competitive eligibles from the Office of Personnel Management or the Department's special examining units. Contact the Office of Human Capital Management. Phone, 202–586–1234.

Freedom of Information Act To obtain administrative and technical support in matters involving the Freedom of Information, Privacy, and Computer Matching Acts, call 202–586–5955.

Inspector General Hotline Persons who wish to raise issues of concern regarding departmental operations, processes, or practices or who may be aware of or suspect illegal acts or noncriminal violations should contact the hotline. Phone, 202–586–4073 or 800–541–1625.

Public Information Issuances, Press Releases, and Publications For media contacts, call 202–586–5575.

Public Reading Room For information materials on DOE and public access to DOE records, call 202–586–3142.

Scientific and Technical Information The Office manages a system for the centralized collection, announcement, and dissemination of and historical reference to the Department's scientific and technical information and worldwide energy information. Contact the Office of Scientific and Technical Information, 175 Oak Ridge Turnpike, Oak Ridge, TN 37830–7255. Phone, 423–576–1188.

Whistleblower Assistance Federal or DOE contractor employees wishing to make complaints of alleged wrongdoing against the Department or its contractors should call 202–586–4034.

For further information concerning the Department of Energy, contact the Office of Public Affairs, Department of Energy, 1000 Independence Avenue SW., Washington, DC 20585. Phone, 202–586–4940. Internet, www.energy.gov.

DEPARTMENT OF HEALTH AND HUMAN SERVICES *

200 Independence Avenue SW., Washington, DC 20201
Phone, 202–619–0257. Internet, www.hhs.gov.

SECRETARY OF HEALTH AND HUMAN SERVICES	MICHAEL O. LEAVITT
Deputy Secretary	ALEX M. AZAR II
Chief of Staff	RICH MCKEOWN
Chair, Departmental Appeals Board	CECILIA SPARKS FORD
Director, Intergovernmental Affairs	JACK KALAVRITINOS
Director, Office for Civil Rights	WINSTON WILKINSON
Executive Secretary	ANN AGNEW
Assistant Secretary for Health	JOHN O. AGWUNOBI
Surgeon General	RICHARD CARMONA
Assistant Secretary for Administration and Management	JOE ELLIS
Assistant Secretary for Budget, Technology, and Finance	CHARLES JOHNSON
Assistant Secretary for Legislation	VINCE VENTIMIGLIA
Assistant Secretary for Planning and Evaluation	DONALD YOUNG, *Acting*
Assistant Secretary for Public Affairs	SUZANNE DEFRANCIS
Assistant Secretary for Public Health and Emergency Preparedness	STEWART SIMONSON
General Counsel	PAULA STANNARD, *Acting*
Inspector General	DANIEL R. LEVINSON
National Coordinator, Health Information Technology	DAVID J. BRAILER

ADMINISTRATION ON AGING

One Massachusetts Avenue NW., Washington, DC 20201
Phone, 202–401–4634. Internet, www.aoa.gov.

Assistant Secretary	JOSEFINA CARBONELL

ADMINISTRATION FOR CHILDREN AND FAMILIES

370 L'Enfant Promenade SW., Washington, DC 20447
Phone, 202–401–9200. Internet, www.acf.gov.

Assistant Secretary	WADE F. HORN

AGENCY FOR HEALTHCARE RESEARCH AND QUALITY

540 Gaither Road, Rockville, MD 20850
Phone, 301–427–1889. Internet, www.ahrq.gov.

Director	CAROLYN CLANCY

* **Editorial note:** The Department did not submit an organizational chart.

AGENCY FOR TOXIC SUBSTANCES AND DISEASE REGISTRY

1600 Clifton Road NE., Atlanta, GA 30333
Phone, 404–639–0700. Internet, www.atsdr.cdc.gov.

Administrator	JULIE L. GERBERDING

CENTERS FOR DISEASE CONTROL AND PREVENTION

1600 Clifton Road NE., Atlanta, GA 30333
Phone, 404–639–3311. Internet, www.cdc.gov.

Director	JULIE L. GERBERDING

CENTERS FOR MEDICARE & MEDICAID SERVICES

7500 Security Boulevard, Baltimore, MD 21244
Phone, 410–786–3000. Internet, www.cms.gov.

Administrator	MARK B. MCCLELLAN

FOOD AND DRUG ADMINISTRATION

5600 Fishers Lane, Rockville, MD 20857
Phone, 888–463–6332. Internet, www.fda.gov.

Commissioner	ANDREW VON ESCHENBACH, *Acting*

HEALTH RESOURCES AND SERVICES ADMINISTRATION

5600 Fishers Lane, Rockville, MD 20857
Phone, 301–443–2086. Internet, www.hrsa.gov.

Administrator	ELIZABETH M. DUKE

INDIAN HEALTH SERVICE

Suite 400, 801 Thompson Avenue, Rockville, MD 20852
Phone, 301–443–1083. Internet, www.ihs.gov.

Director	CHARLES W. GRIM

NATIONAL INSTITUTES OF HEALTH

1 Center Lane, Bethesda, MD 20892
Phone, 301–496–4000. Internet, www.nih.gov.

Director	ELIAS A. ZERHOUNI

SUBSTANCE ABUSE AND MENTAL HEALTH SERVICES ADMINISTRATION

1 Choke Cherry Road, Rockville, MD 20857
Phone, 240–276–2130. Internet, www.samhsa.gov.

Administrator	CHARLES G. CURIE

The Department of Health and Human Services is the Cabinet-level department of the Federal executive branch most involved with the Nation's human concerns. In one way or another, it touches the lives of more Americans than any other Federal agency. It is a department of people serving people, from newborn infants to persons requiring health services to our most elderly citizens.

The Department of Health and Human Services (HHS) was created as the Department of Health, Education, and Welfare on April 11, 1953 (5 U.S.C. app.).

Secretary The Secretary of Health and Human Services advises the President on health, welfare, and income security plans, policies, and programs of the Federal Government; and directs Department staff in carrying out the approved programs and activities of the Department and promotes general public understanding of the Department's goals, programs, and objectives.

Public Health and Science The Office serves as the Secretary's primary adviser on matters involving the Nation's public health. It provides assistance in implementing and coordinating Secretarial decisions for the Public Health Service and coordination of population-based health, clinical divisions; provides oversight of research conducted or supported by the Department; implements several programs to provide population-based public health services; and provides direction and policy oversight, through the Surgeon General, for the Public Health Service Commissioned Corps.

Regional Offices—Department of Health and Human Services

Area	Address/Areas Served	Telephone
Atlanta, GA	Atlanta Federal Ctr., 61 Forsyth St. SW., 30303 (AL, FL, GA, KY, MS, NC, SC, TN).	404–562–7888
Boston, MA	Government Ctr., 02203 (CT, MA, ME, NH, RI, VT)	617–565–1500
Chicago, IL	233 N. Michigan Ave., 60601 (IL, IN, MI, OH, WI)	312–353–5160
Dallas, TX	1301 Young St., 75202 (AR, LA, NM, OK, TX)	214–767–3301
Denver, CO	1961 Stout St., 80294 (CO, MT, ND, SD, UT, WY)	303–844–3372
Kansas City, MO	601 E. 12th St., 64106 (IA, KS, MO, NE)	816–426–2821
New York, NY	26 Federal Plz., 10278 (NJ, NY, PR, VI)	212–264–4600
Philadelphia, PA	150 S. Independence Mall W., 19106 (DC, DE, MD, PA, VA, WV)	215–861–4633
San Francisco, CA	50 United Nations Plz., 94102 (AS, AZ, CA, GU, HI, NV)	415–437–8500
Seattle, WA	2201 6th Ave., 98121 (AK, ID, OR, WA)	206–615–2010

Administration on Aging

The Administration on Aging, the principal agency designated to carry out the provisions of the Older Americans Act of 1965, is responsible for all issues involving the elderly. The Administration develops policies, plans, and programs designed to promote the welfare of the elderly; promotes their needs by planning programs and developing policy; and provides policy, procedural direction, and technical assistance to States and Native American tribal governments.

For further information, contact the Administration on Aging, One Massachusetts Avenue NW., Washington, DC 20201. Phone, 202–401–4634. Internet, www.aoa.gov.

Administration for Children and Families

The Administration for Children and Families provides advice to the Secretary on issues pertaining to children, youth, and families; child support enforcement; community services; developmental disabilities; family assistance; Native American assistance; refugee resettlement; and legalized aliens.

For further information, contact the Administration for Children and Families, 370 L'Enfant Promenade SW., Washington, DC 20447. Phone, 202–401–9261. Internet, www.acf.dhhs.gov.

Agency for Healthcare Research and Quality

The Agency for Healthcare Research and Quality (AHRQ) is charged with improving the quality, safety, efficiency, and effectiveness of health care for all Americans. AHRQ supports health services research that will improve the quality of health care and promote evidence-based decisionmaking.

For further information, contact the Agency for Healthcare Research and Quality, 540 Gaither Road, Rockville, MD 20850. Phone, 301–427–1889. Internet, www.ahrq.gov. E-mail, info@ahrq.gov.

Agency for Toxic Substances and Disease Registry

The Agency for Toxic Substances and Disease Registry, as part of the Public Health Service, is charged with the prevention of exposure to toxic substances and the prevention of the adverse health effects and diminished quality of life associated with exposure to hazardous substances from waste sites, unplanned releases, and other sources of pollution present in the environment.

For further information, contact the Agency for Toxic Substances and Disease Registry, MS E–60, 1600 Clifton Road NE., Atlanta, GA 30333. Phone, 404–639–0501. Internet, www.atsdr.cdc.gov.

Centers for Disease Control and Prevention

The Centers for Disease Control and Prevention, as part of the Public Health Service, is charged with protecting the public health of the Nation by providing leadership and direction in the prevention of and control of diseases and other preventable conditions and responding to public health emergencies.

For further information, contact the Centers for Disease Control and Prevention, 1600 Clifton Road NE., Atlanta, GA, 30333. Phone, 404–639–3286, Internet, www.cdc.gov.

Centers for Medicare & Medicaid Services

[For the Health Care Financing Administration statement of reorganization citing their official change of Agency name, see the *Federal Register* of July 5, 2001, 66 FR 35437]

The Centers for Medicare & Medicaid Services was created to combine under one administration the oversight of the Medicare program, the Federal portion of the Medicaid program and State Children's Health Insurance Program, and related quality assurance activities.

For further information, contact the Centers for Medicare & Medicaid Services, Department of Health and Human Services, 7500 Security Boulevard, Baltimore, MD 21244. Phone, 410–786–3000. Internet, www.cms.gov.

Food and Drug Administration

The Food and Drug Administration (FDA) is responsible for protecting the public health by ensuring the safety, efficacy, and security of human and veterinary drugs, biological products, medical devices, the Nation's food supply, cosmetics, and products that emit radiation. FDA is also responsible for advancing the public health by accelerating innovations to make medicines more effective and providing the public with accurate, science-based information on medicines and food to improve their health. FDA plays a significant role in addressing the Nation's counterterrorism capability and ensuring the security of the food supply.

For further information, contact the Food and Drug Administration, 5600 Fishers Lane, Rockville, MD 20857. Phone, 888–463–6332. Internet, www.fda.gov.

Health Resources and Services Administration

The Health Resources and Services Administration (HRSA) provides access to primary healthcare service through its more than 6,500 grantees nationwide, to medically underserved families and individuals who are poor, uninsured, geographically isolated, or vulnerable in some other way. Programs administered by HRSA include maternal and child health services; HIV/AIDS assistance; bioterrorism/hospital emergency preparedness; health information technology; nurse education scholarships and loan repayments; community health center; organ donation/transplantation; vaccine injury compensation; and Hansen's disease. With HRSA funds, community health care center grantees attend to chronic health care needs; health services in rural, isolated areas; and care and treatment of minorities nationwide, and those living along the U.S.-Mexico border. HRSA also administers the national practitioner databank.

For further information, contact the Office of Communications, Health Resources and Services Administration, 5600 Fishers Lane, Rockville, MD 20857. Phone, 301–443–3376. Internet, www.hrsa.gov.

Indian Health Service

The Indian Health Service, as part of the Public Health Service, provides a comprehensive health services delivery system for American Indians and Alaska Natives, with opportunity for maximum tribal involvement in developing and managing programs to meet their health needs. It assists Native American tribes in developing their health programs; facilitates and assists tribes in coordinating health planning, obtaining and utilizing health resources available through Federal, State, and local programs, operating comprehensive health programs, and evaluating health programs; and provides comprehensive healthcare services including hospital and ambulatory medical care, preventive and rehabilitative services, and development of community sanitation facilities.

For further information, contact the Management Policy Support Staff, Indian Health Service, Suite 400, 801 Thompson Avenue, Rockville, MD 20852. Phone, 301–443–2650. Internet, www.ihs.gov.

National Institutes of Health

The National Institutes of Health (NIH), as part of the Public Health Service, supports biomedical and behavioral research domestically and abroad, conducts research in its own laboratories and clinics, trains promising young researchers, and promotes acquisition and distribution of medical knowledge.

Aging The Institute conducts and supports biomedical, social, and behavioral research, training, health information, dissemination, and other programs with respect to the aging process and the diseases and other special problems and needs of the aged.

For further information, contact the National Institute on Aging. Phone, 301–496–1752. Internet, www.nih.gov/nia.

Alcohol Abuse and Alcoholism The Institute leads the national effort to reduce alcohol-related problems by conducting and supporting biomedical and behavioral research into the causes, consequences, prevention, and treatment of alcohol-use disorders.

For further information, contact the National Institute on Alcohol Abuse and Alcoholism. Phone, 301–443–3885 or 301–443–3860. Internet, www.niaaa.nih.gov.

Allergy and Infectious Diseases The Institute conducts and supports research, research training, and clinical evaluations on the causes, treatment, and prevention of a wide variety of infectious, allergic, and immunologic diseases.

For further information, contact the National Institute of Allergy and Infectious Diseases. Phone, 301–496–5717. Internet, www.niaid.nih.gov.

Arthritis and Musculoskeletal and Skin Diseases The Institute supports research into the causes, treatment, and prevention of arthritis and musculoskeletal and skin diseases.

For further information, contact the National Institute of Arthritis and Musculoskeletal and Skin Diseases. Phone, 301–496–4353. Internet, www.niams.nih.gov.

Biomedical Imaging and Bioengineering The Institute conducts, coordinates, and supports research, training, dissemination of health information, and other programs with respect to biomedical imaging, biomedical engineering, and associated technologies and modalities with biomedical applications.

For further information, contact the National Institute of Biomedical Imaging and Bioengineering. Phone, 301–451–6768. Internet, www.nibib.nih.gov.

Cancer The Institute developed a national cancer program to expand existing scientific knowledge on cancer causes and prevention as well as on the diagnosis, treatment, and rehabilitation of cancer patients. Research activities encompass basic biological, clinical, prevention, and behavioral research.

For further information, contact the Cancer Information Service. Phone, 800–422–6237 or 301–435–3848. Internet, www.cancer.gov.

Center for Information Technology The Center provides, coordinates, and manages information technology to advance computational science.

For further information, contact the Center for Information Technology. Phone, 301–496–6203. Internet, www.cit.nih.gov.

Child Health and Human Development The Institute conducts and supports laboratory, clinical, and epidemiological research on the reproductive, neurobiologic, developmental, and behavioral processes that determine and maintain the health of children, adults, families, and populations.

For further information, contact the National Institute of Child Health and Human Development. Phone, 301–496–5133. Internet, www.nichd.nih.gov.

Clinical Center The NIH Clinical Center is the clinical research hospital for NIH. Through clinical research, physician-investigators translate laboratory discoveries into better treatments, therapies, and interventions to improve the Nation's health. Clinical and laboratory research are both conducted at the NIH Clinical Center. This tandem approach drives all aspects of its operations. More than 350,000 patients from across the Nation have participated in clinical research studies since the Center opened in 1953. About 1,300 clinical research studies are currently in progress.

For further information, contact the Clinical Center. Phone, 301–496–2563. Internet, http://clinicalcenter.nih.gov

Complementary and Alternative Medicine The Center is dedicated to exploring complementary and alternative healing practices in the context of rigorous science; educating and training complementary and alternative medicine researchers; and disseminating authoritative information to the public and professionals. Through its programs, the Center seeks to facilitate the integration of safe and effective complementary and alternative practices into conventional medicine.

For further information, call 888–644–6226. Internet, http://nccam.nih.gov.

Deafness and Other Communication Disorders The Institute conducts and supports biomedical and behavioral research and research training on normal and disordered processes of hearing, balance, smell, taste, voice, speech, and language, and provides health information, based on scientific discovery, to the public. The Institute conducts diverse research performed in its own laboratories and funds a program of research and research grants.

For further information, contact the National Institute on Deafness and Other Communication Disorders. Phone, 301–496–7243. Internet, www.nidcd.nih.gov.

Dental and Craniofacial Diseases The Institute conducts and supports research and research training into the causes, prevention, diagnosis, and treatment of craniofacial, oral, and dental diseases and disorders.

For further information, contact the National Institute of Dental and Craniofacial Research. Phone, 301–496–4261. Internet, www.nidcr.nih.gov.

Diabetes and Digestive and Kidney Diseases The Institute conducts, fosters, and supports basic and clinical research into the causes, prevention, diagnosis, and treatment of diabetes, endocrine, and metabolic diseases, digestive diseases and nutrition, kidney and urologic diseases, and blood diseases.

For further information, contact the National Institute of Diabetes and Digestive and Kidney Diseases. Phone, 301–496–3583. Internet, www.niddk.nih.gov.

Drug Abuse The Institute's primary mission is to lead the Nation in bringing the power of science to bear on drug abuse and addiction through the strategic support and conduct of research across a broad range of disciplines and the rapid and effective dissemination and use of the results of that research to significantly improve drug abuse and addiction prevention, treatment, and policy.

For further information, contact the National Institute on Drug Abuse. Phone, 301–443–1124. Internet, www.nida.nih.gov.

Environmental Health Sciences The Institute reduces the burden of human illnesses and disability by understanding how the environment influences the development and progression of human disease. To have the greatest impact on preventing disease and improving human health, Health Sciences focuses on basic science, disease-oriented research, global environmental health, and multidisciplinary training for researchers.

For further information, contact the National Institute of Environmental Health Sciences. Phone, 919–541–3345. Internet, www.niehs.nih.gov.

Fogarty International Center The Center addresses global health challenges through innovative and collaborative research and training programs. It also supports and advances the NIH mission through international partnerships.

For further information, contact the Fogarty International Center. Phone, 301–496–2075. Internet, www.fic.nih.gov.

General Medical Sciences The Institute supports basic biomedical research and research training in areas ranging from cell biology, chemistry, and biophysics to genetics, pharmacology, and systemic response to trauma.

For further information, contact the National Institute of General Medical Sciences. Phone, 301–496–7301. Internet, www.nigms.nih.gov.

Heart, Lung, and Blood Diseases The Institute provides leadership for a national program in diseases of the heart, blood vessels, lung, and blood; sleep disorders; and blood resources. It conducts, fosters, and supports an integrated and coordinated program of basic research, clinical investigations and trials, observational studies, and demonstration and education projects.

For further information, contact the National Heart, Lung, and Blood Institute. Phone, 301–496–0554. Internet, www.nhlbi.nih.gov.

Human Genome Research The Institute, which helped lead the Human Genome Project, leads and supports a broad range of initiatives and studies aimed at understanding the structure and function of the human genome and its role in health and disease.

For further information, contact the National Human Genome Research Institute. Phone, 301–496–0844. Internet, www.genome.gov.

Medical Library The Library of Medicine serves as the Nation's chief medical information source and is authorized to provide medical library services and online bibliographic search capabilities, such as MEDLINE and TOXLINE, to public and private agencies, organizations, institutions, and individuals.

For further information, contact the National Library of Medicine. Phone, 301–496–6308. Internet, www.nlm.nih.gov.

Mental Health The National Institute of Mental Health reduces the burden of mental illness and behavioral disorders through research on mind, brain, and behavior. To fulfill this public health mandate, the Institute uses powerful scientific tools to achieve better understanding of, expand and refine treatment for, and prevent these disabling conditions that affect millions of Americans.

For further information, contact the National Institute of Mental Health. Phone, 301–443–3673. Internet, www.nimh.nih.gov.

Minority Health and Health Disparities The Center advises the NIH Director and the Institute and Center Directors on the development of NIH-wide policy issues related to minority health disparities research, research on other health disparities, and related research training; develops a comprehensive strategic plan governing the conduct and support of all NIH minority health disparities research, research on other health disparities, and related research training activities; and administers funds for the support of that research through grants and through leveraging the programs of NIH.

For further information, contact the National Center for Minority Health and Health Disparities. Phone, 301–402–1366. Internet, www.ncmhd.nih.gov.

Neurological Disorders and Stroke The Institute's mission is to reduce the burden of neurological diseases. It conducts, fosters, coordinates, and guides research on the causes, prevention, diagnosis, and treatment of neurological disorders and strokes, and supports basic research in related scientific areas.

For further information, contact the National Institute of Neurological Disorders and Strokes Brain Resources and Information Network (BRAIN), P.O. Box 5801, Bethesda, MD 20824. Phone, 800–352–9424. Internet, www.ninds.nih.gov.

Nursing Research The Institute supports and conducts clinical and basic research and training on acute and chronic illness across the life span. It focuses on health promotion, disease prevention, health disparities, caregiving, management of symptoms, self-management, and the end of life. The Insitute promotes and improves the health of individuals, families, communities, and populations. It seeks to extend nursing science by integrating the biological and behavioral sciences, applying new technologies to nursing research questions, improving the quality and effectiveness of interventions, and developing nursing research investigators.

For further information, contact the National Institute of Nursing Research. Phone, 301–496–0207. Internet, http://ninr.nih.gov/ninr.

Ophthalmological Diseases The Institute conducts, fosters, and supports research on the causes, natural history, prevention, diagnosis, and treatment of disorders of the eye and visual system. It also directs the National Eye Health Education Program.

For further information, contact the National Eye Institute. Phone, 301–496–5248. Internet, www.nei.nih.gov.

Research Resources The Center provides clinical research facilities for investigators to study a wide range of diseases. It enhances research capabilities in underserved institutions and States and develops and provides access to new technologies that help researchers study virtually every human disease. The Center also develops and provides access to animal models to gain understanding of human genetics, disease mechanisms, and new therapeutic agents. Other grants programs support the purchase of shared instrumentation; provide training and career development for researchers; and educate the public about health issues.

For further information, contact the National Center for Research Resources. Phone, 301–435–0888. Internet, www.ncrr.nih.gov.

Scientific Review The Center for Scientific Review (CSR) organizes the peer review groups that evaluate the majority of grant applications submitted to NIH. These groups include experienced and respected researchers from across the country and abroad. Since 1946, CSR has ensured that NIH grant applications receive fair, independent, expert, and timely reviews—free from inappropriate influences—so NIH can fund the most promising research. CSR also receives all incoming applications and assigns them to the NIH Institutes and Centers that fund grants.

For further information, contact the Center for Scientific Review. Phone, 301–435–1111. Internet, www.csr.nih.gov.

For further information, contact the National Institutes of Health, 1 Center Lane, Bethesda, MD 20892. Phone, 301–496–4000. Internet, www.nih.gov.

Substance Abuse and Mental Health Services Administration

The Substance Abuse and Mental Health Services Administration (SAMHSA) focuses attention, programs, and funding on promoting life in the community with jobs, homes, and meaningful relationships with family and friends for people with, or at risk for, mental or substance abuse disorders. SAMSHA accomplishes this through an action-oriented, measurable mission of building resilience and facilitating recovery. SAMSHA has a matrix management system that outlines and guides its activities in pursuit of this mission. The matrix includes 11 program priority areas. They are co-ocurring disorders, substance abuse treatment capacity, seclusion and restraint, children and families, mental health system transformation, disaster readiness and response, homelessness, older adults, HIV/AIDS and Hepatitis, and criminal and juvenile justice.

For further information, contact the Substance Abuse and Mental Health Services Administration, 1 Choke Cherry Road, Rockville, MD 20857. Phone, 240–276–2130. Internet, www.samhsa.gov.

Sources of Information

Office of the Secretary
Direct inquiries to the appropriate office, Department of Health and Human Services, Hubert H. Humphrey Building, 200 Independence Avenue SW., Washington, DC 20201. Internet, www.hhs.gov.
Civil Rights For information on enforcement of civil rights laws, call 202–205–4344, or 800–368–1019. TDD, 800–537–7697. Internet, www.hhs.gov/ocr. For information on medical records and health information privacy, call 866–627–7748. TDD, 866–788–4989. Internet, www.hhs.gov/ocr/hipaa.
Contracts and Small Business Activities For information concerning programs, contact the Director, Office of Small and Disadvantaged Business Utilization. Phone, 202–690–7300.
Inspector General General inquiries may be directed to the Office of Inspector General, Wilbur J. Cohen Building, 330 Independence Avenue SW., Washington, DC 20201. Phone, 202–619–1142. Internet, www.oig.hhs.gov.
Inspector General Hotline To report fraud, waste, or abuse against Department programs, contact the Office of Inspector General, HHS–TIPS Hotline, P.O. Box 23489, L'Enfant Plaza Station, Washington, DC 20026–3489. Phone, 800–HHS–TIPS (800–447–8477). TTY, 800–377–4950. Fax, 800–223–8164.
Locator For inquiries about the location and telephone numbers of HHS offices, call 202–619–0257.
Program Support For information concerning competitive service-for-fee in the areas of human resources, financial management, and administrative operations, call 301–443–1494.
Public Health and Science Contact the Assistant Secretary for Health, Room 716G, 200 Independence Avenue SW., Washington, DC 20201. Phone, 202–690–7694. Internet, www.hhs.gov/ash.
Surgeon General Phone, 301–443–4000. Internet, www.surgeongeneral.gov.

Administration on Aging

Direct inquiries to the appropriate office, Administration on Aging, One Massachusetts Avenue NW., Washington, DC 20201. Internet, www.aoa.hhs.gov.
Aging Contact the National Aging Information Center. Phone, 202–619–7501. Fax, 202–401–7620.
Elder Care Services Contact the Elder Care Locator. Phone, 800–677–1116.
Public Inquiries/Publications Phone, 202–619–0724. Fax, 202–260–1012. Internet, www.aoa.gov.

Administration for Children and Families

Direct inquiries to the appropriate office, Administration for Children and Families, 370 L'Enfant Promenade SW., Washington, DC 20447. Phone, 202–401–9200. Internet, www.acf.gov.

Agency for Healthcare Research and Quality

Direct inquiries to the appropriate office at the Agency for Healthcare Research and Quality, 540 Gaither Road, Rockville, MD 20850. Phone, 301–427–1200. Internet, www.ahrq.gov.

Agency for Toxic Substances and Disease Registry

Information regarding programs and activities is available electronically through the Internet at www.atsdr.cdc.gov.

Centers for Disease Control and Prevention
Direct inquiries to the appropriate office at the Centers for Disease Control and Prevention, Department of Health and Human Services, 1600 Clifton Road NE., Atlanta, GA 30333.
Electronic Access Information regarding programs, films, publications, employment, and activities is available electronically through the Internet at www.cdc.gov.
Employment The majority of scientific and technical positions are filled through the Commissioned Corps of the Public Health Service, a uniformed service of the U.S. Government.

Centers for Medicare and Medicaid Services
Direct inquiries to the appropriate office, Centers for Medicare & Medicaid Services, 7500 Security Boulevard, Baltimore, MD 21244–1850. Internet, www.cms.gov.
Electronic access General information on Medicare/Medicaid is available on the Internet at www.cms.gov. Beneficiary-specific Medicare/Medicaid information is available at www.medicare.gov. General information on the Insure Kids Now! program is available at www.insurekidsnow.gov.

Food and Drug Administration
Direct inquiries to the appropriate office, Food and Drug Administration, 5600 Fishers Lane, Rockville, MD 20857.
Electronic Access Information on FDA is available through the Internet at www.fda.gov.
Employment FDA uses various civil service examinations and registers in its recruitment for positions. In the Washington, DC, metropolitan area contact the Personnel Officer (HFA–400) (phone, 301–827–4120). Outside the Washington, DC, area contact the appropriate local FDA office. Schools interested in the college recruitment program should contact the Personnel Officer (HFA–400) (phone, 301–827–4120).

Health Resources and Services Administration
Direct inquiries to the appropriate office, Health Resources and Services Administration, 5600 Fishers Lane, Rockville, MD 20857. Internet, www.hrsa.gov.
Employment The majority of positions are in the Federal civil service. Some health professional positions are filled through the Commissioned Corps of the Public Health Service, a uniformed service of the U.S. Government.

Indian Health Service
Direct inquiries to the appropriate office, Indian Health Service, 5600 Fishers Lane, Rockville, MD 20857.
Electronic Access Information on IHS is available through the Internet at www.ihs.gov.
Employment Information about employment opportunities is available at the National Institutes of Health employment Web site at www.jobs.nih.gov.

National Institutes of Health
Public Health Service Commissioned Officer Program Information on the Commissioned Officer programs at NIH is available at the NIH Commissioned Officer Web site at http://hr.od.nih.gov/corps/default.htm.

Substance Abuse and Mental Health Services Administration
Direct inquiries to the appropriate office, Substance Abuse and Mental Health Services Administration, 1 Choke Cherry Road, Rockville, MD 20857.
Electronic Access Information is available through the Internet at www.samhsa.gov, www.mentalhealth.org, or www.health.org.

For further information, contact the Locator, Department of Health and Human Services, 200 Independence Avenue SW., Washington, DC 20201. Phone, 202–619–0257. Internet, www.hhs.gov.

DEPARTMENT OF HOMELAND SECURITY

Washington, DC 20528
Phone, 202–282–8000. Internet, www.dhs.gov.

SECRETARY OF HOMELAND SECURITY	MICHAEL CHERTOFF
Deputy Secretary	MICHAEL P. JACKSON
Chief of Staff	JOHN F. WOOD

Directorates:

Federal Emergency Management

Under Secretary	R. DAVID PAULISON
Director, Mitigation Division	DAVID MAURSTAD
Director, Preparedness Division	GIL JAMIESON, *Acting*
Director, Response Division	MICHAEL LOWDER, *Acting*

Management

Under Secretary	(VACANCY)
Chief Administrative Services Officer	DONALD G. BATHURST
Chief Human Capital Officer	GREGG PRILLAMAN
Chief Information Officer	SCOTT CHARBO
Chief Procurement Officer	ELAINE C. DUKE
Chief Security Officer	DWIGHT M. WILLIAMS

Policy

Assistant Secretary	STEWART A. BAKER
Special Adviser, Asylum and Refugee Affairs	IGOR V. TIMOFEYEV
Executive Director, Homeland Security Advisory Council	DOUGLAS L. HOELSCHER
Director, Immigration Statistics	MICHAEL HOEFER
Assistant Secretary, Office of International Affairs	CRESENCIO ARCOS
Assistant Secretary, Policy	(VACANCY)
Assistant Secretary, Private Sector Coordination	ALFONSO MARTINEZ-FONTS
Assistant Secretary, Strategic Plans	RANDY BEARDSWORTH

Preparedness

Under Secretary	GEORGE W. FORESMAN
Assistant Secretary, Cyber Security and Telecommunications	(VACANCY)
Administrator, United States Fire Administration	CHARLIE DICKINSON, *Acting*
Executive Director, Office of Grants and Training	TRACY A. HENKE
Assistant Secretary, Infrastructure Protection	ROBERT B. STEPHAN
Chief Medical Officer	JEFFREY W. RUNGE
Director, Office for National Capital Region Coordination	THOMAS J. LOCKWOOD
Director, Office of State and Local Government Coordination	CHESTER LUNNER, *Acting*

Science and Technology

Under Secretary	JEFFREY W. RUNGE, *Acting*
Director, Homeland Security Advanced Research Projects Agency	(VACANCY)
Director, Plans, Programs and Requirements	KIRK E. EVANS
Director, Research and Development	MAUREEN MCCARTHY
Director, Office of Systems Engineering and Development	JOHN J. KUBRICKY

Components:

Director, United States Citizenship and Immigration Services	EMILIO T. GONZALEZ
Ombudsman, United States Citizenship and Immigration Services	PRAKASH I. KHATRI
Officer, Civil Rights and Civil Liberties	DANIEL W. SUTHERLAND
Commandant, United States Coast Guard	THAD W. ALLEN
Director, Office of Counternarcotics Enforcement	UTTAM DHILLON
Commissioner, Customs and Border Protection	W. RALPH BASHAM
Director, Domestic Nuclear Detection Office	VAYL OXFORD
Executive Secretary, Executive Secretariat	FRED L. SCHWIEN
Director, Federal Law Enforcement Training Center	CONNIE L. PATRICK
Chief Financial Officer	DAVID L. NORQUIST
General Counsel	PHILIP J. PERRY
Coordinator, Gulf Coast Region Recovery and Rebuilding	DONALD E. POWELL
Assistant Secretary, United States Immigration and Customs Enforcement	JULIE L. MYERS
Inspector General	RICHARD L. SKINNER
Assistant Secretary, Office of Intelligence and Analysis	CHARLES E. ALLEN
Assistant Secretary, Office of Legislative and Intergovernmental Affairs	PAMELA J. TURNER
Senior Military Adviser	TIMOTHY S. SULLIVAN
Director, Office of Operations Coordination	(VACANCY)
Chief Privacy Officer	MAUREEN COONEY, *Acting*
Assistant Secretary, Office of Public Affairs	BRIAN R. BESANCENEY
Director, United States Secret Service	MARK J. SULLIVAN
Assistant Secretary, Transportation Security Administration	EDMUND S. HAWLEY
White House Liaison	ERIC M. LECKEY

The Department of Homeland Security leads the unified national effort to secure America. It will prevent and deter terrorist attacks and protect against and respond to threats and hazards to the Nation. The Department will ensure safe and secure borders, welcome lawful immigrants and visitors, and promote the free-flow of commerce.

The Department of Homeland Security (DHS) was established by the Homeland Security Act of 2002, (6 U.S.C. 101 note). Pursuant to this legislation, the Department came into existence on January 24, 2003, and is administered under the supervision and direction of the Secretary of Homeland Security. It was created to do the following:

DEPARTMENT OF HOMELAND SECURITY

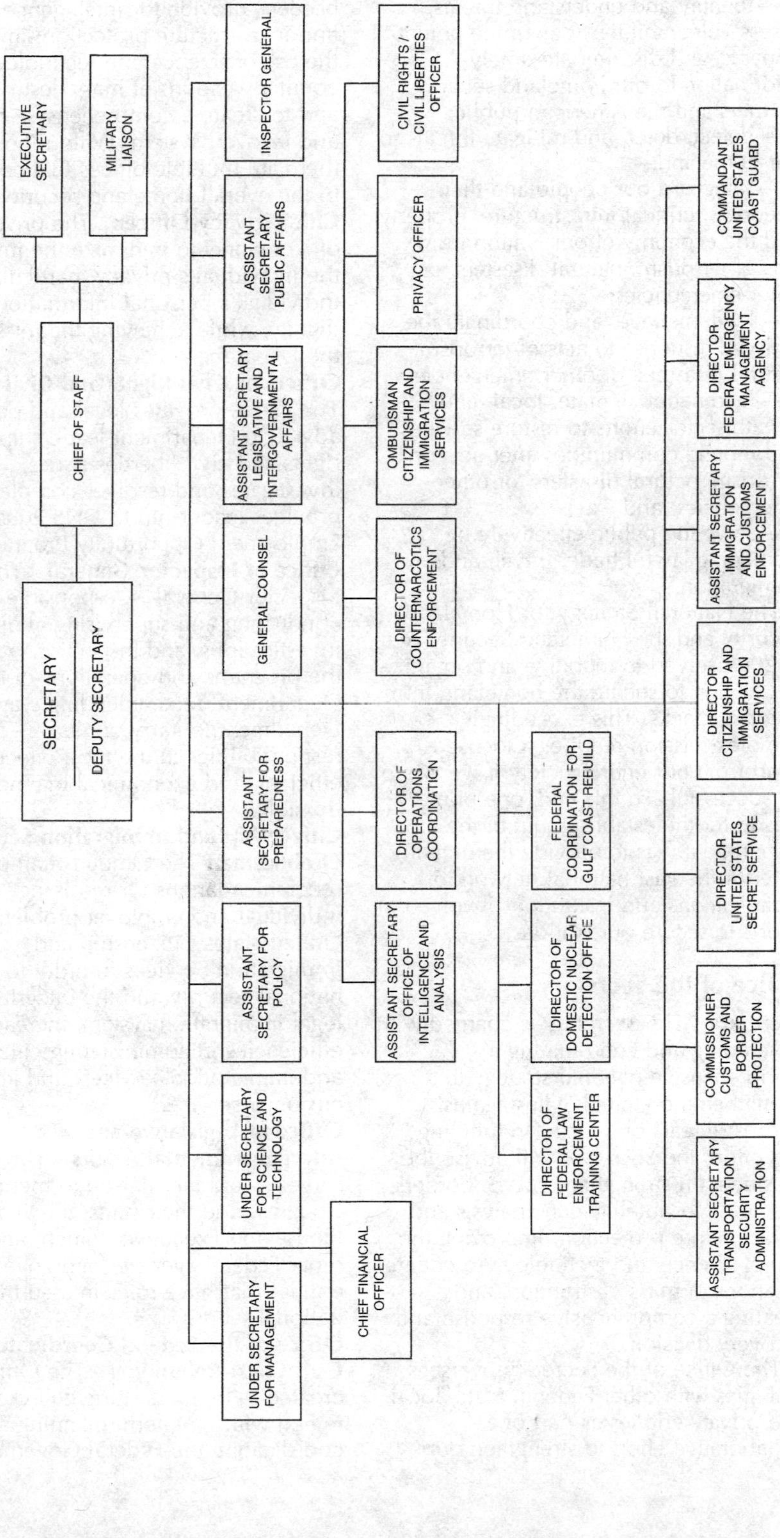

—identify and understand threats, assess vulnerabilities, determine potential impacts, and disseminate timely information to our homeland security partners and the American public;

—detect, deter, and mitigate threats to our homeland;

—safeguard our people and their freedoms, critical infrastructure, property, and the economy of our Nation from acts of terrorism, natural disasters, or other emergencies;

—lead, manage, and coordinate the national response to acts of terrorism, natural disasters, or other emergencies;

—lead national, State, local, and private sector efforts to restore services and rebuild communities after acts of terrorism, natural disasters, or other emergencies; and

—serve the public effectively by facilitating lawful trade, travel, and immigration.

The National Strategy for Homeland Security and the Homeland Security Act of 2002 served to mobilize and organize our Nation to secure the homeland from terrorist attacks. This exceedingly complex mission requires a focused effort from our entire society if we are to be successful. To this end, one primary reason for the establishment of the Department was to provide the unifying core for the vast national network of organizations and institutions involved in efforts to secure our Nation.

Office of the Secretary

Secretary The Secretary is charged with developing and coordinating a comprehensive national strategy to strengthen the United States against terrorist threats or attacks. In fulfilling this effort, the Secretary will advise the President on strengthening U.S. borders, providing for intelligence analysis and infrastructure protection, improving the use of science and technology to counter weapons of mass destruction, and creating a comprehensive response and recovery division.

The Office of the Secretary oversees activities with other Federal, State, local, and private entities as part of a collaborative effort to strengthen our borders, provide for intelligence analysis and infrastructure protection, improve the use of science and technology to counter weapons of mass destruction, and to create a comprehensive response and recovert system. Within the Office, there are multiple offices that contribute to the overall homeland security mission.

Chief Privacy Officer The privacy officer works to minimize the impact on the individual's privacy, particularly the individual's personal information and dignity, while achieving the mission of the Department.

Office for Civil Rights and Civil Liberties The Office provides legal and policy advice to Department leadership on civil rights and civil liberties issues, investigates and resolves complaints, and provides leadership to DHS Equal Employment Opportunity Programs.

Office of Inspector General The Inspector General is responsible for conducting and supervising audits, investigations, and inspections relating to the programs and operations of the Department, recommending ways for the Department to carry out its responsibilities in the most effective, efficient, and economical manner possible.

Citizenship and Immigration Services Ombudsman The Ombudsman provides recommendations for resolving individual and employer problems with United States Citizenship and Immigration Services in order to ensure national security and the integrity of the legal immigration system, increase efficiencies in administering citizenship and immigration services, and improve customer service.

Office of Legislative and Intergovernmental Affairs The Office serves as primary liaison to members of Congress and their staffs, the White House and Executive Branch, and to other Federal agencies and governmental entities that have roles in assuring national security.

Office of the Federal Coordinator for Gulf Coast Rebuilding The Office was created to help assist the gulf coast region with long-term planning and coordinating the Federal Government's response to rebuild the gulf coast region devastated by Hurricanes Katrina and Rita.

Directorates

Federal Emergency Management Federal Emergency Management (FEMA) is responsible for leading the effort to prepare the Nation for all hazards and effectively manage Federal response and recovery efforts following any national incident. FEMA also initiates proactive mitigation activities, trains first responders, and manages the National Flood Insurance Program.

Management Directorate The Directorate for Management is responsible for budget, appropriations, expenditure of funds, accounting and finance; procurement; human resources and personnel; information technology systems; facilities, property, equipment, and other material resources; and identification and tracking of performance measurements relating to the responsibilities of the Department.

The Directorate for Management ensures that the Department's employees have well-defined responsibilities and that managers and their employees have effective means of communicating with one another, with other governmental and nongovernmental bodies, and with the public they serve.

Policy Directorate The Policy Directorate develops and integrates policies, planning, and programs in order to better coordinate the Department's prevention, protection, response, and recovery missions. It is also responsible for the following functions:

—leading coordination of Departmentwide policies, programs, and planning, which will ensure consistency and integration of missions throughout the entire Department;

—providing a central office to develop and communicate policies across multiple components of the homeland security network and strengthens the Department's ability to maintain policy and operational readiness needed to protect the homeland;

—providing the foundation and direction for Departmentwide strategic planning and budget priorities;

—bridging multiple headquarters' components and operating agencies to improve communication among DHS entities, eliminate duplication of effort, and translate policies into timely action; and

—creating a single point of contact for internal and external stakeholders that will allow for streamlined policy management across the Department.

Preparedness Directorate The Directorate for Preparedness bolsters our Nation's security through a multilayered system of preparedness measures based on risk assessment and management. Working with State, local, and private sector partners, the Directorate identifies threats, determines vulnerabilities, and targets resources where risk is greatest. Through grants and training on both national and local levels, the Directorate fosters a layered system of protective measures to safeguard our borders, seaports, bridges and highways, and critical information systems. It is responsible for the following functions:

—consolidating preparedness assets across the Department;

—facilitating grants and oversees nationwide preparedness efforts by supporting first responder training, citizen awareness, public health, infrastructure and cyber security and ensures proper steps are taken to protect high-risk targets;

—focusing on cyber security and telecommunications; and

—addressing threats to our Nation's public health through the Chief Medical Officer, who coordinates preparedness efforts against biological attacks.

—The Directorate is also responsible for infrastructure protection, training and exercises, the U.S. Fire Administration, and the Office of National Capitol Region Coordination.

Science and Technology Directorate The Directorate for Science and Technology is the primary research and development arm of the Department. The Directorate provides Federal, State, and local officials with the technology and capabilities to protect the homeland. Its strategic objectives are as follows:

—developing and deploying state-of-the art, high-performance, low-operating-cost systems to prevent, detect, and mitigate the consequences of chemical, biological, radiological, nuclear, and explosive attacks;

—developing equipment, protocols, and training procedures for response to and recovery from chemical, biological, radiological, nuclear, and explosive attacks;

—enhancing the technical capabilities of the Department's operational elements and other Federal, State, local, and tribal agencies to fulfill their homeland security-related functions;

—developing methods and capabilities to test and assess threats and vulnerabilities, preventing technology surprise, and anticipating emerging threats;

—developing technical standards and establishing certified laboratories to evaluate homeland security and emergency responder technologies, and evaluating technologies for SAFETY Act (6 U.S.C. 101 note) certification; and

—supporting U.S. leadership in science and technology.

Components

United States Citizenship and Immigration Services The United States Citizenship and Immigration Services is responsible for the administration of immigration and naturalization adjudication functions and establishing immigration policies and priorities.

United States Coast Guard The Coast Guard protects the public, the environment, and U.S. economic interests in the Nation's ports and waterways, along the coast, on international waters, or in any maritime region, as required, to support national security.

Customs and Border Protection The United States Customs and Border Protection is responsible for protecting our Nation's borders in order to prevent terrorists and terrorist weapons from entering the United States, while facilitating the flow of legitimate trade and travel.

Domestic Nuclear Detection Office The Office works to enhance the nuclear detection efforts of Federal; State; territorial; tribal; and local governments; and the private sector;and to ensure a coordinated response to such threats.

Federal Law Enforcement Training Center The Center provides career-long training to law enforcement professionals from 81 Federal agencies, and State, local, and international law enforcement agencies to help them fulfill their responsibilities safely and proficiently.

United States Immigration and Customs Enforcement Immigration and Customs Enforcement is the largest investigative arm of DHS. It is responsible for identifying and shutting down vulnerabilities in the Nation's border and for economic, transportation and infrastructure security.

Office of Intelligence and Analysis The Office is responsible for using information and intelligence from multiple sources to identify and assess current and future threats to the United States.

Office of Operations Coordination The Office is responsible for monitoring the security of the United States on a daily basis and coordinating activities within DHS and with Governors, Homeland Security advisors, law enforcement partners, and critical infrastructure operators in all 50 States and more than 50 major urban areas nationwide.

United States Secret Service The Secret Service protects the President and other high-level officials and investigates counterfeiting and other financial crimes, including financial institution fraud, identity theft, and computer fraud; and computer-based attacks on our Nation's financial, banking, and telecommunications infrastructure.

Transportation Security Administration The Transportation Security Administration protects the Nation's transportation systems to ensure freedom of movement for people and commerce.

Sources of Information

Electronic Access Additional information about the Department of Homeland Security is available electronically through the Internet at www.dhs.gov.

For further information concerning the Department of Homeland Security, contact the Office of Public Affairs, Department of Homeland Security, Washington, DC 20528. Phone, 202–282–8000. Internet, www.dhs.gov.

DEPARTMENT OF HOUSING AND URBAN DEVELOPMENT

451 Seventh Street SW., Washington, DC 20410
Phone, 202–708–1422. Internet, www.hud.gov.

SECRETARY OF HOUSING AND URBAN DEVELOPMENT	ALPHONSO R. JACKSON
Deputy Secretary	ROY A. BERNARDI
Assistant Deputy Secretary for Field Policy and Management	JO BAYLOR
Director, Office of Small and Disadvantaged Business Utilization	(VACANCY)
Chair, HUD Board of Contract Appeals and Chief Administrative Judge	DAVID T. ANDERSON
Chief Administrative Law Judge	ARTHUR A. LIBERTY
Assistant Secretary for Administration	KEITH NELSON
Assistant Secretary for Community Planning and Development	PAMELA PATENAUDE
General Deputy Assistant Secretary for Office of General Counsel	KEITH E. GOTTFRIED
Assistant Secretary for Congressional and Intergovernmental Relations	(VACANCY)
Assistant Secretary for Fair Housing and Equal Opportunity	KIM KENDRICK
Assistant Secretary for Housing—Federal Housing Commissioner	BRIAN MONTGOMERY
Assistant Secretary for Policy Development and Research	DARLENE WILLIAMS
Assistant Secretary for Public Affairs	CATHERINE M. MACFARLAND
Assistant Secretary for Public and Indian Housing	ORLANDO J. CABRERA
Director, Office of Departmental Equal Employment Opportunity	(VACANCY)
Chief Financial Officer	JOHN W. COX
Director, Office of Departmental Operations and Coordination	INEZ BANKS-DUBOSE
Director, Office of Healthy Homes and Lead Hazard Control	MIKE HILL, *Acting*
Director, Center for Faith-Based and Community Initiatives	RYAN T. STREETER
Inspector General	KENNETH M. DONAHUE, SR.
President, Government National Mortgage Association	(VACANCY)
Chief Information Officer	LISA SCHLOSSER
Chief Procurement Officer	JOSEPH A. NEURAUTER
Director, Office of Federal Housing Enterprise Oversight	(VACANCY)

The Department of Housing and Urban Development is the principal Federal agency responsible for programs concerned with the Nation's housing needs, fair housing opportunities, and improvement and development of the Nation's communities.

The Department of Housing and Urban Development (HUD) was established in 1965 by the Department of Housing and Urban Development Act (42 U.S.C. 3532–3537). It was created to:

—administer the principal programs that provide assistance for housing and for the development of the Nation's communities;

—encourage the solution of housing and community development problems through States and localities; and

—encourage the maximum contributions that may be made by vigorous private homebuilding and mortgage lending industries, both primary and secondary, to housing, community development, and the national economy.

Although HUD administers many programs, its major functions may be grouped into six categories:

—insuring mortgages for single-family and multi-family dwellings, and extending loans for home improvement and for purchasing mobile homes;

—channeling funds from investors into the mortgage industry through the Government National Mortgage Association;

—making direct loans for construction or rehabilitation of housing projects for the elderly and the handicapped;

—providing Federal housing subsidies for low- and moderate-income families;

—providing grants to States and communities for community development activities; and

—promoting and enforcing fair housing and equal housing opportunity.

Secretary The Secretary formulates recommendations for basic policies in the fields of housing and community development; encourages private enterprise participation in housing and community development; promotes the growth of cities and States and the efficient and effective use of housing and community and economic development resources by stimulating private sector initiatives, public/private sector partnerships, and public entrepreneurship; ensures equal access to housing and affirmatively prevents discrimination in housing; and provides general oversight for the Federal National Mortgage Association.

Federal Housing Finance Board An independent agency in the executive branch, the Board oversees the Federal Home Loan Banks to ensure that they carry out their housing finance mission, remain adequately capitalized, and operate in a safe and sound manner.

Program Areas

Community Planning and Development The Office administers grant programs to help communities plan and finance their growth and development, increase their capacity to govern, and provide shelter and services for homeless people. The Office is responsible for implementing Community Development Block Grant (CDBG) programs for entitlement communities; State- and HUD-administered small cities programs; community development loan guarantees; special purpose grants for insular areas and historically black colleges and universities; Appalachian Regional Commission grants; Home Investment in Affordable Housing (HOME), which provides Federal assistance for housing rehabilitation, tenant-based assistance, assistance to first-time homebuyers, and new construction when a jurisdiction is determined to need new rental housing; the Department's programs to address

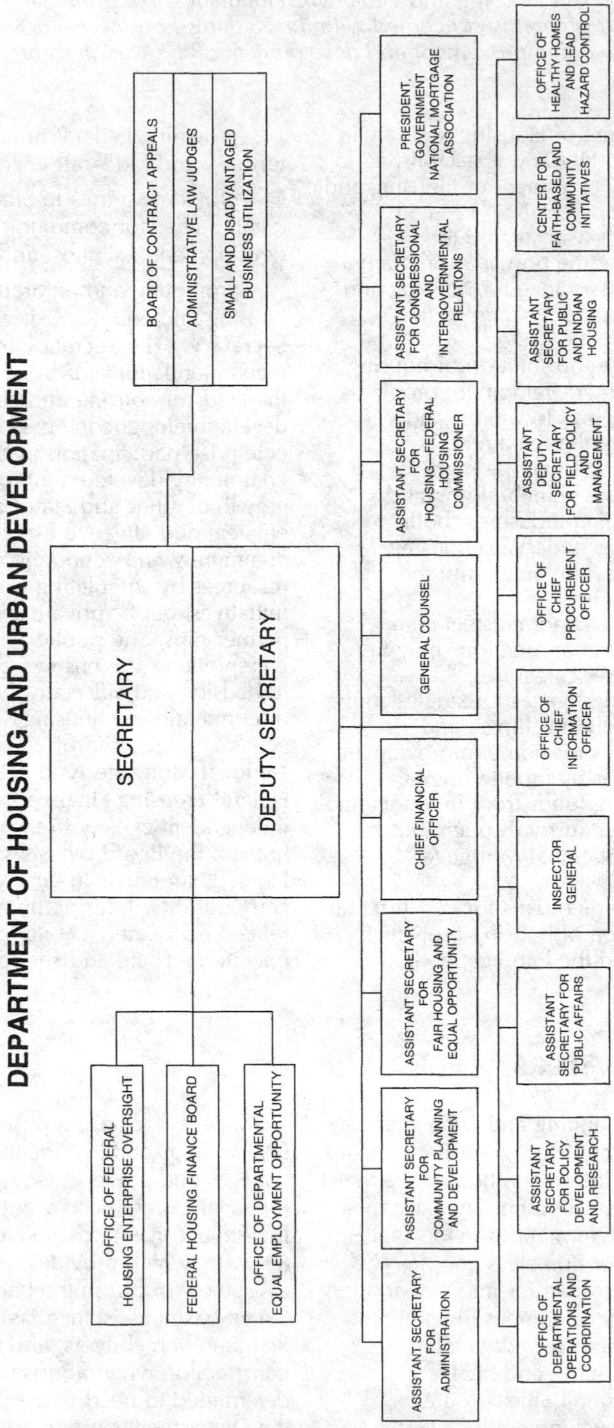
DEPARTMENT OF HOUSING AND URBAN DEVELOPMENT
SECRETARY
DEPUTY SECRETARY
BOARD OF CONTRACT APPEALS
ADMINISTRATIVE LAW JUDGES
SMALL AND DISADVANTAGED BUSINESS UTILIZATION
OFFICE OF FEDERAL HOUSING ENTERPRISE OVERSIGHT
FEDERAL HOUSING FINANCE BOARD
OFFICE OF DEPARTMENTAL EQUAL EMPLOYMENT OPPORTUNITY
ASSISTANT SECRETARY FOR ADMINISTRATION
ASSISTANT SECRETARY FOR COMMUNITY PLANNING AND DEVELOPMENT
ASSISTANT SECRETARY FOR FAIR HOUSING AND EQUAL OPPORTUNITY
CHIEF FINANCIAL OFFICER
GENERAL COUNSEL
ASSISTANT SECRETARY FOR HOUSING—FEDERAL HOUSING COMMISSIONER
ASSISTANT SECRETARY FOR CONGRESSIONAL AND INTERGOVERNMENTAL RELATIONS
PRESIDENT, GOVERNMENT NATIONAL MORTGAGE ASSOCIATION
OFFICE OF DEPARTMENTAL OPERATIONS AND COORDINATION
ASSISTANT SECRETARY FOR POLICY DEVELOPMENT AND RESEARCH
ASSISTANT SECRETARY FOR PUBLIC AFFAIRS
INSPECTOR GENERAL
OFFICE OF CHIEF INFORMATION OFFICER
OFFICE OF CHIEF PROCUREMENT OFFICER
ASSISTANT DEPUTY SECRETARY FOR FIELD POLICY AND MANAGEMENT
ASSISTANT SECRETARY FOR PUBLIC AND INDIAN HOUSING
CENTER FOR FAITH-BASED AND COMMUNITY INITIATIVES
OFFICE OF HEALTHY HOMES AND LEAD HAZARD CONTROL

homelessness; the John Heinz Neighborhood Development Program; community outreach partnerships; the joint community development plan, assisting institutions of higher education working in concert with State and local governments to undertake activities under the CDBG program; community adjustment and economic diversification planning grants; the YouthBuild Program, which provides opportunities and assistance to very low income high school dropouts, ages 16–24; empowerment zones and enterprise communities; efforts to improve the environment; and community planning and development efforts with other departments and agencies, public and private organizations, private industry, financial markets, and international organizations.

For further information, contact the Office of Community Planning and Development. Phone, 202–708–2690.

Fair Housing and Equal Opportunity The Office administers fair housing laws and regulations prohibiting discrimination in public and private housing; equal opportunity laws and regulations prohibiting discrimination in HUD-assisted housing and community development programs; the fair housing assistance grants program to provide financial and technical assistance to State and local government agencies to implement local fair housing laws and ordinances; and the Community Housing Resources Boards program to provide grants for fair housing activities such as outreach and education, identification of institutional barriers to fair housing, and complaint telephone hotlines.

For further information, contact the Office of Fair Housing and Equal Opportunity. Phone, 202–708–4252.

Federal Housing Enterprise Oversight The Office oversees the financial safety and soundness of the Federal National Mortgage Association (Fannie Mae) and the Federal Home Loan Mortgage Corporation (Freddie Mac) to ensure that they are adequately capitalized and operating safely.

For further information, contact the Office of Federal Housing Enterprise Oversight. Phone, 202–414–3800.

Government National Mortgage Association (GNMA) The mission of this Government corporation, also known as Ginnie Mae, is to support expanded affordable housing by providing an efficient Government-guaranteed secondary market vehicle to link the capital markets with Federal housing markets. Ginnie Mae guarantees mortgage-backed securities composed of FHA-insured or VA-guaranteed mortgage loans that are issued by private lenders and guaranteed by GNMA with the full faith and credit of the United States. Through these programs, Ginnie Mae increases the overall supply of credit available for housing by providing a vehicle for channeling funds from the securities market into the mortgage market.

For further information, contact the Government National Mortgage Association. Phone, 202–708–0926.

Housing The Office of Housing is responsible for the Department's housing functions and oversees aid for construction and financing of new and rehabilitated housing and for preservation of existing housing. The Office underwrites single-family, multi-family, property improvement, and manufactured home loans; administers special purpose programs designed specifically for the elderly, the handicapped, and the chronically mentally ill; administers assisted housing programs for low-income families who are experiencing difficulties affording standard housing; administers grants to fund resident ownership of multi-family house properties; and protects consumers against fraudulent practices of land developers and promoters.

For further information, contact the Office of Housing. Phone, 202–708–3600.

Healthy Homes and Lead Hazard Control This Office is responsible for lead hazard control policy development, abatement, training, regulations, and research. Activities of the Office include increasing public and building industry awareness of the dangers of lead-based paint poisoning and the options for detection, risk reduction, and abatement; encouraging the development of safer, more effective, and less costly methods for detection, risk reduction, and abatement; and encouraging State and local governments to develop lead-based paint programs covering contractor certification, hazard reduction, financing, enforcement, and primary prevention, including public education.

For further information, contact the Office of Healthy Homes and Lead Hazard Control. Phone, 202–755–1785.

Public and Indian Housing The Office administers public and Indian housing programs; provides technical and financial assistance in planning, developing, and managing low-income projects; provides operating subsidies for public housing agencies (PHAs) and Indian housing authorities (IHAs), including procedures for reviewing the management of public housing agencies; administers the comprehensive improvement assistance and comprehensive grant programs for modernization of low-income housing projects to upgrade living conditions, correct physical deficiencies, and achieve operating efficiency and economy; administers program for resident participation, resident management, homeownership, economic development and supportive services, and drug-free neighborhood programs; protects tenants from the hazards of lead-based paint poisoning by requiring PHAs and IHAs to comply with HUD regulations for the testing and removal of lead-based paint from low-income housing units; implements and monitors program requirements related to program eligibility and admission of families to public and assisted housing, and tenant income and rent requirements pertaining to continued occupancy; administers the HOPE VI and vacancy reduction programs; administers voucher and certificate programs and the Moderate Rehabilitation Program; coordinates all departmental housing and community development programs for Indian and Alaskan Natives; and awards grants to PHAs and IHAs for the construction, acquisition, and operation of public and Indian housing projects, giving priority to projects for larger families and acquisition of existing units.

For further information, contact the Office of Public and Indian Housing. Phone, 202–708–0950.

Regional Offices—Department of Housing and Urban Development

Region	Address	Regional Director	Telephone
I	Rm. 301, 10 Causeway St., Boston, MA 02222–1092	Taylor Caswell	617–994–8200
II	26 Federal Plz., New York, NY 10278–0068	Sean Moss	212–264–8000
III	100 Penn Sq., Philadelphia, PA 19107–3380	Guy Ciarrochi	215–656–0600
IV	2d Fl., 40 Marietta St., Atlanta, GA 30303–2806	Robert Young	404–331–5001
V	77 W. Jackson Blvd., Chicago, IL 60604–3507	Joseph Galvan	312–353–5680
VI	801 Cherry St., Fort Worth, TX 76113	A. Cynthia Leon	817–978–5540
VII	Rm. 200, 400 State Ave., Kansas City, KS 66101–2406	Macie Houston	913–551–5462
VIII	23d Fl., 1670 Broadway, Denver, CO 80202–4801	John Carson	303–672–5440
IX	450 3d Fl., 600 Harrison St., San Francisco, CA 94107–1300	Richard K. Rainey	415–489–6400
X	Suite 200, 909 1st Ave., Seattle, WA 98104–1000	John Meyers	206–220–5101

Sources of Information

Inquiries on the following subjects should be directed to the nearest regional office or to the specified headquarters office, Department of

Housing and Urban Development, 451 Seventh Street SW., Washington, DC 20410. Phone, 202–708–0614. TDD, 202–708–1455.

Contracts Contact the Contracting Division. Phone, 202–708–1290.

Directory Locator Phone, 202–708–0614. TDD, 202–708–1455.

Employment Inquiries and applications should be directed to the headquarters Office of Human Resources (phone, 202–708–0408); or the Personnel Division at the nearest HUD regional office.

Freedom of Information Act (FOIA) Requests Persons interested in inspecting documents or records under the Freedom of Information Act should contact the Freedom of Information Officer. Phone, 202–708–3054. Written requests should be directed to the Director, Executive Secretariat, Department of Housing and Urban Development, Room 10139, 451 Seventh Street SW., Washington, DC 20410.

HUD Hotline The Hotline is maintained by the Office of the Inspector General as a means for individuals to report activities involving fraud, waste, or mismanagement. Phone, 202–708–4200, or 800–347–3735 (toll free). TDD, 202–708–2451.

Program Information Center The Center provides viewing facilities for information regarding departmental activities, functions, and publications and other literature to headquarters visitors. Phone, 202–708–1420.

Property Disposition For single-family properties, contact the Property Disposition Division (phone, 202–708–0614); or the Chief Property Officer at the nearest HUD regional office. For multifamily properties, contact the Property Disposition Division (phone, 202–708–0614); or the Regional Housing Director at the nearest HUD regional office.

For further information, contact the Office of Public Affairs, Department of Housing and Urban Development, 451 Seventh Street SW., Washington, DC 20410. Phone, 202–708–0980. Internet, www.hud.gov.

DEPARTMENT OF THE INTERIOR

1849 C Street NW., Washington, DC 20240
Phone, 202–208–3100. Internet, www.doi.gov.

SECRETARY OF THE INTERIOR	DIRK KEMPTHORNE
Deputy Secretary	P. LYNN SCARLETT
Chief of Staff	BRIAN WAIDMANN
Deputy Chief of Staff	DOUGLAS W. DOMENECH
Special Trustee for American Indians	ROSS OWEN SWIMMER
Director of Congressional and Legislative Affairs	MATTHEW EAMES
Chief Counselor to the Secretary	(VACANCY)
Counselor to the Secretary	(VACANCY)
White House Liaison	(VACANCY)
Science Adviser to the Secretary	JAMES TATE
Director, Office of Communications	ERNESTINE KREISHER
Director of External and Intergovernmental Affairs	KIT KIMBLE
Director, Office of the Executive Secretariat and Regulatory Affairs	FAY IUDICELLO
Senior Advisor to the Secretary for Alaskan Affairs	DRUE PEARCE
Executive Director, Office of Historical Trust Accounting	BERT T. EDWARDS
Executive Director, Take Pride in America	MARTHA ALLBRIGHT
Solicitor	(VACANCY)
Deputy Solicitor	DAVID BERNHARDT
Counselor to the Solicitor	LAWRENCE JENSEN
Associate Solicitor (Administration)	EDWARD KEABLE
Associate Solicitor (Conservation and Wildlife)	DAVID VERHEY
Associate Solicitor (Land and Water Resources)	EMMA SUAREZ
Associate Solicitor (General Law)	ARTHUR E. GARY
Associate Solicitor (Indian Affairs)	CARL ARTMAN
Associate Solicitor (Mineral Resources)	JAMES HARRIS
Director, Office of Ethics	SHAYLA F. SIMMONS
Inspector General	EARL E. DEVANEY
Deputy Inspector General	MARY KENDALL
Assistant Secretary—Water and Science	MARK LIMBAUGH
Deputy Assistant Secretary	(VACANCY)
Director, U.S. Geological Survey	(VACANCY)
Commissioner, Bureau of Reclamation	JOHN W. KEYS III
Assistant Secretary—Fish and Wildlife and Parks	(VACANCY)
Deputy Assistant Secretaries	MATTHEW J. HOGAN, JULIE MACDONALD, DAVID P. SMITH
Director, U.S. Fish and Wildlife Service	H. DALE HALL
Director, National Park Service	FRAN MAINELLA

Assistant Secretary—Indian Affairs	(VACANCY)
Counselor to the Assistant Secretary	MICHAEL OLSEN
Principal Deputy Assistant Secretary	(VACANCY)
Deputy Assistant Secretary—Policy and Economic Development	(VACANCY)
Deputy Assistant Secretary—Management	DEBBIE CLARK
Deputy Assistant Secretary—Information Resources Management/Chief Information Officer	(VACANCY)
Director, Bureau of Indian Affairs	WILLIAM RAGSDALE
Assistant Secretary—Land and Minerals Management	(VACANCY)
Deputy Assistant Secretary	CHAD CALVERT
Director, Minerals Management Service	R.M. JOHNNIE BURTON
Director, Bureau of Land Management	KATHLEEN B. CLARKE
Director, Office of Surface Mining Reclamation and Enforcement	(VACANCY)
Assistant Secretary—Policy, Management, and Budget	R. THOMAS WEIMER
Chief of Staff	MONICA NOE
Chief Information Officer, Office of the Chief Information Officer	W. HORD TIPTON
Deputy Assistant Secretary—Policy and International Affairs	CHRISTOPHER KEARNEY
Director, Office of Environmental Policy and Compliance	WILLIE R. TAYLOR
Director, Office of Policy Analysis	(VACANCY)
Director, Office of Hawaiian Affairs	(VACANCY)
Deputy Assistant Secretary—Business Management and Wildlife Fire	NINA HATFIELD
Director, Office of Small and Disadvantaged Business Utilization	ROBERT W. FAITHFUL
Director, Office of Budget	JOHN TREZISE
Director, Office of Financial Management	DANIEL FLETCHER
Director, Office of Acquisition and Property	DEBRA SONDERMAN
Director, National Business Center	DOUGLAS BOURGEOIS
Director, Office of Wildland Fire Coordination	(VACANCY)
Deputy Assistant Secretary—Performance, Accountability, and Human Resources	PAUL D. HOFFMAN
Deputy Chief Human Capital Officer	KATHLEEN J.H. WHEELER
Director, Office of Human Resources	MARILIA MATOS
Director, Office of Civil Rights	SHARON ELLER
Director, Office of Occupational Health and Safety	DIANE SCHMITZ
Director, Office of Strategic Development of Human Capital	MICHELLE CHAVEZ
Director, Office of Collaborative Action and Dispute Resolution	ELENA GONZALEZ
Director, Office of Planning and Performance Management	RICHARD T. BECK
Director, Office of Hearings and Appeals	ROBERT S. MORE
Director, Center for Competitive Sourcing Excellence	DONNA KALVELS

Deputy Assistant Secretary—Law Enforcement and Security	LARRY R. PARKINSON
Director, Office of Law Enforcement and Security	STEVEN CALVERY
Deputy Assistant Secretary—Insular Affairs	DAVID COHEN
Director, Office of Insular Affairs	NIKOLAO PULA

The mission of the Department of the Interior is to protect and provide access to our Nation's natural and cultural heritage and honor our trust responsibilities to tribes and our commitments to island communities. The Department manages the Nation's public lands and minerals, national parks, national wildlife refuges, and western water resources and upholds Federal trust responsibilities to Indian tribes and our commitments to island communities. It is responsible for migratory wildlife conservation; historic preservation; endangered species; surface-mined lands protection and restoration; mapping; geological, hydrological, and biological science; and financial and technical assistance for the insular areas.

The Department of the Interior was created by act of March 3, 1849 (43 U.S.C. 1451), which transferred to it the General Land Office, the Office of Indian Affairs, the Pension Office, and the Patent Office. It was reorganized by Reorganization Plan No. 3 of 1950, as amended (5 U.S.C. app.).

Secretary The Secretary of the Interior reports directly to the President and is responsible for the direction and supervision of all operations and activities of the Department. Some areas where public purposes are broadly applied include:

Fish, Wildlife, and Parks The Office of the Assistant Secretary (Fish and Wildlife and Parks) has responsibility for programs associated with the use, management and conservation of natural resources, lands and cultural facilities associated with the National Park and National Refuge Systems, and the conservation and enhancement of fish, wildlife, vegetation, and habitat. The Office represents the Department in the coordination of marine ecosystems and biological resources programs with other Federal agencies. It also exercises secretarial direction and supervision over the United States Fish and Wildlife Service and the National Park Service.

Water and Science The Office of the Assistant Secretary (Water and Science) provides oversight to the U.S. Geological Survey, the Bureau of Reclamation and the Central Utah Project Completion Act Office. It provides policy direction and oversight in program areas related to water project operations, facility security and natural resource management as well as for geologic, hydrologic, cartographic, biologic, and technological research. It provides guidance in developing national water and science policies and environmental improvement.

Land and Minerals Management The Office of the Assistant Secretary (Land and Minerals Management) has responsibility for programs associated with public land management; operations management and leasing for minerals on public lands, including the Outer Continental Shelf to the outer limits of the United States economic jurisdiction; minerals operations management on Indian lands; surface mining reclamation and enforcement functions; and management of revenues from Federal and Indian mineral leases.

Indian Affairs The Office of the Assistant Secretary (Indian Affairs) is responsible for establishing and acting on issues affecting Indian policy and programs; exercising direction and supervision of the Bureau of Indian Affairs, including the Office of Indian Education Programs; directly supervising the Federal acknowledgment of tribes, tribal self-determination and self-governance, Indian gaming management, economic development, and all administrative, financial, and information resources management activities; and maintaining liaison and coordination

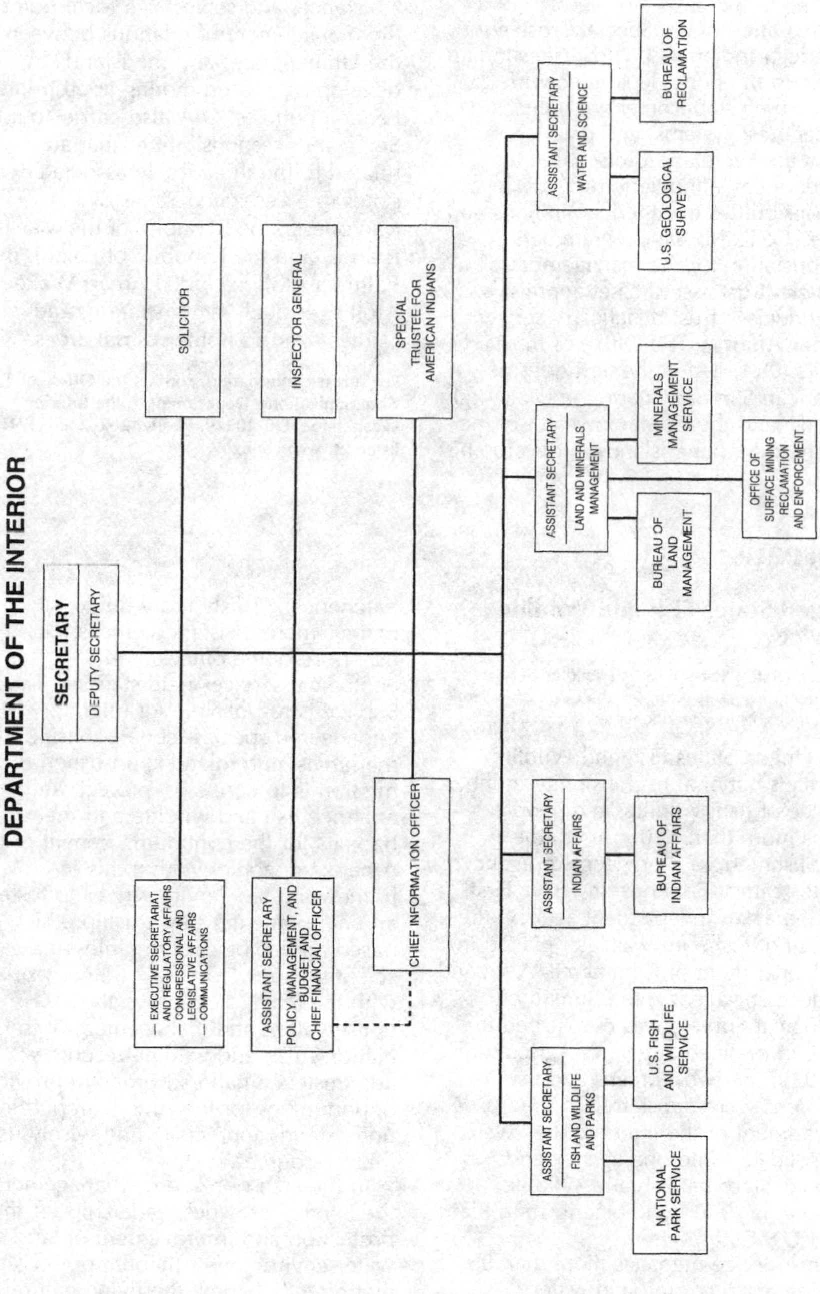
DEPARTMENT OF THE INTERIOR
SECRETARY
DEPUTY SECRETARY
SOLICITOR
INSPECTOR GENERAL
SPECIAL TRUSTEE FOR AMERICAN INDIANS
— EXECUTIVE SECRETARIAT AND REGULATORY AFFAIRS
— CONGRESSIONAL AND LEGISLATIVE AFFAIRS
— COMMUNICATIONS
ASSISTANT SECRETARY
POLICY, MANAGEMENT, AND BUDGET AND CHIEF FINANCIAL OFFICER
CHIEF INFORMATION OFFICER
ASSISTANT SECRETARY
FISH AND WILDLIFE AND PARKS
NATIONAL PARK SERVICE
U.S. FISH AND WILDLIFE SERVICE
ASSISTANT SECRETARY
INDIAN AFFAIRS
BUREAU OF INDIAN AFFAIRS
ASSISTANT SECRETARY
LAND AND MINERALS MANAGEMENT
BUREAU OF LAND MANAGEMENT
MINERALS MANAGEMENT SERVICE
OFFICE OF SURFACE MINING RECLAMATION AND ENFORCEMENT
ASSISTANT SECRETARY
WATER AND SCIENCE
U.S. GEOLOGICAL SURVEY
BUREAU OF RECLAMATION

between the Department and other Federal agencies that provide services or funding to Indians.

The Office of the Special Trustee for American Indians (OST) oversees Indian trust reform efforts departmentwide to ensure the establishment of policies, procedures, systems, and practices to allow the Secretary to discharge the Government's fiduciary trust responsibilities to American Indians and tribes. OST also has programmatic responsibility for the management of financial trust assets, asset appraisals, and fiduciary trust beneficiary services.

Insular Affairs The Office of Insular Affairs (OIA) assists the territories of American Samoa, Guam, the U.S. Virgin Islands, and the Commonwealth of the Northern Mariana Islands in developing more efficient and effective government by providing financial and technical assistance, and serves as a focal point for the management of relations between the United States and the islands by developing and promoting appropriate Federal policies. OIA also carries out the Secretary's responsibilities that are related to the three freely associated states (the Federated States of Micronesia, the Republic of the Marshall Islands, and the Republic of Palau); the Palmyra Atoll Excluded Areas; Wake Atoll's residual administration; and Midway Atoll's nonterrestrial areas.

For further information, contact the Office of Communications, Department of the Interior, Washington, DC 20240. Phone, 202–208–3171. Internet, www.doi.gov.

Bureaus

United States Fish and Wildlife Service

[For the United States Fish and Wildlife Service statement of organization, see the *Code of Federal Regulations,* Title 50, Subchapter A, Part 2]

The United States Fish and Wildlife Service's national responsibility in the service of fish, wildlife, and people spans more than 130 years to the establishment of a predecessor agency, the Bureau of Fisheries, in 1871. First created as an independent agency, the Bureau of Fisheries was later placed in the Department of Commerce. A second predecessor agency, the Bureau of Biological Survey, was established in 1885 in the Department of Agriculture. In 1939, the two Bureaus and their functions were transferred to the Department of the Interior. They were consolidated into one agency and redesignated the Fish and Wildlife Service in 1940 by Reorganization Plan III (5 U.S.C. app.).

The Service manages more than 95 million acres of land and water consisting of more than 540 national wildlife refuges, thousands of small wetlands, and other special management areas. It also operates 69 national fish hatcheries, 63 fish and wildlife management assistance offices, 64 fishery resource offices, and 81 ecological services field stations. The Service is responsible for migratory birds, endangered species, certain marine mammals, and inland sport fisheries. Its mission is to conserve, protect, and enhance fish and wildlife and their habitats for the continuing benefit of the American people. Within this framework, the Service strives to foster an environmental stewardship ethic based on ecological principles and scientific knowledge of wildlife; works with the States to improve the conservation and management of the Nation's fish and wildlife resources; and administers a national program providing opportunities for the American public to understand, appreciate, and wisely use these resources.

In the area of resource management, the Service provides leadership for the protection and improvement of land and water environments (habitat preservation) that directly benefit the living natural resources and add quality to human life. Activities include:

—surveillance of pesticides, heavy metals, and other contaminants;

—studies of fish and wildlife populations;

—ecological studies;

—environmental impact assessment, including hydroelectric dams, nuclear power sites, stream channelization, and dredge-and-fill permits; and

—environmental impact statement review.

The Service is responsible for improving and maintaining fish and wildlife resources by proper management of wildlife and habitat. It also helps fulfill the public demand for recreational fishing while maintaining the Nation's fisheries at a level and in a condition that will ensure their continued survival. Specific wildlife and fishery resources programs include:

—migratory birds (wildlife refuge management for production, migration, and wintering; law enforcement; game; and bird population, production, and harvest surveys);

—mammals and nonmigratory birds (refuge management of resident species, law enforcement, protection of certain marine mammals, and technical assistance);

—coastal anadromous fish (hatchery production and stocking);

—Great Lakes fisheries (hatchery production of lake trout and fishery management in cooperation with Canada and the States); and

—other inland fisheries (hatchery production and stocking of Indian lands, and technical assistance).

The Service provides national and international leadership in identifying, protecting, and restoring endangered species of fish, wildlife, and plants. This program includes:

—developing the Federal Endangered and Threatened Species List, conducting status surveys, preparing recovery plans, and coordinating efforts nationally and internationally;

—operating national wildlife refuges;

—law enforcement;

—foreign importation enforcement; and

—consultation with foreign countries.

Public use and information programs include preparing leaflets and brochures; operating environmental study areas on Service lands; operating visitor centers, self-guided nature trails, observation towers, and display ponds; and providing recreational activities such as hunting, fishing, and wildlife photography.

The Service's Office of Federal Assistance apportions funds for projects designed to conserve and enhance the Nation's fish and wildlife resources. The funds for the projects are generated from excise taxes on sporting arms and fishing equipment.

Regional Offices—United States Fish and Wildlife Service

Region	Address	Telephone
ALBUQUERQUE—AZ, NM, OK, TX	P.O. Box 1306, Albuquerque, NM 87103–1306	505–248–6282
ANCHORAGE—AK	1011 E. Tudor Rd., Anchorage, AK 99503	907–786–3542
ATLANTA—AL, AR, FL, GA, KY, LA, MS, NC, PR, SC, TN, VI	1875 Century Blvd. NE., Atlanta, GA 30345–3301	404–679–4000
HADLEY—CT, DE, MA, ME, MD, NH, NJ, NY, PA, RI, VT, VA, WV	300 Westgate Ctr. Dr., Hadley, MA 01035–9589	413–253–8200
DENVER—CO, KS, MT, NE, ND, SD, UT, WY	P.O. Box 25486, Denver Federal Center, Denver, CO 80225	303–236–7920
PORTLAND—HI, ID, OR, WA, Pacific Islands	911 NE. 11th Ave., Portland, OR 97232–4181	503–231–6118
California/Nevada Operations Office	Suite W–2606, 2800 Cottage Way, Sacramento, CA 95825–1846	916–414–6464
TWIN CITIES—IL, IN, IA, MI, MN, MO, OH, WI	Federal Bldg., Fort Snelling, Twin Cities, MN 55111–4056	612–713–5300

For further information, contact the Office of Public Affairs, Fish and Wildlife Service, Department of the Interior, Washington, DC 20240. Phone, 202–208–5634. Internet, www.fws.gov.

National Park Service

The National Park Service was established in the Department of the Interior on August 25, 1916 (16 U.S.C. 1).

The National Park Service is dedicated to conserving unimpaired the natural and cultural resources and values of the National Park System for the enjoyment, education, and inspiration of this and future generations. There are 390 units in the National Park System, including national parks, monuments and memorials, scenic parkways, preserves, reserves, trails, riverways, wild and scenic rivers, seashores, lakeshores, recreation areas, battlefields and battlefield parks and sites, national military parks, international historic sites, and historic sites associated with important movements, events, and personalities of the American past.

The National Park Service has a Service Center in Denver that provides planning, architectural, engineering, and other professional services. The Service is also responsible for managing a great variety of national and international programs designed to help extend the benefits of natural and cultural resource conservation and outdoor recreation throughout this country and the world.

Activities The National Park Service develops and implements park management plans and staffs the areas under its administration. It relates the natural values and historical significance of these areas to the public through talks, tours, films, exhibits, publications, and other interpretive media. It operates campgrounds and other visitor facilities and provides lodging, food, and transportation services in many areas.

The National Park Service also administers the following programs: the State portion of the Land and Water Conservation Fund, nationwide outdoor recreation coordination and information, State comprehensive outdoor recreation planning, planning and technical assistance for the national wild and scenic rivers system, the national trails system, natural area programs, the National Register of Historic Places, national historic landmarks, historic preservation, technical preservation services, the historic American buildings survey, the historic American engineering record, and interagency archeological services.

Regional Offices—National Park Service

Regions	Address	Telephone
ALASKA—AK	Suite 114, 240 West 5th Ave., Anchorage, AK 99501	907–644–3510
INTERMOUNTAIN—AZ, CO, MT, NM, OK, TX, UT, WY	P.O. Box 25287, 12795 W. Alameda Pkwy., Denver, CO 80225–0287	303–969–2500
MIDWEST—AR, IL, IN, IA, KS, MI, MN, MO, ND, NE, OH, SD, WI	1709 Jackson St., Omaha, NE 68102–2571	402–221–3431
NATIONAL CAPITAL—Washington, DC, and nearby MD, VA, and WV	1100 Ohio Dr. SW., Washington, DC 20242–0001	202–619–7000
NORTHEAST—CT, DE, ME, MA, MD, NH, NJ, NY, PA, RI, VT, VA, WV	5th Fl., 200 Chestnut St., Philadelphia, PA 19106–2818	215–597–7013
PACIFIC WEST—CA, HI, ID, NV, OR, WA, American Samoa, Guam	Suite 700, 1111 Jackson St., Oakland, CA 94607–1372	510–817–1304
SOUTHEAST—AL, FL, GA, KY, LA, MS, NC, SC, TN, PR, VI	1924 Bldg., 100 Alabama St. SW., Atlanta, GA 30303	404–562–3100

For further information, contact the Chief, Office of Communications, National Park Service, Department of the Interior, 1849 C Street NW., Washington, DC 20240. Phone, 202–208–4747. Internet, www.nps.gov.

United States Geological Survey

The U.S. Geological Survey (USGS) was established by the Organic Act of March 3, 1879 (43 U.S.C. 31). USGS classifies public lands, examines the geological structure, and assesses the energy, mineral, and biology resources and products within and outside the national domain.

USGS provides relevant, objective scientific studies and information used to help address issues and solve problems dealing with natural resources, natural hazards, and the environmental effects on human and wildlife health. It is responsible for:

—investigating and assessing the Nation's water, energy, biological, and mineral resources;

—conducting research on global change;

—providing information to land and resource managers in the Department to help them assess and manage the biological and environmental consequences of management practices;

—investigating natural hazards and providing real-time information about the Earth and minimizing loss of life and property from earthquakes, volcanoes, floods, droughts, coastal erosion, and wildland fires;

—maintaining an archive of land-remote sensing data for historical, scientific, and technical purposes, including long-term global environmental monitoring;

—ensuring production and availability of basic biologic, hydrologic, geologic, and geographical spatial data of the Nation; and

—maintaining and analyzing databases of natural resource information.

To attain these objectives, USGS prepares maps and digital and cartographic data; collects and interprets data on energy, mineral, and biological resources; conducts nationwide assessments of the quality, quantity, and use of the Nation's water resources; performs fundamental and applied research in the sciences and techniques involved; and publishes the results of its investigations through maps, technical reports, and fact sheets.

For further information, contact the U.S. Geological Survey, Department of the Interior, 12201 Sunrise Valley Drive, Reston, VA 20192. Phone, 703–648–4000. Internet, www.usgs.gov. E-mail, ASK@usgs.gov.

Office of Surface Mining Reclamation and Enforcement

The Office of Surface Mining Reclamation and Enforcement (OSM) was established in the Department of the Interior by the Surface Mining Control and Reclamation Act of 1977 (30 U.S.C. 1211).

The Office's primary goal is to assist States in operating a nationwide program that protects society and the environment from the adverse effects of coal mining, while ensuring that surface coal mining can be done without permanent damage to land and water resources. With most coal mining States responsible for regulating coal mining and reclamation activities within their borders, OSM's main objectives are to oversee State mining regulatory and abandoned-mine reclamation programs, assist States in meeting the objectives of the surface mining law, and regulate mining and reclamation activities on Federal and Indian lands, and in those States choosing not to assume primary responsibility.

Activities The Office establishes national policy for the surface mining control and reclamation program provided for in the surface mining law, reviews and approves amendments to previously approved State programs, and reviews and recommends approval of new State program submissions. Other activities include:

—managing the collection, disbursement, and accounting for abandoned- mine land reclamation fees;

—administering civil penalties programs;

—establishing technical standards and regulatory policy for reclamation and enforcement efforts;

—providing guidance for environmental considerations, research, training, and technology transfer for State, tribal, and Federal regulatory and abandoned-mine land reclamation programs;

—monitoring and evaluating State and tribal regulatory programs, cooperative agreements, and abandoned-mine land reclamation programs; and

—coordinating the Appalachian clean streams initiative, a public-private joint effort, at the Federal, State, and local levels, to clean up streams and rivers polluted by acid mine drainage.

For further information, contact the Office of Communications, Office of Surface Mining Reclamation and Enforcement, Department of the Interior, Washington, DC 20240. Phone, 202–208–2565. TDD, 202–208–2694. Internet, www.osmre.gov.

Bureau of Indian Affairs

The Bureau of Indian Affairs (BIA) was created as part of the War Department in 1824 and transferred to the Department of the Interior when the latter was established in 1849. The mission of BIA is to fulfill its trust responsibilities and promote self-determination on behalf of tribal governments, American Indians, and Alaska Natives. BIA provides services directly or through contracts, grants, or compacts to approximately 1.4 million American Indians and Alaska Natives, members of 561 federally recognized Indian tribes in the 48 contiguous United States and Alaska. The scope of BIA's programs is extensive, covering virtually the entire range of State and local governmental services. The programs administered by either tribes or BIA include: an education system for over 48,000 elementary and secondary students; 25 tribally controlled community colleges; social service programs; management of natural resources on 56 million acres of trust land; fire protection; emergency natural disaster relief; economic development programs in some of the most isolated and economically depressed areas of the United States; law enforcement; administration of tribal courts and detention centers; implementation of legislated land and water claim settlements; replacement and repair of schools; repair and maintenance of roads and bridges; repair of structural deficiencies on high-hazard dams; and Federal acknowledgment of Indian tribes.

BIA works with Indian and Alaska Native people, tribal governments, Native American organizations, other Federal agencies, State and local governments, and other interested groups in the development and implementation of effective programs.

Regional Offices—Bureau of Indian Affairs

Region	Address	Telephone
Alaska	P.O. Box 25520, Juneau, AK 99802–5520	800–645–8397
Eastern	545 Marriott Dr., Nashville, TN 37214	615–564–6700
Eastern Oklahoma	P.O. Box 8002, 3100 W. Peak Blvd., Muskogee, OK 74402–8002	918–781–4600
Great Plains	115 4th Ave. SE., Aberdeen, SD 57401–4382	605–226–7343
Midwest	Rm. 550, 1 Federal Dr., Ft. Snelling, MN 55111–4007	612–713–4400
Navajo	P.O. Box 1060, Gallup, NM 87305	505–863–8314
Northwest	911 NE. 11th Ave., Portland, OR 97232–4169	503–231–6702
Pacific	2800 Cottage Way, Sacramento, CA 95825	916–978–6000
Rocky Mountain	316 N. 26th St., Billings, MT 59101–1362	406–247–7943
Southern Plains	WCD Office Complex, Anadarko, OK 73005–0368	405–247–6673
Southwest	P.O. Box 26567, 1001 Indian School Rd. NW., Albuquerque, NM 87125–6567.	505–563–3100
Western	P.O. Box 10, Phoenix, AZ 85001–0010	602–379–6600

For further information, contact the Office of the Assistant Secretary—Indian Affairs, Public Affairs, Department of the Interior, 1849 C Street NW., MS–2415 MIB, Washington, DC 20240. Phone, 202–208–3710.

Minerals Management Service

The Minerals Management Service was established on January 19, 1982, by Secretarial order. The Service assesses the nature, extent, recoverability, and value of leasable minerals on the Outer Continental Shelf. It ensures the orderly and timely inventory and development and the efficient recovery of mineral resources; encourages utilization of the best available and safest technology; and safeguards against fraud, waste, and abuse.

Offshore Minerals Management The Service is responsible for resource assessment and evaluation; environmental review; leasing and permitting activities (including public liaison and planning functions), management of leases, easements, and rights-of-way; and inspection and enforcement programs for Outer Continental Shelf lands.

Programs are developed for energy, mineral, and related activities on the Outer Continental Shelf in consultation with the Congress, affected States, local governments, environmental groups, industry, and the public.

The Service conducts extensive environmental studies and consultations with State officials prior to issuing leases, easements, or rights-of-way. Once permits or other approvals have been issued, inspectors conduct frequent inspections of offshore operations, and environmental studies personnel collect data to ensure that marine and coastal environments are kept free of pollutants.

Minerals Revenue Management The Service is responsible for collecting, accounting for, and disbursing revenues associated with minerals produced on Federal and Indian-leased lands. The Service also conducts a comprehensive compliance program to ensure that fair market value is received for the mineral assets and that royalties are timely and accurately paid.

The basic organization of the Service consists of a headquarters in Washington, DC, with program components located in Herndon, VA, and Lakewood, CO; three Outer Continental Shelf regional offices; and two administrative service centers.

Field Offices—Minerals Management Service

Office	Address	Telephone
Minerals Revenue Management	P.O. Box 25165, Denver, CO 80225–0165	303–231–3162
	OCS Regional Offices	
Alaska Region	Suite 500, 3801 Centerpoint Dr., Anchorage, AK 99503–5820	907–334–5200
Gulf of Mexico Region	1201 Elmwood Park Blvd., New Orleans, LA 70123–2394	504–736–2589
Pacific Region	770 Paseo Camarillo, Camarillo, CA 93010–6064	805–389–7502
	Administrative Service Centers	
Western Service Center	P.O. Box 25165, Denver, CO 80225–0165	303–231–3900
Southern Service Center	1201 Elmwood Park Blvd., New Orleans, LA 70123–2394	504–736–2616

For further information, contact the Chief, Public Affairs, Minerals Management Service, Department of the Interior, Room 4259, (MS 4230), 1849 C Street NW., Washington, DC 20240–7000. Phone, 202–208–3985. Internet, www.mms.gov.

Bureau of Land Management

The Bureau of Land Management (BLM) was established July 16, 1946, by the consolidation of the General Land Office (created in 1812) and the Grazing Service (formed in 1934).

The Bureau manages more land—262 million surface acres—than any other Federal Government agency. Most of this public land is located in 12 western States, including Alaska. There are also small, scattered parcels in States east of the Mississippi River. The Bureau also administers more than 700 million acres of subsurface mineral estate throughout the Nation. It preserves open space in the fast-growing, fast-changing West by managing the public lands for multiple uses and by conserving resources so that current and future generations may use and enjoy them.

Resources managed by the Bureau include timber, solid minerals, oil and gas, geothermal energy, wildlife habitat, endangered plant and animal species, rangeland vegetation, recreation and cultural values, wild and scenic rivers, designated conservation and wilderness areas, and open space. Bureau programs provide for the protection (including fire suppression), orderly development, and use of the public lands and resources under principles of multiple use and sustained yield. Land use plans are developed with public involvement to provide orderly use and development while maintaining and enhancing the quality of the environment. The Bureau also manages watersheds to protect soil and enhance water quality; develops recreational opportunities on public lands; administers programs to protect and manage wild horses and burros; and under certain conditions, makes land available for sale to individuals, organizations, local governments, and other Federal agencies when such transfer is in the public interest. Lands may be leased to State and local government agencies and to nonprofit organizations for certain purposes.

The Bureau oversees and manages the development of energy and mineral leases and ensures compliance with applicable regulations governing the extraction of these resources. It has responsibility to issue rights-of-way, leases, and permits.

The Bureau is also responsible for the survey of Federal lands and establishes and maintains public land records and mining claims records. It administers a program of payments in lieu of taxes based on the amount of federally owned lands in counties and other units of local government.

Field Offices—Bureau of Land Management

State Office	Address	Telephone
Alaska—AK	No. 13, 222 W. 7th Ave., Anchorage, 99513–7599	907–271–5080
Arizona—AZ	222 N. Central Ave., Phoenix, 85004–2203	602–417–9500
California—CA	Suite W–1834, 2800 Cottage Way, Sacramento, 95825–0451.	916–978–4600
Colorado—CO	2850 Youngfield St., Lakewood, 80215–7093	303–239–3700
Eastern States—All States bordering on and east of the Mississippi River.	7450 Boston Blvd., Springfield, VA 22153–1711	703–440–1711
Idaho—ID	1387 S. Vinnell Way, Boise, 83709–1657	208–373–4001
Montana—MT, ND, SD	P.O. Box 36800, 5001 Southgate Dr., Billings, MT 59101–6800.	406–896–5012
Nevada—NV	P.O. Box 12000, 1340 Financial Way, Reno, 89520–0006	775–861–6590
New Mexico—KS, NM, OK, TX	P.O. Box 27115, 1474 Rodeo Rd., Santa Fe, NM 87502–0115.	505–438–7501
Oregon—OR, WA	P.O. Box 2965, 333 SW 1st Ave, Portland, OR	503–808–6026
Utah—UT	P.O. Box 45155, 324 S. State St., Salt Lake City, 84145–0155.	801–539–4010
Wyoming—NE, WY	P.O. Box 1828, 5353 Yellowstone Rd., Cheyenne, WY 82003.	307–775–6001
	Service and Support Offices	
National Office of Fire and Aviation	3833 S. Development Ave., Boise, ID 83705–5354	208–387–5446
National Training Center	9828 N. 31st Ave., Phoenix, AZ 85051–2517	602–906–5500
National Business Center	Bldg. 50, BC–600, P.O. Box 25047, Denver, CO 80225–0047.	303–236–8857
National Human Resources Management Center.	Bldg. 50, HR–200, P.O. Box 25047, Denver, CO 80225–0047.	303–236–6503
National Science and Technology Center	Bldg. 50, RS–100, P.O. Box 25047, Denver, CO 80225–0047.	303–236–6454
National Information Resources Management Center.	Bldg. 40, NI–100, P.O. Box 25047, Denver, CO 80225–0047.	303–236–6965
Washington Office Headquarters Directorate	1849 C St. NW., Washington, DC 20240	202–452–7732
National Law Enforcement Office	1849 C St. NW., Washington, DC 20240	202–208–3269

For further information, contact the Office of Public Affairs, Bureau of Land Management, Department of the Interior, LS–406, 1849 C Street NW., Washington, DC 20240. Phone, 202–452–5125. Internet, www.blm.gov.

Bureau of Reclamation

The Bureau of Reclamation was established pursuant to the Reclamation Act of 1902 (43 U.S.C. 371 *et seq.*). The Bureau is the largest wholesale water supplier and the second largest producer of hydroelectric power in the United States, with operations and facilities in the 17 Western States. Its facilities also provide substantial flood control, recreation, and fish and wildlife benefits.

Major Offices—Bureau of Reclamation

Office/Region	Address	Telephone
Commissioner	Rm. 7654, Dept. of the Interior, Washington, DC 20240–0001.	202–513–0575
Denver Office	Bldg. 67, Box 25007, Denver, CO 80225	303–445–2797
Great Plains Region	Box 36900, 316 N. 26th St., Billings, MT 59107	406–247–7610
Lower Colorado Region	Box 61470, Boulder City, NV 89006–1470	702–293–8000
Mid-Pacific Region	2800 Cottage Way, Sacramento, CA 95825	916–978–5100
Pacific Northwest Region	1150 N. Curtis Rd., Boise, ID 83706	208–378–5021
Upper Colorado Region	Rm. 6107, 125 S. State St., Salt Lake City, UT 84138	801–524–3793

For further information, contact the Public Affairs Office, Bureau of Reclamation, Department of the Interior, Washington, DC 20240–0001. Phone, 202–513–0575. Internet, www.usbr.gov.

Sources of Information

Inquiries on the following subjects should be directed to the specified office, Department of the Interior, Washington, DC 20240.

Contracts Contact the Office of Acquisition and Property Management, Room 2607. Phone, 202–208–6352.

Electronic Access Information is available electronically from the Department of the Interior. Internet, www.doi.gov (or see listings for specific Department components).

Employment Direct general inquiries to the Personnel Liaison Staff, 202–208–6702, the personnel office of a specific bureau or office, or visit any of the field personnel offices.

Museum The Interior Museum presents exhibits on the history and missions of the Department. Programs and changing exhibits highlight Bureau management of cultural and natural resources and trust responsibilities to tribes. The museum staff coordinates tours of the art and architecture of the Interior headquarters. For more information, contact the museum staff. Phone, 202–208–4743.

Publications Most departmental publications are available from the Superintendent of Documents, Government Printing Office, Washington, DC 20402. Information regarding bibliographies on select subjects is available from the Natural Resources Library. Phone, 202–208–5815. All other inquiries regarding publications should be directed to the individual bureau or office's publications or public affairs office.

Reading Room Visit the Natural Resources Library, Main Interior Building. Phone, 202–208–5815.

Employee Locator To locate an employee of the Department of the Interior, call 202–208–3100.

United States Fish and Wildlife Service

Inquiries on the following subjects should be directed to the specified office, U.S. Fish and Wildlife Service, Department of the Interior, Washington, DC 20240.

Congressional/Legislative Services Congressional staffers and persons seeking information about specific legislation should call the Congressional/Legislative Services Office. Phone, 202–208–5403.

Contracts Contact the Washington, DC, headquarters Division of Contracting and General Services (phone, 703–358–1728) or any of the regional offices.

Electronic Access The Fish and Wildlife Service offers a range of information through the Internet at www.fws.gov.

Employment For information regarding employment opportunities with the U.S. Fish and Wildlife Service, contact the Headquarters Personnel Office (phone, 703–358–1743) or the regional office within the area you are seeking employment.

Import/Export Permits To obtain CITES permits for importing and exporting wildlife, contact the Office of Management Authority. Phone, 800–358–2104 or 703–358–2104.

Law Enforcement To obtain information about the enforcement of wildlife laws or to report an infraction of those laws, contact the Division of Law Enforcement (phone, 703–358–1949) or the nearest regional law enforcement office.

National Wildlife Refuges For general information about the National Wildlife Refuge System, as well as information about specific refuges, contact the Division of Refuges (phone, 703–358–2029) or the nearest national wildlife refuge or regional refuge office.

News Media Inquiries Specific information about the U.S. Fish and Wildlife Service and its activities is available from the Office of Media Services (phone, 202–208–5634) or the public affairs officer in each of the Service's regional offices.

Publications The U.S. Fish and Wildlife Service has publications available on subjects ranging from the National Wildlife Refuge System to endangered species. Some publications are only available as sales items from the Superintendent of Documents, Government Printing Office, Washington, DC 20402. Further information is available from the Publications Unit, U.S. Fish and Wildlife Service, Mail Stop NCTC Washington, DC 20240. Phone, 800–344–WILD.

National Park Service

Contracts Contact the nearest regional office; Administrative Services Division, National Park Service, 1849 C Street NW., Washington, DC 20240 (phone, 202–354–1950); or the Denver Service Center, P.O. Box 25287, 12795 West Alameda Parkway, Denver, CO 80225 (phone, 303–969–2110).

Employment Employment inquiries and applications may be sent to the Human Resources Office, National Park Service, Department of the Interior, Washington, DC, and to the regional offices and individual parks. Applications for temporary employment should be sent to the Division of Human Resources, National Park Service, 1849 C Street NW., Washington, DC 20240. Phone, 202–513–7280. Schools interested in the recruitment program should write to: Chief Human Resources Officer, National Park Service, 1849 C Street NW., Washington, DC 20240. Phone, 202–513–7280.

Grants For information on grants authorized under the Land and Water Conservation Fund and the Urban Park and Recreation Recovery Program, contact the National Park Service, 1849 C Street NW., Washington, DC 20240. Phone, 202–354–6900. For information on grants authorized under the Historic Preservation Fund, contact the National Park Service, 1849 C Street NW, Washington, DC 20240. Phone, 202–354–2054.

Publications Items related to the National Park Service are available from the Superintendent of Documents, Government Printing Office, Washington, DC 20402. Phone, 202–512–1800. Items available for sale include the *National Park System Map and Guide* (stock no. 024–005–01135–8); *The National Parks: Index 2001–2003* (stock no. 024–005–01209–5); and *National Parks: Lesser Known Areas* (stock no. 024–005–01152–8). Contact the Consumer Information Center, Pueblo, CO 81009, for other publications about the National Park Service available for sale. For general park and camping information, write to the National Park Service, Office of Public Inquiries, 1849 C Street NW., Washington, DC 20240.

United States Geological Survey

Contracts, Grants, and Cooperative Agreements Write to the Office of Acquisition and Grants, 12201 Sunrise Valley Drive, National Center, Mail Stop 205G, Reston, VA 20192. Phone, 703–648–7485.

Employment Visit USGS Jobs at www.usgs.gov/ohr/oars/, or contact one of the following Personnel Offices:

USGS Headquarters Personnel Operations, National Center, Mail Stop 601, Reston, VA 20192. Phone, 703–648–6131.

USGS Eastern Region Personnel Office, National Center, Mail Stop 157, Reston, VA 20192 (phone, 703–648–5804) or 3850 Holcomb Bridge Road, Suite 160, Norcross, GA 30092 (phone, 770–409–7750).

USGS Central Region Personnel Office, Mail Stop 603, Box 25046, Denver, CO 80225. Phone, 303–236–9562.

USGS Western Region Personnel Office, 345 Middlefield Road, MS 612, Menlo Park, CA 94025 or 7801 Folsom Boulevard, Suite 103, Sacramento, CA 95826. Phone, 650–329–4071.

Communications For news media and congressional inquiries, arranging interviews, and obtaining news releases and other informational products pertaining to USGS programs and activities, contact the Office of Communications at:

USGS Headquarters, Office of Communications, National Center, Mail Stop 119, Reston, VA 20192. Phone, 703–648–4460.

USGS Eastern Region, Office of Communications. Phone, 703–648–4463.

USGS Central Region, Office of

Communications. Phone, 303–202–4744.

USGS Western Region, Office of Communications. Phone, 206–220–4573.

General Inquiries, Maps, Publications, Scientific Reports, and Water Data
Contact USGS at 888–ASK–USGS, or e-mail ASK@usgs.gov.

Publications and Thematic Maps USGS scientific publications and thematic maps are available to the public through the USGS Publications Warehouse (pubs.usgs.gov), with more than 61,000 bibliographic citations for USGS reports and thematic maps. USGS technical and scientific reports and maps and nontechnical general interest publications are described in the quarterly online periodical *New Publications of the U.S. Geological Survey* at pubs.usgs.gov/publications.

Maps and Reports Customers can now browse and purchase online thousands of USGS maps and reports. The USGS Store (store.usgs.gov) is an online catalog that presents thumbnail images of more than 58,000 topographic maps along with larger images of other selected maps.

Water Data Information on the availability of and access to water data acquired by the USGS and other local, State, and Federal agencies can be obtained by calling USGS. Phone, 888–ASK–USGS. Internet, water.usgs.gov.

Maps, Aerial Photographs, Geodetic Control Data or Index Material, Digital Cartographic Data, and USGS Products Purchases Write to or visit the following network of USGS Earth Science Information Centers:

Alaska—4230 University Drive, Rm. 101, Anchorage, 99508–4664. Phone, 907–786–7011.

California—345 Middlefield Road, Bldg. 3, Rm. 3128, Menlo Park, 94025. Phone, 650–329–4309.

Colorado—Denver Federal Center, Bldg. 810, Box 25286, Denver, 80225. Phone, 303–202–4200.

Missouri—1400 Independence Road, Mail Stop 231, Rolla, 65401. Phone, 573–308–3500.

South Dakota—EROS Data Center, Sioux Falls, 57198 (also for spacecraft and aircraft remote sensor data). Phone, 605–594–6151.

Virginia—12201 Sunrise Valley Drive, Rm. 1C100, Reston, 20192. Phone, 703–648–5953.

Libraries and Reading Rooms Reports, maps, publications, and a variety of Earth science information resources and historical documents are available through the USGS library system. Locations, directions, and resources are found at www.usgs.gov/library, or ask a librarian. The main USGS libraries are located at:

John Wesley Powell Bldg., Rm. 1D100
12201 Sunrise Valley Drive, Reston, VA 20192.

Denver Federal Center, Bldg. 20, Rm. C–2002, Denver, CO 80225–0046.

345 Middlefield Road, Bldg. 15, Foyer, Menlo Park, CA 94025–3591.

2255 N. Gemini Drive, Bldg. 6, Rm. 670, Flagstaff, AZ 86001

Office of Surface Mining Reclamation and Enforcement

Contracts Contact the Procurement Branch, Office of Surface Mining, Department of the Interior, 1951 Constitution Avenue NW., Washington, DC 20240. Phone, 202–208–2839. TDD, 202–208–2737.

Employment For information on OSM employment opportunities throughout the United States, go to the jobs Web site, at https://jobs.quickhire.com/scripts/smart.exe.

Bureau of Indian Affairs

Inquiries regarding the Bureau of Indian Affairs may be obtained by calling the Office of the Assistant Secretary—Indian Affairs, Public Affairs, at 202–208–3710, or writing to the Office of the Assistant Secretary—Indian Affairs, Public Affairs, 1849 C Street NW., MS 2415 MIB, Washington, DC 20240.

Minerals Management Service

Information about the Minerals Management Service and its activities is available from the Chief, Public Affairs, 1849 C Street NW., Room 4259, MS 4230, Washington, DC 20240. Phone, 202–208–3985.

Bureau of Land Management

Contracts The Bureau of Land Management (BLM) and the Department of the Interior (DOI) are now acquiring goods and services through the Internet Web site at http://ideasec.nbc.gov. Requirements that are valued over $25,000 are also published on the Government Web site at www.eps.gov. To take advantage of future business opportunities with BLM, you must (1) obtain a valid Dun & Bradstreet number from Dun & Bradstreet at www.dnb.com, or by calling them at 800–333–0505; or (2) register your firm on the Central Contractor Registration System at www.ccr.gov.

Also, for information about BLM's purchases, how to do business with BLM, and the BLM acquisition offices and contacts, visit the BLM National Acquisition Web site at www.blm.gov/natacq. You may also view BLM's projected purchases of goods and services, known as the Advanced Procurement Plan.

Employment Inquiries should be directed to the National Human Resources Management Center, any Bureau of Land Management State Office, or the Personnel Officer, Bureau of Land Management, Eastern States Office, Department of the Interior, Washington, DC. Phone, 202–452–5072.

General Inquiries For information about parcels of land that the Bureau occasionally sells, contact any of the State offices or the Bureau of Land Management, Office of Public Affairs, Department of the Interior, Washington, DC 20240. Phone, 202–452–5125. Fax, 202–452–5124.

Publications The annual publication *Public Land Statistics,* which relates to public lands, is available from the Superintendent of Documents, Government Printing Office, Washington, DC 20402.

Reading Rooms All State offices provide facilities for individuals who wish to examine status records, tract books, or other records relating to the public lands and their resources.

Small Business Activities The Bureau has four major buying offices that provide contacts for small business activities: the Headquarters Office in Washington, DC (phone, 202–452–5177); the national business center in Lakewood, CO (phone, 303–236–9447); and the Oregon State office (phone, 503–808–6216). The acquisition plan and procurement office contacts are available through the Internet at www.blm.gov/natacq.

Speakers Local Bureau offices will arrange for speakers to explain Bureau programs upon request from organizations within their areas of jurisdiction.

Bureau of Reclamation

Contracts Information is available to contractors, manufacturers, and suppliers from Acquisition and Assistance Management Division, Building 67, Denver Federal Center, Denver, CO 80225. Phone, 303–445–2499.

Employment Information on engineering and other positions is available from the Diversity and Human Resources Office, Denver, CO (phone, 303–445–2670) or from the nearest regional office.

Publications Publications for sale are available through the National Technical Information Service. Phone, 703–605–6585.

For further information, contact the U.S. Department of the Interior, 1849 C Street NW., Washington, DC 20240. Phone, 202–208–3171. Internet, www.doi.gov.

DEPARTMENT OF JUSTICE

950 Pennsylvania Avenue NW., Washington, DC 20530
Phone, 202–514–2000. Internet, www.usdoj.gov.

THE ATTORNEY GENERAL	ALBERTO GONZALES
Chief of Staff	KYLE SAMPSON
Deputy Chief of Staff and Counsel	COURTNEY ELWOOD
Deputy Attorney General	PAUL J. MCNULTY
Associate Attorney General	ROBERT D. MCCALLUM, JR.
Senior Counsel, Office of Dispute Resolution	LINDA CINCIOTTA
Solicitor General	PAUL D. CLEMENT
Inspector General	GLENN A. FINE
Assistant Attorney General, Office of Legal Counsel	STEVEN BRADBURY, *Acting*
Assistant Attorney General, Office of Legislative Affairs	WILLIAM E. MOSCHELLA
Assistant Attorney General, Office of Legal Policy	RACHEL BRAND
Assistant Attorney General for Administration	PAUL R. CORTS
Assistant Attorney General, Antitrust Division	THOMAS O. BARNETT
Assistant Attorney General, Civil Division	PETER D. KEISLER
Assistant Attorney General, Civil Rights Division	WAN J. KIM
Assistant Attorney General, Criminal Division	ALICE S. FISHER
Assistant Attorney General, Environment and Natural Resources Division	SUE ELLEN WOOLDRIDGE
Assistant Attorney General, Tax Division	EILEEN J. O'CONNOR
Assistant Attorney General, Office of Justice Programs	REGINA B. SCHOFIELD
Director, Office of Public Affairs	TASIA SCALINOS
Director, Office of Information and Privacy	DANIEL J. METCALFE
Director, Office of Intergovernmental and Public Liaison	CRYSTAL JEZIERSKI
Director, Executive Office for U.S. Attorneys	MICHAEL A. BATTLE
Director, Bureau of Prisons	HARLEY G. LAPPIN
Director, Federal Bureau of Investigation	ROBERT S. MUELLER III
Director, United States Marshals Service	JOHN F. CLARK
Director, Bureau of Alcohol, Tobacco, Firearms, and Explosives	CARL J. TRUSCOTT
Director, Executive Office for Immigration Review	KEVIN D. ROONEY
Director, Executive Office for United States Trustees	CLIFFORD J. WHITE, *Acting*
Director, Community Relations Service	SHAREE M. FREEMAN
Director, Community Oriented Policing Services	CARL R. PEED

Director, Office on Violence Against Women	DIANE STUART
Administrator, Drug Enforcement Administration	KAREN P. TANDY
Chairman, United States Parole Commission	EDWARD F. REILLY, JR.
Chairman, Foreign Claims Settlement Commission	MAURICIO J. TAMARGO
Chief, INTERPOL–U.S. National Central Bureau	JAMES M. SULLIVAN
Counsel, Office of Intelligence Policy and Review	JAMES A. BAKER
Counsel, Office of Professional Responsibility	H. MARSHALL JARRETT
Director, Professional Responsibility Advisory Office	BARBARA KAMMERMAN, *Acting*
Pardon Attorney	ROGER C. ADAMS
Director, National Drug Intelligence Center	MICHAEL F. WALTHER
Trustee, Office of the Federal Detention Trustee	STACIA HYLTON

[For the Department of Justice statement of organization, see the *Code of Federal Regulations,* Title 28, Chapter I, Part 0]

The Department of Justice serves as counsel for its citizens. It represents them in enforcing the law in the public interest. Through its thousands of lawyers, investigators, and agents, the Department plays the key role in protection against criminals and subversion, ensuring healthy business competition, safeguarding the consumer, and enforcing drug, immigration, and naturalization laws.

The Department of Justice was established by act of June 22, 1870 (28 U.S.C. 501, 503, 509 note), with the Attorney General as its head. The affairs and activities of the Department of Justice are generally directed by the Attorney General.

Attorney General The Attorney General represents the United States in legal matters generally and gives advice and opinions to the President and to the heads of the executive departments of the Government when so requested. The Attorney General appears in person to represent the Government before the U.S. Supreme Court in cases of exceptional gravity or importance.

Community Relations Service The Service offers assistance to communities in resolving disputes relating to race, color, or national origin and facilitates the development of viable agreements as alternatives to coercion, violence, or litigation. It also assists and supports communities in developing local mechanisms as proactive measures to prevent or reduce racial/ethnic tensions.

For further information, contact any regional office or the Director, Community Relations Service, Department of Justice, Suite 2000, 600 E Street NW., Washington, DC 20530. Phone, 202–305–2935.

Regional Offices—Community Relations Service

Address	Director	Phone/FTS
Atlanta, GA (75 Piedmont Ave. NE., 30303)	Ozell Sutton	404–331–6883
Boston, MA (Suite 222, 308 Atlantic Ave., 02201)	Martin A. Walsh	617–424–5715
Chicago, IL (55 W. Monroe St., 60603)	Jesse Taylor	312–353–4391
Dallas, TX (1420 W. Mockingbird Ln., 75247)	Richard Sombrano, *Acting*	214–655–8175
Denver, CO (1244 Speer Blvd., 80204–3584)	Philip Arreda	303–844–2973
Kansas City, MO (323 W. 8th St., 64105)	Atkins Warren	816–426–7434
Los Angeles, CA (888 S. Figuera St., 90017)	Ron Wakabayashi	213–894–2941
New York, NY (26 Federal Plz., 10278)	Moses Jones, *Acting*	212–264–0700
Philadelphia, PA (2d & Chestnut Sts., 19106)	Henry Mitchum, *Acting*	215–597–2344

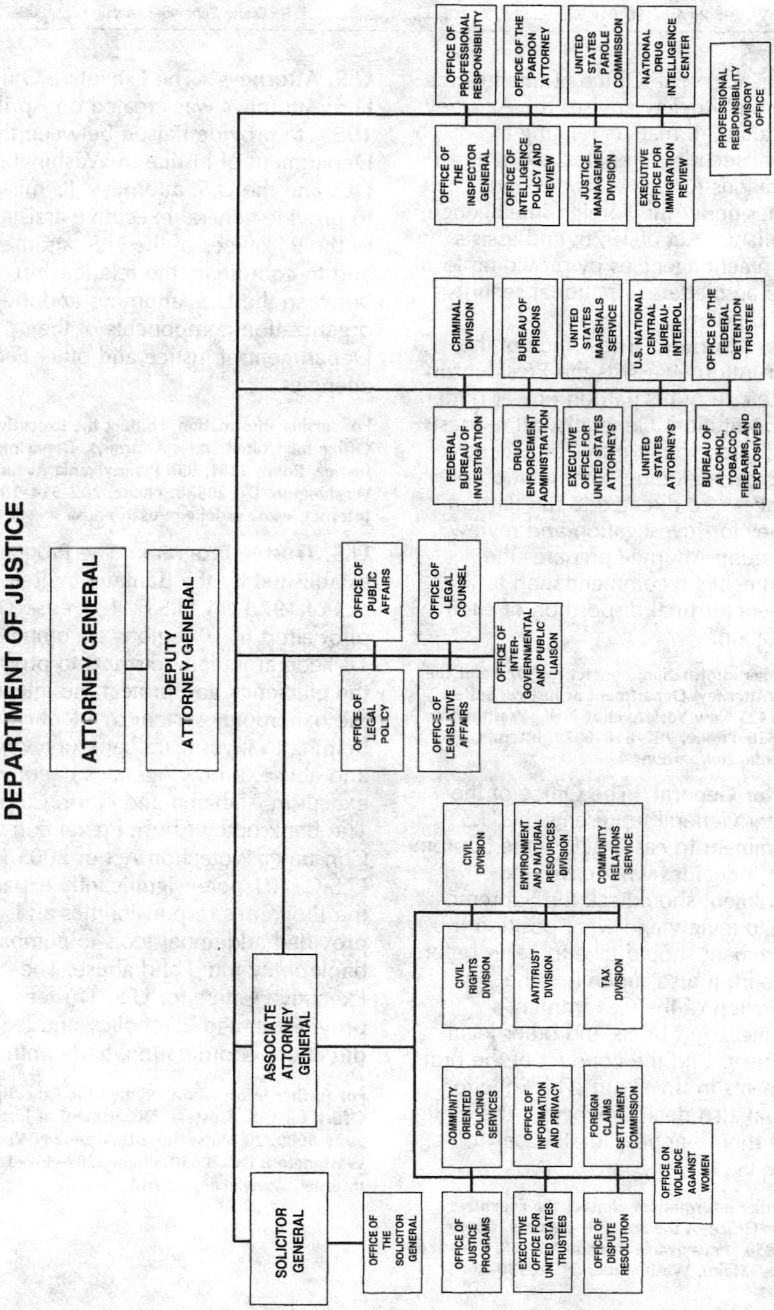
DEPARTMENT OF JUSTICE
ATTORNEY GENERAL
DEPUTY ATTORNEY GENERAL
OFFICE OF PUBLIC AFFAIRS
OFFICE OF LEGAL COUNSEL
OFFICE OF LEGAL POLICY
OFFICE OF LEGISLATIVE AFFAIRS
OFFICE OF INTER-GOVERNMENTAL AND PUBLIC LIAISON
FEDERAL BUREAU OF INVESTIGATION
DRUG ENFORCEMENT ADMINISTRATION
EXECUTIVE OFFICE FOR UNITED STATES ATTORNEYS
UNITED STATES ATTORNEYS
BUREAU OF ALCOHOL, TOBACCO, FIREARMS, AND EXPLOSIVES
CRIMINAL DIVISION
BUREAU OF PRISONS
UNITED STATES MARSHALS SERVICE
U.S. NATIONAL CENTRAL BUREAU-INTERPOL
OFFICE OF THE FEDERAL DETENTION TRUSTEE
OFFICE OF THE INSPECTOR GENERAL
OFFICE OF INTELLIGENCE POLICY AND REVIEW
JUSTICE MANAGEMENT DIVISION
EXECUTIVE OFFICE FOR IMMIGRATION REVIEW
OFFICE OF PROFESSIONAL RESPONSIBILITY
OFFICE OF THE PARDON ATTORNEY
UNITED STATES PAROLE COMMISSION
NATIONAL DRUG INTELLIGENCE CENTER
PROFESSIONAL RESPONSIBILITY ADVISORY OFFICE
ASSOCIATE ATTORNEY GENERAL
CIVIL DIVISION
ENVIRONMENT AND NATURAL RESOURCES DIVISION
COMMUNITY RELATIONS SERVICE
CIVIL RIGHTS DIVISION
ANTITRUST DIVISION
TAX DIVISION
COMMUNITY ORIENTED POLICING SERVICES
OFFICE OF INFORMATION AND PRIVACY
FOREIGN CLAIMS SETTLEMENT COMMISSION
OFFICE ON VIOLENCE AGAINST WOMEN
OFFICE OF JUSTICE PROGRAMS
EXECUTIVE OFFICE FOR UNITED STATES TRUSTEES
OFFICE OF DISPUTE RESOLUTION
SOLICITOR GENERAL
OFFICE OF THE SOLICITOR GENERAL

Regional Offices—Community Relations Service—Continued

Address	Director	Phone/FTS
Seattle, WA (915 2d Ave., 98101)	P. Diane Schneider, *Acting*	206–220–6700

Intelligence The Office of Intelligence Policy and Review advises the Attorney General on all matters relating to national security; prepares and files all applications for surveillances and searches under the Foreign Intelligence Surveillance Act of 1978; and assists Government agencies by providing legal advice on matters of national security law and policy.

Pardon Attorney The Office of the Pardon Attorney assists the President in the exercise of his pardon power under the Constitution. Generally, all requests for pardon or other forms of executive clemency, including commutation of sentences, are directed to the Pardon Attorney for investigation and review. The Pardon Attorney prepares the Department's recommendation to the President for final disposition of each application.

For further information, contact the Office of the Pardon Attorney, Department of Justice, Suite 1100, 1425 New York Avenue NW., Washington, DC 20530. Phone, 202–616–6070. Internet, www.usdoj.gov/pardon.

Solicitor General The Office of the Solicitor General represents the U.S. Government in cases before the Supreme Court. It decides what cases the Government should ask the Supreme Court to review and what position the Government should take in cases before the Court. It also supervises the preparation of the Government's Supreme Court briefs and other legal documents and the conduct of the oral arguments in the Court. The Solicitor General also decides whether the United States should appeal in all cases it loses before the lower courts.

For further information, contact the Executive Officer, Office of the Solicitor General, Room 5142, 950 Pennsylvania Avenue NW., RFK Justice Building (Main), Washington, DC 20530–0001.

U.S. Attorneys The Executive Office for U.S. Attorneys was created on April 6, 1953, to provide liaison between the Department of Justice in Washington, DC, and the U.S. attorneys. Its mission is to provide general executive assistance to the 94 offices of the U.S. attorneys and to coordinate the relationship between the U.S. attorneys and the organization components of the Department of Justice and other Federal agencies.

For further information, contact the Executive Office for United States Attorneys, Department of Justice, Room 2261, 950 Pennsylvania Avenue NW., Washington, DC 20530. Phone, 202–514–1020. Internet, www.usdoj.gov/usao/eousa.

U.S. Trustee Program The Program was established by the Bankruptcy Reform Act of 1978 (11 U.S.C. 101 *et seq.*) as a pilot effort in 10 regions encompassing 18 Federal judicial districts to promote the efficiency and protect the integrity of the bankruptcy system by identifying and helping to investigate bankruptcy fraud and abuse. It now operates nationwide except in Alabama and North Carolina. The Bankruptcy Abuse Prevention and Consumer Protection Act of 2005 (11 U.S.C. 101 note) significantly expanded the Program's responsibilities and provided additional tools to combat bankruptcy fraud and abuse. The Executive Office for U.S. Trustees provides day-to-day policy and legal direction, coordination, and control.

For further information, contact the Executive Office for U.S. Trustees, Department of Justice, Suite 8000, 20 Massachusetts Avenue NW., Washington, DC 20530. Phone, 202–307–1391. Internet, www.usdoj.gov/ust.

Divisions

Antitrust Division

The Assistant Attorney General in charge of the Antitrust Division is responsible for promoting and maintaining competitive markets by enforcing the Federal antitrust laws. This involves investigating possible antitrust violations, conducting grand jury proceedings, reviewing proposed mergers and acquisitions, preparing and trying antitrust cases, prosecuting appeals, and negotiating and enforcing final judgments. The Division prosecutes serious and willful violations of antitrust laws by filing criminal suits that can lead to large fines and jail sentences. Where criminal prosecution is not appropriate, the Division seeks a court order forbidding future violations of the law and requiring steps by the defendant to remedy the anticompetitive effects of past violations.

The Division also is responsible for acting as an advocate of competition within the Federal Government as well as internationally. This involves formal appearances in Federal administrative agency proceedings, development of legislative initiatives to promote deregulation and eliminate unjustifiable exemptions from the antitrust laws, and participation on executive branch policy task forces and in multilateral international organizations. The Division provides formal advice to other agencies on the competitive implications of proposed transactions requiring Federal approval, such as mergers of financial institutions.

For further information, contact the FOIA Unit, Antitrust Division, Department of Justice, 325 Seventh Street NW., Washington, DC 20530. Phone, 202–514–2692.

Civil Division

The Civil Division represents the United States, its departments and agencies, Members of Congress, Cabinet officers, and other Federal employees. Its litigation reflects the diversity of Government activities involving, for example, the defense of challenges to Presidential actions; national security issues; benefit programs; energy policies; commercial issues such as contract disputes, banking, insurance, fraud, and debt collection; all manner of accident and liability claims; and violations of the immigration and consumer protection laws. The Division confronts significant policy issues, which often rise to constitutional dimensions, in defending and enforcing various Federal programs and actions. Each year, Division attorneys handle thousands of cases that collectively involve billions of dollars in claims and recoveries.

The Division litigates cases in the following areas:

—Commercial litigation, litigation associated with the Government's diverse financial involvements including all monetary suits involving contracts, express or implied; actions to foreclose on Government mortgages and liens; bankruptcy and insolvency proceedings; suits against guarantors and sureties; actions involving fraud against the Government, including false or fraudulent claims for Federal insurance, loans, subsidies, and other benefits such as Medicare, false or fraudulent claims for payment under Federal contracts, whistleblower suits, and Government corruption; patent, copyright, and trademark cases and suits arising out of construction, procurement, service contracts, and claims associated with contract terminations; claims for just compensation under the fifth amendment; claims for salary or retirement by civilian and military personnel; cases assigned by congressional reference or special legislation; and litigation involving interests of the United States in any foreign court, whether civil or criminal in nature.

—Consumer litigation, including civil and criminal litigation and related matters arising under various consumer protection and public health statutes.

—Federal programs, including constitutional challenges to statutes, suits to overturn Government policies and programs, challenges to the legality of Government decisions, allegations that the President has violated the Constitution or Federal law, suits to enforce regulatory statutes and to remedy or prevent statutory or regulatory violations. The areas of litigation include: suits against the heads of Federal departments and agencies and other government officials to enjoin official actions, as well as suits for judicial review of administrative decisions, orders, and regulations; suits involving national security, including suits to protect sensitive intelligence sources and materials; suits to prevent interference with Government operations; litigation concerning the constitutionality of Federal laws; and suits raising employment discrimination claims and Government personnel issues.

—Immigration litigation, involving civil litigation under the Immigration and Nationality Act and related laws; district court litigation, habeas corpus review and general advice; petitions for removal order review and immigration-related appellate matters; cases pertaining to the issuance of visas and passports; and litigation arising under the legalization and employer sanction provisions of the immigration laws.

—Torts, including the broad range of tort litigation arising from the operation of the Federal Government, constitutional tort claims against Federal Government officials throughout the Government, aviation disasters, environmental and occupational disease, and radiation and toxic substance exposure. It defends petitions filed pursuant to the Vaccine Injury Compensation Program and is responsible for administering the Radiation Exposure Compensation Program. It also handles maritime litigation and suits that seek personal monetary judgments against individual officers or employees.

—Appellate, having primary responsibility for the litigation of Civil Division cases in the courts of appeal, and on occasion, State appeal courts. The Appellate Staff prepares Government briefs and presents oral arguments for these cases. Additionally, the Appellate Staff works with the Solicitor General's office to prepare documents filed for these cases in the Supreme Court, including briefs on the merits, petitions for certiorari, and jurisdictional statements. The Appellate Staff also works with the Solicitor General's office to obtain authorization for appellate review.

For further information, contact the Office of the Assistant Attorney General, Civil Division, Department of Justice, Tenth Street and Pennsylvania Avenue NW., Washington, DC 20530. Phone, 202–514–3301.

Civil Rights Division

The Civil Rights Division, headed by an Assistant Attorney General, was established in 1957 to secure effective Federal enforcement of civil rights. The Division is the primary institution within the Federal Government responsible for enforcing Federal statutes prohibiting discrimination on the basis of race, sex, disability, religion, citizenship, and national origin. The Division has responsibilities in the following areas:

—Coordination and review of various civil rights statutes that prohibit discrimination on the basis of race, color, national origin, sex, and religion in programs and activities that receive Federal financial assistance by Federal agencies.

—Criminal cases involving conspiracies to interfere with federally protected rights; deprivation of rights under color of law; the use of force or threat of force to injure or intimidate someone in their enjoyment of specific rights (such as voting, housing, employment, education, public facilities, and accommodations); interference with the free exercise of religious beliefs or damage to religious property; the holding of a worker in a condition of slavery or involuntary servitude; and interference with persons seeking to obtain or provide reproductive services.

—Disability rights cases, achieving equal opportunity for people with disabilities in the United States by implementing the Americans with Disabilities Act (ADA). The section's enforcement, certification, regulatory, coordination, and technical assistance activities, combined with an innovative mediation program and a technical assistance grant program, provide an approach for carrying out the ADA's mandates. The section also carries out responsibilities under sections 504 and 508 of the Rehabilitation Act, the Help American Vote Act, the Small Business Regulatory Enforcement Fairness Act, and Executive Order 12250.

—Educational opportunities litigation, involving title IV of the Civil Rights Act of 1964, the Equal Educational Opportunities Act of 1974, and title III of the Americans with Disabilities Act. In addition, the section is responsible for enforcing other statutes such as title VI of the Civil Rights Act of 1964, title IX of the Education Amendments of 1972, section 504 of the Rehabilitation Act of 1973, title II of the Americans with Disabilities Act, and the Individuals with Disabilities Education Act upon referral from other governmental agencies.

—Employment litigation enforcing against State and local government employers the provisions of title VII of the Civil Rights Act of 1964, as amended, and other Federal laws prohibiting employment practices that discriminate on grounds of race, sex, religion, and national origin. The section also enforces against State and local government and private employers the provisions of the Uniformed Services Employment and Reemployment Rights Act of 1994, which prohibits employers from discriminating or retaliating against an employee or applicant for employment because of such person's past, current or future military obligation.

—Housing and Civil Enforcement statutes enforcing the Fair Housing Act, which prohibits discrimination in housing; the Equal Credit Opportunity Act, which prohibits discrimination in credit; title II of the Civil Rights Act of 1964, which prohibits discrimination in certain places of public accomodation, such as hotels, restaurants, nightclubs and theaters; title III of the Civil Rights Act of 1964, which prohibits discrimination in public facilities; and the Religious Land Use and Institutionalized Persons Act, which prohibits local governments from adopting or enforcing land use regulations that discriminate against religious assemblies and institutions or which unjustifiably burden religious exercise.

—Immigration-related unfair employment practices enforcing the antidiscrimination provisions of the Immigration and Nationality Act, which protect U.S. citizens and legal immigrants from employment discrimination based upon citizenship or immigration status and national origin, unfair documentary practices relating to the employment eligibility verification process, and retaliation.

—Special litigation protecting the constitutional and statutory rights of persons confined in certain institutions owned or operated by State or local governments, including facilities for individuals with mental and developmental disabilities, nursing homes, prisons, jails, and juvenile detention facilities where a pattern or practice of violations exist; civil enforcement of statutes prohibiting a pattern or practice of conduct by law enforcement agencies that violates Federal law; and protection against a threat of force and physical obstruction that injures, intimidates, or interferes with a person seeking to obtain or provide reproductive health services, or to exercise the first amendment right of religious freedom at a place of worship.

—Voting cases enforcing the Voting Rights Act, the Help America Vote Act, the National Voter Registration Act, the Voting Accessibility for the Elderly and Handicapped Act, the Uniformed and Overseas Citizens Absentee Voting Act, and other Federal statutes designed to safeguard citizen's right to vote. This includes racial and language minorities, illiterate persons, individuals with disabilities, overseas citizens, persons who change their residence shortly before a Presidential election, and persons 18 to 20 years of age.

For further information, contact the Executive Officer, Civil Rights Division, Department of Justice, 950 Pennsylvania Avenue NW., Washington, DC 20035. Phone, 202–514–4224. Internet, www.usdoj.gov/crt.

Criminal Division

The Criminal Division develops, enforces, and supervises the application of all Federal criminal laws, except those specifically assigned to other divisions. In addition to its direct litigation responsibilities, the Division formulates and implements criminal enforcement policy and provides advice and assistance, including representing the United States before the United States Courts of Appeal. The Division engages in and coordinates a wide range of criminal investigations and prosecutions, such as those targeting individuals and organizations that commit domestic and extraterritorial terrorist acts or assist in the financing of those acts, and international and national drug trafficking and money laundering systems or organizations and organized crime groups. The Division also approves or monitors sensitive areas of law enforcement such as participation in the Witness Security Program and the use of electronic surveillance; advises the Attorney General, Congress, the Office of Management and Budget, and the White House on matters of criminal law; provides legal advice, assistance, and training to Federal, State, and local prosecutors and investigative agencies; provides leadership for coordinating international and national law enforcement matters; and provides training and development assistance to foreign criminal justice systems. Areas of responsibility include:

—Asset forfeiture and money laundering, including the prosecution of complex, sensitive, multidistrict and international cases; formulating policy and conducting training in the money laundering and forfeiture areas; developing legislation and regulations; ensuring the uniform application of forfeiture and money laundering statutes; participating in bilateral and multilateral initiatives to develop international forfeiture and money laundering policy and promote international cooperation; adjudicating petitions for remission or mitigation of forfeited assets; distributing forfeited funds and properties to appropriate domestic and foreign law enforcement agencies and community groups within the United States; and ensuring that such agencies comply with proper usage of received funds.

—Child exploitation and obscenity, including providing prosecutorial and forensic assistance to Federal prosecutors and law enforcement agents in investigating and prosecuting violators of Federal criminal statutes relating to the manufacture, distribution, receipt, or possession, of child pornography; selling, buying, or transporting women and children to engage in sexually explicit conduct; interstate or international travel to sexually abuse children; abusing children on Federal and Indian lands; transporting obscene materials in interstate or foreign commerce; international parental abduction; nonpayment of certain court-ordered child support; and contributing to the development of policy and legislative efforts related to these areas.

—Computer crime and intellectual property, including cyber-attacks on critical information systems, improving domestic and international infrastructure to pursue network criminals most effectively; and initiating and participating in international efforts to combat computer crime.

—Enforcement, overseeing the use of the most sophisticated investigative tools at the Department's disposal; reviewing all Federal electronic surveillance requests and requests to apply for court orders permitting the use of video surveillance; authorizing or denying the entry of applicants into the Federal Witness Security Program (WSP) and coordinating and administering matters relating to all aspects of the WSP among all program components; reviewing requests for witness immunity; transfer of prisoners to and from foreign countries to serve the remainder of their prison sentences; attorney and press subpoenas; applications for S-visa status; and disclosure of grand jury information.

—Fraud, including cases that focus on corporate and securities fraud schemes, financial institution fraud, insurance fraud, fraud involving Government programs such as Medicare, and international criminal activities including the bribery of foreign government officials in violation of the Foreign Corrupt Practices Act.

—Internal security, including cases affecting national security, foreign relations, and the export of military and strategic commodities and technology.

—International affairs, including requests for international extradition and foreign evidence on behalf of Federal, State, and local prosecutors and investigators, fulfilling foreign requests for fugitives and evidence, and negotiating and implementing law enforcement treaties.

—Narcotics and dangerous drugs, including statutes pertaining to controlled substances; developing and implementing domestic and international narcotics law enforcement policies and programs; developing and administering other cooperative drug enforcement strategies, such as the Bilateral Case Initiative, and projects conducted by the law enforcement and intelligence communities.

—Organized crime and racketeering efforts against traditional groups and emerging groups from Asia and Europe.

—Organized Crime Drug Enforcement Task Forces, combining the resources and expertise of several Federal agencies in cooperation with the Tax Division, U.S. Attorneys Offices, and State and local law enforcement, to identify, disrupt, and dismantle major drug supply and money laundering organizations through coordinated, nationwide investigations targeting the entire infrastructure of these enterprises.

—Overseas prosecutorial development, assistance, and training for prosecutors and judicial personnel in other countries to develop and sustain democratic criminal justice institutions.

—Policy and legislation, developing legislative proposals and reviewing pending legislation affecting the Federal criminal justice system; reviewing and developing proposed changes to the Federal sentencing guidelines and rules; and analyzing crime policy and program issues.

—Public integrity efforts to combat corruption of elected and appointed public officials at all levels of Government.

—Special investigations of individuals who took part in Nazi-sponsored acts of persecution abroad before and during World War II and who subsequently entered or seek to enter the United States illegally and/or fraudulently, and interagency investigation into assets looted from victims of Nazi persecution.

—Terrorism, involving design, implementation, and support of law enforcement efforts, legislative initiatives, policies, and strategies relating to international and domestic terrorism.

—Domestic security, enforcing Federal criminal laws relating to violent crimes, the illegal use of firearms and explosives, and alien smuggling and other immigration-related offenses.

For further information, contact the Office of the Assistant Attorney General, Criminal Division, Department of Justice, Tenth Street and Pennsylvania Avenue NW., Washington, DC 20530. Phone, 202–514–2601.

Environment and Natural Resources Division

The Environment and Natural Resources Division is the Nation's environmental lawyer. The Division's responsibilities include enforcing civil and criminal environmental laws that protect America's health and environment. It also defends environmental challenges to Government activities and programs and ensures that environmental laws are implemented in a fair and consistent manner nationwide. It also represents the United States in all matters concerning the protection, use, and development of the Nation's natural resources and public lands, wildlife protection, Indian rights and claims, and the acquisition of Federal property. To carry out this broad mission, the Division litigates in the following areas:

—Environmental crimes, prosecuting individuals and corporate entities violating laws designed to protect the environment.

—Civil environmental enforcement, on behalf of EPA; claims for damages to natural resources filed on behalf of the Departments of the Interior, Commerce, and Agriculture; claims for contribution against private parties for contamination of public land; and recoupment of money spent to clean up certain oil spills on behalf of the U.S. Coast Guard.

—Environmental defense, representing the United States in suits challenging the Government's administration of Federal environmental laws including claims that regulations are too strict or lax, and claims alleging that Federal agencies are not complying with environmental standards.

—Wildlife and marine resources protection, including prosecution of smugglers and black-market dealers in protected wildlife.

—Use and protection of federally owned public lands and natural resources across a broad spectrum of laws.

—Indian resources protection, including establishing water rights, establishing and protecting hunting and fishing rights, collecting damages for trespass on Indian lands, and establishing reservation boundaries and rights to land.

—Land acquisition for use by the Federal Government for purposes ranging from establishing public parks to building Federal courthouses.

For further information, contact the Office of the Assistant Attorney General, Environment and Natural Resources Division, Department of Justice, Tenth Street and Pennsylvania Avenue NW., Washington, DC 20530. Phone, 202–514–2701.

Tax Division

Tax Division ensures the uniform and fair enforcement of Federal tax laws in Federal and State courts. The Division conducts enforcement activities to deter specific taxpayers, as well as the taxpaying public at large, from conduct that deprives the Federal Government of its tax-related revenue. It represents the United States and its officers in all civil and criminal litigation arising under the internal revenue laws, other than proceedings in the United States Tax Court. Tax Division attorneys frequently join with Assistant U.S. Attorneys in prosecuting tax cases. Some criminal tax grand jury investigations and prosecutions are handled solely by Tax Division prosecutors, while others are delegated to Assistant U.S. Attorneys. Division attorneys evaluate requests by the Internal Revenue Service or United States Attorneys to initiate grand jury investigations or prosecutions of tax crimes.

The Division handles a wide array of civil tax litigation including the following:

—Suits to enjoin the promotion of abusive tax shelters and to enjoin activities relating to aiding and abetting the understatement of tax liabilities of others;

—Suits to enforce Internal Revenue Service administrative summonses that seek information essential to determine and collect taxpayers' liabilities, including summonses for records of corporate tax shelters and offshore transactions;

—Suits brought by the United States to set aside fraudulent conveyances and to collect assets held by nominees and alter egos;

—Tax refund suits challenging the Internal Revenue Service's determination of taxpayers' Federal income, employment, excise, and estate liabilities;

—Bankruptcy litigation raising issues of the validity, dischargeability, and priority of Federal tax claims, and the feasibility of reorganization plans;

—Suits brought by taxpayers challenging determinations made in the collection due process proceedings before the Internal Revenue Service's Office of Appeals; and

—Suits against the United States for damages for the unauthorized disclosure of tax return information or for damages claimed because of alleged injuries caused by Internal Revenue Service employees in the performance of their official duties.

The Division also collects judgments in tax cases. To this end, the Division directs collection efforts and coordinates with, monitors the efforts of, and provides assistance to the various United States Attorneys' offices in collecting outstanding judgments in tax cases.

The Division also works with the Internal Revenue Service, United States Attorneys, and other Government agencies on policy and legislative proposals to enhance tax administration and handling tax cases assigned to those offices.

For further information, contact the Office of the Assistant Attorney General, Tax Division, Department of Justice, Tenth Street and Pennsylvania Avenue NW., Washington, DC 20530. Phone, 202–514–2901. Internet, www.usdoj.gov/tax.

Bureaus

Federal Bureau of Investigation

935 Pennsylvania Avenue NW., Washington, DC 20535. Phone, 202–324–3000. Internet, www.fbi.gov.

The Federal Bureau of Investigation (FBI) is the principal investigative arm of the United States Department of Justice. It is primarily charged with gathering and reporting facts, locating witnesses, and compiling evidence in cases involving Federal jurisdiction. It also provides law enforcement leadership and assistance to State and international law enforcement agencies.

The Federal Bureau of Investigation was established in 1908 by the Attorney General, who directed that Department of Justice investigations be handled by its own staff. The Bureau is charged with investigating all violations of Federal law except those that have been assigned by legislative enactment or otherwise to another Federal agency. Its jurisdiction includes a wide range of responsibilities in the national security, criminal, and civil fields. Priority has been assigned to areas such as counterterrorism, counterintelligence, cyber-crimes, internationally and nationally organized crime/drug matters, and financial crimes.

The FBI also offers cooperative services to local, State, and international law enforcement agencies. These services include fingerprint identification, laboratory examination, police training, the Law Enforcement Online communication and information service for use by the law enforcement community, the National Crime Information Center, and the National Center for the Analysis of Violent Crime.

For further information, contact the Office of Public and Congressional Affairs, Federal Bureau of Investigation, J. Edgar Hoover FBI Building, 935 Pennsylvania Avenue NW., Washington, DC 20535. Phone, 202–317–2727.

Bureau of Prisons

320 First Street NW., Washington, DC 20534. Phone, 202–307–3198. Internet, www.bop.gov.

The mission of the Bureau of Prisons is to protect society by confining offenders in the controlled environments of prisons and community-based facilities that are safe, humane, cost-efficient, and appropriately secure, and that provide work and other self-improvement opportunities to assist offenders in becoming law-abiding citizens. The Bureau has its headquarters, or Central Office, in Washington, DC. The Central Office is divided into nine divisions, including the National Institute of Corrections.

The Correctional Programs Division (CPD) is responsible for inmate classification and programming, including psychology and religious services, substance abuse treatment, case management, and programs for special needs offenders. It provides policy direction and daily operational oversight of institution security, emergency preparedness, intelligence gathering, inmate discipline, inmate sentence computations, receiving and discharge, and inmate transportation, as well as coordinating international treaty transfers and overseeing the special security needs of inmates placed in the Federal Witness Protection Program. CPD administers contracts and intergovernmental agreements for the confinement of offenders in community-based programs, community corrections centers, and other facilities, including privately managed facilities. The CPD staff is also involved in the Bureau's privatization efforts.

The Industries, Education, and Vocational Training Division oversees Federal Prison Industries, or UNICOR, which is a wholly owned Government corporation that provides employment and training opportunities for inmates confined in Federal correctional facilities. Additionally, it is responsible for oversight of educational, occupational, and vocational training, and leisure-time programs, as well as those related to inmate release preparation.

The National Institute of Corrections (NIC) provides technical assistance, training, and information to State and local corrections agencies throughout the country, as well as the Bureau. It also provides research assistance and documents through the NIC Information Center.

For further information, contact the Public Information Office, Bureau of Prisons, 320 First Street NW., Washington, DC 20534. Phone, 202–514–6551.

United States Marshals Service

Washington, DC 20530. Phone, 202–307–9000

The United States Marshals Service is the Nation's oldest Federal law enforcement agency, having served as a vital link between the executive and judicial branches of the Government since 1789. The Marshals Service performs tasks that are essential to the operation of virtually every aspect of the Federal justice system. The Service has these responsibilities:

—providing support and protection for the Federal courts, including security for 800 judicial facilities and nearly 2,000 judges and magistrates, as well as countless other trial participants such as jurors and attorneys;

—apprehending the majority of Federal fugitives;

—operating the Federal Witness Security Program and ensuring the safety of endangered Government witnesses;

—maintaining custody of and transporting thousands of Federal prisoners annually;

—executing court orders and arrest warrants;

—managing and selling seized property forfeited to the Government by drug traffickers and other criminals and assisting the Justice Department's asset forfeiture program;

—responding to emergency circumstances, including civil disturbances, terrorist incidents, and other crisis situations through its Special Operations Group, and restoring order in riot and mob-violence situations; and

—operating the U.S. Marshals Service Training Academy.

For further information, contact the Office of Public Affairs, U.S. Marshals Service, Department of Justice, Washington, DC 20530. Phone, 202–307–9065. Internet, www.usmarshals.gov.

International Criminal Police Organization–United States National Central Bureau

Washington, DC 20530. Phone, 202–616–9000. Fax, 202–616–8400.

The U.S. National Central Bureau (USNCB) is the United States' representative to INTERPOL, the International Criminal Police Organization. Also known as INTERPOL-Washington, the USNCB provides an essential communications link between the U.S. police community and their counterparts in the foreign member countries. The USNCB also serves as the United States' point of contact for the European Police Office (EUROPOL), the European Union's law enforcement organization.

INTERPOL is an association of 182 countries dedicated to promoting mutual assistance among law enforcement authorities in the prevention and suppression of international crime. With no police force of its own, INTERPOL has no powers of arrest or search and seizure and therefore relies on the law enforcement authorities of its member countries. Each member country is required to have a national central bureau, such as the USNCB, to act as the primary point of contact for police matters. INTERPOL serves as a channel of communication for its member countries to cooperate in the investigation and prosecution of crime, provides a forum for discussions, working group meetings, and symposia to enable police to focus on specific areas of criminal activity affecting their countries, and issues and maintains information and databases on crime, fugitives, stolen passports and vehicles, missing persons, and humanitarian concerns, which are supplied by and can be used as a source by its member countries.

The USNCB is staffed by a permanent staff and detailed special agents from numerous Federal law enforcement agencies. The USNCB is organized into the Terrorism and Violent Crimes Division, the Economic Crimes Division, the Drug Division, the Fugitive Division, the Investigative Support Division, the Administrative Services Division, the Office of the General Counsel, and the State and Local Liaison Division (SLLD).

SLLD coordinates INTERPOL requests with 62 INTERPOL State liaison offices established in each State and the cities of New York, Boston, Chicago, Washington, DC, Miami-Dade, San Diego (city and county), Los Angeles, San Francisco, and Seattle. The USNCB has three sub-bureaus which serve to more effectively address the law enforcement needs of U.S. territories. The sub-bureaus are located in Puerto Rico, American Samoa, and the U.S. Virgin Islands. SLLD provides the primary means of communication between foreign law enforcement authorities and domestic State and local police for the purpose of pursuing international investigations. International leads developed in criminal investigations being conducted by a State or local police entity can be pursued through their liaison office.

For further information, contact the INTERPOL–U.S. National Central Bureau, Department of Justice, Washington, DC 20530. Phone, 202–616–9000.

Drug Enforcement Administration

600–700 Army Navy Drive, Arlington, VA 22202. Phone, 202–307–1000. FTS, 367–1000

The Drug Enforcement Administration (DEA) is the lead Federal agency in enforcing narcotics and controlled substances laws and regulations. DEA also enforces the Federal money laundering and bulk currency smuggling statutes when the funds involved in the transactions or smuggling are derived from the sale of narcotics. It was created in July 1973, by Reorganization Plan No. 2 of 1973 (5 U.S.C. app.).

DEA enforces the provisions of the controlled substances and chemical diversion and trafficking laws and regulations of the United States, and operates on a worldwide basis. It presents cases to the criminal and civil justice systems of the United States—or any other competent jurisdiction—on those significant organizations and their members involved in cultivation, production, smuggling, distribution, laundering of proceeds, or diversion of controlled substances appearing in or destined for illegal traffic in the United States. DEA disrupts and dismantles these organizations by arresting their members, confiscating their drugs, and seizing their assets; and creates, manages, and supports enforcement-related programs—domestically and internationally—aimed at reducing the availability of and demand for illicit controlled substances.

DEA's responsibilities include:

—investigation of major narcotic, chemical, drug-money laundering, and bulk currency smuggling violators who operate at interstate and international levels;

—seizure and forfeiture of assets derived from, traceable to, or intended to be used for illicit drug trafficking;

—seizure and forfeiture of assets derived from or traceable to drug-money laundering or the smuggling of bulk currency derived from illegal drugs;

—enforcement of regulations governing the legal manufacture, distribution, and dispensing of controlled substances;

—management of an intelligence program that supports drug investigations, initiatives, and operations worldwide;

—coordination with Federal, State, and local law enforcement authorities and cooperation with counterpart agencies abroad;

—assistance to State and local law enforcement agencies in addressing their most significant drug and drug-related violence problems;

—leadership and influence over international counterdrug and chemical policy and support for institution building in host nations;

—training, scientific research, and information exchange in support of drug traffic prevention and control; and

—education and assistance to the public community on the prevention, treatment, and dangers of drugs.

DEA maintains liaison with the United Nations, INTERPOL, and other organizations on matters relating to international narcotics control programs. It has offices throughout the United States and in 62 foreign countries.

For further information, contact the Public Affairs Section, Drug Enforcement Administration, Department of Justice, Washington, DC 20537. Phone, 202–307–7977.

Office of Justice Programs

810 Seventh Street NW., Washington, DC 20531. Phone, 202–307–0703

The Office of Justice Programs (OJP) was established by the Justice Assistance Act of 1984 and reauthorized in 1994 to provide Federal leadership, coordination, and assistance needed to make the Nation's justice system more efficient and effective in preventing and controlling crime. OJP is responsible for collecting statistical data and conducting analyses; identifying emerging criminal justice issues; developing and testing promising approaches to address these issues; evaluating program results, and disseminating these findings and other information to State and local governments.

The Office is comprised of the following bureaus and offices:

—The Bureau of Justice Assistance provides funding, training, and technical assistance to State and local governments to combat violent and drug-related crime and help improve the criminal justice system.

—The Bureau of Justice Statistics is responsible for collecting and analyzing data on crime, criminal offenders, crime victims, and the operations of justice systems at all levels of government.

—The National Institute of Justice sponsors research and development programs, conducts demonstrations of innovative approaches to improve criminal justice, and develops new criminal justice technologies.

—The Office of Juvenile Justice and Delinquency Prevention provides grants and contracts to States to help them improve their juvenile justice systems and sponsors innovative research, demonstration, evaluation, statistics, replication, technical assistance, and training programs to help improve the Nation's understanding of and response to juvenile violence and delinquency.

—The Office for Victims of Crime administers victim compensation and assistance grant programs and provides funding, training, and technical assistance to victim service organizations, criminal justice agencies, and other professionals to improve the Nation's response to crime victims.

—The Violence Against Women Office coordinates legislative and other initiatives relating to violence against women and administers grant programs to help prevent, detect, and stop violence against women, including domestic violence, sexual assault, and stalking.

—The Drug Courts Program Office supports the development, implementation, and improvement of drug courts through technical assistance and training and grants to State, local, or tribal governments and courts.

—The Corrections Program Office provides financial and technical assistance to State and local governments to implement corrections-related programs including correctional facility construction and corrections-based drug treatment programs.

—The Executive Office for Weed and Seed helps communities build stronger, safer neighborhoods by implementing the weed and seed strategy, a community-based, multidisciplinary approach to combating crime.

—The Office for State and Local Domestic Preparedness Support is responsible for enhancing the capacity of State and local jurisdictions to prepare for and respond to incidents of domestic terrorism involving chemical and biological agents, radiological and explosive devices, and other weapons of mass destruction.

—The Office of the Police Corps and Law Enforcement Education provides college educational assistance to students who commit to public service in law enforcement, and scholarships with no service commitment to dependents of law enforcement officers who died in the line of duty.

For further information, contact the Department of Justice Response Center. Phone, 800–421–6770. Internet, www.ojp.usdoj.gov. E-mail, askojp@ojp.usdoj.gov.

Bureau of Alcohol, Tobacco, Firearms and Explosives

650 Massachusetts Avenue NW., Washington, DC 20226. Phone, 202–927–8500

The Bureau of Alcohol, Tobacco, Firearms and Explosives (ATF) is responsibile for enforcing Federal criminal laws and regulating the firearms and explosives industries. ATF, formerly known as the Bureau of Alcohol, Tobacco, and Firearms, was initially established by Department of Treasury Order No. 221, effective July 1, 1972, which transferred the functions, powers, and duties arising under laws relating to alcohol, tobacco, firearms, and explosives from the Internal Revenue Service to ATF. The Homeland Security Act of 2002 (6 U.S.C. 531) transferred certain functions and authorities of ATF to the Department of Justice and established it under its current name. ATF works, directly and through partnerships, to investigate and reduce violent crime involving firearms and explosives, acts of arson, and illegal trafficking of alcohol and tobacco products. The Bureau provides training and support to its Federal, State, local, and international law enforcement partners and works primarily in 23 field divisions across the 50 States, Puerto Rico, the U.S. Virgin Islands, and Guam. It also has foreign offices in Mexico, Canada, Colombia, and France.

For further information, contact the Office of Public Affairs, Bureau of Alcohol, Tobacco, Firearms and Explosives. Phone, 202–927–8500. Internet, www.atf.gov.

Boards

Executive Office for Immigration Review

Falls Church, VA 22041. Phone, 703–305–0289. Internet, www.usdoj.gov/eoir.

The Executive Office for Immigration Review, under a delegation of authority from the Attorney General, is charged with adjudicating matters brought under various immigration statutes to its three administrative tribunals: the Board of Immigration Appeals, the Office of the Chief Immigration Judge, and the Office of the Chief Administrative Hearing Officer.

The Board of Immigration Appeals has nationwide jurisdiction to hear appeals from certain decisions made by immigration judges and by district directors of the Department of Homeland Security (DHS). In addition, the Board is responsible for hearing appeals involving disciplinary actions against attorneys and representatives before DHS and the Board.

Decisions of the Board are binding on all DHS officers and immigration judges unless modified or overruled by the Attorney General or a Federal court. All Board decisions are subject to judicial review in Federal court. The majority of appeals reaching the Board involve orders of removal and applications for relief from removal. Other cases before the Board include the removal of aliens applying for admission to the United States, petitions to classify the status of alien relatives for the issuance of preference immigrant visas, fines imposed upon carriers for the violation of the immigration laws, and motions for reopening and reconsideration of decisions previously rendered.

The Office of the Chief Immigration Judge provides overall direction for more than 200 immigration judges located in 53 immigration courts throughout the Nation. Immigration judges are responsible for conducting formal administrative proceedings and act independently in their decisionmaking capacity. Their decisions are administratively final, unless appealed or certified to the Board.

In removal proceedings, an immigration judge determines whether an individual from a foreign country should be admitted or allowed to stay in the United States or be removed. Judges are located throughout the United States, and each judge has jurisdiction to consider various forms of relief available under the law, including applications for asylum.

The Office of the Chief Administrative Hearing Officer is responsible for the general supervision and management of administrative law judges who preside at hearings which are mandated by provisions of immigration law concerning allegations of unlawful employment of aliens, unfair immigration-related employment practices, and immigration document fraud.

For further information, contact the Office of Legislative and Public Affairs, Executive Office for Immigration Review, Department of Justice, Falls Church, VA 22041. Phone, 703–305–0289. Internet, www.usdoj.gov/eoir.

United States Parole Commission

Friendship Boulevard, Chevy Chase, MD 20815. Phone, 301–492–5990

The United States Parole Commission (USPC) makes parole release decisions for eligible Federal and District of Columbia prisoners; authorizes methods of release and conditions under which release occurs; prescribes, modifies, and monitors compliance with the terms and conditions governing offenders' behavior while on parole or mandatory or supervised release; issues warrants for violation of supervision; determines probable cause for the revocation process; revokes parole, mandatory, or supervised release; releases from supervision those offenders who are no longer a risk to public safety; and promulgates the rules, regulations, and guidelines for the exercise of the USPC's authority and the implementation of a national parole policy.

The USPC has sole jurisdiction over the following: Federal offenders who committed offenses before November 1, 1987; D.C. Code offenders who committed offenses before August 5, 2000; D.C. Code offfenders sentenced to a term of supervised release; Uniform Code of Military Justice offenders who are in Bureau of Prison's custody; transfer treaty cases; and State probationers and parolees in the Federal Witness Protection Program.

For further information, contact the United States Parole Commission, Department of Justice, 5550 Friendship Boulevard, Chevy Chase, MD 20815. Phone, 301–492–5990. Internet, www.usdoj.gov/uspc/parole.htm.

Office of Community Oriented Policing Services

The Office of Community Oriented Policing Services (COPS) was established to assist law enforcement agencies in enhancing public safety through the implementation of community policing strategies. COPS does so by providing training to enhance law enforcement officers' problem-solving and community interaction skills; encouraging law enforcement and community members to develop initiatives to prevent crime; substantially increasing the number of law enforcement officers directly interacting with the community; and supporting the development of new technologies to shift law enforcement's focus to preventing crime and disorder within their communities.

The COPS Office includes the following program divisions:

—The grants administration division is responsible for developing and designing new programs to provide resources for the hiring of new officers and to further the adoption and implementation of community policing, reviewing grant applications, and assisting grantees in the implementation of their grants.

—The grants monitoring division is responsible for tracking grantees' compliance with the conditions of their grants. The Division conducts site visits and reviews grantee files to ensure that COPS funds are properly used to hire officers and implement community policing. The Division also provides onsite technical assistance to grantees, office-based grant reviews, alleged noncompliance reviews, audit resolution, and collects and disseminates examples of successful community policing strategies.

—The training and technical assistance division is responsible for coordinating the provision of training and technical assistance to advance the adoption, implementation, and sustaining of community policing in the thousands of communities served by the COPS Office.

—The compliance division is responsible for the monitoring and coordination of the Office of Inspector General (OIG) audits and independent audits required by the Single Audit Act and serves as the liaison between grantees and auditors in the conduct and resolution of OIG audits.

For further information, contact the Office of Community Oriented Policing Services (COPS), Department of Justice, 1100 Vermont Avenue NW., Washington, DC 20530. Phone, 202–514–2058. Internet, www.cops.usdoj.gov.

Foreign Claims Settlement Commission of the United States

The Foreign Claims Settlement Commission of the United States is a quasi-judicial, independent agency within the Department of Justice which adjudicates claims of U.S. nationals against foreign governments, either under specific jurisdiction conferred by Congress or pursuant to international claims settlement agreements. The decisions of the Commission are final and are not reviewable under any standard by any court or other authority. Funds for payment of the Commission's awards are derived from congressional appropriations, international claims settlements, or the liquidation of foreign assets in the United States by the Departments of Justice and the Treasury.

The Commission also has authority to receive, determine the validity and amount, and provide for the payment of claims by members of the U.S. armed services and civilians held as prisoners of war or interned by a hostile force in Southeast Asia during the Vietnam conflict, or by the survivors of such service members and civilians.

The Commission is also responsible for maintaining records and responding to inquiries related to the various claims programs it has conducted against the Governments of Albania, Bulgaria, China, Cuba, Czechoslovakia, Egypt, Ethiopia, the Federal Republic of Germany, the German Democratic Republic, Hungary, Iran, Italy, Panama, Poland, Romania, the Soviet Union, Vietnam, and Yugoslavia, as well as those authorized under the War Claims Act of 1948 and other statutes.

For further information, contact the Office of the Chairman, Foreign Claims Settlement Commission of the United States, Department of Justice, Suite 6002, 600 E Street NW., Washington, DC 20579. Phone, 202–616–6975. Fax, 202–616–6993.

Sources of Information

Controlled Substances Act Registration Information about registration under the Controlled Substances Act may be obtained from the Registration Section of the Drug Enforcement Administration, P.O. Box 28083, Central Station, Washington, DC 20038. Phone, 202–307–7255.

Disability-Related Matters Contact the Civil Rights Division's ADA Hotline. Phone, 800–514–0301. TDD, 800–514–0383. Internet, www.usdoj.gov/crt/ada/adahom1.htm.

Drugs and Crime Clearinghouse Phone, 800–666–3332 (toll free).

Electronic Access Information concerning Department of Justice programs and activities is available electronically through the Internet, at www.usdoj.gov.

The NCJRS Electronic Bulletin Board may be accessed by calling 301–738–8895 (modem).

Employment The Department maintains an agencywide job line. Phone, 202–514–3397.

Attorneys' applications: Director, Office of Attorney Personnel Management, Department of Justice, Room 6150, Tenth Street and Constitution Avenue NW., Washington, DC 20530. Phone, 202–514–1432. Assistant U.S. attorney applicants should apply to individual U.S. attorneys.

United States Marshals Service: Field Staffing Branch, United States Marshals Service, Department of Justice, 600 Army Navy Drive, Arlington, VA 22202–4210.

Federal Bureau of Investigation: Director, Washington, DC 20535, or any of the field offices or resident agencies whose addresses are listed in the front of most local telephone directories.

Drug Enforcement Administration: regional offices, laboratories, or Washington Headquarters Office of Personnel.

Bureau of Prisons: Central Office, 320 First Street NW., Washington, DC 20534 (phone, 202–307–3082); or any regional or field office.

Office of Justice Programs: 633 Indiana Avenue NW., Washington, DC 20531. Phone, 202–307–0730.

United States Trustee Program, Room 770, 901 E Street NW., Washington, DC 20530. Phone, 202–616–1000.

Foreign Claims Settlement Commission: Attorneys: Office of the Chief Counsel, Suite 6002, 600 E Street NW., Washington, DC 20579 (phone, 202–616–6975); Other: Administrative Officer, same address and phone.

Housing Discrimination Matters Contact the Civil Rights Division's Housing and Civil Enforcement Section. Phone, 800–896–7743.

Immigration-Related Employment Matters The Civil Rights Division maintains a worker hotline. Phone, 800–255–7688. TDD, 800–237–2515. It also offers information for employers. Phone, 800–255–8155. TDD, 800–362–2735.

Publications and Films The *FBI Law Enforcement Bulletin* and *Uniform Crime Reports—Crime in the United States* are available from the Superintendent of Documents, Government Printing Office, Washington, DC 20402.

The Annual Report of the Attorney General of the United States is published each year by the Department of Justice, Washington, DC 20530.

Textbooks on citizenship consisting of teachers manuals and student textbooks at various reading levels are distributed free to public schools for applicants for citizenship and are on sale to all others from the Superintendent of Documents, Government Printing Office, Washington, DC 20402. Public schools or organizations under the supervision of public schools which are entitled to free textbooks should make their requests to the appropriate Immigration and Naturalization Service Regional Office. For general information, call 202–514–3946.

The Freedom of Information Act Guide and Privacy Act Overview and the *Freedom of Information Case List,* both published annually, are available from the Superintendent of Documents, Government Printing Office, Washington, DC 20530.

FOIA Update (Stock No. 727–002–00000–6), published quarterly, is available free of charge to FOIA offices and other interested offices Governmentwide. This publication is also available from the Superintendent of Documents, Government Printing Office, Washington, DC 20402.

Guidelines for Effective Human Relations Commissions, Annual Report of the Community Relations Service, Community Relations Service Brochure, CRS Hotline Brochure, Police Use of Deadly Force: A Conciliation Handbook for Citizens and Police, Principles of Good Policing: Avoiding Violence Between Police and Citizens, Resolving Racial Conflict: A Guide for Municipalities, and *Viewpoints and Guidelines on Court-Appointed Citizens Monitoring Commissions in School Desegregation* are available upon request from the Public Information Office, Community Relations Service, Department of Justice, Washington, DC 20530.

A limited number of drug educational films are available, free of charge, to civic, educational, private, and religious groups.

A limited selection of pamphlets and brochures is available. The most widely requested publication is *Drugs of Abuse,* an identification manual intended for professional use. Single copies are free.

Copies of the Foreign Claims Settlement Commission's semiannual (through December 1966) and annual (from January 1967) reports to the Congress concerning its activities are available at the Commission in limited quantities.

Copies of the *Program Plan* and other Office of Justice Programs publications and documents are available by calling the National Criminal Justice Reference Service (phone, 303–251–5500 or 800–851–3420 (toll free); Internet, www.ncjrs.org). Some documents are also available from the Office's Web site, (Internet, www.ojp.usdoj.gov).

Reading Rooms Located in Washington, DC, at the following locations:

Department of Justice, Room 6505, Tenth Street and Constitution Avenue NW., Washington, DC 20530. Phone, 202–514–3775.

Bureau of Prisons, 320 First Street NW., 20534. Phone, 202–307–3029.

Foreign Claims Settlement Commission, 600 E Street NW., 20579. Phone, 202–616–6975.

U.S. Parole Commission, 5550 Friendship Boulevard, Chevy Chase, MD 20815. Phone, 301–492–5959.

Board of Immigration Appeals, Suite 2400, 5107 Leesburg Pike, Falls Church, VA 22041. Phone, 703–305–0168.

National Institute of Justice, 9th Floor, 633 Indiana Avenue NW., Washington, DC 20531 (phone, 202–307–5883).

Redress for Wartime Relocation/ Internment Contact the Civil Rights Division's Office of Redress Administration. Helpline phone, 202–219–6900. TDD, 202–219–4710. Internet, www.usdoj.gov.

Small Business Activities Contract information for small businesses can be obtained from the Office of Small and Disadvantaged Business Utilization, Department of Justice, Tenth Street and Pennsylvania Avenue NW., Washington, DC 20530. Phone, 202–616–0521.

For further information concerning the Department of Justice, contact the Office of Public Affairs, Department of Justice, Tenth Street and Constitution Avenue NW., Washington, DC 20530. Phone, 202–514–2007. TDD, 202–786–5731. Internet, www.usdoj.gov.

DEPARTMENT OF LABOR

200 Constitution Avenue NW., Washington, DC 20210
Phone, 202–693–5000. Internet, www.dol.gov.

SECRETARY OF LABOR	ELAINE L. CHAO
Chief of Staff	PAUL T. CONWAY
Executive Secretary	RUTH KNOUSE
Deputy Secretary	STEVEN J. LAW
Chief Administrative Law Judge	JOHN M. VITTONE
Chief Administrative Appeals Judge, Benefits Review Board	NANCY S. DOLDER
Chief Economist	(VACANCY)
Chief Financial Officer	SAMUEL T. MOK
Chief Administrative Appeals Judge, Administrative Review Board	M. CYNTHIA DOUGLASS
Chairman, Employees Compensation Appeals Board	ALEC J. KOROMILAS
Director, Center for Faith-Based and Community Initiatives	JEDD MEDEFIND
Director, Office of Small Business Programs	JOSE A. LIRA
Director, Office of the 21st Century Workforce	KAREN CZARNECKI
Director, Women's Bureau	SHINAE CHUN
Assistant Secretary for Administration and Management	PATRICK PIZZELLA
Assistant Secretary for Congressional and Intergovernmental Affairs	KRISTINE IVERSON
Assistant Secretary for Employment and Training	EMILY STOVER DEROCCO
Assistant Secretary for Employment Standards	VICTORIA A. LIPNIC
Administrator, Wage and Hour Division	ALFRED B. ROBINSON, JR., *Acting*
Assistant Secretary for Mine Safety and Health	DAVID G. DYE, *Acting*
Assistant Secretary of Disability Employment Policy	W. ROY GRIZZARD, JR.
Assistant Secretary for Occupational Safety and Health	EDWIN G. FOULKE, JR.
Deputy Assistant Secretary	JONATHAN L. SNARE
Assistant Secretary for Employee Benefit Security Administration	ANN L. COMBS
Assistant Secretary for Policy	VERONICA VARGAS STIDVENT
Assistant Secretary for Public Affairs	LISA M. KRUSKA
Assistant Secretary for Veterans' Employment and Training	CHARLES S. CICCOLELLA
Commissioner of Labor Statistics	KATHLEEN P. UTGOFF
Deputy Under Secretary for International Labor Affairs	JAMES CARTER

Inspector General	GORDON S. HEDDELL
Solicitor of Labor	HOWARD M. RADZELY

The purpose of the Department of Labor is to foster, promote, and develop the welfare of the wage earners of the United States, to improve their working conditions, and to advance their opportunities for profitable employment. In carrying out this mission, the Department administers a variety of Federal labor laws guaranteeing workers' rights to safe and healthful working conditions, a minimum hourly wage and overtime pay, freedom from employment discrimination, unemployment insurance, and workers' compensation. The Department also protects workers' retirement and health care benefits; provides for job training programs; helps workers find jobs; works to strengthen free collective bargaining; and keeps track of changes in employment, prices, and other national economic measurements. As the Department seeks to assist all Americans who need and want to work, special efforts are made to meet the unique job market problems of older workers, youths, minority group members, women, individuals with disabilities, and other groups.

The present Department of Labor (DOL) was created by act of March 4, 1913 (29 U.S.C. 551). A Bureau of Labor was first created by Congress by act of June 24, 1884, in the Interior Department. The Bureau of Labor later became independent as a Department of Labor without executive rank by act of June 13, 1888. It again returned to bureau status in the Department of Commerce and Labor, which was created by act of February 14, 1903 (15 U.S.C. 1501; 29 U.S.C. 1 note).

Secretary The Secretary is the principal adviser to the President on the development and execution of policies and the administration and enforcement of laws relating to wage earners, their working conditions, and their employment opportunities.

Employees' Compensation Appeals Board The Board is a three-member quasi-judicial body appointed by the Secretary which has been delegated exclusive jurisdiction by Congress to hear and make final decisions on workers' compensation appeals of Federal employees from determinations of the Office of Workers' Compensation Programs (Office) arising under the Federal Employees' Compensation Act. The Employees' Compensation Appeals Board (Board) was created by Reorganization Plan No. 2 of 1946 (60 Stat. 1095). The Board is independent of the Office, and its jurisdiction is strictly appellate and extends to questions of fact and law. The Board's decisions are not reviewable and are binding upon the Office.

For further information, contact the Clerk of the Employees' Compensation Board. Phone, 202–693–6360. Internet, www.dol.gov.

Small Business Programs The Office of Small Business Programs ensures procurement opportunities for small businesses, small disadvantaged businesses, women-owned businesses, HUBZone businesses, and businesses owned by service-disabled veterans. It serves as the Department's ombudsman under the Small Business Regulatory Enforcement Fairness Act (SBREFA) and is the Department's central referral point for inquiries and complaints arising under SBREFA. It is also active in the Department of Labor's compliance assistance activities. The Office manages the Department's programs for minority colleges and universities and Asian American and Pacific Islanders. Additionally, the Office conducts national outreach activities to raise awareness of the growing opportunities and services available to small businesses and minority colleges and universities.

For further information, call 202–693–6460.

The Solicitor of Labor The Office of the Solicitor provides necessary legal services to accomplish the Department's mission and goals. The Solicitor directs a broad-scale litigation effort in the Federal

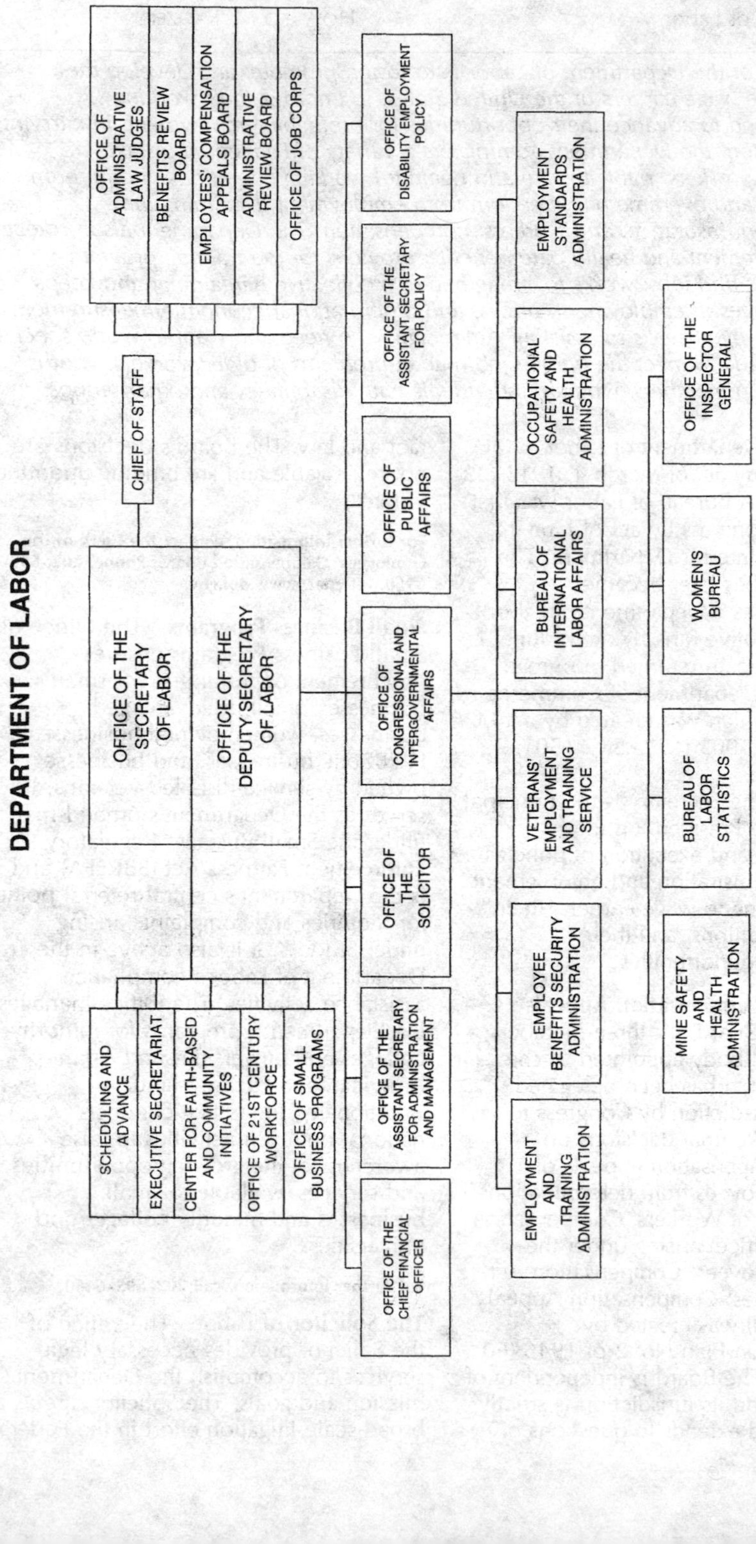
DEPARTMENT OF LABOR
OFFICE OF THE SECRETARY OF LABOR
OFFICE OF THE DEPUTY SECRETARY OF LABOR
CHIEF OF STAFF
OFFICE OF ADMINISTRATIVE LAW JUDGES
BENEFITS REVIEW BOARD
EMPLOYEES' COMPENSATION APPEALS BOARD
ADMINISTRATIVE REVIEW BOARD
OFFICE OF JOB CORPS
SCHEDULING AND ADVANCE
EXECUTIVE SECRETARIAT
CENTER FOR FAITH-BASED AND COMMUNITY INITIATIVES
OFFICE OF 21ST CENTURY WORKFORCE
OFFICE OF SMALL BUSINESS PROGRAMS
OFFICE OF DISABILITY EMPLOYMENT POLICY
OFFICE OF THE ASSISTANT SECRETARY FOR POLICY
OFFICE OF PUBLIC AFFAIRS
OFFICE OF CONGRESSIONAL AND INTERGOVERNMENTAL AFFAIRS
OFFICE OF THE SOLICITOR
OFFICE OF THE ASSISTANT SECRETARY FOR ADMINISTRATION AND MANAGEMENT
OFFICE OF THE CHIEF FINANCIAL OFFICER
EMPLOYMENT STANDARDS ADMINISTRATION
OCCUPATIONAL SAFETY AND HEALTH ADMINISTRATION
BUREAU OF INTERNATIONAL LABOR AFFAIRS
VETERANS' EMPLOYMENT AND TRAINING SERVICE
EMPLOYEE BENEFITS SECURITY ADMINISTRATION
EMPLOYMENT AND TRAINING ADMINISTRATION
OFFICE OF THE INSPECTOR GENERAL
WOMEN'S BUREAU
BUREAU OF LABOR STATISTICS
MINE SAFETY AND HEALTH ADMINISTRATION

courts pertaining to various labor statutes administered by the Department, ranging from workers' compensation to employment discrimination.

For further information, contact the Office of the Solicitor, Department of Labor, 200 Constitution Avenue NW., Washington, DC 20210. Phone, 202–693–5260.

Regional Offices—Office of the Solicitor

(RS: Regional Solicitor; ARS: Associate Regional Solicitor)

Region	Address	Solicitor
Atlanta, GA (AL, FL, GA, KY, MS, NC, SC, TN).	Rm. 7T10, 61 Forsyth St. SW., 30303	Stanley E. Keen (RS)
Branch Office	Suite 230, 618 Church St., Nashville, TN 37219.	Theresa Ball (ARS)
Boston, MA (CT, ME, MA, NH, RI, VT)	Rm. E–375, JFK Federal Office Bldg., 02203.	Frank V. McDermott (RS)
Chicago, IL (IL, IN, MI, MN, OH, WI).	Rm. 844, 230 S. Dearborn St., 60604	Joan Gestrin (RS)
Branch Office	Rm. 881, 1240 E. 9th St., Cleveland, OH 44199.	Benjamin Chinni (ARS)
Dallas, TX (AR, LA, NM, OK, TX)	Suite 501, 525 S. Griffin St., 75202	William E. Everheart (RS)
Kansas City, MO (CO, IA, KS, MO, MT, NE, ND, SD, UT, WY).	Suite 1210, 1100 Main St., 64105	Michael A. Stabler (RS)
Branch Office	Suite 1600, 1999 Broadway, Denver, CO 80201–6550.	Ann M. Noble (ARS)
New York, NY (NJ, NY, PR, VI)	Rm. 983, 201 Varick St., 10014	Patricia M. Rodenhausen (RS)
Philadelphia, PA (DE, DC, MD, PA, VA, WV).	Suite 630 East, 170 S. Independence Mall West, 19106.	Catherine O. Murphy (RS)
Branch Office	1100 Wilson Blvd., 22nd Floor West, Arlington, VA 22209.	Douglas N. White (ARS)
San Francisco, CA (AK, AZ, CA, HI, ID, NV, OR, WA, GU, MP, AS).	Suite 1110, 71 Stevenson St., 94105	Lawrence Brewster, *Acting* (RS)
Branch Offices	Suite 370, 350 S. Figueroa St., Los Angeles, CA 90071.	Pamela McKee (ARS)
	Suite 945, 1111 3d Ave., Seattle, WA 98101.	Rochelle Kleinberg (ARS)

Women's Bureau The Women's Bureau is responsible for promoting the status of wage-earning women, improving their working conditions, increasing their efficiency, and advancing their opportunities for profitable employment.

For further information, call 202–693–6710.

Regional Offices—Women's Bureau

Address (Areas Served)	Administrator
Atlanta, GA (Suite 7T95, 61 Forsyth St. SW., 30303) (AL, FL, GA, KY, MS, NC, SC, TN)	Delores L. Crockett
Boston, MA (Rm. E–270, JFK Federal Bldg., 02203) (CT, MA, ME, NH, RI, VT)	Jacqueline Cooke
Chicago, IL (Rm. 1022, 230 S. Dearborn St., 60604) (IL, IN, MI, MN, OH, WI)	Nancy Chen
Dallas, TX (Suite 735, 525 Griffin St., 75202) (AR, LA, NM, OK, TX)	Beverly Lyle
Denver, CO (Suite 1620, 1999 Broadway, 80202–6550) (CO, MT, ND, SD, UT, WY)	Frances Jefferson
Kansas City, MO (Suite 845, 1100 Main St., 64105) (IA, KS, MO, NE)	(Vacancy)
New York, NY (Rm. 708, 201 Varick St., 10014) (NJ, NY, PR, VI)	Cornelia Moore
Philadelphia, PA (Suite 880 W., 170 S. Independence Mall W., 19106–3318) (DC, DE, MD, PA, VA, WV).	Cornelia Moore
San Francisco, CA (Suite 927, 71 Stevenson St., 94105) (AZ, CA, GU, HI, NV)	Jenny Erwin
Seattle, WA (Rm. 925, 1111 3d Ave., 98101) (AK, ID, OR, WA)	Jenny Erwin

International Affairs The Bureau of International Labor Affairs is mandated to carry out the Secretary's international responsibilities, develop departmental policy and programs relating to international activities, and coordinate departmental international activities involving other U.S. Government agencies, intergovernmental and nongovernmental organizations.

Employment and Training Administration

The Employment and Training Administration (ETA) provides quality job training, employment, labor market information, and income maintenance services primarily through State and local workforce development systems. ETA also administers programs to enhance employment opportunities and business prosperity.

Office of Workforce Investment The Office of Workforce Investment provides national leadership, oversight, policy guidance, and technical assistance to the one-stop career center systems, the Business Relations Group, and the youth and adult employment and training programs funded under the Workforce Investment Act. It oversees the development and implementation of the Nation's labor market information system and programs authorized under the Workforce Investment Act.

For further information, call 202–693–3980

Business Relations Group The Business Relations Group (BRG) implements the President's High Growth Job Training initiative. The initiative is an effort to prepare workers to take advantage of new and increasing job opportunities in high-growth/high-demand and economically vital industries and sectors of the American economy. It also provides workers with training and career development resources to help them gain the skills and competencies they need. The BRG also oversees the Partnerships for Jobs initiative, which was designed to connect national businesses and the public workforce and work collaboratively with Federal, State, and local partners.

For further information, call 202–693–3949.

Office of Workforce Security The Office of Workforce Security determines which States administer the Work Opportunity and Welfare-to-Work Tax Credit Program; interprets Federal legislative requirements; and provides national leadership, oversight, policy guidance, and technical assistance to the Federal-State unemployment compensation system.

For more information, call 202–692–3029. Internet, workforcesecurity.doleta.gov.

Office of National Response The Office of National Response is responsible for national leadership, oversight, policy guidance, funding allocations, and technical assistance for Trade Adjustment Assistance and National Emergency Grant programs for dislocated workers.

For more information, call 202–693–3500.

Office of Apprenticeship The Office of Apprenticeship administers the Registered Apprenticeship Training System. The Office also promotes the adoption by employers, labor, and other organizers of structured training programs, and enhances opportunities for women and minorities to participate in such programs.

For more information, call 202–693–2796. Internet, www.doleta.gov/atels_bat.

Office of Foreign Labor Certification The Office of Foreign Labor Certification provides national leadership and policy guidance to carry out the responsibilities of the Secretary of Labor, under the Immigration and Nationality Act, as amended, concerning foreign workers seeking admission to the United States for employment.

For more information, call 202–693–3840. Internet, www.ows.doleta.gov/foreign/

Office of Performance, Results, and Technology The Office of Performance, Results, and Technology (PROTECH) is responsible for the construction, maintenance, and improvement of ETA's technology infrastructure for its national and regional offices. PROTECH provides executive leadership for the Agency in the development of its strategic plan, measurement of performance and results, and increased accountability of the workforce investment system to customers, partners, and stakeholders. PROTECH ensures that ETA has a 21st century information technology infrastructure supporting the Agency's mission and all its business lines.

For further information, call 202–693–3165.

Office of Policy Development and Research The Office of Policy Development and Research (OPDR) assists ETA in supporting its goal to inform workforce investment policies and investments, and support improvement of the public workforce system by analyzing, formulating, and recommending legislative changes and options for policy initiatives. OPDR provides ETA with strategic approaches to improve performance and outcomes through its research and demonstration projects as well as its evaluation of major ETA programs.

For further information, call 202–693–3700.

Office of Financial Administration Management The Office of Financial and Administrative Management (OFAM) provides ETA with leadership, guidance, and direction, both internally and externally, for human resource, administrative, financial, and management systems and services in order to build and maintain our Nation's workforce. OFAM works collaboratively with ETA program and administrative officers to ensure that necessary support services are provided and maintained, and that they are responsive to the needs of the larger workforce investment system.

For further information, call 202–693–2800.

Office of Field Operations The Office of Field Operations (OFO), through its six regional offices, supports the development and operation of the workforce investment system through oversight of and assistance to States and other agency grant recipients. These activities protect Federal taxpayer investment, maximize program return-on-investment, improve the administration and outcome of ETA-funded grants and programs, and better meets the needs of businesses and workers in the 21st century economy.

For further information, call 202–693–2742.

The Employment and Training Administration has six regional offices responsible for the oversight and grants administration of employment and training programs operated by State governments.

Regional Offices—Employment and Training Administration

Address (Areas Served)	Administrator	Telephone	Fax
Atlanta, GA (Rm. 6M12, 61 Forsyth St. SW., 30303) (AL, FL, GA, KY, MS, NC, SC, TN).	Helen Parker	404–562–2092	404–562–2149
Boston, MA (Rm. E–350, JFK Federal Bldg., 02203) (CT, NJ, NY, MA, ME, NH, PR, RI, VI, VT).	William Carlson	617–788–0170	617–788–0101
Chicago, IL (Rm. 628, 230 S. Dearborn St., 60604) (IA, IL, IN, KS, MI, MN, MO, NE, OH, WI, MO, NE).	Byron Zudiema	312–596–5400	312–596–5401
Dallas, TX (Rm. 317, 525 Griffin St., 75202) (AR, CO, LA, MT, ND, NM, OK, SD, TX, UT, WY).	Joseph C. Juarez	214–767–8263	214–767–5113
Philadelphia, PA (Suite 825 E., 170 Independence Mall West, 19106–3315) (DC, DE, MD, PA, VA, WV).	Lenita Jacobs-Simmons.	215–861–5205	215–861–5260
San Francisco, CA (Rm. 830, 71 Stevenson St., 94119–3767) (AK, AZ, CA, HI, ID, NV, OR, WA, American Samoa, Saipan-CNMI, Federated States of Micronesia, Republic of Marshall Islands, Territory of Guam).	Richard Trigg	415–975–4610	415–975–4612

For further information, contact the Employment and Training Administration. Phone, 202–693–2700. Internet, www.eta.gov.

Employee Benefits Security Administration

The Employee Benefits Security Administration (EBSA) promotes and protects the pension, health, and other benefits of the over 150 million participants and beneficiaries in over 6 million private sector employee benefit plans. In administering its responsibilities, EBSA assists workers in understanding their rights and protecting their benefits; facilitates compliance by plan sponsors, plan officials, service providers, and other members of the regulated community; encourages the growth of employment-based benefits; and deters and corrects violations of the relevant statutes. The Employee Retirement Income Security Act (ERISA) is enforced through 15 EBSA field offices nationwide and the national office in Washington, DC.

Field Offices—Employee Benefits Security Administration

Area/Address	Director
Atlanta, GA (Suite 7B54, 61 Forsyth St. SW., 30303)	Howard Marsh
Boston, MA (Rm. 575, John F. Kennedy Bldg., 02203)	James Benages
Chicago, IL (Suite 1600, 200 W. Adams St., 60606)	Kenneth Bazar
Cincinnati, OH (Suite 210, 1885 Dixie Hwy., Fort Wright, KY 41011)	Joseph Menez
Detroit, MI (Suite 1310, 211 W. Fort St., 48226–3211)	Patrick Kawa (DS)
Dallas, TX (Rm. 900, 525 S. Griffin St., 75202)	Roger Hilburn
Kansas City, MO (Suite 1200, 1100 Main St., 64105)	Steve Eischen
Los Angeles, CA (Suite 200, 1055 E. Colorado Blvd., Pasadena, CA 91106–2341)	Billy Beaver
Miami, FL (Suite 104, Bldg. H, 8040 Peters Rd., Plantation, FL 33324)	Isabel Colon (DS)
New York, NY (Suite 1200, 12th Fl., 33 Whitehall St., 10004)	Jonathan Kay
Philadelphia, PA (Suite 870 W., 170 S. Independence Mall W., 19106)	Mabel Capolongo
St. Louis, MO (Rm. 6310, Robert A. Young Federal Bldg., 1222 Spruce St., 63103–2818)	Gary Newman (DS)
San Francisco, CA (Suite 915, 71 Stevenson St., 94105)	Francis Clisham
Seattle, WA (Suite 860, 1111 3d Ave., 98101–3212)	Duane Peterson (DS)
Washington, DC (Suite 200, 1335 East-West Highway, Silver Spring, MD 20910)	Elizabeth Bond (DS)

For further information, contact the Employee Benefits Security Administration. Phone, 866–444–3272. Internet, www.dol.gov/ebsa.

Employment Standards Administration

The Employment Standards Administration (ESA) manages and directs employment standards programs. It handles minimum wage and overtime standards; registration of farm labor contractors; determining prevailing wage rates to be paid on Government contracts and subcontracts; nondiscrimination and affirmative action for minorities, women, veterans, and handicapped Government contract and subcontract workers; and workers' compensation programs for Federal and certain private employers and employees. ESA also safeguards the financial integrity and internal democracy of labor unions and administers statutory programs to certify employee protection provisions for various federally sponsored transportation programs.

Contracts The Office of Federal Contract Compliance Programs (OFCCP) administers and enforces three equal opportunity mandates: Executive Order 11246, as amended; section 503 of the Rehabilitation Act of 1973, as amended; and the Vietnam Era Veterans' Readjustment Assistance Act of 1974, as amended, 38 U.S.C. 4212. These mandates prohibit Federal contractors and subcontractors from discriminating on the basis of race, color, religion, sex, national origin, disability, or veteran status. They also require Federal contractors and subcontractors to take affirmative steps to ensure equal opportunity in their employment processes. OFCCP also shares responsibility with the U.S. Equal Opportunity Employment Commission in enforcing Title I of the Americans with Disabilities Act.

For further information, contact the Office of Federal Contract Compliance Programs help desk. Phone, 800–397–6251. Internet, www.dol.gov/esa/ofccp/index.htm.

Regional Directors—Office of Federal Contract Compliance Programs

Address (Areas Served)	Director
Southeast (61 Forsyth St. SW., Atlanta, GA 30303) (AL, FL, GA, KY, MS, NC, SC, TN)	Evelyn Y. Teague
Midwest (230 S. Dearborn St., Chicago, IL 60604) (IA, IL, IN, KS, MI, MN, MO, NE, OH, WI).	Sandra S. Zeigler
Southwest and Rocky Mtns. (525 S. Griffin St., Dallas, TX 75202) (AR, CO, LA, MT, ND, NM, OK, SD, TX, UT, WY).	Fred A. Azua, Jr.
Northeast (201 Varick St., New York, NY 10014) (CT, MA, ME, NH, NJ, NY, PR, RI, VI, VT).	(Vacancy)
Mid-Atlantic (170 S. Independence Mall West, Philadelphia, PA 19106) (DC, DE, MD, PA, VA, WV).	Patsy B. Blackshear
Pacific (71 Stevenson St., San Francisco, CA 94105) (AK, AZ, CA, HI, ID, NV, OR, WA).	Woodrow Gilliand

Wages The Wage and Hour Division is responsible for planning, directing, and administering programs dealing with a variety of Federal labor legislation. These programs are designed to protect low-wage incomes; safeguard the health and welfare of workers by discouraging excessively long work hours; safeguard the health and well-being of minors; prevent curtailment of employment and earnings for students, trainees, and handicapped workers; minimize losses of income and job rights caused by indebtedness; and direct a program of farm labor contractor registration designed to protect the health, safety, and welfare of migrant and seasonal agricultural workers.

For further information, contact the Office of the Administrator, Wage and Hour Division, Department of Labor, Room S–3502, 200 Constitution Avenue NW., Washington, DC 20210. Phone, 202–693–0051.

Regional Administrators—Wage and Hour Division

Address (Areas Served)	Regional Administrator
Northeast Region (850W, 170 S. Independence Mall West, Philadelphia, PA 19106)	Corlis L. Sellers
Southeast Region (Rm. 7M40, 61 Forsyth St. SW., Atlanta, GA 30303)	John L. McKeon
Midwest Region (Rm. 530, 230 S. Dearborn St., Chicago, IL 60604–1591)	Timothy Reardon
Southwest Region (Rm. 800, 525 S. Griffin St., Dallas, TX 75202–5007)	Cynthia Watson
Western Region (Suite 930, 71 Stevenson St., San Francisco, CA 94105)	George Friday, Jr.

Labor-Management Standards The Office of Labor-Management Standards conducts criminal and civil investigations to safeguard the financial integrity of unions and to ensure union democracy, and conducts investigative audits of labor unions to uncover and remedy criminal and civil violations of the Labor-Management Reporting and Disclosure Act and related statutes.

For Labor-Management Reporting and Disclosure Act assistance, phone, 202–693–0123. For electronic forms software technical support, phone, 866–487–2365. For transit employee protections assistance, phone, 202–693–0126. Internet, www.dol.gov/esa/olms_org.htm.

Regional Offices—Office of Labor-Management Standards

Region	Address	Director
Atlanta, GA	Suite 8B85, 61 Forsyth St. SW., 30303	Carol Carter
Chicago, IL	Suite 774, 230 S. Dearborn St., 60604	Ronald Lehman
Philadelphia, PA	Suite 760W, S. Independence Mall West, 19106	Eric Feldman
Pittsburgh, PA	Suite 801, 1000 Liberty Ave., 15222	John Pegula
San Francisco, CA	Suite 440, 71 Stevenson St., 94105	Antoinette Dempsey, *Acting*

Workers' Compensation The Office of Workers' Compensation Programs is responsible for programs providing workers' compensation for Federal employees, benefits to employees in private enterprise while engaged in maritime employment on navigable waters in the United States, and benefits to coal miners who are totally disabled due to pneumoconiosis, a respiratory disease contracted after prolonged inhalation of coal mine dust, and to their survivors when the miner's death is due to pneumoconiosis.

For further information, contact the Office of the Director, Office of Workers' Compensation Programs, Department of Labor, Room S–3524, 200 Constitution Avenue NW., Washington, DC 20210. Phone, 202–693–0031.

Regional/District Offices—Office of Workers' Compensation Programs

Area	Address	Director
Regional Offices		
Chicago, IL (IL, IN, MI, OH, WI)	230 S. Dearborn St., 60604	Nancy Jenson
Dallas, TX (AR, LA, NM, OK, TX)	525 S. Griffin St., 75202	E. Martin Walker
Jacksonville, FL (AL, FL, GA, KY, MS, NC, SC, TN).	214 N. Hogan St., 32202	Richard Brettell
New York, NY (CT, MA, ME, NH, PR, RI, NJ, NY, VI, VT).	201 Varick St., 10014	Jaye Weisman
Philadelphia, PA (DC, DE, MD, PA, PR, VA, VI, WV).	170 S. Independence Mall W., 19106	R. David Lotz
San Francisco, CA (AZ, CA, Guam, HI, NV)	71 Stevenson St., 94105	Edward Bound
District Offices		
Division of Federal Employees' Compensation		
Boston, MA	Rm. E–260, JFK Federal Bldg., 02203	Michael Harvill
Chicago, IL	230 S. Dearborn St., 60604	Joan Rosel
Cleveland, OH	1240 E. 9th St., 44199	Robert M. Sullivan
Dallas, TX	525 S. Griffin St., 75202	Frances Memmolo
Denver, CO	1999 Broadway, 80202	Shirley Bridge
Jacksonville, FL	214 N. Hogan St., 32202	Magdalena Fernandez
Kansas City, MO	Suite 750, 1100 Main St., 64105	Lois Maxwell
New York, NY	201 Varick St., 10014	Louis Cruz
Philadelphia, PA	170 S. Independence Mall W., 19106	William Staarman
San Francisco, CA	71 Stevenson St., 94105	Andrew Tharp
Seattle, WA	1111 3d Ave., 98101–3212	Marcus Tapia
Washington, DC	800 N. Capitol St. NW., 20211	Patricia Green
Division of Longshore and Harbor Workers' Compensation		
Baltimore, MD	31 Hopkins Plz., 21201	Emma Riley
Boston, MA	Rm. E–260, JFK Federal Bldg., 02103	David B. Groeneveld
Honolulu, HI	300 Ala Moana Blvd., 96850	R. Todd Bruininks
Houston, TX	Suite 140, 8866 Gulf Freeway, 77017	Chris Gleasman
Jacksonville, FL	214 N. Hogan St., 32202	Charles Lee
Long Beach, CA	401 E. Ocean Blvd., 90802	Eric Richardson
New Orleans, LA	701 Loyola St., 70113	David A. Duhon
New York, NY	201 Varick St., 10014	Richard V. Robilotti
Norfolk, VA	200 Granby Mall, 23510	Basil E. Voultsides
San Francisco, CA	71 Stevenson St., 94105	R. Todd Bruininks
Seattle, WA	1111 3d Ave., 98101–3212	Karen Staats
Division of Coal Mine Workers' Compensation		
Charleston, WV	Suite 110, 500 Quarrice St., 25301	Richard Hanna
Columbus, OH	Suite 300, 1160 Dublin Rd., 43215	Don Dopps
Denver, CO	1999 Broadway, 80201	Debra Thurston
Greensburg, PA	1225 S. Main St., 15601	Colleen Smalley
Johnstown, PA	Rm. 226, 319 Washington St., 15901	Stuart Glassman
Pikeville, KY	164 Main St., 41501	Harry Skidmore
Wilkes-Barre, PA	Rm. 300A, 100 N. Wilkes-Barre Blvd., 18702.	Marybeth Girton

District Offices—Division of Energy Employees Occupational Illness Compensation

Area	Address	Director
Jacksonville, FL	Suite 910, 214 N. Hogan St., 32202	William Franson
Cleveland, OH	Suite 350, 1001 Lakeside Dr., 44114	Annette Prindle
Denver, CO	Suite 1120, 1999 Broadway, 80201	Robert Mansanares
Seattle, WA	Suite 601, 719 2nd Ave., 6th Fl., 98104	Christy Long

For further information, contact the Employment Standards Administration, Department of Labor, Room S–3524, 200 Constitution Avenue NW., Washington, DC 20210. Phone, 202–693–0001. Internet, www.dol.gov/dol/esa.

Occupational Safety and Health Administration

The Administration, headed by the Assistant Secretary for Occupational Safety and Health, sets and enforces workplace safety and health standards and assists employers in complying with those standards. The Occupational Safety and Health Administration (OSHA), created pursuant to the Occupational Safety and Health Act of 1970 (29 U.S.C. 651 et seq.), has established a four-fold focus: firm and fair enforcement of safety and health rules; partnership with States running their own OSHA-approved programs and with employers and employees interested in developing effective workplace safety and health programs; efficient promulgation of new rules that are clear and easy to understand and follow; and increased outreach and training to help employers and employees eliminate safety and health hazards.

Regional Offices—Occupational Safety and Health Administration

Address	Administrator	Telephone
Atlanta, GA (61 Forsyth St. SW., 30303) (AL, FL, GA, KY, MS, NC, SC, TN)	Cindy Coe Laseter	404–562–2300
Boston, MA (Rm. E–340, JFK Federal Bldg., 02203) (CT, MA, ME, NH, RI, VT)	Marthe Kent	617–565–9860
Chicago, IL (230 S. Dearborn St., 60604) (IL, IN, MI, OH, WI)	Michael Connors	312–353–2220
Dallas, TX (525 Griffin St., 75202) (AR, LA, NM, OK, TX)	Frank Strasheim, *Acting.*	972–850–4145
Denver, CO (1999 Broadway, 80202) (CO, MT, ND, SD, UT, WY)	Greg Baxter	720–264–6551
Kansas City, MO (1100 Main St., 64105) (IA, KS, MO, NE)	Charles Adkins	816–426–5861
New York, NY (201 Varick St., 10014) (NJ, NY)	Patricia Clark	212–337–2378
Philadelphia, PA (3535 Market St., 19104) (DC, DE, MD, PA, PR, VA, VI, WV)	Richard Soltan	215–861–4900
San Francisco, CA (71 Stevenson St., 94105) (AZ, CA, HI, NV)	Christopher Lee, *Acting.*	415–975–4310
Seattle, WA (1111 3d Ave., 98101) (AK, ID, OR, WA)	Richard Terrill	206–553–5930

For further information, contact the Occupational Safety and Health Administration, Department of Labor, 200 Constitution Avenue NW., Washington, DC 20210. Phone, 202–693–1999.

Mine Safety and Health Administration

The Mine Safety and Health Administration is responsible for safety and health in the Nation's mines. The Administration develops and promulgates mandatory safety and health standards, ensures compliance with such standards, assesses civil penalties for violations, and investigates accidents. It cooperates with and provides assistance to the States in the development of effective State mine safety and health programs; improves and expands training programs in cooperation with the States and the mining industry; and contributes to the improvement and expansion of mine safety and health research and development. All of these activities are aimed at preventing and reducing mine accidents and occupational diseases in the mining industry.

District Offices—Mine Safety and Health Administration

District/Address	Telephone
Coal Mine Safety and Health	
Barbourville, KY (3837 S. U.S. Hwy., 25 E, 40906)	606–546–5123
Birmingham, AL (Suite 213, 135 Gemini Cir., 35209–4896)	205–290–7300
Denver, CO (6th & Kipling, 2nd St., Bldg. 25, E-16, 80225)	303–231–5458
Hunker, PA (319 Paintersville Rd., 15639–1034)	724–925–5150
Madisonville, KY (100 YMCA Dr., 42431–9019)	270–821–4180
Morgantown, WV (604 Cheat Rd., 26508)	304–225–6800
Mount Hope, WV (100 Bluestone Rd., 25880)	304–877–3900
Norton, VA (P.O. Box 560, 24273)	540–679–0230
Pikeville, KY (100 Fae Ramsey Ln., 41501)	606–432–0943
Vincennes, IN (Suite 200, 2300 Old Decker Rd., 47591)	812–882–7617

District Offices—Mine Safety and Health Administration—Continued

District/Address	Telephone
Wilkes-Barre, PA (Suite 034, 7 N. Wilkes-Barre Blvd., 18702)	570–826–6321
Metal/Nonmetal Mine Safety and Health	
Northeastern (547 Keystone Dr., Warrendale, PA 15086–7573)	724–772–2333
Southeastern (Suite 212, 135 Gemini Cir., Birmingham, AL 35209–4896)	205–290–7294
North Central (515 W. 1st St., Duluth, MN 55802–1302)	218–720–5448
South Central (Rm. 462, 1100 Commerce St., Dallas, TX 75242–0499)	214–767–8401
Rocky Mountain (P.O. Box 25367, Denver, CO 80225–0367)	303–231–5465
Western (Suite 610, 2060 Peabody Rd., Vacaville, CA 95687)	707–447–9844
Additional Offices	
Pittsburgh Safety and Health Technology Center (P.O. Box 18233, Pittsburgh, PA 15236)	412–386–6901
Approval and Certification Center (R.R. 1, Box 251, Triadelphia, WV 26059)	304–547–0400
National Mine Health and Safety Academy (1301 Airport Rd., Beaver, WV 25813–9426)	304–256–3100

For further information, contact the Office of Program, Education and Outreach Services, Mine Safety and Health Administration, Department of Labor, Room 2317, 1100 Wilson Boulevard, Arlington, VA 22209–3939. Phone, 202–693–9400.

Office of Disability Employment Policy

The Office of Disability Employment Policy (ODEP) provides national disability employment policy leadership by developing and influencing the implementation of disability employment policies and practices affecting the employment of people with disabilities. ODEP's response to low employment rates among such a large group of Americans is unique, comprehensive, and aggressive, and includes the active involvement and cooperation of Federal, State, and local public and private entities, including employers. ODEP also leads efforts to achieve the employment-related goals of the President's New Freedom Initiative.

ODEP addresses the significant barriers to employment faced by individuals with disabilities by developing and disseminating national, State, and local disability employment policy; by fostering implementation of innovative strategies and practices among employers and throughout the various systems serving people with disabilities; by conducting disability-related research to build knowledge to inform policy development; and by providing technical assistance to service delivery systems and employers to increase employment opportunities and the recruitment, retention, and promotion of people with disabilities.

For further information, call 202–693–7880. TTY, 202–693–7881. Internet, www.dol.gov/odep.

Bureau of Labor Statistics

The Bureau of Labor Statistics (BLS) is the principal fact-finding agency of the Federal Government in the broad field of labor economics and statistics. The Bureau is an independent national statistical agency that collects, processes, analyzes, and disseminates essential statistical data to the American public, Congress, other Federal agencies, State and local governments, businesses, and labor. BLS also serves as a statistical resource to the Department of Labor. Data are available relating to employment, unemployment, and other characteristics of the labor force; consumer and producer prices, consumer expenditures, and import and export prices; wages and employee benefits; productivity and technological change; employment projections; occupational illness and injuries; and international comparisons of labor statistics. Most of the data are collected in surveys conducted by the Bureau, the Bureau of the Census (on a contract basis), or on a cooperative basis with State agencies.

The Bureau strives to have its data satisfy a number of criteria, including: relevance to current social and economic issues, timeliness in reflecting today's rapidly changing economic conditions, accuracy and consistently high statistical quality, and impartiality in both subject matter and presentation.

The basic data are issued in monthly, quarterly, and annual news releases; bulletins, reports, and special publications; and periodicals. Data are also made available through an electronic news service, magnetic tape, diskettes, and microfiche, as well as on the Internet at stats.bls.gov. Regional offices issue additional reports and releases usually presenting locality or regional detail.

Regional Offices—Bureau of Labor Statistics

Region	Address	Commissioner
Atlanta, GA (AL, FL, GA, KY, MS, NC, SC, TN)	61 Forsyth St. SW., 30303	Janet S. Rankin
Boston, MA (CT, ME, MA, NH, NY, PR, RI, VT)	JFK Federal Bldg., 02203	Denis S. McSweeney
Chicago, IL (IA, IL, IN, MI, MN, ND, NE, OH, SD, WI)	230 S. Dearborn St., 60604	Jay Mousa
Dallas, TX (AR, CO, KS, LA, MO, MT, NM, OK, TX, UT, WY).	525 Griffin Sq. Bldg., 75202	Stan Suchman
Philadelphia, PA (DE, DC, MD, NJ, PA, VA, WV)	3535 Market St., 19104	Sheila Watkins
San Francisco, CA (AK, AS, AZ, CA, GU, HI, ID, NV, OR, Pacific Islands, WA).	71 Stevenson St., 94119–3766	Richard Holden

For further information, contact the Associate Commissioner, Office of Publications and Special Studies, Bureau of Labor Statistics, Department of Labor, Room 4110, 2 Massachusetts Avenue NE., Washington, DC 20212. Phone, 202–691–5200.

Veterans' Employment and Training Service

The Veterans' Employment and Training Service (VETS) is responsible for administering veterans' employment and training programs and activities to ensure that legislative and regulatory mandates are accomplished. The field staff works closely with and provides technical assistance to State employment security agencies and Workforce Investment Act grant recipients to ensure that veterans are provided the priority services required by law. They also coordinate with employers, labor unions, veterans service organizations, and community organizations through planned public information and outreach activities. VETS provides training to separating servicemembers through its transition assistance program. Federal contractors are provided management assistance in complying with their veterans affirmative action and reporting obligations. Staff also administer the veterans reemployment rights program and investigate complaints from veterans concerning denial of Federal veterans preference. They provide assistance to help restore job, seniority, and pension rights to veterans following absences from work for active military service and to protect employment and reemployment rights of members of the Reserve or National Guard.

Regional Administrators/State Directors—Veterans' Employment and Training Service

(RA: Regional Administrator; D: Director)

Region/Address	Director	Telephone
Aberdeen, SD (420 S. Roosevelt St., 57402–4730)	Earl R. Schultz (D)	605–626–2325
Albany, NY (Rm. 518, Bldg. 12, Harriman State Campus, 12240)	J. Frank Merges (D)	518–457–7465
Albuquerque, NM (501 Mountain Rd. NE., 87102)	Sharon Mitchell (D)	505–346–7502

Regional Administrators/State Directors—Veterans' Employment and Training Service—Continued

(RA: Regional Administrator; D: Director)

Region/Address	Director	Telephone
Atlanta, GA (Rm. 6–T85, 61 Forsyth St. SW., 30303)	William Bolls (RA)	404–562–2305
Atlanta, GA (Suite 203, 151 Ellis St. NE., 30303)	Ed Gresham (D)	404–656–3127
Austin, TX (Suite 516–T, 1117 Trinity St., 78701)	John McKinny (D)	512–463–2814
Baltimore, MD (Rm. 205, 1100 N. Eutaw St., 21201)	Stan Seidel (D)	410–767–2110
Baton Rouge, LA (Rm. 184, 1001 N. 23d St., 70802)	Lester Parmenter (D)	225–389–0339
Bismarck, ND (1000 E. Divide Ave., 58501)	Jerry Meske (D)	701–250–4337
Boise, ID (Suite 101, 413 Idaho St., 83702)	Dale Langford (D)	208–332–8947
Boston, MA (5th Fl., 19 Staniford St., 02114–2502)	Paul Desmond (D)	617–626–6699
Boston, MA (Rm. E–315, JFK Federal Bldg., 02203)	David Houle (RA)	617–565–2080
Carson City, NV (1925 N. Carson St., 89701)	Darrol Brown (D)	775–687–4632
Casper, WY (100 W. Midwest Ave., 82602–2760)	David McNulty (D)	307–261–5454
Charleston, WV (Rm. 205, 112 California Ave., 25305–0112)	Charles Stores (D)	304–558–4001
Chicago, IL (Rm. 1064, 230 S. Dearborn St., 60604)	Ronald G. Bachman (RA)	312–353–4932
Chicago, IL (8th Fl., Rm. 8174, 33 S. State St., 60605)	Patrick Winfrey (D)	312–793–3433
Columbia, SC (Suite 141, 631 Hampton St., 29201)	William C. Plowden, Jr. (D)	803–765–5195
Columbus, OH (Rm. 523, 145 S. Front St., 43215)	Rob Creel (D)	614–466–2768
Concord, NH (Rm. 3602, 53 Pleasant St., James C. Cleveland Federal Bldg., 03301).	Dennis Viola (D)	603–225–1424
Dallas, TX (Rm. 858, 525 Griffin St., 75202)	Lester L. Williams, Jr. (RA)	214–767–4987
Denver, CO (Suite 700, 633 17th St., 80202)	Mark A. McGinty (D)	303–844–2151
Des Moines, IA (150 Des Moines St., 50309–5563)	Anthony Smithart (D)	515–281–9061
Detroit, MI (Suite 9-550, 3032 W. Grand Blvd., 48202)	Kim Fulton (D)	313–456–3182
Frankfort, KY (2d. Fl. W., 275 E. Main St., 40621–2339)	Charles R. Netherton (D)	502–564–7062
Harrisburg, PA (Rm. 1108, 7th & Forster Sts., 17121)	Randall Wright (D)	717–787–5834
Hato Rey, PR (No. 198, Calle Guayama, 00917)	Angel Mojica (D)	787–754–5391
Helena, MT (301 South Park, No. 578, 59604)	H. Polly LaTray-Holmes (D)	406–841–2005
Honolulu, HI (Rm. 315, 830 Punch Bowl St., 96813)	Tom Rosenswike (D)	808–522–8216
Indianapolis, IN (Rm. SE–103, 10 N. Senate Ave., 46204)	Bruce Redman (D)	317–232–6804
Jackson, MS (1235 Echelon Pkwy., 39213–1699)	Benjamin McCaffery (D)	601–321–6078
Jefferson City, MO (421 E. Dunklin St., 65101–3138)	Mickey J. Jones (D)	573–751–3921
Juneau, AK (1111 W. 8th St., 99802–5509)	Thomas Hall (D)	907–465–2723
Lewiston, ME (Suite 104, 5 Mollison Way, 04240)	Jon Guay (D)	207–753–9090
Lincoln, NE (1030 O St., 68508)	Richard Nelson (D)	402–437–5289
Little Rock, AR (Rm. 1208, No. 1 Pershing Cir., BMH, 72114)	Bryan Gallup (D)	501–682–3786
Madison, WI (Rm. G–201A, 201 E. Washington Ave., 53702)	Dan Schmitz (D)	608–266–3110
Montgomery, AL (Rm. 2218, 649 Monroe St., 36131–6300)	Thomas M. Karrh (D)	334–223–7677
Montpelier, VT (Rm. 303, 87 State St., 05602)	Richard Gray (D)	802–828–4441
Nashville, TN (2232 Metro Center Blvd., 37228–1306)	Richard E. Ritchie (D)	615–736–7680
Oklahoma City, OK (Room 304–2, 2401 N. Lincoln Blvd., 73105)	Joe Dyer (D)	405–231–5088
Olympia, WA (3d Fl., 605 Woodview Sq. Loop SE., 98503–1040)	Tom Pearson (D)	360–438–4600
Philadelphia, PA (770 West, 170 S. Independence Mall, 19106–3310)	Joseph W. Hortiz, Jr. (RA)	215–861–5390
Phoenix, AZ (1400 W. Washington St., 85005)	Michael Espinosa (D)	602–379–4961
Raleigh, NC (Bldg. M, 700 Wade Ave., 27605)	Harry E. Payne, Jr.)	919–733–7546
Richmond, VA (Rm. 118, 703 E. Main St., 23219)	Paul Hinkhouse (D)	804–786–7270
Sacramento, CA (Rm. W1142, 800 Capitol Mall, 94280–0001)	William F. Beal (D)	916–654–8178
St. Paul, MN (1st Bank, 332 Minneapolis St., E 200, 5501–1361)	Kevin Nagel (D)	651–296–3665
Salt Lake City, UT (Suite 209, 140 E. 300 South St., 84111–2333)	Dale Brockbank (D)	801–524–5703
San Francisco, CA (Suite 705, 71 Stevenson St., 94105)	Rosendo A. Cuevas (RA)	415–975–4702
Seattle, WA (Suite 900, 1111 3d Ave., 98101–3212)	Rosendo A. Cuevas (RA)	206–553–4831
Tallahassee, FL (Suite B30, 107 E. Madison St., 32399)	Derek Taylor (D)	850–245–7199
Topeka, KS (Suite 509, 900 SW. Jackson St., 66612–1220)	Mark Bryant (D)	785–296–5032
Trenton, NJ (11th Fl., CN–058, Labor Bldg., 08625)	Alan E. Grohs (D)	609–292–2930
Wakefield, RI (4808 Tower Hill Rd., 02879)	Steven Durst (D)	401–528–5134
Washington, DC (Rm. 3156, 64 New York Ave. NE., 20002)	Stanley Williams (D)	202–671–2143
Wethersfield, CT (200 Follybrook Blvd., 06109)	Louis Kennedy (D)	860–263–6490
Wilmington, DE (Rm. 420, 4425 N. Market St., 19809–0828)	David White (D)	302–761–8138

For further information, contact the Assistant Secretary for Veterans' Employment and Training, Department of Labor, 200 Constitution Avenue NW., Washington, DC 20210. Phone, 202–693–4700.

Sources of Information

Contracts General inquiries may be directed to the Procurement Services Center, OASAM, Room N–5416, 200 Constitution Avenue NW., Washington, DC 20210. Phone, 202–693–4570.

Inquiries on doing business with the Job Corps should be directed to the job corps regional director in the appropriate Employment and Training Administration regional office listed in the preceding text.

Electronic Access Information concerning Department of Labor agencies, programs, and activities is available electronically through the Internet at www.dol.gov.

Employment The Department of Labor's Web site (www.dol.gov) provides detailed information about job opportunities with the Department, including the address and telephone numbers of the Department's personnel offices in the regions and in Washington, DC.

Publications The Office of Public Affairs distributes fact sheets which describe the activities of the major agencies within the Department.

The Employment and Training Administration issues periodicals such as *Area Trends in Employment and Unemployment* available by subscription through the Superintendent of Documents, Government Printing Office, Washington, DC 20402. Information about publications may be obtained from the Administration's Information Office. Phone, 202–219–6871.

The Office of Labor-Management Standards publishes the text of the Labor-Management Reporting and Disclosure Act and pamphlets that explain the reporting, election, bonding, and trusteeship provisions of the act. The pamphlets and reporting forms used by persons covered by the act are available free in limited quantities from the OLMS National Office at Room N–5616, 200 Constitution Avenue NW., Washington, DC 20210, and from OLMS field offices listed in the telephone directory under United States Government, Department of Labor.

The Employee Benefit Security Administration distributes fact sheets, pamphlets, and booklets on employer obligations and employee rights under ERISA. A list of publications is available by writing to the Office of Participant Assistance, Employee Benefit Security Administration, Room N–5625, 200 Constitution Avenue NW., Washington, DC 20210. Phone, 202–693–8664, or 866–444–EBSA (3272). Internet, www.dol.gov/ebsa.

The Bureau of Labor Statistics has an information office at 2 Massachusetts Avenue NE., Room 2850, Washington, DC 20212. Phone, 202–606–5886. Periodicals include the *Monthly Labor Review, Consumer Price Index, Producer Prices and Price Indexes, Employment and Earnings, Current Wage Developments, Occupational Outlook Handbook,* and *Occupational Outlook Quarterly*. Publications are both free and for sale, but for-sale items must be obtained from the Superintendent of Documents, Government Printing Office. Inquiries may be directed to the Washington Information Office or to the Bureau's regional offices.

Publications of the Employment Standards Administration, such as *Handy Reference Guide to the Fair Labor Standards Act,* and *OFCCP, Making Affirmative Action Work,* are available from the nearest area office. Single copies are free.

Reading Rooms Department of Labor Library, Room N2439, 200 Constitution Avenue NW., Washington, DC 20210. Phone, 202–219–6992.

The Office of Labor-Management Standards maintains a Public Disclosure Room at Room N–5616, 200 Constitution Avenue NW., Washington, DC 20210. Reports filed under the Labor-Management Reporting and Disclosure Act may be examined there and purchased for 15 cents per page. Reports also may be obtained by calling the Public Disclosure Room at 202–219–7393, or by contacting an Office field office listed in the telephone directory under United States Government, Department of Labor.

The Employee Benefit Security Administration maintains a Public Disclosure Room at Room N–1513, 200 Constitution Avenue NW., Washington, DC 20210. Reports filed under the Employee Retirement Income Security Act may be examined there and purchased for 15 cents per page or by calling the Public Disclosure Room at 202–693–8678.

The Office of Small Business Programs maintains a clearinghouse and inventory of compliance-assistance materials, which may be examined in Room C–2313, 200 Constitution Avenue NW., Washington, DC 20210. Phone, 888–9–SBREFA. Internet, www.dol.gov/dol/osbp.

Inspector General Hotline To report waste, fraud, or abuse in Department programs, contact the Office of Inspector General Hotline, at OIG, U.S. Department of Labor, 200 Constitution Avenue, NW., Rm. S–5506, Washington, DC 20210. Phone, 202–639–6999 or 800–347–3756. Fax, 202–693–7020. E-mail, hotline@oig.dol.gov.

For further information concerning the Department of Labor, contact the Office of Public Affairs, Department of Labor, Room S–1032, 200 Constitution Avenue NW., Washington, DC 20210. Phone, 202–693–4650. Internet, www.dol.gov.

DEPARTMENT OF STATE

2201 C Street NW., Washington, DC 20520
Phone, 202–647–4000. Internet, www.state.gov.

SECRETARY OF STATE	CONDOLEEZZA RICE
Deputy Secretary of State	ROBERT B. ZOELLICK
Ambassador-at-Large and Coordinator for Counterterrorism	HENRY A. CRUMPTON
U.S. Global AIDS Coordinator	MARK DYBUL, *Acting*
Assistant Secretary for Intelligence and Research	(VACANCY)
Assistant Secretary for Legislative Affairs	JEFFREY T. BERGNER
Chairman, Foreign Service Grievance Board	EDWARD REIDY
Chief of Protocol	DONALD B. ENSENAT
Chief of Staff	BRIAN GUNDERSON
Civil Service Ombudsman	FREDERICK A. WHITTINGTON
Counselor of the Department of State	PHILIP ZELIKOW
Director of the Office of Civil Rights	(VACANCY)
Director, Policy Planning Staff	STEPHEN KRASNER
Inspector General	HOWARD J. KRONGARD
Legal Adviser	JOHN B. BELLINGER III
Special Assistant to the Secretary and Executive Secretary of the Department	HARRY K. THOMAS, JR.
Under Secretary for Arms Control and International Security Affairs	ROBERT JOSEPH
Assistant Secretary for Arms Control and Nonproliferation	STEPHEN G. RADEMAKER, *Acting*
Assistant Secretary for Political-Military Affairs	JOHN HILLEN
Assistant Secretary for Verification,Compliance, and Implementation	PAULA A. DESUTTER
Under Secretary for Economic, Business, and Agricultural Affairs	JOSETTE S. SHINER
Assistant Secretary for Economic and Business Affairs	DANIEL S. SULLIVAN
Under Secretary for Democracy and Global Affairs	PAULA J. DOBRIANSKY
Assistant Secretary for Democracy, Human Rights, and Labor	BARRY F. LOWENKRON
Assistant Secretary for Oceans and International Environmental and Scientific Affairs	CLAUDIA A. MCMURRAY
Assistant Secretary for Population, Refugees, and Migration	ELLEN SAUERBREY
Under Secretary for Management	HENRIETTA H. FORE
Assistant Secretary for Administration	RAJKUMAR CHELLARAJ
Assistant Secretary for Consular Affairs	MAURA HARTY

Assistant Secretary for Diplomatic Security and Director of the Office of Foreign Missions	RICHARD J. GRIFFIN
Assistant Secretary for Information Resource Management and Chief Information Officer	JAMES VAN DERHOFF
Assistant Secretary for Resource Management and Chief Financial Officer	BRADFORD R. HIGGINS
Director and Chief Operating Officer of Overseas Buildings Operations	CHARLES E. WILLIAMS
Director General of the Foreign Service and Director of Human Resources	GEORGE M. STAPLES
Director of the Foreign Service Institute	RUTH A. WHITESIDE
Director, Office of Medical Services	LAURENCE G. BROWN
Under Secretary for Political Affairs	R. NICHOLAS BURNS
Assistant Secretary for African Affairs	JENDAYI E. FRAZER
Assistant Secretary for East Asian and Pacific Affairs	CHRISTOPHER R. HILL
Assistant Secretary for European and Eurasian Affairs	DANIEL FRIED
Assistant Secretary for International Narcotics and Law Enforcement Affairs	ANNE W. PATTERSON
Assistant Secretary for Western Hemisphere Affairs	THOMAS A. SHANNON, JR.
Assistant Secretary for Near Eastern Affairs	C. DAVID WELCH
Assistant Secretary for South and Central Asian Affairs	RICHARD A. BOUCHER
Ambassador and Coordinator for Afghanistan	MAUREEN E. QUINN
Assistant Secretary for International Organization Affairs	KRISTEN SILVERBERG
Under Secretary for Public Diplomacy and Public Affairs	KAREN P. HUGHES
Assistant Secretary for Public Affairs and Spokesman for the Department of State	SEAN IAN MCCORMACK
Assistant Secretary for Educational and Cultural Affairs	DINA HABIB POWELL
Coordinator, International Information Programs	ALEXANDER C. FELDMAN
Permanent Representative of the United States of America to the Organization of American States	RICHARD C. HOLBROOKE

United States Mission to the United Nations [1]

799 United Nations Plaza, New York, NY 10017

United States Permanent Representative to the United Nations and Representative in the Security Council	JOHN R. BOLTON
Deputy United States Representative to the United Nations	ALEJANDRO DANIEL WOLFF

United States Representative for Special Political Affairs in the United Nations	JACKIE W. SANDERS
United States Representative on the Economic and Social Council	RICHARD T. MILLER
United States Representative for U.N. Management and Reform	MARK D. WALLACE

[For the Department of State statement of organization, see the *Code of Federal Regulations,* Title 22, Part 5]

The Department of State advises the President in the formulation and execution of foreign policy and promotes the long-range security and well-being of the United States. The Department determines and analyzes the facts relating to American overseas interests, makes recommendations on policy and future action, and takes the necessary steps to carry out established policy. In so doing, the Department engages in continuous consultations with the American public, the Congress, other U.S. departments and agencies, and foreign governments; negotiates treaties and agreements with foreign nations; speaks for the United States in the United Nations and other international organizations in which the United States participates; and represents the United States at international conferences.

The Department of State was established by act of July 27, 1789, as the Department of Foreign Affairs and was renamed Department of State by act of September 15, 1789 (22 U.S.C. 2651 note).

Secretary of State The Secretary of State is responsible for the overall direction, coordination, and supervision of U.S. foreign relations and for the interdepartmental activities of the U.S. Government abroad. The Secretary is the first-ranking member of the Cabinet, is a member of the National Security Council, and is in charge of the operations of the Department, including the Foreign Service.

Regional Bureaus Foreign affairs activities worldwide are handled by the geographic bureaus, which include the Bureaus of African Affairs, European and Eurasian Affairs, East Asian and Pacific Affairs, Near East Affairs, South and Asian Affairs, and Western Hemisphere Affairs.

Administration The Bureau of Administration provides support programs to the Department of State and U.S. embassies and consulates, including management of owned or leased facilities in the United States; procurement; supply and transportation; diplomatic pouch and small mail services; official records, publishing, and library services; language services; support to the schools abroad that educate dependents of U.S. Government employees; and small and disadvantaged business utilization. Direct services to the public and other Government agencies include: authenticating documents used abroad for legal and business purposes; responding to requests under the Freedom of Information and Privacy Acts and providing the electronic reading room for public reference to State Department records; and determining use of the diplomatic reception rooms of the Harry S. Truman headquarters building in Washington, DC.

For further information, contact the Bureau of Administration at 703–875–7000.

Consular Affairs The Bureau of Consular Affairs is responsible for the protection and welfare of American citizens and interests abroad; the administration and enforcement of the provisions of the immigration and nationality laws insofar as they concern the Department of State and Foreign Service; and the issuance of passports and visas and related services. Approximately 10 million passports a year are issued by the Office of Passport Services of the Bureau at the processing centers in Portsmouth, NH, and Charleston, SC, and the regional agencies in Boston, MA; Chicago, IL; Aurora, Colorado; Honolulu, HI;

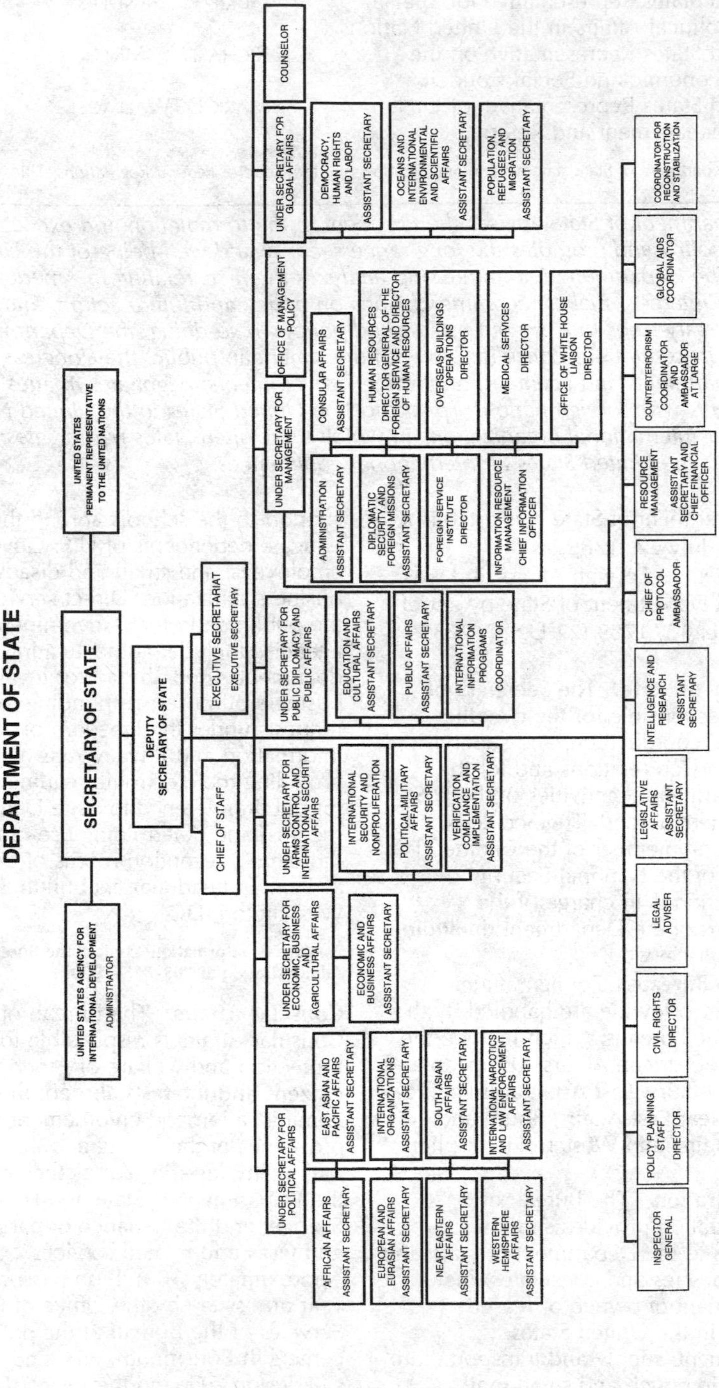
DEPARTMENT OF STATE
SECRETARY OF STATE
UNITED STATES AGENCY FOR INTERNATIONAL DEVELOPMENT ADMINISTRATOR
UNITED STATES PERMANENT REPRESENTATIVE TO THE UNITED NATIONS
DEPUTY SECRETARY OF STATE
CHIEF OF STAFF
EXECUTIVE SECRETARIAT EXECUTIVE SECRETARY
UNDER SECRETARY FOR POLITICAL AFFAIRS
AFRICAN AFFAIRS ASSISTANT SECRETARY
EAST ASIAN AND PACIFIC AFFAIRS ASSISTANT SECRETARY
EUROPEAN AND EURASIAN AFFAIRS ASSISTANT SECRETARY
INTERNATIONAL ORGANIZATIONS ASSISTANT SECRETARY
NEAR EASTERN AFFAIRS ASSISTANT SECRETARY
SOUTH ASIAN AFFAIRS ASSISTANT SECRETARY
WESTERN HEMISPHERE AFFAIRS ASSISTANT SECRETARY
INTERNATIONAL NARCOTICS AND LAW ENFORCEMENT AFFAIRS ASSISTANT SECRETARY
UNDER SECRETARY FOR ECONOMIC, BUSINESS AND AGRICULTURAL AFFAIRS
ECONOMIC AND BUSINESS AFFAIRS ASSISTANT SECRETARY
UNDER SECRETARY FOR ARMS CONTROL AND INTERNATIONAL SECURITY AFFAIRS
INTERNATIONAL SECURITY AND NONPROLIFERATION
POLITICAL-MILITARY AFFAIRS ASSISTANT SECRETARY
VERIFICATION COMPLIANCE AND IMPLEMENTATION ASSISTANT SECRETARY
UNDER SECRETARY FOR PUBLIC DIPLOMACY AND PUBLIC AFFAIRS
EDUCATION AND CULTURAL AFFAIRS ASSISTANT SECRETARY
PUBLIC AFFAIRS ASSISTANT SECRETARY
INTERNATIONAL INFORMATION PROGRAMS COORDINATOR
UNDER SECRETARY FOR MANAGEMENT
ADMINISTRATION ASSISTANT SECRETARY
CONSULAR AFFAIRS ASSISTANT SECRETARY
DIPLOMATIC SECURITY AND FOREIGN MISSIONS ASSISTANT SECRETARY
HUMAN RESOURCES DIRECTOR GENERAL OF THE FOREIGN SERVICE AND DIRECTOR OF HUMAN RESOURCES
FOREIGN SERVICE INSTITUTE DIRECTOR
OVERSEAS BUILDINGS OPERATIONS DIRECTOR
INFORMATION RESOURCE MANAGEMENT CHIEF INFORMATION OFFICER
MEDICAL SERVICES DIRECTOR
OFFICE OF WHITE HOUSE LIAISON DIRECTOR
OFFICE OF MANAGEMENT POLICY
UNDER SECRETARY FOR GLOBAL AFFAIRS
DEMOCRACY, HUMAN RIGHTS AND LABOR ASSISTANT SECRETARY
OCEANS AND INTERNATIONAL ENVIRONMENTAL AND SCIENTIFIC AFFAIRS ASSISTANT SECRETARY
POPULATION, REFUGEES AND MIGRATION ASSISTANT SECRETARY
COUNSELOR
INSPECTOR GENERAL
POLICY PLANNING STAFF DIRECTOR
CIVIL RIGHTS DIRECTOR
LEGAL ADVISER
LEGISLATIVE AFFAIRS ASSISTANT SECRETARY
INTELLIGENCE AND RESEARCH ASSISTANT SECRETARY
CHIEF OF PROTOCOL AMBASSADOR
RESOURCE MANAGEMENT ASSISTANT SECRETARY AND CHIEF FINANCIAL OFFICER
COUNTERTERRORISM COORDINATOR AND AMBASSADOR AT LARGE
GLOBAL AIDS COORDINATOR
COORDINATOR FOR RECONSTRUCTION AND STABILIZATION

Houston, TX; Los Angeles, CA; Miami, FL; New Orleans, LA; New York, NY; Philadelphia, PA; San Francisco, CA; Seattle, WA; Norwalk, CT; Stamford, CT; and Washington, DC. In addition, the Bureau helps secure America's borders against entry by terrorists or narco-traffickers, facilitates international adoptions, and supports parents whose children have been abducted abroad.

For further information, visit the Bureau of Consular Affairs Web site at www.travel.state.gov.

Democracy, Human Rights, and Labor The Bureau of Democracy, Human Rights, and Labor (DRL) is responsible for developing and implementing U.S. policy on democracy, human rights, labor, and religious freedom. The Bureau undertakes dialog with foreign governments and builds partnerships in multilateral organizations in order to build global consensus in support of democratic rule and universal human rights principles. It is responsible for preparing the annual *Country Reports on Human Rights Practices* which are regarded as the most comprehensive and objective assessment of human rights conditions around the world. Through the Human Rights and Democracy Fund, DRL provides comprehensive technical and financial support for democracy and human rights, which helps prosecute war criminals, promote religious freedom, monitor free and fair elections, support workers' rights, encourage the establishment of the rule of law, and facilitate the growth of civil society.

For further information, contact the Bureau of Democracy, Human Rights, and Labor at 202–647–2126.

Diplomatic Security The Bureau of Diplomatic Security provides a secure environment to promote U.S. interests at home and abroad. The Bureau's mission includes the protection of the Secretary of State and other senior Government officials, residents, and visiting foreign dignitaries and foreign missions in the United States; the conduct of criminal, counterintelligence, and personnel security investigations; ensuring the integrity of international travel documents, sensitive information, classified processing equipment, and management information systems; the physical and technical protection of domestic and overseas facilities of the Department of State; providing professional law enforcement and security training to U.S. and foreign personnel; and a comprehensive, multifaceted overseas security program servicing the needs of U.S. missions and the resident U.S. citizens and business communities. Through the Office of Foreign Missions, the Bureau regulates the domestic activities of the foreign diplomatic community in the areas of taxation, real property acquisitions, motor vehicle operation, domestic travel, and customs processing.

For further information, contact the Bureau of Diplomatic Security. Phone, 571–345–2499. Fax, 571–345–2527. Internet, www.ds.state.gov.

Economic and Business Affairs The Bureau of Economic and Business Affairs has overall responsibility for formulating and implementing policy regarding international development and reconstruction, trade, investment, intellectual property enforcement, international energy issues, terrorism financing and economic sanctions, international communications and information policy, and aviation and maritime affairs.

For further information, contact the Bureau of Economic and Business Affairs. Phone, 202–647–7971. Fax, 202–647–5713.

Educational and Cultural Affairs The Bureau of Educational and Cultural Affairs administers the principal provisions of the Mutual Educational and Cultural Exchange Act (the Fulbright-Hays Act), including U.S. international educational and cultural exchange programs. These programs include the prestigious Fulbright Program for students, scholars, and teachers; the International Visitor Program, which brings leaders and future leaders from other countries to the United States for consultation with their professional colleagues; and citizen exchanges through cooperative relationships with

U.S. nongovernmental organizations that support the Bureau's mission.

For further information, contact the Bureau of Educational and Cultural Affairs. Phone, 202–203–5118. Fax, 202–203–5115. Internet, http://exchanges.state.gov/.

Foreign Missions The Office of Foreign Missions (OFM) operates the motor vehicles, tax, customs, real property, and travel programs to regulate and serve the 175 foreign missions in the United States and approximately 55,000 foreign mission members and dependents. The Office is also an advocate for improved treatment of U.S. missions and personnel abroad. It guards the U.S. public against abuses of diplomatic privilege and preserves U.S. security interests. OFM maintains regional offices in New York, Chicago, San Francisco, Los Angeles, Miami, and Honolulu.

For further information, contact the Office of Foreign Missions. Phone, 202–647–3417. Fax, 202–647–1919.

Foreign Service Institute The Foreign Service Institute of the Department of State is the Federal Government's primary training institution for foreign affairs related training. In addition to the Department of State, the Institute provides training for more than 47 other governmental agencies. The Institute's more than 475 courses, including some 60 foreign language courses, range in length from 1 day to 2 years. The courses are designed to promote successful performance in each professional assignment, to ease the adjustment to other countries and cultures, and to enhance the leadership and management capabilities of the foreign affairs community.

For further information, contact the Foreign Service Institute. Phone, 703–302–6729. Fax, 703–302–7227.

Information Resource Management The Bureau of Information Resource Management (IRM) provides the Department with the information technology it needs to carry out U.S. diplomacy in the information age. The IRM Bureau is lead by the Department's Chief Information Officer. IRM establishes effective information resource management planning and policies; ensures availability of information technology systems and operations, including information technology contingency planning, to support the Department's diplomatic, consular, and management operations; excercises management responsibility for ensuring that the Department's information resources meet the business requirements of the Department and provide an effective basis for knowledge sharing and collaboration within the Department and with other foreign affairs agencies and partners; excercises delegated approving authority for the Secretary of State for development and administration of the Department's computer and information security programs and policies.

Inspector General The Office of Inspector General (OIG) conducts independent audits, inspections, and investigations to promote effective management, accountability, and positive change in the Department of State, the Broadcasting Board of Governors (BBG), and the foreign affairs community. OIG provides leadership to promote integrity, efficiency, effectiveness, and economy; prevent and detect waste, fraud, abuse, and mismanagement; identify vulnerabilities and recommend constructive solutions; offer expert assistance to improve Department and BBG operations; communicate timely, useful information that facilitates decisionmaking and achieves measurable gains; and keep the Department, BBG, and Congress informed.

For further information, contact the Office of Inspector General. Phone, 202–663–0340.

Intelligence and Research The Bureau coordinates the activities of U.S. intelligence agencies to ensure that their overseas activities are consistent with U.S. foreign policy objectives and interests. It also provides all-source analysis which gives the Department insights and information to foreign policy questions. It organizes seminars on topics of high interest to policymakers and the intelligence community and monitors and analyzes foreign public and media opinion on key issues.

For further information, call 202–647–1080.

International Information Programs The Bureau of International Information Programs (IIP) informs, engages, and influences international audiences about U.S. policy and society to advance America's interests. IIP is a leader in developing and implementing public diplomacy strategies that measurablly influence international audiences through quality programs and cutting-edge technologies. IIP provides localized contact for U.S. policies and messages, reaching millions worldwide in English, Arabic, Chinese, French, Persian, Russian, and Spanish. IIP delivers America's message to the world through a number of key products and services. These programs reach, and are created strictly for, key international audiences, such as U.S. diplomatic missions abroad, the media, government officials, opinion leaders, and the general public in more than 140 countries around the world. They include Web and print publications, speaker programs—both traveling (live) and electronic— and information resource services. IIP orchestrates the State Department's efforts to counter anti-American disinformation/propaganda and serves as the Department's chief link with other agencies in coordinating international public diplomacy programs.

For further information, contact the Bureau of International Information Programs. Phone, 202–453–8358. Fax, 202–453–8356. Internet, www.state.gov/r/iip/.

International Narcotics and Law Enforcement The Bureau of International Narcotics and Law Enforcement Affairs is responsible for developing, coordinating, and implementing international narcotics control and anticrime assistance activities of the Department of State. It provides advice on international narcotics control matters for the Office of Management and Budget, the National Security Council, and the White House Office of National Drug Control Policy and ensures implementation of U.S. policy in international narcotics matters. The Bureau also provides guidance on narcotics control and anticrime matters to chiefs of missions and directs narcotics control coordinators at posts abroad. It communicates or authorizes communication, as appropriate, with foreign governments on drug control and anticrime matters including negotiating, concluding, and terminating agreements relating to international narcotics control and anticrime programs.

For further information, contact the Bureau of International Narcotics and Law Enforcement Affairs. Phone, 202–776–8750. Fax, 202–776–8775.

International Organizations The Bureau of International Organization Affairs provides guidance and support for U.S. participation in international organizations and conferences and formulates and implements U.S. policy toward international organizations, with particular emphasis on those organizations which make up the United Nations system. It provides direction in the development, coordination, and implementation of U.S. multilateral policy.

For further information, call 202–647–9326. Fax, 202–647–2175.

International Security and Nonproliferation The Bureau of International Security and Nonproliferation (ISN), is responsible for managing a broad range of nonproliferation, counterproliferation, and arms control functions. ISN leads U.S. efforts to prevent the spread of weapons of mass destruction (nuclear, chemical, and biological weapons) and their delivery systems. It is also responsible for the following functions:

—spearheading effort to promote international consensus on weapons of mass destruction proliferation through bilateral and multilateral diplomacy;

—addressing weapons of mass destruction proliferation threats posed by non-state actors and terrorist groups by improving physical security, using interdiction and sanctions, and actively participating in the Proliferation Security Initiative;

—coordinating the implementation of key international treaties and arrangements, working to make them relevant to today's security challenges;

—working closely with the UN, the G–8, NATO, the Organization for the Prohibition of Chemical Weapons, the International Atomic Energy Agency and other international institutions and organizations to reduce and eliminate the threat posed by weapons of mass destruction; and

—supporting efforts of foreign partners to prevent, protect against, and respond to the threat or use of weapons of mass destruction by terrorists.

For further information, contact the Bureau of International Security and Nonproliferation. Phone, 202–647–9868. Fax, 202–736–4863. Internet, www.state.gov/t/isn.

Legal Adviser The Office of the Legal Adviser advises the Secretary of State and other Department officials on all domestic and international legal matters relating to the Department of State, the Foreign Service, and the diplomatic and consular posts abroad. The Office lawyers draft, negotiate, and interpret treaties, international agreements, domestic statutes, Departmental regulations, Executive orders, and other legal documents; provide guidance on international and domestic law; represent the United States in meetings of international organizations and in international negotiations; work on domestic and foreign litigation affecting the Department's interests; and represent the United States before international tribunals, including the International Court of Justice.

For further information, contact the Office of the Legal Adviser. Phone, 202–647–9598. Fax, 202–647–7096. Internet, www.state.gov/s/l/.

Medical Services The Office of Medical Services develops, manages, and staffs a worldwide primary health care system for U.S. citizen employees and their eligible dependents residing overseas. In support of its overseas operations, the Office approves and monitors the medical evacuation of patients, conducts pre-employment and in-service physical examinations, and provides clinical referral and advisory services. The Office also provides for emergency medical response in the event of a crisis at an overseas post.

For further information, fax 202–663–1613.

Oceans, International Environmental, and Scientific Affairs The Bureau of Oceans, and International Environmental and Scientific Affairs (OES) serves as the foreign policy focal point for international oceans, environmental, and scientific efforts. OES projects, protects, and promotes U.S. global interests in these areas by articulating U.S. foreign policy, encouraging international cooperation, and negotiating treaties and other instruments of international law. The Bureau serves as the principal adviser to the Secretary of State on international environment, science, and technology matters and takes the lead in coordinating and brokering diverse interests in the interagency process, where the development of international policies or the negotiation and implementation of relevant international agreements are concerned. The Bureau seeks to promote the peaceful exploitation of outer space, develop and coordinate policy on international health issues, encourage government to government scientific cooperation, and prevent the destruction and degradation of the planet's natural resources and the global environment.

For further information, contact the Bureau of Oceans and International Environmental and Scientific Affairs. Phone, 202–647–0978. Fax, 202–647–0217.

Overseas Building Operations The Bureau of Overseas Buildings Operations (OBO) directs the worldwide overseas buildings program for the Department of State and the U.S. Government community serving abroad under the authority of the chiefs of mission. Along with the input and support of other State Department bureaus, foreign affairs agencies, and Congress, OBO sets worldwide priorities for the design, construction, acquisition, maintenance, use, and sale of real properties and the use of sales proceeds. OBO also serves as the Single Real Property Manager of all overseas facilities under the authority of the chiefs of mission.

For further information, contact the Bureau of Overseas Buildings Operations. Phone, 703–875–4131. Fax, 703–875–5043. Internet, www.state.gov/obo.

Political-Military Affairs The Bureau of Political-Military Affairs is the principal link between the Departments of State and Defense and is the Department of State's lead on operational military matters regarding the global war on terror. The Bureau provides policy direction in the areas of international security, security assistance, military operations, post-conflict stabilization, and defense trade. Its responsibilities include securing base access to support U.S. military forces overseas, coordinating coalition combat and stabilization forces, promoting critical infrastructure protection, regulating arms transfers, promoting responsible U.S. defense trade, combating illegal trafficking in small arms and light weapons, facilitating the education and training of international peacekeepers and foreign military personnel, managing humanitarian mine action programs, and coordinating U.S. Government response to chemical, biological, radiological, and natural events and crises overseas.

For further information, contact the Bureau of Political-Military Affairs. Phone, 202–647–5104. Fax, 202–736–4413. Internet, www.state.gov/t/pm.

Population, Refugees, and Migration The Bureau of Population, Refugees, and Migration directs the Department's population, refugee, and migration policy development. It administers U.S. contributions to international organizations for humanitarian assistance- and protection-related programs on behalf of refugees, conflict victims, and internally displaced persons and provides U.S. contributions to nongovernmental organizations which provide assistance and protection to refugees abroad. The Bureau oversees the annual admissions of refugees to the United States for permanent resettlement, working closely with the Department of Homeland Security, the Department of Health and Human Services, and various State and private voluntary agencies. It coordinates U.S. international population policy and promotes its goals through bilateral and multilateral cooperation. It works closely with the U.S. Agency for International Development, which administers U.S. international population programs. The Bureau also coordinates the Department's international migration policy through bilateral and multilateral diplomacy. The Bureau oversees efforts to encourage greater participation in humanitarian assistance and refugee resettlement on the part of foreign governments and uses humanitarian diplomacy to increase access and assistance to those in need in the absence of political solutions.

For further information, contact the Bureau of Population, Refugees, and Migration. Phone, 202–663–1071. Fax, 202–663–1002. Internet, www.state.gov/g/prm.

Protocol The Chief of Protocol is the principal adviser to the U.S. Government, the President, the Vice President, and the Secretary of State on matters of diplomatic procedure governed by law or international custom and practice. The Office is responsible for the following activities:

—arranging visits of foreign chiefs of state, heads of government, and other high officials to the United States;

—organizing credential presentations of newly arrived Ambassadors, as presented to the President and to the Secretary of State;

—operating the President's guest house, Blair House;

—organizing delegations representing the President at official ceremonies abroad;

—conducting official ceremonial functions and public events;

—interpreting the official order of precedence;

—conducting outreach programs of cultural enrichment and substantive briefings of the Diplomatic Corps;

—accrediting of over 100,000 embassy, consular, international organization, and other foreign government personnel, members of their families, and domestics throughout the United States;

—determining entitlement to diplomatic or consular immunity;

—publishing of diplomatic and consular lists;

—resolving problems arising out of diplomatic or consular immunity, such as legal and police matters; and

—approving the opening of embassy and consular offices in conjunction with the Office of Foreign Missions.

For further information, contact the Office of the Chief of Protocol. Phone, 202–647–2663. Fax, 202–647–1560.

Verification and Compliance The Bureau of Verification and Compliance provides oversight, with respect to both policy and resources, on all matters relating to ensuring and verifying compliance with international arms control, nonproliferation, and disarmament agreements and commitments. In this regard, the Bureau develops verification proposals and assessments for prospective arms control, nonproliferation, and disarmament agreements and commitments, and supports and participates in such negotiations and related consultations. The Bureau is responsible for the preparation of the President's Annual Report to Congress on Adherence to and Compliance with Arms Control, Nonproliferation, and Disarmament Agreements and Commitments, for verifiability assessments for international arms control and non proliferation agreements, and for specialized compliance reports required by Senate resolutions of ratification. The Bureau participates in interagency groups and organizations that assess, analyze, or review U.S. planned or ongoing policies, programs, and resources that have a direct bearing on verification or compliance matters, and it advocates directly with the intelligence community and others on verification and compliance related policy issues. The Bureau also assists in the evaluation of transfers related to weapons of mass destruction (including WMD-capable delivery systems) by foreign entities that are potentially contrary to U.S. sanctions, laws, and Executive orders, and advises on determinations of sanctionability.

For further information, contact the Bureau of Verification and Compliance and Implementation. Phone, 202–647–5315. Fax, 202–647–1321. Internet, www.state.gov/t/vc.

Foreign Service To a great extent the future of our country depends on the relations we have with other countries, and those relations are conducted principally by the U.S. Foreign Service. Trained representatives stationed worldwide provide the President and the Secretary of State with much of the raw material from which foreign policy is made and with the recommendations that help shape it.

Ambassadors are the personal representatives of the President and report to the President through the Secretary of State. Ambassadors have full responsibility for implementation of U.S. foreign policy by any and all U.S. Government personnel within their country of assignment, except those under military commands. Their responsibilities include negotiating agreements between the United States and the host country, explaining and disseminating official U.S. policy, and maintaining cordial relations with that country's government and people.

A listing of Foreign Service posts, together with addresses and telephone numbers and key personnel, appears in *Key Officers of Foreign Service Posts—Guide for Business Representatives,* which is for sale by the Superintendent of Documents, Government Printing Office, Washington, DC 20402.

United States Diplomatic Offices—Foreign Service

(C: Consular Office; N: No Embassy or Consular Office)

Country/Capitol	Chief of Mission
Afghanistan/Kabul	Ronald E. Newman
Albania/Tirana	Marcie B. Ries
Algeria/Algiers	Robert S. Ford
Andorra/Andorra La Vella	Eduardo Aguirre, Jr.
Angola/Luanda	Cynthia G. Efird
Antigua and Barbuda/St. John's (N).	Mary Elizabeth Kramer
Argentina/Buenos Aires	Lino Gutierrez
Armenia/Yerevan	John M. Evans
Australia/Canberra	(Vacancy)
Austria/Vienna	Susan Rasinski McCaw
Azerbaijan/Baku	Anne E. Derse
Bahamas/Nassau	John D. Rood
Bahrain/Manama	William Monroe

United States Diplomatic Offices—Foreign Service—Continued

(C: Consular Office; N: No Embassy or Consular Office)

Country/Capitol	Chief of Mission
Bangladesh/Dhaka	(Vacancy)
Barbados/Bridgetown	Mary Elizabeth Kramer
Belarus/Minsk	George A. Krol
Belgium/Brussels	Tom C. Korologos
Belize/Belize City	Robert J. Dieter
Benin/Cotonou	Wayne E. Neill
Bolivia/La Paz	David N. Greenlee
Bosnia and Herzegovina/Sarajevo.	Douglas L. McElhaney
Botswana/Gaborone	Katherine H. Canavan
Brazil/Brasilia	Phil Chicola
Brunei Darussalam/Bandar Seri Begawan.	Emil M. Skodon
Bulgaria/Sofia	Jon Ross Beyrle
Burkina Faso/Ouagadougou	Jeanine E. Jackson
Burma/Rangoon	Sharon E. Villarosa
Burundi/Bujumbura	Patricia Moller
Cambodia/Phnom Penh	Joseph A. Mussomeli
Cameroon/Yaounde	R. Niles Marquardt
Canada/Ottawa	David Horton Wilkins
Cape Verde/Praia	Roger D. Pierce
Central African Republic/Bangui	James Panos
Chad/N'Djamena	Marc McGowan Wall
Chile/Santiago	Craig A. Kelly
China/Beijing	Clark T. Randt, Jr.
Colombia/Bogota	William B. Wood
Comoros/Moroni (N)	(Vacancy)
Congo, Democratic Republic of the/Kinshasa.	Roger A. Meece
Congo, Republic of the/Brazzaville.	Robert I. Weisburg
Costa Rica/San Jose	Mark Langdale
Cote d'Ivoire/Abidjan	Aubrey Hooks
Croatia/Zagreb	Robert A. Bradtke
Cuba/Havana (U.S. Interests Section).	Michael Parmly
Curacao/Willemstad	Robert E. Sorenson
Cyprus/Nicosia	Ronald L. Schlicher
Czech Republic/Prague	William J. Cabaniss, Jr.
Denmark/Copenhagen	James Cain
Djibouti, Republic of/Djibouti	Marguerita D. Ragsdale
Dominican Republic/Santo Domingo.	Hans H. Hertell
East Timor/Dili	Grover Joseph Rees III
Ecuador/Quito	Linda Jewell
Egypt/Cairo	Francis Joseph Ricciardone, Jr.
El Salvador/San Salvador	H. Douglas Barclay
Equatorial Guinea/Malabo	R. Niles Marquardt
Eritrea, State of/Asmara	Scott H. DeLisi
Estonia/Tallinn	Aldona Wos
Ethiopia/Addis Ababa	(Vacancy)
Fiji Islands, Republic of/Suva	Larry Miles Dinger
Finland/Helsinki	(Vacancy)
France/Paris	Craig Roberts Stapleton
Gabonese Republic/Libreville	R. Barrie Walkley
Gambia/Banjul	Joseph D. Stafford
Georgia/Tbilisi	John F. Tefft
Germany/Berlin	William Robert Timken, Jr.
Ghana/Accra	Pamela E. Bridgewater
Greece/Athens	Charles P. Ries
Grenada/St. George (N)	Mary Elizabeth Kramer
Guatemala/Guatemala	James M. Derham
Guinea/Conakry	Jackson C. McDonald
Guinea-Bissau/Bissau (N)	Janice Jacobs
Guyana/Georgetown	David M. Robinson
Haiti/Port-au-Prince	Janet E. Sorenson
Holy See/Vatican City	Francis Rooney
Honduras/Tegucigalpa	Charles Ford
Hong Kong/Hong Kong (C)	James B. Cunningham
Hungary/Budapest	April H. Foley
Iceland/Reykjavik	Carol Van Voorst
India/New Delhi	David C. Mulford
Indonesia/Jakarta	B. Lynn Pascoe
Iraq/Baghdad	Zalmay Khalilazad
Ireland/Dublin	James Kenny
Israel/Tel Aviv	Richard Henry Jones
Italy/Rome	Ronald Spogli
Jamaica/Kingston	Brenda La Grange Johnson
Japan/Tokyo	John Thomas Schieffer
Jerusalem (C)	Jacob Walles
Jordan/Amman	David M. Hale
Kazakhstan/Almaty	John M. Ordway
Kenya/Nairobi	William M. Bellamy
Kiribati/Tarawa (N)	Larry Miles Dinger
Korea/Seoul	Alexander R. Vershbow
Kosovo/Pristina	Philip S. Goldberg
Kuwait/Kuwait	Richard LeBaron
Kyrgyz Republic/Bishkek	Marie L. Yovanovitch
Laos/Vientiane	Patricia M. Haslach
Latvia/Riga	Catherine Todd Bailey
Lebanon/Beirut	Jeffrey D. Feltman
Lesotho/Maseru	June Carter Perry
Liberia/Monrovia	Donald E. Booth
Liechtenstein/Vaduz	Pamela Willeford
Lithuania/Vilnius	John A. Cloud
Luxembourg/Luxembourg	Ann Louise Wagner
Macedonia/Skopje	Gillian Arlette Milovanovic
Madagascar/Antananarivo	James D. McGee
Malawi/Lilongwe	Alan W. Eastham
Malaysia/Kuala Lumpur	Christopher J. LaFleur
Maldives/Male (N)	Jeffrey Lunstead
Mali/Bamako	Terence P. McCulley
Malta/Valletta	Molly Hering Bordonaro
Marshall Islands/Majuro	Greta N. Morris
Mauritania/Nouakchott	Joseph E. LeBaron
Mauritius/Port Louis	(Vacancy)
Mexico/Mexico City	Antonio O. Garza, Jr.
Micronesia/Kolonia	Suzanne K. Hale
Moldova/Chisinau	Michael D. Kirby
Mongolia/Ulaanbaatar	Mark Clements Minton
Morocco/Rabat	Thomas T. Riley
Mozambique/Maputo	Helen R. Meagher La Lime
Namibia/Windhoek	Joyce A. Barr
Nauru/Yaren (N)	Larry Miles Dinger
Nepal/Kathmandu	James Moriarty
Netherlands/The Hague	(Vacancy)
New Zealand/Wellington	William Paul McCormick
Nicaragua/Managua	Paul A. Trivelli
Niger/Niamey	(Vacancy)
Nigeria/Abuja	John Campbell
Norway/Oslo	Benson K. Withney
Oman/Muscat	Gary Grappo
Pakistan/Islamabad	Ryan Crocker
Panama/Panama	William Alan Eaton
Papua New Guinea/Port Moresby.	Robert W. Fitts
Paraguay/Asuncion	James C. Cason
Peru/Lima	James Curtis Struble
Philippines/Manila	(Vacancy)
Poland/Warsaw	Victor Henderson Ashe
Portugal/Lisbon	Alfred Hoffman
Qatar/Doha	Charles Untermeyer
Romania/Bucharest	Nicholas F. Taubman
Russian Federation/Moscow	William J. Burns
Rwanda/Kigali	Michael R. Arietti
St. Kitts and Nevis/Basseterre (N).	Mary Elizabeth Kramer
St. Lucia/Castries (N)	Mary Elizabeth Kramer
St. Vincent and the Grenadines/Kingstown (N).	Mary Elizabeth Kramer

United States Diplomatic Offices—Foreign Service—Continued

(C: Consular Office; N: No Embassy or Consular Office)

Country/Capitol	Chief of Mission
Samoa/Apia	William Paul McCormick
Sao Tome and Principe/Sao Tome (N).	R. Barrie Walkley
Saudi Arabia/Riyadh	James C. Oberwetter
Senegal/Dakar	Janice Jacobs
Serbia and Montenegro/Belgrade.	Michael Christian Polt
Seychelles/Victoria	(Vacancy)
Sierra Leone/Freetown	Thomas Neil Hull III
Singapore/Singapore	Patricia Louise Herbold
Slovak Republic/Bratislava	Rodolphe M. Vallee
Slovenia/Ljubljana	Thomas Bolling Robertson
Solomon Islands/Honiara	Robert W. Fitts
South Africa/Pretoria, Cape Town.	(Vacancy)
Spain/Madrid	Eduardo Aguirre, Jr.
Sri Lanka/Colombo	Jeffrey Lunstead
Sudan/Khartoum	Cameron Hume (charge d'affaires)
Suriname/Paramaribo	Lisa Hughes
Swaziland/Mbabane	Lewis W. Lucke
Sweden/Stockholm	Michael M. Wood
Switzerland/Bern	Pamela Willeford
Syrian Arab Republic/Damascus	Margaret Scobey
Tajikistan/Dushanbe	Richard Hoagland
Tanzania/Dar es Salaam	Michael Retzer
Thailand/Bangkok	Ralph Leo Boyce, Jr.
Togolese, Republic/Lome	David B. Dunn
Tonga/Nuku'alofa (N)	Larry Miles Dinger
Trinidad and Tobago/Port-of-Spain.	Roy Leslie Austin
Tunisia/Tunis	Robert F. Godec
Turkey/Ankara	Ross Wilson
Turkmenistan/Ashgabat	Tracey Jacobson
Tuvalu/Funafuti (N)	Larry Miles Dinger
Uganda/Kampala	Steven A. Browning
Ukraine/Kiev	William B. Taylor
United Arab Emirates/Abu Dhabi	Michele J. Sison
United Kingdom/London	Robert H. Tuttle
Uruguay/Montevideo	James D. Nealon
Uzbekistan/Tashkent	Jon Purnell
Vanuatu/Port Vila (N)	Robert W. Fitts
Venezuela/Caracas	William Brownfield
Vietnam/Hanoi	Michael W. Marine
Yemen/Sanaa	Thomas Charles Krajeski
Zambia/Lusaka	Carmen M. Martinez
Zimbabwe/Harare	Christopher W. Dell

United States Permanent Diplomatic Missions to International Organizations

Organization	Ambassador
African Union/Addis Ababa	(Vacancy)
European Union/Brussels	C. Boyden Gray
International Civil Aviation Organization.	Edward Stimpson
North Atlantic Treaty Organization/Brussels.	Victoria Nuland
Organization of American States/ Washington, DC.	John Maisto
Organization for Economic Co-operation and Development/ Paris.	Connie Morella
Organization for Security and Co-operation in Europe/Vienna.	Julie Finley
United Nations/Geneva	Kevin E. Moley
United Nations/New York	John Robert Bolton
United Nations/Vienna	Gregory L. Schulte
U.S. Mission to United Nations Agencies for Food and Agriculture.	Tony P. Hall
U.S. Mission to United Nations Economic, Scientific and Cultural Organization/Paris.	Louise V. Oliver

Sources of Information

Contracts General inquiries may be directed to the Office of Acquisitions Management (A/LM/AQM), Department of State, P.O. Box 9115, Arlington, VA 22219. Phone, 703–875–6060. Fax, 703–875–6085.

Diplomatic and Official Passports Inquirers for these types of passports should contact their respective travel offices. The U.S. Government only issues these types of passports to individuals traveling abroad in connection with official employment. For additional information, please refer to the Consular Affairs Web site at www.travel.state.gov. Internet, www.travel.state.gov.

Electronic Access The Department's Bureau of Public Affairs, Office of Public Communication, coordinates the dissemination of public electronic information for the Department. The main Web site (Internet, www.state.gov) and the Secretary's Web site (Internet, secretary.state.gov) provide comprehensive, up-to-date information on foreign policy, support for U.S. businesses and careers and the counterterrorism rewards program and much more.

The Bureau of Consular Affairs Web site (Internet, www.travel.state.gov) provides travel warnings and other information designed to help Americans travel safely abroad, as well as information on U.S. passports and visas and downloadable applications. The

Bureau of Intelligence and Research has established a geographic learning Web site (Internet, geography.state.gov), to assist in teaching geography and foreign affairs to students in grades K–12.

The State Department Electronic Reading Room at foia.state.gov uses new information technologies to enable access to unique historical records of international significance which have been made available to the public under the Freedom of Information Act or as a special collection.

Employment Inquiries about employment in the Foreign Service should be directed to HR/REE, Room H–518, 2401 E Street NW., Washington, DC 20522. Phone, 202–261–8888. Internet, www.careers.state.gov. Information about civil service positions in the Department of State and copies of civil service job announcements can be accessed through the Internet, at www.careers.state.gov. Individual questions may be directed to cspapps@state.gov. Job information staff is also available to answer questions from 8:30 a.m. to 4:30 p.m. eastern time on Federal workdays. Phone, 202–663–2176.

Freedom of Information Act and Privacy Act Requests Requests from the public for Department of State records should be addressed to the Director, Office of IRM Programs and Services, Department of State, SA–2, 515 Twenty-second Street NW., Washington, DC 20522–6001. Phone, 202–261–8300. Individuals are requested to indicate on the outside of the envelope the statute under which they are requesting access: FOIA REQUEST or PRIVACY REQUEST.

A public reading room, where unclassified and declassified documents may be inspected, is located in the Department of State, SA–2, 515 Twenty-second Street NW., Washington, DC 20522–6001. Phone, 202–261–8484. Directions to the reading room may be obtained from receptionists at public entrances to the Department.

Additional information about the Department's FOIA program can be found on the FOIA electronic reading room (Internet, foia.state.gov).

Missing Persons, Emergencies, Deaths of Americans Abroad For information concerning missing persons, emergencies, travel warnings, overseas voting, judicial assistance, and arrests or deaths of Americans abroad, contact the Office of American Citizens Services and Crisis Management, Department of State. Phone, 888–407–4747 or 317–472–2328 (international). Internet, www.travel.state.gov. Correspondence should be directed to this address: Overseas Citizens Services, Bureau of Consular Affairs, Department of State, Washington, DC 20520.

Inquiries regarding international parental child abduction or adoption of foreign children by private U.S. citizens should be directed to the Office of Children's Issues, CA/OCS/CI, Department of State, 2201 C Street NW., Washington, DC 20520–4818. Phone, 888–407–4747 or 317–472–2328 (international). Internet, www.travel.state.gov.

Passports Passport information is available through the Internet, at travel.state.gov. For recorded general passport information, contact any of the Regional Passport Agencies at the telephone numbers listed in the following table. For passport assistance and information, you may call the National Passport Information Center (phone, 900–225–5674; TDD, 900–225–7778), and you will be charged $0.35 per minute to listen to automated messages and $1.05 per minute to speak with an operator. You may also call the National Passport Information Center using a major credit card at a flat rate of $4.95 (phone, 888–362–8668; TDD, 888–498–3648). These rates are subject to change. Correspondence should be directed to the appropriate regional agency or the Correspondence Branch, Passport Services, Room 510, 1111 Nineteenth Street NW., Washington, DC 20524.

Regional Passport Agencies

City	Address	Telephone
Boston, MA	Suite 247, 10 Causeway St., 02222	617–878–0900
Charleston, SC	Bldg. 643, 1269 Holland St., 29405	843–308–5501
Chicago, IL	Suite 1803, 230 S. Dearborn St., 60604	312–341–6020
Honolulu, HI	Suite I-330, Box 50185, 300 Ala Moana Blvd., 96850	808–522–8283
Houston, TX	Suite 1400, 1919 Smith St., 77002	713–751–0294
Los Angeles, CA	Suite 1000, 11000 Wilshire Blvd., 90024	310–575–5700
Miami, FL	3d Fl., 51 SW. 1st Ave., 33130	305–539–3600
New Orleans, LA	Suite 1300, 365 Canal St., 70130	504–412–2600
New York, NY	10th Fl., 376 Hudson St., 10014	212–206–3500
Norwalk, CT	50 Washington St., 06856	203–299–5443
Philadelphia, PA	Rm. 103, 200 Chestnut St., 19106	215–418–5937
Portsmouth, NH	National Passport Center, 31 Rochester Ave., 03801	603–334–0500
San Francisco, CA	5th Fl., 95 Hawthorne St., 94105–3901	415–538–2700
Seattle, WA	Suite 992, 915 2d Ave., 98174	206–808–5700
Washington, DC	Suite 300, 1111 19th St. NW., 20524	202–647–0518

Public Affairs The Bureau of Public Affairs carries out the Secretary's foreign policy objectives and helps American and foreign audiences understand the importance of foreign affairs. Led by the Assistant Secretary, who also serves as Department spokesman, the Bureau pursues the State Department's mission to inform the American people and foreign audiences and to feed their concerns and comments back to policymakers. Phone, 202–647–6575.

Publications Publications that are produced on a regular basis include *Background Notes* and the *Foreign Relations* series. The Bureau of Public Affairs also occasionally publishes brochures and other publications to inform the public of U.S. diplomatic efforts. All publications are available on the Internet at www.state.gov.

Small Business Information Information about doing business with the Department of State is available from the Office of Small and Disadvantaged Business Utilization. Phone, 703–875–6822. Internet, www.statebuy.gov/home.htm.

Telephone Directory The Department's telephone directory is available for sale by the Superintendent of Documents, Government Printing Office, Washington, DC 20402.

Tips for U.S. Travelers Abroad The following pamphlets from the Bureau of Consular Affairs are posted on the Internet at travel.state.gov and are for sale for $1–$3 (except where noted) by the Superintendent of Documents, U.S. Government Printing Office, Washington, DC 20402:

Travel Warning on Drugs Abroad contains important facts on the potential dangers of being arrested for illegal drugs abroad and the type of assistance that U.S. consular officers can and cannot provide. This booklet is free from the Department of State, Consular Affairs/Public Affairs Staff, Room 6831, Washington, DC 20520.

Travel Tips for Older Americans contains basic information on passports, currency, health, aid for serious problems, and other useful travel tips for senior citizens.

Your Trip Abroad contains basic information on passports, vaccinations, unusual travel requirements, dual nationality, drugs, modes of travel, customs, legal requirements, and many other topics for the American tourist, business representative, or student traveling overseas.

A Safe Trip Abroad contains helpful precautions to minimize one's chances of becoming a victim of terrorism and also provides other safety tips.

Tips for Americans Residing Abroad contains advice for almost 4 million Americans living in foreign countries. These publications cost between $1.25 and $1.75 each.

Regional Tips for Travelers cover customs, currency regulations, dual nationality, and other local conditions. Currently available are publications for the following countries/regions: Canada; the Caribbean, Central and South America; Mexico; Sub-Saharan Africa;

the Middle East and North Africa; Russia; China; and South Asia and Korea.

Foreign Entry Requirements; Passports: Applying for Them the Easy Way; Advance Fee Business Scams; Travel Tips for Students; Tips for Women Traveling Alone; and *Travel Smart/Travel Safe* are available from the Consumer Information Center, Pueblo, CO 81009 (50 cents each).

Visas To obtain information on visas for foreigners wishing to enter the United States, call 202–663–1225. Internet, www.travel.state.gov.

For further information, contact the Office of Public Communication, Public Information Service, Bureau of Public Affairs, Department of State, Washington, DC 20520. Phone, 202–647–6575. Internet, www.state.gov.

DEPARTMENT OF TRANSPORTATION

400 Seventh Street SW., Washington, DC 20590
Phone, 202–366–4000. Internet, www.dot.gov.

SECRETARY OF TRANSPORTATION	NORMAN Y. MINETA
Chief of Staff	JOHN A. FLAHERTY
White House Liaison	LORI MCMAHON
Deputy Secretary	MARIA CINO
Under Secretary for Policy	JEFFREY N. SHANE
Assistant to the Secretary and Director of Public Affairs	ROBERT JOHNSON
Chairman, Board of Contract Appeals	JAMES L. STERN
Chief Information Officer	JAQUELYN PATILLO, *Acting*
Director, Executive Secretariat	J. RICHARD HENRY
Director of Civil Rights	J. MICHAEL TRUJILLO
Director of Drug and Alcohol Policy and Compliance	JOHN BOBO
Director of Small and Disadvantaged Business Utilization	JOHN BOBO, *Acting*
Advisor of Intelligence, Security, and Emergency Response	ROGER BOHNERT, *Acting*
General Counsel	JEFFREY ROSEN
Inspector General	TODD J. ZINSER, *Acting*
Assistant Secretary for Administration	LINDA J. WASHINGTON, *Acting*
Assistant Secretary for Aviation and International Affairs	MICHAEL REYNOLDS, *Acting*
Assistant Secretary for Budget and Programs and Chief Financial Officer	PHYLLIS SCHEINBERG
Assistant Secretary for Governmental Affairs	ROGER S. KARR
Assistant Secretary for Transportation Policy	TYLER DUVALL

FEDERAL AVIATION ADMINISTRATION

800 Independence Avenue SW., Washington, DC 20591
Phone, 202–366–4000. Internet, www.faa.gov.

Administrator	MARION C. BLAKEY
Deputy Administrator	ROBERT A. STURGELL
Associate Administrator for Airports	WOODIE WOODWARD
Chief Counsel	ANDREW B. STEINBERG
Chief Operating Officer, Air Traffic Organization	RUSSELL G. CHEW
Assistant Administrator for Information and Chief Information Officer	WALTER IWANOW, *Acting*
Assistant Administrator for Civil Rights	FANNY RIVERA
Associate Administrator for Commercial Space Transportation	PATRICIA GRACE SMITH

Assistant Administrator for Government and Industry Affairs	DAVID BALLOFF
Assistant Administrator for Financial Services/Chief Financial Officer	RAMESH K. PUNWANI
Assistant Administrator for Human Resource Management	VENTRIS C. GIBSON
Assistant Administrator for Policy, Planning, and Environment	SHARON L. PINKERTON
Assistant Administrator for Public Affairs	GREG MARTIN
Assistant Administrator for Region and Center Operations	RUTH A. LEVERENZ
Assistant Administrator for Security and Hazardous Materials	LYNNE A. OSMUS
Associate Administrator for Aviation Safety	NICHOLAS A. SABATINI
Assistant Administrator for International Aviation	JOSEPH BOGOSIAN

FEDERAL HIGHWAY ADMINISTRATION

400 Seventh Street SW., Washington, DC 20590
Phone, 202–366–0650. Internet, www.fhwa.dot.gov.

Administrator	J. RICHARD CAPKA, *Acting*
Deputy Administrator	J. RICHARD CAPKA
Executive Director	FREDERICK G. WRIGHT, JR.
Chief Counsel	JAMES D. RAY
Associate Administrator for Administration	MICHAEL J. VECCHIETTI
Associate Administrator for Civil Rights	FREDERICK D. ISLER
Associate Administrator for Policy	CHARLES D. NOTTINGHAM
Associate Administrator for Public Affairs	BRIAN KEETER
Associate Administrator for Professional and Corporate Development	JOSEPH S. TOOLE
Associate Administrator for Research, Development, and Technology	DENNIS C. JUDYCKI
Associate Administrator for Federal Lands Highway	ARTHUR E. HAMILTON
Associate Administrator for Infrastructure	KING W. GEE
Associate Administrator for Operations	JEFFERY F. PANIATI
Associate Administrator for Planning, Environment, and Realty	CYNTHIA J. BURBANK
Associate Administrator for Safety	(VACANCY)

FEDERAL RAILROAD ADMINISTRATION

1120 Vermont Avenue NW., Washington, DC 20590
Phone, 202–493–6000. Internet, www.fra.dot.gov.

Administrator	JOSEPH H. BOARDMAN
Deputy Administrator	CLIFFORD EBY
Associate Administrator for Congressional and Public Affairs	STEVE KLUM
Associate Administrator for Financial Management/Chief Financial Officer and Administration	PEGGY REID
Associate Administrator for Policy and Program Development	(VACANCY)

Associate Administrator for Railroad Development	MARK YACHMETZ
Associate Administrator for Safety	JO STRANG
Chief Counsel	S. MARK LINDSEY
Director, Office of Civil Rights	CARL MARTIN RUIZ

NATIONAL HIGHWAY TRAFFIC SAFETY ADMINISTRATION

400 Seventh Street SW., Washington, DC 20590
Phone, 202–366–9550. Internet, www.nhtsa.gov.

Administrator	NICOLE NASON
Senior Policy Advisor to the Administrator	(VACANCY)
Senior Advisor to the Administrator	(VACANCY)
Staff Assistant	(VACANCY)
Deputy Administrator	JACQUELINE GLASSMAN
Director of External Affairs	MICHAEL W. HARRINGTON
Chief Counsel	(VACANCY)
Director, Office of Civil Rights	GEORGE B. QUICK
Director, Executive Correspondence	TAMMIE O. WHITE
Senior Associate Administrator for Policy and Operations	GREGORY WALTER
Associate Administrator for Administration	(VACANCY)
Associate Administrator for Plans, Evaluation and Budget	(VACANCY)
Director, Communications and Consumer Information	SUSAN GORCOWSKI
Chief Information Officer	MARGARET O'BRIEN
Director, National Center for Statistics and Analysis	JOSEPH CARA
Senior Associate Administrator for Traffic Injury Control	BRIAN MCLAUGHLIN
Associate Administrator for Program Development and Delivery	MARILENA AMONI
Associate Administrator for Injury Control Operations and Resources	MARLENE MARKISON
Senior Associate Administrator for Vehicle Safety	RONALD MEDFORD
Associate Administrator for Rulemaking	STEPHEN R. KRATZKE
Associate Administrator for Enforcement	DANIEL SMITH
Associate Administrator for Applied Vehicle Safety Research	JOSEPH KANIANTHRA

FEDERAL TRANSIT ADMINISTRATION

400 Seventh Street SW., Washington, DC 20590
Phone, 202–366–4043. Internet, www.fta.dot.gov.

Administrator	(VACANCY)
Deputy Administrator	SANDRA BUSHUE
Associate Administrator for Administration	RITA WELLS
Associate Administrator for Budget and Policy	ROBERT J. TUCCILLO
Associate Administrator for Planning	(VACANCY)
Associate Administrator for Program Management	SUSAN E. SCHRUTH

Associate Administrator for Research, Demonstration, and Innovation	BARBARA A. SISSON
Chief Counsel	DAVID HORNER
Director, Office of Civil Rights	MICHAEL A. WINTER
Director, Office of Public Affairs	JOHN IRVIN

MARITIME ADMINISTRATION

400 Seventh Street SW., Washington, DC 20590
Phone, 202–366–5807. Internet, www.marad.dot.gov.

Administrator	(VACANCY)
Deputy Administrator for Inland Waterways and Great Lakes	(VACANCY)
Deputy Administrator	JULIE A. NELSON, *Acting*
Associate Administrator for Administration	EILEEN ROBDERSON
Associate Administrator for Policy and International Trade	BRUCE J. CARLTON
Associate Administrator for National Security	JAMES E. CAPONITI
Associate Administrator for Port, Intermodal, and Environmental Activities	MARGARET D. BLUM
Associate Administrator for Shipbuilding	JEAN E. MCKEEVER
Associate Administrator for Financial Approvals and Cargo Preference	JAMES J. ZOK
Chief Counsel	JULIE A. BELSON
Director of Congressional and Public Affairs	SHANNON M. RUSSELL
Director, Office of Maritime Labor, Training, and Safety	TAYLOR E. JONES II
Secretary, Maritime Administration/ Maritime Subsidy Board	JOEL C. RICHARD
Superintendent, United States Merchant Marine Academy	JOSEPH D. STEWART

SAINT LAWRENCE SEAWAY DEVELOPMENT CORPORATION

400 Seventh Street SW., Washington, DC 20590
Phone, 202–366–0091; 800–785–2779 (toll free). Fax, 202–366–7147. Internet, www.seaway.dot.gov.

180 Andrews Street, Massena, NY 13662
Phone, 315–764–3200

Administrator	ALBERT S. JACQUEZ
Deputy Administrator	CRAIG H. MIDDLEBROOK
Chief of Staff	ANITA K. BLACKMAN
Chief Counsel	(VACANCY)
Director of Trade Development and Congressional and Public Affairs	REBECCA A. MCGILL
Director of Budget, Strategic Planning, and Information Technology	KEVIN P. O'MALLEY
Associate Administrator	SALVATORE L. PISANI
Deputy Associate Administrator	CAROL A. FENTON
Director of Financial Management and Administration	MARY ANN HAZEL

Director of Engineering	THOMAS A. LAVIGNE
Chief Financial Officer	EDWARD MARGOSIAN
Director of Lock Operations and Marine Services	LORI K. CURRAN
Director of Maintenance	JESSE HINOJOSA

PIPELINE AND HAZARDOUS MATERIALS SAFETY ADMINISTRATION

400 Seventh Street SW., Washington, DC 20590
Phone, 202–366–4433. Internet, www.phmsa.dot.gov.

Administrator	THOMAS J. BARRETT
Deputy Administrator	ERIC PETERSON
Assistant Administrator/Chief Safety Officer	STACEY GERARD, *Acting*
Chief Counsel	JOSEPH AHERN, *Acting*
Director, Office of Civil Rights	HELEN HAGIN
Associate Administrator for Management and Administration	EDWARD A. BRIGHAM
Associate Administrator for Pipeline Safety	STACEY GERARD
Associate Administrator for Hazardous Materials Safety	ROBERT A. MCGUIRE
Director, Office of Government, International, and Public Affairs	JAMES WIGGINS

RESEARCH AND INNOVATIVE TECHNOLOGY ADMINISTRATION

400 Seventh Street SW., Washington, DC 20590
Phone, 202–366–7582. Internet, www.rita.dot.gov. E-mail, info.rita@dot.gov.

Administrator	ASHOK G. KAVEESHWAR
Deputy Administrator	ERIC PETERSON
Chief Counsel	VICTORIA SUTTON
Deputy Chief Counsel	ROBERT MONNIERE
Associate Administrator, Office of Government, International and Public Affairs	PAUL FEENSTRA
Associate Administrator for Administraton	MARIE SAVOY, *Acting*
Public Affairs Contact	ROGER LOTZ
Associate Administrator for Research, Development and Technology	RICHARD BITER, *Acting*
Director, Bureau of Transportation Statistics	(VACANCY)
Deputy Director, Bureau of Transportation Statistics	MARY HUTZLER, *Acting*
Director, Volpe National Transportation Systems Center	CURTIS TOMPKINS
Director, Transportation Safety Institute	FRANK TUPPER

FEDERAL MOTOR CARRIER SAFETY ADMINISTRATION

400 Seventh Street, SW., Washington, DC 20590
Phone, 202–366–2519. Internet, www.fmcsa.dot.gov.

Administrator	(VACANCY)
Deputy Administrator	WARREN E. HOEMANN
Assistant Administrator (Chief Safety Officer)	JOHN H. HILL
Associate Administrator for Administration	D. MARLENE THOMPSON

Associate Administrator for Enforcement and Program Delivery	WILLIAM PADEN
Associate Administrator for Research, Technology, and Information Management	TERRY SHELTON
Associate Administrator for Policy and Program Development	ROSE A. MCMURRAY
Chief Counsel	SUZANNE TEBEAU
Director, Office of Civil Rights	KENNIE MAY
Director, Office of Communications	IAN GROSSMAN

SURFACE TRANSPORTATION BOARD

1925 K Street NW., Washington, DC 20423–0001
Phone, 202–565–1500

Chairman	ROGER NOBER
Vice Chairman	W. DOUGLAS BUTTERY
Commissioner	FRANCIS MULVEY
Director, Office of Compliance and Enforcement	MELVIN F. CLEMENS, JR.
Director, Office of Congressional and Public Services	DAN G. KING
Director, Office of Economics, Environmental Analysis, and Administration	LELAND L. GARDNER
Director, Office of Proceedings	DAVID M. KONSCHNIK
General Counsel	ELLEN D. HANSON
Secretary	VERNON A. WILLIAMS

[For the Department of Transportation statement of organization, see the *Code of Federal Regulations,* Title 49, Part 1, Subpart A]

The U.S. Department of Transportation establishes the Nation's overall transportation policy. Under its umbrella are 11 administrations whose jurisdictions include highway planning, development, and construction; motor carrier safety; urban mass transit; railroads; aviation; and the safety of waterways, ports, highways, and oil and gas pipelines. Decisions made by the Department in conjunction with the appropriate State and local officials strongly affect other programs such as land planning, energy conservation, scarce resource utilization, and technological change.

The Department of Transportation (DOT) was established by act of October 15, 1966, as amended (49 U.S.C. 102 and 102 note), "to assure the coordinated, effective administration of the transportation programs of the Federal Government" and to develop "national transportation policies and programs conducive to the provision of fast, safe, efficient, and convenient transportation at the lowest cost consistent therewith." It became operational in April 1967 and was comprised of elements transferred from eight other major departments and agencies.

Secretary The Department of Transportation is administered by the Secretary of Transportation, who is the principal adviser to the President in all matters relating to Federal transportation programs.

Aviation and International Affairs The Office of the Assistant Secretary for Aviation and International Affairs has principal responsibility for the development, review, and coordination of policy for international transportation, and for development, coordination, and implementation of policy relating to

DEPARTMENT OF TRANSPORTATION

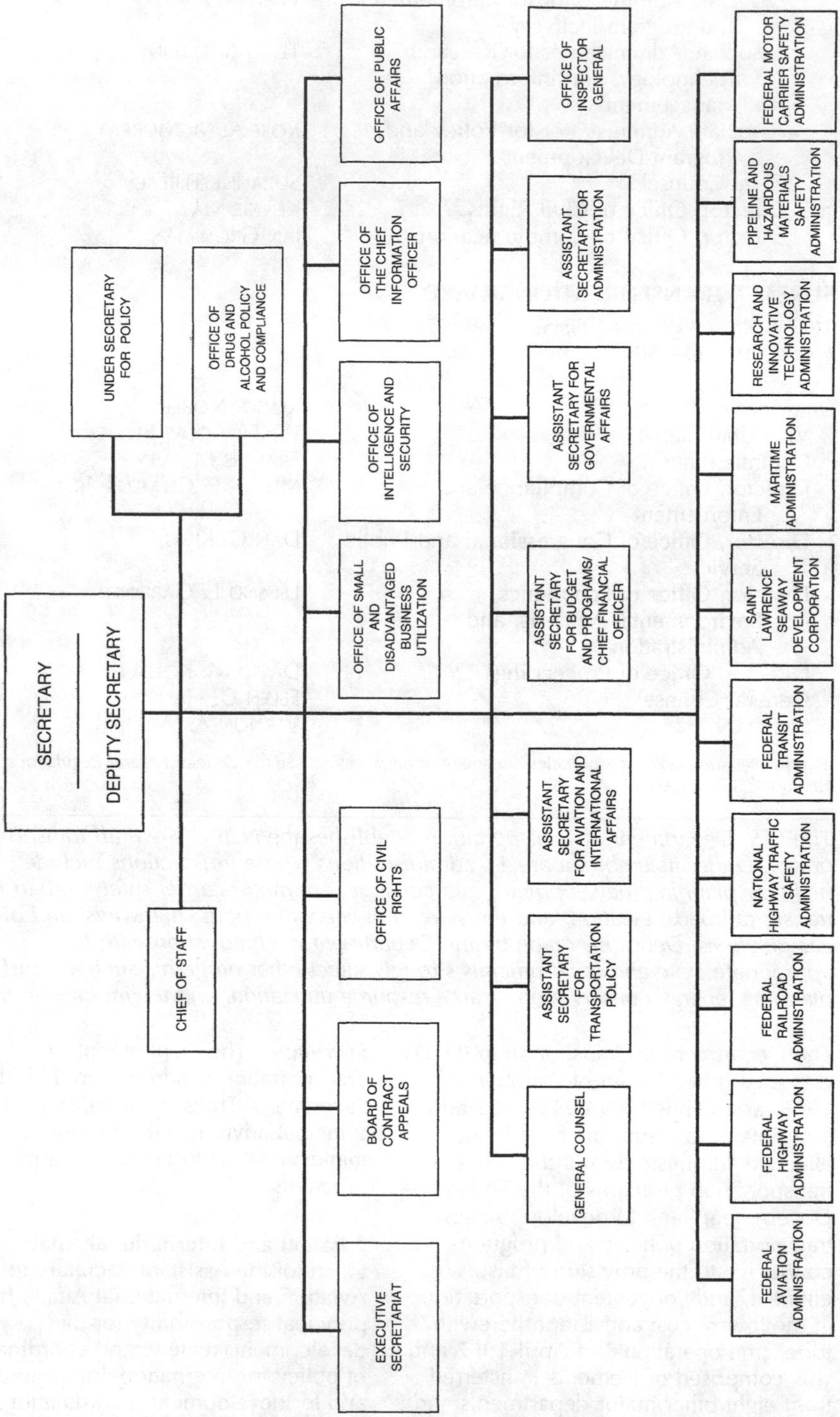

economic regulation of the airline industry. The Office:

—licenses U.S. and foreign carriers to serve in international air transportation and conducts carrier fitness determinations for carriers serving the United States;

—develops policies to support the Department in aviation and maritime multilateral and bilateral negotiations with foreign governments and participates on the U.S. negotiating delegations;

—develops policies on a wide range of international transportation and trade matters;

—arranges and coordinates cooperative agreements with foreign governments for the exchange of state-of-the-art scientific and technical information;

—processes and resolves complaints concerning unfair competitive practices in domestic and international air transportation;

—establishes international and intra-Alaska mail rates;

—determines the disposition of requests for approval and immunization from the antitrust laws of international aviation agreements; and

—administers the essential air service program.

For further information, call 202–366–8822.

Drug and Alcohol Policy and Compliance The Office ensures that the national and international drug and alcohol policies and goals of the Secretary are developed and carried out in a consistent, efficient, and effective manner within the transportation industries. The Office provides expert advice, counsel, and recommendations to the Secretary regarding drugs and alcohol as it pertains to the Department of Transportation and testing within the transportation industry.

For further information, contact the Office of Drug and Alcohol Policy and Compliance. Phone, 202–366–3784.

Intelligence and Security The Office advises the Secretary on domestic and international intelligence and security matters; coordinates the development and implementation of long-term strategic plans, information management systems, and integrated research and development programs affecting the security of the traveling public and cargo; serves as the focal point in the Department for intelligence and security policy, weapons of mass destruction, critical infrastructure protection, and drug and illegal immigrant interdiction effects on transportation systems; and provides oversight of transportation security and intelligence programs.

For further information, contact the Office of Intelligence and Security. Phone, 202–366–6525.

Transportation Policy The Office of the Assistant Secretary for Transportation Policy has principal responsibility for analysis, development, articulation, and review of policies and plans for all modes of transportation. The Office:

—develops, coordinates, and evaluates public policy related to the transportation industries, and maintains policy and economic oversight of regulatory programs and legislative initiatives of the Department;

—reviews transportation matters involving the public and private sectors, analyzes current and emerging transportation policy issues, and assesses their economic and institutional implications;

—provides departmental policy leadership and coordination on safety, energy, and environmental initiatives which affect air, surface, marine, and pipeline transportation; and

—provides leadership on questions involving the financing of transportation infrastructure projects, and provides economic analyses of new transportation technologies; and

—coordinates the development of intermodal transportation solutions that move people and goods in an energy-efficient manner, provide the foundation for improved productivity growth, strengthen the Nation's ability to compete in the global economy, and obtain the optimum yield from the Nation's transportation resources.

For further information, contact the Office of Transportation Policy. Phone, 202–366–4416.

Federal Aviation Administration

The Federal Aviation Administration (FAA), formerly the Federal Aviation Agency, was established by the Federal Aviation Act of 1958. The agency became a component of the Department of Transportation in 1967 pursuant to the Department of Transportation Act (49 U.S.C. 106). The mission of the Federal Aviation Administration involves safety considerations and activities in the public interest, including:

—assigning, maintaining, and enhancing safety and security as the highest priorities in air commerce;

—regulating air commerce in a way that best promotes safety and fulfills national defense requirements;

—encouraging and developing civil aeronautics, including new aviation technology;

—controlling the use of the navigable airspace and regulating civil and military operations in that airspace in the interest of safety and efficiency of both of those operations;

—consolidating research and development for air navigation facilities and the installation and operation of those facilities;

—developing and operating a common system of air traffic control and navigation for military and civil aircraft;

—providing assistance to law enforcement agencies in the enforcement of laws related to regulation of controlled substances, to the extent consistent with aviation safety;

—developing and implementing a program to solve the aircraft noise and sonic boom problem; and

—regulating U.S. commercial space transportation.

Activities

Air Navigation Facilities The agency is responsible for the location, construction or installation, maintenance, operation, and quality assurance of Federal visual and electronic aids to air navigation. The agency operates and maintains voice/data communications equipment, radar facilities, computer systems, and visual display equipment at flight service stations, airport traffic control towers, and air route traffic control centers.

Airport Programs The agency maintains a national plan of airport requirements, administers a grant program for development of public use airports to assure and improve safety and to meet current and future airport capacity needs, evaluates the environmental impacts of airport development, and administers an airport noise compatibility program with the goal of reducing noncompatible uses around airports. It also develops standards and technical guidance on airport planning, design, safety, and operations and provides grants to assist public agencies in airport system and master planning and airport development and improvement.

Airspace and Air Traffic Management The safe and efficient utilization of the navigable airspace is a primary objective of the agency. To meet this objective, it operates a network of airport traffic control towers, air route traffic control centers, and flight service stations. It develops air traffic rules and regulations and allocates the use of the airspace. It also provides for the security control of air traffic to meet national defense requirements.

Civil Aviation Abroad Under the Federal Aviation Act of 1958 and the International Aviation Facilities Act (49 U.S.C. app. 1151), the agency encourages aviation safety and civil aviation abroad by exchanging aeronautical information with foreign aviation authorities; certifying foreign repair stations, airmen, and mechanics; negotiating bilateral airworthiness agreements to facilitate the import and export of aircraft and components; and providing technical assistance and training in all areas of the agency's expertise. It provides technical representation at international conferences, including participation in the International Civil Aviation Organization and other international organizations.

Commercial Space Transportation The agency regulates and encourages the U.S. commercial space transportation industry. It licenses the private sector launching of space payloads on expendable launch vehicles and commercial space launch facilities. It also sets insurance requirements for the protection of persons and property and ensures that space transportation activities comply with U.S. domestic and foreign policy.

Registration The agency provides a system for registering aircraft and recording documents affecting title or interest in the aircraft, aircraft engines, propellers, appliances, and spare parts.

Research, Engineering, and Development The research, engineering, and development activities of the agency are directed toward providing the systems, procedures, facilities, and devices needed for a safe and efficient system of air navigation and air traffic control to meet the needs of civil aviation and the air defense system. The agency also performs an aeromedical research function to apply knowledge gained from its research program and the work of others to the safety and promotion of civil aviation and the health, safety, and efficiency of agency employees. The agency also supports development and testing of improved aircraft, engines, propellers, and appliances.

Safety Regulation The Administration issues and enforces rules, regulations, and minimum standards relating to the manufacture, operation, and maintenance of aircraft, as well as the rating and certification (including medical) of airmen and the certification of airports serving air carriers. It performs flight inspection of air navigation facilities in the U.S. and, as required, abroad.

Test and Evaluation The agency conducts tests and evaluations of specified items such as aviation systems, subsystems, equipment, devices, materials, concepts, or procedures at any phase in the cycle of their development from conception to acceptance and implementation, as well as assigned independent testing at key decision points.

Other Programs The agency administers the aviation insurance program. It is an allotting agency under the defense materials system with respect to priorities and allocation for civil aircraft and civil aviation operations. The agency develops specifications for the preparation of aeronautical charts. It publishes current information on airways and airport service and issues technical publications for the improvement of safety in flight, airport planning and design, and other aeronautical activities. It serves as the executive administration for the operation and maintenance of the Department of Transportation automated payroll and personnel systems.

Major Field Organizations—Federal Aviation Administration

Region/Field Office	Address	Administrator/Director
Alaskan—AK	No. 14, 222 W. 7th Ave., Anchorage, AK 99513	Patrick N. Poe
Central—IA, KS, MO, NE	901 Locust, Kansas City, MO 64106	Christopher Blum
Eastern—DE, MD, NJ, NY, PA, VA, WV	1 Aviation Plz., Jamaica, NY 11434	Arlene B. Feldman
Great Lakes—IL, IN, MI, MN, ND, OH, SD, WI	2300 E. Devon Ave., Des Plaines, IL 60018	Christopher Blum, *Acting*
New England—CT, MA, ME, NH, RI, VT	12 New England Executive Park, Burlington, MA 01803	Amy Lind Corbett
Northwest Mountain—CO, ID, MT, OR, UT, WA, WY	1601 Lind Ave. SW., Renton, WA 98055	Douglas R. Murphy
Southern—AL, FL, GA, KY, MS, NC, PR, SC, TN	1701 Columbia Ave., College Park, GA 30337	Carolyn C. Blum
Southwest—AR, LA, NM, OK, TX	2601 Meacham Blvd., Fort Worth, TX 76137–4298	Ava L. Wilkerson
Western-Pacific—AZ, CA, HI, NV	15000 Aviation Blvd., Hawthorne, CA 90261	William C. Withycombe
Europe, Africa, and Middle East	15, Rue de la Loi B–1040, Brussels, Belgium	Paul Feldman
Asia-Pacific	U.S. Embassy, FAA, Singapore	Elizabeth E. Erickson
Latin America-Caribbean	8600 NW. 36th St., Miami, FL 33166	Joaquin Archilla
William J. Hughes Technical Center	Atlantic City, NJ 08405	Anne Harlan
Mike Monroney Aeronautical Center	6500 S. MacArthur, Oklahoma City, OK 73125	Lindy Ritz

For further information, contact the Office of Public Affairs, Federal Aviation Administration, Department of Transportation, 800 Independence Avenue SW., Washington, DC 20591. Phone, 202–267–3883. Fax, 202–267–5039.

Federal Highway Administration

The Federal Highway Administration (FHWA) was established as an agency of the Department of Transportation by the Department of Transportation Act (49 U.S.C. 104). It administers the Department's highway transportation programs. The Administration is responsible for:

—carrying out the Federal-aid highway program, in partnership with State transportation departments and metropolitan planning organizations, local governments, and the private sector;

—providing grants to assist State departments of transportation and metropolitan planning organizations in developing statewide and metropolitan intermodal transportation plans and programs;

—providing technical support grants to States for safety activities;

—working with other Federal agencies to design and build roads in national forests, parks, wildlife refuges, and Indian reservations; and

—cooperating with foreign governments through technology exchange and technical assistance.

FHWA administers programs for:

—planning, preserving, improving, and expanding the surface transportation system and enhancing its safety;

—providing national leadership for the operations, efficiency, and intermodal integration for the surface transportation system;

—providing technical training and professional development programs to public and private transportation entities;

—providing innovative and effective research and development and developing means to market and deploy this technology;

—providing oversight and accountability for public resources and ensuring appropriate uniformity;

—providing for efficient and safe freight and passenger mobility to strengthen economic and social linkages;

—protecting and enhancing the environment;

—improving highway-related aspects of surface transportation safety in coordination with the other DOT operating administrations; and

—enhancing overall transportation safety by addressing the FHWA's "vital few" priorities, i.e., safety, environmental stewardship and streamlining, and congestion mitigation.

Activities

Infrastructure The Administration manages the majority of the Federal-aid programs and engineering policies and standards, and provides technical expertise and assistance relating to the design, construction, and maintenance of the Nation's highways, pavements, bridges, tunnels, hydraulic/geotechnical structures, and other related engineering activities.

Federal Lands Programs The Administration manages the Federal lands highway program, the emergency relief program for federally owned roads, and the defense access roads program. It also provides transportation services, planning, design, procurement, and construction oversight to Federal agencies, serves as an advocate for safe public access to Federal and Indian lands, and develops and disseminates technology relative to transportation access to Federal and Indian lands. The Federal lands highway program is administered by three division offices.

Field Operations FHWA's field structure is comprised of a resource center operating out of four locations. The resource center provides specialized program expertise and support to the 52 State-level division offices. The division offices provide Federal-aid program assistance to partners and customers in highway transportation and safety services, including planning and research, preliminary engineering, technology transfer, right-of-way, bridges, highway safety, traffic operations, environment, civil rights, design, construction and maintenance, engineering coordination, highway beautification, and management.

Field Offices—Federal Highway Administration

Office	Address	Manager or Equivalent	Telephone
	Resource Centers		
Baltimore, MD	Suite 4000, 10 S. Howard St., 21201–2819	Joyce A. Curtis	410–962–0093
Olympia Fields, IL	Suite 301, 19900 Governors Dr., 60461–1021	William R. Gary White	708–283–3510
Atlanta, GA	Suite 17T26, 61 Forsyth St. SW., 30303–3104	Garrett Corino	404–562–3570
San Francisco, CA	Suite 2100, 201 Mission St., 94105	William R. Gary White, *Acting*	415–744–3102
	Metropolitan Offices		
Los Angeles, CA	Suite 1850, 888 S. Figueroa St., 90017–5467	Sandra Balmir	213–202–3950
Chicago, IL	Rm. 320, 200 W. Adams, 60606–5232	Steven Call	312–886–1616
New York, NY	Rm. 428, 1 Bowling Green, 10004–1415	Arthur O'Connor	212–668–2206
Philadelphia	Suite 900, 1760 Market St., 19103	Carmine Fiscina	215–656–7070
	Federal Lands Highway Divisions		
Central	Suite 390, 12300 W. Dakota Ave., Lakewood, CO 80228–1010	Larry C. Smith	702–963–3500
Eastern	Loudoun Tech. Ctr., 21400 Ridgetop Cir., Sterling, VA 20166–6511	Melissa L. Ridenour	703–404–6201
Western	610 E. 5th St., Vancouver, WA 98661–3801	Ronald W. Carmichael	360–619–7700

For further information, contact the Department of Transportation, Federal Highway Administration, Office of Information and Management Services, 400 Seventh Street SW., Washington, DC 20590. Phone, 202–366–0534.

Federal Railroad Administration

The Federal Railroad Administration was created pursuant to section 3(e)(1) of the Department of Transportation Act of 1966 (49 U.S.C. 103). The purpose of the Administration is to promulgate and enforce rail safety regulations, administer railroad financial assistance programs, conduct research and development in support of improved railroad safety and national rail transportation policy, provide for the rehabilitation of Northeast Corridor rail passenger service, and consolidate government support of rail transportation activities.

Activities

Passenger and Freight Services The Administration oversees and provides financial assistance to Amtrak and administers financial assistance programs to demonstrate high-speed rail technology, to reduce grade crossing hazards in high-speed rail corridors, to provide for investments in small freight railroads and other rail projects, to plan for high-speed rail projects, and to plan and deploy magnetic levitation technology.

Railroad Safety The Administration administers and enforces the Federal laws and related regulations designed to promote safety on railroads; exercises jurisdiction over all areas of rail safety under the Rail Safety Act of 1970, such as track maintenance, inspection standards, equipment standards, and operating practices. Railroad and related industry equipment, facilities, and records are inspected and required reports reviewed. In addition, the administration educates the public about safety at highway-rail grade crossings and the danger of trespassing on rail property.

Research and Development The Administration's ground transportation research and development program seeks to advance all aspects of intercity ground transportation and railroad safety pertaining to the physical sciences and engineering, in order to improve railroad safety and ensure that railroads continue to be a viable national transportation resource.

Transportation Test Center FRA tests and evaluates conventional and advanced railroad systems and components at the Transportation Test Center near Pueblo, CO. Private sector companies and the Governments of the United States, Canada, and Japan use the facility to explore the operation of conventional and advanced systems under controlled conditions. It is used by Amtrak for the testing of new high-speed locomotives and trains and by the Federal Transit Administration for testing urban rapid transit vehicles.

For further information, contact the Transportation Technology Center, Pueblo, CO 81001. Phone, 719–584–0507.

Major Field Organizations—Federal Railroad Administration

Region	Address	Administrator	Telephone
Northeastern—CT, MA, ME, NH, NJ, NY, RI, VT	Rm. 1077, 55 Broadway, Cambridge, MA 02142	Mark H. McKeon	617–494–2302
Eastern—DC, DE, MA, OH, PA, VA, WV	Suite 550, 2 International Plz., Philadelphia, PA 19113	David R. Myers	610–521–8200
Southern—AL, FL, GA, KY, MS, NC, SC, TN	Suite 16T20, 61 Forsyth St. SW., Atlanta, GA 30303–3104	Fred Dennin II	404–562–3800
Central—IL, IN, MI, MN, WI	Suite 310, 200 W. Adam St., Chicago, IL 60606	Laurence A. Hasvold	312–353–6203
Southwestern—AR, LA, NM, OK, TX	Suite 450, 4100 International Plz., Fort Worth, TX, 76109–4820	Bonnie Murphy	817–862–2200
Midwestern—CO, IA, KS, MO, NE	Suite 464, 901 Locust St., Kansas City, MO 64106	Darrell J. Tisor	816–392–3840
Western—AZ, CA, NV, UT	Suite 466, 801 I St., Sacramento, CA 95814	Alvin Settje	916–498–6540
Northwestern—AK, ID, MT, ND, OR, SD, WA, WY	Suite 650, 703 Broadway, Vancouver, WA 98660	Dave Brooks	360–696–7536

For further information, contact the Office of Congressional and Public Affairs, Federal Railroad Administration, Department of Transportation, 1120 Vermont Avenue NW., Washington, DC 20590. Phone, 202–493–6024. Internet, www.fra.dot.gov.

National Highway Traffic Safety Administration

[For the National Highway Traffic Safety Administration statement of organization, see the *Code of Federal Regulations,* Title 49, Part 501]

The National Highway Traffic Safety Administration (NHTSA) was established by the Highway Safety Act of 1970 (23 U.S.C. 401 note) to help reduce the mounting number of deaths, injuries, and economic losses resulting from motor vehicle crashes on the Nation's highways.

The Administration carries out programs relating to the safety performance of motor vehicles and related equipment; administers the Nation's State and community highway safety program (administered jointly with the Federal Highway Administration); carries out the National Driver Register (NDR) Program to facilitate the interstate exchange of State records on problem drivers; conducts studies and operates programs aimed at reducing economic losses in motor vehicle crashes and repairs through general motor vehicle programs; administers the corporate average fuel economy program; administers the Federal odometer law; and issues theft prevention standards for passenger and nonpassenger motor vehicles.

Activities

Research and Development The Administration provides a foundation for the development of motor vehicle and highway safety program standards by researching, developing, testing, and evaluating motor vehicles, motor vehicle equipment, and advanced technologies, and collecting and analyzing crash data.

The research program covers numerous areas affecting safety problems and includes providing laboratory testing facilities to obtain necessary basic data. The objectives are to encourage industry to adopt advanced motor vehicle safety designs, stimulate public awareness of safety potentials, and provide a base for vehicle safety information.

The Administration maintains a collection of scientific and technical information related to motor vehicle safety, and operates the National Center for Statistics and Analysis, whose activities include the development and maintenance of highway crash data collection systems and related analysis efforts. These comprehensive motor vehicle safety information resources serve as documentary reference points for Federal, State, and local agencies, as well as industry, universities, and the public.

Safety Assurance The Office of Safety Assurance identifies and investigates problems with motor vehicles and motor vehicle equipment. If the Office determines that the vehicle or item of equipment contains a defect which is safety related or that it does not meet all applicable Federal motor vehicle safety standards, the Office will seek a recall in which owners are notified and the vehicles or equipment are remedied free of charge. The Office monitors recalls to ensure that owners are being notified, that the notifications are done in a timely manner, and that the scope of the recall and the remedy are adequate to correct the problem.

The Office operates the toll-free auto safety hotline to identify safety problems in motor vehicles and motor vehicle equipment. Consumers can call the hotline (phone, 888–DASH–2–DOT, or 888–327–4236; TDD, 800–424–9153, or 202–366–7800 in the Washington, DC, area) 24 hours a day, 7 days a week, to report safety-related problems. English- and Spanish-speaking representatives are available between 8 a.m. and 10 p.m. eastern standard time, Monday through Friday, except Federal holidays. Consumers can also reach the hotline via the Internet at www.nhtsa.dot.gov/hotline. These calls form the basis for investigations and, ultimately, recalls if safety-related defects are identified. The hotline also provides information and literature to consumers about vehicle and child-seat recalls, New Car Assessment Program test results, and a variety of other highway safety information.

Safety Performance Standards The Administration manages motor vehicle safety programs to reduce the occurrence of highway crashes and the severity of resulting injuries; reduce the economic losses in crashes; and provide consumer information in the areas of crash test results, rollover resistance, proper usage of vehicle safety features, and tire grading for treadwear, temperature resistance, and traction.

The Administration issues Federal motor vehicle safety standards that prescribe safety features and levels of safety-related performance for vehicles and items of motor vehicle equipment. It conducts the New Car Assessment Program, under which high-speed crash tests are conducted on passenger cars, light trucks, and vans to assess their frontal and side impact safety performance; separate tests are conducted to assess the vehicles' resistance to rollovers. Results from these tests are provided to the public to assist them in selecting and purchasing safer motor vehicles. The Administration also informs consumers on how to properly use vehicle safety features. It manages a fuel economy program that establishes and revises fleet average fuel economy standards for passenger car and light truck manufacturers to ensure that maximum feasible fuel economy is attained. The Administration also carries out a theft program, issuing rules requiring the designation of likely high-theft vehicles that must comply with parts-marking requirements, and calculating and publishing annual motor vehicle theft rates.

State and Community Services The Administration administers approximately $2.3 billion in State highway safety grant programs, authorized by the Transportation Equity Act for the 21st Century. The State and Community Highway Safety formula grant program provides funds to the States, Indian nations, and the territories each year to support safety programs, particularly in the following national priority program areas: occupant protection, impaired driving, police traffic services, emergency medical services, data/traffic records, motorcycle safety, pedestrian and bicycle safety, speed control, and roadway safety. Incentive grant programs are also used to encourage States to implement effective impaired driving, occupant protection, and data improvement programs.

Traffic Safety Programs The Administration leads the national traffic safety and emergency services efforts in order to save lives, reduce injuries, and lessen medical and other costs. In accomplishing these tasks, it utilizes behavioral research, demonstration, and evaluation, in addition to developing safety programs and strategies, for use by a variety of public and private agencies and organizations. The Administration maintains a national register of information on individuals whose licenses to operate a motor vehicle have been revoked, suspended, canceled, or denied; or who have been convicted of certain traffic-related violations such as driving while impaired by alcohol or other drugs. The information obtained from the register assists State driver licensing officials in determining whether or not to issue a license.

Regional Offices—National Highway Traffic Safety Administration

Region/Address	Administrator
Atlanta, GA (Rm. 17T30, 61 Forsyth St. SW., 30303–3104)	Terrance D. Schiavone
Baltimore, MD (Suite 6700, 10 S. Howard St., 21201)	Elizabeth A. Baker
Cambridge, MA (55 Broadway, Kendall Sq., Code 903, 02142)	Philip J. Weiser
Fort Worth, TX (Rm. 8a38, 819 Taylor St., 76102–6177)	Georgia S. Chakiris
Kansas City, MO (466 Locust St., 64106)	Romell W. Cooks
Lakewood, CO (Rm 430, 555 Zang St., 80228)	Bill Watada
Olympia Fields, IL (Suite 201, 19900 Governors Dr., 60461)	Donald J. McNamara
San Francisco, CA (Suite 2230, 201 Mission St., 94105)	David Manning
Seattle, WA 98174 (3140 Jackson Federal Bldg., 915 2d Ave., 98174)	Curtis A. Winston
White Plains, NY (Suite 204, 222 Mamaroneck Ave., 10605)	Thomas M. Louizou

For further information, contact the Office of Public and Consumer Affairs, National Highway Traffic Safety Administration, Department of Transportation, 400 Seventh Street SW., Washington, DC 20590. Phone, 202–366–9550. Internet, www.nhtsa.dot.gov.

Federal Transit Administration

[For the Federal Transit Administration statement of organization, see the *Code of Federal Regulations,* Title 49, Part 601]

The Federal Transit Administration (FTA) (formerly the Urban Mass Transportation Administration) was established as an operating administration of the Department of Transportation by section 1 of Reorganization Plan No. 2 of 1968 (5 U.S.C. app. 1), effective July 1, 1968. The missions of the Administration are:

—to assist in developing improved mass transportation equipment, facilities, techniques, and methods with the cooperation of public and private mass transportation companies;

—to encourage the planning and establishment of areawide mass transportation systems needed for economical and desirable development with the cooperation of public and private mass transportation companies;

—to assist State and local governments and their authorities in financing areawide mass transportation systems that are to be operated by public or private mass transportation companies as decided by local needs;

—to provide financial assistance to State and local governments and their authorities to help carry out national goals related to mobility for elderly individuals, individuals with disabilities, and economically disadvantaged individuals; and

—to establish a partnership that allows a community, with financial assistance from the Government, to satisfy its mass transportation requirements.

Programs

Capital Investment Grants are authorized to assist in financing the acquisition, construction, reconstruction, and improvement of facilities and equipment for use in mass transportation service in urban areas. There are three categories of funds available under the capital investment program: fixed guideway modernization, rolling stock renewal, safety-related improvements, and signal and power modernization; new starts funds for construction of new fixed guideway service; and bus funds for acquiring buses and rolling stock, ancillary equipment, and the construction of bus facilities.

For further information, call 202–366–2053.

Elderly and Persons With Disabilities The program provides financial assistance to private nonprofit agencies to meet the transportation needs of elderly persons and persons with disabilities where services provided by public operators are unavailable, insufficient, or inappropriate; to public bodies approved by the State to coordinate services for elderly persons or persons with disabilities; or to public bodies which certify to the Governor that no nonprofit corporation or association is readily available in an area to provide the service. Funds are allocated by formula to the States. Local organizations apply for funding through a designated State agency.

For further information, call 202–366–2053.

Job Access and Reverse Commute Grants The program makes funding available to public agencies and nonprofit organizations to pay the capital and operating costs of delivering new or expanded job access or reverse commute services, and to promote the use of transit during non-traditional work hours, as well as encourage employer-based transportation strategies and use of transit pass programs. The program provides competitive grants for two kinds of projects:

—job access projects implementing new or expanded transportation services for transporting welfare recipients and low-income persons to and from jobs and needed employment support services such as child care; and

—reverse commute projects implementing new or expanded general-purpose public transportation services to transport residents of urban, rural, and suburban areas to suburban employment centers.

For further information, call 202–366–0176. Internet, www.fta.dot.gov/wtw.

Non-Urbanized Area Assistance The Administration provides capital and operating assistance for public transportation in non-urbanized areas. Funds are allocated to the Governor, and the program is administered at the State level by the designated transportation agency. Assistance is provided for planning, administrative, and program development activities; coordination of public transportation programs; vehicle acquisition; and other capital investments in support of transit services tailored to the needs of elderly individuals and individuals with disabilities and other individuals who depend upon transit for their basic mobility.

Planning The program provides financial assistance in meeting the transportation planning needs of metropolitan planning organizations by allocating funds to States which, in turn, they allocate to the metropolitan planning organizations. Assistance is available for transportation planning, technical assistance studies, demonstrations, management training, and cooperative research.

For further information, call 202–366–1626.

Research and Technology The Administration seeks to improve public transportation for America's communities by delivering products and services that are valued by its customers and by assisting transit agencies in better meeting the needs of their customers. To accomplish these goals, it partners with the transportation industry to undertake research, development, and education that will improve the quality, reliability, and cost-effectiveness of transit in America and that leads to increases in transit ridership.

Transit research and technology efforts are categorized as follows:

Joint Partnership The Administration enters into agreements with both public and private research organizations, transit providers, and industry to promote the early deployment of innovation in public transportation services, management, operational practices, and technology of broad applicability.

Advanced Technologies The Administration assists the study, design, and demonstration of fixed-guideway technologies, bus and bus rapid transit technologies, fuel-cell-powered transit buses, advanced propulsion control for rail transit, and other types of technologies in development.

International Mass Transportation Program The Administration promotes American transit products and services overseas, and cooperates with foreign public sector entities on research and development in the public transportation industries. Trade missions and other international gatherings enable American vendors to showcase their products and services and facilitate technology transfer and information diffusion for developing nations.

For further information, call 202–366–4052. Internet, www.fta.dot.gov/research.

Rural Transportation Assistance The Rural Transportation Assistance Program allocates funds annually to the States to provide assistance for transit research, technical assistance, training, and related support activities for transit providers serving non-urbanized areas. Additional funds are used at the national level for developing training materials, developing and maintaining a national clearinghouse on rural transit activities and information, and providing technical assistance through peer practitioners to promote exemplary techniques and practices.

For further information, call 202–366–2053.

Safety The Administration's safety program supports State and local agencies in fulfilling their responsibility for the safety and security of urban mass transportation facilities and services, through the encouragement and sponsorship of safety and security planning, training, information collection and analysis, drug control programs, system/safety assurance reviews, generic research, and other cooperative government/industry activities.

For further information, call 202–366–2896.

Training and Technical Assistance Through the National Transit Institute (NTI), the Administration develops and offers training courses for improving transit planning, operations, workforce performance, and productivity. NTI courses are conducted at sites across the United States on a wide variety of subjects, ranging from multimodal planning to management development, third-party contracting, safety, and security. Current NTI course offerings are available online at www.ntionline.com.

For further information, call 202–366–5741.

Field Organization—Federal Transit Administration

Region/Address	Telephone
Atlanta, GA (Suite 17T50, 61 Forsyth St. SW., 30303)	404–562–3500
Cambridge, MA (Suite 920, 55 Broadway, 02142)	617–494–2055
Chicago, IL (Suite 320, 200 W. Adams St., 60606)	312–353–2789
Denver, CO (Suite 650, 216 16th St., 80202)	303–844–3242
Fort Worth, TX (Suite 8A36, 819 Taylor St., 76102)	817–978–0550
Kansas City, MO (Suite 404, 901 Locust St., 64106)	816–329–3920
New York, NY (Suite 429, 1 Bowling Green, 10004–1415)	212–668–2170
Philadelphia, PA (Suite 500, 1760 Market St., 19103)	215–656–7100
San Francisco, CA (Suite 2210, 201 Mission St., 94105)	415–744–3133
Seattle, WA (Suite 3142, 915 2d Ave., 98174)	206–220–7954

Metropolitan Offices—Federal Transit Administration

Office/Address	Telephone
Chicago, IL (Suite 320, 200 W. Adams St., 60606–5232)	312–886–1616
Los Angeles, CA (Suite 1460, 210 Figueroa, 90012)	213–202–3950
New York, NY (Suite 428, 1 Bowling Green, 10004–1415)	212–668–2201
Philadelphia, PA (Suite 903, 1760 Market St., 19103–4142)	215–656–7070
Washington, DC (Suite 510, 1990 K St., NW, 20006)	202–219–3562

For further information, contact the Office of Communications and Congressional Affairs, Federal Transit Administration, Department of Transportation, 400 Seventh Street SW., Washington, DC 20590. Phone, 202–366–4043. Internet, www.fta.dot.gov.

Maritime Administration

The Maritime Administration was established by Reorganization Plan No. 21 of 1950 (5 U.S.C. app.). The Maritime Act of 1981 (46 U.S.C. 1601) transferred the Maritime Administration to the Department of Transportation. The Administration manages programs to aid in the development, promotion, and operation of the U.S. merchant marine. It is also charged with organizing and directing emergency merchant ship operations.

The Maritime Administration administers subsidy programs to pay the difference between certain costs of operating ships under the U.S. flag and foreign competitive flags on essential services, and the difference between the costs of constructing ships in U.S. and foreign shipyards. It provides financing guarantees for the construction, reconstruction, and reconditioning of ships; and enters into capital construction fund agreements that grant tax deferrals on moneys to be used for the acquisition, construction, or reconstruction of ships.

The Administration constructs or supervises the construction of merchant-type ships for the Federal Government. It helps industry generate increased business for U.S. ships and conducts programs to develop ports, facilities, and intermodal transport, and to promote domestic shipping.

It conducts program and technical studies and administers a war risk insurance program that insures operators and seamen against losses caused by hostile action if domestic commercial insurance is not available.

Under emergency conditions the Maritime Administration charters Government-owned ships to U.S. operators, requisitions or procures ships owned by U.S. citizens, and allocates them to meet defense needs.

It maintains a national defense reserve fleet of Government-owned ships that it operates through ship managers and general agents when required in national defense interests. An element of this activity is the Ready Reserve force consisting of a number of ships available for quick-response activation.

The Administration regulates sales to aliens and transfers to foreign registry of ships that are fully or partially owned by U.S. citizens. It also disposes of Government-owned ships found nonessential for national defense.

The Administration operates the U.S. Merchant Marine Academy, Kings Point, NY, where young people are trained to become merchant marine officers, and conducts training in shipboard firefighting at Earle, NJ, and Toledo, OH. It also administers a Federal assistance program for the maritime academies operated by California, Maine, Massachusetts, Michigan, New York, and Texas.

Field Organization—Maritime Administration

Region	Address	Director	Telephone
Central	Rm. 1223, 501 Magazine St., New Orleans, LA 70130–3394	John W. Carnes	504–589–2000
Great Lakes	Suite 185, 2860 South River Rd., Des Plaines, IL 60018–2413.	Alpha H. Ames, Jr.	847–298–4535
North Atlantic	Rm. 418, 1 Bowling Green, New York, NY 10004–1415	Robert McKeon	212–668–3330
South Atlantic	Rm. 211, 7737 Hampton Blvd., Norfolk, VA 23505	Mayank Jain	757–441–6393
Western	Suite 2200, 201 Mission St., San Francisco, CA 94105–1905	Francis X. Johnston	415–744–3125
Merchant Marine Academy.	Kings Point, NY 11024–1699	Joseph D. Stewart	516–773–5000

For further information, contact the Office of Congressional and Public Affairs, Maritime Administration, Department of Transportation, 400 Seventh Street SW., Washington, DC 20590. Phone, 202–366–5807 or 800–996–2723. Internet, www.marad.dot.gov.

Saint Lawrence Seaway Development Corporation

The Saint Lawrence Seaway Development Corporation was established by the Saint Lawrence Seaway Act of May 13, 1954 (33 U.S.C. 981–990) and became an operating administration of the Department of Transportation in 1966.

The Corporation, working cooperatively with the Saint Lawrence Seaway Management Corporation (SLSMC) of Canada, is dedicated to operating and maintaining a safe, reliable, and efficient deep draft waterway between the Great Lakes and the Atlantic Ocean. It ensures the safe transit of commercial and noncommercial vessels through the two U.S. locks and the navigation channels of the Saint Lawrence Seaway System. The Corporation works jointly with SLSMC on all matters related to rules and regulations, overall operations, vessel inspections, traffic control, navigation aids, safety, operating dates, and trade development programs.

The Great Lakes/Saint Lawrence Seaway System extends from the Atlantic Ocean to the Lake Superior ports of Duluth/Superior, a distance of 2,342 miles. The Corporation's main customers are vessel owners and operators, Midwest States and Canadian provinces, Great Lakes port communities, shippers and receivers of domestic and international cargo, and the Lakes/Seaway maritime and related services industries. International and domestic commerce through the Seaway contributes to the economic prosperity of the entire Great Lakes region.

For further information, contact the Director of Trade Development and Public Affairs, Saint Lawrence Seaway Development Corporation, Department of Transportation, 400 Seventh Street SW., Washington, DC 20590. Phone, 202–366–0091. Fax, 202–366–7147. Internet, www.greatlakes-seaway.com.

Pipeline and Hazardous Materials Safety Administration

The Pipeline and Hazardous Materials Administration (PHMSA) was established on February 20, 2005. It is responsible for hazardous materials transportation and pipeline safety.

Hazardous Materials The Office of Hazardous Materials Safety develops and issues regulations for the safe and secure transportation of hazardous materials by all modes, excluding bulk transportation by water. The regulations cover shipper and carrier operations, packaging and container specifications, and hazardous materials definitions. The Office provides training and outreach to help shippers and carriers meet the requirements of the hazardous material regulations. The Office is also responsible for the enforcement of regulations other than those applicable to a single mode of transportation. The Office manages a fee-funded grant program to assist States in planning for hazardous materials emergencies and to assist States and Indian tribes with training for hazardous materials emergencies. Additionally, the Office maintains a national safety program to safeguard food and certain other products from contamination during motor or rail transportation.

For further information, call 202–366–0656. Internet, hazmat.dot.gov.

Regional Offices—Office of Hazardous Materials Safety

Region	Address	Chief
Central—IA, IL, IN, KY, MI, MN, MO, ND, NE, OH, SD, WI	Suite 478, 2350 E. Devon Ave., Des Plaines, IL 60018	Kevin Boehne
Eastern—CT, DC, DE, MA, MD, ME, NH, NJ, NY, PA, RI, VA, VT, WV	Suite 306, 820 Bear Tavern Rd., W. Trenton, NJ 08628	Colleen Abbenhaus
Southern—AL, FL, GA, MS, NC, PR, SC, TN	Suite 602, 233 Peachtree St. NE., Atlanta, GA 30303	John Heneghan
Southwest—AR, CO, KS, LA, NM, OK, TX	Suite 1110, 8701 S. Gessner Rd., Houston, TX 77004	Billy Hines
Western—AK, AZ, CA, HI, ID, MT, NV, OR, UT, WA, WY	Suite 550B, 3401 Centrelake Dr., Ontario, CA 91761	Daniel Derwey

Pipelines The Office of Pipeline Safety's (OPS) mission is to ensure the safety, security, and environmental protection of the Nation's pipeline transportation system. The Office establishes and enforces safety and environmental standards for transportation of gas and hazardous liquids by pipeline. OPS also analyzes data, conducts education and training, promotes damage prevention, and conducts research and development for pipeline safety. Through OPS-administered grants-in-aid, States that voluntarily assume regulatory jurisdiction of pipelines can receive funding for up to 50 percent of the costs for their intrastate pipeline safety programs. OPS engineers inspect most interstate pipelines and other facilities not covered by the State programs. The Office also implements the Oil Pollution Act of 1990 by providing approval for and testing of oil pipeline spill response plans.

For further information, call 202–366–4595.

Regional Offices—Office of Pipeline Safety

Region	Address	Chief
Central—IA, IL, IN, KS, MI, MN, MO, ND, NE, OH, SD, WI	Rm. 462, 901 Locust St., Kansas City, MO 64106	Ivan Huntoon
Eastern—CT, DC, DE, MA, MD, ME, NH, NJ, NY, PA, RI, VA, VT, WV	Rm. 7128, 400 7th St. SW., Washington, DC 20590	William Gute
Southern—AL, AR, FL, GA, KY, MS, NC, PR, SC, TN	Suite 602, 223 Peachtree St. NE., Atlanta, GA 30303	Linda Daugherty
Southwest—AZ, LA, NM, OK, TX	Suite 1110, 8701 S. Gessner Rd., Houston, TX 77074	Rodrick M. Seeley
Western—AK, CA, CO, HI, ID, MT, NV, OR, UT, WA, WY	Suite 110, 12300 W. Dakota Ave., Lakewood, CO 80215	Chris Hoidal

For further information, contact the Office of Governmental, International and Public Affairs, Pipeline and Hazardous Materials Safety Administration, Department of Transportation, Suite 8406, 400 Seventh Street SW., Washington, DC 20590. Phone, 202–366–4831. Internet, www.phmsa.dot.gov.

Research and Innovative Technology Administration

The Research and Innovative Technology Administration (RITA) was created under the Norman Y. Mineta Research and Special Programs Improvement Act (118

Stat. 2425). RITA is dedicated to the advancement of DOT priorities for innovation and research in transportation technologies and concepts that will improve DOT mobility, promote economic growth, and deliver a better integrated transportation system.

RITA will:

—coordinate and advance transportation research efforts within DOT;

—support transportation professionals in their research efforts through grants and consulting services, as well as professional development through training centers; and

—inform transportation decisionmakers on intermodal and multimodal transportation topics through release of statistics, research reports, and a variety of information products via the Internet, publications, and in-person venues such as conferences.

RITA is composed of the staff from the Office of Research, Development, and Technology, the Volpe National Transportation Systems Center, the Transportation Safety Institute, and the Bureau of Transportation Statistics.

For further information, contact the Research and Innovative Technology Administration, Department of Transportation, 400 Seventh Street SW., Washington, DC 20590. Phone, 202–366–7582. Internet, www.rita.dot.gov. E-mail, info.rita@dot.gov.

Federal Motor Carrier Safety Administration

The Federal Motor Carrier Safety Administration was established within the Department of Transportation on January 1, 2000, pursuant to the Motor Carrier Safety Improvement Act of 1999 (49 U.S.C. 113).

Formerly a part of the Federal Highway Administration, the Federal Motor Carrier Safety Administration's primary mission is to prevent commercial motor vehicle-related fatalities and injuries. Activities of the Administration contribute to ensuring safety in motor carrier operations through strong enforcement of safety regulations, targeting high-risk carriers and commercial motor vehicle drivers; improving safety information systems and commercial motor vehicle technologies; strengthening commercial motor vehicle equipment and operating standards; and increasing safety awareness. To accomplish these activities, the Administration works with Federal, State, and local enforcement agencies, the motor carrier industry, labor safety interest groups, and others.

Activities

Commercial Drivers' Licenses The Administration develops standards to test and license commercial motor vehicle drivers.

Data and Analysis The Administration collects and disseminates data on motor carrier safety and directs resources to improve motor carrier safety.

Regulatory Compliance and Enforcement The Administration operates a program to improve safety performance and remove high-risk carriers from the Nation's highways.

Research and Technology The Administration coordinates research and development to improve the safety of motor carrier operations and commercial motor vehicles and drivers.

Safety Assistance The Administration provides States with financial assistance for roadside inspections and other commercial motor vehicle safety programs. It promotes motor vehicle and motor carrier safety.

Other Activities The Administration supports the development of unified motor carrier safety requirements and procedures throughout North America. It participates in international technical organizations and committees to help share the best practices in motor carrier safety throughout North America and the rest of the world. It enforces regulations ensuring safe highway transportation of hazardous materials and has established a task force to identify and investigate those carriers of household goods which have exhibited a substantial pattern of consumer abuse.

Field Organization—Federal Motor Carrier Safety Administration Administration

Region	Address	Telephone
Eastern	Suite 4000, 10 S. Howard St., Baltimore, MD 21201–2819	410–962–0077
Southern	Suite 17T75, 61 Forsyth St., SW., Atlanta, GA 30303–3104	404–562–3600
Midwestern	Suite 210, 19900 Governors Dr., Olympia Fields, IL 60461–1021	708–283–3577
Western	Suite 2100, 201 Mission St., San Francisco, CA 94105	415–744–3088

For further information, contact the Federal Motor Carrier Safety Administration, 400 Seventh Street SW., Washington, DC 20590. Phone, 202–366–2519. Internet, www.fmcsa.dot.gov.

Surface Transportation Board

The Surface Transportation Board was established in 1996 by the Interstate Commerce Commission (ICC) Termination Act of 1995 (49 U.S.C. 10101 *et seq.*) as an independent adjudicatory body organizationally housed within the Department of Transportation with jurisdiction over certain surface transportation economic regulatory matters formerly under ICC jurisdiction. The Board consists of three members, appointed by the President with the advice and consent of the Senate for 5-year terms.

The Board adjudicates disputes and regulates interstate surface transportation through various laws pertaining to the different modes of surface transportation. The Board's general responsibilities include the oversight of firms engaged in transportation in interstate and foreign commerce to the extent that it takes place within the United States, or between or among points in the contiguous United States and points in Alaska, Hawaii, or U.S. territories or possessions. Surface transportation matters under the Board's jurisdiction in general include railroad rate and service issues, rail restructuring transactions (mergers, line sales, line construction, and line abandonments), and labor matters related thereto; certain trucking company, moving van, and noncontiguous ocean shipping company rate matters; certain intercity passenger bus company structure, financial, and operational matters; and certain pipeline matters not regulated by the Federal Energy Regulatory Commission.

In performing its functions, the Board is charged with promoting, where appropriate, substantive and procedural regulatory reform and providing an efficient and effective forum for the resolution of disputes. Through the granting of exemptions from regulations where warranted, the streamlining of its decisionmaking process and the regulations applicable thereto, and the consistent and fair application of legal and equitable principles, the Board seeks to provide an effective forum for efficient dispute resolution and facilitation of appropriate market-based business transactions. Through rulemakings and case disposition, it strives to develop new and better ways to analyze unique and complex problems, to reach fully justified decisions more quickly, to reduce the costs associated with regulatory oversight, and to encourage private sector negotiations and resolutions to problems, where appropriate.

For further information, contact the Office of Congressional and Public Services, Surface Transportation Board, Suite 840, 1925 K Street NW., Washington, DC 20423–0001. Phone, 202–565–1594. Internet, www.stb.dot.gov.

Sources of Information

Inquiries for information on the following subjects should be directed to the specified office, Department of Transportation, Washington, DC 20590, or to the address indicated.

Civil Rights For information on equal employment opportunity, nondiscrimination in DOT employment and transportation services, or DOT's Disadvantaged Business Enterprise certification appeals program, contact the Director, Departmental Office of Civil Rights. Phone, 202–366–4648. Internet, www.dot.gov/ost/docr.

Consumer Activities For information about air travelers' rights or for assistance in resolving consumer problems with providers of commercial air transportation services, contact the Consumer Affairs Division (phone, 202–366–2220).

To report vehicle safety problems, obtain information on motor vehicle and highway safety, or to request consumer information publications, call the National Highway Traffic Safety Administration's 24-hour auto safety hotline. Phone, 202–366–0123 (Washington, DC, area) or 800–424–9393 (toll free except Alaska and Hawaii).

Contracts Contact the Office of the Senior Procurement Executive. Phone, 202–366–4263.

Employment The principal occupations in the Department are air traffic controller, aviation safety specialist, electronics maintenance technician, engineer (civil, aeronautical, automotive, electronic, highway, and general), administrative/management, and clerical. For further information, contact the Transportation Administrative Service Center (TASC) DOT Connection, Room PL–402, 400 Seventh Street SW., Washington, DC 20590. Phone, 202–366–9391 or 800–525–2878.

Environment Inquiries on environmental activities and programs should be directed to the Assistant Secretary for Transportation Policy, Office of Transportation Policy Development, Washington, DC 20590. Phone, 202–366–4416.

Films Many films on transportation subjects are available for use by educational institutions, community groups, private organizations, etc. Requests for specific films relating to a particular mode of transportation may be directed to the appropriate operating administration.

Fraud, Waste, and Abuse To report, contact the Office of Inspector General hotline, P.O. Box 23178, Washington, DC 20026–0178. Phone, 202–366–1461 or 800–424–9071.

Publications The Department and its operating agencies issue publications on a wide variety of subjects. Many of these publications are available from the issuing agency or for sale from the Government Printing Office and the National Technical Information Service, 5285 Port Royal Road, Springfield, VA 22151. Contact the Department or the specific agency at the addresses indicated in the text.

Reading Rooms Contact the Department of Transportation TASC Dockets, PL–401, 400 Seventh Street SW., Washington, DC 20590. Phone, 800–647–5527. Administrations and their regional offices maintain reading rooms for public use. Contact the specific administration at the address indicated in the text.

Other reading rooms include: TASC Department of Transportation Library, Room 2200, 400 Seventh Street SW., Washington, DC 20590 (phone, 202–366–0745); Department of Transportation/TASC Law Library, Room 2215, 400 Seventh Street SW., Washington, DC 20590 (phone, 202–366–0749); Department of Transportation/TASC Library, FB–10A Branch, Room 930, 800 Independence Avenue SW., Washington, DC 20591 (phone, 202–267–3115); and Department of Transportation/TASC Library, Transpoint Branch, B–726, 2100 Second Street SW., Washington, DC 20593 (phone, 202–267–2536).

Speakers The Department of Transportation and its operating administrations and regional offices make speakers available for civic, labor, and community groups. Contact the specific agency or the nearest regional office at the address indicated in the text.

Surface Transportation Board Proceedings and Public Records Requests for public assistance with pending or potential proceedings of the Board should be addressed to the Office of Public Services, Surface Transportation Board, Suite 840, 1925 K Street NW., Washington, DC 20423–0001. Phone, 202–565–1592.

Requests for access to the Board's public records should be made to the Office of the Secretary, Surface Transportation Board, Suite 700, 1925 K Street NW., Washington, DC 20423–0001. Phone, 202–565–1674.

Telephone Directory The Department of Transportation telephone directory is available for sale by the Superintendent of Documents, Government Printing Office, Washington, DC 20402.

For further information concerning the Department of Transportation, contact the Office of Public Affairs, Department of Transportation, 400 Seventh Street SW., Washington, DC 20590. Phone, 202–366–5580. Internet, www.dot.gov.

DEPARTMENT OF THE TREASURY

1500 Pennsylvania Avenue NW., Washington, DC 20220
Phone, 202–622–2000. Internet, www.treas.gov.

SECRETARY OF THE TREASURY	JOHN W. SNOW
Chief of Staff	CHRISTOPHER SMITH
Executive Secretary	JONATHAN WEINBERGER
Deputy Secretary	ROBERT M. KIMMITT
Treasury Inspector General for Tax Administration	J. RUSSELL GEORGE
Deputy Inspector General for Audit	MICHAEL R. PHILLIPS
Deputy Inspector General for Investigations	STEVEN M. JONES
General Counsel	ARNOLD HAVENS
Deputy General Counsel	JAMES CARROLL
Assistant Secretary (Economic Policy)	MARK WARSHAWSKY
Deputy Assistant Secretary (Macroeconomics)	ROBERT STEIN
Deputy Assistant Secretary for Policy Coordination	JAMES CARTER
Deputy Assistant Secretary (Microeconomic Analysis)	NADA EISSA
Assistant Secretary (Legislative Affairs and Public Liaison)	KEVIN FROMER
Deputy Assistant Secretary (Appropriation and Management)	ANDREW FISHBURN
Deputy Assistant Secretary (Public Liaison)	BECKY RELIC
Assistant Secretary for Management/Chief Financial Officer	SANDRA L. PACK
Deputy Assistant Secretary for Chief Human Resources and Chief Human Capital Officer	ROCHELLE GRANAT
Deputy Chief Financial Officer	RICHARD HOLCOMB
Chief Information Officer	IRA L. HOBBS
Deputy Assistant Secretary for Management and Budget	WESLEY FOSTER
Deputy Assistant Secretary for Headquarters Operations and Senior Procurement Executive	THOMAS SHARPE, JR.
DC Pension	(VACANCY)
Assistant Secretary (Public Affairs)	SALVATORE FRATTO
Deputy Assistant Secretary (Public Affairs)	(VACANCY)
Assistant Secretary (Tax Policy)	(VACANCY)
Deputy Assistant Secretary (Regulatory Affairs)	ERIC SOLOMAN
Deputy Assistant Secretary (Tax Analysis)	ROBERT CARROLL
Deputy Assistant Secretary (Tax Policy)	(VACANCY)
Treasurer of the United States	ANNA ESCOBEDO CABRAL
Under Secretary (Domestic Finance)	RANDAL K. QUARLES

Deputy Assistant Secretary for Financial Education	DAN IANNICOLA
Deputy Assistant Secretary for Critical Infrastructure Protection and Compliance	JESSE VILLARREAL
Director, Community Development Financial Institutions Fund	ARTHUR GARCIA
Assistant Secretary (Financial Institutions)	EMIL HENRY
Deputy Assistant Secretary (Financial Institutions Policy)	DAVID NASON
Assistant Secretary (Financial Markets)	(VACANCY)
Deputy Assistant Secretary (Federal Finance)	JAMES CLOUSE
Deputy Assistant Secretary (Government Financial Policy)	ROGER KODAT
Fiscal Assistant Secretary	DONALD V. HAMMOND
Deputy Assistant Secretary (Accounting Policy)	ROBERT N. REID
Deputy Assistant Secretary (Fiscal Operations and Policy)	KENNETH CARFINE
Under Secretary (Terrorism and Financial Crimes)	STUART LEVEY
Assistant Secretary (Terrorism and Financial Crimes)	PATRICK O'BRIEN
Deputy Assistant Secretary (Terrorist Financing and Financial Crimes)	DANNY GLASER
Assistant Secretary (Intelligence and Analysis)	JANICE GARDNER
Deputy Assistant Secretary for Tax, Trade and Tariff Policy	TIMOTHY E. SKUD
Director, Office of Financial Crimes Enforcement Network (FinCEN)	ROBERT T. WERNER
Under Secretary (International Affairs)	TIM ADAMS
Assistant Secretary (International Affairs)	CLAY LOWERY
Deputy Assistant Secretary for International Monetary and Financial Policy	MARK SOBEL
Deputy Assistant Secretary for Asia, the Americas, and Africa	DAVID LOVEINGER
Deputy Assistant Secretary for Multilateral Development Bank and Specialized Development Institution	KENNETH PEEL
Deputy Assistant Secretary for Eurasia and Latin America	NANCY LEE
Deputy Assistant Secretary for Technical Assistance Policy	W. LARRY MACDONALD
Deputy Assistant Secretary for Trade and Investment Policy	CHARLES SCHOTT

ALCOHOL AND TOBACCO TAX AND TRADE BUREAU

1310 G Street NW., Washington, DC 20220
Phone, 202–927–5000. Fax, 202–927–5611. Internet, www.ttb.gov.

Administrator	JOHN MANFREDA
Deputy Administrator	VICKY MCDOWELL

Assistant Administrator (Field Operations)	MARY RYAN
Assistant Administrator (Headquarters)	BILL FOSTER
Associate Chief Counsel	ROBERT TOBIASSEN

OFFICE OF THE COMPTROLLER OF THE CURRENCY

250 E Street SW., Washington, DC 20219
Phone, 202–874–5000. Internet, www.occ.treas.gov.

Comptroller	JOHN C. DUGAN
Chief of Staff	JOHN G. WALSH
Chief Information Officer	JACKIE FLETCHER
Deputy to the Federal Deposit Insurance Corporation Director (Comptroller of the Currency)	(VACANCY)
Ombudsman	SAMUEL P. GOLDEN
First Senior Deputy Comptroller	JULIE L. WILLIAMS
Senior Deputy Comptroller for the Office of Management and Chief Financial Officer	THOMAS R. BLOOM
Senior Deputy Comptroller for Midsize Community Bank Supervision	TIMOTHY W. LONG
Senior Deputy Comptroller and Chief National Bank Examiner	EMORY WAYNE RUSHTON
Senior Deputy Comptroller for International and Economic Affairs	JEFFERY A. BROWN
Senior Deputy Comptroller for Large Bank Supervision	DOUGLAS W. ROEDER
Executive Officer for Leadership, Learning, and Workplace Fairness	MARK A. NISHAN

BUREAU OF ENGRAVING AND PRINTING

Fourteenth and C Streets SW., Washington, DC 20228
Phone, 202–874–3019. Internet, www.moneyfactory.com.

Director	LARRY R. FELIX
Deputy Director	(VACANCY)
Associate Director (Chief Financial Officer)	LEONARD R. OLIJAR, *Acting*
Associate Director (Chief Information Officer)	ROBERT P. SCHERER, *Acting*
Associate Director (Chief Operating Officer)	KIT REGONE
Associate Director (Management)	PAMELA J. GARDINER
Associate Director (Technology)	JUDITH DIAZ MYERS
Chief Counsel	MICHAEL DAVIDSON

FINANCIAL MANAGEMENT SERVICE

401 Fourteenth Street SW., Washington, DC 20227
Phone, 202–874–6740. Internet, www.fms.treas.gov.

Commissioner	RICHARD L. GREGG
Deputy Commissioner	KENNETH R. PAPAJ
Director, Legislative and Public Affairs	ALVINA A. MCHALE
Chief Counsel	MARGARET MARQUETTE
Assistant Commissioner, Debt Management Services	MARTY MILLS
Assistant Commissioner, Federal Finance	GARY GRIPPO

Assistant Commissioner, Financial Operations	WANDA ROGERS
Assistant Commissioner, Governmentwide Accounting and Agency Services	D. JAMES STURGILL
Assistant Commissioner, Information Resources	CHARLES SIMPSON
Assistant Commissioner, Management (Chief Financial Officer)	SCOTT JOHNSON
Assistant Commissioner, Regional Operations	JUDY TILLMAN

INTERNAL REVENUE SERVICE

1111 Constitution Avenue NW., Washington, DC 20224
Phone, 202–622–5000. Internet, www.irs.gov.

Commissioner of Internal Revenue	MARK W. EVERSON
Commissioner, Large and Midsize Business Division	DEBORAH NOLAN
Commissioner, Small Business/Self-Employed Division	KEVIN BROWN
Commissioner, Tax Exempt and Government Entities Division	STEVE T. MILLER
Commissioner, Wage and Investment Division	HENRY O. LAMAR, JR.
Deputy Commissioner Operations Support	JOHN M. DALRYMPLE
Deputy Commissioner Services and Enforcement	MARK E. MATTHEWS
Chief Counsel	DONALD KORB
Chief Financial Officer	JANICE LAMBERT
Chief, Agency-Wide Shared Services	CARL FROEHLICH
Chief, Appeals	DAVID ROBISON
Chief, Communications and Liaison	FRANK M. KEITH
Chief, Criminal Investigation	NANCY JARDINI
Chief, Information Officer	W. TODD GRAMS
National Taxpayer Advocate	NINA E. OLSON

UNITED STATES MINT

801 Ninth Street NW., Washington, DC 20220
Phone, 202–354–7200. Internet, www.usmint.gov.

Director	DAVID A. LEBRYK, *Acting*
Deputy Director	JERRY HORTON, *Acting*
Chief Counsel	DAN SHAVER
Associate Director, Chief Financial Officer	ROBERT BYRD
Associate Director, Chief Information Officer	JERRY HORTON
Associate Director, Manufacturing Strategic Business Unit	R. SCOTT MYERS
Associate Director, Sales and Marketing Strategic Business Unit	GLORIA ESKRIDGE
Associate Director, Protection Strategic Business Unit	WILLIAM F. DADDIO

BUREAU OF THE PUBLIC DEBT

999 E Street NW., Washington, DC 20239–0001
Phone, 202–504–3500. Internet, www.publicdebt.treas.gov.

Commissioner	VAN ZECK

Deputy Commissioner	NANCY FLEETWOOD
Chief Counsel	PAUL WOLFTEICH
Assistant Commissioner (Financing)	MICHAEL W. SUNNER, *Acting*
Assistant Commissioner (Information Technology)	CYNTHIA Z. SPRINGER
Assistant Commissioner (Public Debt Accounting)	DEBRA HINES
Assistant Commissioner (Securities Operations)	JOHN R. SWALES III
Assistant Commissioner (Investor Services)	FRED PYATT
Assistant Commissioner (Management Services)	GLENN E. BALL
Executive Director (Administration Resource Center)	FRED PHILLIPS
Executive Director (Government Securities Regulation Staff)	LORI SANTAMORENA
Executive Director (Investor Education and Communications Staff)	KIM TREAT, *Acting*

OFFICE OF THRIFT SUPERVISION

1700 G Street NW., Washington, DC 20552
Phone, 202–906–6000. Internet, www.ots.treas.gov.

Director	JOHN M. REICH
Deputy Director	SCOTT N. POLAKOFF
Chief Counsel	JOHN E. BOWMAN
Managing Director, Chief Information Officer and Chief Financial Officer	TIMOTHY T. WARD
Managing Director, External Affairs	KEVIN PETRASIC
Managing Director, Examinations, Supervision and Consumer Protection	SCOTT M. ALBINSON
Associate Director	WALTER B. MASON
Managing Director, Human Resources and Administrative Services	SUE A. RENDLEMAN

The Department of the Treasury performs four basic functions: formulating and recommending economic, financial, tax, and fiscal policies; serving as financial agent for the U.S. Government; enforcing the law; and manufacturing coins and currency.

The Treasury Department was created by act of September 2, 1789 (31 U.S.C. 301 and 301 note). Many subsequent acts have figured in the development of the Department, delegating new duties to its charge and establishing the numerous bureaus and divisions that now comprise the Treasury.

Secretary As a major policy adviser to the President, the Secretary has primary responsibility for formulating and recommending domestic and international financial, economic, and tax policy; participating in the formulation of broad fiscal policies that have general significance for the economy; and managing the public debt. The Secretary also oversees the activities of the Department in carrying out its major law enforcement responsibility; in serving as the financial agent for the U.S. Government; and in manufacturing coins, currency, and other products for customer agencies. The Secretary also serves as the Government's chief financial officer.

DEPARTMENT OF THE TREASURY

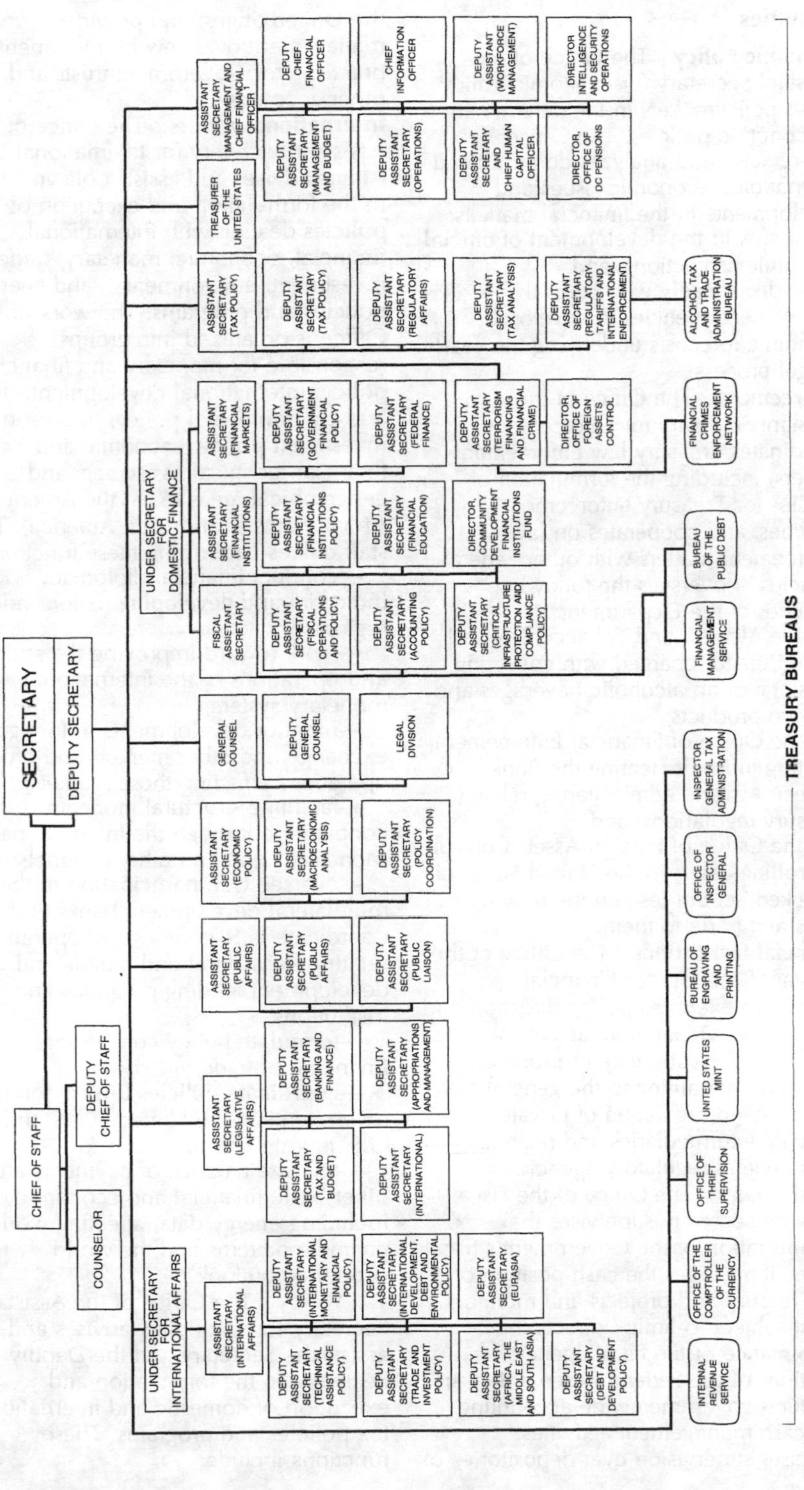

1 Assistant Secretary (Management) and Chief Financial Officer is Treasury's Chief Operating Officer.

Activities

Economic Policy The Office of the Assistant Secretary for Economic Policy assists policymakers in the determination of economic policies. The Office:

—reviews and analyzes domestic and international economic issues and developments in the financial markets;

—assists in the development of official economic projections; and

—works closely with Federal Government agencies to develop economic forecasts underlying the yearly budget process.

Enforcement The Office of the Assistant Secretary for Enforcement coordinates Treasury law enforcement matters, including the formulation of policies for Treasury enforcement activities, and cooperates on law enforcement matters with other Federal agencies. It oversees the following branches of the Department:

—the Alcohol and Tobacco Tax and Trade Bureau, charged with collecting excise taxes on alcoholic beverages and tobacco products;

—the Office of Financial Enforcement, assisting in implementing the Bank Secrecy Act and administering related Treasury regulations; and

—the Office of Foreign Assets Control, controlling assets in the United States of "blocked" countries and the flow of funds and trade to them.

Financial Institutions The Office of the Assistant Secretary for Financial Institutions exercises policy direction and control over Department activities relating to the substance of proposed legislation pertaining to the general activities and regulation of private financial intermediaries and relating to other Federal regulatory agencies.

Fiscal Affairs The Office of the Fiscal Assistant Secretary supervises the administration of the Government's fiscal affairs. It manages the cash position of the Treasury and projects and monitors "debt subject-to-limit;" directs the performance of the fiscal agency functions of the Federal Reserve Banks; conducts governmentwide accounting and cash management activities; exercises supervision over depositories of the United States; and provides management overview of investment practices for Government trusts and other accounts.

International Affairs The Office of the Assistant Secretary for International Affairs advises and assists policymakers in the formulation and execution of policies dealing with international financial, economic, monetary, trade, investment, environmental, and energy policies and programs. The work of the Office is organized into groups responsible for monetary and financial policy; international development, debt, and environmental policy; trade and investment policy; economic and financial technical assistance; and geographical areas (Asia, the Americas, Africa, Eurasia, and Latin America). The staff offices performing these functions:

—conduct financial diplomacy with industrial and developing nations and regions;

—work toward improving the structure and operations of the international monetary system;

—monitor developments in foreign exchange and other markets and official operations affecting those markets;

—facilitate structural monetary cooperation through the International Monetary Fund and other channels;

—oversee U.S. participation in the multilateral development banks and coordinate U.S. policies and operations relating to bilateral and multilateral development lending programs and institutions;

—formulate policy concerning financing of trade;

—coordinate policies toward foreign investments in the United States and U.S. investments abroad; and

—analyze balance of payments and other basic financial and economic data, including energy data, affecting world payment patterns and the world economic outlook.

Tax Policy The Office of the Assistant Secretary for Tax Policy advises and assists the Secretary and the Deputy Secretary in the formulation and execution of domestic and international tax policies and programs. These functions include:

—analysis of proposed tax legislation and tax programs;

—projections of economic trends affecting tax bases;

—studies of effects of alternative tax measures;

—preparation of official estimates of Government receipts for the President's annual budget messages;

—legal advice and analysis on domestic and international tax matters;

—assistance in the development and review of tax legislation and domestic and international tax regulations and rulings; and

—participation in international tax treaty negotiations and in maintenance of relations with international organizations on tax matters.

Treasurer of the United States The Office of the Treasurer of the United States was established on September 6, 1777. The Treasurer was originally charged with the receipt and custody of Government funds, but many of these functions have been assumed by different bureaus of the Department of the Treasury. In 1981, the Treasurer was assigned responsibility for oversight of the Bureau of Engraving and Printing and the United States Mint. The Treasurer reports to the Secretary through the Assistant Secretary for Management/Chief Financial Officer.

Treasury Inspector General The Treasury Inspector General for Tax Administration (TIGTA) was established in January 1999, in accordance with the Internal Revenue Service Restructuring and Reform Act of 1998, to provide independent oversight of the Internal Revenue Service programs and activities. TIGTA is charged with monitoring the Nation's tax laws to ensure the IRS acts with efficiency, economy, and effectiveness toward program accomplishment; ensuring compliance with applicable laws and regulations, preventing, detecting, and deterring fraud, waste, and abuse; investigating activities or allegations related to fraud, waste, and abuse by IRS personnel; and protecting the IRS against attempts to corrupt or threaten its employees.

For further information concerning the departmental offices, contact the Public Affairs Office, Department of the Treasury, 1500 Pennsylvania Avenue NW., Washington, DC 20220. Phone, 202–622–2960.

Alcohol and Tobacco Tax and Trade Bureau

The Alcohol and Tobacco Tax and Trade Bureau (TTB) administers and enforces the existing Federal laws and Tax Code provisions related to the production and taxation of alcohol and tobacco products. TTB also collects all excise taxes on the manufacture of firearms and ammunition.

For further information, contact the Office of Public and Governmental Affairs, Alcohol and Tobacco Tax and Trade Bureau. Phone, 202–927–5000. Internet, www.ttb.gov.

Office of the Comptroller of the Currency

[For the Office of the Comptroller of the Currency statement of organization, see the *Code of Federal Regulations,* Title 12, Part 4]

The Office of the Comptroller of the Currency was created February 25, 1863 (12 Stat. 665), as a bureau of the Department of the Treasury. Its primary mission is to regulate national banks. The Office is headed by the Comptroller, who is appointed for a 5-year term by the President with the advice and consent of the Senate.

The Office regulates national banks by its power to examine banks; approves or denies applications for new bank charters, branches, or mergers; takes enforcement action—such as bank closures—against banks that are not in compliance with laws and regulations;

and issues rules, regulations, and interpretations on banking practices.

The Office supervises approximately 2,100 national banks, including their trust activities and overseas operations. Each bank is examined annually through a nationwide staff of approximately 1,900 bank examiners supervised in 4 district offices. The Office is independently funded through assessments of the assets of national banks.

For further information, contact the Communications Division, Office of the Comptroller of the Currency, 250 E Street SW., Mail Stop 3-2, Washington, DC 20219. Phone, 202–874–4700.

Bureau of Engraving and Printing

The Bureau of Engraving and Printing operates on basic authorities conferred by act of July 11, 1862 (31 U.S.C. 303) and additional authorities contained in past appropriations made to the Bureau that are still in force. Operations are financed by a revolving fund established in 1950 in accordance with Public Law 81–656. The Bureau is headed by a Director who is selected by the Secretary of the Treasury.

The Bureau designs, prints, and finishes all of the Nation's paper currency and many other security documents, including White House invitations and military identification cards. It also is responsible for advising and assisting Federal agencies in the design and production of other Government documents that, because of their innate value or for other reasons, require security or counterfeit-deterrence characteristics.

The Bureau also operates a second currency manufacturing plant in Fort Worth, TX (9000 Blue Mound Road, 76131). Phone, 817–231–4000.

For further information, contact the Office of External Relations, Bureau of Engraving and Printing, Department of the Treasury, Room 533-M, Fourteenth and C Streets SW., Washington, DC 20228. Phone, 202–874–3019. Fax, 202–874–3177. Internet, www.moneyfactory.com.

Financial Management Service

The Financial Management Service (FMS) provides central payment services to Federal program agencies, operates the Federal Government's collections and deposit systems, provides governmentwide accounting and reporting services, and manages the collection of delinquent debt owed to the Federal Government. FMS has four Regional Financial Centers located in Texas, Missouri, Pennsylvania, and California; and one Debt Collection Center in Alabama.

Accounting The Service gathers and publishes Governmentwide financial information that is used by the public and private sectors to monitor the Government's financial status and establish fiscal and monetary policies. These publications include the *Daily Treasury Statement*, the *Monthly Treasury Statement*, the *Treasury Bulletin*, the *U.S. Government Annual Report*, and the *Financial Report of the U.S. Government.*

Collections FMS administers the world's largest collection system, gathering more than $2.2 trillion annually through a network of more than 10,000 financial institutions. It also manages the collection of Federal revenues such as individual and corporate income tax deposits, customs duties, loan repayments, fines, and proceeds from leases.

FMS and IRS launched the Electronic Federal Tax Payment System (www.eftps.gov), which allows individuals and businesses to pay Federal taxes through the Internet. EFTPS-OnLine also provides such features as an instant, printable acknowledgment for documenting each transaction, the ability to schedule advance payments, and access to payment history.

The Treasury Offset Program is one of the methods used to collect delinquent debt. FMS uses the program to withhold Federal payments, such as Federal income tax refunds, Federal salary payments, and Social Security benefits, to recipients with delinquent debts, including past-due child support obligations and State and Federal income tax debt.

Electronic Commerce Through its electronic money program, FMS tests new payments and collection technologies using the Internet and card technology, as well as related technologies such as digital signatures and biometrics. FMS has initiated electronic money pilot programs to help Federal agencies modernize their payments and collection activities. Examples include stored-value cards used on military bases and in Government hospitals, electronic checks, point-of-sale check truncations, and Internet credit card collection programs.

Payments Each year, FMS disburses nearly 1 billion with an access dollar value of more than 1.7 trillion, to a wide variety of recipients, such as those who receive Social Security, IRS tax refunds, and veterans' benefits. For fiscal year 2004, nearly 75 percent of these transactions were issued by electronic funds transfer. The remainder of FMS payments are disbursed by check.

Regional Financial Centers—Financial Management Service

Center/Address	Director
Austin, TX (P.O. Box 149058, 78741)	Robert Mange
Kansas City, MO (P.O. Box 12599, 64116)	Gary Beets
Philadelphia, PA (P.O. Box 8676, 19101)	Michael Colarusso
San Francisco, CA (P.O. Box 193858, 94119)	Philip Belisle

For further information, contact the Office of Legislative and Public Affairs, Financial Management Service, Department of the Treasury, Room 555, 401 Fourteenth Street SW., Washington, DC 20227. Phone, 202–874–6740. Internet, www.fms.treas.gov.

Internal Revenue Service

The Office of the Commissioner of Internal Revenue was established by act of July 1, 1862 (26 U.S.C. 7802). The Internal Revenue Service (IRS) is responsible for administering and enforcing the internal revenue laws and related statutes, except those relating to alcohol, tobacco, firearms, and explosives. Its mission is to collect the proper amount of tax revenue, at the least cost to the public, by efficiently applying the tax law with integrity and fairness. To achieve that purpose, the IRS:

—strives to achieve the highest possible degree of voluntary compliance in accordance with the tax laws and regulations;

—advises the public of their rights and responsibilities;

—determines the extent of compliance and the causes of noncompliance;

—properly administers and enforces the tax laws; and

—continually searches for and implements new, more efficient ways of accomplishing its mission.

Basic activities include

—ensuring satisfactory resolution of taxpayer complaints, providing taxpayer service and education;

—determining, assessing, and collecting internal revenue taxes;

—determining pension plan qualifications and exempt organization status; and

—preparing and issuing rulings and regulations to supplement the provisions of the Internal Revenue Code.

The source of most revenues collected is the individual income tax and the social insurance and retirement taxes. Other major sources are corporate income, excise, estate, and gift taxes. Congress first received authority to levy taxes on the income of individuals and corporations in 1913, pursuant to the 16th amendment of the Constitution.

For further information, contact the Internal Revenue Service, Department of the Treasury, 1111 Constitution Avenue NW., Washington, DC 20224. Phone, 202–622–5000.

United States Mint

The establishment of a mint was authorized by act of April 2, 1792 (1 Stat. 246). The Bureau of the Mint was established by act of February 12, 1873 (17 Stat. 424) and recodified on September 13, 1982 (31 U.S.C. 304, 5131). The name was changed to United States Mint by Secretarial order dated January 9, 1984.

The primary mission of the Mint is to produce an adequate volume of circulating coinage for the Nation to conduct its trade and commerce. The Mint also produces and sells numismatic coins, American Eagle gold and silver bullion coins, and national medals. In addition, the Fort Knox Bullion Depository is the primary storage facility for the Nation's gold bullion.

The U.S. Mint maintains sales centers at the Philadelphia and Denver Mints, and at Union Station in Washington, DC. Public tours are conducted, with free admission, at the Philadelphia and Denver Mints.

Field Facilities

(PM: Plant Manager; O: Officer in Charge)

Facility/Address	Facility Head
Bullion Depository, Fort Knox, KY 40121	Bert Barnes (O)
Denver, CO 80204	Tim Riley (PM)
Philadelphia, PA 19106	Robert Robidoux (PM)
San Francisco, CA 94102	Larry Eckerman (PM)
West Point, NY 10996	Ellen McCullom (PM)

For further information, contact the United States Mint, Department of the Treasury, 801 Ninth Street NW., Washington, DC 20220. Phone, 202–354–7222.

Bureau of the Public Debt

The Bureau of the Public Debt was established on June 30, 1940, pursuant to the Reorganization Act of 1939 (31 U.S.C. 306).

Its mission is to borrow the money needed to operate the Federal Government; account for the resulting public debt; and to issue and buy back Treasury securities to implement debt management policy. The Bureau fulfills its mission through four programs: wholesale securities, Government agency investment, retail securities services, and summary debt accounting.

The Bureau auctions and issues Treasury bills, notes, and bonds and manages the U.S. Savings Bond Program. It issues, services, and redeems bonds through a nationwide network of issuing and paying agents. It provides daily and other periodic reports to account for the composition and size of the debt. In addition, the Bureau implements the regulations for the Government securities market. These regulations provide for investor protection while maintaining a fair and liquid market for Government securities.

For more information, contact the Director, Legislative and Public Affairs, Office of the Commissioner, Bureau of the Public Debt, Washington, DC 20239–0001. Phone, 202–504–3502. Internet, www.publicdebt.treas.gov.

Office of Thrift Supervision

The Office of Thrift Supervision (OTS) regulates Federal and State-chartered savings institutions. Created by the Financial Institutions Reform, Recovery, and Enforcement Act of 1989, its mission is to effectively and efficiently supervise Thrift institutions in a manner that encourages a competitive industry to meet housing and other credit and financial services needs and ensure access to financial services for all Americans.

The Office is headed by a Director appointed by the President, with the advice and consent of the Senate, for a 5-year term. The Director is responsible for the overall direction and policy of the agency. OTS is responsible for:

—examining and supervising thrift institutions in the four OTS regions to ensure the safety and soundness of the industry;

—ensuring that thrifts comply with consumer protection laws and regulations;

—conducting a regional quality assurance program to ensure consistent applications of policies and procedures;

—developing national policy guidelines to enhance statutes and regulations and to establish programs to implement new policy and law;

—issuing various financial reports, including the quarterly report on the financial condition of the thrift industry;

—preparing regulations, bulletins, other policy documents, congressional testimony, and official correspondence on matters relating to the condition of the thrift industry, interest rate risk, financial derivatives, and economic issues; and

—prosecuting enforcement actions relating to thrift institutions.

For further information, contact External Affairs, Office of Thrift Supervision, 1700 G Street NW., Washington, DC 20552. Phone, 202–906–6677. Fax, 202–906–7849. Internet, www.ots.treas.gov.

Sources of Information

Departmental Offices

Contracts Write to the Director, Office of Procurement, Suite 400–W, 1310 G Street NW., Washington, DC 20220. Phone, 202–622–0203.

Environment Environmental statements prepared by the Department are available for review in the Departmental Library. Information on Treasury environmental matters may be obtained from the Office of the Assistant Secretary of the Treasury for Management and Chief Financial Officer, Treasury Department, Washington, DC 20220. Phone, 202–622–0043.

General Inquiries For general information about the Treasury Department, including copies of news releases and texts of speeches by high Treasury officials, write to the Office of the Assistant Secretary (Public Affairs and Public Liaison), Room 3430, Departmental Offices, Treasury Department, Washington, DC 20220. Phone, 202–622–2920.

Inspector General For general information, contact the Assistant Inspector General for Management at 202–927–5200, or visit the Office of Inspector General Web site at www.treas.gov/inspector-general. To report the possible existence of a Treasury activity (not including the Internal Revenue Service, which reports to the Treasury Inspector General for Tax Administration) constituting a violation of law, rules, regulations, or mismanagement, gross waste of funds, abuse of authority, or a substantial and specific danger to the public health and safety, phone, 800–359–3898; fax, 202–927–5799; e-mail, Hotline@oig.treas.gov; or write to Treasury OIG Hotline, Office of Inspector General, 1500 Pennsylvania Avenue NW., Washington, DC 20220. For Freedom of Information Act/Privacy Act requests, write to Freedom of Information Act Request, Treasury OIG, Office of Counsel, Suite 510, 740 15th Street NW., Washington, DC 20220.

Reading Room The Reading Room is located in the Treasury Library, Room 1428, Main Treasury Building, 1500 Pennsylvania Avenue NW., Washington, DC 20220. Phone, 202–622–0990.

Small and Disadvantaged Business Activities Write to the Director, Office of Small and Disadvantaged Business Utilization, Suite 400–W, 1310 G Street NW., Washington, DC 20220. Phone, 202–622–0530.

Tax Legislation Information on tax legislation may be obtained from the Assistant Secretary (Tax Policy), Departmental Offices, Treasury Department, Washington, DC 20220. Phone, 202–622–0050.

Telephone Directory The Treasury Department telephone directory is available for sale by the Superintendent of Documents, Government Printing Office, Washington, DC 20402.

Treasury Inspector General Individuals wishing to report fraud, waste, or abuse against or by IRS employees should write to the Treasury Inspector General for Tax Administration, P.O. Box 589, Ben Franklin Station, Washington, DC 20044–0589. Phone, 800–366–4484. E-mail, complaints@TIGTA.TREAS.gov.

Comptroller of the Currency For Freedom of Information Act Requests, contact the Manager, Disclosure Services and Administrative Operations, Communications Division, 250 E Street SW., Mail Stop 3–2, Washington, DC 20219 (phone, 202–874–4700; fax, 202–874–5274). For information about contracts, contact the Acquisition Management Division at 250 E Street SW., Washington, DC 20219 (phone, 202–874–5040; fax, 202–874–5625). For information regarding national bank examiner employment opportunities (generally hired at the entry level through a college recruitment program), contact the Director for Human Resources Operations, 250 E Street SW., Washington, DC 20219 (phone, 202–874–4500; fax, 202–874–4655). Publications are available from the Communications Division, 250 E Street SW., Washington, DC 20219 (phone, 202–874–4700; fax, 202–874–5263).

Bureau of Engraving and Printing

Address inquiries on the following subjects to the specified office, Bureau of Engraving and Printing.

Contracts and Small Business Activities Information relating to contracts and small business activity may be obtained by contacting the Office of Procurement. Phone, 202–874–1981.

Employment Information regarding employment opportunities and required qualifications is available from the Office of Human Resources. Phone, 202–874–2633.

Freedom of Information Act Requests Inquiries should be directed to 202–874–2058.

General Inquiries Requests for information about the Bureau, its products, or numismatic and philatelic interests should be directed to 202–874–3019.

Mail Order Sales Uncut sheets of currency, engraved Presidential portraits, historical engravings of national landmarks, and other souvenirs and mementos are available for purchase by phone at 800–456–3408 and the Internet at www.moneyfactory.com.

Tours Tours of the Bureau's facilities are provided throughout the year according to the following schedules:

Washington, DC—

Peak season, March through August, 9 a.m. until 10:45 a.m. and 12:30 p.m. until 2 p.m. Tickets are required for all tours. Tours begin every 15 minutes, with the last tour beginning at 2 p.m. The times between 11 a.m. and 12:15 p.m. are reserved for school and other groups. The ticket booth is located on Raoul Wallenberg Place (formerly Fifteenth Street) and opens at 8 a.m. Tour tickets are free. The ticket booth remains open for the morning and evening tours until all tickets have been distributed. Lines form early and tickets go quickly, typically by 9 a.m. during peak season. Tickets are distributed on a first-come, first-serve basis. Lines organize on Raoul Wallenberg Place.

Evening tours, May through August, 5 p.m. until 7 p.m. Tours are offered every 15 minutes.

Non-peak season, September through February, 9 a.m. until 2 p.m. No tickets are necessary for tours during this time. Lines organize on Fourteenth Street.

Fort Worth, TX—

Non-peak season, September through May, 9 a.m. until 2 p.m. The Visitors Center is open from 8:30 a.m. until 3:30 p.m.

In June and July, tour hours are every 30 minutes, from 11 a.m. until 5 p.m. The Visitors Center is open from 10:30 a.m. until 6:30 p.m.

No tours are given at either facility on weekends, Federal holidays, or between Christmas and New Year's Day.

Up-to-the-minute tour information is available on the Bureau's Web site at www.moneyfactory.com. Information about the Washington, DC, tour and visitors center can also be obtained by calling 202–874–2330 or 866–874–2330. Information about the Fort Worth tour and visitor center can be obtained by calling 817–231–4000 or 866–865–1194.

Financial Management Service

Inquiries on the following subjects should be directed to the specified office, Financial Management Service, 401 Fourteenth Street SW., Washington, DC 20227. Fax, 202–874–7016.

Contracts Write to the Director, Acquisition Management Division, Room 428 LCB. Phone, 202–874–6910.

Employment Inquiries may be directed to the Human Resources Division, Room 170A, 3700 East-West Highway, Hyattsville, MD 20782. Phone, 202–874–8090. TDD, 202–874–8825.

Internal Revenue Service

Audiovisual Materials Films providing information on the American tax system, examination and appeal rights, and the tax responsibilities of running a small business are available. Some of the films are also available in Spanish. The films can be obtained by contacting any territory office.

Also available are audio and video cassette tapes that provide step-by-step instructions for preparing basic individual income tax forms. These tapes are available in many local libraries.

Contracts Write to the Internal Revenue Service, 1111 Constitution Avenue NW. (M:P:C), Washington, DC 20224 (phone, 202–283–1710); or the Director of Support Services, at any of the Internal Revenue territory offices.

Customer Account Service The Internal Revenue Service provides year-round tax information and assistance to taxpayers, primarily through its toll-free telephone system, which also includes telephone assistance to deaf and hearing-impaired taxpayers who have access to a teletypewriter or television/phone. The toll-free numbers are listed in local telephone directories and in the annual tax form packages. Taxpayers may also visit agency offices for help with their tax problems. The Service provides return preparation assistance to taxpayers by guiding groups of individuals line by line on the preparation of their returns. Individual preparation is available for handicapped or other individuals unable to use the group preparation method.

Foreign language tax assistance also is available at many locations.

Educational Programs The Service provides, free of charge, general tax information publications and booklets on specific tax topics. Taxpayer information materials also are distributed to major television networks and many radio and television stations, daily and weekly newspapers, magazines, and specialized publications. Special educational materials and films are provided for use in high schools and colleges. Individuals starting a new business are given specialized materials and information at small business workshops, and community colleges provide classes based on material provided by the Service. The community outreach tax assistance program provides assistance, through agency employees, to community groups.

Through the volunteer income tax assistance program and the tax counseling for the elderly program, the Service recruits, trains, and supports volunteers who offer free tax assistance to low-income, elderly, military, and non-English-speaking taxpayers.

Materials, films, and information on the educational programs can be obtained by contacting any territory office.

Employment For information, write to the recruitment coordinator at any of the territory offices.

Publications The *Annual Report—Commissioner of Internal Revenue,* the *Internal Revenue Service Data Book,* and periodic reports of statistics of income are available from the Superintendent of Documents, Government Printing Office, Washington, DC 20402.

Audit of Returns, Appeal Rights, and Claims for Refund, Your Federal Income Tax, Farmers Tax Guide, Tax Guide for Small Business, and other publications are available at Internal Revenue Service offices free of charge.

Reading Rooms Public reading rooms are located in the national office and in each territory office.

Speakers Arrangements for speakers on provisions of the tax law and operations of the Internal Revenue Service for professional and community groups may be made by writing to the Senior Commissioner's Representative or, for national organizations only, to the Communications Division at the IRS National Headquarters in Washington, DC.

Taxpayer Advocate Each district has a problem resolution staff which attempts to resolve taxpayer complaints not satisfied through regular channels.

United States Mint

Contracts and Employment Inquiries should be directed to the facility head of the appropriate field office or to the Director of the Mint.

Numismatic Services The United States Mint maintains public exhibit and sales areas at the Philadelphia and Denver Mints, and at Union Station in Washington, DC. Brochures and order forms for official coins, medals, and other numismatic items are available through the Internet, at www.usmint.gov.

Publications The *CFO Annual Financial Report* is available from the United States Mint, Department of the Treasury, 801 Ninth Street NW., Washington, DC 20220. Phone, 202–354–7800.

Bureau of the Public Debt

Electronic Access Information about the public debt, U.S. Savings Bonds, Treasury bills, notes, and bonds, and other Treasury securities is available through the Internet, at www.treasurydirect.gov. Forms and publications may be ordered electronically at the same address.

Employment General employment inquiries should be addressed to the Bureau of the Public Debt, Division of Personnel Management, Employment and Classification Branch, Parkersburg, WV 26106–1328. Phone, 304–480–6144.

Savings Bonds Savings bonds are continuously on sale at more than 40,000 financial institutions and their branches in virtually every locality in the United States. Information about bonds is provided by such issuing agents. Current rate information is available toll free by calling 800–4US–BOND.

Requests for information about all series of savings bonds, savings notes, and retirement plans or individual retirement bonds should be addressed to the Bureau of the Public Debt, Department of the Treasury, 200 Third Street, Parkersburg, WV 26106–1328. Phone, 304–480–6112.

Treasury Securities Information inquiries regarding the purchase of Treasury bills, bonds, and notes should be addressed to a Treasury direct contact center, or to the Bureau of the Public Debt, 200 Third Street, Parkersburg, WV 26106–1328. Phone, 800–722–2678.

Office of Thrift Supervision

Electronic Access Information about OTS and institutions regulated by OTS is available through the Internet, at www.ots.treas.gov.

Employment Inquiries about employment opportunities with the Office of Thrift Supervision should be directed to the Human Resources Office. Phone, 202–906–6061.

Freedom of Information Act/Privacy Act Requests For information not readily available from the Web site, please submit to the Office of Thrift Supervision, Dissemination Branch, 1700 G Street NW., Washington, DC 20552. E-mail, publicinfo@ots.treas.gov. Fax, 202–906–7755.

General Information General information about OTS may be obtained by calling 202–906–6000.

Publications Publications that provide information and guidance regarding the thrift industry are available at the "Public Information" link on the Web site.

For further information, contact the Public Affairs Office, Department of the Treasury, 1500 Pennsylvania Avenue NW., Washington, DC 20220. Phone, 202–622–2960. Internet, www.treas.gov.

DEPARTMENT OF VETERANS AFFAIRS

810 Vermont Avenue NW., Washington, DC 20420
Phone, 202–273–4800. Internet, www.va.gov.

SECRETARY OF VETERANS AFFAIRS	R. JAMES NICHOLSON
Chief of Staff	THOMAS G. BOWMAN
Deputy Secretary	GORDON H. MANSFIELD
General Counsel	TIM S. MCCLAIN
Chairman, Board of Contract Appeals	GARY KRUMP
Chairman, Board of Veterans' Appeals	(VACANCY)
Vice Chairman, Board of Veterans' Appeals	(VACANCY)
Director, Office of Small and Disadvantaged Business Utilization	SCOTT F. DENNISTON
Director, Center for Minority Veterans	LUCRETIA MCCLENNEY
Director, Center for Women Veterans	IRENE TROWELL-HARRIS
Director, Office of Employment Discrimination Complaint Adjudication	CHARLES R. DELOBE
Assistant to the Secretary, Office of Regulation Policy and Management	ROBERT C. MCFETRIDGE, *Acting*
Inspector General	RICHARD J. GRIFFIN
Veterans' Service Organizations Liaison	KEVIN S. SECOR
Under Secretary for Health, Veterans Health Administration	JONATHAN B. PERLIN
Deputy Under Secretary for Health	MICHAEL J. KUSSMAN, *Acting*
Deputy Under Secretary for Health for Operations and Management	WILLIAM F. FEELEY
Under Secretary for Benefits, Veterans Benefits Administration	DANIEL L. COOPER
Deputy Under Secretary for Benefits	RONALD R. AUMENT
Under Secretary for Memorial Affairs, National Cemetery Administration	RICHARD A. WANNEMACHER, JR., *Acting*
Deputy Under Secretary for Memorial Affairs	RICHARD A. WANNEMACHER, JR.
Assistant Secretary for Management	ROBERT J. HENKE
Principal Deputy Assistant Secretary	RITA A. REED
Deputy Assistant Secretary for Budget	DANIEL A. TUCKER
Deputy Assistant Secretary for Finance	EDWARD J. MURRAY
Deputy Assistant Secretary for Acquisition and Materiel Management	JAN R. FRYE
Assistant Secretary for Information and Technology	(VACANCY)
Deputy Assistant Secretary for Information and Technology	PEDRO CADENAS, JR., *Acting*
Associate Deputy Assistant Secretary for Information Technology Enterprise Architecture	SCOTT CRAGG
Associate Deputy Assistant Secretary for Policies, Portfolio Oversight, and Execution	(VACANCY)

Associate Deputy Assistant Secretary for Information Technology Operations	(VACANCY)
Associate Deputy Assistant Secretary for e-Government/Records Management	SALLY WALLACE
Associate Deputy Assistant Secretary for Cyber and Information Security	PEDRO CARDENAS, JR.
Deputy Chief Information Officer for National Cemetary Administration	JOE NOSARI
Deputy Chief Information Officer for Veterans Health Administration	(VACANCY)
Deputy Chief Information Officer for Veterans Benefits Administration	DON WILLIAMS
Director, Austin Automation Center	LINDA VOGES
Assistant Secretary for Policy, Planning, and Preparedness	DENNIS DUFFY, *Acting*
Principal Deputy Assistant Secretary for Policy and Planning	DENNIS DUFFY
Deputy Assistant Secretary for Policy and Planning	MICHAEL MCLENDON
Deputy Assistant Secretary for Planning and Evaluation	(VACANCY)
Director, Office of Emergency Management	KEVIN HANRETTA
Deputy Assistant Secretary for Security and Law Enforcement	JOHN H. BAFFA
Assistant Secretary for Human Resources and Administration	R. ALLEN PITTMAN
Principal Deputy Assistant Secretary for Human Resources and Administration	GARY A. STEINBERG
Director, Office of Administration	CONSTANTINE G. VERENES
Deputy Director, Office of Administration	CATHERINE BIGGS-SILVERS
Deputy Assistant Secretary for Diversity Management and Equal Employment Opportunity	SUSAN C. MCHUGH
Deputy Assistant Secretary for Human Resources Management and Labor Relations	THOMAS J. HOGAN
Associate Deputy Assistant for Human Resources Management and Labor Relations	WILLIE L. HENSLEY, *Acting*
Associate Deputy Assistant Secretary for Human Resources Management and Labor Relations	(VACANCY)
Associate Deputy Assistant Secretary for Labor Management Relations	RONALD E. COWLES
Deputy Assistant Secretary for Resolution Management	GARY A. STEINBERG, *Acting*
Assistant Secretary for Public and Intergovernmental Affairs	LISETTE M. MONDELLO
Deputy Assistant Secretary for Public Affairs	SCOTT A. HOGENSON
Deputy Assistant Secretary for Intergovernmental and International Affairs	WILLIAM W. MCLEMORE
Director, Center for Faith-Based and Community Initiatives	DARIN S. SELNICK

Assistant Secretary for Congressional and Legislative Affairs	THOMAS E. HARVEY, *Acting*
Deputy Assistant Secretary for Congressional and Legislative Affairs	CHRISTINE O. HILL

The Department of Veterans Affairs operates programs to benefit veterans and members of their families. Benefits include compensation payments for disabilities or death related to military service; pensions; education and rehabilitation; home loan guaranty; burial; and a medical care program incorporating nursing homes, clinics, and medical centers.

The Department of Veterans Affairs (VA) was established as an executive department by the Department of Veterans Affairs Act (38 U.S.C. 201 note). It is comprised of three organizations that administer veterans programs: the Veterans Health Administration, the Veterans Benefits Administration, and the National Cemetery Administration. Each organization has field facilities and a central office component.

Activities

Cemeteries The National Cemetery Administration (NCA) is responsible for more than 120 national cemeteries nationwide. Burial in a national cemetery is available to veterans, their spouses, and dependent children. At no cost to the family, a national cemetery burial includes the gravesite, grave-liner, opening and closing of the grave, headstone or marker, and perpetual care as part of a national shrine. If a veteran is buried in a private cemetery, anywhere in the world, NCA will provide a headstone or marker. NCA's State Cemetery Grants Program provides funds to establish, expand, or improve State-operated veterans cemeteries. Presidential Memorial Certificates honoring the veteran may be requested from NCA.

Center for Minority Veterans The Center for Minority Veterans was established under Public Law 103–446 (108 Stat. 4645) and is responsible for promoting the use of VA benefits, programs, and services by minority veterans and assessing the needs of minority group members. The work of the Center focuses on the unique and special needs of five distinct groups of veterans: African-Americans, Hispanics, Asian-Americans, Pacific Islanders, and Native Americans, which include American Indians, Native Hawaiians, and Alaskan Natives.

Center for Women Veterans The Center for Women Veterans was established under Public Law 103–446 (108 Stat. 4645) and acts as the Secretary's primary adviser on women veterans issues and evaluates VA programs, policies, legislation, and practices to ensure that they are responsive and accessible to eligible women veterans.

Health Services The Veterans Health Administration provides hospital, nursing home, and domiciliary care, and outpatient medical and dental care to eligible veterans of military service in the Armed Forces. It conducts both individual medical and health-care delivery research projects and multi-hospital research programs, and it assists in the education of physicians and dentists and with training of many other health care professionals through affiliations with educational institutions and organizations.

Veterans Benefits The Veterans Benefits Administration provides information, advice, and assistance to veterans, their dependents, beneficiaries, representatives, and others applying for VA benefits. It also cooperates with the Department of Labor and other Federal, State, and local agencies in developing employment opportunities for veterans and referral for assistance in resolving socioeconomic, housing, and other related problems.

The Compensation and Pension Service is responsible for claims for disability compensation and pension,

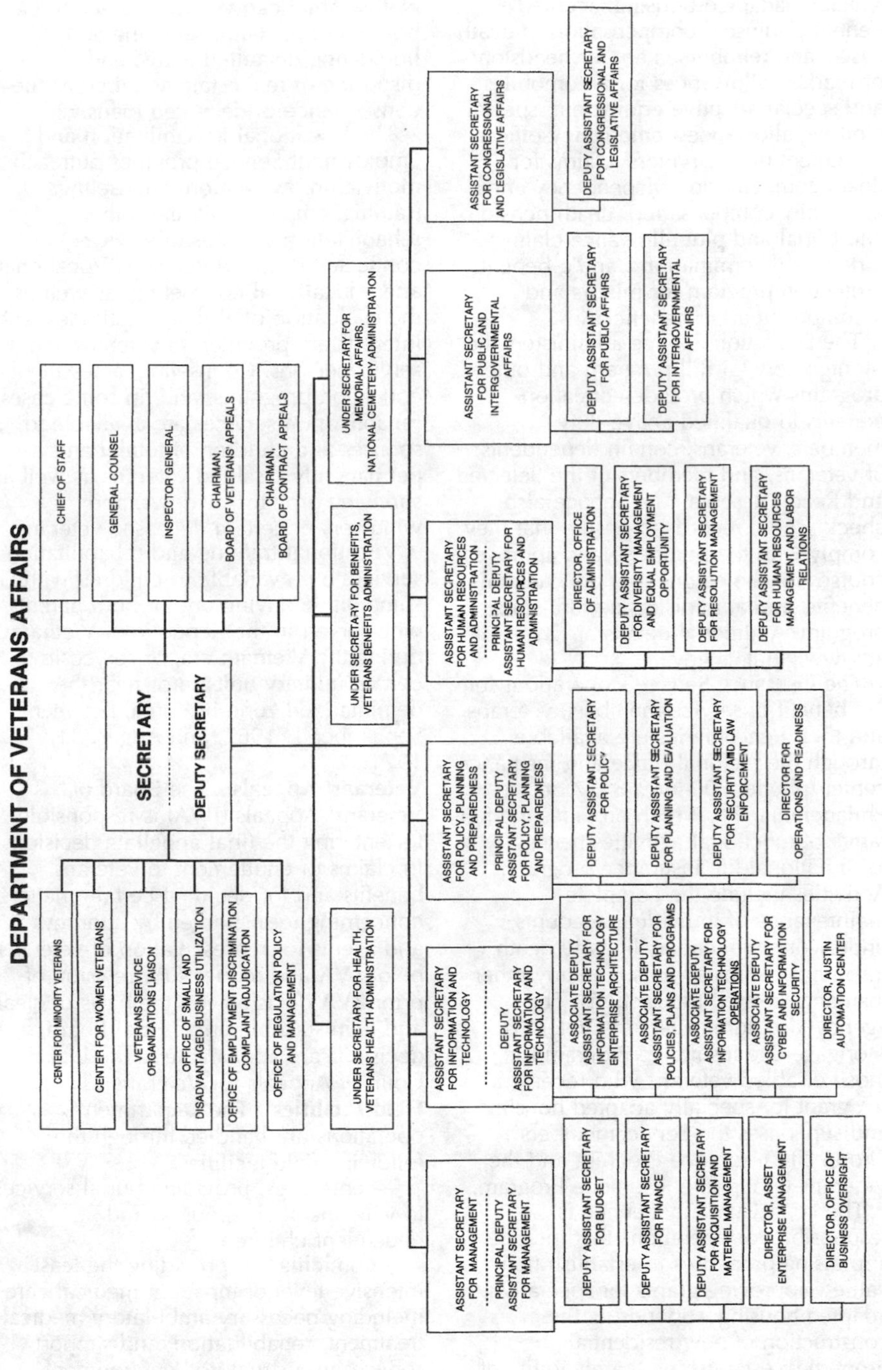
DEPARTMENT OF VETERANS AFFAIRS
SECRETARY
DEPUTY SECRETARY
CHIEF OF STAFF
GENERAL COUNSEL
INSPECTOR GENERAL
CHAIRMAN, BOARD OF VETERANS' APPEALS
CHAIRMAN, BOARD OF CONTRACT APPEALS
CENTER FOR MINORITY VETERANS
CENTER FOR WOMEN VETERANS
VETERANS SERVICE ORGANIZATIONS LIAISON
OFFICE OF SMALL AND DISADVANTAGED BUSINESS UTILIZATION
OFFICE OF EMPLOYMENT DISCRIMINATION COMPLAINT ADJUDICATION
OFFICE OF REGULATION POLICY AND MANAGEMENT
UNDER SECRETARY FOR HEALTH, VETERANS HEALTH ADMINISTRATION
UNDER SECRETARY FOR BENEFITS, VETERANS BENEFITS ADMINISTRATION
UNDER SECRETARY FOR MEMORIAL AFFAIRS, NATIONAL CEMETERY ADMINISTRATION
ASSISTANT SECRETARY FOR MANAGEMENT
PRINCIPAL DEPUTY ASSISTANT SECRETARY FOR MANAGEMENT
DEPUTY ASSISTANT SECRETARY FOR BUDGET
DEPUTY ASSISTANT SECRETARY FOR FINANCE
DEPUTY ASSISTANT SECRETARY FOR ACQUISITION AND MATERIEL MANAGEMENT
DIRECTOR, ASSET ENTERPRISE MANAGEMENT
DIRECTOR, OFFICE OF BUSINESS OVERSIGHT
ASSISTANT SECRETARY FOR INFORMATION AND TECHNOLOGY
DEPUTY ASSISTANT SECRETARY FOR INFORMATION AND TECHNOLOGY
ASSOCIATE DEPUTY ASSISTANT SECRETARY FOR INFORMATION TECHNOLOGY ENTERPRISE ARCHITECTURE
ASSOCIATE DEPUTY ASSISTANT SECRETARY FOR POLICIES, PLANS AND PROGRAMS
ASSOCIATE DEPUTY ASSISTANT SECRETARY FOR INFORMATION TECHNOLOGY OPERATIONS
ASSOCIATE DEPUTY ASSISTANT SECRETARY FOR CYBER AND INFORMATION SECURITY
DIRECTOR, AUSTIN AUTOMATION CENTER
ASSISTANT SECRETARY FOR POLICY, PLANNING AND PREPAREDNESS
PRINCIPAL DEPUTY ASSISTANT SECRETARY FOR POLICY, PLANNING AND PREPAREDNESS
DEPUTY ASSISTANT SECRETARY FOR POLICY
DEPUTY ASSISTANT SECRETARY FOR PLANNING AND EVALUATION
DEPUTY ASSISTANT SECRETARY FOR SECURITY AND LAW ENFORCEMENT
DIRECTOR FOR OPERATIONS AND READINESS
ASSISTANT SECRETARY FOR HUMAN RESOURCES AND ADMINISTRATION
PRINCIPAL DEPUTY ASSISTANT SECRETARY FOR HUMAN RESOURCES AND ADMINISTRATION
DIRECTOR, OFFICE OF ADMINISTRATION
DEPUTY ASSISTANT SECRETARY FOR DIVERSITY MANAGEMENT AND EQUAL EMPLOYMENT OPPORTUNITY
DEPUTY ASSISTANT SECRETARY FOR RESOLUTION MANAGEMENT
DEPUTY ASSISTANT SECRETARY FOR HUMAN RESOURCES MANAGEMENT AND LABOR RELATIONS
ASSISTANT SECRETARY FOR PUBLIC AND INTERGOVERNMENTAL AFFAIRS
DEPUTY ASSISTANT SECRETARY FOR PUBLIC AFFAIRS
DEPUTY ASSISTANT SECRETARY FOR INTERGOVERNMENTAL AFFAIRS
ASSISTANT SECRETARY FOR CONGRESSIONAL AND LEGISLATIVE AFFAIRS
DEPUTY ASSISTANT SECRETARY FOR CONGRESSIONAL AND LEGISLATIVE AFFAIRS

specially adapted housing, accrued benefits, adjusted compensation in death cases, and reimbursement for headstone or marker; allowances for automobiles and special adaptive equipment; special clothing allowances; emergency officers' retirement pay; survivors' claims for death compensation, dependency and indemnity compensation, death pension, and burial and plot allowance claims; forfeiture determinations; and a benefits protection program for minors and incompetent adult beneficiaries.

The Education Service administers the Montgomery GI Bill program and other programs which provide education benefits to qualified active-duty members, veterans, certain dependents of veterans, and members of the Selected and Ready Reserve. The Service also check school records to ensure that they comply with the pertinent law, approves courses for the payment of educational benefits, and administers a work-study program. Additional details are available at www.gibill.va.gov.

The Insurance Service's operations for the benefit of service members, veterans, and their beneficiaries are available through the regional office and insurance center (phone, 800–669–8477) in Philadelphia, PA, which provides the full range of functional activities necessary for a national life insurance program. Activities include the complete maintenance of individual accounts, underwriting functions, life and death insurance claims awards, and any other insurance-related transactions. The agency also administers the Veterans Mortgage Life Insurance Program for those disabled veterans who receive a VA grant for specially adapted housing and supervises the Servicemembers' Group Life Insurance Program and the Veterans Group Life Insurance Program.

The Loan Guaranty Service is responsible for operations that include appraising properties to establish their values; approving grants for specially adapted housing; supervising the construction of new residential properties; establishing the eligibility of veterans for the program; evaluating the ability of a veteran to repay a loan and the credit risk; making direct loans to Native American veterans to acquire a home on trust land; servicing and liquidating defaulted loans; and disposing of real estate acquired as the consequence of defaulted loans.

The Vocational Rehabilitation and Employment Service provides outreach, motivation, evaluation, counseling, training, employment, and other rehabilitation services to service-connected disabled veterans. Vocational and educational counseling, as well as the evaluation of abilities, aptitudes, and interests are provided to veterans and servicepersons. Counseling, assessment, education programs, and, in some cases, rehabilitation services are available to spouses and children of totally and permanently disabled veterans as well as surviving orphans, widows, and widowers of certain deceased veterans.

Vocational training and rehabilitation services are available to children with spina bifida having one or both parents who served in the Republic of Vietnam during the Vietnam era, or served in certain military units in or near the demilitarized zone in Korea, between September 1, 1967, and August 31, 1971.

Veterans' Appeals The Board of Veterans' Appeals (BVA) is responsible for entering the final appellate decisions in claims of entitlement to veterans' benefits and for deciding certain matters concerning fees charged by attorneys and agents for representation of veterans before VA and requests for revision of prior BVA decisions on the basis of clear and unmistakable error. Final Board decisions are appealable to the U.S. Court of Appeals for Veterans Claims.

Field Facilities The Department's operations are handled through the following field facilities:

—cemeteries, providing burial services to veterans, their spouses, and dependent children;

—domiciliaries, providing the least intensive level of inpatient medical care including necessary ambulatory medical treatment, rehabilitation, and support services in a structured environment to veterans who are unable because of their disabilities to provide adequately for themselves in the community;

—medical centers, providing eligible beneficiaries with medical and other health care services equivalent to those provided by private-sector institutions, augmented in many instances by services to meet the special requirements of veterans;

—outpatient clinics to provide eligible beneficiaries with ambulatory care; and

—regional offices to grant benefits and services provided by law for veterans, their dependents, and beneficiaries within an assigned territory; furnish information regarding VA benefits and services; adjudicate claims and make awards for disability compensation and pension; conduct outreach and information dissemination and provide support and assistance to various segments of the veteran population to include former prisoners of war (POW), minority veterans, homeless veterans, women veterans and elderly veterans; supervise payment of VA benefits to incompetent beneficiaries; provide vocational rehabilitation and employment training; administer educational benefits; guarantee loans for purchase, construction, or alteration of homes; process grants for specially adapted housing; process death claims; and assist veterans in exercising rights to benefits and services.

National Facilities—Department of Veterans Affairs

Address	Type of facility	Director
ALABAMA:		
Birmingham (700 S. 19th St., 35233)	Medical Center	Y.C. Parris
Central Alabama Health Care System (215 Perry Hill Rd., Montgomery, 36109–3798).	Medical Center	Robert Ratliff
Mobile (1202 Virginia St., 36604)	National Cemetary	
Montgomery (345 Perry Hill Rd., 36109)	Regional Office	Montgomery Watson
Seale (Fort Mitchell, 553 Hwy. 165, 36856)	National Cemetary	
Tuscaloosa (35404)	Medical Center	Robert Malone
ALASKA:		
Anchorage (2925 Debarr Rd., 99508)	Outpatient Clinic and Regional Office.	Alex Spector
Fort Richardson (Bldg. 997, Davis Hwy., 99505–5498).	National Cemetery	
Sitka (803 Sawmill Creek Rd., 99835)	National Cemetery	
ARIZONA:		
Northern Arizona Health Care System (500 N. Hwy. 89, Prescott, 86313).	Medical Center (medical and domiciliary).	Deborah Thompson
Phoenix (7th St. & Indian School Rd., 85012)	Medical Center	(Vacancy)
Phoenix (3225 N. Central Ave., 85012)	Regional Office	Sandra D. Flint
Phoenix (23029 N. Cave Creek Rd., 85024) (National Memorial Cemetery of Arizona).	National Cemetery	
Prescott (500 Hwy. 89 N., 86301)	National Cemetery	
Southern Arizona Health Care System (3601 S. 6th Ave., Tucson, 85723).	Medical Center	Jonathan H. Gardner
ARKANSAS:		
Fayetteville (72701)	Medical Center	Michael Winn
Fayetteville (700 Government Ave., 72701)	National Cemetery	
Fort Smith (522 Garland Ave., 72901)	National Cemetery	
Little Rock (2523 Confederate Blvd., 72206)	National Cemetery	
Little Rock (300 Roosevelt Rd., 72205) (John L. McClellan Memorial Veterans Hospital). Little Rock Division North Little Rock Division	Medical Center	Tim Shea
North Little Rock (P.O. Box 1280, Bldg. 65, Ft. Roots, 72115).	Regional Office	William Nicholas
CALIFORNIA:		
Central California Health Care System (2615 Clinton Ave., Fresno, 93703).	Medical Center	Alan S. Perry
Gustine (San Joaquin Valley National Cemetery, 32053 W. McCabe Rd., 95322).	National Cemetery	
Loma Linda (Jerry L. Pettis Memorial Veterans Hospital, 11201 Benton St., 92357).	Medical Center	Dean R. Stordahl
Long Beach (5901 E. 7th St., 90822)	Medical Center	Ron Norby
Los Angeles (11301 Wilshire Blvd., 90073)	Medical Center	Charles Dorman
Los Angeles (11000 Wilshire Blvd., 90024)	Regional Office	Stewart F. Liff
Los Angeles (950 S. Sepulveda Blvd., 90049)	National Cemetery	
Northern California Health Care System (150 Muir Rd., Benicia, 94523).	Medical Center	Larry Sandler
Oakland (Oakland Federal Bldg., 1301 Clay St., 94612–5209).	Regional Office	Cathy L. Smith

National Facilities—Department of Veterans Affairs—Continued

Address	Type of facility	Director
Palo Alto Health Care System (3801 Miranda Ave., 94304).	Medical Center	Elisabeth J. Freeman
Riverside (22495 Van Buren Blvd., 92518)	National Cemetery	
San Bruno (Golden Gate National Cemetery, 1300 Sneath Ln., 94066).	National Cemetery	
San Diego (3350 La Jolla Village Dr., 92161)	Medical Center	Gary Rossio
San Diego (8810 Rio San Diego Dr., 92108)	Regional Office	Lily Fetzer
San Diego (Fort Rosecrans National Cemetery, P.O. Box 6237, Point Loma, 92106).	National Cemetery	
San Francisco (4150 Clement St., 94121)	Medical Center	Sheila Cullen
San Francisco (P.O. Box 29012, Presidio of San Francisco, 94129).	National Cemetery	
COLORADO:		
Denver (1055 Clermont St., 80220)	Medical Center	Lynette Roff
Denver (80225)	Denver Distribution Center	Jim Sandman
Denver (Fort Logan National Cemetery, 3698 S. Sheridan Blvd., 80235).	National Cemetery	
Fort Lyon (81038)	National Cemetery	
Grand Junction (81501)	Medical Center	Michael Murphy
Lakewood (P.O. Box 25126, 155 Van Gordon St., 80228).	Regional Office	Jeffrey Alger
CONNECTICUT:		
Connecticut Health Care System (950 Campbell Ave., West Haven, 06516).	Medical Center	Roger Johnson
Hartford (450 Main St., 06103)	Regional Office	Linda Walker
DELAWARE:		
Wilmington (1601 Kirkwood Hwy., 19805)	Medical Center	Richard Citron
DISTRICT OF COLUMBIA:		
Washington (50 Irving St. NW., 20422)	Medical Center	Sanford M. Garfunkel
Washington (1120 Vermont Ave. NW., 20421)	Regional Office	Judy Reyes-Maggio
FLORIDA:		
Bay Pines (1000 Bay Pines Blvd. N., 33504)	Medical Center (medical and domiciliary).	Wallace M. Hopkins
Bay Pines (10000 Bay Pines Blvd., North Bay Pines, 33504–0477).	National Cemetery	
Bushnell (Florida National Cemetery, 6502 SW. 102d Ave., 33513).	National Cemetery	
Miami (1201 NW. 16th St., 33125)	Medical Center	Stephen Lucas
Northern Florida/Southern Georgia Health Care System (1601 SW. Archer Rd., Gainesville, 32608–1197).	Medical Center	Fred Malphrus
Orlando (5201 Raymond St., Orlando, 32803)	Medical Center	(Vacancy)
Pensacola (Barrancas National Cemetery, Naval Air Station, 80 Hovey Rd. 32508–1099).	National Cemetery	
St. Augustine (104 Marine St., 32084)	National Cemetery	
St. Petersburg (P.O. Box 1437, 33731)	Regional Office	Barry Baker
Tampa (James A. Haley Veterans Hospital, 13000 Bruce B. Downs Blvd., 33612).	Medical Center	Forest Farley, Jr.
West Palm Beach (7305 N. Military Trail, 33410–6400).	Medical Center	Edward H. Seiler
West Palm Beach (South Florida National Cemetery, 7305 N. Military Trail, 33410).	National Cemetery	
GEORGIA:		
Atlanta (1670 Clairmont Rd., 30033)	Medical Center	Thomas A. Cappello
Atlanta (P.O. Box 100026, 1700 Clairmont Rd., Decatur, 30033).	Regional Office	Larry Burks
Augusta (2460 Wrightsboro Rd., 30904–6285)	Medical Center	James Trusley
Forest Hills Division		
Lenwood Division		
Canton (Georgia National Cemetery, 2025 Mount Carmel Church Ln., 30114).	National Cemetery	
Dublin (31021)	Medical Center (medical and domiciliary).	Richard W. Fry
Marietta (500 Washington Ave., 30060)	National Cemetery	
HAWAII:		
Honolulu (P.O. Box 29020, 96850)	Medical Center	James Hastings
Honolulu (National Memorial Cemetery of the Pacific, 2177 Puowaina Dr., 96813–1729).	National Cemetery	
IDAHO:		
Boise (805 W. Franklin St., 83702)	Regional Office	James Vance
Boise (500 W. Fort St., 83702–4598)	Medical Center	Wayne Tippets
ILLINOIS:		
Alton (600 Pearl St., 62003)	National Cemetery	
Chicago Health Care System (333 E. Huron St., 60611).	Medical Center	James Jones

National Facilities—Department of Veterans Affairs—Continued

Address	Type of facility	Director
Chicago (P.O. Box 8136, 536 S. Clark St., 60680)	Regional Office	Michael Olson
Danville (61832)	Medical Center	Susan P. Bowers
Danville (1900 E. Main St., 61832)	National Cemetery	
Elwood (Abraham Lincoln National Cemetery, 27034 S. Diagonal Rd., 60421).	National Cemetery	
Hines (Lock Box 66303, AMF O'Hare, 60666–0303)	Finance Center	Billy R. Barker
Hines (Edward Hines, Jr., Hospital, 60141)	Medical Center	Jack Hetrick
Hines (P.O. Box 76, 60141)	VA National Acquisition Center	Efrain Fernandez
Hines (P.O. Box 27, 60141)	Service and Distribution Center	George Moore
Marion (2401 W. Main St., 62959)	Medical Center	Kathy Spivey-Paul
Moline (Rock Island National Cemetery, Bldg. 118, Rock Island Arsenal, 61299–7090).	National Cemetery	
Mound City (Junction Hwys. 37 and 51, 62963)	National Cemetery	
North Chicago (60064)	Medical Center	Patrick L. Sullivan
Quincy (36th and Maine Sts., 62301)	National Cemetery	
Springfield (Camp Butler National Cemetery, 5063 Camp Butler Rd., 62707).	National Cemetery	
INDIANA:		
Indianapolis (1481 W. 10th St., 46202) Cold Spring Road Division Tenth Street Division	Medical Center	Susan P. Bowers
Indianapolis (575 N. Pennsylvania St., 46204)	Regional Office	Dennis Kuewa
Indianapolis (Crown Hill National Cemetery, 700 W. 38th St., 46208).	National Cemetery	
Marion (1700 E. 38th St., 46952)	National Cemetery	
New Albany (1943 Ekin Ave., 47150)	National Cemetery	
Northern Indiana Health Care System (2121 Lake Ave., Fort Wayne, 46805).	Medical Center	Kathy Spivey-Paul
IOWA:		
Central Iowa Health Care System (30th and Euclid Ave., Des Moines, 50310–5774).	Medical Center	Donald Cooper
Des Moines (210 Walnut St., 50309)	Regional Office	Richard Braley
Iowa City (Hwy. 6 W., 52246–5774)	Medical Center	Peter Henry, *Acting*
Keokuk (1701 J St., 52632)	National Cemetery	
KANSAS:		
Eastern Kansas Health Care System (Leavenworth, 66048).	Medical Center (medical and domiciliary).	(Vacancy)
Fort Leavenworth (66027)	National Cemetery	
Fort Scott (P.O. Box 917, 900 E. National, 66701)	National Cemetery	
Leavenworth (P.O. Box 1694, 66048)	National Cemetery	
Topeka (Bldg. 9, 3401 SW. 21st St., 66604)	Health Revenue Center	Matthew Kelly, *Acting*
Wichita (5500 E. Kellogg, 67218)	Medical Center	Thomas J. Sanders
Wichita (5500 E. Kellogg, 67218)	Regional Office and Medical Center	Charlie Wolford
KENTUCKY:		
Danville (277 N. 1st St., 40442)	National Cemetery	
Lebanon (20 Hwy. 208E, 40033)	National Cemetery	
Lexington (40511) Cooper Drive Division Leestown Division	Medical Center	Sandy J. Nielson
Lexington (833 W. Main St., 40508)	National Cemetery	
Louisville (545 S. 3d St., 40202)	Regional Office	Keith Thompson
Louisville (800 Zorn Ave., 40202)	Medical Center	Wayne L. Pfeffer
Louisville (Cave Hill National Cemetery, 701 Baxter Ave., 40204).	National Cemetery	
Louisville (Zachary Taylor National Cemetery, 4701 Brownsboro Rd., 40207).	National Cemetery	
Nancy (Mill Springs National Cemetery, 9044 W. Hwy. 80, 42544).	National Cemetery	
Nicholasville (Camp Nelson National Cemetery, 6980 Danville Rd., 40356).	National Cemetery	
LOUISIANA:		
Alexandria (71301)	Medical Center	Barbara Watkins
Baton Rouge (220 N. 19th St., 70806)	National Cemetery	
New Orleans (1601 Peridido St., 70146)	Medical Center	John D. Church, Jr.
New Orleans (701 Loyola Ave., 70113)	Regional Office	Rowland Christian
Pineville (Alexandria National Cemetery, 209 E. Shamrock St., 71360).	National Cemetery	
Shreveport (510 E. Stoner Ave., 71101)	Medical Center	George Moore
Zachary (20978 Port Hickey Rd., 70791) (Port Hudson National Cemetery).	National Cemetery	
MAINE:		
Togus (1 VA Ctr., 04330)	Medical and Regional Office Center	Dale Demurs
Togus (1 VA Ctr., 04330)	National Cemetery	
MARYLAND:		
Annapolis (800 West St., 21401)	National Cemetery	

National Facilities—Department of Veterans Affairs—Continued

Address	Type of facility	Director
Baltimore (31 Hopkins Plz., 21201)	Regional Office	George Wolohojian
Baltimore (5501 Frederick Ave., 21228)	National Cemetery	
Baltimore (Loudon Park National Cemetery, 3445 Frederick Ave., 21228).	National Cemetery	
Maryland Health Care System (10 N. Green St., Baltimore, 21201).	Medical Center	Dennis Smith
MASSACHUSETTS:		
Bedford (Edith Nourse Rogers Memorial Veterans Hospital, 200 Springs Rd., 01730).	Medical Center	Karen Waghorn
Boston Health Care Center (150 S. Huntington Ave., 02130).	Medical Center	Michael Lawson
Boston (John F. Kennedy Federal Bldg., 02203)	Regional Office	(Vacancy)
Bourne (Massachusetts National Cemetery, Connery Ave., 02532).	National Cemetery	
Brockton (940 Belmont St., 02301)	Medical Center	Michael Lawson
Northampton (01060)	Medical Center	Joanne Carney, *Acting*
MICHIGAN:		
Ann Arbor (2215 Fuller Rd., 48105)	Medical Center	Gabriel Perez, *Acting*
Augusta (Fort Custer National Cemetery, 15501 Dickman Rd., 49012).	National Cemetery	
Battle Creek (49106)	Medical Center	(Vacancy)
Detroit (48101–1932)	Medical Center	(Vacancy)
Detroit (477 Michigan Ave., 48226)	Regional Office	(Vacancy)
Holly (Great Lakes National Cemetery, 4200 Belford Rd., 48442).	National Cemetery	
Iron Mountain (49801)	Medical Center	Janice M. Boss
Saginaw (1500 Weiss St., 48602)	Medical Center	Gabriel Perez
MINNESOTA:		
Minneapolis (1 Veterans Dr., 55417)	Medical Center	Steven Kleinglass
Minneapolis (Fort Snelling National Cemetery, 7601 34th Ave. S., 55450).	National Cemetery	
St. Cloud (4801 8th St. N., 56303)	Medical Center	Barry I. Bahl
St. Paul (Bishop Henry Whipple Federal Bldg., Fort Snelling, 55111) (Remittances: P.O. Box 1820, 55111).	Regional Office & Insurance Center	(Vacancy)
St. Paul (Bishop Henry Whipple Federal Bldg., Fort Snelling, 55111).	Debt Management Center	Dan Osendorf
MISSISSIPPI:		
Biloxi (39531)	Medical Center (medical and domiciliary).	Charles Sepich
Biloxi Hospital and Domiciliary Division		
Gulfport Hospital Division		
Biloxi (P.O. Box 4968, 400 Veterans Ave., 39535–4968).	National Cemetery	
Corinth (1551 Horton St., 38834)	Medical Center (medical and domiciliary).	Mary Dill
Corinth (1551 Horton St., 38834)	National Cemetary	
Jackson (1500 E. Woodrow Wilson Dr., 39216)	Medical Center	Richard Baltz
Jackson (1600 E. Woodrow Wilson Ave., 39216)	Regional Office	Jospeh Adair
Natchez (41 Cemetery Rd., 39120)	National Cemetery	
MISSOURI:		
Columbia (Harry S. Truman Memorial Veterans Hospital, 800 Hospital Dr., 65201).	Medical Center	Mary Weldon, *Acting*
Jefferson City (1024 E. McCarthy, 65101)	National Cemetery	
Kansas City (4801 Linwood Blvd., 64128)	Medical Center	Kent D. Hill
Poplar Bluff (63901)	Medical Center	Nancy Arnold
Springfield (1702 E. Seminole St., 65804)	National Cemetery	
St. Louis (63125)	Medical Center	Glen Struchtemeyer
John J. Cochran Division, 63106		
St. Louis (P.O. Box 5020, Bldg. 104, 4300 Goodfellow Blvd., 63115).	Records Management Center	(Vacancy)
St. Louis (400 S. 18th St., 63103–2271)	Regional Office	Kim Graves
St. Louis (Jefferson Barracks National Cemetery, 2900 Sheridan Dr., 63125).	National Cemetery	
MONTANA:		
Montana Health Care System (Fort Harrison, 59636).	Medical and Regional Office Center	Joseph M. Underkofler
NEBRASKA:		
Greater Nebraska Health Care System (600 S. 70th St., Lincoln, 68510).	Medical Center	Albert Washko
Lincoln (5631 S. 48th St., 68516)	Regional Office	Willie Clark
Maxwell (Fort McPherson National Cemetery, 12004 S. Spur 56A, 69151–1031).	National Cemetery	
NEVADA:		
Las Vegas (102 Lake Mead Dr., 89106)	Outpatient Clinic	John Bright

National Facilities—Department of Veterans Affairs—Continued

Address	Type of facility	Director
Reno (1000 Locust St., 89520)	Medical Center	Kurt Schlegelmilch
Reno (1201 Terminal Way, 89520)	Regional Office	Don Iddings
NEW HAMPSHIRE:		
Manchester (718 Smyth Rd., 02104)	Medical Center	Mark F. Levenson
Manchester (275 Chestnut St., 03101)	Regional Office	Marybeth Cully
NEW JERSEY:		
Beverly (916 Bridgeboro Rd., 08010)	National Cemetery	
Hillsborough (08844)	Asset Management Service	John Snow
Newark (20 Washington Pl., 07102)	Regional Office	John McCourt
New Jersey Health Care System (East Orange, 07018).	Medical Center	Kenneth Mizrach
Salem (Finn's Point National Cemetery, R.F.D. 3, Fort Mott Rd., Box 542, 08079).	National Cemetery	
Somerville (08876)	Asset Management Service	Sharon Dufour
NEW MEXICO:		
Albuquerque (2100 Ridgecrest Dr. SE., 87108–5138).	Medical Center	Mary A. Dowling
Albuquerque (500 Gold Ave. SW., 87102)	Regional Office	(Vacancy)
Fort Bayard (Fort Bayard National Cemetery, P.O. Box 189, 88036).	National Cemetery	
Santa Fe (501 N. Guadalupe St., 87501)	National Cemetery	
NEW YORK:		
Albany (113 Holland Ave., 12208)	Medical Center	Mary Ellen Piche
Bath (14810)	Medical Center (medical and domiciliary).	Craig Howard, *Acting*
Bath (San Juan Ave., 14810)	National Cemetery	
Bronx (130 W. Kingsbridge Rd., 10468) Brooklyn Division St. Albans Division	Medical Center	MaryAnn Musumeci
Brooklyn (Cypress Hills National Cemetery, 625 Jamaica Ave., 11208).	National Cemetery	
Buffalo (111 W. Huron St., 14202)	Regional Office	(Vacancy)
Calverton (210 Princeton Blvd., 11933–1031)	National Cemetery	
Canandaigua (14424)	Medical Center	W. Craig Howard
Elmira (Woodlawn National Cemetery, 1825 Davis St., 14901).	National Cemetery	
Farmingdale (Long Island National Cemetery, 2040 Wellwood Ave., 11735–1211).	National Cemetery	
Hudson Valley Health Care System (Franklin Delano Roosevelt Hospital, Montrose, 10548).	Medical Center	Michael Sabo
New York (245 W. Houston St., 10014)	Regional Office	Pat Amberg-Blyskal
New York Harbor Health Care System (Brooklyn, 11209).	Medical Center	John J. Donnellan, Jr.
Northport (Long Island, 11768)	Medical Center	Robert Schuster
Schuylerville (General B.H. Soloman Saratoga National Cemetery, 200 Duell Rd., 12871–1721).	National Cemetery	
Syracuse (Irving Ave. & University Pl., 13210)	Medical Center	James Cody
Western New York Health Care System (3495 Bailey Ave., Buffalo, 14215).	Medical Center	Tim Leizert, *Acting*
NORTH CAROLINA:		
Asheville (28805)	Medical Center	Susan Pendergrass
Durham (508 Fulton St. & Erwin Rd., 27705)	Medical Center	Michael Phaup
Fayetteville (2300 Ramsey St., 28301)	Medical Center	Janet Stout
New Bern (1711 National Ave., 28560)	National Cemetery	
Raleigh (501 Rock Quarry Rd., 27610)	National Cemetery	
Salisbury (1601 Brenner Ave., 28144)	Medical Center	Don Moore
Salisbury (202 Government Rd., 28144)	National Cemetery	
Wilmington (2011 Market St., 28403)	National Cemetery	
Winston-Salem (251 N. Main St., 27155)	Regional Office	John Montgomery
NORTH DAKOTA:		
Fargo (655 1st Ave., 58102)	Medical and Regional Office Center	Rosalyn Cole, *Acting*
OHIO:		
Chillicothe (45601)	Medical Center	Linda Smith
Cincinnati (3200 Vine St., 45220)	Medical Center	Carlos B. Lott
Cleveland (10701 East Blvd., 44106–3800) Brecksville Division Wade Park Division	Medical Center	William Montague
Cleveland (1240 E. 9th St., 44199)	Regional Office	Phillip J. Ross
Columbus (2090 Kenny Rd., 43221)	Outpatient Clinic	Lilian T. Thome
Dayton (VA Medical Center, 4100 W. 3d St., 45428–1008).	Medical Center (medical and domiciliary).	Guy Richardson
Dayton (VA Medical Center, 4100 W. 3d St., 45428–1008).	National Cemetery	
Rittman (Ohio Western Reserve National Cemetery, P.O. Box 8, 10175 Rawiga Rd., 44270).	National Cemetery	

National Facilities—Department of Veterans Affairs—Continued

Address	Type of facility	Director
OKLAHOMA:		
Elgin (Fort Sill National Cemetery, 2648 Jake Dunn Rd., 73538).	National Cemetery	
Fort Gibson (1423 Cemetery Rd., 74434)	National Cemetery	
Muskogee (Memorial Station, Honor Heights Dr., 74401).	Medical Center	Adam Walmus
Muskogee (125 S. Main St., 74401)	Regional Office	Sam Jarvis
Oklahoma City (921 NE. 13th St., 73104)	Medical Center	Steve J. Gentling
OREGON:		
Eagle Point (2763 Riley Rd., 97524)	National Cemetery	
Portland (3710 SW. U.S. Veterans Hospital Rd., 97207).	Medical Center	James Tuchschmidt
Portland (1220 SW. 3d Ave., 97204)	Regional Office	Gerry Lorang
Portland (Willamette National Cemetery, 11800 SE. Mt. Scott Blvd., 66147, 97266–6937).	National Cemetery	
Roseburg (97470–6513)	Medical Center	George Marnell
Roseburg (913 Garden Valley Blvd., 97470)	National Cemetery	
PENNSYLVANIA:		
Altoona (16602–4377)	Medical Center	Gerald L. Williams
Annville (Indiantown Gap National Cemetery, Rural Rte. 2, Box 484, 17003–9618).	National Cemetery	
Butler (16001–2480)	Medical Center	David Wood
Coatesville (19320)	Medical Center	Gary W. Devansky
Erie (135 E. 38th St. Blvd., 16504)	Medical Center	Meg O'Shea-Caplan, *Acting*
Lebanon (17042)	Medical Center	Terry Gerigk
Philadelphia (5000 Wissahickon Ave., 19101) (Insurance remittances: P.O. Box 7787). (Mail: P.O. Box 42954).	Regional Office & Insurance Center	Thomas M. Lastowka
Philadelphia (University & Woodland Aves., 19104)	Medical Center	Michael Sullivan
Philadelphia (Haines St. & Limekiln Pike, 19138)	National Cemetery	
Pittsburgh (1000 Liberty Ave., 15222)	Regional Office	(Vacancy)
Pittsburgh Health Care System (University Dr. C, 15240).	Medical Center	Michael Moreland
Aspinwall Division		
Pittsburgh Division		
Wilkes-Barre (1111 E. End Blvd., 18711)	Medical Center	Roland Moore
PHILIPPINE REPUBLIC:		
Manila (1131 Roxas Blvd., FPO AP96515–1110)	Regional Office & Outpatient Clinic	Jon Skelly
PUERTO RICO:		
Bayamon (Puerto Rico National Cemetery, Avenue Cementerio Nacional No. 50, 00960).	National Cemetery	
Hato Rey (U.S. Courthouse & Federal Bldg., Carlos E. Chardon St., 00918).		
San Juan (Barrio Monacillos G.P.O., Box 364867, 00927–5800).	Medical Center	Rafael E. Ramirez
San Juan (U.S. Courthouse & Federal Bldg., Carlos E. Chardon St., G.P.O. Box 364867, Hato Rey, 00936).	Regional Office	Sonia Moreno
RHODE ISLAND:		
Providence (380 Westminster Mall, 02903)	Regional Office	Kerrie Witty
Providence (Davis Park, 02908)	Medical Center	Vincent Ng
SOUTH CAROLINA:		
Beaufort (1601 Boundary St., 29902–3947)	National Cemetery	
Charleston (109 Bee St., 29401–5799)	Medical Center	Flo Hutchison, *Acting*
Columbia (William Jennings Bryan Dorn Veterans Hospital, 29209).	Medical Center	Brian Heckert
Columbia (1801 Assembly St., 29201)	Regional Office	Carl W. Hawkins
Florence (803 E. National Cemetery Rd., 29501)	National Cemetery	
SOUTH DAKOTA:		
Black Hills Health Care System (113 Comanche Rd., Fort Meade, 57741).	Medical Center	Steve DiStasio, *Acting*
Hot Springs (500 N. 5th St., 57747)	National Cemetery	
Sioux Falls (Royal C. Johnson Veterans Memorial Hospital, P.O. Box 5046, 25051 W. 22d St., 57117).	Medical Center and Regional Office	Joe Dalpiaz
Sioux Falls (2501 West 2nd St., Sioux Falls, SD 57117).	Regional Office	John Smith
Sturgis (Fort Meade National Cemetery, P.O. Box 640, Old Stone Rd. 57785).	National Cemetery	
Sturgis (Black Hills National Cemetery, 20901 Pleasant Valley Dr., 57785).	National Cemetery	
TENNESSEE:		
Chattanooga (1200 Bailey Ave., 37404)	National Cemetery	
Knoxville (939 Tyson St. NW., 37917)	National Cemetery	

National Facilities—Department of Veterans Affairs—Continued

Address	Type of facility	Director
Madison (1420 Gallatin Rd. S., 37115–4619) (Nashville National Cemetery).	National Cemetery	
Memphis (1030 Jefferson Ave., 38104)	Medical Center	Patricia Pittman
Memphis (3568 Townes Ave., 38122)	National Cemetery	
Mountain Home (Johnson City, 37684)	Medical Center (medical and domiciliary).	(Vacancy)
Mountain Home (P.O. Box 8, VA Medical Center, Bldg. 117, 37684).	National Cemetery	
Tennessee Valley HCS.		
Murfreesboro (37129–1236)	Medical Center	David N. Pennington
Nashville (1310 24th Ave. S., 37212–2637)	Medical Center	David N. Pennington
Nashville (110 9th Ave. S., 37203)	Regional Office	Brian Corley
TEXAS:		
Amarillo (6010 Amarillo Blvd. W., 79106)	Medical Center	Bryan Jaqua
Austin (1615 E. Woodward St., 78772)	Automation Center	Robert Evans
Austin (P.O. Box 149975, 78714–9575)	Financial Services Center	Rodney W. Wood
Austin (1615 E. Woodward St., 78772)	Mortgage Loan Accounting Center	Allen Sartain
Big Spring (79720)	Medical Center	Lou Ann Atkins
Central Texas Health Care System (Olin E. Teague Veterans Center, Temple, 76504).	Medical Center (medical and domiciliary).	Bruce Gordon
Dallas (Dallas-Fort Worth National Cemetery, 2000 Mountain Creek Pkwy., 75211).	National Cemetery	
El Paso Health Care System (5919 Brook Hollow Dr., 79925).	Medical Center	Bruce Stewart
Fort Bliss (5200 Fred Wilson Rd., P.O. Box 6342, 79906).	National Cemetery	
Houston (2002 Holcombe Blvd., 77030)	Medical Center	Edgar L. Tucker
Houston (6900 Almeda Rd., 77030)	Regional Office	Ursula Henderson
Houston (10410 Veterans Memorial Dr., 77038)	National Cemetery	
Kerrville (VA Medical Center, 3600 Memorial Blvd., 78028).	National Cemetery	
North Texas Health Care System (4500 S. Lancaster Rd., 75216).	Medical Center	Betty Brown
San Antonio (517 Paso Hondo St., 78202)	National Cemetery	
San Antonio (1520 Harry Wurzbach Rd., 78209) (Fort Sam Houston National Cemetery).	National Cemetery	
South Texas Veterans Health Care System (Audie L. Murphy Memorial Veterans Hospital, 7400 Merton Minter Blvd., San Antonio, 78284).	Medical Center	Jose R. Coronado
Waco (701 Clay Ave., 76799)	Regional Office	Carl E. Lowe II
UTAH:		
Salt Lake City (125 S. State St., 84147)	Regional Office	Douglas B. Wadsworth
Salt Lake City (500 Foothill Blvd., 84148)	Medical Center	James Floyd
VERMONT:		
White River Junction (215 N. Main St., 05009)	Medical and Regional Office Center	Gary M. DeGasta
VIRGINIA:		
Alexandria (1450 Wilkes St., 22314)	National Cemetery	
Culpeper (305 U.S. Ave., 22701)	National Cemetery	
Danville (721 Lee St., 24541)	National Cemetery	
Hampton (23667)	Medical Center (medical and domiciliary).	Joseph Williams
Hampton (Cemetery Rd. at Marshall Ave., 23667)	National Cemetery	
Hampton (VA Medical Center, Emancipation Dr., 23667).	National Cemetery	
Hopewell (10th Ave. & Davis St., 23860) (City Point National Cemetery).	National Cemetery	
Leesburg (Balls Bluff National Cemetery, Rte. 7, 22075).	National Cemetery	
Mechanicsville (Cold Harbor National Cemetery, Rte. 156 N., 23111).	National Cemetery	
Richmond (1201 Broad Rock Rd., 23249)	Medical Center	(Vacancy)
Richmond (1701 Williamsburg Rd., 23231)	National Cemetery	
Richmond (Fort Harrison National Cemetery, 8620 Varina Rd., 23231).	National Cemetery	
Richmond (Glendale National Cemetery, 8301 Willis Church Rd., 23231).	National Cemetery	
Roanoke (210 Franklin Rd. SW., 24011)	Regional Office	John W. Smith
Salem (24153)	Medical Center	Stephen Lemons
Sandston (Seven Pines National Cemetery, 400 E. Williamsburg Rd., 23150).	National Cemetery	
Staunton (901 Richmond Ave., 24401)	National Cemetery	
Triangle (Quantico National Cemetery, P.O. Box 10, 18424 Joplin Rd., Rte. 619, 22172).	National Cemetery	
Winchester (401 National Ave., 22601)	National Cemetery	

National Facilities—Department of Veterans Affairs—Continued

Address	Type of facility	Director
WASHINGTON:		
Kent (Tahoma National Cemetery, 18600 SE. 240th St., 98042–4868).	National Cemetery	
Puget Sound Health Care System (4435 Beacon Ave. S., Seattle, 98108).	Medical Center	Timothy Williams
Seattle (915 2d Ave., 98174)	Regional Office	Carol Batten-Fillman
Spokane (N. 4815 Assembly St., 99205)	Medical Center	Joseph M. Manley
WEST VIRGINIA:		
Beckley (200 Veterans Ave., 25801)	Medical Center	Gerard Husson
Clarksburg (26301)	Medical Center	Glen Struchtemeyer
Grafton (West Virginia National Cemetery, Rt. 2, Box 127, 26354).	National Cemetery	
Grafton (Grafton National Cemetery, 431 Walnut St., 26354).	National Cemetery	
Huntington (1540 Spring Valley Dr., 25704)	Medical Center	(Vacancy)
Huntington (640 4th Ave., 25701)	Regional Office	Cheryl Rawls
Martinsburg (25401)	Medical Center (medical and domiciliary).	(Vacancy)
WISCONSIN:		
Madison (William S. Middleton Memorial Veterans Hospital, 2500 Overlook Ter., 53705).	Medical Center	Nathan L. Geraths
Milwaukee (5000 W. National Ave., 53295–4000)	Medical Center (medical and domiciliary).	Glen Grippen
Milwaukee (5000 W. National Ave., Bldg. 6, 53295–4000).	Regional Office	Jon A. Baker
Milwaukee (Wood National Cemetery, 5000 W. National Ave., Bldg. 1301, 53295–4000).	National Cemetery	
Tomah (54660)	Medical Center	Stanley Q. Johnson
WYOMING:		
Cheyenne (2360 E. Pershing Blvd., 82001)	Medical Center	David M. Kilpatrick
Sheridan (82801)	Medical Center	Gary Morton, *Acting*

Sources of Information

Audiovisuals Persons interested in the availability of VA video productions or exhibits for showing outside of VA may write to the Chief, Media Services Division (032B), Department of Veterans Affairs, 810 Vermont Avenue NW., Washington, DC 20420. Phone, 202–273–9781 or 9782.

Contracts Persons interested in business opportunities with the Department of Veterans Affairs (VA) may contact the Director, Acquisition Resources Service (049A5), 810 Vermont Avenue NW., Washington, DC 20420. Phone, 202–273–8815. Information on business opportunities with the VA can be found on the Internet at www.va.gov/oamm/busopp/doingbusiness.htm. Additional information is available at the Office of Acquisition and Material Management Web site at www.va.gov/oamm. Information on solicitations issued by VA is available at www.va.gov/oamm/busopp/index.htm.

Small Business Programs Persons seeking information on VA's small business programs may call 800–949–8387 or 202–565–8124. The Office of Small and Disadvantaged Business Utilization Web site (Internet, www.va.gov/osdbu) contains a considerable amount of information about these programs.

Veterans Business Ownership Services The Center for Veterans Enterprise assists veterans who want to open or expand a business. This Center is a component of the Office of Small and Disadvantaged Business Utilization. Phone, 866–584–2344. Internet, www.vetbiz.gov. E-mail, vacve@mail.va.gov.

Electronic Access Information concerning the Department of Veterans Affairs is available electronically through the Internet, at www.va.gov.

Employment The Department of Veterans Affairs employs physicians, dentists, podiatrists, optometrists, nurses, nurse anesthetists, physician assistants, expanded-function dental auxiliaries, registered respiratory therapists, certified respiratory technicians, licensed physical therapists, occupational therapists, pharmacists, and licensed practical or vocational nurses under VA's excepted merit system. This system does not require civil service eligibility. Other professional, technical, administrative, and clerical occupations, such as veterans claims examiners, secretaries, and management analysts, exist in VA that do require civil service eligibility. Persons interested in employment should contact the human resources services office at their nearest VA facility or search the VA Web site, www.va.gov/jobs. All qualified applicants will receive consideration for appointments without regard to race, religion, color, national origin, sex, political affiliation, or any nonmerit factor.

Freedom of Information Act Requests Inquiries should be directed to the Assistant Secretary for Information and Technology, Information Management Service (045A4), 810 Vermont Avenue NW., Washington, DC 20420. Phone, 202–273–8135.

Inspector General Inquiries and Hotline Publicly available documents and information on the VA Office of Inspector General are available electronically through the Internet, at www.va.gov/oig/homepage.htm. Complaints may be sent by mail to the VA Inspector General (53E), P.O. Box 50410, Washington, DC 20091–0410. Hotline phone, 800–488–8244. E-mail, vaoighotline@va.gov.

Medical Center (Hospital) Design, Construction, and Related Services Construction projects for VA medical centers and other facilities in excess of $4 million are managed and controlled at the VA central office, located in Washington, DC. Projects requiring design, construction, and other related services are advertised on the Internet FirstGov site, at www.firstgov.gov. Submit project-specific qualifications (SF 254 and SF 255) to the Director, A/E Evaluation and Program Support Team (181A), 810 Vermont Avenue NW., Washington, DC 20420. Phone, 202–565–4181. Additional information regarding the selection process can be found on the VA Office of Facilities Management Internet site, at www.va.gov/facmgt.

Construction projects for VA medical centers and other facilities which are less than $4 million are managed and controlled at the individual medical centers. For information regarding these specific projects, contact the Acquisition and Materiel Management Office at each individual VA medical center. Addresses and additional information on VA medical centers can be found on the VA Internet site, www.va.gov/facilities.

News Media Representatives may contact VA through the nearest regional Office of Public Affairs:

Atlanta (404–929–5880)
Chicago (312–980–4235)
Dallas (817–385–3720)
Denver (303–914–5855)
Los Angeles (310–268–4207)
New York (212–807–3429)
Washington, DC (202–530–9360)

National media may contact the Office of Public Affairs in the VA Central Office, 810 Vermont Avenue NW., Washington, DC 20420. Phone, 202–273–6000.

Publications The *Annual Performance and Accountability Report* may be obtained (in single copies), without charge, from the Office of Budget (041H), 810 Vermont Avenue NW., Washington, DC 20420.

The 2005 VA pamphlet *Federal Benefits for Veterans and Dependents* (80–98–1) is available for sale by the Superintendent of Documents, Government Printing Office, Washington, DC 20402.

The *Board of Veterans Appeals Index* (I–01–1), an index to appellate decisions, is available on microfiche in annual cumulation from July 1977 through December 1994. The quarterly indexes may be purchased for $7 and annual cumulative indexes for $22.50. The VADEX/CITATOR of Appellate Research Materials is a complete printed quarterly looseleaf cumulation of research material which may be purchased for $175 with binder and for $160 without binder. The Vadex Infobase, a computer-searchable version of the VADEX, is also available on diskettes for $100 per copy. These publications may be obtained by contacting Promisel and Korn, Inc. Phone, 301–986–0650. Archived decisions of the Board of Veterans'

Appeals are available through the VA Web site at www.va.gov.

A January 2000 VA pamphlet entitled *Understanding the Appeal Process* (01–00–1) is available for sale from the Superintendent of Documents, Government Printing Office, Washington, DC 20402.

The VA pamphlet, *A Summary of Department of Veteran Affairs Benefits* (27–82–2), may be obtained, without charge, from any VA regional office.

Interments in VA National Cemeteries, VA NCA–IS–1, details eligibility information and contains a list of both national and State veterans cemeteries. Copies may be obtained without charge from the National Cemetery Administration (41C1), 810 Vermont Avenue NW., Washington, DC 20420. Call 800–827–1000 or visit www.cem.va.gov for more information.

For further information, contact the Office of Public and Intergovernmental Affairs, Department of Veterans Affairs, 810 Vermont Avenue NW., Washington, DC 20420. Phone, 202–273–6000. Internet, www.va.gov/opa.

Independent Establishments and Government Corporations

AFRICAN DEVELOPMENT FOUNDATION

1400 I Street NW., Washington, DC 20005
Phone, 202–673–3916. Internet, www.adf.gov.

Board of Directors:

Chairman	EDWARD BREHM
Vice Chair	(VACANCY)
Members of the Board	EPHRAIM BATAMBUZE, JENDAYI E. FRAZER, JACK LESLIE, LLOYD O. PIERSON, (VACANCY)

Staff:

President	RODNEY J. MACALISTER
Vice President	(VACANCY)
Vice President and Chief Executive Officer for Africa Operations	NATHANIEL FIELDS
General Counsel	DORIS MASON MARTIN

[For the African Development Foundation statement of organization, see the *Code of Federal Regulations,* Title 22, Part 1501]

The African Development Foundation's goals are to alleviate poverty and promote broad-based sustainable development and empowerment in Africa; to expand local capacity to promote and support grassroots, participatory development; and to enhance and strengthen U.S. relations with Africa through effective development assistance.

The African Development Foundation was established by the African Development Foundation Act (22 U.S.C. 290h) as a Government corporation to support the self-help efforts of the poor in Africa.

The Foundation awards grants and cooperative agreements to African private organizations to do the following:

—promote micro- and small-enterprise development that will generate income and employment;

—improve community-based natural resource management for sustainable rural development;

—increase participation of African grassroots enterprises and producer groups in trade and investment relationships with the U.S. and within Africa; and

—promote community-based HIV/AIDS intervention programs.

In addition, the Foundation works within Africa to perform the following tasks:

—build self-supporting, sustainable, local community development agencies that provide technical assistance and support to grassroots groups;

—develop and replicate new models for community reinvestment; and

—establish strategic partnerships with national and local governments, other donor agencies, and the local private sector, to support sustainable, grassroots development.

Finally, the Foundation works within the United States to gather resources for grassroots development through strategic partnerships with the U.S. private sector, American philanthropic organizations, and other U.S. Government agencies, and to expand U.S. funding for grassroots development activities.

For further information, contact the Communications Manager, African Development Foundation, 1400 I Street NW., 10th Floor, Washington, DC 20005. Phone, 202–673–3916. Fax, 202–673–3810. E-mail, info@adf.gov. Internet, www.adf.gov.

BROADCASTING BOARD OF GOVERNORS

330 Independence Avenue SW., Washington, DC 20237
Phone, 202–203–4545. Internet, www.bbg.gov

Chairman	KENNETH Y. TOMLINSON
Members	JOAQUIN F. BLAYA, BLANQUITA WALSH CULLUM, D. JEFFREY HIRSCHBERG, EDWARD E. KAUFMAN, NORMAN J. PATTIZ, STEVEN J. SIMMONS
(Secretary of State, *ex officio*)	CONDOLEEZZA RICE
Executive Director	BRIAN T. CONNIFF
Legal Counsel	CAROL M. BOOKER
Chief Financial Officer	JANET STORMES
Congressional Coordinator	SUSAN ANDROSS
Communications Coordinator	LARRY HART
Strategic Planning Manager	BRUCE SHERMAN
Policy and Program Coordinator	JOHN GIAMBALVO
Special Projects Officer	OANH TRAN
Chief Information Officer	RONALD LINZ, *Acting*
General Counsel	CAROL M. BOOKER, *Acting*
Director, International Broadcasting Bureau	(VACANCY)
Chief of Staff	JANICE BRAMBILLA
Director, Office of Civil Rights	DELIA L. JOHNSON
Associate Director for Management	STEPHEN S. SMITH
Associate Director for Program Support	GARY THATCHER
Director, Office of Engineering and Technical Services	GEORGE A. MOORE
Director, Voice of America	DAVID S. JACKSON
Chief of Staff	MARIE LENNON
Associate Director for Language Programming	KELU CHAO
Associate Director for Central Programming	(VACANCY)
Associate Director for Operations	MARK L. PRAHL
Director, Office of Cuba Broadcasting	PEDRO V. ROIG
President, Radio Free Europe/Radio Liberty	JEFFREY TRIMBLE, *Acting*
President, Radio Free Asia	LIBBY LIU
President, Middle East Broadcasting Networks	BERT KLEINMAN

The Broadcasting Board of Governors' mission is to promote freedom and democracy and to enhance understanding by broadcasting accurate, objective, and balanced news and information about the United States and the world to audiences abroad.

The Broadcasting Board of Governors (BBG) became an independent agency on October 1, 1999, by authority of the Foreign Affairs Reform and Restructuring Act of 1998 (22 U.S.C. 6501 note).

The BBG serves as the governing body for all nonmilitary U.S. broadcasting and provides programming in 56 languages via radio, television, and the Internet. The BBG broadcast services include: the Voice of America (VOA), the Office of Cuba Broadcasting (OCB), Radio Free Europe/Radio Liberty (RFE/RL), Radio Free Asia (RFA), and the Middle East Broadcasting Networks (MBN).

All BBG broadcast services adhere to the broadcasting standards and principles of the International Broadcasting Act of 1994, which include reliable, accurate, and comprehensive news; balanced and comprehensive presentations of U.S. thought, institutions, and policies, as well as discussions about those policies; information about developments throughout the world; and a variety of opinions from nations around the world.

Activities

Voice of America The Voice of America (VOA) broadcasts on radio, television, and the Internet (www.VOAnews.com) in 44 languages. The VOA Charter requires that broadcasts be accurate, objective, and comprehensive; that they represent all segments of American society and present a balanced and comprehensive view of significant American thought and institutions; and that they clearly present the policies of the United States. VOA broadcasts more than 1,000 hours a week and includes U.S. and international news, features, call-in shows, roundtable decisions, and other programming that is delivered directly or through affiliated stations to audiences around the world.

Middle East Broadcasting Networks, Inc. The Middle East Broadcasting Networks, Inc. (MBN) is a nonprofit corporation that is financed by the U.S. Government through a grant from the Broadcasting Board of Governors. MBN operates the Arabic-language Radio Sawa (www.radiosawa.com) and Alhurra television networks (www.alhurra.com).

—*Alhurra* Alhurra, Arabic for "The Free One," is a commercial-free Arabic-language satellite television channel in the Middle East devoted primarily to news and information. In addition to reporting on regional and international events, the channel broadcasts a diverse schedule of news, talk shows, debates, documentaries, and entertaining information programs on a wide variety of subjects from sports to fashion to technology, to millions of viewers every day.

—*Radio Sawa* Radio Sawa is the popular radio network that provides news, information, and a mix of Western and Arabic popular music on its 24-hour, 7-day-a-week FM and medium-wave radio stations throughout the Middle East. The Arabic-language network broadcasts objective, balanced, up-to-the-minute news and news analysis along with interviews, opinion pieces, sports, and features on a wide variety of political and social issues.

Radio Free Europe/Radio Liberty Radio Free Europe/Radio Liberty (RFE/RL) is a nonprofit, international communications organization broadcasting to Eastern and Southeastern Europe, Russia, the Caucasus, Central Asia, the Middle East, and Southwestern Asia. Listeners rely on RFE/RL's daily news, analysis, and current affairs programming to provide a coherent, objective account of events in their region and the world. RFE/RL broadcasts in 27 languages with more than 1,000 hours of radio programming a week from its operations center in Prague, Czech Republic, and 23 bureaus in its broadcast region. Its corporate headquarters are located in Washington, DC. All RFE/RL broadcasts are also

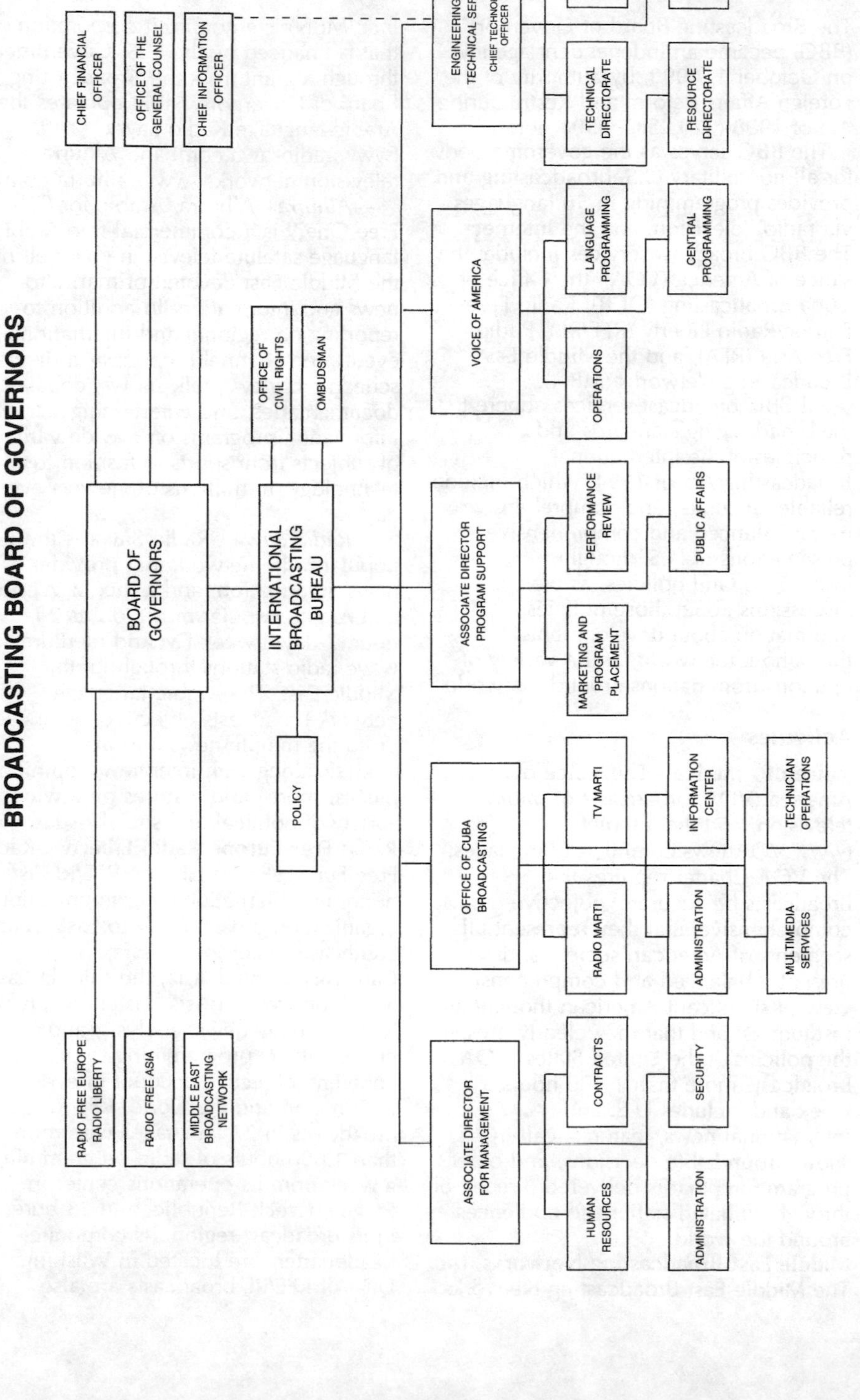
BROADCASTING BOARD OF GOVERNORS
CHIEF FINANCIAL OFFICER
OFFICE OF THE GENERAL COUNSEL
CHIEF INFORMATION OFFICER
BOARD OF GOVERNORS
RADIO FREE EUROPE RADIO LIBERTY
RADIO FREE ASIA
MIDDLE EAST BROADCASTING NETWORK
OFFICE OF CIVIL RIGHTS
OMBUDSMAN
INTERNATIONAL BROADCASTING BUREAU
POLICY
ENGINEERING AND TECHNICAL SERVICES
CHIEF TECHNOLOGY OFFICER
VOICE OF AMERICA
ASSOCIATE DIRECTOR PROGRAM SUPPORT
OFFICE OF CUBA BROADCASTING
ASSOCIATE DIRECTOR FOR MANAGEMENT
INFORMATION TECHNOLOGY DIRECTORATE
OPERATIONS DIRECTORATE
TECHNICAL DIRECTORATE
RESOURCE DIRECTORATE
LANGUAGE PROGRAMMING
CENTRAL PROGRAMMING
OPERATIONS
PERFORMANCE REVIEW
PUBLIC AFFAIRS
MARKETING AND PROGRAM PLACEMENT
TV MARTI
INFORMATION CENTER
TECHNICIAN OPERATIONS
RADIO MARTI
ADMINISTRATION
MULTIMEDIA SERVICES
CONTRACTS
SECURITY
HUMAN RESOURCES
ADMINISTRATION

streamed live and on-demand over the Internet; audio, video, and text in English and the broadcast languages are available from its web site at www.rferl.org.

RFE/RL also broadcasts Radio Free Iraq and Radio Free Afghanistan. In a joint effort with the Voice of America, RFE/RL broadcasts a Persian-language radio service called Radio Farda, which means "Radio Tomorrow." Operated from Washington, DC, and Prague, Czech Republic, Radio Farda produces current news and information at least twice an hour, with longer news programming in the morning and the evening. Radio Farda also broadcasts a combination of Persian and Western music. The station operates 24 hours a day on medium wave (AM 1593 and AM 1539), digital audio satellite, and the Internet, as well as 21 hours a day on shortwave. Radio Farda complements the VOA's Persian-language radio and television broadcasts in Iran.

Radio Free Asia Radio Free Asia (RFA) is a private, nonprofit news organization providing daily broadcasts in nine languages to listeners in Asia whose governments restrict freedom of information and expression. RFA broadcasts accurate and timely news and information, along with a range of voices and opinions from within Asia, with the aim of demonstrating freedom of expression over the airwaves and online.

RFA focuses primarily on news and features of unique and specific relevance to its target countries. Through shortwave transmission and the Internet at www.rfa.org, RFA broadcasts in Mandarin, Cantonese, Uyghur, three dialects of Tibetan, Burmese, Vietnamese, Korean, Lao, and Khmer. All broadcasts originate from RFA's Washington, DC, headquarters.

Office of Cuba Broadcasting The Office of Cuba Broadcasting (OCB) oversees the operations of Radio Marti and TV Marti from its headquarters in Miami, Florida. In accordance with the Broadcasting to Cuba Act of 1983, Radio Marti follows Voice of America journalistic standards and guidelines for presenting a variety of news and information in an accurate and objective manner and is guided by the standards and principles of the U.S. International Broadcasting Act.

Radio Marti broadcasts 7 days a week, 24 hours a day. TV Marti produces 8 hours of original programming daily, including a 30-minute newscast each day. Primary areas of coverage include the Cuban economy, news relating to the independent human rights and dissident movement, U.S.-Cuban relations, and international stories such as elections around the world.

In addition to broadcasting via shortwave, AM, aerostat, and airborne transmissions, OCB broadcasts TV Marti on HispaSat, a direct-to-home satellite television service, and is working to establish a permanent airborne platform for TV and Radio Marti. Radio and TV Marti programming can also be accessed on the Internet at www.martinoticias.com.

For further information, contact the Office of Public Affairs, Broadcasting Board of Governors, 330 Independence Avenue SW., Washington, DC 20237. Phone, 202–401–7000. Fax, 202–619–1241. Internet, www.bbg.gov.

CENTRAL INTELLIGENCE AGENCY

Washington, DC 20505
Phone, 703–482–0623. Internet, www.cia.gov.

Director — MICHAEL V. HAYDEN

[For the Central Intelligence Agency statement of organization, see the *Code of Federal Regulations,* Title 32, Part 1900]

The Central Intelligence Agency collects, evaluates, and disseminates vital information on political, military, economic, scientific, and other developments abroad needed to safeguard national security.

The Central Intelligence Agency was established by the National Security Act of 1947, as amended (50 U.S.C. 401 *et seq.*). It now functions under that statute, Executive Order 12333 of December 4, 1981, the Intelligence Reform and Terrorism Prevention Act of 2004 (50 U.S.C. 401 note), and other laws, Executive orders, regulations, and directives.

The Central Intelligence Agency is headed by a Director, who is appointed by the President with the advice and consent of the Senate.

The Central Intelligence Agency does the following:

—collects intelligence through human sources and by other appropriate means, except that the Central Intelligence Agency exercises no police, subpoena, or law enforcement powers or internal security functions;

—correlates and evaluates intelligence related to national security and provides appropriate dissemination of such intelligence;

—provides overall direction for and coordination of the collection of national intelligence outside the United States through human sources by elements of the Intelligence Community authorized to undertake such collection. In coordination with other departments, agencies, or elements of the United States Government authorized to undertake such human source collection, ensures that the most effective use is made of resources and that appropriate account is taken of the risks to the United States and those involved in such collection;

—performs such other functions and duties related to intelligence affecting national security as the President or the Director of National Intelligence may direct; and

—under the direction of the Director of National Intelligence and in a manner consistent with section 207 of the Foreign Service Act of 1980 (22 U.S.C. 3927), coordinate the relationships between elements of the Intelligence Community and the intelligence or security services of foreign governments or international organizations on all matters involving intelligence related to national security or involving intelligence acquired through clandestine means.

For further information, contact the Central Intelligence Agency, Washington, DC 20505. Phone, 703–482–0623. Internet, www.cia.gov.

COMMODITY FUTURES TRADING COMMISSION

1155 Twenty-first Street NW., Washington, DC 20581
Phone, 202–418–5000. Fax, 202–418–5521. Internet, www.cftc.gov.

Chairman	REUBEN JEFFERY III
Commissioners	MICHAEL V. DUNN, FREDERICK W. HATFIELD, SHARON BROWN-HRUSKA, WALTER L. LUKKEN
General Counsel	NANETTE EVERSON
Executive Director	MADGE BOLINGER
Director, Division of Market Oversight	RICHARD SHILTS
Director, Division of Clearing and Intermediary Oversight	ANANDA RADHAKRISHNAN
Director, Division of Enforcement	GREGORY MOCEK
Chief Economist	JAMES OVERDAHL

[For the Commodity Futures Trading Commission statement of organization, see the *Code of Federal Regulations,* Title 17, Part 140]

The mission of the Commodity Futures Trading Commission is to protect market users and the public from fraud, manipulation, and abusive practices related to the sale of commodity futures and options, and to foster open, competitive, and financially sound commodity futures and option markets.

The Commodity Futures Trading Commission (CFTC) , the Federal regulatory agency for futures trading, was established by the Commodity Futures Trading Commission Act of 1974 (7 U.S.C. 4a). The Commission began operation in April 1975, and its authority to regulate futures trading was renewed by Congress in 1978, 1982, 1986, 1992, 1995, and 2000.

The Commission consists of five Commissioners who are appointed by the President, with the advice and consent of the Senate. One Commissioner is designated by the President to serve as Chairman. The Commissioners serve staggered 5-year terms, and by law no more than three Commissioners can belong to the same political party.

The Commission has six major operating components: the Divisions of Market Oversight, Clearing and Intermediary Oversight, and Enforcement, and the Offices of the Executive Director, General Counsel, and Chief Economist.

Activities

The Commission regulates trading on the U.S. futures markets, which offer commodity futures and options contracts. It regulates these markets in order to ensure the operational integrity of the futures markets. The Commission regulates two tiers of markets: designated contract markets and registered derivatives transaction execution facilities. It also exercises more limited regulatory or enforcement authority over other types of markets. Additionally, the Commission regulates derivatives clearing organizations. Each board of trade that operates a designated contract market must own or have a relationship with a derivatives clearing organization which provides clearing services for each futures contract executed.

The Commission also regulates the activities of numerous commodity trading professionals, including brokerage houses (futures commission merchants), futures industry salespersons (associated persons), commodity trading advisers, commodity pool operators, and floor brokers and traders.

COMMODITY FUTURES TRADING COMMISSION

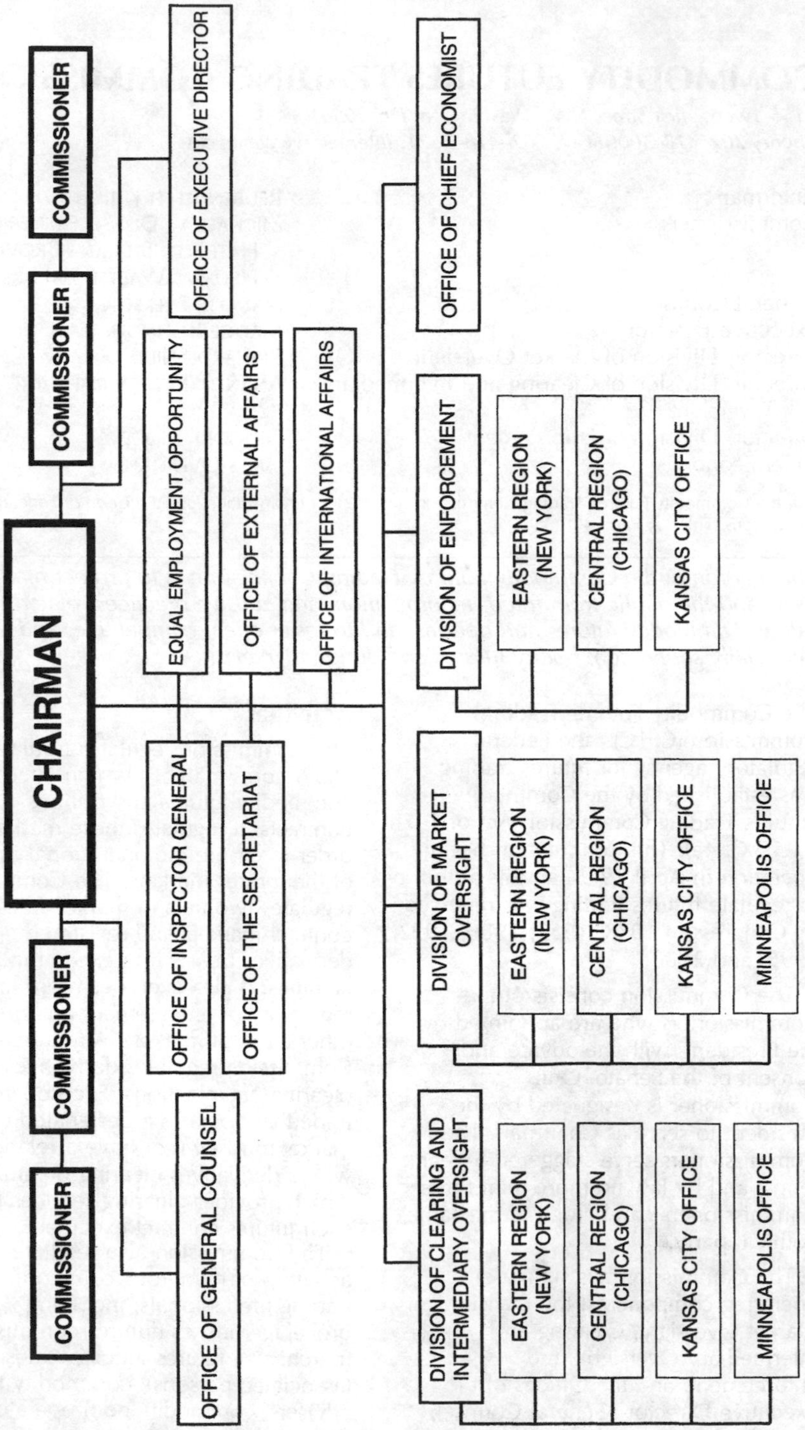

The Commission's regulatory and enforcement efforts are designed to foster transparent and financially sound markets, encourage market competition and efficiency, ensure market integrity, and protect market participants and the public from fraud, manipulation, and abusive practices. It oversees the rules under which designated contract markets and derivatives clearing organizations operate and monitors enforcement of those rules. The Commission reviews the terms of futures contracts and registers firms and individuals who handle customer funds or give trading advice. It also protects the public by enforcing rules that require customer funds be kept in separate accounts, away from accounts maintained by firms for their own use or maintained on behalf of the firm, and that such customer accounts be marked to present market value at the close of trading each day.

The Commission maintains regional offices in Chicago, IL, and New York, NY, where many of the Nation's designated contract markets are located. Additional regional offices are located in Kansas City, MO, and Minneapolis, MN.

For further information, contact the Office of External Affairs, Commodity Futures Trading Commission, 1155 Twenty-first Street NW., Washington, DC 20581. Phone, 202–418–5080. Internet, www.cftc.gov.

CONSUMER PRODUCT SAFETY COMMISSION

4330 East-West Highway, Bethesda, MD 20814
Phone, 301–504–7908. Internet, www.cpsc.gov.

Chairman	HAL STRATTON
Commissioners	THOMAS H. MOORE, NANCY NORD
General Counsel	PAGE C. FAULK
Director, Office of Congressional Relations	JOHN HORNER
Director, Office of the Secretary	TODD A. STEVENSON
Freedom of Information Officer	SANDRA K. BRADSHAW
Director, Office of Equal Employment Opportunity and Minority Enterprise	KATHLEEN V. BUTTREY
Executive Director	PATRICIA M. SEMPLE
Deputy Executive Director	LOWELL MARTIN
Inspector General	CHRISTOPHER W. DENTEL
Director, Office of Human Resources Management	DONNA M. SIMPSON
Director, Office of International Programs and Intergovernmental Affairs	JOSEPH MOHOROVIC
Assistant Executive Director, Office of Information and Technology Services	PATRICK D. WEDDLE
Director, Office of Information and Public Affairs	JULIE VALLESE
Director, Office of Financial Management, Planning and Evaluation	EDWARD E. QUIST
Assistant Executive Director for Compliance and Field Operations	JOHN GIBSON MULLAN
Deputy Assistant Executive Director, Office of Compliance	MARC J. SCHOEM
Assistant Executive Director for Hazard Identification and Reduction	JACQUELINE ELDER
Associate Executive Director for Economics	GREGORY B. RODGERS

Associate Executive Director for Engineering Sciences	HUGH M. MCLAURIN
Associate Executive Director for Epidemiology	RUSSELL H. ROEGNER
Associate Executive Director for Health Sciences	MARY ANN DANELLO
Associate Executive Director for Laboratory Sciences	ANDREW G. STADNIK

[For the Consumer Product Safety Commission statement of organization, see the *Code of Federal Regulations,* Title 16, Part 1000]

The Consumer Product Safety Commission protects the public against unreasonable risks of injury from consumer products; assists consumers in evaluating the comparative safety of consumer products; develops uniform safety standards for consumer products and minimizes conflicting State and local regulations; and promotes research and investigation into the causes and prevention of product-related deaths, illnesses, and injuries.

The Consumer Product Safety Commission is an independent Federal regulatory agency established by the Consumer Product Safety Act (15 U.S.C. 2051 *et seq.*). The Commission consists of five Commissioners, appointed by the President with the advice and consent of the Senate, one of whom is appointed Chairman.

The Commission is responsible for implementing provisions of the Flammable Fabrics Act (15 U.S.C. 1191), the Poison Prevention Packaging Act of 1970 (15 U.S.C. 1471), the Federal Hazardous Substances Act (15 U.S.C. 1261), and the act of August 2, 1956 (15 U.S.C. 1211), which prohibits the transportation of refrigerators without door safety devices.

Activities

To help protect the public from unreasonable risks of injury associated with consumer products, the Commission performs the following functions:

—requires manufacturers to report defects in products that could create substantial hazards;

—requires, where appropriate, corrective action with respect to specific substantially hazardous consumer products already in commerce;

—collects information on consumer product-related injuries and maintains a comprehensive Injury Information Clearinghouse;

—conducts research on consumer product hazards;

—encourages and assists in the development of voluntary standards related to the safety of consumer products;

—establishes, where appropriate, mandatory consumer product standards;

—bans, where appropriate, hazardous consumer products; and

—conducts outreach programs for consumers, industry, and local governments.

Offices

The Commission's headquarters is located at 4330 East-West Highway, Bethesda, MD 20814.

Sources of Information

Consumer Information The Commission operates a toll-free Consumer Product Safety Hotline, 800–638–CPSC (English and Spanish); and a teletypewriter for the hearing-impaired, 800–638–8270 (or in Maryland only, 800–492–8140).

General Inquiries Information on Commission activities may be obtained from the Office of Information and Public Affairs, Consumer Product Safety Commission, 4330 East-West Highway, Bethesda, MD 20814. Phone, 301–504–7908.

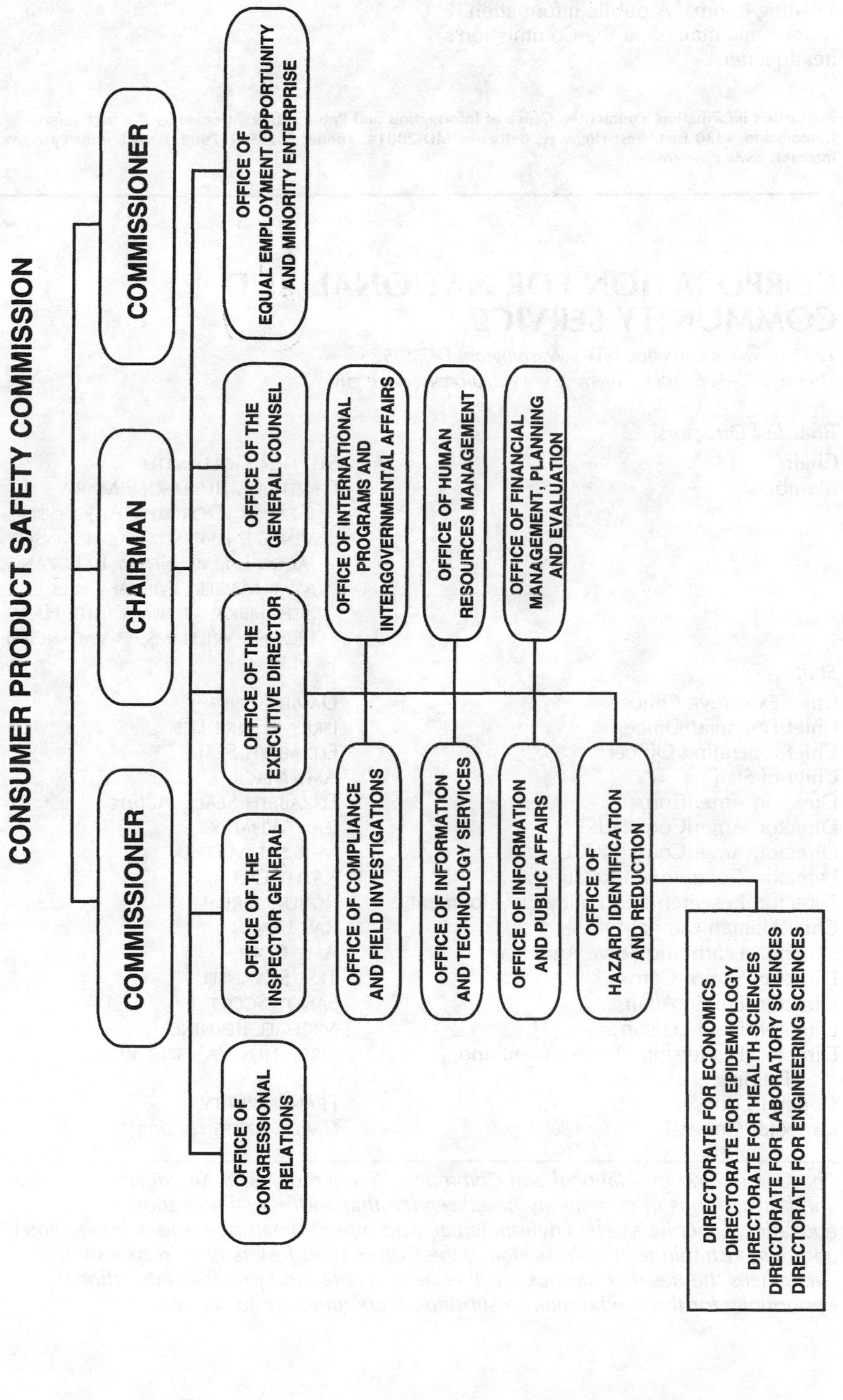
CONSUMER PRODUCT SAFETY COMMISSION
COMMISSIONER
CHAIRMAN
COMMISSIONER
OFFICE OF CONGRESSIONAL RELATIONS
OFFICE OF THE INSPECTOR GENERAL
OFFICE OF THE EXECITIVE DIRECTOR
OFFICE OF THE GENERAL COUNSEL
OFFICE OF EQUAL EMPLOYMENT OPPORTUNITY AND MINORITY ENTERPRISE
OFFICE OF INTERNATIONAL PROGRAMS AND INTERGOVERNMENTAL AFFAIRS
OFFICE OF HUMAN RESOURCES MANAGEMENT
OFFICE OF FINANCIAL MANAGEMENT, PLANNING AND EVALUATION
OFFICE OF COMPLIANCE AND FIELD INVESTIGATIONS
OFFICE OF INFORMATION AND TECHNOLOGY SERVICES
OFFICE OF INFORMATION AND PUBLIC AFFAIRS
OFFICE OF HAZARD IDENTIFICATION AND REDUCTION
DIRECTORATE FOR ECONOMICS
DIRECTORATE FOR EPIDEMIOLOGY
DIRECTORATE FOR HEALTH SCIENCES
DIRECTORATE FOR LABORATORY SCIENCES
DIRECTORATE FOR ENGINEERING SCIENCES

Reading Room A public information room is maintained at the Commission's headquarters.

For further information, contact the Office of Information and Public Affairs, Consumer Product Safety Commission, 4330 East-West Highway, Bethesda, MD 20814. Phone, 301–504–7908. E-mail, info@cpsc.gov. Internet, www.cpsc.gov.

CORPORATION FOR NATIONAL AND COMMUNITY SERVICE

1201 New York Avenue NW., Washington, DC 20525
Phone, 202–606–5000. Internet, www.nationalservice.gov.

Board of Directors:

Chair	Stephen Goldsmith
Members	Cynthia J. Burleson, Mark Gearan, Dorothy A. Johnson, Vince J. Juaristi, Carol Kinsley, Jacob J. Lew, Henry L. Lozano, Mimi Mager, William Schambra, Leona White Hat, Donna Williams, (3 vacancies)

Staff:

Chief Executive Officer	David Eisner
Chief Financial Officer	Jerry G. Bridges
Chief Operating Officer	Elizabeth Seale
Chief of Staff	Amy Mack
Director, AmeriCorps	Elizabeth Seale, *Acting*
Director, AmeriCorps*VISTA	Jean Whaley
Director, AmeriCorps*NCCC	Merlene Mazyck
Director, Government Relations	Kathy Ott
Director, Research and Policy Development	Robert Grimm
Chief Human Capital Officer	Ray Limon
Director, Learn and Serve America	Amy Cohen
Director, Senior Corps	Tess Scannell
Director, Public Affairs	Sandy Scott
Director, Field Liaison	Michael Berning
Director, Leadership Development and Training	Gretchen Van der Veer
General Counsel	Frank Trinity
Inspector General	Carol Bates, *Acting*

The Corporation for National and Community Service engages Americans of all ages and backgrounds in community-based service that addresses the Nation's educational, public safety, environmental, and other human needs to achieve direct and demonstrable results. In so doing, the Corporation fosters civic responsibility, strengthens the ties that bind us together as a people, and provides educational opportunity for those who make a substantial commitment to service.

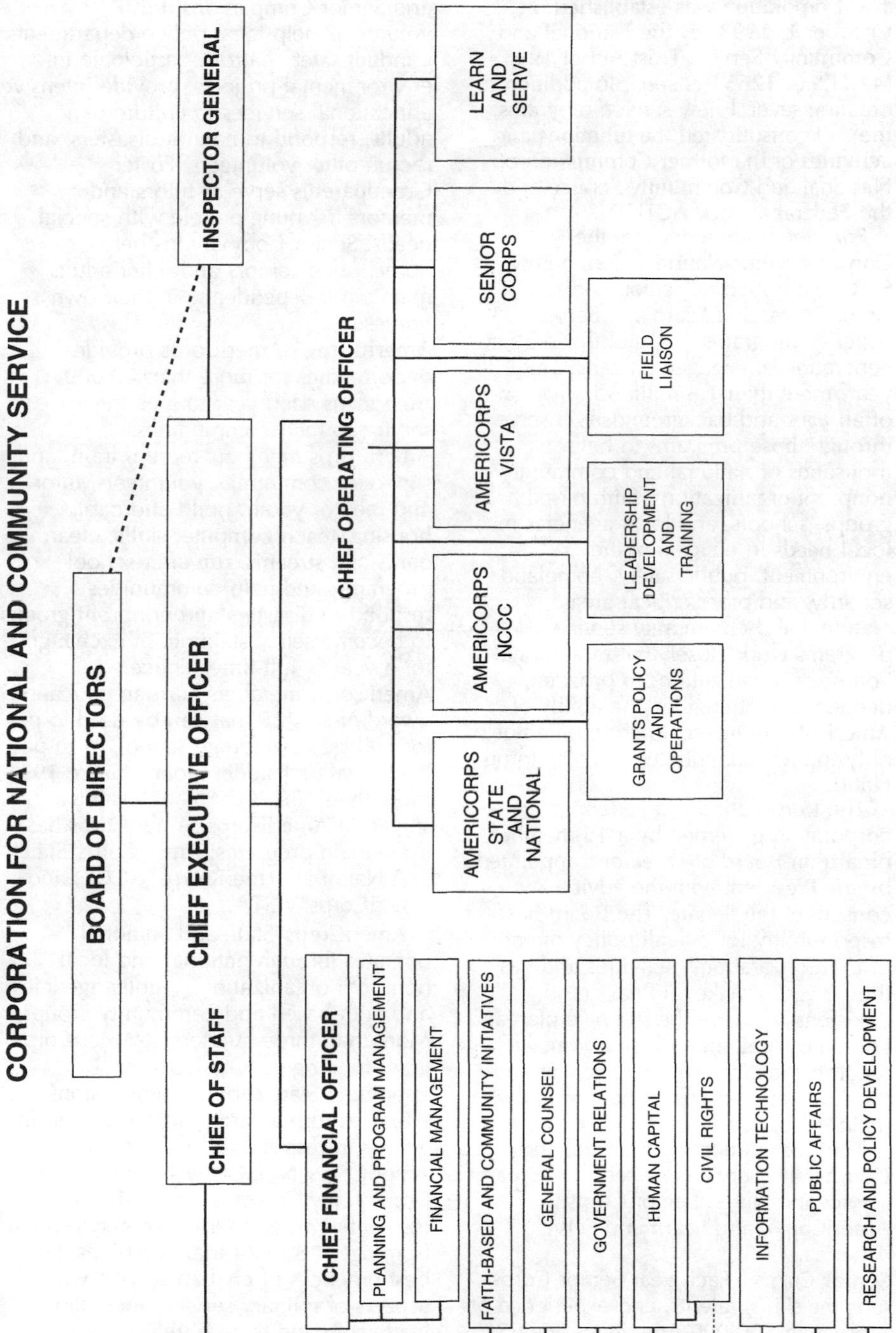
CORPORATION FOR NATIONAL AND COMMUNITY SERVICE
BOARD OF DIRECTORS
INSPECTOR GENERAL
CHIEF EXECUTIVE OFFICER
CHIEF OF STAFF
CHIEF OPERATING OFFICER
LEARN AND SERVE
SENIOR CORPS
AMERICORPS VISTA
AMERICORPS NCCC
AMERICORPS STATE AND NATIONAL
FIELD LIAISON
LEADERSHIP DEVELOPMENT AND TRAINING
GRANTS POLICY AND OPERATIONS
CHIEF FINANCIAL OFFICER
PLANNING AND PROGRAM MANAGEMENT
FINANCIAL MANAGEMENT
FAITH-BASED AND COMMUNITY INITIATIVES
GENERAL COUNSEL
GOVERNMENT RELATIONS
HUMAN CAPITAL
CIVIL RIGHTS
INFORMATION TECHNOLOGY
PUBLIC AFFAIRS
RESEARCH AND POLICY DEVELOPMENT

The Corporation was established on October 1, 1993, by the National and Community Service Trust Act of 1993 (42 U.S.C. 12651 *et seq.*). In addition to creating several new service programs, the Act consolidated the functions and activities of the former Commission on National and Community Service and the Federal agency ACTION.

For more than a decade, the Corporation for National Community Service, through its Senior Corps, AmeriCorps, and Learn and Serve America programs, has mobilized a new generation of engaged citizens. This year, more than 1.6 million individuals of all ages and backgrounds will serve through those programs to help thousands of national and community nonprofit organizations, faith-based groups, schools, and local agencies meet local needs in education, the environment, public safety, homeland security, and other critical areas. National and community service programs work closely with traditional volunteer organizations to broaden, deepen, and strengthen the ability of America's volunteers to contribute not only to their community, but also to our Nation.

The Corporation is a Federal corporation governed by a 15-member bipartisan Board of Directors, appointed by the President with the advice and consent of the Senate. The Board has responsibility for overall policy direction of the Corporation's activities and has the power to make all final grant decisions, approve the strategic plan and annual budget, and advise and make recommendations to the President and the Congress regarding changes in the national service laws.

The Corporation for National and Community Service oversees three major service initiatives: Senior Corps, AmeriCorps, and Learn and Serve America.

Senior Corps Each year Senior Corps taps the skills, talents, and experience of more than 500,000 Americans age 55 and older to meet a wide range of community challenges through three programs: Retired and Senior Volunteers Program (RSVP), Foster Grandparents, and Senior Companions. RSVP volunteers help local police departments conduct safety patrols, participate in environmental projects, provide intensive educational services to children and adults, respond to natural disasters, and recruit other volunteers. Foster Grandparents serve as tutors and mentors to young people with special needs. Senior Companions help homebound seniors and other adults maintain independence in their own homes.

AmeriCorps AmeriCorps provides opportunities for more than 70,000 Americans each year to give intensive service to their communities. AmeriCorps members recruit, train, and supervise community volunteers, tutor and mentor youth, build affordable housing, teach computer skills, clean parks and streams, run after-school programs, and help communities respond to disasters and nonprofit groups to become self-sustaining. In exchange for a year of full-time service, AmeriCorps members earn an education award of $4,725 that can be used to pay for college or graduate school, or to pay back qualified student loans. Since 1994 more than 400,000 Americans have served in AmeriCorps. AmeriCorps has three main programs: AmeriCorps*State and National, AmeriCorps*NCCC, and AmeriCorps*VISTA.

AmeriCorps*State and National operates through national and local nonprofit organizations, public agencies, and faith-based and community groups. More than three-quarters of AmeriCorps grant funding goes to Governor-appointed State service commissions, which in turn award grants to nonprofit groups to respond to local needs. AmeriCorps*NCCC (National Civilian Community Corps) is a team-based, residential program for men and women from ages 18 to 24 that combines the best practices of civilian service with aspects of military service, including leadership and team building. AmeriCorps*VISTA (Volunteers in Service to America) members serve full-time, for 1 year, in nonprofits, public agencies, and faith-based organizations to fight illiteracy, improve health services, create and expand business, increase housing opportunities, and bridge the digital divide.

Learn and Serve America Learn and Serve America engages more than one million students in community service linked to academic achievement and the development of civic skills. This type of learning, called service learning, improves communities while preparing young people for a lifetime of responsible citizenship.

Learn and Serve America provides grants to schools, colleges, and nonprofit groups to support its efforts. Grants are awarded through the Corporation and State educational agencies and commissions, nonprofit organizations, and higher education associations. School-based programs receive grants through State educational agencies or nonprofits, while community-based programs apply for funding through the same State commissions that coordinate AmeriCorps grants or through nonprofits. Higher education institutions and associations apply directly to the Corporation for grants. In addition to providing grants, Learn and Serve America serves as a resource on service and service-learning to teachers, faculty members, schools, and community groups and promotes student service through the Presidential Freedom Scholarships.

Other Initiatives Other programs and special initiatives administered by the Corporation's umbrella include: Next Generation Grants, which provide seed money to help startup organizations that have not previously received funds from the Corporation plan and implement new service programs that have the potential to become national in scope; Challenge Grants, a matching grant program designed to help nonprofit organizations secure previously untapped sources of private funds in order to build sustainable service and volunteer programs; King Day of Service Grants, which support community organizations in their efforts to engage local citizens in service on the Martin Luther King, Jr., Federal holiday; and the President's Council on Service and Civic Participation, which presents the President's Volunteer Service Award to citizens of all ages and backgrounds who have demonstrated a sustained commitment to service. The Corporation also provides extensive training and technical assistance to support and assist State service commissions and local service programs.

The Corporation and its programs work with the USA Freedom Corps, established on January 29, 2002, by Executive Order 13254. USA Freedom Corps is a White House initiative to foster a culture of citizenship, service, and responsibility, and help all Americans answer the President's call to service.

Sources of Information

Electronic Access Information regarding the Corporation's programs and activities is available on the Internet at www.nationalservice.gov. Information for persons interested in joining AmeriCorps is available at www.americorps.gov. Information for persons interested in joining Senior Corps is at www.seniorcorps.gov. Information on the USA Freedom Corps is available at www.usafreedomcorps.gov.

General Information To obtain additional information regarding AmeriCorps, call 800–942–2677. For Senior Corps programs, call 800–424–8867. TDD, 202–565–2799. For USA Freedom Corps, call 877–872–2677.

Grants All notices of available funds are made through the grants.gov Web site. State program offices and commissions on national and community service are located in most States and are the best source of information on programs in specific States or communities. To contact State offices or State commissions, visit www.nationalservice.gov/contactus.html.

For further information, contact the Corporation for National and Community Service, 1201 New York Avenue NW., Washington, DC 20525. Phone, 202–606–5000. Internet, www.nationalservice.gov.

DEFENSE NUCLEAR FACILITIES SAFETY BOARD

Suite 700, 625 Indiana Avenue NW., Washington, DC 20004
Phone, 202–694–7000. Fax, 202–208–6518. Internet, www.dnfsb.gov.

Chairman	A.J. EGGENBERGER
Vice Chairman	(VACANCY)
Members	JOSEPH F. BADER, JOHN E. MANSFIELD, (VACANCY)
General Counsel	RICHARD A. AZZARO
General Manager	BRIAN GROSNER, *Acting*
Technical Director	J. KENTON FORTENBERRY

The Defense Nuclear Facilities Safety Board reviews and evaluates the content and implementation of standards relating to the design, construction, operation, and decommissioning of defense nuclear facilities of the Department of Energy.

The Defense Nuclear Facilities Safety Board was established as an independent agency on September 29, 1988, by the Atomic Energy Act of 1954, as amended (42 U.S.C. 2286–2286i).

The Board is composed of five members appointed by the President with the advice and consent of the Senate. Members of the Board are appointed from among United States citizens who are respected experts in the field of nuclear safety.

Activities

The Defense Nuclear Facilities Safety Board reviews and evaluates the content and implementation of standards for defense nuclear facilities of the Department of Energy (DOE); investigates any event or practice at these facilities which may adversely affect public health and safety; and reviews and monitors the design, construction, and operation of facilities. The Board makes recommendations to the Secretary of Energy concerning DOE defense nuclear facilities to ensure adequate protection of public health and safety. In the event that any aspect of operations, practices, or occurrences reviewed by the Board is determined to present an imminent or severe threat to public health and safety, the Board transmits its recommendations directly to the President.

For further information, contact the Defense Nuclear Facilities Safety Board, Suite 700, 625 Indiana Avenue NW., Washington, DC 20004. Phone, 202–694–7000. Internet, www.dnfsb.gov.

ENVIRONMENTAL PROTECTION AGENCY

1200 Pennsylvania Avenue NW., Washington, DC 20460–0001
Phone, 202–272–0167. Internet, www.epa.gov.

Administrator	STEPHEN L. JOHNSON
Deputy Administrator	MARCUS PEACOCK
Associate Administrator for Public Affairs	LISA LYBBERT

DEFENSE NUCLEAR FACILITIES SAFETY BOARD

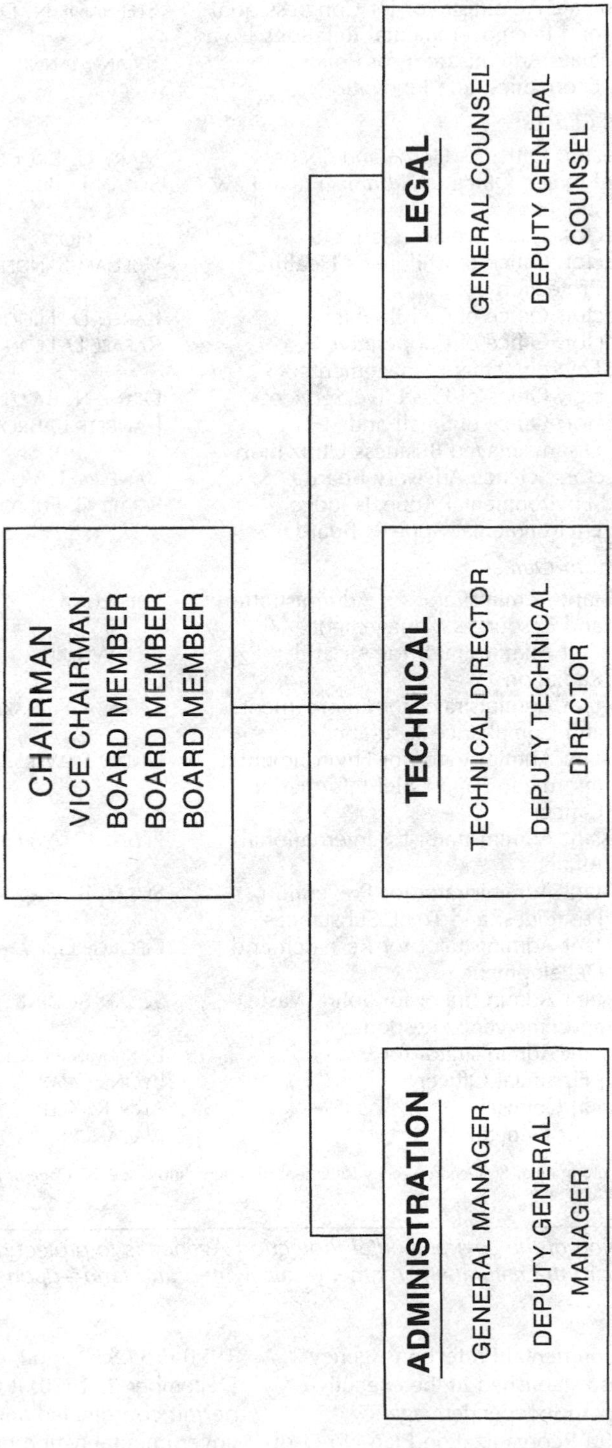

Associate Administrator for Congressional and Intergovernmental Relations	STEPHANIE N. DAIGLE
Associate Administrator for Policy, Economics, and Innovation	BRIAN MANNI
Staff Offices:	
Director, Office of Homeland Security	MARY U. KRUGER
Chief Judge, Office of Administrative Law Judges	SUSAN L. BIRO
Director, Executive Secretariat	BRIAN HOPE
Director, Office of Children's Health Protection	WILLIAM SANDERS, *Acting*
Director, Office of Civil Rights	KAREN D. HIGGINBOTHAM
Director, Office of Cooperative Environmental Management	RAFAEL DELEON
Director, Office of Executive Services	DIANE N. BAZZLE
Director, Office of Small and Disadvantaged Business Utilization	JEANETTE L. BROWN
Director, Science Advisory Board	VANESSA T. VU
Lead Environmental Appeals Judge, Environmental Appeals Board	SCOTT C. FULTON
Program Offices:	
Assistant Administrator for Administration and Resources Management	LUIS LUNA
Assistant Administrator for Air and Radiation	BILL WEHRUM
Assistant Administrator for Enforcement and Compliance Assurance	GRANTA Y. NAKAYAMA
Assistant Administrator for Environmental Information and Chief Information Officer	LINDA TRAVERS, *Acting*
Assistant Administrator for International Affairs	JUDITH E. AYRES
Assistant Administrator for Prevention, Pesticides, and Toxic Substances	SUSAN B. HAZEN, *Acting*
Assistant Administrator for Research and Development	GEORGE GRAY
Assistant Administrator for Solid Waste and Emergency Response	SUSAN BODINE
Assistant Administrator for Water	BENJAMIN H. GRUMBLES
Chief Financial Officer	LYONS GRAY
General Counsel	ANN R. KLEE
Inspector General	(VACANCY)

[For the Environmental Protection Agency statement of organization, see the *Code of Federal Regulations,* Title 40, Part 1]

The mission of the Environmental Protection Agency is to protect human health and to safeguard the natural environment—air, water, and land—upon which life depends.

The Environmental Protection Agency (EPA) was established in the executive branch as an independent agency pursuant to Reorganization Plan No. 3 of 1970 (5 U.S.C. app.), effective December 2, 1970. It was created to permit coordinated and effective governmental action on behalf of the

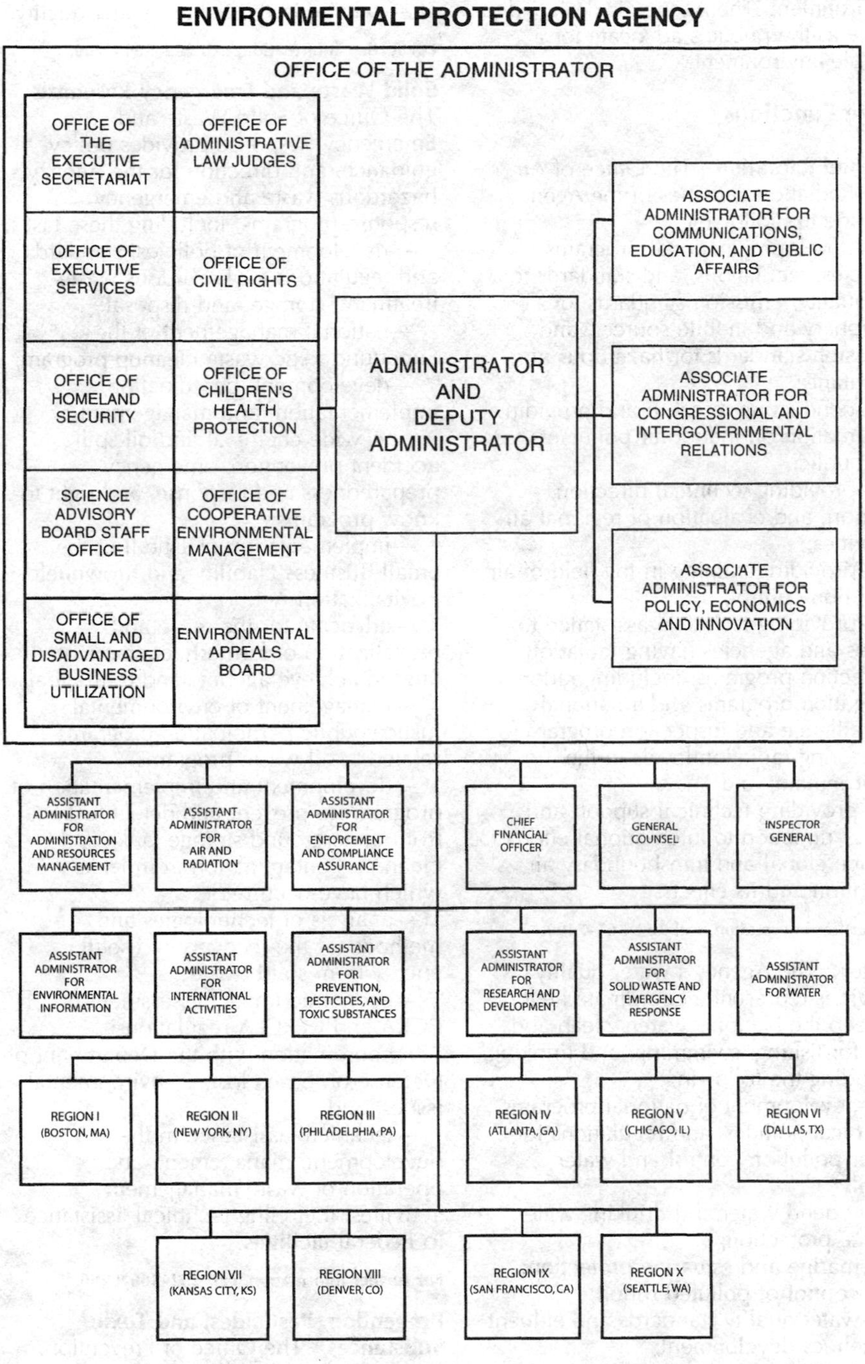
ENVIRONMENTAL PROTECTION AGENCY
OFFICE OF THE ADMINISTRATOR
OFFICE OF THE EXECUTIVE SECRETARIAT
OFFICE OF ADMINISTRATIVE LAW JUDGES
OFFICE OF EXECUTIVE SERVICES
OFFICE OF CIVIL RIGHTS
OFFICE OF HOMELAND SECURITY
OFFICE OF CHILDREN'S HEALTH PROTECTION
SCIENCE ADVISORY BOARD STAFF OFFICE
OFFICE OF COOPERATIVE ENVIRONMENTAL MANAGEMENT
OFFICE OF SMALL AND DISADVANTAGED BUSINESS UTILIZATION
ENVIRONMENTAL APPEALS BOARD
ADMINISTRATOR AND DEPUTY ADMINISTRATOR
ASSOCIATE ADMINISTRATOR FOR COMMUNICATIONS, EDUCATION, AND PUBLIC AFFAIRS
ASSOCIATE ADMINISTRATOR FOR CONGRESSIONAL AND INTERGOVERNMENTAL RELATIONS
ASSOCIATE ADMINISTRATOR FOR POLICY, ECONOMICS AND INNOVATION
ASSISTANT ADMINISTRATOR FOR ADMINISTRATION AND RESOURCES MANAGEMENT
ASSISTANT ADMINISTRATOR FOR AIR AND RADIATION
ASSISTANT ADMINISTRATOR FOR ENFORCEMENT AND COMPLIANCE ASSURANCE
CHIEF FINANCIAL OFFICER
GENERAL COUNSEL
INSPECTOR GENERAL
ASSISTANT ADMINISTRATOR FOR ENVIRONMENTAL INFORMATION
ASSISTANT ADMINISTRATOR FOR INTERNATIONAL ACTIVITIES
ASSISTANT ADMINISTRATOR FOR PREVENTION, PESTICIDES, AND TOXIC SUBSTANCES
ASSISTANT ADMINISTRATOR FOR RESEARCH AND DEVELOPMENT
ASSISTANT ADMINISTRATOR FOR SOLID WASTE AND EMERGENCY RESPONSE
ASSISTANT ADMINISTRATOR FOR WATER
REGION I (BOSTON, MA)
REGION II (NEW YORK, NY)
REGION III (PHILADELPHIA, PA)
REGION IV (ATLANTA, GA)
REGION V (CHICAGO, IL)
REGION VI (DALLAS, TX)
REGION VII (KANSAS CITY, KS)
REGION VIII (DENVER, CO)
REGION IX (SAN FRANCISCO, CA)
REGION X (SEATTLE, WA)

environment. The Agency is designed to serve as the public's advocate for a livable environment.

Core Functions

Air and Radiation The Office of Air and Radiation activities of the Agency include the following:

—developing national programs, policies, regulations, and standards for air quality, emission standards for stationary and mobile sources, and emission standards for hazardous air pollutants;

—conducting research and providing information on indoor air pollutants to the public;

—providing technical direction, support, and evaluation of regional air activities;

—providing training in the field of air pollution control;

—providing technical assistance to States and agencies having radiation protection programs, including radon mitigation programs and a national surveillance and inspection program for measuring radiation levels in the environment; and

—providing technical support and policy direction to international efforts to reduce global and transboundary air pollution and its effects.

For further information, call 202–564–7400.

Water The Agency's water quality activities represent a coordinated effort to keep the Nation's waters clean and safe for fishing, swimming, and drinking, including the following:

—development of national programs, technical policies, and regulations for water pollution control and water supply;

—ground water and drinking water source protection;

—marine and estuarine protection;

—control of polluted runoff;

—water quality standards and effluent guidelines development;

—support of regional water activities;

—development of programs for technical assistance and technology transfer; and

—training in the field of water quality.

For further information, call 202–564–5700.

Solid Waste and Emergency Response The Office of Solid Waste and Emergency Response provides policy, guidance, and direction for the Agency's hazardous waste and emergency response programs, including these tasks:

—development of policies, standards, and regulations for hazardous waste treatment, storage, and disposal;

—national management of the Superfund toxic waste cleanup program;

—development, coordination, implementation, and management of Agencywide chemical and oil spill accident prevention, emergency preparedness and response, and right-to-know programs;

—implementation of Title II of the Small Business Liability and Brownfields Revitalization Act;

—advocate for the reuse and revitalization of formerly contaminated land to achieve agency land reuse goals;

—management of environmental justice/public participation programs related to all waste programs;

—development and implementation of programs to prevent and detect leakage from underground storage tanks and to clean up contamination from leaks which have occurred;

—analysis of technologies and methods for the recovery of useful energy from solid waste;

—economic impact assessment of RCRA and CERCLA regulations;

—coordination with the Department of Defense on base closure environmental issues; and

—technical assistance in the development, management, and operation of waste management activities, including technical assistance to Federal facilities.

For further information, call 202–566–0200.

Prevention, Pesticides, and Toxic Substances The Office of Prevention, Pesticides, and Toxic Substances is responsible for the following tasks:

—promoting the public's right to know about industrial chemicals;

—promoting pollution prevention through innovative strategies;

—evaluating and regulating pesticides and industrial chemicals to safeguard all Americans;

—reviewing and regulating emerging technology, including biotechnology-derived products;

—developing, evaluating, and implementing science policies both domestically and internationally;

—establishing safe levels for pesticide residues on food;

—developing national strategies for control of persistent, bioaccumulative, and toxic substances;

—developing scientific criteria for assessing chemical substances, standards for test protocols for chemicals, rules and procedures for industry reporting, and scientific information for the regulation of pesticides and toxic chemicals to ensure protection of people or the environment; and

—evaluating and assessing the impact of existing chemicals, new chemicals, and chemicals with new uses to determine the hazard and develop appropriate restrictions.

The Office also coordinates its activities with States and other agencies during the assessment and control of toxic substances and pesticides.

For further information, call 202–564–2902.

Research and Development The Office of Research and Development (ORD) provides the scientific foundation for the Agency's environmental protection mission. ORD's chief role is to conduct and support high quality research targeted to understanding and resolving the Nation's most serious environmental threats. In addition, ORD develops methods and technologies to reduce exposures to pollution and prevent its creation. The Office is also a major player in sharing information on technological innovations to protect people and the environment. ORD prepares health and ecological risk assessments and makes recommendations for sound risk management strategies in order to assure that highest risk pollution problems receive optimum remediation. The Office manages a vital extramural grants program entitled Science To Achieve Results (STAR), which awards research grants to scientists in universities and students in environmental science. All ORD extramural and intramural research is carefully aligned to support Agency environmental goals and strategic priorities.

For further information, call 202–564–6620.

Enforcement and Compliance Assurance The Office of Enforcement and Compliance Assurance (OECA) is the lead agency office for matters pertaining to the Agency's enforcement and compliance assurance programs. OECA manages a national criminal enforcement, forensics, and training program. OECA also manages the Agency's regulatory, site remediation, and Federal facilities enforcement and compliance assurance programs, as well as the Agency's environmental justice program, and Federal activities program responsibilities under the National Environmental Policy Act.

For further information, call 202–564–2440.

Regional Offices

The Agency's 10 regional offices represent its commitment to the development of strong local programs for pollution abatement. The Regional Administrators are responsible for accomplishing, within their regions, the national program objectives established by the Agency. They develop, propose, and implement an approved regional program for comprehensive and integrated environmental protection activities.

Regional Offices—Environmental Protection Agency

Region/Address/Areas Served	Regional Administrator
Region I (Suite 1100, 1 Congress St., Boston, MA 02114–2023) (CT, MA, ME, NH, RI, VT)	Robert W. Varney
Region II (290 Broadway, New York, NY 10007–1866) (NJ, NY, PR, VI)	Alan J. Steinberg
Region III (1650 Arch St., Philadelphia, PA 19103–2029) (DC, DE, MD, PA, VA, WV)	Donald S. Welsh

Regional Offices—Environmental Protection Agency—Continued

Region/Address/Areas Served	Regional Administrator
Region IV (61 Forsyth St. SW, Atlanta GA 30303–3104) (AL, FL, GA, KY, MS, NC, SC, TN)	James I. Palmer, Jr.
Region V (77 W. Jackson Blvd., Chicago, IL 60604–3507) (IL, IN, MI, MN, OH, WI)	Thomas V. Skinner
Region VI (Suite 1200, 1445 Ross Ave., Dallas, TX 75202–2733) (AR, LA, NM, OK, TX)	Richard E. Greene
Region VII (901 N. 5th St., Kansas City, KS 66101) (IA, KS, MO, NE)	James B. Gulliford
Region VIII (Suite 500, 999 18th St., Denver, CO 80202–2466) (CO, MT, ND, SD, UT, WY)	Robert E. Roberts
Region IX (75 Hawthorne St., San Francisco, CA 94105) (AZ, CA, HI, NV, and U.S. affiliated Pacific Islands).	Wayne H. Nastri
Region X (1200 6th Ave., Seattle, WA 98101) (AK, ID, OR, WA)	Michael Bogert

Sources of Information

Information inquiries for the following subjects should be directed to the respective organization listed below by telephone; by mail to 1200 Pennsylvania Avenue NW., Washington, DC 20460; or through the Internet at (www.epa.gov).

Contracts and Procurement Office of Acquisition Management. Phone, 202–564–4310.

Employment Office of Human Resources. Phone, 202–564–3300.

Freedom of Information Act Requests Freedom of Information Officer. Phone, 202–566–1667. E-mail, hq.foia@epa.epa.gov.

Information Resources Phone, 202–564–6665.

Telephone Directory Available for sale by the Superintendent of Documents, Government Printing Office, P.O. Box 37194, Pittsburgh, PA 15250–7954.

For further information, contact the Office of Public Affairs, Environmental Protection Agency, 1200 Pennsylvania Avenue NW., Washington, DC 20460–0001. Phone, 202–564–4355. Internet, www.epa.gov.

EQUAL EMPLOYMENT OPPORTUNITY COMMISSION

1801 L Street NW., Washington, DC 20507

Phone, 202–663–4900. TTY, 202–663–4494. Internet, www.eeoc.gov.

Chair	Cari M. Dominguez
Vice Chair	Naomi C. Earp
Commissioners	Christine M. Griffin, Stuart J. Ishimaru, Leslie Silverman
Executive Officer	Stephen Llewellyn, *Acting*
Chief Operating Officer	Leonora L. Guarraia
General Counsel	(vacancy)
Inspector General	Aletha L. Brown
Deputy Director, Office of Communications and Legislative Affairs	Karin Pedrick
Director, Office of Equal Opportunity	Jean Watson
Director, Office of Federal Operations	Carlton M. Hadden
Legal Counsel	Peggy R. Mastroianni, *Acting*
Director, Office of Field Programs	Nicholas Inzeo
Director, Office of Financial and Resource Management	Jeffrey Smith
Director, Office of Human Resources	Angelica Ibarguen
Director, Office of Information Resources Management	Sallie T. Hsieh

Director, Office of Research, Information, and Planning — DEIDRE FLIPPEN

The Equal Employment Opportunity Commission enforces laws which prohibit discrimination based on race, color, religion, sex, national origin, disability, or age in hiring, promoting, firing, setting wages, testing, training, apprenticeship, and all other terms and conditions of employment. The Commission conducts investigations of alleged discrimination; makes determinations based on gathered evidence; attempts conciliation when discrimination has taken place; files lawsuits; and conducts voluntary assistance programs for employers, unions, and community organizations. The Commission also has adjudicatory and oversight responsibility for all compliance and enforcement activities relating to equal employment opportunity among Federal employees and applicants, including discrimination against individuals with disabilities.

The Equal Employment Opportunity Commission (EEOC) was created by title VII of the Civil Rights Act of 1964 (42 U.S.C. 2000e–4), and became operational July 2, 1965. The Commission is comprised of five Commissioners appointed by the President, with the advice and consent of the Senate, for 5-year staggered terms. The President designates a Chairman and a Vice Chairman. The Commission operates through 50 field offices, each of which processes charges.

Activities

Enforcement The Commission's field offices receive charges of job discrimination under title VII of the Civil Rights Act, the Americans with Disabilities Act, the Equal Pay Act, and the Age Discrimination in Employment Act. Field offices may initiate investigations to find violations of the acts.

Charges Under Title VII Title VII prohibits employment discrimination based on race, color, religion, sex, or national origin by private employers, State and local governments, and educational institutions with 15 or more employees, or by the Federal Government, private and public employment agencies, labor organizations, and joint labor-management committees for apprenticeship and training.

If there is reasonable cause to believe a charge filed is true, the district, area, or local office attempts to remedy the alleged unlawful practices through informal methods of conciliation, conference, and persuasion. If an acceptable conciliation agreement is not secured, the case is considered for possible litigation. If litigation is approved, the Commission will bring suit in an appropriate Federal district court.

Americans with Disabilities Act Charges Employment discrimination charges based on disability may be filed at any of the Commission's field offices. The Commission will investigate and attempt to conciliate the charges.

Age Discrimination in Employment Act or Equal Pay Act Charges and Complaints When a discrimination charge is filed, the Commission will attempt to eliminate the unlawful practice through informal methods of conciliation, conference, and persuasion. A lawsuit may be brought by the Commission if conciliation fails, or individuals may file suit on their own. A lawsuit under the EPA may be filed by the Commission or by the complainant.

Complaints Against the Federal Government The Commission's Federal sector processing regulations guide Federal employees or job applicants who want to file complaints of job discrimination based on race, color, national origin, sex, religion, age, or physical or mental disability. Informal mediation of the matter is required before filing a charge. An accepted complaint is investigated by the respondent agency, and there is a right to a hearing before an EEOC administrative judge before the agency

EQUAL EMPLOYMENT OPPORTUNITY COMMISSION

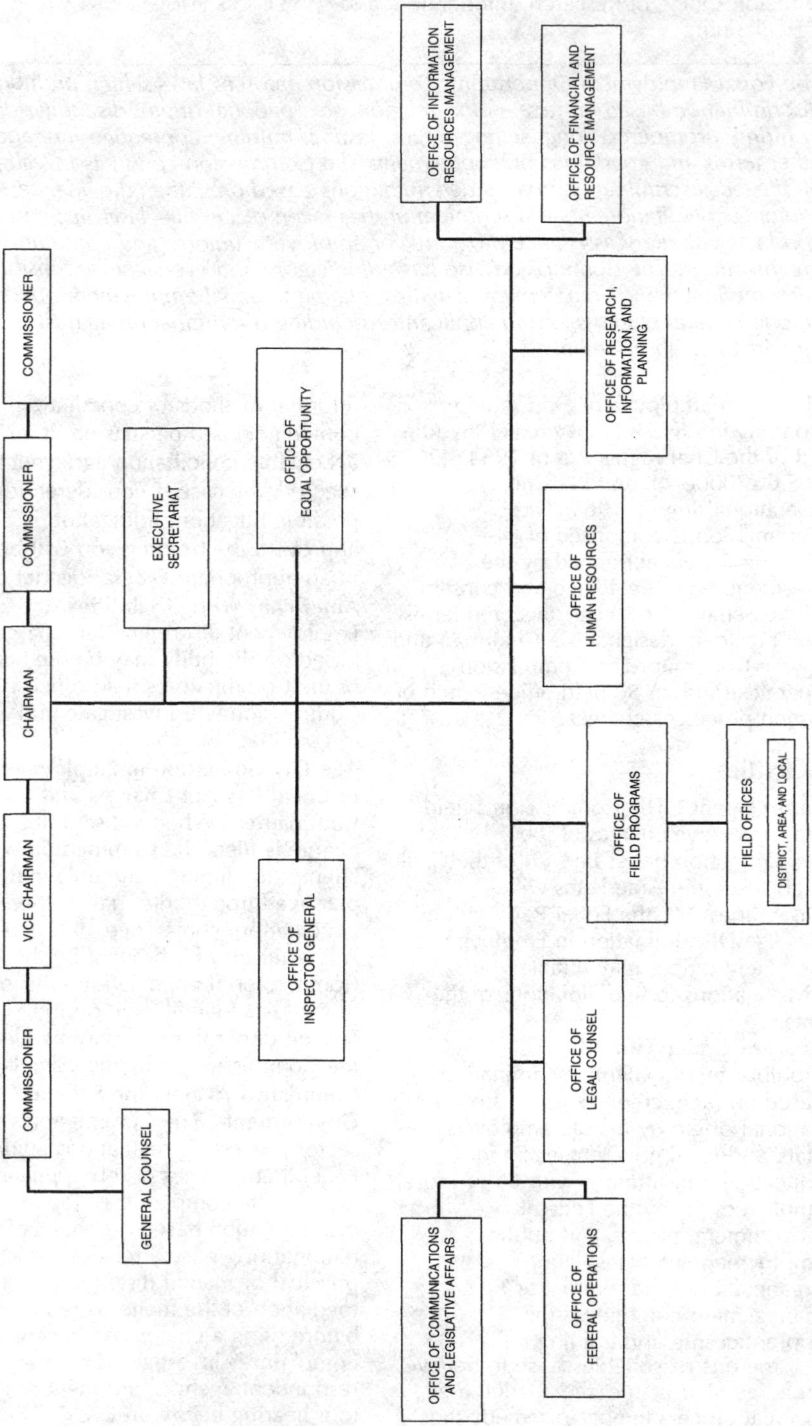

issues its final decision. Final decisions may be appealed.

Other Activities The Commission actively promotes voluntary compliance with equal employment opportunity statutes through a variety of educational and technical assistance activities. A distinct activity of the Commission is the Voluntary Assistance Program. This outreach program is designed to provide educational and technical assistance to small and midsize employers and unions—through 1-day seminars on equal employment opportunity laws—about their rights and obligations under all the statutes that the Commission enforces.

Another activity initiated by the Commission is the Expanded Presence Program, which is designed to make the Commission accessible in areas identified as underserved by Commission offices.

Through its Educational Technical Assistance and Training Revolving Fund, the Commission is also able to provide its constituency with advanced and specialized technical assistance offerings. Fees charged for Revolving Fund products are not to exceed the cost of producing the materials or services provided, are to bear a direct relationship to the cost of providing such outreach, and are to be imposed on a uniform basis.

The Commission participates in the development of employment discrimination law through the issuance of guidelines, publication of significant Commission decisions, and involvement in litigation brought under the relevant statutes.

The Commission has direct liaison with Federal, State, and local governments, employers and union organizations, trade associations, civil rights organizations, and other agencies and organizations concerned with employment of minority group members and women.

The Commission develops and implements affirmative employment policies designed to enhance the occupational status of minorities, women, and persons with disabilities in the Federal Government.

The Commission also publishes data on the employment status of minorities and women. Through six employment surveys covering private employers, apprenticeship programs, labor unions, State and local governments, elementary and secondary schools, and colleges and universities, the Commission tabulates and stores data on the ethnic, racial, and sex composition of employees at all job levels within the reported groups.

This collection of research information is shared with selected Federal agencies and is made available, in appropriate form, for public use.

Field Offices—Equal Employment Opportunity Commission

(DO: District Office; AO: Area Office; LO: Local Office; FO: Field Office)

Office	Address/Telephone	Director
Albuquerque, NM (AO)	Suite 900, 505 Marquette NW., 87102. Ph., 505–248–5201. Fax, 505–248–5233. TTY, 505–248–5240.	Georgia Marchbanks
Atlanta, GA (DO)	Suite 4R30, 100 Alabama St. NW., 30303. Ph., 404–562–6800. Fax, 404–562–6909. TTY, 404–562–6801.	Bernice Williams-Kimbrough
Baltimore, MD (FO)	3d Fl., City Crescent Bldg., 10 S. Howard St., 21201. Ph., 410–962–3932. Fax, 410–962–4270. TTY, 410–962–6065.	Gerald Kiel
Birmingham, AL (DO)	Suite 200, 1130 22d St. S., 35205. Ph., 205–731–0082. Fax, 205–731–2101. TTY, 205–731–0175.	Bernice Williams-Kimbrough, *Acting*
Boston, MA (AO)	Rm. 475, John F. Kennedy Fed. Bldg., 02203. Ph., 617–565–3200. Fax, 617–565–3196. TTY, 617–565–3204.	Robert L. Sanders
Buffalo, NY (LO)	Suite 350, 6 Fountain Plz., 14202. Ph., 716–551–4441. Fax, 716–551–4387. TTY, 716–551–5923.	Elizabeth Cadle
Charlotte, NC (DO)	Suite 400, 129 W. Trade St., 28202. Ph., 704–344–6682. Fax, 704–344–6734. TTY, 704–334–6684.	Reuben Daniels, Jr.
Chicago, IL (DO)	Suite 2800, 500 W. Madison St., 60661. Ph., 312–353–2713. Fax, 312–353–4041. TTY, 312–353–2421.	John P. Rowe
Cincinnati, OH (AO)	Suite 10019, 550 Main St., 45202–5202. Ph., 513–684–2851. Fax, 513–684–2361. TTY, 513–684–2074.	Wilma Javey
Cleveland, OH (FO)	Suite 850, 1660 W. 2d St., 44113–1454. Ph., 216–522–2001. Fax, 216–522–7395. TTY, 216–522–8441.	Daniel Cabot
Dallas, TX (DO)	3d Fl., 207 S. Houston St., 75202–4726.	Michael Fetzer

Field Offices—Equal Employment Opportunity Commission—Continued

(DO: District Office; AO: Area Office; LO: Local Office; FO: Field Office)

Office	Address/Telephone	Director
	Ph., 214–253–2700. Fax, 214–253–2720. TTY, 214–253–2710.	
Denver, CO (FO)	Suite 510, 303 E. 17th Ave., 80203. Ph., 303–866–1300. Fax, 303–866–1386. TTY, 303–866–1950.	Nancy Sienko
Detroit, MI (FO)	Rm. 865, 477 Michigan Ave., 48226–2523. Ph., 313–226–4600. Fax, 313–226–2778. TTY, 313–226–7599.	Gail Cober
El Paso, TX (AO)	Suite 500, 300 E. Main Dr., 79901–1331. Ph., 915–534–6700. Fax, 915–534–6701. TTY, 915–534–6710.	Robert Calderon
Fresno, CA (LO)	Suite 103, 1265 W. Shaw Ave., 93711. Ph., 559–487–5793. Fax, 559–487–5053. TTY, 559–487–5837.	Olophius Perry, *Acting*
Greensboro, NC (LO)	Suite 201, 2303 W. Meadowview Rd., 27407. Ph., 336–547–4188. Fax, 336–547–4032. TTY, 336–547–4035.	Thomas Colclough
Greenville, SC (LO)	Suite 1402, 301 N. Main St., 29601. Ph., 864–241–4400. Fax, 864–241–4416. TTY, 864–241–4403.	Patricia Fuller
Honolulu, HI (LO)	Rm. 7–127, 300 Ala Moana Blvd., P.O. Box 50082, 96850–0051. Ph., 808–541–3120. Fax, 808–541–3390. TTY, 808–541–3131.	Timothy A. Riera
Houston, TX (DO)	7th Fl., 1919 Smith St., 77002–8049. Ph., 713–209–3320. Fax, 713–209–3381. TTY, 713–209–3439.	Jeanette Leino
Indianapolis, IN (DO)	Suite 1900, 101 W. Ohio St., 46204–4203. Ph., 317–226–7212. Fax, 317–226–7953. TTY, 317–226–5162.	Danny G. Harter
Jackson, MS (AO)	Suite 207, 100 W. Capitol St., 39269. Ph., 601–965–4537. Fax, 601–965–5272. TTY, 601–965–4915.	Wilma Scott
Kansas City, KS (AO)	Suite 905, 400 State Ave., 66101. Ph., 913–551–5655. Fax, 913–551–6956. TTY, 913–551–5657.	James Neely, Jr., *Acting*
Little Rock, AR (AO)	Suite 200, 820 S. Louisiana Ave., 72201. Ph., 501–324–5060. Fax, 501–324–5991. TTY, 501–324–5481.	Katherine Kores
Los Angeles, CA (DO)	4th Fl., 255 E. Temple St., 90012. Ph., 213–894–1000. Fax, 213–894–1118. TTY, 213–894–1121.	Olophius Perry
Louisville, KY (AO)	Suite 268, 600 Dr. Martin Luther King Jr. Pl., 40202. Ph., 502–582–6082. Fax, 502–582–5895. TTY, 502–582–6285.	Marcia Hall Craig
Memphis, TN (DO)	Suite 621, 1407 Union Ave., 38104. Ph., 901–544–0115. Fax, 901–544–0111. TTY, 901–544–0112.	Katherine Kores
Miami, FL (DO)	Suite 2700, 2 S. Biscayne Blvd., 33131. Ph., 305–536–4491. Fax, 305–536–4011. TTY, 305–536–5721.	Federico Costales
Milwaukee, WI (AO)	Suite 800, 310 W. Wisconsin Ave., 53203–2292. Ph., 414–297–1111. Fax, 414–297–4133. TTY, 414–297–1115.	John P. Rowe, *Acting*
Minneapolis, MN (AO)	Suite 430, 330 S. 2d Ave., 55401–2224. Ph., 612–335–4040. Fax, 612–335–4044. TTY, 612–335–4045.	John P. Rowe, *Acting*
Nashville, TN (AO)	Suite 202, 50 Vantage Way, 37228–9940. Ph., 615–736–5820. Fax, 615–736–2107. TTY, 615–736–5870.	Sarah Smith
New Orleans, LA (FO)	Suite 600, 701 Loyola Ave., 70113–9936. Ph., 504–589–2329. Fax, 504–589–6861. TTY, 504–589–2958.	Keith Hill, *Acting*
New York, NY (DO)	5th Fl., 33 Whitehall St., 10004. Ph., 212–336–3620. Fax, 212–336–3625. TTY, 212–336–3622.	Spencer H. Lewis, Jr.
Newark, NJ (AO)	21st Fl., One Newark Ctr., 07102–5233. Ph., 973–645–6383. Fax, 973–645–4524. TTY, 973–645–3004.	Corrado Gigante
Norfolk, VA (AO)	Suite 739, 200 Granby St., 23510. Ph., 757–441–3470. Fax, 757–441–6720. TTY, 757–441–3578.	Herbert Brown
Oakland, CA (LO)	Suite 1170–N, 1301 Clay St., 94612–5217. Ph., 510–637–3230. Fax, 510–637–3235. TTY, 510–637–3234.	Joyce A. Hendy
Oklahoma City, OK (AO)	Suite 1350, 210 Park Ave., 73102. Ph., 405–231–4911. Fax, 405–231–4140. TTY, 405–231–5745.	Donald T. Stevens
Philadelphia, PA (DO)	Suite 400, 21 S. 5th St., 19106–2515. Ph., 215–440–2600. Fax, 215–440–2632. TTY, 215–440–2610.	Marie Tomasso
Phoenix, AZ (DO)	Suite 690, 3300 N. Central Ave., 85012–2504. Ph., 602–640–5000. Fax, 602–640–5071. TTY, 602–640–5072.	Chester Bailey
Pittsburgh, PA (AO)	Suite 300, 1001 Liberty Ave., 15222–4187. Ph., 412–644–3444. Fax, 412–644–2664. TTY, 412–644–2720.	Joseph Hardiman
Raleigh, NC (AO)	1309 Annapolis Dr., 27608–2129. Ph., 919–856–4064. Fax, 919–856–4151. TTY, 919–856–4296.	Richard E. Walz
Richmond, VA (LO)	Suite 600, 803 E. Main St., 23219. Ph., 804–771–2200. Fax, 804–771–2222. TTY, 804–278–2227.	Patricia Glisson, *Acting*
San Antonio, TX (FO)	Suite 200, 5410 Fredericksburg Rd., 78229–3555. Ph., 210–281–7600. Fax, 210–281–7690. TTY, 210–281–7610.	Pedro Esquivel
San Diego, CA (AO)	Suite 510, 401 B St., 92101. Ph., 619–557–7235. Fax, 619–557–7274. TTY, 619–557–5748.	Bettie Isiaka, *Acting*
San Francisco, CA (DO)	Suite 500, 350 Embarcadero, 94105–1687. Ph., 415–625–5600. Fax, 415–625–5609. TTY, 415–625–5610.	Joan Ehrlich
San Jose, CA (LO)	Suite 200, 96 N. 3d St., 95112. Ph., 408–291–7352. Fax, 408–291–4539. TTY, 408–291–7374.	Hae Jung Atkins
San Juan, PR (AO)	Suite 1202, 525 F.D. Roosevelt Ave., Plz. Las Americas, 00918–8001. Ph., 787–771–1464. Fax, 787–771–1485. TTY, 787–771–1484.	Ozzie Black, *Acting*
Savannah, GA (LO)	Suite G, 410 Mall Blvd., 31406–4821. Ph., 912–652–4234. Fax, 912–652–4248. TTY, 912–652–4439.	John Smith, *Acting*

Field Offices—Equal Employment Opportunity Commission—Continued
(DO: District Office; AO: Area Office; LO: Local Office; FO: Field Office)

Office	Address/Telephone	Director
Seattle, WA (FO)	Suite 400, 909 First Ave., 98104–1061. Ph., 206–220–6883. Fax, 206–220–6911. TTY, 206–220–6882.	Luis Lucero
St. Louis, MO (DO)	Rm. 8.100, 1222 Spruce St., 63103. Ph., 314–539–7800. Fax, 314–539–7893. TTY, 314–539–7803.	James Neely, Jr.
Tampa, FL (AO)	Rm. 1000, 501 E. Polk St., 33602. Ph., 813–228–2310. Fax, 813–228–2841. TTY, 813–228–2003.	Manuel Zurita
Washington, DC (FO)	Suite 200, 1400 L St. NW., 20005. Ph., 202–275–7377. Fax, 202–275–6834. TTY, 202–275–7518.	Dana Hutter, *Acting*

Sources of Information

Electronic Access Information regarding the programs, publications, and activities of the Commission is available through the Internet, at www.eeoc.gov.

Employment The Commission selects its employees from various examinations and registers, including mid- and senior-level registers, secretarial, typing, and stenographic registers, and the Equal Opportunity Specialist register. Employment inquiries or applications for positions in the headquarters office should be directed to the Office of Human Resources, Equal Employment Opportunity Commission, 1801 L Street NW., Washington, DC 20507 (phone, 202–663–4306), or contact the appropriate district office for district office positions.

General Inquiries A nationwide toll-free telephone number links callers with the appropriate field office where charges may be filed. Phone, 800–669–4000. TTY, 800–669–6820.

Information About Survey Forms (EEO–1, 2, 3, 4, 5, and 6). Phone, 202–663–4958.

Media Inquiries Office of Communications and Legislative Affairs, 1801 L Street NW., Washington, DC 20507. Phone, 202–663–4900.

Publications Phone, 800–669–3362. TTY, 800–800–3302. Fax, 513–489–8692.

Reading Room EEOC Library, 1801 L Street NW., Washington, DC 20507. Phone, 202–663–4630.

Speakers Office of Communications and Legislative Affairs, 1801 L Street NW., Washington, DC 20507. Phone, 202–663–4900.

For further information, contact the Equal Employment Opportunity Commission, 1801 L Street NW., Washington, DC 20507. Phone, 202–663–4900. Internet, www.eeoc.gov.

EXPORT–IMPORT BANK OF THE UNITED STATES

811 Vermont Avenue NW., Washington, DC 20571
Phone, 202–565–3946 or 800–565–EXIM. Internet, www.exim.gov.

President and Chairman	JAMES LAMBRIGHT, *Acting*
Vice Chairman	(VACANCY)
Directors	MAX CLELAND, LINDA CONLIN, (VACANCY)
Executive Vice President	(VACANCY)
Senior Vice President and Chief Financial Officer	MICHAEL DISCENZA
Deputy Chief Financial Officer	ALICE MCNUTT MILLER
Director, Administrative Services	JONATHAN T. MCMULLEN

Director, Equal Opportunity and Diversity Programs and Training	PATREASE JONES-BROWN
Director, Human Resources	ELLIOTT DAVIS
Vice President, Trade Finance and Insurance	JEFFREY ABRAMSON
General Counsel	HOWARD SCHWEITZER, *Acting*
Senior Vice President, Resource Management	MICHAEL CUSHING
Senior Vice President, Small Business	JOHN EMENS
Senior Vice President, Export Finance	JOHN MCADAMS
Senior Vice President, Credit and Risk Management	KENNETH M. TINSLEY
Vice President, Export Finance Operations	RAY ELLIS
Vice President, Asset Management	FRANCES NWACHUKU
Senior Vice President, Communications	BRETT M. DECKER
Senior Vice President, Congressional Affairs	THOMAS MONTGOMERY
Vice President, Country Risk and Economics	WILLIAM MARSTELLAR
Vice President, Engineering and Environment	JAMES A. MAHONEY, JR.
Chief Information Officer	FERNANDA YOUNG
Vice President, Planning and International Relations	PIPER STARR
Senior Vice President, Policy	JAMES CRUSE
Vice President, Structured Finance	BARBARA O'BOYLE
Vice President, Transportation	ROBERT MORIN
Vice President, Credit Underwriting	DAVID CARTER, *Acting*
Vice President, Short-Term Trade Finance	BRUCE HUNT

The Export-Import Bank of the United States helps the private sector to create and maintain U.S. jobs by financing exports of the Nation's goods and services. To accomplish this mission, the Bank offers a variety of loan, guarantee, and insurance programs to support transactions that would not be awarded to U.S. companies without the Bank's assistance.

The Export-Import Bank of the United States (Ex-Im Bank), established in 1934, operates as an independent agency of the U.S. Government under the authority of the Export-Import Bank Act of 1945, as amended (12 U.S.C. 635 *et seq.*). Its Board of Directors consists of a President and Chairman, a First Vice President and Vice Chairman, and three other Directors, all of whom are appointed by the President with the advice and consent of the Senate.

Ex-Im Bank's mission is to help American exporters meet government-supported financing competition from other countries, so that U.S. exports can compete for overseas business on the basis of price, performance, and service, and in doing so help create and sustain U.S. jobs. The Bank also fills gaps in the availability of commercial financing for creditworthy export transactions.

Ex-Im Bank is required to find a reasonable assurance of repayment for each transaction it supports. Its legislation requires it to meet the financing terms of competitor export credit agencies, but not to compete with commercial lenders. Legislation restricts the Bank's operation in some countries and its support for military goods and services.

Activities

Ex-Im Bank is authorized to have outstanding at any one time loans, guarantees, and insurance in aggregate amount not in excess of $100 billion. It supports U.S. exporters through a range of diverse programs, which are offered under four broad categories of export financing, including the following:

—working capital guarantees, provided to lenders, so that they can provide creditworthy small- and medium-sized exporters with working capital they need to buy, build, or assemble products for export sale;

—export credit insurance which protects exporters and lenders against both the commercial and political risks of a foreign buyer defaulting on payment;

—loan guarantees which encourage sales to creditworthy foreign buyers by providing private sector lenders in medium- and long-term transactions with Ex-Im Bank guarantees against the political and commercial risks of nonpayment; and

—direct loans made to provide foreign buyers with competitive, fixed-rate medium- or long-term financing from Ex-Im Bank for their purchases from U.S. exporters.

Ex-Im Bank initiated several changes to enhance its support to small business. It created a new position, Senior Vice President for Small Business, who reports directly to the Bank's President and Chairman. In addition, the Bank's regional offices are now dedicated exclusively to small business outreach and support. The Bank also established a Small Business Committee to coordinate, evaluate, and make recommendations on Bank functions necesary for a successful small business strategy.

Regional Offices

The Export-Import Bank operates five regional offices.

Regional Offices—Export-Import Bank

Region	Address	Telephone	Fax
Regional Offices			
New York	20 Exchange Pl., New York, NY 10005	212–809–2650	212–809–2646
Miami	Suite 203, 5835 Blue Lagoon Dr., Miami, FL 33126	305–526–7436	305–526–7435
Chicago	Suite 2450, 200 W. Adams St., Chicago, IL 60606	312–353–8081	312–353–8098
Houston	Suite 585, 1880 S. Dairy Ashford II, Houston, TX 77077	281–721–0465	281–679–0156
Western Regional Offices			
Long Beach, CA	Suite 1670, 1 World Trade Ctr., Long Beach, CA 90831	562–980–4580	562–980–4590
San Francisco, CA	14th Fl., 250 Montgomery St., San Francisco, CA 94104	415–705–2285	415–705–1156
San Diego, CA	Suite 230, 6363 Greenwich Dr., San Diego, CA 92122	619–557–7091	619–557–6176

For further information, contact the Export-Import Bank, Business Development Office, 811 Vermont Avenue NW., Washington, DC 20571. Phone, 202–565–3946 or 800–565–EXIM. Internet, www.exim.gov.

FARM CREDIT ADMINISTRATION

1501 Farm Credit Drive, McLean, VA 22102–5090
Phone, 703–883–4000. Fax, 703–734–5784. Internet, www.fca.gov.

Farm Credit Administration Board:

Chairman and Chief Executive Officer	NANCY C. PELLETT
Members of the Board	DOUGLAS L. FLORY, DALLAS P. TONSAGER
Secretary to the Board	ROLAND E. SMITH
Staff:	
Chief of Staff	KEITH HEFFERNAN
Director, Office of Congressional and Public Affairs	MARTHA SCHOBER
General Counsel	CHARLES R. RAWLS
Deputy General Counsel	JOY STRICKLAND
Inspector General	CARL A. CLINEFELTER
Director, Office of Examination and Chief Examiner	THOMAS G. MCKENZIE
Director, Office of Regulatory Policy	ANDREW D. JACOB
Director, Office of Secondary Market Oversight	S. ROBERT COLEMAN

Director, Office of Management Services	STEPHEN G. SMITH
Director, Equal Employment Opportunity and Ombudsman	ERIC HOWARD
Designated Agency Ethics Official	KATHLEEN V. BUFFON
Chief Freedom of Information Act Officer	KATHLEEN V. BUFFON

[For the Farm Credit Administration statement of organization, see the *Code of Federal Regulations,* Title 12, Parts 600 and 611]

The Farm Credit Administration is responsible for ensuring the safe and sound operation of the banks, associations, affiliated service organizations, and other entities that collectively comprise what is known as the Farm Credit System, and for protecting the interests of the public and those who borrow from Farm Credit institutions or invest in Farm Credit securities.

The Farm Credit Administration (FCA) was established as an independent financial regulatory agency in the executive branch of the Federal Government by Executive Order 6084 on March 27, 1933. The Administration carries out its responsibilities by conducting examinations of the various Farm Credit lending institutions, which are Farm Credit Banks, the Agricultural Credit Bank, Agricultural Credit Associations, and Federal Land Credit Associations. It also examines the service organizations owned by the Farm Credit lending institutions, as well as the National Consumer Cooperative Bank (also known as the National Cooperative Bank).

FCA policymaking is vested in the Farm Credit Administration Board, whose three full-time members are appointed to 6-year terms by the President, with the advice and consent of the Senate. One member of the Board is designated by the President as Chairman and serves as the Administration's chief executive officer. The Board is responsible for approving rules and regulations, providing for the examination and regulation of and reporting by Farm Credit institutions, and establishing the policies under which the Administration operates. Board meetings are regularly held on the second Thursday of the month and are subject to the Government in the Sunshine Act. Public announcements of these meetings are published in the *Federal Register.*

The lending institutions of the Farm Credit System were established to provide adequate and dependable credit and closely related services to farmers, ranchers, and producers or harvesters of aquatic products; persons engaged in providing on-the-farm services; rural homeowners; and associations of farmers, ranchers, and producers or harvesters of aquatic products, or federations of such associations that operate on a cooperative basis and are engaged in marketing, processing, supply, or business service functions for the benefit of their members. Initially capitalized by the United States Government, the Farm Credit lending institutions are organized as cooperatives and are completely owned by their borrowers. The loan funds provided to borrowers by these institutions are obtained primarily through the sale of securities to investors in the Nation's capital markets.

The Agricultural Credit Act of 1987, as amended (12 U.S.C. 2279aa-1), established the Federal Agricultural Mortgage Corporation (commonly known as "Farmer Mac"). The Corporation, designated as part of the Farm Credit System, is a federally chartered instrumentality of the United States and promotes the development of a secondary market for agricultural real estate and rural housing loans. Farmer Mac also provides guarantees for the timely payment of principal and interest on securities, representing interests in or obligations backed by pools of agricultural real estate loans. The Administration is responsible for the examination and regulation of Farmer Mac to ensure the safety and soundness of its operations.

FARM CREDIT ADMINISTRATION

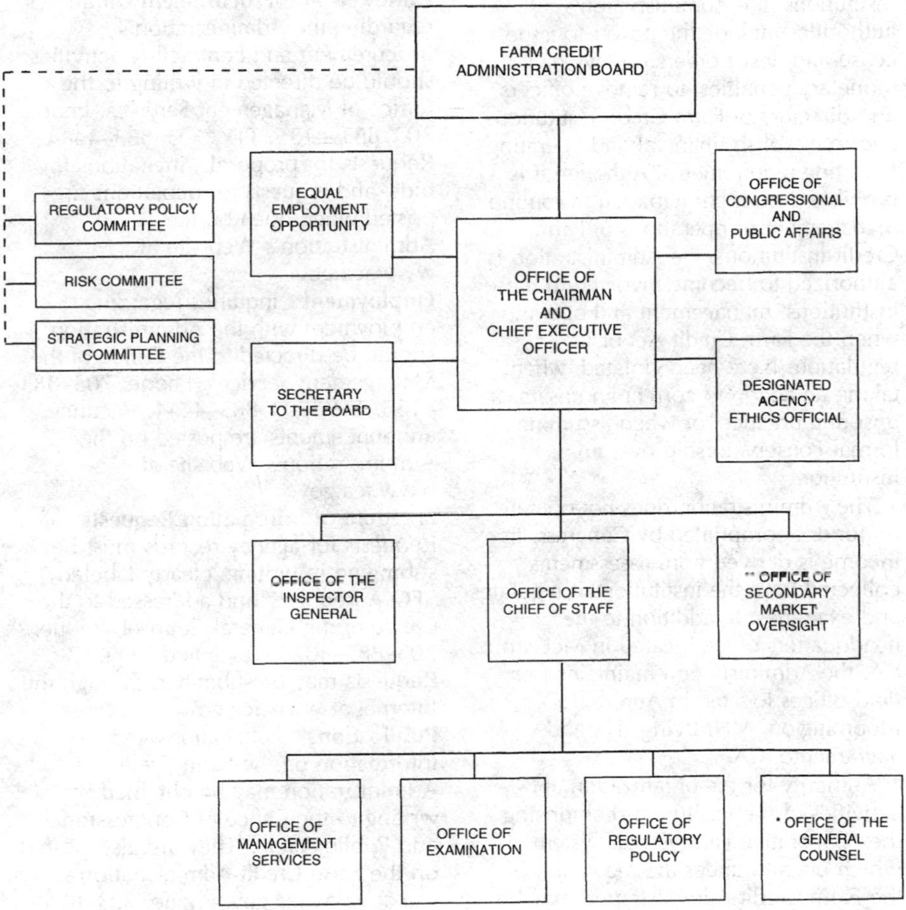

* Maintains a confidential advisory relationship with each of the Board members.

** Reports to the Board for policy and to the Chief Executive Officer for administration.

The Administration manages regulations under which Farm Credit institutions operate. These regulations implement the Farm Credit Act of 1971, as amended (12 U.S.C. 2001), and have the force and effect of law. Similar to other Federal regulators of financial institutions, the Administration's authorities include the power to issue cease-and-desist orders, to levy civil monetary penalties, to remove officers and directors of Farm Credit institutions, and to establish financial and operating reporting requirements. Although it is prohibited from participation in routine management or operations of Farm Credit institutions, the Administration is authorized to become involved in these institutions' management and operations when the Farm Credit Act or its regulations have been violated, when taking an action to correct an unsafe or unsound practice, or when assuming a formal conservatorship over an institution.

The Administration does not operate on funds appropriated by Congress. Its income is derived from assessments collected from the institutions it regulates and examines. In addition to the headquarters office located in McLean, VA, the Administration maintains four field offices located in Aurora, CO; Bloomington, MN; Irving, TX; and Sacramento, CA.

Authority for the organization and activities of the institutions comprising the cooperative Farm Credit System which operate under the regulation of the Farm Credit Administration may be found in the Farm Credit Act of 1971, as amended.

Sources of Information

Inquiries for information on the following subjects may be directed to the specified office, Farm Credit Administration, 1501 Farm Credit Drive, McLean, VA 22102–5090.

Contracts and Procurement Inquiries regarding the Administration's procurement and contracting activities should be directed in writing to the Office of Management Services. Phone, 703–883–4135. TTY, 703–883–4444. Requests for proposals, invitations for bids, and requests for quotations are posted when open on the Administration's Web site at www.fca.gov.

Employment Inquiries regarding employment with the Administration should be directed to the Office of the Management Services. Phone, 703–883–4135. TTY, 703–883–4444. Vacancy announcements are posted on the Administration's Web site at www.fca.gov.

Freedom of Information Requests Requests for agency records must be submitted in writing, clearly labeled "FOIA Request" and addressed to the Office of the General Counsel. Phone, 703–883–4020 (voice and TTY). Requests may be submitted through the Internet at www.fca.gov.

Publications Publications and information on the Farm Credit Administration may be obtained by writing to the Office of Congressional and Public Affairs. They are also posted on the Farm Credit Administration's Web site at www.fca.gov. Phone, 703–883–4056 (voice and TTY). Fax, 703–790–3260. E-mail, info-line@fca.gov.

For further information, contact the Office of Congressional and Public Affairs, Farm Credit Administration, 1501 Farm Credit Drive, McLean, VA 22102–5090. Phone, 703–883–4056 (voice and TTY). E-mail, info-line@fca.gov. Internet, www.fca.gov.

FEDERAL COMMUNICATIONS COMMISSION

445 Twelfth Street SW., Washington, DC 20554
Phone, 888–225–5322. TTY, 888–835–5322. Internet, www.fcc.gov.

Chairman	KEVIN J. MARTIN
Commissioners	JONATHAN S. ADELSTEIN, MICHAEL J. COPPS, ROBERT M. MCDOWELL, DEBORAH TAYLOR TATE
Managing Director	ANDREW S. FISHEL
General Counsel	SAMUEL FEDER, *Acting*
Inspector General	KENT NILSSON, *Acting*
Chief, Consumer and Governmental Affairs Bureau	MONICA DESAI
Chief, Enforcement Bureau	KRIS MONTEITH
Chief, International Bureau	DONALD ABELSON
Chief, Media Bureau	DEONNA GREGG
Chief, Office of Administrative Law Judges	RICHARD L. SIPPEL
Chief, Office of Engineering and Technology	(VACANCY)
Chief, Office of Strategic Planning and Policy Analysis	CATHERINE BOHIGIAN
Chief, Wireless Telecommunications Bureau	CATHERINE W. SEIDEL, *Acting*
Chief, Wireline Competition Bureau	THOMAS NAVIN
Director, Office of Communications Business Opportunities	CAROLYN FLEMING WILLIAMS
Director, Office of Legislative Affairs	S. KEVIN WASHINGTON
Director, Office of Media Relations	DAVID FISKE
Director, Office of Workplace Diversity	P. JUNE TAYLOR

[For the Federal Communications Commission statement of organization, see the *Code of Federal Regulations,* Title 47, Part 0]

The Federal Communications Commission regulates interstate and foreign communications by radio, television, wire, satellite, and cable. It is responsible for the orderly development and operation of broadcast services and the provision of rapid, efficient nationwide and worldwide telephone and telegraph services at reasonable rates. Its responsibilities also include the use of communications for promoting safety of life and property and for strengthening the national defense.

The Federal Communications Commission (FCC) was created by the Communications Act of 1934 (47 U.S.C. 151 *et seq.*) to regulate interstate and foreign communications by wire and radio in the public interest. The scope of FCC regulation includes radio and television broadcasting; telephone, telegraph, and cable television operation; two-way radio and radio operators; and satellite communication.

The Commission is composed of five members, who are appointed by the President with the advice and consent of the Senate. One of the members is designated by the President as Chairman.

Activities

Media The Media Bureau develops, recommends, and administers the policy and licensing programs for the regulation of media, including cable television, multichannel video programming distribution, broadcast television and radio, and satellite services in the United States and its territories. The Bureau's responsibilities include the following:

FEDERAL COMMUNICATIONS COMMISSION

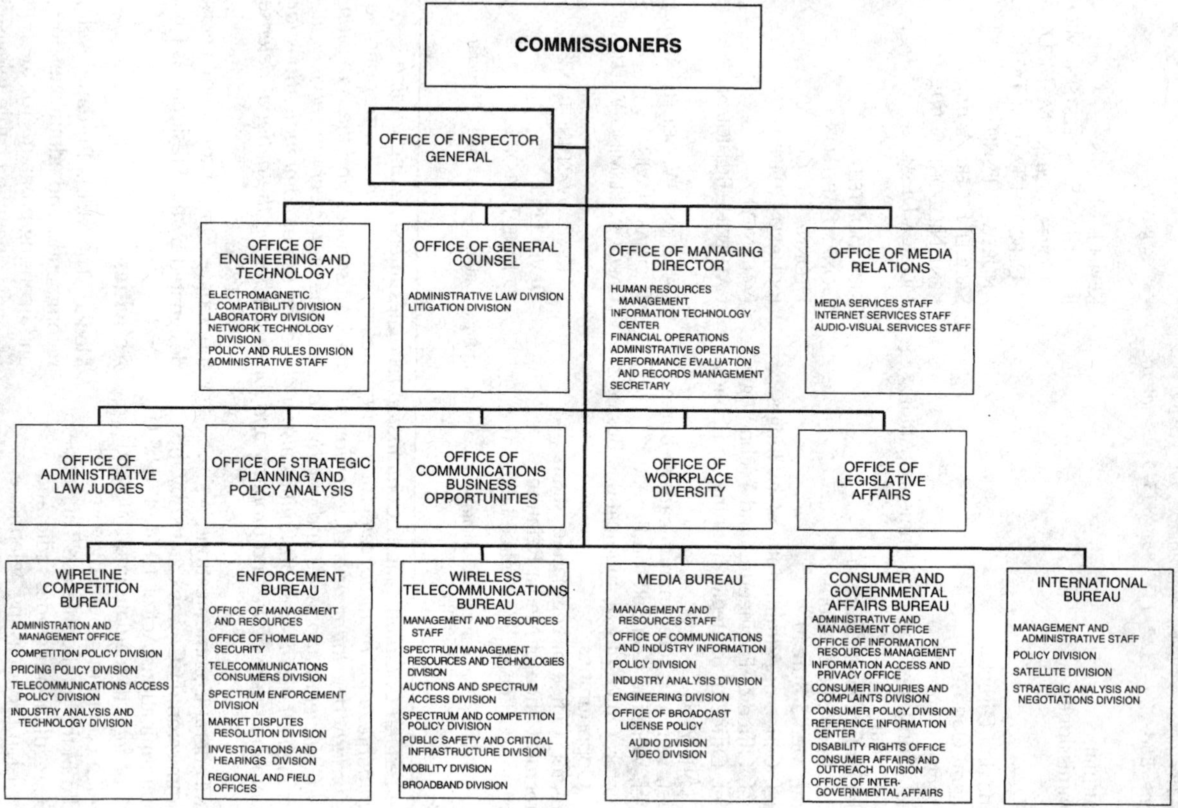

—conducting rulemaking proceedings concerning the legal, engineering, and economic aspects of electronic media services;

—resolving waiver petitions, declaratory rulings, and adjudications related to electronic media services; and

—processing applications for authorization, assignment, transfer, and renewal of media services, including AM, FM, TV, the cable TV relay service, and related matters.

For further information, contact the Media Bureau. Phone, 202–418–7200 or 888–225–5322.

Wireline Competition Bureau The Wireline Competition Bureau advises and makes recommendations to the Commission, or acts for the Commission under delegated authority, in all matters pertaining to the regulation and licensing of communications common carriers and ancillary operations (other than matters pertaining exclusively to the regulation and licensing of wireless telecommunications services and facilities). The Bureau carries out the following duties:

—ensures choice, opportunity, and fairness in the development of wireline telecommunications;

—assesses the present and future wireline telecommunications needs of the Nation and promotes the development and widespread availability of wireline telecommunications;

—promotes economically efficient investment in wireline telecommunications infrastructure; and

—reviews and coordinates orders, programs, and actions initiated by other bureaus and offices in matters affecting wireline telecommunications to ensure consistency with overall Commission policy.

For further information, contact the Wireline Competition Bureau. Phone, 202–418–1500 or 888–225–5322.

Consumer and Governmental Affairs The Consumer and Governmental Affairs Bureau develops and administers the Commission's consumer and governmental affairs policies and initiatives to enhance the public's understanding of the Commission's work and to facilitate its relationship with other governmental agencies and organizations. The Bureau is responsible for the following:

—facilitating public participation in the Commission's decisionmaking process;

—representing the Commission on consumer and government committees, working groups, task forces, and conferences;

—working with public, Federal, State, local, and tribal agencies to develop and coordinate policies;

—overseeing the Consumer Advisory Committee, Federal Advisory Committee, and the Local and State Government Advisory Committee, and providing expert advice and assistance regarding compliance with applicable disability and accessibility requirements, rules, and regulations;

—resolving informal complaints through mediation; and

—conducting consumer outreach and education programs.

For further information, contact the Consumer and Governmental Affairs Bureau. Phone, 202–418–1400 or 888–225–5322.

Enforcement The Enforcement Bureau serves as the Commission's primary entity responsible for the enforcement of the Communications Act and other communications statutes, the Commission's rules, Commission orders and authorizations, and other matters related to pending applications for a license or other authorization. The Office of Homeland Security is located in the Enforcement Bureau and oversees rulemaking proceedings relating to the Emergency Alert System, operates the Communication and Crisis Management Center, and coordinates all agency matters concerning homeland security, emergency preparedness, public warning, and continuity of Government issues. The Bureau's responsibilities include investigating and resolving complaints regarding the following:

—acts or omissions of common carriers (wireline, wireless, and international);

—acts or omissions of noncommon carriers subject to the Commission's jurisdiction under Title II of the Communications Act;

—accessibility to communications services and equipment for persons with disabilities, when filed formally;

—noncompliance with the Commission's Emergency Alert System, the lighting and marking of radio transmitting towers, and pole attachment regulations;

—noncompliance with the broadcast and cable television children's television programming commercial limits; and

—unauthorized construction and operation of communications facilities and false distress signals.

For further information, contact the Enforcement Bureau. Phone, 202–418–7450 or 888–225–5322.

Enforcement Bureau

Office	Address	Director
Regional Offices		
Kansas City, MO	2d Fl., 520 NE. Colbern Rd., Lee's Summit, 64086	Dennis P. Carlton
Park Ridge, IL	Rm. 306, 1550 Northwest Hwy., 60068–1460	Russell D. Monie
San Francisco, CA	Suite 105, 5653 Stoneridge Dr., Pleasanton, 94588–8543	Rebecca Dorch
Field Offices		
Atlanta, GA	Rm. 320, 3575 Koger Blvd., Duluth 30096–4958	Fred L. Broce
Boston, MA	1 Batterymarch Pk., Quincy 02169–7495	ennis Loria
Chicago, IL	Rm. 306, 1550 Northwest Hwy., Park Ridge 60068–1460	George M. Moffitt
Columbia, MD	9300 E. Hampton Dr., Capitol Heights, 20743	Charles C. Magin
Dallas, TX	Rm. 1170, 9330 LBJ Fwy., 75243–3429	James D. Wells
Denver, CO	Suite 303, 215 S. Wadsworth Blvd., Lakewood, 80226–1544.	Nikki Shears, *Acting*
Detroit, MI	24897 Hathaway St., Farmington Hills 48335–1552	James A. Bridgewater
Kansas City, MO	2d Fl., 520 NE. Colbern Rd., Lee's Summit, 64086–4895	Robert C. McKinney
Los Angeles, CA	Rm. 660, 18000 Studebaker Rd., Cerritos 90701–3684	Catherine Deaton
New Orleans, LA	Rm. 460, 2424 Edenborn Ave., Metairie, 70001	James C. Hawkins
New York, NY	Rm. 1151, 201 Varick St., 10014–4870	Daniel W. Noel
Philadelphia, PA	Rm. 404, 2300 E. Lincoln Hwy., Langhorne 19047–1859	John Rahtes
San Francisco, CA	Suite 105, 5653 Stoneridge Dr., Pleasanton, 94588–8543	Thomas N. Van Stavern
San Diego, CA	Rm. 370, 4542 Ruffner St., 92111–2216	Bill Zears
Seattle, WA	Rm. 312, 11410 NE. 122d Way, Kirkland 98034–6927	(Vacancy)
Tampa, FL	Rm. 1215, 2203 N. Lois Ave., 33607–2356	Ralph M. Barlow

International Bureau The International Bureau develops, recommends, and administers policies, standards, procedures, and programs for the regulation of international telecommunications facilities and services and the licensing of satellite facilities under its jurisdiction. The International Bureau assumes the principal representational role for Commission activities in international organizations. The Bureau also has the following duties and responsibilities:

—monitoring compliance with the terms and conditions of authorizations and licenses granted by the Bureau and pursues enforcement actions in conjunction with appropriate bureaus and offices;

—providing advice and technical assistance to U.S. trade officials in the negotiation and implementation of telecommunications trade agreements; and

—promoting the international coordination of spectrum allocation and frequency and orbital assignments in order to minimize cases of international radio interference involving U.S. licenses.

For further information, contact the International Bureau. Phone, 202–418–0437 or 888–225–5322.

Wireless Telecommunications The Wireless Telecommunications Bureau administers all domestic commercial and private wireless telecommunications programs and rules. The commercial wireless services include cellular, paging, personal communications, specialized mobile radio, air-ground, and basic exchange telecommunications services. The private wireless services generally serve the specialized internal communications needs of eligible users, and include the public safety, microwave, aviation, and marine services. Additionally, the Bureau:

—develops, recommends, administers, and coordinates policy matters for the assigned services, including rulemaking, interpretations, and equipment standards;

—explains and advises the public on rules and interpretations and provides rule interpretation material for the Enforcement Bureau;

—serves as the FCC's principal policy and administrative resource with regards to all spectrum auctions;

—implements the compulsory provisions of law and treaties covering the use of radio for the safety of life and property at sea and in the air;

—projects the demand for existing and possible new communications requirements and services; and

—processes applications and licensing for the assigned services.

For further information, contact the Wireless Telecommunications Bureau. Phone, 202–418–0600 or 888–225–5322.

Sources of Information

Inquiries for information on the special subjects listed in the following paragraphs and those concerning licensing/grant requirements in the various services may be directed to the person or office specified or to the Chief of the Bureau or Office listed below as having responsibility for the service, Federal Communications Commission, 445 Twelfth Street SW., Washington, DC 20554. Internet, www.fcc.gov.

Licensing/Grant Responsibility—Federal Communications Commission

Service	Bureau or Office
All broadcasting (except broadcast auxiliary services) Cable TV relay services (CARS) Cable signal leakage Registration of cable systems	Media Bureau
Interstate telecommunications services	Wireline Competition Bureau
Emergency Alert System	Enforcement Bureau
Amateur radio Auxiliary broadcast services Aviation radio Commercial radio operators Common carrier microwave services Interactive video and data services Land mobile radio Marine radio Private microwave radio Broadband radio service Educational broadband service	Wireless Telecommunications Bureau
Direct broadcast satellites (DBS) Foreign carrier affiliation notification International accounting rate change applications International high frequency broadcast stations International public fixed radio communication applications Permit to deliver programs to foreign broadcast stations (Section 325–C applications) Requests for data network identification code (DNIC) assignment Requests for international signalling point code (ISPC) assignment Recognized private operating agencies Satellite Earth stations Satellite space stations (GSO) Satellite space stations (NGSO) Submarine cable landing license applications	International Bureau

Federal Advisory Committee Management Direct inquiries to the Office of Performance Evaluation and Records Management. Phone, 202–418–0444.

Consumer Assistance Inquiries concerning general information on Commission operations should be addressed to the Reference Center, Room CY–B523, 445 Twelfth Street SW., Washington, DC 20554. Phone, 888–225–5322. TTY, 888–835–5322.

Contracts and Procurement Direct inquiries to the Chief, Contracts and Purchasing Center. Phone, 202–418–1952.

Electronic Access Information regarding the Commission is also available electronically through the Internet, at www.fcc.gov.

Employment and Recruitment The Commission's programs require attorneys, electronics engineers, economists, accountants, administrative management and computer specialists, and clerical personnel. Requests for employment information should be directed to the Recruitment and Staffing Service Center. Phone, 202–418–0130.

Equal Employment Practices by Industry Direct inquiries to the Portals Consumer Center. Phone, 888–225–5322.

Internal Equal Employment Practices Direct inquiries to the Office of Workplace Diversity. Phone, 202–418–1799.

Ex-Parte Presentations Information concerning ex-parte presentations should be directed to the Commission's Office of General Counsel. Phone, 202–418–1720.

Fees Inquiries concerning the Commission's fee program should be addressed to the Portals Consumer Center, Room CY–B523, 445 Twelfth Street SW., Washington, DC 20554. Phone, 888–225–5322.

Freedom of Information Act Requests Requests should be directed to the Managing Director. Phone, 202–418–1919.

Information Available for Public Inspection At the Commission's headquarters office in Washington, DC, dockets concerning rulemaking and adjudicatory matters, copies of applications for licenses and grants, and reports required to be filed by licensees and cable system operators are maintained in the public reference rooms (some reports are held confidentially by law). The Library has Commission rules and regulations on file (phone, 202–418–0450). General information is also available through the Commission's fax-on-demand (phone, 202–418–2805).

In addition to the information available at the Commission, each broadcasting station makes available for public reference certain information pertaining to the operation of the station, a current copy of the application filed for license, and nonconfidential reports filed with the Commission.

Publications The Office of Media Relations distributes publications, public notices, and press releases. Phone, 202–418–0500.

For further information, contact the Consumer Center, Federal Communications Commission, 445 Twelfth Street SW., Washington, DC 20554. Phone, 888–225–5322. TTY, 888–835–5322. Internet, www.fcc.gov.

FEDERAL DEPOSIT INSURANCE CORPORATION

550 Seventeenth Street NW., Washington, DC 20429
Phone, 202–736–6000. Internet, www.fdic.gov.

Board of Directors:	
Chairman	MARTIN J. GRUENBERG, *Acting*
Vice Chairman	MARTIN J. GRUENBERG
Directors:	
(Comptroller of the Currency)	JOHN C. DUGAN
(Director, Office of Thrift Supervision)	JOHN M. REICH
Appointive Director	THOMAS J. CURRY
Officials:	
Deputy to the Chairman and Chief Operating Officer	JOHN F. BOVENZI

Deputy to the Chairman and Chief Financial Officer	STEVEN O. APP
Deputy to the Vice Chairman	BARBARA A. RYAN, *Acting*
Deputy to the Director (Comptroller of the Currency)	WILLIAM A. ROWE III
Deputy to the Director (Office of Thrift Supervision)	CLAUDE A. ROLLIN
Special Assistant to the Director	JOHN F. VOGEL
General Counsel	DOUGLAS H. JONES, *Acting*
Director, Division of Administration	ARLEAS UPTON KEA
Director, Division of Finance	FREDERICK S. SELBY
Director, Division of Information Technology and Chief Information Officer	MICHAEL E. BARTELL
Director, Division of Insurance and Research	ARTHUR J. MURTON
Director, Division of Resolutions and Receiverships	MITCHELL L. GLASSMAN
Director, Division of Supervision and Consumer Protection	SANDRA L. THOMPSON, *Acting*
Director, Office of Diversity and Economic Opportunity	D. MICHAEL COLLINS
Director, Office of Enterprise Risk Management	JAMES H. ANGEL, JR.
Director, Office of Legislative Affairs	ALICE C. GOODMAN
Ombudsman	COTTRELL L. WEBSTER
Director, Office of Public Affairs	D.J. NORDQUIST
Chief Learning Officer	DAVID C. COOKE
Inspector General	PATRICIA M. BLACK, *Acting*

The Federal Deposit Insurance Corporation promotes and preserves public confidence in U.S. financial institutions by insuring bank and thrift deposits up to the legal limit of $100,000; by periodically examining State-chartered banks that are not members of the Federal Reserve System for safety and soundness as well as compliance with consumer protection laws; and by liquidating assets of failed institutions to reimburse the insurance funds for the cost of failures.

The Federal Deposit Insurance Corporation (FDIC) was established under the Banking Act of 1933 in response to numerous bank failures during the Great Depression. FDIC began insuring banks on January 1, 1934. As of April 1, 2006, the deposit insurance coverage on certain retirement accounts at a bank or savings institution was raised to $250,000. The basic insurance coverage for other deposit accounts remains at $100,000.

FDIC does not operate on funds appropriated by Congress. Its income is derived from insurance premiums on deposits held by insured banks and savings associations and from interest on the required investment of the premiums in U.S. Government securities. It also has authority to borrow from the Treasury up to $30 billion for insurance purposes.

Management of FDIC consists of a Board of Directors that includes the Chairman, Vice Chairman, and Appointive Director. The Comptroller of the Currency, whose office supervises national banks, and the Director of the Office of Thrift Supervision, which supervises federally or State-chartered savings associations, are also members of the Board. All five Board members are appointed by the President and confirmed by the Senate, with no more than three being from the same political party.

Activities

FDIC insures about $3.9 trillion of U.S. bank and thrift deposits. The insurance fund is composed of insurance premiums

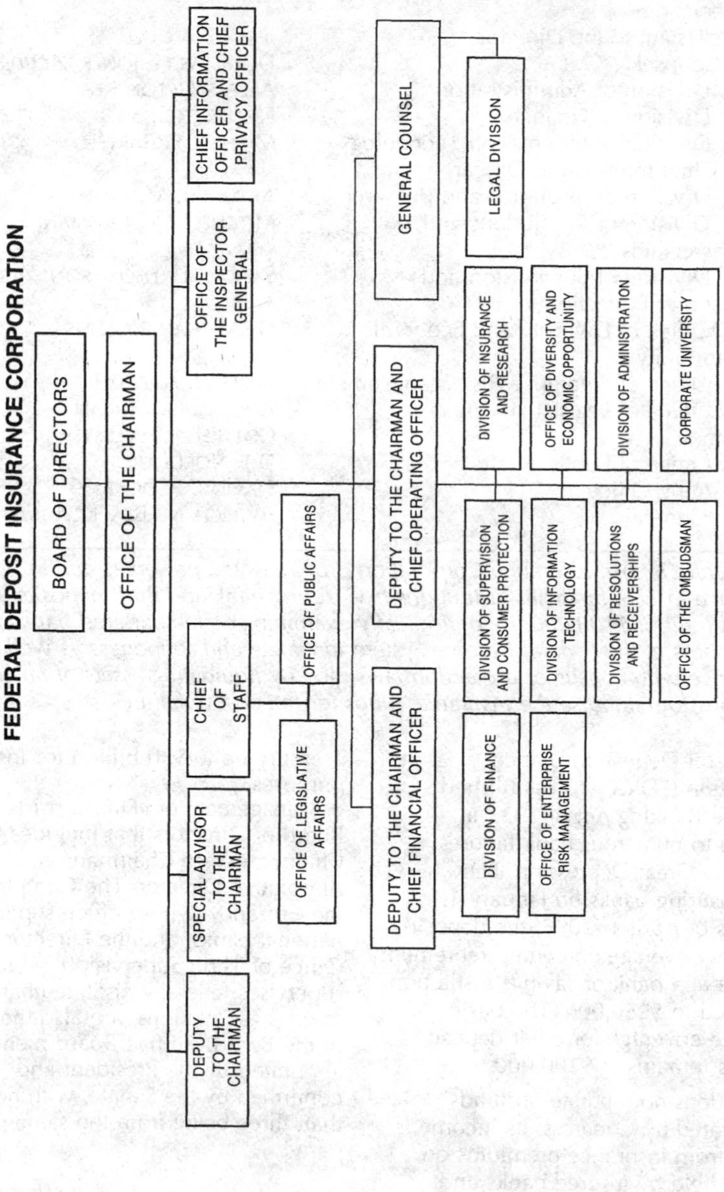
FEDERAL DEPOSIT INSURANCE CORPORATION
BOARD OF DIRECTORS
OFFICE OF THE CHAIRMAN
CHIEF INFORMATION OFFICER AND CHIEF PRIVACY OFFICER
OFFICE OF THE INSPECTOR GENERAL
CHIEF OF STAFF
SPECIAL ADVISOR TO THE CHAIRMAN
DEPUTY TO THE CHAIRMAN
OFFICE OF PUBLIC AFFAIRS
OFFICE OF LEGISLATIVE AFFAIRS
GENERAL COUNSEL
LEGAL DIVISION
DEPUTY TO THE CHAIRMAN AND CHIEF OPERATING OFFICER
DIVISION OF INSURANCE AND RESEARCH
OFFICE OF DIVERSITY AND ECONOMIC OPPORTUNITY
DIVISION OF ADMINISTRATION
CORPORATE UNIVERSITY
DIVISION OF SUPERVISION AND CONSUMER PROTECTION
DIVISION OF INFORMATION TECHNOLOGY
DIVISION OF RESOLUTIONS AND RECEIVERSHIPS
OFFICE OF THE OMBUDSMAN
DEPUTY TO THE CHAIRMAN AND CHIEF FINANCIAL OFFICER
DIVISION OF FINANCE
OFFICE OF ENTERPRISE RISK MANAGEMENT

paid by banks and savings associations and the interest on the investment of those premiums in U.S. Government securities, as required by law. Premiums are determined by an institution's level of capitalization and potential risk to the insurance fund.

FDIC examines about 5,245 State-chartered commercial and savings banks that are not members of the Federal Reserve System, called State nonmember banks. FDIC also has authority to examine other types of FDIC-insured institutions for deposit insurance purposes. The two types of examinations conducted are for safety and soundness, and for compliance with applicable consumer laws such as the Truth in Lending Act, the Home Mortgage Disclosure Act, the Equal Credit Opportunity Act, the Fair Housing Act, and the Community Reinvestment Act. Examinations are performed on the institution's premises and off-site through computer data analysis.

A failed bank or savings association is generally closed by its chartering authority, and FDIC is named receiver. FDIC is required to resolve the closed institution in a manner that is least costly to FDIC. Ordinarily, FDIC attempts to locate a healthy institution to acquire the failed entity. If such an entity cannot be found, FDIC pays depositors the amount of their insured funds, usually by the next business day following the closing. Depositors with funds that exceed the insurance limit often receive an advance dividend, which is a portion of their uninsured funds that is determined by an estimate of the future proceeds from liquidating the failed institution's remaining assets. Depositors with funds in a failed institution that exceed the insurance limit receive a receivership certificate for those funds and partial payments of their uninsured funds as asset disposition permits.

As part of its insurance, supervisory, and receivership responsibilities, FDIC also performs other functions relating to State nonmember banks, including:

—approval or disapproval of mergers, consolidations, and acquisitions where the resulting bank is an insured State nonmember;

—approval or disapproval of a proposal by a bank to establish and operate a new branch, close an existing branch, or move its main office from one location to another;

—approval or disapproval of requests to engage as principal in activities and investments that are not permissible for a national bank;

—issuance of enforcement actions, including cease-and-desist orders, for specific violations or practices requiring corrective action; and

—review of changes in ownership or control of a bank.

Regional Offices—Federal Deposit Insurance Corporation

Region/Address	Telephone
Atlanta, GA (Suite 800, 10 Tenth St. NE., 30309)	678–916–2200
Chicago, IL (Suite 3500, 500 W. Monroe St., 60661)	312–382–7500
Dallas, TX (Suite 1900, 1910 Pacific Ave., 75201)	214–754–0098
Kansas City, MO (Suite 1200, 2345 Grand Blvd., 64108)	816–234–8000
New York, NY (4th Fl., 20 Exchange Pl., 10005)	917–320–2500
San Francisco, CA (Suite 2300, 25 Jessie St., 94105)	808–546–1810

Sources of Information

Consumer Information Telephone inquiries about deposit insurance and other consumer matters can be directed to the FDIC call center at 877–ASK–FDIC (275–3342), from 8 a.m. to 8 p.m. eastern time, Monday through Friday. For credit card complaints, call 800–378–9581, from 8:30 a.m. to 4:30 p.m. central time, Monday through Friday. Written inquiries can be sent to the Division of Supervision and Consumer Protection at the regional offices listed above or to FDIC headquarters. E-mail inquiries can be sent to the FDIC web site at www.fdic.gov. The online FDIC customer assistance form for submitting an inquiry or a complaint is available at www2.fdic.gov/starsmail/index.asp. A copy of a bank's quarterly Report of

Condition is available from the call center at cost, or free from the FDIC web site at www2.fdic.gov/Call_TFR_Rpts/.

General Inquiries Written requests for general information may be directed to the Office of Public Affairs, Federal Deposit Insurance Corporation, 550 Seventeenth Street NW., Washington, DC 20429.

Public Records Many FDIC records are available on the FDIC web site. Inquiries about other types of records available to the public, including records available under the Freedom of Information Act, should be directed to the Chief, FOIA/PA Group 550 17th St. NW., Washington, DC 20429 or any regional office.

Publications Publications, press releases, congressional testimony, directives to financial institutions, and other documents are available through the Public Information Center. Phone, 877–275–3342 (option 4). E-mail, publicinfo@fdic.gov. Internet, www.fdic.gov.

For further information, contact the Office of Public Affairs, Federal Deposit Insurance Corporation, 550 Seventeenth Street NW., Washington, DC 20429. Phone, 202–898–6993. Internet, www.fdic.gov.

FEDERAL ELECTION COMMISSION

999 E Street NW., Washington, DC 20463
Phone, 202–694–1100 or 800–424–9530 (toll free). Internet, www.fec.gov.

Chairman	MICHAEL E. TONER
Vice Chairman	ROBERT D. LENHARD
Commissioners	DAVID M. MASON, HANS A. VON SPAKOVSKY, STEVEN T. WALTHER, ELLEN L. WEINTRAUB
Staff Director	ROBERT J. COSTA, *Acting*
General Counsel	LAWRENCE NORTON
Inspector General	LYNNE A. MCFARLAND

The Federal Election Commission has exclusive jurisdiction in the administration and civil enforcement of laws regulating the acquisition and expenditure of campaign funds to ensure compliance by participants in the Federal election campaign process. Its chief mission is to provide public disclosure of campaign finance activities and effect voluntary compliance by providing the public with information on the laws and regulations concerning campaign finance.

The Federal Election Commission is an independent agency established by section 309 of the Federal Election Campaign Act of 1971, as amended (2 U.S.C. 437c). It is composed of six Commissioners appointed by the President with the advice and consent of the Senate. The act also provides for three statutory officers—the Staff Director, the General Counsel, and the Inspector General—who are appointed by the Commission.

Activities

The Commission administers and enforces the Federal Election Campaign Act of 1971, as amended (2 U.S.C. 431 *et seq.*), and the Revenue Act, as amended (26 U.S.C. 1 *et seq.*). These laws provide for the public funding of Presidential elections, public disclosure of the financial activities of political committees involved in Federal elections, and limitations and prohibitions on contributions and expenditures made to influence Federal elections (Presidency, Senate, and House of Representatives).

Public Funding of Presidential Elections The Commission oversees the public financing of Presidential elections by certifying Federal payments to primary candidates, general election nominees, and national nominating conventions. It also audits recipients of Federal funds and may require repayments to the U.S. Treasury if a committee makes nonqualified campaign expenditures.

Disclosure The Commission ensures the public disclosure of the campaign finance activities reported by political committees supporting Federal candidates. Committee reports, filed regularly, disclose where campaign money comes from and how it is spent. The Commission places reports on the public record within 48 hours after they are received and computerizes the data contained in the reports.

Sources of Information

Congressional Affairs Office This Office serves as primary liaison with Congress and executive branch agencies. The Office is responsible for keeping Members of Congress informed about Commission decisions and, in turn, for informing the Commission on legislative developments. For further information, call 202–694–1006 or 800–424–9530.

Employment Inquiries regarding employment opportunities should be directed to the Director, Human Resources and Labor Relations. Phone, 202–694–1080 or 800–424–9530.

General Inquirics The Information Services Division provides information and assistance to Federal candidates, political committees, and the general public. This division answers questions on campaign finance laws, conducts workshops and seminars on the law, and provides publications and forms. For information or materials, call 202–694–1100 or 800–424–9530.

Media Inquiries The Press Office answers inquiries from print and broadcast media sources around the country, issues press releases on Commission actions and statistical data, responds to informational requests, and distributes other materials. All persons representing media should direct inquiries to the Press Office. Phone, 202–694–1220 or 800–424–9530.

Public Records The Office of Public Records, located at 999 E Street NW., Washington, DC, provides space for public inspection of all reports and statements relating to campaign finance since 1972. It is open weekdays from 9 a.m. to 5 p.m. and has extended hours during peak election periods. The public is invited to visit the Office or obtain information by calling 202–694–1120 or 800–424–9530.

Reading Room The library contains a collection of basic legal research resources, with emphasis on political campaign financing, corporate and labor political activity, and campaign finance reform. It is open to the public on weekdays between 9 a.m. and 5 p.m. For further information, call 202–694–1600 or 800–424–9530.

For further information, contact Information Services, Federal Election Commission, 999 E Street NW., Washington, DC 20463. Phone, 202–694–1100 or 800–424–9530. Internet, www.fec.gov.

FEDERAL HOUSING FINANCE BOARD

1625 I Street NW., Washington, DC 20006
Phone, 202–408–2500. Internet, www.fhfb.gov.

Board of Directors:

Chairman RONALD A. ROSENFELD

Members:	ALICIA R. CASTANEDA, FRANZ S. LEICHTER, ALLAN I. MENDELOWITZ
Secretary of Housing and Urban Development, *ex officio*	ALPHONSO R. JACKSON
Special Assistant to the Chairman	DARIS D. MEEKS
Special Assistants to Board of Directors	CHRISTOPHER BOSLAND, CHARLES D. JONES
Officials:	
Inspector General	EDWARD KELLEY
General Counsel and Secretary of the Board	JOHN P. KENNEDY
Director, Office of Supervision	STEPHEN M. CROSS
Director, Office of Management	JUDITH L. HOFMANN

[For the Federal Housing Finance Board statement of organization, see the *Code of Federal Regulations,* Title 12, Part 900]

The Federal Housing Finance Board is responsible for the administration and enforcement of the Federal Home Loan Bank Act, as amended.

The Federal Housing Finance Board (Finance Board) was established by the Federal Home Loan Bank Act, as amended by the Financial Institutions Reform, Recovery, and Enforcement Act of 1989 (FIRREA) (12 U.S.C. 1421 *et seq.*), as an independent regulatory agency in the executive branch. The Finance Board succeeded the Federal Home Loan Bank Board for those functions transferred to it by FIRREA.

The Finance Board is managed by a five-member Board of Directors. Four members are appointed by the President with the advice and consent of the Senate for 7-year terms; one of the four is designated as Chairperson. The Secretary of the Department of Housing and Urban Development is the fifth member and serves in an *ex officio* capacity.

The Finance Board supervises the 12 Federal Home Loan Banks created in 1932 by the Federal Home Loan Bank Act and issues regulations and orders for carrying out the purposes of the provisions of that act. Savings associations, commercial banks, savings banks, credit unions, insurance companies, and other institutions specified in section 4 of the act that make long-term home-mortgage loans are eligible to become members of the Federal Home Loan Banks. The Finance Board supervises the Federal Home Loan Banks and ensures that they carry out their housing finance and community investment mission and remain adequately capitalized and able to raise funds in the capital markets. The functions of the Finance Board include the following:

—prescribing rules and regulations governing the Bank System's capital, lending, financial management, and investment activities;

—maintaining Bank System financial and membership databases and preparing reports on a regular basis;

—overseeing the implementation of the community investment and affordable housing programs;

—conducting a biennial review of each member's community support performance;

—annually examining each Federal Home Loan Bank and the Office of Finance;

—requiring an independent financial audit of each Bank, the Office of Finance, the Financing Corporation, and the Bank System;

—appointing public interest directors to the board of directors of each Bank and establishing the rules by which the Banks elect the remaining directors; and

—setting standards for the review and approval of applications for Bank membership.

Regional Banks

The System includes 12 regional Federal Home Loan Banks, each of which is a

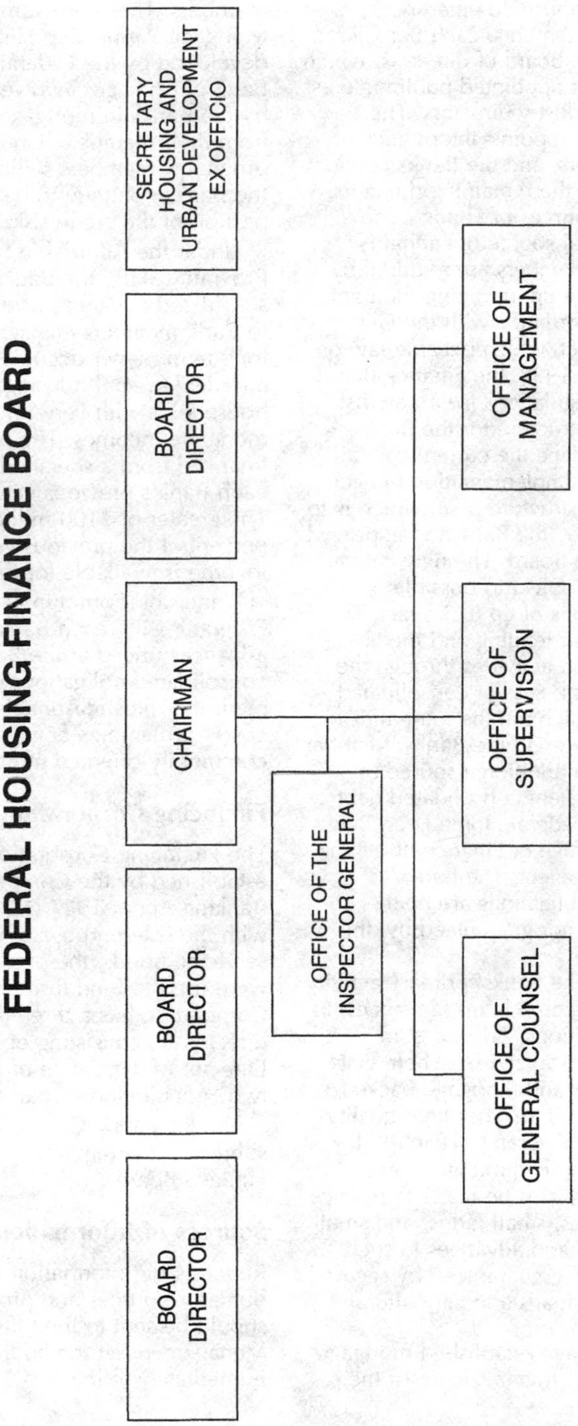
FEDERAL HOUSING FINANCE BOARD
SECRETARY HOUSING AND URBAN DEVELOPMENT EX OFFICIO
BOARD DIRECTOR
CHAIRMAN
BOARD DIRECTOR
BOARD DIRECTOR
OFFICE OF THE INSPECTOR GENERAL
OFFICE OF MANAGEMENT
OFFICE OF SUPERVISION
OFFICE OF GENERAL COUNSEL

Government-sponsored enterprise, owned by its members. Each Bank is managed by its board of directors, which is comprised of appointed public interest and elected industry directors. The Finance Board appoints the public interest directors, and the Banks conduct the election of the remaining directors.

Capital and Sources of Funds The Banks' principal source of capital is stock, which members are required by law to purchase upon joining the Bank System. In accordance with the Gramm-Leach-Bliley Act, which became law on November 12, 1999, the Finance Board has adopted regulations for a new risk-based capital structure for the Banks, which will replace the current capital structure upon implementation of each Bank's capital structure plan, which is to be developed by the Bank and approved by the Finance Board. The new capital structures are subject to possible transition periods of up to 3 years. The Banks fund their lending and member asset acquisition activities through the issuance of Bank System consolidated obligations, which are the joint-and-several liability of all the Banks. Member deposits are an additional source of funds. Bank System consolidated debt is issued by the Federal Home Loan Banks through the Office of Finance, the Bank System's fiscal agent. The Banks' consolidated obligations are neither obligations of, nor guaranteed by, the United States.

Operations The Banks' primary activity is extending secured loans (advances) to member institutions. Advances are generally collateralized by whole first mortgage loans and mortgage-backed securities, as well as other high-quality assets. Under the Gramm-Leach-Bliley Act, advances to community financial institutions may also be made to finance small businesses, small farms, and small agribusinesses, and advances to such members may be guaranteed by secured small business loans and agricultural loans.

The Banks have established mortgage asset purchase programs to assist their members. These programs, such as the Mortgage Partnership Finance program developed by the Federal Home Loan Bank of Chicago, involve the investment by the Banks in mortgages they acquire from their members. Under these programs, members selling mortgages to the Banks continue to bear a significant portion of the credit risk.

Under the Affordable Housing Program (AHP), the Banks provide subsidized advances or direct subsidies to Bank members engaged in lending for long-term owner-occupied and affordable rental housing targeted to households with very low, low, or moderate incomes. The program is financed from a specified percentage of each Bank's previous year's net income. The greater of $100 million or 10 percent of the previous year's net income is available for the program.

Under the Community Investment Program (CIP), each Bank provides advances priced at the Bank's cost of consolidated obligations of comparable maturities plus reasonable administrative costs, to members engaged in community-oriented mortgage lending.

Financing Corporation

The Financing Corporation (FICO) was established by the Competitive Equality Banking Act of 1987 (12 U.S.C. 1441) with the sole purpose of issuing and servicing bonds, the proceeds of which were used to fund thrift resolutions. The Corporation has a three-member directorate, consisting of the Managing Director of the Office of Finance and two Federal Home Loan Bank presidents.

The Financing Corporation operates subject to the regulatory authority of the Finance Board.

Sources of Information

Requests for information relating to human resources and procurement should be sent to the Office of Resource Management, at the address that immediately follows.

For further information, contact the Executive Secretariat, Federal Housing Finance Board, 1625 I Street NW., Washington, DC 20006. Phone, 202–408–2500. Fax, 202–408–2895. Internet, www.fhfb.gov.

FEDERAL LABOR RELATIONS AUTHORITY

1400 K Street NW., Washington, DC 20005
Phone, 202–218–7770. Internet, www.flra.gov.

Chairman	DALE CABANISS
Executive Director	JILL M. CRUMPACKER
Chief Counsel	KIRK UNDERWOOD
Director, Case Control Office and Legal Publications	GAIL D. REINHART
Solicitor	WILLIAM TOBEY, *Acting*
Inspector General	FRANCINE C. EICHLER
Chief Administrative Law Judge	CHARLES CENTER
Members	CAROL WALLER POPE, (VACANCY)
Chief Counsels	SUSAN D. MCCLUSKEY, (VACANCY)
General Counsel	COLLEEN DUFFY KIKO
Deputy General Counsel	DONALD S. HARRIS
Federal Service Impasses Panel	
Chairman	BECKY NORTON DUNLOP
Members	RICHARD B. AINSWORTH, MARK A. CARTER, JOHN G. CRUZ, ANDREA FISCHER NEWMAN, GRACE FLORES-HUGHES, JOSEPH C. WHITAKER
Special Assistant to Federal Service Impasses Panel Chairman	VICTORIA L. DUTCHER
Executive Director	H. JOSEPH SCHIMANSKY
Foreign Service Labor Relations Board	
Chairman	DALE CABANISS
Members	RICHARD BLOCH, (VACANCY)
General Counsel	COLLEEN DUFFY KIKO
Foreign Service Impasse Disputes Panel	
Chairman	PETER TREDICK
Members	BECKY NORTON DUNLOP, JUDY ROLPH EBNER, HOLLY HIGGINS, JOSE A. LIRA

The Federal Labor Relations Authority oversees the Federal service labor-management relations program. It administers the law that protects the right of employees of the Federal Government to organize, bargain collectively, and participate through labor organizations of their own choosing in decisions affecting them. The Authority also ensures compliance with the statutory rights and obligations of Federal employees and the labor organizations that represent them in their dealings with Federal agencies.

FEDERAL LABOR RELATIONS AUTHORITY

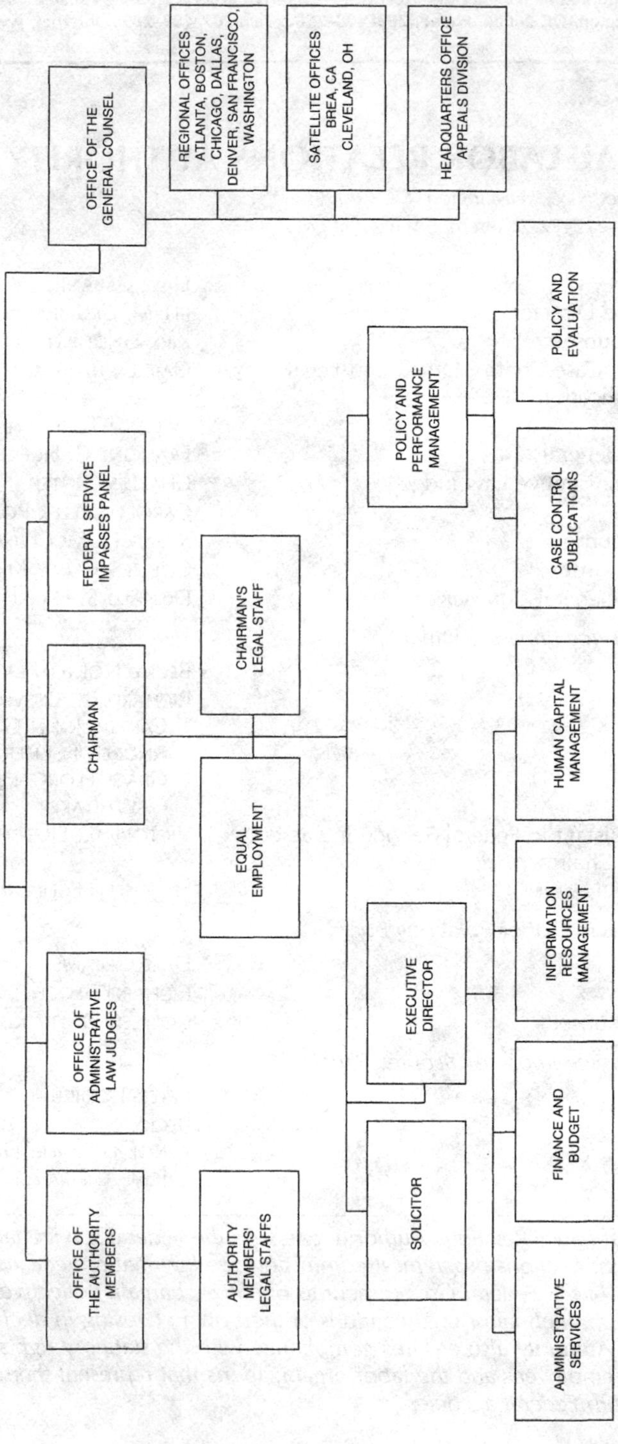

The Federal Labor Relations Authority (Authority) was created as an independent establishment by Reorganization Plan No. 2 of 1978 (5 U.S.C. app.), effective January 1, 1979, pursuant to Executive Order 12107 of December 28, 1978, to consolidate the central policymaking functions in Federal labor-management relations. Its duties and authority are specified in title VII (Federal Service Labor-Management Relations) of the Civil Service Reform Act of 1978 (5 U.S.C. 7101–7135).

Activities

The Authority adjudicates disputes arising under the Federal labor-management relations program, deciding cases concerning the negotiability of collective bargaining agreement proposals, appeals concerning unfair labor practices and representation petitions, and exceptions to grievance arbitration awards. Consistent with its statutory charge to provide leadership in establishing policies and guidance to participants in the Federal labor-management relations program, it also assists Federal agencies and unions in understanding their rights and responsibilities under the program through training. The Chairman of the Authority serves as the chief executive and administrative officer. The Chairman also chairs the Foreign Service Labor Relations Board.

The General Counsel of the Authority investigates alleged unfair labor practices, files and prosecutes unfair labor practice complaints before the Authority, and exercises such other powers as the Authority may prescribe.

The Federal Service Impasses Panel, an entity within the Authority, is assigned the function of providing assistance in resolving negotiation impasses between agencies and unions. After investigating an impasse, the Panel can either recommend procedures to the parties for the resolution of the impasse or assist the parties in resolving the impasse through whatever methods and procedures, including factfinding and recommendations, it considers appropriate. If the parties do not arrive at a settlement after assistance by the Panel, the Panel may hold hearings and take whatever action is necessary to resolve the impasse.

The Foreign Service Labor Relations Board and the Foreign Service Impasse Disputes Panel administer provisions of chapter 2 of the Foreign Service Act of 1980 (22 U.S.C. 3921), concerning labor-management relations. This chapter establishes a statutory labor-management relations program for Foreign Service employees of the U.S. Government. Administrative and staff support is provided by the Federal Labor Relations Authority and the Federal Service Impasses Panel.

Regional Offices—Federal Labor Relations Authority

City/Address	Director	Telephone
Atlanta, GA (Suite 701, 285 Peachtree Ctr. Ave., 30303–1270)	Nancy A. Speight	404–331–5300
Boston, MA (Suite 472, Thomas P. O'Neill Federal Bldg., 10 Causeway St., 02222).	Richard D. Zaiger	671–565–5100
Chicago, IL (Suite 1150, 55 W. Monroe, 60603–9729)	Peter A. Sutton	312–886–3465
Dallas, TX (Suite 926, LB–107, 525 S. Griffin St., 75202–1906)	James Petrucci	214–767–6266
Denver, CO (Suite 100, 1244 Speer Blvd., 80204–3581)	Matthew Jarvinen	303–844–5224
San Francisco, CA (Suite 220, 901 Market St., 94103–1791)	Gerald M. Cole	415–356–5000
Washington, DC (2nd Fl., 1400 K St. NW., 20424-0001)	Robert P. Hunter	202–357–6029

Sources of Information

Employment Employment inquiries and applications may be sent to the Human Resources Division. Phone, 202–218–7963. Internet, www.flra.gov/29-jobs.html.

Public Information and Publications The Authority will assist in arranging reproduction of documents and ordering transcripts of hearings. Requests for publications should be submitted to the Director, Case Control and Legal Publications. Phone, 202–218–7780. Internet, www.flra.gov.

For further information, contact the Office of the Executive Director, Federal Labor Relations Authority, 1400 K Street NW., Washington, DC 20005. Phone, 202–218–7949. E-mail, flraexecutivedirector@flra.gov. Internet, www.flra.gov.

FEDERAL MARITIME COMMISSION

800 North Capitol Street NW., Washington, DC 20573–0001
Phone, 202–523–5707. Internet, www.fmc.gov.

Chairman	STEVEN R. BLUST
Commissioners	A. PAUL ANDERSON, JOSEPH E. BRENNAN, HAROLD J. CREEL, JR., REBECCA F. DYE
General Counsel	AMY W. LARSON
Secretary	BRYANT L. VANBRAKLE
Director, Consumer Affairs and Dispute Resolution Services	RONALD D. MURPHY
Administrative Law Judge	KENNETH A. KRANTZ
Director, Office of Equal Employment Opportunity	CARMEN G. CANTOR
Inspector General	BRIDGETTE S. HICKS, *Acting*
Director, Office of Administration	BRUCE A. DOMBROWSKI
Director, Officer of Operations	AUSTIN L. SCHMITT
Director, Bureau of Certification and Licensing	SANDRA L. KUSUMOTO
Director, Bureau of Enforcement	VERN W. HILL
Director, Bureau of Trade Analysis	FLORENCE A. CARR

The Federal Maritime Commission is responsible for regulating the waterborne foreign commerce of the United States. It ensures that U.S. oceanborne trades are open to all on fair and equitable terms and protects against concerted activities and unlawful practices. This is accomplished by reviewing and monitoring agreements between persons subject to the Shipping Act of 1984, as amended by the Ocean Shipping Reform Act of 1998; licensing ocean transportation intermediaries; monitoring the activities of common carriers and ocean transportation intermediaries; enforcing prohibitions against unjustly discriminatory acts and other prohibited practices of shippers, carriers, and other persons subject to the shipping statutes; and ensuring that passenger vessel operators maintain adequate levels of financial responsibility for the indemnification of passengers for nonperformance or casualty.

The Federal Maritime Commission was established by Reorganization Plan No. 7 of 1961 (5 U.S.C. app.), effective August 12, 1961. It is an independent agency that regulates shipping under the following statutes: the Shipping Act of 1984, as amended (46 U.S.C. app. 1701–1720); the Merchant Marine Act, 1920 (46 U.S.C. app. 861 *et seq.*); the Foreign Shipping Practices Act of 1988 (46 U.S.C. app. 1710a); the Merchant Marine Act, 1936 (46 U.S.C. app. 1101 *et seq.*); and certain provisions of the Act of November 6, 1966 (46 U.S.C. app. 817(d) and 817(e)).

Activities

Agreements The Commission reviews agreements by and among ocean common carriers and/or marine terminal operators, filed under section 5 of the Shipping Act of 1984, for statutory compliance as well as for likely impact on competition. It also monitors activities under all effective agreements

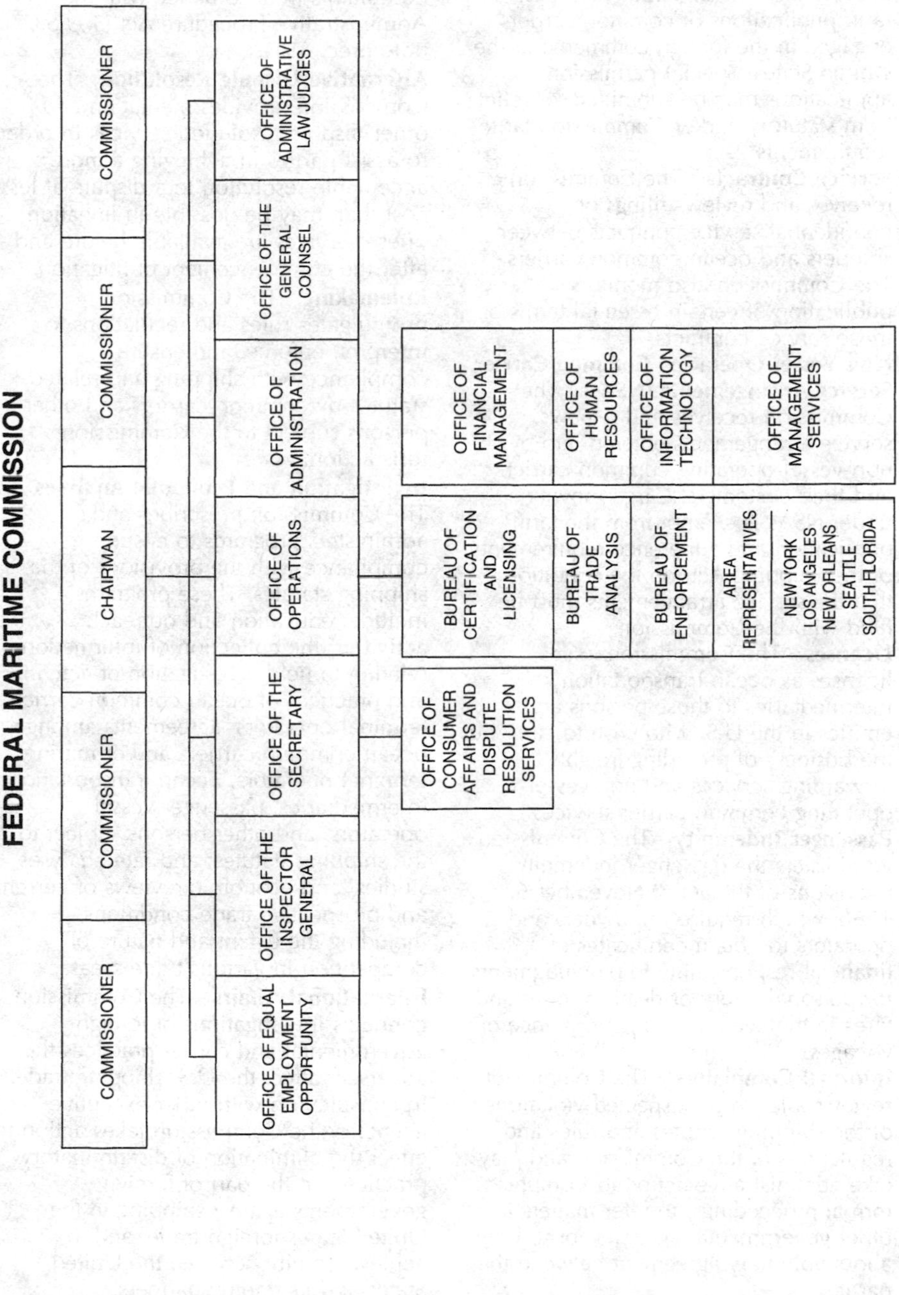
FEDERAL MARITIME COMMISSION
COMMISSIONER
COMMISSIONER
CHAIRMAN
COMMISSIONER
COMMISSIONER
OFFICE OF EQUAL EMPLOYMENT OPPORTUNITY
OFFICE OF THE INSPECTOR GENERAL
OFFICE OF THE SECRETARY
OFFICE OF OPERATIONS
OFFICE OF ADMINISTRATION
OFFICE OF THE GENERAL COUNSEL
OFFICE OF ADMINISTRATIVE LAW JUDGES
OFFICE OF CONSUMER AFFAIRS AND DISPUTE RESOLUTION SERVICES
BUREAU OF CERTIFICATION AND LICENSING
BUREAU OF TRADE ANALYSIS
BUREAU OF ENFORCEMENT
AREA REPRESENTATIVES
NEW YORK
LOS ANGELES
NEW ORLEANS
SEATTLE
SOUTH FLORIDA
OFFICE OF FINANCIAL MANAGEMENT
OFFICE OF HUMAN RESOURCES
OFFICE OF INFORMATION TECHNOLOGY
OFFICE OF MANAGEMENT SERVICES

for compliance with the provisions of law and its rules, orders, and regulations.

Tariffs The Commission monitors and prescribes requirements to ensure accessibility and accuracy of electronic tariff publications of common carriers engaged in the foreign commerce of the United States. Special permission applications may be submitted for relief from statutory and/or Commission tariff requirements.

Service Contracts The Commission receives and reviews filings of confidential service contracts between shippers and ocean common carriers. The Commission also monitors publication of certain essential terms of those service contracts.

Non-Vessel-Operating Common Carrier Service Arrangements (NSAs) The Commission receives and reviews service arrangements entered into by non-vessel-operating common carriers and their customers. Cargo moving under NSAs is exempt from the tariff publication and adherence requirements of the Shipping Act, on the condition that the service arrangements must be filed with the Commission.

Licenses The Commission issues licenses as ocean transportation intermediaries to those persons and entities in the U.S. who wish to carry out the business of providing freight forwarding services and non-vessel-operating common carrier services.

Passenger Indemnity The Commission administers the passenger indemnity provisions of the act of November 6, 1966, which require shipowners and operators to obtain certificates of financial responsibility to pay judgments for personal injury or death or to refund fares in the event of nonperformance of voyages.

Informal Complaints The Commission reviews alleged or suspected violations of the shipping statutes and rules and regulations of the Commission and may take administrative action to institute formal proceedings, to refer matters to other governmental agencies, or to bring about voluntary agreement between the parties.

Formal Adjudicatory Procedures The Commission conducts formal investigations and hearings on its own motion and adjudicates formal complaints in accordance with the Administrative Procedure Act (5 U.S.C. note prec. 551).

Alternative Dispute Resolution The Commission provides mediation and other dispute resolution services in order to assist parties in achieving a more acceptable resolution to a dispute at less cost than may be possible in litigation. These services are available before and after the commencement of litigation.

Rulemaking The Commission promulgates rules and regulations to interpret, enforce, and ensure compliance with shipping and related statutes by common carriers and other persons subject to the Commission's jurisdiction.

Investigation and Economic Analyses The Commission prescribes and administers programs to ensure compliance with the provisions of the shipping statutes. These programs include: education and outreach activities; the collection of information relating to field investigation of activities and practices of ocean common carriers, terminal operators, agreements among ocean common carriers and/or marine terminal operators, ocean transportation intermediaries, passenger vessel operators, and other persons subject to the shipping statutes; and rate analyses, studies, and economic reviews of current and prospective trade conditions, including the extent and nature of competition in various trade areas.

International Affairs The Commission conducts investigations of foreign governmental and carrier practices that adversely affect the U.S. shipping trade. In consultation with other executive agencies, the Commission takes action to effect the elimination of discriminatory practices on the part of foreign governments against shipping in the United States foreign trade, and to achieve comity between the United States and its trading partners.

Area Representatives—Federal Maritime Commission

Area	Address/Phone	Representative
Los Angeles	Rm. 320, 839 S. Beacon St., San Pedro, CA 90733–0230.	
	Phone, 310–514–4905. Fax, 310–514–3931. E-mail, oclark@fmc.gov	Oliver E. Clark
South Florida	P.O. Box 813609, Hollywood, FL 33081–3609.	
	Phone, 954–963–5362. Fax, 954–963–5630. E-mail, amargolis@fmc.gov	Andrew Margolis
	Phone, 954–963–5284. Fax, 954–963–5630. E-mail, emintz@fmc.gov	Eric O. Mintz
New Orleans	P.O. Box 7806, Metarie, LA 70010–7806.	
	Phone, 504–589–6662. Fax, 504–589–6663. E-mail, akellogg@fmc.gov	Alvin N. Kellogg
New York	JFK Int'l Airport, Bldg. 75, Rm. 205B, Jamaica, NY 11430.	
	Phone, 718–553–2228. Fax, 718–553–2229. E-mail, emingione@fmc.gov	Emanuel J. Mingione
Seattle	Suite 100, 7 S. Nevada St., Seattle, WA 98134.	
	Phone, 206–553–0221. Fax, 206–553–0222. E-mail, mmoneck@fmc.gov	Michael A. Moneck

Sources of Information

Electronic Access Information about the Federal Maritime Commission is available in electronic form through the Internet, at www.fmc.gov.

Employment Employment inquiries may be directed to the Office of Human Resources, Federal Maritime Commission, 800 North Capitol Street NW., Washington, DC 20573–0001. Phone, 202–523–5773.

Informal Complaints Phone, 202–523–5807. E-mail, complaints@fmc.gov.

Publications The *Performance and Accountability Report (2005)* and the *2005 Management Discussion and Analysis Report* are recent publications of the Federal Maritime Commission.

For further information, contact the Office of the Secretary, Federal Maritime Commission, 800 North Capitol Street NW., Washington, DC 20573–0001. Phone, 202–523–5725. Fax, 202–523–0014. Internet, www.fmc.gov. E-mail, secretary@fmc.gov.

FEDERAL MEDIATION AND CONCILIATION SERVICE

2100 K Street NW., Washington, DC 20427
Phone, 202–606–8100. Internet, www.fmcs.gov.

Director — Arthur F. Rosenfeld

The Federal Mediation and Conciliation Service assists labor and management in resolving disputes in collective bargaining contract negotiation through voluntary mediation and arbitration services; provides training to unions and management in cooperative processes to improve long-term relationships under the Labor Management Cooperation Act of 1978; provides alternative dispute resolution services and training to Government agencies, including the facilitation of regulatory negotiations under the Administrative Dispute Resolution Act and the Negotiated Rulemaking Act of 1996; and awards competitive grants to joint labor-management committees to encourage innovative approaches to cooperative efforts.

The Federal Mediation and Conciliation Service (FMCS) was created by the Labor Management Relations Act, 1947 (29 U.S.C. 172). The Director is appointed by the President with the advice and consent of the Senate.

Activities

The Federal Mediation and Conciliation Service helps prevent disruptions in the flow of interstate commerce caused by labor-management disputes by providing mediators to assist disputing parties in the resolution of their differences.

Mediators have no law enforcement authority and rely wholly on persuasive techniques.

The Service offers its facilities in labor-management disputes to any industry affecting interstate commerce with employees represented by a union, either upon its own motion or at the request of one or more of the parties to the dispute, whenever in its judgment such dispute threatens to cause a substantial interruption of commerce. The Labor Management Relations Act requires that parties to a labor contract must file a dispute notice if agreement is not reached 30 days in advance of a contract termination or reopening date. The notice must be filed with the Service and the appropriate State or local mediation agency. The Service is required to avoid the mediation of disputes that would have only a minor effect on interstate commerce if State or other conciliation services are available to the parties.

For further information, contact one of the regional offices listed below.

Mediation Efforts of FMCS mediators are directed toward the establishment of sound and stable labor-management relations on a continuing basis, thereby helping to reduce the incidence of work stoppages. The mediator's basic function is to encourage and promote better day-to-day relations between labor and management, so that issues arising in negotiations may be faced as problems to be settled through mutual effort rather than issues in dispute.

For further information, contact the Office of Public Affairs. Phone, 202–606–8100.

Arbitration The Service, on the joint request of employers and unions, will also assist in the selection of arbitrators from a roster of private citizens who are qualified as neutrals to adjudicate matters in dispute.

For further information, contact the Office of Arbitration Services. Phone, 202–606–5111.

For further information, contact the Public Affairs Office, Federal Mediation and Conciliation Service, 2100 K Street NW., Washington, DC 20427. Phone, 202–606–8100. Internet, www.fmcs.gov.

FEDERAL MINE SAFETY AND HEALTH REVIEW COMMISSION

601 New Jersey Avenue NW., Suite 9500, Washington, DC 20001–2021
Phone, 202–434–9900. E-mail, info@fmshrc.gov. Internet, www.fmshrc.gov.

Chairman	MICHAEL F. DUFFY
Commissioners	MARY LU JORDAN, STANLEY C. SUBOLESKI, MICHAEL G. YOUNG, (VACANCY)
Chief Administrative Law Judge	ROBERT J. LESNICK
General Counsel	THOMAS A. STOCK
Executive Director	RICHARD L. BAKER

The Federal Mine Safety and Health Review Commission ensures compliance with occupational safety and health standards in the Nation's surface and underground coal, metal, and nonmetal mines.

The Federal Mine Safety and Health Review Commission is an independent, adjudicative agency established by the Federal Mine Safety and Health Act of 1977 (30 U.S.C. 801 *et seq.*) that provides administrative trial and

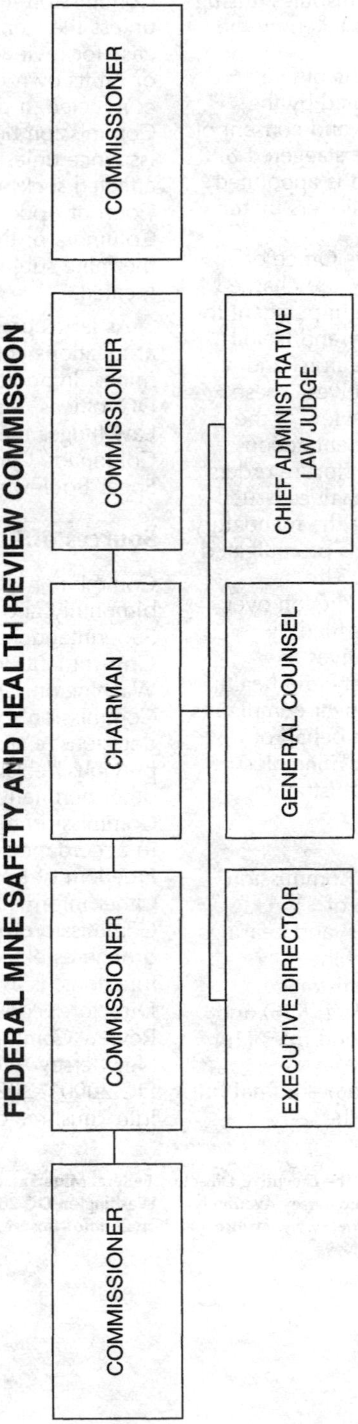
FEDERAL MINE SAFETY AND HEALTH REVIEW COMMISSION
COMMISSIONER
COMMISSIONER
CHAIRMAN
COMMISSIONER
COMMISSIONER
CHIEF ADMINISTRATIVE LAW JUDGE
GENERAL COUNSEL
EXECUTIVE DIRECTOR

appellate review of legal disputes arising from enforcement actions taken by the Department of Labor.

The Commission consists of five members who are appointed by the President with the advice and consent of the Senate and who serve staggered 6-year terms. The Chairman is appointed from among the Commissioners by the President.

The Commission and its Office of Administrative Law Judges are charged with deciding cases brought pursuant to the act by the Mine Safety and Health Administration, mine operators, and miners or their representatives. These cases generally involve review of the Administration's enforcement actions including citations, mine closure orders, and proposals for civil penalties issued for violations of the act or the mandatory safety and health standards promulgated by the Secretary of Labor. The Commission also has jurisdiction over discrimination complaints filed by miners or their representatives in connection with their safety and health rights under the act, and over complaints for compensation filed on behalf of miners idled as a result of mine closure orders issued by the Administration.

Activities

Cases brought before the Commission are assigned to the Office of Administrative Law Judges, and hearings are conducted pursuant to the requirements of the Administrative Procedure Act (5 U.S.C. 554, 556) and the Commission's procedural rules (29 CFR Part 2700).

A judge's decision becomes a final but nonprecedential order of the Commission 40 days after issuance unless the Commission has directed the case for review in response to a petition or on its own motion. If a review is conducted, a decision of the Commission becomes final 30 days after issuance unless a party adversely affected seeks review in the U.S. Circuit Court of Appeals for the District of Columbia or the Circuit within which the mine subject to the litigation is located.

As far as practicable, hearings are held at locations convenient to the affected mines. In addition to its Washington, DC, offices, the Office of Administrative Law Judges maintains an office in the Colonnade Center, Room 280, 1244 Speer Boulevard, Denver, CO 80204.

Sources of Information

Commission decisions are published bimonthly and are available through the Superintendent of Documents, U.S. Government Printing Office, Washington, DC 20402. The Commission's web site includes recent decisions, a searchable database of previous decisions, procedural rules, and other pertinent information. Requests for Commission records should be submitted in accordance with the Commission's Freedom of Information Act regulations. Other information, including Commission rules of procedure and brochures explaining the Commission's functions, is available from the Executive Director, Federal Mine Safety and Health Review Commission, Suite 9500, 601 New Jersey Avenue NW., Washington, DC 20001–2021. E-mail, info@fmshrc.gov.

For further information, contact the Executive Director, Federal Mine Safety and Health Review Commission, Suite 9500, 601 New Jersey Avenue NW., Washington DC 20001–2021. Phone, 202–434–9905. Fax, 202–434–9906. Internet, www.fmshrc.gov. E-mail, info@fmshrc.gov.

FEDERAL RESERVE SYSTEM

Board of Governors of the Federal Reserve System
Twentieth Street and Constitution Avenue NW., Washington, DC 20551
Phone, 202–452–3000. Internet, www.federalreserve.gov.

Board of Governors

Chairman	BEN S. BERNANKE
Vice Chair	(VACANCY)
Members	SUSAN SCHMIDT BIES, DONALD L. KOHN, RANDALL S. KROSZNER, MARK W. OLSON, KEVIN M. WARSH

Staff:

Director, Division of Board Members	MICHELLE A. SMITH
Congressional Liaison	WINTHROP P. HAMBLEY
General Counsel	SCOTT G. ALVAREZ
Secretary	JENNIFER J. JOHNSON
Director, Division of Banking Supervision and Regulation	RICHARD SPILLENKOTHEN
Director, Division of Consumer and Community Affairs	SANDRA F. BRAUNSTEIN
Director, Division of Federal Reserve Bank Operations and Payment Systems	LOUISE L. ROSEMAN
Director, Division of Information Technology	MARIANNE M. EMERSON
Director, Division of International Finance	KAREN H. JOHNSON
Director, Management Division	H. FAY PETERS
Director, Division of Monetary Affairs	VINCENT R. REINHART
Director, Division of Research and Statistics	DAVID J. STOCKTON
Staff Director, Office of Staff Director for Management	STEPHEN R. MALPHRUS
Inspector General	BARRY R. SNYDER

Officers of the Federal Reserve Banks

Federal Reserve Bank Chairmen:

Boston, MA	BLENDA J. WILSON
New York, NY	JOHN E. SEXTON
Philadelphia, PA	DORIS M. DAMM
Cleveland, OH	CHARLES E. BUNCH
Richmond, VA	THOMAS J. MACKELL, JR.
Atlanta, GA	DAVID M. RATCLIFFE
Chicago, IL	MILES D. WHITE
St. Louis, MO	WALTER L. METCALFE, JR.
Minneapolis, MN	FRANK L. SIMS
Kansas City, MO	ROBERT A. FUNK
Dallas, TX	RAY L. HUNT
San Francisco, CA	DAVID K. TANG

Presidents:

Atlanta, GA	JACK GUYNN
Boston, MA	CATHY E. MINEHAN
Chicago, IL	MICHAEL H. MOSKOW
Cleveland, OH	SANDRA PIANALTO
Dallas, TX	RICHARD FISHER

Kansas City, MO	THOMAS M. HOENIG
Minneapolis, MN	GARY H. STERN
New York, NY	TIMOTHY F. GEITHNER
Philadelphia, PA	ANTHONY M. SANTOMERO
Richmond, VA	JEFFERY M. LACKER
St. Louis, MO	WILLIAM POOLE
San Francisco, CA	JANET L. YELLEN

Federal Open Market Committee

Chairman	BEN S. BERNANKE
Vice Chairman	TIMOTHY F. GEITHNER
Members	SUSAN SCHMIDT BIES, JACK GUYNN, DONALD L. KOHN, RANDALL S. KROSZNER, JEFFREY M. LACKER, MARK W. OLSON, SANDRA PIANALTO, KEVIN M. WARSH, JANET L. YELLEN
Staff:	
Secretary and Economist	VINCENT R. REINHART
Deputy Secretary	DEBORAH DANKER
Assistant Secretary	DAVID SKIDMORE
General Counsel	SCOTT G. ALVAREZ
Economists	KAREN H. JOHNSON, DAVID J. STOCKTON
Federal Advisory Councils:	
Secretary, Federal Advisory Council	THOMAS A. RENYI
Chairman, Consumer Advisory Council	LORI R. SWANSON
President, Thrift Institutions Advisory Council	ROY M. WHITEHEAD

The Federal Reserve System, the central bank of the United States, is charged with administering and formulating the Nation's credit and monetary policy. Through its supervisory and regulatory banking functions, the Federal Reserve maintains the safety and soundness of the Nation's economy, responding to the Nation's domestic and international financial needs and objectives.

The Federal Reserve System was established by the Federal Reserve Act (12 U.S.C. 221), approved December 23, 1913. The System serves as the Nation's central bank. As such, its major responsibility is in the execution of monetary policy. It also performs other functions, such as the transfer of funds, handling Government deposits and debt issues, supervising and regulating banks, and acting as lender of last resort.

It is the responsibility of the Federal Reserve System to contribute to the strength and vitality of the U.S. economy. By influencing the lending and investing activities of depository institutions and the cost and availability of money and credit, the Federal Reserve System helps promote the full use of human and capital resources, the growth of productivity, relatively stable prices, and equilibrium in the Nation's international balance of payments. Through its supervisory and regulatory banking functions, the Federal Reserve System helps maintain a commercial banking system that is responsive to the Nation's financial needs and objectives.

The System consists of the Board of Governors in Washington, DC; the 12 Federal Reserve Banks and their 25 branches and other facilities situated throughout the country; the Federal Open Market Committee; the Federal Advisory Council; the Consumer Advisory Council; the Thrift Institutions Advisory Council; and the Nation's financial institutions, including commercial banks, savings and loan associations, mutual savings banks, and credit unions.

Board of Governors

The Board is composed of seven members appointed by the President with the advice and consent of the Senate. The Chairman of the Board of Governors is a member of the National Advisory Council on International Monetary and Financial Policies. The Board determines general monetary, credit, and operating policies for the System as a whole and formulates the rules and regulations necessary to carry out the purposes of the Federal Reserve Act. The Board's principal duties consist of monitoring credit conditions; supervising the Federal Reserve Banks, member banks, and bank holding companies; and regulating the implementation of certain consumer credit protection laws.

Power To Influence Credit Conditions The Board has the power, within statutory limitations, to fix the requirements concerning reserves to be maintained by depository institutions on transaction accounts or nonpersonal time deposits. The Board of Governors reviews and determines the discount rate charged by the Federal Reserve Banks. For the purpose of preventing excessive use of credit for the purchase or carrying of securities, the Board is authorized to regulate the amount of credit that may be initially extended and subsequently maintained on any security (with certain exceptions).

Supervision of Federal Reserve Banks The Board is authorized to make examinations of the Federal Reserve Banks, to require statements and reports from such Banks, to supervise the issue and retirement of Federal Reserve notes, to require the establishment or discontinuance of branches of Reserve Banks, and to exercise supervision over all relationships and transactions of those Banks with foreign branches.

Supervision of Bank Holding Companies The Federal Reserve has primary responsibility for supervising and regulating the activities of bank holding companies. The main objectives of this activity are to control the expansion of bank holding companies by avoiding the creation of monopoly or restraining trade in banking, and to limit the expansion of bank holding companies to those nonbanking activities that are closely related to banking, thus maintaining a separation between banking and commerce. A company that seeks to become a bank holding company must obtain the prior approval of the Federal Reserve. Any company that qualifies as a bank holding company must register with the Federal Reserve System and file reports with the System.

Supervision of Banking Organizations The Federal Reserve is responsible for the supervision and regulation of domestic and international activities of U.S. banking organizations. It supervises State-chartered banks that are members of the System, all bank holding companies, and Edge Act and agreement corporations (corporations chartered to engage in international banking).

The Board has jurisdiction over the admission of State banks and trust companies to membership in the Federal Reserve System, the termination of membership of such banks, the establishment of branches by such banks, and the approval of bank mergers and consolidations where the resulting institution will be a State member bank. It receives copies of condition reports submitted to the Federal Reserve Banks. It has power to examine all member banks and the affiliates of member banks and to require condition reports from them. It has authority to require periodic and other public disclosure of information with respect to an equity security of a State member bank that is held by 500 or more persons. It establishes minimum standards with respect to installation, maintenance, and operation of security devices and procedures by State member banks. Also, it has authority to issue cease-and-desist orders in connection with violations of law or unsafe or unsound banking practices by State member banks and to remove directors or officers of such banks in certain circumstances, and it may suspend member banks from the use of the credit facilities of the Federal Reserve System for making undue use of bank credit for speculative purposes or for any other purpose inconsistent with the maintenance of sound credit conditions.

The Board may grant authority to member banks to establish branches in foreign countries or dependencies or insular possessions of the United States, to invest in the stocks of banks or corporations engaged in international or foreign banking, or to invest in foreign banks. It also charters, regulates, and supervises certain corporations that engage in foreign or international banking and financial activities.

The Board is authorized to issue general regulations permitting interlocking relationships in certain circumstances between member banks and organizations dealing in securities or between member banks and other banks.

Other Activities The Board reviews other bank stock acquisitions, as listed below.

The Board prescribes regulations to ensure a meaningful disclosure by lenders of credit terms so that consumers will be able to compare more readily the various credit terms available and will be informed about rules governing credit cards, including their potential liability for unauthorized use.

The Board has authority to impose reserve requirements and interest rate ceilings on branches and agencies of foreign banks in the United States, to grant loans to them, to provide them access to Federal Reserve services, and to limit their interstate banking activities.

Federal Open Market Committee

The Federal Open Market Committee is comprised of the Board of Governors and five of the presidents of the Reserve Banks. The Chairman of the Board of Governors is traditionally the Chairman of the Committee. The president of the Federal Reserve Bank of New York serves as a permanent member of the Committee. Four of the twelve Reserve Bank presidents rotate annually as members of the Committee.

Open market operations of the Reserve Banks are conducted under regulations adopted by the Committee and pursuant to specific policy directives issued by the Committee, which meets in Washington at frequent intervals. Purchases and sales of securities in the open market are undertaken to supply bank reserves to support the credit and money needed for long-term economic growth, to offset cyclical economic swings, and to accommodate seasonal demands of businesses and consumers for money and credit. These operations are carried out principally in U.S. Government obligations, but they also include purchases and sales of Federal agency obligations. All operations are conducted in New York, where the primary markets for these securities are located; the Federal Reserve Bank of New York executes transactions for the Federal Reserve System Open Market Account in carrying out these operations.

Under the Committee's direction, the Federal Reserve Bank of New York also undertakes transactions in foreign currencies for the Federal Reserve System Open Market Account. The purposes of these operations include helping to safeguard the value of the dollar in international exchange markets and facilitating growth in international liquidity in accordance with the needs of an expanding world economy.

Federal Reserve Banks

The 12 Federal Reserve Banks are located in Atlanta, GA; Boston, MA; Chicago, IL; Cleveland, OH; Dallas, TX; Kansas City, MO; Minneapolis, MN; New York, NY; Philadelphia, PA; Richmond, VA; San Francisco, CA; and St. Louis, MO. Branch banks are located in Baltimore, MD; Birmingham, AL; Buffalo, NY; Charlotte, NC; Cincinnati, OH; Denver, CO; Detroit, MI; El Paso, TX; Helena, MT; Houston, TX; Jacksonville, FL; Little Rock, AR; Los Angeles, CA; Louisville, KY; Memphis, TN; Miami, FL; Nashville, TN; New Orleans, LA; Oklahoma City, OK; Omaha, NE; Pittsburgh, PA; Portland, OR; Salt Lake City, UT; San Antonio, TX; and Seattle, WA.

Reserves on Deposit The Reserve Banks receive and hold on deposit the reserve or clearing account deposits of depository institutions. These banks are permitted to count their vault cash as part of their required reserve.

Extensions of Credit The Federal Reserve is required to open its discount window to any depository institution that is subject to Federal Reserve reserve requirements on transaction accounts or nonpersonal time deposits. Discount window credit provides for Federal Reserve lending to eligible depository institutions under two basic programs. One is the adjustment credit program; the other supplies more extended credit for certain limited purposes.

Short-term adjustment credit is the primary type of Federal Reserve credit. It is available to help borrowers meet temporary requirements for funds. Borrowers are not permitted to use adjustment credit to take advantage of any spread between the discount rate and market rates.

Extended credit is provided through three programs designed to assist depository institutions in meeting longer term needs for funds. One provides seasonal credit—for periods running up to 9 months—to smaller depository institutions that lack access to market funds. A second program assists institutions that experience special difficulties arising from exceptional circumstances or practices involving only that institution. Finally, in cases where more general liquidity strains are affecting a broad range of depository institutions—such as those whose portfolios consist primarily of longer term assets—credit may be provided to address the problems of particular institutions being affected by the general situation.

Currency Issue The Reserve Banks issue Federal Reserve notes, which constitute the bulk of money in circulation. These notes are obligations of the United States and are a prior lien upon the assets of the issuing Federal Reserve Bank. They are issued against a pledge by the Reserve Bank with the Federal Reserve agent of collateral security including gold certificates, paper discounted or purchased by the Bank, and direct obligations of the United States.

Other Powers The Reserve Banks are empowered to act as clearinghouses and as collecting agents for depository institutions in the collection of checks and other instruments. They are also authorized to act as depositories and fiscal agents of the United States and to exercise other banking functions specified in the Federal Reserve Act. They perform a number of important functions in connection with the issue and redemption of United States Government securities.

Sources of Information

Employment Written inquiries regarding employment should be addressed to the Director, Division of Personnel, Board of Governors of the Federal Reserve System, Washington, DC 20551.

Procurement Firms seeking business with the Board should address their inquiries to the Director, Division of Support Services, Board of Governors of the Federal Reserve System, Washington, DC 20551.

Publications Among the publications issued by the Board are *The Federal Reserve System—Purposes and Functions,* and a series of pamphlets including *Guide to Business Credit and the Equal Credit Opportunity Act; Consumer Handbook; Making Deposits: When Will Your Money Be Available;* and *When Your Home Is On the Line: What You Should Know About Home Equity Lines of Credit.* Copies of these pamphlets are available free of charge. Information regarding publications may be obtained in Room MP–510 (Martin Building) of the Board's headquarters. Phone, 202–452–3244.

Reading Room A reading room where persons may inspect records that are available to the public is located in Room B–1122 at the Board's headquarters, Twentieth Street and Constitution Avenue NW., Washington, DC. Information regarding the availability of records may be obtained by calling 202–452–3684.

For further information, contact the Office of Public Affairs, Board of Governors, Federal Reserve System, Washington, DC 20551. Phone, 202–452–3204 or 202–452–3215. Internet, www.federalreserve.gov.

FEDERAL RETIREMENT THRIFT INVESTMENT BOARD

1250 H Street NW., Washington, DC 20005
Phone, 202–942–1600. Fax, 202–942–1676. Internet, www.tsp.gov.

Chairman	ANDREW M. SAUL
Members	TERRENCE A. DUFFY, THOMAS A. FINK, ALEJANDRO M. SANCHEZ, GORDON J. WHITING
Officials:	
Executive Director	GARY A. AMELIO
Chief Investment Officer	TRACEY A. RAY
Participant Services Director	PAMELA-JEANNE MORAN
Director of External Affairs	THOMAS J. TRABUCCO
General Counsel	(VACANCY)
Chief Information Officer	MARK A. HAGERTY
Chief Financial Officer	JAMES B. PETRICK
Product Development Director	GREGORY T. LONG

The Federal Retirement Thrift Investment Board administers the Thrift Savings Plan, which provides Federal employees the opportunity to save for additional retirement security.

The Federal Retirement Thrift Investment Board was established as an independent agency by the Federal Employees' Retirement System Act of 1986 (5 U.S.C. 8351 and 8401–79). The act vests responsibility for the agency in six named fiduciaries: the five Board members and the Executive Director. The five members of the Board, one of whom is designated as Chairman, are appointed by the President with the advice and consent of the Senate and serve on the Board on a part-time basis. The members appoint the Executive Director, who is responsible for the management of the agency and the Plan.

Activities

The Thrift Savings Plan is a tax-deferred, defined contribution plan that was established as one of the three parts of the Federal Employees' Retirement System. For employees covered under the System, savings accumulated through the Plan make an important addition to the retirement benefits provided by Social Security and the System's Basic Annuity. Civil Service Retirement System employees and members of the Uniformed Services may also take advantage of the Plan to supplement their annuities.

The Board operates the Thrift Savings Plan and manages the investments of the Thrift Savings Fund solely for the benefit of participants and their beneficiaries. As part of these responsibilities, the Board maintains an account for each Plan participant, makes loans, purchases annuity contracts, and provides for the payment of benefits.

For further information, contact the Director of External Affairs, Federal Retirement Thrift Investment Board, 1250 H Street NW., Washington, DC 20005. Phone, 202–942–1640. Internet, www.tsp.gov.

FEDERAL TRADE COMMISSION

600 Pennsylvania Avenue NW., Washington, DC 20580
Phone, 202–326–2222. Internet, www.ftc.gov.

Chairman	DEBORAH P. MAJORAS
Chief of Staff	MARYANNE KANE
Commissioners	PAMELA JONES HARBOUR, WILLIAM E. KOVACIC, JONATHAN LEIBOWITZ, J. THOMAS ROSCH
Executive Director	CHARLES SCHNEIDER
Deputy Executive Director	JUDITH BAILEY
Chief Information Officer	STEPHEN WARREN
Chief Financial Officer	STEVEN FISHER
Director, Bureau of Competition	JEFFREY SCHMIDT
Director, Bureau of Consumer Protection	LYDIA B. PARNES
Deputy Directors	EILEEN HARRINGTON, C. LEE PEELER
Director, Bureau of Economics	MICHAEL SALINGER
Deputy Directors	MARK FRANKENA, PAUL A. PAUTLER
General Counsel	WILLIAM BLUMENTHAL
Principal Deputy General Counsel	JOHN D. GRAUBERT
Director, Office of Congressional Relations	ANNA H. DAVIS
Director, Office of Public Affairs	NANCY NESS JUDY
Director, Office of Policy Planning	MAUREEN K. OHLHAUSEN
Secretary of the Commission	DONALD S. CLARK
Chief Administrative Law Judge	STEPHEN J. MCGUIRE
Inspector General	HOWARD L. SRIBNICK

[For the Federal Trade Commission statement of organization, see the *Code of Federal Regulations,* Title 16, Part 0]

The Federal Trade Commission has jurisdiction to enhance consumer welfare and protect competition in broad sectors of the economy. The Commission enforces the laws that prohibit business practices that are anticompetitive, deceptive, or unfair to consumers; promotes informed consumer choice and public understanding of the competitive process; and seeks to accomplish its mission without impeding legitimate business activity.

The Federal Trade Commission was established in 1914 by the Federal Trade Commission Act (15 U.S.C. 41–58). The Commission is composed of five members appointed by the President, with the advice and consent of the Senate, for a term of 7 years. Not more than three of the Commissioners may be members of the same political party. One Commissioner is designated by the President as Chairman of the Commission and is responsible for its administrative management.

Activities

The Commission's principal functions include the following:

—promoting competition through the prevention of general trade restraints such as price-fixing agreements, boycotts, illegal combinations of competitors, and other unfair methods of competition;

FEDERAL TRADE COMMISSION

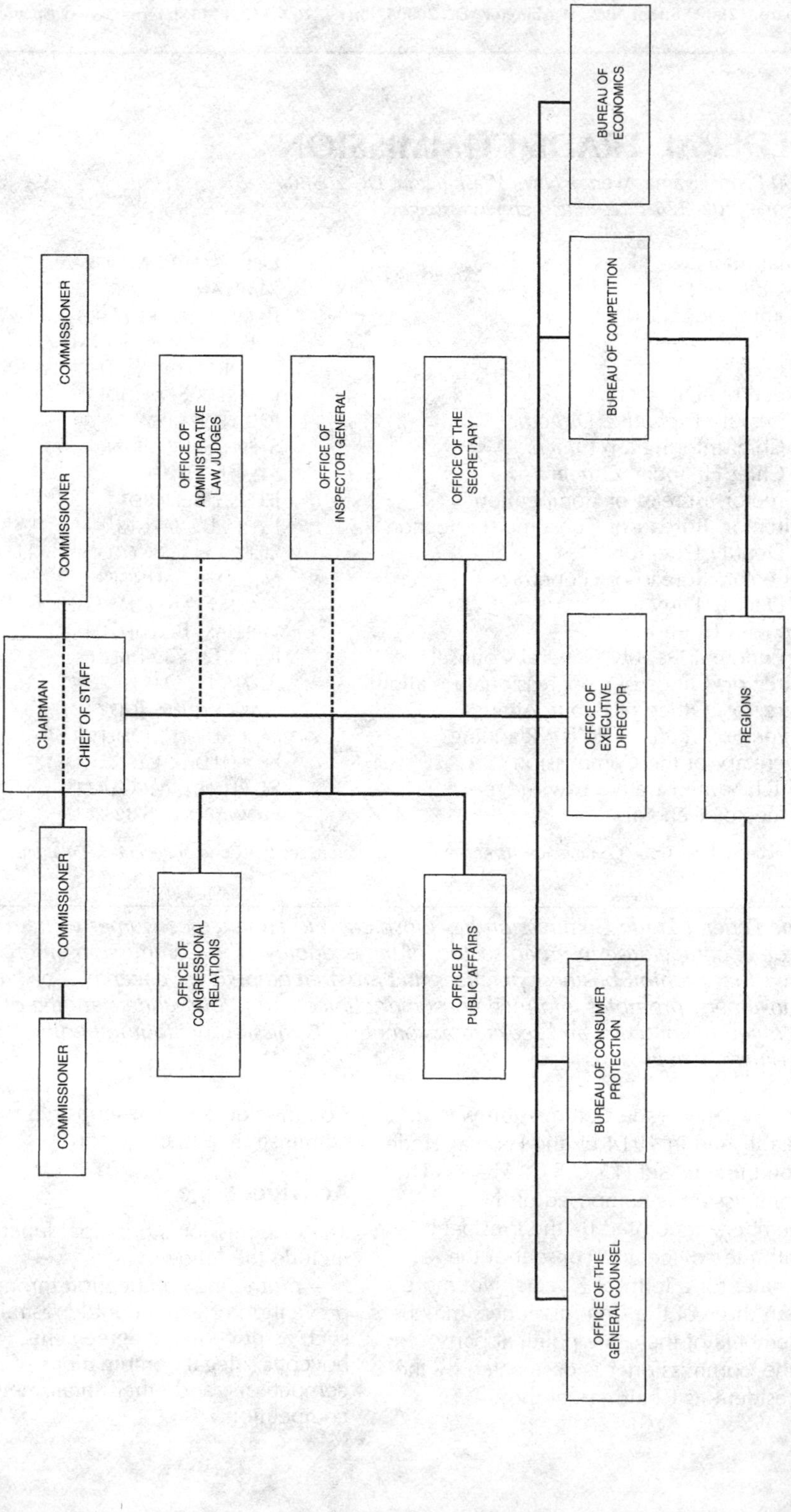

—stopping corporate mergers, acquisitions, or joint ventures that may substantially lessen competition or tend to create a monopoly;

—preventing pricing discrimination, exclusive dealing, tying arrangements, and discrimination among competing customers by sellers;

—preventing interlocking directorates or officers' positions that may restrain competition;

—preventing the dissemination of false or deceptive advertisements of consumer products and services as well as other unfair or deceptive practices;

—promoting electronic commerce by stopping fraud on the Internet and working with other domestic and foreign agencies to develop and promote policies to safeguard online privacy of personal information;

—protecting the privacy of consumers' personal information to prevent illegal or unwanted use of financial or other data;

—stopping various fraudulent telemarketing schemes and protecting consumers from abusive, deceptive, or unwanted telephone tactics; and enforcing the National Do Not Call Registry;

—ensuring truthful labeling of textile, wool, and fur products;

—requiring creditors to disclose in writing certain cost information, such as the annual percentage rate, before consumers enter into credit transactions, as required by the Truth in Lending Act;

—protecting consumers against circulation of inaccurate or obsolete credit reports and ensuring that credit bureaus, consumer reporting agencies, credit grantors, and bill collectors exercise their responsibilities in a manner that is fair and equitable;

—educating consumers and businesses about their rights and responsibilities under Commission rules and regulations; and

—gathering factual data concerning economic and business conditions and making it available to the Congress, the President, and the public.

Competition One of the two major missions of the Commission is to encourage competition in the American economy. The Commission seeks to prevent unfair practices that undermine competition and attempts to prevent mergers of companies if the result may be to lessen competition. Under some circumstances, companies planning to merge must first give notice to the Commission and the Department of Justice's Antitrust Division and provide certain information concerning the operations of the companies involved.

The Commission also enforces the provisions of the Robinson-Patman Act, a part of the Clayton Act prohibiting companies from discriminating among their customers in terms of price or other services provided.

Consumer Protection Consumer protection is the second of the two main missions of the Commission. The Commission, therefore, works to accomplish the following:

—increase the usefulness of advertising by ensuring that it is truthful and not misleading;

—reduce instances of fraudulent, deceptive, or unfair marketing practices;

—prevent creditors from using unlawful practices when granting credit, maintaining credit information, collecting debts, and operating credit systems; and

—educate the public about Commission activities.

The Commission initiates investigations in areas of concern to consumers. It has issued and enforces many trade regulation rules in areas important to consumers, including health and nutrition claims in advertising; environmental advertising and labeling; general advertising issues; health care, telemarketing and electronic commerce, business opportunity, and franchise and investment fraud; mortgage lending and discrimination; enforcement of Commission orders; and enforcement of credit statutes and trade regulation rules.

Competition and Consumer Advocacy To promote competition, consumer protection, and the efficient allocation of resources, the Commission also advocates consumer interest in a competitive marketplace by encouraging courts, legislatures, and government administrative bodies to consider efficiency and consumer welfare as important elements in their deliberations. The Commission uses these opportunities to support procompetitive means of regulating the Nation's economy, including the elimination of anticompetitive restrictions that reduce the welfare of consumers and the implementation of regulatory programs that protect the public and preserve as much as possible the discipline of competitive markets.

Compliance Activities Through systematic and continuous review, the Commission obtains and maintains compliance with its cease-and-desist orders. All respondents against whom such orders have been issued are required to file reports with the Commission to substantiate their compliance. In the event compliance is not obtained, or if the order is subsequently violated, civil penalty proceedings may be instituted.

Cooperative Procedures In carrying out the statutory directive to prevent unfair methods of competition or unfair or deceptive practices, the Commission makes extensive use of voluntary and cooperative procedures. Through these procedures, business and industry may obtain authoritative guidance and a substantial measure of certainty as to what they may do under the laws administered by the Commission.

The Commission issues administrative interpretations in plain language of laws enforced by the Commission. Guides provide the basis for voluntary abandonment of unlawful practices by members of a particular industry or by an industry in general. Failure to comply with the guides may result in corrective action by the Commission under applicable statutory provisions.

Enforcement The Commission's law enforcement work falls into two general categories: actions to foster voluntary compliance with the law, and formal administrative or Federal court litigation leading to mandatory orders against offenders.

Compliance with the law may be obtained through voluntary and cooperative action by private companies in response to nonbinding staff advice, formal advisory opinions by the Commission, and guides and policy statements delineating legal requirements as to particular business practices.

Formal litigation is instituted either by issuing an administrative complaint or by filing a Federal district court complaint charging a person, partnership, or corporation with violating one or more of the statutes administered by the Commission. If the charges in an administrative matter are not contested or if the charges are found to be true after an administrative hearing in a contested case, an order may be issued requiring discontinuance of the unlawful practices.

Investigations Investigations by the Commission may originate through complaint by a consumer or a competitor, the Congress, or from Federal, State, or municipal agencies. Also, the Commission itself may initiate an investigation into possible violations of the laws it administers. No formality is required in submitting a complaint. A letter giving the facts in detail, accompanied by all supporting evidence in possession of the complaining party, is sufficient. The Commission also maintains electronic complaint systems that are accessible through its Web site. It is the general policy of the Commission not to disclose the identity of any complainant, except as required by law or Commission rules.

Upon receipt of a complaint, various criteria are applied in determining whether the particular matter should be investigated.

An order issued after an administrative proceeding that requires the respondent to cease and desist or take other corrective action may be appealed. Appeals processes may go as far as the Supreme Court.

In addition to or in lieu of the administrative proceeding initiated by a formal complaint, the Commission may request that a U.S. district court issue a preliminary or permanent injunction to halt the use of allegedly unfair or deceptive practices, to prevent an anticompetitive merger or unfair methods of competition from taking place, or to prevent violations of any statute enforced by the Commission.

Reports The Commission prepares studies of conditions and problems affecting the marketplace. Such reports may be used to inform legislative proposals in response to requests of the Congress and statutory directions, or for the information and guidance of the Commission, the executive branch of the Government, and the public. Such reports have provided the basis for significant legislation and have also led to voluntary changes in the conduct of business, with resulting benefits to the public.

Regional Offices—Federal Trade Commission

Region	Address	Director
East Central (DC, DE, MD, MI, OH, PA, VA, WV)	Suite 200, 1111 Superior Ave., Cleveland, OH 44114	John Mendenhall
Midwest (IA, IL, IN, KS, KY, MN, MO, ND, NE, SD, WI)	Suite 1860, 55 E. Monroe St., Chicago, IL 60603	C. Steven Baker
Northeast (CT, MA, ME, NH, NJ, NY, RI, VT, PR, VI)	Suite 318, One Bowling Green, New York, NY 10004	Barbara Anthony
Northwest (AK, ID, MT, OR, WA, WY)	Suite 2896, 915 2d Ave., Seattle, WA 98174	Charles A. Harwood
Southeast (AL, FL, GA, MS, NC, SC, TN)	Suite 1500, 225 Peachtree St., NE., Atlanta, GA 30303	Bradley Elbein
Southwest (AR, LA, NM, OK, TX)	Suite 2150, 1999 Bryan St., Dallas, TX 75201	(Vacancy)
Western (AZ, CA, CO, HI, NV, UT)	Suite 570, 901 Market St., San Francisco, CA 94103	Jeffrey A. Klurfeld
	Suite 700, 10877 Wilshire Blvd., Los Angeles, CA 90024	

Sources of Information

Contracts and Procurement Persons seeking to do business with the Federal Trade Commission should contact the Assistant CFO for Acquisitions, Federal Trade Commission, Washington, DC 20580. Phone, 202–326–3068. Fax, 202–326–3529. Internet, www.ftc.gov.

Employment Civil service registers are used in filling positions for economists, accountants, investigators, and other professional, administrative, and clerical personnel. The Federal Trade Commission employs a sizable number of attorneys under the excepted appointment procedure. All employment inquiries should be directed to the Director of Human Resources Management, Federal Trade Commission, Washington, DC 20580. Phone, 202–326–2021. Fax, 202–326–2328. Internet, www.ftc.gov.

General Inquiries Persons desiring information on consumer protection or restraint of trade questions, or to register a complaint, should contact the Federal Trade Commission (phone, 202–326–2222 or 877–382–4357) or the nearest regional office. Complaints may also be filed on the Internet at www.ftc.gov.

Publications Consumer and business education publications of the Commission are available through the Consumer Response Center, Federal Trade Commission, Washington, DC 20580. Phone, 877–382–4357. TTY, 866–653–4261. Internet, www.ftc.gov.

For further information, contact the Office of Public Affairs, Federal Trade Commission, 600 Pennsylvania Avenue NW., Washington, DC 20580. Phone, 202–326–2180. Fax, 202–326–3366. Internet, www.ftc.gov.

GENERAL SERVICES ADMINISTRATION

1800 F Street NW., Washington, DC 20405
Phone, 202–708–5082. Internet, www.gsa.gov.

Administrator of General Services — LURITA A. DOAN

Deputy Administrator	David L. Bibb
Chief of Staff	Alan R. Swendiman, *Acting*
Chairman, GSA Board of Contract Appeals	Stephen M. Daniels
Inspector General	Brian D. Miller
General Counsel	Alan R. Swendiman
Associate Administrator for Civil Rights	Madeline C. Caliendo
Associate Administrator for Citizen Services and Communications	Mary J. Pizzella
Associate Administrator for Congressional and Intergovernmental Affairs	Tom Dryer, *Acting*
Associate Administrator for Small Business Utilization	Felipe Mendoza
Associate Administrator for Performance Improvement	Emily W. Murphy, *Acting*
Chief Financial Officer	Kathleen M. Turco
Chief Information Officer	Michael W. Carleton
Chief People Officer	Gail T. Lovelace
Chief Acquisition Officer	Emily W. Murphy

FEDERAL ACQUISITION SERVICE

2200 Crystal Drive, Room 1100, Arlington, VA 22202
Phone, 703–605–5400. Fax, 703–605–9955.

Commissioner	G. Martin Wagner, *Acting*
Deputy Commissioner	(vacancy)
Chief Information Officer	Casey Coleman, *Acting*
Assistant Commissioner for Customer Accounts and Research	Mary A. Davie, *Acting*
Assistant Commissioner for Acquisition Management	Jeffrey A. Koses, *Acting*
Assistant Commissioner for Integrated Technology Services	James A. Williams, *Acting*
Assistant Commissioner for General Supplies and Services	Joseph H. Jeu
Assistant Commissioner for Travel, Motor Vehicle and Card Services	Barnaby L. Brasseux
Assistant Commissioner for Administration	Brenda K. Maxson, *Acting*
Controller	Jon A. Jordan

PUBLIC BUILDINGS SERVICE

1800 F Street NW., Washington, DC 20405
Phone, 202–501–1100

Commissioner	David L. Winstead
Deputy Commissioner	Anthony Costa
Chief of Staff	Cathleen C. Kronopolus, *Acting*
Assistant Commissioner for Organizational Resources	Kay L. McNew
Assistant Commissioner for Real Property Asset Management	William H. Matthews
Assistant Commissioner for Applied Science	Glen S. Hunter
Assistant Commissioner for Customer Service Management	Christopher Reutershan

Chief Architect	LESLIE L. SHEPHERD, *Acting*
Chief Financial Officer	WILLIAM E. BRADY

OFFICE OF GOVERNMENTWIDE POLICY

1800 F Street NW., Washington, DC 20405
Phone, 202–501–8880

Associate Administrator for Governmentwide Policy	JOHN G. SINDELAR, *Acting*
Deputy Associate Administrator	STANLEY F. KACZMARCZYK, *Acting*
Director, GSA Administrative Policy	JAMES L. DEAN
Deputy Associate Administrator for Technology Strategy	MARY J. MITCHELL
Director, Regulatory Information Service Center	JOHN C. THOMAS
Deputy Associate Administrator for Real Property Management	STANLEY F. KACZMARCZYK
Deputy Associate Administrator for Travel, Transportation and Asset Management	REBECCA R. RHODES

[For the General Services Administration statement of organization, see the *Code of Federal Regulations,* Title 41, Part 105–53]

The General Services Administration establishes policy for and provides economical and efficient management of Government property and records, including construction and operation of buildings; procurement and distribution of supplies; utilization and disposal of real and personal property; transportation, traffic, and communications management; and management of the governmentwide automatic data processing resources program.

The General Services Administration (GSA) was established by section 101 of the Federal Property and Administrative Services Act of 1949 (40 U.S.C. 751).

Contract Appeals The General Services Administration Board of Contract Appeals is responsible for resolving disputes arising out of contracts with the General Services Administration and other Government agencies. The Board is also empowered to hear and decide requests for review of transportation audit rate determinations; claims by Federal civilian employees regarding travel and relocation expenses; and claims for the proceeds of the sale of property of certain Federal civilian employees. In addition, the Board provides alternative dispute resolution services to executive agencies in both contract disputes which are the subject of a contracting officer's decision and other contract-related disputes. Although the Board is located within the agency, it functions as an independent tribunal.

For further information, contact the Board of Contract Appeals, General Services Administration, Washington, DC 20405. Phone, 202–501–0585.

Governmentwide Policy The Office of Governmentwide Policy (OGP) collaborates with the Federal community to develop policies and guidelines for the management of Government property, technology, and administrative services. OGP's policymaking authority and policy support activities encompass the areas covering electronic government and information technology, real property and the workplace, travel, transportation, personal property, aircraft, Federal motor vehicle fleet, mail, regulatory information and use of Federal advisory committees. OGP also provides leadership to interagency groups and facilities governmentwide management reform through the effective

GENERAL SERVICES ADMINISTRATION

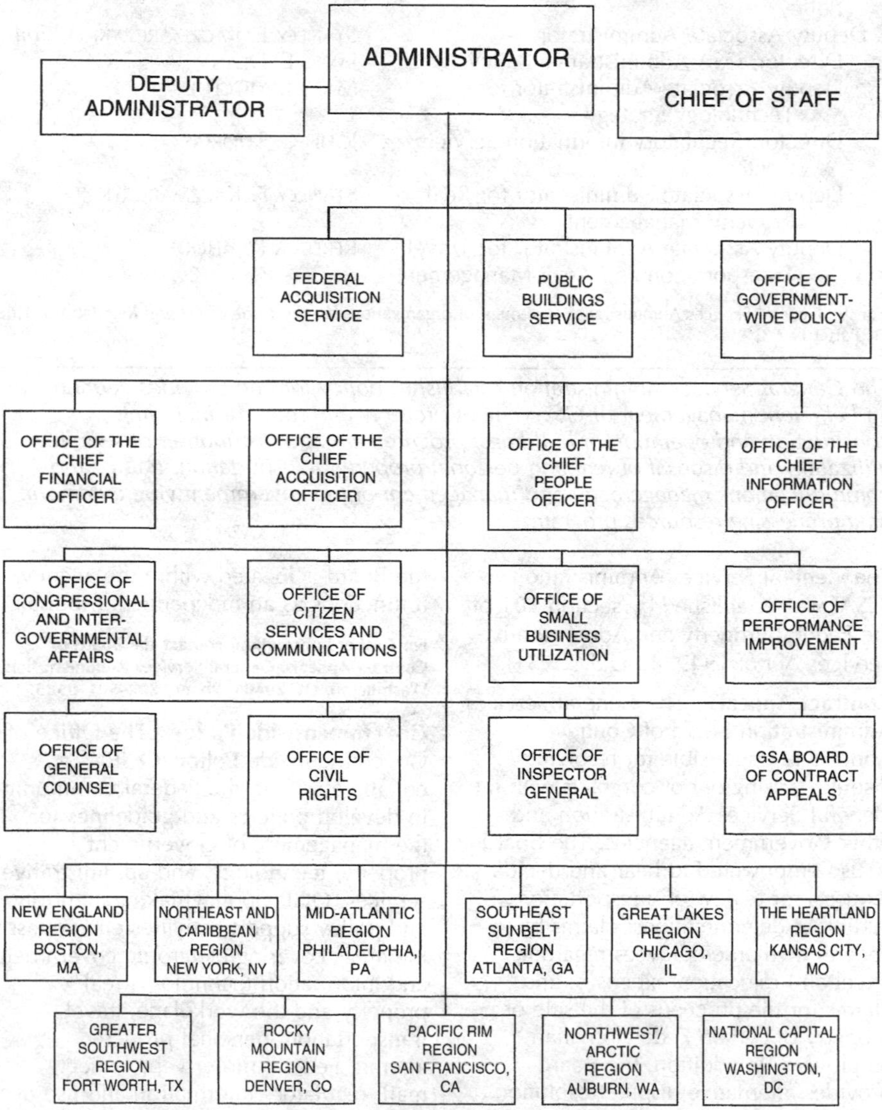

use of performance measures and best practices.

The Office of Technology Strategy provides policy guidance on issues pertaining to electronic business and technology and coordinates information technology strategies to improve Government effectiveness and efficiency. The Office fosters interagency collaboration on IT management policies and assists agencies on IT policy matters such as IT accommodation, security, smart cards, and electronic signatures. For further information, call 202–501–0202.

The Office of Real Property provides policy guidance in the responsible management of the Federal Government's real property assets and in the development of quality workplaces. It develops and issues Governmentwide management regulations and standards that relate to real property asset management and workplace development. Real property programs include real estate management, acquisition, disposal, design, construction, performance standards, delegations, safety and environmental issues, and sustainable design. For further information, call 202–501–0856.

The Office of Travel, Transportation and Asset Management develops Governmentwide policies to ensure the economical and efficient management of Government assets including aircraft and motor vehicles, transportation, traffic and audits, mail, passenger travel, and relocation allowances. It develops regulations, collects and analyzes Governmentwide data, manages interagency policy committees, and collaborates with customers and stakeholders to address and facilitate Governmentwide improvements. For further information, call 202–501–1777.

The Regulatory Information Services Center compiles and analyzes data on Governmentwide regulatory information and activities. The principal publication of the Center is the *Unified Agenda of Federal Regulatory and Deregulatory Actions,* which is published in the *Federal Register* every spring and fall and is available online at www.reginfo.gov. For further information, call 202–482–7345.

The Office of GSA Administrative Policy has nationwide responsibility for developing policies relating to the management of GSA's internal mail, fleet, space, personal property, forms and printing management, and governmentwide Standard and Optional Forms. In addition, the Office develops policy, training, evaluation, and performance metrics for the Federal Advisory Committee Program to maximize public participation in Federal decisionmaking through Federal Advisory Committees.

For further information, contact the Office of Governmentwide Policy. Phone, 202–501–8880. Internet, www.gsa.gov.

Citizen Services and Communications

The Office of Citizen Services and Communications (OCSC) serves as a central Federal gateway for citizens, businesses, other governments, and the media to easily obtain information and services from the Government on the Web, in print, over the telephone, or by e-mail. OCSC is organized into two components Citizen Services and Communications.

Citizen Services comprises the Federal Citizen Information Center which serves citizens, businesses, and other Government agencies by providing information and services via Firstgov.gov, 1–800–FED–INFO, and print publications through Pueblo, Colorado. It also develops and implements innovative technologies that improve the delivery of Government information and services to citizens through the Office of E-Gov Solutions Support. OCSC also collaborates with Federal, State, local, and foreign governments and intergovernmental organizations to promote more effective use of information technology and E-Gov solutions through the Office of Intergovernmental Solutions.

Communications, the other component of OCSC, plans, administers, and coordinates GSA media relations, develops and executes internal and external communications efforts, and responds to Freedom of Information Act requests and official agency correspondence. It also coordinates GSA-wide strategic marketing activities, events planning, graphics and audiovisual production, and writing and editing support services for the entire agency.

For further information, contact the Office of Citizen Services and Communications. Phone, 202–501–0705. Internet, www.gsa.gov.

Acquisitions The Office of the Chief Acquisition Officer is responsible for strengthening GSA's acquisition activities and ensuring that acquisition services are delivered to Federal agency customers in support of their missions of service, while balancing an emphasis on compliance, ethics, and integrity. It is also responsible for managing a broad range of acquisition activities including: ensuring compliance with applicable laws, regulations, and policies; fostering full and open competition for contract awards; developing the acquisition workforce; and accountability for acquisition decisionmaking.

Excellence in acquisition is the top priority for GSA. The "Get It Right" Plan affirms GSA's commitment to ensuring the proper use of GSA contracting vehicles and services.

For further information, contact the Office of the Chief Acquisition Officer. Phone, 202–501–1043.

Domestic Assistance Catalog The Federal Domestic Assistance Catalog Program collects and disseminates information on all federally operated domestic assistance programs such as grants, loans, and insurance. This information is published annually in the Catalog of Federal Domestic Assistance and electronically at www.cfda.gov.

Small Business Utilization The Office of Small Business Utilization focuses on programs, policy, and outreach to assist the small business community nationwide in doing business with GSA.

For further information, call 202–501–1021. Internet, www.gsa.gov/smallbusiness.

Small Business Centers—General Services Administration

Region	Address	Telephone
National Capital—Washington, DC	Rm. 1050, 7th & D Sts. SW., 20407	202–708–5804
New England—Boston, MA	Rm. 901, 10 Causeway St., 02222	617–565–8100
Northeast and Caribbean—New York, NY	Rm. 18–130, 26 Federal Plz., 10278	212–264–1234
Mid-Atlantic—Philadelphia, PA	9th Fl., 20 N. Eighth Street, 19107	215–466–4918
Southeast Sunbelt—Atlanta, GA	Suite 600, 77 Forsyth St., 30303	404–331–5103
Great Lakes—Chicago, IL	Rm. 3714, 230 S. Dearborn St., 60604	312–353–5383
Heartland—Kansas City, MO	Rm. 1161, 1500 E. Bannister Rd., 64131	816–926–7203
Southwest—Fort Worth, TX	Rm. 1E13A, 819 Taylor St., 76102	817–978–0800
Rocky Mountain—Denver, CO	Rm. 210, Denver Federal Ctr., 80225–0006	303–236–7409
Pacific Rim—San Francisco, CA	Rm. 5–6535, 450 Golden Gate Ave., 94102	415–522–2705
Satellite office—Los Angeles, CA	Rm. 3108, 300 N. Los Angeles St., 90012	213–894–3210
Northwest/Arctic—Auburn, WA	400 15th St. SW., 98001	253–931–7956

Federal Acquisition Service

The Federal Acquisition Service (FAS) offers services to customer agencies by providing innovative, compliant, and integrated solutions to today's acquisition challenges. Its key goal is to deliver excellent acquisition services that provide the best value, in terms of cost, quality, and service, for Federal agencies and taxpayers. This includes acquisition of products and services and full-service programs in information technology, telecommunications, professional services, supplies, motor vehicles, travel and transportation, charge cards, and personal property utilization and disposal.

FAS provides multiple channels for customers to acquire the products, services, and solutions they need. Key acquisition programs include multiple awards schedules and Governmentwide area contracts that provide customers easy access to a wide range of information technology, telecommunications, and professional products and services. It also provides its customers with access to the products and services they need through online Web sites such as GSA *Advantage!*, e-Buy, Schedules e-Library, GSA Auctions,

Transportation Management Services Solutions, and a myriad of other electronic tools.

For further information, contact the Office of the Commissioner, Federal Acquisition Service. Phone, 703–605–5400. Internet, www.gsa.gov.

Public Buildings Service

The Public Buildings Service (PBS) is the landlord for the civilian Federal Government. PBS provides a superior workplace for the Federal worker and superior value to the American taxpayer.

PBS designs, builds, leases, manages, and maintains space in office buildings, courthouses, laboratories, border stations, data processing centers, warehouses, and child care centers. It also repairs, alters, and renovates existing facilities and disposes of surplus Government properties. PBS is a leader in energy conservation, build green, and recycling. It preserves and maintains more than 400 historic properties in the Federal Government's inventory. PBS also commissions our country's most talented artists to create artwork for new Federal buildings and conserves a substantial inventory of artwork from the past.

PBS collects rent from Federal tenants, which is deposited into the Federal Buildings Fund, the principal funding mechanism for PBS.

For further information, contact the Office of the Commissioner, Public Buildings Service. Phone, 202–501–1100. Internet, www.gsa.gov/pbs.

Regional Offices—General Services Administration

Region	Address	Administrator
New England	Boston, MA (10 Causeway St., 02222)	Dennis R. Smith
Northeast and Caribbean	New York, NY (26 Federal Plz., 10278)	Eileen Long-Chelales
Mid-Atlantic	Philadelphia, PA (20 N. Eighth St., 19107–3191)	Barbara L. Shelton
Southeast Sunbelt	Atlanta, GA (Suite 600, 77 Forsyth St., 30303)	Edwin E. Fielder, Jr.
Great Lakes	Chicago, IL (230 S. Dearborn St., 60604)	James C. Handley
The Heartland	Kansas City, MO (1500 E. Bannister Rd., 64131)	Bradley Scott
Greater Southwest	Fort Worth, TX (819 Taylor St., 76102)	Scott Armey
Rocky Mountain	Denver, CO (Bldg. 41, Denver Federal Ctr., 80225–0006)	Larry E. Trujillo, Sr.
Pacific Rim	San Francisco, CA (5th Fl., 450 Golden Gate Ave., 94102)	Peter G. Stamison
Northwest/Arctic	Auburn, WA (GSA Ctr., 400 15th St. SW., 98002)	Jon R. Kvistad
National Capital	Washington, DC (7th & D Sts. SW., 20407)	Annie W. Everett, *Acting*

Sources of Information

Contracts Individuals seeking to do business with the General Services Administration may obtain detailed information from the Small Business Centers listed in the preceding text.

Electronic Access Information about GSA is available electronically through the Internet, at www.gsa.gov.

Employment Inquiries and applications should be directed to the Central Office Human Resources Division (CPS), Office of Human Resources Services, General Services Administration, Washington, DC 20405. Phone, 202–501–0370. Internet, www.gsa.gov (click "GSAjobs" to search for current job openings).

Fraud and Waste Contact the Inspector General's Hotline. Phone, 202–501–1780, or 800–424–5210.

Freedom of Information Act Requests Inquiries concerning policies pertaining to Freedom of Information Act matters should be addressed to the GSA FOIA Officer, FOIA/Correspondence Coordination Team (XAP), General Services Administration, Room 7126, Washington, DC 20405. Phone, 202–501–2262. Fax, 202–501–2727.

Privacy Act Requests Inquiries concerning policies pertaining to Privacy Act matters should be addressed to GSA Privacy Act Officer, Information Resources and Privacy Management Division (CIB), General Services Administration, Room 6224, Washington, DC 20405. Phone, 202–501–1452.

Property Disposal Inquiries about the redistribution or competitive sale of surplus real property should be directed to the Office of Property Disposal, Public Buildings Service, 1800 F Street NW., Washington, DC 20405. Phone, 202–501–0084.

Public and News Media Inquiries Inquiries from both the general public and news media should be directed to the Office of Communications, General Services Administration, 1800 F Street NW., Washington, DC 20405. Phone, 202–501–1231.

Publications Many GSA publications are available at moderate prices through the bookstores of the Government Printing Office (http://bookstore.gpo.gov). Orders and inquiries concerning publications and subscriptions for sale by the Government Printing Office should be directed to the Superintendent of Documents, Government Printing Office, Washington, DC 20401. Others may be obtained free or at cost from a Small Business Center. If a publication is not distributed by any of the stores, inquiries should be directed to the originating agency's service or office. The addresses for GSA inquiries are:

Public Buildings Service (P), General Services Administration, Washington, DC 20405

Federal Acquisition Service (F), General Services Administration, 2200 Crystal Drive, Room 1100, Arlington, VA 22202

Office of Finance (BC), General Services Administration, Washington, DC 20405

For a free copy of the *U.S. Government TTY Directory*, contact the Federal Citizen Information Center, Department TTY, Pueblo, CO 81009. Phone, 888–878–3256. Internet, www.gsa.gov/frs. For a free copy of the quarterly *Consumer Information Catalog,* including information on food, nutrition, employment, Federal benefits, the environment, fraud, privacy and Internet issues, investing and credit, and education, write to the Federal Citizen Information Center, Pueblo, CO 81009. Phone, 888–878–3256. Internet, www.pueblo.gsa.gov.

For information about Federal programs and services, call the Federal Citizen Information Center's National Contact Centers at 800–333–4636, Monday through Friday from 8 a.m. to 8 p.m. eastern standard time.

For a free copy of the *Federal Relay Service Brochure*, call 877–387–2001. TTY, 202–585–1840.

Small Business Activities Inquiries concerning programs to assist small businesses should be directed to one of the Small Business Centers listed in the preceding text.

Speakers Inquiries and requests for speakers should be directed to the Office of Citizen Services and Communications (X), General Services Administration, Washington, DC 20405 (phone, 202–501–0705); or contact the nearest regional office.

For further information concerning the General Services Administration, contact the Office of Citizen Services and Communications (X), General Services Administration, Washington, DC 20405. Phone, 202–501–0705. Internet, www.gsa.gov.

INTER–AMERICAN FOUNDATION

901 North Stuart Street, Arlington, VA 22203
Phone, 703–306–4301. Internet, www.iaf.gov.

Board of Directors:

Chair	Roger W. Wallace
Vice Chair	Nadine M. Hogan
Directors	Kay Kelley Arnold, Adolfo A. Franco, Nadine M. Hogan, Roger W. Wallace, (5 vacancies)

Staff:

President	Larry L. Palmer

General Counsel	JENNIFER HODGES
Vice President for Programs	RAMÓN DAUBÓN
Vice President for External Affairs	PATRICK BRESLIN
Vice President for Operations	LINDA B. KOLKO

The Inter-American Foundation is an independent Federal agency that supports social and economic development in Latin America and the Caribbean. It makes grants primarily to private, local, and community organizations that carry out self-help projects.

The Inter-American Foundation (IAF) was created in 1969 (22 U.S.C. 290f) as an experimental U.S. foreign assistance program. IAF works in Latin America and the Caribbean to promote equitable, participatory, and sustainable self-help development by awarding grants directly to local organizations throughout the region. It also enters into partnerships with public and private sector entities to scale up support and mobilize local, national, and international resources for grassroots development. From all of its innovative funding experiences, IAF extracts lessons learned and best practices to share with other donors and development practitioners throughout the hemisphere.

IAF is governed by a nine-person Board of Directors appointed by the President with the advice and consent of the Senate. Six members are drawn from the private sector and three from the Federal Government. The Board of Directors appoints the President of IAF.

For further information, contact the Office of the President, Inter-American Foundation, 901 North Stuart Street, Arlington, VA 22203. Phone, 703–306–4301. Internet, www.iaf.gov.

MERIT SYSTEMS PROTECTION BOARD

1615 M Street NW., Fifth Floor, Washington, DC 20419
Phone, 202–653–7200. Internet, www.mspb.gov.

Chairman	NEIL A.G. MCPHIE
Vice Chair	MARY M. ROSE
Member	BARBARA J. SAPIN
Chief of Staff	TRACEY WATKINS
Clerk of the Board	BENTLEY M. ROBERTS, JR.
Director, Financial and Administrative Management	CHARLIE ROCHE
Director, Information Resources Management	TOMMY HWANG
Director, Office of Appeals Counsel	LYNORE CARNES
Director, Office of Equal Employment Opportunity	JULIO MATTA
Director, Office of Policy and Evaluation	STEVE NELSON
Director, Office of Regional Operations	DEBORAH MIRON
General Counsel	MARTHA SCHNEIDER

[For the Merit Systems Protection Board statement of organization, see the *Code of Federal Regulations,* Title 5, Part 1200]

The Merit Systems Protection Board protects the integrity of the Federal personnel merit systems and the rights of Federal employees. In overseeing the personnel practices of the Federal Government, the Board conducts special studies of the merit systems, hears and decides charges of wrongdoing and employee appeals of adverse agency actions, and orders corrective and disciplinary actions when appropriate.

The Merit Systems Protection Board is a successor agency to the United States Civil Service Commission, established by act of January 16, 1883 (22 Stat. 403). Reorganization Plan No. 2 of 1978 (5 U.S.C. app.) redesignated part of the Commission as the Merit Systems Protection Board.

Activities

The Board has responsibility for hearing and adjudicating appeals by Federal employees of adverse personnel actions, such as removals, suspensions, and demotions. It also resolves cases involving reemployment rights, the denial of periodic step increases in pay, actions against administrative law judges, and charges of prohibited personnel practices, including charges in connection with whistleblowing. The Board has the authority to enforce its decisions and to order corrective and disciplinary actions. An employee or applicant for employment involved in an appealable action that also involves an allegation of discrimination may ask the Equal Employment Opportunity Commission to review a Board decision. Final decisions and orders of the Board can be appealed to the U.S. Court of Appeals for the Federal Circuit.

The Board reviews regulations issued by the Office of Personnel Management and has the authority to require agencies to cease compliance with any regulation that could constitute a prohibited personnel practice. It also conducts special studies of the civil service and other executive branch merit systems and reports to the President and the Congress on whether the Federal work force is being adequately protected against political abuses and prohibited personnel practices.

Regional Offices—Merit Systems Protection Board

Region	Address	Director	Telephone
Atlanta Regional Office	401 W. Peachtree St. NW., Atlanta, GA 30308	Thomas J. Lanphear	404–730–2755
Central Regional Office	31st Fl., 230 S. Dearborn St., Chicago, IL 60604	Martin W. Baumgaertner	312–353–2923
Dallas Regional Office	Rm. 620, 1100 Commerce St., Dallas, TX 75242	Sharon F. Jackson	214–767–0555
Northeastern Regional Office.	Rm. 501, 2d & Chestnut Sts., Philadelphia, PA 19106.	William L. Boulden	215–597–9960
Washington Regional Office.	Suite 205, 1800 Diagonal Rd., Alexandria, VA 22314.	P.J. Winzer	703–756–6250
Western Regional Office	Suite 400, 4th Fl., 250 Montgomery St., San Francisco, CA 94104.	Amy Dunning	415–705–2935

Field Offices—Merit Systems Protection Board

Region	Address	Chief Administrative Judge	Telephone
Denver, CO	Suite 318, 165 S. Union Blvd., 80228.	Maxanne Witkin	303–969–5101
New York, NY	Rm. 3137A, 26 Federal Plz., 10278	Arthur S. Joseph	212–264–9372

For further information, contact the Merit Systems Protection Board, 1615 M Street NW., Washington, DC 20419. Phone, 202–653–7200 or 800–209–8960. TDD, 800–209–8960. Fax, 202–653–7130. E-mail, mspb@mspb.gov. Internet, www.mspb.gov.

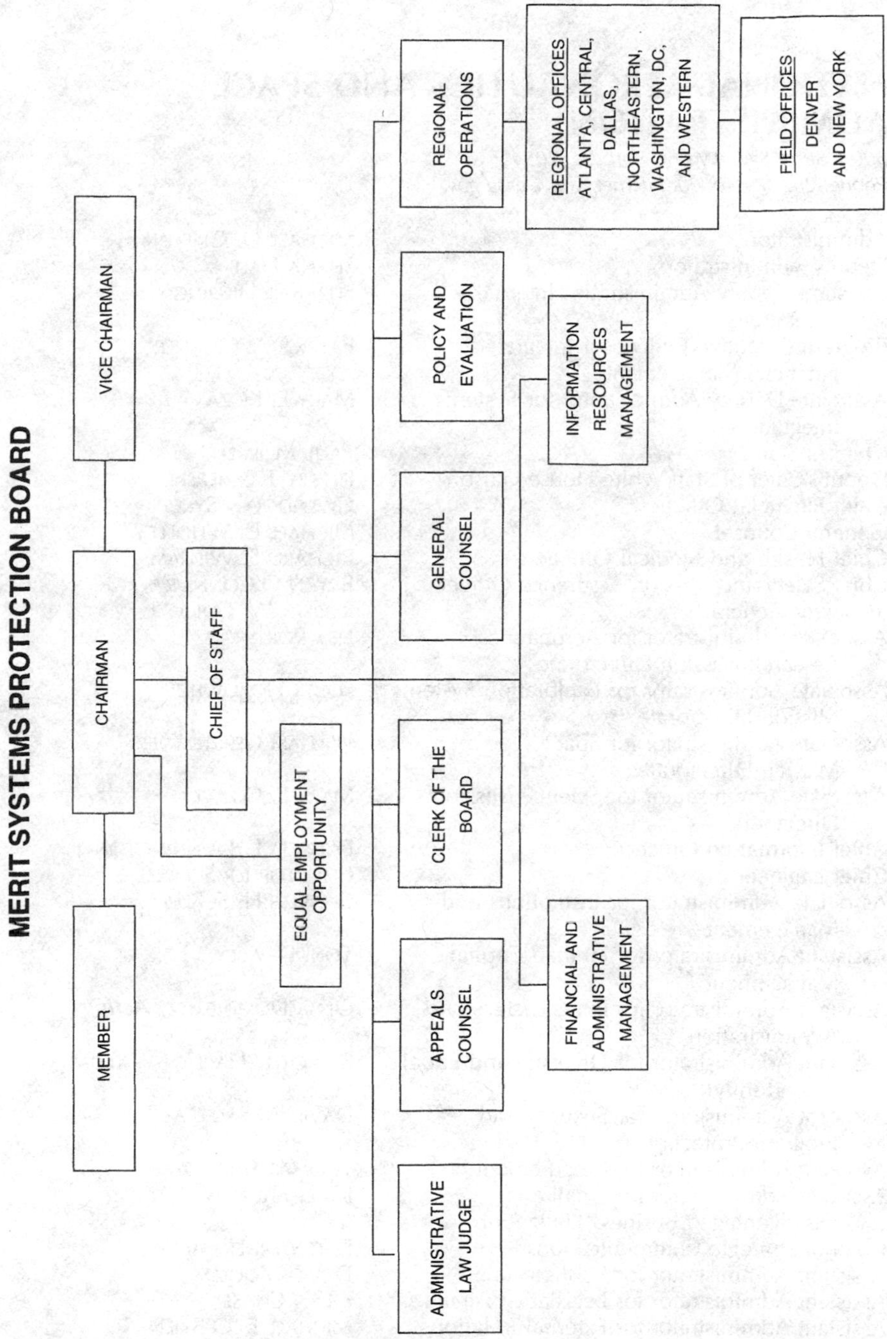
MERIT SYSTEMS PROTECTION BOARD
MEMBER
CHAIRMAN
VICE CHAIRMAN
CHIEF OF STAFF
EQUAL EMPLOYMENT OPPORTUNITY
ADMINISTRATIVE LAW JUDGE
APPEALS COUNSEL
CLERK OF THE BOARD
GENERAL COUNSEL
POLICY AND EVALUATION
REGIONAL OPERATIONS
FINANCIAL AND ADMINISTRATIVE MANAGEMENT
INFORMATION RESOURCES MANAGEMENT
REGIONAL OFFICES
ATLANTA, CENTRAL, DALLAS, NORTHEASTERN, WASHINGTON, DC, AND WESTERN
FIELD OFFICES
DENVER AND NEW YORK

NATIONAL AERONAUTICS AND SPACE ADMINISTRATION

300 E Street SW., Washington, DC 20546
Phone, 202–358–0000. Internet, www.nasa.gov.

Administrator	MICHAEL D. GRIFFIN
Deputy Administrator	SHANA DALE
Assistant Deputy Administrator, Internal Operations	SUZANNE HILDING
Program Executive Officer for Integrated Financial Management	PATRICK A. CIGANER
Associate Deputy Administrator for Systems Integration	MARY E. KICZA
Chief of Staff	PAUL MORRELL
Deputy Chief of Staff/White House Liaison	JEFFREY T. JEZIERSKI
Chief Financial Officer	GWENDOLYN SYKES
General Counsel	MICHAEL C. WHOLLEY
Chief Health and Medical Officer	RICHARD S. WILLIAMS
Chief Safety and Mission Assurance Officer	BRYAN O'CONNOR
Inspector General	ROBERT W. COBB
Associate Administrator for Aeronautics Research Mission Directorate	LISA PORTER
Associate Administrator for Exploration Systems Mission Directorate	SCOTT HOROWITZ
Associate Administrator for Space Operations Mission Directorate	WILLIAM GERSTEMAIER
Associate Administrator for Science Mission Directorate	MARY L. CLEAVE
Chief Information Officer	PATRICIA L. DUNNINGTON
Chief Engineer	CHRISTOPHER SCOLESE
Associate Administrator for Institutions and Management	CHARLES H. SCALES
Assistant Administrator for Human Capital Management	TONI DAWSEY
Assistant Administrator for Infrastructure and Administration	OLGA DOMINGUEZ, *Acting*
Assistant Administrator for Diversity and Equal Opportunity	DOROTHY HAYDEN-WATKINS
Assistant Administrator for Security and Program Protection	DAVID A. SALEEBA
Assistant Administrator for Procurement	THOMAS S. LUEDTKE
Assistant Administrator for Small and Disadvantaged Business Utilization	JAMES BALINSKAS, *Acting*
Chief of Strategic Communications	ERIC STERNER, *Acting*
Assistant Administrator for Public Affairs	DAVID MOULD
Assistant Administrator for Legislative Affairs	BRIAN CHASE
Assistant Administrator for External Relations	MICHAEL F. O'BRIEN

NASA Centers

Director, Ames Research Center	MARVIN CHRISTENSEN, *Acting*
Director, Dryden Flight Research Center	KEVIN L. PETERSEN
Director, John H. Glenn Research Center	WOODROW WHITLOW

Director, Goddard Space Flight Center	Edward J. Weiler
Director, Lyndon B. Johnson Space Center	Michael Coats
Director, John F. Kennedy Space Center	James W. Kennedy
Director, Langley Research Center	Lesa Roe
Director, George C. Marshall Space Flight Center	David A. King
Director, John C. Stennis Space Center	Richard Gilbrech
Director, Jet Propulsion Laboratory	Charles Elachi

[For the National Aeronautics and Space Administration statement of organization, see the *Code of Federal Regulations,* Title 14, Part 1201]

The National Aeronautics and Space Administration maintains the United States' role as a leader in aeronautical and space science technology by improving the usefulness, performance, speed, safety, and efficiency of aeronautical and space vehicles and by conducting space flight research. It also conducts space exploration activities with manned and unmanned vehicles and utilizes the aeronautical and space resources of the United States and other nations for peaceful purposes.

The National Aeronautics and Space Administration (NASA) was established by the National Aeronautics and Space Act of 1958, as amended (42 U.S.C. 2451 *et seq.*).

Activities

Aeronautics Research Directorate The Aeronautics Research Mission Directorate conducts research and technology activities to develop the knowledge, tools, and technologies to support the development of future air and space vehicles and to support the transformation of the Nations's air transportation system. The Directorate's programs focus on cutting-edge, fundamental research in traditional aeronautical disciplines, as well as emerging fields with promising applications to aeronautics, and are conducted in conjunction with industry, academia, and other U.S. Government departments and agencies, including the Federal Aviation Administration and the Department of Defense.

For further information, call 202–358–5241.

Space Operations The Office of Space Operations (OSO) provides the foundation for NASA's space program—space travel for human and robotic missions, in-space laboratories, and the means to return data to Earth. OSO is responsible for many critical enabling capabilities that make possible much of the science, research, and exploration achievements of the rest of NASA. This is done through three themes: the International Space Station, Space Shuttle, and Space and Flight Support.

The International Space Station supports activities for establishing a permanent human presence in Earth's orbit. It provides a long-duration, habitable laboratory for science and research activities.

The Space Shuttle, first launched in 1981, provides the only current capability in the United States for human access to space. The Shuttle's focus over the next several years will be the assembly of the International Space Station after which it will be phased out of service.

The Space and Flight Support theme encompasses space communications, launch services, and rocket propulsion testing. Space communications consists of three programs: Tracking and Data Relay Satellite System, NASA's spectrum allocation, and Integrated Services Network. The launch services program focuses on NASA's launch and payload processing requirements for payloads not requiring the Space Shuttle. The rocket propulsion testing program supports the flight readiness of various liquid propulsion engines and acts as a test bed for rocket engines of the future.

For further information, call 202–358–2015.

NATIONAL AERONAUTICS AND SPACE ADMINISTRATION

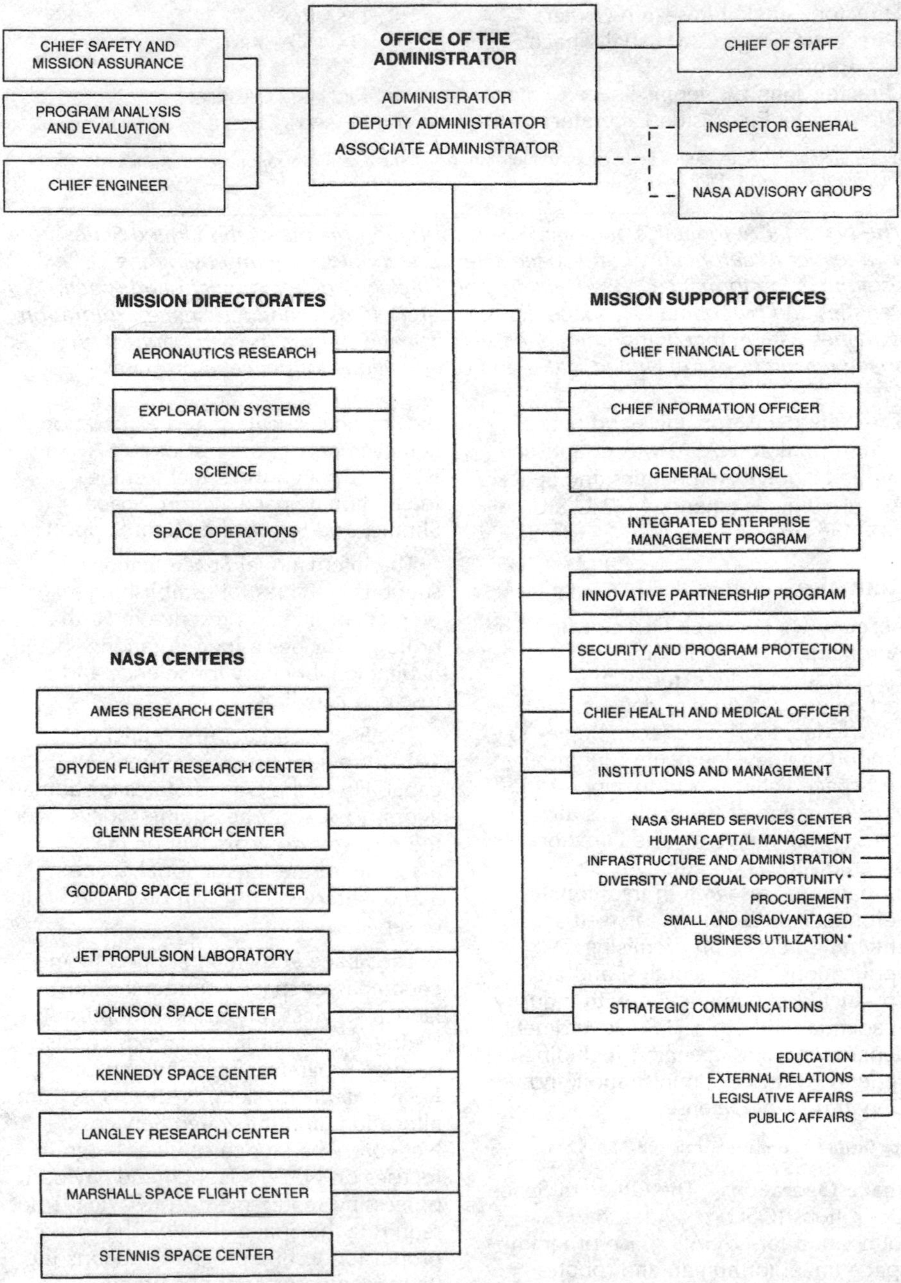

* In accordance with law, the offices of Diversity and Equal Opportunity and Small and Disadvantaged Business Utilization maintain reporting relationships to the Deputy Administrator and Administrator.

Science Mission Directorate The Science Mission Directorate carries out the scientific exploration of the Earth, Moon, Mars, and beyond, charting the best route of discovery. The mission directorate manages and sponsors research, flight missions, advanced technology development, and related activities. It works to expand our understanding of the Earth and the Sun and the Sun's effect on the solar system environments; explore the solar system with robots to study its origins and evolution including the origins of life within it; and explore the universe beyond, from the search for planets and life in other solar systems to the origin, evolution, and destiny of the universe itself.

For further information, call 202–358–1409.

NASA Centers

Ames Research Center The Ames Research Center, located in California's Silicon Valley, provides solutions to NASA's exploration questions through interdisciplinary scientific discovery and innovative technology systems. The Center provides leadership in astrobiology, information science, nanotechnology, advanced thermal protection systems, human factors, and the development of new tools for a safer and more efficient national airspace. It also develops unique partnerships and collaborations, exemplified by NASA's Astrobiology Institute and Research Park and the University Affiliated Research Center.

Dryden Flight Research Center The Dryden Flight Research Center, located at Edwards, CA, is NASA's primary installation for flight research. Since 1946, Dryden's researchers have led the way in major advancements to the design and capabilities of many civilian and military aircraft. Dryden's workforce expertise in aeronautics and in the development of flight research tools and techniques, coupled with the suite of specialized laboratories and facilities needed for flight validation, are key to the development and maturation of new vehicles.

Glenn Research Center The John H. Glenn Research Center at Lewis Field, located in Cleveland, OH, provides customer-focused technology solutions that enable the NASA mission and other national goals. Our products range from basic research through flight systems, based on our world-class capabilities in aeronautics and space.

Goddard Space Flight Center The Goddard Space Flight Center, located in Greenbelt, MD, expands the knowledge of Earth and its environment, the solar system, and the universe through observations from space. The Center also conducts scientific investigations, develops and operates space systems, and advances essential technologies.

Johnson Space Center The Lyndon B. Johnson Space Center, located in Houston, TX, leads the United States in the human exploration of space. The Center has made major advances in science, technology, engineering, and medicine and has led the Nation's human space flight programs and projects. It strives to advance the Nation's exploration of the universe with its expertise in medical, biomedical, and life sciences, lunar and planetary geosciences, crew and mission operations, crew health and safety, project management, and space systems engineering. The Center also leads worldwide research in extraterrestrial materials curation and the interaction between humans and robotics, as well as the biology and physiology of humans in space.

Kennedy Space Center The John F. Kennedy Center, located in Florida, is responsible for NASA's space launch operation and spaceport and range technologies. Home to the Space Shuttle fleet and the launch services program, it carries out its primary mission by managing the processing and launch of astronaut crews; the Space Shuttle and associated payloads; International Space Station elements, research experiments, and supplies; and enabling the payload processing of a wide variety of robotics payloads launched on commercial services into space. The Center supports the Space Shuttle and International

Space Station programs and serves as NASA's focal point for spaceport and range technology development efforts to provide advanced technologies, systems, and techniques to increase safety and security and reduce the cost of access to space.

Langley Research Center The Langley Research Center, located in Hampton, VA, is renowned for its scientific and technological expertise in aerospace research, systems integration, and atmospheric science. Since 1917, the Center's staff has undertaken research in aeronautics, and more recently, space technology. Langley leads NASA's initiative in aviation safety and security, quiet-aircraft technology, small-aircraft transportation systems, and aerospace vehicles systems technology. It also supports space programs with atmospheric research and technology testing and development. Researchers have developed and validated technologies to improve the effectiveness, capability, comfort, efficiency, and safety of the Nation's air transportation system. The Center continues to have a principal role in understanding and protecting our planet through atmospheric measurement, instruments, missions, and prediction algorithms. In 2003, NASA's Engineering and Safety Center was established at Langley to improve mission safety by performing independent engineering assessments, testing, analysis, and evaluation to determine appropriate preventative and corrective action for problems, trends, or issues across NASA programs and projects.

Marshall Space Flight Center The George C. Marshall Space Flight Center, located in Huntsville, AL, provides and maintains NASA core competencies in the areas of space transportation and propulsion systems development; large complex systems and infrastructure development and integration; and applied materials and manufacturing process development. The Center manages key propulsion system hardware and technologies for the Space Shuttle program; develops next generation space transportation and propulsion systems; and develops hardware and provides payload operation services for the International Space Station. It also maintains state-of-the-art facilities that support ongoing Agency programs and projects. Other key programs include the Chandra X-Ray Observatory, Gravity Probe-B, Demonstration of Autonomous Rendezvous Technology, Discovery and New Frontiers, Multipurpose Logistics Modules, Environmental Control and Life Support Systems, and Nodes for the International Space Station.

Stennis Space Center The John C. Stennis Center, located near Bay St. Louis, MS, has served as NASA's rocket propulsion testing ground for more than four decades. Today, the Center provides test services not only for America's space program, but also for the Department of Defense and the private sector. The Center's Earth Science Applications Directorate leads NASA's efforts to help solve problems on Earth related to homeland security, agricultural efficiency, disaster preparedness, and coastal management. Through the use of NASA's Earth science research, remote sensing, and other technical capabilities, the Directorate bridges the gap between Earth science research results and the use of its data to help its partner agencies.

Government-Owned/Contractor-Operated Facility

Jet Propulsion Laboratory The Laboratory, which is operated under contract by the California Institute of Technology in Pasadena, CA, develops spacecraft and space sensors and conducts mission operations and ground-based research in support of solar system exploration, Earth science and applications, Earth and ocean dynamics, space physics and astronomy, and life science and information systems technology. It is also responsible for the operation of the Deep Space Network in support of NASA projects.

Sources of Information

Contracts and Small Business Activities Inquiries regarding contracting for small business opportunities with NASA should be directed to the Assistant Administrator for Small and Disadvantaged Business Utilization, NASA Headquarters, 300 E Street SW., Washington, DC 20546. Phone, 202–358–2088.

Employment Direct all inquiries to the Personnel Director of the nearest NASA Center or, for the Washington, DC, metropolitan area, to the Chief, Headquarters Personnel Branch, NASA Headquarters, Washington, DC 20546. Phone, 202–358–1543.

OIG Hotline An individual may report crimes, fraud, waste, and abuse in NASA programs and operations by calling the OIG Hotline (phone, 800–424–9183); by writing to the NASA Inspector General, P.O. Box 23089, L'Enfant Plaza Station, Washington, DC 20026; or by sending an electronic message from the OIG's Web site (Internet, www.hq.nasa.gov/office/org/hq/hotline.html).

Publications, Speakers, Films, and Exhibit Services Several publications concerning these services can be obtained by contacting the Public Affairs Officer of the nearest NASA Center. Publications include *NASA Directory of Services for the Public, NASA Film List,* and *NASA Educational Publications List.* The headquarters telephone directory and certain publications and picture sets are available for sale from the Superintendent of Documents, Government Printing Office, Washington, DC 20402. Telephone directories for NASA Centers are available only from the Centers. Publications and documents not available for sale from the Superintendent of Documents or the National Technical Information Service (Springfield, VA 22151) may be obtained from NASA Center's Information Center in accordance with the NASA regulation concerning freedom of information.

Reading Room NASA Headquarters Information Center, Room 1H23, 300 E Street SW., Washington, DC 20546. Phone, 202–358–0000.

For further information, contact the Headquarters Information Center, National Aeronautics and Space Administration, Washington, DC 20546. Phone, 202–358–0000. Internet, www.nasa.gov.

NATIONAL ARCHIVES AND RECORDS ADMINISTRATION

8601 Adelphi Road, College Park, Maryland 20740–6001
Phone, 866–272–6272. Internet, www.archives.gov.

Archivist of the United States	Allen Weinstein
Deputy Archivist of the United States	Lewis J. Bellardo
Assistant Archivist for Administration Services	Adrienne C. Thomas
Assistant Archivist for Information Services	Martha Morphy, *Acting*
Assistant Archivist for Presidential Libraries	Sharon K. Fawcett
Assistant Archivist for Records Services—Washington, DC	Michael J. Kurtz
Assistant Archivist for Regional Records Services	Thomas E. Mills
Director of the Federal Register	Raymond A. Mosley
Director, Congressional Affairs and Communications Staff	John A. Constance
Director, Equal Employment Opportunity and Diversity Programs	Robert Jew

Director, Information Security Oversight Office	J. William Leonard
Director, Policy and Planning Staff	Susan M. Ashtianie
Executive Director, National Historical Publications and Records Commission	Max J. Evans
General Counsel	Gary M. Stern
Inspector General	Paul Brachfeld

[For the National Archives and Records Administration statement of organization, see the *Federal Register* of June 25, 1985, 50 FR 26278]

The National Archives and Records Administration ensures, for citizens and Federal officials, ready access to essential evidence that documents the rights of American citizens, the actions of Federal officials, and the national experience. It establishes policies and procedures for managing U.S. Government records; manages the Presidential Libraries system; and publishes the laws, regulations, and Presidential and other public documents.

The National Archives and Records Administration (NARA) is the successor agency to the National Archives Establishment, which was created in 1934 and subsequently incorporated into the General Services Administration as the National Archives and Records Service in 1949. NARA was established as an independent agency in the executive branch of the Government by act of October 19, 1984 (44 U.S.C. 2101 *et seq.*), effective April 1, 1985.

Activities

Archival Program The National Archives and Records Administration maintains the historically valuable records of the U.S. Government dating from the Revolutionary War era to the recent past; arranges and preserves records and prepares finding aids to facilitate their use; makes records available for use in research rooms in its facilities and via the Internet; answers written and oral requests for information contained in its holdings; and, for a fee, provides copies of records. In addition, many important records are available on microfilm and on the NARA Web site, at www.archives.gov. Historically valuable records created in the Washington, DC, area and in the custody of NARA are maintained in NARA facilities in the Washington, DC, area. Historically valuable records of high regional or local interest in the custody of NARA are maintained in the NARA regional archives (see the "Regional Records Services" section). NARA also has eight affiliated archives that hold NARA-owned records on behalf of NARA and make them available to the public.

For further information concerning records in the custody of NARA, contact the Customer Services Division. Phone, 202–357–5400 or 866–272–6272. Fax, 301–837–0483. E-mail, inquire@nara.gov.

Washington Area Records Facilities—National Archives and Records Administration

Facility	Address	Director	Telephone
National Archives	700 Pennsylvania Ave. NW., Washington, DC 20408.	James Hastings	202–357–5393
National Archives at College Park	8601 Adelphi Rd., College Park, MD 20740.	Sharon Gibbs Thibodeau	301–837–3400
Washington National Records Center.	4205 Suitland Rd., Suitland, MD 20746.	Alan Kramer	301–778–1600

Laws, Regulations, and Presidential Documents The Office of the Federal Register prepares and publishes a wide variety of public documents. Upon issuance, acts of Congress are published in slip law (pamphlet) form and then cumulated and published for each session of Congress in the *United States Statutes at Large*.

Each Federal workday, the *Federal Register* is published, containing current Presidential proclamations and Executive

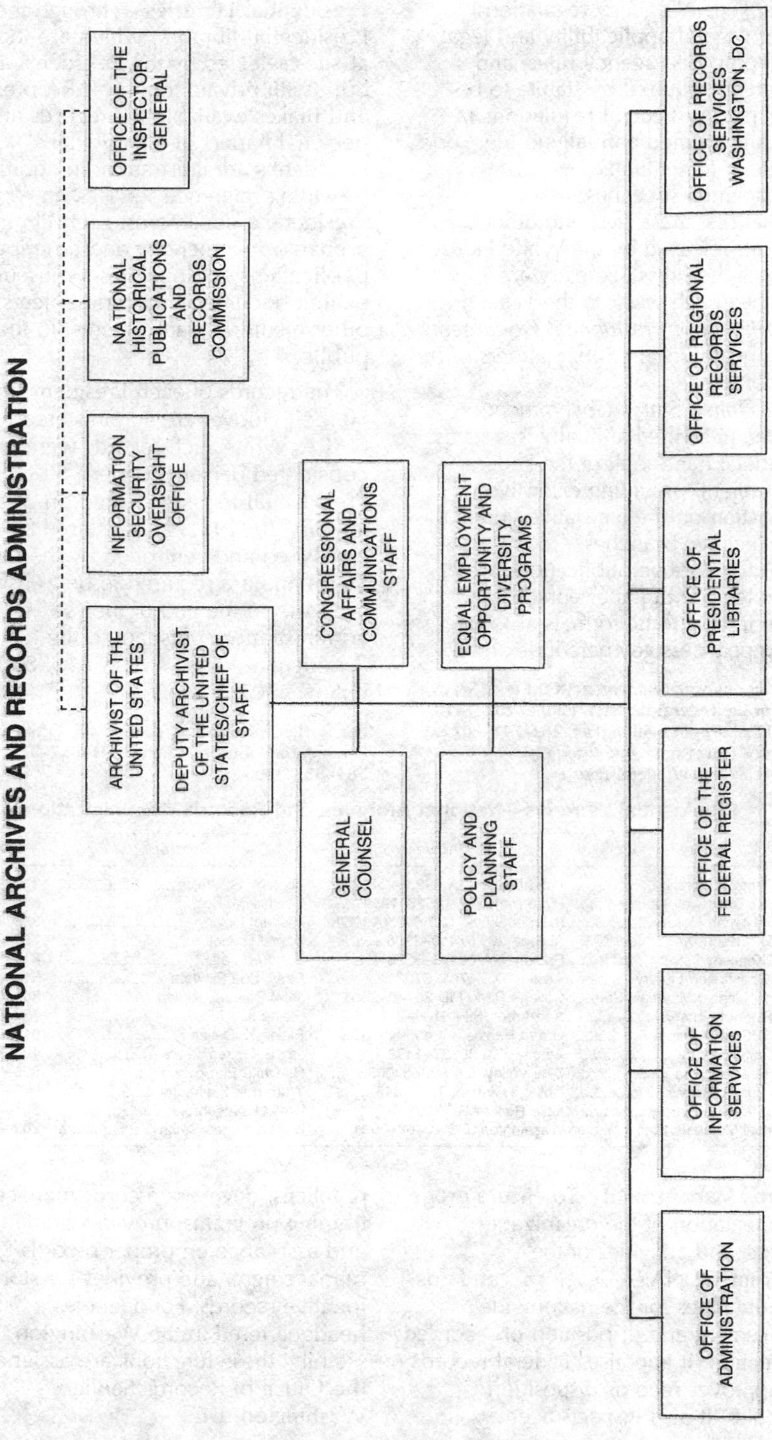
NATIONAL ARCHIVES AND RECORDS ADMINISTRATION
ARCHIVIST OF THE UNITED STATES
DEPUTY ARCHIVIST OF THE UNITED STATES/CHIEF OF STAFF
INFORMATION SECURITY OVERSIGHT OFFICE
NATIONAL HISTORICAL PUBLICATIONS AND RECORDS COMMISSION
OFFICE OF THE INSPECTOR GENERAL
CONGRESSIONAL AFFAIRS AND COMMUNICATIONS STAFF
GENERAL COUNSEL
EQUAL EMPLOYMENT OPPORTUNITY AND DIVERSITY PROGRAMS
POLICY AND PLANNING STAFF
OFFICE OF RECORDS SERVICES WASHINGTON, DC
OFFICE OF REGIONAL RECORDS SERVICES
OFFICE OF PRESIDENTIAL LIBRARIES
OFFICE OF THE FEDERAL REGISTER
OFFICE OF INFORMATION SERVICES
OFFICE OF ADMINISTRATION

orders, Federal agency regulations having general applicability and legal effect, proposed agency rules, and documents required by statute to be published. All Federal regulations in force are codified annually in the *Code of Federal Regulations.*

Presidential speeches, news conferences, messages, and other materials released by the White House Office of the Press Secretary are published each week in the *Weekly Compilation of Presidential Documents* and annually in the *Public Papers of the Presidents.*

The United States Government Manual, published annually, serves as the official handbook of the Federal Government, providing extensive information on the legislative, judicial, and executive branches.

All of the above publications are available in both paper editions and online in electronic formats at www.gpoaccess.gov/nara/index.html.

For further information, contact Customer Service, Office of the Federal Register. Phone, 202–741–6000. TTY, 202–741–6086. Fax, 202–741–6012. E-mail, info@fedreg.nara.gov. Internet, www.archives.gov/federal-register.

Presidential Libraries Through the Presidential libraries, which are located at sites selected by the Presidents and built with private funds, NARA preserves and makes available the records and personal papers of a particular President's administration. In addition to providing reference services on Presidential documents, each library prepares documentary and descriptive publications and operates a museum to exhibit documents, historic objects, and other memorabilia of interest to the public.

The records of each President since Herbert Hoover are administered by NARA. While such records were once considered personal papers, all Presidential records created on or after January 20, 1981, are declared by law to be owned and controlled by the United States and are required to be transferred to NARA at the end of the administration, pursuant to the Presidential Records Act of 1978 (44 U.S.C. 2201 *et seq.*).

For further information, contact the Office of Presidential Libraries. Phone, 301–837–3250. Fax, 301–837–3199.

Presidential Libraries—National Archives and Records Administration

Library	City/Address	Director	Telephone
Herbert Hoover Library	West Branch, IA 52358–0488	Timothy G. Walch	319–643–5301
Franklin D. Roosevelt Library	Hyde Park, NY 12538–1999	Cynthia M. Koch	845–486–7770
Harry S. Truman Library	Independence, MO 64050–1798	Michael Devine	816–268–8200
Dwight D. Eisenhower Library	Abilene, KS 67410–2900	Daniel D. Holt	785–263–6700
John F. Kennedy Library	Boston, MA 02125–3398	Deborah Leff	617–514–1600
Lyndon B. Johnson Library	Austin, TX 78705–5702	Betty Sue Flowers	512–721–0200
Nixon Presidential Materials Staff	College Park, MD 20740–6001	John Powers, *Acting*	301–837–3290
Gerald R. Ford Library	Ann Arbor, MI 48109–2114	Elaine K. Didier	734–205–0555
Gerald R. Ford Museum	Grand Rapids, MI 49504–5353	Elaine K. Didier	616–254–0400
Jimmy Carter Library	Atlanta, GA 30307–1498	Jay E. Hakes	404–865–7100
Ronald Reagan Library	Simi Valley, CA 93065–0666	R. Duke Blackwood	805–577–4000
George Bush Library	College Station, TX 77845	Warren L. Finch, Jr.	979–691–4000
William J. Clinton Library	Little Rock, AR 72201	David E. Alsobrook	501–374–4242
Presidential Materials Staff	Washington, DC 20408–0001	Nancy Kegan Smith	202–357–5200

Records Management To ensure proper documentation of the organization, policies, and activities of the Government, NARA develops standards and guidelines for the nationwide management and disposition of recorded information. It appraises Federal records and approves records disposition schedules. It also inspects agency records and records management practices, develops records management training programs, provides guidance and assistance on proper records management, and provides for storage of inactive records. For agencies headquartered in the Washington, DC, vicinity, these functions are assigned to the Office of Records Services—Washington, DC.

The Office of Records Services (Washington, DC)

Modern Records Program The Modern Records Program improves the life cycle management of Federal records in all media for Government agencies; provides formal training in Federal records management; and coordinates technical assistance to Federal agencies on records creation, management, and disposition to agencies in the Washington, DC, area. For more information, go to: www.archives.gov/records-mgmt.

The Washington National Records Center offers a wide range of records storage and servicing options as described below under Regional Records Services and also offers customized workshops and records management assistance upon request and will assist agencies with their records storage problems.

For further information on records center services in the Washington, DC, area (West Virginia, Virginia, and Maryland), contact the Washington National Records Center. Phone, 301–778–1600.

Regional Records Services

Regional Records Services The Regional Records Services Office provides services to agencies outside the Washington, DC, area. NARA has nine regions and the National Personnel Records Center. Each region operates a full life cycle records program including records management operations, records centers, and regional archives.

Records Management Outside of the Washington, DC, area, NARA maintains information about the records managment programs of Federal agencies in the region; conducts inspections, evaluations, or surveys of records and records management programs in agencies; reports on findings; and recommends improvements or necessary corrective actions. NARA also furnishes guidance and technical assistance to Federal agencies on records creation, management, and disposition; develops and conducts training aimed at improving agency records management and disposition practices; and appraises Federal records to determine whether they warrant preservation by the U.S. Government.

Federal Records Centers These Centers are for the storage and servicing of non-current and certain active records of Federal agencies. Services include the storage of textual and special media records; storage for non-classified and classified records; retrieval of records to fulfill statutory requirements and conduct daily business; special projects to respond to sudden shifts in customer demands; expedited response to congressional inquiries, litigation, and urgent business needs; and disposition services, providing disposal for records that have reached their required retention period or transfer to the holdings of the National Archives for permanent records.

Regional Archives Historically valuable records of high regional significance are maintained in most of these facilities. Many important original records held in NARA facilities in the Washington, DC, area, are available in microform in most of these regional facilities. These facilities arrange and preserve the records and prepare finding aids to facilitate their use; make the records available for use in research rooms; answer written or oral requests for information contained in the holdings; and for a fee, provide copies of the records.

National Personnel Records Center The Center directs activities for storing, servicing, and disposing civilian (personnel, medical, and pay records of former U.S. Civil Service employees) and military records (personnel and medical records of inactive military personnel); and provides Federal agencies with a full range of services and technical advice relating to records disposition, filing and classification schemes, and protection of vital civilian and military records.

For further information, contact the Office of Regional Records Services. Phone, 301–837–2950. Fax, 301–837–1617. Internet, www.archives.gov/locations/records-management.html.

Regional Records Services Facilities—National Archives and Records Administration

(HQ: Headquarters facility; A: Facility holding archival records)

City	Address	Director	Telephone
Northeast Region (HQ)	380 Trapelo Rd., Waltham, MA 02154–6399	Diane LeBlanc	781–663–0130
Boston, MA (A)	380 Trapelo Rd., Waltham, 02154–6399		781–663–0121
Pittsfield, MA	100 Conte Dr., 01201–8230		413–236–3600
New York City, NY (A)	201 Varick St., 10014–4811		212–401–1620
Mid-Atlantic Region (HQ)	900 Market St., Philadelphia, PA 19107–4292	V. Chapman Smith	215–597–0921
Center City Philadelphia, PA (A).	900 Market St., 19107–4292		215–597–0921
Northeast Philadelphia, PA	14700 Townsend Rd., 19154–1096		215–305–2003
Southeast Region (HQ) (A)	5780 Jonesboro Rd., Morrow, GA 30260–3806	James McSweeney	404–968–2100
Ellenwood, GA	4712 Southpark Blvd., 30294–3595		404–736–2820
Great Lakes Region (HQ)	7358 S. Pulaski Rd., Chicago, IL 60629–5898	David E. Kuehl	773–581–7816
Chicago, IL (A)	7358 S. Pulaski Rd., 60629–5898		773–581–7816
Dayton, OH	3150 Springboro Rd., 45439–1883		937–225–2852
Central Plains Region (HQ)	2312 E. Bannister Rd., Kansas City, MO 64131–3011.	R. Reed Whitaker	816–926–6920
Kansas City, MO (A)	2312 E. Bannister Rd., 64131–3011		816–926–6272
Lee's Summit, MO	200 Space Ctr. Dr., 64064–1182		816–478–7089
Lenexa, KS	17501 West 98th St., 66219–1735		913–825–7809
Southwest Region (HQ) (A)	501 W. Felix St., Fort Worth, TX 76115–3405	Kent C. Carter	817–334–5515
Rocky Mountain Region (HQ) (A).	Bldg. 48, Denver Federal Ctr., Denver, CO 80225–0307.	Barbara Voss	303–236–0801
Pacific Region (HQ)	1000 Commodore Dr., San Bruno, CA 94066	Shirley J. Burton	650–876–9249
Laguna Niguel, CA (A)	1st Fl. E., 24000 Avila Rd., 92607–3497		949–360–2618
San Francisco, CA (A)	1000 Commodore Dr., San Bruno, 94066		415–876–9009
Riverside County, CA	23123 Cajalco Rd., Perris, CA 92570–7298		951–956–2000
Pacific Alaska Region (HQ)	6125 Sand Point Way NE., Seattle, WA 98115–7999.	Steven M. Edwards	206–526–6501
Seattle, WA (A)	6125 Sand Point Way NE., 98115–7999		206–526–6501
Anchorage, AK (A)	654 W. 3d Ave., 99501–2145		907–271–2443
National Personnel Records Center (HQ).	9700 Page Ave., St. Louis, MO 63132	Ronald L. Hindman	314–538–4201

Affiliated Archives Facilities—National Archives and Records Administration

Facility	Address	Telephone	Fax
Library of Congress	Prints and Photographs Division, Rm. 339, James Madison Bldg., Washington, DC 20540–4730.	202–707–6394	202–707–6647
New Mexico State Records Center and Archives.	Archives and Historical Services Division, New Mexico Commission of Public Records, 1205 Camino Carlos Rey, Sante Fe, NM 87505.	505–476–7948	505–476–7909
Oklahoma Historical Society	Wiley Post Historical Bldg., 2100 N. Lincoln Blvd., Oklahoma City, OK 73105–4997.	405–522–5206	405–521–2492
Pennsylvania State Archives	Bureau of Archives and History, Pennsylvania Historical and Museum Commission, 350 North St., Harrisburg, PA 17120.	717–783–3281	717–787–4822
U.S. Government Printing Office	Superintendent of Documents, 732 N. Capitol St. NW, Washington, DC 20401.	202–512–1800	202–512–2104
U.S. Military Academy	Special Collections and Archives Division, U.S. Military Academy Library, Jefferson and Collum Rd., West Point, NY 10996–1711.	845–938–3259	845–938–6444
U.S. Naval Academy	William W. Jeffries Memorial Archives, Rm. 320, Nimitz Library, 589 McNair Rd., Annapolis, MD 21402.	410–293–6922	410–293–4926
Yellowstone National Park Archives.	P.O. Box 168, Yellowstone National Park, WY 82190	307–344–2261	307–344–2323

National Archives Trust Fund Board

The National Archives Trust Fund Board receives funds from the sale of reproductions of historic documents and publications about the records, as well as from gifts and bequests. The Board invests these funds and uses income to support archival functions such as the preparation of publications that make information about historic records more widely available. Members of the Board are the Archivist of the United States, the Secretary of the Treasury, and the Chairman of the National Endowment for the Humanities.

For further information, contact the Secretary, National Archives Trust Fund Board. Phone, 301–837–3550.

National Historical Publications and Records Commission The National Historical Publications and Records Commission (NHPRC) is the grant-making affiliate of the National Archives and Records Administration. Its mission is to promote the preservation and use of America's documentary heritage essential to understanding our democracy, history, and culture. NHPRC grants help State and local archives, universities, historical societies, and other nonprofit organizations solve preservation problems dealing with electronic records, improve training and techniques, strengthen archival programs, preserve and process records collections, and provide access to them through the publication of finding aids and documentary editions of the papers of the Founding Era and other themes and historical figures in American history. The NHPRC works in partnership with a national network of State historical records advisory boards. It also provides Federal leadership in public policy for the preservation of, and access to, America's documentary heritage.

For further information, contact the National Historical Publications and Records Commission. Phone, 202–357–5010. E-mail, nhprc@archives.gov. Internet, www.archives.gov/nhprc.

Information Security Oversight Office The Information Security Oversight Office (ISOO) oversees the security classification programs in both Government and industry and reports to the President annually on their status. Two Executive orders serve as the authority for ISOO, and the Office receives its policy and program guidance from the National Security Council. An organizational component of the National Archives and Records Administration, ISOO's goals are to hold classification activity to the minimum necessary to protect the national security; to ensure the safeguarding of classified national security information in both Government and industry in a cost-effective and efficient manner; and to promote declassification and public access to information as soon as national security considerations permit.

For further information, contact the Information Security Oversight Office. Phone, 202–357–5250.

Sources of Information

Calendar of Events To be added to the mailing list for the monthly *National Archives Calendar of Events,* call 202–357–5000. For a recorded announcement of events at the National Archives building and the National Archives at College Park, call 202–357–5000. TDD, 301–837–0482.

Congressional Affairs The Congressional Affairs staff maintains contact with and responds to inquiries from congressional offices. Phone, 202–357–5100. Fax, 202–357–5959.

Contracts Information on business opportunities with NARA are available electronically at www.fedbizopps.gov.

Educational Opportunities NARA offers several courses on archival and records management principles and on using NARA resources for research and in the classroom. For information on public programs and workshops, contact the Center for the National Archives Experience Education Office at 202–357–5439. Fax, 202–357–5925.

For information about the "Modern Archives Institute," contact the Modern Archives Institute, Room 301, National Archives Building, 700 Pennsylvania Avenue NW., Washington, DC 20408–0001. Phone 202–357–5259.

For information about records management workshops, contact the Life Cycle Management Division (phone, 301–837–3560), any regional records services facility, or the Office of Regional Records Services (phone, 301–837–2950) or Internet, www.archives.gov/records-mgmt/training/index.html.

For information about "The Federal Register: What It Is and How To Use It," call 202–741-6000.

For information about the "Institute for the Editing of Historical Documents" at the University of Wisconsin, Madison, or fellowships in documentary editing and archival administration, contact NHPRC, National Archives and Records

Administration, 700 Pennsylvania Avenue NW., Washington, DC 20408–0001. Phone, 202–357–5010. E-mail, nhprc@archives.gov. Internet, www.archives.gov/grants.

Electronic Access Information about NARA and its holdings and publications is available electronically (Internet, www.archives.gov. E-mail, inquire@nara.gov).

Employment For job opportunities nationwide, contact the nearest NARA facility or the Human Resources Operations Branch, Room 2004, 9700 Page Avenue, St. Louis, MO 63132. Phone, 800–827–4898. TDD, 314–538–4799. Internet, www.archives.gov/careers/jobs.

Fax-on-Demand To use the fax-on-demand service, call 301–837–0990 from a fax machine handset and follow the voice instructions. One of the options that can be selected is a list of the available documents. There is no charge for using fax-on-demand, other than for any long distance telephone charges users may incur.

Freedom of Information Act/Privacy Act Requests Requests should be directed as follows:

For operational records of the National Archives and Records Administration, contact the NARA Freedom of Information Act/Privacy Act Officer, General Counsel Staff, National Archives and Records Administration, 8601 Adelphi Road, College Park, MD 20740–6001. Phone, 301–837–FOIA (3642). Fax, 301–837–0293.

For historically valuable records in the custody of the Office of Records Services—Washington, DC, contact the Special Access/FOIA Staff, National Archives and Records Administration, 8601 Adelphi Road, College Park, MD 20740–6001. Phone, 301–837–3190. Fax, 301–837–1864.

For historically valuable records in the custody of a regional archives, contact the facility serving the appropriate region (see the "Regional Records Services Facilities" section) or the Office of Regional Records Services. Phone, 301–837–2950. Fax, 301–837–1617.

For historical records in the custody of a Presidential library, contact the library that has custody of the records (see the "Presidential Libraries" section).

For records in the physical custody of the Washington National Records Center or the regional Federal records centers, contact the Federal agency that transferred the records to the facility.

Grants For NHPRC grants, contact NHPRC, National Archives and Records Administration, 700 Pennsylvania Avenue NW., Washington, DC 20408–0001. Phone, 202–357–5010. E-mail, nhprc@archives.gov. Internet, www.archives.gov/grants.

Museum Shops Publications, document facsimiles, and document-related souvenirs are available for sale at the National Archives shop in Washington, DC, each Presidential library, and some regional archives.

Public Affairs The Public Affairs staff maintains contact with and responds to inquiries from the media, issues press releases and other literature, and maintains contact with organizations representing the archival profession, scholarly organizations, and other groups served by NARA. Phone, 202–357–5300.

Museum Programs Contact the Center for the National Archives Experience, National Archives and Records Administration, Washington, DC 20408. Phone, 202–357–5210. Fax, 202–357–5926.

Publications Agency publications, including facsimiles of certain documents, finding aids to records, and *Prologue*, a scholarly journal published quarterly, are available from the Customer Service Center (NWCC2), NARA, Room 1000, National Archives at College Park, 8601 Adelphi Road, College Park, MD 20740–6001. Phone, 800–234–8861. Fax, 301–837–0483. Internet, www.archives.gov/publications.

Most records management publications are available electronically on the NARA Web site. Limited quantities of some records management publications and posters are available in hard copy format from the Life Cycle Management Division, NARA, 8601 Adelphi Road, College Park, MD 20740–6001. Phone, 301–837–3560. Fax, 301–837–3699. E-mail, records.mgt@nara.gov. Internet, www.archives.gov/publications/lists/topic-records-mgt.html.

Information about laws, regulations, and Presidential documents is available from the Office of the Federal Register, NARA, Washington, DC 20408. Phone, 202–741–6000. E-mail, info@fedreg.nara.gov. Internet, www.archives.gov/federal-register. To subscribe to the *Federal Register* table of contents electronic mailing list, go to http://listserv.access.gpo.gov and select online mailing list archives, FEDREGTOC–L. To receive e-mail notification of new public laws, subscribe to PENS (Public Law Electronic Notification Service) at www.archives.gov/federal-register, ''New Public Laws.''

NHPRC guidelines are available from the NHPRC, National Archives and Records Administration, 700 Pennsylvania Avenue NW., Washington, DC 20408–0001. Phone, 202–357–5010. E-mail, nhprc@archives.gov. Internet, www.archives.gov/grants.

Reference Services Records are available for research purposes in reading rooms at the National Archives building, 700 Pennsylvania Avenue NW., Washington, DC (phone, 202–357–5400); at the National Archives at College Park, 8601 Adelphi Road, College Park, MD (phone, 866–272–6272); and at each Presidential library and at regional archives. Written requests for information may be sent to any of these units, or they may be addressed to the Customer Services Division, National Archives at College Park, Room 1000, 8601 Adelphi Road, College Park, MD 20740–6001. Phone, 866–272–6272. E-mail, inquire@nara.gov.

The Nixon Presidential Materials Staff is located in Room 1320 at the National Archives at College Park. Some Nixon materials are available for public inspection, but researchers are advised to contact the staff in advance to arrange for the use of materials before visiting the facility. Phone, 301–837–3290.

The Public Inspection Desk of the Office of the Federal Register is open every Federal businessday for public inspection of documents scheduled for publication in the next day's *Federal Register,* at Suite 700, 800 North Capitol Street NW., Washington, DC. Phone, 202–741–6000. The list of documents on public inspection may be viewed at: www.archives.gov/federal-register/public-inspection.

Speakers and Presentations The National Archives conducts regular public programs featuring authors, films, and symposia related to National Archives holdings. For programs in the Washington, DC, area, more information is available on the calendar update line. Phone, 202–357–5000. The Calendar of Events is also available by sending an e-mail to reservations.nwe@nara.gov.

Teacher Workshops and Teaching Materials The National Archives' education specialists have developed programs to train teachers in the use of primary source material in the classroom and can provide information on how to obtain documentary teaching materials for classroom use. For further information, contact the education staff of the Center for the National Archives Experience. Phone, 202–357–5439.

Docent Tours Individuals or groups may request general or specialty visits behind the scenes at the National Archives building. Tours are given by reservation only, and individuals are requested to make reservations at least 6 weeks in advance. Tours are usually scheduled for 9:45 a.m., 10:15 a.m., and 1:15 p.m., Monday through Friday. Tours of the National Archives at College Park, MD, may also be arranged. For information and reservations, contact the Visitor and Volunteer Services Office between 9 a.m. and 4 p.m., Monday through Friday. Phone, 202–357–5450.

Volunteer Service Opportunities A wide variety of opportunities is available for volunteers. At the National Archives building and the National Archives at College Park, MD, volunteers conduct tours, provide information in the exhibit halls, work with staff archivists in processing historic documents, and serve as genealogical aides in the genealogical orientation room. For further information, call 202–357–5450. Similar opportunities exist in the Presidential libraries and at the regional archives. If outside the Washington, DC, area, contact the facility closest to you for further information on volunteer opportunities.

For further information, write or visit the National Archives and Records Administration, 700 Pennsylvania Avenue NW., Washington, DC 20408–0001. Phone, 202–357–5400. Internet, www.archives.gov. E-mail, inquire@nara.gov.

NATIONAL CAPITAL PLANNING COMMISSION

401 Ninth Street NW., Suite 500, Washington, DC 20576
Phone, 202–482–7200. Internet, www.ncpc.gov.

Chairman	JOHN V. COGBILL III
Vice Chairman	PATRICIA ELWOOD
Members	ARRINGTON DIXON, JOSE L. GALVEZ III, HERBERT A. AMES
Ex Officio:	
(Secretary of the Interior)	DIRK KEMPTHORNE
(Secretary of Defense)	DONALD H. RUMSFELD
(Administrator of General Services)	LURITA A. DOAN
(Chairman, Senate Committee on Homeland Security and Governmental Affairs)	SUSAN M. COLLINS
(Chairman, House Committee on Government Reform)	TOM DAVIS
(Mayor of the District of Columbia)	ANTHONY A. WILLIAMS
(Chairman, Council of the District of Columbia)	LINDA W. CROPP
Staff:	
Executive Director	PATRICIA E. GALLAGHER
Deputy Executive Director	MARCEL C. ACOSTA
Chief Operating Officer	BARRY S. SOCKS
Director, Planning Research and Policy Division	JULIA A. KOSTER
Director, Plan and Project Implementation Division	WILLIAM G. DOWD
Director, Urban Design and Plan Review Division	CHRISTINE SAUM
Director, Technology Development and Applications Support	MICHAEL SHERMAN
General Counsel and Congressional Liaison	LOIS SCHIFFER
Director, Office of Public Affairs	LISA N. MACSPADDEN
Secretariat	DEBORAH B. YOUNG

[For the National Capital Planning Commission statement of organization, see the *Code of Federal Regulations,* Title 1, Part 456.2]

The National Capital Planning Commission is the central agency for conducting planning and development activities for Federal lands and facilities in the National Capital Region. The region includes the District of Columbia and all land areas within the boundaries of Montgomery and Prince George's Counties in Maryland and

NATIONAL CAPITAL PLANNING COMMISSION

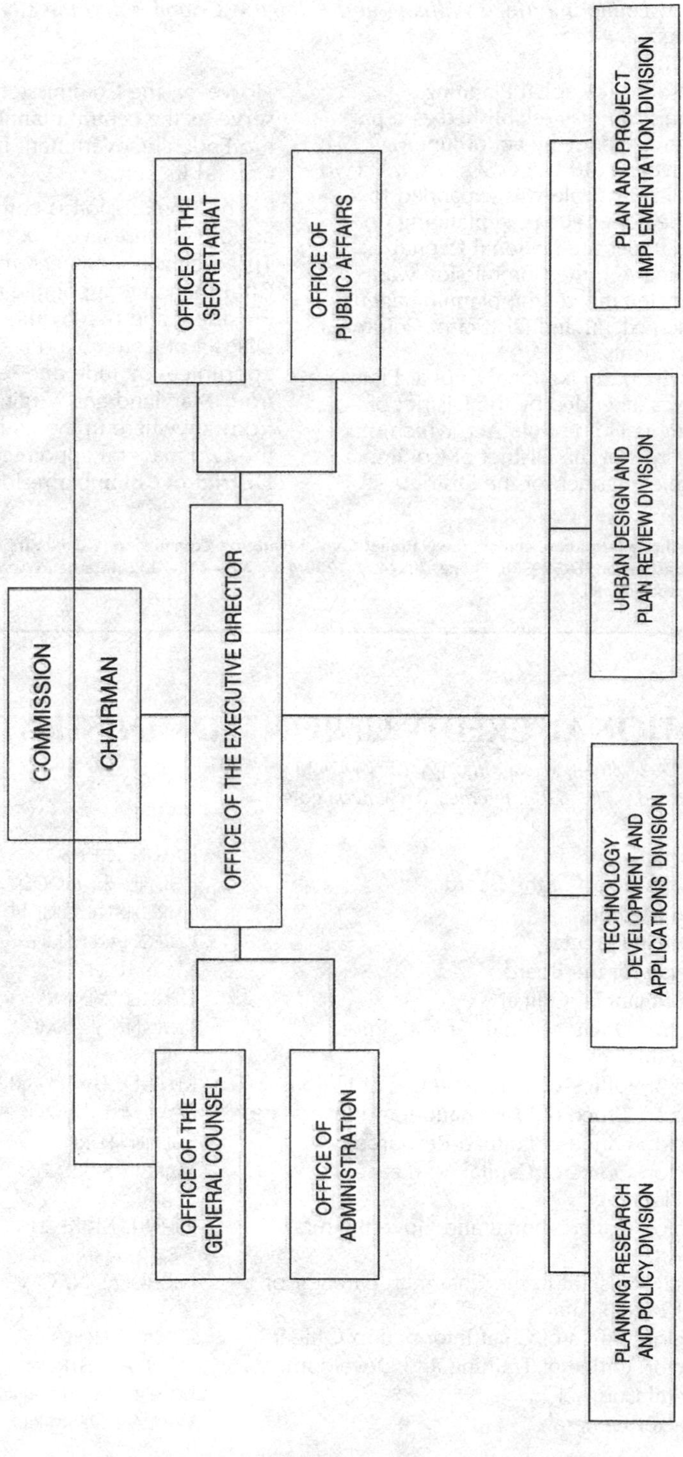

Fairfax, Loudoun, Prince William, and Arlington Counties and the city of Alexandria in Virginia.

The National Capital Planning Commission was established as a park planning agency by act of June 6, 1924, as amended (40 U.S.C. 71 *et seq.*). Two years later its role was expanded to include comprehensive planning. In 1952, under the National Capital Planning Act, the Commission was designated the central planning agency for the Federal and District of Columbia governments.

In 1973, the National Capital Planning Act was amended by the District of Columbia Home Rule Act, which made the Mayor of the District of Columbia the chief planner for the District. However, the Commission continues to serve as the central planning agency for the Federal Government in the National Capital Region.

The Commission is composed of five appointed and seven *ex officio* members. Three citizen members, including the Chairman, are appointed by the President and two by the mayor of the District of Columbia. Presidential appointees include one resident each from Maryland and Virginia and one from anywhere in the United States, but the two mayoral appointees must be District of Columbia residents.

For further information, contact the National Capital Planning Commission, 401 Ninth Street NW., Suite 500, Washington, DC 20576. Phone, 202–482–7200. Fax, 202–482–7272. Internet, www.ncpc.gov. E-mail, info@ncpc.gov.

NATIONAL CREDIT UNION ADMINISTRATION

1775 Duke Street, Alexandria, VA 22314–3428
Phone, 703–518–6300. Internet, www.ncua.gov.

Chairman	JoAnn Johnson
Vice Chairman of the Board	Rodney E. Hood
Board Member	Christiane Gigi Hyland
Executive Director	J. Leonard Skiles
Secretary of the Board	Mary Rupp
Chief Financial Officer	Dennis Winans
Director, Office of Small Credit Union Initiatives	Tawana Y. James
Director, Office of Corporate Credit Unions	Kent D. Buckham
Director, Office of Examination and Insurance	David M. Marquis
Director, Office of Human Resources	Sherry Turpenoff
Director, Office of Capital Markets and Planning	Marcia Sarrazin
Director, Congressional and Governmental Affairs	John J. McKechnie III
Special Assistant to the Chairman/Director of External Affairs	Nicholas N. Owens
Director, Office of Chief Information Officer	Doug Verner
Director, Office of Training and Development	Leslie Armstrong
General Counsel	Robert M. Fenner
Inspector General	Willian DeSarno

President, Asset Management and Assistance Center	MIKE BARTON

[For the National Credit Union Administration statement of organization, see the *Code of Federal Regulations*, Title 12, Part 720]

The National Credit Union Administration is responsible for chartering, insuring, supervising, and examining Federal credit unions and administering the National Credit Union Share Insurance Fund. The Administration also administers the Community Development Revolving Loan Fund and manages the Central Liquidity Facility, a mixed-ownership Government corporation whose purpose is to supply emergency loans to member credit unions.

The National Credit Union Administration (NCUA) was established by act of March 10, 1970 (12 U.S.C. 1752), and reorganized by act of November 10, 1978 (12 U.S.C. 226), as an independent agency in the executive branch of the Federal Government. It regulates and insures all Federal credit unions and insures State-chartered credit unions that apply and qualify for share insurance.

Activities

Chartering The Administration grants Federal credit union charters to groups sharing a common bond of occupation or association or groups within a well-defined neighborhood, community, or rural district. A preliminary investigation is made to determine if certain standards are met before granting a Federal charter.

For further information, contact the appropriate regional office listed in the following table.

Examinations The Administration regularly examines Federal credit unions to determine their solvency and compliance with laws and regulations and to assist credit union management and operations.

For further information, contact the Director, Office of Examination and Insurance. Phone, 703–518–6360.

Share Insurance The act of October 19, 1970 (12 U.S.C. 1781 *et seq.*), provides for a program of share insurance. The insurance is mandatory for Federal credit unions. State-chartered credit unions in many States are required to have Federal share insurance, and it is optional for other State-chartered credit unions. Credit union members' accounts are insured up to $100,000. The National Credit Union Share Insurance Fund requires each insured credit union to place and maintain a 1-percent deposit of its insured savings with the Fund.

For further information, contact the Director, Office of Examination and Insurance. Phone, 703–518–6360.

Supervision Supervisory activities are carried out through regular examiner contacts and through periodic policy and regulatory releases from the Administration. The Administration also identifies emerging problems and monitors operations between examinations.

Regional Offices—National Credit Union Administration

Region	Address	Director	Telephone	Fax
CT, MA, ME, NH, NY, MI, RI, VT	9 Washington Sq., Washington Ave. Ext., Albany, NY 12205	Mark A. Treichel	518–862–7400	518–862–7420
DC, DE, MD, NJ, PA, VA, WV	Suite 4206, 1775 Duke St., Alexandria, VA 22314	Edward Dupcak	703–519–4600	703–519–6674
AL, FL, GA, IN, KY, MS, NC, OH, PR, SC, TN, VI	Suite 1600, 7000 Central Pkwy., Atlanta, GA 30328	Alonzo A. Swann III	678–443–3000	678–443–3020
AR, IA, IL, LA, KS, MN, MO, ND, NE, OK, SD, TX, WI	Suite 5200, 4807 Spicewood Springs Rd., Austin, TX 78759–8490	Jane Walters	512–342–5600	512–342–5620

Regional Offices—National Credit Union Administration—Continued

Region	Address	Director	Telephone	Fax
AK, AS, AZ, CA, CO, GU, HI, ID, MT, NV, NM, OR, WA, WY	Suite 301, West Washington St., Tempe, AZ 85281	Melinda Love	602–302–6000	602–302–6024

Sources of Information

Consumer Complaints The Administration investigates the complaints of members unable to resolve problems with their Federal credit unions. Complaints should be sent to the Office of Public and Congressional Affairs, National Credit Union Administration, 1775 Duke Street, Alexandria, VA 22314–3428.

Employment Inquiries and applications for employment should be directed to the Office of Human Resources, National Credit Union Administration, 1775 Duke Street, Alexandria, VA 22314–3428.

Federally Insured Credit Unions A list of federally insured credit union names, addresses, asset levels, and number of members is available for review at NCUA's central and regional offices. Copies of the listing are available at a nominal fee from NCUA, Publications, 1775 Duke Street, Alexandria, VA 22314–3428. Phone, 703–518–6340. A listing is also available electronically through the Internet at www.ncua.gov/indexdata.html.

Publications A listing and copies of NCUA publications are available from NCUA, Publications, 1775 Duke Street, Alexandria, VA 22314–3428. Phone, 703–518–6340. Publications are also available electronically through the Internet at www.ncua.gov.

Starting a Federal Credit Union Groups interested in forming a Federal credit union may obtain free information by writing to the appropriate regional office.

For further information concerning the National Credit Union Administration, contact the Office of Public and Congressional Affairs, National Credit Union Administration, 1775 Duke Street, Alexandria, VA 22314–3428. Phone, 703–518–6330. Internet, www.ncua.gov.

NATIONAL FOUNDATION ON THE ARTS AND THE HUMANITIES

The purpose of the National Foundation on the Arts and Humanities is to develop and promote a broadly conceived national policy of support for the humanities and the arts in the United States, and for institutions which preserve the cultural heritage of the United States.

The National Foundation on the Arts and the Humanities was created as an independent agency by the National Foundation on the Arts and the Humanities Act of 1965 (20 U.S.C. 951). The Foundation consists of the National Endowment for the Arts, the National Endowment for the Humanities, the Federal Council on the Arts and the Humanities, and the Institute of Museum and Library Services. The Federal Council on the Arts and the Humanities assists the Endowments in coordinating their programs and other activities with those of Federal agencies. Each Endowment is advised on its respective grantmaking and related policies, programs, and procedures by its own National Council, composed of the Endowment Chairman and other members appointed by the President and confirmed by the Senate. Members of

Congress, appointed by the leadership of the House and the Senate, serve in an *ex officio*, non-voting capacity on the National Council on the Arts. The Federal Council's membership comprises the Chairmen of the two Endowments, the Director of Museum and Library Services, and other key Federal cultural officials. Excluding participation by certain of its members, the Federal Council makes agreements to indemnify—against loss or damage—items eligible under the Arts and Artifacts Indemnity Act (20 U.S.C. 971).

[For the National Foundation on the Arts and the Humanities statement of organization, see the *Code of Federal Regulations*, Title 45, Part 1100]

National Endowment for the Arts

1100 Pennsylvania Avenue NW., Washington, DC 20506–0001
Phone, 202–682–5400. TDD, 202–682–5496. Internet, www.arts.gov.

Chairman	DANA GIOIA
Senior Deputy Chairman	EILEEN B. MASON
Deputy Chairman, Management and Budget	LAURENCE M. BADEN
Deputy Chairman, Grants and Awards	TONY CHAUVEAUX
Government Affairs Director	ANN GUTHRIE HINGSTON
Council Operations Director and Deputy Director, Office of Government Affairs	MICHAEL FAUBION
Federal Partnerships Coordinator	TONY TIGHE
International Activities Coordinator	PENNIE OJEDA
Chief Information Officer	MICHAEL BURKE
AccessAbility Coordinator	PAULA TERRY
Administrative Services Director	MURRAY R. WELSH
Arts Education Director	SARAH B. CUNNINGHAM
Budget Officer	JOHN SOTELO, *Acting*
Challenge America/Local Arts Agencies Director	PATRICE WALKER POWELL
Civil Rights, Equal Employment Opportunity Director	ANGELIA RICHARDSON
Communications Director	FELICIA K. KNIGHT
Design Director	JEFF B. SPECK
Finance Officer	SANDRA STUECKLER
Folk/Traditional Arts Director	BARRY BERGEY
General Counsel	CLAUDIA NADIG
Grants and Contracts Officer	NICKI JACOBS
Guidelines and Panel Operations Director	JILLIAN L. MILLER
Human Resources Director	CRAIG M. MCCORD, SR.
Indemnity Program Administrator	ALICE M. WHELIHAN
Inspector General	DANIEL SHAW
Literature Director	DAVID KIPEN
Media Arts Director	TED LIBBEY
Museum/Visual Arts Director	ROBERT FRANKEL
Music/Opera Director	WAYNE BROWN
National Initiatives and Dance Director	DOUGLAS SONNTAG
Presenting Director	MARIO GARCIA DURHAM
Research and Analysis Director	KAREN PAINTER
State and Regional Director	JOHN OSTROUT
Theater/Musical Theater Director	MARIO GARCIA DURHAM, *Acting*

The National Endowment for the Arts, established by Congress in 1965 as an independent Federal agency, is the official arts organization of the United States Government. It is dedicated to supporting excellence in the arts, both new and established; bringing the arts to all Americans; and providing leadership in arts education.

Through its grants and programs, the Arts Endowment brings great art to all 50 States and 6 U.S. jurisdictions including rural areas, inner cities, and military bases. The Arts Endowment awards competitive matching grants to nonprofit organizations, units of State or local government, and federally recognized tribal communities or tribes, for projects, programs, or activities in the fields of dance, design, folk and traditional arts, literature, media arts, museums, music, musical theater, opera, presenting, theater, and visual arts. In addition, it awards competitive nonmatching individual fellowships in literature and honorary fellowships in jazz and the folk and traditional arts. Forty percent of the Arts Endowment's funds go to the 56 State and jurisdictional arts agencies and their 6 regional arts organizations in support of arts projects in thousands of communities across the country.

Sources of Information

Grants For information about Arts Endowment funding opportunities, contact the Communications Office. Phone, 202–682–5400. TDD, 202–682–5496. Internet, www.arts.gov/grants.

Publications To obtain a copy of the Arts Endowment's annual report, funding guidelines, or other publications, contact the Communications Office. Phone, 202–682–5400. TDD, 202–682–5496. Internet, www.arts.gov.

For further information, contact the Communications Office, National Endowment for the Arts, 1100 Pennsylvania Avenue NW., Washington, DC 20506–0001. Phone, 202–682–5400. TDD, 202–682–5496. Internet, www.arts.gov.

National Endowment for the Humanities

1100 Pennsylvania Avenue NW., Washington, DC 20506
Phone, 202–606–8400. Internet, www.neh.gov. E-mail, info@neh.gov.

Chairman	BRUCE COLE
Deputy Chairman	THOMAS MALLON
Adviser to the Chairman	ANDREW HAZLETT
Assistant Chairman for Planning and Operations	JEFF THOMAS
Assistant Chairman for Partnership and National Affairs	CAROLE WATSON
Director, We the People Program	THOMAS LINDSAY
Director, Communications	NOEL MILAN, *Acting*
General Counsel	MICHAEL MCDONALD
Director, Congressional Affairs	BRIAN LEE
Inspector General	SHELDON BERNSTEIN
Administrative Services Officer	BARRY MAYNES
Chief Information Officer	BRETT BOBLEY
Director, Division of Education Programs	MICHAEL POLIAKOFF
Director, Division of Preservation and Access	RALPH CANEVALI, *Acting*

Director, Division of Public Programs	NANCY ROGERS
Director, Division of Research Programs	JOYCE LEE MALCOLM
Director, Federal/State Partnership	EDYTHE MANZA
Director, Office of Challenge Grants	STEPHEN M. ROSS
Director, Office of Human Resources	TIMOTHY G. CONNELLY
Director, Office of Strategic Planning	LARRY MYERS
Director, Office of Grants Management	SUSAN DAISEY
Director, Office of Public Affairs	NOEL MILAN
Director, Office of Publications	MARY LOU BEATTY
Equal Employment Opportunity Officer	WILLIE MCGHEE

The National Endowment for the Humanities is an independent, grantmaking agency established by Congress in 1965 to support research, education, preservation, and public programs in the humanities.

According to the agency's authorizing legislation, the term "humanities" includes, but is not limited to, the study of the following: language, both modern and classical; linguistics; literature; history; jurisprudence; philosophy; archeology; comparative religion; ethics; the history, criticism, and theory of the arts; and those aspects of the social sciences that employ historical or philosophical approaches.

The Endowment makes grants to individuals, groups, or institutions—schools, colleges, universities, museums, public television stations, libraries, public agencies, and nonprofit private groups to increase understanding and appreciation of the humanities.

Challenge Grants Nonprofit institutions interested in developing new sources of long-term support for educational, scholarly, preservation, and public programs in the humanities may be assisted in these efforts by a challenge grant.

For further information, call 202–606–8309.

Education Through grants to educational institutions and fellowships to scholars and teachers, this division strengthens sustained thoughtful study of the humanities at all levels of education.

For further information, call 202–606–8500.

Federal/State Partnership Humanities committees in each of the 50 States, the Virgin Islands, Puerto Rico, the District of Columbia, the Northern Mariana Islands, American Samoa, and Guam receive grants from the Endowment, which they, in turn, grant to support humanities programs at the local level.

For further information, call 202–606–8254.

Preservation and Access This division supports projects that will create, preserve, and increase the availability of resources important for research, education, and public programming in the humanities.

For further information, call 202–606–8570.

Public Programs This division strives to fulfill the Endowment's mandate "to increase public understanding of the humanities" by supporting those institutions and organizations that develop and present humanities programming for general audiences.

For further information, call 202–606–8269.

Research This division promotes original research in the humanities by providing grants for significant research projects.

For further information, call 202–606–8200.

We the People Program This office coordinates programs throughout the agency on American history, culture, and principles.

For further information, call 202–606–8310.

Sources of Information

Employment For employment information, contact the NEH Job Line. Phone, 202–606–8281.

Grants Those interested in applying for a grant in the humanities should request

NATIONAL ENDOWMENT FOR THE HUMANITIES

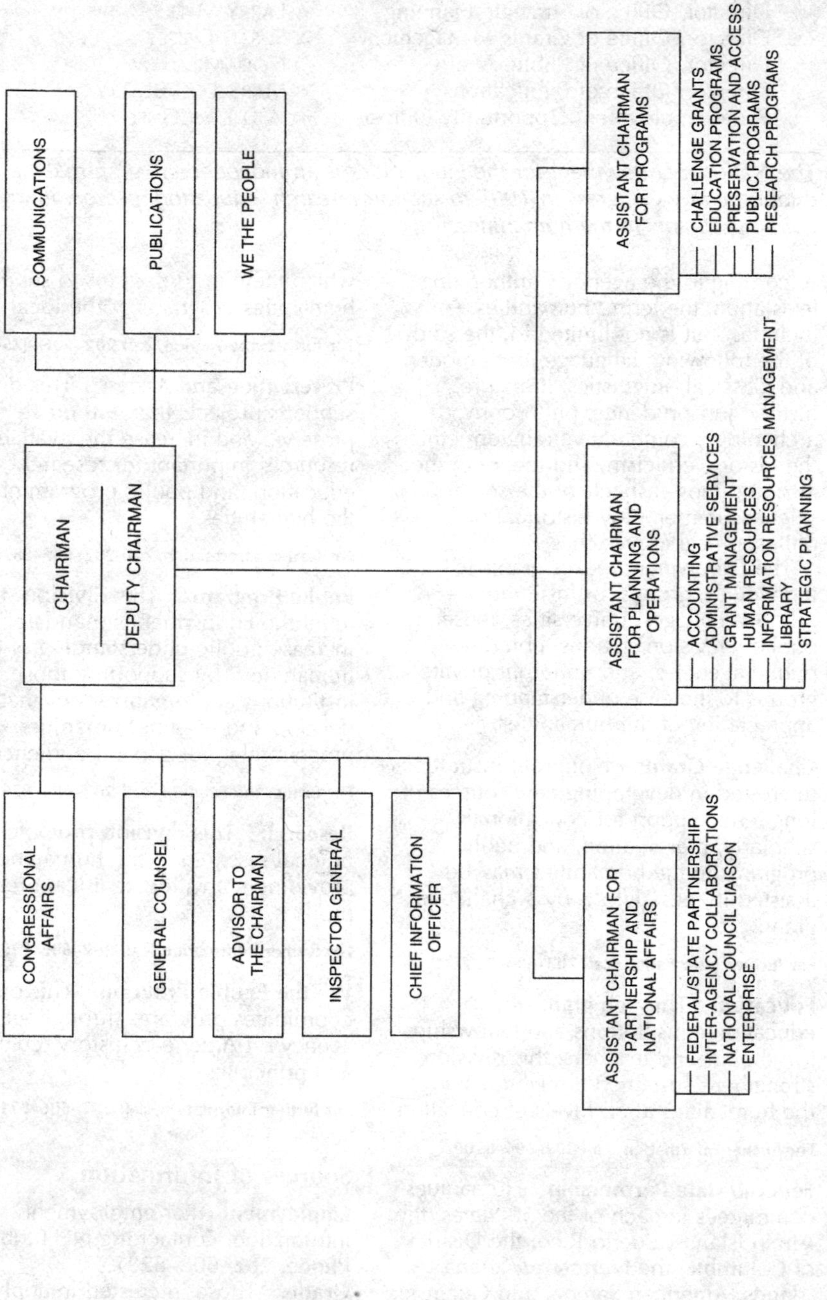

information, guidelines, and application forms from the Endowment's Office of Public Affairs, Room 402, 1100 Pennsylvania Avenue NW., Washington, DC 20506. Phone, 202–606–8400, or visit our Web site.

Publications The "Pocket Guide to NEH" provides a convenient overview of NEH's mission, history, funded projects, current initiatives, and grant opportunities. It and other publications may be obtained from the Office of Public Affairs, National Endowment for the Humanities, Room 402, 1100 Pennsylvania Avenue NW., Washington, DC 20506. Phone, 202–606–8400, or visit our Web site.

The bimonthly review of issues in the humanities, entitled *Humanities,* is available by subscription ($24 domestic, $33.60 foreign) through the Superintendent of Documents, P.O. Box 371954, Pittsburgh, PA 15250–7954 or by phone at 202-512-1800.

For further information, contact the Office of Public Affairs, National Endowment for the Humanities, Room 402, 1100 Pennsylvania Avenue NW., Washington, DC 20506. Phone, 202–606–8400 or 800–NEH–1121. TDD, 202–606–8282 or 866–372–2930. Internet, www.neh.gov. E-mail, info@neh.gov.

Institute of Museum and Library Services

1800 M Street NW., 9th Floor, Washington, DC 20036
Phone, 202–653–IMLS (4657). Internet, www.imls.gov. E-mail, imlsinfo@imls.gov.

Director	Anne-Imelda M. Radice
Deputy Director for Library Services	Mary L. Chute
Deputy Director for Museum Services	Marsha Semmel
Chief of Staff	Kate Fernstrom
Counselors to the Director	Schroeder Cherry, Carol A. Scannelli
Director, Public and Legislative Affairs	Mamie Bittner
Director, Administration and Budget	Teresa M. LaHaie
Director, Research and Technology	Rebecca Danvers
Director, Strategic Partnerships	Marsha Semmel
Associate Deputy Director for Library Services	Joyce Ray
Associate Deputy Director, State Programs	George Smith
Associate Deputy Director for Museum Services	Mary Estelle Kennelly
General Counsel	Nancy E. Weiss

The Institute of Museum and Library Services is the primary source of Federal support for the Nation's 122,000 libraries and 15,000 museums. Its mission is to grow and sustain a nation of learners. Through its grantmaking, convenings, research, and publications, the Institute empowers museums and libraries nationwide to provide leadership and services to enhance learning in families and communities, sustain cultural heritage, build 21st-century skills, and increase civic participation.

The Institute of Museum and Library Services (IMLS) was established within the National Foundation on the Arts and the Humanities by the Museum and Library Services Act of September 30, 1996 (110 Stat. 3009–293), which amended the Museum Services Act (20 U.S.C. 961 *et seq.*). The Institute combines administration of Federal museum programs formerly carried out by the Institute of Museum Services and Federal library programs formerly carried out by the Department of Education. The Institute's Director is appointed by the President with the advice and consent of the Senate and is authorized to make grants to museums and libraries. The Director receives policy advice on museum and library programs from the National Museum and Library Services Board, which is comprised of 20 Presidentially appointed members, the Director, the Deputy Director for the Office of Museum Services, and the Deputy Director for the Office of Library Services.

In addition to providing distinct programs of support for museums and libraries, IMLS encourages collaboration between these community resources. The Institute's library programs help libraries use new technologies to identify, preserve, and share library and information resources across institutional, local, and State boundaries and to reach those for whom library use requires extra effort or special materials. Museum programs strengthen museum operations, improve care of collections, increase professional development opportunities, and enhance the community service role of museums.

IMLS awards grants to all types of museums and libraries. Eligible museums include art, history, general, children's, natural history, science and technology, as well as historic houses, zoos and aquariums, botanical gardens and arboretums, nature centers, and planetariums. Eligible libraries include public, school, academic, research, and special libraries. The Institute makes grants in 10 program categories.

States These grants improve electronic sharing of information and expand public access to an increasing wealth of information and services.

Native American Library Services This program provides small grants to tribes and Alaska Native villages for core library operations, technical assistance, and enhancement grants to promote innovative practices.

Native Hawaiian Library Services This program provides grants to nonprofit organizations that primarily serve and represent Native Hawaiians.

National Leadership Grants This program provides grants to enhance the quality of library and museum services nationwide. Awarded projects demonstrate national impact and generate results—whether new tools, research, models, services, practices, or alliances—that can be widely adapted or replicated to extend the benefit of Federal support.

Museums for America This program provides funds to aid museums in advancing their capacity to serve a wider, more diverse public through education, partnerships, and technology.

Laura Bush 21st-Century Librarians Program This program supports efforts to recruit and educate the next generation of librarians and the faculty who will prepare them for careers in library science.

21st Century Museum Professionals This program supports the preparation of museum professionals for the future by updating and expanding their knowledge and skills.

Native American/Native Hawaiian Museum Services This program enables Native American tribes and organizations that primarily serve Native Hawaiians to benefit their communities and audiences through strengthened museum services in the areas of programming, professional development, and enhancement of museum services.

Conservation Project Support This program awards matching grants to help museums identify conservation needs and priorities and perform activities to ensure the safekeeping of their collections.

Museum Assessment Program IMLS helps support the cost of the Museum Assesment Program through a cooperative agreement with the American Association of Museums. The program is designed to help museums assess their strengths and weaknesses and plan for the future.

Conservation Assessment Program IMLS helps support the costs of the Conservation Assesment Program through a cooperative agreement with Heritage Preservation. The program is designed to support a 2-day site visit by a conservation professional to perform the assesment and up to 3 days to write the report.

National Awards for Museum and Library Service This program recognizes outstanding museums and libraries that provide meaningful public service for their communities.

Sources of Information

Electronic Access Information about IMLS programs, application guidelines, and lists of grantees are available electronically. Internet, www.imls.gov. E-mail, imlsinfo@imls.gov.

Grants, Contracts, and Cooperative Agreements For information about applying for IMLS funding, contact the appropriate program office. Museums should contact the Office of Museum Services, Institute of Museum and Library Services, 1800 M Street NW., 9th Floor, Washington, DC 20036 (phone, 202–653–4798). Libraries should contact the Office of Library Services, Institute of Museum and Library Services, 1800 M Street NW., Washington, DC 20036 (phone, 202–653–4700).

For further information, contact the Office of Public and Legislative Affairs, Institute of Museum and Library Services, 1800 M Street NW., Washington, DC 20036. Phone, 202–653–4757. Internet, www.imls.gov. E-mail, imlsinfo@imls.gov.

NATIONAL LABOR RELATIONS BOARD

1099 Fourteenth Street NW., Washington, DC 20570
Phone, 202–273–1000. TDD, 202–273–4300. Internet, www.nlrb.gov.

Chairman	ROBERT J. BATTISTA
Members	WILMA B. LIEBMAN, PETER C. SCHAUMBER, (2 VACANCIES)
Executive Secretary	LESTER A. HELTZER
Solicitor	HANK BREITENEICHER, *Acting*
Inspector General	JANE E. ALTENHOFEN
Representation Appeals	LAFE E. SOLOMON
Associate Director, Division of Information	PATRICIA M. GILBERT
Chief Administrative Law Judge	ROBERT A. GIANNASI
Chief, Information Technology	RICHARD WESTFIELD
General Counsel	RONALD MEISBURG
Director, Equal Employment Opportunity	ROBERT J. POINDEXTER
Associate General Counsel, Division of Operations-Management	RICHARD A. SIEGEL
Associate General Counsel, Division of Advice	BARRY J. KEARNEY
Associate General Counsel, Division of Enforcement Litigation	JOHN H. FERGUSON
Director, Division of Administration	GLORIA J. JOSEPH

[For the National Labor Relations Board statement of organization, see the *Federal Register* of June 14, 1979, 44 FR 34215]

The National Labor Relations Board is vested with the power to prevent and remedy unfair labor practices committed by private sector employers and unions and to safeguard employees' rights to organize and determine whether to have unions as their bargaining representative.

NATIONAL LABOR RELATIONS BOARD

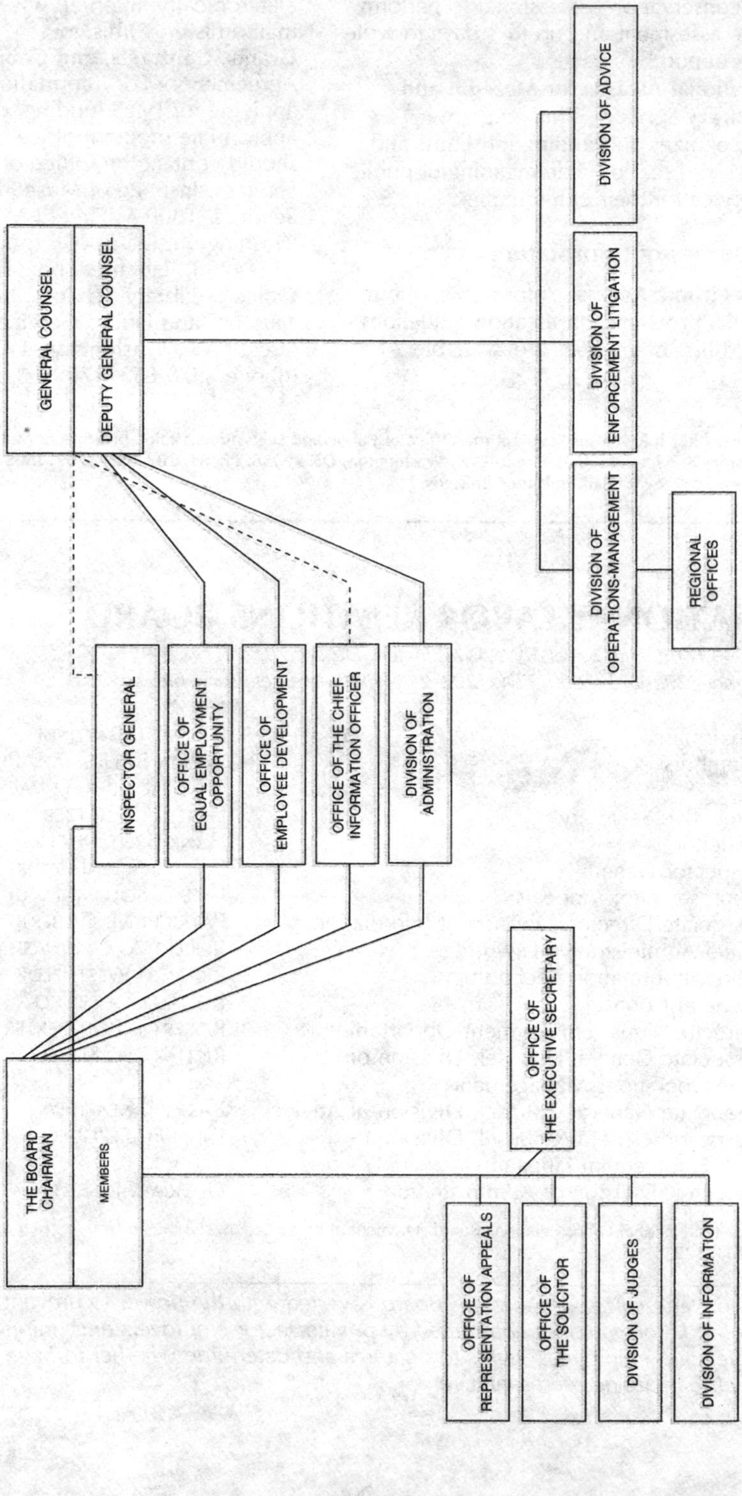

The National Labor Relations Board (NLRB) is an independent agency created by the National Labor Relations Act of 1935 (Wagner Act; 29 U.S.C. 167). The Board is authorized to designate appropriate units for collective bargaining and to conduct secret ballot elections to determine whether employees desire representation by a labor organization.

Activities

NLRB has two principal functions: preventing and remedying unfair labor practices by employers and labor organizations or their agents, and conducting secret ballot elections among employees in appropriate collective-bargaining units to determine whether or not they desire to be represented by a labor organization in bargaining with employers about their wages, hours, and working conditions. The agency also conducts secret ballot elections among employees who have been covered by a union-security agreement to determine whether or not they wish to revoke their union's authority to make such agreements. In jurisdictional disputes between two or more unions, the Board determines which competing group of workers is entitled to perform the work involved.

The regional directors and their staffs process representation, unfair labor practice, and jurisdictional dispute cases. They issue complaints in unfair labor practice cases; seek settlement of unfair labor practice charges; obtain compliance with Board orders and court judgments; and petition district courts for injunctions to prevent or remedy unfair labor practices. The regional directors direct hearings in representation cases; conduct elections pursuant to the agreement of the parties or the decision-making authority delegated to them by the Board or pursuant to Board directions; and issue certifications of representatives when unions win or certify the results when unions lose employee elections. They process petitions for bargaining unit clarification, for amendment of certification, and for rescission of a labor organization's authority to make a union-shop agreement. They also conduct national emergency employee referendums.

Administrative law judges conduct hearings in unfair labor practice cases, make findings of fact and conclusions of law, and recommend remedies for violations found. Their decisions can be appealed to the Board for a final agency determination. The Board's decisions are subject to review in the U.S. courts of appeals.

Field Offices—National Labor Relations Board
(RO: Resident Office; SR: Subregion)

Office/Address	Director	Telephone	Fax
Region 1, Rm. 601, 10 Causeway St., Boston, MA 02222–1072	Rosemary Pye	617–565–6700	617–565–6725
Region 2, Rm. 3614, 26 Federal Plz., New York, NY 10278–0104.	Celeste J. Mattina	212–264–0300	212–264–2450
Region 3			
Suite 630, 130 S. Elmwood Ave., Buffalo, NY 14202	Helen E. Marsh	716–551–4931	716–551–4972
Rm. 342, Clinton Ave. at N. Pearl St., Albany, NY 12207–2350 (RO).	Jon Mackle	518–431–4155	518–431–4157
Region 4, 7th Fl., 615 Chestnut St., Philadelphia, PA 19106–4404.	Dorothy L. Moore-Duncan	215–597–7601	215–597–7658
Region 5			
8th Fl., 103 S. Gay St., Baltimore, MD 21202–4026	Wayne R. Gold	410–962–2822	410–962–2198
Suite 5530, 1099 14th St., Washington, DC 20570–0001 (RO)	Mark Baptiste-Kalaris	202–208–3000	202–208–3013
Region 6, Rm. 510, 112 Washington Pl., Pittsburgh, PA 15219	Gerald Kobell	412–395–4400	412–395–5986
Region 7			
Rm. 300, 477 Michigan Ave., Detroit, MI 48226–2569	Stephen M. Glasser	313–226–3200	313–226–2090
Rm. 330, 82 Ionia NW., Grand Rapids, MI 49503–3022 (RO)	Chet H. Byerly, Jr.	616–456–2679	616–456–2596
Region 8, Rm. 1695, 1240 E. 9th St., Cleveland, OH 44199–2086.	Frederick Calatrello	216–522–3716	216–522–2418
Region 9, Rm. 3003, 550 Main St., Cincinnati, OH 45202–3271	Gary Muffley	513–684–3686	513–684–3946
Region 10			
Suite 1000, Harris Twr., 233 Peachtree St. NE., Atlanta, GA 30303.	Martin M. Arlook	404–331–2896	404–331–2858
Suite 3400, 1130 South 22d St., Birmingham, AL 35205–2870 (RO).	C. Douglas Marshall	205–731–1062	205–731–0955

Field Offices—National Labor Relations Board—Continued
(RO: Resident Office; SR: Subregion)

Office/Address	Director	Telephone	Fax
Region 11, Suite 200, 4035 University Pkwy., Winston-Salem, NC 27106–3323.	Willie L. Clark, Jr.	336–631–5201	336–631–5210
Region 12			
Suite 530, 201 E. Kennedy Blvd., Tampa, FL 33602–5824	Rochelle Kentov	813–228–2641	813–228–2874
Suite 340, 550 Water St., Jacksonville, FL 32202–5177 (RO)	Thomas J. Blabey	904–232–3768	904–232–3146
Rm. 1320, 51 SW. 1st Ave., Miami, FL 33130–1608 (RO)	Hector O. Nava	305–536–5391	305–536–5320
Region 13, Suite 900, The Rockery Bldg., 209 S. LaSalle St., Chicago, IL 60604–5208.	Roberto G. Chavarry	312–353–7570	312–886–1341
Region 14, Rm. 8.302, 1222 Spruce St., St. Louis, MO 63103–2829.	Ralph R. Tremain	314–539–7770	314–539–7794
Suite 200, 300 Hamilton Blvd., Peoria, IL 61602–1246 (SR 33)	Will Vance	309–671–7080	309–671–7095
Region 15, Rm. 610, 1515 Poydras St., New Orleans, LA 70112–3723.	Rodney D. Johnson	504–589–6361	504–589–4069
Region 16			
Rm. 8A24, 819 Taylor St., Fort Worth, TX 76102–6178	(Vacancy)	817–978–2921	817–978–2928
Suite 1545, 1919 Smith St., Houston, TX 77002 (RO)	Nadine Littles	713–209–4888	713–209–4890
Suite 705, 711 Navarro St., San Antonio, TX 78205–1711 (RO)	Steve E. Martinez	210–472–6140	210–472–6143
Region 17			
Suite 100, 8600 Farley St., Overland Park, KS 66212–4677	D. Michael McConnell	913–967–3000	913–967–3010
Rm. 318, 224 S. Boulder Ave., Tulsa, OK 74103–3027 (RO)	Charles T. Hoskin	918–581–7951	918–581–7970
Region 18			
Suite 790, 330 S. 2d Ave., Minneapolis, MN 55401–2221	(Vacancy)	612–348–1757	612–348–1785
Rm. 439, 210 Walnut St., Des Moines, IA 50309–2103 (RO)	David T. Garza	515–284–4391	515–284–4713
Region 19			
Rm. 2948, 915 2d Ave., Seattle, WA 98174–1078	Richard L. Ahearn	206–220–6300	206–220–6305
Suite 206, 1007 W. 3d Ave., Anchorage, AK 99501–1936 (RO)	Minoru N. Hayashi	907–271–5015	907–271–3055
Suite 1910, 601 SW. 2d Ave., Portland, OR 97204–3170 (SR 36).	Cathleen C. Callahan	503–326–3085	503–326–5387
Region 20			
Suite 400, 901 Market St., San Francisco, CA 94103–1735	Joseph P. Norelli	415–356–5130	415–356–5156
Rm. 7–245, 300 Ala Moana Blvd., Honolulu, HI 96850–4980 (SR 37).	Thomas W. Cestare	808–541–2814	808–541–2818
Region 21			
9th Fl., 888 S. Figueroa St., Los Angeles, CA 90017–5449	Victoria E. Aguayo	213–894–5200	213–894–2778
Suite 418, 555 W. Beech St., San Diego, CA 92101–2939 (RO)	Steven J. Sorensen	619–557–6184	619–557–6358
Region 22, 5th Floor, 20 Washington Pl., Newark, NJ 07102–3110.	Gary T. Kendellen	973–645–2100	973–645–3852
Region 24, Suite 1002, 525 F.D. Roosevelt Ave., Hato Rey, PR 00918–1002.	Marta Figueroa	787–766–5347	787–766–5478
Region 25, Rm. 238, 575 N. Pennsylvania St., Indianapolis, IN 46204–1577.	Rik Lineback	317–226–7382	317–226–5103
Region 26			
Suite 350, The Brinkley Plaza Bldg., 80 Monroe Ave., Memphis, TN 38103–2481.	Ronald K. Hooks	901–544–0018	901–544–0008
Suite 800, 425 W. Capitol Ave., Little Rock, AR 72201–3489 (RO).	Bruce D. Hill	501–324–6311	501–324–5009
Suite 320, 810 Broadway, Nashville, TN 37203–3816 (RO)	Joseph H. Artilles	615–736–5921	615–736–7761
Region 27, 7th Fl. N. Twr., 600 17th St., Denver, CO 80202–5433.	B. Allan Benson	303–844–3551	303–844–6249
Region 28			
Suite 1800, 2600 N. Central Ave., Phoenix, AZ 85004–3099	Cornele A. Overstreet	602–640–2160	602–640–2178
Suite 1820, 505 Marquette Ave. NW., Albuquerque, NM 87102–2181 (RO).	Kathleen L. McCorkell	505–248–5125	505–248–5134
P.O. Box 971187, El Paso, TX 79997–1187 (RO)	(Vacancy)	915–592–6571	915–592–6572
Suite 400, 600 Las Vegas Blvd. S., Las Vegas, NV 89101–6637 (RO).	(Vacancy)	702–388–6416	702–388–6248
Region 29, 10th Fl., Jay St. & Myrtle Ave., Brooklyn, NY 11201–4201.	Alvin B. Blyer	718–330–7713	718–330–7579
Region 30, Suite 700, 310 W. Wisconsin Ave., Milwaukee, WI 53203–2211.	Irving E. Gottschalk, *Acting*	414–297–3861	414–297–3880
Region 31, Suite 700, 11150 W. Olympic Blvd., Los Angeles, CA 90064–1824.	James J. McDermott	310–235–7351	310–235–7420
Region 32, Suite 300N, 1301 Clay St., Oakland, CA 94612–5211.	Alan B. Reichard	510–637–3300	510–637–3315
Region 34, 21st Fl., 280 Trumbull St., Hartford, CT 06103–3503	Peter B. Hoffman	860–240–3522	860–240–3564

Sources of Information

Contracts Prospective suppliers of goods and services may inquire about agency procurement and contracting practices by writing to the Chief, Procurement and Facilities Branch, National Labor Relations Board,

Washington, DC 20570. Phone, 202–273–4040.

Electronic Access Information about the Board's programs and activities is available through the Internet at www.nlrb.gov.

Employment The Board appoints administrative law judges from a register established by the Office of Personnel Management. The agency hires attorneys, stenographers, and typists for all its offices; field examiners for its field offices; and administrative personnel for its Washington office. Inquiries regarding college and law school recruiting programs should be directed to the nearest regional office. Employment inquiries and applications may be sent to any regional office or the Washington Human Resources office.

Publications Anyone desiring to inspect formal case documents or read agency publications may use facilities of the Washington or field offices. The agency will assist in arranging reproduction of documents and order transcripts of hearings. The Board's offices offer free informational leaflets in limited quantities: *The National Labor Relations Board and YOU (Unfair Labor Practices), The National Labor Relations Board and YOU (Representation Cases), Your Government Conducts an Election for You on the Job,* and *The National Labor Relations Board—What It Is, What It Does.* The Superintendent of Documents, Government Printing Office, Washington, DC 20402, sells *A Guide to Basic Law and Procedures Under the NLRA,* the *Annual Report,* the *Classified Index of National Labor Relations Board Decisions and Related Court Decisions,* volumes of Board decisions, and a number of subscription services, including the *NLRB Casehandling Manual* (in three parts), the *Weekly Summary of NLRB Cases,* the *NLRB Election Report,* and *An Outline of Law and Procedure in Representation Cases.*

Speakers To give the public and persons appearing before the agency a better understanding of the National Labor Relations Act and the Board's policies, procedures, and services, Washington and regional office personnel participate as speakers or panel members before bar associations, labor, educational, civic, or management organizations, and other groups. Requests for speakers or panelists may be made to Washington officials or to the appropriate regional director.

For further information, contact the Information Division, National Labor Relations Board, 1099 Fourteenth Street NW., Washington, DC 20570. Phone, 202–273–1991. Internet, www.nlrb.gov.

NATIONAL MEDIATION BOARD

1301 K Street NW., Suite 250 East, Washington, DC 20572
Phone, 202–692–5000. Internet, www.nmb.gov.

Chairman	READ VAN DE WATER
Members	EDWARD J. FITZMAURICE, JR., HARRY R. HOGLANDER
Director, Mediation Services	LARRY GIBBONS
Senior Mediators	LES PARMELEE, PATRICIA SIMS
Director, Alternative Dispute Resolution	DANIEL RAINEY
Senior Mediator (Alternative Dispute Resolution)	LINDA PUCHALA
General Counsel, Office of Legal Affairs	MARY JOHNSON
Associate General Counsel	KATE DOWLING
Director, Arbitration Services	ROLAND WATKINS
Director, Administration	JUNE KING

The National Mediation Board assists in maintaining a free flow of commerce in the railroad and airline industries by resolving labor-management disputes that could disrupt travel or imperil the economy. The Board also handles railroad and airline employee representation disputes and provides administrative and financial support in adjusting grievances in the railroad industry.

The National Mediation Board (NMB), established by the 1934 amendments to the Railway Labor Act (RLA) of 1926 (45 U.S.C. 151–158, 160–162, 1181–1188), is an independent agency performing a central role in facilitating harmonious labor-management relations within two of the Nation's key transportation sectors—the railroads and airlines. Pursuant to the RLA, NMB programs provide an integrated dispute resolution process that effectively meets the NMB's statutory mandate to minimize work stoppages by securing voluntary agreements.

The RLA has five general purposes, as follows:

—to avoid interruptions to interstate commerce in the airline and railroad industries;

—to ensure the right of employees to freely determine whether they wish to be represented for collective bargaining purposes;

—to ensure the independence of labor and management for self-organization to carry out the purposes of the act;

—to provide for the settlement of collective bargaining disputes; and

—to provide for the settlement of disputes over the interpretation of existing collective bargaining agreements.

The Railway Labor Act of 1926 provided for mandatory mediation and interest arbitration in contract negotiations, as well as for section 10 Presidential Emergency Boards to enhance dispute resolution. Key amendments to the act in 1934 established a three-member National Mediation Board and authorized it to resolve employee representation disputes. In 1936, jurisdiction was expanded to include the airline industry. The act's most recent substantive amendment, in 1981, permitted the creation of specialized section 9a Presidential Emergency Board for disputes at certain commuter railroads.

Activities

Mediation and Alternative Dispute Resolution The RLA requires labor and management to make every reasonable effort to make and maintain collective bargaining agreements. Initially, the parties negotiate directly in an effort to reach an agreement. Should the parties fail to do so, either party or both may apply to the Board for mediation.

The Board is obligated under the act to use its "best efforts" to bring about a peaceful resolution of the dispute. NMB mediators apply a variety of dispute resolution techniques, including traditional mediation, interest-based problem solving, and facilitation, to resolve the dispute. If after such efforts the Board determines that mediation will not settle the dispute, the NMB offers voluntary arbitration (interest arbitration) as an alternative approach to resolve the remaining issues. This option is rarely exercised by the parties. In situations where the parties agree to use interest arbitration, an arbitrator's decision is final and binding with very narrow ground for judicial review. If either party rejects this offer of arbitration, the Board promptly releases the parties from formal mediation. This release triggers a 30-day cooling off period. During this 30-day period, the Board will continue to work with the parties to achieve a mutually agreeable settlement. However, if an agreement has not been reached by the end of the 30-day period, the parties are free to exercise lawful self-help, unless a Presidential Emergency Board is established. Examples of lawful self-help include carrier-imposed working conditions or lock-outs, or union-initiated strikes and job actions.

Presidential Emergency Board The RLA authorizes the NMB to recommend the

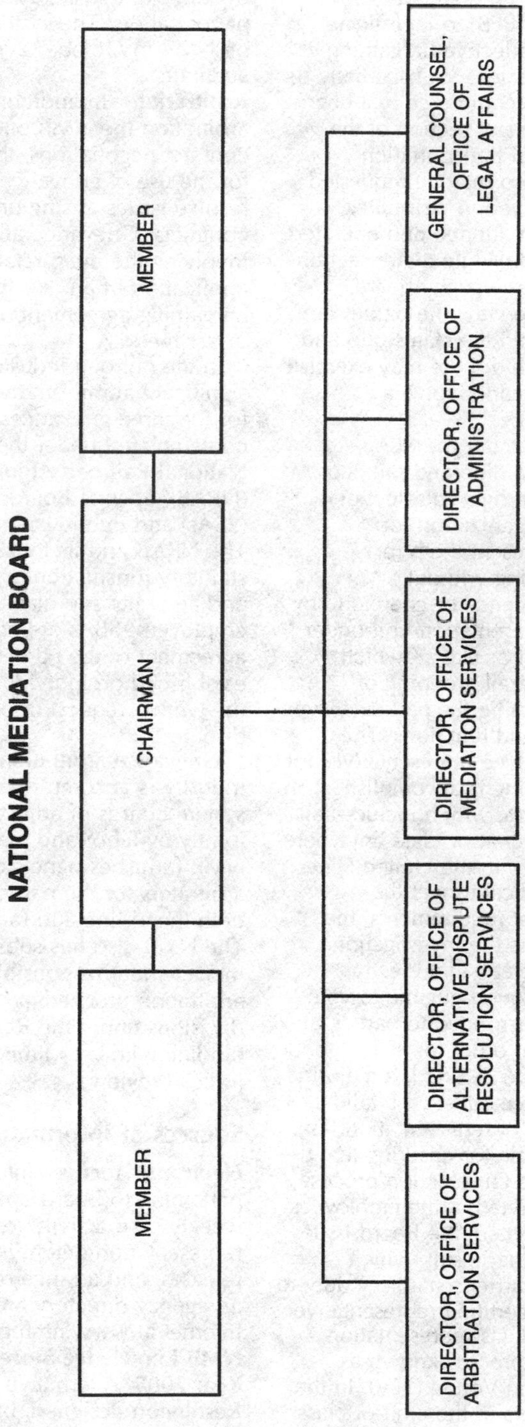
NATIONAL MEDIATION BOARD
MEMBER
CHAIRMAN
MEMBER
DIRECTOR, OFFICE OF ARBITRATION SERVICES
DIRECTOR, OFFICE OF ALTERNATIVE DISPUTE RESOLUTION SERVICES
DIRECTOR, OFFICE OF MEDIATION SERVICES
DIRECTOR, OFFICE OF ADMINISTRATION
GENERAL COUNSEL, OFFICE OF LEGAL AFFAIRS

establishment of a Presidential Emergency Board (PEB) to investigate and report on a collective bargaining dispute which threatens "substantially to interrupt interstate commerce to a degree such as to deprive any section of the country of essential transportation service." A PEB also may be requested by any party involved in a dispute affecting a publicly funded and operated commuter railroad. While either section 10 or section 9a emergency board processes are underway, the parties are required to maintain the status quo and neither party to the dispute may exercise self-help which could involve a disruption of service.

Representation Under the RLA, employees in the airline and railroad industries have the right to select or decline a labor organization, or individual, to represent them for collective bargaining without "interference, influence or coercion" by the carrier. A representation unit under the RLA is a "craft or class," which consists of the overall grouping of employees performing the particular type of related duties and functions. The selection of employee representatives for collective bargaining is accomplished on a system wide basis, which includes all employees in the craft or class anywhere the carrier operates in the United States.

Should the applicant meet the showing of interest requirements, the NMB will continue the investigation, usually with a secret ballot election. Only employees found eligible to vote by the NMB are permitted to participate in the elections. In order for a representative to be certified, a majority of the eligible voters must cast valid ballots in support of representation. The Board is responsible for ensuring that the requirements for a fair election process have been maintained. If the employees vote to be represented, the Board issues a certification of that result, which commences the carrier's statutory duty to bargain with the certified representative.

The NMB conducts representation elections using a process known as Telephone Election Voting (TEV). In the TEV process, voters in the craft or class use two secret passwords to cast ballots by telephone instead of using mail-in paper ballots. The system, inaugurated by NMB in October 2002, is secure and accurate.

Arbitration In addition to interest arbitration the NMB offers to parties in contract negotiations, the RLA provides for the use of grievance arbitration to resolve issues arising under existing contracts. Grievance arbitration, involving the interpretation or application of an existing collective bargaining agreement, is mandatory under the RLA.

In the railroad industry, the NMB has significant administrative responsibilities for the three grievance-arbitration forums contemplated under the RLA: the National Railroad Adjustment Board (NRAB), Special Boards of Adjustment (SBAs) and Public Law Boards (PLBs). The NRAB and its four divisions have statutory jurisdiction over all rail carrier's and all crafts and classes of railroad employees. SBAs are created by mutual agreement of the parties, and PLBs are established on individual railroads upon the written request of either party to a dispute.

Grievance arbitration in the airline industry is accomplished at the various system boards of adjustment created jointly by labor and management. The NMB furnishes panels of prospective arbitrators for the parties' selection on both the airline and railroad industries. The NMB also has substantial financial management responsibilities for railroad arbitration proceedings. Arbitration decisions under the RLA are final and binding with very limited grounds for judicial review.

Sources of Information

Electronic Access Information pertaining to Board operations including weekly case activity reports, representation determinations, press releases, and a range of documents and an agency directory are available on the Internet at www.nmb.gov.

NMB Knowledge Store During Fiscal Year 2005, Alternative Dispute Resolution designed, built, and implemented a public archive, available through the NMB web site, containing public documents related to the agency's operations back to its inception in 1934. Currently, the Knowledge Store contains over 90,000 documents in an easily searchable format, including arbitration awards, representation decisions, annual reports, PEB reports, industry contracts, and union constitutions and bylaws.

Publications The following documents are available for public distribution: *Determinations of the National Mediation Board* and *Annual Reports of the National Mediation Board.* Phone, 202–692–5031

Reading Room Copies of collective-bargaining agreements between labor and management of various rail and air carriers are available for public inspection at the Board's headquarters in Washington, DC, by appointment. Phone, 202-692-5031.

For further information, visit the National Mediation Board's Web site at www.nmb.gov; write the Public Information Officer, National Mediation Board, Suite 250 East, 1301 K Street NW., Washington, DC 20572; or call the NMB hotline at 202–692–5050.

NATIONAL RAILROAD PASSENGER CORPORATION (AMTRAK)

60 Massachusetts Avenue NE., Washington, DC 20002
Phone, 202–906–3000. Internet, www.amtrak.com.

Board of Directors:

Chairman	DAVID LANEY
Members	NORMAN Y. MINETA (SECRETARY OF TRANSPORTATION), FLOYD HALL, ENRIQUE SOSA, (3 VACANCIES)

Officers:

President and Chief Executive Officer	DAVID J. HUGHES, *Acting*
Chief Financial Officer	DAVID N. SMITH
Vice President, Labor Relations	JOSEPH M. BRESS
Senior Vice President, Operations	WILLIAM L. CROSBIE
Vice President, Human Resources	LORRAINE A. GREEN
Vice President, Business Diversity	GERRI MASON HALL
Vice President, Planning and Contract Administration	GILBERT O. MALLERY
Vice President, Government Affairs and Policy	JOSEPH H. MCHUGH
Vice President, Planning and Analysis	PAUL NISSENBAUM
Vice President, Marketing and Sales	BARBARA J. RICHARDSON
Vice President, Procurement and Materials Management	MICHAEL J. RIENZI
General Counsel and Corporate Secretary	ALICIA M. SERFATY
Inspector General	FRED E. WEIDERHOLD

[For the National Railroad Passenger Corporation statement of organization, see the *Code of Federal Regulations,* Title 49, Part 700]

The National Railroad Passenger Corporation was established by Congress to meet the Nation's intercity passenger transportation needs.

The National Railroad Passenger Corporation (Amtrak) was created by the Rail Passenger Service Act of 1970, as amended (49 U.S.C. 241), and was incorporated under the laws of the District of Columbia to provide a balanced national transportation system by developing, operating, and improving U.S. intercity rail passenger service.

Amtrak operates approximately 275 trains per day, serving over 520 stations in 46 States, over a system of nearly 21,800 route miles. Of this route system, Amtrak owns about 525 track miles in the Northeast Corridor, and several other small track segments elsewhere in the country.

Amtrak owns or leases its stations and owns its own repair and maintenance facilities. The Corporation employs a total workforce of approximately 19,200 and provides all reservation, station, and on-board service staffs, as well as train and engine operating crews. Outside the Northeast Corridor, Amtrak contracts with privately or publicly owned railroads for the right to operate over their track. Under contract, these railroads are responsible for the condition of the roadbed and for coordinating the flow of traffic.

In fiscal year 2005, Amtrak transported over 25 million people with 69,000 passengers traveling on Amtrak per day. Also, Amtrak runs commuter trains under contract with several commuter agencies.

Although Amtrak's basic route system was originally designated by the Secretary of Transportation in 1971, modifications have been made to the Amtrak system and to individual routes that have resulted in more efficient and cost-effective operations. Currently, in the face of ongoing budget constraints, new service will only be added if a State agrees to share any operating losses.

For further information, contact the Government Affairs Department, Amtrak, 60 Massachusetts Avenue NE., Washington, DC 20002. Phone, 202–906–3918. Internet, www.amtrak.com.

NATIONAL SCIENCE FOUNDATION

4201 Wilson Boulevard, Arlington, VA 22230
Phone, 703–292–5111. Internet, www.nsf.gov.

National Science Board

Chairman	Steven C. Beering
Vice Chairman	Kathryn D. Sullivan
Members	Dan E. Arvizu, Barry C. Barish, Steven C. Beering, Ray M. Bowen, G. Wayne Clough, Kelvin K. Droegemeier, Nina V. Fedoroff, Kenneth M. Ford, Daniel E. Hastings, Elizabeth Hoffman, Louis J. Lanzerotti, Alan I. Leshner, Diana S. Natalico, Douglas D. Randall, Michael G. Rossmann, Daniel Simberloff, Jon C. Strauss, Kathryn D. Sullivan, JoAnne Vasquez, Warren M. Washington, Mark S. Wrighton
(*Ex officio*)	Arden L. Bement, Jr.
Executive Officer	Michael P. Crosby
Inspector General	Christine C. Boesz

Officials:

Director	ARDEN L. BEMENT, JR.
Deputy Director	KATHIE L. OLSEN
Assistant Director for Biological Sciences	JAMES COLLINS
Assistant Director for Computer and Information Science and Engineering	PETER A. FREEMAN
Assistant Director for Education and Human Resources	DONALD E. THOMPSON, *Acting*
Assistant Director for Engineering	RICHARD BUCKIUS, *Acting*
Assistant Director for Geosciences	MARGARET S. LEINEIN
Assistant Director for Mathematical and Physical Sciences	JUDITH S. SUNLEY, *Acting*
Assistant Director for Social, Behavioral, and Economic Sciences	DAVID W. LIGHTFOOT
Chief Financial Officer and Director, Office of Budget, Finance, and Award Management	THOMAS N. COOLEY
Director, Office of Information and Resource Management	ANTHONY ARNOLIE
Director, Office of Integrative Activities	NATHANIEL G. PITTS
Director, Office of Legislative and Public Affairs	JEFF NESBIT
Director, Office of Polar Programs	KARL A. ERB
General Counsel	LAWRENCE RUDOLPH

[For the National Science Foundation statement of organization, see the *Federal Register* of February 8, 1993, 58 FR 7587–7595; May 27, 1993, 58 FR 30819; May 2, 1994, 59 FR 22690; and Oct. 6, 1995, 60 FR 52431]

The National Science Foundation promotes the progress of science and engineering through the support of research and education programs. Its major emphasis is on high-quality, merit-selected research—the search for improved understanding of the fundamental laws of nature upon which our future well-being as a nation depends. Its educational programs are aimed at ensuring increased understanding of science and engineering at all educational levels, maintaining an adequate supply of scientists, engineers, and science educators to meet our country's needs.

The National Science Foundation (NSF) is an independent agency created by the National Science Foundation Act of 1950, as amended (42 U.S.C. 1861–1875).

The purposes of the Foundation are to increase the Nation's base of scientific and engineering knowledge and strengthen its ability to conduct research in all areas of science and engineering; to develop and help implement science and engineering education programs that can better prepare the Nation for meeting the challenges of the future; and to promote international cooperation through science and engineering. In its role as a leading Federal supporter of science and engineering, the agency also has an important role in national policy planning.

The Director and the Deputy Director are appointed by the President, with the advice and consent of the Senate, to a 6-year term and an unspecified term, respectively. The Foundation's activities are guided by the National Science Board. The National Science Board is composed of 24 members and the Director *ex officio.* Members are appointed by the President with the advice and consent of the Senate for 6-year terms, with one-third appointed every 2 years. They are selected because of their records of distinguished service in science, engineering, education, research management, or public affairs to be broadly representative of the views

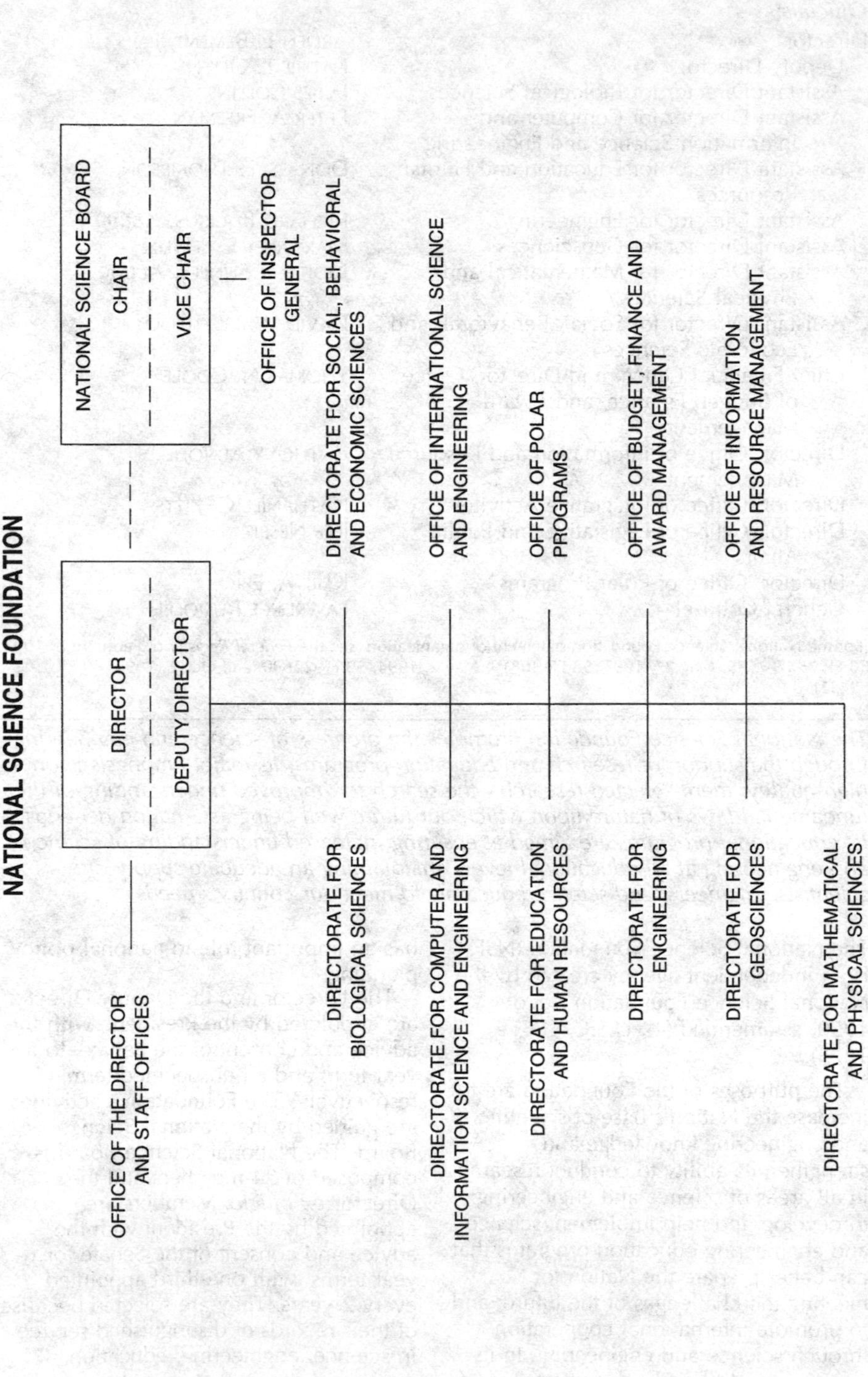
NATIONAL SCIENCE FOUNDATION
NATIONAL SCIENCE BOARD
CHAIR
VICE CHAIR
OFFICE OF INSPECTOR GENERAL
DIRECTOR
DEPUTY DIRECTOR
OFFICE OF THE DIRECTOR AND STAFF OFFICES
DIRECTORATE FOR SOCIAL, BEHAVIORAL AND ECONOMIC SCIENCES
OFFICE OF INTERNATIONAL SCIENCE AND ENGINEERING
OFFICE OF POLAR PROGRAMS
OFFICE OF BUDGET, FINANCE AND AWARD MANAGEMENT
OFFICE OF INFORMATION AND RESOURCE MANAGEMENT
DIRECTORATE FOR BIOLOGICAL SCIENCES
DIRECTORATE FOR COMPUTER AND INFORMATION SCIENCE AND ENGINEERING
DIRECTORATE FOR EDUCATION AND HUMAN RESOURCES
DIRECTORATE FOR ENGINEERING
DIRECTORATE FOR GEOSCIENCES
DIRECTORATE FOR MATHEMATICAL AND PHYSICAL SCIENCES

of national science and engineering leadership. The Board also has a broad national policy responsibility to monitor and make recommendations to promote the health of U.S. science and engineering research and education.

The Foundation's Office of Inspector General is responsible for conducting and supervising audits, inspections, and investigations relating to the programs and operations of the Foundation, including allegations of misconduct in science.

Activities

The National Science Foundation initiates and supports fundamental, long-term, merit-selected research in all the scientific and engineering disciplines. This support is made through grants, contracts, and other agreements awarded to universities, colleges, academic consortia, and nonprofit and small business institutions. Most of this research is directed toward the resolution of scientific and engineering questions concerning fundamental life processes, natural laws and phenomena, fundamental processes influencing the human environment, and the forces affecting people as members of society as well as the behavior of society as a whole.

The Foundation encourages cooperative efforts by universities, industries, and government. It also promotes the application of research and development for better products and services that improve the quality of life and stimulate economic growth.

The Foundation promotes the development of research talent through support of undergraduate and graduate students, as well as postdoctoral researchers. It administers special programs to identify and encourage participation by groups underrepresented in science and technology and to strengthen research capability at smaller institutions, small businesses, undergraduate colleges, and universities.

The Foundation supports major national and international science and engineering activities, including the U.S. Antarctic Program, the Ocean Drilling Program, global geoscience studies, and others. Cooperative scientific and engineering research activities support exchange programs for American and foreign scientists and engineers, execution of jointly designed research projects, participation in the activities of international science and engineering organizations, and travel to international conferences.

Support is provided through contracts and cooperative agreements with national centers where large facilities are made available for use by qualified scientists and engineers. Among the types of centers supported by the Foundation are astronomy and atmospheric sciences, biological and engineering research, science and technology, supercomputers, and long-term ecological research sites.

The Foundation's science and engineering education activities include grants for research and development activities directed to model instructional materials for students and teachers and the application of advanced technologies to education. Grants also are available for teacher preparation and enhancement and informal science education activities. Funding is also provided for college science instrumentation, course and curriculum improvement, faculty and student activities, and minority resource centers. In addition, studies of the status of math, science, and engineering education are supported.

The National Science Board presents the Vannevar Bush Award annually to a person who, through public service activities in science and technology, has made an outstanding contribution toward the welfare of mankind and the Nation. It also presents the Public Service Award to an individual and to a company, corporation, or organization who, through contributions to public service in areas other than research, have increased the public understanding of science or engineering. The National Science Foundation annually presents the Alan T. Waterman Award to an outstanding young scientist or engineer for support of research and study. The Foundation also provides administrative support for the President's Committee on the National Medal of Science.

Information on these awards is available through the Internet at www.nsf.gov/home/nsb/start.htm.

Sources of Information

Board and Committee Minutes Summary minutes of the open meetings of the Board may be obtained from the National Science Board Office. Phone, 703–292–7000. Information on NSB meetings, minutes, and reports is available through the Internet at www.nsf.gov/home/nsb/start.htm. Summary minutes of the Foundation's advisory groups may be obtained from the contacts listed in the notice of meetings published in the *Federal Register* or under "News and Media" on the Foundation's Web site. General information about the Foundation's advisory groups may be obtained from the Division of Human Resource Management, Room 315, Arlington, VA 22230. Phone, 703–292–8180.

Contracts The Foundation publicizes contracting and subcontracting opportunities in the *Commerce Business Daily* and other appropriate publications. Organizations seeking to undertake contract work for the Foundation should contact either the Division of Contracts, Policy, and Oversight (phone, 703–292–8240) or the Division of Administrative Services (phone, 703–292–8190), National Science Foundation, Arlington, VA 22230.

Electronic Access Information regarding NSF programs and services is available through the Internet at www.nsf.gov.

Employment Inquiries may be directed to the Division of Human Resource Management, National Science Foundation, Room 315, Arlington, VA 22230. Phone, 703–292–8180. TDD, 703–292–8044. Internet, www.nsf.gov/jobs.

Fellowships Consult the *NSF Guide to Programs* and appropriate announcements and brochures for postdoctoral fellowship opportunities that may be available through some Foundation divisions. Beginning graduate and minority graduate students wishing to apply for fellowships should contact the Directorate for Education and Human Resources. Phone, 703–292–8601.

Freedom of Information Act Requests Requests for agency records should be submitted in accordance with the Foundation's FOIA regulation at 45 CFR 612. Such requests should be clearly identified with "FOIA REQUEST" and be addressed to the FOIA Officer, Office of General Counsel, National Science Foundation, Room 1265, Arlington, VA 22230. Phone, 703–292–8060. Fax, 703–292–9041. E-mail, foia@nsf.gov.

Grants Individuals or organizations who plan to submit grant proposals should refer to the *NSF Guide to Programs, Grant Proposal Guide* (NSF–01–2), and appropriate program brochures and announcements that may be obtained as indicated in the Publications section. Grant information is also available through the Internet at www.nsf.gov.

Office of Inspector General General inquiries may be directed to the Office of Inspector General, National Science Foundation, Room 1135, Arlington, VA 22230. Phone, 703–292–7100.

Privacy Act Requests Requests for personal records should be submitted in accordance with the Foundation's Privacy Act regulation at 45 CFR 613. Such requests should be clearly identified with "PRIVACY ACT REQUEST" and be addressed to the Privacy Act Officer, National Science Foundation, Room 1265, Arlington, VA 22230. Phone, 703–292–8060.

Publications The National Science Board assesses the status and health of science and its various disciplines, including such matters as human and material resources, in reports submitted to the President for submission to the Congress. The most recent report is *Science and Engineering Indicators, 2004* (NSB–04–04).

The National Science Foundation issues publications that announce and describe new programs, critical dates, and application procedures for competitions. Single copies of these publications can be ordered by writing to NSF Clearinghouse, P.O. Box 218, Jessup, MD 20794–0218. Phone, 301–947–2722. E-mail, pubinfo@nsf.gov. Internet, www.nsf.gov.

Other Foundation publications include: the *Grant Policy Manual* (NSF–01–2), which contains comprehensive statements of Foundation grant administration policy, procedures, and guidance; *Guide to Programs,* which summarizes information about support programs; the quarterly *Antarctic Journal of the United States* and its annual review issue; and the *NSF Annual Report.* These publications are available from the Superintendent of Documents, Government Printing Office, Washington, DC 20402. Internet, www.nsf.gov.

Reading Room A collection of Foundation policy documents and staff instructions, as well as current indexes, are available to the public for inspection and copying during regular business hours, 8:30 a.m. to 5 p.m., Monday through Friday, in the National Science Foundation Library, Room 225, Arlington, VA 22230. Phone, 703–292–7830.

Small Business Activities The Office of Small Business Research and Development provides information on opportunities for Foundation support to small businesses with strong research capabilities in science and technology. Phone, 703–292–8330. The Office of Small and Disadvantaged Business Utilization oversees agency compliance with the provisions of the Small Business Act and the Small Business Investment Act of 1958, as amended (15 U.S.C. 631, 661, 683). Phone, 703–292–8330.

For further information, contact the National Science Foundation Information Center, 4201 Wilson Boulevard, Arlington, VA 22230. Phone, 703–292–5111. TDD, 703–292–5090. E-mail, info@nsf.gov. Internet, www.nsf.gov.

NATIONAL TRANSPORTATION SAFETY BOARD

490 L'Enfant Plaza SW., Washington, DC 20594
Phone, 202–314–6000. Internet, www.ntsb.gov.

Chairman	MARK V. ROSENKER, *Acting*
Vice Chairman	MARK V. ROSENKER
Members	DEBORAH HERSMAN, KATHRYN O'LEARY HIGGINS, (2 VACANCIES)
Executive Director	(VACANCY)
Managing Director	JOSEPH OSTERMAN
Chief Financial Officer	STEVEN GOLDBERG
Chief Administrative Law Judge	WILLIAM E. FOWLER, JR.
General Counsel	GARY HALBERT
Deputy General Counsel	KAREN LANIER
Director, Office of Aviation Safety	JOHN C. CLARK
Deputy Director	THOMAS HAUETER, *Acting*
Chief, Major Investigations	JOHN DELISI
Chief Advisor for International Safety Affairs	ROBERT MACINTOSH
Deputy Director, Regional Operations	JEFF GUZZETTI
Director, Office of Government and Industry Affairs	(VACANCY)
Deputy Director for Government Affairs	CHERYL MCCULLOUGH
Director, Office of Transportation Disaster Assistance	SHARON BRYSON
Assistant to the Director	ERIC GROSOF

Director, Office of Public Affairs	Ted Lopatkiewicz
Director, Office of Highway Safety	Bruce Magladry, *Acting*
Deputy Director	Dwight Foster, *Acting*
Director, Office of Marine Safety	John Spencer
Director, Office of Railroad, Pipeline, and Hazardous Materials Investigations	Robert J. Chipkevich
Deputy Director	James Ritter
Associate Director for Railroad Investigations	(vacancy)
Associate Director for Hazardous Materials Investigations	Robert Trainor
Associate Director for Pipeline Investigations	Rod Dyck
Director, Office of Research and Engineering	Vernon Ellingstad
Deputy Director	Joseph Kolly
Director, Office of Safety Recommendations and Communications	Elaine Weinstein
Deputy Director for Operations	Jim Rosenberg
Director, Office of the Academy	Donald Chupp, *Acting*

[For the National Transportation Safety Board statement of organization, see the *Code of Federal Regulations,* Title 49, Part 800]

The National Transportation Safety Board seeks to ensure that all types of transportation in the United States are conducted safely. The Board investigates accidents, conducts studies, and makes recommendations to Government agencies, the transportation industry, and others on safety measures and practices.

The National Transportation Safety Board (NTSB) was established in 1967 and became totally independent on April 1, 1975, by the Independent Safety Board Act of 1974 (49 U.S.C. 1111).

NTSB consists of five members appointed by the President with the advice and consent of the Senate for 5-year terms. The President designates two of these members as Chairman and Vice Chairman of the Board for 2-year terms. The designation of the Chairman is made with the advice and consent of the Senate.

Activities

Accident Investigation NTSB is responsible for investigating, determining probable cause, making safety recommendations, and reporting the facts and circumstances of incidents in the following areas:

—U.S. civil aviation and certain public-use aircraft accidents;

—railroad accidents in which there is a fatality or substantial property damage, or that involve a passenger train;

—pipeline accidents in which there is a fatality, substantial property damage, or significant injury to the environment;

—highway accidents, including railroad grade-crossing accidents, that the Board selects in cooperation with the States;

—major marine casualties and marine accidents involving a public vessel and a nonpublic vessel, in accordance with regulations prescribed jointly by the Board and the U.S. Coast Guard;

—certain accidents involving hazardous materials; and

—other transportation accidents that are catastrophic, involve problems of a recurring character, or otherwise should be investigated in the judgment of the Board.

Safety Problem Identification NTSB makes recommendations on matters pertaining to transportation safety and is a catalyst for transportation accident prevention by conducting safety studies and special investigations; assessing techniques of accident investigation and publishing recommended procedures; establishing regulatory requirements for reporting accidents; evaluating the transportation safety consciousness and efficacy of other Government agencies in the prevention of accidents; evaluating the adequacy of safeguards and

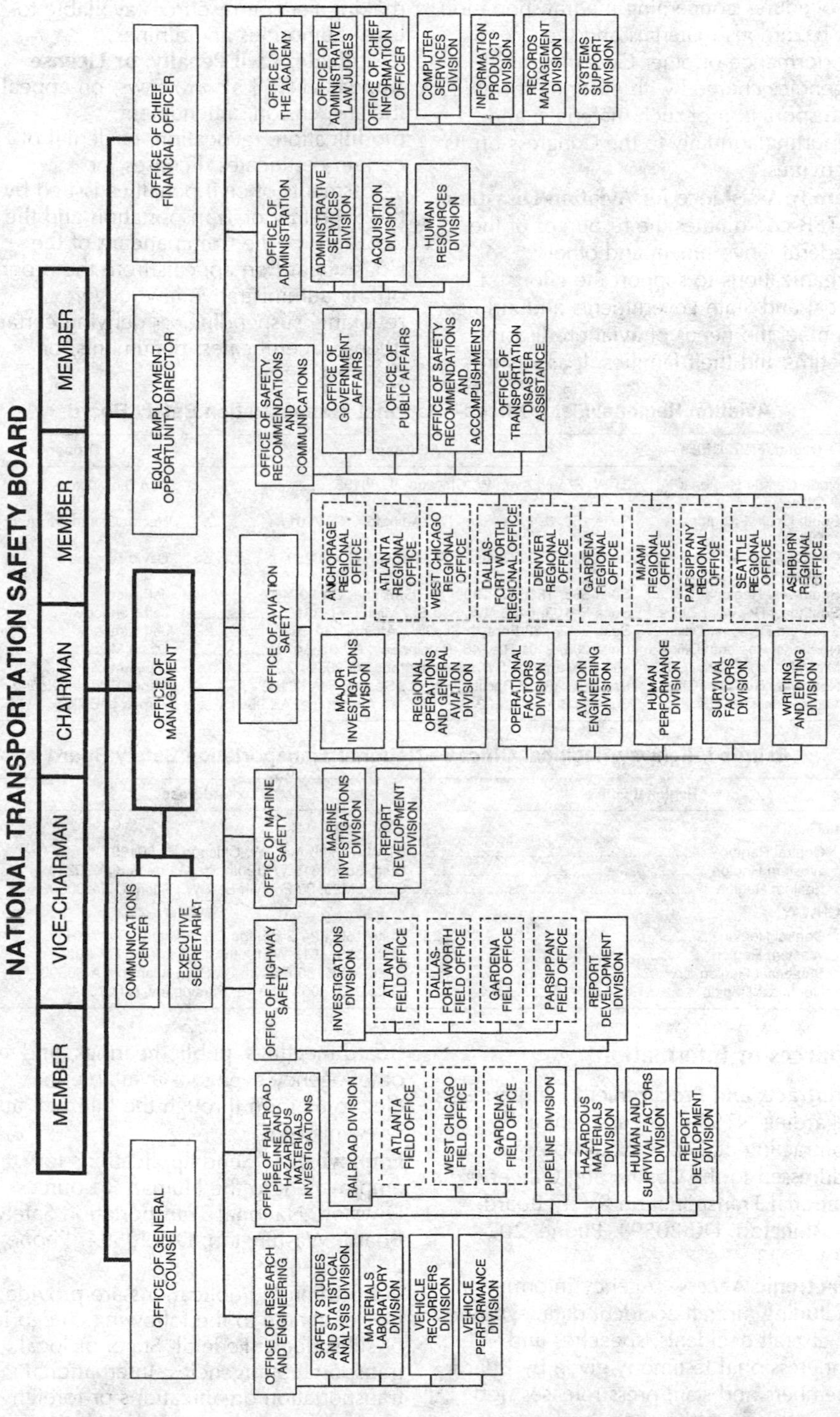
NATIONAL TRANSPORTATION SAFETY BOARD
MEMBER
VICE-CHAIRMAN
CHAIRMAN
MEMBER
MEMBER
OFFICE OF GENERAL COUNSEL
COMMUNICATIONS CENTER
EXECUTIVE SECRETARIAT
OFFICE OF MANAGEMENT
EQUAL EMPLOYMENT OPPORTUNITY DIRECTOR
OFFICE OF CHIEF FINANCIAL OFFICER
OFFICE OF RESEARCH AND ENGINEERING
SAFETY STUDIES AND STATISTICAL ANALYSIS DIVISION
MATERIALS LABORATORY DIVISION
VEHICLE RECORDERS DIVISION
VEHICLE PERFORMANCE DIVISION
OFFICE OF RAILROAD, PIPELINE AND HAZARDOUS MATERIALS INVESTIGATIONS
RAILROAD DIVISION
ATLANTA FIELD OFFICE
WEST CHICAGO FIELD OFFICE
GARDENA FIELD OFFICE
PIPELINE DIVISION
HAZARDOUS MATERIALS DIVISION
HUMAN AND SURVIVAL FACTORS DIVISION
REPORT DEVELOPMENT DIVISION
OFFICE OF HIGHWAY SAFETY
INVESTIGATIONS DIVISION
ATLANTA FIELD OFFICE
DALLAS-FORT WORTH FIELD OFFICE
GARDENA FIELD OFFICE
PARSIPPANY FIELD OFFICE
REPORT DEVELOPMENT DIVISION
OFFICE OF MARINE SAFETY
MARINE INVESTIGATIONS DIVISION
REPORT DEVELOPMENT DIVISION
OFFICE OF AVIATION SAFETY
MAJOR INVESTIGATIONS DIVISION
REGIONAL OPERATIONS AND GENERAL AVIATION DIVISION
OPERATIONAL FACTORS DIVISION
AVIATION ENGINEERING DIVISION
HUMAN PERFORMANCE DIVISION
SURVIVAL FACTORS DIVISION
WRITING AND EDITING DIVISION
ANCHORAGE REGIONAL OFFICE
ATLANTA REGIONAL OFFICE
WEST CHICAGO REGIONAL OFFICE
DALLAS-FORT WORTH REGIONAL OFFICE
DENVER REGIONAL OFFICE
GARDENA REGIONAL OFFICE
MIAMI REGIONAL OFFICE
PARSIPPANY REGIONAL OFFICE
SEATTLE REGIONAL OFFICE
ASHBURN REGIONAL OFFICE
OFFICE OF SAFETY RECOMMENDATIONS AND COMMUNICATIONS
OFFICE OF GOVERNMENT AFFAIRS
OFFICE OF PUBLIC AFFAIRS
OFFICE OF SAFETY RECOMMENDATIONS AND ACCOMPLISHMENTS
OFFICE OF TRANSPORTATION DISASTER ASSISTANCE
OFFICE OF ADMINISTRATION
ADMINISTRATIVE SERVICES DIVISION
ACQUISITION DIVISION
HUMAN RESOURCES DIVISION
OFFICE OF THE ACADEMY
OFFICE OF ADMINISTRATIVE LAW JUDGES
OFFICE OF CHIEF INFORMATION OFFICER
COMPUTER SERVICES DIVISION
INFORMATION PRODUCTS DIVISION
RECORDS MANAGEMENT DIVISION
SYSTEMS SUPPORT DIVISION

procedures concerning the transportation of hazardous materials and the performance of other Government agencies charged with ensuring the safe transportation of such materials; and reporting annually to the Congress on its activities.

Family Assistance for Aviation Disasters NTSB coordinates the resources of the Federal Government and other organizations to support the efforts of local and State governments and airlines to meet the needs of aviation disaster victims and their families. It assists in making Federal resources available to local authorities and airlines.

Certificate, Civil Penalty, or License Appeal NTSB also reviews, on appeal, the suspension, amendment, modification, revocation, or denial of certain certificates, licenses, or assessments of civil penalties issued by the Secretary of Transportation and the decisions of the Commandant of the Coast Guard on appeals from the orders of any administrative law judge, revoking, suspending, or denying certain licenses, certificates, documents, or registers.

Aviation Regional/Field Offices—National Transportation Safety Board

Region/Field Office	Address	Officer
North Central Regional Office.	31 W. 775 N. Ave., W. Chicago, IL 60185	Carl Dinwiddie
South Central Regional Office.	Suite 150, 624 Six Flags Dr., Arlington, TX 76011	Hector Casanova, *Acting*
Central Mountain Regional Office.	Suite 500, 4760 Oakland St., Denver, CO 80239	David Bowling
Southwest Regional Office	Suite 555, 1515 W. 190th St., Gardena, CA 90248	Jeff Rich
Southeast Regional Office	Suite B–103, 8405 NW. 53d St., Miami, FL 33166	Jeff Kennedy
Southern Regional Office	Suite 3M25, 60 Forsyth St. SW., Atlanta, GA 30303	Jeff Kennedy
Northeast Regional Office	Suite 203, 2001 Rte. 46, Parsippany, NJ 07054	David Muzio
Mid-Atlantic Regional Office	490 L'Enfant Plz. SW., Washington, DC 20594	David Muzio
Northwest Regional Office	Rm. 201, 19518 Pacific Hwy. S., Seattle, WA 98188	Debra Eckrote, *Acting*
Alaska Regional Office	Box 11, Rm. 216, 222 W. 7th Ave., Anchorage, AK 99513	James LaBelle

Railroad/Highway Regional Offices—National Transportation Safety Board

Regional Office	Address
RAILROAD:	
Central Region	31 W. 775 N. Ave., W. Chicago, IL 60185
Western Region	Suite 555, 1515 W. 190th St., Gardena, CA 90248
Eastern Region	Suite 3M25, 60 Forsyth St. SW., Atlanta, GA 30303
HIGHWAY:	
Central Region	Suite 150, 624 Six Flags Dr., Arlington, TX 76011
Western Region	Suite 555, 1515 W. 190th St., Gardena, CA 90248
Southeast Region	Suite 3M25, 60 Forsyth St. SW., Atlanta, GA 30303
Northeast Region	Suite 203, 2001 Rte. 46, Parsippany, NJ 07054

Sources of Information

Contracts and Procurement Inquiries regarding NTSB's procurement and contracting activities should be addressed to the Contracting Officer, National Transportation Safety Board, Washington, DC 20594. Phone, 202–314–6223.

Electronic Access Agency information, including aircraft accident data, synopses of aircraft accidents, speeches and congressional testimony given by Board members and staff, press releases, job vacancy announcements, and notices of Board meetings, public hearings, and other agency events, is available in electronic form through the Internet, at www.ntsb.gov.

Employment Send applications for employment to the Human Resources Division, National Transportation Safety Board, Washington, DC 20594. Phone, 202–314–6239.

Publications Publications are provided free of charge to the following categories of subscribers: Federal, State, or local transportation agencies; international transportation organizations or foreign governments; educational institutions or public libraries; nonprofit public safety organizations; and the news media. Persons in these categories who are interested in receiving copies of Board publications should contact the Records Management Branch, National Transportation Safety Board, Washington, DC 20594. Phone, 202–314–6551. All other persons interested in receiving publications must purchase them from the National Technical Information Service, 5285 Port Royal Road, Springfield, VA 22161. Orders may be placed by telephone to the Subscription Unit at 703–487–4630, or the sales desk at 703–487–4768.

Reading Room The Board's Public Reference Room is available for record inspection or photocopying. It is located in Room 6500 at the Board's Washington, DC, headquarters and is open from 8:45 a.m. to 4:45 p.m. every business day. Requests for access to public records should be made in person at Room 6500, or by writing the Records Management Branch, National Transportation Safety Board, Washington, DC 20594. Phone, 202–314–6551.

For further information, contact the Office of Public Affairs, National Transportation Safety Board, 490 L'Enfant Plaza SW., Washington, DC 20594. Phone, 202–314–6100. Fax, 202–314–6110. Internet, www.ntsb.gov.

NUCLEAR REGULATORY COMMISSION

Washington, DC 20555
Phone, 301–415–7000. Internet, www.nrc.gov.

Chairman	DALE E. KLEIN
Commissioners	GREGORY B. JACZKO, PETER B. LYONS, EDWARD MCGAFFIGAN, JR., JEFFREY S. MERRIFIELD
Chief Administrative Judge, Atomic Safety and Licensing Board Panel	E. ROY HAWKINS
Director, Office of Commission Appellate Adjudication	JOHN F. CORDES, JR.
Director, Office of International Programs	JANICE DUNN LEE
General Counsel	KAREN D. CYR
Secretary of the Commission	ANNETTE L. VIETTI-COOK
Chairman, Advisory Committee on Nuclear Waste	MICHAEL T. RYAN
Chairman, Advisory Committee on Reactor Safeguards	GRAHAM B. WALLIS
Chief Financial Officer	JESSE L. FUNCHES
Deputy Executive Director for Information Services and Administration	JACQUELINE E. SILBER
Director, Office of Congressional Affairs	REBECCA L. SCHMIDT
Director, Office of Public Affairs	ELIOT B. BRENNER
Inspector General	HUBERT T. BELL, JR.

[For the Nuclear Regulatory Commission statement of organization, see the *Code of Federal Regulations,* Title 10, Part I]

The Nuclear Regulatory Commission licenses and regulates civilian use of nuclear energy to protect public health and safety and the environment. This is achieved by licensing persons and companies to build and operate nuclear reactors and other facilities and to own and use nuclear materials. The Commission makes rules and sets standards for these types of licenses. It also carefully inspects the activities of the persons and companies licensed to ensure compliance with the safety rules of the Commission.

The Nuclear Regulatory Commission (NRC) was established as an independent regulatory agency under the provisions of the Energy Reorganization Act of 1974 (42 U.S.C. 5801 *et seq.*) and Executive Order 11834 of January 15, 1975. All licensing and related regulatory functions formerly assigned to the Atomic Energy Commission were transferred to the Commission.

The Commission's major program components are the Office of Nuclear Reactor Regulation, the Office of Nuclear Material Safety and Safeguards, and the Office of Nuclear Regulatory Research. Headquarters offices are located in suburban Maryland, and there are four regional offices.

The Commission ensures that the civilian uses of nuclear materials and facilities are conducted in a manner consistent with the public health and safety, environmental quality, national security, and the antitrust laws. Most of the Commission's effort is focused on regulating the use of nuclear energy to generate electric power.

Activities

The Nuclear Regulatory Commission is primarily responsible for the following functions:

—licensing the construction, operation, and closure of nuclear reactors and other nuclear facilities, such as nuclear fuel cycle facilities, low-level radioactive waste disposal sites under NRC jurisdiction, the geologic repository for high-level radioactive waste, and nonpower test and research reactors;

—licensing the possession, use, processing, handling, and export of nuclear material;

—licensing the operators of nuclear power and nonpower test and research reactors;

—inspecting licensed facilities and activities;

—conducting the U.S. Government research program on light-water reactor safety;

—developing and implementing rules and regulations that govern licensed nuclear activities;

—investigating nuclear incidents and allegations concerning any matter regulated by the NRC;

—maintaining the NRC Incident Response Program;

—collecting, analyzing, and disseminating information about the operational safety of commercial nuclear power reactors and certain nonreactor activities; and

—developing effective working relationships with the States regarding reactor operations and the regulation of nuclear material, and assuring that adequate regulatory programs are maintained by those States that exercise regulatory control over certain nuclear materials in the State.

Sources of Information

Freedom of Information Act Requests Requests for copies of records should be directed to the FOIA/Privacy Act Officer, Mail Stop T–5 F11, Nuclear Regulatory Commission, Washington, DC 20555–0001. Phone, 301–415–7169. Fax, 301–415–5130. Requests may also be submitted using the form on our Web site at www.nrc.gov.

Publications NRC publishes scientific, technical, and administrative information dealing with licensing and regulation of civilian nuclear facilities and materials, as well as periodic reports including the annual *Report to Congress on Abnormal Occurrences,* the annual *Accountability and Performance Report,* the quarterly *Licensee, Contractor, and Vendor Inspection Status Report,* the annual *NRC Information Digest,* the *NRC Strategic Plan,* and *Nuclear Regulatory Commission Issuances.*

Some publications and documents are available on the Internet, at www.nrc.gov. The U.S. Government Printing Office (GPO) and the National Technical Information Service (NTIS) sell

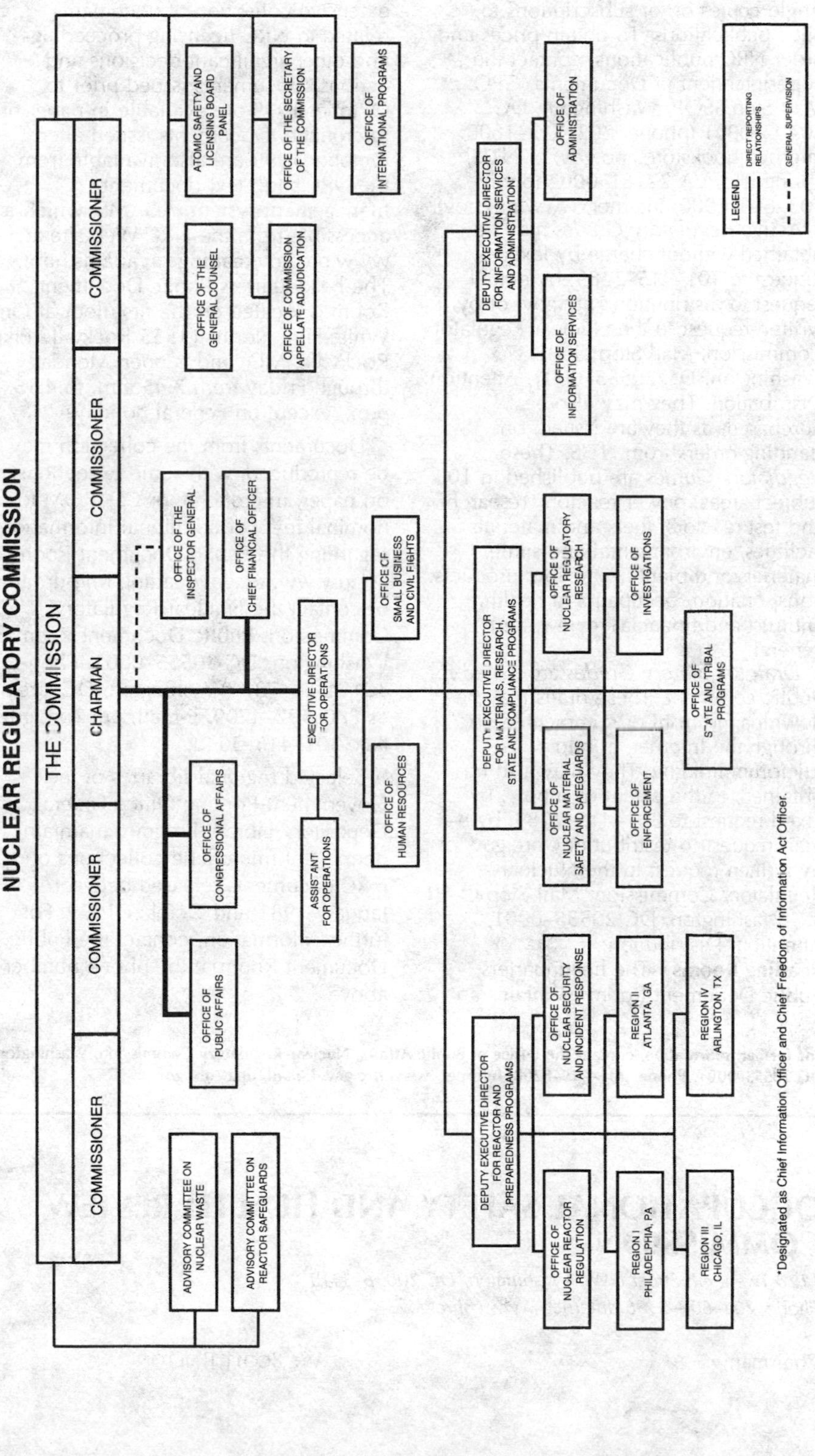
NUCLEAR REGULATORY COMMISSION
THE COMMISSION
COMMISSIONER
COMMISSIONER
CHAIRMAN
COMMISSIONER
COMMISSIONER
ADVISORY COMMITTEE ON NUCLEAR WASTE
ADVISORY COMMITTEE ON REACTOR SAFEGUARDS
OFFICE OF PUBLIC AFFAIRS
OFFICE OF CONGRESSIONAL AFFAIRS
ASSISTANT FOR OPERATIONS
OFFICE OF HUMAN RESOURCES
EXECUTIVE DIRECTOR FOR OPERATIONS
OFFICE OF THE INSPECTOR GENERAL
OFFICE OF CHIEF FINANCIAL OFFICER
OFFICE OF SMALL BUSINESS AND CIVIL RIGHTS
OFFICE OF THE GENERAL COUNSEL
OFFICE OF COMMISSION APPELLATE ADJUDICATION
ATOMIC SAFETY AND LICENSING BOARD PANEL
OFFICE OF THE SECRETARY OF THE COMMISSION
OFFICE OF INTERNATIONAL PROGRAMS
DEPUTY EXECUTIVE DIRECTOR FOR REACTOR AND PREPAREDNESS PROGRAMS
DEPUTY EXECUTIVE DIRECTOR FOR MATERIALS, RESEARCH, STATE AND COMPLIANCE PROGRAMS
DEPUTY EXECUTIVE DIRECTOR FOR INFORMATION SERVICES AND ADMINISTRATION*
OFFICE OF NUCLEAR REACTOR REGULATION
OFFICE OF NUCLEAR SECURITY AND INCIDENT RESPONSE
OFFICE OF NUCLEAR MATERIAL SAFETY AND SAFEGUARDS
OFFICE OF NUCLEAR REGULATORY RESEARCH
OFFICE OF INFORMATION SERVICES
OFFICE OF ADMINISTRATION
REGION I PHILADELPHIA, PA
REGION II ATLANTA, GA
OFFICE OF ENFORCEMENT
OFFICE OF INVESTIGATIONS
REGION III CHICAGO, IL
REGION IV ARLINGTON, TX
OFFICE OF STATE AND TRIBAL PROGRAMS
LEGEND
DIRECT REPORTING RELATIONSHIPS
GENERAL SUPERVISION
*Designated as Chief Information Officer and Chief Freedom of Information Act Officer.

single copies of, or subscriptions to, NRC publications. To obtain prices and order NRC publications, contact the Superintendent of Documents, GPO, Mail Stop SSOP, Washington, DC 20402–0001 (phone, 202–512–1800; Internet, bookstore.gpo.gov) or NTIS, Springfield, VA 22161–0002 (phone, 703–605–6000; Internet, www.ntis.gov).

Active *Regulatory Guides* may be obtained without charge by faxed request to 301–415–2289, by e-mail request to distribution@nrc.gov, or by written request to the Nuclear Regulatory Commission, Mail Stop O–P1 37, Washington, DC 20555–0001, Attention: Distribution. They may also be purchased, as they are issued, on standing orders from NTIS. These *Regulatory Guides* are published in 10 subject areas: power reactors, research and test reactors, fuels and materials facilities, environmental and siting, materials and plant protection, products, transportation, occupational health, antitrust and financial review, and general.

Draft Regulatory Guides are issued for public comment. These drafts may be downloaded from or commented on through the Internet, at http://ruleforum.llnl.gov. They may also be obtained, to the extent of supply, by faxed request to 301–415–2289, by e-mail request to distribution@nrc.gov, or by written request to the Nuclear Regulatory Commission, Mail Stop O–P1 37, Washington, DC 20555–0001, Attention: Distribution.

Reading Rooms The headquarters Public Document Room maintains an extensive collection of documents related to NRC licensing proceedings and other significant decisions and actions. Documents issued prior to October 1999 are available in paper or microfiche. Documents issued after October 1999 are also available from the NRC's full-text document management system, ADAMS, which is accessible from the NRC Web site at www.nrc.gov/reading-rm/adams.html. The headquarters Public Document Room is located on the first floor at One White Flint North, 11555 Rockville Pike, Rockville, MD, and is open Monday through Friday from 7:45 a.m. to 4:15 p.m., except on Federal holidays.

Documents from the collection may be reproduced, with some exceptions, on paper, microfiche, or CD–ROM for a nominal fee. For additional information regarding the Public Document Room, go to www.nrc.gov/reading-rm/pdr.html or contact the Nuclear Regulatory Commission, Public Document Room, Washington, DC 20555–0001. Phone, 301–415–4737 (Washington, DC, area), or 800–397–4209. E-mail, pdr@nrc.gov. Fax, 301–415–3548.

Selected regional libraries of the Government Printing Office Federal Depository Library Program maintain permanent microfiche collections of NRC documents released between January 1981 and October 1999. For further information, contact the Public Document Room at the phone number above.

For further information, contact the Office of Public Affairs, Nuclear Regulatory Commission, Washington, DC 20555–0001. Phone, 301–415–8200. Internet, www.nrc.gov. E-mail, opa@nrc.gov.

OCCUPATIONAL SAFETY AND HEALTH REVIEW COMMISSION

1120 Twentieth Street NW., Washington, DC 20036–3419
Phone, 202–606–5398. Internet, www.oshrc.gov.

Chairman — W. Scott Railton

Commissioners	THOMASINA V. ROGERS, HORACE A. THOMPSON
General Counsel	ALEXANDER FERNÁNDEZ
Chief Administrative Law Judge	IRVING SOMMER
Special Assistant and Counsel to the Chairman	RICHARD C. LOEB
Director, Office of Administration	MERRITT C. BROWN, *Acting*
Executive Secretary	RAY H. DARLING, JR.

The Occupational Safety and Health Review Commission works to ensure the timely and fair resolution of cases involving the alleged exposure of American workers to unsafe or unhealthy working conditions.

The Occupational Safety and Health Review Commission is an independent, quasi-judicial agency established by the Occupational Safety and Health Act of 1970 (29 U.S.C. 651–678).

The Commission is charged with ruling on cases forwarded to it by the Department of Labor when disagreements arise over the results of safety and health inspections performed by the Department's Occupational Safety and Health Administration. Employers have the right to dispute any alleged job safety or health violation found during the inspection by the Administration, the penalties it proposed, and the time given by the agency to correct any hazardous situation. Employees and representatives of employees may initiate a case by challenging the propriety of the time the Administration has allowed for correction of any violative condition.

The Occupational Safety and Health Act covers virtually every employer in the country. Enforced by the Secretary of Labor, the act is an effort to reduce the incidence of personal injuries, illness, and deaths among working men and women in the United States that result from their employment. It requires employers to furnish to each of their employees a working environment free from recognized hazards that are causing or likely to cause death or serious physical harm to the employees and to comply with occupational safety and health standards promulgated under the act.

Activities

The Commission was created to adjudicate enforcement actions initiated under the act when they are contested by employers, employees, or representatives of employees. A case arises when a citation is issued against an employer as the result of an Occupational Safety and Health Administration inspection and it is contested within 15 working days.

The Commission is more of a court system than a simple tribunal, for within the Commission there are two levels of adjudication. All cases are assigned to an administrative law judge, who decides the case. Ordinarily the hearing is held in the community where the alleged violation occurred or as close as possible. At the hearing, the Secretary of Labor will generally have the burden of proving the case. After the hearing, the judge must issue a decision, based on findings of fact and conclusions of law.

A substantial number of the decisions of the judges become final orders of the Commission. However, each decision is subject to discretionary review by the three members of the Commission upon the direction of any one of the three, if done within 30 days of the filing of the decision. When that occurs, the Commission issues its own decision.

Once a case is decided, any party to the case adversely affected or aggrieved thereby may seek a review of the decision in the United States Courts of Appeals.

The Commission's principal office is in Washington, DC. There are also two regional offices where Commission judges are stationed.

OCCUPATIONAL SAFETY AND HEALTH REVIEW COMMISSION

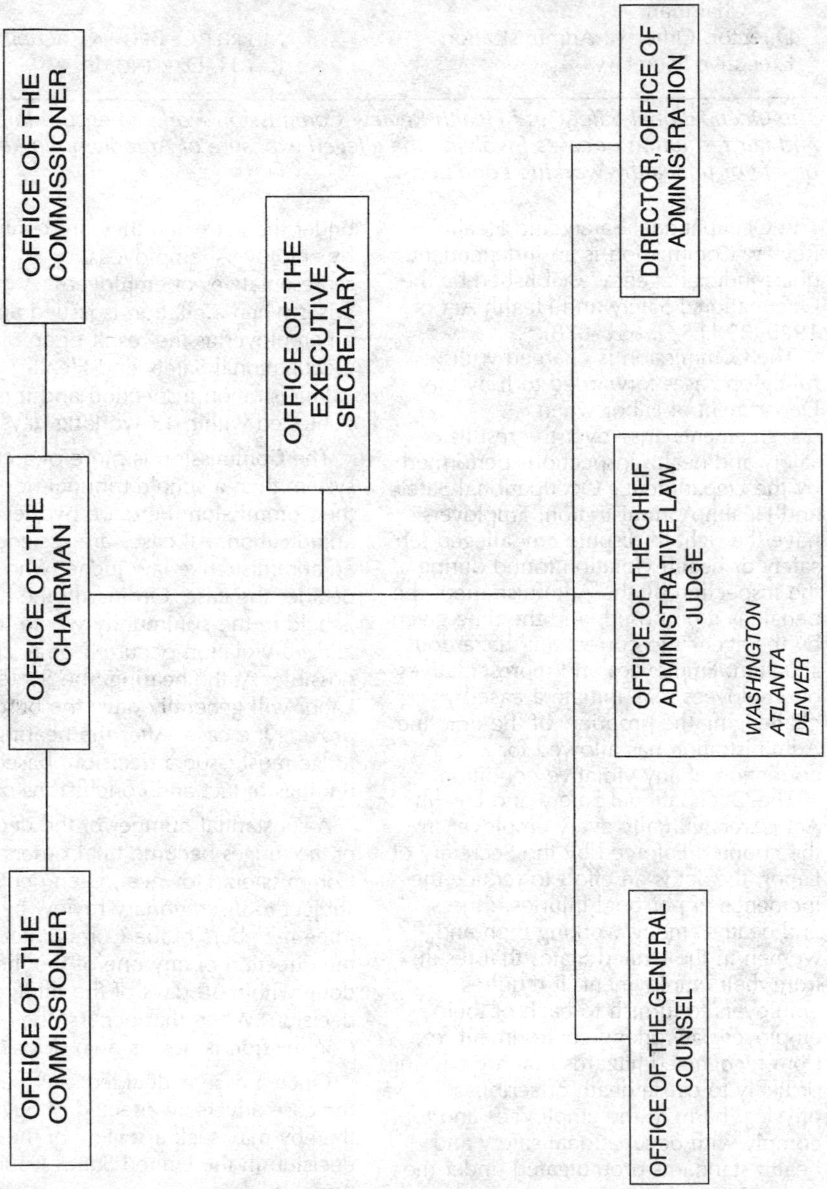

Review Commission Judges—Occupational Safety and Health Review Commission

City/Address	Telephone
Atlanta, GA (Rm. 2R90, Bldg. 1924, 100 Alabama St. SW., 30303–3104)	404–562–1640
Denver, CO (Rm. 250, 1244 N. Speer Blvd., 80204)	303–844–3409

Sources of Information

Publications Copies of the Commission's *Rules of Procedure, Guide to Review Commission Procedures, Guide to Simplified Proceedings,* and *Employee Guide to Review Commission Procedures: Supplement to the Guide to Review Commission Procedures,* decisions, and pamphlets explaining the functions of the Commission are available from the Public Information Office at the Commission's Washington, DC, office and on the Internet at www.oshrc.gov.

For further information, contact the Director, Office of Administration, Occupational Safety and Health Review Commission, 1120 Twentieth Street NW., Washington, DC 20036–3419. Phone, 202–606–5398. Fax, 202–606–5050. Internet, www.oshrc.gov.

OFFICE OF THE DIRECTOR OF NATIONAL INTELLIGENCE

Washington, DC 20511
Phone, 202–201–1111. Internet, www.dni.gov.

Director	John D. Negroponte
Principal Deputy Director	Gen. Michael V. Hayden, USAF
Deputy Director (Collection)	Mary Margaret Graham
Deputy Director (Analysis)	Thomas Fingar
Deputy Director (Management)	Patrick F. Kennedy
Deputy Director (Customer Outcomes)	Lt. Gen. Ronald Burgess, Jr., USA
Associate Director of National Intelligence and Chief of Staff	David Shedd
Associate Director of National Intelligence for Science and Technology	Eric Haseltine
Associate Director of National Intelligence and Chief Information Officer	Dale Meyerrose
Program Manager for Information Sharing Environment	Thomas E. McNamara
Inspector General	Edward Maguire
Chief of Equal Employment Opportunity	John M. Robinson
Executive Secretary	Don Nau
General Counsel	Benjamin A. Powell
Director of Public Affairs	Judith Emmel
Chief of Protocol	Nancy Pilon
Director of Legislative Affairs	Darlene Connelly
Assistant Deputy Director of National Intelligence for Open Source	Eliot A. Jardines
Civil Liberties Protection Officer	Alexander W. Joel
National Counterterrorism Center	Vice Adm. John Redd, USN (Ret.)
National Counterproliferation Center	Kenneth Brill
National Counterintelligence Executive	Eric Boswell, *Acting*

Mission Manager for North Korea	JOSEPH DETRANI
Mission Manager for Iran	S. LESLIE IRELAND

As head of the Intelligence Community, the Director of National Intelligence oversees and coordinates the foreign and domestic activities of the Intelligence Community across the Federal Government.

The Director of National Intelligence (DNI) is a Cabinet-level post established by section 1011 of the Intelligence Reform and Terrorism Prevention Act of 2004 (50 U.S.C. 403). The DNI is responsible for overseeing and coordinating elements of the Intelligence Community and is the principal intelligence adviser to the President. The DNI reports directly to the President of the United States.

The DNI's responsibilities are:

—coordinating collection, processing, analysis, and dissemination of intelligence information required by the President, the National Security Council, the Secretaries of State and Defense, and other executive branch officials in performing their duties and responsibilities;

—ensuring the sharing of intelligence information within the Intelligence Community;

—establishing personnel policies and programs applicable to the Intelligence Community; and

—determining the annual National Intelligence Program budget and directing the expenditure of those funds.

For further information, contact the Office of the Director of National Intelligence, Washington, DC 20511. Phone, 202–201–1111. Internet, www.dni.gov.

OFFICE OF GOVERNMENT ETHICS

1201 New York Avenue NW., Suite 500, Washington, DC 20005–3917
Phone, 202–482–9300. Internet, www.usoge.gov.

Director	ROBERT I. CUSICK
Deputy Director for the Office of Administration and Information Management	DANIEL D. DUNNING
Deputy Director for the Office of Agency Programs	JOSEPH E. GANGLOFF
Deputy Director to the Office of International Assistance and Governance Initiatives	JANE S. LEY
General Counsel	MARILYN L. GLYNN
Deputy General Counsel	SUSAN PROPPER

[For the Office of Government Ethics statement of organization, see the *Code of Federal Regulations,* Title 5, Part 2600]

The Office of Government Ethics exercises leadership in the executive branch to prevent conflicts of interest on the part of Government employees and to resolve those conflicts of interest that do occur. In partnership with executive branch agencies and departments, the Office fosters high ethical standards for employees and strengthens the public's confidence that the Government's business is conducted with impartiality and integrity. The Office is the principal agency for administering the Ethics in Government Act for the executive branch.

The Office of Government Ethics is a separate executive agency established under the Ethics in Government Act of 1978, as amended (5 U.S.C. app. 401).

The Director of the Office is appointed by the President with the advice and consent of the Senate for a 5-year term.

Activities

The chief responsibilities of the Office are as follows:

—developing rules and regulations pertaining to standards of ethical conduct of executive branch officials, public and confidential financial disclosure of executive branch officials, executive agency ethics training programs, and the identification and resolution of conflicts of interest;

—monitoring and investigating compliance with the executive branch financial disclosure requirements of the Ethics in Government Act of 1978, as amended;

—providing ethics program assistance and information to executive branch agencies through a desk officer system;

—conducting periodic reviews of the ethics programs of executive agencies;

—ordering corrective action on the part of agencies and employees, including orders to establish or modify an agency's ethics program;

—providing guidance on and promoting understanding of ethical standards in executive agencies through an extensive program of Government ethics advice, education, and training;

—evaluating the effectiveness of the Ethics Act, the conflict of interest laws, and other related statutes; and

—recommending appropriate new legislation or amendments.

Sources of Information

Electronic Access Information regarding Office of Government Ethics services and programs is available in electronic format on the Internet, at www.usoge.gov.

Publications The Office of Government Ethics periodically updates its publication, *The Informal Advisory Letters and Memoranda and Formal Opinions of the United States Office of Government Ethics,* available from the Government Printing Office. In addition, the Office has ethics publications and instructional videotapes available. Upon request, the Office also provides copies of executive branch public financial disclosure reports (SF 278s) in accordance with the Ethics Act and the Office's regulations.

For further information, contact the Office of Government Ethics, Suite 500, 1201 New York Avenue NW., Washington, DC 20005–3917. Phone, 202–482–9300. TDD, 202–482–9293. Fax, 202–482–9237. Internet, www.usoge.gov.

OFFICE OF PERSONNEL MANAGEMENT

1900 E Street NW., Washington, DC 20415–0001
Phone, 202–606–1800. Internet, www.opm.gov.

Director	LINDA M. SPRINGER
Deputy Director	DAN G. BLAIR
Chief of Staff	TRICIA HOLLIS
Senior Advisor for Homeland Security	(VACANCY)
Director, Office of Human Resources Line of Business	NORMAN ENGER
Chair, Federal Prevailing Rate Advisory Committee	(VACANCY)
Inspector General	PATRICK E. MCFARLAND
Director, Office of Congressional Relations	JOHN C. GARTLAND

Associate Director, Strategic Human Resources Policy	RONALD SANDERS
Associate Director, Human Resources Products and Services	ROBERT F. DANBECK
Associate Director, Human Capital and Merit Systems	MARTA BRITO PEREZ
Director, Communications and Public Liaison	SCOTT HATCH
Associate Director, Management and Chief Financial Officer	CLARENCE C. CRAWFORD
General Counsel	KATHIE A. WHIPPLE, *Acting*

[For the Office of Personnel Management statement of organization, see the *Federal Register* of Jan. 5, 1979, 44 FR 1501]

The Office of Personnel Management administers a merit system to ensure compliance with personnel laws and regulations and assists agencies in recruiting, examining, and promoting people on the basis of their knowledge and skills, regardless of their race, religion, sex, political influence, or other nonmerit factors. Its role is to provide guidance to agencies in operating human resources programs which effectively support their missions and to provide an array of personnel services to applicants and employees. The Office supports Government program managers in their human resources management responsibilities and provides benefits to employees, retired employees, and their survivors.

The Office of Personnel Management (OPM) was created as an independent establishment by Reorganization Plan No. 2 of 1978 (5 U.S.C. app.), pursuant to Executive Order 12107 of December 28, 1978. Many of the functions of the former United States Civil Service Commission were transferred to OPM.

Activities

Employee Benefits OPM manages numerous activities that directly affect the well-being of the Federal employee and indirectly enhance employee effectiveness. These include health benefits, life insurance, and retirement benefits.

Examining and Staffing The Office of Personnel Management is responsible for providing departments and agencies with technical assistance and guidance in examining competitive positions in the Federal civil service for General Schedule grades 1 through 15 and Federal Wage system positions. In addition, OPM is responsible for the following duties:

—providing testing and examination services, at the request of an agency, on a reimbursable basis;

—establishing basic qualification standards for all occupations;

—certifying agency delegated examining units to conduct examining;

—providing employment information for competitive service positions; and

—providing policy direction and guidance on promotions, reassignments, appointments in the excepted and competitive services, reinstatements, temporary and term employment, veterans preference, workforce planning and reshaping, organizational design, career transition, and other staffing provisions.

Executive Resources OPM leads in the selection, management, and development of Federal executives. OPM provides policy guidance, consulting services, and technical support on Senior Executive Service (SES) recruitment, selection, succession planning, mobility performance, awards, and removals. It reviews agency nominations for SES career appointments and administers the Qualifications Review Boards that certify candidates' executive qualifications. It manages SES, senior-level, and scientific and professional space allocations to agencies, administers the Presidential Rank Awards program, and conducts orientation sessions for newly appointed

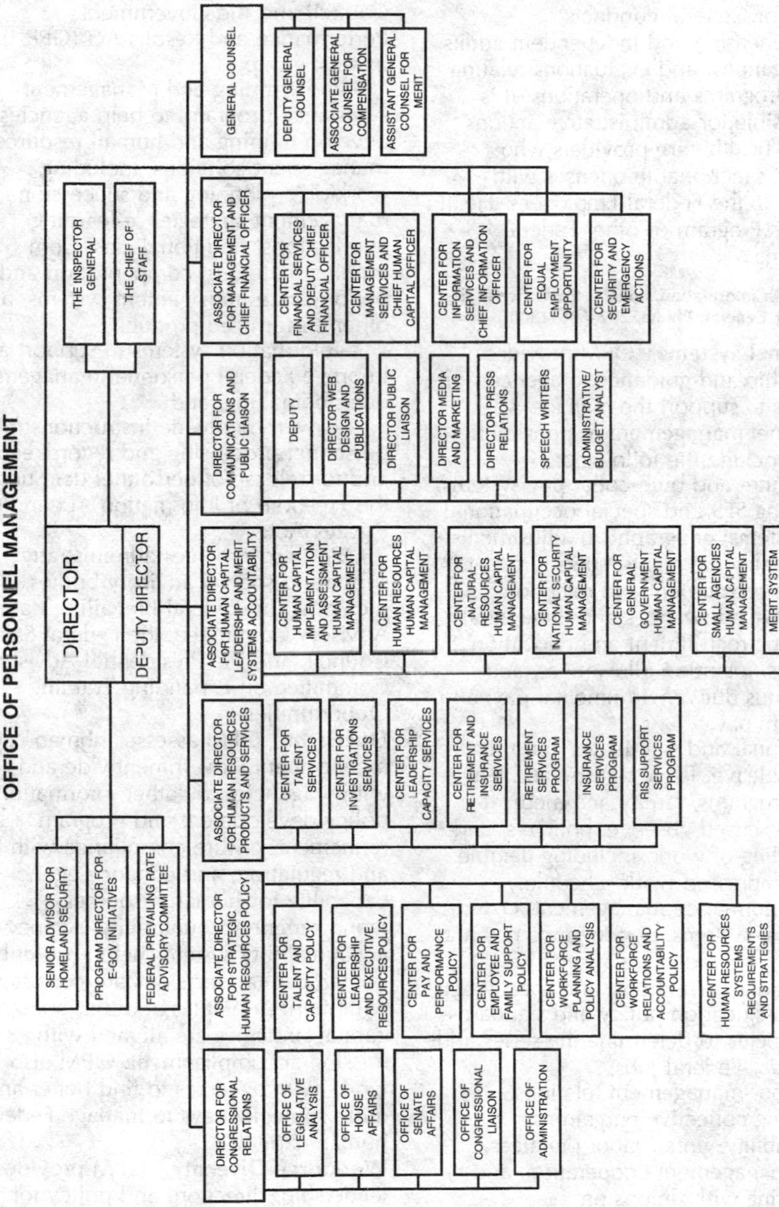
OFFICE OF PERSONNEL MANAGEMENT
DIRECTOR
DEPUTY DIRECTOR
THE INSPECTOR GENERAL
THE CHIEF OF STAFF
SENIOR ADVISOR FOR HOMELAND SECURITY
PROGRAM DIRECTOR FOR E-GOV INITIATIVES
FEDERAL PREVAILING RATE ADVISORY COMMITTEE
GENERAL COUNSEL
DEPUTY GENERAL COUNSEL
ASSOCIATE GENERAL COUNSEL FOR COMPENSATION
ASSISTANT GENERAL COUNSEL FOR MERIT
ASSOCIATE DIRECTOR FOR MANAGEMENT AND CHIEF FINANCIAL OFFICER
CENTER FOR FINANCIAL SERVICES AND DEPUTY CHIEF FINANCIAL OFFICER
CENTER FOR MANAGEMENT SERVICES AND CHIEF HUMAN CAPITAL OFFICER
CENTER FOR INFORMATION SERVICES AND CHIEF INFORMATION OFFICER
CENTER FOR EQUAL EMPLOYMENT OPPORTUNITY
CENTER FOR SECURITY AND EMERGENCY ACTIONS
DIRECTOR FOR COMMUNICATIONS AND PUBLIC LIAISON
DEPUTY
DIRECTOR WEB DESIGN AND PUBLICATIONS
DIRECTOR PUBLIC LIAISON
DIRECTOR MEDIA AND MARKETING
DIRECTOR PRESS RELATIONS
SPEECH WRITERS
ADMINISTRATIVE/ BUDGET ANALYST
ASSOCIATE DIRECTOR FOR HUMAN CAPITAL LEADERSHIP AND MERIT SYSTEMS ACCOUNTABILITY
CENTER FOR HUMAN CAPITAL IMPLEMENTATION AND ASSESSMENT HUMAN CAPITAL MANAGEMENT
CENTER FOR HUMAN RESOURCES HUMAN CAPITAL MANAGEMENT
CENTER FOR NATURAL RESOURCES HUMAN CAPITAL MANAGEMENT
CENTER FOR NATIONAL SECURITY HUMAN CAPITAL MANAGEMENT
CENTER FOR GENERAL GOVERNMENT HUMAN CAPITAL MANAGEMENT
CENTER FOR SMALL AGENCIES HUMAN CAPITAL MANAGEMENT
MERIT SYSTEM COMPLIANCE GROUP
ASSOCIATE DIRECTOR FOR HUMAN RESOURCES PRODUCTS AND SERVICES
CENTER FOR TALENT SERVICES
CENTER FOR INVESTIGATIONS SERVICES
CENTER FOR LEADERSHIP CAPACITY SERVICES
CENTER FOR RETIREMENT AND INSURANCE SERVICES
RETIREMENT SERVICES PROGRAM
INSURANCE SERVICES PROGRAM
RIS SUPPORT SERVICES PROGRAM
ASSOCIATE DIRECTOR FOR STRATEGIC HUMAN RESOURCES POLICY
CENTER FOR TALENT AND CAPACITY POLICY
CENTER FOR LEADERSHIP AND EXECUTIVE RESOURCES POLICY
CENTER FOR PAY AND PERFORMANCE POLICY
CENTER FOR EMPLOYEE AND FAMILY SUPPORT POLICY
CENTER FOR WORKFORCE PLANNING AND POLICY ANALYSIS
CENTER FOR WORKFORCE RELATIONS AND ACCOUNTABILITY POLICY
CENTER FOR HUMAN RESOURCES SYSTEMS REQUIREMENTS AND STRATEGIES
DIRECTOR FOR CONGRESSIONAL RELATIONS
OFFICE OF LEGISLATIVE ANALYSIS
OFFICE OF HOUSE AFFAIRS
OFFICE OF SENATE AFFAIRS
OFFICE OF CONGRESSIONAL LIAISON
OFFICE OF ADMINISTRATION

executives. In addition, OPM manages three interagency residential development and training centers for executives and managers.

Investigations The Office of the Inspector General conducts comprehensive and independent audits, investigations, and evaluations relating to OPM programs and operations. It is responsible for administrative actions against health care providers who commit sanctionable offenses with respect to the Federal Employees' Health Benefits Program or other Federal programs.

For further information, contact the Office of the Inspector General. Phone, 202–606–1200.

Personnel Systems OPM provides leadership and guidance to agencies on systems to support the manager's personnel management responsibilities. These include the following:

—white- and blue-collar pay systems, including SES and special occupational pay systems; geographical adjustments and locality payments; special rates to address recruitment and retention problems; allowances and differentials, including recruitment and relocation bonuses, retention allowances, and hazardous duty/environmental pay; and premium pay;

—annual and sick leave, court leave, military leave, leave transfer and leave bank programs, family and medical leave, excused absence, holidays, and scheduling of work, including flexible and compressed work schedules;

—performance management, covering appraisal systems, performance pay and awards, and incentive awards for suggestions, inventions, and special acts;

—classification policy and standards for agencies to determine the series and grades for Federal jobs;

—labor-management relations, including collective bargaining, negotiability, unfair labor practices, labor-management cooperation, and consulting with unions on Governmentwide issues;

—systems and techniques for resolving disputes with employees;

—quality of worklife initiatives, such as employee health and fitness, work and family, AIDS in the workplace, and employee assistance programs;

—human resources development, including leadership and administration of the Human Resources Development Council and the Government Performance and Results Act (GPRA) interest group;

—the Training and Management Assistance program, to help agencies develop training and human resources management solutions, including workforce planning and succession management strategies, e-learning applications, traditional classroom training materials, compensation and performance management systems, and other customized products;

—information systems to support and improve Federal personnel management decisionmaking; and

—Governmentwide instructions for personnel processing and recordkeeping, and for release of personnel data under the Freedom of Information Act and the Privacy Act.

OPM also provides administrative support to special advisory bodies, including the Federal Prevailing Rate Advisory Committee, the Federal Salary Council, and the Presidential Advisory Committee on Expanding Training Opportunities.

Oversight OPM assesses human capital management Governmentwide and within agencies to gather information for policy development and program refinement, ensure compliance with law and regulation, and enhance agency capability for human resources management accountability. Agency accountability systems help ensure that human capital decisions are consistent with merit principles and that human capital strategies are aligned with mission accomplishment. OPM also works with agencies to find better and more strategic ways to manage Federal human capital.

Workforce Diversity OPM provides leadership, direction, and policy for Governmentwide affirmative recruiting programs for women, minorities, individuals with disabilities, and veterans. It also provides leadership, guidance, and technical assistance to promote merit and equality in systemic workforce recruitment, employment, training, and retention. In addition, OPM gathers, analyzes, and maintains statistical data on the diversity of the Federal workforce, and prepares evaluation reports for Congress and others on individual agency and Governmentwide progress toward full workforce representation for all Americans in the Federal sector.

Other Personnel Programs OPM coordinates the temporary assignment of employees between Federal agencies and State, local, and Indian tribal governments; institutions of higher education; and other eligible nonprofit organizations for up to 2 years, for work of mutual benefit to the participating organizations. It administers the Presidential Management Intern Program, which provides 2-year, excepted appointments with Federal agencies to recipients of graduate degrees in appropriate disciplines. In addition, the Office of Personnel Management administers the Federal Merit System Standards, which apply to certain grant-aided State and local programs.

Federal Executive Boards Federal Executive Boards (FEBs) were established by Presidential memorandum on November 10, 1961, to improve internal Federal management practices and to provide a central focus for Federal participation in civic affairs in major metropolitan centers of Federal activity. They carry out their functions under OPM supervision and control.

FEBs serve as a means for disseminating information within the Federal Government and for promoting discussion of Federal policies and activities of importance to all Federal executives in the field. Each Board is composed of heads of Federal field offices in the metropolitan area. A chairman is elected annually from among the membership to provide overall leadership to the Board's operations. Committees and task forces carry out interagency projects consistent with the Board's mission.

Federal Executive Boards are located in 28 metropolitan areas that are important centers of Federal activity. These areas are as follows: Albuquerque-Santa Fe, NM; Atlanta, GA; Baltimore, MD; Boston, MA; Buffalo, NY; Chicago, IL; Cincinnati, OH; Cleveland, OH; Dallas-Fort Worth, TX; Denver, CO; Detroit, MI; Honolulu, HI-Pacific; Houston, TX; Kansas City, MO; Los Angeles, CA; Miami, FL; New Orleans, LA; New York, NY; Newark, NJ; Oklahoma City, OK; Philadelphia, PA; Pittsburgh, PA; Portland, OR; St. Louis, MO; San Antonio, TX; San Francisco, CA; Seattle, WA; and the Twin Cities (Minneapolis-St. Paul, MN).

Federal Executive Associations or Councils have been locally organized in approximately 65 other metropolitan areas to perform functions similar to the Federal Executive Boards but on a lesser scale of organization and activity.

For further information, contact the Director for Federal Executive Board Operations, Office of Personnel Management, Room 5524, 1900 E Street NW., Washington, DC 20415–0001. Phone, 202–606–1000.

Sources of Information

Contracts For information, contact the Chief, Contracting Division, Office of Personnel Management, Washington, DC 20415–0071. Phone, 202–606–2240. Internet, www.opm.gov/procure/index.htm.

Employment Information about Federal employment and current job openings is available from USAJobs (phone, 478–757–3000; TTY, 478–744–2299; Internet, www.usajobs.opm.gov). Contact information for your local OPM office is available in the blue pages of the phone book under U.S. Government, Office of Personnel Management. For information about employment opportunities within the Office of Personnel Management, contact the Director of Human Resources. Phone, 202–606–2400.

Publications The Chief, Publications Services Division, can provide information about Federal personnel management publications. Phone, 202–606–1822. Internet, http://apps.opm.gov/publications

For further information, contact the Office of Communications, Office of Personnel Management, 1900 E Street NW., Washington, DC 20415–0001. Phone, 202–606–1800. Internet, www.opm.gov.

OFFICE OF SPECIAL COUNSEL

1730 M Street NW., Suite 218, Washington, DC 20036–4505
Phone, 202–254–3600 or 800–872–9855. Fax, 202–653–5151. Internet, www.osc.gov.

Special Counsel	Scott J. Bloch
Deputy Special Counsel	James McVay
Associate Special Counsel for Investigation and Prosecution Division	Leonard Dribinsky
Director of Field Operations	William Reukauf
Outreach Director and Counsel	Rebecca McGinley
Associate Special Counsel for Legal Counsel and Policy Division	Erin M. McDonnell
Director, Congressional and Public Affairs	Loren Smith

The Office of Special Counsel investigates allegations of certain activities prohibited by civil service laws, rules, or regulations and litigates before the Merit Systems Protection Board.

Activities

The Office of Special Counsel (OSC) was established on January 1, 1979, by Reorganization Plan No. 2 of 1978 (5 U.S.C. app.). The Civil Service Reform Act of 1978 (5 U.S.C. 1101 note), which became effective on January 11, 1979, enlarged its functions and powers. Pursuant to provisions of the Whistleblower Protection Act of 1989 (5 U.S.C. 1211 *et seq.*), OSC functions as an independent investigative and prosecutorial agency within the executive branch which litigates before the Merit Systems Protection Board.

The primary role of OSC is to protect employees, former employees, and applicants for employment from prohibited personnel practices, especially reprisal for whistleblowing. Its basic areas of statutory responsibility are to do the following:

—receive and investigate allegations of prohibited personnel practices and other activities prohibited by civil service law, rule, or regulation and, if warranted, initiating corrective or disciplinary action;

—provide a secure channel through which information evidencing a violation of any law, rule, or regulation, gross mismanagement, gross waste of funds, abuse of authority, or substantial and specific danger to public health or safety may be disclosed without fear of retaliation and without disclosure of identity, except with the employee's consent; and

—enforce the provisions of the Hatch Act and the Uniformed Services Employment and Reemployment Rights Act.

Sources of Information

Field offices are located in Dallas, TX (525 Griffin Street, Room 824, Box 103, Dallas, TX 75202. Phone, 214–747–1519. Fax, 214–767–2764); Oakland, CA (Suite 365S, 1301 Clay Street, 94612–5217. Phone, 510–637–3460. Fax, 510–637–3474); and Detroit, MI (477 Michigan Avenue, Suite 495, Detroit, MI 48226. Phone, 313-226-4496. Fax, 313-226-5606).

For further information, contact the Office of Special Counsel, 1730 M Street NW., Suite 218, Washington, DC 20036–4505. Phone, 202–254–3600 or 800–872–9855. Fax, 202–653–5151. Internet, www.osc.gov.

OVERSEAS PRIVATE INVESTMENT CORPORATION

1100 New York Avenue NW., Washington, DC 20527
Phone, 202–336–8400. Fax, 202–408–9859. Internet, www.opic.gov.

President and Chief Executive Officer	ROBERT A. MOSBACHER, JR.
Executive Vice President	JOHN A. SIMON
Vice President of External Affairs	CHRISTOPHER COUGHLIN
Vice President of Investment Policy	CHRISTINE V. EMERY
Vice President of Structured Finance	ROBERT B. DRUMHELLER
Vice President of Small and Medium Enterprise Finance	JAMES C. POLAN
Vice President of Insurance	EDITH P. QUINTRELL, *Acting*
Vice President of Economic Development	DANIEL A. NICHOLS
Vice President of Investment Funds	CYNTHIA HOSTETLER
Vice President and General Counsel	MARK A. GARFINKEL
Vice President and Chief Financial Officer	HOWARD L. BURRIS

[For the Overseas Private Investment Corporation statement of organization, see the *Code of Federal Regulations,* Title 22, Chapter VII]

The Overseas Private Investment Corporation is a self-sustaining Federal agency whose purpose is to promote economic growth in developing countries and emerging markets by encouraging U.S. private investment in those nations.

The Overseas Private Investment Corporation (OPIC) was established in 1971 as an independent agency by the Foreign Affairs Reform and Restructuring Act (112 Stat. 2681–790). OPIC helps U.S. businesses invest overseas, fosters economic development in new and emerging markets, complements the private sector in managing risks associated with foreign direct investment, and supports U.S. foreign policy. OPIC charges market-based fees for its products, and it operates on a self-sustaining basis at no net cost to taxpayers.

OPIC helps U.S. businesses compete in emerging markets when private sector support is not available. OPIC offers up to $250 million in long-term financing and/or political risk insurance to U.S. companies investing in over 150 emerging markets and developing countries. Backed by the full faith and credit of the U.S. Government, OPIC advocates for U.S. investment, offers experience in risk management, and draws on an outstanding record of success.

OPIC mobilizes America's private sector to advance U.S. foreign policy and development initiatives. Projects supported by OPIC expand economic development, which encourages political stability and free market reforms. Since 1971, OPIC has supported $164 billion in investments that have helped developing countries to generate over 732,000 jobs. OPIC projects have also generated $69 billion in U.S. exports and supported more than 264,000 American jobs. OPIC promotes U.S. best practices by requiring projects to adhere to international standards on the environment, worker rights, and human rights.

Activities

OPIC insures U.S. investors, contractors, exporters, and financial institutions against political violence, expropriation of assets by foreign governments, and the inability to convert local currencies into U.S. dollars. OPIC can insure up to $250 million per project and has no minimum investment size requirements. Insurance is available for investments in new ventures, expansions of existing enterprises, privatizations, and acquisitions with positive developmental benefits.

OPIC provides financing through direct loans and loan guaranties for medium- and long-term private investment. Loans range from $100,000 to $250 million for projects sponsored by U.S. companies, and financing can be provided on a project finance or corporate finance basis. In most cases, the U.S. sponsor is expected to contribute at least 25 percent of the project equity, have a track record in the industry, and have the means to contribute to the financial success of the project.

To address the lack of sufficient equity investment in emerging markets, OPIC has supported the creation of privately owned and managed investment funds that make direct equity and equity-related investments in new, expanding, or privatizing companies. These funds, which have a regional or sectoral focus, provide the long-term growth capital that can serve as a catalyst for private sector economic activity in developing countries and the creation of new markets and opportunities for American companies.

Helping America's small businesses grow through investments in emerging markets is an important OPIC priority. Any small business with annual revenues less than $35 million is eligible for small business center programs. For businesses with annual revenues over $35 million and under $250 million, OPIC's regular small business programs are available. OPIC provides direct loans to U.S. small businesses, and offers insurance products to meet the special needs of small businesses. Other client services include streamlined applications and processing procedures, and a small business hotline.

Sources of Information

General Inquiries Inquiries should be directed to the Information Officer, Overseas Private Investment Corporation, 1100 New York Avenue NW., Washington, DC 20527. Phone, 202–336–8799. E-mail, info@opic.gov. Internet, www.opic.gov.

Publications OPIC programs are further detailed in the *Annual Report* and the *Program Handbook.* These publications are available free of charge and on the Web site.

For further information, contact the Overseas Private Investment Corporation, 1100 New York Avenue NW., Washington, DC 20527. Phone, 202–336–8400. Fax, 202–408–9859. Internet, www.opic.gov.

PEACE CORPS

1111 Twentieth Street NW., Washington, DC 20526
Phone, 202–692–2000. Fax, 202–692–2231. Internet, www.peacecorps.gov.

Director	GADDI H. VASQUEZ
Deputy Director	JODY OLSEN
Chief of Staff/Chief of Operations	JAY KATZEN, *Acting*
Deputy Chief of Staff/Chief of Operations	DAVID LINER
Director of Congressional Relations	MICHELLE BROOKS
General Counsel	TYLER POSEY
Director of Communications	RICHARD PARKER
Director of Press Relations	BARBARA DALY
Director of Office of Planning, Policy, and Analysis	KYO (PAUL) JHIN

American Diversity Program Manager	SHIRLEY EVEREST
Director of Private Sector Initiatives	NANCI BRANNAN
Inspector General	DAVID KOTZ
Director of the Crisis Corps	MARY ANGELINI
Regional Director/Africa Operations	HENRY MCKOY
Regional Director/Europe, Mediterranean, and Asia Operations	JAY KATZEN
Regional Director/Inter-American and the Pacific Operations	ALLENE ZANGER
Director, Center for Field Assistance and Applied Research	BETSI SHAYS
Chief Financial Officer	GEORGE SCHUTTER
Associate Director for Management	WIL BRYANT
Associate Director for Volunteer Support	STEVEN WEINBERG
Chief Information Officer	ED ANDERSON
Associate Director for Volunteer Recruitment and Selection	CHUCK BROOKS
Associate Director for Safety and Security	PATRICK HOGAN
Chief Acquisition Officer	CAREY FOUNTAIN
Chief Compliance Officer	COURTNEY SANTONICOLA
AIDS Relief Coordinator	RONALD CAMPBELL

The mission of the Peace Corps is to help the people of interested countries in meeting their need for trained men and women, and to help promote better mutual understanding between Americans and citizens of other countries.

The Peace Corps was established by the Peace Corps Act of 1961, as amended (22 U.S.C. 2501), and was made an independent agency by title VI of the International Security and Development Cooperation Act of 1981 (22 U.S.C. 2501–1).

The Peace Corps consists of a Washington, DC, headquarters; 11 area offices; and overseas operations in 75 countries, utilizing more than 7,800 volunteers.

Activities

To fulfill the Peace Corps mandate, men and women are trained for a 9-to-14 week period in the appropriate local language, the technical skills necessary for their particular jobs, and the cross-cultural skills needed to adjust to a society with traditions and attitudes different from their own. Volunteers serve for a period of 2 years, living among the people with whom they work. Volunteers are expected to become a part of the community through their voluntary service.

Thousands of volunteers serve throughout the world, working in six program areas: education, health and HIV/AIDS, environment, information technology, agriculture, and business development. Community-level projects are designed to incorporate the skills of volunteers with the resources of host-country agencies and other international assistance organizations to help solve specific development problems, often in conjunction with private volunteer organizations.

In the United States, the Peace Corps is working to promote an understanding of people in other countries. Through its World Wise Schools Program, volunteers are matched with elementary and junior high schools in the United States to encourage an exchange of letters, pictures, music, and artifacts. Participating students increase their knowledge of geography, languages, and different cultures, while gaining an appreciation for volunteerism.

The Peace Corps offers other domestic programs involving former volunteers, universities, local public school systems, and private businesses and foundations in a partnership to help solve some of

PEACE CORPS

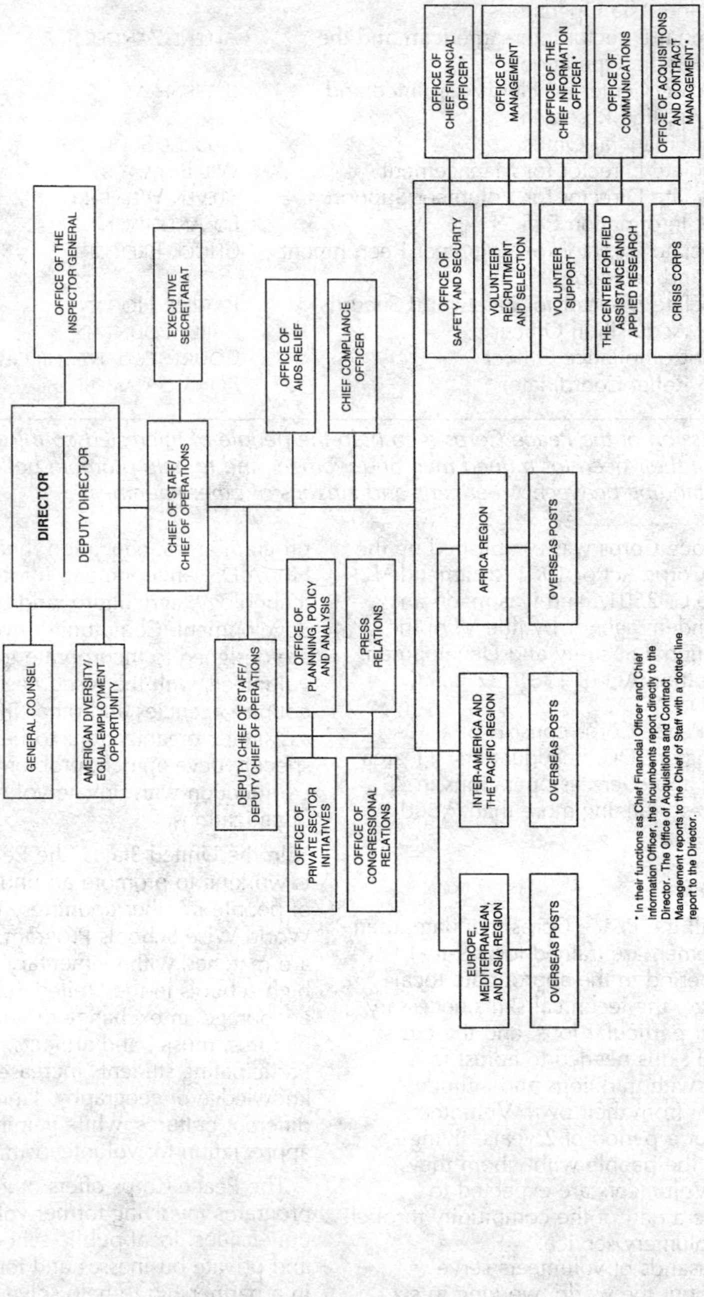

DIRECTOR
DEPUTY DIRECTOR
OFFICE OF THE INSPECTOR GENERAL
GENERAL COUNSEL
AMERICAN DIVERSITY/ EQUAL EMPLOYMENT OPPORTUNITY
EXECUTIVE SECRETARIAT
CHIEF OF STAFF/ CHIEF OF OPERATIONS
DEPUTY CHIEF OF STAFF/ DEPUTY CHIEF OF OPERATIONS
OFFICE OF AIDS RELIEF
CHIEF COMPLIANCE OFFICER
OFFICE OF PLANNING, POLICY AND ANALYSIS
PRESS RELATIONS
OFFICE OF PRIVATE SECTOR INITIATIVES
OFFICE OF CONGRESSIONAL RELATIONS
OFFICE OF CHIEF FINANCIAL OFFICER*
OFFICE OF MANAGEMENT
OFFICE OF THE CHIEF INFORMATION OFFICER*
OFFICE OF COMMUNICATIONS
OFFICE OF ACQUISITIONS AND CONTRACT MANAGEMENT*
OFFICE OF SAFETY AND SECURITY
VOLUNTEER RECRUITMENT AND SELECTION
VOLUNTEER SUPPORT
THE CENTER FOR FIELD ASSISTANCE AND APPLIED RESEARCH
CRISIS CORPS
AFRICA REGION
OVERSEAS POSTS
INTER-AMERICA AND THE PACIFIC REGION
OVERSEAS POSTS
EUROPE, MEDITERRANEAN, AND ASIA REGION
OVERSEAS POSTS
* In their functions as Chief Financial Officer and Chief Information Officer, the incumbents report directly to the Director. The Office of Acquisitions and Contract Management reports to the Chief of Staff with a dotted line report to the Director.

the United States' most pressing domestic problems.

The Peace Corps Office of Private Sector Initiatives works with schools, civic groups, businesses, and neighborhood and youth organizations in the United States to facilitate their support of Peace Corps initiatives here and abroad.

Area Offices—Peace Corps

Office	Address	Telephone
Atlanta, GA (AL, FL, GA, MS, PR, SC, TN)	Suite 2R70, Bldg. 1924, 100 Alabama St., 30303	404–562–3456
Boston, MA (MA, ME, NH, RI, VT)	Suite 450, 10 Causeway St., 02222	617–565–5555
Chicago, IL (IL, IN, KY, MI, MO, OH)	Suite 450, 55 W. Monroe St., 60603	312–353–4990
Dallas, TX (AR, LA, NM, OK, TX)	Rm. 527, 207 S. Houston St., 75202	214–767–5435
Denver, CO (CO, KS, NE, UT, WY)	Suite 2205, 1999 Broadway, 80202	303–844–7020
Los Angeles, CA (AZ, southern CA)	Suite 155, 2361 Rosecrans Ave., El Segundo, CA 90245.	310–356–1100
Minneapolis, MN (IA, MN, ND, SD, WI)	Suite 420, 330 2d Ave. S., 55401	612–348–1480
New York, NY (CT, NJ, NY, PA)	Suite 1025, 201 Varick St., 10014	212–352–5440
San Francisco, CA (northern CA, HI, NV)	Suite 600, 333 Market St., 94105	415–977–8800
Seattle, WA (AK, ID, MT, OR, WA)	Rm. 1776, 2001 6th Ave., 98121	206–553–5490
Washington, DC (DC, DE, MD, NC, VA, WV)	Suite 250, 1525 Wilson Blvd., Arlington, VA 22209	703–235–9191

Sources of Information

Becoming a Peace Corps Volunteer Contact the nearest area office. Phone, 800–424–8580. Internet, www.peacecorps.gov.

Employment Contact the Peace Corps, Office of Human Resource Management, Washington, DC 20526. Phone, 202–692–1200. For recorded employment opportunities, call 800–818–9579 (toll free).

General Inquiries Information or assistance may be obtained by contacting the Peace Corps Washington, DC, headquarters or any of its area offices.

For further information, contact the Press Office, Peace Corps, 1111 Twentieth Street NW., Washington, DC 20526. Phone, 202–692–2230 or 800–424–8580. Fax, 202–692–2201. Internet, www.peacecorps.gov.

PENSION BENEFIT GUARANTY CORPORATION

1200 K Street NW., Washington, DC 20005
Phone, 202–326–4000; 800–400–7242. Internet, www.pbgc.gov.

Board of Directors:

Chairman (Secretary of Labor)	ELAINE L. CHAO
Members:	
(Secretary of the Treasury)	JOHN W. SNOW
(Secretary of Commerce)	CARLOS M. GUTIERREZ

Officials:

Executive Director	VINCE K. SNOWBARGER, *Acting*
Office of Risk Assessment	JUSTEN CARTER, *Acting*
Chief Technology Officer	RICK HARTT
Chief Administrative Officer	STEPHEN E. BARBER
Director, Budget Department	HENRY R. THOMPSON
Director, Facilities and Services Department	PATRICIA DAVIS
Director, Human Resources Department	MICHELE PILIPOVICH
Director, Procurement Department	ROBERT W. HERTING
Director, Strategic Planning and Evaluation Department	WILMER GRAHAM

Chief Operating Officer	WILLIAM HULTENG, *Acting*
Director, Benefits Administration and Payment Department	BENNIE L. HAGANS
Director, Insurance Program Department	TERRENCE M. DENEEN
Chief Financial Officer	JAMES GERBER
Director, Contracts and Controls Review Department	MARTIN BOEHM
Director, Financial Operations Department	THEODORE J. WINTER, JR.
General Counsel	JUDITH STARR
Deputy Executive Director, Office of Policy and External Affairs	VINCENT K. SNOWBARGER
Director, Communications and Public Affairs Department	RANDY CLERIHUE
Director, Legislative and Regulatory Department	JOHN HANLEY
Director, Policy, Research, and Analysis Department	DAVE GUSTAFSON, *Acting*
Inspector General	ROBERT L. EMMONS

The Pension Benefit Guaranty Corporation protects the pension benefits of more than 44 million Americans who participate in defined-benefit pension plans sponsored by private-sector employees.

The Pension Benefit Guaranty Corporation (PBGC) is a self-financing, wholly owned Government corporation subject to the Government Corporation Control Act (31 U.S.C. 9101–9109). The Corporation, established by Title IV of the Employee Retirement Income Security Act of 1974 (29 U.S.C. 1301–1461), is governed by a Board of Directors consisting of the Secretaries of Labor, Commerce, and the Treasury. The Secretary of Labor is Chairman of the Board. A seven-member Advisory Committee, composed of two labor, two business, and three public members appointed by the President, advises the agency on investment issues.

Activities

Coverage The Corporation insures most private-sector defined benefit pension plans, which provide a pension benefit based on factors such as age, years of service, and salary.

The Corporation administers two insurance programs separately covering single-employer and multiemployer plans. More than 44 million workers and retirees participate in more than 30,300 covered plans.

Single-Employer Insurance Under the single-employer program, the Corporation guarantees payment of basic pension benefits if an insured plan terminates without sufficient assets to pay those benefits. However, the law limits the total monthly benefit that the agency may guarantee for one individual to $3,971.59 per month for a 65-year-old individual in a pension plan that terminates in 2006. The law also sets other restrictions on PBGC's gaurantee, including limits on the insured amount of recent benefit increases. In certain cases, the Corporation may also pay some benefits above the guaranteed amount depending on the funding level of the plan and amounts recovered from employers.

A plan sponsor may terminate a single-employer plan in a standard termination if the plan has sufficient assets to purchase private annuities to cover all benefit liabilities. If a plan does not have sufficient assets, the sponsor may seek to transfer the pension liabilities to the PBGC by demonstrating that it meets the legal criteria for a distress termination. In either termination, the plan administrator must inform participants in writing at least 60 days prior to the date the administrator proposes to terminate the plan. Only a plan that has sufficient assets to pay all benefit liabilities may terminate in a standard termination. The Corporation also may institute termination of underfunded plans in certain specified circumstances.

Multiemployer Insurance Under title IV, as revised in 1980 by the Multiemployer Pension Plan Amendments Act (29 U.S.C. 1001 note) which changed the insurable event from plan termination to plan insolvency, the Corporation provides financial assistance to multiemployer plans that are unable to pay nonforfeitable benefits. The plans are obligated to repay such assistance. The act also made employers withdrawing from a plan liable to the plan for a portion of its unfunded vested benefits.

Premium Collections All defined benefit pension plans insured by PBGC are required to pay premiums to the Corporation according to rates set by Congress. The annual premium per plan participant for multiemployer pension plans is $8 for plan years beginning after September 26, 1988. The basic premium for all single-employer plans is $30 per participant per year. Underfunded single-employer plans must also pay an additional premium equal to $9 per $1,000 of unfunded vested benefits. A termination premium of $1,250 per participant per year applies to certain distress and involuntary plan terminations occurring on or after January 1, 2006, payable for 3 years after the termination.

Sources of Information

Access to the Pension Benefit Guaranty Corporation is available through the Internet at www.pbgc.gov.

TTY/TDD users may call the Federal Relay Service toll free at 800–877–8339 and ask to be connected to 202–326–4000.

For further information, contact the Pension Benefit Guaranty Corporation, 1200 K Street NW., Washington, DC 20005–4026. Phone, 202–326–4000 or 800–400–7242. Internet, www.pbgc.gov.

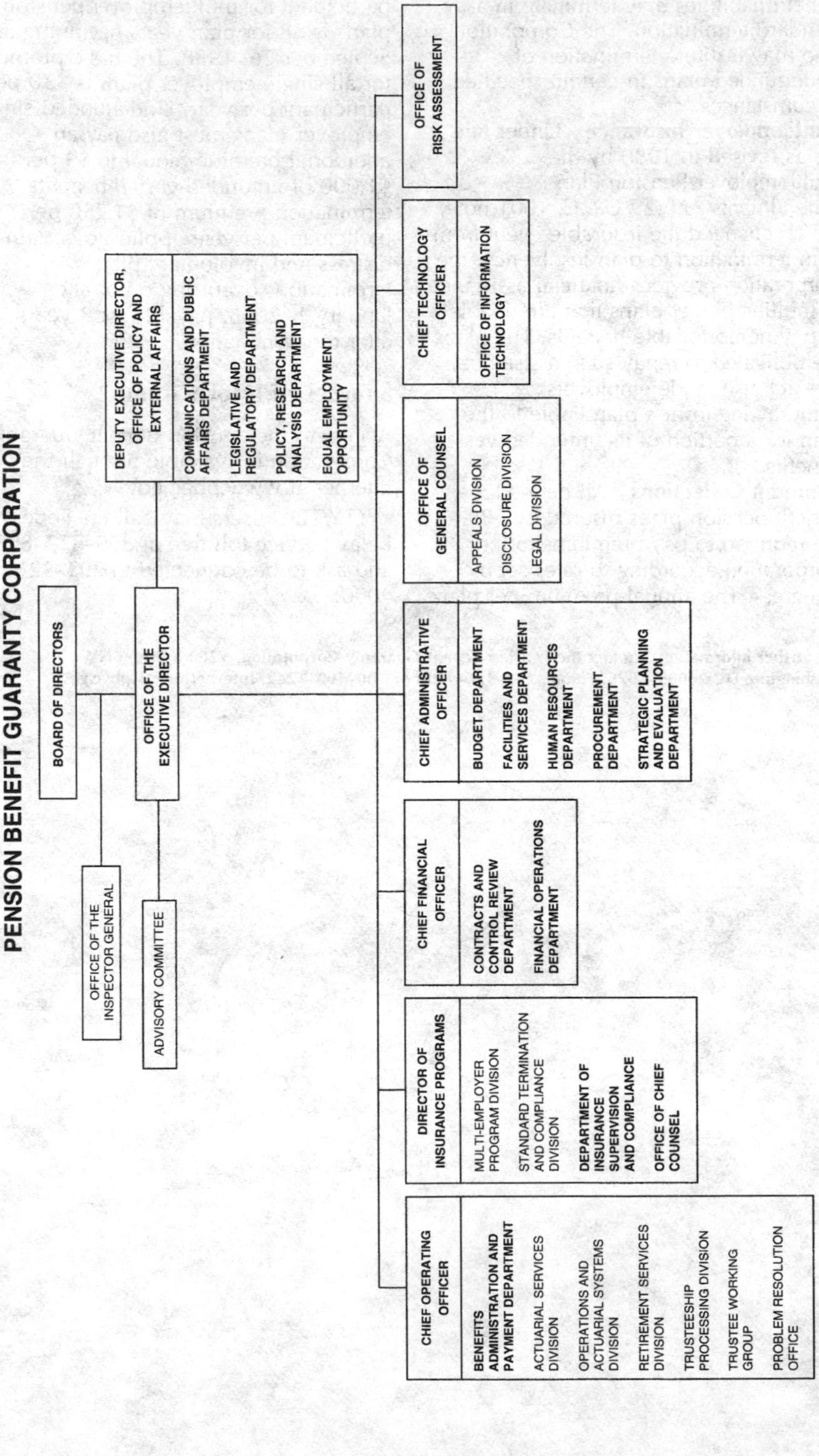
PENSION BENEFIT GUARANTY CORPORATION
BOARD OF DIRECTORS
OFFICE OF THE INSPECTOR GENERAL
OFFICE OF THE EXECUTIVE DIRECTOR
ADVISORY COMMITTEE
DEPUTY EXECUTIVE DIRECTOR, OFFICE OF POLICY AND EXTERNAL AFFAIRS
COMMUNICATIONS AND PUBLIC AFFAIRS DEPARTMENT
LEGISLATIVE AND REGULATORY DEPARTMENT
POLICY, RESEARCH AND ANALYSIS DEPARTMENT
EQUAL EMPLOYMENT OPPORTUNITY
OFFICE OF RISK ASSESSMENT
CHIEF TECHNOLOGY OFFICER
OFFICE OF INFORMATION TECHNOLOGY
OFFICE OF GENERAL COUNSEL
APPEALS DIVISION
DISCLOSURE DIVISION
LEGAL DIVISION
CHIEF ADMINISTRATIVE OFFICER
BUDGET DEPARTMENT
FACILITIES AND SERVICES DEPARTMENT
HUMAN RESOURCES DEPARTMENT
PROCUREMENT DEPARTMENT
STRATEGIC PLANNING AND EVALUATION DEPARTMENT
CHIEF FINANCIAL OFFICER
CONTRACTS AND CONTROL REVIEW DEPARTMENT
FINANCIAL OPERATIONS DEPARTMENT
DIRECTOR OF INSURANCE PROGRAMS
MULTI-EMPLOYER PROGRAM DIVISION
STANDARD TERMINATION AND COMPLIANCE DIVISION
DEPARTMENT OF INSURANCE SUPERVISION AND COMPLIANCE
OFFICE OF CHIEF COUNSEL
CHIEF OPERATING OFFICER
BENEFITS ADMINISTRATION AND PAYMENT DEPARTMENT
ACTUARIAL SERVICES DIVISION
OPERATIONS AND ACTUARIAL SYSTEMS DIVISION
RETIREMENT SERVICES DIVISION
TRUSTEESHIP PROCESSING DIVISION
TRUSTEE WORKING GROUP
PROBLEM RESOLUTION OFFICE

POSTAL RATE COMMISSION

901 New York Avenue NW., Washington, DC 20268–0001
Phone, 202–789–6800. Fax, 202–789–6861. Internet, www.prc.gov.

Chairman	GEORGE A. OMAS
Vice Chairman	DAWN A. TISDALE
Commissioners	RUTH Y. GOLDWAY, TONY HAMMOND, (VACANCY)
Special Assistant to the Chairman	MARK ACTON
Chief Administrative Officer and Secretary	STEVEN W. WILLIAMS
General Counsel	STEPHEN L. SHARFMAN
Director, Office of Rates, Analysis and Planning	JOHN D. WALLER
Director, Office of the Consumer Advocate	SHELLEY S. DREIFUSS
Deputy Chief Administrative Officer and Personnel Officer	GARRY SIKORA

[For the Postal Rate Commission statement of organization, see the *Code of Federal Regulations,* Title 39, Part 3002]

The major responsibility of the Postal Rate Commission is to submit recommended decisions to the United States Postal Service Governors on postage rates, fees, and mail classifications.

The Postal Rate Commission is an independent agency created by the Postal Reorganization Act, as amended (39 U.S.C. 3601–3604). It is composed of five Commissioners, appointed by the President with the advice and consent of the Senate, one of whom is designated as Chairman.

The Commission promulgates rules and regulations, establishes procedures, and takes other actions necessary to carry out its obligations. Acting upon requests from the U.S. Postal Service or on its own initiative, the Commission recommends and issues advisory opinions to the Governors of the U.S. Postal Service on changes in rates or fees in each class of mail or type of service. It studies and submits recommended decisions on establishing or changing the mail classification schedule and holds on-the-record hearings that are lawfully required to attain sound and fair recommendations. It initiates studies on postal matters, such as cost theory and operations.

The Commission also receives, studies, and conducts hearings and issues recommended decisions and reports to the Postal Service on complaints received from interested persons relating to postage rates, postal classifications, and problems of national scope regarding postal services. It has appellate jurisdiction to review Postal Service determinations to close or consolidate small post offices. The Commission also prepares an annual report on international mail.

Sources of Information

Employment The Commission's programs require attorneys, economists, statisticians, accountants, industrial engineers, marketing specialists, and administrative and clerical personnel to fulfill its responsibilities. Requests for employment information should be directed to the Personnel Officer.

Electronic Access Electronic access to current docketed case materials is available through the Internet at www.prc.gov. E-mail can be sent to the Commission at prc-admin@prc.gov and prc-dockets@prc.gov.

Reading Room Facilities for inspection and copying of records, viewing automated daily lists of docketed materials, and accessing the Commission's Internet site are located at Suite 200, 901 New York Avenue NW., Washington, DC. The room is open from 8 a.m. to 4:30 p.m., Monday through Friday, except legal holidays.

Rules of Practice and Procedure The Postal Rate Commission's Rules of Practice and Procedure governing the conduct of proceedings before the Commission may be found in part 3001 of title 39 of the *Code of Federal Regulations.*

For further information, contact the Secretary, Postal Rate Commission, 901 New York Avenue NW., Washington, DC 20268–0001. Phone, 202–789–6840. Internet, www.prc.gov.

RAILROAD RETIREMENT BOARD

844 North Rush Street, Chicago, IL 60611–2092
Phone, 312–751–4777. Fax, 312–751–7154. Internet, www.rrb.gov.

Chairman	MICHAEL S. SCHWARTZ
Labor Member	V.M. SPEAKMAN, JR.
Management Member	JEROME F. KEVER
Inspector General	MARTIN J. DICKMAN
Director, Administration and Senior Executive Officer	HENRY M. VALIULIS
Director, Equal Opportunity	LYNN E. COUSINS
Director, Human Resources	KEITH B. EARLEY
Supervisor, Public Affairs	ANITA J. ROGERS
Supervisor, Acquisition Management	PAUL T. AHERN
General Counsel	STEVEN A. BARTHOLOW
Director, Legislative Affairs	MARGARET STANLEY
Director, Hearings and Appeals	ARTHUR A. ARFA
Secretary to the Board	BEATRICE E. EZERSKI
Chief Actuary	FRANK J. BUZZI
Chief Information Officer	TERRI S. MORGAN
Chief Financial Officer	KENNETH P. BOEHNE
Director, Programs	DOROTHY A. ISHERWOOD
Director, Assessment and Training	CATHERINE A. LEYSER
Director, Field Service	MARTHA M. BARRINGER
Director, Operations	ROBERT J. DUDA
Director, Policy and Systems	RONALD RUSSO
Director, Resource Management Center	CECILIA A. FREEMAN

[For the Railroad Retirement Board statement of organization, see the *Code of Federal Regulations,* Title 20, Part 200]

The Railroad Retirement Board administers comprehensive retirement-survivor and unemployment-sickness benefit programs for the Nation's railroad workers and their families.

The Railroad Retirement Board was originally established by the Railroad Retirement Act of 1934, as amended (45 U.S.C. 201 through 228z–1).

The Board derives statutory authority from the Railroad Retirement Act of 1974 (45 U.S.C. 231–231u) and the Railroad Unemployment Insurance Act

RAILROAD RETIREMENT BOARD

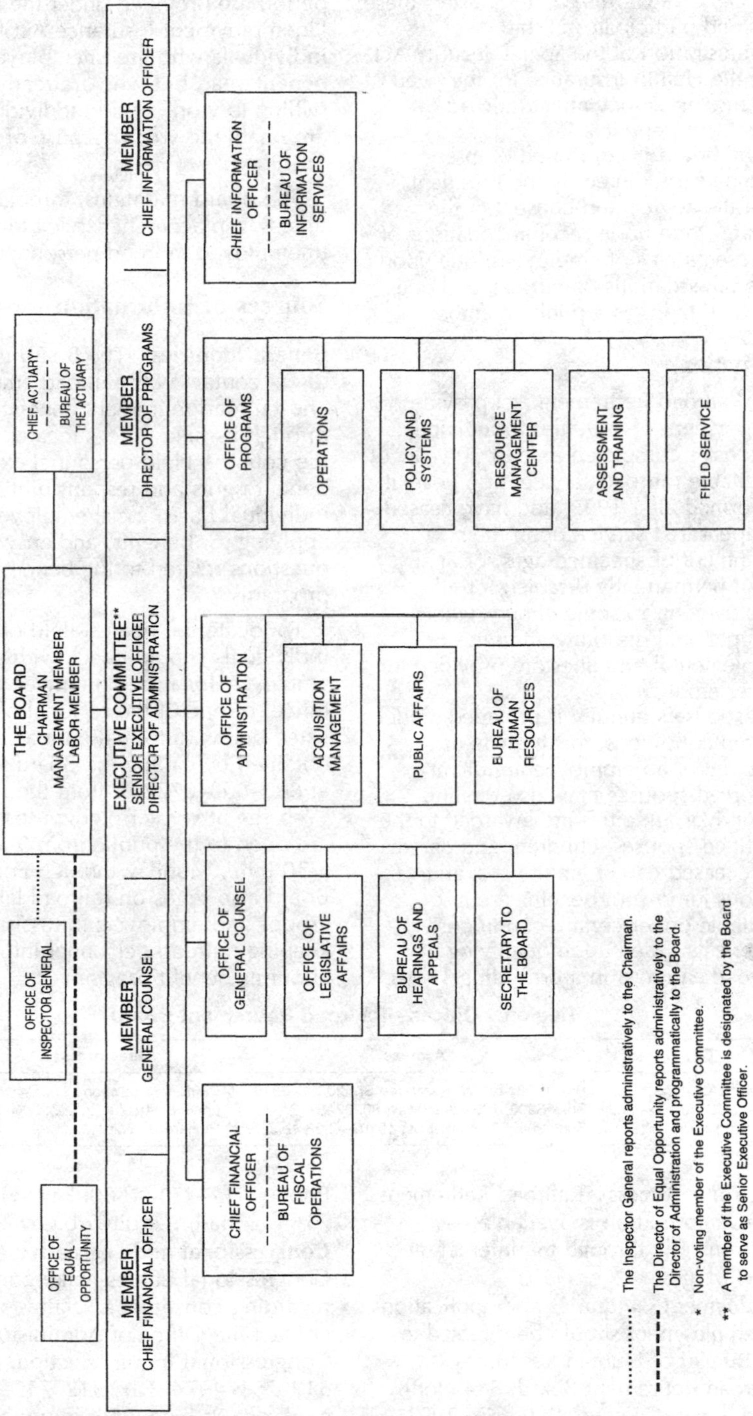
THE BOARD
CHAIRMAN
MANAGEMENT MEMBER
LABOR MEMBER
OFFICE OF INSPECTOR GENERAL
OFFICE OF EQUAL OPPORTUNITY
CHIEF ACTUARY*
BUREAU OF THE ACTUARY
EXECUTIVE COMMITTEE**
SENIOR EXECUTIVE OFFICER
DIRECTOR OF ADMINISTRATION
MEMBER
CHIEF FINANCIAL OFFICER
MEMBER
GENERAL COUNSEL
MEMBER
DIRECTOR OF PROGRAMS
MEMBER
CHIEF INFORMATION OFFICER
CHIEF FINANCIAL OFFICER
BUREAU OF FISCAL OPERATIONS
OFFICE OF GENERAL COUNSEL
OFFICE OF LEGISLATIVE AFFAIRS
BUREAU OF HEARINGS AND APPEALS
SECRETARY TO THE BOARD
OFFICE OF ADMINISTRATION
ACQUISITION MANAGEMENT
PUBLIC AFFAIRS
BUREAU OF HUMAN RESOURCES
OFFICE OF PROGRAMS
OPERATIONS
POLICY AND SYSTEMS
RESOURCE MANAGEMENT CENTER
ASSESSMENT AND TRAINING
FIELD SERVICE
CHIEF INFORMATION OFFICER
BUREAU OF INFORMATION SERVICES
The Inspector General reports administratively to the Chairman.
The Director of Equal Opportunity reports administratively to the Director of Administration and programmatically to the Board.
* Non-voting member of the Executive Committee.
** A member of the Executive Committee is designated by the Board to serve as Senior Executive Officer.

(45 U.S.C. 351–369). It administers these acts and participates in the administration of the Social Security Act and the Health Insurance for the Aged Act insofar as they affect railroad retirement beneficiaries.

The Board is composed of three members appointed by the President with the advice and consent of the Senate—one upon recommendations of representatives of employees; one upon recommendations of carriers; and one, the Chairman, as a public member.

Activities

The Railroad Retirement Act provides for the payment of annuities to individuals who have completed at least 10 years of creditable railroad service, or 5 years if performed after 1995, and have ceased compensated service upon their attainment of specified ages, or at any age if permanently disabled for all employment. In some circumstances occupational disability annuities or supplemental annuities are provided for career employees.

A spouse's annuity is provided, under certain conditions, for the wife or husband of an employee annuitant. Divorced spouses may also qualify.

Survivor annuities are awarded to the qualified spouses, children, and parents of deceased career employees, and various lump-sum benefits are also available under certain conditions.

Benefits based upon qualifying railroad earnings in a preceding 1-year period are provided under the Railroad Unemployment Insurance Act to individuals who are unemployed in a benefit year, but who are ready and willing to work, and to individuals who are unable to work because of sickness or injury.

The Board maintains, through its field offices, a placement service for unemployed railroad personnel.

Sources of Information

Benefit Inquiries The Board maintains direct contact with railroad employees and railroad retirement beneficiaries through its field offices located across the country. Field personnel explain benefit rights and responsibilities on an individual basis, assist employees applying for benefits, and answer questions related to the benefit programs.

To locate the nearest field office, individuals should check with their rail employer, local union official, local post office, or one of the regional offices listed below. Information may also be obtained by calling the Board's helpline at 800–808–0772 or from the Board's Web site at www.rrb.gov. Most offices are open to the public from 9 a.m. to 3:30 p.m., Monday through Friday. The Board also relies on railroad labor groups and employers for assistance in keeping railroad personnel informed about its benefit programs.

Regional Offices—Railroad Retirement Board

City	Address	Director	Telephone
Atlanta, GA	Rm. 1703, 401 W. Peachtree St., 30308–3519	Patricia R. Lawson	404–331–2691
Denver, CO	Suite 3300, 1999 Broadway, 80202–5737	Louis E. Austin	303–844–0800
Philadelphia, PA	Suite 304, 900 Market St., 19107–4228	Richard D. Baird	215–597–2647

Electronic Access Railroad Retirement Board information is available electronically through the Internet, at www.rrb.gov.

Employment Inquiries and applications for employment should be directed to the Bureau of Human Resources, Railroad Retirement Board, 844 North Rush Street, Chicago, IL 60611–2092. Phone, 312–751–4580. Fax, 312–751–7164. E-mail, recruit@rrb.gov

Congressional and Legislative Assistance Congressional offices making inquiries regarding constituents' claims should contact the Office of Administration, Congressional Inquiry Section. Phone, 312–751–4974. Fax, 312–751–7154. E-mail, opa@rrb.gov. For information regarding legislative matters, contact the

Office of Legislative Affairs, Suite 500, 1310 G Street NW., Washington, DC 20005–3004. Phone, 202–272–7742. Fax, 202–272–7728. E-mail, ola@rrb.gov.

Publications General information pamphlets on benefit programs may be obtained from the Board's field offices or Chicago headquarters. Requests for annual reports or statistical data should be directed to Public Affairs at the Chicago headquarters. Phone, 312–751–4777. Fax, 312–751–7154. E-mail, opa@rrb.gov.

Telecommunications Devices for the Deaf (TDD) The Board provides TDD services. Phone, 312–751–4701 for beneficiary inquiries or 312–751–4334 for equal opportunity inquiries.

For further information, contact Public Affairs, Railroad Retirement Board, 844 North Rush Street, Chicago, IL 60611–2092. Phone, 312–751–4777. E-mail, opa@rrb.gov. Internet, www.rrb.gov.

SECURITIES AND EXCHANGE COMMISSION

100 F Street NE., Washington, DC 20549
Phone, 202–551–7500. Internet, www.sec.gov.

Chairman	CHRISTOPHER COX
Commissioners	PAUL ATKINS, ROEL CAMPOS, CYNTHIA GLASSMAN, ANNETTE L. NAZARETH
Senior Advisers to the Chairman	PETER UHLMANN, PAUL WILKINSON, BENEDICT S. COHEN
Director, Office of Legislative Affairs	JANE COBB
Director, Office of Public Affairs	JOHN NESTER
Director, Office of Investor Education and Assistance	SUSAN FERRIS-WYDERKO
Secretary	NANCY M. MORRIS
Executive Director	JAMES M. MCCONNELL
Associate Executive Director, Office of Human Resources	JEFFREY RISINGER
Associate Executive Director, Office of Administrative Services	ANNE O'DONOGHUE
Associate Executive Director, Office of Financial Management	MARGARET J. CARPENTER
Associate Executive Director, Office of Filings and Information Services	KENNETH A. FOGASH
General Counsel	BRIAN G. CARTWRIGHT
Director, Division of Corporation Finance	JOHN W. WHITE
Director, Division of Enforcement	LINDA CHATMAN THOMSEN
Director, Division of Investment Management	ANDREW DONOHUE
Director, Division of Market Regulation	(VACANCY)
Director, Office of Compliance Inspections and Examinations	LORI A. RICHARDS
Chief Accountant	(VACANCY)
Chief Administrative Law Judge	BRENDA P. MURRAY
Chief Economist	CHESTER SPATT
Chief Information Officer, Office of Information Technology	R. COREY BOOTH
Director, Office of International Affairs	ETHIOPIS TAFARA

Director, Office of Equal Employment Opportunity	DEBORAH K. BALDUCCHI
Director, Office of Risk Assessment	CHARLES FISHKIN
Inspector General	WALTER J. STACHNIK

[For the Securities and Exchange Commission statement of organization, see the *Code of Federal Regulations*, Title 17, Part 200]

The Securities and Exchange Commission administers Federal securities laws that seek to provide protection for investors; to ensure that securities markets are fair and honest; and, when necessary, to provide the means to enforce securities laws through sanctions.

The Securities and Exchange Commission (SEC) was created under authority of the Securities Exchange Act of 1934 (15 U.S.C. 78a–78jj) and was organized on July 2, 1934. The Commission serves as adviser to United States district courts in connection with reorganization proceedings for debtor corporations in which there is a substantial public interest. The Commission also has certain responsibilities under section 15 of the Bretton Woods Agreements Act of 1945 (22 U.S.C. 286k–1) and section 851(e) of the Internal Revenue Code of 1954 (26 U.S.C. 851(e)).

The Commission is vested with quasi-judicial functions. Persons aggrieved by its decisions in the exercise of those functions have a right of review by the United States courts of appeals.

Activities

Full and Fair Disclosure The Securities Act of 1933 (15 U.S.C. 77a) requires issuers of securities and their controlling persons making public offerings of securities in interstate commerce or through the mail to file with the Commission registration statements containing financial and other pertinent data about the issuer and the securities being offered. There are limited exemptions, such as government securities, nonpublic offerings, and intrastate offerings, as well as certain offerings not exceeding $1.5 million. The effectiveness of a registration statement may be refused or suspended after a public hearing if the statement contains material misstatements or omissions, thus barring sale of the securities until it is appropriately amended.

Regulation of Investment Advisers
Persons who, for compensation, engage in the business of advising others with respect to securities must register with the Commission. The Commission is authorized to define what practices are considered fraudulent or deceptive and to prescribe means to prevent those practices.

Regulation of Mutual Funds and Other Investment Companies The Commission registers investment companies and regulates their activities to protect investors. The regulation covers sales load, management contracts, composition of boards of directors, and capital structure. The Commission must also determine the fairness of various transactions of investment companies before these actually occur.

The Commission may institute court action to enjoin the consummation of mergers and other plans of reorganization of investment companies if such plans are unfair to securities holders. It also may impose sanctions by administrative proceedings against investment company management for violations of the act and other Federal securities laws and file court actions to enjoin acts and practices of management officials involving breaches of fiduciary duty and personal misconduct and to disqualify such officials from office.

Regulation of Securities Markets The Securities Exchange Act of 1934 assigns to the Commission broad regulatory responsibilities over the securities markets, the self-regulatory organizations within the securities industry, and persons conducting a business in securities. Persons who execute

SECURITIES AND EXCHANGE COMMISSION

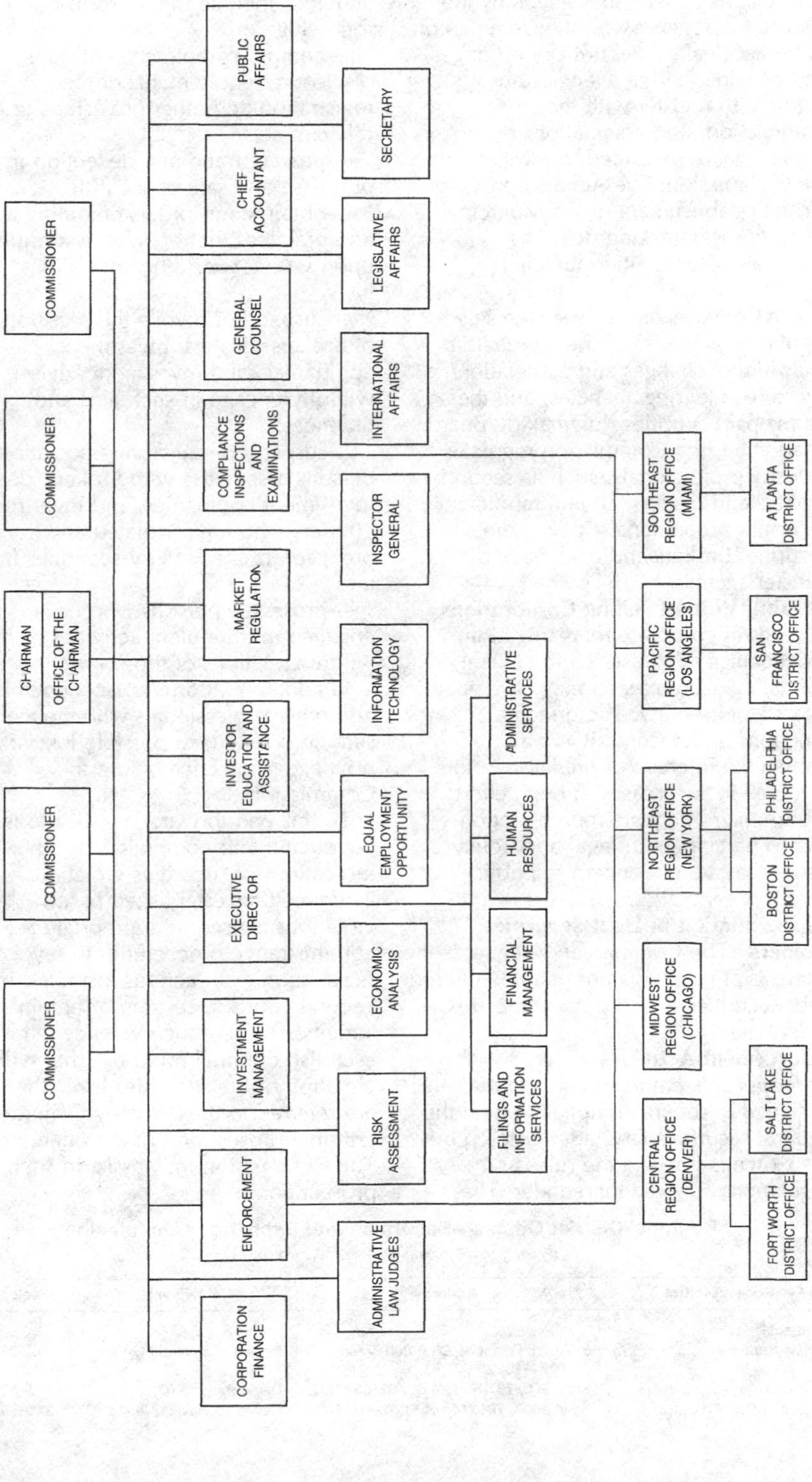

transactions in securities generally are required to register with the Commission as broker-dealers. Securities exchanges and certain clearing agencies are required to register with the Commission, and associations of brokers or dealers are permitted to register with the Commission. The Act also provides for the establishment of the Municipal Securities Rulemaking Board to formulate rules for the municipal securities industry.

The Commission oversees the self-regulatory activities of the national securities exchanges and associations, registered clearing agencies, and the Municipal Securities Rulemaking Board. In addition, the Commission regulates industry professionals, such as securities brokers and dealers, certain municipal securities professionals, government securities brokers and dealers, and transfer agents.

Rehabilitation of Failing Corporations In cases of corporate reorganization proceedings administered in Federal courts, the Commission may participate as a statutory party. The principal functions of the Commission are to protect the interests of public investors involved in such cases through efforts to ensure their adequate representation, and to participate in legal and policy issues that are of concern to public investors generally.

Representation of Debt Securities Holders The Commission safeguards the interests of purchasers of publicly offered debt securities issued pursuant to trust indentures.

Enforcement Activities The Commission's enforcement activities are designed to secure compliance with the Federal securities laws administered by the Commission and the rules and regulations adopted thereunder. These activities include measures to do the following:

—compel compliance with the disclosure requirements of the registration and other provisions of the relevant acts;

—prevent fraud and deception in the purchase and sale of securities;

—obtain court orders enjoining acts and practices that operate as a fraud upon investors or otherwise violate the laws;

—suspend or revoke the registrations of brokers, dealers, investment companies, and investment advisers who willfully engage in such acts and practices;

—suspend or bar from association persons associated with brokers, dealers, investment companies, and investment advisers who have violated any provision of the Federal securities laws; and

—prosecute persons who have engaged in fraudulent activities or other willful violations of those laws.

In addition, attorneys, accountants, and other professionals who violate the securities laws face possible loss of their privilege to practice before the Commission.

To this end, private investigations are conducted into complaints or other indications of securities violations. Evidence thus established of law violations is used in appropriate administrative proceedings to revoke registration or in actions instituted in Federal courts to restrain or enjoin such activities. Where the evidence tends to establish criminal fraud or other willful violation of the securities laws, the facts are referred to the Attorney General for criminal prosecution of the offenders. The Commission may assist in such prosecutions.

Regional/District Offices—Securities and Exchange Commission

(R: Regional Director; D: District Administrator)

Region/District	Address	Official	Telephone
Northeast			
New York, NY	3 World Financial Ctr., 200 Vesey St., 10281–1022	Mark K. Schonfeld (R)	212–336–1020
Boston, MA	Suite 600, 73 Tremont St., 02108–3912	David Bergers (D)	617–573–8900
Philadelphia, PA	Suite 2000, 701 Market St., 19106–1532	Daniel M. Hawke, *Acting* (D)	215–597–3100

Regional/District Offices—Securities and Exchange Commission—Continued

(R: Regional Director; D: District Administrator)

Region/District	Address	Official	Telephone
Southeast			
Miami, FL	Suite 1800, 801 Brickell Ave., 33131	David P. Nelson (R)	305–982–6300
Atlanta, GA	Suite 1000, 3475 Lenox Rd. NE., 30326–1232	Richard P. Wessel (D)	404–842–7600
Midwest			
Chicago, IL	Suite 900, 175 W. Jackson Blvd., 60604	Merri Jo Gillette (R)	312–353–7390
Central			
Denver, CO	Suite 1500, 1801 California St., 80202–2656	Vacancy (R)	303–844–1000
Fort Worth, TX	Burnett Plaza, Suite 1900, 801 Cherry St. Unit 18, 76102–6882	Rose Romero (D)	817–978–3821
Salt Lake City, UT	Suite 1800, 15 W. South Temple St., 84101	Kenneth D. Israel, Jr. (D)	801–524–5796
Pacific			
Los Angeles, CA	11th Fl., 5670 Wilshire Blvd., 90036–3648	Randall R. Lee (R)	323–965–3998
San Francisco, CA	Suite 2600, 44 Montgomery St., 94104	Helane Morrison (D)	415–705–2500

Sources of Information

Inquiries regarding the following matters should be directed to the appropriate office, Securities and Exchange Commission, 100 F Street NE., Washington, DC 20549.

Contracts Inquiries regarding SEC procurement and contracting activities should be directed to the Office of Administrative Services. Phone, 202–551–7400.

Electronic Access Information on the Commission is available through the Internet at www.sec.gov.

Employment With the exception of the attorney category, positions are in the competitive civil service, which means applicants must apply for consideration for a particular vacancy and go through competitive selection procedures. The Commission operates a college and law school recruitment program, including on-campus visitations for interview purposes. Inquiries should be directed to the Office of Human Resources. Phone, 202–942–7500. Fax, 703–914–0592.

Investor Assistance and Complaints The Office of Investor Education and Assistance answers questions from investors, assists investors with specific problems regarding their relations with broker-dealers and companies, and advises the Commission and other offices and divisions regarding problems frequently encountered by investors and possible regulatory solutions to such problems. Phone, 202–551–6551. Consumer information line, 800–SEC–0330. Fax, 202–772–9295. Complaints and inquiries may also be directed to any regional or district office.

Publications Blank copies of SEC forms and other publications are available in the Publications Unit. Phone, 202–551–4040.

Reading Rooms The Commission maintains a public reference room (phone, 202–551–8090) in Washington, DC, where registration statements and other public documents filed with the Commission are available for public inspection. Copies of public material may be purchased from the Commission's contract copying service at prescribed rates. The Commission also maintains a library (phone, 202–551–5450; fax, 202–772–9326) where additional information may be obtained.

Small Business Activities Information on securities laws that pertain to small businesses in relation to securities offerings may be obtained from the Commission. Phone, 202–551–3460.

For further information, contact the Office of Public Affairs, Securities and Exchange Commission, 100 F Street NE., Washington, DC 20549. Phone, 202–551–4120. Fax, 202–777–1026. Internet, www.sec.gov.

SELECTIVE SERVICE SYSTEM

National Headquarters, Arlington, VA 22209–2425
Phone, 703–605–4000. Internet, www.sss.gov.

Director	WILLIAM A. CHATFIELD
Deputy Director	S. ERIC BENSON
Chief of Staff	ERNEST E. GARCIA
Special Assistant	CARLO VERDINO
General Counsel	RUDY SANCHEZ
Director for Mobilization	WILLIE C. BLANDING, JR.
Director for Public and Intergovernmental Affairs	RICHARD S. FLAHAVAN
Director for Support Services	EDWARD A. BLACKADAR, JR.
Director for Information Technology	SCOTT CAMPBELL
Director for Financial Management	WILLIAM REESE

[For the Selective Service System statement of organization, see the *Code of Federal Regulations,* Title 32, Part 1605]

The Selective Service System provides manpower to the Armed Forces in an emergency and operates an Alternative Service Program during a draft for men classified as conscientious objectors.

The Selective Service System was established by the Military Selective Service Act (50 U.S.C. app. 451–471a). The act requires the registration of male citizens of the United States and all other male persons who are in the United States and who are ages 18 to 26. The act exempts members of the active Armed Forces and nonimmigrant aliens. Proclamation 4771 of July 20, 1980, requires male persons born on or after January 1, 1960, and who have attained age 18 but have not attained age 26 to register. Registration is conducted at post offices within the United States, at U.S. embassies and consulates outside the United States, and online at www.sss.gov.

The act imposes liability for training and service in the Armed Forces upon registrants who are ages 18 to 26, except those who are exempt or deferred. Persons who have been deferred remain liable for training and service until age 35. Aliens are not liable for training and service until they have remained in the United States for more than 1 year. Conscientious objectors who are found to be opposed to all service in the Armed Forces are required to perform civilian work in lieu of induction into the Armed Forces.

The authority to induct registrants, including doctors and allied medical specialists, expired July 1, 1973.

Regional Offices—Selective Service System

Region/Address	Director	Telephone
North Chicago, IL (Suite 276, 2834 Green Bay Rd., 60064–9983)	Thomas White	847–688–7985
Smyrna, GA (Suite 270, 2400 Lake Park Dr., 30080)	Keith A. Scragg	770–319–6036
Denver, CO (Suite 1014, 3401 Quebec St., 80207–2323)	Debbie Bielanski	720–941–1670

Sources of Information

Employment Inquiries and applications should be directed to the Director, Selective Service System, Attn: SPT/HR, Arlington, VA 22209–2425. Phone, 703–605–4056.

Procurement Inquiries should be directed to the Director, Selective

SELECTIVE SERVICE SYSTEM

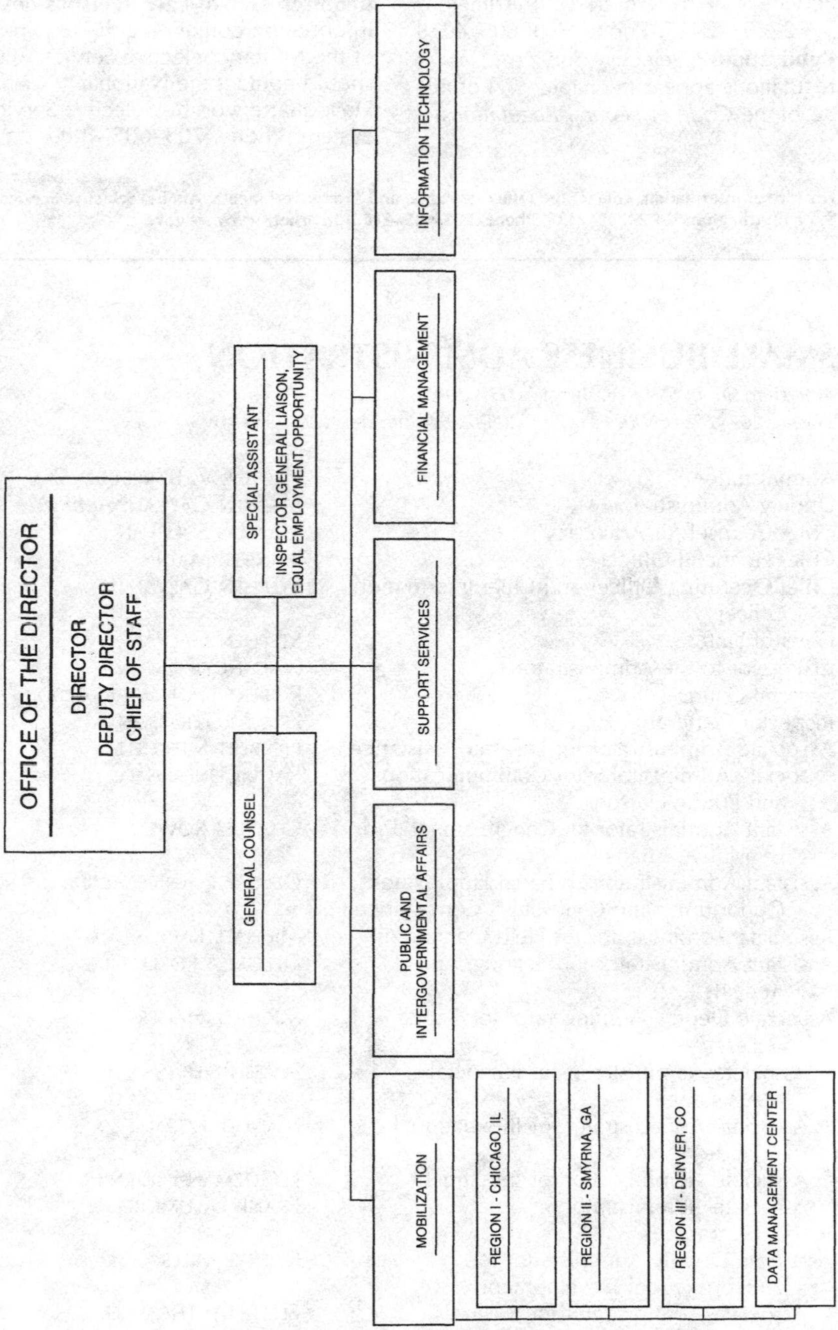

Service System, Attn: STP/LO, Arlington, VA 22209–2425. Phone, 703–605–4038.

Publications Selective Service regulations appear in chapter XVI of title 32 of the *Code of Federal Regulations.*

Requirements of Law Persons desiring information concerning the requirements of the Military Selective Service Act should contact the National Headquarters of the Selective Service System. Phone, 703–605–4000.

For further information, contact the Office of Public and Intergovernmental Affairs, Selective Service System, Arlington, VA 22209–2425. Phone, 703–605–4100. Internet, www.sss.gov.

SMALL BUSINESS ADMINISTRATION

409 Third Street SW., Washington, DC 20416
Phone, 202–205–6600. Fax, 202–205–7064. Internet, www.sba.gov.

Administrator	Hector V. Barreto
Deputy Administrator	Stephen Galvan, *Acting*
Chief Counsel for Advocacy	Thomas Sullivan
Chief Financial Officer	Jennifer Main
Chief Operating Officer and Chief Information Officer	Stephen Galvan
Chief of Staff	Stephen Galvan
Counselor to the Administrator	(vacancy)
General Counsel	Robert Gangwere, *Acting*
Inspector General	Eric M. Thorson
Associate Administrator for Disaster Assistance	Herbert Mitchell
Associate Administrator for Communications and Public Liaison	Raul Cisneros
Assistant Administrator for Congressional and Legislative Affairs	Charles Rowe
Assistant Administrator for Equal Employment Opportunity and Civil Rights Compliance	Delorice Ford, *Acting*
Associate Administrator for Field Operations	Michael Pappas
Assistant Administrator for Hearings and Appeals	Delorice Ford
Associate Deputy Administrator for Capital Access	Michael Hager
Associate Administrator for Financial Assistance	James Rivera
Associate Administrator for International Trade	Manuel Rosales
Associate Administrator for Investment	J. Guzman-Fournier
Associate Administrator for Surety Guarantees	Frank Lalumiere
Associate Deputy Administrator for Entrepreneurial Development	Cheryl Mills
Associate Administrator for Business Initiatives	Ellen M. Thrasher
National Director for Native American Affairs	Holly Schick, *Acting*
Associate Administrator for Small Business Development Centers	Antonio Doss

Associate Administrator for Veterans Business Development	WILLIAM ELMORE
Associate Administrator for Women's Business Ownership	WILMA GOLDSTEIN
Associate Deputy Administrator for Government Contracting and Business Development	CALVIN JENKINS, *Acting*
Associate Administrator for Government Contracting	KAREN HONTZ
Associate Administrator for Business Development	(VACANCY)
Associate Administrator for HUBZone Empowerment Contracting	MICHAEL MCHALE
Associate Deputy Administrator for Management and Administration	LEWIS ANDREWS
Assistant Administrator for Administration	DARRYL HAIRSTON
Chief Human Capital Officer	RICHARD BRECHBIEL
Director, Executive Secretariat	DONALD SWAIN

[For the Small Business Administration statement of organization, see the *Code of Federal Regulations,* Title 13, Part 101]

The fundamental purposes of the Small Business Administration are to aid, counsel, assist, and protect the interests of small business; ensure that small business concerns receive a fair portion of Government purchases, contracts, and subcontracts, as well as of the sales of Government property; make loans to small business concerns, State and local development companies, and the victims of floods or other catastrophes, or of certain types of economic injury; and license, regulate, and make loans to small business investment companies.

The Small Business Administration (SBA) was created by the Small Business Act of 1953 and derives its present existence and authority from the Small Business Act (15 U.S.C. 631 *et seq.*) and the Small Business Investment Act of 1958 (15 U.S.C. 661).

Activities

Advocacy The Office of Advocacy is mandated by Congress to serve as an independent voice within the Federal Government for the approximately 23.7 million small businesses throughout the country. The Office is headed by the Chief Counsel for Advocacy, appointed by the President from the private sector with the advice and consent of the Senate, who advances the views, concerns, and interests of small business before the Congress, the White House, and Federal and State regulatory agencies.

The Office monitors the compliance of Federal agencies with the Regulatory Flexibility Act—the law that requires agencies to analyze the impact of their regulations on small entities and consider less burdensome alternatives. The Office is one of the leading national sources for information on the state of small business and the issues that affect small business success and growth. It conducts economic and statistical research into matters affecting the competitive strength of small business and jobs created by small business, and analyzes the impact of Federal laws, regulations, and programs on small businesses, making recommendations to policymakers for appropriate adjustments to meet the special needs of small business.

Additionally, regional advocates enhance communication between the small business community and the Chief Counsel. As the Chief Counsel's direct link to local business owners, State and local government agencies, State legislatures, and small business organizations, they help identify new

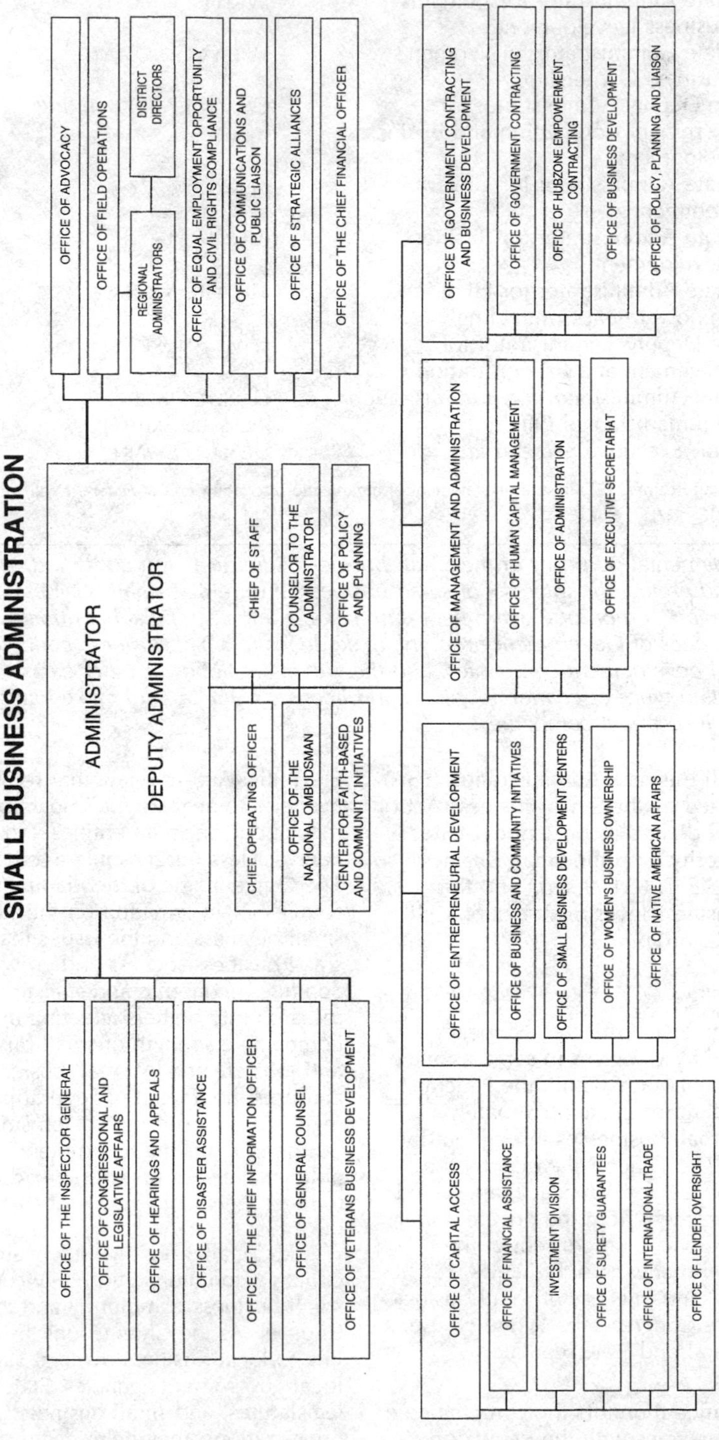
SMALL BUSINESS ADMINISTRATION
ADMINISTRATOR
DEPUTY ADMINISTRATOR
OFFICE OF ADVOCACY
OFFICE OF FIELD OPERATIONS
REGIONAL ADMINISTRATORS
DISTRICT DIRECTORS
OFFICE OF EQUAL EMPLOYMENT OPPORTUNITY AND CIVIL RIGHTS COMPLIANCE
OFFICE OF COMMUNICATIONS AND PUBLIC LIAISON
OFFICE OF STRATEGIC ALLIANCES
OFFICE OF THE CHIEF FINANCIAL OFFICER
CHIEF OF STAFF
COUNSELOR TO THE ADMINISTRATOR
OFFICE OF POLICY AND PLANNING
CHIEF OPERATING OFFICER
OFFICE OF THE NATIONAL OMBUDSMAN
CENTER FOR FAITH-BASED AND COMMUNITY INITIATIVES
OFFICE OF THE INSPECTOR GENERAL
OFFICE OF CONGRESSIONAL AND LEGISLATIVE AFFAIRS
OFFICE OF HEARINGS AND APPEALS
OFFICE OF DISASTER ASSISTANCE
OFFICE OF THE CHIEF INFORMATION OFFICER
OFFICE OF GENERAL COUNSEL
OFFICE OF VETERANS BUSINESS DEVELOPMENT
OFFICE OF GOVERNMENT CONTRACTING AND BUSINESS DEVELOPMENT
OFFICE OF GOVERNMENT CONTRACTING
OFFICE OF HUBZONE EMPOWERMENT CONTRACTING
OFFICE OF BUSINESS DEVELOPMENT
OFFICE OF POLICY, PLANNING AND LIAISON
OFFICE OF MANAGEMENT AND ADMINISTRATION
OFFICE OF HUMAN CAPITAL MANAGEMENT
OFFICE OF ADMINISTRATION
OFFICE OF EXECUTIVE SECRETARIAT
OFFICE OF ENTREPRENEURIAL DEVELOPMENT
OFFICE OF BUSINESS AND COMMUNITY INITIATIVES
OFFICE OF SMALL BUSINESS DEVELOPMENT CENTERS
OFFICE OF WOMEN'S BUSINESS OWNERSHIP
OFFICE OF NATIVE AMERICAN AFFAIRS
OFFICE OF CAPITAL ACCESS
OFFICE OF FINANCIAL ASSISTANCE
INVESTMENT DIVISION
OFFICE OF SURETY GUARANTEES
OFFICE OF INTERNATIONAL TRADE
OFFICE OF LENDER OVERSIGHT

issues and problems of small business by monitoring the effect of Federal and State regulations and policies on the local business communities within their regions.

For further information, contact the Office of Advocacy. Phone, 202–205–6533. E-mail, advocacy@sba.gov.

Business and Community Initiatives The Office of Business and Community Initiatives (OBCI) develops and cosponsors counseling, education, training, and information resources for small businesses. It has partnered with the private sector to promote entrepreneurial development. OBCI directs the national program of the Service Corps of Retired Executives (SCORE), a resource partner of SBA. SCORE provides free counseling, mentoring, training seminars, and specialized assistance to veterans and active military. For more information, visit www.score.org. OBCI also offers young entrepreneurs a teen business site at www.sba.gov/teens.

The Office of International Visitors briefs foreign delegations, business organizations, and international nongovernmental organizations (NGOs) on the SBA model.

In addition to education and training events, SBA offers an online management series on business growth and sustainability at www.sba.gov/library/pubs.

For further information, contact the Office of Business and Community Initiatives. Phone, 202–205–6665.

Capital Access The Office of the Associate Deputy Administrator for Capital Access provides overall direction for SBA's financial programs. They offer a comprehensive array of debt and equity programs for startup and expanding businesses. In addition to lending to businesses which sell their products and services domestically, the Office provides financial assistance programs for small business exporters, in the form of loan programs and technical assistance. The Office also oversees a surety bond guarantee program for small business contractors and SBA's lender oversight programs.

For further information, contact the Office of Capital Access. Phone, 202–205–6657.

Disaster Assistance The Administration serves as the Federal disaster bank for nonfarm, private sector losses. It lends money to help the victims of disasters repair or replace most disaster-damaged property. Direct loans with subsidized interest rates are made to assist individuals, homeowners, businesses of all sizes, and nonprofit organizations.

For further information, contact the Office of Disaster Assistance. Phone, 202–205–6734.

Financial Assistance SBA provides its guarantee to lending institutions and certified development companies which make loans to small-business concerns, which in turn use the loans to provide working capital and help finance the acquisition of land and buildings; the construction, conversion, or expansion of facilities; and the purchase of machinery and equipment.

SBA provides loan guarantees to finance commercial construction or building rehabilitation. It makes loans to qualified employee trusts and may finance small firms that manufacture, sell, install, service, or develop specific energy measures, including engineering, architectural, consulting, or other professional services connected with eligible energy measures. SBA also makes loans for the installation of pollution control measures.

The Administration also provides small-scale financial and technical assistance to very small businesses through loans and grants to nonprofit organizations that act as intermediaries under SBA's microloan program.

For further information, contact the nearest Small Business Administration district office listed at the end of this writeup.

Government Contracting and Policy, Planning and Liaison SBA helps small businesses, including small disadvantaged businesses, women-owned small business, HUBZone-certified firms, and service-disabled veteran-owned small businesses obtain a fair share of Government procurement through a variety of programs and services. The contracting liaison helps small businesses secure an equitable share of natural resources sold by the Federal Government. It works closely with Federal agencies and the Office of Management and Budget to establish policy and regulations concerning small business access to Government contracts. It assists in the formulation of small business procurement policies as they relate to size standards, the Small Business Innovation Research Program, and the Small Business Technology Transfer Program.

For further information, contact the nearest Office of Government Contracting or visit our Web site. Phone, 202–205–6459. Internet, www.sba.gov/GC/indexcontacts.html.

International Trade The Office of International Trade (OIT) supports small business access to export markets and participates in broader U.S. Government activities related to trade policy and international commercial affairs to encourage an environment of trade and international economic policies favorable to small businesses. These activities are designed to facilitate both entrance and growth into the international marketplace, including educational initiatives, technical assistance programs and services, and risk management and trade finance products.

SBA's export promotion activities for small business combine financial and technical assistance through a nationwide delivery system. Export-finance products include long-term, short-term, and revolving lines of credit through SBA's 7(a) program administered by a staff of field-based export specialists located in U.S. Export Assistance Centers (USEAC). They work with the U.S. Department of Commerce and the Export Import Bank of the United States and the effort is leveraged through close collaboration with commercial lenders, Small Business Development Centers, and local business development organizations.

Available financial assistance can provide a business with up to $1.25 million with terms as long as 25 years for real estate and 15 years for equipment. Export Working Capital program loans generally provide 12 months of renewable financing. For smaller loan amounts SBA Export Express has a streamlined, quick approval process for businesses needing up to $250,000. Technical assistance includes making available to current and potential small business exporters, export training, export legal assistance, collaboration with the 30 Small Business Development Centers with international trade expertise and to the Government's USA Trade Information Center.

SBA is required to work with the Government's international trade agencies to ensure that small business is adequately represented in bilateral and multilateral trade negotiations. OIT represents SBA and the Government on two official U.S. Government-sponsored multilateral organizations concerned with small business—the Organization for Economic Cooperation and Development and Asia-Pacific Economic Cooperation. SBA's trade policy involvement is carried out with the U.S. Trade Representative and the Commerce Department's International Trade Administration. Private sector input on trade policy is achieved through participation with the small business industry sector advisory committee on international trade. OIT also lends support to the Government's key trade initiatives such as Trade Promotion Authority, the Central American Free Trade Area, and the Free Trade Area of the Americas. The Commerce and State Departments, Agency for International Development, and the U.S. Trade Representative look to the SBA to share ideas and provide small business technical expertise to certain countries.

OIT's office in Washington, DC, coordinates SBA's participation/operation of USEACs, including budget, policy and administration. It participates in a variety of interagency trade efforts and financial programs. OIT provides representations to the cabinet-level Trade Promotion Coordinating Committee concerning trade and international economic policy. It also participates on the Industry Sector

Advisory Council on Small Business International Trade and the congressionally sponsored Task Force on Small Business International Trade. SBA's Administrator is also a sitting member of the President's Export Council.

OIT's field offices provide a nationwide network of service delivery for small business exporters. Full-time SBA export specialists staff 16 USEACs. Their outreach efforts are supplemented by the 70 SBA district offices by employees with collateral duties as international trade officers.

For further information, contact the Office of International Trade. Phone, 202–205–6720. Internet, www.sba.gov/oit.

Venture Capital The Small Business Investment Company (SBIC) program was created in 1958 to fill the gap between the availability of venture capital and the needs of small businesses in startup and growth situations. The structure of the program is unique in that SBICs are privately owned and managed venture capital funds licensed and regulated by the SBA that use their own capital, plus funds borrowed with an SBA guarantee to make equity and debt investments in qualifying small businesses. The New Markets Venture Capital (NMVC) program is a sister program focused on low-income areas, which augments the contribution made by SBICs to U.S. small businesses.

The Goverment itself does not make direct investments or target specific industries in the SBIC program. Fund portfolio management and investment decisions are left to qualified private fund managers. To obtain an SBIC license, an experienced team of private equity managers must secure minimum commitments from private investors of either $5 million (for a debenture fund) or $10 million (for an equity fund). SBICs may only invest in "small businesses" having net worth of less than $18 million and prior 2 years' average after-tax income of less than $6 million.

For further information, contact the Investment Division. Phone, 202–205–6510. Internet, www.sba.gov/inv.

HUBZone Program The HUBZone program provides Federal contracting assistance for qualified small businesses located in historically underutilized business zones in an effort to increase employment, capital investment, and economic development in these areas, including Indian reservations. The Office coordinates efforts with other Federal agencies and local municipal governments to leverage resources to assist qualified small businesses located in HUBZone areas. The program provides for set-asides, sole source awards, and price evaluation preferences for HUBZone small businesses and establishes goals for awards to such firms.

For further information, visit our Web site at www.sba.gov/hubzone. Phone, 202–205–6731.

Business Development The Office of Business Development manages the 8(a) Business Development Program and the Small Disadvantaged Business Certification Program that help eligible small disadvantaged business concerns compete in the Nation's mainstream economy. Specifically, it provides business counseling and training, management and technical assistance, Mentor-Protégé Agreements, surplus property, technology transfer, and access to procurement opportunities. Its responsibilities include issuing program policies and plans, marketing and evaluating program implementation, coordinating with other SBA offices to ensure program integration, and making program eligibility decisions.

For further information, visit our Web site at www.sba.gov/gcbd. Phone, 202–205–5180.

Native American Affairs The Office of Native American Affairs was established to assist and encourage the creation, development, and expansion of Native American-owned small businesses by developing and implementing initiatives designed to address those difficulties encountered by Native Americans in their quest to start, develop, and expand small businesses. In addition, in an effort to address the unique conditions encountered by reservation-based entrepreneurs, SBA has established the

Tribal Business Information Centers (TBIC) pilot project. The project is a partnership arrangement between a tribe or tribal college and SBA.

TBICs offer community access to business-related computer software technology, provide one-on-one business counseling, and hold business workshops on an ongoing basis. Additionally, all TBIC managers/ facilitators have received extensive training in all SBA entrepreneurial development programs, lending programs, and procurement programs. Currently there are 16 centers located in California, Minnesota, Montana, North Carolina, North Dakota, and South Dakota.

In addition to the TBIC project, the Office actively participates with other SBA program offices and other Federal agencies to ensure that Native American entrepreneurs are being actively encouraged to participate. Also, the Office maintains liaisons with tribal governments, business organizations, and Native American community organizations.

For further information, contact the Office of Native American Affairs. Phone, 202–205–7364.

Regulatory Fairness Program Congress established the national ombudsman and 10 Regulatory Fairness Boards in 1996 as part of the Small Business Regulatory Enforcement Fairness Act (SBREFA). Section 222 of SBREFA was designed to ensure that small businesses, small government entities, and small nonprofit organizations that experience unfair regulatory enforcement action by Federal agencies have a means to register their comments about such actions. Comments from small business concerns are received by e-mail, fax, regular mail, or by testifting at ombudsman hearings that are held across the country. The ombudsman acts as a neutral liaison between small business concerns and affected agencies to include comments for the report. Each of the Regulatory Fairness Boards (RegFair) has five volunteer members who are owners, operators or officers of small business concerns that are appointed by the SBA Administrator for terms of 3 years. Each RegFair Board meets at least annually with the ombudsman on matters of concern to small businesses relating to the enforcement or compliance activities of Federal agencies; report to the ombudsman on substantiated instances of excessive enforcement; and, prior to publication, provide comment on the annual report to Congress.

For further information, contact the Office of the National Ombudsman. Phone, 202–205–2417 or 888–REG–FAIR (888–734–3247). Internet, www.sba.gov/ombudsman.

Small Business Development Centers Small Business Development Centers provide counseling and training to existing and prospective small business owners at approximately 1,000 locations around the country, operating in every State, Puerto Rico, the U.S. Virgin Islands, Guam, and American Samoa. The Small Business Development Center Program is a cooperative effort of the private sector, the educational community, and Federal, State, and local governments. It enhances economic development by providing small businesses with management and technical assistance.

The Office of Small Business Development Centers develops national policies and goals. It establishes standards for the selection and performance of Centers, monitors compliance with applicable Office of Management and Budget circulars and laws, and implements new approaches to improve operations of existing centers.

The Office is responsible for coordinating program efforts with other internal activities of SBA and with the activities of other Federal agencies. It maintains liaison with other Federal, State, and local agencies and private organizations whose activities relate to Small Business Development Centers, and it assesses how the program is affected by substantive developments and policies in other areas of the agency, in other Government agencies, and in the private sector.

For further information, contact the Office of Small Business Development Centers. Phone, 202–205–6766.

Surety Bonds Through its Surety Bond Guarantee Program, SBA helps small and emerging contractors to obtain the bonding necessary for them to bid on and perform contracts up to $2 million. SBA guarantees bonds that are issued by participating surety companies, and reimburses between 70% and 90% of losses and expenses incurred if the contractor defaults. Construction and service contractors are eligible for the program if they meet surety underwriting requirements and their average annual receipts for the last 3 fiscal years, including affiliates, do not exceed $6 million. Manufacturing firms qualify based on their number of employees.

For further information, contact the Office of Surety Guarantees. Phone, 202–205–6540. Internet, www.sba.gov/osg.

Technology The Office of Technology has authority and responsibility for directing and monitoring the governmentwide activities of the Small Business Innovation Research Program (SBIR) and the Small Business Technology Transfer Program (STTR). The Office develops and issues policy directives for the general conduct of the programs within the Federal Government and maintains a source file and information program to provide each interested and qualified small business concern with information on opportunities to compete for SBIR and STTR program awards. The Office also coordinates with each participating Federal agency in developing a master release schedule of all program solicitations; publishes the *Presolicitation Announcement* online quarterly, which contains pertinent facts on upcoming solicitations; and surveys and monitors program operations within the Federal Government and reports on the progress of the programs each year to Congress.

The Office has four main objectives: to expand and improve SBIR and STTR; to increase private sector commercialization of technology developed through Federal research and development; to increase small business participation in Federal research and development; and to improve the dissemination of information concerning SBIR and STTR, particularly with regard to participation by women-owned small business concerns and by socially and economically disadvantaged small business concerns.

For further information, contact the Office of Technology. Phone, 202–205–6450. E-mail, technology@sba.gov.

Veterans Affairs The Office of Veterans Business Development (OVBD) is responsible for the formulation, execution, and promotion of policies and programs that provide assistance to small-business concerns owned and controlled by veterans and service-disabled veterans. This includes reserve component members of the U.S. military. Additionally, OVBD serves as an ombudsman for the full consideration of veterans in all programs of the Administration.

OVBD provides e-counseling and works with every SBA program to ensure that veterans receive special consideration in the operation of that program. OVBD also provides numerous tools such as the *VetGazette* veterans newsletter, the Reserve and Guard business assistance kits, program design assistance, and training events. Additionally, OVBD manages five Veterans Business Outreach Centers to provide outreach, directed referrals, and tailored entrepreneurial development services such as business training, counseling, and mentoring to service-disabled veteran, veterans, and reservist-entrepreneurs. These centers provide an in-depth resource for existing and potential veteran entrepreneurs. The Office also coordinates SBA collaborative efforts with Veterans Service Organizations, the Departments of Defense, Labor, and Veterans Affairs, the National Veterans Business Development Corporation, State Departments of Veterans Affairs, the National Committee for Employer Support of the Guard and Reserve, and other public, civic, and private organizations to ensure that the entrepreneurial needs of veterans, service-disabled veterans, and self-employed members of the Reserve and National Guard are being met.

For further information, contact the Office of Veterans Business Development. Phone, 202–205–6773. Internet, www.sba.gov/vets, or www.sba.gov/reservists.

Women's Business Ownership The Office of Women's Business Ownership (OWBO) provides assistance to current and potential women business owners and acts as their advocate in the public and private sectors. OWBO assists women in becoming full partners in economic development through technical, financial, and management information training, business skills counseling, and research. OWBO offers their services through a network of local SBA offices, Women's Business Centers (WBCs), and mentoring roundtables.

At nearly 100 WBCs, business owners and those interested in starting businesses can receive long-term, in-depth business training and counseling as well as access to SBA's programs and services. Each WBC is tailored to meet the needs of its individual community and places a special emphasis on helping women who are socially and economically disadvantaged. Assistance covers every stage of business from startup to going public. There are WBCs in almost every State and U.S. territory.

The Women's Network for Entrepreneurial Training (WNET) brings experienced and emerging entrepreneurs together with volunteer counselors from SCORE (Service Corps of Retired Executives), in roundtable formats for mentoring and peer support. There are nearly 200 WNET roundtables nationwide, coordinated through SBA district offices, WBCs, and SCORE chapters.

OWBO works with Federal agencies and private sector organizations to leverage its resources and improve opportunities for women-owned businesses to access Federal procurement and international trade opportunities. OWBO also works with the National Women's Business Council and the Department of Labor to maintain the most current research on women's business ownership.

SBA has loan guaranty programs to help women access the credit and capital they need to start and grow successful businesses, including the loan prequalification program and SBA*Express*. Through the loan prequalification program, entrepreneurs get help in packaging and marketing their loan applications. SBA*Express* offers guaranties on loans of up to $150,000, including revolving lines of credit and unsecured smaller loans. The microloan program offers direct small loans, combined with business assistance, through SBA-licensed intermediaries nationwide. The SBA does not offer grants for small businesses.

For further information, contact the Women's Business Ownership representative in your SBA district office, or contact the Office of Women's Business Ownership. Phone, 202–205–6673. E-mail, owbo@sba.gov. Internet, www.onlinewbc.gov.

Field Operations The Office of Field Operations provides management direction and oversight to SBA's 10 regional and 68 district offices, acting as the liaison between the district offices, the agency's program delivery system, and the headquarters administrative and program offices.

For further information, contact the Office of Field Operations. Phone, 202–205–6808.

Field Offices—Small Business Administration

(RO: Regional Office; DO: District Office; BO: Branch Office)

Office	Address	Officer in Charge	Telephone
ATLANTA, GA (RO)	Suite 1800, 233 Peachtree St. NE., 30303	Nuby Fowler	404–331–4999
Atlanta, GA (DO)	Suite 1900, 233 Peachtree St. NE., 30303	Terri Denison	404–331–0100
Birmingham, AL (DO)	Suite 201, 801 Tom Martin Dr., 35211	Michael Ricks	205–290–7101
Charlotte, NC (DO)	Suite 300, 6302 Fairview Rd., 28210–2227	Lee Cornelison	704–344–6563
Columbia, SC (DO)	Rm. 358, 1425 Assembly St., 29201	Elliot Cooper	803–765–5377
Gulfport, MS (BO)	Suite 203, 2909 13th St., 39501	Judith Adcock	228–863–4449
Jackson, MS (DO)	210 E, 210 E. Capital St., 39201	Janita Stewart	601–965–4378
Jacksonville, FL (DO)	Suite 100–B, 7825 Baymeadows Way, 32256–7504.	Wilfredo Gonzalez	904–443–1970
Louisville, KY (DO)	Rm. 188, 600 Dr. M.L. King, Jr. Pl., 40202	Steve Ayers	502–582–5978

Field Offices—Small Business Administration—Continued

(RO: Regional Office; DO: District Office; BO: Branch Office)

Office	Address	Officer in Charge	Telephone
Miami, FL (DO)	7th Fl., 100 S. Biscayne Blvd., 33131	Pancho Marrero	305–536–5533
Nashville, TN (DO)	Suite 201, 50 Vantage Way, 37228–1500	Clint Smith	615–736–5850
BOSTON, MA (RO)	Suite 812, 10 Causeway St., 02222	Charles Summers	617–565–8415
Augusta, ME (DO)	Rm. 512, 68 Sewall St., 04330	Mary McAleney	207–622–8378
Boston, MA (DO)	Suite 265, 10 Causeway St., 02222	Maurice L. Dube	617–565–5561
Concord, NH (DO)	Suite 3101, 55 Pleasant St., 03301	Bill Phillips	603–225–1400
Hartford, CT (DO)	2d Fl., 330 Main St., 06106	Bernard Sweeney	860–240–4700
Montpelier, VT (DO)	Suite 205, 87 State St., 05602	Kenneth Silvia	802–828–4422
Providence, RI (DO)	5th Fl., 380 Westminster Mall, 02903	Mark Hayward	401–528–4561
Springfield, MA (BO)	One Federal St., Bldg. 101, 01105	Bob Nelson	413–785–0484
CHICAGO, IL (RO)	Suite 1250, 500 W. Madison St., 60661	Patrick Rea	312–353–4426
Chicago, IL (DO)	500 W. Madison St., 60661	Judith Roussel	312–353–4508
Cincinnati, OH (BO)	Rm. 2–522, JWP Federal Bldg., 550 Main St., 45202.	Ronald Carlson	513–684–2814
Cleveland, OH (DO)	Suite 211, 1315 Euclid Ave., 44114–2507	Gilbert Goldberg	216–522–4180
Columbus, OH (DO)	Suite 200, 401 N. Front St., 43215–2592	Tom Mueller	614–469–6860
Detroit, MI (DO)	Suite 515, 477 Michigan Ave., 48226	Richard Temkin	313–226–6075
Indianapolis, IN (DO)	Suite 400, 85 Keystone Crossing, 46204–1873	Gail Gessell	317–226–7275
Milwaukee, WI (DO)	Suite 400, 310 W. Wisconsin Ave., 53203	Eric Ness	414–297–1471
Minneapolis, MN (DO)	Suite 210–C, 100 N. 6th St., 55403–1563	Ed Daum	612–370–2306
Springfield, IL (BO)	1st Fl., 3330 Ginger Creek Rd., 62704	Valerie Ross	217–492–4416
DALLAS, TX (RO)	Suite 108, 4300 Amon Carter Blvd., Ft. Worth, TX 76155.	Joseph O. Montes	817–684–5581
Albuquerque, NM (DO)	Suite 320, 625 Silver Ave. SW., 87102	Anthony McMahon	505–346–7909
Corpus Christi, TX (BO)	Suite 411, 3649 Leopard St., 78408	Simon Castillo	361–879–0017
El Paso, TX (DO)	Suite 320, 10737 Gateways West, 79935	Phil Silva, *Acting*	915–633–7001
Fort Worth, TX (DO)	Suite 114, 4300 Amon Carter Blvd., 76155	Lavan Alexander	817–684–5500
Harlingen, TX (DO)	Rm. 500, 222 E. Van Buren St., 78550–6855	Sylvia Zamponi	956–427–8533
Houston, TX (DO)	Suite 1200, 8701 S. Gessner Dr., 77074	Manuel Gonzales, *Acting*	713–773–6500
Little Rock, AR (DO)	Suite 100, 2120 Riverfront Dr., 72202	Linda Nelson, *Acting*	501–324–5871
Lubbock, TX (DO)	Rm. 408, 1205 Texas Ave., 79401–2693	Calvin O. Davis	806–472–7462
New Orleans, LA (DO)	Suite 2820, 365 Canal Pl., 70130	Eugene Cornelius	504–589–6685
Oklahoma City, OK (DO).	Suite 116, 301 N. 8th St., 73102	Dorothy Overal	405–231–5521
San Antonio, TX (DO)	Suite 200, 17319 San Pedro, Bldg. No. 2, 78232	Anthony Alvarez, *Acting*	210–472–5900
DENVER, CO (RO)	Suite 400, 721 19th St., 80202–2599	Elton W. Ringsak	303–844–0503
Casper, WY (DO)	P.O. Box 4001, 100 E. B St., 82601	Steven Despain	307–261–6501
Denver, CO (DO)	Suite 426, 721 19th St., 80202–2599	Patricia Barela Rivera	303–844–6500
Fargo, ND (DO)	Rm. 219, 657 2d Ave. N., 58108–3086	James L. Stai	701–239–5434
Helena, MT (DO)	Suite 1100, 10 W. 15th St., 59626	Michelle Johnston	406–441–1081
Salt Lake City, UT (DO)	Rm. 2237, 125 S. State St., 84138–1195	Stanley Nakano	801–524–3200
Sioux Falls, SD (DO)	Suite 200, 110 S. Phillips Ave., 57104	John Brown	605–330–4243
KANSAS CITY, MO (RO)	Suite 307, 323 W. 8th St., 64105–1500	Samuel C. Jones	816–374–6380
Cedar Rapids, IA (BO)	Suite 350, 2750 1st Ave. NE., 52401–1806	Linda Haus, *Acting*	319–362–6405
Des Moines, IA (DO)	Rm. 350, 2750 1st Ave., NE., 50309–2186	Linda Haus, *Acting*	515–284–4026
Kansas City, MO (DO)	Suite 501, 323 W. 8th St., 64105	Gary Cook	816–374–6708
Omaha, NE (DO)	11145 Mill Valley Rd., 68154	Glenn Davis	402–221–4691
Springfield, MO (BO)	Suite 101, 830 E. Primrose, 65807–5254	Larry Aduddie	417–890–8501
St. Louis, MO (DO)	Suite 1500, 200 N. Broadway, 63102	Dennis Melton	314–539–6600
Wichita, KS (DO)	Suite 2500, 271 W 3d St. N., 67202–1212	Elizabeth Auer	316–269–6566
NEW YORK, NY (RO)	Rm. 31–08, 26 Federal Plz., 10278	William Manger	212–264–1450
Buffalo, NY (DO)	130 S. Elmwood St., 14202	Franklin J. Sciortino	716–551–4301
Elmira, NY (BO)	4th Fl., 333 E. Water St., 14901	Brian Qualey	607–734–1571
Hato Rey, PR (DO)	252 Ponce de Leon Ave., 00918	Carmen Culpeper	787–766–5002
Melville, NY (BO)	Suite 207, 35 Pinelawn Rd., 11747	Norman Hunte, Acting	631–454–0750
New York, NY (DO)	Suite 3100, 26 Federal Plz., 10278	Jose Sifontes	212–264–2454
Newark, NJ (DO)	15th Fl., 2 Gateway Ctr., 07102	Jim Kocsi, *Acting*	973–645–3580
Rochester, NY (BO)	Suite 410, 100 State St., 14614	Victoria Reynolds	716–263–6700
St. Croix, VI (BO)	Suites 5 & 6, Sunny Isle Professional Bldg., 00820.	Carl Christensen	340–778–5380
St. Thomas, VI (BO)	3800 Crown Bay St., 00802	(Vacancy)	809–774–8530
Syracuse, NY (DO)	5th Fl., 401 S. Salina St., 13202	B.J. Paprocki	315–471–9393
PHILADELPHIA, PA (RO)	5th Fl., 900 Market St., 19107	Stefanie Watkins	215–580–2870
Baltimore, MD (DO)	Suite 6220, 10 S. Howard St., 21201–2525	Allan Stephenson	410–962–6195
Charleston, WV (BO)	Suite 412, 405 Capitol St., 25301	(Vacancy)	304–347–5220
Clarksburg, WV (DO)	320 W. Pike St., 26301	Judy McCauley	304–623–5631
Harrisburg, PA (BO)	Suite 850, 228 Walnut St., 17101	(Vacancy)	717–782–3840
Philadelphia, PA (DO)	5th Fl., 900 Market St., 19107	David Dickson	215–580–2700
Pittsburgh, PA (DO)	Suite 1450, 411 7th Ave., 15219	Carl Knoblock	412–395–6560
Richmond, VA (DO)	11th Fl., 400 N. 8th St., 23240	Ron Bew	804–771–2400
Washington, DC (DO)	740 15th St. NW., 20005	Joe Loddo	202–606–4000
Wilkes-Barre, PA (BO)	Suite 407, 7 N. Wilkes-Barre Blvd., 18702	(Vacancy)	570–826–6497
Wilmington, DE (DO)	Suite 1200, 1007 N. Orange St., 19801–1232	Jayne Armstrong	302–573–6294

Field Offices—Small Business Administration—Continued

(RO: Regional Office; DO: District Office; BO: Branch Office)

Office	Address	Officer in Charge	Telephone
SAN FRANCISCO, CA (RO).	Suite 1200, 330 N. Brand Blvd., 94105	Bruce C. Thompson	415–744–2118
Fresno, CA (DO)	Suite 200, 2719 N. Air Fresno Dr., 93727–1547	Carlos G. Mendoza	559–487–5791
Glendale, CA (DO)	Suite 1200, 330 N. Brand Blvd., 91203–2304	Alberto Alvarado	818–552–3201
Hagatna, GU (BO)	Suite 302, 400 Rt. 8, 96910–2003	Kenneth Lujan	671–472–7419
Honolulu, HI (DO)	Rm. 2–235, 300 Ala Moana Blvd., 96850–4981	Andrew Poepoe	808–541–2990
Las Vegas, NV (DO)	Suite 250, 400 S. 4th St., 89101	John Scott	702–388–6611
Phoenix, AZ (DO)	Suite 800, 2828 N. Central Ave., 85004–1025	Robert Blaney	602–745–7200
Sacramento, CA (DO)	Suite 7–500, 650 Capital Mall, 95814	James O'Neal	916–930–3700
San Diego, CA (DO)	Suite 550, 550 W. C St., 92101	Reuben Garcia	619–557–7250
San Francisco, CA (DO)	6th Fl., 455 Market St., 94105	Mark Quinn	415–744–6801
Santa Ana, CA (DO)	Suite 700, 200 W. Santa Ana Blvd., 92701	Adelberto Quijada	714–550–7420
SEATTLE, WA (RO)	Suite 400, 2401 4th Ave., 98121	Norm Proctor	206–553–5676
Anchorage, AK (DO)	Suite 310, 510 L St., 99501	Frank Cox	907–271–4022
Boise, ID (DO)	Suite 330, 380 Parkcenter Blvd., 83702–5745	Thomas Bergdoll	208–334–9004
Portland, OR (DO)	Suite 950, 601 SW. 2d Ave., 97201–6695	Leon Milobar	503–326–2682
Seattle, WA (DO)	Suite 450, 2401 4th Ave., 98121	Nancy Gilbertson	206–553–7310
Spokane, WA (BO)	Suite 200, 801 W. Riverside, 99201	Nancy Gilbertson, *Acting*	509–353–2810

Disaster Area Offices

Office	Address	Telephone
Atlanta, GA	Suite 300, 1 Baltimore Pl., 30308	404–347–3771
Fort Worth, TX	Suite 102, 4400 Amon Carter Blvd., 76155	817–885–7600
Niagara Falls, NY	3d Fl., 360 Rainbow Blvd. S., 14303	716–282–4612
Sacramento, CA	Suite 208, 1825 Bell St., 95825	916–566–7246

Sources of Information

Electronic Access Information on the Small Business Administration is available electronically by various means. Internet, www.sba.gov. FTP, ftp.sbaonline.sba.gov.

Access the U.S. Business Adviser through the Internet, at www.business.gov.

Access the Administration's electronic bulletin board by modem at 800–697–4636 (limited access), 900–463–4636 (full access), or 202–401–9600 (Washington, DC, metropolitan area).

General Information Contact the nearest Small Business Administration field office listed in the preceding text, or call the SBA answer desk. Phone, 800–8–ASK–SBA. Fax, 202–205–7064. TDD, 704–344–6640.

Public Affairs For public inquiries and small-business advocacy affairs, contact the Office of Public Communications and Public Liaison, 409 Third Street SW., Washington, DC 20416. Phone, 202–205–6740. Internet, www.sba.gov.

Publications A free copy of *The Resource Directory for Small Business Management*, a listing of for-sale publications and videotapes, is available from any local SBA office or the SBA answer desk.

For further information, contact the Office of Public Communications and Public Liaison, Small Business Administration, 409 Third Street SW., Washington, DC 20416. Phone, 202–205–6740. Internet, www.sba.gov.

SOCIAL SECURITY ADMINISTRATION

6401 Security Boulevard, Baltimore, MD 21235
Phone, 410–965–1234. Internet, www.socialsecurity.gov.

Commissioner of Social Security	Jo Anne B. Barnhart
Deputy Commissioner	James B. Lockhart III
Chief of Staff	Larry W. Dye
Counselor to the Commissioner	Laurence J. Love
Executive Counselor on Interagency Adjudication	Rita S. Geier
Executive Director for Disability Service Improvement	Mary B. Chatel
Executive Secretary	Veronica B. Henderson
Senior Executive Officer	Nancy A. McCullough
Senior Advisors	Phillip B. Dulaney IV, Michel N. Korbey, Barbara M. Levering
Chief Actuary	Stephen C. Goss
Deputy Chief Actuary (Short Range)	Eli N. Donkar
Deputy Chief Actuary (Long Range)	Alice H. Wade
Chief Information Officer	Thomas P. Hughes
Deputy Chief Information Officer	Gregory C. Pace
Chief Quality Officer	G. Kelly Croft
Chief Strategic Officer	Myrtle S. Habersham
Deputy Chief Strategic Officer	Susan A. Kennedy
Deputy Commissioner for Communications	James J. Courtney
Assistant Deputy Commissioner for Communications	Philip A. Gambino
Deputy Commissioner for Disability and Income Security Programs	Martin H. Gerry
Assistant Deputy Commissioner for Disability and Income Security Programs (Program Policy)	Frederick G. Streckewald
Assistant Deputy Commissioner for Disability and Income Security Programs (Disability Operations)	Patricia A. Jonas
Deputy Commissioner for Finance, Assessment, and Management	Dale W. Sopper
Assistant Deputy Commissioner for Finance, Assessment, and Management	Anthony F. Dinoto
General Counsel	Lisa de Soto
Deputy General Counsel	Thomas W. Crawley
Deputy Commissioner for Human Resources	Reginald F. Wells
Assistant Deputy Commissioner for Human Resources	Felicita Sola-Carter
Inspector General	Patrick P. O'Carroll
Deputy Inspector General	James A. Kissko
Deputy Commissioner for Legislation and Congressional Affairs	Robert M. Wilson
Assistant Deputy Commissioner for Legislation and Congressional Affairs	Diane B. Garro
Deputy Commissioner for Operations	Linda S. McMahon

Assistant Deputy Commissioner for Operations	MARY E. GLENN-CROFT
Deputy Commissioner for Policy	LAURENCE J. LOVE, *Acting*
Assistant Deputy Commissioner for Policy	EDWARD J. DEMARCO
Deputy Commissioner for Systems	WILLIAM E. GRAY
Assistant Deputy Commissioner for Systems	JERRY L. BERSON

[For the Social Security Administration statement of organization, see the Code of Federal Regulations, Title 20, Part 422]

The Social Security Administration manages the Nation's social insurance program—consisting of retirement, survivors, and disability insurance programs—commonly known as Social Security. It also administers the Supplemental Security Income program for the aged, blind, and disabled. The Administration is responsible for studying the problems of poverty and economic insecurity among Americans and making recommendations on effective methods for solving these problems through social insurance. The Administration also assigns Social Security numbers to U.S. citizens and maintains earnings records for workers under their Social Security numbers.

The Social Security Administration (SSA) was established by Reorganization Plan No. 2 of 1946 (5 U.S.C. app.), effective July 16, 1946. It became an independent agency in the executive branch by the Social Security Independence and Program Improvements Act of 1994 (42 U.S.C. 901), effective March 31, 1995.

The Administration is headed by a Commissioner, appointed by the President with the advice and consent of the Senate.

In administering the programs necessary to carry out the agency's mission, by law the Commissioner is assisted by a Deputy Commissioner who performs duties assigned or delegated by the Commissioner, a Chief Financial Officer, a Chief Information Officer, a Chief Strategic Officer, a General Counsel, a Chief Actuary, and an Inspector General.

Programs and Activities

Old-Age, Survivors, and Disability Insurance The agency administers social insurance programs, which provide monthly benefits to retired and disabled workers, their spouses and children, and to survivors of insured workers. Financing is under a system of contributory social insurance, whereby employees, employers, and the self-employed pay contributions that are pooled in special trust funds. When earnings stop or are reduced because the worker retires, dies, or becomes disabled, monthly cash benefits are paid to partially replace the earnings the family has lost.

Supplemental Security Income The agency administers this needs-based program for the aged, blind, and disabled. A basic Federal monthly payment is financed out of general revenue, rather than a special trust fund. Some States, choosing to provide payments to supplement the benefits, have agreements with the Administration under which it administers the supplemental payments for those States.

Medicare While the administration of Medicare is the responsibility of the Centers for Medicare and Medicaid Services, the Social Security Administration provides Medicare assistance to the public through SSA field offices and call centers, and adjudicates requests for hearings and appeals of Medicare claims.

Black Lung By agreement with the Department of Labor, SSA is involved in certain aspects of the administration of the black lung benefits provisions of the Federal Coal Mine Health and Safety Act of 1969, as amended (30 U.S.C. 901).

Regional Offices Social Security Administration operations are decentralized to provide services at the local level. Each of the 10 SSA regions, under the overall direction of its Regional Commissioner, contains a

SOCIAL SECURITY ADMINISTRATION

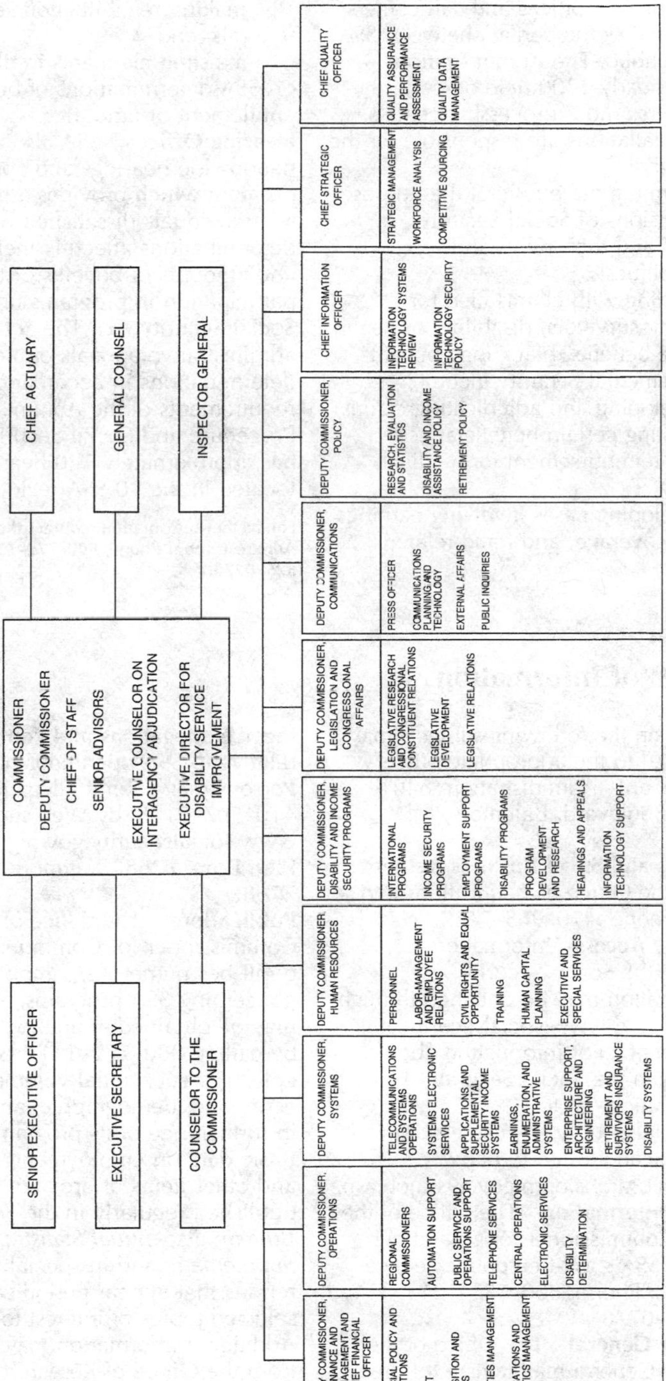

network of field offices and call centers, which serve as the contact between SSA and the public. The Administration operates nearly 1300 field offices, 38 call centers, and 7 processing centers. These installations are responsible for the following:

—informing the public of the purposes and provisions of Social Security programs and their rights and responsibilities;

—assisting with claims filed for retirement, survivors, disability, or health insurance benefits, black lung benefits, or Supplemental Security Income;

—developing and adjudicating claims;

—assisting certain beneficiaries in claiming reimbursement for medical expenses;

—developing cases involving earnings records, coverage, and fraud-related questions;

—making rehabilitation service referrals; and

—assisting claimants in filing appeals on SSA determinations of benefit entitlement or amount.

Hearing Offices SSA also administers a nationwide hearings and appeals program which provides a mechanism for individuals dissatisfied with determinations affecting their rights to and amounts of benefits or their participation in programs under the Social Security Act. The act allows for administrative appeals of these determinations in accordance with the requirements of the Administrative Procedure and Social Security Acts. SSA has approximately 140 hearing offices located in the 10 SSA regions.

For further information, contact the Social Security Administration. Phone, 800–772–1213. TTY, 800–325–0778.

Sources of Information

Inquiries on the following subjects may be directed to the appropriate office, Social Security Administration, 6401 Security Boulevard, Baltimore, MD 21235.

Contracts and Small Business Activities Contact the Office of Acquisitions and Grants. Phone, 410–965–7467.

Electronic Access Information regarding the Social Security Administration may be obtained through the Internet at www.socialsecurity.gov.

Employment For information about careers with the Social Security Administration, go to www.socialsecurity.gov/careers/. For current vacancies, go to http://jobsearch.usajobs.opm.gov.a9ssajob.asp.

General Information The Office of the Deputy Commissioner for Operations manages SSA's toll-free public service telephone. Phone, 800–772–1213. TTY, 800–325–0778.

Inspector General The Office of the Inspector General maintains a toll-free hotline that operates between the hours of 10 am and 4 pm, e.s.t. (phone, 800–269–0271; TTY, 866–501–2101) to receive allegations and complaints relative to SSA operations nationwide. Persons may submit allegations by fax at 410–597–0118, by Web site at www.socialsecurity.gov/oig or by mail at P.O. Box 17768, Baltimore, MD 21235–7768.

Publications The Office of the Deputy Commissioner for Communications publishes numerous pamphlets concerning SSA programs. Single copies may be obtained at any local office or by calling 800–772–1213. SSA also collects a substantial volume of economic, demographic, and other data in furtherance of its program mission. Basic data on employment, payments, and other items of program interest are published regularly in the *Social Security Bulletin,* its *Annual Statistical Supplement,* and in special releases and reports that appear periodically on selected topics of interest to the public. Additional information may be obtained from the Office of Research, Evaluation, and Statistics. E-mail, op.publications@ssa.gov. Phone, 202–358–6274.

Reading Room Requests for information, for copies of records, or to inspect records may be made at any local office or the Headquarters Contact Unit, Room G–44, Altmeyer Building.

Speakers and Films SSA makes speakers, films, and exhibits available to public or private organizations, community groups, schools, etc., throughout the Nation. Requests for this service should be directed to the local Social Security Office.

For further information, contact the Office of Public Inquiries, Social Security Administration, 6401 Security Boulevard, Windsor Park Building, Baltimore, MD 21235. Phone, 410–965–2736. Internet, www.socialsecurity.gov.

TENNESSEE VALLEY AUTHORITY

400 West Summit Hill Drive, Knoxville, TN 37902
Phone, 865–632–2101. Internet, www.tva.com.

One Massachusetts Avenue NW., Washington, DC 20444–0001
Phone, 202–898–2999

Chairman	WILLIAM B. SANSOM
Directors	BILL BAXTER, DENNIS BOTTORFF, DONALD R. DEPRIEST, ROBERT M. (MIKE) DUNCAN, SKILA HARRIS, HOWARD A. THRAILKILL, SUSAN RICHARDSON WILLIAMS, (VACANCY)
Executive Vice President, Administrative Services	JOHN E. LONG, JR.
Senior Vice President, Communications	PEYTON T. HAIRSTON, JR.
President and Chief Operating Officer	TOM D. KILGORE
Chief Executive Officer	TOM D. KILGORE, *Acting*
Chief Nuclear Officer	KARL W. SINGER
Chief Financial Officer	MICHAEL E. RESCOE

The Tennessee Valley Authority conducts a unified program of resource development for the advancement of economic growth in the Tennessee Valley region. The Authority's program of activities includes flood control, navigation, electric power production and transmission, recreation improvement, water supply, water quality, environmental stewardship, and economic development.

The Tennessee Valley Authority (TVA) is a wholly owned Government corporation created by act of May 18, 1933 (16 U.S.C. 831–831dd). All functions of the Authority are vested in its nine-member Board of Directors, the members of which are appointed by the President with the advice and consent of the Senate. The Board designates one member as Chairman.

TVA's electric power program is financially self-supporting and operates as part of an independent system with TVA's system of dams on the Tennessee River and its larger tributaries. These dams provide flood regulation on the Tennessee River and contribute to regulation of the lower Ohio and Mississippi Rivers. The system maintains a continuous 9-foot-draft navigation channel for the length of the 650-mile Tennessee River main stream, from Paducah, KY, to Knoxville, TN. The dams harness the power of the rivers to produce electricity. They also provide other benefits, notably outdoor recreation and water supply.

The Authority operates the river control system and provides assistance to State and local governments in reducing local flood problems. It also works with other agencies to encourage full and effective use of the navigable waterway by industry and commerce.

The Authority is the wholesale power supplier for 158 local municipal and cooperative electric systems serving customers in parts of 7 States. It supplies power to several Federal installations and 61 large companies whose power requirements are large or unusual. Power to meet these demands is supplied from dams, coal-fired powerplants, nuclear powerplants, combustion turbine and diesel installations, solar energy sites, wind turbines, a methane gas facility, and a pumped-storage hydroelectric plant; U.S. Corps of Engineers dams in the Cumberland Valley; and Aluminum Company of America dams, whose operation is coordinated with TVA's system.

Economic development is at the heart of the TVA's mission of making the Tennessee Valley a better place to live. A thriving economy means quality jobs, more investment in the region, sustainable growth, and opportunities for residents in the Southeastern region to build more prosperous lives. TVA Economic Development takes a regional approach on economic growth by partnering with power distributors and both public and private organizations to attract new investments and quality jobs, support retention and growth of existing businesses and industries, prepare communities for leadership and economic growth, and provides financial and technical services.

Sources of Information

Citizen Participation TVA Communications, 400 West Summit Hill Drive, Knoxville, TN 37902–1499. Phone, 865–632–2101.

Contracts Purchasing, WT 3A, 400 West Summit Hill Drive, Knoxville, TN 37902–1499. Phone, 865–632–4796. This office will direct inquiries to the appropriate procurement officer.

Economic Development OCP 2A–NST, One Century Place, 26 Century Boulevard., Suite 100, Nashville, TN 37214. Mailing address: P.O. Box 292409, Nashville, TN 37229–2409. Phone, 615–232–6051.

Electric Power Supply 1101 Market Street, Chattanooga, TN 37402. Phone, 423–751–6000.

Electric Rates One Century Plaza, 26 Century Boulevard, Suite 100, Nashville, TN 37214–3685.

Employment For employment inquiries, visit www.tva.com.

Research Technology and Applications TVA Reservation, P.O. Box 1010, Muscle Shoals, AL 35661–1010. Phone, 256–386–2026.

Library Services TVA Research Library, 400 West Summit Hill Drive, Knoxville, TN 37902–1499. Phone, 865–632–3464. Chattanooga Office Complex, LP4A–C, 1101 Market Street, Chattanooga, TN 37402–2791. Phone, 423–751–4913. P.O. Box 1010, CTR 1E–M, Muscle Shoals, AL 35662. Phone, 256–386–2872.

Maps Maps Information and Photo Records, HV 1C–C, 2837 Hickory Valley Road, Chattanooga, TN 37421. Phone, 423–499–6285; 800–627–7882.

Publications TVA Communications, WT 7D, 400 West Summit Hill Drive, Knoxville, TN 37902–1499. Phone, 865–632–6000.

For further information, contact Tennessee Valley Authority Communications, 400 West Summit Hill Drive, Knoxville, TN 37902–1499; phone, 865–632–3199. Or Tennessee Valley Authority Washington Office, One Massachusetts Avenue NW., Washington, DC 20044; phone, 202–898–2999; Internet, www.tva.com.

TRADE AND DEVELOPMENT AGENCY

1000 Wilson Boulevard, Suite 1600, Arlington, VA 22209–3901
Phone, 703–875–4357. Fax, 703–875–4009.
Internet, www.ustda.gov. E-mail, info@ustda.gov.

Director	THELMA J. ASKEY
Deputy Director	LEOCADIA I. ZAK
General Counsel	(VACANCY)
Policy and Programs Director	GEOFFREY JACKSON
Chief of Staff	THOMAS R. HARDY
Resource Advisor	MICHAEL HILLIER
Communications/Policy Advisor	DONNA THIESSEN
Congressional Relations Liaison	JENNIFER WOLFF
Regional Directors:	
Asia	HENRY D. STEINGASS
Europe and Eurasia	DANIEL D. STEIN
Latin America and Caribbean	ALBERT W. ANGULO
Middle East, North Africa, and South Asia	CARL B. KRESS
Sub-Saharan Africa	NED CHABOT
Economist/Evaluation Officer	DAVID DENNY
Financial Manager	NOREEN ST. LOUIS
Contracting Officer	DELLA GLENN
Administrative Officer	CAROLYN HUM
Grants Administrator	PATRICIA DAUGHETEE

The Trade and Development Agency's mission is to advance economic development and U.S. commercial interest in developing and middle-income countries in the following regions of the world: Asia; Europe and Eurasia; Latin America and the Caribbean; Middle East, North Africa, and South Asia; and Sub-Saharan Africa.

The Trade and Development Program was established on July 1, 1980, as a component organization of the International Development Cooperation Agency. Section 2204 of the Omnibus Trade and Competitiveness Act of 1988 (22 U.S.C. 2421) made it a separate component agency. The organization was renamed the Trade and Development Agency and made an independent agency within the executive branch of the Federal Government on October 28, 1992, by the Jobs Through Exports Act of 1992 (22 U.S.C. 2421).

The Trade and Development Agency (TDA) is a foreign assistance agency that delivers its program commitments through overseas grants, contracts with U.S. firms, and the use of trust funds at several multilateral development bank groups. The projects supported by TDA activities represent strong and measurable development priorities in host countries and offer opportunities for commercial participation by U.S. firms. Public and private sector project sponsors, in developing and middle-income countries, request TDA support to assist them in implementing their development priorities.

TDA's program is designed to help countries establish a favorable trading environment and a modern infrastructure that promotes sustainable economic development. To this end, the Agency funds overseas projects and sponsors access to U.S. private sector expertise in the areas of project definition and investment analysis and trade capacity building and sector development. Project definition and investment analysis involves activities that support large

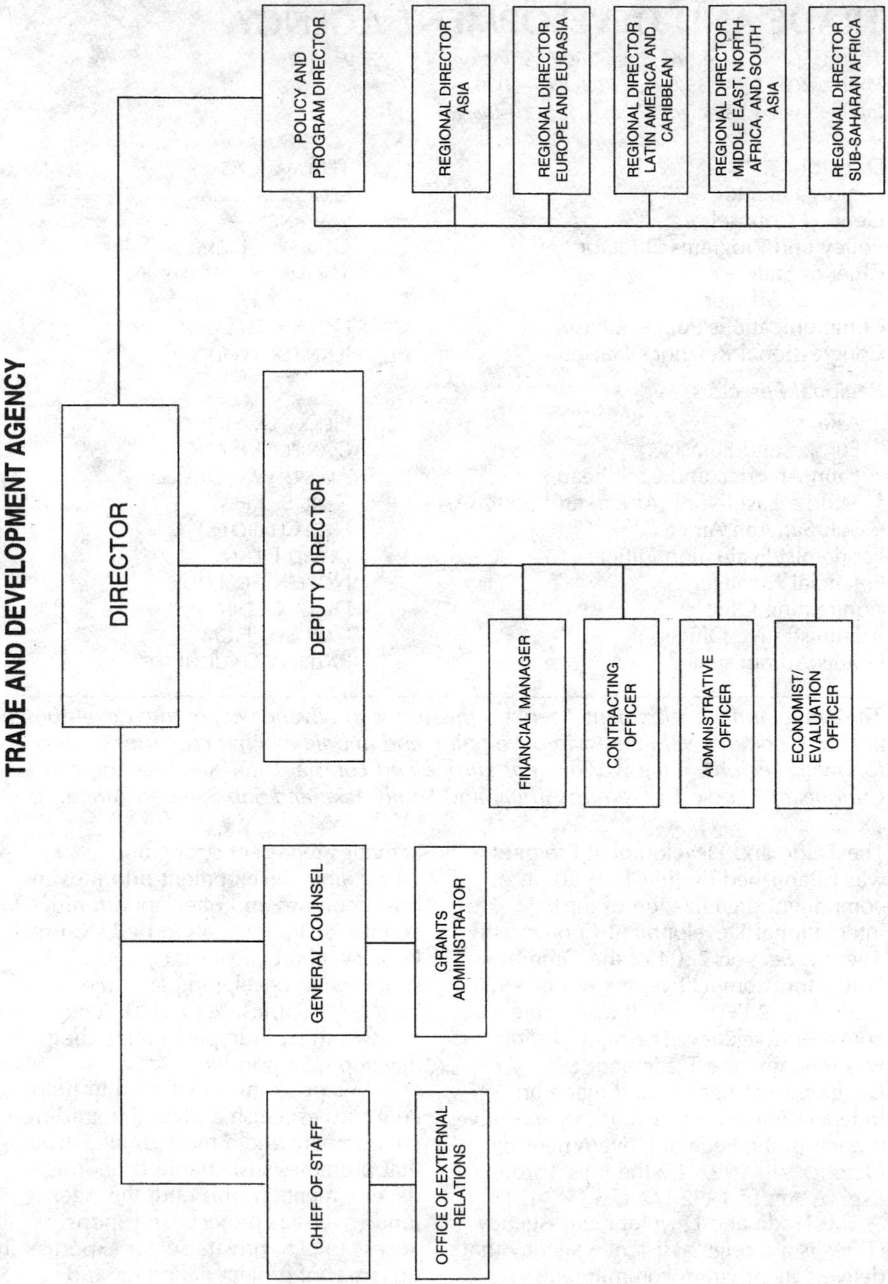
TRADE AND DEVELOPMENT AGENCY
DIRECTOR
POLICY AND PROGRAM DIRECTOR
REGIONAL DIRECTOR ASIA
REGIONAL DIRECTOR EUROPE AND EURASIA
REGIONAL DIRECTOR LATIN AMERICA AND CARIBBEAN
REGIONAL DIRECTOR MIDDLE EAST, NORTH AFRICA, AND SOUTH ASIA
REGIONAL DIRECTOR SUB-SAHARAN AFRICA
DEPUTY DIRECTOR
FINANCIAL MANAGER
CONTRACTING OFFICER
ADMINISTRATIVE OFFICER
ECONOMIST/ EVALUATION OFFICER
GENERAL COUNSEL
GRANTS ADMINISTRATOR
CHIEF OF STAFF
OFFICE OF EXTERNAL RELATIONS

capital investments that contribute to overseas infrastructure development. Trade capacity building and sector development supports the establishment of industry standards, rules and regulations, trade agreements, market liberalization, and other policy reform.

TDA works with other U.S. Government agencies to bring their particular expertise and resources to a development objective. These agencies include the Departments of State, the Treasury, Commerce, Transportation, Energy, Agriculture, and Homeland Security; the Office of the U.S. Trade Representative; the Export-Import Bank of the United States; and the Overseas Private Investment Corporation.

Activities

TDA funds various forms of technical assistance, training, feasibility studies, orientation visits, and business workshops that support the development of a modern infrastructure and a fair and open trading environment. Working closely with a foreign project sponsor, TDA makes its funds available on the condition that the foreign entity contract with a U.S. firm to perform the activity funded. This affords American firms market entry, exposure, and information, thus helping them to establish a position in markets that are otherwise difficult to penetrate. TDA is involved in many sectors, including transportation, energy, telecommunications, environment, health care, mining and minerals development, biotechnology, and agriculture.

TDA-funded studies evaluate the technical, economic, and financial aspects of a development project. They also advise the host nation about the availability of U.S. goods and services and can be used by financial institutions in assessing the creditworthiness of an undertaking. Grants are based on an official request for assistance made by the sponsoring government or private sector organization of a developing or middle-income nation. Study costs typically are shared between TDA and the U.S. firm developing the project.

The Agency makes decisions on funding requests based on the recommendations contained in definitional mission (DM) or desk study (DS) reports, the advice of the U.S. Embassy, and its own internal analysis.

Sources of Information

Requests for proposals (RFPs) to conduct TDA-funded technical assistance and feasibility studies, or DMs involving review of projects under consideration for TDA support are listed on the Federal Business Opportunities Web site at www.fbo.gov.

Small and minority U.S. firms that wish to be included in TDA's consultant database and considered for future DM and DS solicitations should register with the Online Consultant database through the Internet at www.ustda.gov.

In an effort to provide timely information on Agency-supported projects, TDA publishes the *Pipeline* and a calendar of events on a biweekly basis. For a paper subscription, call CIB Publications at 703–516–4801. For an e-mail subscription, visit the guest book at www.ustda.gov. A quarterly publication, *TDA Update,* contains current items of interest on a variety of program activities. Region- or sector-specific fact sheets and case studies also are available. An annual report summarizes the Agency's activities.

Agency news, reports, and lists of upcoming conferences, orientation visits, and business briefings are available through the Internet at www.ustda.gov.

Regional program inquiries should be directed to the assigned Country Manager. Phone, 703–875–4357. Fax, 703–875–4009. E-mail, info@ustda.gov.

TDA's library maintains final reports on all Agency activities. The reports are available for public review Monday through Friday from 8:30 a.m. to 5:30 p.m. Copies of completed studies may be purchased through the Department of Commerce's National Technical Information Service.

For further information, contact the Trade and Development Agency, Suite 1600, 1000 Wilson Boulevard, Arlington, VA 22209–3901. Phone, 703–875–4357. Fax, 703–875–4009. E-mail, info@ustda.gov. Internet, www.ustda.gov.

UNITED STATES AGENCY FOR INTERNATIONAL DEVELOPMENT

1300 Pennsylvania Avenue NW., Washington, DC 20523–0001
Phone, 202–712–0000. Internet, www.usaid.gov.

Administrator	RANDALL L. TOBIAS
Deputy Administrator	FREDERICK SCHIECK
Counselor	MOSINA JORDAN
Executive Secretary and Chief of Staff	DOUGLAS J. ALLER
Assistant Administrator for Africa	LLOYD O. PIERSON
Assistant Administrator for Asia and the Near East	JAMES KUNDER
Assistant Administrator for Democracy, Conflict and Humanitarian Assistance	MICHAEL HESS
Assistant Administrator for Economic Growth, Agriculture and Trade	JACQUELINE E. SCHAFER
Assistant Administrator for Europe and Eurasia	DREW LUTEN
Assistant Administrator for Global Health	KENT R. HILL
Assistant Administrator for Latin America and the Caribbean	ADOLFO A. FRANCO
Assistant Administrator for Legislative and Public Affairs	J. EDWARD FOX
Assistant Administrator for Management	MOSINA JORDAN, *Acting*
Assistant Administrator for Policy and Program Coordination	DOUGLAS MENARCHIK
Director of the Global Development Alliance Secretariat	DAN RUNDE
Director of Security	HARRY MANCHESTER
Director of Equal Opportunity Programs	JESSALYN L. PENDARVIS
Director of Small and Disadvantaged Business Utilization/Minority Resource Center	MARILYN MARTON
General Counsel	ARNOLD J. HAIMAN, *Acting*
Inspector General	DONALD A. GAMBATESA

[For the Agency for International Development statement of organization, see the *Federal Register* of Aug. 26, 1987, 52 FR 32174]

The U.S. Agency for International Development administers U.S. foreign economic and humanitarian assistance programs worldwide in the developing world, Central and Eastern Europe, and Eurasia.

The United States Agency for International Development (USAID) is an independent Federal agency established by 22 U.S.C. 6563. Its principal statutory authority is the Foreign Assistance Act of 1961, as amended (22 U.S.C. 2151 *et seq.*). USAID serves as the focal point within the Government for economic matters affecting U.S. relations with developing countries. USAID administers international economic and humanitarian assistance programs. The Administrator is under the direct

UNITED STATES AGENCY FOR INTERNATIONAL DEVELOPMENT

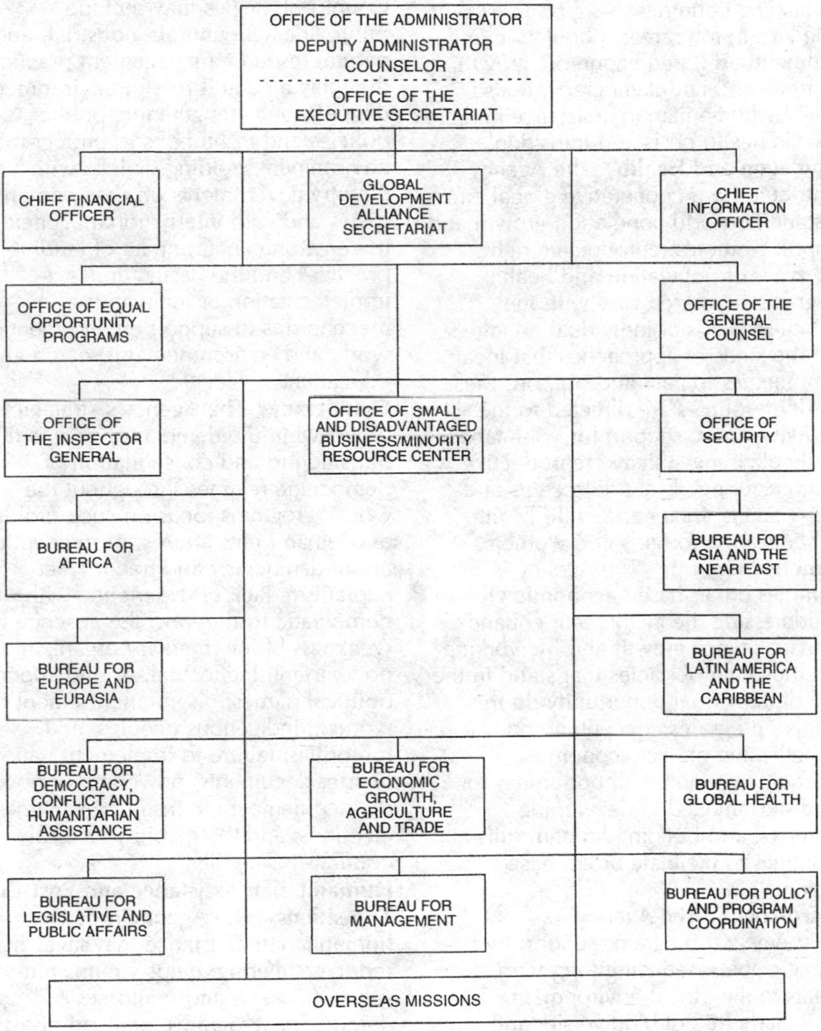

authority and foreign policy guidance of the Secretary of State.

Programs

The Agency meets its post-cold war era challenges by utilizing its strategy for achieving sustainable development in developing countries. It supports programs in four areas: population and health, broad-based economic growth, environment, and democracy. It also provides humanitarian assistance and aid to countries in crisis and transition.

Population and Health The Agency contributes to a cooperative global effort to stabilize world population growth and support women's reproductive rights. The types of population and health programs supported vary with the particular needs of individual countries and the kinds of approaches that local communities initiate and support. Most USAID resources are directed to the following areas: support for voluntary family planning systems, reproductive health care, needs of adolescents and young adults, infant and child health, and education for girls and women.

Economic Growth The Agency promotes broad-based economic growth by addressing the factors that enhance the capacity for growth and by working to remove the obstacles that stand in the way of individual opportunity. In this context, programs concentrate on strengthening market economies, expanding economic opportunities for the disadvantaged in developing countries, and building human skills and capacities to facilitate broad-based participation.

Environment The Agency's environmental programs support two strategic goals: reducing long-term threats to the global environment, particularly loss of biodiversity and climate change; and promoting sustainable economic growth locally, nationally, and regionally by addressing environmental, economic, and developmental practices that impede development and are unsustainable. Globally, Agency programs focus on reducing sources and enhancing sinks of greenhouse gas emissions and on promoting innovative approaches to the conservation and sustainable use of the planet's biological diversity. The approach to national environmental problems differs on a country-by-country basis, depending on a particular country's environmental priorities. Country strategies may include improving agricultural, industrial, and natural resource management practices that play a central role in environmental degradation; strengthening public policies and institutions to protect the environment; holding dialogs with country governments on environmental issues and with international agencies on the environmental impact of lending practices and the design and implementation of innovative mechanisms to support environmental work; and environmental research and education.

Democracy The Agency's strategic objective in the democracy area is the transition to and consolidation of democratic regimes throughout the world. Programs focus on such problems as: human rights abuses; misperceptions about democracy and free-market capitalism; lack of experience with democratic institutions; the absence or weakness of intermediary organizations; nonexistent, ineffectual, or undemocratic political parties; disenfranchisement of women, indigenous peoples, and minorities; failure to implement national charter documents; powerless or poorly defined democratic institutions; tainted elections; and the inability to resolve conflicts peacefully.

Humanitarian Assistance and Post-Crisis Transitions The Agency provides humanitarian assistance that saves lives, reduces suffering, helps victims return to self-sufficiency, and reinforces democracy. Programs focus on disaster prevention, preparedness, and mitigation; timely delivery of disaster relief and short-term rehabilitation supplies and services; preservation of basic institutions of civil governance during disaster crisis; support for democratic institutions during periods of national transition; and building and reinforcement of local capacity to anticipate and handle disasters and their aftermath.

Overseas Organizations

U.S. Agency for International Development country organizations are located in countries where a bilateral program is being implemented. The in-country organizations are subject to the direction and guidance of the chief U.S. diplomatic representative in the country, usually the Ambassador. The organizations report to the Agency's Assistant Administrators for the four geographic bureaus: the Bureaus for Africa, Asia and Near East, Europe and the New Independent States, and Latin America and the Caribbean.

The overseas program activities that involve more than one country are administered by regional offices. These offices may also perform country organizational responsibilities for assigned countries. Generally, the offices are headed by a regional development officer.

Development Assistance Coordination and Representative Offices provide liaison with various international organizations and represent U.S. interests in development assistance matters. Such offices may be only partially staffed by Agency personnel and may be headed by employees of other U.S. Government agencies.

Country Organizations—U.S. Agency for International Development

Country	Officer in Charge [1]
Afghanistan	Alonzon Fulgham (MD)
Albania	Harry Birnholz (MD)
Angola	Diana Swain (MD)
Armenia	Robin Phillips (MD)
Azerbaijan	James Goggin (CPO)
Bangladesh	Gene George (MD)
Belarus	Earl Gast (CPO)
Benin	Rudy Thomas (MD)
Bolivia	Michael Yates (MD)
Bosnia	Howard Sumka (MD)
Brazil	Richard Goughnour (MD)
Bulgaria	Michael Fritz (MD)
Cambodia	Jonathan Addleton (MD)
Colombia	Michael Deal (MD)
Croatia	William Jeffers (MD)
Cyprus	Thomas Dailey (MD)
Democratic Republic of the Congo.	Robert Hellyer (MD)
Dominican Republic	Elena Brineman (MD)
East Timor	Flynn Fuller (MD)
Ecuador	Alexandra Panehal (MD)
Egypt	Kenneth Ellis (MD)
El Salvador	Mark Silverman (MD)
Ethiopia	William Hammink (MD)
Georgia	Denny Robertson (MD)
Ghana	Sharon Cromer (MD)
Guatemala	Glenn Anders (MD)
Guinea	Annette Adams (MD)
Guyana	Fenton Sands (MD)
Haiti	Erna Kerst (MD)
Honduras	Paul Tuebner (MD)
India	George Deikun (MD)
Indonesia	William Frej (MD)
Iraq	Dawn Liberi (MD)
Jamaica	Karen Turner (MD)
Jordan	Anne Aarnes (MD)
Kenya	Kiert Toh (MD)
Kosovo	Ken Yamashita (MD)
Kyrgyzstan	Clifford Brown (CPO)
Lebanon	Raoul Youseff (AID R)
Liberia	Wilbur Thomas (MD)
Macedonia, FRY	Richard Goldman (MD)
Madagascar	Stephen Haykin (MD)
Malawi	Roger Yochelson (MD)
Mali	Pam White (MD)
Mexico	Edward Kadunc (MD)
Moldova	John Starnes (CPO)
Mongolia	Leon Waskin (MD)
Montenegro	Joseph Taggart (CPO)
Morocco	Monica Stein-Olson (MD)
Mozambique	Jay Knott (MD)
Namibia	Gary Newton (MD)
Nepal	Donald Clark (MD)
Nicaragua	Alexander Dickie (MD)
Nigeria	Patrick Fleuret (MD)
Panama	Kermit Moh (AID R)
Pakistan	Lisa Chiles (MD)
Paraguay	Wayne Nilsestuen (MD)
Peru	Hilda Arellano (MD)
Philippines	Jon Lindborg (MD)
Romania	Rodger Garner (MD)
Russia	Terry Myers (MD)
Rwanda	James Anderson (MD)
Senegal	Olivier Carduner (MD)
Serbia	Keith Simmons (MD)
Sri Lanka	Carol Becker (MD)
Tajikistan	Peter Argo (MD)
Tanzania	Derrick Brown (MD)
Turkmenistan	Ashley Moretz (CPO)
Uganda	Vicki Moore (MD)
Uzbekistan	Joanne Hale (CPO)
West Bank/Gaza in Israel	Larry Garber (MD)
Yemen	Douglas Heisler (MD)
Zambia	James Bednar (MD)
Zimbabwe	Paul Weisenfeld (MD)

[1] MD: Mission Director; CPO: Country Program Officer; RD: Regional Director; AAO: AID Affairs Officer for Section of Embassy; CO: Coordinator in Washington; AID R: USAID Representative; FFP: Food for Peace Officer

International Organizations—U.S. Agency for International Development

(Selected Regional Organizations)

(A: Adviser; C: Counselor; D: Director; ED: Executive Director; MD: Mission Director; AID R: USAID Representative; RD: Regional Director)

Office	Officer in Charge
Regional Offices	
Regional Center for Southern Africa—Gaborone, Botswana	Gerald Cashion (RD)
Regional Economic Development Services Offices—Nairobi, Kenya	Andrew Sission (RD)
Regional Mission to Central Asia—Almaty, Kazakhstan	Chris Crowley (RD)
Regional Mission to Ukraine, Belarus and Moldova—Kiev, Ukraine	Earl Gast (RD)
Regional Support Center—Budapest, Hungary	Hilda Arellano (RD)
USAID Mission to Southern Africa	Dirk Dijkerman (RD)
West Africa Regional Program	Carleene Dei (MD)
International Organizations and USAID Contacts	
Office for Humanitarian Assistance, World Food Program Affairs—Rome, Italy	Richard Newberg (FFP)
Office of the U.S. Representative to the Development Assistance Committee of the Organization for Economic Cooperation and Development—Paris, France.	George Carner (AID R)
U.S. Mission to the European Office of the United Nations and Other International Organizations—Geneva, Switzerland.	Nance Kyloh (AID R)
AID Office for Development Cooperation—Tokyo, Japan	Charles Aaenenson (AID R)
Office of AID Coordination Representative—Brussels, Belgium	Patricia Lerner (AID R)

Sources of Information

General Inquiries Inquiries may be directed to the Bureau for Legislative and Public Affairs, USAID/LPA, Washington, DC 20523–0001. Phone, 202–712–4810. Fax, 202–216–3524.

Congressional Affairs Congressional inquiries may be directed to the Bureau for Legislative and Public Affairs, USAID/LPA, Washington, DC 20523–0001. Phone, 202–712–4810.

Contracting and Small Business Inquiries For information regarding contracting opportunities, contact the Office of Small and Disadvantaged Business Utilization, U.S. Agency for International Development, Washington, DC 20523–0001. Phone, 202–712–1500. Fax, 202–216–3056.

Employment For information regarding employment opportunities, contact the Workforce Planning, Recruitment, and Personnel Systems Division, Office of Human Resources, U.S. Agency for International Development, Washington, DC 20523–0001. Internet, www.usaid.gov.

General Inquiries General inquiries may be directed to the Bureau for Legislative and Public Affairs, USAID/LPA, Washington, DC 20523–0001. Phone, 202–712–4810. Fax, 202–216–3524.

News Media Inquiries from the media only should be directed to the Press Relations Division, Bureau for Legislative and Public Affairs, USAID/LPA, Washington, DC 20523–0001. Phone, 202–712–4320.

For further information, contact the United States Agency for International Development, 1300 Pennsylvania Avenue NW., Washington, DC 20523–0001. Phone, 202–712–0000. Internet, www.usaid.gov.

UNITED STATES COMMISSION ON CIVIL RIGHTS

624 Ninth Street NW., Washington, DC 20425
Phone, 202–376–8177. Internet, www.usccr.gov.

Chairperson	GERALD A. REYNOLDS

Vice Chairman	ABIGAIL THERNSTROM
Commissioners	JENNIFER C. BRACERAS, PETER KIRSANOW, ARLAN D. MELENDEZ, ASHLEY TAYLOR, MICHAEL YAKI
Staff Director	KENNETH L. MARCUS
Deputy Staff Director	(VACANCY)
Associate Deputy Staff Director	DEBRA A. CARR
General Counsel	(VACANCY)
Deputy General Counsel	(VACANCY)
Assistant Staff Director for Civil Rights Evaluation	(VACANCY)
Assistant Staff Director for Congressional Affairs	(VACANCY)
Assistant Staff Director for Management	(VACANCY)
Chief, Public Affairs Unit	(VACANCY)
Chief, Regional Programs Coordination	IVY DAVIS, *Acting*

[For the Commission on Civil Rights statement of organization, see the *Code of Federal Regulations,* Title 45, Part 701]

The Commission on Civil Rights collects and studies information on discrimination or denials of equal protection of the laws because of race, color, religion, sex, age, disability, national origin, or in the administration of justice in such areas as voting rights, enforcement of Federal civil rights laws, and equal opportunity in education, employment, and housing.

The Commission on Civil Rights was first created by the Civil Rights Act of 1957, as amended, and reestablished by the United States Commission on Civil Rights Act of 1994, as amended (42 U.S.C. 1975).

Activities

The Commission makes findings of fact but has no enforcement authority. Findings and recommendations are submitted to the President and Congress, and many of the Commission's recommendations have been enacted, either by statute, Executive order, or regulation. The Commission evaluates Federal laws and the effectiveness of Government equal opportunity programs. It also serves as a national clearinghouse for civil rights information.

Regional Programs The Commission maintains six regional divisions.

Regional Divisions

Region (Address/Telephone)	Director
Central (Suite 908, 400 State Ave., Kansas City, KS 66101–2406. Phone, 913–551–1400)	(Vacancy)
Eastern (Rm. 500, 624 9th St. NW., Washington, DC 20425. Phone, 202–376–7533)	(Vacancy)
Midwestern (Suite 410, 55 W. Monroe St., Chicago, IL 60603. Phone, 312–353–8311)	Constance M. Davis
Rocky Mountain (Suite 710, 1700 Broadway, Denver, CO 80290. Phone, 303–866–1040)	John Foster Dulles
Southern (Suite 184OT, 61 Forsyth St. SW, Atlanta, GA 30303. Phone, 404–562–7000)	Peter Minarik
Western (Suite 2010, 300 N. Los Angeles, Los Angeles, CA 90012. Phone, 213–894–3437)	(Vacancy)

Sources of Information

Complaints Complaints alleging denials of civil rights may be reported to Complaints Referral, 624 Ninth Street NW., Washington, DC 20425. Phone, 202–376–8513 or 800–552–6843. Internet, www.usccr.gov.

Employment Human Resources Office, Room 510, 624 Ninth Street NW., Washington, DC 20425. Phone, 202–376–8364.

Publications Commission publications are made available upon request from the Administrative Services and Clearinghouse Division, Room 550, 624 Ninth Street NW., Washington, DC 20425. Phone, 202–376–8105. A catalog

UNITED STATES COMMISSION ON CIVIL RIGHTS

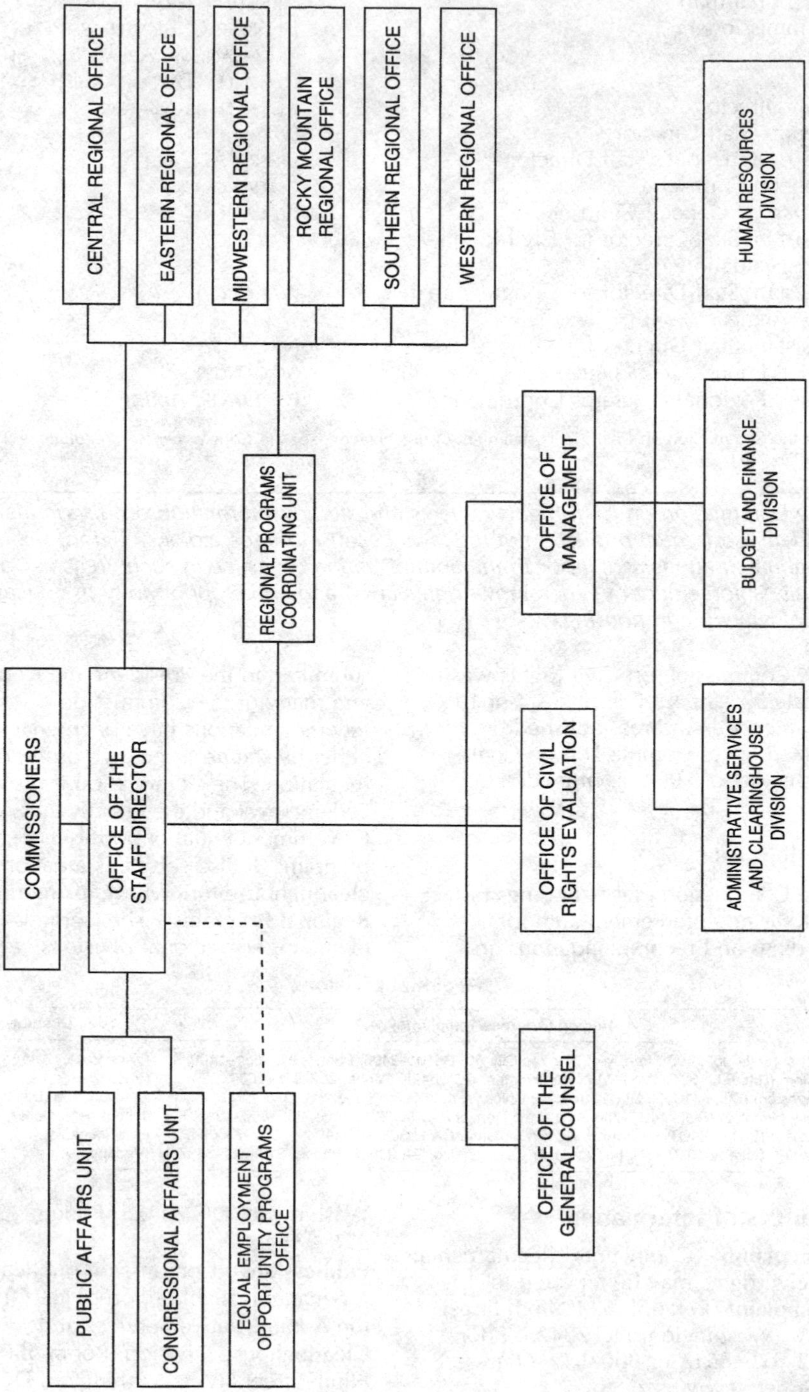

of publications may be obtained from this office.

Reading Room The National Civil Rights Clearinghouse Library is located in Room 602, 624 Ninth Street NW., Washington, DC 20425. Phone, 202–376–8110.

For further information, contact the Office of the Staff Director, United States Commission on Civil Rights, Room 730, 624 Ninth Street NW., Washington, DC 20425. Phone, 202–376–7700. TTY, 202–376–8116. Internet, www.usccr.gov.

UNITED STATES INTERNATIONAL TRADE COMMISSION

500 E Street SW., Washington, DC 20436
Phone, 202–205–2000. Internet, www.usitc.gov.

Chairman	STEPHEN KOPLAN
Vice Chairman	DEANNA TANNER OKUN
Commissioners	SHARA L. ARANOFF, JENNIFER A. HILLMAN, CHARLOTTE R. LANE, DANIEL R. PEARSON
Administrative Law Judges	ROBERT L. BARTON, JR., CHARLES E. BULLOCK, SIDNEY HARRIS, PAUL J. LUCKERN
Director, Office of Administration/Chief Information Officer	STEPHEN MCLAUGHLIN
Deputy Chief Information Officer	PAMELA C. DYSON
Director, Office of Economics	ROBERT B. KOOPMAN
Director, Office of External Relations	LYN M. SCHLITT
Congressional Relations Officer	NANCY M. CARMAN
Public Affairs Officer	MARGARET M. O'LAUGHLIN
Trade Remedy Assistance Program Manager	JOHN J. GREER
Director, Office of Equal Employment Opportunity	JACQUELINE A. WATERS
Director, Office of Industries	KAREN LANEY-CUMMINGS
Division Chief, Agriculture and Fisheries	CATHY L. JABARA
Division Chief, Natural Resources and Metals	(VACANCY)
Division Chief, Chemicals and Textiles	DENNIS RAPKINS
Division Chief, Advanced Technology and Machinery	MICHAEL ANDERSON
Division Chief, Services	RICHARD W. BROWN
Director, Office of Investigations	ROBERT G. CARPENTER
Director, Office of Operations	ROBERT ROGOWSKY
Director, Office of Tariff Affairs and Trade Agreements	DAVID BECK, *Acting*
Director, Office of Unfair Import Investigations	LYNN LEVINE
General Counsel	JAMES M. LYONS
Inspector General	JEAN SMITH, *Acting*
Secretary	MARILYN R. ABBOTT

The United States International Trade Commission furnishes studies, reports, and recommendations involving international trade and tariffs to the President, the U.S.

Trade Representative, and congressional committees. The Commission also conducts a variety of investigations pertaining to international trade relief.

The United States International Trade Commission is an independent agency created by act of September 8, 1916 (39 Stat. 795), and originally named the United States Tariff Commission. The name was changed to the United States International Trade Commission by section 171 of the Trade Act of 1974 (19 U.S.C. 2231).

Six Commissioners are appointed by the President with the advice and consent of the Senate for 9-year terms, unless appointed to fill an unexpired term. The Chairman and Vice Chairman are designated by the President for 2-year terms, and succeeding Chairmen may not be of the same political party. The Chairman generally is responsible for the administration of the Commission. Not more than three Commissioners may be members of the same political party (19 U.S.C. 1330).

Activities

The Commission performs a number of functions pursuant to the statutes referred to above. Under the Tariff Act of 1930, the Commission is given broad powers of investigation relating to the customs laws of the United States and foreign countries; the volume of importation in comparison with domestic production and consumption; the conditions, causes, and effects relating to competition of foreign industries with those of the United States; and all other factors affecting competition between articles of the United States and imported articles. The Commission is required, whenever requested, to make available to the President, the House Committee on Ways and Means, and the Senate Committee on Finance all information at its command, and is directed to make such investigations and reports as may be requested by the President, said committees, or Congress.

In order to carry out these responsibilities, the Commission is required to engage in extensive research, conduct specialized studies, and maintain a high degree of expertise in all matters relating to the commercial and international trade policies of the United States.

Imported Articles Subsidized or Sold at Less Than Fair Value The Commission conducts preliminary-phase investigations to determine whether imports of foreign merchandise allegedly being subsidized or sold at less than fair value injure or threaten to injure an industry in the United States. If the Commission's determination is affirmative, and the Secretary of Commerce determines there is reason to believe or suspect such unfair practices are occurring, then the Commission conducts final-phase investigations to determine the injury or threat of injury to an industry because of such imports.

Under the Uruguay Round Agreements Act, the Commission also conducts sunset reviews. In these reviews, the Commission evaluates whether material injury to a U.S. industry would continue or recur if the antidumping duty or countervailing duty order under review was revoked. Such injury reviews must be conducted on all antidumping duty and countervailing duty orders every 5 years as long as the orders remain in effect.

Unfair Practices in Import Trade The Commission applies U.S. statutory and common law of unfair competition to the importation of products into the United States and their sale. If the Commission determines that there is a violation of law, it is to direct that the articles involved be excluded from entry into the United States, or it may issue cease-and-desist orders directing the person engaged in such violation to cease and desist from engaging in such unfair methods or acts.

Trade Negotiations The Commission advises the President as to the probable economic effect on the domestic industry and consumers of modification of duties and other barriers to trade that may be considered for inclusion in any proposed trade agreement with foreign countries.

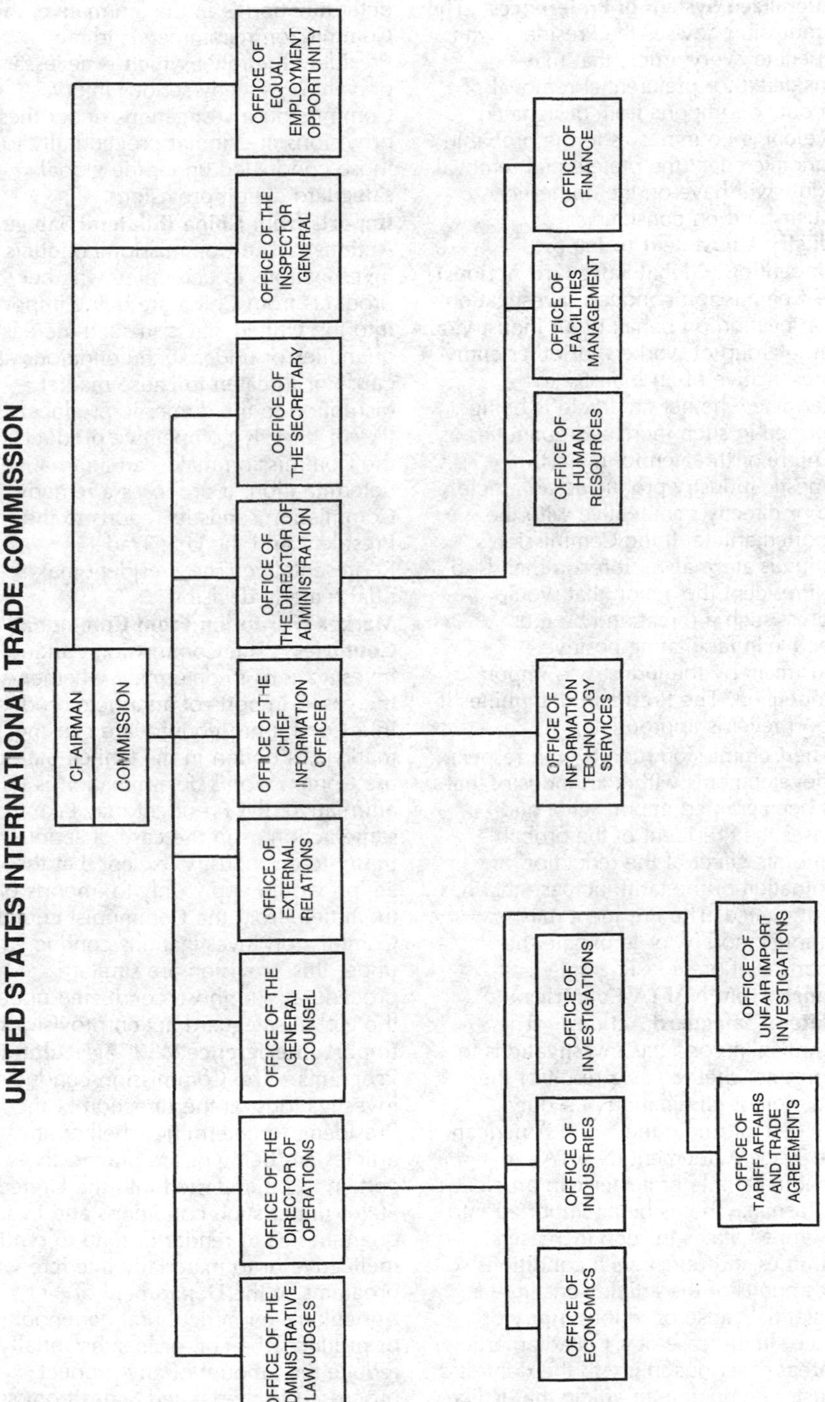
UNITED STATES INTERNATIONAL TRADE COMMISSION
CHAIRMAN
COMMISSION
OFFICE OF EQUAL EMPLOYMENT OPPORTUNITY
OFFICE OF THE INSPECTOR GENERAL
OFFICE OF THE SECRETARY
OFFICE OF THE DIRECTOR OF ADMINISTRATION
OFFICE OF THE CHIEF INFORMATION OFFICER
OFFICE OF EXTERNAL RELATIONS
OFFICE OF THE GENERAL COUNSEL
OFFICE OF THE DIRECTOR OF OPERATIONS
OFFICE OF THE ADMINISTRATIVE LAW JUDGES
OFFICE OF FINANCE
OFFICE OF FACILITIES MANAGEMENT
OFFICE OF HUMAN RESOURCES
OFFICE OF INFORMATION TECHNOLOGY SERVICES
OFFICE OF INVESTIGATIONS
OFFICE OF INDUSTRIES
OFFICE OF ECONOMICS
OFFICE OF UNFAIR IMPORT INVESTIGATIONS
OFFICE OF TARIFF AFFAIRS AND TRADE AGREEMENTS

Generalized System of Preferences The Commission advises the President with respect to every article that may be considered for preferential removal of the duty on imports from designated developing countries as to the probable economic effect the preferential removal of duty will have on the domestic industry and on consumers.

Industry Adjustment to Import Competition (Global Safeguard Actions) The Commission conducts investigations upon petition on behalf of an industry, a firm, a group of workers, or other entity representative of an industry to determine whether an article is being imported in such increased quantities as to injure or threaten to injure the domestic industry producing an article like or directly competitive with the imported article. If the Commission's finding is affirmative, it recommends to the President the action that would address such a threat and be most effective in facilitating positive adjustment by the industry to import competition. The President determines if import relief is appropriate.

The Commission reports with respect to developments within an industry that has been granted import relief and advises the President of the probable economic effect of the reduction or elimination of the tariff increase that has been granted. The President may continue, modify, or terminate the import relief previously granted.

Imports From NAFTA Countries (Bilateral Safeguard Actions) The Commission conducts investigations to determine whether, as a result of the reduction or elimination of a duty provided for under the North American Free Trade Agreement (NAFTA), a Canadian article or a Mexican article, as the case may be, is being imported into the United States in such increased quantities and under such conditions so that imports of the article constitute a substantial cause of serious injury or (except in the case of a Canadian article) a threat of serious injury to the domestic industry producing an article that is like or directly competitive with the imported article. If the Commission's determination is in the affirmative, the Commission recommends to the President the relief which is necessary to prevent or remedy serious injury. Commission investigations under these provisions are similar procedurally to those conducted under the global safeguard action provisions.

Imports from China (Bilateral Safeguard Actions) The Commission conducts investigations to determine whether products from China are being imported into the United States in such increased quantities or under such conditions as to cause or threaten to cause market disruption to the domestic producers of like or directly competitive products. If the Commission makes an affirmative determination, it proposes a remedy. The Commission sends its reports to the President and the U.S. Trade Representative. The President makes the final remedy decision.

Market Disruption From Communist Countries The Commission conducts investigations to determine whether increased imports of an article produced in a Communist country are causing market disruption in the United States. If the Commission's determination is in the affirmative, the President may take the same action as in the case of serious injury to an industry, except that the action would apply only to imports of the article from the Communist country. Commission investigations conducted under this provision are similar procedurally to those conducted under the global safeguard action provisions.

Import Interference With Agricultural Programs The Commission conducts investigations, at the direction of the President, to determine whether any articles are being or are practically certain to be imported into the United States under such conditions and in such quantities as to render or tend to render ineffective or to materially interfere with programs of the Department of Agriculture for agricultural commodities or products thereof, or to substantially reduce the amount of any product processed in the United States from such commodities or products, and makes findings and recommendations. The

President may restrict the imports in question by imposition of either import fees or quotas. Such fees or quotas may be applied only against countries that are not members of the World Trade Organization.

Uniform Statistical Data The Commission, in cooperation with the Secretary of the Treasury and the Secretary of Commerce, establishes for statistical purposes an enumeration of articles imported into the United States and exported from the United States, and seeks to establish comparability of such statistics with statistical programs for domestic production.

Harmonized Tariff Schedule of the United States, Annotated The Commission issues a publication containing the U.S. tariff schedules and related matters and considers questions concerning the arrangement of such schedules and the classification of articles.

International Trade Studies The Commission conducts studies, investigations, and research projects on a broad range of topics relating to international trade, pursuant to requests of the President, the House Ways and Means Committee, the Senate Finance Committee, either branch of the Congress, or on its own motion. Public reports of these studies, investigations, and research projects are issued in most cases.

The Commission also keeps informed of the operation and effect of provisions relating to duties or other import restrictions of the United States contained in various trade agreements. Occasionally the Commission is required by statute to perform specific trade-related studies.

Industry and Trade Summaries The Commission prepares and publishes a series of summaries of trade and tariff information. These summaries contain descriptions (in terms of the Harmonized Tariff Schedule of the United States) of the thousands of products imported into the United States, methods of production, and the extent and relative importance of U.S. consumption, production, and trade, together with certain basic factors affecting the competitive position and economic health of domestic industries.

Sources of Information

Inquiries should be directed to the specific organizational unit or to the Secretary, United States International Trade Commission, 500 E Street SW., Washington, DC 20436. Phone, 202–205–2000.

Contracts The Procurement Executive has responsibility for contract matters. Phone, 202–205–2745.

Electronic Access Commission publications, news releases, *Federal Register* notices, scheduling information, the Commission's interactive Trade and Tariff DataWeb, and general information about ITC are available for electronic access. Investigation-related public inspection files are available through the Electronic Document Imaging System (EDIS). Internet, www.usitc.gov.

Employment Information on employment can be obtained from the Director, Office of Human Resources. The Agency employs international economists, attorneys, accountants, commodity and industry specialists and analysts, and clerical and other support personnel. Phone, 202–205–2651.

Publications The Commission publishes results of investigations concerning various commodities and subjects. Other publications include *Industry and Trade Summaries*, an annual report to the Congress on the operation of the trade agreements program, and an annual review of Commission activities. Specific information regarding these publications can be obtained from the Office of the Secretary.

Reading Rooms Reading rooms are open to the public in the Office of the Secretary, the ITC Main Library, and the ITC law library.

For further information, contact the Secretary, United States International Trade Commission, 500 E Street SW., Washington, DC 20436. Phone, 202–205–2000. Internet, www.usitc.gov.

UNITED STATES POSTAL SERVICE

475 L'Enfant Plaza SW., Washington, DC 20260–0010
Phone, 202–268–2000. Internet, www.usps.gov.

Board of Governors:	
Chairman of the Board	JAMES C. MILLER III
Vice Chairman of the Board	ALAN C. KESSLER
Secretary of the Board	WENDY A. HOCKING
Inspector General	DAVID C. WILLIAMS
Governors	CAROLYN LEWIS GALLAGHER, JOHN S. GARDNER, LOUIS J. GIULIANO, (4 VACANCIES)
Postmaster General, Chief Executive Officer	JOHN E. POTTER
Deputy Postmaster General and Chief Operating Officer	PATRICK R. DONAHOE
Management:	
Postmaster General, Chief Executive Officer	JOHN E. POTTER
Vice President, Strategic Planning	LINDA A. KINGSLEY
Deputy Postmaster General	PATRICK R. DONAHOE
Executive Vice President, Chief Marketing Officer	ANITA J. BIZZOTO
Chief Postal Inspector	LEE HEATH
Chief Financial Officer and Executive Vice President	RICHARD J. STRASSER, JR.
Senior Vice President, Government Relations	TOM DAY
Executive Vice President, Chief Human Resources Officer	ANTHONY VEGLIANTE
Senior Vice President, Intelligent Mail and Address Quality	CHARLES E. BRAVO
Senior Vice President, General Counsel	MARY ANNE GIBBONS
Senior Vice President, Operations	WILLIAM GALLIGAN
Area Operations:	
Vice President, Eastern Area	ALEXANDER LAZAROFF
Vice President, Great Lakes Area	JO ANN FEINDT
Vice President, New York Metro Area	DAVID L. SOLOMON
Vice President, Northeast Area	MEGAN BRENNAN
Vice President, Pacific Area	AL INIGUEZ
Vice President, Southeast Area	WILLIAM J. BROWN
Vice President, Southwest Area	GEORGE L. LOPEZ
Vice President, Western Area	SYLVESTER BLACK
Capital Metro Operations Manager	JERRY LANE

[For the United States Postal Service statement of organization, see the *Code of Federal Regulations,* Title 39, Part 221]

The United States Postal Service provides mail processing and delivery services to individuals and businesses within the United States. The Service is committed to serving customers through the development of efficient mail-handling systems and operates its own planning and engineering programs. It also protects the mails from loss or theft and apprehends those who violate postal laws.

The Postal Service was created as an independent establishment of the executive branch by the Postal Reorganization Act (39 U.S.C. 101 *et seq.*), approved August 12, 1970. The present United States Postal Service commenced operations on July 1, 1971.

The Postal Service has approximately 705,000 career employees and handles about 212 billion pieces of mail annually. The chief executive officer of the Postal Service, the Postmaster General, is appointed by the nine Governors of the Postal Service, who are appointed by the President with the advice and consent of the Senate for overlapping 9-year terms. The Governors and the Postmaster General appoint the Deputy Postmaster General, and these 11 people constitute the Board of Governors.

In addition to the national headquarters, there are area and district offices supervising more than 37,000 post offices, branches, stations, and community post offices throughout the United States.

Activities

In order to expand and improve service to the public, the Postal Service is engaged in customer cooperation activities, including the development of programs for both the general public and major customers. The Consumer Advocate, a postal ombudsman, represents the interest of the individual mail customer in matters involving the Postal Service by bringing complaints and suggestions to the attention of top postal management and solving the problems of individual customers. To provide postal services responsive to public needs, the Postal Service operates its own planning, research, engineering, real estate, and procurement programs specially adapted to postal requirements, and maintains close ties with international postal organizations.

The Postal Service is the only Federal agency whose employment policies are governed by a process of collective bargaining under the National Labor Relations Act. Labor contract negotiations, affecting all bargaining unit personnel, as well as personnel matters involving employees not covered by collective bargaining agreements, are administered by Labor Relations or Human Resources.

The U.S. Postal Inspection Service is the Federal law enforcement agency which has jurisdiction in criminal matters affecting the integrity and security of the mail. Postal Inspectors enforce more than 200 Federal statutes involving mail fraud, mail bombs, child pornography, illegal drugs, mail theft, and other postal crimes, as well as being responsible for the protection of all postal employees. Information on the Postal Inspection Service is available on the Internet at www.usps.gov/postalinspectors.

Postal Inspection Service—United States Postal Service

Division	Address	Telephone
Atlanta	P.O. Box 16489, Atlanta, GA 30321–0489	404–608–4500
Boston	495 Summer St., Boston, MA 02210–2214	617–556–4400
Charlotte	2901 Scott Futrell Dr., Charlotte, NC 28228–3000	704–329–9120
Chicago	Fl. 6, 433 W. Harrison St., Chicago, IL 60669–2201	312–983–7900
Denver	Suite 900, 1745 Stout St., Denver, CO 80202–3034	303–313–5320
Detroit	P.O. Box 330119, Detroit, MI 48232–6119	313–226–8184
Fort Worth	14800 Trinity Blvd., Fort Worth, TX 76161–2929	817–359–2700
Houston	650 N. Sam Houston Pkwy, Houston, TX 77251–1276	713–238–4400
Los Angeles	P.O. Box 2000, Pasadena, CA 91102–2000	626–405–1200
Miami	6th Fl., 3400 Lakeside Dr., Miramar, FL 33027–3242	954–436–7200
New Jersey/Caribbean	P.O. Box 509, Newark, NJ 07101–0509	973–693–5400
New York	P.O. Box 555, New York, NY 10116–0555	212–330–3844
Philadelphia	Rm. 400, 2970 Market St., Philadelphia, PA 19101–9000	215–895–8450
Pittsburgh	Rm. 2101, 1001 California Ave., Pittsburgh, PA 15290–9000	412–359–7900
San Francisco	P.O. Box 882528, San Francisco, CA 94188–2528	415–778–5800
Seattle	P.O. Box 400, Seattle, WA 98111–4000	206–442–6300

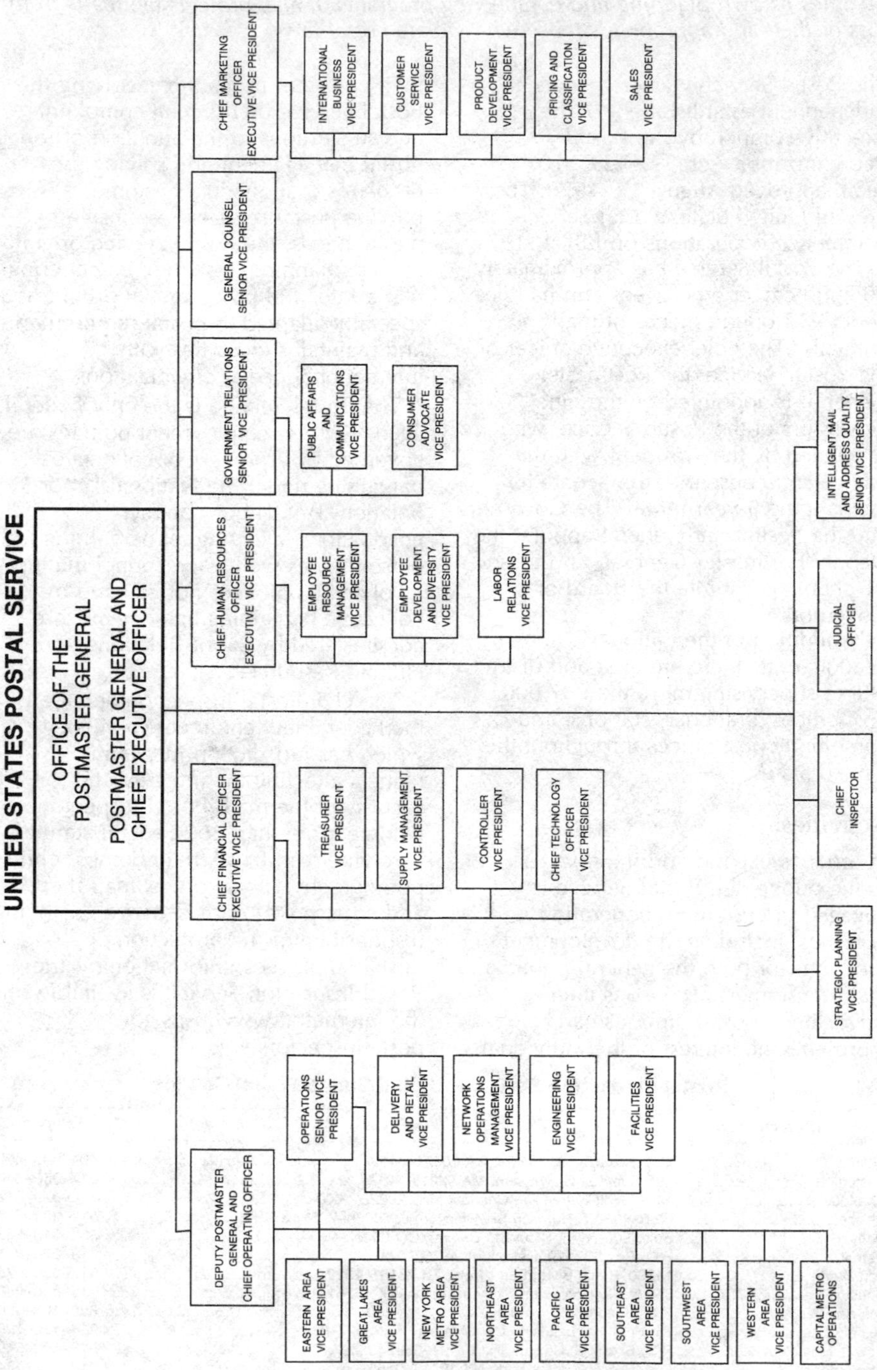
UNITED STATES POSTAL SERVICE
OFFICE OF THE POSTMASTER GENERAL
POSTMASTER GENERAL AND CHIEF EXECUTIVE OFFICER
DEPUTY POSTMASTER GENERAL AND CHIEF OPERATING OFFICER
EASTERN AREA VICE PRESIDENT
GREAT LAKES AREA VICE PRESIDENT
NEW YORK METRO AREA VICE PRESIDENT
NORTHEAST AREA VICE PRESIDENT
PACIFIC AREA VICE PRESIDENT
SOUTHEAST AREA VICE PRESIDENT
SOUTHWEST AREA VICE PRESIDENT
WESTERN AREA VICE PRESIDENT
CAPITAL METRO OPERATIONS
OPERATIONS SENIOR VICE PRESIDENT
DELIVERY AND RETAIL VICE PRESIDENT
NETWORK OPERATIONS MANAGEMENT VICE PRESIDENT
ENGINEERING VICE PRESIDENT
FACILITIES VICE PRESIDENT
CHIEF FINANCIAL OFFICER EXECUTIVE VICE PRESIDENT
TREASURER VICE PRESIDENT
SUPPLY MANAGEMENT VICE PRESIDENT
CONTROLLER VICE PRESIDENT
CHIEF TECHNOLOGY OFFICER VICE PRESIDENT
CHIEF HUMAN RESOURCES OFFICER EXECUTIVE VICE PRESIDENT
EMPLOYEE RESOURCE MANAGEMENT VICE PRESIDENT
EMPLOYEE DEVELOPMENT AND DIVERSITY VICE PRESIDENT
LABOR RELATIONS VICE PRESIDENT
GOVERNMENT RELATIONS SENIOR VICE PRESIDENT
PUBLIC AFFAIRS AND COMMUNICATIONS VICE PRESIDENT
CONSUMER ADVOCATE VICE PRESIDENT
GENERAL COUNSEL SENIOR VICE PRESIDENT
CHIEF MARKETING OFFICER EXECUTIVE VICE PRESIDENT
INTERNATIONAL BUSINESS VICE PRESIDENT
CUSTOMER SERVICE VICE PRESIDENT
PRODUCT DEVELOPMENT VICE PRESIDENT
PRICING AND CLASSIFICATION VICE PRESIDENT
SALES VICE PRESIDENT
STRATEGIC PLANNING VICE PRESIDENT
CHIEF INSPECTOR
JUDICIAL OFFICER
INTELLIGENT MAIL AND ADDRESS QUALITY SENIOR VICE PRESIDENT

Postal Inspection Service—United States Postal Service—Continued

Division	Address	Telephone
St. Louis	1106 Walnut St., St. Louis, MO 63199–2201	314–539–9300
Washington, DC	Suite 200, 10500 Little Patuxent Pkwy., Columbia, MD 21044–3509	410–715–7700

Sources of Information

Consumer Information For general information, call 800–275–8777 (800–ASK–USPS) 24 hours a day. Express Mail, Priority Mail, and Package Support Line, 800–222–1811. Information on past and present schemes used to defraud the public is available through Congressional and Public Affairs, Postal Inspection Service. Phone, 202–268–5400.

Contracts and Small Business Activities Contact Supplier Diversity. Phone, 202–268–4633.

Employment General information about jobs such as clerk, letter carrier, etc., including information about programs for veterans, may be obtained by contacting the nearest post office.

Individuals interested in working at Postal Headquarters in Washington, DC, may obtain information by calling the U.S. Postal Service information hotline. Phone, 800–562–8777 (800–JOB–USPS). Current vacancy announcements are also listed in the Postal Service Web site, at www.usps.gov/employment.

Information about Postal Inspector employment may be obtained from the Office of Recruitment. Phone, 301–983–7400.

Inspector General The Office of Inspector General maintains a toll-free hotline as a means for individuals to report activities involving fraud, waste, or mismanagement. Phone, 888–877–7644 (888–USPS–OIG). Fax, 703–248–2259. Complaints may be sent by mail to the United States Postal Service, Office of Inspector General Hotline, 10th Floor, 1735 North Lynn Street, Arlington, VA 22209–2020. Publicly available documents and information on the Office of Inspector General and some Freedom of Information Act documents are available electronically through the Internet at www.uspsoig.gov.

Philatelic Sales Contact Stamp Fulfillment Services, Kansas City, MO 64179–1009. Phone, 800–782–6724 (800–STAMP–24).

Publications Pamphlets on mailability, postage rates and fees, and many other topics may be obtained free of charge from the nearest post office.

Most postal regulations are contained in Postal Service manuals covering domestic mail, international mail, postal operations, administrative support, employee and labor relations, financial management, and procurement. These manuals and other publications including the *National Five-Digit ZIP Code and Post Office Directory* (Publication 65) may be purchased from the Superintendent of Documents, Government Printing Office, Washington, DC 20402–0001. The *National Five-Digit ZIP Code and Post Office Directory* is also available through local post offices.

Reading Rooms Located on the 11th Floor North, Library. Phone, 202–268–2900.

For further information, contact the U.S. Postal Service, 475 L'Enfant Plaza SW., Washington, DC 20260. Phone, 202–268–2000. Internet, www.usps.gov.

Boards, Commissions, and Committees

Note: This is a listing of Federal boards, commissions, councils, etc., not listed elsewhere in the *Manual,* which were established by congressional or Presidential action, whose functions are not strictly limited to the internal operations of a parent department or agency and which are authorized to publish documents in the *Federal Register.* While the editors have attempted to compile a complete and accurate listing, suggestions for improving coverage of this guide are welcome. Please address your comments to the Office of the Federal Register, National Archives and Records Administration, Washington, DC 20408. Phone, 202–741–6040. Internet, www.archives.gov/federal-register.

Federal advisory committees, as defined by the Federal Advisory Committee Act, as amended (5 U.S.C. app.), have not been included here. Information on Federal advisory committees may be obtained from the Committee Management Secretariat, General Services Administration, General Services Building (MC), Room G–230, Washington, DC 20405. Phone, 202–273–3556. Internet, www.gsa.gov/committeemanagement.

Administrative Committee of the Federal Register

National Archives and Records Administration, Washington, DC 20408. Phone, 202–741–6010. Internet, www.archives.gov/federal-register.

Advisory Council on Historic Preservation

1100 Pennsylvania Avenue NW., Suite 809, Washington, DC 20004. Phone, 202–606–8503. Fax, 202–606–5073. E-mail, achp@achp.org. Internet, www.achp.gov.

American Battle Monuments Commission

Court House Plaza Two, Suite 500, 2300 Clarendon Boulevard, Arlington, VA 22201. Phone, 703–696–6900. Internet, www.abmc.gov.

Appalachian Regional Commission

1666 Connecticut Avenue NW., Suite 700, Washington, DC 20009–1068. Phone, 202–884–7700. E-mail, info@arc.gov. Internet, www.arc.gov.

Architectural and Transportation Barriers Compliance Board [1]

1331 F Street NW., Suite 1000, Washington, DC 20004–1111. Phone, 202–272–0080 or TTY, 202–272–0082. Fax, 202–272–0081. Internet, www.access-board.gov.

Arctic Research Commission

4350 North Fairfax Drive, Suite 510, Arlington, VA 22203. Phone, 703–525–0111. Fax, 703–525–0114. Internet, www.arctic.gov.

[1] Also known as the Access Board.

Arthritis and Musculoskeletal Interagency Coordinating Committee
National Institutes of Health/NIAMS, Building 31, Room 4C02, 31 Center Drive, Bethesda, MD 20892–2350. Phone, 301–496–8190. Internet, www.niams.nih.gov.

Barry M. Goldwater Scholarship and Excellence in Education Foundation
6225 Brandon Avenue, Suite 315, Springfield, VA 22150–2519. Phone, 703–756–6012. Fax, 703–756–6015. E-mail, goldh2o@vacoxmail.com. Internet, www.act.org/goldwater.

Chemical Safety and Hazard Investigation Board
2175 K Street NW., Suite 400, Washington, DC 20037–1809. Phone, 202–261–7600. Fax, 202–261–7650. E-mail, info@csb.gov. Internet, www.csb.gov.

Citizens' Stamp Advisory Committee
United States Postal Service, Room 5013, 1735 N. Lynn Street, Arlington, VA 22209–6432. Phone, 703–292–3810. Fax, 703–292–3634.

Commission of Fine Arts
401 F Street NW., Suite 312, Washington, DC 20001. Phone, 202–504–2200. Fax, 202–504–2195. E-mail, staff@cfa.gov. Internet, www.cfa.gov.

Committee on Foreign Investment in the United States
Department of the Treasury, 1500 Pennsylvania Avenue NW., Room 5221, Washington, DC 20220. Phone, 202–622–1860. Internet, www.treas.gov/offices/international-affairs/exon-florio/.

Committee for the Implementation of Textile Agreements
Department of Commerce, Room 3001A, Fourteenth Street and Constitution Avenue NW., Washington, DC 20230. Phone, 202–482–3737.

Committee for Purchase From People Who Are Blind or Severely Disabled
1421 Jefferson Davis Highway, Jefferson Plaza 2, Suite 10800, Arlington, VA 22202–3259. Phone, 703–603–7740. E-mail, info@jwod.gov. Internet, www.jwod.gov.

Coordinating Council on Juvenile Justice and Delinquency Prevention

Department of Justice, Office of Juvenile Justice and Delinquency Prevention, 810 7th Street NW., Washington, DC 20531. Phone, 202–307–9963. Fax, 202–907–9093. Internet, www.juvenilecouncil.gov.

Delaware River Basin Commission

25 State Police Drive, P.O. Box 7360, West Trenton, NJ 08628–0360. Phone, 609–883–9500. Fax, 609–883–9522. Internet, www.drbc.net.

Endangered Species Committee

4401 N. Fairfax Drive, Room 420, Arlington, VA 22203. Phone, 703–358–2390. Fax 703–358–1735. Internet, http://endangered.fws.gov.

Export Administration Operating Committee

Department of Commerce, Room 3889, Herbert C. Hoover Building, Fourteenth Street and Pennsylvania Avenue NW., Washington, DC 20230. Phone, 202–482–5863. Fax, 202–501–2815.

Federal Financial Institutions Examination Council

2000 K Street NW., Suite 310, Washington, DC 20006. Phone, 202–872–7500. Fax, 202–872–7501. Internet, www.ffiec.gov.

Federal Financing Bank

Department of the Treasury, Pennsylvania Avenue NW., Washington, DC 20220. Phone, 202–622–2470. Fax, 202–622–0707. Internet, www.ustreas.gov/ffb.

Federal Interagency Committee on Education

Department of Education, Federal Office Building 6, Room 5E222, 400 Maryland Avenue SW., Washington, DC 20202–3572. Phone, 202–401–3673.

Federal Laboratory Consortium for Technology Transfer

1629 K Street NW., Suite 220, Washington, DC 20006-7602. Phone, 202–296–7201. Fax, 202–296–7203. Internet, www.federallabs.org.

Federal Library and Information Center Committee

Library of Congress, 101 Independence Avenue SE., Adams Building, Room 217, Washington, DC 20540–4935. Phone, 202–707–4800. Fax, 202–707–4818. Internet, www.loc.gov/flicc/.

Harry S. Truman Scholarship Foundation

712 Jackson Place NW., Washington, DC 20006. Phone, 202–395–4831. Fax, 202–395–6995. E-mail, office@truman.gov. Internet, www.truman.gov.

Indian Arts and Crafts Board

Department of the Interior, Room MS 2058–MIB, 1849 C Street NW., Washington, DC 20240. Phone, 202–208–3773. E-mail, iacb@ios.doi.gov. Internet, www.iacb.doi.gov.

J. William Fulbright Foreign Scholarship Board

Office of Academic Exchange Programs, Bureau of Educational and Cultural Affairs, Department of State (SA–44), 301 4th Street SW., Room 234, Washington, DC 20547. Phone, 202–453–8135. Internet, http://exchanges.state.gov/education/fulbright.

James Madison Memorial Fellowship Foundation

2000 K Street NW., Suite 303, Washington, DC 20006–1809. Phone, 202–653–8700. Fax, 202–653–6045. E-mail, madison@act.org. Internet, www.jamesmadison.com.

Japan-United States Friendship Commission

1201 15th Street, Suite 330, Washington, DC 20005. Phone, 202–653–9800. Fax, 202–653–9802. E-mail, justice@justfc.gov. Internet, www.jusfc.gov.

Joint Board for the Enrollment of Actuaries

Internal Revenue Service, SE: OPR, 1111 Constitution Avenue NW., Washington, DC 20224. Phone, 202–622–8229. Fax, 202–622–8300.

Marine Mammal Commission

4340 East-West Highway, Suite 905, Bethesda, MD 20814. Phone, 301–504–0087. Fax, 301–504–0099. E-mail, mmc@mmc.gov. Internet, www.mmc.gov.

Medicare Payment Advisory Commission

601 New Jersey Avenue NW., Suite 9000, Washington, DC 20001. Phone, 202–220–3700. Internet, www.medpac.gov.

Migratory Bird Conservation Commission

United States Fish and Wildlife Service Division of Realty, Mail Stop ARLSQ–622, 4401 North Fairfax Drive, Arlington, VA 22203–1610. Phone, 703–358–1716. Internet, realty.fws.gov.

Mississippi River Commission

United States Army Corps of Engineers, Mississippi Valley Division, 1400 Walnut Street, Vicksburg, MS 39180–0080. Phone, 601–634–5760. Fax, 601–634–7110. Internet, www.mvd.usace.army.mil.

Morris K. Udall Scholarship and Excellence in National Environmental Policy Foundation

130 South Scott Avenue, Tucson, AZ 85701. Phone, 520–670–5529. Fax, 520–670–5530. Internet, www.udall.gov.

National Commission on Libraries and Information Science

1800 M Street NW., Suite 350, North Tower, Washington, DC 20036–5841. Phone, 202–606–9200. Fax, 202–606–9203. E-mail, info@nclis.gov. Internet, www.nclis.gov.

National Council on Disability

1331 F Street NW., Suite 850, Washington, DC 20004. Phone, 202–

272–2004. TTY, 202–272–2074. Fax, 202–272–2022. E-mail, ncd@ncd.gov. Internet, www.ncd.gov.

National Indian Gaming Commission
1441 L Street NW., Suite 9100, Washington, DC 20005. Phone, 202–632–7003. Fax, 202–632–7066. Internet, www.nigc.gov.

National Park Foundation
11 Dupont Circle NW., Suite 600, Washington, DC 20036. Phone, 202–238–4200. Fax, 202–234–3103. E-mail, ask-npf@nationalparks.org. Internet, www.nationalparks.org.

Northwest Power and Conservation Council
851 SW. Sixth Avenue, Suite 1100, Portland, OR 97204. Phone, 503–222–5161 or 800–452–5161. Fax, 503–820–2370. Internet, www.nwcouncil.org.

Office of Navajo and Hopi Indian Relocation
201 East Birch Street, Flagstaff, AZ 86001. Phone, 928–779–2721 or 800–321–3114. Fax, 928–774–1977.

Permanent Committee for the Oliver Wendell Holmes Devise
Library of Congress, Manuscript Division, Washington, DC 20540–4680. Phone, 202–707–1082.

President's Council on Integrity and Efficiency
Office of Management and Budget, New Executive Office Building, Room 260, Washington, DC 20503. Internet, www.ignet.gov.

President's Foreign Intelligence Advisory Board
New Executive Office Building, Room 5020, Washington, DC 20502. Phone, 202–456–2352. Fax, 202–395–3403.

Presidio Trust
34 Graham Street, P.O. Box 29052, San Francisco, CA 94129–0052. Phone, 415–561–5300. TTY, 415–561–5301. Fax, 415–561–5315. E-mail, presidio@presidiotrust.gov. Internet, www.presidio.gov.

Social Security Advisory Board
400 Virginia Avenue SW., Suite 625, Washington, DC 20024. Phone, 202–475–7700. Fax, 202–475–7715. E-mail, info@ssab.gov. Internet, www.ssab.gov.

Susquehanna River Basin Commission
1721 North Front Street, Harrisburg, PA 17102–2391. Phone, 717–238–0423. Fax, 717–238–2436. E-mail, srbc@srbc.net. Internet, www.srbc.net.

Trade Policy Staff Committee
Office of the United States Trade Representative, 1724 F Street NW., Washington, DC 20508. Phone, 202–395–3475. Fax, 202–395–5141.

United States Holocaust Memorial Museum
100 Raoul Wallenberg Place SW., Washington, DC 20024–2126. Phone, 202–488–0400. TTY, 202–488–0406. Internet, www.ushmm.org.

United States Nuclear Waste Technical Review Board
2300 Clarendon Boulevard, Suite 1300, Arlington, VA 22201. Phone, 703–235–4473. Fax, 703–235–4495. Internet, www.nwtrb.gov.

Veterans Day National Committee
Department of Veterans Affairs (002C), 810 Vermont Avenue NW., Washington, DC 20420. Phone, 202–273–4849. Fax, 202–273–5717. Internet, www.va.gov/vetsday

White House Commission on Presidential Scholars
Department of Education, 400 Maryland Avenue SW., Washington, DC 20202–8173. Phone, 202–401–0961. Fax, 202–260–7464. Internet, www.ed.gov/programs/psp/index.html

QUASI–OFFICIAL AGENCIES

Note: This section contains organizations that are not Executive agencies under the definition in 5 U.S.C. 105 but that are required by statute to publish certain information on their programs and activities in the *Federal Register.*

LEGAL SERVICES CORPORATION

3333 K Street NW., Washington, DC 20007–3522
Phone, 202–295–1500. Fax, 202–337–6797. Internet, www.lsc.gov.

President	HELAINE M. BARNETT
Vice President for Legal Affairs, General Counsel, and Corporate Secretary	VICTOR M. FORTUNO
Vice President for Programs and Compliance	KAREN J. SARJEANT
Director, Office of Compliance and Enforcement	DANILO CARDONA
Director, Office of Information Management	JOHN MEYER
Director, Office of Program Performance	MICHAEL GENZ
Chief Administrative Officer	CHARLES JEFFRESS
Comptroller/Treasurer	DAVID RICHARDSON
Director, Office of Human Resources	ALICE DICKERSON
Director, Office of Information Technology	JEFF MORNINGSTAR
Director, Government Relations and Public Affairs	THOMAS C. POLGAR
Inspector General	RICHARD WEST

[For the Legal Services Corporation statement of organization, see the *Code of Federal Regulations,* Title 45, Part 1601]

The Legal Services Corporation's mission is to promote equal access to justice in our Nation and to provide high quality civil legal assistance to low-income persons.

The Legal Services Corporation (LSC) is a private, nonprofit corporation established by the Legal Services Act of 1974, as amended (42 U.S.C. 2996) to seek to ensure equal access to justice under the law for all Americans.

LSC is headed by an 11-member Board of Directors, appointed by the President and confirmed by the Senate. By law, the Board is bipartisan; no more than six members may be of the same political party. LSC is funded through congressional appropriations and provides legal services through grants to independent local programs selected through a system of competition. In

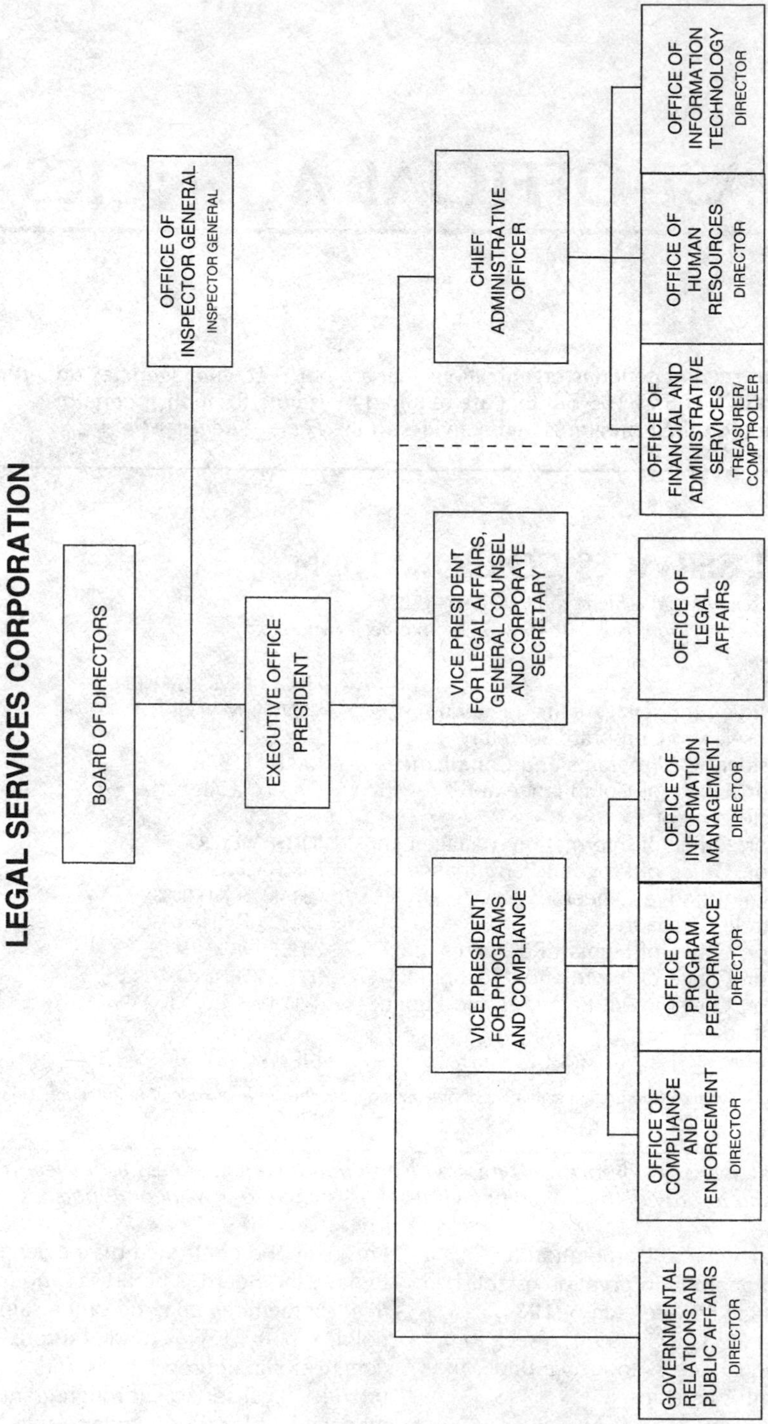
LEGAL SERVICES CORPORATION
BOARD OF DIRECTORS
OFFICE OF INSPECTOR GENERAL
INSPECTOR GENERAL
EXECUTIVE OFFICE
PRESIDENT
VICE PRESIDENT FOR PROGRAMS AND COMPLIANCE
VICE PRESIDENT FOR LEGAL AFFAIRS, GENERAL COUNSEL AND CORPORATE SECRETARY
CHIEF ADMINISTRATIVE OFFICER
GOVERNMENTAL RELATIONS AND PUBLIC AFFAIRS
DIRECTOR
OFFICE OF COMPLIANCE AND ENFORCEMENT
DIRECTOR
OFFICE OF PROGRAM PERFORMANCE
DIRECTOR
OFFICE OF INFORMATION MANAGEMENT
DIRECTOR
OFFICE OF LEGAL AFFAIRS
OFFICE OF FINANCIAL AND ADMINISTRATIVE SERVICES
TREASURER/ COMPTROLLER
OFFICE OF HUMAN RESOURCES
DIRECTOR
OFFICE OF INFORMATION TECHNOLOGY
DIRECTOR

2005, LSC funded 138 programs. Together they serve every county and congressional district in the nation, as well as the U.S. territories. Special service areas also address the needs of Native Americans and migrant farmworkers.

The legal services delivery is based on several principles: local priorities; national accountability; competition for grants; and a strong public-private partnership. Local programs are governed by their own boards of directors, which set priorities and determine the types of cases that will be handled subject to restrictions set by Congress. A majority of each local Board is appointed by local bar associations and one-third of each local Board is composed of client representatives appointed by client groups. Each Board hires its own Executive Director.

Programs may supplement their LSC grants with additional funds from State and local governments and other sources. They further leverage Federal funds by involving private attorneys in the delivery of legal services for the poor, mostly through volunteer pro bono work.

LSC funded programs do not handle criminal cases, nor do they accept fee-generating cases that private attorneys are willing to accept on a contingency basis. In addition, in 1996 a series of new limitations were placed upon activities in which LSC-funded programs may engage on behalf of their clients, even with non-LSC funds. All Legal Services' programs must comply with laws enacted by Congress and the implementing regulations promulgated by the Legal Services Corporation.

For further information, contact the Office of Government Relations and Public Affairs, Legal Services Corporation, 3333 K Street NW., Washington, DC 20007–3522. Phone, 202–295–1500. Fax, 202–337–6797. Internet, www.lsc.gov.

SMITHSONIAN INSTITUTION

1000 Jefferson Drive SW., Washington, DC 20560
Phone, 202–633–1000. Internet, www.smithsonian.org.

Board of Regents:

The Chief Justice of the United States (*Chancellor*)	JOHN G. ROBERTS, JR.
The Vice President of the United States	DICK CHENEY
Members of the Senate	THAD COCHRAN, WILLIAM FRIST, PATRICK J. LEAHY
Members of the House of Representatives	SAMUEL JOHNSON, XAVIER BECERRA, RALPH REGULA
Citizen Members	ELI BROAD, ANNE D'HARNONCOURT, MANUEL L. IBAÑEZ, SHIRLEY ANN JACKSON, ROBERT P. KOGOD, WALTER MASSEY, ROGER SANT, ALAN G. SPOON, PATTY STONESIFER

Officials:

Secretary	LAWRENCE M. SMALL
Inspector General	DEBRA S. RITT
Director of External Affairs	VIRGINIA CLARK
Director, Office of Policy and Analysis	CAROLE P. NEVES
Executive Assistant to the Secretary	JAMES M. HOBBINS

Deputy Secretary and Chief Operating Officer	SHEILA BURKE
Director, Asian/Pacific-American Program	FRANKLIN ODO
Chief, Renwick Gallery	ROBYN KENNEDY
Director of National Programs	RICHARD KURIN, *Acting*
Director, Anacostia Museum and Center for African American History and Culture	CAMILLE AKEJU
Director, Archives of American Art	NED RIFKIN, *Acting*
Director, Center for Folklife and Cultural Heritage	RICHARD KURIN
Director, Cooper-Hewitt National Design Museum	PAUL WARWICK THOMPSON
Director, National Air and Space Museum	GEN. JOHN R. DAILEY, USMC (RET.)
Director, National Museum of American History	BRENT GLASS
Director, National Museum of the American Indian	W. RICHARD WEST, JR.
Director, National Museum of African American History and Culture	LONNIE BUNCH
Director, National Portrait Gallery	MARC PACHTER
Director, National Postal Museum	ALLEN KANE
Director, Office of Communications/Public Affairs	EVELYN LIEBERMAN
Director, Office of Exhibits Central	MICHAEL HEADLEY
Director, Office of Government Relations	NELL PAYNE
Director, Office of Special Events and Protocol	NICOLE L. KRAKORA
Director, Smithsonian American Art Museum	ELIZABETH BROUN
Director, Smithsonian Center for Education and Museum Studies	STEPHANIE NORBY
Director, Smithsonian Latino Center	PILAR O'LEARY
Director, Smithsonian Institution Traveling Exhibition Service (SITES)	ANNA R. COHN
Director, Smithsonian Affiliations	HAROLD CLOSTER
Director, The Smithsonian Associates	BARBARA TUCELING, *Acting*
Editor, Joseph Henry Papers	MARC ROTHENBERG
Under Secretary for Science	DAVID L. EVANS
Management Officer, Museum Support Center	ELIZABETH DIETRICH
Director, National Museum of Natural History	CRISTIAN SAMPER
Executive Director, National Science Resources Center	SALLY SHULER
Director, National Zoological Park	JOHN BERRY
Director, Office of Fellowships	CATHERINE HARRIS
Director, Smithsonian Astrophysical Observatory	CHARLES ALCOCK
Director, Smithsonian Center for Materials Research and Education	ROBERT KOESTLER
Director, Smithsonian Environmental Research Center	ANSON H. HINES
Director, Smithsonian Marine Station	VALERIE PAUL

Director, Smithsonian Tropical Research Institute	IRA RUBINOFF
Chief Information Officer	DENNIS SHAW
Chief Financial Officer	ALICE C. MARONI
Comptroller	ANDREW ZINO
Director, Office of Equal Employment and Minority Affairs	ERA MARSHALL
Director, Office of Human Resources	JAMES DOUGLAS
Director, Office of International Relations	FRANCINE BERKOWITZ
Director, Smithsonian Institution Archives	THOMAS SOAPES, *Acting*
Director, Smithsonian Institution Libraries	NANCY E. GWINN
General Counsel	JOHN E. HUERTA
Ombudsman	CHANDRA HEILMAN
Director of Facilities Engineering and Operations	WILLIAM W. BRUBAKER
Under Secretary for Art	NED RIFKIN
Director, Freer Gallery of Art and Arthur M. Sackler Gallery	JULIAN RABY
Director, Hirshhorn Museum and Sculpture Garden	OLGA VISO
Director, National Museum of African Art	SHARON PATTON
Chief Executive Officer of Smithsonian Business Ventures	GARY BEER
Editor-in-Chief, Smithsonian Magazine	CAREY WINFRFY
Publisher, Smithsonian Magazine	AMY P. WILKINS

The John F. Kennedy Center for the Performing Arts [1]

Chairman	STEPHEN A. SCHWARZMAN
President	MICHAEL M. KAISER

National Gallery of Art [1]

President	VICTORIA P. SANT
Director	EARL A. POWELL III

Woodrow Wilson International Center for Scholars [1]

Director	LEE H. HAMILTON
Deputy Director	MICHAEL H. VAN DUSEN
Chairman, Board of Trustees	JOSEPH GILDENHORN

The Smithsonian Institution is an independent trust instrumentality of the United States which comprises the world's largest museum and research complex. The Smithsonian includes 19 museums and galleries, the National Zoo, and research facilities in several States and the Republic of Panama. It holds more than 136 million artifacts and specimens in its trust for the American people. The Smithsonian is dedicated to public education, national service, and scholarship in the arts, sciences, history, and culture.

The Smithsonian Institution was created by an act of Congress on August 10, 1846 (20 U.S.C. 41 *et seq.*), to carry out the terms of the will of British scientist James Smithson (1765–1829), who in 1826 had bequeathed his entire estate to the United States "to found at Washington, under the name of the Smithsonian Institution, an establishment for the increase and diffusion of

[1] Administered under a separate Board of Trustees.

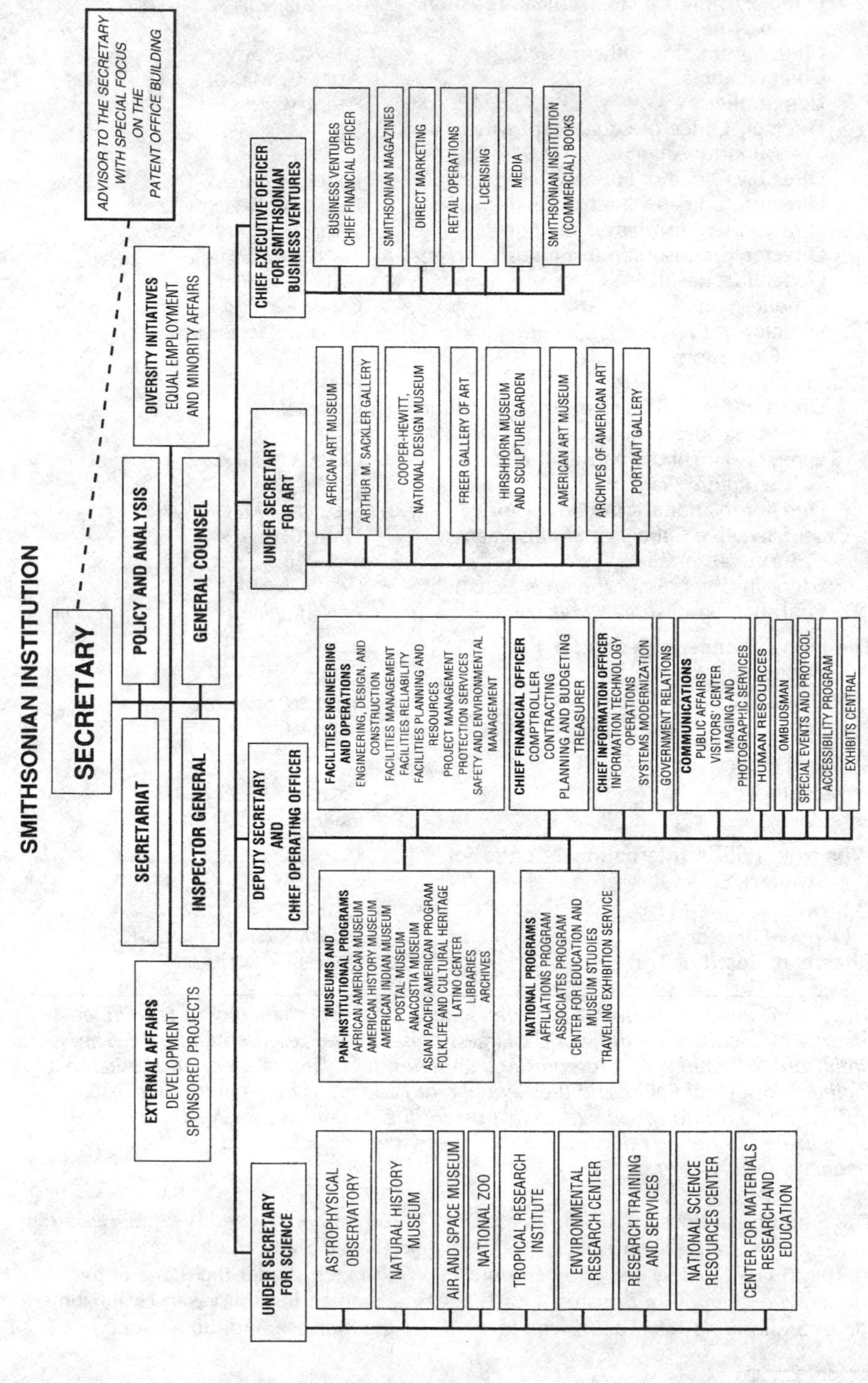
SMITHSONIAN INSTITUTION
SECRETARY
ADVISOR TO THE SECRETARY WITH SPECIAL FOCUS ON THE PATENT OFFICE BUILDING
SECRETARIAT
POLICY AND ANALYSIS
INSPECTOR GENERAL
GENERAL COUNSEL
EXTERNAL AFFAIRS
DEVELOPMENT
SPONSORED PROJECTS
DIVERSITY INITIATIVES
EQUAL EMPLOYMENT AND MINORITY AFFAIRS
UNDER SECRETARY FOR SCIENCE
ASTROPHYSICAL OBSERVATORY
NATURAL HISTORY MUSEUM
AIR AND SPACE MUSEUM
NATIONAL ZOO
TROPICAL RESEARCH INSTITUTE
ENVIRONMENTAL RESEARCH CENTER
RESEARCH TRAINING AND SERVICES
NATIONAL SCIENCE RESOURCES CENTER
CENTER FOR MATERIALS RESEARCH AND EDUCATION
DEPUTY SECRETARY AND CHIEF OPERATING OFFICER
MUSEUMS AND PAN-INSTITUTIONAL PROGRAMS
AFRICAN AMERICAN MUSEUM
AMERICAN HISTORY MUSEUM
AMERICAN INDIAN MUSEUM
POSTAL MUSEUM
ANACOSTIA MUSEUM
ASIAN PACIFIC AMERICAN PROGRAM
FOLKLIFE AND CULTURAL HERITAGE
LATINO CENTER
LIBRARIES
ARCHIVES
NATIONAL PROGRAMS
AFFILIATIONS PROGRAM
ASSOCIATES PROGRAM
CENTER FOR EDUCATION AND MUSEUM STUDIES
TRAVELING EXHIBITION SERVICE
FACILITIES ENGINEERING AND OPERATIONS
ENGINEERING, DESIGN, AND CONSTRUCTION
FACILITIES MANAGEMENT
FACILITIES RELIABILITY
FACILITIES PLANNING AND RESOURCES
PROJECT MANAGEMENT
PROTECTION SERVICES
SAFETY AND ENVIRONMENTAL MANAGEMENT
CHIEF FINANCIAL OFFICER
COMPTROLLER
CONTRACTING
PLANNING AND BUDGETING
TREASURER
CHIEF INFORMATION OFFICER
INFORMATION TECHNOLOGY OPERATIONS
SYSTEMS MODERNIZATION
GOVERNMENT RELATIONS
COMMUNICATIONS
PUBLIC AFFAIRS
VISITORS' CENTER
IMAGING AND PHOTOGRAPHIC SERVICES
HUMAN RESOURCES
OMBUDSMAN
SPECIAL EVENTS AND PROTOCOL
ACCESSIBILITY PROGRAM
EXHIBITS CENTRAL
UNDER SECRETARY FOR ART
AFRICAN ART MUSEUM
ARTHUR M. SACKLER GALLERY
COOPER-HEWITT, NATIONAL DESIGN MUSEUM
FREER GALLERY OF ART
HIRSHHORN MUSEUM AND SCULPTURE GARDEN
AMERICAN ART MUSEUM
ARCHIVES OF AMERICAN ART
PORTRAIT GALLERY
CHIEF EXECUTIVE OFFICER FOR SMITHSONIAN BUSINESS VENTURES
BUSINESS VENTURES CHIEF FINANCIAL OFFICER
SMITHSONIAN MAGAZINES
DIRECT MARKETING
RETAIL OPERATIONS
LICENSING
MEDIA
SMITHSONIAN INSTITUTION (COMMERCIAL) BOOKS

knowledge among men.'' On July 1, 1836, Congress accepted the legacy and pledged the faith of the United States to the charitable trust.

In September 1838, Smithson's legacy, which amounted to more than 100,000 gold sovereigns, was delivered to the mint at Philadelphia. Congress vested responsibility for administering the trust in the Secretary of the Smithsonian and the Smithsonian Board of Regents, composed of the Chief Justice, the Vice President, three Members of the Senate, three Members of the House of Representatives, and nine citizen members appointed by joint resolution of Congress. To carry out Smithson's mandate, the Institution executes the following functions:

—conducts scientific and scholarly research;

—publishes the results of studies, explorations, and investigations;

—preserves for study and reference more than 136 million artifacts, works of art, and scientific specimens;

—organizes exhibits representative of the arts, the sciences, and American history and culture;

—shares Smithsonian resources and collections with communities throughout the Nation; and

—engages in educational programming and national and international cooperative research.

Smithsonian activities are supported by its trust endowments and revenues; gifts, grants, and contracts; and funds appropriated to it by Congress. Admission to the museums in Washington, DC, is free.

Activities

Anacostia Museum The Museum, located in the historic Fort Stanton neighborhood of southeast Washington, serves as a national resource for exhibitions, historical documentation, and interpretive and educational programs relating to African-American history and culture.

For further information, contact the Anacostia Museum, 1901 Fort Place SE., Washington, DC 20020. Phone, 202–633–1000. Internet, www.si.edu/anacostia.

Archives of American Art The Archives contains the Nation's largest collection of documentary materials reflecting the history of visual arts in the United States. On the subject of art in America, it is the largest archives in the world, holding more than 16 million documents. The Archives gathers, preserves, and microfilms the papers of artists, craftsmen, collectors, dealers, critics, and art societies. These papers include manuscripts, letters, diaries, notebooks, sketchbooks, business records, clippings, exhibition catalogs, transcripts of tape-recorded interviews, and photographs of artists and their work. The Archives are housed at 750 9th Street NW., in Washington, DC.

For further information, contact the Archives of American Art, Smithsonian Institution, Washington, DC 20560. Phone, 202–275–2156. Internet, http://archivesofamericanart.si.edu/askus.htm.

Cooper-Hewitt National Design Museum The Museum is the only museum in the country devoted exclusively to historical and contemporary design. Collections include objects in such areas as applied arts and industrial design, drawings and prints, glass, metalwork, wallcoverings, and textiles. Changing exhibits and public programs seek to educate by exploring the role of design in daily life. The Museum is open daily except Mondays and holidays. The general admission fee is $12, $7 for students and senior citizens with ID, and free for members and children under 12.

For further information, contact Cooper-Hewitt National Design Museum, 2 East Ninety-First Street, New York, NY 10128. Phone, 212–849–8400. Internet, www.si.edu/ndm.

Freer Gallery of Art The building, the original collection, and an endowment were the gift of Charles Lang Freer (1854–1919). The Gallery houses one of the world's most renowned collections of Asian art, an important group of ancient Egyptian glass, early Christian manuscripts, and works by 19th and early 20th century American artists. The objects in the Asian collection represent the arts of East Asia, the Near East, and South and Southeast Asia, including paintings, manuscripts, scrolls, screens, ceramics, metalwork, glass, jade, lacquer, and sculpture. Members of the staff conduct research on objects in the collection and publish results in scholarly journals and books for general and scholarly audiences.

For further information, contact the Freer Gallery of Art, Jefferson Drive at Twelfth Street SW., Washington, DC 20560. Phone, 202–633–1000. Internet, www.asia.si.edu.

Hirshhorn Museum and Sculpture Garden From cubism to minimalism, the Museum houses major collections of modern and contemporary art. The nucleus of the collection is the gift and bequest of Joseph H. Hirshhorn (1899–1981). Supplementing the permanent collection are loan exhibitions. The Museum houses a collection research facility, a specialized art library, and a photographic archive, available for consultation by prior appointment. The outdoor sculpture garden is located nearby on the National Mall. There is an active program of public service and education, including docent tours, lectures on contemporary art and artists, and films of historic and artistic interest.

For further information, contact the Hirshhorn Museum and Sculpture Garden, Seventh Street and Independence Avenue SW., Washington, DC 20560. Phone, 202–633–1000. Internet, www.hirshhorn.si.edu.

National Air and Space Museum Created to memorialize the development and achievements of aviation and space flight, the Museum collects, displays, and preserves aeronautical and space flight artifacts of historical significance as well as documentary and artistic materials related to air and space. Among its artifacts are full-size planes, models, and instruments. Highlights of the collection include the Wright brothers' *Flyer,* Charles Lindbergh's *Spirit of St. Louis,* a Moon rock, and Apollo spacecraft. The exhibitions and study collections record human conquest of the air from its beginnings to recent achievements. The principal areas in which work is concentrated include flight craft of all types, space flight vehicles, and propulsion systems. Recent blockbuster exhibitions at this most popular museum have included "Star Wars: The Magic of Myth" and "Star Trek." The Museum's IMAX Theater and the 70-foot domed Einstein Planetarium are popular attractions. The Museum's Steven F. Udvar-Hazy Center at Washington Dulles International Airport, opened in December 2003. Its featured artifacts include a space shuttle and the *Enola Gay* B–29 World War II bomber.

For further information, contact the National Air and Space Museum, Sixth Street and Independence Avenue SW., Washington, DC 20560. Phone, 202–633–1000. Internet, www.nasm.si.edu.

National Museum of African Art This is the only art museum in the United States dedicated exclusively to portraying the creative visual traditions of Africa. Its research components, collection, exhibitions, and public programs establish the Museum as a primary source for the examination and discovery of the arts and culture of Africa. The collection includes works in wood, metal, fired clay, ivory, and fiber. The Eliot Elisofon Photographic Archives includes slides, photos, and film segments on Africa. There is also a specialized library.

For further information, contact the National Museum of African Art, 950 Independence Avenue SW., Washington, DC 20560. Phone, 202–633–1000. Internet, www.nmafa.si.edu.

National Museum of African American History and Culture The Museum was established in 2003 and will be the only national museum devoted exclusively to the documentation of African American life, art, history, and culture.

For further information, contact the National Museum of African American History and Culture, 470 L'Enfant Plaza SW., Washington, DC 20560. Phone, 202–633–1000. Internet, www.nmaahc.si.edu.

Smithsonian American Art Museum The Museum's art collection spans centuries of American painting, sculpture, folk art, photography, and graphic art. A major center for research in American art, the Museum has contributed to such resources as the Inventory of American Paintings Executed Before 1914; the Smithsonian Art Index; and the Inventory of American

Sculpture. The library, shared with the National Portrait Gallery, contains volumes on art, history, and biography, with special emphasis on the United States. The Old Patent Office Building, home to both the Smithsonian American Art Museum and the National Portrait Gallery, is currently closed for major renovation, during which time the museums are sponsoring traveling exhibits around the country. The Museum will reopen on July 1, 2006. Hundreds of images from the collection and extensive information on its collections, publications, and activities are available electronically (Internet, www.saam.si.edu).

For further information, contact the Smithsonian American Art Museum, Eighth and G Streets NW., Washington, DC 20560. Phone, 202–633–1000. Internet, www.americanart.si.edu.

Renwick Gallery The Gallery is dedicated to exhibiting crafts of all periods and to collecting 20th century American crafts. It offers changing exhibitions of American crafts and decorative arts, both historical and contemporary, and a rotating selection from its permanent collection. The Gallery's grand salon is elegantly furnished in the Victorian style of the 1860's and 1870's.

For further information, contact the Renwick Gallery, Seventeenth Street and Pennsylvania Avenue NW., Washington, DC 20560. Phone, 202–633–1000. Internet, www.saam.si.edu/collections/exhibits/renwick25.

National Museum of American History In pursuit of its fundamental mission to inspire a broader understanding of the United States and its people, the Museum provides learning opportunities, stimulates the imagination of visitors, and presents challenging ideas about the Nation's past. The Museum's exhibits provide a unique view of the American experience. Emphasis is placed upon innovative individuals representing a wide range of cultures, who have shaped our heritage, and upon science and the remaking of our world through technology. Exhibits draw upon strong collections in the sciences and engineering, agriculture, manufacturing, transportation, political memorabilia, costumes, musical instruments, coins, Armed Forces history, photography, computers, ceramics, and glass. Classic cars, icons of the American Presidency, First Ladies' gowns, musical instruments, the Star-Spangled Banner flag, Whitney's cotton gin, Morse's telegraph, the John Bull locomotive, Dorothy's ruby slippers from "The Wizard of Oz," and other American icons are highlights of the collection.

For further information, contact the National Museum of American History, Fourteenth Street and Constitution Avenue NW., Washington, DC 20560. Phone, 202–633–1000. Internet, www.americanhistory.si.edu.

National Museum of the American Indian The Museum was established in 1989, and the building on the National Mall opened September 2004. The collection of the Museum is comprised of the collection of the Museum of the American Indian, Heye Foundation, in New York City. It is an institution of living cultures dedicated to the collection, preservation, study, and exhibition of the life, languages, literature, history, and arts of the Native peoples of the Americas. Highlights include Northwest Coast carvings; dance masks; pottery and weaving from the Southwest; painted hides and garments from the North American Plains; goldwork of the Aztecs, Incas, and Maya; and Amazonian featherwork.

For further information, contact the National Museum of the American Indian, Fourth Street and Independence Avenue SW., Washington, DC 20560. Phone, 202–633–1000. Internet, www.nmai.si.edu.

National Museum of Natural History Dedicated to understanding the natural world and the place of humans in it, the Museum's permanent exhibits focus on human cultures, Earth sciences, biology, and anthropology, with the most popular displays featuring gemstones such as the Hope diamond, dinosaurs, insects, marine ecosystems, birds, and mammals. To celebrate the millennial anniversary of the journey of Leif Ericson to America, the Museum mounted a special exhibition titled Vikings: The North Atlantic Saga; the exhibition is now traveling around the Nation. A new IMAX theater offers large-format nature films. The Museum's encyclopedic collections comprise nearly 126 million specimens, making the Museum one of the world's foremost facilities for natural history research. The museum's four departments are anthropology, mineral sciences, paleobiology, and systematic biology. Doctorate-level staff researchers ensure the continued growth and value of the collection by conducting studies in the field and laboratory.

For further information, contact the National Museum of Natural History, Tenth Street and Constitution Avenue NW., Washington, DC 20560. Phone, 202–633–1000. Internet, www.mnh.si.edu.

National Portrait Gallery The Gallery was established in 1962 for the exhibition and study of portraiture depicting men and women who have made significant contributions to the history, development, and culture of the United States. The Gallery contains more than 19,000 works, including photographs and glass negatives. The first floor of the Gallery is devoted to changing exhibitions from the Gallery's collection of paintings, sculpture, prints, photographs, and drawings as well as to special portrait collections. On the second floor are featured the permanent collection of portraits of eminent Americans and the Hall of Presidents, including the famous Gilbert Stuart portrait-from-life of George Washington. The two-story American Victorian Renaissance Great Hall on the third floor of the gallery houses a Civil War exhibit, and is used for special events and public programs. A large library is shared with the Smithsonian American Art Museum and the Archives of American Art. The education department offers public programs; outreach programs for schools, senior adults, hospitals, and nursing homes; and walk-in and group tours. The Gallery is currently closed for renovation and will reopen July 1, 2006.

For further information, contact the National Portrait Gallery, Eighth and F Streets NW., Washington, DC 20560. Phone, 202–633–1000. Internet, www.npg.si.edu.

National Postal Museum The Museum houses the Nation's postal history and philatelic collection, the largest of its kind in the world, with more than 13 million objects. The Museum is devoted to the history of America's mail service, and major galleries include exhibits on mail service in Colonial times and during the Civil War, the Pony Express, modern mail service, automation, mail transportation, and the art of letters, as well as displays of the Museum's priceless stamp collection. Highlights include three mail planes, a replica of a railway mail car, displays of historic letters, handcrafted mail boxes, and rare U.S. and foreign issue stamps and covers.

For further information, contact the National Postal Museum, 2 Massachusetts Avenue NE., Washington, DC 20560. Phone, 202–633–1000. Internet, www.si.edu/postal.

National Zoological Park The National Zoo encompasses 163 acres along Rock Creek Park in Northwest Washington, DC. Established in 1889, the Zoo is developing into a biopark with live animals, botanic gardens and aquaria, and artworks with animal themes. The collection today has animals ranging in size and diversity from leaf-cutter ants to giraffes. The zoo recently acquired a new pair of young giant pandas, Mei Xiang and Tian Tian. In July 2005, Mei Xiang gave birth to a cub, Tia Shan. Recent exhibits include "Amazonia," a simulated tropical rain forest; the "Pollinarium" exhibit; and the Reptile Discovery Center, featuring the world's largest lizards, Komodo dragons. Research on genetics, animal behavior, and reproductive studies has given the National Zoo a leadership role among the Nation's conservation institutions.

For further information, contact the National Zoo, 3000 Connecticut Avenue NW., Washington, DC 20008. Phone, 202–673–4717. Internet, www.si.edu/natzoo.

Center for Folklife and Cultural Heritage The Center is responsible for research, documentation, and presentation of grassroots cultural traditions. It maintains a documentary collection and produces Smithsonian Folkways Recordings, educational materials, documentary films, publications, and traveling exhibits, as well as the annual

Smithsonian Folklife Festival on the National Mall. Recent Folklife Festivals have featured a range of American music styles, a number of State tributes, and performers from around the world. Admission to the festival is free. The 2-week program includes Fourth of July activities on the National Mall.

For further information, contact the Center for Folklife and Cultural Heritage, Suite 4100, 750 9th Street NW., Washington, DC 20560. Phone, 202–633–1000. Internet, www.folklife.si.edu.

International Center The International Center supports Smithsonian activities abroad and serves as liaison for the Smithsonian's international interests. The Smithsonian seeks to encourage a broadening of public understanding of the histories, cultures, and natural environments of regions throughout the world. The International Center provides a meeting place and an organizational channel to bring together the world's scholars, museum professionals, and the general public, to attend and participate in conferences, public forums, lectures, and workshops.

For further information, contact the Office of International Relations, MRC 705, 1100 Jefferson Drive SW., Washington, DC 20560. Phone, 202–633–1000.

Arthur M. Sackler Gallery This Asian art museum opened in 1987 on the National Mall. Changing exhibitions drawn from major collections in the United States and abroad, as well as from the permanent holdings of the Sackler Gallery, are displayed in the distinctive below-ground museum. The Gallery's growing permanent collection is founded on a group of art objects from China, South and Southeast Asia, and the ancient Near East that was given to the Smithsonian by Arthur M. Sackler (1913–1987). The Museum's current collection features Persian manuscripts; Japanese paintings; ceramics, prints, and textiles; sculptures from India; and paintings and metalware from China, Korea, Japan, and Southeast Asia. The Sackler Gallery is connected by an underground exhibition space to the neighboring Freer Gallery.

For further information, contact the Arthur M. Sackler Gallery, 1050 Independence Avenue SW., Washington, DC 20560. Phone, 202–633–1000. Internet, www.asia.si.edu.

Smithsonian Institution Archives The Smithsonian Institution Archives acquires, preserves, and makes available for research the official records of the Smithsonian Institution and the papers of individuals and organizations associated with the Institution or with its work. These holdings document the growth of the Smithsonian and the development of American science, history, and art.

For further information, contact the Smithsonian Institution Archives, MRC 414, 900 Jefferson Drive SW., Washington, DC 20560. Phone, 202–633–1000.

Smithsonian Astrophysical Observatory The Smithsonian Astrophysical Observatory and the Harvard College Observatory have coordinated research activities under a single director in a cooperative venture, Harvard-Smithsonian Center for Astrophysics. The Center's research activities are organized in the following areas of study: atomic and molecular physics, radio and geoastronomy, high-energy astrophysics, optical and infrared astronomy, planetary sciences, solar and stellar physics, and theoretical astrophysics. Research results are published in the *Center Preprint Series* and other technical and nontechnical bulletins, and distributed to scientific and educational institutions around the world.

For more information, contact the Smithsonian Astrophysical Observatory, 60 Garden Street, Cambridge, MA 02138. Phone, 617–495–7461. Internet, www.cfa.harvard.edu/saohome.

Smithsonian Center for Materials Research and Education The Center researches preservation, conservation, and technical study and analysis of collection materials. Its researchers investigate the chemical and physical processes that are involved in the care of art, artifacts, and specimens, and attempt to formulate conditions and procedures for storage, exhibit, and stabilization that optimize the preservation of these objects. In interdisciplinary collaborations with archeologists, anthropologists, and art historians, natural and physical scientists study and analyze objects from the collections and related materials to expand knowledge and understanding of their historical and scientific context.

For further information, contact the Smithsonian Center for Materials Research and Education, Museum Support Center, Suitland, MD 20746. Phone, 301–238–1240.

Smithsonian Environmental Research Center (SERC) The Center is the leading national research center for understanding environmental issues in the coastal zone. SERC is dedicated to increasing knowledge of the biological and physical processes that sustain life on Earth. The Center, located near the Chesapeake Bay, trains future generations of scientists to address ecological questions of the Nation and the globe.

For further information, contact the Smithsonian Environmental Research Center, 647 Contees Wharf Road, Edgewater, MD 21037. Phone, 443–482–2200. Internet, www.serc.si.edu.

Smithsonian Institution Libraries The Smithsonian Institution Libraries include more than one million volumes (among them 40,000 rare books) with strengths in natural history, art, science, humanities, and museology. Many volumes are available through interlibrary loan.

For further information, contact the Smithsonian Institution Libraries, Tenth Street and Constitution Avenue NW., Washington, DC 20560. Phone, 202–633–2240. Internet, www.sil.si.edu. E-mail, libhelp@sil.si.edu.

Smithsonian Institution Traveling Exhibition Service (SITES) Since 1952, SITES has been committed to making Smithsonian exhibitions available to millions of people who cannot view them firsthand at the Smithsonian museums. Exhibitions on art, history, and science (including such exhibits as "Full Deck Art Quilts," "Red, Hot, and Blue: A Salute to American Musicals," and "Hubble Space Telescope") travel to more than 250 locations each year.

For further information, contact the Smithsonian Institution Traveling Exhibition Service, Suite 7103, 470 L'Enfant Plaza SW., Washington, DC 20024. Phone, 202–633–1000. Internet, www.si.edu/organiza/offices/sites.

Smithsonian Marine Station The research institute features a state-of-the-art laboratory where Station scientists catalog species and study marine plants and animals. Among the most important projects being pursued at the site is the search for possible causes of fish kills including *pfiesteria* and other organisms.

For further information, contact the Smithsonian Marine Station, 701 Seaway Drive, Fort Pierce, FL 34946. Phone, 772–465–6630. Internet, www.sms.si.edu.

Smithsonian Tropical Research Institute (STRI) The Institute is a research organization for advanced studies of tropical ecosystems. Headquartered in the Republic of Panama, STRI maintains extensive facilities in the Western Hemisphere tropics. It is the base of a corps of tropical researchers who study the evolution, behavior, ecology, and history of tropical species of systems ranging from coral reefs to rain forests.

For further information, contact the Smithsonian Tropical Research Institute, 1100 Jefferson Drive SW., Suite 3123, Washington, DC 20560. Phone, 202–633–4016. Phone (Panama), 011–507–212–8000. Internet, www.stri.org.

The John F. Kennedy Center for the Performing Arts The Kennedy Center is the only official memorial in Washington, DC, to President Kennedy. Since its opening in 1971, the Center has presented a year-round program of the finest in music, dance, and drama from the United States and abroad. The Kennedy Center box offices are open daily, and general information and tickets may be obtained by calling 202–467–4600 or 202–416–8524 (TDD). Full-time students, senior citizens over the age of 65, enlisted personnel of grade E–4 and below, fixed low-income groups, and the disabled may purchase tickets for most performances at a 50-percent discount through the Specially Priced Ticket Program. This program is designed to make the Center accessible to all, regardless of economic circumstance. Visitor services are provided by the Friends of the Kennedy Center volunteers. Tours are available free of charge between 10 a.m. and 5 p.m. on weekdays and between 10 a.m. and 1 p.m. on weekends. Free performances are given everyday at 6 p.m. on the Millennium Stage in the Grand Foyer.

For further information, contact the Kennedy Center. Phone, 202–467–4600. Internet, www.kennedy-center.org.

National Gallery of Art The Gallery houses one of the finest collections in the world, illustrating Western man's achievements in painting, sculpture, and the graphic arts. The West Building includes European (13th–early 20th century) and American (18th–early 20th century) works. An extensive survey of Italian painting and sculpture, including the only painting by Leonardo da Vinci in the Western Hemisphere, is presented here. Rich in Dutch masters and French impressionists, the collection offers superb surveys of American, British, Flemish, Spanish, and 15th and 16th century German art, as well as Renaissance medals and bronzes, Chinese porcelains, and about 90,000 works of graphic art from the 12th to the 20th centuries. The East Building collections and Sculpture Garden include important works by major 20th century artists. The Gallery represents a partnership of Federal and private resources. Its operations and maintenance are supported through Federal appropriations, and all of its acquisitions of works of art, as well as numerous special programs, are made possible through private donations and funds. Graduate and postgraduate research is conducted under a fellowship program; education programs for schoolchildren and the general public are conducted daily; and an extension service distributes loans of audiovisual materials, including films, slide lectures, and slide sets.

For further information, contact the National Gallery of Art. Phone, 202–737–4215. TTY, 202–842–6176. Internet, www.nga.gov.

Woodrow Wilson International Center for Scholars The Center was established by Congress in 1968 as the Nation's official memorial to its 28th President. The Center is a nonpartisan institution of advanced study that promotes scholarship in public affairs. The Center convenes scholars and policymakers, businesspeople, and journalists in a neutral forum for open, serious, and informed dialogue. The Center supports research in social sciences and humanities, with an emphasis on history, political science, and international relations.

For further information, contact the Scholar Selection and Services Office, Woodrow Wilson Center, One Woodrow Wilson Plaza, 1300 Pennsylvania Avenue NW., Washington, DC 20004–3027. Phone, 202–691–4170. Fax, 202–691–4001. Internet, www.wilsoncenter.org.

Sources of Information

Smithsonian Institution

Contracts and Small Business Activities Information regarding procurement of supplies, property management and utilization services for Smithsonian Institution organizations, and contracts for construction, services, etc., may be obtained from the Director, Office of Contracting, Smithsonian Institution, Washington, DC 20560. Phone, 202–275–1600.

Education and Research Write to the Directors of the following offices at the Smithsonian Institution, Washington, DC 20560: Office of Fellowships and Grants, Center for Folklife and Cultural Heritage, National Science Resources Center; and Smithsonian Center for Education and Museum Studies.

Electronic Access Information about the Smithsonian Institution is available electronically through the Internet at www.si.edu or www.smithsonian.org.

Employment Employment information for the Smithsonian is available from the Office of Human Resources, Smithsonian Institution, Suite 6100, 750 Ninth Street NW., Washington, DC 20560. Phone, 202–275–1102. Recorded message, 202–287–3102.

Media Affairs Members of the press may contact the Smithsonian Office of

Public Affairs, 1000 Jefferson Drive SW., Washington, DC 20560. Phone, 202–633–2400. Internet, http://newsdesk.si.edu.

Memberships For information about Smithsonian membership (Resident Program), write to the Smithsonian Associates, MRC 701, 1100 Jefferson Drive SW., Washington, DC 20560. Phone, 202–357–3030. For information about Smithsonian membership (National Program), call 202–357–4800. For information about the Contributing Membership, call 202–357–1699. For information about the Young Benefactors, call 202–786–9049.

Information about activities of the Friends of the National Zoo and their magazine, *The Zoogoer,* is available by writing to FONZ, National Zoological Park, Washington, DC 20008. Phone, 202–673–4950.

Photographs Color and black-and-white photographs and slides are available to Government agencies, research and educational institutions, publishers, and the general public from the Smithsonian photographic archives. A searchable database of images is available through the Internet. Information, order forms, and price lists may be obtained from the Office of Imaging, Printing, and Photographic Services, MAH CB–054, Smithsonian Institution, Washington, DC 20560. Internet, http://photos.si.edu. E-mail, psdmx@sivm.si.edu.

Publications To purchase the Smithsonian Institution's annual report, *Smithsonian Year,* call 202–633–2400. The Smithsonian Institution Press publishes a range of books and studies related to the sciences, technology, history, culture, air and space, and the arts. A book catalog is available from Publications Sales, Smithsonian Books or Smithsonian Institution University Press, 1111 North Capitol Street, Washington, DC 20002. Phone, 800–782–4612. To purchase a recording of the *Smithsonian Folkways Recordings,* call 800–410–9815. Internet, www.si.edu/folkways.

A free brochure providing a brief guide to the Smithsonian Institution is published in English and several foreign languages. For a copy, call Visitor Information, 202–633–1000, or pick up a copy at the information desks in the museums. A visitor's guide for individuals with disabilities is also available.

Smithsonian Institution Research Reports, containing news of current research projects in the arts, sciences, and history that are being conducted by Smithsonian staff, is produced by the Smithsonian Office of Public Affairs, Smithsonian Institution Building, 1000 Jefferson Drive SW., Washington, DC 20560. Phone, 202–633–2400.

To request a copy of *Smithsonian Runner,* a newsletter about Native American-related activities at the Smithsonian, contact the National Museum of the American Indian, Smithsonian Institution, Washington, DC 20560. Phone, 800–242–NMAI.

For the newsletter *Art to Zoo* for teachers of fourth through eighth graders, write to the Smithsonian Center for Education and Museum Studies, Room 1163, MRC 402, Arts and Industries Building, Washington, DC 20560. Phone, 202–357–2425.

Telephone *Dial-A-Museum,* 202–633–1000 provides a taped message with daily announcements on new exhibits and special events. For a Spanish listing of Smithsonian events, call 202–633–9126.

Tours For information about museum and gallery tours, contact the Smithsonian Information Center, 1000 Jefferson Drive SW., Washington, DC 20560. Phone, 202–633–1000. School groups are welcome. Special behind-the-scenes tours are offered through the various memberships.

Visitor Information The Smithsonian Information Center, located in the original Smithsonian building, commonly known as "The Castle," provides general orientation, through films, computer interactive programs, and visitor information specialists, to help members and the public learn about the national collections, museum events, exhibitions, and special programs. Write to the Smithsonian Information Center, 1000 Jefferson Drive SW., Washington, DC

20560. Phone, 202–633–1000. TTY, 202–357–1729.

Volunteer Service Opportunities The Smithsonian Institution welcomes volunteers and offers a variety of interesting service opportunities. For information, write to the Visitor Information and Associates' Reception Center, 1000 Jefferson Drive SW., Washington, DC 20560. Phone, 202–633–1000. TTY, 202–357–1729.

John F. Kennedy Center for the Performing Arts

Contracts and Small Business Activities Contact the John F. Kennedy Center for the Performing Arts, Washington, DC 20566.

Education and Research For information regarding Kennedy Center education programs, contact the John F. Kennedy Center for the Performing Arts, Washington, DC 20566. Phone, 202–416–8000.

Electronic Access Information on the John F. Kennedy Center for the Performing Arts is available through the Internet at www.kennedy-center.org.

Employment For information on employment opportunities at the John F. Kennedy Center for the Performing Arts, contact the Human Resources Department, Washington, DC 20566. Phone, 202–416–8610.

Memberships Information about the national and local activities of Friends of the Kennedy Center (including the bimonthly *Kennedy Center News* for members) is available at the information desks within the Center or by writing to Friends of the Kennedy Center, Washington, DC 20566.

Special Functions Inquiries regarding the use of Kennedy Center facilities for special functions may be directed to the Office of Special Events, John F. Kennedy Center for the Performing Arts, Washington, DC 20566. Phone, 202–416–8000.

Theater Operations Inquiries regarding the use of the Kennedy Center's theaters may be addressed to the Booking Coordinator, John F. Kennedy Center for the Performing Arts, Washington, DC 20566. Phone, 202–416–8000.

Volunteer Service Opportunities For information about volunteer opportunities at the Kennedy Center, write to Friends of the Kennedy Center, Washington, DC 20566. Phone, 202–416–8000.

National Gallery of Art

Calendar of Events To access on the Web, go to www.nga.gov/ginfo/calendar.htm. To receive e-mail notices when new calendars go online, send your name, street address, and e-mail address to calendar@nga.gov.

Concerts Concerts by world-renowned musicians are presented Sunday evenings from October through June. For information, call the Concert Line at 202–842–6941. Internet, www.nga.gov/programs/music.htm.

Contracts and Small Business Activities Contact National Gallery of Art, Office of Procurement and Contracts, 2000B South Club Drive, Landover, MD 20785. Phone, 202–842–6745.

Educational Resources The National Gallery of Art circulates slide programs, teaching packets, videos, CD–ROMs, videodiscs, and DVDs at no charge to individuals, schools and civic organizations throughout the country. Contact the Department of Education Resources, National Gallery of Art, 2000B South Club Drive, Landover, MD 20785. Phone, 202–842–6273. Internet, www.nga.gov/education/classroom/loanfinder. Please write or e-mail EdResources@nga.gov to request a free catalog of programs.

Electronic Access Information on the National Gallery of Art is available through the Internet at www.nga.gov. NGAkids (www.nga.gov/kids) includes interactive activities and adventures with works of art in the Gallery's collection and an animated tale set in the Gallery's Sculpture Garden.

Employment For information on employment opportunities at the National Gallery, contact the Personnel Office, National Gallery of Art, 601 Pennsylvania Avenue South NW., 2nd Floor, Washington, DC 20004. Phone, 202–842–6282. TDD, 202–842–6176.

Internet, www.nga.gov/resources/employ.htm.

Family Programs The Gallery offers a full range of free family programs suitable for children ages 4 and up, including workshops, children's films, music performances, and storytelling. Phone, 202–789–3030. For detailed information, visit www.nga.gov/kids.

Fellowships For information about research fellowship programs, contact the Center for Advanced Study in the Visual Arts. Phone, 202–842–6482. Fax, 202–842–6733. Internet, www.nga.gov/resources/casva.htm.

Films An ongoing free program of independent films, major retrospectives, classic cinema, and area premieres are presented. Visiting filmmakers and scholars are often invited to discuss films with the audience following screenings. The auditorium is equipped with an FM wireless listening system for the hearing impaired. Receivers, ear phones, and neck loops are available at the East Building Art Information Desk near the main entrance. Call 202–842–6799 for current information. Internet, www.nga.gov/programs/film.htm.

Internships For information about National Gallery internship programs for college graduates, master's degree students, and Ph.D. candidates, contact the Department of Academic Programs, National Gallery of Art, 2000B South Club Drive, Landover, MD 20785. E-mail, intern@nga.gov. Phone, 202–842–6257. Fax, 202–842–6935.

Lectures An ongoing schedule of lectures, symposia, and works in progress are free and open to the public on a first-come, first-serve basis. For more information, please visit our Web site at www.nga.gov/programs/lecture.htm.

Library The Gallery's collection of more than 300,000 books and periodicals on the history, theory, and criticism of art and architecture emphasizes Western art from the Middle Ages to the present, and American art from the Colonial era to the present. The library is open by appointment on Monday (from 12 noon to 4:30 p.m.) and Tuesday through Friday (from 10 a.m. to 4:30 p.m.), and is closed on all Federal holidays. Adult researchers may gain access to the library by calling 202–842–6511. Internet, www.nga.gov/resources/dldesc.htm.

Library Image Collections The Department of Image Collections is the study and research center for images of Western art and architecture at the National Gallery of Art. The collection now numbers nearly 10 million photographs, slides, negatives, and microform images, making it one of the largest resources of its kind. The Department serves the Gallery's staff, members of the Center for Advanced Study in the Visual Arts, visiting scholars, and serious adult researchers. The library is open by appointment on Monday (from 12 noon to 4:30 p.m.) and Tuesday through Friday (from 10 a.m. to 4:30 p.m.), and is closed on all Federal holidays. Phone, 202–842–6026. Internet, www.nga.gov/resources/dlidesc.htm.

Memberships The Circle of the National Gallery of Art is a membership program which provides support for special projects for which Federal funds are not available. For more information about membership in the Circle of the National Gallery of Art, please write to The Circle, National Gallery of Art, Washington, DC 20565. Phone, 202–842–6450. Internet, www.nga.gov/ginfo/involved.htm.

Publications The National Gallery shop makes available quality reproductions and publications about the Gallery's collections. To order, call 202–842–6002. Selected items are also available for sale on the Web site at www.nga.gov/shop. The Office of Press and Public Information offers a free bimonthly calendar of events, which can be ordered by calling 202–842–6662, or through e-mail at calendar@nga.gov. The calendar and *Brief Guide to the National Gallery of Art* are also available at art information desks throughout the Gallery or by calling Visitor Services at 202–842–6691.

Radio A 3-minute program, "This Week at the National Gallery," airs Sundays at 10:43 a.m. on WGMS, 103.5

FM, Washington, and Saturday at 12:55 p.m. on WBJC, 91.5 FM, Baltimore. It features interviews with art experts, artists, and museum specialists about exhibitions, the permanent collection, and various Gallery activities.

Tours The Education Division of the National Gallery of Art offers gallery talks and lectures. For further information about tours for adults, please call 202–842–6247. For information about school tours, please see our Web site at www.nga.gov/education/school.htm. Information about all tours can be found at www.nga.gov/programs/tours.htm.

Visitor Services The Visitor Services Office of the National Gallery of Art provides individual assistance to those with special needs, responds to written and telephone requests, and provides information to those planning to visit the Washington, DC, area. For more information, write to the National Gallery of Art, Office of Visitor Services, Washington, DC 20565. Phone, 202–842–6691. Internet, www.nga.gov/ginfo/disabled.htm.

Volunteer Opportunities For information about volunteering as a docent or as an Art Information Desk volunteer, please call Volunteer Opportunities at 202–789–3013. You may also visit our Web site at www.nga.gov/education/volunteer.htm.

Library Volunteering Phone, 202–842–6510. Internet, www.nga.gov/ginfo/involved.htm.

Horticulture Volunteers Phone, 202–842–6844.

Works on Paper Works of art on paper that are not on view may be seen by appointment on weekdays by calling 202–842–6380. The Matisse cutouts are on view in the Tower from 10 a.m. to 2 p.m., Monday through Saturday, and from 11 a.m. to 3 p.m. on Sunday.

Woodrow Wilson Center for International Scholars

Electronic Access Information on the Woodrow Wilson Center for International Scholars is available through the Internet at www.wilsoncenter.org.

Employment For information on employment opportunities at the Woodrow Wilson Center, contact the Office of Human Resources, One Woodrow Wilson Plaza, 1300 Pennsylvania Avenue NW., Washington, DC 2004–3027. Internet, www.wilsoncenter.org/hr/index.htm.

Fellowships and Internships The Woodrow Wilson Center offers residential fellowships that allow academics, public officials, journalists, business professionals, and others to pursue their research and writing at the Center, while interacting with policymakers in Washington. The Center also invites public policy scholars and senior scholars from a variety of disciplines to conduct research for varying lengths of time in residence. For more information, call 202–691–4213. The Center also has a year-round need for interns to assist the program and projects staff and to act as research assistants for scholars and fellows. For more information, call 202–691–4053.

Media Affairs Members of the press may contact the Woodrow Wilson Center at 202–691–4016.

Publications The Woodrow Wilson Center publishes a monthly newsletter *Centerpoint*, and books written by staff and visiting scholars and fellows, through the Wilson Center Press. It also produces *Dialogue*, a weekly radio and television program about national and international affairs, history, and culture. For more information, call 202–691–4016.

Visitor Services To hear a listing of events at the Woodrow Wilson Center, call 202–691–4188. All events, unless otherwise noted, are free and open to the public. Please note that a photo identification is required for entry.

For further information, contact the Smithsonian Information Center, 1000 Jefferson Drive SW., Washington, DC 20560. Phone, 202–633–1000. TDD, 202–357–1729. Internet, www.smithsonian.org.

STATE JUSTICE INSTITUTE

Suite 600, 1650 King Street, Alexandria, VA 22314
Phone, 703–684–6100. Internet, www.statejustice.org.

Board of Directors:

Chairman	ROBERT A. MILLER
Vice Chairman	JOSEPH F. BACA
Secretary	SANDRA A. O'CONNOR
Executive Committee Member	KEITH MCNAMARA
Members	TERRENCE B. ADAMSON, ROBERT N. BALDWIN, CARLOS R. GARZA, SOPHIA H. HALL, TOMMY JEWELL, ARTHUR MCGIVERIN, (VACANCY)

Officers:

Executive Director	KEVIN LINSKEY
Deputy Director	KATHY SCHWARTZ

The State Justice Institute awards grants to improve judicial administration in the State courts of the United States.

The State Justice Institute was created by the State Justice Institute Act of 1984 (42 U.S.C. 10701) as a private, nonprofit corporation to further the development and improvement of judicial administration in the State courts.

The Institute is supervised by a Board of Directors consisting of 11 members appointed by the President with the advice and consent of the Senate. The Board is statutorily composed of six judges, a State court administrator, and four members of the public, of whom no more than two can be of the same political party.

The goals of the Institute are to fulfill the following duties:

—direct a national program of assistance to ensure that all U.S. citizens have ready access to a fair and effective judicial system;

—foster coordination and cooperation with the Federal Judiciary;

—serve as a clearinghouse and information center for the dissemination of information regarding State judicial systems; and

—encourage education for judges and support personnel of State court systems.

To accomplish these broad objectives, the Institute is authorized to provide funds, through grants, cooperative agreements, and contracts, to State courts and organizations that can assist in the achievement of improving judicial administration of the State courts.

Sources of Information

Inquiries concerning the following programs and activities should be directed to the specified office of the State Justice Institute, Suite 600, 1650 King Street, Alexandria, VA 22314. Phone, 703–684–6100.

Grants—Deputy Director.

Publications, consumer information, speakers, Privacy Act/Freedom of Information Act requests—Executive Director.

Information regarding the programs and services of the State Justice Institute is also available through the Internet, at www.statejustice.org.

For further information, contact the State Justice Institute, Suite 600, 1650 King Street, Alexandria, VA 22314. Phone, 703–684–6100. Internet, www.statejustice.org.

UNITED STATES INSTITUTE OF PEACE

Suite 200, 1200 Seventeenth Street NW., Washington, DC 20036–3011
Phone, 202–457–1700. Fax, 202–429–6063. Internet, www.usip.org.

Board of Directors:	
Public Members:	
Chairman	J. ROBINSON WEST
Vice Chairman	MARIA OTERO
Members	BETTY F. BUMPERS, HOLLY J. BURKHALTER, CHESTER A. CROCKER, LAURIE S. FULTON, CHARLES HORNER, SEYMOUR MARTIN LIPSET, MORA L. MCLEAN, BARBARA W. SNELLING, (2 VACANCIES)
Ex officio:	
Assistant Secretary of State for Democracy, Human Rights, and Labor	BARRY F. LOWENKRON
President, National Defense University	MICHAEL M. DUNN
Under Secretary of Defense for International Security Affairs	PETER W. RODMAN
President, U.S. Institute of Peace	RICHARD H. SOLOMON
Officials:	
President	RICHARD H. SOLOMON
Vice President, Management	PATRICIA THOMSON
Senior Counselor/Vice President for Headquarters Project	CHARLES E. NELSON
Vice President, Education Program	PAMELA AALL
Vice President, Grants and Fellowships	JUDITH M. BARSALOW
Director, Jeannette Rankin Library Program	(VACANCY)
Director, Jennings Randolph Fellowship Program for International Peace	(VACANCY)
Vice President for the Center for Conflict Analysis and Prevention	PAUL B. STARES
Associate Vice President, Rule of Law	NEIL J. KRITZ
Vice President, Professional Training Program	MICHAEL LEKSON
Vice President, Center for Postconflict Peacebuilding	DANIEL P. SERWER
Vice President, Center for Mediation and Conflict Resolution	DAVID R. SMOCK
Director, Virtual Diplomacy Initiative	(VACANCY)
Director, Office of Public Affairs and Communications	PAMELA KEETON
Director, Office of Publications	(VACANCY)

The United States Institute of Peace promotes research, policy analysis, education, and training on international peace and conflict resolution.

The United States Institute of Peace is an independent Federal institution created and funded by Congress to develop and disseminate knowledge about international peace and conflict resolution. The Institute addresses this mandate in three principal ways:

—by expanding basic and applied knowledge about the origins, nature, and processes of peace and war, encompassing the widest spectrum of approaches and insights;

—by disseminating this knowledge to officials, policymakers, diplomats, and others engaged in efforts to promote international peace; and

—by supporting education and training programs and providing information for secondary and university-level teachers and students and the general public.

Programs

The Education Program supports educational activities and curricula that help teachers and students, in the United States and abroad, understand international conflict resolution and build the capacities of future peacemakers.

The Jennings Randolph Program for International Peace each year awards Senior Fellowships to 12–15 foreign policy scholars, policymakers, and journalists who conduct research on aspects of international conflict and peace. The Fellowship Program also awards nonresident Peace Scholar Dissertation Fellowships to students and U.S. universities researching and writing doctoral dissertations on international peace and conflict.

In addition to its in-house collections, the Jeannette Rankin Library has placed online the full texts of numerous peace agreements and documents relating to truth commissions plus annotated links to related Web sites.

The Grants Program administers the Institute's program of financial support for research, education, training, and the dissemination of information on international peace and conflict resolution. Grants are made for both solicited and unsolicited components.

The Office of Public Outreach helps provide the work of the Institute to a range of audiences through the media, convening public events, and scheduling speaking engagements by Institute specialists.

The Office of Publications oversees the publication of a broad range of products concerned with various aspects of international conflict and its resolution. Institute publications are available by request, or by free subscription while other items are available for purchase.

The Research and Studies Program develops and disseminates knowledge on the prevention, management, and peaceful resolution of conflicts through working groups, public meetings, written products, and other forms of research and analysis.

The Rule of Law Program refines principles of the rule of law articulated by various international bodies and provides governments and policymakers with practical guidance for their implementation.

The Training Program offers interactive programs that help government officials, military and police personnel, international organization representatives, and others interested acquire skills to handle all phases of conflict.

The Office of Peace and Stability Operations applies the knowledge and lessons learned from other conflict resolution experiences to active zones of conflict abroad that are of highest priority to U.S. interests.

Special Initiatives

The Balkans Initiative works to promote peace and reconciliation in the former Yugoslavia and to build consensus on Balkans policy and the U.S. role in maintaining peace.

The Special Initiative on the Muslim World addresses a broad range of political, social, cultural, and religious questions. It explores the prospects for long-term understanding between the Western and Islamic worlds, and develops crisis management strategies for resolving conflicts.

The Religion and Peacemaking Initiative enhances the capacity of faith communities to be forces for peace. It focuses on the role of religion in world conflicts and the applicability of human rights.

The Virtual Diplomacy Initiative helps scholars and practitioners better understand and apply information and communications technologies in preventing, managing, and resolving international conflict.

Sources of Information

Electronic access to the Institute is available through the Internet at www.usip.org.

For further information, contact the Office of Congressional and Public Affairs, United States Institute of Peace, 1200 Seventeenth Street NW., Suite 200, Washington, DC 20036–3011. Phone, 202–457–1700. Internet, www.usip.org.

SELECTED MULTILATERAL ORGANIZATIONS

MULTILATERAL INTERNATIONAL ORGANIZATIONS IN WHICH THE UNITED STATES PARTICIPATES

Explanatory note: The United States participates in the organizations named below in accordance with the provisions of treaties, other international agreements, congressional legislation, or executive arrangements. In some cases, no financial contribution is involved.

Various commissions, councils, or committees subsidiary to the organizations listed here are not named separately on this list. These include the international bodies for narcotics control, which are subsidiary to the United Nations.

I. United Nations, Specialized Agencies, and International Atomic Energy Agency

Food and Agricultural Organization
International Agency for Research in Cancer
International Atomic Energy Agency
International Civil Aviation Organization
International Fund for Agriculture Development
International Labor Organization
International Maritime Organization
International Telecommunication Union
United Nations Educational, Scientific and Cultural Organization (UNESCO)
Universal Postal Union
World Health Organization
World Intellectual Property Organization
World Meteorological Organization

II. Peacekeeping

United Nations Disengagement Observer Force (Golan Heights)
United Nations Force in Cyprus
United Nations Interim Force in Lebanon
United Nations International Criminal Tribunal—Rwanda
United Nations International Criminal Tribunal—Yugoslavia
United Nations Iraq-Kuwait Observer Mission
United Nations Mission in Bosnia-Herzegovina
United Nations Mission in the Democratic Republic of Congo
United Nations Mission in Kosovo
United Nations Mission of Observers in Tajikistan
United Nations Mission for the Referendum in Western Sahara
United Nations Observer Mission in Angola
United Nations Observer Mission in Georgia
United Nations Observer Mission in Sierra Leone
United Nations Prevention Deployment Force
United Nations Transitional Administration in East Timor
United Nations Transitional Administration in Eastern Slovenia

III. Inter-American Organizations

Border Environment Cooperation Commission
Inter-American Center of Tax Administrators
Inter-American Indian Institute
Inter-American Institute for Cooperation on Agriculture

Inter-American Institute for Global Change Research
Inter-American Tropical Tuna Commission
Organization of American States
Pan American Health Organization (PAHO)
Pan American Institute of Geography and History
Pan American Railway Congress Association
Postal Union of the Americas and Spain and Portugal (PUASP)

IV. Regional Organizations

Asia Pacific Energy Research Center
Colombo Plan Council
Great Lakes Fishery Commission
International Energy Agency
North Atlantic Assembly
North Atlantic Treaty Organization (NATO)
Nuclear Energy Agency
Organization for Economic Cooperation and Development (OECD)
South Pacific Commission

V. Other International Organizations

Center for International Forestry Research
Commission for Labor Cooperation
Commission for the Conservation of Antarctic Marine Living Resources
Convention on International Trade in Endangered Species of Wild Fauna and Flora
Global Biodiversity Information Facility
Hague Conference on Private International Law
International Agreement on the Maintenance of Certain Lights in the Red Sea
International Bureau for the Permanent Court of Arbitration
International Bureau for the Protection of Industrial Property
International Bureau for the Publication of Customs Tariffs
International Bureau of Weights and Measures
International Center for Agriculrural Research in the Dry Areas
International Center for the Study of the Preservation and the Restoration of Cultural Property (ICCROM)
International Coffee Organization
International Committee of the Red Cross
International Cotton Advisory Committee
International Council for the Exploration of the Seas (ICES)
International Council of Scientific Unions and Its Associated Unions (20)
International Criminal Police Organization (INTERPOL)
International Crops Research Institute for the Semi-Arid Tropics
International Development Law Institute
International Fertilizer Development Center
International Grain Council
International Human Frontier Science Program Organization
International Hydrographic Organization
International Institute for Cotton
International Institute for the Unification of Private Law
International Mobile Satellitte Organization
International North Pacific Fisheries Commission
International Organization for Legal Metrology (IOLM)
International Organization for Migration
International Organization of Supreme Audit Institutions
International Plant Genetics Resources Institute
International Rubber Study Group
International Science and Technology Center
International Seed Testing Association
International Service for National Agriculture Research
International Sugar Council
International Tropical Timber Organization
International Union of Credit and Investment Insurers
International Whaling Commission
Interparliamentary Union
Iran-United States Claims Tribunal
Korean Peninsula Energy Development Organization
Multinational Force Observers
Organization for the Prohibition of Chemical Weapons
Pacific Aviation Safety Office
Permanent International Association of Navigation Congresses
Preparatory Commission for the Comprehensive Nuclear Test-Ban Treaty

Regional Environmental Center for Central and Eastern Europe
Science and Technology Center in Ukraine
Sierra Leone Special Court
World Heritage Fund
World Customs Organization
World Trade Organization (WTO)

VI. Special Voluntary Programs

African Institute for Prevention of Crime and Treatment of Offenders
Asian Vegetable Research and Development Center
Convention on International Trade in Endangered Species of Wild Fauna and Flora (CITES)
International Center for Research in Agroforestry
International Council of Science
International Crop Research Institute for Semi-Arid Tropics
International Federation of the Red Cross
International Food Policy Research Institute
International Fund for Agricultural Development (IFAD)
International Institute of Tropical Agriculture
International Organization for Migration (IOM)
Joint United Nations Programme on HIV/AIDS (UNAIDS)
Korean Peninsula Energy Development Organization
Montreal Protocol Multilateral Fund
Organization of American States Fund for Strengthening Democracy
Organization of American States Special Development Assistance Fund
Permanent Interstate Committee for Drought Control in the Sahel
Ramsar Convention on Wetlands
United Nations Afghanistan Emergency Trust Fund
United Nations Children's Fund (UNICEF)
United Nations Development Fund for Women (UNIFEM)
United Nations Development Program (UNDP)
United Nations Environment Program (UNEP)
United Nations/Food and Agricultural Organization World Food Program (WFP)
United Nations High Commissioner for Refugees Program (UNHCR)
United Nations Relief and Works Agency (UNRWA)
United Nations Voluntary Fund for the Victims of Torture
World Health Organization Special Programs

African Development Bank

Headquarters (temporary): Angle des Trois Rues, Avenue Du Ghana, Rue Pierre De Coubertin, Rue Hedi Nouira, BP. 323, 1002 Tunis Belvedere, Tunisia. Internet, www.afdb.org. E-mail, afdb@afdb.org.

President: Omar Kabbaj

The African Development Bank (AFDB) was established in 1964 and, by charter amendment, opened its membership to non-African countries in 1982. Its mandate is to contribute to the economic development and social progress of its regional members. Bank members total 77, including 53 African countries and 24 nonregional countries. With the September 1999 ratification of the agreement on the fifth general capital increase, Bank ownership is 60 percent African and 40 percent nonregional.

The African Development Fund (AFDF), the concessional lending affiliate, was established in 1973 to complement AFDB operations by providing concessional financing for high-priority development projects in the poorest African countries. The Fund's membership consists of 25 nonregional member countries, South Africa, and AFDB, which represents its African members and is allocated half of the votes.

In February 2003, security concerns resulted in AFDB headquarters temporarily relocating to Tunis, Tunisia.

Asian Development Bank

Headquarters: 6 ADB Avenue, Mandaluyong City, 0401 Metro Manila, Philippines. Phone, 632–632–4444. Fax, 632–636–2444. Internet, www.adb.org.

President: Tadao Chino

The Asian Development Bank commenced operations on December

19, 1966. It now has 63 member countries—45 from Asia and 18 from outside the region.

The purpose of the Bank is to foster sustainable economic development, poverty alleviation, and cooperation among its developing member countries in the Asia/Pacific region.

For further information, contact the Asian Development Bank, P.O. Box 789, 0980 Manila, Philippines. E-mail, information@adb.org. Or contact the ADB North American Representative Office, 815 Connecticut Avenue NW., Washington, DC 20006. Phone, 202-728-1500. E-mail, adbnaro@adb.org.

Inter-American Defense Board

2600 Sixteenth Street NW., Washington, DC 20441. Phone, 202-939-6600. Internet, www.jid.org. E-mail, pao@jid.org.

Chairman: Maj. Gen. Keith M. Huber, USA

The Inter-American Defense Board is the oldest permanently constituted, international military organization in the world. It was founded by Resolution XXXIX of the Meeting of Foreign Ministers at Rio de Janeiro in January 1942. Senior army, navy, and air force officers from 27 member nations staff the various agencies of the Board. Its four major components are the Council of Delegates, the decisionmaking body; the International Staff; the Inter-American Defense College; and the Secretariat, which provides administrative and logistical support.

The Board studies and recommends to member governments measures necessary for close military collaboration in preparation for the collective defense and security of the hemisphere. It also acts as a technical military adviser for the Organization of American States, and is involved in projects such as disaster relief planning and demining programs in Central and South America.

The Inter-American Defense College, founded in 1962, prepares senior military officers and civilian functionaries for positions in their respective governments. The College's multidisciplinary program uses four annual seminars to focus on the Western Hemisphere's most pressing defense and security issues.

Inter-American Development Bank

Headquarters: 1300 New York Avenue NW., Washington, DC 20577. Phone, 202-623-1000. Internet, www.iadb.org.

President: Enrique V. Iglesias

The Inter-American Development Bank (IDB) was established in 1959 to help accelerate economic and social development in Latin America and the Caribbean. It is based in Washington, DC.

The Bank has 28 member countries in the Western Hemisphere and 18 outside of the region.

Inter-American Investment Corporation

Headquarters: 1350 New York Avenue NW., Washington, DC 20577. Phone, 202-623-3900

Chairman of Board of Directors: Enrique V. Iglesias

General Manager: Jacques Rogozinski

The Inter-American Investment Corporation (IIC), an affiliate of the Inter-American Development Bank, was established in 1984 to promote the economic development of its Latin American and Caribbean members by financing small- and medium-size private enterprises. IIC makes direct loans and equity investments and grants lines of credit to local financial intermediaries. It is based in Washington, DC.

IIC has 37 member countries, of which 27 are in the Western Hemisphere, including the United States, and 10 are outside the region.

International Bank for Reconstruction and Development

Headquarters: 1818 H Street NW., Washington, DC 20433. Phone, 202-473-1000

President: Paul D. Wolfowitz

The International Bank for Reconstruction and Development (IBRD), also known as the World Bank, officially came into existence on December 27, 1945.

The Bank's purpose is to promote economic, social, and environmental progress in developing nations by reducing poverty so that their people may live better and fuller lives. The Bank lends funds at market-determined interest rates, provides advice, and serves as a catalyst to stimulate outside investments. Its resources come primarily from funds raised in the world capital markets, its retained earnings, and repayments on its loans.

International Development Association The International Development Association (IDA) came into existence on September 24, 1960, as an affiliate of IBRD. The Association's resources consist of subscriptions and supplementary resources in the form of general replenishments, mostly from its more industrialized and developed members; special contributions by its richer members; repayments on earlier credits; and transfers from IBRD's net earnings.

The Association promotes economic development, reduces poverty, and raises the standard of living in the least developed areas of the world. It does this by financing their developmental requirements on concessionary terms, which are more flexible and bear less heavily on the balance of payments than those of conventional loans, thereby furthering the objectives of IBRD and supplementing its activities.

International Finance Corporation

Headquarters: 2121 Pennsylvania Avenue NW., Washington, DC 20433. Phone, 202–473–3800. Internet, www.ifc.org.

President: Paul D. Wolfowitz
Executive Vice President: Peter Woicke

The International Finance Corporation (IFC), an affiliate of the World Bank, was established in July 1956, to promote productive private enterprise in developing member countries.

The Corporation pursues its objective principally through direct debt and equity investments in projects that establish new businesses or expand, modify, or diversify existing businesses. It also encourages cofinancing by other investors and lenders.

Additionally, advisory services and technical assistance are provided by IFC to developing member countries in areas such as capital market development, privatization, corporate restructuring, and foreign investment.

International Monetary Fund

700 Nineteenth Street NW., Washington, DC 20431. Phone, 202–623–7000. Fax, 202–623–4661. Internet, www.imf.org.

Managing Director and Chairman of the Executive Board: Rodrigo de Rato y Figaredo
First Deputy Managing Director: Anne O. Krueger
Deputy Managing Directors: Augustín Carstens, Takatoshi Kato

The Final Act of the United Nations Monetary and Financial Conference, signed at Bretton Woods, NH, on July 22, 1944, set forth the original Articles of Agreement of the International Monetary Fund (IMF). The Agreement became effective on December 27, 1945, when the President, authorized by the Bretton Woods Agreements Act (22 U.S.C. 286), accepted membership for the United States in IMF, the Agreement having thus been accepted by countries whose combined financial commitments (quotas) equaled approximately 80 percent of IMF's total commitments. The inaugural meeting of the Board of Governors was held in March 1946, and the first meeting of the Executive Directors was held May 6, 1946.

On May 31, 1968, the Board of Governors approved an amendment to the Articles of Agreement for the establishment of a facility based on Special Drawing Rights (SDR) in IMF and for modification of certain IMF rules and practices. The amendment became effective on July 28, 1969, and the Special Drawing Account became operative on August 6, 1969. United States acceptance of the amendment and participation in the Special Drawing Account were authorized by the Special Drawing Rights Act (22 U.S.C. 286 *et seq.*).

On April 30, 1976, the Board of Governors approved a second

amendment to the Articles of Agreement, which entered into force on April 1, 1978. This amendment gave members the right to adopt exchange arrangements of their choice while placing certain obligations on them regarding their exchange rate policies, over which IMF was to exercise firm surveillance. The official price of gold was abolished and the SDR account was promoted as the principal reserve asset of the international monetary system. United States acceptance of this amendment was authorized by the Bretton Woods Agreements Act Amendments (22 U.S.C. 286e–5).

On June 28, 1990, the Board of Governors approved a third amendment to the Articles of Agreement, which became effective on November 11, 1992. Under this amendment, a member's voting rights and certain related rights may be suspended by a 70-percent majority of the executive board if the member, having been declared ineligible to use the general resources of the Fund, persists in its failure to fulfill any of its obligations under the Articles.

As of January 31, 2006, IMF had 184 member countries. Total quotas at the end of January 2006 were SDR 213 billion (about $310 billion).

The purposes of IMF are to promote international monetary cooperation through a permanent forum for consultation and collaboration on international monetary problems; to facilitate the expansion and balanced growth of international trade; to promote exchange rate stability; to assist in the establishment of an open multilateral system of payments for current transactions between members; and to give confidence to members by making IMF resources temporarily available to them under adequate safeguards.

In accordance with these purposes, IMF seeks to help its members correct imbalances in their international balances of payments. It periodically examines the economic developments and policies of its member countries, offers policy advice, and at member's request and upon executive board approval, provides financial assistance through a variety of financial facilities designed to address specific problems. These lending mechanisms include stand-by and extended arrangements, a supplemental reserve facility to provide short-term assistance for difficulties related to crises of market confidence, a facility to provide compensatory and contigency financing to countries suffering temporary declines in their export earnings, a concessional (low-interest rate) poverty reduction and growth facility to support structural adjustment and promote growth in the poorest countries, and emergency assistance for countries recovering from natural disasters or armed conflict. IMF also provides technical assistance and training to its members. As of January 31, 2006, IMF usable resources were SDR 152.1 billion ($221 billion), and one-year forward commitment capacity was SDR 117.3 billion ($170.6 billion).

For further information, contact the Chief, Public Affairs Division, External Relations Department, International Monetary Fund, 700 Nineteenth Street NW., Washington, DC 20431. Phone, 202–623–7300. Fax, 202–623–6278. E-mail, publicaffairs@imf.org. Internet, www.imf.org.

International Organization for Migration

Headquarters: 17 Route des Morillons, Grand-Saconnex, Geneva. Mailing address, P.O. Box 71, CH–1211, Geneva 19, Switzerland. Phone, 011–41–22–717–9111. Fax, 011–41–22–798–6150. Internet, www.iom.int.

Director General: Brunson McKinley (United States)

Deputy Director General: Ndioro Ndiaye (Senegal)

Washington Office: Suite 700, 1752 N Street NW., Washington, DC 20036. Phone, 202–862–1826. Fax, 202–862–1879. E-mail, MRFWashington@iom.int.
Regional Representative: Frances Sullivan (United States)

New York Office: Suite 1610, 122 E. 42d Street, New York, NY 10168. Phone, 212–681–7000. Fax, 212–867–5887. E-mail, newyork@iom.int
Chief of Mission: Michael Gray (United States)

Permanent Observer to the United Nations: Luca Dall'Oglio (Italy)

The International Organization for Migration (IOM) was formed in 1951 as the Intergovernmental Committee for European Migration (ICEM) to help solve the postwar problems of refugees and displaced persons in Europe and to assist in orderly trans-Atlantic migration. It adopted its current name in 1989 to reflect its progressively global outreach. Since its creation, IOM has assisted more than 12 million refugees and migrants in over 125 countries. As of December 2005, 116 governments are members of IOM, and 21 others have observer status. IOM has observer status at the United Nations.

IOM's guiding principle is that humane and orderly migration benefits migrants and societies. In carrying out its mandate, IOM helps migrants, governments, and civil society plan and operate international and national migration programs at the request of its member states and in cooperation with other international orgaanizations. Its major objectives are the processing and movement of migrants and refugees to countries offering them permanent resettlement opportunities; the promotion of orderly migration to meet the needs of both emigration and immigration communities; counter-trafficking activities; the transfer of technology through migration in order to promote the economic, educational, and social advancement of developing countries; the provision of a forum for states and other partners to exchange views; the promotion of cooperation and coordination on migration issues; and technical cooperation and advisory services on migration policies and legislation.

Multilateral Investment Guarantee Agency

Headquarters: 1818 H Street NW., Washington, DC 20433. Phone, 202–458–9292. Internet, www.miga.org.

President: Paul D. Wolfowitz
Executive Vice President: Yukiko Omura

The Multilateral Investment Guarantee Agency (MIGA), an affiliate of the World Bank, was formally constituted in April 1988.

Its basic purpose is to facilitate the flow of foreign private investment for productive purposes to developing member countries by offering long-term political risk insurance in the areas of expropriation, transfer restriction, breach of contract, and war and civil disturbance; and by providing advisory and consultative services. The Agency cooperates with national investment insurance schemes, such as OPIC, and with private insurers.

Organization of American States

Headquarters: Seventeenth Street and Constitution Avenue NW., Washington, DC 20006. Phone, 202–458–3000. Fax, 202–458–3967. Internet, www.oas.org.

Secretary General: José Miguel Insulza
Assistant Secretary General: Albert Ramdi

The Organization of American States (OAS) brings together the countries of the Western Hemisphere to strengthen cooperation and advance commmon interests. At the core of the OAS mission is a commitment to democracy. Building on this foundation, OAS works to promote good governance, strengthen human rights, foster peace and security, expand trade, and address the complex problems caused by poverty, drugs, and corruption. Though decisions made by its political bodies and programs carried out by its General Secretariat, OAS promotes greater inter-American cooperation and understanding.

OAS member states have intensified their cooperation since the end of the cold war, taking on new and important challenges. In 1994, the region's 34 democratically elected presidents and prime ministers met in Miami for the First Summit of the Americas, where they established broad political, economic and social development goals. They have continued to meet periodically since then to examine common interests and priorities. Through the ongoing Summits of the Americas process, the region's leaders have entrusted the OAS with a growing number of responsibilities to help advance the countries' shared vision.

With four official languages—English, Spanish, Portugese, and French—the OAS reflects the rich diversity of peoples and cultures across the Americas. The OAS has 35 member states, the independent nations of North, Central and South America and the Caribbean. Since 1962, Cuba has been barred from participation by resolution of the Eight Meeting of Ministers of Foreign Affairs. Countries from all around the world are permanent observers, closely following the issues that are critical to the Americas and often providing key financial support for OAS programs.

The member states set major policies and goals through the General Assembly, which gathers the hemisphere's foreign ministeres once a year in regular session. The Permanent Council, made up of ambassadors appointed by member states, meets regularly, at OAS headquarters in Washington, DC, to guide ongoing policies and actions. The chairmanship of the Permanent Council rotates every three months, in alphabetical order of countries. Each member state has an equal voice, and most decisions are made through consensus.

Also under the OAS umbrella are several specialized agencies that have considerable autonomy. Those agencies are the Pan American Health Organization in Washington, DC; the Inter-American Children's Institute in Montevideo, Uruguay; the Inter-American Institute for Cooperation on Agriculture in San José, Costa Rica; and the Pan American Institute of Geography and History and the Inter-American Indian Institute, both in Mexico City.

In 1948, 21 nations of the hemisphere signed the OAS Charter at the Ninth International Conference of American States. They were Argentina, Bolivia, Brazil, Chile, Colombia, Costa Rica, Cuba (barred from participation), Dominican Republic, Ecuador, El Salvador, Guatemala, Haiti, Honduras, Mexico, Nicaragua, Panama, Paraguay, Peru, United States of America, Uruguay and Venezuela.

Subsequently, 14 other American States joined the OAS by signing and ratifying the Charter. They were Barbados and Trinidad and Tobago, Jamaica, Grenada, Suriname, Dominica and Saint Lucia, Antigua and Barbuda and Saint Vincent and the Grenadines, Bahamas, St. Kitts and Nevis, Canada, and Belize and Guyana. This brings to 35 the number of member states.

For further information, contact the Director, Department of Press and Communications, OAS, 1889 F Street NW., Washington, DC 20006. Phone, 202-458-3760. Fax, 202-458-6421.

United Nations

United Nations, New York, NY 10017. Phone, 212-963-1234. Internet, www.un.org.

Secretary-General: Kofi A. Annan

United Nations Office at Geneva: Palais des Nations, 1211 Geneva 10, Switzerland

Director-General: Sergi Ordzhonikidze

United Nations Office at Vienna: Vienna International Centre, P.O. Box 500, A-1400, Vienna, Austria

Director-General: Antonio Maria Costa

Washington, DC, Office: U.N. Information Centre, Suite 400, 1775 K Street NW., Washington, DC 20006. Phone, 202-331-8670. Fax, 202-331-9191. Internet, www.unicwash.org.

Director: Will Davis

The United Nations is an international organization that was set up in accordance with the Charter [1] drafted by governments represented at the Conference on International Organization meeting at San Francisco. The Charter was signed on June 26, 1945, and came into force on October 24, 1945, when the required number of ratifications and accessions had been made by the signatories. Amendments increasing membership of the Security Council and the Economic and Social

[1] Charter of the United Nations, together with the Statute of the International Court of Justice (Department of State Publication No. 2353, International Organization and Conference Series III, 21), June 26, 1945. Available for sale from the Superintendent of Documents, Government Printing Office, Washington, DC 20402. Phone, 202-512-1800.

Council came into effect on August 31, 1965.

The United Nations now consists of 191 member states, of which 51 are founding members.

The purposes of the United Nations set out in the Charter are to maintain international peace and security; to develop friendly relations among nations; to achieve international cooperation in solving international problems of an economic, social, cultural, or humanitarian character and in promoting respect for human rights; and to be a center for harmonizing the actions of nations in the attainment of these common ends.

The principal organs of the United Nations are as follows:

General Assembly All states that are members of the United Nations are members of the General Assembly. Its functions are to consider and discuss any matter within the scope of the Charter of the United Nations and to make recommendations to the members of the United Nations and other organs. It approves the budget of the organization, the expenses of which are borne by the members as apportioned by the General Assembly.

The General Assembly may call the attention of the Security Council to situations likely to endanger international peace and security, may initiate studies, and may receive and consider reports from other organs of the United Nations. Under the "Uniting for Peace" resolution adopted by the General Assembly in November 1950, if the Security Council fails to act on an apparent threat to or breach of the peace or act of aggression because of lack of unanimity of its five permanent members, the Assembly itself may take up the matter within 24 hours—in emergency special session—and recommend collective measures, including, in case of a breach of the peace or act of aggression, use of armed force when necessary to maintain or restore international peace and security.

The General Assembly normally meets in regular annual session from September through December. It also has met in special sessions and emergency special sessions.

Security Council The Security Council consists of 15 members, of which 5—the People's Republic of China, France, Russia, the United Kingdom, and the United States of America—are permanent members. The 10 nonpermanent members are elected for 2-year terms by the General Assembly. The primary responsibility of the Security Council is to act on behalf of the members of the United Nations in maintenance of international peace and security. Measures that may be employed by the Security Council are outlined in the Charter.

The Security Council, together with the General Assembly, also elects the judges of the International Court of Justice and makes a recommendation to the General Assembly on the appointment of the Secretary-General of the organization.

The Security Council first met in London on January 17, 1946, and is so organized as to be able to function continuously.

Economic and Social Council This organ is responsible, under the authority of the General Assembly, for the economic and social programs of the United Nations. Its functions include making or initiating studies, reports, and recommendations on international economic, social, cultural, educational, health, and related matters; promoting respect for and observance of human rights and fundamental freedoms for all; calling international conferences and preparing draft conventions for submission to the General Assembly on matters within its competence; negotiating agreements with the specialized agencies and defining their relationship with the United Nations; coordinating the activities of the specialized agencies; and consulting with nongovernmental organizations concerned with matters within its competence. The Council consists of 54 members of the United Nations elected by the General Assembly for 3-year terms; 18 are elected each year.

The Council usually holds two regular sessions a year. It has also held a number of special sessions.

Trusteeship Council The Trusteeship Council was initially established to consist of any member states that administered trust territories, permanent members of the Security Council that did not administer trust territories, and enough other nonadministering countries elected by the General Assembly for 3-year terms to ensure that membership would be equally divided between administering and nonadministering members. Under authority of the General Assembly, the Council considered reports from members administering trust territories, examined petitions from trust territory inhabitants, and provided for periodic inspection visits to trust territories.

With the independence of Palau, the last remaining U.N. trust territory, the Trusteeship Council formally suspended operations after nearly half a century. The council will henceforth meet only on an extraordinary basis, as the need may arise.

International Court of Justice The International Court of Justice is the principal judicial organ of the United Nations. It has its seat at The Hague, The Netherlands. All members of the United Nations are *ipso facto* parties to the Statute of the Court. Nonmembers of the United Nations may become parties to the Statute of the Court on conditions prescribed by the General Assembly on the recommendation of the Security Council.

The jurisdiction of the Court comprises all cases that the parties refer to it and all matters specially provided for in the Charter of the United Nations or in treaties and conventions in force.

The Court consists of 15 judges known as "members" of the Court. They are elected for 9-year terms by the General Assembly and the Security Council, voting independently, and may be reelected.

Secretariat The Secretariat consists of a Secretary-General and "such staff as the Organization may require." The Secretary-General, who is appointed by the General Assembly on the recommendation of the Security Council, is the chief administrative officer of the United Nations. He acts in that capacity for the General Assembly, the Security Council, the Economic and Social Council, and the Trusteeship Council. Under the Charter, the Secretary-General "may bring to the attention of the Security Council any matter that in his opinion may threaten the maintenance of international peace and security."

SELECTED BILATERAL ORGANIZATIONS

International Boundary Commission, United States and Canada

United States Section: 1250 23d Street NW., Suite 100, Washington, DC 20037. Phone, 202–736–9100. Internet, www.internationalboundary commission.org.

Canadian Section: Room 575, 615 Booth Street, Ottawa, ON K1A 0E9. Phone, 613–992–1294.

International Boundary and Water Commission, United States and Mexico

United States Section: Suite C–100, 4171 North Mesa Street, El Paso, TX 79902. Phone, 800–262–8857 or 915–832–4100. Fax, 915–832–4190. Internet, www.ibwc.state.gov.

Mexican Section: Universidad Numero 2180, Zona Chamizal, C.P. 32310, Ciudad Juárez, Chihuahua, Mexico; or P.O. Box 10525, El Paso, TX 79995. Phone, 011–52–656–613–7311 or 011–52–656–613–7363. Internet, www.sre.gob.mx/cila.

International Joint Commission—United States and Canada

United States Section: 1250 23rd Street NW., Suite 100, Washington, DC 20440. Phone, 202–736–9024. Fax, 202–467–0746. Internet, www.ijc.org.

Canadian Section: 22nd Floor, 234 Laurier Avenue West, Ottawa, ON K1P 6K6. Phone, 613–995–0088. Fax, 613–993–5583.

Regional Office: 100 Ouellette Avenue, 8th Floor, Windsor, ON N9A 6T3; or P.O. Box 32869, Detroit MI 48232. Phone, 519–257–6700. Fax, 519–257–6741.

Joint Mexican-United States Defense Commission

United States Section: 5134 Joint Staff, Room 2D967, The Pentagon, Washington, DC 20318. Phone, 703–695–8164.

Mexican Section: 1911 Pennsylvania Avenue NW., Mexican Embassy, Suite 600, Washington, DC 20006. Phone, 202–728–1748.

Permanent Joint Board on Defense—United States and Canada

United States Section: Room 2D967, The Pentagon, Washington, DC 20318-5000. Phone, 703–695–4477. Fax, 703–614–8945.

Canadian Section: National Defense Headquarters, 125 Sussex Drive, Ottawa, ON K1A 0K2. Phone, 613–996–0407.

Appendices

APPENDIX A: Commonly Used Abbreviations and Acronyms

ADA	Americans with Disabilities Act of 1990
ADB	Asian Development Bank
AFDB	African Development Bank
AFDF	African Development Fund
AFIS	American Forces Information Service (Defense)
AGRICOLA	Agricultural Online Access
AmeriCorps* NCCC	National Civilian Community Corps
AmeriCorps* VISTA	Volunteers in Service to America
AMS	Agricultural Marketing Service
Amtrak	National Railroad Passenger Corporation
APH	American Printing House for the Blind (Education)
APHIS	Animal and Plant Health Inspection Service
ARS	Agricultural Research Service
ATF	Bureau of Alcohol, Tobacco, Firearms, and Explosives
BBG	Broadcasting Board of Governors
BEA	Bureau of Economic Analysis
BIA	Bureau of Indian Affairs
BIC	Business Information Center (SBA)
BIF	Bank Insurance Fund
BIS	Bureau of Industry and Security (Commerce)
BLM	Bureau of Land Management
BLS	Bureau of Labor Statistics
BRS	Biotechnology Regulatory Services (Agriculture)
BTA	Business Transformation Agency (Defense)
BTS	Bureau of Transportation Statistics
	Directorate of Border and Transportation Security (Homeland Security)
BVA	Board of Veterans' Appeals
CBO	Congressional Budget Office
CBP	Customs and Border Protection
CCC	Commodity Credit Corporation
CDBG	Community Development Block Grant
CEA	Council of Economic Advisers
CEQ	Council on Environmental Quality
CFR	*Code of Federal Regulations*
CFTC	Commodity Futures Trading Commission
COPS	Office of Community Oriented Policing Services (Justice)
CRS	Congressional Research Service
CSR	Center for Scientific Review (HHS)
CSREES	Cooperative State Research, Education, and Extension Service
CSS	*See* NSA/CSS
DAU	Defense Acquisition University

DDESS	Department of Defense Domestic Dependent Elementary and Secondary Schools
DEA	Drug Enforcement Administration
DHS	Department of Homeland Security
DIA	Defense Intelligence Agency
DISA	Defense Information Systems Agency
DLA	Defense Logistics Agency
DNFSB	Defense Nuclear Facilities Safety Board
DNI	Director of National Intelligence
DOD	Department of Defense
DODDS	Department of Defense Dependent Schools
DODEA	Department of Defense Education Activity
DOE	Department of Energy
DOL	Department of Labor
DOT	Department of Transportation
DPMO	Defense Prisoner of War/ Missing Personnel Office
DRL	Bureau of Democracy, Human Rights, and Labor (State)
DSS	Defense Security Service
DTIC	Defense Technical Information Center
DTRA	Defense Threat Reduction Agency
DTSA	Defense Technology Security Administration
EBSA	Employee Benefits Security Administration
EDA	Economic Development Administration
EEOC	Equal Employment Opportunity Commission
EO	Executive order
EPA	Environmental Protection Agency
EP&R	Emergency Preparedness and Response Directorate
ERS	Economic Research Service (Agriculture)
ESA	Economics and Statistics Administration (Commerce)
	Employee Standards Administration (Labor)
ETA	Employment Training Administration (Labor)
EUCOM	U.S. European Command
EUROPOL	European Police Office
Ex-Im Bank	Export-Import Bank of the United States
FAA	Federal Aviation Administration
Fannie Mae	Federal National Mortgage Association
Farmer Mac	Federal Agricultural Mortgage Corporation
FAS	Foreign Agricultural Service
	Federal Acquisition Service (GSA)
FBI	Federal Bureau of Investigation
FCA	Farm Credit Administration
FCC	Federal Communications Commission
FCIC	Federal Crop Insurance Corporation
FDA	Food and Drug Administration
FDIC	Federal Deposit Insurance Corporation
FEB	Federal Executive Boards
FERC	Federal Energy Regulatory Commission
FFB	Federal Financing Bank
FHWA	Federal Highway Administration
FICO	Financing Corporation
Finance Board	Federal Housing Finance Board
FMCS	Federal Mediation and Conciliation Service
FMS	Financial Management Service
FNS	Food and Nutrition Service
FOIA	Freedom of Information Act
FR	*Federal Register*
Freddie Mac	Federal Home Loan Corporation
FSA	Farm Service Agency
FSIS	Food Safety and Inspection Service
FSS	Federal Supply Service
FTA	Federal Transit Administration
FTS	Federal Technology Service
GAO	Government Accountability Office

GATT	General Agreement on Tariffs and Trade
GC	Office of Goverment Contracting (SBA)
Ginnie Mae	Government National Mortgage Association
GIPSA	Grain Inspection, Packers, and Stockyards Administration
GNMA	Government National Mortgage Association
GPO	Government Printing Office
GPS	Global Positioning System
GSA	General Services Administration
HHS	Department of Health and Human Services
HIV/AIDS	Human Immunodeficiency Virus/ Acquired Immunodeficiency Syndrome
HRSA	Health Resources and Services Administration
HUD	Department of Housing and Urban Development
IAF	Inter-American Foundation
IAIP	Information Analysis and Infrastructure Protection Directorate
IBRD	International Bank for Reconstruction and Development (World Bank)
IDA	International Development Association
IDB	Inter-American Development Bank
IFC	International Finance Corporation
IHA	Indian Housing Authority
IIC	Inter-American Investment Corporation
IMF	International Monetary Fund
IMLS	Institute of Museum and Library Services
INTERPOL	International Criminal Police Organization
IOLM	International Organization for Legal Metrology
IOM	International Organization for Migration
IRM	Information Resources Management College
IRS	Internal Revenue Service
ISN	Bureau of International Security and Nonproliferation (State)
ISOO	Information Security Oversight Office (NARA)
IT	Information technology
ITA	International Trade Administration
JAG	Judge Advocate General
JFSC	Joint Forces Staff College
LSC	Legal Services Corporation
MBDA	Minority Business Development Agency
MBN	Middle East Broadcasting Networks
MDA	Missile Defense Agency
MDW	U.S. Military District of Washington
MIGA	Multilateral Investment Guarantee Agency
NAFTA	North American Free Trade Agreement
NAL	National Agricultural Library
NARA	National Archives and Records Administration
NASA	National Aeronautics and Space Administration
NASS	National Agricultural Statistics Service
NATO	North Atlantic Treaty Organization
NCA	National Cemetery Administration
NCCC	*See* AmeriCorps*NCCC
NCR	National Capital Region
NCUA	National Credit Union Administration
NEH	National Endowment for the Humanities
NESDIS	National Environmental Satellite, Data, and Information Service
NGA	National Geospatial-Intelligence Agency
NGO	Non-Governmental Organization
NHPRC	National Historical Publications and Records Commission
NHTSA	National Highway Traffic Safety Administration
NIC	National Institute of Corrections

NIH National Institutes of Health
NIST National Institute of Standards and Technology
NLRB National Labor Relations Board
NMAO NOAA Marine and Aviation Operations
NMB National Mediation Board
NMFS National Marine Fisheries Service (Commerce)
NNSA National Nuclear Security Administration
NOAA National Oceanic and Atmospheric Administration
NOS National Ocean Service (Commerce)
NPS National Park Service
NRC Nuclear Regulatory Commission
NRCS Natural Resources Conservation Service
NSA/CSS National Security Agency/Central Security Service
NSF National Science Foundation
NTI National Transit Institute (Transportation)
NTIA National Telecommunications and Information Administration
NTID National Technical Institute for the Deaf
NTIS National Technical Information Service (Commerce)
NTSB National Transportation Safety Board
NWS National Weather Service (Commerce)
OAR Office of Oceanic and Atmospheric Research (Commerce)
OAS Organization of American States
OBCI Office of Business and Community Initiatives (SBA)
OBO Bureau of Overseas Building Operations
OCB Office of Cuba Broadcasting
OCSC Office of Citizen Services and Communications
ODEP Office of Disability Employment Policy (Labor)
OECA Office of Enforcement and Compliance Assurance (EPA)
OECD Organization for Economic Cooperation and Development
OES Bureau of Oceans and International Environmental and Scientific Affairs (State)
OFAM Office of Financial and Administrative Management
OFCCP Office of Federal Contract Compliance Programs (Labor)
OFM Office of Foreign Missions (State)
OFO Office of Field Operations (Labor)
OGP Office of Governmentwide Policy
OIE World Organization for Animal Health (Office International des Epizooties)
OIG Office of Inspector General
OIT Office of International Trade (SBA)
OJP Office of Justice Programs
OMB Office of Management and Budget
OPDR Office of Policy Development and Research (Labor)
OPE Office of Postsecondary Education
OPIC Overseas Private Investment Corporation
OPM Office of Personnel Management
OPS Office of Pipeline Safety (Transportation)
ORD Office of Research and Development (EPA)
OSC Office of Special Counsel
OSDFS Office of Safe and Drug-Free Schools
OSERS Office of Special Education and Rehabilitative Services

OSHA Occupational Safety and Health Administration
OSM Office of Surface Mining Reclamation and Enforcement
OSO Office of Space Operations
OST Office of the Special Trustee for American Indians (Interior)
OTP Office of Technology Policy (Commerce)
OTS Office of Thrift Supervision
OVBD Office of Veterans Business Development (SBA)
OWBO Office of Women's Business Ownership (SBA)
PBGC Pension Benefit Guaranty Corporation
PBS Public Buildings Service
PFPA Pentagon Force Protection Agency
PHA Public Housing Agency
PHMSA Pipeline and Hazardous Materials Administration
POW/MIA Prisoner of War/Missing in Action
PPQ Plant Protection and Quarantine
PROTECH Office of Performance, Results, and Training (Labor)
PTO Patent and Trademark Office
PUASP Postal Union of the Americas and Spain and Portugal
RFA Radio Free Asia
RFE/RL Radio Free Europe/Radio Liberty
RHS Rural Housing Service
RITA Research and Innovative Technology Administration (Transportation)
RMA Risk Management Agency (Agriculture)
RSVP Retired and Senior Volunteers Program
SAIF Savings Association Insurance Fund
SAMHSA Substance Abuse and Mental Health Services Administration
SBA Small Business Administration
SCORE Service Corps of Retired Executives
SEC Securities and Exchange Commission
SFH Single Family Homes
SERC Smithsonian Environmental Research Center
SES Senior Executive Service
SITES Smithsonian Institution Traveling Exhibit Service
SSA Social Security Administration
S&T Science and Technology Directorate (DHS)
Stat. *United States Statutes at Large*
STRI Smithsonian Tropical Research Institute
TA Technology Administration (Commerce)
TBIC Tribal Business Information Centers (SBA)
TDA Trade and Development Agency
TIGTA Treasury Inspector General for Tax Administration
TMA TRICARE Management Activity (Defense)
TTB Alcohol and Tobacco Tax and Trade Bureau
TVA Tennessee Valley Authority
U.N. United Nations[1]
UNAIDS Joint United Nations Programme on HIV/AIDS
UNESCO United Nations Educational, Scientific and Cultural Organization
UNHCR United Nations High Commissioner for Refugees Program
UNICEF United Nations Children's Fund (formerly United Nations International Children's Emergency Fund)
UNICOR Federal Prison Industries

[1] Acronyms for U.N. agencies can be found under *Selected Multilateral Organizations* in the preceding text.

UNSCEAR United Nations Scientific Committee on the Effects of Atomic Radiation
USA United States Army
USACE United States Army Corps of Engineers
USAF United States Air Force
USAID United States Agency for International Development
USAREUR U.S. Army Europe
U.S.C. United States Code
USCG United States Coast Guard
USCIS U.S. Citizenship and Immigration Services (Homeland Security)
USDA United States Department of Agriculture
USEAC United States Export Assistance Centers (SBA)
USGS United States Geological Survey
USMC United States Marine Corps
USMS United States Maritime Service
USN United States Navy
USNCB U.S. National Central Bureau (Justice)
VA Department of Veterans Affairs
VETS Veterans' Employment and Training Service
VISTA *See* AmeriCorps*VISTA
VOA Voice of America
WBC Women's Business Center (SBA)
WFP United Nations/Food and Agricultural Organization World Food Program
WHS Washington Headquarters Services (DOD)
WIC Special Supplemental Food Program for Women, Infants, and Children
WNET Women's Network for Entrepreneurial Training (SBA)
World Bank *See* IBRD
WSP Federal Witness Security Program
WTO World Trade Organization

APPENDIX B: Federal Executive Agencies Terminated, Transferred, or Changed in Name Subsequent to March 4, 1933

NOTE: Italicized terms indicate obsolete agencies, organizations, and entities. In most instances, explanatory remarks are written at those terms elsewhere in this appendix. Dates prior to March 4, 1933, are included to provide additional information about the agencies.

This appendix is indexed in a format considered to be useful to the reader. Entries are carried at the most significant term in their titles, or when there is more than one significant term, the entry is carried at the first significant term. Thus, **Bureau of the Budget** is found at **Budget, Bureau of the,** and **Annual Assay Commission** is found at **Assay Commission, Annual.** Reader comments on the format are encouraged and should be sent to the address shown on page iv of the *Manual*.

Accounting Office, General Established by act of June 10, 1921 (42 Stat. 20). Renamed Government Accountability Office by act of July 7, 2004 (118 Stat. 814).

ACTION Established by Reorg. Plan No. 1 of 1971 (5 U.S.C. app.), effective July 1, 1971. Reorganized by act of Oct. 1, 1973 (87 Stat. 405). Functions relating to SCORE and ACT programs transferred to Small Business Administration by EO 11871 of July 18, 1975 (40 FR 30915). Functions exercised by the Director of ACTION prior to Mar. 31, 1995, transferred to the Corporation for National and Community Service (107 Stat. 888 and Proclamation 6662 of Apr. 4, 1994 (57 FR 16507)).

Acts of Congress *See* **State, Department of**

Administrative Conference of the United States Established by act of Aug. 30, 1964 (78 Stat. 615). Terminated by act of Nov. 19, 1995 (109 Stat. 480).

Advanced Research Projects Agency *See* Defense Advanced Research Projects Agency

Advisory Board. *See other part of title*

Aeronautical Board Organized in 1916 by agreement of *War* and Navy Secretaries. Placed under supervision of President by military order of July 5, 1939. Dissolved by Secretary of Defense letter of July 27, 1948, and functions transferred to *Munitions Board* and *Research and Development Board.* Military order of July 5, 1939, revoked by military order of Oct. 18, 1948.

Aeronautics, Bureau of Established in the Department of the Navy by act of July 12, 1921 (42 Stat. 140). Abolished by act of Aug. 18, 1959 (73 Stat. 395) and functions transferred to *Bureau of Naval Weapons.*

Aeronautics, National Advisory Committee for Established by act of Mar. 3, 1915 (38 Stat. 930). Terminated by act of July 29, 1958 (72 Stat. 432), and functions transferred to National Aeronautics and Space Administration, established by same act.

Aeronautics Administration, Civil *See* **Aeronautics Authority, Civil**

Aeronautics Authority, Civil Established under act of June 23, 1938 (52 Stat. 973). Renamed *Civil Aeronautics Board* and Administrator transferred to the Department of Commerce by Reorg. Plan Nos. III and IV of 1940, effective June 30, 1940. Office of Administrator designated *Civil Aeronautics Administration* by Department Order 52 of Aug. 29, 1940. *Administration* transferred to *Federal Aviation Agency* by act of Aug. 23, 1958 (72 Stat. 810). Functions of *Board* under act of Aug. 23, 1958 (72 Stat. 775), transferred to National Transportation Safety Board by act of Oct. 15, 1966 (80 Stat. 931). Functions of *Board* terminated or transferred—effective in part Dec. 31, 1981; in part Jan. 1, 1983; and in part Jan. 1, 1985—by act of Aug. 23, 1958 (92 Stat. 1744). Most remaining functions transferred to Secretary of Transportation, remainder to U.S. Postal Service. Termination of *Board* finalized by act of Oct. 4, 1984 (98 Stat. 1703).

Aeronautics Board, Civil *See* **Aeronautics Authority, Civil**

Aeronautics Branch Established in the Department of Commerce to carry out provisions of act of May 20, 1926 (44 Stat. 568). Renamed *Bureau of Air Commerce* by Secretary's administrative order of July 1, 1934. Personnel and property transferred to *Civil Aeronautics Authority* by EO 7959 of Aug. 22, 1938.

Aeronautics and Space Council, National Established by act of July 29, 1958 (72 Stat. 427). Abolished by Reorg. Plan No. 1 of 1973, effective June 30, 1973.

Aging, Administration on Established by *Secretary of Health, Education, and Welfare* on Oct. 1, 1965, to carry out provisions of act of July 14, 1965 (79 Stat. 218). Reassigned to *Social and Rehabilitation Service* by Department reorganization of Aug. 15, 1967. Transferred to Office of Assistant Secretary for Human Development by Secretary's order of June 15, 1973. Transferred to the Office of the Secretary of Health and Human Services by Secretary's reorganization notice dated Apr. 15, 1991.

Aging, Federal Council on Established by Presidential memorandum of Apr. 2, 1956. Reconstituted at Federal level by Presidential letter of Mar. 7, 1959, to *Secretary of Health, Education, and Welfare.* Abolished by EO 11022 of May 15, 1962, which established *President's Council on Aging.*

Aging, Office of Established by *Secretary of Health, Education, and Welfare* June 2, 1955, as *Special Staff on Aging.* Terminated Sept. 30, 1965, and functions assumed by Administration on Aging.

Aging, President's Council on Established by EO 11022 of May 14, 1962. Terminated by EO 11022, which was revoked by EO 12379 of Aug. 17, 1982.

Agricultural Adjustment Administration Established by act of May 12, 1933 (48 Stat. 31). Consolidated into *Agricultural Conservation and Adjustment Administration* as *Agricultural Adjustment Agency,* Department of Agriculture, by EO 9069 of Feb. 23, 1942. Grouped with other agencies to form *Food Production Administration* by EO 9280 of Dec. 5, 1942. Transferred to *War Food Administration* by EO 9322 of Mar. 26, 1943. Administration terminated by EO 9577 of June 29, 1945, and functions transferred to Secretary of Agriculture. Transfer made permanent by Reorg. Plan No. 3 of 1946, effective July 16, 1946. Functions of *Agricultural Adjustment Agency* consolidated with *Production and Marketing Administration* by Secretary's Memorandum 1118 of Aug. 18, 1945.

Agricultural Adjustment Agency *See* **Agricultural Adjustment Administration**

Agricultural Advisory Commission, National Established by EO 10472 of July 20, 1953. Terminated Feb. 4, 1965, on resignation of members.

Agricultural Chemistry and Engineering, Bureau of *See* **Agricultural Engineering, Bureau of**

Agricultural Conservation and Adjustment Administration Established by EO 9069 of Feb. 23, 1942, consolidating *Agricultural Adjustment Agency, Sugar Agency, Federal Crop Insurance Corporation,* and *Soil Conservation Service.* Consolidated into *Food Production Administration* by EO 9280 of Dec. 5, 1942.

Agricultural Conservation Program Service Established by Secretary of Agriculture Jan. 21, 1953, from part of *Production and Marketing Administration.* Merged with *Commodity Stabilization Service* by Secretary's Memorandum 1446, supp. 2, of Apr. 19, 1961.

Agricultural Developmental Service, International Established by Secretary of Agriculture memorandum of July 12, 1963. Functions and delegations of authority transferred to Foreign Agricultural Service by Secretary's memorandum of Mar. 28, 1969. Functions transferred by Secretary to *Foreign Economic Development Service* Nov. 8, 1969.

Agricultural Economics, Bureau of Established by act of May 11, 1931 (42 Stat. 532). Functions transferred to other units of the Department of Agriculture, including *Consumer and Marketing Service* and Agricultural Research Service, under Secretary's Memorandum 1320, supp. 4, of Nov. 2, 1953.

Agricultural Engineering, Bureau of Established by act of Feb. 23, 1931 (46 Stat. 1266). Merged with *Bureau of Chemistry and Soils* by Secretarial order of Oct. 16, 1938, to form *Bureau of Agricultural Chemistry and Engineering.*

Agricultural and Industrial Chemistry, Bureau of *Bureau of Chemistry* and *Bureau of Soils,* created in 1901, combined into *Bureau of Chemistry and Soils* by act of Jan. 18, 1927 (44 Stat. 976). Soils units transferred to other agencies of the Department of Agriculture and remaining units of *Bureau of Chemistry and Soils* and *Bureau of Agricultural Engineering* consolidated with *Bureau of Agricultural Chemistry and Engineering* by Secretary's order of Oct. 16, 1938. In February 1943 agricultural engineering research made part of *Bureau of Plant Industry, Soils, and Agricultural Engineering,* and organization for continuing agricultural chemistry research relating to crop utilization named *Bureau of Agricultural and Industrial Chemistry,* in accordance with *Research Administration* Memorandum 5 issued pursuant to EO 9069 of Feb. 23, 1942, and in conformity with Secretary's Memorandums 960 and 986. Functions transferred to *Agricultural Research Service* under Secretary's Memorandum 1320, supp. 4, of Nov. 2, 1953.

Agricultural Library, National Established by Secretary of Agriculture Memorandum 1496 of Mar. 23, 1962. Consolidated into *Science and Education Administration* by Secretary's order of Jan. 24, 1978. Reestablished as National Agricultural Library by Secretary's order of June 16, 1981. Became part of Agricultural Research Service in 1994 under Department of Agriculture reorganization.

Agricultural Marketing Administration Established by EO 9069 of Feb. 23, 1942, consolidating *Surplus Marketing Administration, Agricultural Marketing Service,* and *Commodity Exchange Administration. Division of Consumers' Counsel* transferred to *Administration* by Secretary's memorandum of Feb. 28, 1942. Consolidated into *Food Distribution Administration* in the Department of Agriculture by EO 9280 of Dec. 5, 1942.

Agricultural Marketing Service Established by the Secretary of Agriculture pursuant to act of June 30, 1939 (53 Stat. 939). Merged into *Agricultural Marketing Administration* by EO 9069 of Feb. 23, 1942. Renamed *Consumer and Marketing Service* by Secretary's Memorandum 1567, supp. 1, of Feb. 8, 1965. Reestablished as Agricultural Marketing Service by the Secretary of Agriculture on Apr. 2,

1972, under authority of Reorg. Plan No. 2 of 1953 (67 Stat. 633).

Agricultural Relations, Office of Foreign *See* **Agricultural Service, Foreign**

Agricultural Research Administration Established by EO 9069 of Feb. 23, 1942. Superseded by Agricultural Research Service.

Agricultural Research Service Established by Secretary of Agriculture Memorandum 1320, supp. 4, of Nov. 2, 1953. Consolidated into *Science and Education Administration* by Secretary's order of Jan. 24, 1978. Reestablished as Agricultural Research Service by Secretarial order of June 16, 1981.

Agricultural Service, Foreign Established by act of June 5, 1930 (46 Stat. 497). Economic research and agricultural attaché activities administered by *Foreign Agricultural Service Division, Bureau of Agricultural Economics,* until June 29, 1939. Transferred by Reorg. Plan No. II of 1939, effective July 1, 1939, from the Department of Agriculture to the Department of State. Economic research functions of *Division* transferred to *Office of Foreign Agricultural Relations* June 30, 1939. Functions of *Office* transferred to Foreign Agricultural Service Mar. 10, 1953. Agricultural attachés placed in the Department of Agriculture by act of Aug. 28, 1954 (68 Stat. 908).

Agricultural Stabilization and Conservation Service Established June 5, 1961, by the Secretary of Agriculture under authority of revised statutes (5 U.S.C. 301) and Reorg. Plan No. 2 of 1953 (5 U.S.C. app.). Abolished and functions assumed by the *Farm Service Agency* by Secretary's Memorandum 1010 1 dated Oct. 20, 1994 (59 FR 60297, 60299).

Agricultural Statistics Division Transferred to *Bureau of Agricultural Economics* by EO 9069 of Feb. 23, 1942.

Agriculture, Division of *See* **Farm Products, Division of**

Air Commerce, Bureau of *See* **Aeronautics Branch**

Air Coordinating Committee Established Mar. 27, 1945, by interdepartmental memorandum; formally established by EO 9781 of Sept. 19, 1946. Terminated by EO 10883 of Aug. 11, 1960, and functions transferred for liquidation to *Federal Aviation Agency.*

Air Force Management Engineering Agency Established in 1975 in Air Force as separate operating unit. Made subordinate unit of Air Force Military Personnel Center (formerly Air Force Manpower and Personnel Center) in 1978. Reestablished as separate operating unit of Air Force, effective Mar. 1, 1985, by Secretarial order.

Air Force Manpower and Personnel Center Certain functions transferred on activation of Air Force Management Engineering Agency, which was made separate operating unit from Air Force Manpower and Personnel Center (later Air Force Military Personnel Center) in April 1985 by general order of Chief of Staff.

Air Force Medical Service Center Renamed Air Force Office of Medical Support by Program Action Directive 85–1 of Mar. 6, 1985, approved by Air Force Vice Chief of Staff.

Air Mail, Bureau of Established in Interstate Commerce Commission to carry out provisions of act of June 12, 1934 (48 Stat. 933). Personnel and property transferred to *Civil Aeronautics Authority* by EO 7959 of Aug. 22, 1938.

Air Patrol, Civil Established in *Civilian Defense Office* by Administrative Order 9 of Dec. 8, 1941. Transferred to *Department of War* as auxiliary of Army Air Forces by EO 9339 of Apr. 29, 1943. Transferred to the Department of the Air Force by Secretary of Defense order of May 21, 1948. Established as civilian auxiliary of U.S. Air Force by act of May 26, 1948 (62 Stat. 274).

Air Safety Board Established by act of June 23, 1938 (52 Stat. 973). Functions transferred to *Civil Aeronautics Board* by Reorg. Plan No. IV of 1940, effective June 30, 1940.

Airways Modernization Board Established by act of Aug. 14, 1957 (71 Stat. 349). Transferred to *Federal Aviation Agency* by EO 10786 of Nov. 1, 1958.

Alaska, Board of Road Commissioners for Established in *Department of War* by act of Jan. 27, 1905 (33 Stat. 616). Functions transferred to the Department of Interior by act of June 30, 1932 (47 Stat. 446), and delegated to *Alaska Road Commission.* Functions transferred to the Department of Commerce by act of June 29, 1956 (70 Stat. 377), and terminated by act of June 25, 1959 (73 Stat. 145).

Alaska, Federal Field Committee for Development Planning in Established by EO 11182 of Oct. 2, 1964. Abolished by EO 11608 of July 19, 1971.

Alaska, Federal Reconstruction and Development Planning Commission for Established by EO 11150 of Apr. 2, 1964. Abolished by EO 11182 of Oct. 2, 1964, which established *President's Review Committee for Development Planning in Alaska* and *Federal Field Committee for Development Planning in Alaska.*

Alaska, President's Review Committee for Development Planning in Established by EO 11182 of Oct. 2, 1964. Superseded by *Federal Advisory Council on Regional Economic Development* established by EO 11386 of Dec. 28, 1967. EO 11386 revoked by EO 12553 of Feb. 25, 1986.

Alaska Communication System Operational responsibility vested in Secretary of the Army by act of May 26, 1900 (31 Stat. 206). Transferred to Secretary of the Air Force by Secretary of Defense reorganization order of May 24, 1962.

Alaska Engineering Commission *See* **Alaska Railroad**

Alaska Game Commission Established by act of Jan. 13, 1925 (43 Stat. 740). Expired Dec. 31, 1959, pursuant to act of July 7, 1958 (72 Stat. 339).

Alaska International Rail and Highway Commission Established by act of Aug. 1, 1956 (70 Stat. 888). Terminated June 30, 1961, under terms of act.Alaska Natural Gas Transporation System, Office of Federal Inspector of Construction for the Established by Reorg. Plan No. 1 of 1979 (5 U.S.C. app.), effective July 1, 1979. Abolished by act of Oct. 24, 1992 (106 Stat. 3128) and functions and authority vested in the Inspector transferred to the Secretary of Energy. Functions vested in the Secretary of Energy transferred to the Federal Coordinator, Office of the Federal Coordinator for Alaska Natural Gas Transportation Projects by act of Oct. 13, 2004 (118 Stat. 1261).

Alaska Power Administration Established by the Secretary of the Interior in 1967. Transferred to the Department of Energy by act of Aug. 4, 1977 (91 Stat. 578).

Alaska Railroad Built pursuant to act of Mar. 12, 1914 (38 Stat. 305), which created *Alaska Engineering Commission.* Placed under the Secretary of the Interior by EO 2129 of Jan. 26, 1915, and renamed Alaska Railroad by EO 3861 of June 8, 1923. Authority to regulate tariffs granted to Interstate Commerce Commission by EO 11107 of Apr. 25, 1963. Authority to operate Railroad transferred to the Secretary of Transportation by act of Oct. 15, 1966 (80 Stat. 941), effective Apr. 1, 1967. Railroad purchased by State of Alaska, effective Jan. 5, 1985.

Alaska Road Commission *See* **Alaska, Board of Road Commissioners for**

Alcohol, Bureau of Industrial Established by act of May 27, 1930 (46 Stat. 427). Consolidated into *Bureau of Internal Revenue* by EO 6166 of June 10, 1933. Consolidation deferred until May 11, 1934, by EO 6639 of Mar. 10, 1934. Order also transferred to Internal Revenue Commissioner certain functions imposed on Attorney General by act of May 27, 1930, with relation to enforcement of criminal laws concerning intoxicating liquors remaining in effect after repeal of 18th amendment; personnel of, and appropriations for, *Bureau of Industrial Alcohol;* and necessary personnel and appropriations of *Bureau of Prohibition,* Department of Justice.

Alcohol, Drug Abuse, and Mental Health Administration Established by the *Secretary of Health, Education, and Welfare* by act of May 21, 1972 (88 Stat. 134). Redesignated as an agency of the Public Health Service from the *National Institute of Mental Health* Sept. 25, 1973, by the Secretary of Health, Education, and Welfare. Functions transferred to the Department of Health and Human Services by act of Oct. 17, 1979 (93 Stat. 695). Established as an agency of the Public Health Service by act of Oct. 27, 1986 (100 Stat. 3207–106). Renamed Substance Abuse and Mental Health Services Administration by act of July 10, 1992 (106 Stat. 325).

Alcohol Abuse and Alcoholism, National Institute on Established within the National Institute of Mental Health, *Department of Health, Education, and Welfare* by act of Dec. 31, 1970 (84 Stat. 1848). Removed from within the National Institute of Mental Health and made an entity within the Alcohol, Drug Abuse, and Mental Health Administration by act of May 14, 1974 (88 Stat. 1356). Functions transferred to the Department of Health and Human Services by act of Oct. 17, 1979 (93 Stat. 695). (*See also* act of Oct. 27, 1986; 100 Stat. 3207–106.) Abolished by act of July 10, 1992 (106 Stat. 331). Reestablished by act of July 10, 1992 (106 Stat. 359).

Alcohol Administration, Federal *See* **Alcohol Control Administration, Federal**

Alcohol Control Administration, Federal Established by EO 6474 of Dec. 4, 1933. Abolished Sept. 24, 1935, on induction into office of Administrator, *Federal Alcohol Administration,* as provided in act of Aug. 29, 1935 (49 Stat. 977). Abolished by Reorg. Plan No. III of 1940, effective June 30, 1940, and functions consolidated with activities of Internal Revenue Service.

Alcohol, Tobacco, and Firearms, Bureau of Established within Treasury Department by Treasury Order No. 221, eff. July 1, 1972. Transferred to Bureau of Alcohol, Tobacco, Firearms, and Explosives in Justice Department by act of Nov. 25, 2002, except some authorities, functions, personnel, and assets relating to administration and enforcement of certain provisions of the Internal Revenue Code of 1986 and title 27 of the U.S. Code (116 Stat. 2275).

Alexander Hamilton Bicentennial Commission Established by act of Aug. 20, 1954 (68 Stat. 746). Terminated Apr. 30, 1958.

Alien Property Custodian Appointed by President Oct. 22, 1917, under authority of act of Oct. 6, 1917 (40 Stat. 415). Office transferred to *Alien Property Division,* Department of Justice, by EO 6694 of May 1, 1934. Powers vested in President by act delegated to Attorney General by EO 8136 of May 15, 1939. Authority vested in Attorney General by EO's 6694 and 8136 transferred by EO 9142 of Apr. 21, 1942, to *Office of Alien Property Custodian, Office for Emergency Management,* as provided for by EO 9095 of Mar. 11, 1942.

American Republics, Office for Coordination of Commercial and Cultural Relations between the Established by *Council of National Defense* order approved by President Aug. 16, 1940. Succeeded by *Office of the Coordinator of Inter-American Affairs, Office for Emergency Management,* established by EO 8840 of July 30, 1941. Renamed *Office of Inter-American Affairs* by EO 9532 of Mar. 23, 1945. Information functions transferred to the Department of State by EO 9608 of Aug. 31, 1945. Terminated by EO 9710 of Apr. 10, 1946, and functions transferred to the Department of State, functioning as *Institute of Inter-American Affairs.* Transferred to *Foreign Operations Administration* by Reorg. Plan No. 7, effective Aug. 1, 1953.

American Revolution Bicentennial Administration *See* **American Revolution Bicentennial Commission**

American Revolution Bicentennial Commission Established by act of July 4, 1966 (80 Stat. 259). *American Revolution Bicentennial Administration* established by act of Dec. 11, 1973 (87 Stat. 697), to replace *Commission. Administration* terminated June 30, 1977, pursuant to terms of act. Certain continuing functions transferred to the Secretary of the Interior by EO 12001 of June 29, 1977.

Anacostia Neighborhood Museum Renamed Anacostia Museum by Smithsonian Institution announcement of Apr. 3, 1987.

Animal Industry, Bureau of Established in the Department of Agriculture by act of May 29, 1884 (23 Stat. 31). Functions transferred to Agricultural Research Service by Secretary's Memorandum 1320, supp. 4, of Nov. 2, 1953.

Apprenticeship, Federal Committee on Previously known as *Federal Committee on Apprentice Training,* established by EO 6750–C of June 27, 1934. Functioned as part of *Division of Labor Standards,* Department of Labor, pursuant to act of Aug. 16, 1937 (50 Stat. 664). Transferred to *Office of Administrator, Federal Security Agency,* by EO 9139 of Apr. 18, 1942. Transferred to *Bureau of Training, War Manpower Commission,* by EO 9247 of Sept. 17, 1942. Returned to the Department of Labor by EO 9617 of Sept. 19, 1945.

Archive of Folksong Renamed Archive of Folk Culture by administrative order of Deputy Librarian of Congress, effective Sept. 21, 1981.

Archives Council, National Established by act of June 19, 1934 (48 Stat. 1122). Transferred to General Services Administration by act of June 30, 1949 (63 Stat. 378). Terminated on establishment of Federal Records Council by act of Sept. 5, 1950 (64 Stat. 583).

Archives Establishment, National *Office of Archivist of the U.S.* and *National Archives* created by act of June 19, 1934 (48 Stat. 1122). Transferred to General Services Administration by act of June 30, 1949 (63 Stat. 381), and incorporated as *National Archives and Records Service* by order of General Services Administrator, together with functions of *Division of the Federal Register, National Archives Council, National Historical Publications Commission,* National Archives Trust Fund Board, *Trustees of the Franklin D. Roosevelt Library,* and Administrative Committee of the Federal Register. Transferred from General Services Administration to National Archives and Records Administration by act of Oct. 19, 1984 (98 Stat. 2283), along with certain functions of Administrator of General Services transferred to Archivist of the United States, effective Apr. 1, 1985.

Archives and Records Service, National *See* **Archives Establishment, National**

Archives Trust Fund Board, National *See* **Archives Establishment, National**

Area Redevelopment Administration Established May 8, 1961, by the Secretary of Commerce pursuant to act of May 1, 1961 (75 Stat. 47) and Reorg. Plan No. 5 of 1950, effective May 24, 1950. Terminated Aug. 31, 1965, by act of June 30, 1965 (79 Stat. 195). Functions transferred to Economic Development Administration in the Department of Commerce by Department Order 4–A, effective Sept. 1, 1965.

Arlington Memorial Amphitheater Commission Established by act of Mar. 4, 1921 (41 Stat. 1440). Abolished by act of Sept. 2, 1960 (74 Stat. 739), and functions transferred to the Secretary of Defense.

Arlington Memorial Bridge Commission Established by act of Mar. 4, 1913 (37 Stat. 885; D.C. Code (1951 ed.) 8–158). Abolished by EO 6166 of June 10, 1933, and functions transferred to *Office of National Parks, Buildings, and Reservations.*

Armed Forces, U.S. Court of Appeals for the *See* **Military Appeals, United States Court of**

Armed Forces Medical Library Founded in 1836 as *Library of the Surgeon General's Office,* U.S. Army. Later known as *Army Medical Library,* then *Armed Forces Medical Library* in 1952. Personnel and property transferred to National Library of Medicine established in Public Health Service by act of Aug. 3, 1956 (70 Stat. 960).

Armed Forces Museum Advisory Board, National Established by act of Aug. 30, 1961 (75 Stat. 414). Functions discontinued due to lack of funding.

Armed Forces Staff College Renamed Joint Forces Staff College by act of Oct. 30, 2000 (144 Stat. 165A–230).

Armed Services Renegotiation Board Established by Secretary of Defense directive of July 19, 1948. Abolished by Secretary's letter of Jan. 18, 1952, and functions transferred to *Renegotiation Board.*

Arms Control and Disarmament Agency, U.S. Established by act of Sept. 26, 1961 (75 Stat. 631). Abolished by act of Oct. 21, 1998 (112 Stat. 2681–767) and functions transferred to the Secretary of State.

Army Communications Command, U.S. Renamed U.S. Army Information Systems Command by Department General Order No. 26 of July 25, 1984.

Army Materiel Development and Readiness Command, U.S. Renamed U.S. Army Materiel Command by Department General Order No. 28 of Aug. 15, 1984.

Army and Navy, Joint Board Placed under direction of President by military order of July 5, 1939. Abolished Sept. 1, 1947, by joint letter of Aug. 20, 1947, to President from Secretaries of *War* and Navy.

Army and Navy Staff College Established Apr. 23, 1943, and operated under Joint Chiefs of Staff. Redesignated the National War College, effective July 1, 1946.

Army Specialist Corps Established in *Department of War* by EO 9078 of Feb. 26, 1942. Abolished by the *Secretary of War* Oct. 31, 1942, and functions merged into central *Officer Procurement Service.*

Arts, National Collection of Fine Established within Smithsonian Institution by act of Mar. 24, 1937 (50 Stat. 51). Renamed *National Museum of American Art* in Smithsonian Institution by act of Oct. 13, 1980 (94 Stat. 1884).

Arthritis, Diabetes, and Digestive and Kidney Diseases, National Institute of *See* **Arthritis, Metabolism, and Digestive Diseases, National Institute of**

Arthritis, Metabolism, and Digestive Diseases, National Institute of Renamed *National Institute of Arthritis, Diabetes, and Digestive and Kidney Diseases* by Secretary's order of June 15, 1981, pursuant to act of Dec. 19, 1980 (94 Stat. 3184). Renamed National Institute of Diabetes and Digestive and Kidney Diseases and National Institute of Arthritis and Musculoskeletal and Skin Diseases by act of Nov. 20, 1985 (99 Stat. 820).

Arts, Advisory Committee on the Established under authority of act of Sept. 20, 1961 (75 Stat. 527). Terminated July 1973 by act of Oct. 6, 1972. Formally abolished by Reorg. Plan No. 2 of 1977, effective Apr. 1, 1978.

Arts, National Council on the Established in Executive Office of the President by act of Sept. 3, 1964 (78 Stat. 905). Transferred to National Foundation on the Arts and the Humanities by act of Sept. 29, 1965 (79 Stat. 845).

Assay Commission, Annual Established initially by act of Apr. 2, 1792 (1 Stat. 250) and by act of Feb. 12, 1873 (Revised Statute sec. 3647; 17 Stat. 432). Terminated and functions transferred to the Secretary of the Treasury by act of Mar. 14, 1980 (94 Stat. 98).

Assistance, Bureau of Public Renamed *Bureau of Family Services* by order of the *Secretary of Health, Education, and Welfare,* effective Jan. 1, 1962. Functions redelegated to *Social and Rehabilitation Service* by Secretary's reorganization of Aug. 15, 1967.

Assistance Coordinating Committee, Adjustment Established by act of Jan. 3, 1975 (88 Stat. 2040). Inactive since 1981.

Assistance Payments Administration Established by *Secretary of Health, Education, and Welfare* reorganization of Aug. 15, 1967. Transferred by *Secretary's* reorganization of Mar. 8, 1977 (42 FR 13262), from *Social and Rehabilitation Service* to Social Security Administration.

Athletics, Interagency Committee on International Established by EO 11117 of Aug. 13, 1963. Terminated by EO 11515 of Mar. 13, 1970.

Atlantic-Pacific Interoceanic Canal Study Commission Established by act of Sept. 22, 1964 (78 Stat. 990). Terminated Dec. 1, 1970, pursuant to terms of act.

Atomic Energy Commission Established by act of Aug. 1, 1946 (60 Stat. 755). Abolished by act of Oct. 11, 1974 (88 Stat. 1237) and functions transferred to *Energy Research and Development Administration* and Nuclear Regulatory Commission.

Aviation, Interdepartmental Committee on Civil International Established by Presidential letter of June 20, 1935. Terminated on organization of *Civil Aeronautics Authority.*

Aviation Agency, Federal Established by act of Aug. 23, 1958 (72 Stat. 731). Transferred to Secretary of Transportation by act of Oct. 15, 1966 (80 Stat. 931). *Agency* reestablished as Federal Aviation Administration by act of Jan 12, 1983 (96 Stat. 2416).

Aviation Commission, Federal Established by act of June 12, 1934 (48 Stat. 938). Terminated Feb. 1, 1935, under provisions of act.

Beltsville Research Center Established to operate with other agencies of the Department of Agriculture under *Agricultural Research Administration.* Consolidated into *Agricultural Research Administration,* the Department of Agriculture, by EO 9069 of Feb. 23, 1942.

Biological Service, National Established in the Department of the Interior in 1995 by Secretarial order. Transferred to U.S. Geological Survey as new Biological Resources Division by Secretarial Order No. 3202, Sept. 30, 1996.

Biological Survey, Bureau of Established by Secretary's order July 1, 1885, as part of *Division of Entomology,* Department of Agriculture. Made separate bureau by act of Apr. 23, 1904 (33 Stat. 276). Transferred to the Department of the Interior by Reorg. Plan No. II of 1939, effective July 1, 1939. Consolidated with *Bureau of Fisheries* into *Fish and Wildlife Service* by Reorg. Plan No. III of 1940, effective June 30, 1940.

Biological Survey, National Established in the the Department of the Interior by Secretarial Order 3173 of Sept. 29, 1993. Renamed *National Biological Service* by Secretarial order in 1995.

Blind, Inc., American Printing House for the Established in 1858 as privately owned institution in Louisville, KY. Functions of the Secretary of the Treasury, except that relating to perpetual trust funds, transferred to *Federal Security Agency* by Reorg. Plan No. II of 1939, effective July 1, 1939. Functions performed by *Department of Health, Education, and Welfare* transferred to the Department of Education.

Blind-made Products, Committee on Purchases of Established by act of June 25, 1938 (52 Stat. 1196). Renamed *Committee for Purchase of Products and Services of the Blind and Other Severely Handicapped* by act of June 23, 1971 (85 Stat. 77). Renamed *Committee for Purchase from the Blind and Other Severely Handicapped* by act of July 25, 1974 (88 Stat. 392). Renamed Committee for Purchase From People Who Are Blind or Severely Disabled by act of Oct. 29, 1992 (106 Stat. 4486).

Blind and Other Severely Handicapped, Committee for Purchase of Products and Services of the *See* **Blind-made Products, Committee on Purchases of**

Board. *See other part of title*

Bond and Spirits Division Established as *Taxes and Penalties Unit,* as announced by Assistant to Attorney General in departmental circular of May 25, 1934, pursuant to EO 6639 of May 10, 1934. Abolished by administrative order of October 1942, and functions transferred to Tax, Claims, and Criminal Divisions, Department of Justice.

Bonneville Power Administration Established by the Secretary of the Interior pursuant to act of Aug. 20, 1937 (50 Stat. 731). Transferred to the Department of Energy by act of Aug. 4, 1977 (91 Stat. 578).

Boston National Historic Sites Commission Established by joint resolution of June 16, 1955 (69 Stat. 137). Terminated June 16, 1960, by act of Feb. 19, 1957 (71 Stat. 4).

Brazil-U.S. Defense Commission, Joint Established in May 1942 by agreement between the U.S. and Brazil. Terminated in September 1977 at direction of Brazilian Government.

Broadcast Bureau Merged with *Cable Television Bureau* to form Mass Media Bureau by Federal Communications Commission order, effective Nov. 30, 1982.

Broadcast Intelligence Service, Foreign *See* **Broadcast Monitoring Service, Foreign**

Broadcast Monitoring Service, Foreign Established in Federal Communications Commission by Presidential directive of Feb. 26, 1941. Renamed *Foreign Broadcast Intelligence Service* by FCC order of July 28, 1942. Transferred to *Department of War* by Secretarial order of Dec. 30, 1945. Act of May 3, 1945 (59 Stat. 110), provided for liquidation 60 days after Japanese armistice. Transferred to *Central Intelligence Group* Aug. 5, 1946, and renamed *Foreign Broadcast Information Service.*

Budget, Bureau of the Established by act of June 10, 1921 (42 Stat. 20), in the Department of the Treasury under immediate direction of President. Transferred to Executive Office of the President by Reorg. Plan No. I of 1939, effective July 1, 1939. Reorganized by Reorg. Plan No. 2 of 1970, effective July 1, 1970, and renamed Office of Management and Budget.

Buildings Administration, Public Established as part of *Federal Works Agency* by Reorg. Plan No. I of 1939, effective July 1, 1939. Abolished by act of June 30, 1949 (63 Stat. 380), and functions transferred to General Services Administration.

Buildings Branch, Public Organized in *Procurement Division,* established in the Department of the Treasury by EO 6166 of June 10, 1933. Consolidated with *Branch of Buildings Management,* National Park Service, to form *Public Buildings Administration, Federal Works Agency,* under Reorg. Plan No. I of 1939, effective July 1, 1939.

Buildings Commission, Public Established by act of July 1, 1916 (39 Stat. 328). Abolished by EO 6166 of June 10, 1933, and functions transferred to *Office of National Parks, Buildings, and Reservations,* Department of the Interior. Functions transferred to *Public Buildings Administration, Federal Works Agency,* under Reorg. Plan No. I of 1939, effective July 1, 1939.

Buildings Management, Branch of Functions of National Park Service (except those relating to monuments and memorials) consolidated with *Public Buildings Branch, Procurement Division,* Department of the Treasury, to form *Public Buildings Administration, Federal Works Agency,* in accordance with Reorg. Plan No. I of 1939, effective July 1, 1939.

Buildings and Public Parks of the National Capital, Office of Public Established by act of Feb. 26, 1925 (43 Stat. 983), by consolidation of *Office of Public Buildings and Grounds* under Chief of Engineers, U.S. Army, and *Office of Superintendent of State, War, and Navy Department Buildings.* Abolished by EO 6166 of June 10, 1933, and functions transferred to *Office of National Parks, Buildings, and Reservations,* Department of the Interior.

Bureau. *See other part of title*

Business, Cabinet Committee on Small Established by Presidential letter of May 31, 1956. Dissolved January 1961.

Business Administration, Domestic and International *See* **Business and Defense Services Administration**

Business and Defense Services Administration Established by the Secretary of Commerce Oct. 1, 1953, and operated under Department Organization Order 40–1. Abolished by Department Organization Order 40–1A of Sept. 15, 1970, and functions transferred to *Bureau of Domestic Commerce.* Functions transferred to *Domestic and International Business Administration,* effective Nov. 17, 1972. *Administration* terminated by Secretary's order of Dec. 4, 1977, and functions assumed by *Industry and Trade Administration.*

Business Economics, Office of Established by the Secretary of Commerce Jan. 17, 1946. Renamed *Office of Economic Analysis* Dec. 1, 1953. Transferred to the *Administration of Social and Economic Statistics* along with Bureau of the Census and renamed Bureau of Economic Analysis on Jan. 1, 1972.

Business Operations, Bureau of International Established by the Secretary of Commerce Aug. 8, 1961, by Departmental Orders 173 and 174. Abolished by Departmental Order 182 of Feb. 1, 1963, which established *Bureau of International Commerce.* Functions transferred to *Domestic and International Business Administration,* effective Nov. 17, 1972.

Cable Television Bureau Merged with *Broadcast Bureau* by Federal Communications Commission order to form Mass Media Bureau, effective Nov. 30, 1982.

California Debris Commission Established by act of Mar. 1, 1893 (27 Stat. 507). Abolished by act of Nov. 17, 1986 (100 Stat. 4229), and functions transferred to the Secretary of the Interior.

Canal Zone Government Established by act of Aug. 24, 1912 (37 Stat. 561). Abolished by act of Sept. 27, 1979 (93 Stat. 454).

Capital Housing Authority, National Established by act of June 12, 1934 (48 Stat. 930). Made agency of District of Columbia government by act of Dec. 24, 1973 (87 Stat. 779), effective July 1, 1974.

Capital Park Commission, National Established by act of June 6, 1924 (43 Stat. 463). *National Capital Park and Planning Commission* named successor by act of Apr. 30, 1926 (44 Stat. 374). Functions transferred to National Capital Planning Commission by act of July 19, 1952 (66 Stat. 781).

Capital Park and Planning Commission, National *See* **Capital Park Commission, National**

Capital Regional Planning Council, National Established by act of July 19, 1952 (66 Stat. 785). Terminated by Reorg. Plan No. 5 of 1966, effective Sept. 8, 1966.

Capital Transportation Agency, National Established by act of July 14, 1960 (74 Stat 537). Authorized to establish rapid rail transit system by act of Sept. 8, 1965 (79 Stat. 663). Functions transferred to Washington Metropolitan Area Transit Authority by EO 11373 of Sept. 20, 1967.

Career Executive Board Established by EO 10758 of Mar. 4, 1958. Terminated July 1, 1959, and EO 10758 revoked by EO 10859 of Feb. 5, 1960.

Caribbean Organization Act of June 30, 1961 (75 Stat. 194), provided for acceptance by President of Agreement for the Establishment of the Caribbean Organization, signed at Washington, June 21, 1960. Article III of Agreement provided for termination of *Caribbean Commission,* authorized by Agreement signed Oct. 30, 1946, on first meeting of Caribbean Council, governing body of *Organization.* Terminated, effective Dec. 31, 1965, by resolution adopted by Council.

Cemeteries and Memorials in Europe, National Supervision transferred from *Department of War* to American Battle Monuments Commission by EO 6614 of Feb. 26, 1934, which transfer was deferred to May 21, 1934, by EO 6690 of Apr. 25, 1934.

Cemeteries and Parks, National *Department of War* functions regarding National Cemeteries and Parks located in continental U.S. transferred to *Office of National Parks, Buildings, and Reservations,* Department of the Interior, by EO 6166 of June 10, 1933.

Cemetery System, National Established in the *Veterans' Administration* by act of June 18, 1973 (87 Stat. 75). Redesignated as the National Cemetery Administration by act of Nov. 11, 1998 (112 Stat. 3337).

Censorship, Office of Established by EO 8985 of Dec. 19, 1941. Terminated by EO 9631 of Sept. 28, 1945.

Censorship Policy Board Established by EO 8985 of Dec. 19, 1941. Terminated by EO 9631 of Sept. 28, 1945.

Census, Bureau of the *See* **Census Office**

Census Office Established temporarily within the the Department of the Interior in accordance with act of Mar. 3, 1899. Established as a permanent office by act of Mar. 6, 1902. Transferred from the Department of the Interior to *Department of Commerce and Labor* by act of Feb. 14, 1903. Remained in the Department of Commerce under provisions of Reorganization Plan No. 5 of May 24, 1950, effective May 24, 1950

Center. *See other part of title*

Central. *See other part of title*

Chemistry and Soils, Bureau of *See* **Agricultural and Industrial Chemistry, Bureau of**

Chesapeake Bay Center for Environmental Studies Established in 1965 in Annapolis, MD, as part of Smithsonian Institution by Secretarial order. Merged with *Radiation Biology Laboratory* by Secretarial Order July 1, 1983, to form Smithsonian Environmental Research Center.

Child Development, Office of *See* **Children's Bureau**

Children's Bureau Established by act of Apr. 9, 1912 (37 Stat. 79). Placed in the Department of Labor by act of Mar. 4, 1913 (37 Stat. 737). Transferred, with exception of child labor functions, to *Social Security Administration, Federal Security Agency,* by Reorg. Plan No. 2 of 1946, effective July 16, 1946. Continued under *Administration* when *Agency* functions assumed by the *Department of Health, Education, and Welfare.* Reassigned to *Welfare Administration* by Department reorganization of Jan. 28, 1963. Reassigned to *Social and Rehabilitation Service* by Department reorganization of Aug. 15, 1967. Reassigned to *Office of Child Development* by Department reorganization order of Sept. 17, 1969.

China, U.S. Court for Established by act of June 30, 1906 (34 Stat. 814). Transferred to the Department of Justice by EO 6166 of June 10, 1933, effective Mar. 2, 1934. Act of June 30, 1906, repealed effective Sept. 1, 1948 (62 Stat. 992).

Christopher Columbus Quincentenary Jubilee Commission Established by act of Aug. 7, 1984 (98 Stat. 1257). Terminated pursuant to terms of act.

Civil defense. *See* **Defense**

Civil Rights, Commission on Established by act of Sept. 9, 1957 (71 Stat. 634). Terminated in 1983 and reestablished by act of Nov. 30, 1983 (97 Stat. 1301). Renamed United States Commission on Civil Rights by act of Nov. 2, 1994 (108 Stat. 4683).

Civil Service Commission, U.S. Established by act of Jan. 16, 1883 (22 Stat. 403). Redesignated as Merit Systems Protection Board and functions transferred to Board and Office of Personnel Management by Reorg. Plan No. 2 of 1978, effective Jan. 1, 1979.

Civil War Centennial Commission Established by act of Sept. 7, 1957 (71 Stat. 626). Terminated May 1, 1966, pursuant to terms of act.

Civilian Conservation Corps Established by act of June 28, 1937 (50 Stat. 319). Made part of *Federal Security Agency* by Reorg. Plan No. I of 1939, effective July 1, 1939. Liquidation provided for by act of July 2, 1942 (56 Stat. 569), not later than June 30, 1943.

Civilian Health and Medical Program of the United States, Office of Established as field activity in the Department of Defense in 1974. Functions consolidated into the TRICARE Management Activity in November 1997 by Defense Reform Initiative.

Civilian Production Administration Established by EO 9638 of Oct. 4, 1945. Consolidated with other agencies to form *Office of Temporary Controls, Office for Emergency Management,* by EO 9809 of Dec. 12, 1946.

Civilian Service Awards Board, Distinguished Established by EO 10717 of June 27, 1957. Terminated by EO 12014 of Oct. 19, 1977, and functions transferred to *U.S. Civil Service Commission.*

Claims, U.S. Court of Established Feb. 25, 1855 (10 Stat. 612). Abolished by act of Apr. 2, 1982 (96 Stat. 26) and trial jurisdiction transferred to *U.S. Claims Court* and appellate functions merged with those of *U.S. Court of Customs and Patent Appeals* to form U.S. Court of Appeals for the Federal Circuit. *U.S. Claims Court* renamed U.S. Court of Federal Claims by act of Oct. 29, 1992 (106 Stat. 4516).

Claims Commission of the United States, International Established in the Department of State by act of Mar. 10, 1950 (64 Stat. 12). Abolished by Reorg. Plan No. 1 of 1954, effective July 1, 1954, and functions transferred to Foreign Claims Settlement Commission of the United States.

Claims Settlement Commission of the United States, Foreign Established by Reorg. Plan No. 1 of 1954, effective July 1, 1954. Transferred to the Department of Justice by act of Mar. 14, 1980 (94 Stat. 96).

Clark Sesquicentennial Commission, George Rogers Established by Public Resolution 51 (45 Stat. 723). Expenditures ordered administered by the Department of the Interior by EO 6166 of June 10, 1933.

Classification Review Committee, Interagency Established by EO 11652 of Mar. 8, 1972. Abolished by EO 12065 of June 28, 1978.

Clemency Board, Presidential Established in Executive Office of the President by EO 11803 of Sept. 16, 1974. Final recommendations submitted to President Sept. 15, 1975, and *Board* terminated by EO 11878 of Sept. 10, 1975.

Coal Commission, National Bituminous Established under authority of act of Aug. 30, 1935 (49 Stat. 992). Abolished by Reorg. Plan No. II of 1939, effective July 1, 1939, and functions transferred to *Bituminous Coal Division,* Department of the Interior.

Coal Consumers' Counsel, Office of the Bituminous Established by act of Apr. 11, 1941 (55 Stat. 134), renewing provisions of act of Apr. 23, 1937 (50 Stat. 72) for 2 years to continue functions of *Consumers' Counsel Division,* Department of the Interior. Functions continued by acts of Apr. 24, 1943 (57 Stat. 68), and May 21, 1943 (57 Stat. 82). Terminated Aug. 24, 1943.

Coal Division, Bituminous Established July 1, 1939, by Secretary of the Interior Order 1394 of June 16, 1939, as amended by Order 1399, of July 5, 1939, pursuant to act of Apr. 3, 1939 (53 Stat. 562) and Reorg. Plan No. II of 1939, effective July 1, 1939. Administered functions vested in *National Bituminous Coal Commission* by act of Apr. 23, 1937 (50 Stat. 72). Act extended to Aug. 24, 1943, on which date it expired.

Coal Labor Board, Bituminous Established by act of July 12, 1921 (42 Stat. 140). Abolished as result of U.S. Supreme Court decision, May 18, 1936, in case of *Carter* v. *Carter Coal Company et al.*

Coal Mine Safety Board of Review, Federal Established by act of July 16, 1952 (66 Stat. 697). Inactive after Mar. 30, 1970, pursuant to act of Dec. 30, 1969 (83 Stat. 803).

Coal Mines Administration Established by the Secretary of the Interior July 1, 1943. Abolished by Secretary's Order 1977 of Aug. 16, 1944, as amended by Order 1982 of Aug. 31, 1944, and functions assumed by *Solid Fuels Administration for War. Administration* reestablished in the Department of the Interior by EO 9728 of May 21, 1946. Terminated June 30, 1947, by act of Mar. 27, 1942 (56 Stat. 176).

Coal Research, Office of Established in the Department of the Interior by act of July 7, 1960 (74 Stat. 336). Functions transferred to *Energy Research and Development Administration* by act of Oct. 11, 1974 (88 Stat. 1237).

Coalition Provisional Authority, Inspector General of the Established by act of Nov. 6, 2003 (117 Stat. 1234). Renamed Special Inspector General for Iraq Reconstruction by act of Oct. 28, 2004 (118 Stat. 2078.)

Coalition Provisional Authority, Office of the Inspector General of the Established by act of Nov. 6, 2003 (117 Stat. 1234). Renamed Office of the Special Inspector General for Iraq Reconstruction by act of Oct. 28, 2004 (118 Stat. 2078).

Coast and Geodetic Survey *See* **Coast Survey**

Coast Guard, U.S. Established by act of Jan. 28, 1915 (38 Stat. 800) as a military service and branch of the U.S. Armed Forces at all times and as a service in Treasury Department, except when operating as a service in the Navy. Transferred from the Department of the Treasury to the Department of the Navy by EO 8929 of Nov. 1, 1941. Returned to the Department of the Treasury by EO 9666 of Dec. 28, 1945. Transferred to the Department of Transportation by act of Oct. 15, 1966 (80 Stat. 931). Transferred to Homeland Security Department by act of Nov. 25, 2002 (116 Stat. 2249) with related authorities and functions of the Secretary of Transportation.

Coast Survey Established by act of Feb. 10, 1807 (2 Stat. 413). Redesignated as *Coast and Geodetic Survey* by act of June 20, 1878 (20 Stat. 206). Transferred to *Environmental Science Services*

Administration by Reorg. Plan No. 2 of 1965, effective July 13, 1965.

Codification Board Established by act of June 19, 1937 (50 Stat. 304). Abolished by Reorg. Plan No. II of 1939, effective July 1, 1939, and functions transferred to *Division of the Federal Register.*

Coinage, Joint Commission on the Established by act of July 23, 1965 (79 Stat. 258). Expired Jan. 4, 1975, pursuant to act of Oct. 6, 1972 (88 Stat. 776).

Columbia Institution for the Instruction of the Deaf and Dumb, and the Blind Established by act of Feb. 16, 1857 (11 Stat. 161). Renamed *Columbia Institution for the Instruction of the Deaf and Dumb* by act of Feb. 23, 1865 (13 Stat. 436). Renamed *Columbia Institution for the Deaf* by act of Mar. 4, 1911 (36 Stat. 1422). Renamed *Gallaudet College* by act of June 18, 1954 (68 Stat. 265). Functions of the *Department of Health, Education, and Welfare* transferred to the Department of Education by act of Oct. 17, 1979 (93 Stat. 695). Renamed Gallaudet University by act of Aug. 4, 1986 (100 Stat. 781).

Commander in Chief, U.S. Fleet, and Chief of Naval Operations Duties of two positions prescribed by EO 8984 of Dec. 18, 1941. Combined under one officer by EO 9096 of Mar. 12, 1942.

Commerce, Bureau of Domestic *See* **Business and Defense Services Administration**

Commerce, Bureau of Foreign Established by the Secretary of Commerce Oct. 12, 1953, by Reorg. Plan No. 5 of 1950, effective May 24, 1950. Abolished by department order of Aug. 7, 1961, and functions vested in *Bureau of International Programs* and *Bureau of International Business Operations.*

Commerce, Bureau of Foreign and Domestic Established by act of Aug. 23, 1912 (37 Stat. 407). Functions reassigned to other offices of the Department of Commerce due to internal reorganizations.

Commerce, Bureau of International *See* **Business Operations, Bureau of International**

Commerce Service, Foreign Established in *Bureau of Foreign and Domestic Commerce,* Department of Commerce, by act of Mar. 3, 1927 (44 Stat. 1394). Transferred to the Department of State as part of Foreign Service by Reorg. Plan No. II of 1939, effective July 1, 1939.

Commercial Company, U.S. Established Mar. 27, 1942, as subsidiary of *Reconstruction Finance Corporation.* Transferred to *Office of Economic Warfare* by EO 9361 of July 15, 1943. *Office* consolidated into *Foreign Economic Administration* by EO 9380 of Sept. 25, 1943. Functions returned to *Corporation* by EO 9630 of Sept. 27, 1945, until June 30, 1948.

Commercial Policy, Executive Committee on Established by Presidential letter of Nov. 11, 1933, to Secretary of State. Abolished by EO 9461 of Aug. 7, 1944.

Commercial Standards Division Transferred with *Division of Simplified Trade Practice* from *National Bureau of Standards* to the Secretary of Commerce by Reorg. Plan No. 3 of 1946, effective July 16, 1946, to permit reassignment to *Office of Domestic Commerce.* Functions transferred to *National Bureau of Standards* by the Department of Commerce Order 90, June 7, 1963, pursuant to Reorg. Plan No. 5 of 1950, effective May 24, 1950.

Commission. *See other part of title*

Committee. *See also other part of title*

Committee Management Secretariat Established in the Office of Management and Budget Jan. 5, 1973, by act of Oct. 6, 1972 (86 Stat. 772). Functions transferred to General Services Administrator by Reorg. Plan No. 1 of 1977, effective Apr. 1, 1978. Reassigned to the *National Archives and Records Service* by GSA order of Feb. 22, 1979. Transferred in Archives to Office of the Federal Register by GSA order of Oct. 14, 1980. Transferred to Office of the Archivist of the United States by GSA order of Sept. 24, 1982. Reassigned to Office of Program Initiatives, GSA, by GSA order of May 18, 1984. Transferred to Office of Management Services, GSA, by GSA order of Apr. 7, 1986.

Commodities Corporation, Federal Surplus *See* **Relief Corporation, Federal Surplus**

Commodity Credit Corporation Organized by EO 6340 of Oct. 16, 1933, and managed in close affiliation with *Reconstruction Finance Corporation.* Transferred to the Department of Agriculture by Reorg. Plan No. I of 1939, effective July 1, 1939.

Commodity Exchange Administration *See* **Grain Futures Administration**

Commodity Exchange Authority *See* **Grain Futures Administration**

Commodity Exchange Commission Established by act of Sept. 21, 1922 (42 Stat. 998). Functions transferred to Commodity Futures Trading Commission by act of Oct. 23, 1974 (88 Stat. 1414).

Commodity Stabilization Service Established in the Department of Agriculture Nov. 2, 1953, by Secretary's Memorandum 1320, supp. 4. Renamed Agricultural Stabilization and Conservation Service by Secretary's Memorandum 1458 of June 14, 1961, effective June 5, 1961.

Communication Agency, International *See Information Agency, U.S.*

Communications Program, Joint Tactical Combined with *Joint Interoperability of the Tactical Command and Control Systems Programs* to form Joint Tactical Command, Control, and Communications Agency in July 1984, pursuant to DOD Directive 5154.28.

Community Development Corporation Established in the Department of Housing and Urban Development by act of Dec. 31, 1970 (84 Stat. 1791). Renamed *New Community Development Corporation* by act of Aug. 22, 1974 (88 Stat. 725). Abolished Nov. 30, 1983, by act of Nov. 30, 1983 (97 Stat. 1238), and functions transferred to Assistant Secretary for Community Planning and

Development, Department of Housing and Urban Development.

Community Development Corporation, New *See* **Community Development Corporation**

Community Facilities, Bureau of Established in 1945 by *Federal Works Administrator.* Transferred by act of June 30, 1949 (63 Stat. 380), to General Services Administration, functioning as *Community Facilities Service.* Certain functions transferred to various agencies, including the Department of the Interior, *Housing and Home Finance Agency,* and *Federal Security Agency* by Reorg. Plans Nos. 15, 16, and 17 of 1950, effective May 24, 1950.

Community Facilities Administration Established in *Housing and Home Finance Agency* by Administrator's Organizational Order 1 of Dec. 23, 1954. Terminated by act of Sept. 9, 1965 (79 Stat. 667), and functions transferred to the Department of Housing and Urban Development.

Community Organization, Committee on Established in *Office of Defense Health and Welfare Services* Sept. 10, 1941. Functions transferred to *Federal Security Agency* by EO 9338 of Apr. 29, 1943.

Community Relations Service Established in the Department of Commerce by act of July 2, 1964 (78 Stat. 241). Transferred to the Department of Justice by Reorg. Plan No. 1 of 1966, effective Apr. 22, 1966.

Community Service, Commission on National and Established by act of Nov. 16, 1990 (104 Stat. 3168). Abolished by act of Sept. 21, 1993, and functions vested in the Board of Directors or the Executive Director prior to Oct. 1, 1993, transferred to the Corporation for National and Community Service (107 Stat. 873, 888).

Community Services Administration Established by act of Jan. 4, 1975 (88 Stat. 2291) as successor to *Office of Economic Opportunity.* Abolished as independent agency through repeal of act of Aug. 20, 1964 (except titles VIII and X of such act) by act of Aug. 13, 1981 (95 Stat. 519).

Community Services Administration Functions concerning Legal Services Program transferred to Legal Services Corporation by act of July 25, 1974 (88 Stat. 389). Renamed *Public Services Administration* by *Health, Education, and Welfare* departmental notice of Nov. 3, 1976. Transferred to *Office of Human Development* by Secretary's reorganization of Mar. 8, 1977 (42 FR 13262).

Community War Services Established in *Office of the Administrator* under EO 9338 of Apr. 29, 1943, and *Federal Security Agency* order. Terminated Dec. 31, 1946, by act of July 26, 1946 (60 Stat. 695).

Conciliation Service, U.S. Established by act of Mar. 4, 1913 (37 Stat. 738). Functions transferred to Federal Mediation and Conciliation Service, established by act of June 23, 1947 (61 Stat. 153).

Conference on Security and Cooperation in Europe Renamed Organization for Security and Cooperation in Europe by EO 13029, Dec. 3, 1996 (61 FR 64591).

Consolidated Farm Service Agency Established by act of Oct. 13, 1994 (108 Stat. 3214). Renamed Farm Service Agency (61 FR 1109), effective Jan. 16, 1996.

Constitution, Commission on the Bicentennial of the United States Established by act of Sept. 29, 1983, as amended (97 Stat. 722). Terminated by act of Dec. 3, 1991 (105 Stat. 1232).

Constitution, transfer of functions *See* **Statutes at Large and other matters**

Construction, Collective Bargaining Committee in Established by EO 11849 of Apr. 1, 1975. Inactive since Jan. 7, 1976. Formally abolished by EO 12110 of Dec. 28, 1978.

Construction, Equipment and Repairs, Bureau of Established in the Department of the Navy by act of Aug. 31, 1842 (5 Stat. 579). Abolished by act of July 5, 1862 (12 Stat. 510), and functions distributed among *Bureau of Equipment and Recruiting, Bureau of Construction and Repair,* and *Bureau of Steam Engineering.*

Construction Branch Established in the Department of the Treasury in 1853 and designated *Bureau of Construction* under control of *Office of Supervising Architect* by Sept. 30, 1855. *Office* incorporated into *Public Buildings Branch, Procurement Division,* by EO 6166 of June 10, 1933. Transferred to *Federal Works Agency* by Reorg. Plan No. I of 1939, effective July 1, 1939, when *Public Buildings Branch* of *Procurement Division, Bureau of Buildings Management,* National Park Service, Department of the Interior—so far as latter concerned with operation of public buildings for other departments or agencies—and *U.S. Housing Corporation* consolidated with *Public Buildings Administration, Federal Works Agency.*

Construction Industry Stabilization Committee Established by EO 11588 of Mar. 29, 1971. Abolished by EO 11788 of June 18, 1974.

Construction and Repair, Bureau of Established by act of July 5, 1862 (12 Stat. 510), replacing *Bureau of Construction, Equipment and Repairs.* Abolished by act of June 20, 1940 (54 Stat. 492), and functions transferred to *Bureau of Ships.*

Consumer Advisory Council Established by EO 11136 of Jan. 3, 1964. *Office of Consumer Affairs* established in Executive Office of the President by EO 11583 of Feb. 24, 1971, and Council reestablished in *Office.*

Consumer Affairs, Office of Established by EO 11583 of Feb. 24, 1971. Transferred to the *Department of Health, Education, and Welfare* by EO 11702 of Jan. 25, 1973.

Consumer Affairs Staff, National Business Council for Established in the Department of Commerce by departmental organization order of Dec. 16, 1971. Terminated by departmental order of Dec. 6, 1973, due to lack of funding.

Consumer agencies Consumer agencies of *National Emergency Council* and *National Recovery Administration* reorganized and functions transferred, together with those of *Consumers' Advisory Board, NRA,* and *Cabinet Committee on Price Policy,* to *Consumers' Division, NRA,* by EO 7120 of July 30, 1935. *Division* transferred to the Department of Labor by EO 7252 of Dec. 21, 1935. Transferred to *Division of Consumers' Counsel, Agricultural Adjustment Administration,* Department of Agriculture, by Secretary of Labor letter of Aug. 30, 1938, to the Secretary of Agriculture. Continued as *Consumer Standards Project* until June 30, 1941. Research on consumer standards continued by *Consumer Standards Section, Consumers' Counsel Division,* transferred to *Agricultural Marketing Administration* by administrative order of Feb. 28, 1942. Other project activities discontinued.

Consumer Cooperative Bank, National Established by act of Aug. 20, 1978 (92 Stat. 499). Removed from mixed-ownership, Government corporation status by acts of Sept. 13, 1982 (96 Stat. 1062) and Jan. 12, 1983 (96 Stat. 2478).

Consumer Interests, President's Committee on Established by EO 11136 of Jan. 3, 1964. Abolished by EO 11583 of Feb. 24, 1971.

Consumer and Marketing Service Established by the Secretary of Agriculture Feb. 2, 1965. Renamed Agricultural Marketing Service Apr. 2, 1972, by Secretary's order and certain functions transferred to Animal and Plant Health Inspection Service.

Consumers' Counsel Established in *National Bituminous Coal Commission* by act of Aug. 30, 1935 (49 Stat. 993). Office abolished by Reorg. Plan No. II of 1939, effective July 1, 1939, and functions transferred to Office of Solicitor, Department of the Interior, to function as *Consumers' Counsel Division* under direction of the Secretary of the Interior. Functions transferred to *Office of the Bituminous Coal Consumers' Counsel* June 1941 by act of Apr. 11, 1941 (55 Stat. 134).

Consumers' Counsel Division *See* **Consumers' Counsel**

Consumers' Counsel, Division of Established by act of May 12, 1933 (48 Stat. 31). Transferred by order of the Secretary of Agriculture from *Agricultural Adjustment Administration* to supervision of *Director of Marketing,* effective Feb. 1, 1940. Transferred to *Agricultural Marketing Administration* by administrative order of Feb. 28, 1942.

Consumers' Problems, Adviser on *See* **Consumer agencies**

Contract Committee Government *See* **Contract Compliance, Committee on Government**

Contract Compliance, Committee on Government Established by EO 10308 of Dec. 3, 1951. Abolished by EO 10479 of Aug. 13, 1953, which established successor *Government Contract Committee.* Abolished by EO 10925 of Mar. 6, 1961, and records and property transferred to *President's Committee on Equal Employment Opportunity.*

Contract Settlement, Office of Established by act of July 1, 1944 (58 Stat. 651). Transferred to *Office of War Mobilization and Reconversion* by act of Oct. 3, 1944 (58 Stat. 785). Terminated by EO 9809 of Dec. 12, 1946, and Reorg. Plan No. 1 of 1947, effective July 1, 1947, and functions transferred to the Department of the Treasury. Functions transferred to General Services Administration by act of June 30, 1949 (63 Stat. 380).

Contract Settlement Advisory Board Established by act of July 1, 1944 (58 Stat. 651). Transferred to the Department of the Treasury by EO 9809 of Dec. 12, 1946, and by Reorg. Plan No. 1 of 1947, effective July 1, 1947. Transferred to General Services Administration by act of June 30, 1949 (63 Stat. 380) and established as *Contract Review Board.* Renamed Board of Contract Appeals in 1961 by Administrator's order. Board established as independent entity within General Services Administration Feb. 27, 1979, pursuant to act of Nov. 1, 1978 (92 Stat. 2383).

Contract Settlement Appeal Board, Office of Established by act of July 1, 1944 (58 Stat. 651). Transferred to the Department of the Treasury by EO 9809 of Dec. 12, 1946, and by Reorg. Plan No. 1 of 1947, effective July 1, 1947. Functions transferred to General Services Administration by act of June 30, 1949 (63 Stat. 380). Abolished by act of July 14, 1952 (66 Stat. 627).

Contract Termination Board, Joint Established Nov. 12, 1943, by *Director of War Mobilization.* Functions assumed by *Office of Contract Settlement.*

Contracts Division, Public Established in the Department of Labor to administer act of June 30, 1936 (49 Stat. 2036). Consolidated with Wage and Hour Division by Secretarial order of Aug. 21, 1942. Absorbed by Wage and Hour Division by Secretarial order of May 1971.

Cooperation Administration, International Established by Department of State Delegation of Authority 85 of June 30, 1955, pursuant to EO 10610 of May 9, 1955. Abolished by act of Sept. 4, 1961 (75 Stat. 446), and functions redelegated to Agency for International Development pursuant to Presidential letter of Sept. 30, 1961, and EO 10973 of Nov. 3, 1961.

Cooperative State Research Service Established in the Department of Agriculture. Incorporated into Cooperative State, Research, Education, and Extension Service under Department of Agriculture reorganization in 1995.

Coordinating Service, Federal *Office of Chief Coordinator* created by Executive order promulgated in *Bureau of the Budget* Circular 15, July 27, 1921, and duties enlarged by other *Bureau* circulars. Abolished by EO 6166 of June 10, 1933. Contract form, Federal traffic, and surplus property functions transferred to *Procurement Division* by order of the Secretary of the Treasury, approved by President Oct. 9, 1933, issued pursuant to EO's 6166 of June 10, 1933, and 6224 of July 27, 1933.

Copyright Royalty Tribunal Established as an independent entity within the legislative branch by act of Oct. 19, 1976 (90 Stat. 2594). Abolished by act of Dec. 17, 1993 (107 Stat. 2304), and functions transferred to copyright arbitration royalty panels.

Copyrighted Works, National Commission on New Technological Uses of Established by act of Dec. 31, 1974 (88 Stat. 1873). Terminated Sept. 29, 1978, pursuant to terms of act.

Corporate Payments Abroad, Task Force on Questionable Established by Presidential memorandum of Mar. 31, 1976. Terminated Dec. 31, 1976, pursuant to terms of memorandum.

Corporation, Federal Facilities Established in the Department of the Treasury by EO 10539 of June 22, 1954. Placed under supervision of Director appointed by General Services Administrator by EO 10720 of July 11, 1957. Dissolved by act of Aug. 30, 1961 (75 Stat. 418), and functions transferred to Administrator of General Services.

Corregidor-Bataan Memorial Commission Established by act of Aug. 5, 1953 (67 Stat. 366). Terminated May 6, 1967, by act of Dec. 23, 1963 (77 Stat. 477).

Cost Accounting Standards Board Established by act of Aug. 15, 1970 (84 Stat. 796). Terminated Sept. 30, 1980, due to lack of funding. Reestablished by act of Nov. 17, 1988 (102 Stat. 4059).

Cost of Living Council Established by EO 11615 of Aug. 15, 1971. Abolished by EO 11788 of June 18, 1974.

Cotton Stabilization Corporation Organized June 1930 under laws of Delaware by *Federal Farm Board* pursuant to act of June 15, 1929 (46 Stat. 11). Certificate of dissolution filed with Corporation Commission of Delaware Dec. 27, 1934.

Cotton Textile Industry, Board of Inquiry for the Established by EO 6840 of Sept. 5, 1934. Abolished by EO 6858 of Sept. 26, 1934.

Council. *See other part of title*

Counterintelligence, Office of Established within the Department of Energy by Public Law 106–65 of Oct. 5, 1999 (113 Stat. 955). Merged with *Office of Intelligence* to form *Office of Intelligence and Counterintelligence* by memorandum of March 9, 2006 of the Secretary of Energy.

Courts Under act of Aug. 7, 1939 (53 Stat. 1223), and revised June 25, 1948 (62 Stat. 913), to provide for administration of U.S. courts, administrative jurisdiction over all continental and territorial courts transferred to Administrative Office of the U.S. Courts, including U.S. courts of appeals and district courts, District Court for the Territory of Alaska, U.S. District Court for the District of the Canal Zone, District Court of Guam, District Court of the Virgin Islands, Court of Claims, Court of Customs and Patent Appeals, and Customs Courts.

Credit Unions, Bureau of Federal *See* **Credit Union System, Federal**

Credit Union System, Federal Established by act of June 26, 1934 (48 Stat. 1216), to be administered by *Farm Credit Administration.* Transferred to Federal Deposit Insurance Corporation by EO 9148 of Apr. 27, 1942, and Reorg. Plan No. 1 of 1947, effective July 1, 1947. Functions transferred to *Bureau of Federal Credit Unions, Federal Security Agency,* established by act of June 29, 1948 (62 Stat. 1091). Functions transferred to the *Department of Health, Education, and Welfare* by Reorg. Plan No. 1 of 1953, effective Apr. 11, 1953. Functions transferred to National Credit Union Administration by act of Mar. 10, 1970 (84 Stat. 49).

Crime, National Council on Organized Established by EO 11534 of June 4, 1970. Terminated by EO 12110 of Dec. 28, 1978.

Critical Materials Council, National Established within Executive Office of the President by act of July 31, 1984 (98 Stat. 1250). *Office* abolished in September 1993 due to lack of funding and functions transferred to the Office of Science and Technology Policy.

Crop Insurance Corporation, Federal Established by act of Feb. 16, 1938. Consolidated with the *Agricultural Stabilization and Conservation Service* and *Farmers' Home Administration* in 1995 to form the *Farm Service Agency* pursuant to act of Oct. 13, 1994 (108 Stat. 3178).

Crop Production Loan Office Authorized by Presidential letters of July 26, 1918, and July 26, 1919, to the Secretary of Agriculture. Further authorized by act of Mar. 3, 1921 (41 Stat. 1347). Transferred to Farm Credit Administration by EO 6084 of Mar. 27, 1933.

Cultural Center, National Established in Smithsonian Institution by act of Sept. 2, 1958 (72 Stat. 1698). Renamed John F. Kennedy Center for the Performing Arts by act of Jan. 23, 1964 (78 Stat. 4).

Customs, Bureau of Established under sec. 1 of act of Mar. 3, 1927 (19 U.S.C. 2071) in Treasury Department. Functions relating to award of numbers to undocumented vessels, vested in *Collectors of Customs,* transferred to Commandant of Coast Guard by EO 9083 of Feb. 27, 1942. Transfer made permanent by Reorg. Plan No. 3 of 1946, effective July 16, 1946. Redesignated U.S. Customs Service by the Department of the Treasury Order 165–23 of Apr. 4, 1973. Functions transferred to and agency established within Homeland Security Department by act of Nov. 25, 2002 (116 Stat. 2178).

Customs Court, U.S. Formerly established as Board of General Appraisers by act of June 10, 1890 (26 Stat. 136). Renamed *U.S. Customs Court* by act of May 26, 1926 (44 Stat. 669). Renamed U.S. Court of International Trade by act of Oct. 10, 1980 (94 Stat. 1727).

Customs and Patent Appeals, U.S. Court of Established by act of Mar. 2, 1929 (45 Stat. 1475). Abolished by act of Apr. 2, 1982 (96 Stat. 28) and functions merged with appellate functions of *U.S. Court of Claims* to form U.S. Court of Appeals for the Federal Circuit.

Dairy Industry, Bureau of *Bureau of Dairying* established in the Department of Agriculture by act of May 29, 1924 (43 Stat. 243). *Bureau of Dairy Industry* designation first appeared in act of May 11,

1926 (44 Stat. 499). Functions transferred to Agricultural Research Service by Secretary's Memorandum 1320, supp. 4, of Nov. 2, 1953.

Defense, Advisory Commission to the Council of National *See* **Defense, Council of National**

Defense, Council of National Established by act of Aug. 29, 1916 (39 Stat. 649). *Advisory Commission*—composed of Advisers on Industrial Production, Industrial Materials, Employment, Farm Products, Price Stabilization, Transportation, and Consumer Protection—established by *Council* pursuant to act and approved by President May 29, 1940. *Commission* decentralized by merging divisions with newly created national defense units. Agencies evolved from *Commission,* except *Office of Agricultural War Relations* and *Office of Price Administration,* made units of *Office for Emergency Management. Council* inactive.

Defense, Office of Civilian Established in *Office for Emergency Management* by EO 8757 of May 20, 1941. Terminated by EO 9562 of June 4, 1945.

Defense Administration, Federal Civil Established in *Office for Emergency Management* by EO 10186 of Dec. 1, 1950; subsequently established as independent agency by act of Jan. 12, 1951 (64 Stat. 1245). Functions transferred to *Office of Defense and Civilian Mobilization* by Reorg. Plan No. 1 of 1958, effective July 1, 1958.

Defense Advanced Research Projects Agency Established as a separate agency of the Department of Defense by DOD Directive 5105.41 dated July 25, 1978. Renamed *Advanced Research Projects Agency* by order of the Secretary of Defense dated July 13, 1993. Reestablished by act of Feb. 10, 1996 (110 Stat. 406).

Defense Advisory Council, Civil Established by act of Jan. 12, 1951 (64 Stat. 1245). Transferred to *Office of Defense and Civilian Mobilization* by Reorg. Plan No. 1 of 1958, effective July 1, 1958.

Defense Aid Reports, Division of Established in *Office for Emergency Management* by EO 8751 of May 2, 1941. Abolished by EO 8926 of Oct. 28, 1941, which created *Office of Lend-Lease Administration.*

Defense Air Transportation Administration Established Nov. 12, 1951, by Department of Commerce Order 137. Abolished by Amendment 3 of Sept. 13, 1962, to Department Order 128 (revised) and functions transferred to *Office of the Under Secretary of Commerce for Transportation.*

Defense Atomic Support Agency Renamed *Defense Nuclear Agency* by General Order No. 1 of July 1, 1971.

Defense Audiovisual Agency Established by DOD Directive 5040.1 of June 12, 1979. Abolished by Secretary's memorandum of Apr. 19, 1985, and functions assigned to the military departments.

Defense Audit Service Established by DOD Directive of Oct. 14, 1976. Abolished by Deputy Secretary's memorandum of Nov. 2, 1982, and functions transferred to Office of the Inspector General.

Defense Civil Preparedness Agency Functions transferred from the Department of Defense to the Federal Emergency Management Agency by EO 12148 of July 20, 1979.

Defense and Civilian Mobilization Board Established by EO 10773 of July 1, 1938. Redesignated *Civil and Defense Mobilization Board* by act of Aug. 26, 1958 (72 Stat. 861). Abolished by *Office of Emergency Preparedness* Circular 1200.1 of Oct. 31, 1962.

Defense Communications Agency Established by direction of the Secretary of Defense on May 12, 1960. Renamed Defense Information Systems Agency by DOD Directive 5105.19 dated June 25, 1991.

Defense Communications Board Established by EO 8546 of Sept. 24, 1940. Renamed *Board of War Communications* by EO 9183 of June 15, 1942. Abolished by EO 9831 of Feb. 24, 1947, and property transferred to Federal Communications Commission.

Defense Coordinating Board, Civil Established by EO 10611 of May 11, 1955. EO 10611 revoked by EO 10773 of July 1, 1958.

Defense Electric Power Administration Established by Order 2605 of Dec. 4, 1950 of the Secretary of the Interior. Abolished June 30, 1953, by Secretary's Order 2721 of May 7, 1953. Reestablished by Departmental Manual Release No. 253 of Aug. 6, 1959. Terminated by Departmental Manual Release No. 1050 of Jan. 10, 1977.

Defense Fisheries Administration Established by Order 2605 of Dec. 4, 1950 of the Secretary of the Interior. Abolished June 30, 1953, by Secretary's Order 2722 of May 13, 1953.

Defense Health and Welfare Services, Office of Established by EO 8890 of Sept. 3, 1941. Terminated by EO 9338 of Apr. 29, 1943, and functions transferred to *Federal Security Agency.*

Defense Homes Corporation Incorporated pursuant to President's letter to the Secretary of the Treasury of Oct. 18, 1940. Transferred to *Federal Public Housing Authority* by EO 9070 of Feb. 24, 1942.

Defense Housing Coordinator Office established July 21, 1940, by *Advisory Commission to Council of National Defense.* Functions transferred to *Division of Defense Housing Coordination, Office for Emergency Management,* by EO 8632 of Jan. 11, 1941.

Defense Housing Division, Mutual Ownership Established by Administrator of *Federal Works Agency* under provisions of act of June 28, 1941 (55 Stat. 361). Functions transferred to *Federal Public Housing Authority, National Housing Agency,* by EO 9070 of Feb. 24, 1942.

Defense Investigative Service Established by the Secretary of Defense Jan. 1, 1972. Renamed Defense

Security Service in November 1997 by Defense Reform Initiative.

Defense Manpower Administration Established by the Secretary of Labor by General Order 48, pursuant to EO 10161 of Sept. 9, 1950, and Reorg. Plan No. 6 of 1950, effective May 24, 1950. General Order 48 revoked by General Order 63 of Aug. 25, 1953, which established *Office of Manpower Administration* in Department.

Defense Mapping Agency Established as a the Department of Defense agency in 1972. Functions transferred to the National Imagery and Mapping Agency by act of Sept. 23, 1996 (110 Stat. 2677).

Defense Materials Procurement Agency Established by EO 10281 of Aug. 28, 1951. Abolished by EO 10480 of Aug. 14, 1953, and functions transferred to General Services Administration.

Defense Materials Service *See* **Emergency Procurement Service**

Defense Mediation Board, National Established by EO 8716 of Mar. 19, 1941. Terminated on creation of *National War Labor Board, Office for Emergency Management* by EO 9017 of Jan. 12, 1942. Transferred to the Department of Labor by EO 9617 of Sept. 19, 1945. *Board* terminated by EO 9672 of Dec. 31, 1945, which established *National Wage Stabilization Board* in the Department of Labor. Terminated by EO 9809 of Dec. 12, 1946, and functions transferred to the Secretary of Labor and the Department of the Treasury, effective Feb. 24, 1947.

Defense Medical Programs Activity Functions consolidated into the TRICARE Management Activity in November 1997 by Defense Reform Initiative.

Defense Minerals Administration Established by Order 2605 of Dec. 4, 1950 of the Secretary of the Interior. Functions assigned to *Defense Materials Procurement Agency.* Functions of exploration for critical and strategic minerals redelegated to the Secretary of the Interior and administered by *Defense Minerals Exploration Administration* by Secretary's Order 2726 of June 30, 1953. Termination of program announced by Secretary June 6, 1958. Certain activities continued in *Office of Minerals Exploration,* Department of the Interior.

Defense Minerals Exploration Administration *See* **Defense Minerals Administration**

Defense Mobilization, Office of Established in Executive Office of the President by EO 10193 of Dec. 16, 1950. Superseded by *Office of Defense Mobilization* established by Reorg. Plan No. 3 of 1953, effective June 12, 1953, which assumed functions of former *Office, National Security Resources Board,* and critical materials stockpiling functions of Army, Navy, Air Force, and Interior Secretaries and of *Army and Navy Munitions Board.* Consolidated with *Federal Civil Defense Administration* into *Office of Defense and Civilian Mobilization* by Reorg. Plan No. 1 of 1958, effective July 1, 1958, and offices of Director and Deputy Director terminated.

Defense Mobilization Board Established by EO 10200 of Jan. 3, 1951, and restated in EO 10480 of Aug. 14, 1953. Terminated by EO 10773 of July 1, 1958.

Defense Nuclear Agency Established in 1971. Renamed *Defense Special Weapons Agency* by DOD Directive 5105.31 of June 14, 1995.

Defense Plant Corporation Established by act of June 25, 1940 (54 Stat. 572). Transferred from *Federal Loan Agency* to the Department of Commerce by EO 9071 of Feb. 24, 1942. Returned to *Federal Loan Agency* pursuant to act of Feb. 24, 1945 (59 Stat. 5). Dissolved by act of June 30, 1945 (59 Stat. 310), and functions transferred to *Reconstruction Finance Corporation.*

Defense Plants Administration, Small Established by act of July 31, 1951 (65 Stat. 131). Terminated July 31, 1953, by act of June 30, 1953 (67 Stat. 131). Functions relating to liquidation transferred to Small Business Administration by EO 10504 of Dec. 1, 1953.

Defense Production Administration Established by EO 10200 of Jan. 3, 1951. Terminated by EO 10433 of Feb. 4, 1953, and functions transferred to *Office of Defense Mobilization.*

Defense Property Disposal Service Renamed Defense Reutilization and Marketing Service by Defense Logistics Agency General Order 10–85, effective July 1, 1985.

Defense Prisoner of War/Missing in Action Office Established by DOD Directive 5110.10, July 16, 1993. Renamed Defense Prisoner of War/Missing Personnel Office by Secretary of Defense memorandum of May 30, 1996.

Defense Public Works Division Established in *Public Works Administration.* Transferred to *Office of Federal Works Administrator* by administrative order of July 16, 1941. Abolished by administrative order of Mar. 6, 1942, and functions transferred to *Office of Chief Engineer, Federal Works Agency.*

Defense Purchases, Office for the Coordination of National Established by order of *Council of National Defense,* approved June 27, 1940. Order revoked Jan. 7, 1941, and records transferred to Executive Office of the President.

Defense Research Committee, National Established June 27, 1940, by order of *Council of National Defense.* Abolished by order of *Council* June 28, 1941, and reestablished in *Office of Scientific Research and Development* by EO 8807 of June 28, 1941. *Office* terminated by EO 9913 of Dec. 26, 1947, and property and records transferred to *National Military Establishment.*

Defense Resources Committee Established by Administrative Order 1496 of June 15, 1940. Replaced by *War Resources Council* by Administrative Order 1636 of Jan. 14, 1942. Inactive.

Defense Security Assistance Agency Established on Sept. 1, 1971. Renamed the Defense Security Cooperation Agency by DOD Directive 5105.38.

Defense Solid Fuels Administration Established by Order 2605 of Dec. 4, 1950 of the Secretary of the Interior. Abolished June 29, 1954, by Secretary's Order 2764.

Defense Special Weapons Agency Established by General Order No. 1 of July 1, 1971. Functions transferred to the Defense Threat Reduction Agency by DOD Directive 5105.62 of Sept. 30, 1998.

Defense Stockpile Manager, National Established by act of Nov. 14, 1986 (100 Stat. 4067). Functions transferred from the Administrator of General Services to the Secretary of Defense by EO 12626 of Feb. 25, 1988.

Defense Supplies Corporation Established under act of June 25, 1940 (54 Stat. 572). Transferred from *Federal Loan Agency* to the Department of Commerce by EO 9071 of Feb. 24, 1942. Returned to *Federal Loan Agency* by act of Feb. 24, 1945 (59 Stat. 5). Dissolved by act of June 30, 1945 (59 Stat. 310), and functions transferred to *Reconstruction Finance Corporation.*

Defense Supply Agency Renamed Defense Logistics Agency by DOD Directive 5105.22 of Jan. 22, 1977.

Defense Supply Management Agency Established in the Department of Defense by act of July 1, 1952 (66 Stat. 318). Abolished by Reorg. Plan No. 6 of 1953, effective June 30, 1953, and functions transferred to the Secretary of Defense.

Defense Technology Security Administration Established on May 10, 1985. Functions transferred to the Defense Threat Reduction Agency by DOD Directive 5105.62 of Sept. 30, 1998.

Defense Transport Administration Established Oct. 4, 1950, by order of Commissioner of *Interstate Commerce Commission* in charge of *Bureau of Service,* pursuant to EO 10161 of Sept. 9, 1950. Terminated by DTA Commissioner's order, effective July 1, 1955, and functions transferred to *Bureau of Safety and Service, Interstate Commerce Commission.*

Defense Transportation, Office of Established in *Office for Emergency Management* by EO 8989 of Dec. 18, 1941. Terminated by EO 10065 of July 6, 1949.

Director. *See other part of title*

Disarmament Administration, U.S. Established in the Department of State. Functions transferred to *U.S. Arms Control and Disarmament Agency* by act of Sept. 26, 1961 (75 Stat. 638).

Disarmament Problems, President's Special Committee on Established by President Aug. 5, 1955. Dissolved in February 1958.

Disaster Assistance Administration, Federal Functions transferred from the Department of Housing and Urban Development to the Federal Emergency Management Agency by EO 12148 of July 20, 1979.

Disaster Loan Corporation Grouped with other agencies to form *Federal Loan Agency* by Reorg. Plan No. I of 1939, effective July 1, 1939. Transferred to the Department of Commerce by EO 9071 of Feb. 24, 1942. Returned to *Federal Loan Agency* by act of Feb. 24, 1945 (59 Stat. 5). Dissolved by act of June 30, 1945 (59 Stat. 310), and functions transferred to *Reconstruction Finance Corporation.*

Disease Control, Center for Established within the Public Health Service by the *Secretary of Health, Education, and Welfare* on July 1, 1973. Renamed *Centers for Disease Control* by Health and Human Services Secretary's notice of Oct. 1, 1980 (45 FR 67772). Renamed Centers for Disease Control and Prevention by act of Oct. 27, 1992 (106 Stat. 3504).

Displaced Persons Commission Established by act of June 25, 1948 (62 Stat. 1009). Terminated Aug. 31, 1952, pursuant to terms of act.

District of Columbia Established by acts of July 16, 1790 (1 Stat. 130), and Mar. 3, 1791. *Corporations of Washington and Georgetown* and *levy court of Washington County* abolished in favor of territorial form of government in 1871. Permanent commission government established July 1, 1878. District Government created as municipal corporation by act of June 11, 1878 (20 Stat. 102). Treated as branch of U.S. Government by various statutory enactments of Congress. District Government altered by Reorg. Plan No. 3 of 1967, effective Nov. 3, 1967. Charter for local government in District of Columbia provided by act of Dec. 24, 1973 (87 Stat. 774).

District of Columbia, Highway Commission of the Established by act of Mar. 2, 1893 (27 Stat 532). *National Capital Park and Planning Commission* named successor by act of Apr. 30, 1926 (44 Stat. 374). Functions transferred to National Capital Planning Commission by act of July 19, 1952 (66 Stat. 781).

District of Columbia, Reform-School of the Established by act of May 3, 1876 (19 Stat. 49). Renamed *National Training School for Boys* by act of May 27, 1908 (35 Stat. 380). Transferred to the Department of Justice by Reorg. Plan No. II of 1939, effective July 1, 1939, to be administered by Director of Bureau of Prisons.

District of Columbia Auditorium Commission Established by act of July 1, 1955 (69 Stat. 243). Final report submitted to Congress Jan. 31, 1957, pursuant to act of Apr. 27, 1956 (70 Stat. 115).

District of Columbia Redevelopment Land Agency Established by act of Aug. 2, 1946 (60 Stat. 790). Agency established as instrumentality of District Government by act of Dec. 24, 1973 (87 Stat. 774), effective July 1, 1974.

District of Columbia-Virginia Boundary Commission Established by act of Mar. 21, 1934 (48 Stat. 453). Terminated Dec. 1, 1935, to which date it had been extended by Public Resolution 9 (49 Stat. 67).

Division. *See other part of title*

Domestic Council Established in Executive Office of the President by Reorg. Plan No. 2 of 1970, effective July 1, 1970. Abolished by Reorg. Plan No. 1 of 1977, effective Mar. 26, 1978, and functions transferred to President and staff designated as *Domestic Policy Staff.* Pursuant to EO 12045 of Mar. 27, 1978, *Staff* assisted President in performance of transferred functions. Renamed Office of Policy Development in 1981. Abolished in February 1992 by President's reorganizational statement, effective May 1992.

Domestic Policy Staff *See* **Domestic Council**

Dominican Customs Receivership Transferred from *Division of Territories and Island Possessions,* Department of the Interior, to the Department of State by Reorg. Plan No. IV of 1940, effective June 30, 1940.

Drug Abuse, National Institute on Established within the National Institute of Mental Health, *Department of Health, Education, and Welfare* by act of Mar. 21, 1972 (86 Stat. 85). Removed from within the National Institute of Mental Health and made an entity within the Alcohol, Drug Abuse, and Mental Health Administration by act of May 14, 1974 (88 Stat. 136). Functions transferred to the Department of Health and Human Services by act of Oct. 17, 1979 (93 Stat. 695). (*See also* act of Oct. 27, 1986; 100 Stat. 3207–106.) Abolished by act of July 10, 1992 (106 Stat. 331). Reestablished by act of July 10, 1992 (106 Stat. 361).

Drug Abuse, President's Advisory Commission on Narcotic and Established by EO 11076 of Jan. 15, 1963. Terminated November 1963 under terms of order.

Drug Abuse Control, Bureau of Established in Food and Drug Administration, Department of Health and Human Services, to carry out functions of act of July 15, 1965 (79 Stat. 226). Functions transferred to *Bureau of Narcotics and Dangerous Drugs,* Department of Justice, by Reorg. Plan No. 1 of 1968, effective Apr. 8, 1968. Abolished by Reorg. Plan No. 2 of 1973, effective July 1, 1973, and functions transferred to Drug Enforcement Administration.

Drug Abuse Law Enforcement, Office of Established by EO 11641 of Jan. 28, 1972. Terminated by EO 11727 of July 6, 1973, and functions transferred to Drug Enforcement Administration.

Drug Abuse Policy, Office of Established in Executive Office of the President by act of Mar. 19, 1976 (90 Stat. 242). Abolished by Reorg. Plan No. 1 of 1977, effective Mar. 26, 1978, and functions transferred to President.

Drug Abuse Prevention, Special Action Office for Established by EO 11599 of June 17, 1971, and act of Mar. 21, 1972 (86 Stat. 65). Terminated June 30, 1975, pursuant to terms of act.

Drug Abuse Prevention, Treatment, and Rehabilitation, Cabinet Committee on Established Apr. 27, 1976, by Presidential announcement. Terminated by Presidential memorandum of Mar. 14, 1977.

Drug Law Enforcement, Cabinet Committee for Established Apr. 27, 1976, pursuant to Presidential message to Congress of Apr. 27, 1976. Abolished by Presidential memorandum of Mar. 14, 1977.

Drugs, Bureau of Narcotics and Dangerous *See* **Drug Abuse Control, Bureau of**

Drugs and Biologics, National Center for Renamed *Center for Drugs and Biologics* by Food and Drug Administration notice of Mar. 9, 1984 (49 FR 10166). Reestablished as Center for Drug Evaluation and Research and Center for Biologics Evaluation and Research by Secretary's notice of Oct. 6, 1987 (52 FR 38275).

Drunk Driving, Presidential Commission on Established by EO 12358 of Apr. 14, 1982. Terminated Dec. 31, 1983, by EO 12415 of Apr. 5, 1983.

Dryden Research Center, Hugh L. Formerly separate field installation of National Aeronautics and Space Administration. Made component of Ames Research Center by NASA Management Instruction 1107.5A of Sept. 3, 1981.

Economic Administration, Foreign Established in *Office for Emergency Management* by EO 9380 of Sept. 25, 1943. Functions of *Office of Lend-Lease Administration, Office of Foreign Relief and Rehabilitation Operations, Office of Economic Warfare* (together with *U.S. Commercial Company, Rubber Development Corporation, Petroleum Reserves Corporation,* and *Export-Import Bank of Washington* and functions transferred thereto by EO 9361 of July 15, 1943), and foreign economic operations of *Office of Foreign Economic Coordination* transferred to *Administration.* Foreign procurement activities of *War Food Administration* and Commodity Credit Corporation transferred by EO 9385 of Oct. 6, 1943. Terminated by EO 9630 of Sept. 27, 1945, and functions redistributed to the Departments of State, Commerce, and Agriculture and the *Reconstruction Finance Corporation.*

Economic Analysis, Office of *See* **Business Economics, Office of**

Economic Cooperation Administration Established by act of Apr. 3, 1948 (62 Stat. 138). Abolished by act of Oct. 10, 1951 (65 Stat. 373), and functions transferred to *Mutual Security Agency* pursuant to EO 10300 of Nov. 1, 1951.

Economic Coordination, Office of Foreign *See* **Board of Economic Operations**

Economic Defense Board Established by EO 8839 of July 30, 1941. Renamed *Board of Economic Warfare* by EO 8982 of Dec. 17, 1941. *Board* terminated by EO 9361 of July 15, 1943, and *Office of Economic Warfare* established in *Office for Emergency Management. Office of Economic Warfare* consolidated with *Foreign Economic Administration* by EO 9380 of Sept. 25, 1943.

Economic Development, Office of Regional Established by the Secretary of Commerce Jan. 6, 1966, pursuant to act of Aug. 26, 1965 (79 Stat. 552). Abolished by Department Order 5A, Dec. 22, 1966, and functions vested in Economic Development Administration.

Economic Development Service, Foreign Established by order of the Secretary of Agriculture Nov. 8, 1969. Abolished by order of Secretary Feb. 6, 1972, and functions transferred to Economic Research Service.

Economic Growth and Stability, Advisory Board on Established by Presidential letter to Congress of June 1, 1953. Superseded by *National Advisory Board on Economic Policy* by Presidential direction Mar. 12, 1961. *Cabinet Committee on Economic Growth* established by President Aug. 21, 1962, to succeed *Board.*

Economic Management Support Center Established by Secretary of Agriculture Memorandum 1836 of Jan. 9, 1974. Consolidated with other Department units into *Economics, Statistics, and Cooperatives Service* by Secretary's Memorandum 1927, effective Dec. 23, 1977.

Economic Operations, Board of Established by Department of State order of Oct. 7, 1941. Abolished by departmental order of June 24, 1943, and functions transferred to *Office of Foreign Economic Coordination* established by same order. *Office* abolished by departmental order of Nov. 6, 1943, pursuant to EO 9380 of Sept. 25, 1943.

Economic Opportunity, Office of Established in Executive Office of the President by act of Aug. 20, 1964 (78 Stat. 508). All OEO programs except three transferred by administrative action to the Departments of *Health, Education, and Welfare,* Labor, and Housing and Urban Development July 6, 1973. Community Action, Economic Development, and Legal Services Programs transferred to *Community Services Administration* by act of Jan. 4, 1975 (88 Stat. 2310).

Economic Policy, Council on Established by Presidential memorandum of Feb. 2, 1973. Functions absorbed by *Economic Policy Board* Sept. 30, 1974.

Economic Policy, Council on Foreign Established Dec. 22, 1954, by Presidential letter of Dec. 11, 1954. Abolished by President Mar. 12, 1961, and functions transferred to Secretary of State.

Economic Policy, Council on International Established in Executive Office of the President by Presidential memorandum of January 1971. Reestablished by act of Aug. 29, 1972 (86 Stat. 646). Terminated Sept. 30, 1977, on expiration of statutory authority.

Economic Policy, National Advisory Board on *See* **Economic Growth and Stability, Advisory Board on**

Economic Policy Board, President's Established by EO 11808 of Sept. 30, 1974. Terminated by EO 11975 of Mar. 7, 1977.

Economic Research Service Established by Secretary of Agriculture Memorandum 1446, supp. 1, of Apr. 3, 1961. Consolidated with other Department of Agriculture units into *Economics, Statistics, and Cooperatives Service* by Secretary's Memorandum 1927, effective Dec. 23, 1977. Redesignated as Economic Research Service by Secretarial order of Oct. 1, 1981.

Economic Security, Advisory Council on Established by EO 6757 of June 29, 1934. Terminated on approval of act of Aug. 14, 1935 (49 Stat. 620) Aug. 14, 1935.

Economic Security, Committee on Established by EO 6757 of June 29, 1934. Terminated as formal agency in April 1936, as provided in act, but continued informally for some time thereafter.

Economic Stabilization, Office of Established in *Office for Emergency Management* by EO 9250 of Oct. 3, 1942. Terminated by EO 9620 of Sept. 20, 1945, and functions transferred to *Office of War Mobilization and Reconversion.* Reestablished in *Office for Emergency Management* by EO 9699 of Feb. 21, 1946. Transferred by EO 9762 of July 25, 1946, to *Office of War Mobilization and Reconversion.* Consolidated with other agencies to form *Office of Temporary Controls* by EO 9809 of Dec. 12, 1946.

Economic Stabilization Agency Established by EO 10161 of Sept. 9, 1950, and EO 10276 of July 31, 1951. Terminated, except for liquidation purposes, by EO 10434 of Feb. 6, 1953. Liquidation completed Oct. 31, 1953, pursuant to EO 10480 of Aug. 14, 1953.

Economic Stabilization Board Established by EO 9250 of Oct. 3, 1942. Transferred to *Office of War Mobilization and Reconversion* by EO 9620 of Sept. 20, 1945. Returned to *Office of Economic Stabilization* on reestablishment by EO 9699 of Feb. 21, 1946. *Board* returned to *Office of War Mobilization and Reconversion* by EO 9762 of July 25, 1946. Functions terminated by EO 9809 of Dec. 12, 1946.

Economic Warfare, Board of *See* **Economic Defense Board**

Economic Warfare, Office of *See* **Economic Defense Board**

Economics, Bureau of Industrial Established by the Secretary of Commerce Jan. 2, 1980, in conjunction with Reorg. Plan No. 3 of 1979, effective Oct. 1, 1980, and operated under Department Organization Order 35–5B. Abolished at bureau level by Secretarial order, effective Jan. 22, 1984 (49 FR 4538). Industry-related functions realigned and transferred from Under Secretary for Economic Affairs to Under Secretary for International Trade. Under Secretary for Economic Affairs retained units to support domestic macroeconomic policy functions.

Economics, Statistics, and Cooperatives Service Renamed *Economics and Statistics Service* by Secretary of Agriculture Memorandum 2025 of Sept. 17, 1980. Redesignated as Economic Research Service and *Statistical Reporting Service* by Secretarial order of Oct. 1, 1981.

Economy Board, Joint Placed under direction of President by military order of July 5, 1939. Abolished Sept. 1, 1947, by joint letter of Aug. 20, 1947, from Secretaries of *War* and Navy to President.

Education, Federal Board for Vocational Established by act of Feb. 23, 1917 (39 Stat. 929). Functions transferred to the Department of the Interior by EO 6166 of June 10, 1933. Functions assigned to *Commissioner of Education* Oct. 10, 1933. *Office of Education* transferred from the Department of the Interior to the *Federal Security Agency* by Reorg. Plan No. I of 1939, effective July 1, 1939. *Board* abolished by Reorg. Plan No. 2 of 1946, effective July 16, 1946.

Education, National Institute of Established by act of June 23, 1972 (86 Stat. 327). Transferred to Office of Educational Research and Improvement, Department of Education, by act of Oct. 17, 1979 (93 Stat. 678), effective May 4, 1980.

Education, Office of Established as independent agency by act of Mar. 2, 1867 (14 Stat. 434). Transferred to the Department of the Interior by act of July 20, 1868 (15 Stat. 106). Transferred to *Federal Security Agency* by Reorg. Plan No. I of 1939, effective July 1, 1939. Functions of *Federal Security Administrator* administered by *Office of Education* relating to student loans and defense-related education transferred to *War Manpower Commission* by EO 9247 of Sept. 17, 1942.

Education, Office of Bilingual Abolished by act of Oct. 17, 1979 (93 Stat. 675), and functions transferred to Office of Bilingual Education and Minority Languages Affairs, Department of Education.

Education Beyond the High School, President's Committee on Established by act of July 26, 1956 (70 Stat. 676). Terminated Dec. 31, 1957. Certain activities continued by *Bureau of Higher Education, Office of Education.*

Education Division Established in the *Department of Health, Education, and Welfare* by act of June 23, 1972 (86 Stat. 327). Functions transferred to the Department of Education by act of Oct. 17, 1979 (93 Stat. 677).

Education Goals Panel, National Terminated by Congressional mandate, March 15, 2002.

Education Statistics, National Center for Established in the Office of the Assistant Secretary, Department of Health and Human Services, by act of Aug. 21, 1974 (88 Stat. 556). Transferred to the Office of Educational Research and Improvement, Department of Education, by act of Oct. 17, 1979 (93 Stat. 678), effective May 4, 1980. Renamed *Center for Education Statistics* by act of Oct. 17, 1986 (100 Stat. 1579). Renamed National Center for Education Statistics by act of Apr. 28, 1988 (102 Stat. 331).

Educational and Cultural Affairs, Bureau of Established by Secretary of State in 1960. Terminated by Reorg. Plan No. 2 of 1977, effective July 1, 1978, and functions transferred to *International Communication Agency,* effective Apr. 1, 1978.

Educational and Cultural Affairs, Interagency Council on International Established Jan. 20, 1964, by Foreign Affairs Manual Circular, under authority of act of Sept. 21, 1961 (75 Stat. 527). Terminated Oct. 1973 following creation of Subcommittee on International Exchanges by National Security Council directive.

Educational Exchange, U.S. Advisory Commission on Established by act of Jan. 27, 1948 (62 Stat. 10). Abolished by act of Sept. 21, 1961 (75 Stat. 538), and superseded by U.S. Advisory Commission on International Educational and Cultural Affairs.

Efficiency, Bureau of Organized under act of Feb. 28, 1916 (39 Stat. 15). Abolished by act of Mar. 3, 1933 (47 Stat. 1519), and records transferred to *Bureau of the Budget.*

Elderly, Committee on Mental Health and Illness of the Established by act of July 29, 1975 (89 Stat. 347). Terminated Sept. 30, 1977.

Electoral votes for President and Vice President, transfer of functions *See* **State, Department of**

Electric Home and Farm Authority Incorporated Aug. 1, 1935, under laws of District of Columbia. Designated as U.S. agency by EO 7139 of Aug. 12, 1935. Continued by act of June 10, 1941 (55 Stat. 248). Grouped with other agencies in *Federal Loan Agency* by Reorg. Plan. No. I of 1939, effective July 1, 1939. Functions transferred to the Department of Commerce by EO 9071 of Feb. 24, 1942. Terminated by EO 9256 of Oct. 13, 1942.

Electric Home and Farm Authority, Inc. Organized Jan. 17, 1934, under laws of State of Delaware by EO 6514 of Dec. 19, 1933. Dissolved Aug. 1, 1935, and succeeded by *Electric Home and Farm Authority.*

Electricity Transmission and Distribution, Office of Renamed *Office of Electricity Delivery and Energy Reliability* by the Secretary of Energy's memo of Feb. 15, 2005.

Emergency Administration of Public Works, Federal Established by act of June 16, 1933 (48 Stat. 200). Operation continued by subsequent legislation, including act of June 21, 1938 (52 Stat. 816). Consolidated with *Federal Works Agency* as *Public Works Administration* by Reorg. Plan No. I of 1939, effective July 1, 1939. Functions transferred to *Office of Federal Works Administrator* by EO 9357 of June 30, 1943.

Emergency Conservation Work Established by EO 6101 of Apr. 5, 1933. Succeeded by *Civilian Conservation Corps.*

Emergency Council, National Established by EO 6433–A of Nov. 17, 1933. Consolidated with *Executive Council* by EO 6889–A of Oct. 29, 1934. Abolished by Reorg. Plan No. II of 1939, effective July 1, 1939, and functions (except those relating to *Radio Division* and *Film Service*) transferred to Executive Office of the President.

Emergency Council, Office of Economic Adviser to National Established by EO 6240 of Aug. 3, 1933, in connection with *Executive Council,* which later consolidated with *National Emergency Council.* Records and property used in preparation of statistical and economic summaries transferred to

Central Statistical Board by EO 7003 of Apr. 8, 1935.

Emergency Management, Office for Established in Executive Office of the President by administrative order of May 25, 1940, in accordance with EO 8248 of Sept. 8, 1939. Inactive.

Emergency Management Agency, Federal Established in EO 12127 of Mar. 31, 1979. Functions transferred to Department of Homeland Security by act of Nov. 25, 2002 (116 Stat. 2213).

Emergency Mobilization Preparedness Board Established Dec. 17, 1981, by the President. Abolished by Presidential directive of Sept. 16, 1985.

Emergency Planning, Office of Established as successor to *Office of Civil and Defense Mobilization* by act of Sept. 22, 1961 (75 Stat. 630). Renamed *Office of Emergency Preparedness* by act of Oct. 21, 1968 (82 Stat. 1194). Terminated by Reorg. Plan No. 2 of 1973, effective July 1, 1973, and functions transferred to the the Departments of the Treasury and Housing and Urban Development and the General Services Administration.

Emergency Preparedness, Office of *See* **Emergency Planning, Office of**

Emergency Procurement Service Established Sept. 1, 1950, by Administrator of General Services. Renamed *Defense Materials Service* Sept. 7, 1956. Functions transferred to *Property Management and Disposal Service* July 29, 1966. *Service* abolished July 1, 1973, and functions transferred to Federal Supply Service, Public Buildings Service, and Federal Property Resources Service.

Emergency Relief Administration, Federal Established by act of May 12, 1933 (48 Stat. 55). Expired June 30, 1938, having been liquidated by *Works Progress Administrator* pursuant to act of May 28, 1937 (50 Stat. 352).

Employee-Management Relations Program, President's Committee on the Implementation of the Federal Established by EO 10988 of Jan. 17, 1962. Terminated upon submission of report to President June 21, 1963.

Employees' Compensation, Bureau of Transferred from *Federal Security Agency* to the Department of Labor by Reorg. Plan No. 19 of 1950, effective May 24, 1950. Functions absorbed by Employment Standards Administration Mar. 13, 1972.

Employees' Compensation Appeals Board Transferred from *Federal Security Agency* to the Department of Labor by Reorg. Plan No. 19 of 1950, effective May 24, 1950.

Employees' Compensation Commission, U.S. Established by act of Sept. 7, 1916 (39 Stat. 742). Abolished by Reorg. Plan No. 2 of 1946, effective July 16, 1946, and functions transferred to *Federal Security Administrator.*

Employment Board, Fair Established by *U.S. Civil Service Commission* pursuant to EO 9980 of July 26, 1948. Abolished by EO 10590 of Jan. 18, 1955.

Employment of People With Disabilities, President's Committee on Created by EO 12640 of May 10, 1988. Duties subsumed by the Office of Disability Employment within the Department of Labor as directed by Public Law 106–554 of Dec. 21, 2000.

Employment of the Physically Handicapped, President's Committee on Established by EO 10640 of Oct. 10, 1955, continuing *Committee* established by act of July 11, 1949 (63 Stat. 409). Superseded by President's Committee on Employment of the Handicapped established by EO 10994 of Feb. 14, 1962.

Employment Policy, President's Committee on Government Established by EO 10590 of Jan. 18, 1955. Abolished by EO 10925 of Mar. 6, 1961, and functions transferred to *President's Committee on Equal Employment Opportunity.*

Employment Practice, Committee on Fair Established in *Office of Production Management* by EO 8802 of June 25, 1941. Transferred to *War Manpower Commission* by Presidential letter effective July 30, 1942. Committee terminated on establishment of *Committee on Fair Employment Practice, Office for Emergency Management,* by EO 9346 of May 27, 1943. Terminated June 30, 1946, by act of July 17, 1945 (59 Stat. 743).

Employment Security, Bureau of Transferred from *Federal Security Agency* to the Department of Labor by Reorg. Plan No. 2 of 1949, effective Aug. 20, 1949. Abolished by order of Mar. 14, 1969 of the Secretary of Labor, and functions transferred to *Manpower Administration.*

Employment Service, U.S. Established in the Department of Labor in 1918 by departmental order. Abolished by act of June 6, 1933 (48 Stat. 113), and created as bureau with same name. Functions consolidated with unemployment compensation functions of *Social Security Board, Bureau of Employment Security,* and transferred to *Federal Security Agency* by Reorg. Plan No. I of 1939, effective July 1, 1939. *Service* transferred to *Bureau of Placement, War Manpower Commission,* by EO 9247 of Sept. 17, 1942. Returned to the Department of Labor by EO 9617 of Sept. 19, 1945. Transferred to *Federal Security Agency* by act of June 16, 1948 (62 Stat. 443), to function as part of *Bureau of Employment Security,* Social Security Administration. *Bureau,* including *U.S. Employment Service,* transferred to the Department of Labor by Reorg. Plan No. 2 of 1949, effective Aug. 20, 1949. Abolished by reorganization of *Manpower Administration,* effective Mar. 17, 1969, and functions assigned to *U.S. Training and Employment Service.*

Employment Stabilization Board, Federal Established by act of Feb. 10, 1931 (46 Stat. 1085). Abolished by EO 6166 of June 10, 1933. Abolition deferred by EO 6623 of Mar. 1, 1934, until functions of *Board* transferred to *Federal Employment Stabilization Office,* established in the Department of Commerce by same order. *Office* abolished by Reorg. Plan No. I of 1939, effective July 1, 1939, and functions transferred from the Department of Commerce to *National Resources Planning Board,* Executive Office of the President.

Employment Stabilization Office, Federal. *See* **Employment Stabilization Board, Federal**

Employment and Training, Office of Comprehensive Established in the Department of Labor. Terminated due to expiration of authority for appropriations after fiscal year 1982. Replaced by *Office of Employment and Training Programs.*

Employment and Training Programs, Office of Renamed Office of Job Training Programs by Employment and Training Administration reorganization in the Department of Labor, effective June 1984.

Endangered Species Scientific Authority Established by EO 11911 of Apr. 13, 1976. Terminated by act of Dec. 28, 1979 (93 Stat. 1228), and functions transferred to the Secretary of the Interior.

Energy Administration, Federal Established by act of May 7, 1974 (88 Stat. 96). Assigned additional responsibilities by acts of June 22, 1974 (88 Stat. 246), Dec. 22, 1975 (89 Stat. 871), and Aug. 14, 1976 (90 Stat. 1125). Terminated by act of Aug. 4, 1977 (91 Stat. 577), and functions transferred to the Department of Energy.

Energy Assurance, Office of Abolished pursuant to Conference Report No. 108-729 on H.R. 4818, Consolidated Appropriations Act. Functions merged with *Office of Electricity Delivery and Energy Reliability.*

Energy Conservation, Office of Established by Interior Secretarial Order 2953 May 7, 1973. Functions transferred to *Federal Energy Administration* by act of May 7, 1974 (88 Stat. 100).

Energy Data and Analysis, Office of Established by Interior Secretarial Order 2953 of May 7, 1973. Functions transferred to *Federal Energy Administration* by act of May 7, 1974 (88 Stat. 100).

Energy Policy Office Established in Executive Office of the President by EO 11726 of June 29, 1973. Abolished by EO 11775 of Mar. 26, 1974.

Energy Programs, Office of Established by Department of Commerce Organization Order 25–7A, effective Sept. 24, 1975. Terminated by act of Aug. 4, 1977 (91 Stat. 581), and functions transferred to the Department of Energy.

Energy Research and Development Administration Established by act of Oct. 11, 1974 (88 Stat. 1234). Assigned responsibilities by acts of Sept. 3, 1974 (88 Stat. 1069, 1079), Oct. 26, 1974 (88 Stat. 1431), and Dec. 31, 1974 (88 Stat. 1887). Terminated by act of Aug. 4, 1977 (91 Stat. 577), and functions transferred to the Department of Energy.

Energy Resources Council Established in Executive Office of the President by act of Oct. 11, 1974 (88 Stat. 1233). Establishing authority repealed by act of Aug. 4, 1977 (91 Stat. 608), and *Council* terminated.

Energy Supplies and Resources Policy, Presidential Advisory Committee on Established July 30, 1954, by President. Abolished Mar. 12, 1961, by President and functions transferred to the Secretary of the Interior.

Enforcement Commission, National Established by General Order 18 of *Economic Stabilization Administrator,* effective July 30, 1952. Functions transferred to Director, *Office of Defense Mobilization,* and Attorney General by EO 10494 of Oct. 14, 1953.

Engineering, Bureau of *See* **Steam Engineering, Bureau of**

Entomology, Bureau of *See* **Entomology and Plant Quarantine, Bureau of**

Entomology and Plant Quarantine, Bureau of *Bureau of Entomology* and *Bureau of Plant Quarantine* created by acts of Apr. 23, 1904 (33 Stat. 276), and July 7, 1932 (47 Stat. 640), respectively. Consolidated with disease control and eradication functions of *Bureau of Plant Industry* into *Bureau of Entomology and Plant Quarantine* by act of Mar. 23, 1934 (48 Stat. 467). Functions transferred to Agricultural Research Service by Secretary's Memorandum 1320, supp. 4, of Nov. 2, 1953.

Environment, Cabinet Committee on the *See* **Environmental Quality Council**

Environmental Financing Authority Established by act of Oct. 18, 1972 (86 Stat. 899). Expired June 30, 1975, pursuant to terms of act.

Environmental Quality Council Established by EO 11472 of May 29, 1969. Renamed *Cabinet Committee on the Environment* by EO 11514 of Mar. 5, 1970. EO 11514 terminated by EO 11541 of July 1, 1970.

Environmental Science Services Administration Established in the Department of Commerce by Reorg. Plan No. 2 of 1965, effective July 13, 1965, by consolidating *Weather Bureau* and *Coast and Geodetic Survey.* Abolished by Reorg. Plan No. 4 of 1970, effective Oct. 3, 1970, and functions transferred to National Oceanic and Atmospheric Administration.

Equal Employment Opportunity, President's Committee on Established by EO 10925 of Mar. 6, 1961. Abolished by EO 11246 of Sept. 24, 1965, and functions transferred to the Department of Labor and *U.S. Civil Service Commission.*

Equal Opportunity, President's Council on Established by EO 11197 of Feb. 5, 1965. Abolished by EO 11247 of Sept. 24, 1965, and functions transferred to the Department of Justice.

Equipment, Bureau of Established as *Bureau of Equipment and Recruiting* by act of July 5, 1862 (12 Stat. 510), replacing *Bureau of Construction, Equipment and Repairs.* Designated as *Bureau of Equipment* in annual appropriation acts commencing with fiscal year 1892 (26 Stat. 192) after cognizance over enlisted personnel matters transferred, effective July 1, 1889, to *Bureau of Navigation.* Functions distributed among bureaus and offices in the Department of the Navy by act of June 24, 1910 (61

Stat. 613). Abolished by act of June 30, 1914 (38 Stat. 408).

Ethics, Office of Government Established in the Office of Personnel Management by act of Oct. 26, 1978 (92 Stat. 1862). Became a separate executive agency status by act of Nov. 3, 1988 (102 Stat. 3031).

European Migration, Intergovernmental Committee for Renamed Intergovernmental Committee for Migration by Resolution 624, passed by Intergovernmental Committee for European Migration Council, effective Nov. 11, 1980.

Evacuation, Joint Committee on *See* **Health and Welfare Aspects of Evacuation of Civilians, Joint Committee on**

Exchange Service, International Established in 1849 in Smithsonian Institution. Renamed Office of Publications Exchange by Secretary's internal directive of Jan. 11, 1985.

Executive Branch of the Government, Commission on Organization of the Established by act of July 7, 1947 (61 Stat. 246). Terminated June 12, 1949, pursuant to terms of act. Second *Commission on Organization of the Executive Branch of the Government* established by act of July 10, 1953 (67 Stat. 142). Terminated June 30, 1955, pursuant to terms of act.

Executive Council Established by EO 6202–A of July 11, 1933. Consolidated with *National Emergency Council* by EO 6889–A of Oct. 29, 1934.

Executive Exchange, President's Commission on *See* **Personnel Interchange, President's Commission on**

Executive orders *See* **State, Department of**

Executive Organization, President's Advisory Council on Established by President Apr. 5, 1969. Terminated May 7, 1971.

Executive Protective Service *See* **Secret Service Division**

Executives, Active Corps of Established in ACTION by act of Oct. 1, 1973 (87 Stat. 404). Transferred to Small Business Administration by EO 11871 of July 18, 1975.

Export Administration, Bureau of Established as a seperate agency within the Department of Commerce on Oct. 1, 1987 (50 USC app. 2401 *et seq.*). Renamed Bureau of Industry and Security by Department of Commerce internal organization order of Apr. 18, 2002 (67 FR 20630).

Export Control, Administrator of Functions delegated to Administrator by Proc. 2413 of July 2, 1940, transferred to *Office of Export Control, Economic Defense Board,* by EO 8900 of Sept. 15, 1941. Renamed *Board of Economic Warfare* by EO 8982 of Dec. 17, 1941. *Board* terminated by EO 9361 of July 15, 1943.

Export Control, Office of *See* **Export Control, Administrator of**

Export-Import Bank of Washington Organization of District of Columbia banking corporation directed by EO 6581 of Feb. 2, 1934. Certificate of incorporation filed Feb. 12, 1934. Grouped with other agencies to form *Federal Loan Agency* by Reorg. Plan No. I of 1939, effective July 1, 1939. Transferred to the Department of Commerce by EO 9071 of Feb. 24, 1942. Functions transferred to *Office of Economic Warfare* by EO 9361 of July 15, 1943. Established as permanent independent agency by act of July 31, 1945 (59 Stat. 526). Renamed Export-Import Bank of the U.S. by act of Mar. 13, 1968 (82 Stat. 47).

Export-Import Bank of Washington, DC, Second Authorized by EO 6638 of Mar. 9, 1934. Abolished by EO 7365 of May 7, 1936, and records transferred to *Export-Import Bank of Washington,* effective June 30, 1936.

Export Marketing Service Established by the Secretary of Agriculture Mar. 28, 1969. Merged with Foreign Agricultural Service by Secretary's memorandum of Dec. 7, 1973, effective Feb. 3, 1974.

Exports and Requirements, Division of Established in *Office of Foreign Economic Coordination* by the Department of State order of Feb. 1, 1943. Abolished by departmental order of Nov. 6, 1943, pursuant to EO 9380 of Sept. 25, 1943.

Extension Service Established by act of May 14, 1914 (38 Stat. 372). Consolidated into *Science and Education Administration* by Secretary's order of Jan. 24, 1978. Reestablished as *Extension Service* by Secretarial order of June 16, 1981. Became part of Cooperative State, Research, Education, and Extension Service under Department of Agriculture's reorganization in 1995.

Facts and Figures, Office of Established in *Office for Emergency Management* by EO 8922 of Oct. 24, 1941. Consolidated with *Office of War Information* in *Office for Emergency Management* by EO 9182 of June 13, 1942.

Family Security Committee Established in *Office of Defense Health and Welfare Services* Feb. 12, 1941, by administrative order. Terminated Dec. 17, 1942.

Family Services, Bureau of *See* **Assistance, Bureau of Public**

Family Support Administration Established on Apr. 4, 1986, in the Department of Health and Human Services under authority of section 6 of Reorganization Plan No. 1 of 1953, effective Apr. 11, 1953 (*see also* 51 FR 11641). Merged into Administration for Children and Families by Secretary's reorganization notice dated Apr. 15, 1991.

Farm Board, Federal Established by act of June 15, 1929 (46 Stat. 11). Renamed Farm Credit Administration and certain functions abolished by EO 6084 of Mar. 27, 1933. Administration placed under the Department of Agriculture by Reorg. Plan No. I of 1939, effective July 1, 1939. Made independent agency in the executive branch of the Government, to be housed in the Department of Agriculture, by act of Aug. 6, 1953 (67 Stat. 390).

Removed from the Department of Agriculture by act of Dec. 10, 1971 (85 Stat. 617).

Farm Credit Administration *See* **Farm Board, Federal**

Farm Loan Board, Federal Established in the Department of the Treasury to administer act of July 17, 1916 (39 Stat. 360). Offices of appointed members of *Board,* except member designated as *Farm Loan Commissioner,* abolished by EO 6084 of Mar. 27, 1933, and *Board* functions transferred to *Farm Loan Commissioner,* subject to jurisdiction and control of Farm Credit Administration. Title changed to *Land Bank Commissioner* by act of June 16, 1933. Abolished by act of Aug. 6, 1953 (67 Stat. 393).

Farm Loan Bureau, Federal Established in the Department of the Treasury under supervision of *Federal Farm Loan Board* and charged with execution of act of July 17, 1916 (39 Stat. 360). Transferred to *Farm Credit Administration* by EO 6084 of Mar. 27, 1933.

Farm Loan Commissioner *See* **Farm Loan Board, Federal**

Farm Mortgage Corporation, Federal Established by act of Jan. 31, 1934 (48 Stat. 344). Transferred to the Department of Agriculture by Reorg. Plan No. I of 1939, effective July 1, 1939, to operate under supervision of Farm Credit Administration. Abolished by act of Oct. 4, 1961 (75 Stat. 773).

Farm Products, Division of (Also known as *Division of Agriculture*) Established by *Advisory Commission to Council of National Defense* pursuant to act of Aug. 29, 1916 (39 Stat. 649). *Office of Agricultural Defense Relations* (later known as *Office for Agricultural War Relations*) established in the Department of Agriculture by Presidential letter of May 5, 1941, which transferred to the Secretary of Agriculture functions previously assigned to *Division of Agriculture.* Functions concerned with food production transferred to *Food Production Administration* and functions concerned with food distribution transferred to *Food Distribution Administration* by EO 9280 of Dec. 5, 1942.

Farm Security Administration *See* **Resettlement Administration**

Farm Service Agency Established by Secretary's Memorandum 1010–1 dated Oct. 20, 1994, under authority of the act of Oct. 13, 1994 (7 U.S.C. 6901), and assumed certain functions of the *Agricultural Stabilization and Conservation Service,* the *Farmers' Home Administration,* and the *Federal Crop Insurance Corporation.* Renamed *Consolidated Farm Service Agency* by Acting Administrator on Dec. 19, 1994.

Farmer Cooperative Service Established by Secretary of Agriculture Memorandum 1320, supp. 4, of Dec. 4, 1953. Consolidated with other Department of Agriculture units into *Economics, Statistics, and Cooperatives Service* by Secretary's Memorandum 1927, effective Dec. 23, 1977.

Farmers' Home Administration. *See* **Resettlement Administration**

Federal. *See also other part of title*

Federal Advisory Council Established in *Federal Security Agency* by act of June 6, 1933 (48 Stat. 116). Transferred to the Department of Labor by Reorg. Plan No. 2 of 1949, effective Aug. 20, 1949.

Federal Register, Administrative Committee of the *See* **Archives Establishment, National**

Federal Register, Division of the Established by act of July 26, 1935 (49 Stat. 500). Transferred to General Services Administration as part of *National Archives and Records Service* by act of June 30, 1949 (63 Stat. 381). Renamed Office of the Federal Register by order of General Services Administrator, Feb. 6, 1959. Transferred to National Archives and Records Administration by act of Oct. 19, 1984 (98 Stat. 2283).

Federal Register, Office of the *See* **Federal Register, Division of the**

Federal Reserve Board Renamed Board of Governors of the Federal Reserve System, and Governor and Vice Governor designated as Chairman and Vice Chairman, respectively, of Board by act of Aug. 23, 1935 (49 Stat. 704).

Field Services, Office of Established by the Secretary of Commerce Feb. 1, 1963, by Department Organization Order 40–3. Terminated by Department Organization Order 40–1A of Sept. 15, 1970, and functions transferred to *Bureau of Domestic Commerce.*

Filipino Rehabilitation Commission Established by act of June 29, 1944 (58 Stat. 626). Inactive pursuant to terms of act.

Film Service, U.S. Established by *National Emergency Council* in September 1938. Transferred to *Office of Education, Federal Security Agency,* by Reorg. Plan No. II of 1939, effective July 1, 1939. Terminated June 30, 1940.

Films, Coordinator of Government Director of *Office of Government Reports* designated *Coordinator of Government Films* by Presidential letter of Dec. 18, 1941. Functions transferred to *Office of War Information* by EO 9182 of June 13, 1942.

Financial Operations, Bureau of Government Renamed Financial Management Service by Order 145–21 of the Secretary of the Treasury, effective Oct. 10, 1984.

Fire Administration, U.S. *See* **Fire Prevention and Control Administration, National**

Fire Council, Federal Established by EO 7397 of June 20, 1936. Transferred July 1, 1939, to *Federal Works Agency* by EO 8194 of July 6, 1939, with functions under direction of *Federal Works Administrator.* Transferred with *Federal Works Agency* to General Services Administration by act of June 30, 1949 (63 Stat. 380). Transferred to the Department of Commerce by EO 11654 of Mar. 13, 1972.

Fire Prevention and Control, National Academy for Established in the Department of Commerce by act of Oct. 29, 1974 (88 Stat. 1537). Transferred to Federal Emergency Management Agency by Reorg. Plan No. 3 of 1978, effective Apr. 1, 1979.

Fire Prevention and Control Administration, National Renamed U.S. Fire Administration by act of Oct. 5, 1978 (92 Stat. 932). Transferred to Federal Emergency Management Agency by Reorg. Plan No. 3 of 1978, effective Apr. 1, 1979.

Fish Commission, U.S. *Commissioner of Fish and Fisheries* established as head of *U.S. Fish Commission* by joint resolution of Feb. 9, 1871 (16 Stat. 594). *Commission* established as *Bureau of Fisheries* in *Department of Commerce and Labor* by act of Feb. 14, 1903 (32 Stat. 827). Department of Labor created by act of Mar. 4, 1913 (37 Stat. 736), and *Bureau* remained in the Department of Commerce. Transferred to the Department of the Interior by Reorg. Plan No. II of 1939, effective July 1, 1939. Consolidated with *Bureau of Biological Survey* into *Fish and Wildlife Service* by Reorg. Plan No. III of 1940, effective June 30, 1940.

Fish and Wildlife Service Established by Reorg. Plan No. III of 1940, effective June 30, 1940, consolidating *Bureau of Fisheries* and *Bureau of Biological Survey*. Succeeded by U.S. Fish and Wildlife Service.

Fisheries, Bureau of *See* **Fish Commission, U.S.**

Fisheries, Bureau of Commercial Organized in 1959 under U.S. Fish and Wildlife Service, the Department of the Interior. Abolished by Reorg. Plan No. 4 of 1970, effective Oct. 3, 1970, and functions transferred to National Oceanic and Atmospheric Administration.

Fishery Coordination, Office of Established in the Department of the Interior by EO 9204 of July 21, 1942. Terminated by EO 9649 of Oct. 29, 1945.

Flood Indemnity Administration, Federal Established in *Housing and Home Finance Agency* by Administrator's Organizational Order 1, effective Sept. 28, 1956, redesignated as Administrator's Organizational Order 2 on Dec. 7, 1956, pursuant to act of Aug. 7, 1956 (70 Stat. 1078). Abolished by Administrator's Organizational Order 3, effective July 1, 1957, due to lack of funding.

Food, Cost of Living Council Committee on Established by EO 11695 of Jan. 11, 1973. Abolished by EO 11788 of June 18, 1974.

Food, Drug, and Insecticide Administration Established by act of Jan. 18, 1927 (44 Stat. 1002). Renamed Food and Drug Administration by act of May 27, 1930 (46 Stat. 422). Transferred from the Department of Agriculture to *Federal Security Agency* by Reorg. Plan No. IV of 1940, effective June 30, 1940. Transferred to *Department of Health, Education, and Welfare* by Reorg. Plan No. 1 of 1953, effective Apr. 11, 1953.

Food Distribution Administration Established in the Department of Agriculture by EO 9280 of Dec. 5, 1942, consolidating *Agricultural Marketing Administration, Sugar Agency,* distribution functions of *Office for Agricultural War Relations,* regulatory work of *Bureau of Animal Industry,* and food units of *War Production Board.* Consolidated with other agencies by EO 9322 of Mar. 26, 1943, to form *Administration of Food Production and Distribution.*

Food and Drug Administration *See* **Food, Drug, and Insecticide Administration**

Food Industry Advisory Committee Established by EO 11627 of Oct. 15, 1971. Abolished by EO 11781 of May 1, 1974.

Food and Nutrition Service Established Aug. 8, 1969, by Secretary of Agriculture under authority of 5 U.S.C. 301 and Reorg. Plan No. 2 of 1953 (5 U.S.C. app.). Abolished by Secretary's Memorandum 1010–1 dated Oct. 20, 1994. Functions assumed by Food and Consumer Service.

Food Production Administration Established in the Department of Agriculture by EO 9280 of Dec. 5, 1942, which consolidated *Agricultural Adjustment Agency,* Farm Credit Administration, *Farm Security Administration,* Federal Crop Insurance Corporation, Soil Conservation Service, and food production activities of *War Production Board, Office of Agricultural War Relations,* and *Division of Farm Management and Costs, Bureau of Agricultural Economics.* Consolidated with other agencies by EO 9322 of Mar. 26, 1943, to form *Administration of Food Production and Distribution.*

Food Production and Distribution, Administration of Established by consolidation of *Food Production Administration, Food Distribution Administration,* Commodity Credit Corporation, and Extension Service, Department of Agriculture, by EO 9322 of Mar. 26, 1943, under direction of Administrator, directly responsible to President. Renamed *War Food Administration* by EO 9334 of Apr. 19, 1943. Terminated by EO 9577 of June 29, 1945, and functions transferred to the Secretary of Agriculture. Transfer made permanent by Reorg. Plan No. 3 of 1946, effective July 16, 1946.

Food Safety and Quality Service Renamed Food Safety and Inspection Service by Agriculture Secretary's memorandum of June 19, 1981.

Foods, Bureau of Renamed Center for Food Safety and Applied Nutrition by Food and Drug Administration notice of Mar. 9, 1984 (49 FR 10166).

Foreign. *See also other part of title*

Foreign Aid, Advisory Committee on Voluntary Established by President May 14, 1946. Transferred from the Department of State to the Director of the *Mutual Security Agency,* and later to Director of the *Foreign Operations Administration,* by Presidential letter of June 1, 1953.

Foreign Operations Administration Established by Reorg. Plan No. 7 of 1953, effective Aug. 1, 1953, and functions transferred from *Office of Director of Mutual Security, Mutual Security Agency, Technical Cooperation Administration, Institute of Inter-American Affairs.* Abolished by EO 10610 of May 9, 1955, and functions and offices transferred to the Departments of State and Defense.

Foreign Scholarships, Board of Renamed J. William Fulbright Foreign Scholarship Board by act of Feb. 16, 1990 (104 Stat. 49).

Forest Reservation Commission, National Established by act of Mar. 1, 1911 (36 Stat. 962). Terminated by act of Oct. 22, 1976 (90 Stat. 2961), and functions transferred to the Secretary of Agriculture.

Forests, Director of Established by Administrative Order 1283 of May 18, 1938. Made part of *Office of Land Utilization,* Department of the Interior, by Administrative Order 1466 of Apr. 15, 1940.

Freedmen's Hospital Established by act of Mar. 3, 1871 (16 Stat. 506; T. 32 of D.C. Code). Transferred from the Department of the Interior to *Federal Security Agency* by Reorg. Plan No. IV of 1940, effective June 30, 1940.

Fuel Yards Established by act of July 1, 1918 (40 Stat. 672). Transferred from *Bureau of Mines,* Department of Commerce, to *Procurement Division,* Department of the Treasury, by EO 6166 of June 10, 1933, effective Mar. 2, 1934.

Fuels Coordinator for War, Office of Solid *See* **Fuels Administration for War, Solid**

Fuels Corporation, U.S. Synthetic Established by act of June 30, 1980 (94 Stat. 636). Terminated Apr. 18, 1986, by act of Dec. 19, 1985 (99 Stat. 1249), and functions transferred to the Secretary of the Treasury.

Fund-Raising Within the Federal Service, President's Committee on Established by EO 10728 of Sept. 6, 1957. Abolished by EO 10927 of Mar. 18, 1961, and functions transferred to *U.S. Civil Service Commission.*

Gallaudet College *See* **Columbia Institution for the Instruction of the Deaf and Dumb, and the Blind**

General Programs, Office of Renamed Office of Public Programs by the Chairman, National Endowment for the Humanities, in January 1991.

Geographic Board, U.S. Established by EO 27–A of Sept. 4, 1890. Abolished by EO 6680 of Apr. 17, 1935, and duties transferred to *U.S. Board on Geographical Names,* Department of the Interior, effective June 17, 1934. *Board* abolished by act of July 25, 1947 (61 Stat. 457), and duties assumed by *Board on Geographic Names.*

Geographical Names, U.S. Board on *See* **Geographic Board, U.S.**

Geography, Office of Function of standardizing foreign place names placed in the Department of the Interior conjointly with the *Board on Geographic Names* by act of July 25, 1947 (61 Stat. 456). Functions transferred to the Department of Defense by memorandum of understanding by the Departments of the Interior and Defense and the *Bureau of the Budget* Mar. 9, 1968.

Geological Survey Established in the the Department of the Interior by act of Mar. 3, 1879 (20 Stat. 394). Renamed United States Geological Survey by acts of Nov. 13, 1991 (105 Stat. 1000) and May 18, 1992 (106 Stat. 172).

Germany, Mixed Claims Commission, U.S. and Established by agreement of Aug. 10, 1922, between U.S. and Germany. Duties extended by agreement of Dec. 31, 1928. Time limit for filing claims expired June 30, 1928. All claims disposed of by Oct. 30, 1939. Terminated June 30, 1941.

Global Communications, Office of Established within the White House Office by EO 13283 of Jan. 21, 2003. Abolished by EO 13385 of Sept. .

Goethals Memorial Commission Established by act of Aug. 4, 1935 (49 Stat. 743). Placed under jurisdiction of *Department of War* by EO 8191 of July 5, 1939.

Government. *See other part of title*

Grain Futures Administration Established in the Department of Agriculture under provisions of act of Sept. 21, 1922 (42 Stat. 998). Superseded by *Commodity Exchange Administration* by order of Secretary, effective July 1, 1936. Consolidated with other agencies into *Commodity Exchange Branch, Agricultural Marketing Administration,* by EO 9069 of Feb. 23, 1942. Functions transferred to the Secretary of Agriculture by EO 9577 of June 29, 1945. Transfer made permanent by Reorg. Plan No. 3 of 1946, effective July 16, 1946. Functions transferred to *Commodity Exchange Authority* by Secretary's Memorandum 1185 of Jan. 21, 1947. Functions transferred to Commodity Futures Trading Commission by act of Oct. 23, 1974 (88 Stat. 1414).

Grain Inspection Service, Federal Established in the Department of Agriculture by act of Oct. 21, 1976 (90 Stat. 2868). Abolished by Secretary's Memorandum 1010–1 dated Oct. 20, 1994, and program authority and functions transferred to the Grain Inspection, Packers and Stockyards Administration.

Grain Stabilization Corporation Organized as Delaware corporation to operate in connection with *Federal Farm Board* pursuant to act of June 15, 1929 (46 Stat. 11). Terminated by filing of certificate of dissolution with Corporation Commission of State of Delaware Dec. 14, 1935.

Grants and Program Systems, Office of Abolished and functions transferred to Cooperative State Research Service, Department of Agriculture, by Secretarial Memorandum 1020–26 of July 1, 1986.

Grazing Service Consolidated with *General Land Office* into Bureau of Land Management, Department of the Interior, by Reorg. Plan No. 3 of 1946, effective July 16, 1946.

Great Lakes Basin Commission Established by EO 11345 of Apr. 20, 1967. Terminated by EO 12319 of Sept. 9, 1981.

Great Lakes Pilotage Administration Established in the Department of Commerce to administer act of June 30, 1960 (74 Stat. 259). Administration of act transferred to the Secretary of Transportation by act of Oct. 15, 1966 (80 Stat. 931).

Handicapped, National Center on Education Media and Materials for the Established by agreement between the *Secretary of Health, Education, and Welfare* and Ohio State University, pursuant to acts of Aug. 20, 1969 (83 Stat. 102) and Apr. 13, 1970 (84 Stat. 187). Authorization deleted by act of Nov. 29, 1975 (89 Stat. 795), and the Secretary was authorized to enter into agreements with non-Federal organizations to establish and operate centers for handicapped.

Handicapped, National Council on the Established in the *Department of Health, Education, and Welfare* by act of Nov. 6, 1978 (92 Stat. 2977). Transferred to the Department of Education by act of Oct. 17, 1979 (93 Stat. 677). Reorganized as independent agency by act of Feb. 22, 1984 (98 Stat. 26).

Handicapped Employees, Interagency Committee on Alternately renamed Interagency Committee on Employment of People with Disabilities by EO 12704 of Feb. 26, 1990.

Handicapped Individuals, White House Conference on Established by act of Dec. 7, 1974 (88 Stat. 1617). Terminated Dec. 30, 1977, pursuant to terms of act.

Handicapped Research, National Institute of Renamed National Institute on Disability and Rehabilitation Research by act of Oct. 21, 1986 (100 Stat. 1820).

Health, Cost of Living Council Committee on Established by EO 11695 of Jan. 11, 1973. Abolished by EO 11788 of June 18, 1974.

Health, Education, and Welfare, Department of Established by Reorganization Plan No. 1 of 1953 (5 U.S.C. app.), effective Apr. 11, 1953. Renamed Department of Health and Human Services by act of Oct. 17, 1979 (93 Stat. 695).

Health, Welfare, and Related Defense Activities, Office of the Coordinator of *Federal Security Administrator* designated as Coordinator of health, welfare, and related fields of activity affecting national defense, including aspects of education under *Federal Security Agency,* by *Council of National Defense,* with approval of President, Nov. 28, 1940. Office of Coordinator superseded by *Office of Defense Health and Welfare Services,* established in *Office for Emergency Services* by EO 8890 of Sept. 3, 1941.

Health Care Technology, National Council on Established by act of July 1, 1944, as amended (92 Stat. 3447). Renamed *Council on Health Care Technology* by act of Oct. 30, 1984 (98 Stat. 2820). Name lowercased by act of Oct. 7, 1985 (99 Stat. 493). Terminated by act of Dec. 19, 1989 (103 Stat. 2205).

Health Facilities, Financing, Compliance, and Conversion, Bureau of Renamed Bureau of Health Facilities by Department of Health and Human Services Secretarial order of Mar. 12, 1980 (45 FR 17207).

Health Industry Advisory Committee Established by EO 11695 of Jan. 11, 1973. Abolished by EO 11781 of May 1, 1974.

Health Manpower, Bureau of Renamed Bureau of Health Professions by Department of Health and Human Services Secretarial order of Mar. 12, 1980 (45 FR 17207).

Health and Medical Committee Established by *Council of National Defense* order of Sept. 19, 1940. Transferred to *Federal Security Agency* by *Council* order approved by President Nov. 28, 1940. Reestablished in *Office of Defense Health and Welfare Services, Office for Emergency Management,* by EO 8890 of Sept. 3, 1941. *Committee* transferred to *Federal Security Agency* by EO 9338 of Apr. 29, 1943.

Health Resources Administration Established in Public Health Service. Abolished by Department of Health and Human Services Secretarial reorganization of Aug. 20, 1982 (47 FR 38409), and functions transferred to Health Resources and Services Administration.

Health Service, Public Originated by act of July 16, 1798 (1 Stat. 605). Transferred from the Department of the Treasury to the *Federal Security Agency* by Reorg. Plan No. I of 1939, effective July 1, 1939.

Health Services Administration Established in Public Health Service. Abolished by Department of Health and Human Services Secretarial reorganization of Aug. 20, 1982 (47 FR 38409), and functions transferred to Health Resources and Services Administration.

Health Services Industry, Committee on the Established by EO 11627 of Oct. 15, 1971. Abolished by EO 11695 of Jan. 11, 1973.

Health Services and Mental Health Administration Established in Public Health Service Apr. 1, 1968. Abolished by *Department of Health, Education, and Welfare* reorganization order and functions transferred to *Centers for Disease Control, Health Resources Administration,* and *Health Services Administration,* effective July 1, 1973.

Health Services Research, National Center for Established by act of July 23, 1974 (88 Stat. 363). Transferred from *Health Resources Administration* to Office of the Assistant Secretary for Health by *Department of Health, Education, and Welfare* reorganization, effective Dec. 2, 1977. Renamed *National Center for Health Services Research and Health Care Technology Assessment* by Secretary's order, pursuant to act of Oct. 30, 1984 (98 Stat. 2817). Terminated by act of Dec. 19, 1989 (103 Stat. 2205).

Health Statistics, National Center for Established by act of July 23, 1974 (88 Stat. 363). Transferred from *Health Resources Administration* to Office of the Assistant Secretary for Health by the *Department of Health, Education, and Welfare* reorganization, effective Dec. 2, 1977. Transferred to *Centers for Disease Control* by Secretary's notice of Apr. 2, 1987 (52 FR 13318).

Health and Welfare Activities, Interdepartmental Committee to Coordinate Appointed by President Aug. 15, 1935, and reestablished by EO 7481 of Oct. 27, 1936. Terminated in 1939.

Health and Welfare Aspects of Evacuation of Civilians, Joint Committee on Established August 1941 as joint committee of *Office of Defense Health and Welfare Services* and *Office of Civilian Defense.* Reorganized in June 1942 and renamed *Joint Committee on Evacuation. Office of Defense Health and Welfare Services* abolished by EO 9388 of Apr. 29, 1943, and functions transferred to *Federal Security Agency. Committee* terminated.

Heart and Lung Institute, National Renamed National Heart, Lung, and Blood Institute by act of Apr. 22, 1976 (90 Stat. 402).

Heritage Conservation and Recreation Service Established by the Secretary of the Interior Jan. 25, 1978. Abolished by Secretarial Order 3060 of Feb. 19, 1981, and functions transferred to National Park Service.

Highway Safety Agency, National Established in the Department of Commerce by act of Sept. 9, 1966 (80 Stat. 731). Functions transferred to the Department of Transportation by act of Oct. 15, 1966 (80 Stat. 931). Functions transferred to *National Highway Safety Bureau* by EO 11357 of June 6, 1967. *Bureau* renamed National Highway Traffic Safety Administration by act of Dec. 31, 1970 (84 Stat. 1739).

Highway Safety Bureau, National *See* **Highway Safety Agency, National**

Home Economics, Bureau of Human Nutrition and *See* **Home Economics, Office of**

Home Economics, Office of Renamed *Bureau of Home Economics* by Secretary's Memorandum 436, effective July 1, 1923, pursuant to act of Feb. 26, 1923 (42 Stat. 1289). Redesignated *Bureau of Human Nutrition and Home Economics* February 1943 in accordance with *Research Administration* Memorandum 5 issued pursuant to EO 9069 of Feb. 23, 1942, and in conformity with Secretary's Memorandums 960 and 986. Functions transferred to Agricultural Research Service by Secretary's Memorandum 1320, supp. 4, of Nov. 2, 1953.

Home Loan Bank Administration, Federal *See* **Home Loan Bank Board, Federal**

Home Loan Bank Board *See* **Home Loan Bank Board, Federal**

Home Loan Bank Board, Federal Established by acts of July 22, 1932 (47 Stat. 725), June 13, 1933 (48 Stat. 128), and June 27, 1934 (48 Stat. 1246). Grouped with other agencies to form *Federal Loan Agency* by Reorg. Plan No. I of 1939, effective July 1, 1939. Functions transferred to *Federal Home Loan Bank Administration, National Housing Agency,* by EO 9070 of Feb. 24, 1942. Abolished by Reorg. Plan No. 3, effective July 27, 1947, and functions transferred to *Home Loan Bank Board, Housing and Home Finance Agency.* Renamed *Federal Home Loan Bank Board* and made independent agency by act of Aug. 11, 1955 (69 Stat. 640). Abolished by act of Aug. 9, 1989 (103 Stat. 354, 415), and functions transferred to Office of Thrift Supervision, Resolution Trust Corporation, Federal Deposit Insurance Corporation, and Federal Housing Finance Board.

Home Loan Bank System, Federal Grouped with other agencies to form *Federal Loan Agency* by Reorg. Plan No. I of 1939, effective July 1, 1939. Functions transferred to *Federal Home Loan Bank Administration, National Housing Agency,* by EO 9070 of Feb. 24, 1942. Transferred to *Housing and Home Finance Agency* by Reorg. Plan No. 3 of 1947, effective July 27, 1947.

Home Mortgage Credit Extension Committee, National Voluntary Established by act of Aug. 2, 1954 (68 Stat 638). Terminated Oct. 1, 1965, pursuant to terms of act.

Home Owners' Loan Corporation Established by act of June 13, 1933 (48 Stat. 128), under supervision of *Federal Home Loan Bank Board.* Grouped with other agencies to form *Federal Loan Agency* by Reorg. Plan No. I of 1939, effective July 1, 1939. Transferred to *Federal Home Loan Bank Administration, National Housing Agency,* by EO 9070 of Feb. 24, 1942. Board of Directors abolished by Reorg. Plan No. 3 of 1947, effective July 27, 1947, and functions transferred, for liquidation of assets, to *Home Loan Bank Board, Housing and Home Finance Agency.* Terminated by order of *Secretary of the Home Loan Bank Board,* effective Feb. 3, 1954, pursuant to act of June 30, 1953 (67 Stat. 121).

Homesteads, Division of Subsistence Established by act of June 16, 1933 (48 Stat. 205). Secretary of the Interior authorized to administer section 208 of act by EO 6209 of July 21, 1933. *Federal Subsistence Homesteads Corporation* created by Secretary's order of Dec. 2, 1933, and organization incorporated under laws of Delaware. Transferred to *Resettlement Administration* by EO 7041 of May 15, 1935.

Homesteads Corporation, Federal Subsistence *See* **Homesteads, Division of Subsistence**

Hospitalization, Board of Federal Organized Nov. 1, 1921. Designated as advisory agency to *Bureau of the Budget* May 7, 1943. Terminated June 30, 1948, by Director's letter of May 28, 1948.

Housing, President's Committee on Equal Opportunity in Established by EO 11063 of Nov. 20, 1962. Inactive as of June 30, 1968.

Housing Administration, Federal Established by act of June 27, 1934 (48 Stat. 1246). Grouped with other agencies to form *Federal Loan Agency* by Reorg. Plan No. I of 1939, effective July 1, 1939. Functions transferred to *Federal Housing Administration, National Housing Agency,* by EO 9070 of Feb. 24, 1942. Transferred to *Housing and Home Finance Agency* by Reorg. Plan No. 3, effective July 27, 1947. Functions transferred to the Department of Housing and Urban Development by act of Sept. 9, 1965 (79 Stat. 667).

Housing Administration, Public Established as constituent agency of *Housing and Home Finance Agency* by Reorg. Plan No. 3 of 1947, effective July 27, 1947. Functions transferred to the Department of Housing and Urban Development by act of Sept. 9, 1965 (79 Stat. 667).

Housing Agency, National Established by EO 9070 of Feb. 24, 1942, to consolidate housing functions relating to *Federal Home Loan Bank Board, Federal Home Loan Bank System, Federal Savings and Loan Insurance Corporation, Home Owners' Loan Corporation, U.S. Housing Corporation, Federal Housing Administration, U.S. Housing Authority, Defense Homes Corporation, Division of Defense Housing Coordination, Central Housing Committee, Farm Security Administration* with respect to nonfarm housing, *Public Buildings Administration, Division of Defense Housing, Mutual Ownership Defense Housing Division, Office of Administrator of Federal Works Agency,* and the Departments of *War* and the Navy with respect to housing located off military installations. Agency dissolved on creation of *Housing and Home Finance Agency* by Reorg. Plan No. 3 of 1947, effective July 27, 1947.

Housing Authority, Federal Public Established by EO 9070 of Feb. 24, 1942. Public housing functions of *Federal Works Agency, the Departments of War* and the Navy (except housing located on military installations), and *Farm Security Administration* (nonfarm housing) transferred to *Authority,* and *Defense Homes Corporation* administered by the Commissioner of the *Authority'.* Functions transferred to *Public Housing Administration, Housing and Home Finance Agency,* by Reorg. Plan No. 3 of 1947, effective July 27, 1947.

Housing Authority, U.S. Established in the Department of the Interior by act of Sept. 1, 1937 (50 Stat. 888). Transferred to *Federal Works Agency* by Reorg. Plan No. I of 1939, effective July 1, 1939. Transferred to *Federal Public Housing Authority, National Housing Agency,* by EO 9070 of Feb. 24, 1942. Office of Administrator abolished by Reorg. Plan No. 3 of 1947, effective July 27, 1947, and functions transferred to *Public Housing Administration, Housing and Home Finance Agency.*

Housing Corporation, U.S. Incorporated July 10, 1918, under laws of New York. Transferred from the Department of Labor to the Department of the Treasury by EO 7641 of June 22, 1937. Transferred from the Department of the Treasury to the *Public Buildings Administration, Federal Works Agency,* by EO 8186 of June 29, 1939. Functions transferred for liquidation to *Federal Home Loan Bank Administration, National Housing Agency,* by EO 9070 of Feb. 24, 1942. Terminated Sept. 8, 1952, by the *Secretary of the Home Loan Bank Board.*

Housing Council, National Established in *Housing and Home Finance Agency* by Reorg. Plan No. 3 of 1947, effective July 27, 1947. Terminated by Reorg. Plan No. 4 of 1965, effective July 27, 1965, and functions transferred to President.

Housing Division Established in *Public Works Administration* by act of June 16, 1933 (48 Stat. 195). Functions transferred to *U.S. Housing Authority* by EO 7732 of Oct. 27, 1937.

Housing Expediter, Office of the Established in *Office of War Mobilization and Reconversion* by Presidential letter of Dec. 12, 1945, to *Housing Expediter.* Functions of *Housing Expediter* defined by EO 9686 of Jan. 26, 1946. *Housing Expediter* confirmed in position of *National Housing Administrator* Feb. 6, 1946. *Office of the Housing Expediter* established by act of May 22, 1946 (60 Stat. 208). Functions of *Office* and *National Housing Administrator* segregated by EO 9820 of Jan. 11, 1947. Housing functions of *Civilian Production Administration* transferred to *Office* by EO 9836 of Mar. 22, 1947, effective Apr. 1, 1947. Rent control functions of *Office of Temporary Controls* transferred to *Office* by EO 9841 of Apr. 23, 1947. *Office* terminated by EO 10276 of July 31, 1951, and functions transferred to *Economic Stabilization Agency.*

Housing and Home Finance Agency Established by Reorg. Plan No. 3 of 1947, effective July 27, 1947. Terminated by act of Sept. 9, 1965 (79 Stat. 667), and functions transferred to the Department of Housing and Urban Development.

Howard University Established by act of Mar. 2, 1867 (14 Stat. 438). Functions of the Department of the Interior transferred to *Federal Security Agency* by Reorg. Plan No. IV of 1940, effective June 30, 1940. Functions of the *Department of Health, Education, and Welfare* transferred to the Department of Education by act of Oct. 17, 1979 (93 Stat. 678).

Human Development, Office of Established in *Department of Health, Education, and Welfare.* Renamed Office of Human Development Services and component units transferred to or reorganized under new administrations in Office by Secretary's reorganization order of July 26, 1977. Merged into the Administration for Children and Families by Secretary of Health and Human Services reorganization notice dated Apr. 15, 1991.

Human Development Services, Office of *See* **Human Development, Office of**

Hydrographic Office Jurisdiction transferred from *Bureau of Navigation* to Chief of Naval Operations by EO 9126 of Apr. 8, 1942, and by Reorg. Plan No. 3 of 1946, effective July 16, 1946. Renamed U.S. Naval Oceanographic Office by act of July 10, 1962 (76 Stat. 154).

Imagery and Mapping Agency, National Established by act of Sept. 23, 1996 (110 Stat. 2677). Renamed National Geospatial-Intelligence Agency by act of Nov. 24, 2003 (117 Stat. 1568).

Imagery Office, Central Established as a Department of Defense agency on May 6, 1992. Functions transferred to National Imagery and Mapping Agency by act of Sept. 23, 1996 (110 Stat. 2677).

Immigration, Bureau of Established as branch of the Department of the Treasury by act of Mar. 3, 1891 (26 Stat. 1085). Transferred to *Department of Commerce and Labor* by act of Feb. 14, 1903 (34 Stat. 596). Made *Bureau of Immigration and Naturalization* by act of June 29, 1906 (37 Stat. 736). Made separate division after the Department of Labor created by act of Mar. 4, 1913 (37 Stat. 736). Consolidated into Immigration and Naturalization Service, Department of Labor, by EO 6166 of June 10, 1933. Transferred to the Department of Justice by Reorg. Plan No. V of 1940, effective June 14, 1940. Abolished by act of Nov. 25, 2002 (116 Stat.

2205) and functions transferred to Homeland Security Department.

Immigration, Commissioners of Offices of commissioners of immigration of the several ports created by act of Aug. 18, 1894 (28 Stat. 391). Abolished by Reorg. Plan No. III of 1940, effective June 30, 1940, and functions transferred to *Bureau of Immigration and Naturalization,* Department of Labor.

Immigration and Naturalization, Bureau of *See* **Immigration, Bureau of**

Immigration and Naturalization, District Commissioner of Created by act of Aug. 18, 1894 (28 Stat. 391). Abolished by Reorg. Plan No. III of 1940, effective June 30, 1940. Functions administered by the Commissioner of Immigration and Naturalization, Department of Justice, through district immigration and naturalization directors.

Immigration and Naturalization Service *See* **Immigration, Bureau of**

Import Programs, Office of Established by the Secretary of Commerce Feb. 14, 1971. Functions transferred to *Domestic and International Business Administration,* effective Nov. 17, 1972.

Indian Claims Commission Established by act of Aug. 13, 1946 (60 Stat. 1049). Terminated by act of Oct. 8, 1976 (90 Stat. 1990), and pending cases transferred to *U.S. Court of Claims* Sept. 30, 1978.

Indian Commissioners, Board of Established by section 2039, Revised Statutes. Abolished by EO 6145 of May 25, 1933.

Indian Medical Facilities Functions transferred from the Department of the Interior to the *Department of Health, Education, and Welfare,* to be administered by the Surgeon General of Public Health Service, by act of Aug. 5, 1954 (68 Stat. 674).

Indian Opportunity, National Council on Established by EO 11399 of Mar. 6, 1968. Terminated Nov. 26, 1974, by act of Nov. 26, 1969 (83 Stat. 220).

Indian Policy Review Commission, American Established by act of Jan. 2, 1975 (88 Stat. 1910). Terminated June 30, 1977, pursuant to terms of act.

Industrial Analysis, Committee of Established by EO 7323 of Mar. 21, 1936. Terminated Feb. 17, 1937.

Industrial Cooperation, Coordinator for Established by EO 7193 of Sept. 26, 1935. Continued by EO 7324 of Mar. 30, 1936. Terminated June 30, 1937.

Industrial Emergency Committee Established by EO 6770 of June 30, 1934. Consolidated with *National Emergency Council* by EO 6889–A of Oct. 29, 1934.

Industrial Pollution Control Council Staff, National Established by Department of Commerce Organization Order 35–3 of June 17, 1970. *Staff* abolished by departmental organization order of Sept. 10, 1973. Council inactive.

Industrial Recovery Board, National Established by EO 6859 of Sept. 27, 1934. Terminated by EO 7075 of June 15, 1935.

Industrial Recovery Board, Special Established by EO 6173 of June 16, 1933. Functions absorbed by *National Emergency Council* under terms of EO 6513 of Dec. 18, 1933.

Industrial Relations, Office of Activated in the Department of the Navy Sept. 14, 1945. Superseded June 22, 1966, by creation of *Office of Civilian Manpower Management.*

Industry and Trade Administration *See* **Business and Defense Services Administration**

Information, Committee for Reciprocity Established by EO 6750 of June 27, 1934; reestablished by EO 10004 of Oct. 5, 1948, which revoked EO 6750. Superseded by EO 10082 of Oct. 5, 1949; abolished by EO 11075 of Jan. 15, 1963, which revoked EO 10082.

Information, Coordinator of Established by Presidential order of July 11, 1941. Functions exclusive of foreign information activities transferred by military order of June 13, 1942, to jurisdiction of Joint Chiefs of Staff, *War Department,* as *Office of Strategic Services.* Foreign information functions transferred to *Office of War Information* by EO 9182 of June 13, 1942.

Information, Division of Established pursuant to Presidential letter of Feb. 28, 1941, to *Liaison Officer, Office of Emergency Management.* Abolished by EO 9182 of June 13, 1942. Functions relating to public information on war effort transferred and consolidated with *Office of War Information,* and publication services relating to specific agencies of OEM transferred to those agencies.

Information, Office of Coordinator of Transferred, exclusive of foreign information activities, to *Office of War Information* by EO 9182 of June 13, 1942. Designated *Office of Strategic Services* and transferred to jurisdiction of Joint Chiefs of Staff by military order of June 13, 1942. Terminated by EO 9621 of Sept. 20, 1945, and functions distributed to the Departments of State and *War.*

Information Administration, International Transferred from the Department of State to the *U.S. Information Agency* by Reorg. Plan No. 8 of 1953, effective Aug. 1, 1953.

Information Agency, U.S. Established by Reorg. Plan No. 8 of 1953, effective Aug. 1, 1953. Abolished by Reorg. Plan No. 2 of 1977, effective Apr. 1, 1978; replaced by and functions transferred to *International Communication Agency.* Redesignated *U.S. Information Agency* by act of Aug. 24, 1982 (96 Stat. 291). Abolished by act of Oct. 21, 1998 (112 Stat. 2681–761), and functions transferred to the Department of State, effective Oct. 1, 1999.

Information and Public Affairs, Office of Merged with *Office of Intergovernmental Affairs* to form Office of Public and Intergovernmental Affairs by Order 1–85 of June 5, 1985 of the Secretary of Labor.

Information Resources Management, Office of *See* **Telecommunications Service, Automated Data**

Information Resources Management Service Established in the General Services Administration. Renamed Information Technology Service in 1995.

Information Security Committee, Interagency Established by EO 12065 of June 28, 1978. Abolished by EO 12356 of Apr. 2, 1982.

Information Security Oversight Office Established in General Services Administration by EO 12065 of June 28, 1978. EO 12065 revoked by EO 12356 of Apr. 2, 1982, which provided for continuation of Office.

Information Service, Government *See* **Information Service, U.S.**

Information Service, Interim International Established in the Department of State by EO 9608 of Aug. 31, 1945. Abolished Dec. 31, 1945, pursuant to terms of order.

Information Service, U.S. Established in March 1934 as division of *National Emergency Council.* Transferred to *Office of Government Reports* by Reorg. Plan No. II of 1939, effective July 1, 1939. Consolidated, along with other functions of *Office,* into *Division of Public Inquiries, Bureau of Special Services, Office of War Information,* by EO 9182 of June 13, 1942. *Bureau of Special Services* renamed *Government Information Service* and transferred to *Bureau of the Budget* by EO 9608 of Aug. 31, 1945. *Service* transferred to *Office of Government Reports* by EO 9809 of Dec. 12, 1946.

Information Systems Council Established by EO 13356 of Aug. 27, 2004. Abolished by EO 13388 of Oct. 25, 2005 (70 FR 62025).

Information Technology Service Established in General Services Administration. Abolished by General Services Administrative Order No. 5440.492, Aug. 21, 1996, and functions transferred to Federal Telecommunications Service.

Insane, Government Hospital for the Established by act of Mar. 3, 1855 (10 Stat. 682). Renamed Saint Elizabeth's Hospital by act of July 1, 1916 (39 Stat. 309). Transferred from the Department of the Interior to *Federal Security Agency* by Reorg. Plan No. IV of 1940, effective June 30, 1940. Transferred to *Department of Health, Education, and Welfare* by Reorg. Plan No. 1 of 1953, effective Apr. 11, 1953. Functions redelegated to National Institute of Mental Health by Secretary's reorganization order of Aug. 9, 1967. Property and administration transferred to District of Columbia Government by act of Nov. 8, 1984 (98 Stat. 3369).

Installations, Director of Established in the Department of Defense by act of July 14, 1952 (66 Stat. 625). Abolished by Reorg. Plan No. 6 of 1953, effective June 30, 1953, and functions transferred to the Secretary of Defense.

Insular Affairs, Bureau of Transferred from *Department of War* to *Division of Territories and Island Possessions,* the Department of the Interior, by Reorg. Plan No. II of 1939, effective July 1, 1939.

Insurance Administrator, Federal Established by act of Aug. 1, 1968 (82 Stat. 567). Functions transferred to Federal Emergency Management Agency by Reorg. Plan No. 3 of 1978, effective Apr. 1, 1979.

Integrity and Efficiency, President's Council on Established by EO 12301 of Mar. 26, 1981 (46 FR 19211). Abolished and reestablished by EO 12625 of Jan 27, 1988 (53 FR 2812). Abolished and reestablished by EO 12805 of May 11, 1992 (57 FR 20627).

Intelligence, Office of Established within the Department of Energy by Public Law 106–65 of Oct. 5, 1999 (113 Stat. 955). Merged with *Office of Counterintelligence* to form Office of Intelligence and Counterintelligence by memorandum of March 9, 2006 of the Secretary of Energy.

Intelligence Activities, President's Board of Consultants on Foreign Established by EO 10656 of Feb. 6, 1956. EO 10656 revoked by EO 10938 of May 4, 1961, and *Board* terminated. Functions transferred to President's Foreign Intelligence Advisory Board.

Intelligence Advisory Board, President's Foreign Established by EO 11460 of Mar. 20, 1969. Abolished by EO 11984 of May 4, 1977. Reestablished by EO 12331 of Oct. 20, 1981.

Intelligence Authority, National Established by Presidential directive of Jan. 22, 1946. Terminated on creation of Central Intelligence Agency under National Security Council by act of July 26, 1947 (61 Stat. 497).

Intelligence Group, Central Terminated on creation of Central Intelligence Agency by act of July 26, 1947 (61 Stat. 497).

Inter-American Affairs, Institute of *See* **American Republics, Office for Coordination of Commercial and Cultural Relations between the**

Inter-American Affairs, Office of *See* **American Republics, Office for Coordination of Commercial and Cultural Relations between the**

Inter-American Affairs, Office of the Coordinator of *See* **American Republics, Office for Coordination of Commercial and Cultural Relations between the**

Interagency. *See other part of title*

Interdepartmental. *See also other part of title*

Interdepartmental Advisory Council Established January 1941 to advise *Coordinator of Health, Welfare, and Related Defense Activities.* Terminated on creation of *Office of Defense Health and Welfare Service* Sept. 3, 1941.

Interest and Dividends, Committee on Established by EO 11695 of Jan. 11, 1973. Abolished by EO 11781 of May 1, 1974.

Intergovernmental Affairs, Office of Merged with *Office of Information and Public Affairs* to form Office of Public and Intergovernmental Affairs by Order 1–85 of June 5, 1985 of the Secretary of Labor.

Intergovernmental and Interagency Affairs, Office of Abolished by decision of March 21, 2005 of the Secretary of Education under authority of section 413 of the Department of Education Organization Act.

Intergovernmental Relations, Advisory Commission on Established by act of Sept. 24, 1959 (73 Stat. 703). Terminated pursuant to act of Nov. 19, 1995 (109 Stat. 480). Continued in existence by act of Oct. 19, 1996 (110 Stat. 4004).

Intergovernmental Relations, Commission on Established by act of July 10, 1953 (67 Stat. 145). Final report submitted to Congress by June 30, 1955, pursuant to act of Feb. 7, 1955 (69 Stat. 7).

Intergovernmental Relations, Office of Established by EO 11455 of Feb. 14, 1969. Functions transferred to *Domestic Council* by EO 11690 of Dec. 14, 1972.

Interim Compliance Panel Established by Dec. 30, 1969 (83 Stat. 774). Terminated June 30, 1976, pursuant to terms of act.

Internal Revenue Service Functions relating to alcohol, tobacco, firearms, and explosives transferred to Bureau of Alcohol, Tobacco, and Firearms by Department of Treasury order of July 1, 1972.

Internal Security Division Established July 9, 1945, by transfer of functions from Criminal Division. Abolished Mar. 22, 1973, and functions transferred to Criminal Division, Department of Justice.

International. *See also other part of title*

International Activities, Office of Renamed *Office of Service and Protocol* by Secretary of the Smithsonian Institution internal directive of Jan. 11, 1985.

International Development, Agency for Transferred from the Department of State to *U.S. International Development Cooperation Agency* by Reorg. Plan No. 2 of 1979, effective Oct. 1, 1979. Continued as agency within *IDCA* by IDCA Delegation of Authority No. 1 of Oct. 1, 1979. By act of Oct. 21, 1998 (112 Stat. 2681–790), became independent agency.

International Development Cooperation Agency, U.S. Established by Reorg. Plan No. 2 of 1979, effective Oct. 1, 1979. Abolished by act of Oct. 21, 1998 (112 Stat. 2681–790) and functions transferred to the Department of State, U.S. Agency for International Development, and Overseas Private Investment Corporation.

Interstate Commerce Commission Created by act of Feb. 4, 1887 (24 Stat. 379). Certain functions as cited in act of Oct. 15, 1966 (80 Stat. 931) transferred to the Secretary of Commerce. Functions relating to railroad and pipeline safety transferred to Federal Railroad Administrator and motor carrier safety to Federal Highway Administrator by act. Abolished by act of Dec. 29, 1995 (109 Stat. 932) and many functions transferred to the newly created Surface Transportation Board within the Department of Transportation.

Investigation, Bureau of Established by act of May 22, 1908 (35 Stat. 235). Functions consolidated with investigative functions of *Bureau of Prohibition, Division of Investigation,* Department of Justice, by EO 6166 of June 10, 1933, effective Mar. 2, 1934.

Investigation, Division of Designated as Federal Bureau of Investigation in the Department of Justice by act of Mar. 22, 1935 (49 Stat. 77).

Investigation and Research, Board of Established by act of Sept. 18, 1940 (54 Stat. 952). Extended to Sept. 18, 1944, by Proc. 2559 of June 26, 1942.

Investigations, Division of Established by administrative order of Apr. 27, 1933. Abolished Jan. 17, 1942, by administrative order and functions transferred to *Branch of Field Examination, General Land Office,* Department of the Interior.

Investments, Office of Foreign Direct Established in the Department of Commerce Jan. 2, 1968, by Departmental Organization Order 25–3 to carry out provisions of EO 11387 of Jan. 1, 1968. Controls on foreign investments terminated Jan. 29, 1974.

Jamestown-Williamsburg-Yorktown National Celebration Commission Established by act of Aug. 13, 1953 (67 Stat. 576). Terminated upon submission of final report to Congress Mar. 1, 1958.

Joint. *See also other part of title*

Joint Resolutions of Congress *See* **State, Department of**

Judicial Procedure, Commission on International Rules of Established by act of Sept. 2, 1958 (72 Stat. 1743). Terminated Dec. 31, 1966, by act of Aug. 30, 1964 (78 Stat. 700).

Justice Assistance, Research, and Statistics, Office of Established in the Department of Justice by act of Dec. 27, 1979 (93 Stat. 1201). Abolished by act of Oct. 12, 1984 (98 Stat. 2091).

Kennedy, Commission To Report Upon the Assassination of President John F. Established by EO 11130 of Nov. 29, 1963. Report submitted Sept. 24, 1964, and *Commission* discharged by Presidential letter of same date.

Labor, President's Committee on Migratory Appointed by Presidential letter of Aug. 26, 1954. Formally established by EO 10894 of Nov. 15, 1960. Terminated Jan. 6, 1964, by the Secretary of Labor in letter to members, with approval of President.

Labor and Commerce, Department of Established by act of Feb. 14, 1903 (32 Stat. 825). Reorganized into separate Departments of Labor and Commerce by act of Mar. 4, 1913 (37 Stat. 736).

Labor Department, Solicitor for Transferred from the Department of Justice to the Department of Labor by EO 6166 of June 10, 1933.

Labor-Management Advisory Committee Established by EO 11695 of Jan. 11, 1973. Abolished by EO 11788 of June 18, 1974.

Labor-Management Policy, President's Advisory Committee on Established by EO 10918 of Feb. 16, 1961. Abolished by EO 11710 of Apr. 4, 1973.

Labor-Management Relations Services, Office of Established by Order 3–84 of May 3, 1984 of the Secretary of Labor. Renamed Bureau of Labor-Management Relations and Cooperative Programs by Secretarial Order 7–84 of Sept. 20, 1984 (49 FR 38374).

Labor-Management Services Administration *Office of Pension and Welfare Benefit Programs* transferred from *Administration* and constituted as separate unit by Order 1–84 of Jan. 20, 1984 of the Secretary of Labor (49 FR 4269). Remaining labor-management relations functions reassigned by Secretarial Order 3–84 of May 3, 1984.

Labor Organization, International Established in 1919 by Treaty of Versailles with U.S. joining in 1934. U.S. membership terminated Nov. 1, 1977, at President's direction.

Labor Relations Council, Federal Established by EO 11491 of Oct. 29, 1969. Abolished by Reorg. Plan No. 2 of 1978, effective Jan. 1, 1979, and functions transferred to Federal Labor Relations Authority.

Labor Standards, Apprenticeship Section, Division of Transferred to *Federal Security Agency* by EO 9139 of Apr. 18, 1942, functioning as *Apprentice Training Service.* Transferred to *War Manpower Commission* by EO 9247 of Sept. 17, 1942, functioning in *Bureau of Training.* Returned to the Department of Labor by EO 9617 of Sept. 19, 1945.

Labor Standards, Bureau of Established by Labor departmental order in 1934. Functions absorbed by Occupational Safety and Health Administration in May 1971.

Land Bank Commissioner *See* **Farm Loan Board, Federal**

Land Law Review Commission, Public Established by act of Sept. 19, 1964 (78 Stat. 982). Terminated Dec. 31, 1970, pursuant to terms of act.

Land Office, General Consolidated with *Grazing Service* into Bureau of Land Management, Department of the Interior, by Reorg. Plan No. 3 of 1946, effective July 16, 1946.

Land Office, Office of Recorder of the General Created in the Department of the Interior by act of July 4, 1836 (5 Stat. 111). Abolished by Reorg. Plan No. III of 1940, effective June 30, 1940, and functions transferred to *General Land Office.*

Land Policy Section Established in 1934 as part of *Program Planning Division, Agricultural Adjustment Administration.* Personnel taken over by *Resettlement Administration* in 1935.

Land Problems, Committee on National Established by EO 6693 of Apr. 28, 1934. Abolished by EO 6777 of June 30, 1934.

Land Program, Director of Basis of program found in act of June 16, 1933 (48 Stat. 200). *Special Board of Public Works* established by EO 6174 of June 16, 1933. Land Program established by *Board* by resolution passed Dec. 28, 1933, and amended July 18, 1934. *Federal Emergency Relief Administration* designated to administer program Feb. 28, 1934. Land Program transferred to *Resettlement Administration* by EO 7028 of Apr. 30, 1935. Functions of *Administration* transferred to the Secretary of Agriculture by EO 7530 of Dec. 31, 1936. Land conservation and land-utilization programs administered by *Administration* transferred to *Bureau of Agricultural Economics* by Secretary's Memorandum 733. Administration of land programs placed under Soil Conservation Service by Secretary's Memorandum 785 of Oct. 6, 1938.

Land Use Coordination, Office of Established by Secretary of Agriculture Memorandum 725 of July 12, 1937. Abolished Jan. 1, 1944, by General Departmental Circular 21 and functions administered by *Land Use Coordinator.*

Land Use and Water Planning, Office of Established in the Department of the Interior by Secretarial Order No. 2953 of May 7, 1973. Abolished by Secretarial Order No. 2988 of Mar. 11, 1976.

Law Enforcement Assistance Administration Established by act of June 19, 1968 (82 Stat. 197). Operations closed out by the Department of Justice due to lack of appropriations and remaining functions transferred to *Office of Justice Assistance, Research, and Statistics.*

Law Enforcement Training Center, Federal *See* **Law Enforcement Training Center, Consolidated Federal**

Law Enforcement Training Center, Consolidated Federal Established by Treasury Order No. 217, Mar. 2, 1970. Renamed Federal Law Enforcement Training Center by Amendment No. 1 to Treasury Order No. 217 on Aug. 14, 1975. Tansferred to Department of Homeland Security by act of Nov. 25, 2002 (116 STat. 2178).

Legislative Affairs, Office of Renamed Office of Intergovernmental and Legislative Affairs Feb. 24, 1984, by Attorney General's Order 1054–84 (49 FR 10177).

Lend-Lease Administration, Office of Established by EO 8926 of Oct. 28, 1941, to replace *Division of Defense Aid Reports.* Consolidated with *Foreign Economic Administration* by EO 9380 of Sept. 25, 1943.

Lewis and Clark Trail Commission Established by act of Oct. 6, 1964 (78 Stat. 1005). Terminated October 1969 by terms of act.

Lighthouses, Bureau of Established in the Department of Commerce by act of Aug. 7, 1789 (1 Stat. 53). Consolidated with U.S. Coast Guard by Reorg. Plan No. II of 1939, effective July 1, 1939.

Lincoln Sesquicentennial Commission Established by joint resolution of Sept. 2, 1957 (71 Stat. 587). Terminated Mar. 1, 1960, pursuant to terms of joint resolution.

Liquidation, Director of Established in *Office for Emergency Management* by EO 9674 of Jan. 4, 1946. Terminated by EO 9744 of June 27, 1946.

Liquidation Advisory Committee Established by EO 9674 of Jan. 4, 1946. Terminated by EO 9744 of June 27, 1946.

Loan Agency, Federal Established by Reorg. Plan No. I of 1939, effective July 1, 1939, by consolidating *Reconstruction Finance Corporation*—including subordinate units of *RFC Mortgage Company, Disaster Loan Corporation, Federal National Mortgage Association, Defense Plant Corporation, Defense Homes Corporation, Defense Supplies Corporation, Rubber Reserve Company, Metals Reserve Company,* and *War Insurance Corporation* (later known as *War Damage Corporation*)—with *Federal Home Loan Bank Board, Home Owners' Loan Corporation, Federal Savings and Loan Insurance Corporation, Federal Housing Administration, Electric Home and Farm Authority,* and *Export-Import Bank of Washington. Federal Home Loan Bank Board, Federal Savings and Loan Insurance Corporation, Home Owners' Loan Corporation, Federal Housing Administration,* and *Defense Homes Corporation* transferred to *National Housing Agency* by EO 9070 of Feb. 24, 1942. *Reconstruction Finance Corporation* and its units (except *Defense Homes Corporation*), *Electric Home and Farm Authority,* and *Export-Import Bank of Washington* transferred to the Department of Commerce by EO 9071 of Feb. 24, 1942. *RFC* and units returned to *Federal Loan Agency* by act of Feb. 24, 1945 (59 Stat. 5). *Agency* abolished by act of June 30, 1947 (61 Stat. 202), and all property and records transferred to *Reconstruction Finance Corporation.*

Loan Fund, Development Established in *International Cooperation Administration* by act of Aug. 14, 1957 (71 Stat. 355). Created as independent corporate agency by act of June 30, 1958 (72 Stat. 261). Abolished by act of Sept. 4, 1961 (75 Stat. 445), and functions redelegated to Agency for International Development.

Loan Policy Board Established by act of July 18, 1958 (72 Stat. 385). Abolished by Reorg. Plan No. 4 of 1965, effective July 27, 1965, and functions transferred to Small Business Administration.

Longshoremen's Labor Board, National Established in the Department of Labor by EO 6748 of June 26, 1934. Terminated by Proc. 2120 of Mar. 11, 1935.

Low-Emission Vehicle Certification Board Established by act of Dec. 31, 1970 (84 Stat. 1701). Terminated by act of Mar. 14, 1980 (94 Stat. 98).

Lowell Historic Canal District Commission Established by act of Jan. 4, 1975 (88 Stat. 2330). Expired January 1977 pursuant to terms of act.

Loyalty Review Board Established Nov. 10, 1947, by *U.S. Civil Service Commission,* pursuant to EO 9835 of Mar. 21, 1947. Abolished by EO 10450 of Apr. 27, 1953.

Management, Budget and Evaluation, Office of Established within the Department of Energy pursuant to the Conference Report No. 107–258 on H.R. 2311, Energy and Water Development Appropriations Act, 2002. Abolished by memorandum of July 28, 2005 of the Secretary of Energy, and various functions transferred within the Department of Energy to the *Office of Management, Office of Chief Financial Officer,* and *Office of Human Capital Management.*

Management Improvement, Advisory Committee on Established by EO 10072 of July 29, 1949. Abolished by EO 10917 of Feb. 10, 1961, and functions transferred to *Bureau of the Budget.*

Management Improvement, President's Advisory Council on Established by EO 11509 of Feb. 11, 1970. Inactive as of June 30, 1973.

Manpower, President's Committee on Established by EO 11152 of Apr. 15, 1964. Terminated by EO 11515 of Mar. 13, 1970.

Manpower Administration Renamed Employment and Training Administration by Order 14–75 of Nov. 12, 1975 of the Secretary of Labor.

Manpower Management, Office of Civilian Renamed Office of Civilian Personnel by Notice 5430 of Oct. 1, 1976 of the Secretary of the Navy.

Marine Affairs, Office of Established by the Secretary of the Interior Apr. 30, 1970, to replace *Office of Marine Resources,* created by Secretary Oct. 22, 1968. Abolished by Secretary Dec. 4, 1970.

Marine Corps Memorial Commission, U.S. Established by act of Aug. 24, 1947 (61 Stat. 724). Terminated by act of Mar. 14, 1980 (94 Stat. 98).

Marine Inspection and Navigation, Bureau of *See* **Navigation and Steamboat Inspection, Bureau of**

Marine Resources and Engineering Development, National Council on Established in Executive Office of the President by act of June 17, 1966 (80 Stat. 203). Terminated Apr. 30, 1971, due to lack of funding.

Maritime Administration Established in the Department of Commerce by Reorg. Plan No. 21 of 1950, effective May 24, 1950. Transferred to the Department of Transportation by act of Aug. 6, 1981 (95 Stat. 151).

Maritime Advisory Committee Established by EO 11156 of June 17, 1964. Terminated by EO 11427 of Sept. 4, 1968.

Maritime Board, Federal *See* **Maritime Commission, U.S.**

Maritime Commission, U.S. Established by act of June 29, 1936 (49 Stat. 1985), as successor agency to *U.S. Shipping Board* and *U.S. Shipping Board Merchant Fleet Corporation.* Training functions transferred to Commandant of Coast Guard by EO 9083 of Feb. 27, 1942. Functions further transferred to *War Shipping Administration* by EO 9198 of July

11, 1942. Abolished by Reorg. Plan No. 21 of 1950, effective May 24, 1950, which established *Federal Maritime Board* and *Maritime Administration* as successor agencies. *Board* abolished, regulatory functions transferred to Federal Maritime Commission, and functions relating to subsidization of merchant marine transferred to the Secretary of Commerce by Reorg. Plan No. 7 of 1961, effective Aug. 12, 1961.

Maritime Labor Board Authorized by act of June 23, 1938 (52 Stat. 968). Mediatory duties abolished by act of June 23, 1941 (55 Stat. 259); title expired June 22, 1942.

Marketing Administration, Surplus Established by Reorg. Plan No. III of 1940, effective June 30, 1940, consolidating functions vested in *Federal Surplus Commodities Corporation* and *Division of Marketing and Marketing Agreements, Agricultural Adjustment Administration.* Consolidated with other agencies into *Agricultural Marketing Administration* by EO 9069 of Feb. 23, 1942.

Marketing and Marketing Agreements, Division of Established in the Department of Agriculture by act of June 3, 1937 (50 Stat. 246). Consolidated with *Federal Surplus Commodities Corporation* into *Surplus Marketing Administration* by Reorg. Plan No. III of 1940, effective June 30, 1940.

Mediation, U.S. Board of Established by act of May 20, 1926 (44 Stat. 577). Abolished by act of June 21, 1934 (48 Stat. 1193), and superseded by National Mediation Board, July 21, 1934.

Medical Information Systems Program Office, Tri-Service Renamed Defense Medical Systems Support Center by memorandum of the Assistant Secretary of Defense (Health Affairs) May 3, 1985.

Medical Services Administration Established by the *Secretary of Health, Education, and Welfare* reorganization of Aug. 15, 1967. Transferred from *Social and Rehabilitation Service* to Health Care Financing Administration by Secretary's reorganization of Mar. 8, 1977 (42 FR 13262).

Medicine and Surgery, Department of Established in the *Veterans Administration* by act of Sept. 2, 1958 (72 Stat. 1243). Renamed *Veterans Health Services and Research Administration* in the the Department of Veterans Affairs by act of Oct. 25, 1988 (102 Stat. 2640). Renamed Veterans Health Administration by act of May 7, 1991 (105 Stat. 187).

Memorial Commission, National Established by Public Resolution 107 of Mar. 4, 1929 (45 Stat. 1699). Terminated by EO 6166 of June 10, 1933, and functions transferred to *Office of National Parks, Buildings, and Reservations,* Department of the Interior.

Mental Health, National Institute of Established by act of July 3, 1946 (60 Stat. 425). Made entity within the Alcohol, Drug Abuse, and Mental Health Administration by act of May 14, 1974 (88 Stat. 135). Functions transferred to the Department of Health and Human Services by act of Oct. 17, 1979 (93 Stat. 695). (*See also* act of Oct. 27, 1986; 100 Stat. 3207–106.) Abolished by act of July 10, 1992 (106 Stat. 331). Reestablished by act of July 10, 1992 (106 Stat. 364).

Metals Reserve Company Established June 28, 1940, by act of Jan. 22, 1932 (47 Stat. 5). Transferred from *Federal Loan Agency* to the Department of Commerce by EO 9071 of Feb. 24, 1942. Returned to *Federal Loan Agency* by act of Feb. 24, 1945 (59 Stat. 5). Dissolved by act of June 30, 1945 (59 Stat. 310), and functions transferred to *Reconstruction Finance Corporation.*

Metric Board, U.S. Established by act of Dec. 23, 1975 (89 Stat. 1007). Terminated Oct. 1, 1982, due to lack of funding.

Mexican-American Affairs, Interagency Committee on Established by Presidential memorandum of June 9, 1967. Renamed *Cabinet Committee on Opportunities for Spanish-Speaking People* by act of Dec. 30, 1969 (83 Stat. 838). Terminated Dec. 30, 1974, pursuant to terms of act.

Mexican Claims Commission, American Established by act of Dec. 18, 1942 (56 Stat. 1058). Terminated Apr. 4, 1947, by act of Apr. 3, 1945 (59 Stat. 59).

Mexican Claims Commission, Special Established by act of Apr. 10, 1935 (49 Stat. 149). Terminated by EO 7909 of June 15, 1938.

Mexico Commission for Border Development and Friendship, U.S.- Established through exchange of notes of Nov. 30 and Dec. 3, 1966, between U.S. and Mexico. Terminated Nov. 5, 1969.

Micronesian Claims Commission Established by act of July 1, 1971 (85 Stat. 92). Terminated Aug. 3, 1976, pursuant to terms of act.

Migration, Intergovernmental Committee for European Renamed Intergovernmental Committee for Migration by Resolution 624, passed by *Intergovernmental Committee for European Migration Council,* effective Nov. 11, 1980.

Migration, International Committee for Created in 1951. Renamed International Organization for Migration pursuant to article 29, paragraph 2, of the ICM constitution, effective Nov. 14, 1989.

Migratory Bird Conservation Commission Chairmanship transferred from the Secretary of Agriculture to the Secretary of the Interior by Reorg. Plan No. II of 1939, effective July 1, 1939.

Military Air Transport Service Renamed *Military Airlift Command* in U.S. Air Force by HQ MATS/MAC Special Order G–164 of Jan. 1, 1966.

Military Airlift Command Inactivated June 1, 1992.

Military Appeals, United States Court of Established under Article I of the Constitution of the United States pursuant to act of May 5, 1950, as amended. Renamed United States Court of Appeals for the Armed Forces by act of Oct. 5, 1994 (108 Stat. 2831).

Military Establishment, National Established as executive department of the Government by act of

July 26, 1947 (61 Stat. 495). Designated Department of Defense by act of Aug. 10, 1949 (63 Stat. 579).

Military Purchases, Interdepartmental Committee for Coordination of Foreign and Domestic Informal liaison committee created on Presidential notification of Dec. 6, 1939, to the Secretaries of the Treasury and *War* and the Acting Secretary of the Navy. Committee dissolved in accordance with Presidential letter to the Secretary of the Treasury Apr. 14, 1941, following approval of act of Mar. 11, 1941 (55 Stat. 31).

Military Renegotiation Policy and Review Board Established by directive of the Secretary of Defense July 19, 1948. Abolished by Secretary's letter of Jan. 18, 1952, which transferred functions to *Renegotiation Board.*

Military Sea Transportation Service Renamed Military Sealift Command in U.S. Navy by COMSC notice of Aug. 1, 1970.

Militia Bureau Established in 1908 as *Division of Militia Affairs, Office of the Secretary of War.* Superseded in 1933 by National Guard Bureau.

Mine Health and Safety Academy, National Transferred from the Department of the Interior to the Department of Labor by act of July 25, 1979 (93 Stat. 111).

Minerals Exploration, Office of Established by act of Aug. 21, 1958 (72 Stat. 700). Functions transferred to *Geological Survey* by Order 2886 of Feb. 26, 1965 of the Secretary of the Interior.

Minerals Mobilization, Office of Established by the Secretary of the Interior pursuant to act of Sept. 8, 1950 (64 Stat. 798) and EO 10574 of Nov. 5, 1954, and by order of *Office of Defense Mobilization.* Succeeded by *Office of Minerals and Solid Fuels* Nov. 2, 1962. *Office of Minerals Policy Development* combined with *Office of Research and Development* in the Department of the Interior May 21, 1976, under authority of Reorg. Plan No. 3 of 1950, to form *Office of Minerals Policy and Research Analysis.* Abolished Sept. 30, 1981, by Secretarial Order 3070 and functions transferred to Bureau of Mines.

Minerals Policy and Research Analysis, Office of *See* **Minerals Mobilization, Office of**

Minerals and Solid Fuels, Office of Established by the Secretary of the Interior Oct. 26, 1962. Abolished and functions assigned to Deputy Assistant Secretary—Minerals and Energy Policy, Office of the Assistant Secretary—Mineral Resources, effective Oct. 22, 1971.

Mines, Bureau of Established in the Department of the Interior by act of May 16, 1910 (36 Stat. 369). Transferred to the Department of Commerce by EO 4239 of June 4, 1925. Transferred to the Department of the Interior by EO 6611 of Feb. 22, 1934. Renamed United States Bureau of Mines by act of May 18, 1992 (106 Stat. 172). Terminated pursuant to act of Jan. 26, 1996 (110 Stat. 32). Certain functions transferred to Secretary of Energy by act of Apr. 26, 1996 (110 Stat. 1321–167).

Mining Enforcement and Safety Administration Established by Order 2953 of May 7, 1973 of the Secretary of the Interior. Terminated by departmental directive Mar. 9, 1978, and functions transferred to Mine Safety and Health Administration, Department of Labor, established by act of Nov. 9, 1977 (91 Stat. 1319).

Minority Business Enterprise, Office of Renamed Minority Business Development Agency by Commerce Secretarial Order DOO–254A of Nov. 1, 1979.

Mint, Bureau of the Renamed U.S. Mint by Treasury Secretarial order of Jan. 9, 1984 (49 FR 5020).

Missile Sites Labor Commission Established by EO 10946 of May 26, 1961. Abolished by EO 11374 of Oct. 11, 1967, and functions transferred to Federal Mediation and Conciliation Service.

Missouri Basin Survey Commission Established by EO 10318 of Jan. 3, 1952. Final report of *Commission* submitted to President Jan. 12, 1953, pursuant to EO 10329 of Feb. 25, 1952.

Missouri River Basin Commission Established by EO 11658 of Mar. 22, 1972. Terminated by EO 12319 of Sept. 9, 1981.

Mobilization, Office of Civil and Defense *See* **Mobilization, Office of Defense and Civilian**

Mobilization, Office of Defense and Civilian Established by Reorg. Plan No. 1 of 1958, effective July 1, 1958. Redesignated as *Office of Civil and Defense Mobilization* by act of Aug. 26, 1958 (72 Stat. 861), consolidating functions of *Office of Defense Mobilization* and *Federal Civil Defense Administration.* Civil defense functions transferred to the Secretary of Defense by EO 10952 of July 20, 1961, and remaining organization redesignated *Office of Emergency Planning* by act of Sept. 22, 1961 (75 Stat. 630).

Mobilization Policy, National Advisory Board on Established by EO 10224 of Mar. 15, 1951. EO 10224 revoked by EO 10773 of July 1, 1958.

Monetary and Financial Problems, National Advisory Council on International Established by act of July 31, 1945 (59 Stat. 512). Abolished by Reorg. Plan No. 4 of 1965, effective July 27, 1965, and functions transferred to President. Functions assumed by National Advisory Council on International Monetary and Financial Policies, established by EO 11269 of Feb. 14, 1966.

Monument Commission, National Established by act of Aug. 31, 1954 (68 Stat. 1029). Final report submitted in 1957, and audit of business completed September 1964.

Monuments in War Areas, American Commission for the Protection and Salvage of Artistic and Historic Established by President June 23, 1943; announced by Secretary of State Aug. 20, 1943. Activities assumed by the Department of State Aug. 16, 1946.

Mortgage Association, Federal National Chartered Feb. 10, 1938, by act of June 27, 1934 (48 Stat. 1246). Grouped with other agencies to form *Federal Loan Agency* by Reorg. Plan No. I of 1939, effective July 1, 1939. Transferred to the Department of Commerce by EO 9071 of Feb. 24, 1942. Returned to *Federal Loan Agency* by act of Feb. 24, 1945 (59 Stat. 5). Transferred to *Housing and Home Finance Agency* by Reorg. Plan No. 22 of 1950, effective July 10, 1950. Rechartered by act of Aug. 2, 1954 (68 Stat. 590) and made constituent agency of *Housing and Home Finance Agency.* Transferred with functions of *Housing and Home Finance Agency* to the Department of Housing and Urban Development by act of Sept. 9, 1965 (79 Stat. 667). Made Government-sponsored, private corporation by act of Aug. 1, 1968 (82 Stat. 536).

Motor Carrier Claims Commission Established by act of July 2, 1948 (62 Stat. 1222). Terminated Dec. 31, 1952, by acts of July 11, 1951 (65 Stat. 116), and Mar. 14, 1952 (66 Stat. 25).

Mount Rushmore National Memorial Commission Established by act of Feb. 25, 1929 (45 Stat. 1300). Expenditures ordered administered by the Department of the Interior by EO 6166 of June 10, 1933. Transferred to National Park Service, Department of the Interior, by Reorg. Plan No. II of 1939, effective July 1, 1939.

Mounted Horse Unit Transferred from the United States Capitol Police to the United States Park Police by Public Law 109–55 of Aug. 2, 2005 (119 Stat. 572).

Munitions Board Established in the Department of Defense by act of July 26, 1947 (61 Stat. 499). Abolished by Reorg. Plan No. 6 of 1953, effective June 30, 1953, and functions vested in the Secretary of Defense.

Munitions Board, Joint Army and Navy Organized in 1922. Placed under direction of President by military order of July 5, 1939. Reconstituted Aug. 18, 1945, by order approved by President. Terminated on establishment of *Munitions Board* by act of July 26, 1947 (61 Stat. 505).

Museum of American Art, National Renamed Smithsonian American Art Museum by Act of October 27, 2000 (114 Stat. 1463).

Museum of History and Technology, National Renamed National Museum of American History in Smithsonian Institution by act of Oct. 13, 1980 (94 Stat. 1884).

Museum Services, Institute of Established by act of June 23, 1972 (86 Stat. 327). Transferred to Office of Educational Research and Improvement, Department of Education, by act of Oct. 17, 1979 (93 Stat. 678), effective May 4, 1980. Transferred to National Foundation on the Arts and the Humanities by act of Dec. 23, 1981 (95 Stat. 1414). Functions transferred to the Institute of Museum and Library Services by act of Sept. 30, 1996 (110 Stat. 3009–307).

Narcotics, Bureau of Established in the Department of the Treasury by act of June 14, 1930 (46 Stat. 585). Abolished by Reorg. Plan No. 1 of 1968, effective Apr. 8, 1968, and functions transferred to *Bureau of Narcotics and Dangerous Drugs,* Department of Justice.

Narcotics, President's Council on Counter- Renamed President's Drug Policy Council by EO 13023, Nov. 6, 1996 (61 FR 57767).

Narcotics Control, Cabinet Committee on International Established by Presidential memorandum of Aug. 17, 1971. Terminated by Presidential memorandum of Mar. 14, 1977.

National. *See other part of title*

Naval Material, Office of Established by act of Mar. 5, 1948 (62 Stat. 68). Abolished by the Department of Defense reorg. order of Mar. 9, 1966, and functions transferred to the Secretary of the Navy (31 FR 7188).

Naval Material Command *See* **Naval Material Support Establishment**

Naval Material Support Establishment Established by Department of the Navy General Order 5 of July 1, 1963 (28 FR 7037). Replaced by *Naval Material Command* pursuant to General Order 5 of Apr. 29, 1966 (31 FR 7188). Functions realigned to form Office of Naval Acquisition Support, and termination of *Command* effective May 6, 1985.

Naval Observatory Jurisdiction transferred from *Bureau of Navigation* to Chief of Naval Operations by EO 9126 of Apr. 8, 1942, and by Reorg. Plan No. 3 of 1946, effective July 16, 1946.

Naval Oceanography Command Renamed Naval Meteorology and Oceanography Command in 1995.

Naval Petroleum and Oil Shale Reserves, Office of Established by the Secretary of the Navy, as required by law (70A Stat. 457). Jurisdiction transferred to the Department of Energy by act of Aug. 4, 1977 (91 Stat. 581).

Naval Reserve Established by act of Mar. 3, 1915 (38 Stat. 940). Redesignated Navy Reserve by Public Law 109–163 of Jan. 6, 2006 (119 Stat. 3233).

Naval Weapons, Bureau of Established by act of Aug. 18, 1959 (73 Stat. 395), to replace *Bureau of Ordnance and Aeronautics.* Abolished by Department of Defense reorg. order of Mar. 9, 1966, and functions transferred to the Secretary of the Navy (31 FR 7188), effective May 1, 1966.

Navigation, Bureau of Created by act of July 5, 1884 (23 Stat. 118), as special service under the Department of the Treasury. Transferred to the *Department of Commerce and Labor* by act of Feb. 4, 1903 (32 Stat. 825). Consolidated with *Bureau of Navigation and Steamboat Inspection* by act of June 30, 1932 (47 Stat. 415).

Navigation, Bureau of Renamed Bureau of Naval Personnel by act of May 13, 1942 (56 Stat. 276).

Navigation and Steamboat Inspection, Bureau of Renamed *Bureau of Marine Inspection and Navigation* by act of May 27, 1936 (49 Stat. 1380). Functions transferred to *Bureau of Customs,* Department of the Treasury, and U.S. Coast Guard by EO 9083 of Feb. 28, 1942. Transfer made permanent and *Bureau* abolished by Reorg. Plan No. 3 of 1946, effective July 16, 1946.

Navy Commissioners, Board of Established by act of Feb. 7, 1815 (3 Stat. 202). Abolished by act of Aug. 31, 1842 (5 Stat. 579).

Navy, Department of Defense housing functions transferred to *Federal Public Housing Authority, National Housing Agency,* by EO 9070 of Feb. 24, 1942.

Neighborhoods, National Commission on Established by act of Apr. 30, 1977 (91 Stat. 56). Terminated May 4, 1979, pursuant to terms of act.

Neighborhoods, Voluntary Associations and Consumer Protection, Office of Abolished and certain functions transferred to Office of the Assistant Secretary for Housing—Federal Housing Commissioner and Office of the Assistant Secretary for Community Planning and Development. Primary enabling legislation, act of Oct. 31, 1978 (92 Stat. 2119), repealed by act of Aug. 13, 1981 (95 Stat. 398). Abolishment of *Office* and transfer of functions carried out by Housing and Urban Development Secretarial order.

New England River Basins Commission Established by EO 11371 of Sept. 6, 1967. Terminated by EO 12319 of Sept. 9, 1981.

Nicaro Project Responsibility for management of Nicaro nickel producing facilities in Oriente Province, Cuba, transferred from *Office of Special Assistant to the Administrator (Nicaro Project)* to *Defense Materials Service* by General Services Administrator, effective July 7, 1959. Facilities expropriated by Cuban Government and nationalized Oct. 26, 1960.

Northern Mariana Islands Commission on Federal Laws Created by joint resolution of Mar. 24, 1976 (90 Stat. 263). Terminated upon submission of final report in August 1985.

Nursing Research, National Center for Renamed National Institute of Nursing Research by act of June 10, 1993 (107 Stat. 178).

Nutrition Division Functions transferred from *Department of Health, Education, and Welfare* to the Department of Agriculture by EO 9310 of Mar. 3, 1943.

Ocean Mining Administration Established by Interior Secretarial Order 2971 of Feb. 24, 1975. Abolished by Department Manual Release 2273 of June 13, 1980.

Oceanography, Interagency Committee on Established by *Federal Council for Science and Technology* pursuant to EO 10807 of Mar. 13, 1959. Absorbed by *National Council on Marine Resources and Engineering Development* pursuant to Vice Presidential letter of July 21, 1967.

Office. *See also other part of title*

Office Space, President's Advisory Commission on Presidential Established by act of Aug. 3, 1956 (70 Stat. 979). Terminated June 30, 1957, by act of Jan. 25, 1957 (71 Stat. 4).

Official Register Function of preparing *Official Register* vested in Director of the Census by act of Mar. 3, 1925 (43 Stat. 1105). Function transferred to *U.S. Civil Service Commission* by EO 6166 of June 10, 1933. Yearly compilation and publication required by act of Aug. 28, 1935 (49 Stat. 956). Act repealed by act of July 12, 1960 (74 Stat. 427), and last *Register* published in 1959.

Ohio River Basin Commission Established by EO 11578 of Jan. 13, 1971. Terminated by EO 12319 of Sept. 9, 1981.

Oil and Gas, Office of Established by the Secretary of the Interior May 6, 1946, in response to Presidential letter of May 3, 1946. Transferred to *Federal Energy Administration* by act of May 7, 1974 (88 Stat. 100).

Oil Import Administration Established in the Department of the Interior by Proc. 3279 of Mar. 10, 1959. Merged into *Office of Oil and Gas* Oct. 22, 1971.

Oil Import Appeals Board Established by the Secretary of Commerce Mar. 13, 1959, and made part of Office of Hearings and Appeals Dec. 23, 1971.

On-Site Inspection Agency Established on Jan. 26, 1988. Functions transferred to the Defense Threat Reduction Agency by DOD Directive 5105.62 of Sept. 30, 1998.

Operations Advisory Group Established by EO 11905 of Feb. 18, 1976. Abolished by Presidential Directive No. 2 of Jan. 20, 1977.

Operations Coordinating Board Established by EO 10483 of Sept. 2, 1953, which was superseded by EO 10700 of Feb. 25, 1957. EO 10700 revoked by EO 10920 of Feb. 18, 1961, and *Board* terminated.

Ordnance, Bureau of *See* **Ordnance and Hydrography, Bureau of**

Ordnance and Hydrography, Bureau of Established in the Department of the Navy by act of Aug. 31, 1842 (5 Stat. 579). Replaced under act of July 5, 1862 (12 Stat. 510), by *Bureau of Ordnance* and *Bureau of Navigation.* Abolished by act of Aug. 18, 1959 (73 Stat. 395), and functions transferred to *Bureau of Naval Weapons.*

Organization, President's Advisory Committee on Government Established by EO 10432 of Jan. 24, 1953. Abolished by EO 10917 of Feb. 10, 1961, and functions transferred to *Bureau of the Budget* for termination.

Organizations Staff, International Functions merged with Foreign Agricultural Service by memorandum of Dec. 7, 1973 of , effective Feb. 3, 1974.

Overseas Private Investment Corporation Transferred as separate agency to *U.S. International Development Cooperation Agency* by Reorg. Plan No. 2 of 1979, effective Oct. 1, 1979. Became an independent agency following the abolition of *IDCA* by act of Oct. 21, 1998 (112 Stat. 2681–790).

Oversight Board (for the Resolution Trust Corporation) Established by act of Aug. 9, 1989 (103 Stat. 363). Renamed *Thrift Depositor Protection Oversight Board* by act of Dec. 12, 1991 (105 Stat. 1767). Abolished by act of July 29, 1998 (112 Stat. 908). Authority and duties transferred to the Secretary of the Treasury.

Pacific Northwest River Basins Commission Established by EO 11331 of Mar. 6, 1967. Terminated by EO 12319 of Sept. 9, 1981.

Packers and Stockyards Administration Established by Memorandum 1613, supp. 1, of May 8, 1967 of the Secretary of Agriculture. Certain functions consolidated into Agricultural Marketing Service by Secretary's Memorandum 1927 of Jan. 15, 1978. Remaining functions incorporated into the Grain Inspection, Packers and Stockyards Administration by Secretary's Memorandum 1010–1 dated Oct. 20, 1994.

Panama Canal Operation of piers at Atlantic and Pacific terminals transferred to *Panama Railroad Company* by EO 7021 of Apr. 19, 1935. Panama Canal reestablished as *Canal Zone Government* by act of Sept. 26, 1950 (64 Stat. 1038).

Panama Canal Commission Established by act of Oct. 1, 1979, as amended (22 U.S.C. 3611). U.S. responsibility terminated by stipulation of the Panama Canal Treaty of 1977, which transferred responsibility for the Panama Canal to the Republic of Panama, effective Dec. 31, 1999. Commission terminated by act of Sept. 30, 2004 (118 Stat. 1140).

Panama Canal Company Established by act of June 29, 1948 (62 Stat. 1076). Abolished and superseded by *Panama Canal Commission* (93 Stat. 454).

Panama Railroad Company Incorporated Apr. 7, 1849, by New York State Legislature. Operated under private control until 1881, when original *French Canal Company* acquired most of its stock. *Company* and its successor, *New Panama Canal Company,* operated railroad as common carrier and also as adjunct in attempts to construct canal. In 1904 their shares of stock in *Panama Railroad Company* passed to ownership of U.S. as part of assets of *New Panama Canal Company* purchased under act of June 28, 1902 (34 Stat. 481). Remaining shares purchased from private owners in 1905. *Panama Railroad Company* reincorporated by act of June 29, 1948 (62 Stat. 1075) pursuant to requirements of act of Dec. 6, 1945 (59 Stat. 597). Reestablished as *Panama Canal Company* by act of Sept. 26, 1950 (64 Stat. 1038). The Secretary of the Army was directed to discontinue commercial operations of *Company* by Presidential letter of Mar. 29, 1961.

Paperwork, Commission on Federal Established by act of Dec. 27, 1974 (88 Stat. 1789). Terminated January 1978 pursuant to terms of act.

Park Service, National Functions in District of Columbia relating to space assignment, site selection for public buildings, and determination of priority in construction transferred to *Public Buildings Administration, Federal Works Agency,* under Reorg. Plan No. I of 1939, effective July 1, 1939.

Park Trust Fund Board, National Established by act of July 10, 1935 (49 Stat. 477). Terminated by act of Dec. 18, 1967 (81 Stat. 656), and functions transferred to National Park Foundation.

Parks, Buildings, and Reservations, Office of National Established in the Department of the Interior by EO 6166 of June 10, 1933. Renamed National Park Service by act of Mar. 2, 1934 (48 Stat. 362).

Parole, Board of Established by act of June 25, 1948 (62 Stat. 854). Abolished by act of Mar. 15, 1976 (90 Stat. 219), and functions transferred to U.S. Parole Commission.

Patent Office Provisions of first patent act administered by the Department of State, with authority for granting patents vested in board comprising Secretaries of State and *War* and Attorney General. Board abolished, authority transferred to Secretary of State, and registration system established by act of Feb. 21, 1793 (1 Stat. 318). *Office* made bureau in the Department of State in October 1802, headed by *Superintendent of Patents. Office* reorganized in 1836 by act of June 4, 1836 (5 Stat. 117) under *Commissioner of Patents. Office* transferred to the Department of the Interior in 1849. *Office* transferred to the Department of Commerce by EO 4175 of Mar. 17, 1925.

Patents Board, Government Established by EO 10096 of Jan. 23, 1950. Abolished by EO 10930 of Mar. 24, 1961, and functions transferred to the Secretary of Commerce.

Pay Board Established by EO 11627 of Oct. 15, 1971. Abolished by EO 11695 of Jan. 11, 1973.

Peace Corps Established in the Department of State by EO 10924 of Mar. 1, 1961, and continued by act of Sept. 22, 1961 (75 Stat. 612), and EO 11041 of Aug. 6, 1962. Functions transferred to ACTION by Reorg. Plan No. 1 of 1971, effective July 1, 1971. Made independent agency in executive branch by act of Dec. 29, 1981 (95 Stat. 1540).

Pennsylvania Avenue, Temporary Commission on Established by EO 11210 of Mar. 25, 1956. Inactive as of Nov. 15, 1969, due to lack of funding.

Pennsylvania Avenue Development Corporation Established by act of Oct. 27, 1972 (86 Stat. 1266). Terminated pursuant to act of Jan. 26, 1996 (110 Stat. 32) and act of Apr. 26, 1996 (110 Stat. 1321–198). Functions transferred to General Services Administration, National Capital Planning Commission, and National Park Service (61 FR 11308), effective Apr. 1, 1996.

Pension and Welfare Benefit Programs, Office of *See* **Labor-Management Services Administration**

Pensions, Commissioner of Provided for by act of Mar. 2, 1833 (4 Stat. 668). Continued by act of Mar. 3, 1835 (4 Stat. 779), and other acts as *Office of the Commissioner of Pensions.* Transferred to the Department of the Interior as bureau by act of Mar. 3, 1849 (9 Stat. 395). Consolidated with other bureaus and agencies into *Veterans Administration* by EO 5398 of July 21, 1930.

Pensions, Office of the Commissioner of *See* **Pensions, Commissioner of**

Perry's Victory Memorial Commission Created by act of Mar. 3, 1919 (40 Stat. 1322). Administration of Memorial transferred to National Park Service by act of June 2, 1936 (49 Stat. 1393). *Commission* terminated by terms of act and membership reconstituted as advisory board to the Secretary of Interior.

Personal Property, Office of *See* **Supply Service, Federal**

Personnel, National Roster of Scientific and Specialized Established by *National Resources Planning Board* pursuant to Presidential letter of June 18, 1940, to the Secretary of the Treasury. After Aug. 15, 1940, administered jointly by *Board* and *U.S. Civil Service Commission.* Transferred to *War Manpower Commission* by EO 9139 of Apr. 18, 1942. Transferred to the Department of Labor by EO 9617 of Sept. 19, 1945. Transferred with *Bureau of Employment Security* to *Federal Security Agency* by act of June 16, 1948 (62 Stat. 443). Transferred to the Department of Labor by Reorg. Plan No. 2 of 1949, effective Aug. 20, 1949, and became inactive. Roster functions transferred to National Science Foundation by act of May 10, 1950 (64 Stat. 154). Reactivated in 1950 as *National Scientific Register* by *Office of Education, Federal Security Agency,* through *National Security Resources Board* grant of funds, and continued by National Science Foundation funds until December 1952, when *Register* integrated into Foundation's National Register of Scientific and Technical Personnel project in Division of Scientific Personnel and Education.

Personnel Administration, Council of Established by EO 7916 of June 24, 1938, effective Feb. 1, 1939. Made unit in *U.S. Civil Service Commission* by EO 8467 of July 1, 1940. Renamed *Federal Personnel Council* by EO 9830 of Feb. 24, 1947. Abolished by act of July 31, 1953 (67 Stat. 300), and personnel and records transferred to *Office of Executive Director, U.S. Civil Service Commission.*

Personnel Council, Federal *See* **Personnel Administration, Council of**

Personnel Interchange, President's Commission on Established by EO 11451 of Jan. 19, 1969. Continued by EO 12136 of May 15, 1979, and renamed *President's Commission on Executive Exchange.* Continued by EO 12493 of Dec. 5, 1984. Abolished by EO 12760 of May 2, 1991.

Personnel Management, Liaison Office for Established by EO 8248 of Sept. 8, 1939. Abolished by EO 10452 of May 1, 1953, and functions transferred to *U.S. Civil Service Commission.*

Petroleum Administration for Defense Established under act of Sept. 8, 1950 (64 Stat. 798) by Order 2591 of Oct. 3, 1950 of the Secretary of the Interior, pursuant to EO 10161 of Sept. 9, 1950. Continued by Secretary's Order 2614 of Jan. 25, 1951, pursuant to EO 10200 of Jan. 3, 1951, and PAD Delegation 1 of Jan. 24, 1951. Abolished by Secretary's Order 2755 of Apr. 23, 1954.

Petroleum Administration for War *See* **Petroleum Coordinator for War, Office of**

Petroleum Administrative Board Established Sept. 11, 1933, by the Secretary of the Interior. Terminated Mar. 31, 1936, by EO 7076 of June 15, 1935. The Secretary of the Interior was authorized to execute functions vested in President by act of Feb. 22, 1935 (49 Stat. 30) by EO 7756 of Dec. 1, 1937. Secretary also authorized to establish *Petroleum Conservation Division* to assist in administering act. Records of *Petroleum Administrative Board* and *Petroleum Labor Policy Board* housed with *Petroleum Conservation Division, Office of Oil and Gas,* acting as custodian for the Secretary of the Interior.

Petroleum Coordinator for War, Office of Secretary of the Interior designated *Petroleum Coordinator for National Defense* pursuant to Presidential letter of May 28, 1941, and approved *Petroleum Coordinator for War* pursuant to Presidential letter of Apr. 20, 1942. *Office* abolished by EO 9276 of Dec. 2, 1942, and functions transferred to *Petroleum Administration for War,* established by same EO. *Administration* terminated by EO 9718 of May 3, 1946.

Petroleum Labor Policy Board Established by the Secretary of the Interior, as *Administrator of Code of Fair Competition for Petroleum Industry,* on recommendation of Planning and Coordination Committee Oct. 10, 1933. Reorganized by Secretary Dec. 19, 1933, and reorganization confirmed by order of Mar. 8, 1935. Terminated Mar. 31, 1936, when *Petroleum Administrative Board* abolished by EO 7076 of June 15, 1935.

Petroleum Reserves Corporation Established June 30, 1943, by *Reconstruction Finance Corporation.* Transferred to *Office of Economic Warfare* by EO 9360 of July 15, 1943. *Office* consolidated into *Foreign Economic Administration* by EO 9380 of Sept. 25, 1943. Functions transferred to *Reconstruction Finance Corporation* by EO 9630 of Sept. 27, 1945. *RFC*'s charter amended Nov. 9, 1945, to change name to *War Assets Corporation. Corporation* designated by *Surplus Property Administrator* as disposal agency for all types of property for which *Reconstruction Finance Corporation* formerly disposal agency. Domestic surplus property functions of *Corporation* transferred to *War Assets Administration* by EO 9689 of Jan. 31, 1946. *Reconstruction Finance Corporation Board of Directors* ordered by President to dissolve *War Assets Corporation* as soon after Mar. 25, 1946, as practicable.

Philippine Alien Property Administration Established in *Office for Emergency Management* by EO 9789 of Oct. 14, 1946. Abolished by EO 10254 of June 15, 1951, and functions transferred to the Department of Justice.

Philippine War Damage Commission Established by act of Apr. 30, 1946 (60 Stat. 128). Terminated Mar. 31, 1951, by act of Sept. 6, 1950 (64 Stat. 712).

Photographic Interpretation Center, National Functions transferred to the National Imagery and Mapping Agency by act of Sept. 23, 1996 (110 Stat. 2677).

Physical Fitness, Committee on Established in *Office of Federal Security Administrator* by EO 9338 of Apr. 29, 1943. Terminated June 30, 1945.

Physical Fitness, President's Council on *See* **Youth Fitness, President's Council on**

Physician Payment Review Commission Established by act of Apr. 7, 1986 (100 Stat. 190). Terminated by act of Aug. 5, 1997 (111 Stat. 354). Assets, staff, and continuing responsibility for reports transferred to the Medicare Payment Advisory Commission.

Planning Board, National Established by *Administrator of Public Works* July 30, 1933. Terminated by EO 6777 of June 30, 1934.

Plant Industry, Bureau of Established by act of Mar. 2, 1902 (31 Stat. 922). Soil fertility and soil microbiology work of *Bureau of Chemistry and Soils* transferred to *Bureau* by act of May 17, 1935. Soil chemistry and physics and soil survey work of *Bureau of Chemistry and Soils* transferred to *Bureau* by Secretary's Memorandum 784 of Oct. 6, 1938. In February 1943 engineering research of *Bureau of Agricultural Chemistry and Engineering* transferred to *Bureau of Plant Industry, Soils, and Agricultural Engineering* by Research Administration Memorandum 5 issued pursuant to EO 9069 of Feb. 23, 1942, and in conformity with Secretary's Memorandums 960 and 986. Functions transferred to Agricultural Research Service by Secretary's Memorandum 1320, supp. 4, of Nov. 2, 1953.

Plant Industry, Soils, and Agricultural Engineering, Bureau of *See* **Plant Industry, Bureau of**

Plant Quarantine, Bureau of *See* **Entomology and Plant Quarantine, Bureau of**

Policy Development, Office of *See* **Domestic Council**

Post Office, Department of *See* **Postal Service**

Postal Savings System Established by act of June 25, 1910 (36 Stat. 814). System closed by act of Mar. 28, 1966 (80 Stat. 92).

Postal Service Created July 26, 1775, by Continental Congress. Temporarily established by Congress by act of Sept. 22, 1789 (1 Stat. 70), and continued by subsequent acts. *Department of Post Office* made executive department under act of June 8, 1872 (17 Stat. 283). Offices of First, Second, Third, and Fourth Assistant Postmasters General abolished and Deputy Postmaster General and four Assistant Postmasters General established by Reorg. Plan No. 3 of 1949, effective Aug. 20, 1949. Reorganized as U.S. Postal Service in executive branch by act of Aug. 12, 1970 (84 Stat. 719), effective July 1, 1971.

Power Commission, Federal Established by act of June 10, 1920 (41 Stat. 1063). Terminated by act of Aug. 4, 1977 (91 Stat. 578), and functions transferred to the Department of Energy.

Preparedness, Office of Renamed *Federal Preparedness Agency* by General Services Administrator's order of June 26, 1975.

Preparedness Agency, Federal Functions transferred from General Services Administration to Federal Emergency Management Agency by EO 12148 of July 20, 1979.

Presidential. *See other part of title*

President's. *See other part of title*

Press Intelligence, Division of Established in August 1933. Made division of *National Emergency Council* July 10, 1935. Continued in *Office of Government Reports* by Reorg. Plan No. II of 1939, effective July 1, 1939. Transferred to *Office of War Information* by EO 9182 of June 13, 1942, functioning in *Bureau of Special Services. Office* abolished by EO 9608 of Aug. 31, 1945, and *Bureau* transferred to *Bureau of the Budget.* Upon reestablishment of *Office of Government Reports,* by EO 9809 of Dec. 12, 1946, *Division of Press Intelligence* made unit of *Office.*

Price Administration, Office of Established by EO 8734 of Apr. 11, 1941, combining *Price Division* and *Consumer Division* of *National Defense Advisory Commission.* Renamed *Office of Price Administration* by EO 8875 of Aug. 28, 1941, which transferred *Civilian Allocation Division* to *Office of Production Management.* Consolidated with other agencies into *Office of Temporary Controls* by EO 9809 of Dec. 12, 1946, except *Financial Reporting Division,* transferred to Federal Trade Commission.

Price Commission Established by EO 11627 of Oct. 15, 1971. Abolished by EO 11695 of Jan. 11, 1973.

Price Decontrol Board Established by act of July 25, 1946 (60 Stat. 669). Effective period of act of Jan. 30, 1942 (56 Stat. 23), extended to June 30, 1947, by joint resolution of June 25, 1946 (60 Stat. 664).

Price Stability for Economic Growth, Cabinet Committee on Established by Presidential letter of Jan. 28, 1959. Abolished by Presidential direction Mar. 12, 1961.

Price Stabilization, Office of Established by General Order 2 of *Economic Stabilization Administrator* Jan. 24, 1951. *Director of Price Stabilization* provided for in EO 10161 of Sept. 9, 1950. Terminated Apr. 30, 1953, by EO 10434 of Feb. 6, 1953, and provisions of acts of June 30, 1952 (66 Stat. 296) and June 30, 1953 (67 Stat. 131).

Prices and Costs, Committee on Government Activities Affecting Established by EO 10802 of Jan. 23, 1959. Abolished by EO 10928 of Mar. 23, 1961.

Priorities Board Established by order of *Council of National Defense,* approved Oct. 18, 1940, and by

EO 8572 of Oct. 21, 1940. EO 8572 revoked by EO 8629 of Jan. 7, 1941.

Prison Industries, Inc., Federal Established by EO 6917 of Dec. 11, 1934. Transferred to the Department of Justice by Reorg. Plan No. II of 1939, effective July 1, 1939.

Prison Industries Reorganization Administration Functioned from Sept. 26, 1935, to Sept. 30, 1940, under authority of act of Apr. 8, 1935 (49 Stat. 115), and of EO's 7194 of Sept. 26, 1935, 7202 of Sept. 28, 1935, and 7649 of June 29, 1937. Terminated due to lack of funding.

Private Sector Programs, Office of Functions transferred to the Office of Citizen Exchanges within the Bureau of Educational and Cultural Affairs, USIA, by act of Feb. 16, 1990 (104 Stat. 56).

Processing tax *Agricultural Adjustment Administration's* function of collecting taxes declared unconstitutional by U.S. Supreme Court Jan. 6, 1936. Functions under acts of June 28, 1934 (48 Stat. 1275), Apr. 21, 1934 (48 Stat. 598), and Aug. 24, 1935 (49 Stat. 750) discontinued by repeal of these laws by act of Feb. 10, 1936 (49 Stat. 1106).

Processing Tax Board of Review Established in the Department of the Treasury by act of June 22, (49 Stat. 1652). Abolished by act of Oct. 21, 1942 (56 Stat. 967).

Proclamations *See* **State, Department of**

Procurement, Commission on Government Established by act of Nov. 26, 1969 (83 Stat. 269). Terminated Apr. 30, 1973, due to expiration of statutory authority.

Procurement and Assignment Service Established by President Oct. 30, 1941. Transferred from *Office of Defense Health and Welfare Services* to *War Manpower Commission* by EO 9139 of Apr. 18, 1942. Transferred to *Federal Security Agency* by EO 9617 of Sept. 19, 1945, which terminated *Commission.*

Procurement Division Established in the Department of the Treasury by EO 6166 of June 10, 1933. Renamed *Bureau of Federal Supply* by Department of the Treasury Order 73 of Nov. 19, 1946, effective Jan. 1, 1947. Transferred to General Services Administration as Federal Supply Service by act of June 30, 1949 (63 Stat. 380).

Procurement Policy, Office of Federal Established within Office of Management and Budget by act of Aug. 30, 1974 (88 Stat. 97). Abolished due to lack of funding and functions transferred to Office of Management and Budget by act of Oct 28, 1993 (107 Stat. 1236).

Product Standards Policy, Office of Formerly separate operating unit under Assistant Secretary for Productivity, Technology, and Innovation, Department of Commerce. Transferred to *National Bureau of Standards* by departmental reorganization order, effective Apr. 27, 1982.

Production Areas, Committee for Congested Established in Executive Office of the President by EO 9327 of Apr. 7, 1943. Terminated Dec. 31, 1944, by act of June 28, 1944 (58 Stat. 535).

Production Authority, National Established in the Department of Commerce Sept. 11, 1950, by EO's 10161 of Sept. 9, 1950, 10193 of Dec. 16, 1950, and 10200 of Jan. 3, 1951. Abolished by order of Oct. 1, 1953 of the Secretary of Commerce, and functions merged into *Business and Defense Services Administration.*

Production Management, Office of Established in *Office for Emergency Management* by EO 8629 of Jan. 7, 1941. Abolished by EO 9040 of Jan. 24, 1942, and personnel and property transferred to *War Production Board.*

Production and Marketing Administration Established by Secretary of Agriculture Memorandum 1118 of Aug. 18, 1945. Functions transferred under Department reorganization by Secretary's Memorandum 1320, supp. 4, of Nov. 2, 1953.

Productivity Council, National Established by EO 12089 of Oct. 23, 1978. EO 12089 revoked by EO 12379 of Aug. 17, 1982.

Programs, Bureau of International Established by the Secretary of Commerce Aug. 8, 1961, by Departmental Orders 173 and 174. Abolished by Departmental Order 182 of Feb. 1, 1963, which established *Bureau of International Commerce.* Functions transferred to *Domestic and International Business Administration,* effective Nov. 17, 1972.

Programs, Office of Public Established in the National Archives and Records Administration. Reorganized by Archivist under Notice 96–260, Sept. 23, 1996, effective Jan. 6, 1997. Functions restructured and transferred to Office of Records Services—Washington, DC.

Prohibition, Bureau of Established by act of May 27, 1930 (46 Stat. 427). Investigative functions consolidated with functions of *Bureau of Investigation* into *Division of Investigation,* Department of Justice. by EO 6166 of June 10, 1933, which set as effective date Mar. 2, 1934, or such later date as fixed by President. All other functions performed by *Bureau of Prohibition* ordered transferred to such division in the Department of Justice as deemed desirable by Attorney General.

Property, Office of Surplus Established in *Procurement Division,* Department of the Treasury, by EO 9425 of Feb. 19, 1944, and act of Oct. 3, 1944 (58 Stat. 765), under general direction of *Surplus Property Board* established by same legislation. Transferred to the Department of Commerce by EO 9541 of Apr. 19, 1945. Terminated by EO 9643 of Oct. 19, 1945, and activities and personnel transferred to *Reconstruction Finance Corporation.*

Property Administration, Surplus *See* **War Property Administration, Surplus**

Property Board, Surplus *See* **War Property Administration, Surplus**

Property Council, Federal Established by EO 11724 of June 25, 1973, and reconstituted by EO 11954 of Jan. 7, 1977. Terminated by EO 12030 of Dec. 15, 1977.

Property Management and Disposal Service *See* **Emergency Procurement Service**

Property Office, Surplus Established in *Division of Territories and Island Possessions,* Department of the Interior, under Regulation 1 of *Surplus Property Board,* Apr. 2, 1945. Transferred to *War Assets Administration* by EO 9828 of Feb. 21, 1947.

Property Review Board Established by EO 12348 of Feb. 25, 1982. EO 12348 revoked by EO 12512 of Apr. 29, 1985.

Protective Service, Federal Functions established in the *Federal Works* Agency by act of June 1, 1948 (62 Stat. 281). Functions transferred to General Services Administrator by act of June 30, 1949 (63 Stat. 380). Established as an agency within General Services Administration by GSA Administrator on Jan. 11, 1971 (ADM. 5440.46). Transferred to Homeland Security Department by act of Nov. 25, 2002 (116 Stat. 2178).

Prospective Payment Assessment Commission Established by act of Apr. 20, 1983 (97 Stat. 159). Terminated by act of Aug. 5, 1997 (111 Stat. 354). Assets, staff, and continuing responsibility for reports transferred to the Medicare Payment Advisory Commission.

Provisions and Clothing, Bureau of Established by acts of Aug. 31, 1842 (5 Stat. 579), and July 5, 1862 (12 Stat. 510). Designated *Bureau of Supplies and Accounts* by act of July 19, 1892 (27 Stat. 243). Abolished by Department of Defense reorg. order of Mar. 9, 1966, and functions transferred to the Secretary of the Navy (31 FR 7188).

Public. *See other part of title*

Publications Commission, National Historical Established by act of Oct. 22, 1968 (82 Stat. 1293). Renamed National Historical Publications and Records Commission by act of Dec. 22, 1974 (88 Stat. 1734).

Puerto Rican Hurricane Relief Commission Established by act of Dec. 21, 1928 (45 Stat. 1067). No loans made after June 30, 1934, and *Commission* abolished June 3, 1935, by Public Resolution 22 (49 Stat. 320). Functions transferred to *Division of Territories and Island Possessions,* Department of the Interior. After June 30, 1946, collection work performed in *Puerto Rico Reconstruction Administration.* Following termination of *Administration,* remaining collection functions transferred to the Secretary of Agriculture by act of July 11, 1956 (70 Stat. 525).

Puerto Rico, U.S.-Puerto Rico Commission on the Status of Established by act of Feb. 20, 1964 (78 Stat. 17). Terminated by terms of act.

Puerto Rico Reconstruction Administration Established in the Department of the Interior by EO 7057 of May 28, 1935. Terminated Feb. 15, 1955, by act of Aug. 15, 1953 (67 Stat. 584).

Radiation Biology Laboratory *See* **Radiation and Organisms, Division of**

Radiation Council, Federal Established by EO 10831 of Aug. 14, 1959, and act of Sept. 23, 1959 (73 Stat. 688). Abolished by Reorg. Plan No. 3 of 1970, effective Dec. 2, 1970, and functions transferred to Environmental Protection Agency.

Radiation and Organisms, Division of Established by Secretarial order of May 1, 1929, as part of Smithsonian Astrophysical Observatory. Renamed *Radiation Biology Laboratory* by Secretarial order of Feb. 16, 1965. Merged with *Chesapeake Center for Environmental Studies* by Secretarial order of July 1, 1983, to form Smithsonian Environmental Research Center.

Radio Commission, Federal Established by act of Feb. 23, 1927 (44 Stat. 1162). Abolished by act of June 19, 1934 (48 Stat. 1102), and functions transferred to Federal Communications Commission.

Radio Division Established by *National Emergency Council* July 1, 1938. Transferred to *Office of Education, Federal Security Agency,* by Reorg. Plan No. II of 1939, effective July 1, 1939. Terminated June 30, 1940, by terms of act of June 30, 1939 (53 Stat. 927).

Radio Propagation Laboratory, Central Transferred from *National Bureau of Standards* to *Environmental Science Services Administration* by the Department of Commerce Order 2–A, effective July 13, 1965.

Radiological Health, National Center for Devices and Renamed Center for Devices and Radiological Health by Food and Drug Administration notice of Mar. 9, 1984 (49 FR 10166).

Rail Public Counsel, Office of Established by act of Feb. 5, 1976 (90 Stat. 51). Terminated Dec. 1, 1979, due to lack of funding.

Railroad Administration, U.S. *See* **Railroads, Director General of**

Railroad and Airline Wage Board Established by *Economic Stabilization Administrator's* General Order 7 of Sept. 27, 1951, pursuant to act of Sept. 8, 1950 (64 Stat. 816). Terminated Apr. 30, 1953, by EO 10434 of Feb. 6, 1953, and acts of June 30, 1952 (66 Stat. 296), and June 30, 1953 (67 Stat. 131).

Railroads, Director General of Established under authority of act of Aug. 29, 1916 (39 Stat. 645). Organization of *U.S. Railroad Administration* announced Feb. 9, 1918. Office abolished by Reorg. Plan No. II of 1939, effective July 1, 1939, and functions transferred to the Secretary of the Treasury.

Railway Association, U.S. Established by act of Jan. 2, 1974 (87 Stat. 985). Terminated Apr. 1, 1987, by act of Oct. 21, 1986 (100 Stat. 1906).

Railway Labor Panel, National Established by EO 9172 of May 22, 1942. EO 9172 revoked by EO 9883 of Aug. 11, 1947.

Real Estate Board, Federal Established by EO 8034 of Jan. 14, 1939. Abolished by EO 10287 of Sept. 6, 1951.

Reclamation, Bureau of *See* **Reclamation Service**

Reclamation Service Established July 1902 in *Geological Survey* by the Secretary of the Interior, pursuant to act of June 17, 1902 (32 Stat. 388). Separated from Survey in 1907 and renamed *Bureau of Reclamation* June 1923. Power marketing functions transferred to the Department of Energy by act of Aug. 4, 1977 (91 Stat. 578). *Bureau* renamed *Water and Power Resources Service* by Secretarial Order 3042 of Nov. 6, 1979. Renamed Bureau of Reclamation by Secretarial Order 3064 of May 18, 1981.

Reconciliation Service Established by Director of Selective Service pursuant to EO 11804 of Sept. 16, 1974. Program terminated Apr. 2, 1980.

Reconstruction Finance Corporation Established Feb. 2, 1932, by act of Jan. 22, 1932 (47 Stat. 5). Grouped with other agencies to form *Federal Loan Agency* by Reorg. Plan No. I of 1939, effective July 1, 1939. Transferred to the Department of Commerce by EO 9071 of Feb. 24, 1942. Returned to *Federal Loan Agency* by act of Feb. 24, 1945 (59 Stat. 5). *Agency* abolished by act of June 30, 1947 (61 Stat. 202), and functions assumed by *Corporation.* Functions relating to financing houses or site improvements, authorized by act of Aug. 10, 1948 (61 Stat. 1275), transferred to *Housing and Home Finance Agency* by Reorg. Plan No. 23 of 1950, effective July 10, 1950. *Corporation* Board of Directors, established by act of Jan. 22, 1932 (47 Stat. 5), abolished by Reorg. Plan No. 1 of 1951, effective May 1, 1951, and functions transferred to Administrator and *Loan Policy Board* established by same plan, effective Apr. 30, 1951. Act of July 30, 1953 (67 Stat. 230), provided for *RFC* succession until June 30, 1954, and for termination of its lending powers Sept. 28, 1953. Certain functions assigned to appropriate agencies for liquidation by Reorg. Plan No. 2 of 1954, effective July 1, 1954. *Corporation* abolished by Reorg. Plan No. 1 of 1957, effective June 30, 1957, and functions transferred to *Housing and Home Finance Agency,* General Services Administration, Small Business Administration, and the Department of the Treasury.

Records Administration, Office of Established in the National Archives and Records Administration. Reorganized by Archivist under Notice 96–260, Sept. 23, 1996, effective Jan. 6, 1997. Functions restructured and transferred to Office of Records Services—Washington, DC.

Records Centers, Office of Federal Established in the National Archives and Records Administration. Reorganized by Archivist under Notice 96–260, Sept. 23, 1996, effective Jan. 6, 1997. Functions restructured and transferred to Office of Regional Records Services.

Records and Information Management, Office of Functions transferred from *National Archives and Records Service* to *Automated Data and Telecommunications Service* by General Services Administrator's decision, effective Jan. 10, 1982, regionally and Apr. 1, 1982, in Washington, DC.

Recovery Administration, Advisory Council, National Established by EO 7075 of June 15, 1935. Transferred to the Department of Commerce by EO 7252 of Dec. 21, 1935, and functions ordered terminated not later than Apr. 1, 1936, by same order. *Committee of Industrial Analysis* created by EO 7323 of Mar. 21, 1936, to complete work of *Council.*

Recovery Administration, National Established by President pursuant to act of June 16, 1933 (48 Stat. 194). Provisions of title I of act repealed by Public Resolution 26 of June 14, 1935 (49 Stat. 375), and extension of *Administration* in skeletonized form authorized until Apr. 1, 1936. *Office of Administrator, National Recovery Administration,* created by EO 7075 of June 15, 1935. *Administration* terminated by EO 7252 of Dec. 21, 1935, which transferred *Division of Review, Division of Business Corporation,* and *Advisory Council* to the Department of Commerce for termination of functions by Apr. 1, 1936. *Consumers' Division* transferred to the Department of Labor by same order.

Recovery Review Board, National Established by EO 6632 of Mar. 7, 1934. Abolished by EO 6771 of June 30, 1934.

Recreation, Bureau of Outdoor Established in the Department of the Interior by act of May 28, 1963 (77 Stat. 49). Terminated by Secretary's order of Jan. 25, 1978, and functions assumed by *Heritage Conservation and Recreation Service.*

Recreation and Natural Beauty, Citizens' Advisory Committee on Established by EO 11278 of May 4, 1966. Terminated by EO 11472 of May 29, 1969.

Recreation and Natural Beauty, President's Council on Established by EO 11278 of May 4, 1966. Terminated by EO 11472 of May 29, 1969.

Recreation Resources Review Commission, Outdoor Established by act of June 28, 1958 (72 Stat. 238). Final report submitted to President January 1962 and terminated Sept. 1, 1962.

Regional Action Planning Commissions Authorized by act of Aug. 26, 1965 (79 Stat. 552). Federal role abolished through repeal by act of Aug. 13, 1981 (95 Stat. 766). At time of repeal, eight commissions—Coastal Plains, Four Corners, New England, Old West Ozarks, Pacific Northwest, Southwest Border, Southwest Border Region, and Upper Great Lakes—affected.

Regional Archives, Office of Special and Established in the National Archives and Records Administration. Reorganized by Archivist under Notice 96–260, Sept. 23, 1996, effective Jan. 6, 1997. Functions restructured and transferred between Office of Records Services—Washington, DC and Office of Regional Records Services.

Regional Councils, Federal Established by EO 12314 of July 22, 1981. Abolished by EO 12407 of Feb. 22, 1983.

Regional Operations, Executive Director of Established in Food and Drug Administration by order of May 20, 1971 of the *Secretary of Health, Education, and Welfare.* Merged into Office of

Regulatory Affairs by order of Nov. 5, 1984 of the Secretary of Health and Human Services.

Regulatory Council, U.S. Disbanded by Vice Presidential memorandum of Mar. 25, 1981. Certain functions continued in Regulatory Information Service Center.

Regulatory Relief, Presidential Task Force on Establishment announced in President's remarks Jan. 22, 1981. Disbanded and functions transferred to Office of Management and Budget in August 1983.

Rehabilitation Services Administration Functions transferred from *Department of Health, Education, and Welfare* to Office of Special Education and Rehabilitative Services, Department of Education, by act of Oct. 17, 1979 (93 Stat. 678), effective May 4, 1980.

Relief Corporation, Federal Surplus Organized under powers granted to President by act of June 16, 1933 (48 Stat. 195). Charter granted by State of Delaware Oct. 4, 1933, and amended Nov. 18, 1935, changing name to *Federal Surplus Commodities Corporation* and naming the Secretary of Agriculture, *Administrator of Agricultural Adjustment Administration,* and *Governor of Farm Credit Administration* as Board of Directors. Continued as agency under the Secretary of Agriculture by acts of June 28, 1937 (50 Stat. 323) and Feb. 16, 1938 (52 Stat. 38). Consolidated with *Division of Marketing and Marketing Agreements* into *Surplus Marketing Administration* by Reorg. Plan No. III of 1940, effective June 30, 1940. Merged into *Agricultural Marketing Administration* by EO 9069 of Feb. 23, 1942.

Relief and Rehabilitation Operations, Office of Foreign Established in the Department of State as announced by White House Nov. 21, 1942. Consolidated with *Foreign Economic Administration* by EO 9380 of Sept. 25, 1943.

Renegotiation Board Established by act of Mar. 23, 1951 (65 Stat. 7). Terminated Mar. 31, 1979, by act of Oct. 10, 1978 (92 Stat. 1043).

Rent Advisory Board Established by EO 11632 of Nov. 22, 1971. Abolished by EO 11695 of Jan. 11, 1973.

Rent Stabilization, Office of Established by General Order 9 of *Economic Stabilization Administrator* July 31, 1951, pursuant to act of June 30, 1947 (61 Stat. 193), and EO' s 10161 of Sept. 9, 1950, and 10276 of July 31, 1951. Abolished by EO 10475 of July 31, 1953, and functions transferred to *Office of Defense Mobilization. Office of Research and Development* combined with *Office of Minerals Policy Development* in the Department of the Interior May 21, 1976, under authority of Reorg. Plan No. 3 of 1950, effective May 24, 1950, to form *Office of Minerals Policy and Research Analysis.* Abolished Sept. 30, 1981, by Secretarial Order 3070 and functions transferred to *Bureau of Mines.*

Reports, Office of Government Established July 1, 1939, to perform functions of *National Emergency Council* abolished by Reorg. Plan No. II of 1939, effective July 1, 1939. Established as administrative unit of Executive Office of the President by EO 8248 of Sept. 8, 1939. Consolidated with *Office of War Information, Office for Emergency Management,* by EO 9182 of June 13, 1942. Reestablished in Executive Office of the President by EO 9809 of Dec. 12, 1946, which transferred to it functions of *Media Programming Division* and *Motion Picture Division, Office of War Mobilization and Reconversion,* and functions transferred from *Bureau of Special Services, Office of War Information,* to *Bureau of the Budget* by EO 9608 of Aug. 31, 1945. Subsequent to enactment of act of July 30, 1947 (61 Stat. 588), functions of *Office* restricted to advertising and motion picture liaison and operation of library. Terminated June 30, 1948.

Research, Office of University Transferred from *Office of Program Management and Administration,* Research and Special Programs Administration, to Office of Economics, Office of the Assistant Secretary for Policy and International Affairs, under authority of the Department of Transportation appropriation request for FY 1985, effective Oct. 1, 1984.

Research and Development Board Established in the Department of Defense by act of July 26, 1947 (61 Stat. 499). Abolished by Reorg. Plan No. 6 of 1953, effective June 30, 1953, and functions vested in the Secretary of Defense.

Research and Development Board, Joint Established June 6, 1946, by charter of Secretaries of *War* and Navy. Terminated on creation of *Research and Development Board* by act of July 26, 1947 (61 Stat. 506).

Research and Intelligence Service, Interim Established in the Department of State by EO 9621 of Sept. 20, 1945. Abolished Dec. 31, 1945, pursuant to terms of order.

Research and Special Programs Administration Established by act of Oct. 24, 1992 (106 Stat. 3310). Abolished and certain duties and powers transferred to both the Pipeline Hazardous Materials Safety Administration and the Administrator of the Research and Innovative Technology Administration, Department of Transportation, by act of Nov. 30, 2004 (118 Stat. 2424–2426).

Research Resources, Division of Established in National Institutes of Health, Department of Health and Human Services. Renamed National Center for Research Resources by Secretarial notice of Feb. 23, 1990 (55 FR 6455) and act of June 10, 1993 (107 Stat. 178).

Research Service, Cooperative State Established by Secretary of Agriculture Memorandum 1462, supp. 1, of Aug. 31, 1961. Consolidated into *Science and Education Administration* by Secretary's order of Jan. 24, 1978. Reestablished as Cooperative State Research Service by Secretarial order of June 16, 1981.

Research and Service Division, Cooperative Functions transferred to the Secretary of Agriculture in *Farmer Cooperative Service* by act of Aug. 6, 1953 (67 Stat. 390).

Resettlement Administration Established by EO 7027 of Apr. 30, 1935. Functions transferred to the Department of Agriculture by EO 7530 of Dec. 31, 1936. Renamed *Farm Security Administration* by Secretary's Memorandum 732 of Sept. 1, 1937. Abolished by act of Aug. 14, 1946 (60 Stat. 1062) and functions incorporated into the *Farmers' Home Administration,* effective Jan. 1, 1947. *Farmers' Home Administration* abolished, effective Dec. 27, 1994, under authority of Secretary's Memorandum 1010–1 dated Oct. 20, 1994 (59 FR 66441). Functions assumed by the *Consolidated Farm Service Agency* and the *Rural Housing and Community Development Service.*

Resolution Trust Corporation Established by act of Aug. 9, 1989 (103 Stat. 369). Board of Directors of the Corporation abolished by act of Dec. 12, 1991 (105 Stat. 1769). Corporation functions terminated pursuant to act of Dec. 17, 1993 (107 Stat. 2369).

Resources Board and Advisory Committee, National Established by EO 6777 of June 30, 1934. Abolished by EO 7065 of June 7, 1935, and functions transferred to *National Resources Committee.*

Resources Committee, National Established by EO 7065 of June 7, 1935. Abolished by Reorg. Plan No. I of 1939, effective July 1, 1939, and functions transferred to *National Resources Planning Board* in Executive Office of the President. *Board* terminated by act of June 26, 1943 (57 Stat. 169).

Resources Planning Board, National *See* **Resources Committee, National**

Retired Executives, Service Corps of Established in ACTION by act of Oct. 1, 1973 (87 Stat. 404). Transferred to Small Business Administration by EO 11871 of July 18, 1975.

Retraining and Reemployment Administration Established by EO 9427 of Feb. 24, 1944, and act of Oct. 3, 1944 (58 Stat. 788). Transferred from *Office of War Mobilization and Reconversion* to the Department of Labor by EO 9617 of Sept. 19, 1945. Terminated pursuant to terms of act.

Revenue Sharing, Office of Established by the Secretary of the Treasury to administer programs authorized by acts of Oct. 20, 1972 (86 Stat. 919), and July 22, 1976 (90 Stat. 999). Transferred from the Office of the Secretary to Assistant Secretary (Domestic Finance) by Department of the Treasury Order 242, rev. 1, of May 17, 1976.

Review, Division of Established in *National Recovery Administration* by EO 7075 of June 15, 1935. Transferred to the Department of Commerce by EO 7252 of Dec. 21, 1935, and functions terminated Apr. 1, 1936. *Committee of Industrial Analysis* created by EO 7323 of Mar. 21, 1936, to complete work of *Division.*

RFC Mortgage Company Organized under laws of Maryland Mar. 14, 1935, pursuant to act of Jan. 22, 1932 (47 Stat. 5). Grouped with other agencies to form *Federal Loan Agency* by Reorg. Plan No. I of 1939, effective July 1, 1939. Transferred to the Department of Commerce by EO 9071 of Feb. 24, 1942. Returned to *Federal Loan Agency* by act of Feb. 24, 1945 (59 Stat. 5). Assets and liabilities transferred to *Reconstruction Finance Corporation* by act of June 30, 1947 (61 Stat. 207).

River Basins, Neches, Trinity, Brazos, Colorado, Guadalupe, San Antonio, Nueces, and San Jacinto, and Intervening Areas, U.S. Study Commission on Established by act of Aug. 28, 1958 (72 Stat. 1058). Terminated June 30, 1962.

River Basins, Savannah, Altamaha, Saint Marys, Apalachicola-Chattahoochee, and Perdido-Escambia, and Intervening Areas, U.S. Study Commission on Established by act of Aug. 28, 1958 (72 Stat. 1090). Terminated Dec. 23, 1962.

Road Inquiry, Office of Established by the Secretary of Agriculture under authority of act of Aug. 8, 1894 (28 Stat. 264). Federal aid for highways to be administered by the Secretary of Agriculture through *Office of Public Roads and Rural Engineering* authorized by act of July 11, 1916 (39 Stat. 355), known as *Bureau of Public Roads* after July 1918. Transferred to *Federal Works Agency* by Reorg. Plan No. I of 1939, effective July 1, 1939, and renamed *Public Roads Administration.* Transferred to General Services Administration as *Bureau of Public Roads* by act of June 30, 1949 (63 Stat. 380). Transferred to the Department of Commerce by Reorg. Plan No. 7 of 1949, effective Aug. 20, 1949. Transferred to the Secretary of Transportation by act of Oct. 15, 1966 (80 Stat. 931), and functions assigned to Federal Highway Administration.

Roads, Bureau of Public *See* **Road Inquiry, Office of**

Roads Administration, Public *See* **Road Inquiry, Office of**

Roads and Rural Engineering, Office of Public *See* **Road Inquiry, Office of**

Rock Creek and Potomac Parkway Commission Established by act of Mar. 14, 1913 (37 Stat. 885). Abolished by EO 6166 of June 10, 1933, and functions transferred to *Office of National Parks, Buildings, and Reservations,* Department of the Interior.

Roosevelt Centennial Commission, Theodore Established by joint resolution of July 28, 1955 (69 Stat. 383). Terminated Oct. 27, 1959, pursuant to terms of act.

Roosevelt Library, Franklin D. Functions assigned to National Park Service by Reorg. Plan No. 3 of 1946, effective July 16, 1946, transferred to General Services Administration by Reorg. Plan No. 1 of 1963, effective July 27, 1963.

Roosevelt Library, Trustees of the Franklin D. Established by joint resolution of July 18, 1939 (53 Stat. 1063). Transferred to General Services Administration by act of June 30, 1949 (63 Stat. 381). Abolished by act of Mar. 5, 1958 (72 Stat. 34), and Library operated by *National Archives and Records Service,* General Services Administration.

Roosevelt Memorial Commission, Franklin Delano Established by joint resolution of Aug. 11, 1955 (69

Stat. 694). Terminated by act of Nov. 14, 1997 (111 Stat. 1601).

Rubber Development Corporation Establishment announced Feb. 20, 1943, by the Secretary of Commerce. Organized under laws of Delaware as subsidiary of *Reconstruction Finance Corporation.* Assumed all activities of *Rubber Reserve Company* relating to development of foreign rubber sources and procurement of rubber therefrom. Functions transferred to *Office of Economic Warfare* by EO 9361 of July 15, 1943. *Office* consolidated into *Foreign Economic Administration* by EO 9380 of Sept. 25, 1943. *Office* returned to *Reconstruction Finance Corporation* by EO 9630 of Sept. 27, 1945. Certificate of incorporation expired June 30, 1947.

Rubber Producing Facilities Disposal Commission Established by act of Aug. 7, 1953 (67 Stat. 408). Functions transferred to *Federal Facilities Corporation* by EO 10678 of Sept. 20, 1956.

Rubber Reserve Company Established June 28, 1940, under act of Jan. 22, 1932 (47 Stat. 5). Transferred from *Federal Loan Agency* to the Department of Commerce by EO 9071 of Feb. 24, 1942. Returned to *Federal Loan Agency* by act of Feb. 24, 1945 (59 Stat. 5). Dissolved by act of June 30, 1945 (59 Stat. 310), and functions transferred to *Reconstruction Finance Corporation.*

Rural Areas Development, Office of Established by Secretary of Agriculture memorandum in 1961 (revised Sept. 21, 1962). Renamed *Rural Community Development Service* by Secretary's Memorandum 1570 of Feb. 24, 1965.

Rural Business and Cooperative Development Service Established within the Department of Agriculture by Secretary's Memorandum 1020–34 dated Dec. 31, 1991. Renamed Rural Business-Cooperative Service (61 FR 2899), effective Jan. 30, 1996.

Rural Community Development Service Established by Secretary of Agriculture Memorandum 1570 of Feb. 25, 1965, to supersede *Office of Rural Areas Development.* Abolished Feb. 2, 1970, by Secretary's Memorandum 1670 of Jan. 30, 1970, and functions transferred to other agencies in the Department of Agriculture.

Rural Development Administration Established within the Department of Agriculture by Secretary's Memorandum 1020–34 dated Dec. 31, 1991. Abolished Dec. 27, 1994 (59 FR 66441) under authority of Secretary's Memorandum 1010–1 dated Oct. 20, 1994. Functions assumed by the Rural Business and Cooperative Development Service.

Rural Development Committee *See* **Rural Development Program, Committee for**

Rural Development Policy, Office of Established initially as *Office of Rural Development Policy Management and Coordination,* Farmers Home Administration, by Secretary of Agriculture Memorandum 1020–3 of Oct. 26, 1981. Abolished in 1986 due to lack of funding.

Rural Development Program, Committee for Established by EO 10847 of Oct. 12, 1959. Abolished by EO 11122 of Oct. 16, 1963, which established *Rural Development Committee. Committee* superseded by EO 11307 of Sept. 30, 1966, and functions assumed by the Secretary of Agriculture.

Rural Development Service Established by Agriculture Secretarial order in 1973. Functions transferred to *Office of Rural Development Coordination and Planning, Farmers Home Administration,* by Secretarial order in 1978.

Rural Electrification Administration Established by EO 7037 of May 11, 1935. Functions transferred by EO 7458 of Sept. 26, 1936, to *Rural Electrification Administration* established by act of May 20, 1936 (49 Stat. 1363). Transferred to the Department of Agriculture by Reorg. Plan No. II of 1939, effective July 1, 1939. Abolished by Secretary's Memorandum 1010–1 dated Oct. 20, 1994, and functions assumed by Rural Utilities Service.

Rural Housing and Community Development Service Established by act of Oct. 13, 1994 (108 Stat. 3219). Renamed Rural Housing Service (61 FR 2899), effective Jan. 30, 1996.

Rural Rehabilitation Division Established April 1934 by act of May 12, 1933 (48 Stat. 55). Functions transferred to *Resettlement Administration* by *Federal Emergency Relief Administrator's* order of June 19, 1935.

Saint Elizabeth's Hospital *See* **Insane, Government Hospital for the**

Saint Lawrence Seaway Development Corporation Established by act of May 13, 1954 (68 Stat. 92). Secretary of Commerce given direction of general policies of *Corporation* by EO 10771 of June 20, 1958. Transferred to the Department of Transportation by act of Oct. 15, 1966 (80 Stat. 931).

Salary Stabilization, Office of *See* **Salary Stabilization Board**

Salary Stabilization Board Established May 10, 1951, by *Economic Stabilization Administrator's* General Order 8. Stabilization program administered by *Office of Salary Stabilization.* Terminated Apr. 30, 1953, by EO 10434 of Feb. 6, 1953, and acts of June 30, 1952 (66 Stat. 296), and June 30, 1953 (67 Stat. 131).

Sales Manager, Office of the General Established by the Secretary of Agriculture Feb. 29, 1976. Consolidated with Foreign Agricultural Service by Secretary's Memorandum 2001 of Nov. 29, 1979.

Savings Bonds, Interdepartmental Committee for the Voluntary Payroll Savings Plan for the Purchase of U.S. Established by EO 11532 of June 2, 1970. Superseded by EO 11981 of Mar. 29, 1977, which established Interagency Committee for the Purchase of U.S. Savings Bonds.

Savings and Loan Advisory Council, Federal Established by act of Oct. 6, 1972 (86 Stat. 770). Continued by act of Dec. 26, 1974 (88 Stat. 1739). Terminated by act of Aug. 9, 1989 (103 Stat. 422).

Savings and Loan Insurance Corporation, Federal Established by act of June 27, 1934 (48 Stat. 1246). Grouped with other agencies to form *Federal Loan Agency* by Reorg. Plan No. I of 1939, effective July 1, 1939. Transferred to *Federal Home Loan Bank Administration, National Housing Agency,* by EO 9070 of Feb. 24, 1942. Board of Trustees abolished by Reorg. Plan No. 3 of 1947, effective July 27, 1947, and functions transferred to *Home Loan Bank Board.* Abolished by act of Aug. 9, 1989 (103 Stat. 354).

Savings Bonds Division, United States Established by Departmental Order 62 of Dec. 26, 1945, as successor to the War and Finance Division, War Savings Staff, and Defense Savings Staff. Functions transferred to Bureau of Public Debt by Departmental Order 101–05 of May 11, 1994, and *Division* renamed Savings Bond Marketing Office.

Science, Engineering, and Technology, Federal Coordinating Council for Established by act of May 11, 1976 (90 Stat. 471). Abolished by Reorg. Plan No. 1 of 1977, effective Feb. 26, 1978, and functions transferred to President. Functions redelegated to Director of the Office of Science and Technology Policy and Federal Coordinating Council for Science, Engineering, and Technology, established by EO 12039 of Feb. 24, 1978.

Science, Engineering, and Technology Panel, Intergovernmental Established by act of May 11, 1976 (90 Stat. 465). Abolished by Reorg. Plan No. 1 of 1977, effective Feb. 26, 1978, and functions transferred to President. Functions redelegated to Director of Office of Science and Technology Policy by EO 12039 of Feb. 24, 1978, which established Intergovernmental Science, Engineering, and Technology Advisory Panel.

Science Advisory Committee, President's Established by President Apr. 20, 1951, and reconstituted Nov. 22, 1957. Terminated with *Office of Science and Technology,* effective July 1, 1973.

Science Exhibit-Century 21 Exposition, U.S. Established Jan. 20, 1960, by Department of Commerce Order 167. Abolished by revocation of order on June 5, 1963.

Science and Technology, Federal Council for *See* **Scientific Research and Development, Interdepartmental Committee on**

Science and Technology, Office of Established by Reorg. Plan No. 2 of 1962, effective June 8, 1962. *Office* abolished by Reorg. Plan No. 1 of 1973, effective June 30, 1973, and functions transferred to National Science Foundation.

Science and Technology, President's Committee on Established by act of May 11, 1976 (90 Stat. 468). Abolished by Reorg. Plan No. 1 of 1977, effective Feb. 26, 1978, and functions transferred to President.

Scientific and Policy Advisory Committee Established by act of Sept. 26, 1961 (75 Stat. 631). Terminated Apr. 30, 1996 under terms of act.

Scientific Research and Development, Interdepartmental Committee on Established by EO 9912 of Dec. 24, 1947. EO 9912 revoked by EO 10807 of Mar. 13, 1959, which established *Federal Council for Science and Technology*. Abolished by act of May 11, 1976 (90 Stat. 472).

Scientific Research and Development, Office of Established in *Office for Emergency Management* by EO 8807 of June 28, 1941. Terminated by EO 9913 of Dec. 26, 1947, and property transferred to *National Military Establishment* for liquidation.

Scientists and Engineers, National Committee for the Development of Established by President Apr. 3, 1956. Renamed *President's Committee on Scientists and Engineers* May 7, 1957. Final report submitted Dec. 17, 1958, and expired Dec. 31, 1958.

Scientists and Engineers, President's Committee on *See* **Scientists and Engineers, National Committee for the Development of**

Screw Thread Commission, National Established by act of July 18, 1918 (40 Stat. 912). Terminated by EO 6166 of June 10, 1933, and records transferred to the Department of Commerce, effective Mar. 2, 1934. Informal Interdepartmental Screw Thread Committee established on Sept. 14, 1939, consisting of representatives of the Departments of *War,* the Navy, and Commerce.

Secret Service, United States *See* **Secret Service Division**

Secret Service Division Established July 5, 1865, as a Bureau under Treasury Department. Acknowledged as distinct agency within Treasury Department in 1883. *White House Police Force* created on October 1, 1922, and placed under supervision of *Secret Service Division* in 1930. *White House Police Force* renamed *Executive Protective Service* by act of June 30, 1970 (84 Stat. 358). *Executive Protective Service* renamed U.S. Secret Service Uniformed Division by act of Nov. 15, 1977 (91 Stat. 1371). *Treasury Police Force* merged into Secret Service on Oct. 5, 1986. U.S. Secret Service transferred to Homeland Security Department by act of Nov. 25, 2002 (116 Stat. 2224)..

Security, Commission on Government Established by act of Aug. 9, 1955 (69 Stat. 595). Terminated Sept. 22, 1957, pursuant to terms of act.

Security, Office of the Director for Mutual *See* **Security Agency, Mutual**

Security Agency, Federal Established by Reorg. Plan No. I of 1939, effective July 1, 1939, grouping under one administration *Office of Education, Public Health Service, Social Security Board, U.S. Employment Service, Civilian Conservation Corps,* and *National Youth Administration.* Abolished by Reorg. Plan No. 1 of 1953, effective Apr. 11, 1953, and functions and units transferred to *Department of Health, Education, and Welfare.*

Security Agency, Mutual Established and continued by acts of Oct. 10, 1951 (65 Stat. 373) and June 20, 1952 (66 Stat. 141). *Agency* and *Office of Director for Mutual Security* abolished by Reorg. Plan No. 7 of 1953, effective Aug. 1, 1953, and functions transferred to *Foreign Operations Administration,* established by same plan.

Security and Individual Rights, President's Commission on Internal Established by EO 10207 of Jan. 23, 1951. Terminated by EO 10305 of Nov. 14, 1951.

Security Resources Board, National Established by act of July 26, 1947 (61 Stat. 499). Transferred to Executive Office of the President by Reorg. Plan No. 4 of 1949, effective Aug. 20, 1949. Functions of *Board* transferred to Chairman and *Board* made advisory to him by Reorg. Plan No. 25 of 1950, effective July 10, 1950. Functions delegated by Executive order transferred to *Office of Defense Mobilization* by EO 10438 of Mar. 13, 1953. *Board* abolished by Reorg. Plan No. 3 of 1953, effective June 12, 1953, and remaining functions transferred to *Office of Defense Mobilization.*

Security Training Commission, National Established by act of June 19, 1951 (65 Stat. 75). Expired June 30, 1957, pursuant to Presidential letter of Mar. 25, 1957.

Seed Loan Office Authorized by Presidential letters of July 26, 1918, and July 26, 1919, to the Secretary of Agriculture. Further authorized by act of Mar. 3, 1921 (41 Stat. 1347). Office transferred to Farm Credit Administration by EO 6084 of Mar. 27, 1933.

Selective Service Appeal Board, National Established by EO 9988 of Aug. 20, 1948. Inactive as of Apr. 11, 1975.

Selective Service Records, Office of *See* **Selective Service System**

Selective Service System Established by act of Sept. 16, 1940 (54 Stat. 885). Placed under jurisdiction of *War Manpower Commission* by EO 9279 of Dec. 5, 1942, and designated *Bureau of Selective Service.* Designated Selective Service System, separate agency, by EO 9410 of Dec. 23, 1943. Transferred for liquidation to *Office of Selective Service Records* established by act of Mar. 31, 1947 (61 Stat. 31). Transferred to Selective Service System by act of June 24, 1948 (62 Stat. 604).

Self-Help Development and Technical Development, Office of Established in *National Consumer Cooperative Bank* by act of Aug. 20, 1978 (92 Stat. 499). Abolished by act of Aug. 13, 1981 (95 Stat. 437), and assets transferred to Consumer Cooperative Development Corporation, Department of Commerce, Dec. 30, 1982.

Services, Bureau of Special *See* **Office of War Information**

Services, Division of Central Administrative Established by *Liaison Officer for Emergency Management* pursuant to Presidential letter of Feb. 28, 1941. Terminated by EO 9471 of Aug. 25, 1944, and functions discontinued or transferred to constituent agencies of *Office for Emergency Management* and other agencies.

Shipbuilding Stabilization Committee Originally organized by *National Defense Advisory Commission* in 1940. Established August 1942 by *War Production Board.* Transferred to the Department of Labor from *Civilian Production Administration,* successor agency to *Board,* by EO 9656 of Nov. 15, 1945. Terminated June 30, 1947.

Shipping Board, U.S. Established by act of Sept. 7, 1916 (39 Stat. 729). Abolished by EO 6166 of June 10, 1933, and functions, including those with respect to *U.S. Shipping Board Merchant Fleet Corporation,* transferred to *U.S. Shipping Board Bureau,* Department of Commerce, effective Mar. 2, 1934. Separation of employees deferred until Sept. 30, 1933, by EO 6245 of Aug. 9, 1933. Functions assumed by *U.S. Maritime Commission* Oct. 26, 1936, pursuant to act of June 29, 1936 (49 Stat. 1985).

Shipping Board Bureau, U.S. *See* **Shipping Board, U.S.**

Shipping Board Emergency Fleet Corporation, U.S. Established Apr. 16, 1917, under authority of act of Sept. 7, 1916 (39 Stat. 729). Renamed *U.S. Shipping Board Merchant Fleet Corporation* by act of Feb. 11, 1927 (44 Stat. 1083). Terminated Oct. 26, 1936, under provisions of act of June 29, 1936 (49 Stat. 1985), and functions transferred to *U.S. Maritime Commission.*

Shipping Board Merchant Fleet Corporation, U.S. *See* **Shipping Board Emergency Fleet Corporation, U.S.**

Ships, Bureau of Established by act of June 20, 1940 (54 Stat. 493), to replace *Bureau of Engineering* and *Bureau of Construction and Repair.* Abolished by Department of Defense reorg. order of Mar. 9, 1966, and functions transferred to the Secretary of the Navy (31 FR 7188).

Simpson Historical Research Center, Albert F. Renamed Headquarters USAF Historical Research Center by special order of Dec. 16, 1983 of the Secretary of Defense.

Small and Disadvantaged Business Utilization, Office of Established within certain Defense Departments by act of Oct. 24, 1978 (92 Stat. 1770). Renamed Office of Small Business Programs by Public Law 109–163 of Jan. 6, 2006 (119 Stat. 3399).

Smithsonian Symposia and Seminars, Office of Renamed Office of Interdisciplinary Studies by Smithsonian Institution announcement of Mar. 16, 1987.

Social Development Institute, Inter-American Established by act of Dec. 30, 1969 (83 Stat. 821). Renamed Inter-American Foundation by act of Feb. 7, 1972 (86 Stat. 34).

Social Protection, Committee on Established in *Office of Defense Health and Welfare Services* by administrative order June 14, 1941. Functions transferred to *Federal Security Agency* by EO 9338 of Apr. 29, 1943.

Social and Rehabilitation Service Established by the *Secretary of Health, Education, and Welfare* reorganization of Aug. 15, 1967. Abolished by Secretary's reorganization of Mar. 8, 1977 (42 FR

13262), and constituent units—*Medical Services Administration, Assistance Payments Administration, Office of Child Support Enforcement, and Public Services Administration*—transferred.

Social Security Administration *See* **Social Security Board**

Social Security Board Established by act of Aug. 14, 1935 (49 Stat. 620). Incorporated into *Federal Security Agency* by Reorg. Plan No. I of 1939, effective July 1, 1939. *Social Security Board* abolished and Social Security Administration established by Reorg. Plan No. 2 of 1946 (5 U.S.C. app.), effective July 16, 1946, and functions of the *Board* transferred to *Federal Security Administrator.* Social Security Administration transferred from the *Federal Security Agency* by Reorganization Plan No. 1 of 1953 (5 U.S.C. app.), effective Apr. 11, 1953, to the *Department of Health, Education, and Welfare.* Social Security Administration became an independent agency in the executive branch by act of Aug. 15, 1994 (108 Stat. 1464), effective Mar. 31, 1995.

Soil Conservation Service *See* **Soil Erosion Service**

Soil Erosion Service Established in the Department of the Interior following allotment made Aug. 25, 1933. Transferred to the Department of Agriculture by Secretary of Interior administrative order of Mar. 25, 1935. Made *Soil Conservation Service* by order of the Secretary of Agriculture, Apr. 27, 1935, pursuant to provisions of act of Apr. 27, 1935 (49 Stat. 163). Certain functions of *Soil Conservation Service* under jurisdiction of the Department of the Interior transferred from the Department of Agriculture to the Department of the Interior by Reorg. Plan No. IV of 1940, effective June 30, 1940. *Soil Conservation Service* abolished by act of Oct. 13, 1994 (108 Stat. 3225) and functions assumed by the Natural Resources Conservation Service.

Soils, Bureau of *See* **Agricultural and Industrial Chemistry, Bureau of** and **Plant Industry, Bureau of**

Solicitor General, Office of Assistant Established in the Department of Justice by act of June 16, 1933 (48 Stat. 307). Terminated by Reorg. Plan No. 2 of 1950, effective May 24, 1950.

Southeastern Power Administration Established by the Secretary of the Interior in 1943 to carry out functions under act of Dec. 22, 1944 (58 Stat. 890). Transferred to the Department of Energy by act of Aug. 4, 1977 (91 Stat. 578).

Southwestern Power Administration Established by the Secretary of the Interior in 1943 to carry out functions under act of Dec. 22, 1944 (58 Stat. 890). Transferred to the Department of Energy by act of Aug. 4, 1977 (91 Stat. 578).

Space Access and Technology, Office of Established in the National Aeronautics and Space Administration. Abolished by Administrator's order of Feb. 24, 1997.

Space Communications, Office of Established in the National Aeronautics and Space Administration. Abolished by Administrator's order of Feb. 24, 1997.

Space Science, Office of *See* **Space and Terrestrial Applications, Office of**

Space Science Board Renamed Space Studies Board by authority of the National Research Council, National Academy of Sciences, effective May 8, 1989.

Space Station, Office of Established in the National Aeronautics and Space Administration. Abolished in 1990 and remaining functions transferred to the Office of Space Flight.

Space Technology Laboratories, National Renamed John C. Stennis Space Center by EO 12641 of May 20, 1988.

Space and Terrestrial Applications, Office of Combined with *Office of Space Science* to form Office of Space Science and Applications by National Aeronautics and Space Administrator's announcement of Sept. 29, 1981.

Space Tracking and Data Systems, Office of Renamed Office of Space Operations by National Aeronautics and Space Administrator's announcement of Jan. 9, 1987.

Space Transportation Operations, Office of Combined with *Office of Space Transportation Systems* to form Office of Space Transportation Systems, National Aeronautics and Space Administration, effective July 1982.

Space Transportation Systems, Office of *See* **Space Transportation Operations, Office of**

Spanish-Speaking People, Cabinet Committee on Opportunities for *See* **Mexican-American Affairs, Interagency Committee on**

Special. *See other part of title*

Specifications Board, Federal Established by *Bureau of the Budget* Circular 42 of Oct. 10, 1921. Transferred from *Federal Coordinating Service* to *Procurement Division* by order of Oct. 9, 1933 of the Secretary of the Treasury. *Board* superseded by *Federal Specifications Executive Committee,* set up by *Director of Procurement* under Circular Letter 106 of July 16, 1935.

Sport Fisheries and Wildlife, Bureau of Established in the Department of the Interior by act of Aug. 8, 1956 (70 Stat. 1119). *Bureau* replaced by U.S. Fish and Wildlife Service pursuant to act of Apr. 22, 1974 (88 Stat. 92).

Standards, National Bureau of *See* **Weights and Measures, Office of Standard**

State, Department of Duty of Secretary of State of procuring copies of all statutes of the States, as provided for in act of Sept. 28, 1789 (R.S. 206), abolished by Reorg. Plan No. 20 of 1950, effective May 24, 1950. Functions of numbering, editing, and distributing proclamations and Executive orders transferred from the Department of State to the *Division of the Federal Register, National Archives,* by EO 7298 of Feb. 18, 1936. Duty of Secretary of State of publishing Executive proclamations and treaties in newspapers in District of Columbia, provided for in act of July 31, 1876 (19 Stat. 105), abolished by Reorg. Plan No. 20 of 1950, effective May 24, 1950. Functions concerning publication of U.S. Statutes at Large, acts and joint resolutions in pamphlet form known as slip laws, and amendments to the Constitution; electoral votes for President and Vice President; and Territorial papers transferred from the Department of State to the Administrator of the General Services Administration by Reorg. Plan No. 20 of 1950. (*See also* **Archives Establishment, National**)

State and Local Cooperation, Division of Established by *Advisory Commission to Council of National Defense* Aug. 5, 1940. Transferred to *Office of Civilian Defense.*

State and Local Government Cooperation, Committee on Established by EO 11627 of Oct 15, 1971. Abolished by EO 11695 of Jan. 11, 1973.

State Technical Services, Office of Established by the Secretary of Commerce Nov. 19, 1965, pursuant to act of Sept. 14, 1965 (79 Stat. 697). Abolished by Secretary, effective June 30, 1970.

Statistical Board, Central Organized Aug. 9, 1933, by EO 6225 of July 27, 1933. Transferred to *Bureau of the Budget* by Reorg. Plan No. I of 1939, effective July 1, 1939. Expired July 25, 1940, and functions taken over by *Division of Statistical Standards, Bureau of the Budget.*

Statistical Committee, Central Established by act of July 25, 1935 (49 Stat. 498). Abolished by Reorg. Plan No. I of 1939, effective July 1, 1939, and functions transferred to *Bureau of the Budget.*

Statistical Policy Coordination Committee Established by EO 12013 of Oct. 7, 1977. Abolished by EO 12318 of Aug. 21, 1981.

Statistical Reporting Service Established by Memorandum 1446, supp. 1, part 3, of 1961 of the Secretary of Agriculture. Consolidated with other departmental units into *Economics, Statistics, and Cooperatives Service* by Secretary's Memorandum 1927, effective Dec. 23, 1977. Redesignated as *Statistical Reporting Service* by Secretary's order of Oct. 1, 1981. Renamed National Agricultural Statistics Service.

Statistics Administration, Social and Economic Established Jan. 1, 1972, by the Secretary of Commerce. Terminated by Department of Commerce Organization Order 10–2, effective Aug. 4, 1975 (40 FR 42765). Bureau of Economic Analysis and Bureau of the Census restored as primary operating units of the Department of Commerce by Organization Orders 35–1A and 2A, effective Aug. 4, 1975.

Statutes at Large *See* **State, Department of**

Statutes of the States *See* **State, Department of**

Steam Engineering, Bureau of Established in the Department of the Navy by act of July 5, 1862 (12 Stat. 510). Redesignated as *Bureau of Engineering* by act of June 4, 1920 (41 Stat. 828). Abolished by act of June 20, 1940 (54 Stat. 492), and functions transferred to *Bureau of Ships.*

Steamboat Inspection Service President authorized to appoint *Service* by act of June 28, 1838 (5 Stat. 252). Secretary of Treasury authorized to establish boards of local inspectors at enumerated ports throughout the U.S. by act of Feb. 28, 1871 (16 Stat. 440). Authority to appoint boards of local inspectors delegated to *Secretary of Commerce and Labor* by act of Mar. 4, 1905 (33 Stat. 1026). Consolidated with *Bureau of Navigation and Steamboat Inspection* by act of June 30, 1932 (47 Stat. 415).

Stock Catalog Board, Federal Standard Originated by act of Mar. 2, 1929 (45 Stat. 1461). Transferred from *Federal Coordinating Service* to *Procurement Division* by order of Oct. 9, 1933 of the Secretary of the Treasury.

Strategic Defense Initiative Organization Established in 1986 as a separate agency of the Department of Defense. Renamed Ballistic Missile Defense Organization by Deputy Secretary's memorandum in May 1993.

Strategic Services, Office of *See* **Information, Office of Coordinator of**

Subversive Activities Control Board Established by act of Sept. 23, 1950 (64 Stat. 987). Terminated June 30, 1973, due to lack of funding.

Sugar Division Created by act of May 12, 1933 (48 Stat. 31), authorized by act of Sept. 1, 1937 (50 Stat. 903). Taken from *Agricultural Adjustment Administration* and made independent division of the Department of Agriculture by Secretary's Memorandum 783, effective Oct. 16, 1938. Placed under *Agricultural Conservation and Adjustment Administration* by EO 9069 of Feb. 23, 1942, functioning as *Sugar Agency.* Functions transferred to *Food Distribution Administration* by EO 9280 of Dec. 5, 1942.

Sugar Rationing Administration Established by Memorandum 1190 of Mar. 31, 1947, of the Secretary of Agriculture under authority of act of Mar. 31, 1947 (61 Stat. 35). Terminated Mar. 31, 1948, on expiration of authority.

Supplies and Accounts, Bureau of *See* **Provisions and Clothing, Bureau of**

Supplies and Shortages, National Commission on Established by act of Sept. 30, 1974 (88 Stat. 1168). Terminated Mar. 31, 1977, pursuant to terms of act.

Supply, Bureau of Federal *See* **Procurement Division**

Supply, Office of Renamed Office of Procurement and Property by Smithsonian Institution announcement of Nov. 4, 1986.

Supply Committee, General Established by act of June 17, 1910 (36 Stat. 531). Abolished by EO 6166 of June 10, 1933, effective Mar. 2, 1934, and functions transferred to *Procurement Division,* the Department of the Treasury.

Supply Priorities and Allocations Board Established in *Office for Emergency Management* by EO 8875 of Aug. 28, 1941. Abolished by EO 9024 of Jan. 16,

1942, and functions transferred to *War Production Board.*

Supply Service, Federal Renamed *Office of Personal Property* by General Services Administration (GSA) order, effective Sept. 28, 1982; later renamed *Office of Federal Supply and Services* by GSA order of Jan. 22, 1983; then redesignated *Federal Supply Service.* Merged with *Federal Technology Service* to form Federal Acquisition Service by GSA Order No. 5440.591 of Sept. 9, 2005.

Surveys and Maps, Federal Board of *See* **Surveys and Maps of the Federal Government, Board of**

Surveys and Maps of the Federal Government, Board of Established by EO 3206 of Dec. 30, 1919. Renamed *Federal Board of Surveys and Maps* by EO 7262 of Jan. 4, 1936. Abolished by EO 9094 of Mar. 10, 1942, and functions transferred to Director, *Bureau of the Budget.*

Space System Development, Office of Established in the National Aeronautics and Space Administration. Renamed Office of Space Access and Technology in 1995.

Tariff Commission, U.S. Established by act of Sept. 8, 1916 (39 Stat. 795). Renamed U.S. International Trade Commission by act of Jan. 3, 1975 (88 Stat. 2009).

Tax Appeals, Board of Established as an independent agency within the executive branch by act of June 2, 1924 (43 Stat. 336). Continued by acts of Feb. 26, 1926 (44 Stat. 105) and Feb. 10, 1939 (53 Stat. 158). Renamed *Tax Court of the United States* by act of Aug. 16, 1954 (68A Stat. 879). Renamed United States Tax Court by act of Dec. 30, 1969 (83 Stat. 730).

Technical Cooperation Administration Transferred from the Department of State to *Mutual Security Agency* by EO 10458 of June 1, 1953. Transferred to *Foreign Operations Administration* by Reorg. Plan No. 7 of 1953, effective Aug. 1, 1953.

Technical Services, Office of Designated unit of Office of the Secretary of Commerce by Department Order 179, July 23, 1962. Functions transferred to *National Bureau of Standards* by Order 90 of Jan. 30, 1964.

Technology Assessment, Office of Created by act of Oct. 13, 1972 (86 Stat. 797). Office inactive as of Sept. 30, 1995.

Technology, Automation, and Economic Progress, National Commission on Established by act of Aug. 19, 1964 (78 Stat. 463). Terminated January 1966 pursuant to terms of act.

Technology Service, Federal Merged with *Federal Supply Service* to form Federal Acquisition Service by General Services Administration Order No. 5440.591 of Sept. 9, 2005.

Telecommunications Adviser to the President Established in Executive Office of the President by EO 10297 of Oct. 9, 1951. EO 10297 revoked by EO 10460 of June 16, 1953, and functions transferred to Director of *Office of Defense Mobilization.*

Telecommunications Management, Director of Established in *Office of Emergency Planning* by EO 10995 of Feb. 16, 1962. Assignment of radio frequencies delegated to Government agencies and foreign diplomatic establishments by EO 11084 of Feb. 16, 1963. Abolished by Reorg. Plan No. 1 of 1970, effective Apr. 20, 1970.

Telecommunications Policy, Office of Established in Executive Office of the President by Reorg. Plan No. 1 of 1970, effective Apr. 20, 1970. Abolished by Reorg. Plan No. 1 of 1977, effective Mar. 26, 1978, and certain functions transferred to President with all other functions transferred to the Department of Commerce.

Telecommunications Service, Automated Data Renamed *Office of Information Resources Management* by General Services Administration order of Aug. 17, 1982. Later renamed Information Resources Management Service.

Temporary Controls, Office of Established in *Office for Emergency Management* by EO 9809 of Dec. 12, 1946, consolidating *Office of War Mobilization and Reconversion, Office of Economic Stabilization, Office of Price Administration,* and *Civilian Production Administration.* Functions with respect to Veterans' Emergency Housing Program transferred to *Housing Expediter* by EO 9836 of Mar. 22, 1947. Functions with respect to distribution and price of sugar products transferred to the Secretary of Agriculture by act of Mar. 31, 1947 (61 Stat. 36). Office terminated by EO 9841 of Apr. 23, 1947, and remaining functions redistributed.

Temporary Emergency Court of Appeals Established by act of Dec. 22, 1971 (85 Stat. 749). Abolished by act of Oct. 29, 1992, effective Apr. 30, 1993 (106 Stat. 4507). Court's jurisdiction and pending cases transferred to the United States Court of Appeals for the Federal Circuit.

Territorial Affairs, Office of Established by Interior Secretarial Order 2951 of Feb. 6, 1973. Abolished by Departmental Manual Release 2270 of June 6, 1980, and functions transferred to Office of Assistant Secretary for Territorial and International Affairs.

Territorial papers *See* **State, Department of**

Territories, Office of Established by the Secretary of the Interior July 28, 1950. Functions reassigned to *Deputy Assistant Secretary for Territorial Affairs* in *Office of the Assistant Secretary—Public Land Management,* Department of the Interior, by Secretarial Order 2942, effective July 1, 1971.

Terrorism, Cabinet Committee To Combat Established by Presidential memorandum of Sept. 25, 1972. Terminated by National Security Council memorandum of Sept. 16, 1977.

Terrorist Threat Integration Center Established on May 1, 2003, pursuant to Presidential initiative. Transferred to the National Counterterrorism Center by act of Dec. 17, 2004 (118 Stat. 3697).

Textile National Industrial Relations Board Established by administrative order of June 28, 1934. Abolished by EO 6858 of Sept. 26, 1934, which created *Textile Labor Relations Board* in connection with the Department of Labor. *Board* terminated July 1, 1937, and functions absorbed by *U.S. Conciliation Service,* Department of Labor.

Textile National Industrial Relations Board, Cotton Established by original Code of Fair Competition for the Cotton Textile Industry, as amended July 10, 1934. Abolished by EO 6858 of Sept. 26, 1934.

Textile Work Assignment Board, Cotton Amendments to Code of Fair Competition for Cotton Textile Industry approved by EO 6876 of Oct. 16, 1934, and *Cotton Textile Work Assignment Board* appointed by *Textile Labor Relations Board. Board* expired June 15, 1935.

Textile Work Assignment Board, Silk Appointed by *Textile Labor Relations Board* following President's approval of amendments to Code of Fair Competition for Silk Textile Industry by EO 6875 of Oct. 16, 1934. Terminated June 15, 1935.

Textile Work Assignment Board, Wool Established by EO 6877 of Oct. 16, 1934. Terminated June 15, 1935.

Textiles, Office of Established by the Secretary of Commerce Feb. 14, 1971. Functions transferred to *Domestic and International Business Administration,* effective Nov. 17, 1972.

Thrift Depositor Protection Oversight Board. *See* **Oversight Board (of the Resolution Trust Corporation).**

Trade, Special Adviser to the President on Foreign Established by EO 6651 of Mar. 23, 1934. Terminated on expiration of *National Recovery Administration.*

Trade Administration, International *See* **Business and Defense Services Administration**

Trade Agreements, Interdepartmental Committee on Established by Secretary of State in 1934 and reestablished by EO 9832 of Feb. 25, 1947. Abolished by EO 11075 of Jan. 15, 1963.

Trade and Development Program Established by act of Sept. 4, 1961, as amended (88 Stat. 1804). Designated separate entity within the *U.S. International Development Cooperation Agency* by act of Sept. 4, 1961, as amended (102 Stat. 1329). Renamed Trade and Development Agency by act of Oct. 28, 1992 (106 Stat. 3657).

Trade Expansion Act Advisory Committee Established by EO 11075 of Jan. 15, 1963. Abolished by EO 11846 of Mar. 27, 1975, and records transferred to Trade Policy Committee established by same EO.

Trade Negotiations, Office of the Special Representative for Renamed Office of the U.S. Trade Representative by EO 12188 of Jan. 4, 1980.

Trade Policy Committee Established by EO 10741 of Nov. 25, 1957. Abolished by EO 11075 of Jan. 15, 1963.

Traffic Safety, President's Committee for Established by Presidential letter of Apr. 14, 1954. Continued by EO 10858 of Jan. 13, 1960. Abolished by EO 11382 of Nov. 28, 1967.

Traffic Safety Agency, National Established in the Department of Commerce by act of Sept. 9, 1966 (80 Stat. 718). Activity transferred to the Department of Transportation by act of Oct. 15, 1966 (80 Stat. 931). Responsibility placed in *National Highway Safety Bureau* by EO 11357 of June 6, 1967.

Training and Employment Service, U.S. Established in *Manpower Administration,* Department of Labor, Mar. 17, 1969. Abolished by Secretary's letter of Dec. 6, 1971, and functions assigned to *Office of Employment Development Programs* and *U.S. Employment Service.*

Training School for Boys, National *See* **District of Columbia, Reform-School of the**

Transportation, Federal Coordinator of Established by act of June 16, 1933 (48 Stat. 211). Expired June 16, 1936, under provisions of Public Resolution 27 (49 Stat. 376).

Transportation, Office of Established in the Department of Agriculture by Secretary's Memorandum 1966 dated Dec. 12, 1978. Abolished by Secretary's Memorandum 1030–25 dated Dec. 28, 1990.

Transportation and Communications Service Established by General Services Administrator Oct. 19, 1961. Abolished by Administrator's order, effective July 15, 1972. Motor equipment, transportation, and public utilities responsibilities assigned to Federal Supply Service; telecommunications function assigned to *Automated Data Telecommunications Service.*

Transportation and Public Utilities Service Abolished by General Services Administration order of Aug. 17, 1982. Functions transferred to various GSA organizations.

Transportation Safety Board, National Established in the Department of Transportation by act of Oct. 15, 1966 (80 Stat. 935). Abolished by act of Jan. 3, 1975 (88 Stat. 2156), which established independent National Transportation Safety Board.

Transportation Security Administration Established by act of Nov. 19, 2001 (115 Stat. 597). Functions transferred from Department of Transportation to Department of Homeland Security by act of Nov. 25, 2002 (116 Stat. 2178).

Transportation Statistics, Bureau of Established by act of Dec. 18, 1991 (105 Stat. 2172). Transferred to Research and Innovative Technology Administration, Transportation Department, by act of Nov. 30, 2004 (118 Stat. 2424).

Travel Service, U.S. Replaced by *U.S. Travel and Tourism Administration,* Department of Commerce, pursuant to act of Oct. 16, 1981 (95 Stat. 1014).

Travel and Tourism Administration, U.S. Established by act of Oct. 16, 1981 (95 Stat. 1014). Abolished by act of Oct. 11, 1996 (110 Stat. 3407).

Travel and Tourism Advisory Board Established by act of Oct. 16, 1981 (95 Stat. 1017). Abolished by act of Oct. 11, 1996 (110 Stat. 3407).

Treasury, Office of the Assistant Secretary of the—Electronics and Information Technology Established by Secretary's Order 114–1 of Mar. 14, 1983. Abolished by Secretary's Order 114–3 of May 17, 1985, and functions transferred to Office of the Assistant Secretary for Management. Certain provisions effective Aug. 31, 1985 (50 FR 23573).

Treasury, Solicitor of the Position established when certain functions of *Solicitor of the Treasury* transferred to the Department of Justice by EO 6166 of June 10, 1933. *Solicitor of the Treasury* transferred from the Department of Justice to the Department of the Treasury by same order. *Office of Solicitor of the Treasury* abolished by act of May 10, 1934 (48 Stat. 758), and functions transferred to General Counsel, the Department of the Treasury.

Treasury Police Force *See* **Secret Service Division**

Treasury Secretary, Assistant Office abolished by Reorg. Plan No. III of 1940, effective June 30, 1940, and functions transferred to Fiscal Assistant Secretary, Department of the Treasury.

Treasury Under Secretary for Enforcement, Office of Established by act of Oct. 28, 1993 (107 Stat. 1234). Office abolished by act of Dec. 8, 2004 (118 Stat. 3245), and functions transferred to the Office of the Under Secretary for Terrorism and Financial Crimes, Department of the Treasury.

Treaties *See* **State, Department of**

Typhus Commission, U.S. of America Established in *Department of War* by EO 9285 of Dec. 24, 1942. Abolished June 30, 1946, by EO 9680 of Jan. 17, 1946.

U.S. *See other part of title*

Uniformed Services University of the Health Sciences, School of Medicine of the Renamed F. Edward Hébert School of Medicine by act of Sept. 24, 1983 (97 Stat. 704).

United Nations Educational, Scientific and Cultural Organization U.S. membership in UNESCO authorized by act of July 30, 1946 (60 Stat. 712). Announcement of U.S. intention to withdraw made Dec. 28, 1983, in accordance with UNESCO constitution. Official U.S. withdrawal effective Dec. 31, 1984, by Secretary of State's letter of Dec. 19, 1984. U.S. maintains status as observer mission in UNESCO.

Upper Mississippi River Basin Commission Established by EO 11659 of Mar. 22, 1972. Terminated by EO 12319 of Sept. 9, 1981.

Urban Affairs, Council for Established in Executive Office of the President by EO 11452 of Jan. 23, 1969. Terminated by EO 11541 of July 1, 1970.

Urban Mass Transportation Administration Functions regarding urban mass transportation established in the Department of Housing and Urban Development by act of July 9, 1964 (78 Stat. 302). Most functions transferred to the Department of Transportation by Reorg. Plan No. 2 of 1968, effective June 30, 1968 (82 Stat. 1369), and joint responsibility assigned to the Departments of Transportation and Housing and Urban Development for functions relating to research, technical studies, and training. Transportation and Housing and Urban Development Under Secretaries agreed in November 1969 that the Department of Transportation should be focal point for urban mass transportation grant administration; at which time functions transferred to the Department of Transportation. Renamed Federal Transit Administration by act of Dec. 18, 1991 (105 Stat. 2088).

Urban Renewal Administration Established in *Housing and Home Finance Agency* by Administrator's Organizational Order 1 of Dec. 23, 1954. Functions transferred to the Department of Housing and Urban Development by act of Sept. 9, 1965 (78 Stat. 667), and *Administration* terminated.

Utilization and Disposal Service Established July 1, 1961, by Administrator of General Services and assigned functions of Federal Supply Service and Public Buildings Service. Functions transferred to *Property Management and Disposal Service* July 29, 1966.

Veterans Administration Legal work in defense of suits against the U.S. arising under act of June 7, 1924 (43 Stat. 607), transferred to the Department of Justice by EO 6166 of June 10, 1933. Transfer deferred to Sept. 10, 1933, by EO 6222 of July 27, 1933. Established as an independent agency under the President by Executive Order 5398 of July 21, 1930, in accordance with the act of July 3, 1930 (46 Stat. 1016) and the act of Sept. 2, 1958 (72 Stat. 1114). Made an executive department in the executive branch and redesignated the Department of Veterans Affairs by act of Oct. 25, 1988 (102 Stat. 2635).

Veterans Appeals, U.S. Court of Established by act of Nov. 18, 1988 (102 Stat. 4113). Renamed U.S. Court of Appeals for Veterans Claims by act of Nov. 11, 1998 (112 Stat. 3341).

Veterans Education Appeals Board *See* **Veterans Tuition Appeals Board**

Veterans Employment Service Renamed Veterans' Employment and Training Service by Order 4–83 of Mar. 24, 1983 of the Secretary of Labor (48 FR 14092).

Veterans Health Administration *See* **Medicine and Surgery, Department of**

Veterans Health Services and Research Administration *See* **Medicine and Surgery, Department of**

Veterans Placement Service Board Established by act of June 22, 1944 (58 Stat. 293). Abolished by Reorg. Plan No. 2 of 1949, effective Aug. 20, 1949, and functions transferred to the Secretary of Labor.

Veterans Tuition Appeals Board Established by act of Aug. 24, 1949 (63 Stat. 654). Functions assumed by *Veterans Education Appeals Board* established by act of July 13, 1950 (64 Stat. 336). *Board* terminated by act of Aug. 28, 1957 (71 Stat. 474).

Veterinary Medicine, Bureau of Established in Food and Drug Administration, *Department of Health, Education, and Welfare.* Renamed Center for Veterinary Medicine by FDA notice of Mar. 9, 1984 (49 FR 10166).

Virgin Islands Public works programs under act of Dec. 20, 1944 (58 Stat. 827), transferred from General Services Administrator to the Secretary of the Interior by Reorg. Plan No. 15 of 1950, effective May 24, 1950.

Virgin Islands Company Established in 1934. Reincorporated as Government corporation by act of June 30, 1949 (63 Stat. 350). Program terminated June 30, 1965, and *Corporation* dissolved July 1, 1966.

Virgin Islands Corporation *See* **Virgin Islands Company**

Visitor Facilities Advisory Commission, National Established by act of Mar. 12, 1968 (82 Stat. 45). Expired Jan. 5, 1975, pursuant to act of Oct. 6, 1972 (86 Stat. 776).

Vocational Rehabilitation, Office of Established to administer provisions of act of July 6, 1943 (57 Stat. 374). Other duties delegated by acts of Aug. 3, 1954 (68 Stat. 652), Nov. 8, 1965 (79 Stat. 1282), July 12, 1960 (74 Stat. 364), and July 10, 1954 (68 Stat. 454). Redesignated *Vocational Rehabilitation Administration* Jan. 28, 1963. Made component of newly created *Social and Rehabilitation Service* as *Rehabilitation Services Administration* by *Department of Health, Education, and Welfare* reorganization of Aug. 15, 1967.

Vocational Rehabilitation Administration *See* **Vocational Rehabilitation, Office of**

Voluntary Citizen Participation, State Office of Renamed State Office of Volunteerism in ACTION by notice of Apr. 18, 1986 (51 FR 13265), effective May 18, 1986.

Volunteer Service, International, Secretariat for Established in 1962 by International Conference on Middle Level Manpower called by President. Terminated Mar. 31, 1976, due to insufficient funding.

Volunteers in Service to America Established by act of Nov. 8, 1966 (80 Stat. 1472). *Service* administered by *Office of Economic Opportunity* and functions transferred to ACTION by Reorg. Plan No. 1 of 1971, effective July 1, 1971.

Wage Adjustment Board Established May 29, 1942, by the Secretary of Labor at Presidential direction of May 14, 1942, to accomplish purpose of act of Mar. 3, 1931 (46 Stat. 1494), as amended by acts of Aug. 30, 1935 (49 Stat. 1011), and Jan. 30, 1942 (56 Stat. 23). Disbanded on termination of *National Wage Stabilization Board.*

Wage and Price Stability, Council on Established in Executive Office of the President by act of Aug. 24, 1974 (88 Stat. 750). Abolished by EO 12288 of Jan. 29, 1981. Funding ceased beyond June 5, 1981, by act of June 5, 1981 (95 Stat. 74), and authorization for appropriations repealed by act of Aug. 13, 1981 (95 Stat. 432).

Wage and Price Stability Program *See* **Wage and Price Stability, Council on**

Wage Stabilization Board Established by EO 10161 of Sept. 9, 1950. Reconstituted by EO 10377 of July 25, 1952. Terminated Apr. 30, 1953, by EO 10434 of Feb. 6, 1953, and acts of June 30, 1952 (66 Stat. 296), and June 30, 1953 (67 Stat. 131).

Wage Stabilization Board, National *See* **Defense Mediation Board, National**

Wallops Flight Center, Wallops Island, VA Formerly separate field installation of National Aeronautics and Space Administration. Made component of Goddard Space Flight Center by NASA Management Instruction 1107.10A of Sept. 3, 1981.

War, Solid Fuels Administration for Established in the Department of the Interior by EO 9332 of Apr. 19, 1943. Absorbed *Office of Solid Fuels Coordinator for War* (originally established as *Office of Solid Fuels Coordinator for National Defense*) pursuant to Presidential letter of Nov. 5, 1941; later changed by Presidential letter of May 25, 1942. Terminated by EO 9847 of May 6, 1947.

War Assets Administration Established in *Office for Emergency Management* by EO 9689 of Jan. 31, 1946. Functions transferred to *Surplus Property Administration* by Reorg. Plan No. 1 of 1947, effective July 1, 1947, and agency renamed *War Assets Administration.* Abolished by act of June 30, 1949 (63 Stat. 738), and functions transferred for liquidation to General Services Administration.

War Assets Corporation *See* **Petroleum Reserves Corporation**

War Claims Commission Established by act of July 3, 1948 (62 Stat. 1240). Abolished by Reorg. Plan No. 1 of 1954, effective July 1, 1954, and functions transferred to Foreign Claims Settlement Commission of the U.S.

War Commodities Division Established in *Office of Foreign Economic Coordination* by Department of State Order of Aug. 27, 1943. *Office* abolished by departmental order of Nov. 6, 1943, pursuant to EO 9380 of Sept. 25, 1943, which established *Foreign Economic Administration* in *Office for Emergency Management.*

War Communications, Board of *See* **Defense Communications Board**

War Contracts Price Adjustment Board Established by act of Feb. 25, 1944 (58 Stat. 85). Abolished by act of Mar. 23, 1951 (65 Stat. 7), and functions transferred to *Renegotiation Board,* established by same act, and General Services Administrator.

War Damage Corporation *See* **War Insurance Corporation**

War, Department of Established by act of Aug. 7, 1789 (1 Stat. 49), succeeding similar department established prior to adoption of the Constitution. Three military departments—Army; Navy, including naval aviation and U.S. Marine Corps; and Air Force—reorganized under *National Military Establishment* by act of July 26, 1947 (61 Stat. 495).

War Finance Corporation Established by act of Apr. 5, 1918 (40 Stat. 506). Functions and obligations transferred by Reorg. Plan No. II of 1939, effective July 1, 1939, to the Secretary of the Treasury for liquidation not later than Dec. 31, 1939.

War Food Administration *See* **Food Production and Distribution, Administration of**

War Information, Office of Established in *Office of Emergency Management* by EO 9182 of June 13, 1942, consolidating *Office of Facts and Figures; Office of Government Reports; Division of Information, Office for Emergency Management;* and *Foreign Information Service—Outpost, Publications, and Pictorial Branches, Coordinator of Information.* Abolished by EO 9608 of Aug. 31, 1945. *Bureau of Special Services* and functions with respect to review of publications of Federal agencies transferred to *Bureau of the Budget.* Foreign information activities transferred to the Department of State.

War Insurance Corporation Established Dec. 13, 1941, by act of June 10, 1941 (55 Stat. 249). Charter filed Mar. 31, 1942. Renamed *War Damage Corporation* by act of Mar. 27, 1942 (56 Stat. 175). Transferred from *Federal Loan Agency* to the Department of Commerce by EO 9071 of Feb. 24, 1942. Returned to *Federal Loan Agency* by act of Feb. 24, 1945 (59 Stat. 5). *Agency* abolished by act of June 30, 1947 (61 Stat. 202), and functions assumed by *Reconstruction Finance Corporation.* Powers of *War Damage Corporation,* except for purposes of liquidation, terminated as of Jan. 22, 1947.

War Labor Board, National *See* **Defense Mediation Board, National**

War Manpower Commission Established in *Office for Emergency Management* by EO 9139 of Apr. 18, 1942. Terminated by EO 9617 of Sept. 19, 1945, and functions, except *Procurement and Assignment Service,* transferred to the Department of Labor.

War Mobilization, Office of Established by EO 9347 of May 27, 1943. Transferred to *Office of War Mobilization and Reconversion* by EO 9488 of Oct. 3, 1944.

War Mobilization and Reconversion, Office of Established by act of Oct. 3, 1944 (58 Stat. 785). Consolidated with other agencies by EO 9809 of Dec. 12, 1946, to form *Office of Temporary Controls. Media Programming Division* and *Motion Picture Division* transferred to *Office of Government Reports,* reestablished by same order. Certain other functions transferred to President and the Secretary of Commerce.

War Mobilization and Reconversion Advisory Board, Office of Established by act of Oct. 3, 1944 (58 Stat. 788). Transferred to *Office of Temporary Controls* by EO 9809 of Dec. 12, 1946.

War Plants Corporation, Smaller Established by act of June 11, 1942 (56 Stat. 351). Functions transferred by EO 9665 of Dec. 27, 1945, to *Reconstruction Finance Corporation* and the Department of Commerce. Abolished by act of June 30, 1947 (61 Stat. 202), and functions transferred for liquidation to General Services Administration by Reorg. Plan No. 1 of 1957, effective July 1, 1957.

War and Post War Adjustment Policies, Advisory Unit on Established in *Office of War Mobilization* by Presidential direction Nov. 6, 1943. Report submitted Feb. 15, 1944, and Unit Director and Assistant Director submitted letter to Director of *War Mobilization* ending their work May 12, 1944.

War Production Board Established in *Office for Emergency Management* by EO 9024 of Jan. 16, 1942. *Board* terminated and successor agency, *Civilian Production Administration,* established by EO 9638 of Oct. 4, 1945.

War Property Administration, Surplus Established in *Office of War Mobilization* by EO 9425 of Feb. 19, 1944. Terminated on establishment of *Surplus Property Board* by act of Oct. 3, 1944 (58 Stat. 768). *Surplus Property Administration* established in *Office of War Mobilization and Reconversion* by act of Sept. 18, 1945 (59 Stat. 533), and *Board* abolished. Domestic functions of *Administration* merged into *War Assets Corporation, Reconstruction Finance Corporation,* by EO 9689 of Jan. 31, 1946. Foreign functions transferred to the Department of State by same order. Transfers made permanent by Reorg. Plan No. 1 of 1947, effective July 1, 1947.

War Refugee Board Established in Executive Office of the President by EO 9417 of Jan. 22, 1944. Terminated by EO 9614 of Sept. 14, 1945.

War Relations, Agricultural, Office for *See* **Farm Products, Division of**

War Relief Agencies, President's Committee on Established by Presidential letter of Mar. 13, 1941. *President's War Relief Control Board* established by EO 9205 of July 25, 1942, to succeed *Committee. Board* terminated by EO 9723 of May 14, 1946, and functions transferred to the Department of State.

War Relief Control Board, President's *See* **President's Committee on War Relief Agencies**

War Relocation Authority Established in *Office for Emergency Management* by EO 9102 of Mar. 18, 1942. Transferred to the Department of the Interior by EO 9423 of Feb. 16, 1944. Terminated by EO 9742 of June 25, 1946.

War Resources Board Established in August 1939 as advisory committee to work with *Joint Army and Navy Munitions Board.* Terminated by President Nov. 24, 1939.

War Resources Council *See* **Defense Resources Committee**

War Shipping Administration Established in *Office for Emergency Management* by EO 9054 Feb. 7, 1942. Terminated by act of July 8, 1946 (60 Stat. 501), and functions transferred to *U.S. Maritime Commission,* effective Sept. 1, 1946.

Water, Office of Saline Established to perform functions vested in the Secretary of the Interior by act of July 29, 1971 (85 Stat. 159). Merged with *Office of Water Resources Research* to form *Office of Water Research and Technology* by Secretary's Order 2966 of July 26, 1974.

Water Commission, National Established by act of Sept. 26, 1968 (82 Stat. 868). Terminated Sept. 25, 1973, pursuant to terms of act.

Water Policy, Office of Established by Department of the Interior Manual Release 2374 of Dec. 29, 1981, under authority of Assistant Secretary. Abolished by Secretarial Order No. 3096 of Oct. 19, 1983, and functions transferred to *Geological Survey* and *Office of Policy Analysis.*

Water Pollution Control Administration, Federal Established under the *Secretary of Health, Education, and Welfare* by act of Oct. 2, 1965 (79 Stat. 903). Transferred to the Department of the Interior by Reorg. Plan No. 2 of 1966, effective May 10, 1966. Renamed *Federal Water Quality Administration* by act of Apr. 3, 1970. Abolished by Reorg. Plan No. 3 of 1970, effective Dec. 2, 1970, and functions transferred to Environmental Protection Agency.

Water and Power Resources Service Renamed Bureau of Reclamation May 18, 1981, by Interior Secretarial Order 3064.

Water Quality Administration, Federal *See* **Water Pollution Control Administration, Federal**

Water Research and Technology, Office of Established by Interior Secretarial Order 2966 of July 26, 1974. Abolished by Secretarial order of Aug. 25, 1982, and functions transferred to Bureau of Reclamation, Geological Survey, and *Office of Water Policy.*

Water Resources Council Established by act of July 22, 1965 (89 Stat 575). Inactive as of Oct. 1, 1982.

Water Resources Research, Office of Established to perform functions vested in the Secretary of the Interior by act of July 17, 1964 (78 Stat. 329). Merged with *Office of Saline Water* to form *Office of Water Research and Technology* by Secretary's Order 2966 of July 26, 1974.

Watergate Special Prosecution Force Established by Attorney General order, effective May 25, 1973. Terminated by Attorney General order, effective June 20, 1977.

Waterways Corporation, Inland Incorporated under act of June 3, 1924 (43 Stat. 360). Transferred from the *Department of War* to the Department of Commerce by Reorg. Plan No. II of 1939, effective July 1, 1939. *Corporation* sold to *Federal Waterways Corporation* under contract of July 24, 1953. Renamed *Federal Barge Lines, Inc.* Liquidated by act of July 19, 1963 (77 Stat. 81).

Weather Bureau Established in the Department of Agriculture by act of Oct. 1, 1890 (26 Stat. 653). Transferred to the Department of Commerce by Reorg. Plan No. IV of 1940, effective June 30, 1940. Functions transferred to *Environmental Science Services Administration* by Reorg. Plan No. 2 of 1965, effective July 13, 1965.

Weather Control, Advisory Committee on Established by act of Aug. 13, 1953 (67 Stat. 559). Act of Aug. 28, 1957 (71 Stat. 426), provided for termination by Dec. 31, 1957.

Weed and Seed, Executive Office of Abolished by Public Law 109–162 of Jan. 5, 2006 (119 Stat. 3107). Functions transferred to Office of Weed and Seed Strategies, Office of Justice Programs, within the Department of Justice.

Weights and Measures, Office of Standard Renamed *National Bureau of Standards* by act of Mar. 3, 1901 (31 Stat. 1449). *Bureau* transferred from the Department of the Treasury to the *Department of Commerce and Labor* by act of Feb. 14, 1903 (32 Stat. 825). *Bureau* established within the Department of Commerce by act of Mar. 4, 1913 (37 Stat. 736). Renamed National Institute of Standards and Technology by act of Aug. 23, 1988 (102 Stat. 1827).

Welfare Administration Established by the *Secretary of Health, Education, and Welfare* reorganization of Jan. 28, 1963. Components consisted of *Bureau of Family Services, Children's Bureau, Office of Juvenile Delinquency and Youth Development,* and *Cuban Refugee Staff.* These functions reassigned to *Social and Rehabilitation Service* by Department reorganization of Aug. 15, 1967.

White House Police Force *See* **Secret Service Divison**

Wilson Memorial Commission, Woodrow Established by act of Oct. 4, 1961 (75 Stat. 783). Terminated on submittal of final report to President and Congress Sept. 29, 1966.

Women, Interdepartmental Committee on the Status of Established by EO 11126 of Nov. 1, 1963. Terminated by EO 12050 of Apr. 4, 1978.

Women, President's Commission on the Status of Established by EO 10980 of Dec. 14, 1961. Submitted final report to President Oct. 11, 1963.

Women's Army Auxiliary Corps Established by act of May 14, 1942 (56 Stat. 278). Repealed in part and superseded by act of July 1, 1943 (57 Stat. 371), which established *Women's Army Corps. Corps* abolished by the Secretary of Defense Apr. 24, 1978, pursuant to provisions of 10 U.S.C. 125A.

Women's Business Enterprise Division Renamed *Office of Women's Business Enterprise* by Small Business Administrator's reorganization, effective Aug. 19, 1981. Renamed Office of Women's Business Ownership Aug. 19, 1982.

Women's Reserve Established in U.S. Coast Guard by act of Nov. 23, 1942 (56 Stat. 1020).

Women's Year, 1975, National Commission on the Observance of International Established by EO 11832 of Jan. 9, 1975. Continued by act of Dec. 23, 1975 (89 Stat. 1003). Terminated Mar. 31, 1978, pursuant to terms of act.

Wood Utilization, National Committee on Established by Presidential direction in 1925. Abolished by EO 6179–B of June 16, 1933.

Work Projects Administration *See* **Works Progress Administration**

Work-Training Programs, Bureau of Abolished by reorganization of *Manpower Administration* and functions assigned to *U.S. Training and Employment Service,* effective Mar. 17, 1969.

Working Life, Productivity and Quality of, National Center for Established by act of Nov. 28, 1975 (89 Stat. 935). Authorized appropriations expired Sept. 30, 1978, and functions assumed by *National Productivity Council.*

Works, Advisory Committee on Federal Public Established by President Oct. 5, 1955. Abolished by President Mar. 12, 1961, and functions assigned to *Bureau of the Budget.*

Works Administration, Federal Civil Established by EO 6420–B of Nov. 9, 1933. Function of employment expired March 1934. Function of settling claims continued under *Works Progress Administration.*

Works Administration, Public *See* **Emergency Administration of Public Works, Federal**

Works Agency, Federal Established by Reorg. Plan No. I of 1939, effective July 1, 1939. Functions relating to defense housing transferred to *Federal Public Housing Authority, National Housing Agency,* by EO 9070 of Feb. 24, 1942. Abolished by act of June 30, 1949 (63 Stat. 380), and functions transferred to General Services Administration.

Works Emergency Housing Corporation, Public Established by EO 6470 of Nov. 29, 1933. Incorporated under laws of State of Delaware. Abolished and liquidated as of Aug. 14, 1935, by filing of certificate of surrender of corporate rights.

Works Emergency Leasing Corporation, Public Incorporated Jan. 3, 1934, under laws of Delaware by direction of Administrator of Public Works. Terminated with filed certificate of dissolution with secretary of state of Delaware Jan. 2, 1935.

Works Progress Administration Established by EO 7034 of May 6, 1935, and continued by subsequent yearly emergency relief appropriation acts. Renamed *Work Projects Administration* by Reorg. Plan No. I of 1939, effective July 1, 1939, which provided for consolidation of *Works Progress Administration* into *Federal Works Agency.* Transferred by President to *Federal Works Administrator* Dec. 4, 1942.

Works, Special Board of Public *See* **Land Program, Director of**

Yards and Docks, Bureau of Established by acts of Aug. 31, 1842 (5 Stat. 579), and July 5, 1862 (12 Stat. 510). Abolished by Department of Defense reorg. order of Mar. 9, 1966, and functions transferred to the Secretary of the Navy (31 FR 7188).

Youth Administration, National Established in *Works Progress Administration* by EO 7086 of June 26, 1935. Transferred to *Federal Security Agency* by Reorg. Plan No. I of 1939, effective July 1, 1939. Transferred to *Bureau of Training, War Manpower Commission,* by EO 9247 of Sept. 17, 1942. Terminated by act of July 12, 1943 (57 Stat. 539).

Youth Crime, President's Committee on Juvenile Delinquency and Established by EO 10940 of May 11, 1961. Terminated by EO 11529 of Apr. 24, 1970.

Youth Fitness, President's Council on Established by EO 10673 of July 16, 1956. Renamed *President's Council on Physical Fitness* by EO 11074 of Jan. 8, 1963. Renamed President's Council on Physical Fitness and Sports by EO 11398 of Mar. 4, 1968. Abolished and reestablished by EO 13265 of June 6, 2002.

Youth Opportunity, President's Council on Established by EO 11330 of Mar. 5, 1967. Inactive as of June 30, 1971; EO 11330 revoked by EO 12379 of Aug. 17, 1982.

Youth Programs, Office of Established in the Department of the Interior by Secretarial Order No. 2985 of Jan. 7, 1965. Functions moved to Office of Historically Black College and University Programs and Job Corps, Office of the Secretary, by Departmental Manual Release 2788 of Mar. 22, 1988.

APPENDIX C: Agencies Appearing in the Code of Federal Regulations

NOTE: This section contains an alphabetical listing of agencies appearing in the *Code of Federal Regulations* (CFR). The listing was revised as of July 1, 2006.

Agency	CFR Title, Subtitle or Chapter
Administrative Committee of the Federal Register	1, I
Advanced Research Projects Agency	32, I
Advisory Council on Historic Preservation	36, VIII
African Development Foundation	22, XV
Federal Acquisition Regulation	48, 57
Agency for International Development, United States	22, II
Federal Acquisition Regulation	48, 7
Agricultural Marketing Service	7, I, IX, X, XI
Agricultural Research Service	7, V
Agriculture Department	5, LXXIII
Agricultural Marketing Service	7, I, IX, X, XI
Agricultural Research Service	7, V
Animal and Plant Health Inspection Service	7, III; 9, I
Chief Financial Officer, Office of	7, XXX
Commodity Credit Corporation	7, XIV
Cooperative State Research, Education, and Extension Service	7, XXXIV
Economic Research Service	7, XXXVII
Energy, Office of	7, XXIX
Environmental Quality, Office of	7, XXXI
Farm Service Agency	7, VII, XVIII
Federal Acquisition Regulation	48, 4
Federal Crop Insurance Corporation	7, IV
Food and Nutrition Service	7, II
Food Safety and Inspection Service	9, III
Foreign Agricultural Service	7, XV
Forest Service	36, II
Grain Inspection, Packers and Stockyards Administration	7, VIII; 9, II
Information Resources Management, Office of	7, XXVII
Inspector General, Office of	7, XXVI
National Agricultural Library	7, XLI
National Agricultural Statistics Service	7, XXXVI
Natural Resources Conservation Service	7, VI
Operations, Office of	7, XXVIII
Procurement and Property Management, Office of	7, XXXII
Rural Business-Cooperative Service	7, XVIII, XLII
Rural Development Administration	7, XLII
Rural Housing Service	7, XVIII, XXXV
Rural Telephone Bank	7, XVI
Rural Utilities Service	7, XVII, XVIII, XLII
Secretary of Agriculture, Office of	7, Subtitle A
Transportation, Office of	7, XXXIII
World Agricultural Outlook Board	7, XXXVIII
Air Force Department	32, VII
Federal Acquisition Regulation Supplement	48, 53
Air Transportation Stabilization Board	14, VI
Alcohol and Tobacco Tax and Trade Bureau	27, I
Alcohol, Tobacco, Firearms, and Explosives, Bureau of	27, II
AMTRAK	49, VII
American Battle Monuments Commission	36, IV
American Indians, Office of the Special Trustee	25, VII

Agency	CFR Title, Subtitle or Chapter
Animal and Plant Health Inspection Service	7, III; 9, I
Appalachian Regional Commission	5, IX
Architectural and Transportation Barriers Compliance Board	36, XI
Arctic Research Commission	45, XXIII
Armed Forces Retirement Home	5, XI
Army Department	32, V
Engineers, Corps of	33, II; 36, III
Federal Acquisition Regulation	48, 51
Benefits Review Board	20, VII
Bilingual Education and Minority Languages Affairs, Office of	34, V
Blind or Severely Disabled, Committee for Purchase From People Who Are	41, 51
Broadcasting Board of Governors	22, V
Federal Acquisition Regulation	48, 19
Census Bureau	15, I
Centers for Medicare & Medicaid Services	42, IV
Central Intelligence Agency	32, XIX
Chief Financial Officer, Office of	7, XXX
Child Support Enforcement, Office of	45, III
Children and Families, Administration for	45, II, III, IV, X
Civil Rights, Commission on	45, VII
Civil Rights, Office for	34, I
Coast Guard	33, I; 46, I; 49, IV
Coast Guard (Great Lakes Pilotage)	46, III
Commerce Department	44, IV
Census Bureau	15, I
Economic Affairs, Under Secretary	37, V
Economic Analysis, Bureau of	15, VIII
Economic Development Administration	13, III
Emergency Management and Assistance	44, IV
Federal Acquisition Regulation	48, 13
Fishery Conservation and Management	50, VI
Foreign-Trade Zones Board	15, IV
Industry and Security, Bureau of	15, VII
International Trade Administration	15, III; 19, III
National Institute of Standards and Technology	15, II
National Marine Fisheries Service	50, II, IV, VI
National Oceanic and Atmospheric Administration	15, IX; 50, II, III, IV, VI
National Telecommunications and Information Administration	15, XXIII; 47, III
National Weather Service	15, IX
Patent and Trademark Office, United States	37, I
Productivity, Technology and Innovation, Assistant Secretary for	37, IV
Secretary of Commerce, Office of	15, Subtitle A
Technology, Under Secretary for	37, V
Technology Administration	15, XI
Technology Policy, Assistant Secretary for	37, IV
Commercial Space Transportation	14, III
Commodity Credit Corporation	7, XIV
Commodity Futures Trading Commission	5, XLI; 17, I
Community Planning and Development, Office of Assistant Secretary for	24, V, VI
Community Services, Office of	45, X
Comptroller of the Currency	12, I
Construction Industry Collective Bargaining Commission	29, IX
Consumer Product Safety Commission	5, LXXI; 16, II
Cooperative State Research, Education, and Extension Service	7, XXXIV
Copyright Office	37, II
Copyright Royalty Board	37, III
Corporation for National and Community Service	45, XII, XXV
Cost Accounting Standards Board	48, 99
Council on Environmental Quality	40, V
Court Services and Offender Supervision Agency for the District of Columbia	28, VIII
Customs and Border Protection Bureau	19, I
Defense Contract Audit Agency	32, I

Agency	CFR Title, Subtitle or Chapter
Defense Department	5, XXVI; 32, Subtitle A; 40, VII
Advanced Research Projects Agency	32, I
Air Force Department	32, VII
Army Department	32, V; 33, II; 36, III, 48, 51
Defense Acquisition Regulations System	48, II
Defense Intelligence Agency	32, I
Defense Logistics Agency	32, I, XII; 48, 54
Engineers, Corps of	33, II; 36, III
National Imagery and Mapping Agency	32, I
Navy Department	32, VI; 48, 52
Secretary of Defense, Office of	32, I
Defense Contract Audit Agency	32, I
Defense Intelligence Agency	32, I
Defense Logistics Agency	32, XII; 48, 54
Defense Nuclear Facilities Safety Board	10, XVII
Delaware River Basin Commission	18, III
District of Columbia, Court Services and Offender Supervision Agency for the	28, VIII
Drug Enforcement Administration	21, II
East-West Foreign Trade Board	15, XIII
Economic Affairs, Under Secretary	37, V
Economic Analysis, Bureau of	15, VIII
Economic Development Administration	13, III
Economic Research Service	7, XXXVII
Education, Department of	5, LIII
Bilingual Education and Minority Languages Affairs, Office of	34, V
Civil Rights, Office for	34, I
Educational Research and Improvement, Office of	34, VII
Elementary and Secondary Education, Office of	34, II
Federal Acquisition Regulation	48, 34
Postsecondary Education, Office of	34, VI
Secretary of Education, Office of	34, Subtitle A
Special Education and Rehabilitative Services, Office of	34, III
Vocational and Adult Education, Office of	34, IV
Educational Research and Improvement, Office of	34, VII
Elementary and Secondary Education, Office of	34, II
Emergency Oil and Gas Guaranteed Loan Board	13, V
Emergency Steel Guarantee Loan Board	13, IV
Employee Benefits Security Administration	29, XXV
Employees' Compensation Appeals Board	20, IV
Employees Loyalty Board	5, V
Employment and Training Administration	20, V
Employment Standards Administration	20, VI
Endangered Species Committee	50, IV
Energy, Department of	5, XXIII; 10, II, III, X
Federal Acquisition Regulation	48, 9
Federal Energy Regulatory Commission	5, XXIV; 18, I
Property Management Regulations	41, 109
Energy, Office of	7, XXIX
Engineers, Corps of	33, II; 36, III
Engraving and Printing, Bureau of	31, VI
Environmental Protection Agency	5, LIV; 40, I, IV, VII
Federal Acquisition Regulation	48, 15
Property Management Regulations	41, 115
Environmental Quality, Office of	7, XXXI
Equal Employment Opportunity Commission	5, LXII; 29, XIV
Equal Opportunity, Office of Assistant Secretary for	24, I
Executive Office of the President	3, I
Administration, Office of	5, XV
Environmental Quality, Council on	40, V
Management and Budget, Office of	5, III, LXXVII; 14, VI; 48, 99
National Drug Control Policy, Office of	21, III
National Security Council	32, XXI; 47, 2

Agency	CFR Title, Subtitle or Chapter
Presidential Documents	3
Science and Technology Policy, Office of	32, XXIV; 47, II
Trade Representative, Office of the United States	15, XX
Export-Import Bank of the United States	5, LII; 12, IV
Family Assistance, Office of	45, II
Farm Credit Administration	5, XXXI; 12, VI
Farm Credit System Insurance Corporation	5, XXX; 12, XIV
Farm Service Agency	7, VII, XVIII
Federal Acquisition Regulation	48, 1
Federal Aviation Administration	14, I
Commercial Space Transportation	14, III
Federal Claims Collection Standards	31, IX
Federal Communications Commission	5, XXIX; 47, I
Federal Contract Compliance Programs, Office of	41, 60
Federal Crop Insurance Corporation	7, IV
Federal Deposit Insurance Corporation	5, XXII; 12, III
Federal Election Commission	11, I
Federal Emergency Management Agency	44, I
Federal Acquisition Regulation	48, 44
Federal Employees Group Life Insurance Federal Acquisition Regulation	48, 21
Federal Employees Health Benefits Acquisition Regulation	48, 16
Federal Energy Regulatory Commission	5, XXIV; 18, I
Federal Financial Institutions Examination Council	12, XI
Federal Financing Bank	12, VIII
Federal Highway Administration	23, I, II
Federal Home Loan Mortgage Corporation	1, IV
Federal Housing Enterprise Oversight Office	12, XVII
Federal Housing Finance Board	12, IX
Federal Labor Relations Authority, and General Counsel of the Federal Labor Relations Authority	5, XIV; 22, XIV
Federal Law Enforcement Training Center	31, VII
Federal Management Regulation	41, 102
Federal Maritime Commission	46, IV
Federal Mediation and Conciliation Service	29, XII
Federal Mine Safety and Health Review Commission	5, LXXIV; 29, XXVII
Federal Motor Carrier Safety Administration	49, III
Federal Prison Industries, Inc.	28, III
Federal Procurement Policy Office	48, 99
Federal Property Management Regulations	41, 101
Federal Railroad Administration	49, II
Federal Register, Administrative Committee of	1, I
Federal Register, Office of	1, II
Federal Reserve System	12, II
Board of Governors	5, LVIII
Federal Retirement Thrift Investment Board	5, VI, LXXVI
Federal Service Impasses Panel	5, XIV
Federal Trade Commission	5, XLVII; 16, I
Federal Transit Administration	49, VI
Federal Travel Regulation System	41, Subtitle F
Fine Arts, Commission on	45, XXI
Fiscal Service	31, II
Fish and Wildlife Service, United States	50, I, IV
Fishery Conservation and Management	50, VI
Food and Drug Administration	21, I
Food and Nutrition Service	7, II
Food Safety and Inspection Service	9, III
Foreign Agricultural Service	7, XV
Foreign Assets Control, Office of	31, V
Foreign Claims Settlement Commission of the United States	45, V
Foreign Service Grievance Board	22, IX
Foreign Service Impasse Disputes Panel	22, XIV
Foreign Service Labor Relations Board	22, XIV
Foreign-Trade Zones Board	15, IV
Forest Service	36, II
General Services Administration	5, LVII; 41, 105
Contract Appeals, Board of	48, 61

Agency	CFR Title, Subtitle or Chapter
Federal Acquisition Regulation	48, 5
Federal Management Regulation	41, 102
Federal Property Management Regulations	41, 101
Federal Travel Regulation System	41, Subtitle F
General	41, 300
Payment From a Non-Federal Source for Travel Expenses	41, 304
Payment of Expenses Connected With the Death of Certain Employees	41, 303
Relocation Allowances	41, 302
Temporary Duty (TDY) Travel Allowances	41, 301
Geological Survey	30, IV
Government Accountability Office	4, I
Government Ethics, Office of	5, XVI
Government National Mortgage Association	24, III
Grain Inspection, Packers and Stockyards Administration	7, VIII; 9, II
Harry S. Truman Scholarship Foundation	45, XVIII
Health and Human Services, Department of	5, XLV; 45, Subtitle A
Centers for Medicare & Medicaid Services	42, IV
Child Support Enforcement, Office of	45, III
Children and Families, Administration for	45, II, III, IV, X
Community Services, Office of	45, X
Defense Acquisition Regulations System	48, 2
Family Assistance, Office of	45, II
Federal Acquisition Regulation	48, 3
Food and Drug Administration	21, I
Human Development Services, Office of	45, XIII
Indian Health Service	25, V; 42, I
Inspector General (Health Care), Office of	42, V
Public Health Service	42, I
Refugee Resettlement, Office of	45, IV
Homeland Security, Department of	6, I
Coast Guard	33, I; 46, I; 49, IV
Coast Guard (Great Lakes Pilotage)	46, III
Customs and Border Protection Bureau	19, I
Federal Emergency Management Agency	44, I
Immigration and Customs Enforcement Bureau	19, IV
Immigration and Naturalization	8, I
Transportation Security Administration	49, XII
Housing and Urban Development, Department of	5, LXV; 24, Subtitle B
Community Planning and Development, Office of Assistant Secretary for	24, V, VI
Equal Opportunity, Office of Assistant Secretary for	24, I
Federal Acquisition Regulation	48, 24
Federal Housing Enterprise Oversight, Office of	12, XVII
Government National Mortgage Association	24, III
Housing—Federal Housing Commissioner, Office of Assistant Secretary for	24, II, VIII, X, XX
Housing, Office of, and Multifamily Housing Assistance Restructuring, Office of	24, IV
Inspector General, Office of	24, XII
Public and Indian Housing, Office of Assistant Secretary for	24, IX
Secretary, Office of	24, Subtitle A, VII
Housing—Federal Housing Commissioner, Office of Assistant Secretary for	24, II, VIII, X, XX
Housing, Office of, and Multifamily Housing Assistance Restructuring, Office of	24, IV
Human Development Services, Office of	45, XIII
Immigration and Customs Enforcement Bureau	19, IV
Immigration and Naturalization	8, I
Immigration Review, Executive Office for	8, V
Independent Counsel, Office of	28, VII
Indian Affairs, Bureau of	25, I, V
Indian Affairs, Office of the Assistant Secretary	25, VI
Indian Arts and Crafts Board	25, II
Indian Health Service	25, V; 42, I
Industry and Security, Bureau of	15, VII
Information Resources Management, Office of	7, XXVII

Agency	CFR Title, Subtitle or Chapter
Information Security Oversight Office, National Archives and Records Administration	32, XX
Inspector General	
Agriculture Department	7, XXVI
Health and Human Services Department	42, V
Housing and Urban Development Department	24, XII
Institute of Peace, United States	22, XVII
Inter-American Foundation	5, LXIII; 22, X
Interior Department	
American Indians, Office of the Special Trustee	25, VII
Endangered Species Committee	50, IV
Federal Acquisition Regulation	48, 14
Federal Property Management Regulations System	41, 114
Fish and Wildlife Service, United States	50, I, IV
Geological Survey	30, IV
Indian Affairs, Bureau of	25, I, V
Indian Affairs, Office of the Assistant Secretary	25, VI
Indian Arts and Crafts Board	25, II
Land Management, Bureau of	43, II
Minerals Management Service	30, II
National Indian Gaming Commission	25, III
National Park Service	36, I
Reclamation, Bureau of	43, I
Secretary of the Interior, Office of	43, Subtitle A
Surface Mining and Reclamation Appeals, Board of	30, III
Surface Mining Reclamation and Enforcement, Office of	30, VII
Internal Revenue Service	26, I
International Boundary and Water Commission, United States and Mexico, United States Section	22, XI
International Development, United States Agency for	22, II
Federal Acquisition Regulation	48, 7
International Development Cooperation Agency, United States	22, XII
International Fishing and Related Activities	50, III
International Investment, Office of	31, VIII
International Joint Commission, United States and Canada	22, IV
International Organizations Employees Loyalty Board	5, V
International Trade Administration	15, III; 19, III
International Trade Commission, United States	19, II
Interstate Commerce Commission	5, XL
James Madison Memorial Fellowship Foundation	45, XXIV
Japan–United States Friendship Commission	22, XVI
Joint Board for the Enrollment of Actuaries	20, VIII
Justice Department	5, XXVIII; 28, I, XI; 40, IV
Alcohol, Tobacco, Firearms, and Explosives, Bureau of	27, II
Drug Enforcement Administration	21, II
Federal Acquisition Regulation	48, 28
Federal Claims Collection Standards	31, IX
Federal Prison Industries, Inc.	28, III
Foreign Claims Settlement Commission of the United States	45, V
Immigration Review, Executive Office for	8, V
Offices of Independent Counsel	28, VI
Prisons, Bureau of	28, V
Property Management Regulations	41, 128
Labor Department	5, XLII
Benefits Review Board	20, VII
Employee Benefits Security Administration	29, XXV
Employees' Compensation Appeals Board	20, IV
Employment and Training Administration	20, V
Employment Standards Administration	20, VI
Federal Acquisition Regulation	48, 29
Federal Contract Compliance Programs, Office of	41, 60
Federal Procurement Regulations System	41, 50
Labor-Management Standards, Office of	29, II, IV
Mine Safety and Health Administration	30, I
Occupational Safety and Health Administration	29, XVII
Public Contracts	41, 50

Agency	CFR Title, Subtitle or Chapter
Secretary of Labor, Office of	29, Subtitle A
Veterans' Employment and Training Service, Office of the Assistant Secretary for	41, 61; 20, IX
Wage and Hour Division	29, V
Workers' Compensation Programs, Office of	20, I
Labor-Management Standards, Office of	29, II, IV
Land Management, Bureau of	43, II
Legal Services Corporation	45, XVI
Library of Congress	36, VII
Copyright Office	37, II
Copyright Royalty Board	37, III
Local Television Loan Guarantee Board	7, XX
Management and Budget, Office of	5, III, LXXVII; 14, VI; 48, 99
Marine Mammal Commission	50, V
Maritime Administration	46, II
Merit Systems Protection Board	5, II
Micronesian Status Negotiations, Office for	32, XXVII
Mine Safety and Health Administration	30, I
Minerals Management Service	30, II
Minority Business Development Agency	15, XIV
Miscellaneous Agencies	1, IV
Monetary Offices	31, I
Morris K. Udall Scholarship and Excellence in National Environmental Policy Foundation	36, XVI
National Aeronautics and Space Administration	5, LIX; 14, V
Federal Acquisition Regulation	48, 18
National Agricultural Library	7, XLI
National Agricultural Statistics Service	7, XXXVI
National and Community Service, Corporation for	45, XII, XXV
National Archives and Records Administration	5, LXVI; 36, XII
Information Security Oversight Office	32, XX
National Bureau of Standards	15, II
National Capital Planning Commission	1, IV
National Commission for Employment Policy	1, IV
National Commission on Libraries and Information Science	45, XVII
National Council on Disability	34, XII
National Counterintelligence Center	32, XVIII
National Credit Union Administration	12, VII
National Crime Prevention and Privacy Compact Council	28, IX
National Drug Control Policy, Office of	21, III
National Foundation on the Arts and the Humanities	45, XI
National Highway Traffic Safety Administration	23, II, III; 49, V
National Imagery and Mapping Agency	32, I
National Indian Gaming Commission	25, III
National Institute for Literacy	34, XI
National Institute of Standards and Technology	15, II
National Labor Relations Board	5, LXI; 29, I
National Marine Fisheries Service	50, II, IV, VI
National Mediation Board	29, X
National Oceanic and Atmospheric Administration	15, IX; 50, II, III, IV, VI
National Park Service	36, I
National Railroad Adjustment Board	29, III
National Railroad Passenger Corporation (AMTRAK)	49, VII
National Science Foundation	5, XLIII; 45, VI
Federal Acquisition Regulation	48, 25
National Security Council	32, XXI
National Security Council and Office of Science and Technology Policy	47, II
National Telecommunications and Information Administration	15, XXIII; 47, III
National Transportation Safety Board	49, VIII
National Weather Service	15, IX
Natural Resources Conservation Service	7, VI
Navajo and Hopi Indian Relocation, Office of	25, IV
Navy Department	32, VI
Federal Acquisition Regulation	48, 52
Neighborhood Reinvestment Corporation	24, XXV

Agency	CFR Title, Subtitle or Chapter
Northeast Interstate Low-Level Radioactive Waste Commission	10, XVIII
Nuclear Regulatory Commission	5, XLVIII; 10, I
Federal Acquisition Regulation	48, 20
Occupational Safety and Health Administration	29, XVII
Occupational Safety and Health Review Commission	29, XX
Offices of Independent Counsel	28, VI
Oklahoma City National Memorial Trust	36, XV
Operations Office	7, XXVIII
Overseas Private Investment Corporation	5, XXXIII; 22, VII
Patent and Trademark Office, United States	37, I
Payment From a Non-Federal Source for Travel Expenses	41, 304
Payment of Expenses Connected With the Death of Certain Employees	41, 303
Peace Corps	22, III
Pennsylvania Avenue Development Corporation	36, IX
Pension Benefit Guaranty Corporation	29, XL
Personnel Management, Office of	5, I, XXXV; 45, VIII
Federal Acquisition Regulation	48, 17
Federal Employees Group Life Insurance Federal Acquisition Regulation	48, 21
Federal Employees Health Benefits Acquisition Regulation	48, 16
Pipeline and Hazardous Materials Safety Administration	49, I
Postal Rate Commission	5, XLVI; 39, III
Postal Service, United States	5, LX; 39, I
Postsecondary Education, Office of	34, VI
President's Commission on White House Fellowships	1, IV
Presidential Documents	3
Presidio Trust	36, X
Prisons, Bureau of	28, V
Procurement and Property Management, Office of	7, XXXII
Productivity, Technology and Innovation, Assistant Secretary	37, IV
Public Contracts, Department of Labor	41, 50
Public and Indian Housing, Office of Assistant Secretary for	24, IX
Public Health Service	42, I
Railroad Retirement Board	20, II
Reclamation, Bureau of	43, I
Refugee Resettlement, Office of	45, IV
Regional Action Planning Commissions	13, V
Relocation Allowances	41, 302
Research and Innovative Technology Administration	49, XI
Rural Business-Cooperative Service	7, XVIII, XLII
Rural Development Administration	7, XLII
Rural Housing Service	7, XVIII, XXXV
Rural Telephone Bank	7, XVI
Rural Utilities Service	7, XVII, XVIII, XLII
Saint Lawrence Seaway Development Corporation	33, IV
Science and Technology Policy, Office of	32, XXIV
Science and Technology Policy, Office of, and National Security Council	47, II
Secret Service	31, IV
Securities and Exchange Commission	17, II
Selective Service System	32, XVI
Small Business Administration	13, I
Smithsonian Institution	36, V
Social Security Administration	20, III; 48, 23
Soldiers' and Airmen's Home, United States	5, XI
Special Counsel, Office of	5, VIII
Special Education and Rehabilitative Services, Office of	34, III
State Department	22, I; 28, XI
Federal Acquisition Regulation	48, 6
Surface Mining and Reclamation Appeals, Board of	30, III
Surface Mining Reclamation and Enforcement, Office of	30, VII
Surface Transportation Board	49, X
Susquehanna River Basin Commission	18, VIII
Technology Administration	15, XI
Technology Policy, Assistant Secretary for	37, IV
Technology, Under Secretary for	37, V

Agency	CFR Title, Subtitle or Chapter
Tennessee Valley Authority	5, LXIX; 18, XIII
Thrift Supervision Office, Department of the Treasury	12, V
Trade Representative, United States, Office of	15, XX
Transportation, Department of	5, L
Commercial Space Transportation	14, III
Contract Appeals, Board of	48, 63
Emergency Management and Assistance	44, IV
Federal Acquisition Regulation	48, 12
Federal Aviation Administration	14, I
Federal Highway Administration	23, I, II
Federal Motor Carrier Safety Administration	49, III
Federal Railroad Administration	49, II
Federal Transit Administration	49, VI
Maritime Administration	46, II
National Highway Traffic Safety Administration	23, II, III; 49, V
Pipeline and Hazardous Materials Safety Administration	49, I
Saint Lawrence Seaway Development Corporation	33, IV
Secretary of Transportation, Office of	14, II; 49, Subtitle A
Surface Transportation Board	49, X
Transportation Statistics Bureau	49, XI
Transportation, Office of	7, XXXIII
Transportation Security Administration	49, XII
Transportation Statistics Bureau	49, XI
Travel Allowances, Temporary Duty (TDY)	41, 301
Treasury Department	5, XXI; 12, XV; 17, IV; 31, IX
Alcohol and Tobacco Tax and Trade Bureau	27, I
Community Development Financial Institutions Fund	12, XVIII
Comptroller of the Currency	12, I
Customs and Border Protection Bureau	19, I
Engraving and Printing, Bureau of	31, VI
Federal Acquisition Regulation	48, 10
Federal Law Enforcement Training Center	31, VII
Fiscal Service	31, II
Foreign Assets Control, Office of	31, V
Internal Revenue Service	26, I
International Investment, Office of	31, VIII
Monetary Offices	31, I
Secret Service	31, IV
Secretary of the Treasury, Office of	31, Subtitle A
Thrift Supervision, Office of	12, V
Truman, Harry S. Scholarship Foundation	45, XVIII
United States and Canada, International Joint Commission	22, IV
United States and Mexico, International Boundary and Water Commission, United States Section	22, XI
Utah Reclamation Mitigation and Conservation Commission	43, III
Veterans Affairs Department	38, I
Federal Acquisition Regulation	48, 8
Veterans' Employment and Training Service, Office of the Assistant Secretary for	41, 61; 20, IX
Vice President of the United States, Office of	32, XXVIII
Vocational and Adult Education, Office of	34, IV
Wage and Hour Division	29, V
Water Resources Council	18, VI
Workers' Compensation Programs, Office of	20, I
World Agricultural Outlook Board	7, XXXVIII

NAME INDEX

NOTE: Separate listings of Senators and Representatives can be found beginning on pages 32 and 34, respectively. Any other references to said persons can be found in this index.

D

E

H

I

L

Q

R

S

T

U

V

W

AGENCY/SUBJECT INDEX

NOTE: This index does not include material appearing in Appendixes A–C.

A

B

C

D

E

F

RECENT CHANGES

Personnel actions brought to the attention of *Manual* editors June 2–July 21, 2006
For current personnel information, please research www.senate.gov; www.whitehouse.gov; www.gpoaccess.gov/wcomp/index.html; and individual department or agency Web sites.

Page	Position	Action
U.S. Courts of Appeals		
69	U.S. Circuit Judge for the Eighth Circuit	Bobby E. Shepherd, confirmed July 20, vice Morris S. Arnold, retiring.
70	U.S. Circuit Judge for the Ninth Circuit	Sandra Segal Ikuta, confirmed June 19, vice James R. Browning, retired.
70	U.S. Circuit Judge for the Tenth Circuit	Neil M. Gorsuch, confirmed July 20, vice David M. Ebel, retired.
White House Office		
86	Assistant to the President for Communications	Kevin Sullivan, appointed July 11.
Office of Management and Budget		
92	General Counsel	Jeffrey A. Rosen, announced June 9, vice Raul F. Yanes
Office of the U.S. Trade Representative		
97	U.S. Trade Representative	Susan C. Schawb, confirmed June 8, vice Robert J. Portman.
Department of Defense		
150	Principal Deputy Under Secretary of Defense for Personnel and Readiness	Michael L. Dominguez, confirmed June 29.
151	Director of Operational Test and Evaluation	Charles E. McQueary, confirmed July 21, vice Thomas P. Christie, resigned.
Department of the Air Force		
160	Assistant Secretary	Sue C. Payton, confirmed July 21, vice Marvin R. Sambur.
National Defense University		
198	President	Frances C. Wilson, assumed position July 14, vice Michael M. Dunn, retiring.
Federal Energy Regulatory Commission		
210	Commissioner	Philip D. Moeller, confirmed July 14, vice Patrick Henry Wood III, resigned.
210	Commissioner	Jon Wellinghoff, confirmed July 14, vice William Lloyd Massey, term expired.
210	Commissioner	Marc Spitzer, confirmed July 14, vice Nora Mead Brownell, resigned.
Housing and Urban Development Department		
236	President, Government National Mortgage Association	Robert M. Couch, confirmed June 15, vice Ronald Rosenfeld.
236	Director, Office of Federal Housing Enterprise Oversight	James B. Lockhart III, confirmed June 15, vice Armando Falcon, Jr., resigned.
Department of State		
300	U.S. Ambassador to Australia	Robert D. McCallum, Jr., confirmed June 29.
300	U.S. Ambassador to Benin	Gayleatha Beatrice Brown, confirmed June 29.
300	U.S. Ambassador to Brazil	Clifford M. Sobel, confirmed June 29.
300	U.S. Ambassador to the Republic of Djibouti	W. Stuart Symington IV, confirmed June 29.
300	U.S. Ambassador to Ireland	Thomas C. Foley, confirmed June 29.

RECENT CHANGES—Continued

Personnel actions brought to the attention of *Manual* editors June 2–July 21, 2006
For current personnel information, please research www.senate.gov; www.whitehouse.gov; www.gpoaccess.gov/wcomp/index.html; and individual department or agency Web sites.

Page	Position	Action
300	U.S. Ambassador to the Republic of Kenya	Michael E. Ranneberger, confirmed June 29.
300	U.S. Ambassador to Papua New Guinea, Solomon Islands, and the Republic of Vanuatu	Leslie V. Rowe, confirmed June 29.
300	U.S. Ambassador to Republic of South Africa	Eric M. Bost, confirmed June 29.
300	U.S. Ambassador to Democratic Socialist Republic of Sri Lanka and Republic of Maldives	Robert O. Blake, Jr., confirmed June 29, vice Jeffrey Lunstead.
300	U.S. Ambassador to Switzerland and Liechtenstein	Peter R. Coneway, confirmed June 29.
Department of the Transportation		
306	Secretary of Transportation	Norman Y. Mineta, resigned June 23 (vol. 42, *Weekly Compilation of Presidential Documents,* p. 1216).
Department of the Treasury		
330	Secretary of the Treasury	Henry M. Paulson, Jr., confirmed June 28, vice John W. Snow, resigned.
Department of Veterans Affairs		
346	Under Secretary for Benefits	Daniel L. Cooper, confirmed June 29, reappointment.
348	Assistant Secretary of Veterans Affairs (Congressional Affairs)	Pamela M. Iovino, resigned.
Environmental Protection Agency		
376	Assistant Administrator for Toxic Substances	James B. Gulliford, confirmed June 29, vice Stephen L. Johnson, resigned.
Federal Deposit Insurance Corporation		
398	Chairman	Sheila C. Bair, confirmed June 15, vice Donald E. Powell, resigned.
398	Member	Sheila C. Bair, confirmed June 15, vice Donald E. Powell, resigned.
398	Inspector General	Jon T. Rymer, confirmed June 22, vice Gaston L. Gianni, Jr.
Federal Reserve System		
417	Vice Chair	Donald L. Kohn, confirmed June 19, vice Roger Walton Ferguson, resigned.
Securities and Exchange Commission		
507	Commissioner	Kathleen L. Casey, confirmed June 15, vice Cynthia A. Glassman, resigned.
Small Business Administration		
514	Administrator	Steven C. Preston, confirmed June 29, vice Hector V. Barreto, Jr., resigned.
United States Institute of Peace		
573	Member, *Ex officio*	Frances C. Wilson, assumed position July 14, vice Michael M. Dunn, retiring.